Praise for Past Access Developer's Handbooks

"**This book characterizes** all that a computer programming book should be... it explained clearly how to program Access 97 and also how to use it effectively. In particular, I liked the many code examples and have used some of those provided on the CD."

Robin Edmonds
Warwick, England

"**This is by far the best** Access book on the market. Tons of information on the guts of Access that you don't get from other books... a necessary addition to the professional Access Developer's library. A must have!"

John Fuex, MCP, MCSD
Austin, Texas

"**After programming in Access** since version 1.1, a developer can be hard pressed to find a book with any information worth learning. This is the first book to come along to change this. In the first 100 pages I learned many new programming methods that would have taken the compilation of 4 or more other books. I would recommend this book to ALL Access, VBA, & VB programmers."

Andrew Ells-O'Brien
Malden, Massachusetts

"**If you do not have this book** in you private library, get it! If you are developing MS-Access applications and have Q's, this is the book that will provide you with the A's you want. Save yourself countless hours. What more can I say? GET IT!"

Michael Borries
Copenhagen, Denmark

"**I have used** the Access Developer's Handbook ar... extremely useful... full of samples, tips and tricks."

Trisha Phoon
Kuala Lumpur, Malaysia

www.sybex.com

Access 2000 Developer's Handbook

Volume 1: Desktop Edition

Access 2000 Developer's Handbook™

Volume 1: Desktop Edition

Ken Getz
Paul Litwin
Mike Gilbert

San Francisco • Paris • Düsseldorf • Soest • London

Associate Publisher: Amy Romanoff
Contracts and Licensing Manager: Kristine O'Callaghan
Acquisitions & Developmental Editor: Melanie Spiller
Editor: Sally Engelfried
Project Editor: Rebecca Rider
Technical Editor: David Shank
Book Designer: Kris Warrenburg
Graphic Illustrators: Tony Jonick, Jerry Williams
Electronic Publishing Specialist: Maureen Forys, Happenstance Type-O-Rama
Project Team Leader: Leslie Higbee
Proofreaders: Lisa King, Camera Obscura, Sandy Young
Indexer: Ted Laux
Companion CD: Ginger Warner
Cover Designer: Design Site
Cover Illustrator/Photographer: Kazuo Kawai/Photonica

Library of Congress Card Number: 99-63320
ISBN: 0-7821-2370-8

Manufactured in the United States of America

10

Software License Agreement: Terms and Conditions

The media and/or any online materials accompanying this book that are available now or in the future contain programs and/or text files (the "Software") to be used in connection with the book. SYBEX hereby grants to you a license to use the Software, subject to the terms that follow. Your purchase, acceptance, or use of the Software will constitute your acceptance of such terms.

The Software compilation is the property of SYBEX unless otherwise indicated and is protected by copyright to SYBEX or other copyright owner(s) as indicated in the media files (the "Owner(s)"). You are hereby granted a single-user license to use the Software for your personal, noncommercial use only. You may not reproduce, sell, distribute, publish, circulate, or commercially exploit the Software, or any portion thereof, without the written consent of SYBEX and the specific copyright owner(s) of any component software included on this media.

In the event that the Software or components include specific license requirements or end-user agreements, statements of condition, disclaimers, limitations or warranties ("End-User License"), those End-User Licenses supersede the terms and conditions herein as to that particular Software component. Your purchase, acceptance, or use of the Software will constitute your acceptance of such End-User Licenses.

By purchase, use, or acceptance of the Software you further agree to comply with all export laws and regulations of the United States as such laws and regulations may exist from time to time.

Reusable Code in This Book

The authors created reusable code in this publication expressly for reuse by readers. Sybex grants readers permission to reuse for any purpose the code found in this publication or its accompanying CD-ROM so long as all three authors are attributed in any application containing the reusable code and the code itself is never sold or commercially exploited as a stand-alone product.

Software Support

Components of the supplemental Software and any offers associated with them may be supported by the specific Owner(s) of that material but they are not supported by SYBEX. Information regarding any available support may be obtained from the Owner(s) using the information provided in the appropriate read.me files or listed elsewhere on the media.

Should the manufacturer(s) or other Owner(s) cease to offer support or decline to honor any offer, SYBEX bears no responsibility. This notice concerning support for the Software is provided for your information only. SYBEX is not the agent or principal of the Owner(s), and SYBEX is in no way responsible for providing any support for the Software, nor is it liable or responsible for any support provided, or not provided, by the Owner(s).

Warranty

SYBEX warrants the enclosed media to be free of physical defects for a period of ninety (90) days after purchase. The Software is not available from SYBEX in any other form or media than that enclosed herein or posted to *www.sybex.com*. If you discover a defect in the media during this warranty period, you may obtain a replacement of identical format at no charge by sending the defective media, postage prepaid, with proof of purchase to:

SYBEX Inc.
Customer Service Department
1151 Marina Village Parkway
Alameda, CA 94501
(510) 523-8233
Fax: (510) 523-2373
e-mail: info@sybex.com
WEB: HTTP://WWW.SYBEX.COM

After the 90-day period, you can obtain replacement media of identical format by sending us the defective disk, proof of purchase, and a check or money order for $10, payable to SYBEX.

Disclaimer

SYBEX makes no warranty or representation, either expressed or implied, with respect to the Software or its contents, quality, performance, merchantability, or fitness for a particular purpose. In no event will SYBEX, its distributors, or dealers be liable to you or any other party for direct, indirect, special, incidental, consequential, or other damages arising out of the use of or inability to use the Software or its contents even if advised of the possibility of such damage. In the event that the Software includes an online update feature, SYBEX further disclaims any obligation to provide this feature for any specific duration other than the initial posting.

The exclusion of implied warranties is not permitted by some states. Therefore, the above exclusion may not apply to you. This warranty provides you with specific legal rights; there may be other rights that you may have that vary from state to state. The pricing of the book with the Software by SYBEX reflects the allocation of risk and limitations on liability contained in this agreement of Terms and Conditions.

Shareware Distribution

This Software may contain various programs that are distributed as shareware. Copyright laws apply to both shareware and ordinary commercial software, and the copyright Owner(s) retains all rights. If you try a shareware program and continue using it, you are expected to register it. Individual programs differ on details of trial periods, registration, and payment. Please observe the requirements stated in appropriate files.

Copy Protection

The Software in whole or in part may or may not be copy-protected or encrypted. However, in all cases, reselling or redistributing these files without authorization is expressly forbidden except as specifically provided for by the Owner(s) therein.

To each reader who took the time to contact us with suggestions, errata, words of encouragement, or complaints. You are the people who made this book better, from version to version.
—KNG

To Suzanne, my soulmate.
—PEL

To Ken and Paul, for inviting me along on what turned out to be a great ride.
—MTG

To Melanie Spiller, who stuck with us through four editions of this book, providing inspiration and support and treating each of us as if we were her only responsibility.
—KNG, PEL, MTG

ACKNOWLEDGMENTS

This book wouldn't have been possible without the concerted effort of many individuals in addition to the authors. First of all, we'd like to thank Melanie Spiller, our acquisitions editor, who's gone to bat for us more times than we care to count. Melanie has been an inspiration, a mentor, and a sensitive, compassionate friend over the past five years.

We'd also like to thank David Shank, our technical editor for the book, for the second time. (He's certainly the only technical person we know who has read every word of the book twice!) David is an excellent technical editor and an accomplished developer and writer—he's one of the authors of *Microsoft Office 2000/Visual Basic Programmer's Guide* from Microsoft Press. David knows this product inside and out and made a nearly superhuman effort to edit the technical content and examples in this book. Because of his tireless attention to detail, this book is that much better. Before working at Microsoft, David developed Visual Basic and Access applications for Applied Information Technologies, Inc.

Very special thanks go out to Greg Reddick, one of the coauthors of the first two editions of this book. Greg's contributions to those editions are still very much a part of the current edition. In addition, we continue to use his RVBA naming standard, which appears in Appendix A. Thanks, Greg, for all your hard work and friendship!

Special thanks also go out to Mike Gunderloy and Michael Kaplan. Mike was the technical editor for the second edition of the book and a contributor to several chapters in the first and second editions. He also provided Chapter 6 for this edition. His support and friendship continues to be invaluable. Michael wrote several sections in the second edition and edited several sections in the third edition. He also supplied lots of early information to use for this edition.

Thanks go to Chris Bell, John Viescas, Mike Hernandez, Mary Chipman, and Andy Baron. Chris helped in deciphering form filter properties and events for the second edition of this book. John provided useful suggestions for examples and helped devise a technique we adopted for carrying forward values to a new row. Mike, a database-design wizard, provided much of the inspiration for the original database design chapter (in the first edition of the book). Mary provided her usual support, suggestions, and ideas, but also helped in doing some research for *Volume II* of this edition. Andy provided an irreplaceable service: he acted as a sounding board for testing new ideas and also provided the subform transactions example in Chapter 8.

We'd also like to thank the folks at Microsoft who supported us during the beta process for the product. In particular, Richard Dickenson, Keith Fink, Eric Gough, and Kevin Mineweaser were especially helpful. We always knew who to run to when a feature didn't work as advertised, or when we couldn't figure out how to use a new part of the product. And, of course, we'd like to thank Tod Nielsen for providing the insightful foreword for the book.

Thanks also go out to the several individuals who helped write chapters for the first edition of this book: Scott Alexander, Brian Randell, and Dan Haught.

Due to their providing satisfaction for some deep-seated chemical need, Mike would like to thank the folks at all the Starbucks outlets (and there are many) in the Greater Puget Sound area.

Thanks to those who helped redesign and test the newest version of the form resizing code in Chapter 8. This is complex code and has gone through several revisions. In particular, thanks to Robert Seso, who not only tested the code, but also provided many suggestions and features that ended up in the final product.

We appreciate the work of the following people who provided ideas or technical editing support for one or more editions of the book: Jürgen Appelo, Dev Ashish, Joe Celko, Mary Chipman, Luke Chung, Jim Ferguson, Steve Forte, Erik Ruthruff, Jürgen Welz, and Brian Wells.

Thanks to all the current and former members of the Access, VBA, and Jet teams at Microsoft. In particular, the following individuals gave us early access to information, answered technical questions, or reviewed chapters: Acey Bunch, Neil Charney, Kevin Collins, Debra Dove, David Gainer, Alyssa Henry, Mark Roberts, Monte Slichter, Doug Stotland, and James Sturms.

Thanks also to all the individuals and companies who contributed content to the companion CD.

Of course, without the hard work and support of the staff at Sybex, this book would be nothing more than a dream. We are especially appreciative of the efforts of our current project editor Rebecca Rider, and those who worked with us on the previous editions: Kim Wimpsett, Lee Ann Pickrell, and Kris Vanberg-Wolff, and our contracts and licensing manager, Kristine O'Callaghan. An extra special thanks goes to Sally Engelfried, our tireless editor, who, after reading every word of this book, knows a lot more about Access than she ever wanted to know.

Finally, we'd like to thank our friends, significant others, and family members who put up with us during yet another long and trying book-writing season.

CONTENTS AT A GLANCE

TABLE OF CONTENTS

Appendices

FOREWORD

It's hard to believe that its been 12 years since I worked on the first version of Access codenamed "Omega." The PC database market was very different in the good old days. I remember how nervous we were trying to develop the first PC Database for Windows. As we were developing the product and talking to users, we were learning all kinds of things ourselves. I guess that is part of the reason it took so long to finally ship what many of us worked on for five years! Many of the developers and users we spoke to back then couldn't understand why anyone would want to use a mouse with a database application, or what a graphical interface would provide for the database developer. Sure, Windows might make sense with spreadsheets and word processors, but not for a PC Database!

When Access 1.0 officially debuted at Comdex in 1992, it was certainly a milestone for many of us at Microsoft, and it was unlike any product that had come before it. The Access team wanted to build a product that could be easy enough for end users to build simple databases yet robust enough to provide a platform for professional developers building data-centric solutions. The "sweet spot" of Access 1.0 was for the experienced database user. These users discovered a tool that enabled them to easily perform complex operations and quickly build types of applications that were too difficult if not impossible to build with other tools.

Access 2.0 addressed many of the areas that needed some polish from the earlier version, and the database developer community embraced it with open arms. I remember many meetings with folks like Ken Getz , Paul Litwin, and Mike Gilbert where they told us what we needed to do in order to make Access better meet their needs. Ken, Paul, and Mike often remind me of my daughter—who is never satisfied, even when she gets what she asks for. There is always more to ask for, more that can be done, more to achieve. In the early days of Access, Ken, Paul, and Mike (the three amigos, for short <g>) would push us to put a specific feature in the product. After some hard work at understanding how to implement their request, we would agree. Upon sharing the good news with them that their feature was going to be included, we expected them to say thanks so we could then move on to building the product. Instead, they told us that the world would come to an end if we didn't fix "just one more" glaring issue in Access. That's the funny thing about the three amigos—they seem to always have "just one more" reason why the world may come to an end…

Over the years, they and the millions of developers working with Access have pushed the Access team and stretched us to do more and build a product that will make all users more productive (and of course, save the world from coming to an end<g>). They continue to do so to this day. I love their persistence and hope that you appreciate the results as you work with the most recent version of Access.

With Access 2000 (our 5th iteration of the product!), we've delivered strong integration with Office applications. We've added a range of new features that will appeal to everyone from the database end user to the top developer.

In Access 2000, developers can link to SQL Server directly, build Web-based solutions with Data Access Pages, and create scaleable solutions with the Microsoft Data Engine (MSDE). That means that the tool you're most familiar with can now help you build seamless solutions that extend from enterprise data to the Web. Access 2000 also fully integrates the Visual Basic for Applications (VBA) 6.0 integrated development environment (IDE) and language. With VBA now integrated throughout the Office suite, you can leverage the skillset you already know across a variety of applications.

On top of that, we've even created an edition of Office specifically for the developer—the Microsoft Office 2000 Developer—in which you'll find everything you need to build solutions with Microsoft Office (including Office 2000 Premium and a whole slew of tools, documentation, and sample code). I have learned over the years, that you can never provide enough samples, code, or documentation on anything to do with Access. That is really where Ken, Paul, and Mike have done a fantastic job. With every new release of Microsoft Office, the three of them have been there to provide the next level of support for developers working with Access. With Office 2000, they've done it again.

In *Access 2000 Developer's Handbook*, (also known as, *The Three Amigos Share Their Deep Dark Secrets with the Access Developer Community*), Ken, Paul and Mike have assembled an enormous collection of information that every Access developer needs to know—database design, fancy form and report tricks, using Automation, Windows API, etc. In addition to providing a strong foundation for building solutions with Access, this book contains great information for taking Access development to the next level.

Class modules, introduced in Access 97, have radically transformed the way developers write code with Access. In fact, if you're not using class modules, you're most likely working too hard. You want classes (and trust me, you do!)? Well, the three amigos deliver—they've got class modules for working with the

Registry, for gathering file version information, and for working with forms, printers, and more, all expertly written and provided along with the book. In fact, there's more code in here than any one could ever possibly need, so feel free to share some with your friends (but make sure they have purchased a copy of this book!).

Whenever I'm on the road talking to developers, I usually start with a top ten list—a sort of "best of" listing of some of the amazing things that go on at Microsoft. If I were putting together my top ten great resources for Access developers, this book would certainly make the list. So, stop reading this foreword (it's really just a foreword, you know) and get to it! Dig into this book and start building those solutions!

—Tod Nielsen
Vice President of Developer Marketing
Microsoft Corporation

ABOUT THE AUTHORS

Ken Getz

Ken Getz (MCSD, MCP) is a senior consultant with MCW Technologies, focusing on the Microsoft suite of products. He has received Microsoft's MVP award (for providing online technical support) since 1993 and has written several books on developing applications using Microsoft products. Ken is a technical editor for *Access-Office-VB Advisor* (Advisor) and a contributing editor for *Microsoft Office & Visual Basic for Applications Developer* (Informant) magazines. Currently, Ken spends a great deal of time traveling around the country for Application Developers Training Company, presenting training classes for Access and Visual Basic developers. Ken co-wrote Access courseware and training videos for AppDev, along with Paul Litwin. He also wrote and recorded AppDev's Visual Basic courseware and training videos. He also speaks at many conferences and trade shows throughout the world, including Microsoft's Tech*Ed, Advisor Publication's DevCon, and Informant's Microsoft Office and VBA Solutions conference. You can reach Ken at `kgetz@developershandbook.com`.

Paul Litwin

Paul Litwin (MCSD, MCP) is a senior consultant with MCW Technologies specializing in application development employing Microsoft Access, Visual Basic, SQL Server, Visual InterDev, Active Server Pages, HTML, and related Microsoft technologies. In addition to the various editions of the *Access Developer's Handbook*, Paul has written books on Internet development and VBA. He has contributed articles to various publications including *Visual Basic Programmer's Journal*, *Smart Access*, *Microsoft Office & Visual Basic for Applications Developer*, and *PC World*. Paul regularly travels around the United States training developers for Application Developers Training Company (AppDev) in Access, VB, SQL Server, and Visual InterDev. Along with Ken Getz, Paul has written and recorded Access courseware and training videos for AppDev. He also developed and recorded AppDev's Visual InterDev courseware and videos. Paul has spoken at a variety of U.S. and international conferences and trade shows, including Microsoft Tech*Ed, Microsoft Office and VBA Solutions, and DevCon 1999. You can reach Paul at `plitwin@developershandbook.com`.

Mike Gilbert

Mike Gilbert works at Microsoft as a program manager designing object models for business productivity and Web collaboration products. Prior to joining Microsoft, he was a senior consultant with MCW Technologies, specializing in application development using Microsoft Access, Visual Basic, SQL Server, and Microsoft Office. He writes for several periodicals and is a contributing editor to *Microsoft Office & Visual Basic for Applications Developer* magazine. He is also a regular speaker at conferences such as Microsoft Tech*Ed and the Microsoft Office and VBA Solutions Conference. You can reach Mike at `mgilbert@developershandbook.com`.

INTRODUCTION

When it was released in late 1992, Microsoft Access took the database world by storm because of its aggressive $99 price. But when the dust settled after the first million were sold, many users and developers were pleasantly surprised to find a *real database* hidden beneath that ridiculously cheap price tag. Access 1.0 and the soon-to-follow modest upgrade, version 1.1, were certainly far from perfect, but users found an instantly usable product that broke down the walls of database accessibility. At the same time, almost overnight, a large and healthy developer community (that included the authors of this book) was born and began to develop professional applications that ran businesses of all sizes throughout the world.

Since its introduction, Microsoft has released four major updates: version 2.0, which hit the streets in May of 1994; Access for Windows 95 (aka Access 95 or Access 7.0), which appeared in November of 1995; Access 97 (aka Access 8.0), which appeared in January of 1997; and Access 2000 (aka Access 9.0), released in June of 1999. These updates have made numerous improvements in the areas of usability, programmability, and extendability. In addition, the last two versions made great strides in making Access a primary candidate for client/server and Internet database development.

Access 2000 is a wonderfully powerful development platform, but like any powerful product, it takes considerable time to master. Fortunately for you, the three of us spent many months and countless hours tearing apart Access 2000, exposing its undocumented secrets, and making it do things that few have imagined were possible—all for your benefit.

About the Book

This book is not a substitute for the Microsoft documentation, nor is it meant as a comprehensive reference manual. Instead, we strove to address the major issues we feel will face most developers. When we had to choose whether to cover a given topic or feature—one has to stop somewhere—we tended to favor the undocumented or poorly documented over the well documented.

In addition to the text, this book includes the usual assortment of figures, examples, and tables. It also includes lots of notes, tips, and warnings to call special attention to certain features or "gotchas."

Because the product has gotten larger and larger over the years, and amazingly, book publishing capabilities haven't grown the same way, we've had to split the book into two volumes for this edition. *Volume I* (this book), covers Access from a desktop developer's point of view. That is, it covers issues pertinent to Access itself—forms, reports, database design, working with the Windows API, creating class modules, and so on. *Volume II*, a separate book, covers Access from an enterprise-wide point of view. It contains chapters on creating multiuser and client/server applications, working with SQL Server/Microsoft Database Engine (MSDE), and publishing data on the Web. The decision of whether to include some chapters in *Volume I* or *Volume II* was somewhat arbitrary, and we hope that this split in the books' chapters makes it possible to include much more information than we could have otherwise.

NOTE

Because of the way we've split the two books, you'll find almost no coverage in this volume of two of the biggest new features in Access 2000: Access Data Projects (ADP files) and Data Access Pages. Aside from some mention in passing in this book, both of these topics are covered in depth in *Volume II*.

NOTE

The authors created reusable code in this publication expressly for reuse by readers in applications that they develop or distribute. Readers cannot publish the code in any way that allows other developers access to the code itself. Sybex grants readers limited permission to reuse the code for applications developed or distributed by the reader so long as all three authors are attributed in any application containing the reusable code and the code itself is never distributed, posted online by electronic transmission, sold or commercially exploited as a stand-alone product.

About This Edition

This edition of the book is a significant rewrite of the best-selling *Microsoft Access 97 Developer's Handbook*. Most chapters have changed in some way, but some chapters have changed more than others. You'll find the largest changes to the chapters in this book in three areas:

- Changes to Jet, requiring substantial rewrites of the chapters discussing Jet: Chapters 5 and 15.
- The addition of ADO, requiring a replacement of Chapter 6 and major modifications to Chapter 8.
- Utilization of class modules. In the Access 97 edition of this book, class modules had just been added to the product around the time we went to press. We quickly added a chapter on creating classes but didn't incorporate the technology into all the existing examples. In this version, we've attempted to use classes wherever appropriate.

One thing you can be sure of: this is *not* an Access 97 book with an Access 2000 cover. It is very much an Access 2000 book—from cover to cover.

Is This Book for You?

This book is for any Access developer or anyone who would like to become one. It doesn't matter whether you develop Access applications full time, as only one component of your job, or in your spare time during the evenings and weekends. What matters is that you take the product seriously and want your applications to be the very best.

If you only care to get your toes wet with Access and are happy to throw together quick-and-dirty applications that are automated with nothing more than a few macros, you probably don't need this book. However, if you're ready to dive into the thick of Access and get down to the business of developing industrial-strength applications that utilize Access to its fullest, you've picked the right book.

If you already own a copy of one of the prior editions of this book, you may be wondering if you should buy this book, too. Yes—if you're planning to develop applications with Access 2000 and you liked the prior editions, we're sure you'll get a lot out of this edition as well. So much in Access has changed for the developer, and we cover it all—okay, not all, but almost all.

What You Need to Know

For you to benefit most from an advanced book such as this, we've had to dispense with the fundamentals and make several assumptions about you. We assume you already have a basic level of familiarity with the product. At a minimum, you should be comfortable creating tables and simple queries, forms, and reports and have at least a rudimentary understanding of Access Basic or Visual Basic for Applications. If you aren't up to speed, you may wish to put down this book for the moment and spend some time with Access and its documentation, the help system, or an introductory text such as *Mastering Access 2000* by Alan Simpson and Celeste Robinson (Sybex, 1999). If you're fluent in Access but need help getting started with programming VBA in Access, you might investigate *Access 2000 VBA Handbook* by Suzann Novalis (Sybex, 1999).

Conventions Used in This Book

It goes without saying that the professional developer must consistently follow *some* standard. We followed several standard conventions in this book to make it easier for you to follow along.

We have used version 6.0 of the Reddick VBA (RVBA) naming conventions for the naming of Access (and other) objects, which have been accepted by many Access and VBA developers as the naming standard to follow. Greg Reddick, a noted Access and Visual Basic developer and trainer, developed the standard, which bears his name. Even if you don't subscribe to the RVBA standard, however, you'll likely appreciate the fact that it has been consistently used throughout the book. These conventions, which were first published in *Smart Access*, are included in their entirety in Appendix A. (In a few places, you'll find we have used tags that differ from those in Appendix A. This happened because Greg finalized version 6.0 of the RVBA standard only weeks before the book went to press. In addition, the RVBA standard is a standard to which we've subscribed but haven't followed slavishly. You'll find many places where we've simplified the rules.)

In addition to following the RVBA standard, we have prefaced all public procedures, user-defined types, and enums that you may wish to use in your own code with the "adh" prefix (which stands for *Access Developer's Handbook*), aliased all public Windows API declarations using an "adh_api" prefix, and prefixed all public constants with "adhc". These conventions should avoid naming conflicts with any existing code in your applications. If, however, you import multiple modules from various chapters' sample databases into a single database, you may find naming conflicts as a result of our using consistent naming throughout the chapters. In that case, you'll need to comment out any conflicting API declarations or user-defined types.

Chapter Walk-Through

This book consists of eighteen chapters and three appendicies. In every chapter you'll find lots of examples, with all but the most trivial included in sample databases you can find on the CD that accompanies this book.

Overview of Access

We begin with a brief history of Access and an overview of what's new in Access 2000 in Chapter 1. In Chapter 2, you'll find a discussion of Access' event model and the sequence of events in Access. Chapter 3 discusses the creation of Access class modules—the only "how-to" coding chapter in the book. We guess that many Access developers that are otherwise proficient in VBA need at least an overview of this important technology, and we've therefore put this near the beginning of the book.

Manipulating Data

When you design your database, you need to follow the principles of relational database design theory, which are detailed in Chapter 4. Here you'll also find a discussion of primary and foreign keys, relationships, the normal forms, and integrity constraints.

You can use Chapter 5 as the Jet SQL reference that Microsoft never provided. This chapter provides the syntax of every Jet SQL statement and clause, with numerous examples, and a discussion of how Jet SQL differs from the ANSI SQL standards.

In Chapter 6, you'll find a discussion of ActiveX Access Objects (ADO), the programmatic interface to OLE DB. Here you'll learn how to programmatically create TableDefs, QueryDefs, Relationships, and other objects; how to set and retrieve object properties; how to manipulate recordsets; and—using collections provided by Access—how to build your own replacement database container. Even if you're an experienced Access developer, you won't want to skip this chapter, as ADO is new to this version of Access.

Managing the User Interface

Chapter 7 presents a comprehensive discussion of controls and their properties and methods, along with numerous examples. In this chapter, you learn about list-filling functions, creating paired multiselect list boxes, using the Tag property, using the tab and subform controls, and creating forms and controls programmatically.

After you've mastered controls, you'll be ready to think about the forms themselves, which is the topic of Chapter 8. In this chapter, you'll find a thorough discussion of advanced ways of using forms in your applications. You'll also find numerous examples and reusable generic routines—some quite extensive, such as the example that shows you how to make any form resolution independent.

Chapter 9 focuses on report design issues. You'll learn how to master sorting and grouping, as well as the myriad of report properties and events. Again, you'll find lots of examples you can use in your applications.

Chapter 10 explains how to programmatically retrieve information about your printer, change print destinations, and perform many other printing wonders by using the prtDevMode, prtDevNames, and prtMip report properties. Although this material is somewhat complex, this edition of the book includes class modules that wrap up the functionality, making it simple to use.

In Chapter 11, you'll learn about three of the shared Office programmable objects. You'll learn how to programmatically control command bars, the object model exposed by the shared Office toolbars and menu bars, and how to programmatically manipulate the shared FileSearch object and the Office Assistant.

Building Applications

In Chapter 12, you'll learn how to manipulate other applications using Automation. This chapter includes examples that demonstrate how to use Automation to control Microsoft Outlook, Word, and Excel. The chapter also covers how to use ActiveX controls.

Chapter 13 presents the flip side of Chapter 12. Here you'll learn how to manipulate Access from Visual Basic, Excel, and other Automation controllers.

In Chapter 14, you'll find a discussion of application debugging strategies and how to handle and recover gracefully from application errors. This chapter includes a generic set of routines for logging errors.

In Chapter 15, you'll learn how to optimize the various Access components, including queries, forms, reports, and VBA code. After you read this chapter, you should be able to make any sluggish application run more quickly.

Advanced Topics

Chapter 16 explains how to use the Windows API and other Dynamic Link Libraries (DLLs) to do things that are otherwise impossible using Access itself. This chapter includes a discussion of the Windows Registry and how to manipulate it using the Windows API, as well as a discussion of 16-bit to 32-bit DLL conversion issues.

In Chapter 17, you'll discover how you can use the undocumented tricks originally included to allow the Wizards to do their work. In this version of Access, most of these "holes" have been closed. This chapter provides replacement techniques for tools provided in previous editions of the book, in addition to other useful tools and techniques you'll need in creating advanced Access applications. In this chapter, you'll find tools for working with files and the Registry; in addition, the chapter includes classes for working with the Windows common dialogs, working with fonts, determining file version information, and retrieving information about the screen. Although this chapter doesn't focus on material that's exclusive to Access, you'll find many useful tips you won't want to miss.

Chapter 18 shows you, with examples, how to build and install Access Wizards, builders, libraries, and other add-ins you can use to enhance your Access applications. The chapter also discusses the practical side of VBA references and examines the new programmatic features of Access modules. Finally, the chapter introduces the concepts involved in creating COM Add-ins for use in Access (and other Office applications).

Appendices

This book contains three appendices.

Appendix A provides a description of the RVBA naming conventions used throughout this book. You'll find this useful both when reading this book and if you wish to use the same naming conventions in your own development work.

Appendix B discusses database startup properties and the GetOption and SetOption methods. This information is crucial for anyone attempting to distribute applications, but it just didn't fit in with any of the other chapters' material. You'll find a number of undocumented options in this appendix, along with several that are documented incorrectly in Access' help system. Check out this appendix when it's time to put the finishing touches on your application or when you need to determine how to control the Access environment programmatically.

Appendix C includes a chapter on Data Access Objects (DAO) from the previous edition of this book. Although ActiveX Data Objects (ADO) provide the latest in data access technology, there are several conditions in Access where you'll still need to interact with DAO, even in this version. Therefore, we've included a slightly modified version of the older chapter for your reference. If you need to support existing applications that use DAO, or you want to work with forms' recordsets, you'll want to read this Appendix, in addition to Chapter 6 (ADO).

About the CD

The accompanying CD is a valuable companion to the book. It includes all the chapter databases discussed in the book, as well as several extra goodies that should make your Access development work more efficient. (For late-breaking information about the CD, including additional files and utilities, see README.TXT in the root directory of the CD.)

What's on the CD?

On the CD, we've included the chapter databases. We've also included white papers, freeware and shareware utilities, and demo versions of several commercial products on the CD. Most of these files have some restrictions on their use; please read the provided supporting documentation and respect the rights of the vendors who were kind enough to provide these files. For shareware programs, please register these programs with the vendor if you find them useful.

The CD files are described here:

- **Chapter Databases:** (\Chapter) Here's where you'll find the chapter databases containing all the examples from the text. Each chapter database includes all the objects discussed in the book so you can try out the examples yourself. These databases also include lots of reusable code and other objects you can copy and paste into your own applications. We've also included several other supporting files in the Chapter folder. If you want to install all the chapter samples, run the program **Chapter.exe** (a self-extracting ZIP file).

- **Converting from DAO to ADO:** (\Microsoft) This white paper from Microsoft should help with your explorations into converting from DAO to ADO. We didn't focus on this particular topic in the book, so if you're converting from DAO to ADO, you'll want to study this useful information.
- **BlueSky Software HTML Help Demo:** (\BlueSky) If you're creating professional applications, you'll need to create help files. BlueSky software provides a popular suite of programs making this arduous task as simple as possible. Check out their limited-time demo by running the **setup.exe** program. For more information, visit `http://www.blue-sky.com`.
- **FMS, Inc. Demonstrations:** (\FMS) Although FMS, Inc., the leading vendor of add-ins and tools for Microsoft Access, hadn't completed their Access 2000 tools at the time we went to print, we wanted to make sure you had a way to find them once their tools are finished. We've included, on the CD, demonstration versions of their Access 97 products, with links to the FMS, Inc. Web site. Run the **FMSDemos.exe** program to investigate the various products. Check their site for information on product availability for Access 2000. For more information, visit `http://www.fmsinc.com`.
- **Win32 API text file:** (\Win32api) From Microsoft. This is a free text file that contains all the declarations for the Win32 API. To use it, copy this text file to a new folder on your hard disk and open it with any text editor. (Notepad, in Windows 95/98, may not be able to handle this file—you'll need to use Wordpad, or some other text editor, in that case.) Note that when you copy this file to your hard drive, it will be read-only. Use Windows Explorer to change its attributes so that it's not read-only.
- **WinZip 7.0:** (\WinZip) From Nico Mak Computing, Inc. This is a shareware evaluation version of WinZip 7.0 SR-1. WinZip is a Windows 95/NT utility for zipping and unzipping files. It includes its own zipping and unzipping routines, but it also can be configured to call PKZip, LHA, and other archiving programs. Run the provided setup program (**winzip70.exe**) to install WinZip.

See the online help for more information on using WinZip and registering the product. For more information, visit `http://www.winzip.com`.

- **ClickBook 2.2 Demo:** (\BlueSquirrel\ClickBook) From Blue Squirrel Software. ClickBook is a Windows printing utility that makes it easy to print two, four, or more logical pages per single printed page. ClickBook also makes it easy to print double-sided booklets, brochures, and other double-sided printouts. Run the provided setup program (**Cbtrial.exe**) to install this program. See the online help for more information on using ClickBook. (The Trial Version of ClickBook prints a "Trial Version" header and footer on each page of your printouts. These headers and footers do not appear on any pages printed by the purchased version.) For more information, visit `http://www.bluesquirrel.com`.
- **Web Whacker 2000 Demo:** (\BlueSquirrel\WebWhacker) From Blue Squirrel Software. Web Whacker provides a complete facility for browsing Web pages offline. If you need to take the Web with you on the road when a dialup connection isn't convenient, you'll want to try out this demo. Run **ww2k.exe** to install the demo. For more information, visit `http://www.bluesquirrel.com`.

Using the Files from the CD

The CD that accompanies this book is organized into several folders (subdirectories) that contain the chapter databases and other files. See the README.TXT file in the root folder of the CD for any late-breaking details on the CD files.

Installing the Chapter Samples

The sample chapter databases are located in the \Chapter folder. The simplest way to get these files onto your hard drive so that you can use them is to run the Chapter.exe program (a self-extracting ZIP file) in that folder. This program will extract the files and place them where you request.

If you want to work with individual files, you can copy them from the \Chapter folder. To install and use the files, follow these instructions:

- Most chapters contain only one database, named CH*xx*.MDB. To use this database, simply copy the file to a new folder on your hard disk and open the database with Access 2000.

- For some chapters, we've included multiple database files, all of which normally begin with the name CH*xx*. In this case, copy all these files to a new folder on your hard disk and open the database with Access 2000. See the description of these files in the text of the chapter for more details.
- A few chapters have other nondatabase supporting files. These include Access add-ins (*xxx*.MDA) and Dynamic Link Libraries (*xxx*.DLL). See the descriptions of these files in the text of the chapters for more details.

WARNING

If you copy files manually, you'll need to also clear the read-only attribute for the files. (All files copied directly from a CD to a hard drive come over as read-only.) After you've copied the files, you'll need to select one or more files in Windows Explorer, right-click the selected files, choose Properties, and then clear the read-only flag manually. If you use the Chapter.exe program that we've provided, you won't need to do this.

How to Use This Book

While you may find it easiest to read the chapters in the order in which they appear in the book, it's not essential. One of our goals as we wrote the book was to make it possible for you to pick up and read any individual chapter without having to read through several other chapters first. Thus, the book is *not* a linear progression that starts with Chapter 1 and ends with Chapter 18. Instead, we have logically grouped together similar chapters, but otherwise (with a few exceptions) the chapters do not particularly build upon each other. To make it easy for you to jump from one chapter to another, we have included cross-references throughout the book.

While we've done a lot of the work for you, you'll get the most benefit from this book by putting the material to real use. Take the examples and generic routines found in the book and expand on them. Add and subtract from them as you incorporate them into your applications. Experiment and enjoy!

Tell Us Who You Are

In order to make it easy for us to contact you with information about updates to the book and other useful information about Access development, we've set up a Web site you can visit: `http://www.developershandbook.com`. At this Web site, you can fill out a form with information about yourself so we can let you know about changes, errata, enhanced examples, and other updates. Be the first person on your block to know about updates to *Access 2000 Developers Handbook*: visit, and sign up now.

CHAPTER

ONE

1

What's New in Access 2000

- Learning the history of Access changes
- Understanding what's new in Access 2000
- Understanding what's new in Jet 4
- Learning about Microsoft Office Developer

Chances are, if you're reading this book, you've already decided that Microsoft Access 2000 (we'll refer to it hereafter as *Access 2000*) is a worthy platform for your development endeavors. Chances are, you're right. Microsoft has created a serious, full-featured, and powerful development environment for creating database applications on single-user and networked personal computers.

A Brief Access History

Access 1.0 really opened the eyes of many database developers. It was one of the first relational database products available for the Windows 3 platform, and it was certainly the first to fill the needs of many developers, both corporate and independent. Besides its ease of use in getting started, Access 1.0 made it very easy to create simple applications. It did have some limitations when developers got past a certain point in their applications, and it had a severe limitation in that databases couldn't be larger than 128MB. Access 1.1 fixed that limitation, expanding the maximum database size to 1GB, and fixed some other limitations as well. Still, many professional features were lacking. Programmers used to Visual Basic's nearly complete flexibility were stymied by Access' inability to change control and form properties at runtime, for example. On the other hand, there was no simpler way to get data in and out of forms than Access, so developers worked around Access 1.1's limitations.

Access 2 offered great gains for developers. Although it also provided numerous improvements for end users, the greatest leap from 1.1 came in the improvements for the developer community. For the professional programmer, Access 2 added features in almost every area of the product, including:

- A vastly extended object and event model
- Runtime access to most form and report properties
- Event procedures
- Cascading updates and deletes for referential integrity
- Engine-level enforcement of rules
- New query types—union, data definition, and pass-through queries—and support for subqueries

- Rushmore query optimization
- Data access objects (DAO), a consistent object model for the manipulation of Jet engine data
- OLE automation client support
- Programmable security
- Support for 16-bit OLE custom controls

Access 95 was a major undertaking. Both Access and Jet were ported from 16-bit Windows to 32-bit Windows. The Access Basic language and integrated development environment (IDE) were replaced with Visual Basic for Applications (VBA) and its enhanced IDE. Numerous other improvements were added, including:

- Support for multi-instance forms
- The addition of the KeyPreview property for forms
- Support for multiselect list boxes and improved combo box performance
- New, lightweight image control
- The ability to detect and alter the type of a control with the ControlType property
- The addition of a built-in query-by-form feature, Filter by Form
- Support for form class modules with public functions (methods) and Let, Get, and Set property procedures
- The ability, with the NoData event of reports, to choose not to print a report if there were no records
- The addition of the RepeatSection property, which lets you repeat a group header at the top of continuation pages
- Replacement of counter fields with the more flexible AutoNumber data type
- The addition of new With…End With and For Each…Next VBA constructs
- The addition of the line continuation character
- Support for named parameters, optional parameters, and parameter arrays
- Support for new Date, Boolean, and Byte data types

- Improvements to the editor and debugger, including Watch variables and color-coded syntax
- Support for replication
- Several concurrency and performance improvements to the Jet 3 Engine
- OLE automation server support
- The addition of startup properties that let you disable access to the database window and change the application's title bar and icon

Access 97 was a minor release in comparison to Access 95. Still, there were lots of new features and improvements to existing features. These changes included:

- A new Hyperlink data type.
- The Publish to the Web Wizard made it easy to publish static or dynamic data on the Internet or a corporate intranet.
- Lightweight forms loaded faster because they didn't have any code behind them.
- The native tab control made it easy to create a tabbed dialog.
- Menus and toolbars were completely programmable using the CommandBars collection and CommandBar object.
- New RecordSetType, FailOnError, and MaxRecords query properties.
- Support for class modules.
- IntelliSense support made writing code much easier. When typing VBA code, the editor displays a list of objects, methods, and properties from which to choose. The VBA editor also displays a list of parameters for built-in and user-defined procedures.
- Support for drag-and-drop meant you could pick up a snippet of code and move it to a new location with the mouse.
- Several debugging enhancements, including the new Locals pane and Data Tips.
- Support for partial replicas and Internet replication.
- Supports for a new client-server connection mode called ODBCDirect.
- Support for the special MDE format that removes all VBA source code.

Access 2000—the Best Access Ever

Access 2000 is a major release. The number of significant changes is staggering. Of those, the most important changes can be grouped into five major areas:

- VBA
- Forms and reports
- Data access
- Internet/intranet
- Other improvements

In the next few sections, we list the most significant changes, grouped by major area.

Access 2000 VBA

The Access module editor has been replaced with the VBA 6 editor. If you're a veteran Access developer, you may find the new editing environment a bit disorienting at first, but with time you'll grow to appreciate the benefits of the new VBA editor. In addition, Access' version of the VBA language, VBA 6, which now brings Access' VBA up to par with Visual Basic 6, has several welcome additions. These changes are summarized here:

- The Access 2000 VBA editor is the same VBA editor that is built into the other Microsoft Office applications as well as third-party VBA hosts.
- You can password-protect all of the VBA code in global modules and the modules behind forms and reports with a single password. VBA code is no longer protected by user-level (workgroup) security.
- The VBA editor has a programmable object model and supports COM add-ins. You can download, purchase, or build add-ins to help you write, analyze, or format your VBA code.
- VBA has several new functions, including StrRev, MonthName, Split, Join, and Replace, to name a few.
- You can use Debug.Assert to place assertions in your code.
- Access supports the AddressOf operator, and class modules support the new Implements keyword.

New class module features are discussed in Chapter 3. Other new language features are scattered about the book. Building add-ins is discussed in Chapter 18.

Access 2000 Forms and Reports

Not a whole lot has changed in Access 2000 forms and reports. The few items that have changed are highlighted here:

- Forms and reports support the grouping and ungrouping of controls.
- Controls that display text allow for a user-specified border around the text, allowing you to move text around within the control.
- You can apply conditional formatting rules to the data in text and combo boxes.
- You can set a form's recordset to point to an arbitrary DAO or ADO recordset. That is, you can now open a recordset and assign it to a form's Recordset property. This means you can finally bind a form to something besides a table, query, or SQL string.
- Because you can assign a recordset to a form, you can wrap transactions around form updates.

New form and report features are discussed in Chapters 7, 8, and 9. In addition, Access 2000's new data access pages allow you to create bound data pages for display within a browser, duplicating some of the same functionality of forms and reports. See the section "Access 2000 Internet and Intranet Features" later in this chapter for more details.

Access 2000 Data Access

Data access in Access 2000 has changed in several big ways. Access 2000 comes with a new database engine option, a new data access model, and a new database format. These and other changes are summarized below:

- Although the Jet engine remains the default database engine, Access also works with the Microsoft Data Engine (MSDE), a limited-connection version of SQL Server 7.
- In addition to being able to create standard Access MDB database files, you can now create Access Data Projects (ADP) files. An ADP file is a "dataless"

database in which you can store forms, reports, macros, and modules, linking to data that is stored in a SQL Server or MSDE database. This means that you can use the same familiar Access user interface you know and love as a lean and mean front-end to SQL Server data!

- Access integrates tightly with ActiveX Data Objects (ADO), Microsoft's preferred data access model. Existing DAO code works just fine, but you'll want to start writing data access code using ADO, because it provides greater flexibility and capabilities.
- The Jet engine stores character data in Unicode. This makes changing languages simpler but also means that strings will now take up twice as much space. Because of this, the maximum size of databases has increased from 1GB to 2GB. In addition, Jet 4 optionally compresses text and memo fields.
- Jet supports row-level locking in addition to the older page-level locking! This means that pessimistic locking is now a much more viable option.
- Jet SQL supports a number of new ANSI-92 SQL extensions. You can take advantage of the new SQL-92 extensions when using ADO and the Jet OLE DB provider.
- Jet provides a user list feature that allows you to determine the machine and user name of all users currently logged into a database. You can use Jet's connection control feature to prevent new users from logging in to a database; this might be useful, for example, if you wished to take a database offline for backup.
- Replication has been improved on several fronts. Previously, synchronizations could produce both conflicts and errors. With Jet 4, everything's a conflict, which makes resolution simpler. In addition, conflict resolution now occurs at the column level rather than the table level. Thus, if different users change different fields within the same record, the record is no longer flagged as a conflict. Jet 4 defines three levels of replica "visibility," which now allows you to create replica hierarchies within a replica set. You can also create special replicas where records cannot be deleted. In addition, Jet supports bidirectional replication with SQL Server.
- Microsoft provides two new object models in the ADO family for working with schemas and replication: ADOX and JRO. You use ADOX to investigate and modify the schema of Access and other ADO providers. JRO, on the other hand, is a Jet-specific object model you can use to compact and repair databases and work with Jet 4's replication features.

ADO and ADOX are discussed in Chapter 6. The new ANSI-92 SQL extensions are discussed in Chapter 5. Multiuser, client-server, and replication features are discussed in *Access 2000 Developer's Handbook, Volume II.*

Access 2000 Internet and Intranet Features

This version of Access replaces the Publish to the Web Wizard with data access pages. A data access page is a Web page that you can use to view or edit data from an Access, MSDE, or SQL Server database using Internet Explorer 5 (or greater). Some facts about data access pages:

- Data access pages take advantage of the client-side data binding capabilities built into IE 5.
- The data in a data access page is embedded in the HTML page using eXtensible Markup Language (XML).
- You can use data access pages from within an MDB database, an ADP project, or IE5.
- Access includes a data access page designer that you can use to design pages.
- You can attach scripting code, written in either VBScript or JavaScript, to your pages. Microsoft has added the Microsoft Script Editor (MSE), a feature-rich script editor based on the Visual InterDev page editor, to Access.
- Data access pages can be created from scratch or can be based on existing Web pages. Access also includes a Wizard that makes it easy to create a page in a hurry.
- You can include the Office Web Components within your pages. The Office Web components are ActiveX controls that componentize features from Microsoft Excel. There are spreadsheet, pivot table, and chart components.
- While you can use data access pages for browsing and editing records, you can also use them for reporting, thanks to built-in grouping features.

Data access pages and Office Web Components are discussed in detail in *Access 2000 Developer's Handbook, Volume II.*

Other Access 2000 Improvements

Additional changes have been made to the product that don't fit neatly into any of the above categories, including the following:

- Object name changes have always been troubling to Access users and developers. That is, until now. Access 2000's Name AutoCorrect feature automatically fixes up object name changes in dependent forms, reports, and queries. There are certain limitations—for example, Name AutoCorrect doesn't correct VBA code references, nor does it work in ADP files or replicated databases—but it can save you a lot of time when you rename objects.
- In the past, you could download an add-in for Access 97 that printed relationships. The print relationships feature is now built into Access 2000.
- The find and replace dialogs are now nonmodal dialogs.
- Access was never big on backward compatibility. Access 2000, however, bucks this trend: select Tools ➢ Database Utilities ➢ Convert Database ➢ To Prior Access Database Versions to save an Access 2000 database to the older Access 97 format.
- Access 2000 lets you compact and repair a database in one step. Plus, there's an option to automatically compact databases when you close them.

Many of these miscellaneous changes are discussed throughout the book.

Microsoft Office Developer Features

Many professional Access developers will want to purchase Microsoft Office Developer (MOD). This version of Microsoft Office includes a copy of Microsoft Office 2000 Premium (the version that comes with everything in Office Professional plus FrontPage, Publisher, and PhotoDraw), plus the following developer tools:

- A runtime distribution license for applications created with Access and either the Jet engine or MSDE
- The COM Add-In designer, a VBA tool for creating add-ins that work across Office 2000

- A licensed copy of the Visual Source Safe (VSS) 6 source code control utility, not just the hooks into VSS that came with Office 97's ODE
- The Package and Deployment Wizard, Office 2000's successor to the Access Setup Wizard
- A number of ActiveX controls, including the ADO Data control, the FlexGrid control, and the Data Repeater control
- Several useful add-ins, including the VBA Code Librarian, the VBA String Editor, the VBA Error Handler, and the VBA Code Commenter
- The Windows API Viewer, a utility for viewing and cutting and pasting Windows API Declare statements, constants, and types
- Microsoft Replication Manager, an updated version of Microsoft's replication administration tool
- Printed copies of the *Microsoft Office 2000 Visual Basic Programmer's Guide* and the *Microsoft Office 2000 Object Model Guide*
- An HTML help authoring tool called the HTML Help Workshop
- The Microsoft Agent Software Development Kit

TIP

If you've already purchased a copy of Microsoft Office, you can get the developer tools that come with MOD by purchasing the Microsoft Office 2000 Developer Tools.

Building COM add-ins is discussed in Chapter 18. Programming the Windows API is discussed in Chapter 16. Source code control, Replication Manager, and the Package and Deployment Wizard are discussed in *Access 2000 Developer's Handbook, Volume II.*

Summary

Access is the best-selling desktop database program on the market today. It has the right mix of features for both users and developers. The changes Microsoft has made to the product for this release make this version the best Access ever.

CHAPTER

TWO

2

The Access Event Model

- Working with objects and events
- Reacting to form and control events
- Handling data events
- Determining the sequence of events

Like many applications that shield you from the details of working with Windows, one of the largest hurdles facing beginning Access developers is finding out how to make something happen. In the golden age of computing before Windows, making things happen was simple. You created a main procedure in your programs that performed tasks in sequential order. When your application needed input from the user, it stopped and waited for a response before continuing. These processes are much more complex today. To create an application in Access, you must write program code that responds to events. An *event* is a change in state that occurs when a user, a program, or the computer does something. For example, an event occurs when you move the mouse, click a button with the mouse, or press a key on the keyboard. An event also occurs when another application attempts to open a form using Automation, or when the time-counting mechanism built into your computer gets to the next increment in time. Once an event occurs and your program code responds to it, Access (or any Windows application, for that matter) enters an idle state and waits for another event to occur.

The Access programming model uses an event-driven programming paradigm. In *event-driven programming,* the programming language operates in response to events that occur, usually in response to some user action. A relatively simple action by the user—moving the mouse over the form and clicking several controls, for example—causes Access to trigger many events, including the MouseMove, MouseDown, MouseUp, GotFocus, LostFocus, Enter, Exit, and Click events. At any of these events, you can step in and perform some action. The code that is activated when an event occurs is called an *event handler.*

NOTE

If you look in the property sheet listing the event properties for an object, you'll see names such as On Mouse Move and On Click. These names (with the spaces removed) are the names of the event properties. The event names themselves do not include the *On*. We'll refer to the MouseMove event (which corresponds to the OnMouseMove event property) or the Click event (which corresponds to the OnClick event property).

So Many Events, So Little Time

The more events Access generates when something happens, the finer the control you have, because you can take control at any point where an event is generated. On the other hand, it takes more work to react to lower-level events than to higher-level events. For example, when you type characters into a text box and press the Tab key, the KeyDown, KeyUp, KeyPress, Change, BeforeUpdate, AfterUpdate, Exit, and LostFocus events all occur. How do you know which event to react to for any specific action you want to take? If you wanted to be able to open a pop-up form when the user pressed and released the Ctrl key twice, you would need to make use of the KeyDown and KeyUp events. If all you cared about were running a validation procedure when the user entered a new value into the text box, you'd be wasting your time working at this low keystroke-by-keystroke level. Instead, you'd likely want to use the BeforeUpdate event, which validates the entire value once the user is finished entering it.

For most of your Access programming, you'll deal with the higher-level events (BeforeUpdate, AfterUpdate), but it's nice to know that the lower-level events (KeyDown, KeyUp, KeyPress, Change, Exit, and LostFocus) are there when you need them.

Hooking In

Events happen continuously in Access, but they're not terribly interesting unless you can react to them. Access provides several ways for you to hook into events and react to them. One option is to place a reference to an event handler in the property sheet of an object. (We'll get to the second option in a moment.) In Table 2.1, you'll find the four kinds of event handlers that you can create through an object's properties sheet, an example of calling each of them, and a description of when you should use them.

TABLE 2.1: Event Handlers

Event Handler	Example	When to Use It
Macro	McrRunMe	In simple prototypes or single-user applications that don't need to be bulletproofed.
Event procedure	[Event Procedure]	When you want VBA code stored in the code module associated with a form or report or when you need parameters that are passed only to event procedures.

Continued on next page

TABLE 2.1 CONTINUED: Event Handlers

Event Handler	Example	When to Use It
Global module function	=GenericFunction	When you want to call generic code or when you want the ability to copy a control to another form or report and want its event handler reference to go with it. You can call only functions (not subroutines) directly from the property sheet.
Form module function	=LocalModuleFunction	When you need to call the same event handler from multiple events or objects and you wish the code to be encapsulated within the form. Again, you can call only functions from here.

The last three event handlers in Table 2.1 use Visual Basic for Applications (VBA) code to respond to events as opposed to the first example, which uses an Access macro. While macros are useful for quickly prototyping applications, we don't recommend their use in professional applications, because macros:

- Can't recover from errors
- Can't easily be used for looping
- Are difficult to debug
- Can't be used to step through recordsets
- Can't be used in transaction processing
- Can't pass parameters
- Can't be used to call DLLs
- Can be halted by users with Ctrl+Break (and this can never be turned off)

The bottom line is that you should program using VBA code for all your Access application development, except when you only need to create a quick-and-dirty prototype or you wish to create a simple application that only you will use. (See Chapter 11 for more information on using macros in applications and for situations in which you don't have any choice about using them.)

Which type of VBA event handler you use depends on your coding style. Many developers use all three or some combination of them. For example, you might create an event procedure that calls a function stored in a global module.

Hooking and Triggering Your Own Events

Most Access developers rely solely on the events exposed by Access itself, but with Access 2000 and VBA 6, you can define and raise your own events. Why would you want to do this? It often simplifies programming tasks by eliminating the need to maintain complex procedure call chains within subroutines. Instead, you raise a useful event in your subroutine and then VBA executes any other part of your program that happens to be "listening" for the event. The question of what a useful event is, and how to define it, is covered in detail in Chapter 3, "Using VBA Class Modules."

A related topic is hooking into events. When you create an Access form and add a few controls, Access does the event "wiring" for you. You just add code to event procedures in the form's module. You can also wire VBA to any object that triggers events using the WithEvents keyword. This is how you react to your own custom events as well as events exposed by other software components through Automation. Using WithEvents with Automation is covered in Chapter 12, "Access as an Automation Client."

NOTE

Report events are not discussed in this chapter. You can find a detailed discussion of these in Chapter 9.

An Alternative to Event Handlers: Hyperlinks

Label, command button, and image controls have a set of properties that allow you to establish hyperlinks to an Internet uniform resource locator (URL), a Microsoft Office document, or an Access object:

- HyperlinkAddress
- HyperlinkSubAddress

Using these properties, you can create a control that, when clicked, jumps to your corporate home page or to a bookmark in a Word document. In addition, you can use these properties to open an Access form or report without using an event handler.

Continued on next page

For example, to create a hyperlink that opens the frmCustomer form in the current database, you would leave the HyperlinkAddress property blank and set the HyperlinkSubAddress to:

```
Form frmCustomer
```

You can also use the hyperlink property Builder by clicking the Builder button (the one with the ellipsis that appears when you highlight a property) in the property window.

Thus, you can use hyperlinks to create codeless switchboard-type forms. This is especially attractive because Access supports something called *lightweight forms*, meaning forms without any code. The advantage of using lightweight forms is that they load and display more quickly than forms containing modules.

You can view or change a form's lightweight status by manipulating the HasModule property of the form. If you set a form's HasModule to No and it has existing code, that code will be deleted when you save the form, so be careful when manipulating this property.

If you attach both a hyperlink and a Click (or MouseUp) event procedure to a control, the processes are executed asynchronously, with the hyperlink jump occurring prior to the event procedure's execution.

Hyperlinks and other Internet/intranet features are discussed in more detail in Chapter 11, "Creating Data Pages," in *Access 2000 Developers Handbook, Volume II*.

Form Events

Although Access supports events in both forms and reports, you will use form events most often. Three types of events can occur for a form:

- Form events
- Section events
- Control events

Form events are those events associated with the form itself. Some form events occur for all forms (for example, Open and Close); others (GotFocus, LostFocus) occur only if the form contains no controls. Still others come into play only in certain situations (for example, the Timer event occurs only when the TimerInterval property is set to a nonzero value; the KeyDown, KeyUp, and KeyPress events occur only when the KeyPreview property is set to True). Table 2.2 provides a description of each of the form events. (For more information on using Form, Section, and Control events, see Chapters 7 and 8.)

TABLE 2.2: Form Events

Event	Occurs	Can Be Canceled?
Current	When a form containing data is first opened and when you move to a different record.	No
BeforeInsert	When a new record is first dirtied.	Yes
AfterInsert	After the new record is saved.	No
Dirty	Just before the current record is changed by the user in any way.	Yes
BeforeUpdate	Just before edits to a record are saved.	Yes
AfterUpdate	Just after edits to a record are saved.	No
Delete	Just before each record is deleted. For multirecord deletes, occurs once per record.	Yes
BeforeDelConfirm	After all records are deleted, but before the confirmation dialog.	Yes
AfterDelConfirm	After the record is deleted or the deletion is canceled.	No
Open	As the form is opened but before data or controls are loaded.	Yes
Load	After the form is loaded and the record source is opened.	No
Resize	As the form is resized. Also occurs during form opening.	No
Unload	When the form close is initiated, but before the form is actually closed.	Yes
Close	When the form is closed, at the moment the form vanishes.	No
Activate	When the form receives focus.	No
Deactivate	When the form loses focus.	No
GotFocus	After the form gets focus. Occurs only when the form contains no controls that can receive the focus.	No
LostFocus	Before the form loses focus. Occurs only when the form contains no controls that can receive the focus.	No
Click	When you click on the form's record selector or dead space* on a form.	No

Continued on next page

TABLE 2.2 CONTINUED: Form Events

Event	Occurs	Can Be Canceled?
DblClick	When you double-click on the form's record selector or dead space* on a form.	Yes**
MouseDown	When you click either mouse button on the form's record selector or dead space* on a form, but before the Click event fires.	No
MouseMove	When you move the mouse over the form's record selector or dead space* on a form.	No
MouseUp	When you release either mouse button on the form's record selector or dead space* on a form, but before the Click event fires.	No
KeyDown	If KeyPreview is True, whenever you depress a key anywhere on the form. (If KeyPreview is False, KeyDown occurs only when you depress a key while the record selector is selected.)	Yes***
KeyUp	If KeyPreview is True, whenever you release a key. (If KeyPreview is False, KeyUp occurs only when you release a key while the record selector is selected.)	No
KeyPress	If KeyPreview is True, whenever you depress and release an ANSI key. (If KeyPreview is False, KeyPress occurs only when you depress and release a key while the record selector is selected.)	Yes†
Error	Occurs when the form causes a runtime data error. This includes validation and datatype errors, as well as most locking errors.	No††
Filter	When you choose to edit a filter using either Records ➢ Filter ➢ Filter By Form or Records ➢ Filter ➢ Advanced Filter/Sort.	Yes
ApplyFilter	When you apply a filter.	Yes
Timer	When the timer interval has elapsed. You set the interval using the TimerInterval property.	No

*Space that occurs when the form is sized larger than the height of its combined sections.

**Canceling this event cancels the second Click event.

***The Keystroke (and KeyPress, Change, and KeyUp events) can be canceled by setting KeyCode to 0.

†The Keystroke (and Change event) can be canceled by setting KeyAscii to 0.

††Although you can't cancel Error, you can suppress the display of Access' error message.

Each section on a form also has events, which are described in Table 2.3. It's unlikely that section events will play a major role in your applications, however, because these events are rather limited, essentially revolving around mouse movement and clicking on the background of sections.

TABLE 2.3: Section Events

Event	Occurs	Can Be Canceled?
Click	When you click on the background of a section	No
DblClick	When you double-click on the background of a section	Yes*
MouseDown	When you click either mouse button on the background of a section, but before the Click event fires	No
MouseMove	When you move the mouse over the background of a section	No
MouseUp	When you release either mouse button on the background of a section, but before the Click event fires	No

*Canceling this event cancels the second Click event

Each type of Access control has a different set of events. Table 2.4 describes the events supported by each type of control. Table 2.5 describes when each control event occurs and whether it can be canceled.

TABLE 2.4: Controls* and Events

Event	Label**, Image, or Rectangle	Text Box	Option Group	Toggle Button, Option Button, or Check Box	Combo Box	List Box	Command Button	Object Frame	Subform
BeforeUpdate		√	√	√***	√	√		√†	
AfterUpdate		√	√	√	√	√		√†	
Updated								√	
Change		√			√				
NotInList					√				
Enter		√	√	√***	√	√	√	√	√
Exit		√	√	√**	√	√	√	√	√

Continued on next page

TABLE 2.4 CONTINUED: Controls* and Events

Event	Label**, Image, or Rectangle	Text Box	Option Group	Toggle Button, Option Button, or Check Box	Combo Box	List Box	Command Button	Object Frame	Subform
GotFocus		√		√	√	√	√		
LostFocus		√		√	√	√	√		
Click	√	√	√	√***	√	√	√	√	
DblClick	√	√	√	√***	√	√	√	√	
MouseDown	√	√	√	√***	√	√	√	√	
MouseMove	√	√	√	√***	√	√	√	√	
MouseUp	√	√	√	√***	√	√	√	√	
KeyDown		√		√	√	√		√†	
KeyUp		√		√	√	√		√†	
KeyPress		√		√	√	√		√†	

*The following controls do not have any events: line and page break.

**Listed events are for freestanding labels. Labels attached to other controls have no events.

***Only independent (when not a member of an option group) toggle button, option button, and check box controls have this event.

†Occurs only for bound object frames.

TABLE 2.5: Control Events

Event	Occurs	Can Be Canceled?
BeforeUpdate	When you commit changes to a control by moving to another control or saving a record.	Yes
AfterUpdate	After changes have been saved to a control.	No
Updated	When you insert or update a source OLE object. May fire multiple times.	No
Change	When data in control changes. May occur because a character was typed or a value was selected from the list.	No
NotInList	When you enter a value in a combo box that is not in the list. Fires only when LimitToList is set to Yes.	No*

Continued on next page

TABLE 2.5 CONTINUED: Control Events

Event	Occurs	Can Be Canceled?
Enter	When you have moved to a control that can receive the focus, but just prior to the control receiving the focus.	No
Exit	When you have moved away from a control, but just prior to the control losing focus.	Yes
GotFocus	After a control gets focus.	No
LostFocus	Before a control loses focus.	No
Click	When you click a control.	No
DblClick	When you double-click a control.	Yes**
MouseDown	When you depress either mouse button on a control, but before the Click event fires.	No
MouseMove	When you move the mouse over a control.	No
MouseUp	When you release either mouse button on a control, but before the Click event fires.	No
KeyDown	When you depress a key while a control has focus.	Yes***
KeyUp	When you release a key while a control has focus.	No
KeyPress	When you depress and release an ANSI key while a control has focus.	Yes†

*While you can't cancel NotInList, you can suppress the display of Access' error message.

**Canceling this event cancels the second Click event.

***The keystroke (and KeyPress, Change, and KeyUp events) can be canceled by setting KeyCode to 0.

†The keystroke (and Change event) can be canceled by setting KeyAscii to 0.

Cancelable Events

Tables 2.2 and 2.5 list events that can be canceled. What does this mean and why is it important? First off, to cancel an event means to suppress the natural result of that event. For instance, a form's Open event can be canceled, thus stopping the form from opening. Likewise, the BeforeUpdate event of a control can be canceled, thus preventing newly modified data in the control from being committed.

In many applications, you will have occasion to cancel events. A control's BeforeUpdate event is a good example. You might want, for instance, to perform some type of complex data validation (something a simple validation rule couldn't handle) and cancel the update if the validation fails.

Any event that can be canceled will define a parameter named Cancel in the associated event procedure. For instance, here's the event procedure associated with a form's Open event:

```
Private Sub Form_Open(Cancel As Integer)

End Sub
```

To cancel the event, simply set the Cancel parameter to True (or any nonzero value) at any point during the procedure. When the procedure terminates, the event will be canceled.

NOTE

Just changing the parameter value does not automatically terminate the event procedure and cancel the event. Any code following a change in the parameter will still run.

The Sequence of Events

Because there are so many events on Access forms, you may find it difficult to determine the event to use for a particular situation. In addition, you may need to know the exact sequence of events for a particular scenario—for example, the opening of a form. In the sections that follow, we describe which events occur for various scenarios. While this is not meant to be comprehensive, we have tried to include the most commonly encountered situations.

Logging Events

One way to determine which events occur, and in what order, is to create a mechanism that will log events as they occur. In the CH02.MDB database, you will find an event-logging facility made up of two forms: frmLog and frmEventTest. These forms allow you to test various scenarios and see the resulting event sequence (see Figure 2.1). To use this facility, load frmLog and adjust the level of event detail by checking and unchecking the FilterEvents check boxes. Then, load frmEventTest and try different actions on the form and its controls, noting the resulting events in frmLog. The other form, frmEventTest, contains several types of controls, including a text box, label, subform, list box, combo box, option group, and others. You can add additional controls if you like.

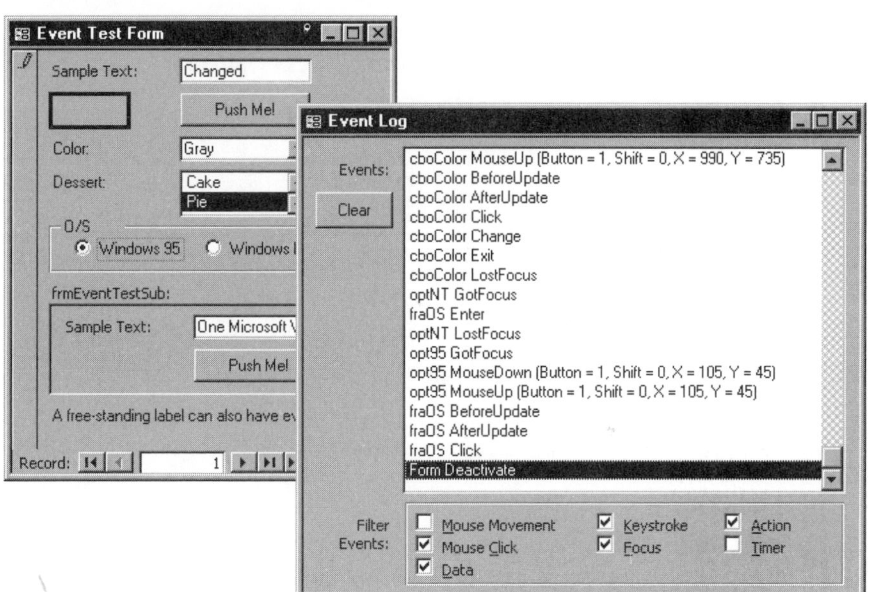

FIGURE 2.1:

Every event that occurs while frmEventTest is active gets logged to frmLog.

How the Event-Logging Facility Works

Many of the components of the event-logging facility are based on topics discussed in later chapters. For this reason, we'll include only a brief overview of how this facility works in this chapter. If you want more information on the inner workings, just dig into the code—it's all there in the sample database.

Figure 2.2 shows frmEventTest in Design view. Notice that we've added event procedures for every event.

FIGURE 2.2:

Event procedures are attached to every event on frmEventTest.

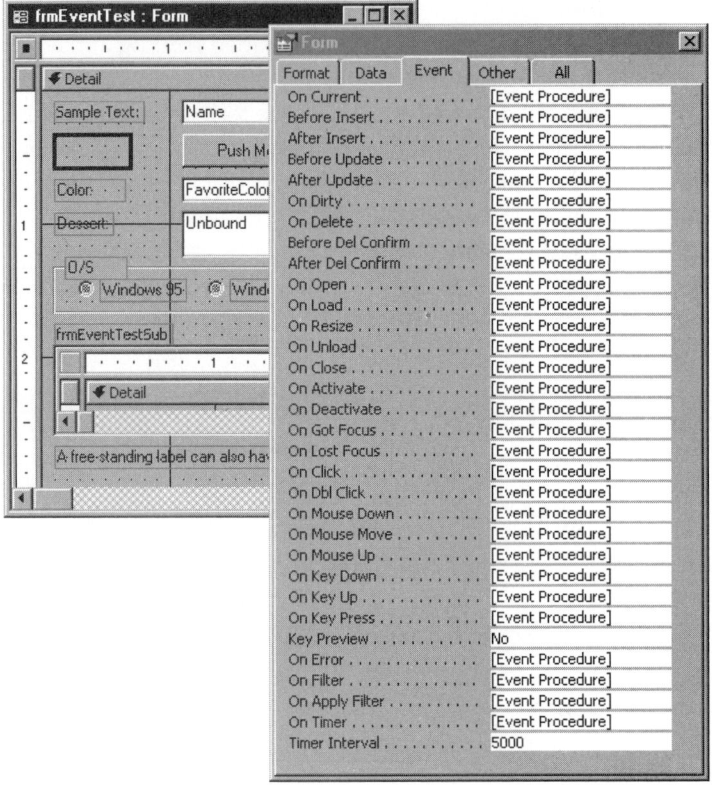

For example, frmEventTest contains this event procedure attached to the Click event of txtSample:

```
Private Sub txtSample_Click()
    adhLogEvent "txtSample Click", conEventMouseClick
End Sub
```

Each event procedure calls the adhLogEvent subroutine found in the basEvents module of the sample database. This procedure serves as the interface between the event-generating form (frmEventTest) and the event-logging form (frmLog). It has two parameters: strEvent, a brief description of the event; and intEventType, the type of event. adhLogEvent calls the AddItem method of frmLog.

The AddItem method of frmLog verifies (by checking the status of the check boxes) that the event passed to it needs to be logged. If the event needs to be logged, AddItem places the event text in a module-level variable and requeries the list box. Finally, the item is added to the list box by a list-filling function attached to the lstLog list box.

NOTE For information on how list-filling functions work and how to create one, see "Filling a List or Combo Box Programmatically" in Chapter 7, "Controlling Controls."

General Form Actions

The following sections describe the sequence of events that occurs when you open and close a form or perform other general form actions.

Opening a Form

When you open a form, the following events occur:

```
Open → Load → Resize → Activate → GotFocus → Current →
1st Control (in tab order) Enter →
1st Control (in tab order) GotFocus
```

You can cancel the opening of the form from the Open event.

If the form contains a subform, the following events for the subform occur *prior* to the main form's Open event:

```
Open → Load → Resize → Current →
1st Control Enter
```

WARNING Note that even though the subform's events are processed in the same manner as the main form's events, the first control in the subform's tab does not trigger a GotFocus event until the subform itself gets the focus—even though it does trigger an Enter event. Beware of this behavior if you use the same form object as a standalone form and a subform.

During the Open event you don't normally have access to the values in the form's controls. If you need the control values, you should use the Load event instead, which occurs immediately after the Open event. But if you can't wait, you can also force the Load event to occur within the Open event procedure by using the following statement in the Open event procedure:

```
Me.SetFocus
```

Closing a Form

When you close a form, the following events occur:

```
Active Control Exit → Active Control LostFocus →
Unload → Deactivate → Close
```

This sequence assumes that any data on the form has already been saved. See the section "Data-Related Actions" later in this chapter for details on data-related events.

If the form contains a subform and one of the *main form's* controls has the focus, the following events occur instead:

```
Active Subform Control Exit → Active Subform Control LostFocus →
Active Form Control Exit →
Active Form Control LostFocus →
Form Unload → Form Deactivate → Form Close →
Subform Unload → Subform Close
```

NOTE If the subform never gets the focus before the main form is closed, then Access will *not* trigger the active subform control's LostFocus event.

If the form contains a subform and one of the *subform's* controls has the focus, the following events occur (notice the addition of the main form's Exit event) instead:

```
Active Subform Control Exit → Active Subform Control LostFocus →
Form Exit → Form Unload → Form Deactivate → Form Close →
Subform Unload → Subform Close
```

Form Resizing Actions

When you minimize a form, the following events occur:

```
Resize → Active Control LostFocus → Deactivate
```

When you restore a minimized form, the following events occur:

```
Activate → Last Active Control GotFocus → Resize
```

When you maximize a form or restore a maximized form, the following form event occurs:

```
Resize
```

When you resize a form, one or more Resize events will fire. The number will be affected by the speed and area of the resize. If the change in area is large or the resize occurs slowly, more resize events will occur than if the change in area is small or the resize occurs quickly.

Changing the Visibility of a Form

When you hide a form, the following events occur:

```
Active Control LostFocus → Deactivate
```

When you unhide a form, the following events occur:

```
Activate → Last Active Control GotFocus
```

Shifting Focus to Another Form

When you shift the focus from one form to another by clicking the title bar of the second form, the following events occur:

```
Active Control on 1st Form LostFocus → 1st Form Deactivate →
2nd Form Activate → Active Control on 2nd Form GotFocus
```

Keyboard Actions

Keyboard event procedures are extremely versatile, providing you with information on exactly which keys the user is using. The event procedures for the three keyboard events are listed below and explained in the following sections.

```
Private Sub Object_KeyDown(KeyCode As Integer, Shift As Integer)

End Sub

Private Sub Object_KeyPress(KeyAscii As Integer)

End Sub

Private Sub Object_KeyUp(KeyCode As Integer, Shift As Integer)

End Sub
```

When you type a character into a control that accepts keystrokes (see Table 2.4), the following events occur:

```
KeyDown → KeyPress → Change → KeyUp
```

When you press a keystroke that causes the focus to move to another control (for example, Tab, BackTab, or Enter), some of the keyboard events will be received by one control and others will be received by the second control:

```
1st Control KeyDown → 1st Control Exit →
1st Control LostFocus → 2nd Control Enter → 2nd Control GotFocus →
2nd Control KeyPress → 2nd Control KeyUp
```

If the first control were updated prior to the navigation keystroke, the first control's BeforeUpdate and AfterUpdate events would also fire between the KeyDown and Exit events.

Using the KeyPreview Property

The form object doesn't normally receive keystrokes unless you have set the KeyPreview property of the form to Yes. When this is set, the form receives all keystrokes typed into controls on the form *prior* to the controls' receiving those same keystrokes. By canceling the keystroke at the form event level (see the next section), you can prevent the controls on the form from also processing the event.

Canceling Keystrokes

If you set the KeyCode parameter passed to your KeyDown event procedure to 0, Access cancels the remaining events, and the keystroke will never appear on the screen.

If you set the KeyAscii parameter passed to your KeyPress event procedure to 0, Access cancels the Change event, and the keystroke will never appear on the screen.

If KeyPreview has been set to Yes and you set KeyCode for the form to 0 in an event procedure attached to the form's KeyDown event, the active control's KeyDown event will receive a KeyCode of 0, and all other keyboard events will be canceled. Similarly, if KeyPreview has been set to Yes and you set KeyAscii for the form to 0 in an event procedure attached to the form's KeyPress event, the control's KeyPress event will receive a KeyAscii of 0, and the control's Change event will be canceled.

Using the KeyCode and Shift Parameters

You can use the KeyDown and KeyUp events to trap all keystrokes, including special non-ANSI keys, such as the function keys and the Ctrl, Shift, and Alt keys. You can determine which keys the user pressed by investigating the KeyCode and Shift parameters that Access passes to your KeyDown and KeyUp event procedures. Microsoft has defined KeyCode constants you can use when checking for various keys. There are constants for alphanumeric keys (for example, vbKeyA and vbKey1) and special keys (for example, vbKeyBack, vbKeySpace, vbNumPad0, and vbKeyF10). You can find these constants and others listed in the KeyCodeConstants class of the VBA type library using the Object Browser (View ➢ Object Browser) or in the Help file by searching on constants, keycode.

If you wish to check whether the Shift, Alt, or Ctrl key has been pressed in combination with another key, use the Shift parameter, applying the appropriate bit mask (acShiftMask, acCtrlMask, or acAltMask) to the passed parameter. For example, the following code sets three Boolean variables to match the state of the three corresponding Shift keys:

```
fShift = (Shift And acShiftMask) <> 0
fCtrl = (Shift And acCtrlMask) <> 0
fAlt = (Shift And acAltMask) <> 0
```

KeyDown and KeyUp versus KeyPress

Unless you need to trap special (non-ANSI) keystrokes, you'll find it easier to react to the KeyPress event in your applications. Access passes the ANSI code of the key that triggered the event via the KeyAscii parameter to the KeyPress event procedure. This parameter is similar to the KeyDown and KeyUp event procedures' KeyCode parameter, except that the KeyPress event never gets triggered for non-ANSI keys. In addition, KeyPress gets distinct codes for lower- and uppercase alphabetic characters. (KeyDown and KeyUp always get the hardware code of the key itself, not of the character that key represents; you must check whether the keystroke is lower- or uppercase by checking the Shift parameter.) Because the KeyPress event receives only ANSI keys, you can use the Chr and Asc functions to convert back and forth between the KeyAscii parameter and the equivalent ANSI character. For example:

```
strKey = Chr(KeyAscii)
KeyAscii = Asc(strKey)
```

Repeating Keyboard Events

If you press and hold down a key, the KeyDown event occurs repeatedly until you release the key, at which point the KeyUp event occurs. If the key is an ANSI key, the KeyPress and Change events also repeat.

Mouse Actions

When you move the mouse cursor over a section, control, or other part of a form, the MouseMove event for that object is triggered. More MouseMove events are triggered the further and more slowly the mouse is moved.

Mouse Click Actions

When you single-click the default (usually defined as the left) mouse button on a control, the background of a section, the record selector, or dead space area of a form (the space that occurs when the form's window is sized larger than the height of its combined sections), the following events occur:

```
MouseDown → MouseUp → Click
```

Mouse event procedures include parameters that indicate which button was clicked (left, right, or middle) as well as the coordinates of the click location in twips. Often you don't care about capturing the individual MouseDown and MouseUp events. In these cases, you'll want to attach code to the Click event.

If one control has the focus and you click a second control, the following events occur:

```
1st Control Exit → 1st Control LostFocus →
2nd Control Enter → 2nd Control GotFocus →
2nd Control MouseDown → 2nd Control MouseUp → 2nd Control Click
```

If the first control were updated prior to the mouse click, the first control's BeforeUpdate and AfterUpdate events would also fire before the Exit event.

NOTE The Click event for list and combo boxes differs from the Click event for other controls. With combo and list boxes, the Click event occurs when a user selects an item from the list, not when the control receives the focus. This means that if you click into the text box area of a combo box or the scroll bar of a list box, the Click event does not fire as you might expect.

Keystrokes That Cause Command Button Click Events

For command buttons, the Click event occurs (in addition to several keyboard events) in the following situations:

- If the command button has the focus and the spacebar is depressed and released

- If the Default property of the command button is set to Yes and the Enter key is depressed and released
- If the Cancel property of the command button is set to Yes and the Esc key is depressed and released
- If you've included an ampersand (&) character in the Caption property of the control to define a command button accelerator key and you depress and release the accelerator key along with the Alt key

Mouse Double-Click Actions

If you double-click the default mouse button on a control other than a command button, the following events occur:

```
MouseDown → MouseUp → Click → DblClick → MouseUp
```

If you double-click a command button, an additional Click event occurs after the second MouseUp event. This makes it virtually impossible for you to assign different actions to the Click and DblClick events of a button because both events occur when you double-click the button. It would be nice if Access was somehow omniscient and could tell when a user was really double-clicking, thus canceling the first Click event, but unfortunately, it can't.

Data-Related Actions

When you change data displayed on forms, Access generates several additional events at various levels.

Access' Data Buffers

When you edit data on a bound form, Access maintains the following two buffers to support two levels of undo:

- Current record buffer
- Current control buffer

These buffers are depicted in Figure 2.3. When you move to a record, Access loads the values from the current record of the form's record source into the current record buffer. Then, as you move from field to field, Access loads the data from the current record buffer into the current control buffer.

FIGURE 2.3:

Access maintains a two-level undo buffer for bound forms.

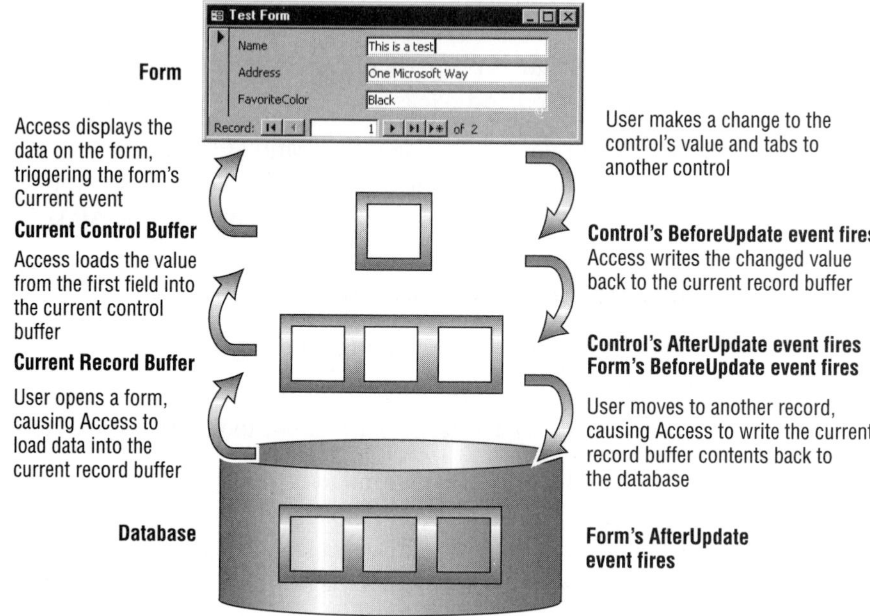
Test Form
Name
This is a test
Address
One Microsoft Way
FavoriteColor
Black
Record: 1 of 2
Form
Access displays the data on the form, triggering the form's Current event
Current Control Buffer
Access loads the value from the first field into the current control buffer
Current Record Buffer
User opens a form, causing Access to load data into the current record buffer
Database
User makes a change to the control's value and tabs to another control
Control's BeforeUpdate event fires
Access writes the changed value back to the current record buffer
Control's AfterUpdate event fires
Form's BeforeUpdate event fires
User moves to another record, causing Access to write the current record buffer contents back to the database
Form's AfterUpdate event fires

When you change the value of a field and tab to another field, the control's BeforeUpdate and AfterUpdate events occur. Between these two events, Access takes the value from the control buffer and uses it to replace the value in the record buffer. Similarly, when you save the current record—by explicitly saving the record, navigating to another record, or closing the form—Access replaces the data in the underlying record with the values in the current record buffer.

If, during the editing of data in a control, you press Esc or select Edit ➢ Undo, Access discards the contents of the current control buffer, refreshing it with the value from the current record buffer. If you press Esc a second time or select Edit ➢ Undo Record, Access discards the contents of the current record buffer, refreshing it with the values from the underlying record.

When using bound forms, you always edit the data in the control buffer; you never directly edit data in the underlying tables.

The Dirty Event

Microsoft has added one new form-level data event to Access 2000, the Dirty event. The Dirty event fires anytime data changes on a bound form. It fires as soon as data in a control is modified and only fires once until you cancel or save any changes. A side effect of the Dirty event is that Access also sets the form's Dirty property to True.

You can cancel the event, which discards the user's changes. The Dirty event is only triggered when changing data in bound controls, however. To monitor changes in unbound controls, you'll still need to write code in the Change or BeforeUpdate events. Finally, Access fires the Dirty event when changes are made by executing VBA code as well as by the user.

NOTE Although Access developers have been asking for a Dirty event since Access 1, its addition doesn't completely solve the problem developers were trying to fix. Yes, it does raise an event when the form's data becomes dirtied (that is, when Access copies the data into an editing buffer), but there's no corresponding event when the form becomes "undirtied." You can react to the BeforeUpdate event if you want to trap the fact that the user has finished editing and has saved the row, but what if the user presses the Escape key? Or chooses the Edit ➢ Undo menu item? Access still provides no event to handle this situation. Basically, what they should have done was provide an event that was raised when the little pencil became visible, and another when it went away. But that's not how it works.

NOTE The following sections that discuss event sequences do not include references to the Dirty event because it only fires once per edit and always fires before any other data-related events.

Changing Data in a Text Box

When you change the data in a text box control and tab to another control, Access triggers the following events (disregarding keyboard events):

```
1st Control Change (one for each typed character) →
1st Control BeforeUpdate → 1st Control AfterUpdate →
1st Control Exit → 1st Control LostFocus →
2nd Control Enter → 2nd Control GotFocus
```

If the current control is the last one in the tab order, Access will move to the next record in the recordset and trigger a Current event between the current control's LostFocus event and the next control's Enter event.

Combo Box Actions

When you select a value from a combo box control that already has the focus, the following events occur (note that for the sake of clarity we've omitted keyboard, MouseDown, and MouseUp events):

```
BeforeUpdate → AfterUpdate → Click → Change
```

The Click event occurs even when you select the value using the keyboard, even though "clicking" is something most people associate with the mouse.

When you type an entry in a combo box and tab to another control, the following events occur:

```
1st Control Change (one for each typed character) →
1st Control BeforeUpdate → 1st Control AfterUpdate →
1st Control Click → 1st Control Exit → 1st Control LostFocus →
2nd Control Enter → 2nd Control GotFocus
```

When the LimitToList property has been set to Yes and you enter a value that is not in the list, the following events occur:

```
Change (one for each typed character) → NotInList → Form Error
```

You may wish to create an event procedure for the NotInList event that adds a new row to the underlying list in this circumstance. You can prevent the form's Error event from occurring by setting the Response parameter of the NotInList event procedure. (See Chapter 7 for more information.)

List Box Actions

When you select a value from a list box control that already has the focus, the following events occur (again, for the sake of clarity we've omitted keyboard, MouseDown, and MouseUp events):

```
BeforeUpdate → AfterUpdate → Click
```

The Click event occurs even when you select the value using the keyboard and when you move from one list item to the next using the arrow keys.

BeforeUpdate versus AfterUpdate for a Control

In many situations, you can use BeforeUpdate and AfterUpdate interchangeably, attaching code to either event. Sometimes, though, it *does* matter to which event you react.

You should use a control's BeforeUpdate event when you need to

- Validate the value entered into a control. You can cancel the committed changes by setting the Cancel parameter to True in the control's Before-Update event procedure.
- Compare the changed value with the previous value (which is available by using the OldValue property of the control).

You should use a control's AfterUpdate event when you need to

- Change the value the user entered
- React to a change in value after Access commits the change

NOTE

The BeforeUpdate and AfterUpdate events are not triggered when you change the value of a control programmatically.

BeforeUpdate versus AfterUpdate for a Form

Similarly, a form's BeforeUpdate and AfterUpdate events have different uses. You should use a form's BeforeUpdate event when you need to

- Validate the data entered for the current record. You can cancel the changes by setting the Cancel parameter to True in the form's BeforeUpdate event procedure.
- Make changes to the data in the current record before the record is saved. For example, you might want to save the current date and time in an event procedure attached to the BeforeUpdate event. (If you made these changes in an event procedure attached to the AfterUpdate event, you could get into an infinite loop because your changes would continue to dirty the record and cause it to trigger the AfterUpdate event repeatedly.)

You should use a form's AfterUpdate event when you need to react to the saving of the record after Access has committed it to the database.

NOTE

Unlike the control's BeforeUpdate and AfterUpdate events, the form's Before-Update and AfterUpdate events are triggered when you change the value of any of the form's controls programmatically.

OLE Control Actions

When you insert an object into an empty bound object frame, the following event occurs:

```
Updated
```

When you change the source object of a bound object frame by double-clicking the control, editing the source, and returning to the form, the following events occur:

```
OLE Control Click → OLE Control DblClick →
OLE Control Updated (may occur multiple times)
```

The Updated event may occur multiple times if the source document changes are extensive.

The following additional events occur when you commit the changes by moving to another control:

```
OLE Control BeforeUpdate → OLE Control AfterUpdate →
OLE Control Click → OLE Control Exit →
OLE Control LostFocus → Other Control Enter →
Other Control GotFocus → OLE Control Updated (three times)
```

NOTE ActiveX controls, as opposed to simple OLE objects like pictures or Word documents, offer a whole new set of events of their own. Access merges ActiveX control events into the event model for a form when you add a control. ActiveX controls are discussed in detail in Chapter 12, "Access as an Automation Client."

Saving and Navigating between Records

When you save the current record by either pressing Shift+Enter or selecting Records ➢ Save Record, the following events occur:

```
Control BeforeUpdate → Control AfterUpdate →
Form BeforeUpdate → Form AfterUpdate
```

If the current record is dirty (contains unsaved changes) and you move to another record, the following events occur:

```
Control BeforeUpdate → Control AfterUpdate →
Form BeforeUpdate → Form AfterUpdate → Control Exit →
Control LostFocus → Form Current → Control Enter →
Control GotFocus
```

When you navigate to another record without changing data in the current record, the following events occur:

```
Control Exit → Control LostFocus → Form Current →
Control Enter → Control GotFocus
```

Inserting a Record

The following events occur when you move to the new record:

```
Control Exit → Control LostFocus → Form Current →
Control Enter → Control GotFocus
```

When you then dirty the new record, the following event occurs (again, we've omitted keyboard, MouseDown, and MouseUp events) prior to other events that would occur when changing data in a control:

```
Form BeforeInsert → Form Dirty
```

Finally, when you save the new record, the following events occur:

```
Control BeforeUpdate → Control AfterUpdate →
Form BeforeUpdate → Form AfterUpdate → Form AfterInsert
```

Deleting a Record

When you delete the current record, the following events occur before the deletion confirmation dialog appears:

```
Control Exit → Control LostFocus → Form Delete →
Form Current → Control Enter → Control GotFocus →
Form BeforeDelConfirm → Form Error
```

For multirecord deletions, the Delete event occurs once per deleted record.

If the deletion is canceled, the following events occur:

```
Control Exit → Control LostFocus → Form Current → Form AfterDelConfirm
```

If you have set the Confirm Record Changes option in the Edit/Find tab of the Tools ➢ Options dialog to False (or have used the SetOption method of the Application object to set the equivalent using VBA code), the BeforeDelConfirm and AfterDelConfirm events are skipped. If you have set off warnings by using the SetWarnings method of the DoCmd object, BeforeDelConfirm and AfterDelConfirm events still occur, but the confirming dialog is skipped.

When the Delete event occurs, Access removes the record and stores it in a temporary buffer. You can cancel the Delete event (and restore the deleted record) by setting its Cancel parameter to True in an event procedure attached to this event. This will serve to cancel the delete operation and all subsequent deletion events.

You can also cancel the BeforeDelConfirm by setting its Cancel event to True. This also cancels the deletion, but the AfterDelConfirm will still occur. If you want to create your own custom deletion message, you should display it from an event procedure attached to the BeforeDelConfirm event. If you wish to continue the delete operation but suppress the built-in deletion message, set the Response parameter to the acDataErrContinue constant.

You can't cancel the deletion from the AfterDelConfirm event. The records have already been deleted (or the deletion has already been canceled). This is a good time to react to the deletion. You can use the Status parameter that is passed to event procedures attached to this event to determine what happened. The following table lists what the value of Status can be.

Constant	Meaning
acDeleteOk	The deletion occurred
acDeleteCancel	The deletion was canceled by your VBA code
acDeleteUserCancel	The deletion was canceled by the user

The Error Event

If you attach an event procedure to the form's Error event, your procedure will be called whenever a trappable error occurs while the form is running. You can use the DataErr parameter passed to your event procedure to determine which error has occurred and react accordingly. For example, you might use the MsgBox statement to provide a custom error message to the user. By setting the response parameter to the acDataErrContinue constant, you can tell Access to skip the display of the built-in error message. (See Chapters 8 and 14 for more information on the Error event. For information on using the Error event in multiuser applications, see Chapter 2 in *Access 2000 Developer's Handbook, Volume II.*)

The Indispensable Timer Event

The form's Timer event occurs only when you have set the TimerInterval property to a value greater than 0. This property—measured in milliseconds—determines how often the Timer interval fires.

The Timer event is useful for performing some action at regular intervals of time. For example, you could create a Timer event procedure that waited ten seconds and then closed the form. You could also use the Timer event to check on a regular basis to see whether some state was true and then to do something when this was the case. For example, you could create an automated import procedure that checked every ten minutes to see whether mainframe data had been downloaded to a certain file.

You can also use the Timer event to simulate user-defined events. The possibilities are endless. For example, you could create a user-defined Locked event by attaching code to the Timer event that checks once a second to see whether the current record has been locked by another user. You can stop Access from triggering a form's Timer event by setting the TimerInterval property back to 0.

Actions That Can't Be Trapped

The following actions cannot be trapped in Access:

- Scrolling
- Discarding changes using the Edit ➢ Undo command
- Another user's locking the current record
- Dragging and dropping an object

As mentioned in the preceding section, you can simulate some of these events by making use of the Timer event.

Summary

In this chapter, we introduced you to the Access event model. We discussed

- The Access event model
- Event handlers
- The different types of events that occur on forms
- The sequence of form events
- Access' data buffers
- Which actions in Access can't be trapped

CHAPTER

THREE

3

Using VBA Class Modules

- Exploring what class modules are and how they work
- Creating your own object classes
- Implementing custom properties and methods
- Establishing a hierarchy of object classes
- Creating and managing collections of objects

With the introduction of VBA in Visual Basic 4, Microsoft endowed Basic developers with a new tool: class modules. While other Basic dialects (Visual Basic and Access Basic) had already introduced object-oriented constructs, class modules gave Basic programmers the ability to create and manipulate their own classes of objects. Access (and other Office applications) did not include class modules until the release of Office 97 with VBA 5. With the release of Office 2000 and VBA 6, Microsoft has enhanced class module capabilities so that they are now on par with Visual Basic.

If you're new to class modules, don't worry. If you have programmed in other object-oriented languages such as SmallTalk or C++, you are familiar with the benefits class modules provide. If you haven't, we hope to surprise you with the power they give you as a programmer. Because examples in this book will use class modules whenever possible, it makes sense at this point to explain what they are and how they work and to demonstrate some examples of how you can use them in your applications.

Because this chapter deals with creating your own objects, it assumes you are familiar with using objects provided by VBA or a host application. That is, you should be comfortable with concepts such as properties and methods and know how to declare and use object variables.

Why Use Class Modules?

If you've been developing applications using Basic for any length of time, you might be thinking, "Why use class modules, anyway? I've been getting along without them for some time." Like any new product feature, class modules have their benefits and costs. The primary cost is the learning curve required to understand them so that you can use them effectively. Although many VBA programmers take working with built-in objects (for example, the Debug and Err objects) for granted, they find the idea of creating their own object types difficult to comprehend. We hope that, after reading this chapter, you won't feel that way.

Once you've mastered the basics of class modules, the benefits become clear. Your code is more manageable, self-documenting, and easier to maintain, especially if you deal with complex sets of related data. The sections that follow examine some reasons for using class modules.

Classes Let You Create Your Own Objects

Class modules allow you to create and use your own object types in your application. Why would you want to do this? Imagine that you want to write an application that tracks information on employees in your company. Using traditional Basic, you might create separate variables to store each employee's name, manager, and salary, among other things. If you're really clever, you might create an array of user-defined data types. It's also likely that you'd write procedures to handle tasks such as hiring or transferring an employee or giving an employee a raise. The problem with this approach is that there is nothing inherent in the program or the language that ties all these bits of information and processes together. We've shown this situation in Figure 3.1. All the data and processes are free-floating. It's up to you, the programmer, to ensure that each element is used correctly.

FIGURE 3.1:

Managing data using traditional Basic constructs—every item stands alone

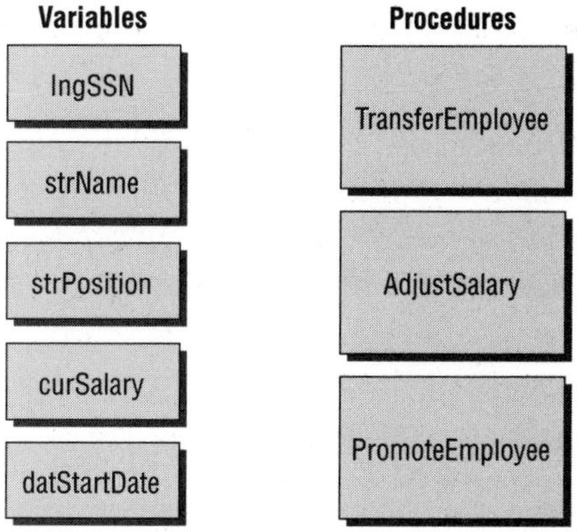

Variables	Procedures
lngSSN	TransferEmployee
strName	AdjustSalary
strPosition	PromoteEmployee
curSalary	
datStartDate	

With nothing enforcing relationships between the items in Figure 3.1, chaos can result. For example, suppose two or more separate procedures modify the salary data using a particular set of rules. Changes to the rules necessitate changes to the program logic in several places.

Encapsulating these data and program components in an object makes the management task much easier. First of all, any references to data (properties) must be associated with a particular object, so you always know what "thing" it is you're operating on. Second, processes that operate on an object are defined as part of that object. In other words, the processes are defined as methods of the object. The consumers of the object—other procedures in your program—are insulated from the inner workings of each method and cannot modify properties directly unless you allow them to. This enforces a degree of control over data that the object represents. Finally, because each property and method is defined in one place (the class module definition), any code modifications need be implemented only once. An object's consumers will benefit automatically from the change. This type of object-oriented development is represented in the diagram shown in Figure 3.2. All data and processes are defined as part of the object, and the application program interacts with them through a central point, a reference to an instance of the object.

FIGURE 3.2:

Managing data using object-oriented techniques

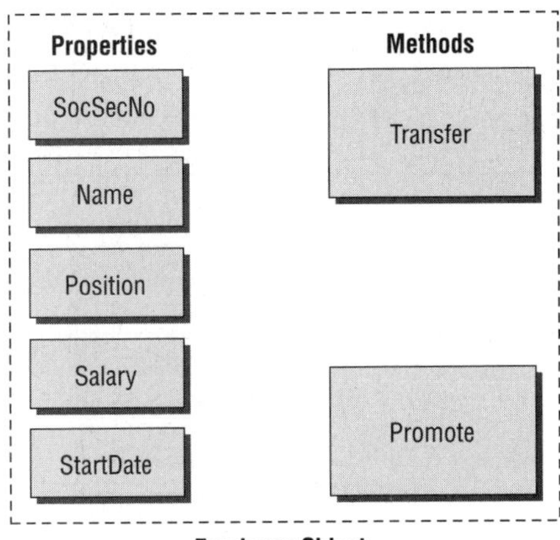

Is VBA Really Object-Oriented?

At this point, many of you who have experience in other object-oriented languages are probably thinking, "What are they talking about? VBA isn't really object-oriented!" Although we concede that VBA does not exhibit some of the characteristics of a "true" object-oriented language, such as polymorphism and implementation inheritance (if you don't know what these are, don't worry), we believe that it just doesn't matter. VBA may not be as feature-rich as C++ or SmallTalk, but for most people it's much easier to understand than those languages. More important, VBA class modules offer concrete benefits to you, the developer, so what difference does it make if VBA is completely object-oriented or not?

Classes Let You Hide Complex Processes

If you find the idea of encapsulating data and processes within an object compelling, you'll be even more excited about the next benefit of using class modules: the ability to hide complex processes. Suppose you are trying to create an application that manages internal purchases within an organization. Determining the amount to charge one department for goods or services received from another (called the *transfer price*) can be a complicated task. If you use traditional programming techniques, the logic for computing the transfer price might be an integral component of the application. Not only does embedding the logic in the application make the program code harder to maintain, it means that every programmer who works with the code must be able to understand the logic.

By using object-oriented techniques, on the other hand, you can create object classes for each good or service being transferred, making the transfer price computation logic part of each object class. This makes the application code easier to understand and write. The programmer using your class need only know that an object is being transferred and that the object knows how to compute the transfer price. The logic for computing that price is maintained separately, perhaps by another programmer more familiar with the intricacies of transfer pricing theory.

When you create an object you define an *interface* to that object. This isn't a user interface, but rather a list of the object's properties, methods, and events. These items are all that consumers of the object (other programmers) need to know in order to use the object. It's then up to you to implement each feature in the object's source code using VBA class modules.

Classes Make Development Simpler

In the preceding example, imagine that another programmer was charged with the task of maintaining the transfer pricing logic encapsulated in the object being transferred. This brings up a continual challenge facing development managers: how to coordinate large, complex programming projects. Object-oriented techniques (which include using VBA class modules) can make the task of managing projects easier. Because objects are autonomous entities that encapsulate their own data and methods, you can develop and test them independently from the overall application. Programmers can create custom objects using VBA class modules and then test them using only a small amount of generic Basic code. After determining that the object behaves as desired, the programmer can use the object in an application simply by importing the appropriate class modules.

How Class Modules Work

We hope that by now we have convinced you that object-oriented techniques in general, and VBA class modules in particular, are worth learning about. In the following sections, we explain how they work by discussing the difference between classes and objects.

Classes Are Like Cookie Cutters

VBA class modules define the properties and methods of an object, but you cannot use them by themselves to manipulate those properties. An object's definition is sometimes called an object *class*. You can think of VBA class modules, and thus object classes, as cookie cutters. A cookie cutter defines what a particular cookie will look like, but it is not itself a cookie. You can't have a cookie, however, without a cookie cutter.

In the case of VBA class modules, you define a set of properties, including their data types and whether they are read-only or read/write, as well as methods, including the data type returned (if any) plus any parameters the methods might require. Figure 3.3 shows a simple example using the cookie analogy. You'll see in the next section how to add a class module to your Access database and how to use it to define properties and methods.

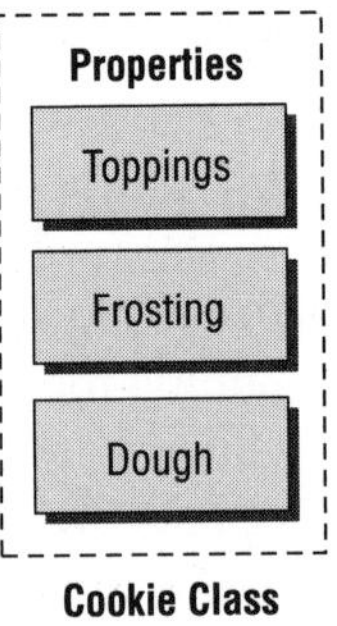

FIGURE 3.3: An imaginary Cookie class, including three properties

Objects Are the Cookies

To actually make use of an object class, you must create a new *instance* of that class. Using the analogy, object instances are the individual cookies. Each has the set of properties and methods defined by the class, but you can also manipulate an instance individually as a real programming entity. When you create a new instance of a class, you can change its properties independently of any other instance of the same class. Figure 3.4 shows several instances of the Cookie class with various property settings.

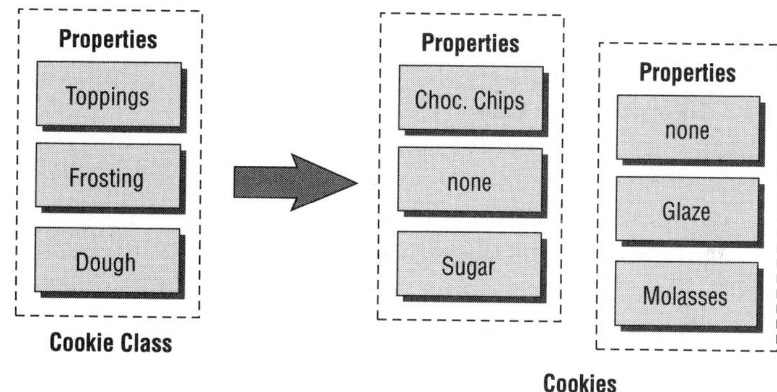

FIGURE 3.4: You can create multiple cookies from the same Cookie class.

A Simple Example: A Text File Class

To demonstrate the basic techniques required to create and use class modules, we'll show you how to create a class that represents a text file. It will include properties that let you manipulate the file name and contents, as well as methods to read and write the contents from and to disk. Not only will this provide a relatively simple example for teaching class module concepts, but it is also a useful class you can add to your Access applications that must work with text files.

Creating an Object Class

As already mentioned, before you can start working with your own custom objects, you must create the object class from which they will be fabricated. You do this simply by adding a new class module to your database.

Inserting a New Class Module

To add a new class module to your database, open the Visual Basic Editor and select the Insert ➢ Class Module menu item. You edit class modules the same way you edit standard VBA code modules. The only difference is that class modules have two events, Initialize and Terminate, associated with the creation and destruction of a class instance. We'll explain these in more detail in the section "The Initialize and Terminate Events" a little later in this chapter.

Naming Your Class

All VBA class modules have a Name property that is integral to the definition of an object class: it determines the class name. Be sure to set the name of the class module to the name you want to use in your VBA programs that use the class. To name a class module, specify the class name when you first save the class module or in the VBA Properties window. Of course, you can alter the name later; but you'll probably want to do that before you write any code that uses the class.

NOTE Although we are strong proponents of using sometimes obscure naming conventions with internal names and variables, you should choose a name for your class that is both easily understood and that identifies the "thing" the object class represents. Typically, developers choose English words in the singular form. Capitalization is used to distinguish word breaks within an object class name. For example, these class names are appropriate: Application, Employee, and DrawingObject. For this example, we've created a class named TextFile.

Creating a Property Using a Public Variable

Most objects have at least one property. Properties store values representing characteristics of the object. Although it's possible to create methods for setting and returning values, we don't recommend this approach. Methods are normally used to implement actions an object can take.

The simplest approach to creating a property is to create a Public variable in the declarations section of the class module. (A second approach is described in the section "Using Property Statements" later in this chapter.) Consumers of your object will then be able to set and retrieve a value stored in that variable. (In other words, the property is read/write.) The variable's name determines the name of the property used by other parts of your program. For this reason, as with class names, choose a name with logical, symbolic meaning.

Although using Public variables to define properties is the simplest approach, this method does have one major drawback. Your class has no way of knowing when an outside process has changed the value of the property. This may be critical to your object for, say, restricting values to a given range or taking other actions in response to a change in value. (To meet these needs, you must use Property procedures.)

Creating a Method

Just as declaring a Public variable creates a property, declaring a Public procedure creates a method. You can create Public functions and subs, the only difference being that a Public function returns a value to the calling process and a sub does not. The TextFile class implements, among other things, a FileOpen method that carries out the task of opening the file specified by the Path property of the class. Listing 3.1 shows the VBA code that makes up the FileOpen method.

TIP

Although you might like to do so, you can't name this method *Open.* This name conflicts with a reserved word in VBA. You may find that VBA reports a syntax error when declaring methods or properties. In these cases, make sure you haven't inadvertently used a reserved word, and change the method or property name if necessary.

Listing 3.1

```
Public Function FileOpen() As Boolean
    On Error GoTo HandleError

    ' If a file is already open, close it
    If Me.IsOpen Then
        Me.FileClose
    End If

    ' Get next available file handle
    mhFile = FreeFile
```

```
    ' Open file based on file open mode property
    Select Case Me.OpenMode
        Case tfOpenReadOnly
            Open Me.Path For Binary Access Read As mhFile
        Case tfOpenReadWrite
            Open Me.Path For Binary Access Read Write As _
             mhFile
        Case tfOpenAppend
            Open Me.Path For Append Access Read Write As _
             mhFile
        Case tfOpenReadOnlyExists
            Open Me.Path For Input Access Read As mhFile
    End Select

' Set IsOpen property variable and return value
    mfIsOpen = True
    FileOpen = True
ExitProc:
    Exit Function

HandleError:
    FileOpen = False
    Resume ExitProc
End Function
```

Although the code shown in Listing 3.1 is not earth shattering by any standard (it uses low-level file I/O functions that have been around for years), you should be able to see the benefits of encapsulating the code in a class. You no longer have to remember all the various forms of the Open statement. All you need to do is set the object's Path and OpenMode properties and call its FileOpen method. The code encapsulated in the class does the rest, including error handling.

One item of note in Listing 3.1 is the use of the reserved word *Me*. You use Me in class modules to refer to the current instance of that class. Just as you use Me in form modules to retrieve a reference to the current form, you use Me in a class module to retrieve a reference to the current object.

NOTE

Perhaps you can now see why we refer to the module containing a form or report's code as its *class module.* In many senses, form or report class modules are equivalent to the class modules presented in this chapter. They both offer encapsulation, and they both use the Me object to refer to the current instance. Stand-alone class modules offer the Initialize and Terminate events, and forms and reports use their Open and Close events instead, but that's one of the few differences between the modules attached to forms and reports and stand-alone class modules.

Table 3.1 lists all the properties and methods of the TextFile class. You may find it useful to follow the table through the class module and see how all the methods and properties have been declared.

TABLE 3.1: Methods and Properties of the Simple TextFile Class

Methods Member	Description
EOF property	Contains True if you've reached the end of the text file (read-only).
Exists method	Determines whether the file exists, based on a directory search. Returns True or False.
FileClose method	Closes the text file.
FileOpen method	Opens the requested file once you've supplied the Path (and optionally, the OpenMode) property. If you don't supply an OpenMode value, the code assumes you want read/write access.
Handle property	Contains the operating system file handle for the opened file (read-only).
IsOpen property	Contains True if the file is currently open, False if not (read-only).
OpenMode property	Contains the file open mode (0 for read-only, 1 for read/write, 2 for append, 3 for read-only for existing files) (read/write until the file is open, read-only after that).
Path property	Contains the path of the text file (read/write until the file has been opened, read-only after that).
ReadNext method	Reads the next line of text into the internal buffer. Use the Text property to retrieve the value.
Text property	Contains the text of the current line from the text file (read-only).

Using the Object Class

Now that you've defined a class and given it a few properties and methods, you can use it in other VBA procedures. The first step in using a class is to create a new instance of the class. This is analogous to cutting a new cookie in the earlier example.

Creating New Class Instances

To create a new class instance, declare an object variable based on the class. You'll use it to store a reference to a new class instance. Variables referencing custom classes adhere to the same rules as those referencing VBA or host application objects. You can declare them using the Dim, Private, Public, or Global reserved word. For example, the following code fragment declares a variable called objFile:

```
Dim objFile As TextFile
```

Note that the data type in this example is the class name defined earlier. The next step is to create a new instance of the object and store a reference to it in the variable. This is called *instantiating* the object. To do this, you use the Set statement in conjunction with the New keyword, as in:

```
Set objFile = New TextFile
```

Although the syntax might seem redundant, you must use the New keyword in the Set statement to create a new instance of the object. Otherwise, VBA will generate runtime errors if you try to use any of the properties or methods of the class. Simply declaring a new object variable in this manner is not enough to create a new object instance.

WARNING

Remember to use the New keyword to create a new instance of a VBA class. If you don't, VBA generates an "Object variable or With block variable not set" error. If you receive this error on a statement involving an instance of your custom class, make sure you've created a new instance using New.

Implicit Instantiation

You can declare a new instance along with the variable declaration by using the New keyword in the declaration statement, as in this example:

```
Dim objFile As New TextFile
```

Immediately after declaring an object variable in this manner, you can start using the object's properties and methods without first using Set. The first time VBA encounters the object variable it will automatically instantiate the object. This method of implicit instantiation saves one line of code, but it does have a drawback—in a complex application, it may not be clear where and when VBA instantiates the object. Knowing when an object is instantiated could be crucial while debugging an application. For this reason, we recommend you use explicit instantiation—that is, use a separate Set New statement—in your applications.

Using Properties and Methods

Once you have a variable storing a reference to a new class instance, you can use the properties and methods defined by the class module. Listing 3.2 shows some sample code that uses the TextFile class to open a file (AUTOEXEC.BAT, in this case) and print out each line using the properties (Path, EOF, Text) and methods (FileOpen, ReadNext, FileClose) of the class. This example is from basTest-TextFile.

NOTE

If you don't have an AUTOEXEC.BAT file on your computer (or it contains no text), you should supply a different, valid file name before running the sample code.

Listing 3.2

```
Function TestFile()
    Dim objFile As TextFile

    ' Create new instance of TextFile class
    Set objFile = New TextFile
```

```
    ' Set the Path property
    objFile.Path = "C:\AUTOEXEC.BAT"

    ' Try to open the file-if successful,
    ' read until the end of the file,
    ' printing each line
    If objFile.FileOpen() Then
        Do Until objFile.EOF
            objFile.ReadNext
            Debug.Print objFile.Text
        Loop
        objFile.FileClose
    End If

    ' Destroy class instance
    Set objFile = Nothing
End Function
```

Certainly, using this class is better than including the low-level I/O routines themselves in your code. In fact, if you've used DAO or ADO, the code should look familiar to you. It's similar to the way you manipulate database data using Recordset objects.

What's Going On?

In just a few lines of code, we've accomplished a number of things. First, the code created a new instance of the object and stored a reference to it in the object variable objFile. It then used the reference to call the object's properties and methods. Programmers trained in other languages, such as C++ or Pascal, are used to calling this type of reference a *pointer.* (Think of a pointer as a variable that holds the memory address of another piece of data. In other words, it *points to* the other piece of data.) VBA doesn't expose the actual value of the pointer, but you don't really need it. All you need to know is that it points to some object you've defined and that you can use it to access that object's properties and methods.

It's important to remember that you can have more than one pointer pointing to the same object, and as long as an object has at least one pointer pointing to it, VBA keeps it in memory. For example, Listing 3.3 demonstrates how you could create two pointers to the same object by setting a second pointer variable equal to the first. You can tell whether two pointers refer to the same object by using the Is operator in a conditional statement.

Listing 3.3

```
Dim objFirst As TextFile
Dim objSecond As TextFile

' Create new instance of TextFile class
Set objFirst = New TextFile

' Create a second pointer to the new instance
Set objSecond = objFirst

' Compare the two pointers
If objFirst Is objSecond Then
    ' Both pointers refer to same object
End If
```

In a sense, VBA keeps the object alive until nothing points to it, that is, until it is no longer needed. When does this happen? It can occur when the last object variable pointing to the object goes out of scope. Also, you can explicitly break the connection between a pointer and the object it points to by setting the pointer variable to the intrinsic constant Nothing. That's what you saw in Listing 3.2. Although doing so was unnecessary (the pointer was local in scope, and VBA automatically sets it to Nothing when it goes out of scope), it is good programming style to explicitly release objects you no longer need rather than to rely on the rules of variable scoping to do it for you.

The Initialize and Terminate Events

Because VBA affords you the opportunity to run code when it creates and/or destroys an object instance, you should carefully consider exactly when those actions occur in your application. Unlike regular VBA modules, which have no events, class modules have Initialize and Terminate events that are triggered when an instance of the class is created and destroyed, respectively. You can use the Initialize event to do such things as setting default property values and creating references to other objects. Use the Terminate event to perform cleanup tasks. Remember that the Initialize event is triggered when VBA first creates a new instance of a class, and Terminate is triggered when the last pointer to the instance is released or destroyed.

Listing 3.4 shows the Initialize and Terminate event code for the TextFile class. During processing of the Initialize event, the code sets the default OpenMode property. In the Terminate event, the code checks to see whether a file is still open (in other words, whether the programmer has not explicitly called the FileClose method) and then closes it. If you want a clear example of when these events are triggered, try inserting a MsgBox statement in each and watching what happens as you use instances of the class.

Listing 3.4

```
Private Sub Class_Initialize()
    ' Set default file open mode property
    Me.OpenMode = tfOpenReadWrite
End Sub

Private Sub Class_Terminate()
    ' If a file is still open then close it
    ' before terminating
    If Me.IsOpen Then
        Me.FileClose
    End If
End Sub
```

Class Modules and Multiple Instances of Forms and Reports

Access forms and reports, like VBA class modules, can have exposed custom properties and methods and allow for multiple instancing. In fact, the rules for defining properties and methods are the same for form and report class modules as they are for VBA class modules. Using Access forms and reports as classes, however, differs slightly.

First, VBA automatically adds the text "Form_" to the beginning of the form's name (and "Report_" to the beginning of a report name) to create the class name used to declare pointer variables. (You can see this by looking at the Project window in the Visual Basic Editor.) For example, to create a new instance of a form named frmTextFile, you would use code like this:

```
Dim objFile As Form_frmTextFile
Set objFile = New Form_frmTextFile
```

Continued on next page

Second, unlike VBA class modules, form modules do not have Initialize and Terminate events. If you need to perform startup and shutdown tasks, use the Load and Close events, respectively.

Finally, creating a new instance of an Access form module creates a new instance of the form. Access adds it to the Forms collection, so beware of any existing code that manipulates this collection. In addition, although it initially loads hidden, the new form instance will show up in the Unhide dialog unless you set its Popup property to Yes.

The example shown in Listing 3.4 uses the keyword Me to refer to the current instance of the class module. As with forms and reports, it is only valid inside a class module, and it returns an object that is the current class instance.

Using Property Procedures

You now know the basic techniques for creating and using class modules in VBA. If you've looked at the complete source code for the sample TextFile class, however, you will have noticed some things we have not yet discussed. The remainder of this chapter is devoted to more advanced class module techniques, beginning with the second way to implement custom properties: Property procedures.

We've already discussed how you can implement properties simply by declaring a Public variable in the declarations section of a class module. Consumers of your class can then reference that property using the *object.property* syntax. The major drawback to this approach is that your class has no way of knowing when the value of the property has changed. Property procedures solve this problem. Property procedures are VBA procedures that are executed when a property value is set or retrieved. During the processing of a Property procedure, you can take action regarding the property.

Property procedures come in three varieties: Property Get, Property Let, and Property Set. You use Property Get statements to retrieve (or get) the values of class instance properties. You use Property Let and Property Set statements, on the other hand, to set the values of properties. The distinction between the two is that you use Property Let for scalar values (Integer, String, and so on), and you use Property Set for object data types. The following sections explain each of these in detail.

Retrieving Values with Property Get

The Property Get procedure is probably the easiest of the three types of Property procedures to understand. Its basic form consists of a declaration, which includes the property name and data type, and a body, just like a normal function. It's up to you to return a property value by setting the procedure name equal to the return value. For example, the following code is the Property Get procedure for the Path property of the sample class:

```
Property Get Path() As String
    ' Return the path of the file from the
    ' Private class variable
    Path = mstrPath
End Property
```

The name of the Property statement, Path, defines the property name, and the return type (String, in this case) defines the property's data type. When another procedure references the property using code like this:

```
Debug.Print objFile.Path
```

VBA calls the procedure, and the value of a Private class module variable (mstrPath) is returned. Of course, you can do anything within a Property procedure that you can do within any VBA procedure (such as performing a calculation or querying a database), so the way you arrive at the value to be returned is completely up to you.

TIP

Use the following technique when you want to control how a program sets and retrieves property values: declare a Private variable in the class module's declarations section to store the property value internally within the class. Then implement Property procedures to set and/or retrieve its value.

In addition to following the simple example just presented, you can create Property Get procedures that accept arguments. Property procedure arguments are declared the same way as arguments of normal VBA procedures. For example, suppose your application requires you to compute weekly payroll dates. You might create a class with a PayDay property that accepts a week number and returns the associated payroll date. The declaration of that property might look like this:

```
Property Get PayDay(ByVal intWeek As Integer) As Date
    '
    ' Insert code here to compute the appropriate payroll date
    '
```

```
    PayDay = datSomeDate
End Property
```

Your program could then access the property by passing the arguments inside parentheses, after the property name:

```
datPayDay = objPayRoll.PayDay(12)
```

Setting Values with Property Let

The counterpart of Property Get is Property Let. You create Property Let procedures to allow consumers of your object to change the value of a property. Listing 3.5 shows the Property Let procedure for the Path property of the TextFile class.

Listing 3.5

```
Property Let Path(ByVal strPath As String)
    ' Set the path property of the file.
    ' If a file is already open, close it
    If Me.IsOpen Then
        Me.FileClose
    End If
    mstrPath = strPath
End Property
```

Notice that the Property Let procedure uses the same name (Path) as the corresponding Property Get. Property procedures (Let/Get, Set/Get) are the only pairs of VBA procedures that can have the same name within a single module. Notice also that VBA passes the value set by the object's consumer in the argument to this procedure, strPath. For example, if another VBA procedure used a statement like this:

```
objFile.Path = "C:\AUTOEXEC.BAT"
```

VBA would pass the string "C:\AUTOEXEC.BAT" to the Property procedure in the strPath argument. In addition, the parameter passed to the Property Let procedure must have exactly the same data type as the value returned from the Property Get procedure.

NOTE

You need not have Property Get and Property Let procedures for each property you wish to implement. By defining only a Property Get procedure, you create, in effect, a read-only property—one that can be retrieved but not set. Likewise, defining only a Property Let procedure produces a write-only property. You'll see that the sample TextFile class makes heavy use of read-only properties. Although consumers of the class can't set the value of read-only properties, procedures inside the class can, by writing directly to the Private variables that store the property values.

Setting Values with Property Set

The Property Set procedure is a variation of the Property Let procedure designed to allow you to create object properties. *Object properties* are properties that are themselves pointers to objects, rather than scalar values. For example, suppose you want to create a property of one class that is itself a pointer to an instance of another class. You would need to define a Property Set procedure to allow consumers of the first class to set the property value.

The code in Listing 3.6 defines a Property Set procedure called SaveFile that might be part of a class representing text documents. The class stores a pointer to the TextFile object used for persistent storage of the document's contents.

Listing 3.6

```
' Private variable used to store a reference
' to the TextFile object associated with this class
Private mobjSaveFile As TextFile

Property Set SaveFile(objFile As TextFile)
    ' Make the private class variable point
    ' to the TextFile object passed to the procedure
    Set mobjSaveFile = objFile
End Property
```

VBA procedures could then set the pointer defined by the SaveFile property to point to another instance of the TextFile class. (Note the use of the Set reserved word.)

```
Set objDoc.SaveFile = New TextFile
```

Once the reference has been established, the procedure could then manipulate properties and call methods of the TextFile object pointed to by the document object's SaveFile property:

```
objDoc.SaveFile.Path = "C:\AUTOEXEC.BAT"
objDoc.SaveFile.FileOpen
```

At this point, you might be wondering how to retrieve the value of an object property if you use Property Set to set it. As it turns out, you can use Property Get procedures for both scalar values and object pointers. You just need to declare the return value as an object data type. For instance, if you wanted to write the corresponding Property Get procedure for the SaveFile property, it might look like this:

```
Property Get SaveFile() As TextFile
    ' Return the pointer contained in the
    ' private class variable
    Set SaveFile = mobjSaveFile
End Property
```

Again, notice the use of the Set reserved word in all assignment statements involving object references.

A Simple Database Example

Although Access makes it trivial to create forms bound directly to data sources, as you start writing more advanced applications, you may need to use unbound forms more and more often. Unbound forms give you better control in client-server and multiuser situations. You may find, in this type of situation, that using a class to represent your data can help make the task less formidable.

The sample Cats class tracks information about, well, cats. The sample form, frmCats (shown in Figure 3.5) demonstrates techniques you can use to load and save data from a table using a class to marshal the data between the table and the form. The Cat class module contains, for the most part, completely ordinary code, providing Property Let and Get statements to set and retrieve the value of each of the properties attributed to each Cat object (Name, Breed, Color, Birthdate, and so on). The class module also contains two routines that handle the transfer of data between the table and the class. The Load and Save methods, shown in Listing 3.7, do all the work and encapsulate data movement in the class module. You can call either method once you've set the ID property for the Cat object. The Load method loads the properties for a specific cat in tblCats. The Save method either saves the current Cat object to the correct row in tblCats or adds a new row and saves the data there (if the cat is new). (For more information on working with data programmatically, see Chapter 6.)

FIGURE 3.5:

frmCats demonstrates using a class module to encapsulate simple data manipulation.

Listing 3.7

```
Public Function Save() As Boolean
    Dim rst As ADODB.Recordset

    On Error GoTo HandleErrors

    Set rst = New ADODB.Recordset
    rst.Open "Select * from tblCats WHERE ID = " & Me.ID, _
     Application.CurrentProject.Connection, adOpenKeyset, _
     adLockPessimistic

    With rst
        If .EOF Then
            .AddNew
            ' Set the ID property for this new cat.
            Me.ID = !ID
        End If
```

```
            !Name = mstrName
            !Birthdate = mdatBirthdate
            !Sex = mstrSex
            !Breed = mstrBreed
            !Color = mstrColor
            !Neutered = mfNeutered
            .Update
        End With
        Save = True

ExitHere:
        If Not rst Is Nothing Then rst.Close
        Set rst = Nothing
        Exit Function

HandleErrors:
        Save = False
        Resume ExitHere
End Function

Public Function Load() As Boolean
        Dim rst As Recordset

        On Error GoTo HandleErrors

        Set rst = New ADODB.Recordset
        rst.Open "Select * from tblCats WHERE ID = " & Me.ID, _
         Application.CurrentProject.Connection
        With rst
            If Not .EOF Then
                mstrName = !Name
                mdatBirthdate = !Birthdate
                mstrSex = !Sex
                mstrBreed = !Breed
                mstrColor = !Color
                mfNeutered = !Neutered
                mlngID = !ID
            End If
        End With
        Load = True
```

```
ExitHere:
    If Not rst Is Nothing Then rst.Close
    Set rst = Nothing
    Exit Function

HandleErrors:
    Load = False
    Resume ExitHere
End Function
```

Although much of the code in the sample form's Class module deals with the particulars of the user interface (disabling and enabling controls at various points in the form's activity), two routines demonstrate a common technique: scattering the elements of an object to various controls on the form and gathering them back up from the form into the object. For examples of this technique, take a look at the ScatterFields and GatherFields procedures in frmCats.

Once you've created the class associated with your unbound form, as well as the routines to move the data between the member of the class and the form, writing the code to load and save the data is simple. For example, to retrieve a row, you can use code like this, from cboCatID_AfterUpdate:

```
Set objCat = New Cat
' Set the new Cat's ID property, so you can
' use the Load method.
objCat.ID = Me!cboCatID
If objCat.Load() Then
    ' Display the loaded fields on the form,
    ' and then select the Name field.
    Call ScatterFields(objCat)
End If
```

The code necessary to save the changes on the form is also simple. The following procedure, called from several places within the form, saves data from the form back to the underlying table:

```
Private Sub SaveCat()
    Dim objCat As New Cat

    Call GatherFields(objCat)
    Call objCat.Save
End Sub
```

By emulating the techniques shown in this example, you can create unbound forms that load and save their data through an object class that mirrors the data in the underlying table. Be aware, however, that the code demonstrated here is missing a vital element: robust error handling. In an attempt to keep the code simple, this example includes very little error handling.

Advanced Class Module Techniques

Now that you've learned the basic principles behind creating and using VBA class modules, you're ready to explore some advanced techniques. The following sections cover these topics:

- Defining enumerated types
- Building class hierarchies
- Creating a Parent property for objects
- Implementing collections of objects
- Raising and sinking custom events

Defining Enumerated Types

Often, when developing custom classes, you'll find yourself needing to define a series of constants for a given property or method. The OpenMode property of our TextFile class is a good example. There are only four discrete values that OpenMode can have, and these are represented by constant values. While normal VBA constants are useful, you can provide even more usability by defining an *enumerated type* for a set of constants. Enumerated types provide you with enhanced developer IntelliSense features when using your class. We've created an enumerated type for OpenMode constants that provides the pop-up list of possible values while coding, shown in Figure 3.6.

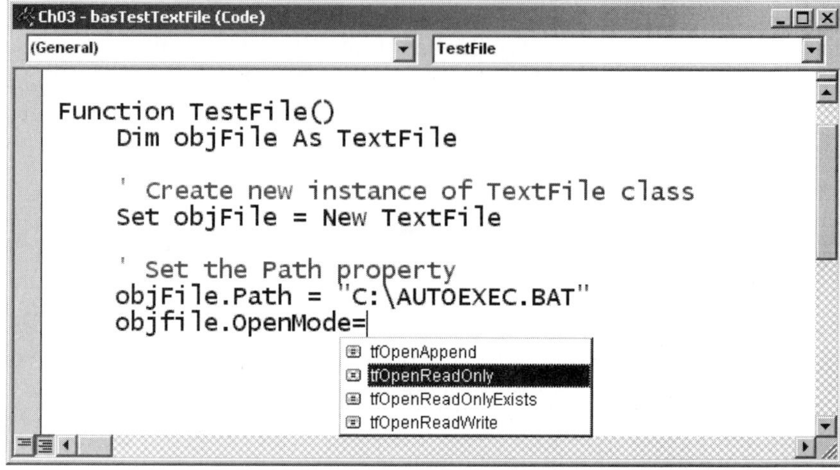

FIGURE 3.6: An enumerated type defines the list of constants displayed while writing code.

Defining an Enumerated Type

You create an enumerated type just like a user-defined type—using a multiline structure. Here's the definition for the enumerated type used by the OpenMode property:

```
' Enumeration for file open mode
Public Enum TextFileOpenMode
    tfOpenReadOnly
    tfOpenReadWrite
    tfOpenAppend
    tfOpenReadOnlyExists
End Enum
```

As you can see, the code block begins with the Enum keyword (optionally modified by Public or Private keywords) and a unique name for the type. Unless you declare the type as Private, the type name must be unique within the scope of the entire project. End Enum terminates the code block. The lines in between represent each enumerated constant value. You'll notice in our example that we've only included constant names and no values. This is perfectly valid, and VBA will assign each constant a long integer value starting at zero and incrementing by one. Therefore, tfOpenReadOnly evaluates to 0, tfOpenReadWrite is 1, and so on. We've omitted values since we only need to distinguish between different constants—the actual numeric values have no intrinsic meaning. If you want or need to, however, you can assign specific values, as in this example:

```
' This uses some specific values
Public Enum TextFileOpenMode
    tfOpenReadOnly = -1
    tfOpenReadWrite = 1
    tfOpenAppend
    tfOpenReadOnlyExists
End Enum
```

In this case, the first two constants have explicitly assigned values. The other two constants are assigned incrementing values starting at the last explicit value.

NOTE Enumerated type constants are limited to Long integers. You cannot create enumerated types using other data types.

Using Enumerated Types with Methods and Properties

Once you've defined an enumerated type, you use it just as you would any other data type, for example, in variable, argument, and return type definitions. It's this usage that provides the IntelliSense features in the Visual Basic Editor. The OpenMode property of our TextFile class uses the TextFileOpenMode type as its return and argument data types:

```
Property Get OpenMode() As TextFileOpenMode
    ' Retrieve the open mode of the file
    OpenMode = mlngOpenMode
End Property
Property Let OpenMode(ByVal lngMode As TextFileOpenMode)
    ' Set the open mode of the file only if
    ' a file is not already open
    If Not Me.IsOpen Then
        mlngOpenMode = lngMode
    End If
End Property
```

Whenever you use an enumerated type in place of a normal data type, VBA displays the list of constant values when it detects that you're editing an assignment or comparison statement. This makes it very easy to remember which choices apply, and it is extremely helpful for other developers using your classes.

WARNING

Simply defining an argument or variable using an enumerated type does not limit the values to those defined as part of the enumerated type. VBA treats the variable or argument internally as a Long integer, and thus you can substitute any Long integer value in place of one of the constants. While we've omitted it for clarity, your procedures that use enumerated types should include code to validate that values passed into procedures are of the right type.

Class Hierarchies

It is almost always the case that when you model an application using object-oriented techniques, you discover relationships between object classes. Sometimes depicted graphically, the relationship between classes is called an application's *object model*. Usually, object relationships form a natural hierarchy. Consider the diagram shown in Figure 3.7, the object model for a fictitious accounting application.

FIGURE 3.7:

Object model for a fictitious accounting application

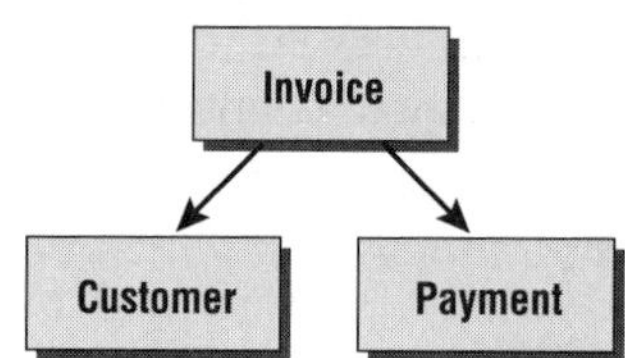

You can see from this figure that a relationship exists between invoice and customer and between invoice and payment. It is generally a good idea to create a sketch like the one in Figure 3.7 before beginning to program an application because it makes very clear which object classes exist and how they relate to one another.

Once you have an object model that represents your application, you can begin constructing class modules—one for each object in the diagram. To represent relationships between objects, declare pointers to child objects in the declarations section of parent class modules. For example, to model the relationship between invoice and customer (assuming classes named Invoice and Customer, respectively), you would declare a Customer variable in the declarations section of the Invoice class:

```
Public Customer As Customer
```

Note that you can, in fact, declare object variables with the same name as the class they're based on. Then, in the Invoice class's Initialize event, you would instantiate the Customer object:

```
Private Sub Class_Initialize()
    Set Customer = New Customer
End Sub
```

When you create a new invoice, VBA creates a new instance of the Customer. You can use the Invoice object to set properties of the customer instance, as the following code fragment demonstrates:

```
Dim objInvoice As Invoice

Set objInvoice = New Invoice
With objInvoice.Customer
    .FirstName = "Jane"
    .LastName = "Smith"
End With
' and so on...
```

The ability to create object hierarchies using class-level pointer variables is a powerful feature of VBA. It lets you develop and test objects (such as the Customer object in this example) separately and then assemble them into a robust, object-oriented representation of your application.

NOTE

The technique just described works great for one-to-one relationships, but what about one-to-many? For example, what if an invoice could have a number of customers associated with it? To model this situation, you need to use a collection. The sections "Collections of Objects" and "Creating Your Own Collections" later in this chapter cover this topic in detail.

Creating a Parent Property

In many object models, objects within the hierarchy implement a Parent property that contains a pointer to the instance of the object immediately above it in the hierarchy. This makes it convenient to traverse the hierarchy using VBA code: you can work your way down the tree using properties of class objects and work your way back up using the Parent property. For example, Excel Worksheet objects have a Parent property that points to the Workbook object in which the worksheets are contained.

You can implement a Parent property in your own classes by creating Property Set and Property Get procedures. For example, suppose you want to be able to reference the Invoice object from the Customer object it contains. Listing 3.8 shows you how to do this.

Listing 3.8

```
' Private variable to store pointer to parent
Private mobjParent As Invoice

Property Set Parent(objParent As Invoice)
    ' If property hasn't been set yet, do so
    If mobjParent Is Nothing Then
        Set mobjParent = objParent
    End If
End Property

Property Get Parent() As Invoice
    ' Return the pointer stored in mobjParent
    Set Parent = mobjParent
End Property
```

In this case, Parent is a *write-once property.* That is, after you set the value of the property, it cannot be set again. This prevents you from changing an object's parent after establishing the initial value. The best place to set the Parent property of the child is in the Class_Initialize event of the parent. The following code would appear in the Invoice class:

```
Private Sub Class_Initialize()
    ' Setup parental reference
    Set Customer.Parent = Me
End Sub
```

NOTE

In this example, we've declared the Property procedures to accept and return a specific object type, Invoice. If you are creating a class that might be used by a number of other classes (and thus have different types of parents), you can use the generic Object data type or use the Implements keyword to define a generic interface class. Using the Implements keyword in custom class modules is beyond the scope of this book, but it is covered in *Visual Basic Language Developer's Handbook*, also published by Sybex.

Collections of Objects

Often, when creating an object model for an application, you will find that the objects are related in a one-to-many relationship, that is, one instance of a class relates to many instances of another class. The set of related objects is typically called a *collection,* and the parent object contains that collection. VBA includes a Collection class you can use to create and manipulate your own custom collections. This section begins with a general discussion of collections and then shows you how to use VBA's Collection object to create your own.

Using Collections

You may already be familiar with collections from your experience using VBA or other Windows applications. For example, Microsoft Excel implements a Workbook object representing the data stored in an XLS file. This object, in turn, contains a collection of unique Worksheet objects. Each Worksheet object represents an individual worksheet tab within the workbook file.

If you're familiar with the way collections of objects work, you already know that you refer to objects in a collection using the collection name along with the name of one of the objects it contains. You can also use the relative position of the object in the collection by specifying a numeric index. For example, to examine the Visible property of a particular worksheet in the active workbook, you could use either of these statements:

```
Debug.Print ActiveWorkbook.Worksheets("Sheet1").Visible
Debug.Print ActiveWorkbook.Worksheets(1).Visible
```

NOTE

Collections are, in some respects, similar to arrays in that both contain a set of similar objects, and you can reference each using a numeric index. However, collections are much more powerful when dealing with sets of objects and when implementing methods for adding, removing, and referencing objects.

Collection Properties and Methods

All collections implement a number of methods and properties designed to help you put other objects into the collection, take them out, and reference particular items. Unfortunately, not all products and components implement these properties and methods the same way. For example, to add a new worksheet to an Excel workbook, you call the Add method of the Worksheets collection. To add a new table to an Access database using ADOX, on the other hand, you first create a new Table object. After setting properties of the new object, you call the Append method of the Tables collection.

If this sounds confusing, don't worry. If you're interested only in creating your own collections of objects using VBA, you need to be concerned with only three methods and one property:

- Use the *Add method* to add objects to a collection. You pass a pointer to the object and an optional unique identifier as parameters.
- Use the *Remove method* to remove objects from a collection. You pass an object's unique identifier (or ordinal position in the collection) as a parameter.
- Use the *Item method* to reference a particular object in the collection and return a pointer to it. You pass an object's unique identifier (or ordinal position in the collection) as a parameter.
- Use the *Count property* to return the number of objects in the collection.

Manipulating Objects in a Collection

Once an object is in a collection, you can manipulate its properties and methods directly. To refer to an object in a collection, you refer to its place in the collection using either a unique identifier (or key) or its ordinal position as a Long integer. You can also capture a pointer to the object in a variable, as in this example:

```
Dim wks As Worksheet
Set wks = ActiveWorkbook.WorkSheets(1)
```

Both of these techniques have been available in Microsoft Basic since the introduction of its object-oriented features. VBA added two new ways to work with objects and collections. The first, the With statement, is not limited to collections, but it can make working with complex object models much easier. The With statement lets you specify an object and then work with that object's properties or methods simply by starting each line with the dot separator character. Consider this example from Microsoft Excel:

```
With Workbooks("BOOK1.XLS").Worksheets("Sheet1"). _
 ChartObjects("Chart1").Chart
    .Rotation = 180
    .Elevation = 30
    .HasLegend = True
End With
```

This method of referring to the Chart object embedded on Sheet1 of BOOK1.XLS is certainly easier than repeating the collection syntax over and over.

Another VBA feature specific to collections is the For Each... loop. Like a regular For...Next loop, a For Each... loop uses a loop variable to iterate through a series of values. The values, however, are pointers to objects in a collection. To use a For Each... loop, you first declare a variable of the appropriate object data type. You then use it in the For Each... statement, along with a reference to the collection you want to loop through. During iterations of the loop, the variable is reset to point to successive objects in the collection. For example, to display all the worksheets in an Excel workbook, you could use code like this:

```
Dim wks As Worksheet
For Each wks In ActiveWorkbook.Worksheets
    wks.Visible = True
Next
```

You can use both of these constructs with collections you create using VBA's Collection object.

Creating Your Own Collections

VBA allows you to create your own collections using a special Collection class. Objects created from the VBA Collection class contain pointers to other objects. To use the Collection object, you must first create a new instance in your VBA code. For example:

```
Dim colSomeObjects As Collection
Set colSomeObjects = New Collection
```

You can then add objects to the collection using the object's Add method. Assuming the variable objSomething contained a pointer to an object, you could use a statement like this:

```
colSomeObjects.Add objSomething
```

When you add an object to a collection in this manner, however, the only way to refer back to it is by its ordinal position in the collection. Typically, you don't want to rely on an object's position, because it might change as other objects are added or removed. Instead, you can specify an alphanumeric identifier as the second parameter to the Add method:

```
colSomeObjects.Add objSomething, "Object1"
```

Having done this, you can refer to the object later on either by its position or by the unique key:

```
Set objSomething = colSomeObjects(1)
' or
Set objSomething = colSomeObjects("Object1")
```

WARNING Setting unique key values for objects can be tricky. See the section "Setting Unique Object Keys" later in this chapter for more information.

Note that the previous examples don't use the Item method to refer to objects in the collection. This is because Item is the default method and can therefore be omitted. When fully qualified, the above statements would look like this:

```
Set objSomething = colSomeObjects.Item(1)
' or
Set objSomething = colSomeObjects.Item("Object1")
```

NOTE Collections created using VBA's Collection object are one-based. There is no way to change this. The first object added is object 1, the second is 2, and so on. As objects are removed from the middle of the collection, higher numbers are adjusted downward to maintain continuity. You can also add objects to a collection at a specific point by specifying either the *before* or *after* parameter of the Add method (see online help for more information). It is for these reasons that you should not depend on an object's position in a collection.

You can represent one-to-many relationships in your object model by creating a collection as a property of an object class. For example, suppose the colSomeObjects collection in the preceding example was declared as the SomeObjects property of a class called Application. To add an object to the collection, you would use a statement like this (assuming objApp contained a pointer to an instance of Application):

```
objApp.SomeObjects.Add objSomething, "Object1"
```

Likewise, referring back to the object would require you to include a reference to the parent class:

```
Set objSomething = objApp.SomeObjects("Object1")
```

Although simple to implement, using public collections does have its drawbacks. The section "Creating a Collection Class" later in this chapter explains what these drawbacks are and how to overcome them.

Collections and Pointer Lifetime

When you add an object to a collection, you create a new pointer to the object. The new pointer is stored as part of the collection. Consider the following code fragment:

```
Dim objSomething As SomeObject

Set objSomething = New SomeObject
SomeObjects.Add objSomething
' Does this terminate the object?
Set objSomething = Nothing
```

What happens to the new instance of SomeObject after you set the objSomething pointer to Nothing? The answer is: nothing. Even though the code explicitly destroyed the pointer contained in objSomething, an implicit pointer exists as part of the SomeObjects collection. Therefore, the new object instance is not terminated until it is removed from the collection.

Also, pay attention to where you declare your new Collection object variable. As a variable, it obeys VBA's rules concerning scope and lifetime. If you declare a Collection object variable in the body of a procedure, for instance, it will disappear when the procedure terminates, destroying all the objects it contains. Typically, you should declare collections as module or global variables.

Creating a Collection Class

VBA makes it simple to create your own collections using the Collection object. The Collection object does have one serious drawback, however. There is no way to limit the types of objects placed into a VBA collection. Traditionally, collections are made up of similar objects, but you can place pointers to any object type into a VBA collection. Unless you are extremely careful, this could lead to problems, especially in large development projects. For example, you can refer to an object's properties or methods using collection syntax, such as:

```
colSomeObjects(1).Amount = 10
```

But what happens if the object represented by colSomeObjects(1) doesn't have an Amount property? VBA generates a runtime error. To control the types of objects that are placed into a collection, you must create a collection class: a VBA class that defines a Private Collection object and implements methods to add, remove, retrieve, and count objects in the collection.

Because the Collection object is Private, you don't have to worry about external procedures cluttering it with invalid object pointers. Using your own class also gives you the ability to create custom replacements for the standard Add, Remove, and Item methods.

Normally, you create two classes to represent a collection of objects in this manner. One defines the object that will be contained in the collection, and the other defines the collection itself. To demonstrate this, we've created a second version of the TextFile class described earlier in the chapter. In the second version, all lines of text are read into a collection when a file is opened, rather than one at a time. Listing 3.9 shows the Line class module that defines a Line object, representing a line of text in the sample TextFile2 object class.

Listing 3.9

```
' Private variables for line of text
Private mstrText As String

' Private ID variable
Private mstrID As String

' Public variable for changed flag
Public Changed As Boolean

Property Get Text() As String
    ' Return value of private variable
    Text = mstrText
End Property

Property Let Text(ByVal strText As String)
    ' Change private variable and set changed flag
    mstrText = strText
    Me.Changed = True
End Property
```

```
Property Get Length() As Long
    ' Use Len function to return string length
    Length = Len(mstrText)
End Property

Property Get ID() As String
    ' Return value of private variable
    ID = mstrID
End Property

Private Sub Class_Initialize()
    ' Set the object's ID property to a random string
    mstrID = "Line" & CLng(Rnd * (2 ^ 31))
End Sub
```

Listing 3.10 shows the class module code for the Lines collection (the Lines class module from CH03.MDB). Note the Private Collection object in the module's declaration section. Note also the Add, Remove, and Item methods, implemented as Public procedures, and the Count Property Get procedure.

TIP

This example also implements a Changed property that indicates whether any of the lines in the collection have been modified. This is another reason for using collection classes: you can create custom properties and methods of your collection, which is not possible with standard VBA Collection objects.

Listing 3.10

```
Option Explicit

' Private collection to store Lines
Private mcolLines As Collection

Private Sub Class_Initialize()
    ' Instantiate the Collection object
    Set mcolLines = New Collection
End Sub

Public Sub Add(ByVal strText As String, _
 Optional ByVal varBefore As Variant)
```

```
    ' Declare new Line object
    Dim objLine As New Line

    ' Set Text property to passed string
    objLine.Text = strText
    ' Add to private collection, using object's
    ' ID property as unique index
    mcolLines.Add objLine, objLine.ID, varBefore
End Sub

Public Sub Remove(ByVal varID As Variant)
    ' Call Remove method of private collection object
    mcolLines.Remove varID
End Sub

Public Function Item(ByVal varID As Variant) As Line
    ' Set return value of property to item within
    ' the private collection object specified by
    ' the passed index value (Note the return type!)
    Set Item = mcolLines(varID)
End Function

Property Get Count() As Long
    ' Return Count property of private collection
    Count = mcolLines.Count
End Property

Property Let Changed(ByVal fChanged As Boolean)
    Dim objLine As Line

    ' Set Changed property of each Line to fChanged
    For Each objLine In mcolLines
        objLine.Changed = fChanged
    Next
End Property

Property Get Changed() As Boolean
    Dim objLine As Line

    ' Loop through all Line objects in collection-
    ' if any Changed property is True then the
```

```
    ' Changed property of the collection is True
    For Each objLine In mcolLines
        If objLine.Changed Then
            Changed = True
            Exit For
        End If
    Next
End Property
```

Implementing the Remove method and the Count property in a custom collection class is straightforward. They are simple wrappers around the Collection object's own method and property. The Add method is a bit more complex, however. Rather than being a simple wrapper, it's declared to accept a string parameter representing a line of text and, optionally, an index of an existing Line object before which to insert the new line. After creating a new instance of the Line class, the code sets the object's Text property to the string passed to the Add method. It then adds the object to the Private Collection object, using the new Line's ID property as the unique index. It's this custom Add method that prevents garbage from getting into the collection. Finally, the Item method returns a particular object from the collection using an index passed to it.

NOTE The arguments to the Add, Remove, and Item methods representing an object index are declared as variants. This is necessary because the index could be either an object's unique alphanumeric identifier or its ordinal position in the collection.

Using a Collection Class

Using a collection class is similar to using any object class. You create a new instance of it and then manipulate its properties and methods. In the case of the Lines class, the TextFile2 class module creates a new instance, in effect producing a Lines collection within the TextFile2 object. The object even has the same name as the class:

```
Public Lines As Lines
```

You can then use the properties and methods of the class to add new instances of Line objects to the collection as you read each line of text from the file. Listing 3.11 shows a portion of the FileOpen method of the TextFile2 class. After reading a line of text into the local variable strLine, the code adds a new object to the Lines collection.

Listing 3.11

```
Dim strLine As String

' ... other statements to open file

' Read all lines into the Lines collection
Set Lines = New Lines
If LOF(mhFile) > 0 Then
    Do Until EOF(mhFile)
        Line Input #mhFile, strLine
        Me.Lines.Add strLine
    Loop
End If
```

Once the collection of lines has been established, printing each one becomes trivial. You simply loop through each element in the collection, as demonstrated in Listing 3.12.

Listing 3.12

```
Dim cLines As Long

' Assume objFile is an open TextFile object

For cLines = 1 To objFile.Lines.Count
    Debug.Print objFile.Lines.Item(cLines).Text
Next cLines
```

WARNING Be careful when using the Remove method inside a loop. Because VBA checks the value of the Count property only as it begins the loop but renumbers the items in the collection as you remove them, you will encounter a runtime error as the loop reaches its halfway point. To remedy this problem, loop backward from the initial Count value back to 1. The sample code in frmTestFile uses this technique to remove blank lines from a file.

Disadvantages of Collection Classes

Although collection classes give you an added level of safety and flexibility, there is a downside to using them: because by default VBA treats your class as a normal object, not a collection, you lose two very handy collection operators.

First, with true collections, you normally don't need to specify the Item method when referring to objects within the collection. That's because Item is a collection's *default method.* For example, in Excel VBA, the following two statements are equivalent:

```
Debug.Print Workbooks.Item(1).Name
Debug.Print Workbooks(1).Name
```

When using a collection class, however, you must always specify the Item method.

The For Each… loop is the second feature that will not work with collection classes. If you wish to enumerate all the objects in your collection, you must use a standard For…Next loop with a numeric variable. Use the Count property to determine the number of objects in the collection and loop from 1 to this number.

You can, however, trick VBA into treating your collection classes as if they were the built-in Collection class using a few undocumented techniques. These techniques rely on features available in Visual Basic 6 that aren't supported in VBA. Specifically, you can set attributes of procedures that define them as default members or enumeration functions, the latter being what makes For Each… loops work. VB offers a dialog for setting these attributes. With VBA, you must edit a class's source file on disk and then import it into a project for the attributes to take effect.

To try this out, follow the steps outlined below:

1. Open the Lines collection class in the Visual Basic Editor and add the following procedure:

   ```
   Public Function NewEnum() As IUnknown
       ' Enumeration function for the collection
       Set NewEnum = mcolLines.[_NewEnum]
   End Function
   ```

2. Select File ➢ Remove Lines from the menu and click the Yes button when prompted to export the file.
3. Save Lines.cls to a disk directory.

4. Open Lines.cls in a text editor like Notepad.
5. Find the NewEnum function and edit it so that it looks like this:

```
Public Function NewEnum() As IUnknown
    Attribute NewEnum.VB_UserMemId = -4
    ' Enumeration function for the collection
    Set NewEnum = mcolLines.[_NewEnum]
End Function
```

6. Find the Item method and edit it so that it looks like this:

```
Public Function Item(ByVal varID As Variant) As Line
    Attribute Item.VB_UserMemId = 0
    ' Set return value of property to item within
    ' the private collection object specified by
    ' the passed index value (Note the return type!)
    Set Item = mcolLines(varID)
End Function
```

7. Save the Lines.cls file.
8. Import the file back into the project by selecting File ➢ Import File and choosing Lines.cls from the Import dialog.

You should be able to treat the Lines collection class just as you would the built-in VBA Collection class. You can now edit the code shown earlier in Listing 3.12 to make it look like that shown in Listing 3.13. We think you'll agree it's much simpler and more intuitive.

Listing 3.13

```
Dim objLine As Line

' Assume objFile is an open TextFile object

For Each objLine in objFile.Lines
    Debug.Print objLine.Text
Next
```

So how does it work? Default members and enumeration functions are defined by procedure attributes stored in the source files. Even though VBA won't let you edit them in the Visual Basic Editor, it will honor them when you import files. Perhaps there'll be an easier way to do this in future versions.

TIP

While enumeration functions are only useful for collection classes, you can use this technique to create a default property or method for any class.

Setting Unique Object Keys

We stated earlier that you should set a unique key for objects added to collections. It's worth noting, however, that this is not always intuitive or easy to do. First, an object's key cannot be numeric, making the generation of arbitrary, incrementing keys cumbersome. Second, once you set the key value, you cannot change it. Your only option is to destroy the object.

Ideally, you would use a property of the object being added. For example, the unique key for Excel Worksheet objects is the name of the worksheet. Unfortunately, you cannot mimic this feature in VBA, because the name of the object might change. If your object has a property that will not change, it's fine to use it. Otherwise, you can create a property of objects added to collections (for example, one called ID) to hold the unique key. Set the value of this property to an arbitrary (random) value during the Initialize event of the class. For example, this code fragment sets the value of a Private variable to a random, alphanumeric value:

```
Private Sub Class_Initialize()
    ' Set the object's ID property to a random string
    mstrID = "Line" & CLng(Rnd * (2 ^ 31))
End Sub
```

By setting this value in the Initialize event, you ensure that it will always have a value—the Initialize event is always triggered when an instance of the class is created. You can then use the value as the object's unique index in a collection. Consider the code shown in Listing 3.14. This code creates a new instance of the Line class and then adds it to a collection named mcolLines. The ID property of the new Line class is used as the unique key.

Listing 3.14

```
Public Sub Add(ByVal strText As String, _
 Optional ByVal varBefore As Variant)

    ' Declare new Line object
    Dim objLine As New Line
```

```
    ' Set Text property to passed string
    objLine.Text = strText

    ' Add to private collection, using object's
    ' ID property as unique index
    mcolLines.Add objLine, objLine.ID, varBefore
End Sub
```

Defining and Using Custom Events

If you've been developing in Access, Office, or Visual Basic for any length of time, you probably don't even think about how easy it is, thanks to support for *event-driven programming*. Event-driven programming creates a coding framework defined around an application's events. All you need to do is pick the event you want to respond to and write some code. In Access applications, you normally respond to events on forms and reports. Starting with VBA 6 in Access 2000, you now have the chance to define your own events in the custom classes you create. This section will explain how and why to do this.

Why Custom Events?

Before explaining how to create your own events, it makes sense to explain why you'd want to do this. You may have noticed that the examples in this chapter are broken up into two components: the class module that implements core functionality and the application (sample code or form) that utilizes the class. The class never interacts with the user interface or processes errors—that's up to the application component. It makes the class module more reusable by not tying it to a specific UI implementation.

Custom events extend this concept even further by exposing an even deeper level of control for the application component. In class modules without events, the interaction between an application component and a class module is unidirectional—the component calls a method or accesses a property and waits for the class to return control. With custom events, the class module can broadcast what's happening during method or property processing and the application component can respond. In effect, the class can say, "Something just happened," and any application component using the class can decide what, if anything, to do.

Defining and Raising Events

Defining and raising events is accomplished using two new VBA keywords—Event and RaiseEvent. You use the Event keyword in a class module's declaration section to define what events a class supports, including any parameters passed to an event procedure. When you want to trigger a defined event, you use the RaiseEvent operator in one or more procedures. While you only define a custom event once, you can raise it multiple times.

NOTE

You can only define, raise, and sink events in VBA class modules. You cannot use standard modules for custom events.

We've created yet another incarnation of the TextFile class that illustrates custom events. This version, TextFile3, includes the following statements in its declaration section:

```
' Event declarations
Public Event LineRead(Text As String, Skip As Boolean)
Public Event LineWrite(Text As String, Skip As Boolean)
```

These statements define two custom events, LineRead and LineWrite, which will be triggered whenever a line of text is read from or written to a text file, respectively. Both define two arguments. Text will contain the line of text about to be read or written. Skip will give the application component responding to the event a chance to tell the class instance to skip the current line.

LineRead and LineWrite are raised in the FileOpen and FileSave methods, respectively. These look almost identical to the methods in TextFile and TextFile2 except for a small bit of extra code. Here's the relevant portion of the FileOpen method:

```
' Fire the LineRead event
If Not mfSuppressEvents Then
    fSkip = False
    RaiseEvent LineRead(strLine, fSkip)
End If

' If no one has asked to skip
' this line then add to collection
If Not fSkip Then
    Me.Lines.Add strLine
End If
```

The FileSave method includes similar code:

```
' Fire the LineWrite event
fSkip = False
RaiseEvent LineWrite(strText, fSkip)

' If no one has asked to skip this
' then write it to the file
If Not fSkip Then
    Print #hFile, strText
End If
```

Both reset a local variable, fSkip, to False prior to raising an event. This variable, along with the string variable storing the current line of text, is passed to the event. If any other part of the application is "listening" to the event, it can modify either argument. That's why the methods both check the value of fSkip after raising the event.

Sinking to Custom Events

Defining and raising custom events is just half the story. You still need to respond to events in some other part of your application. To do this, you need to create an object variable capable of funneling events to your application. This is called creating an *event sink*. Event sinks are extensions to normal object references with one restriction: you can only create an event sink inside a class module. This makes sense if you think about the event sinks that Access provides for you—those for built-in and ActiveX controls. These are only accessible through form and report modules that, as we mentioned earlier, are class modules.

You create an event sink using the VBA keyword WithEvents by modifying a normal object variable declaration. We've illustrated this in the frmCopyFile form included in CH03.MDB. You can use this form to copy the contents of one text file to another. If you open the form's module in the Visual Basic Editor, you'll see these lines of code:

```
' Event sinks for two TextFile3 objects
Private WithEvents mobjFileFrom As TextFile3
Private WithEvents mobjFileTo As TextFile3
```

These lines declare the two TextFile3 objects required for the copy operation. You'll notice that these are just like regular object variable declarations except for the WithEvents keyword. When you use WithEvents, VBA queries the class for any defined events (see the previous section) and provides the event sink and event procedures for you to respond to. Just like event procedures for controls, you access event procedures for custom events through the drop-down lists in the code window. Figure 3.8 shows the form's code window displaying the event procedure list. Notice that the object names are defined by the variable names you use in the declaration.

FIGURE 3.8:

Creating event sinks adds items to the object and procedure lists.

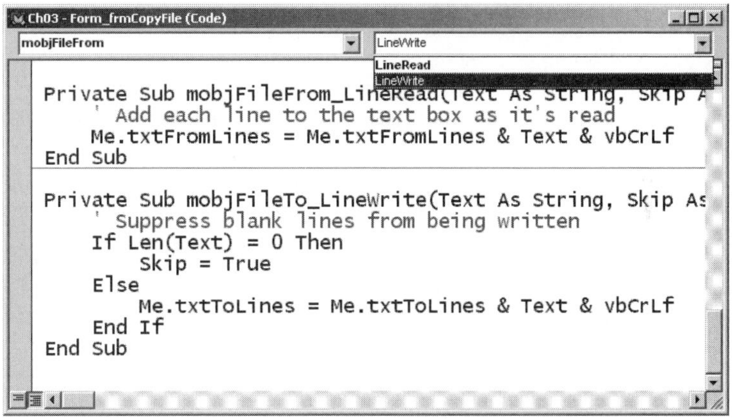

```
Ch03 - Form_frmCopyFile (Code)
mobjFileFrom                    LineWrite
                                LineRead
                                LineWrite
Private Sub mobjFileFrom_LineRead(Text As String, Skip A
    ' Add each line to the text box as it's read
    Me.txtFromLines = Me.txtFromLines & Text & vbCrLf
End Sub

Private Sub mobjFileTo_LineWrite(Text As String, Skip As
    ' Suppress blank lines from being written
    If Len(Text) = 0 Then
        Skip = True
    Else
        Me.txtToLines = Me.txtToLines & Text & vbCrLf
    End If
End Sub
```

Before the event sinks will work, however, you must instantiate both the class in which the sinks are declared as well as the class that raises the events. We accomplish the latter with code behind a command button's Click event. The former is handled automatically by Access when it opens the form.

In our sample form, we respond to the LineRead event of the source file by writing the current line of text to the appropriate text box on the form (see Listing 3.15). Likewise, when the LineWrite of the target file is fired, we respond to it by checking for an empty line and suppress the write operation by setting the procedure's Skip argument to True.

Listing 3.15

```
Private Sub mobjFileFrom_LineRead(Text As String, _
 Skip As Boolean)
    ' Add each line to the text box as it's read
    Me.txtFromLines = Me.txtFromLines & Text & vbCrLf
End Sub
```

```
Private Sub mobjFileTo_LineWrite(Text As String, _
 Skip As Boolean)
    ' Suppress blank lines from being written
    If Len(Text) = 0 Then
        Skip = True
    Else
        Me.txtToLines = Me.txtToLines & Text & vbCrLf
    End If
End Sub
```

Figure 3.9 shows the frmCopyFile form after using it to copy AUTOEXEC.BAT to a test file. The text boxes listing the files' contents were populated by code in the aforementioned event procedures.

FIGURE 3.9:

The text boxes on this form are populated by responding to custom class events.

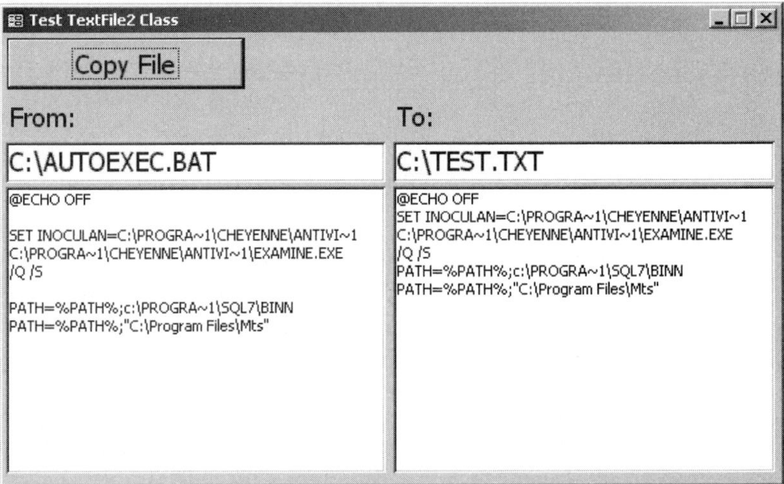

While this is a simple and somewhat trivial example, it does demonstrate the power of custom class events. If you examine the code in the form's module that copies one file into another, you'll see it's very straightforward: open one file, copy each line to another file, save the second file. It does not interact with the user interface at all. That task is left to the event procedures. By breaking the link between program logic and UI, you can increase the flexibility and maintainability of your applications.

NOTE We used a form for our example to simplify coding. Since a form module is a class module, it was automatically instantiated when the form was opened. If you create an event sink in a normal class module, you'll need to instantiate the class before the event sink will work.

Summary

In this chapter, we took a look at VBA class modules, one of the most powerful features of VBA. By encapsulating complex functionality and code in class modules, you can develop applications that are easier to program and maintain. Of course, it all starts with thinking about the problem you're trying to solve in terms of object classes and the relationships between them. Once you've identified the components, it is relatively easy to model them using class modules: simply create one class for each "thing" you want to model. In the case of one-to-many relationships between classes, you'll need an additional class to model a collection.

This chapter also explored class module coding techniques. It demonstrated how to create a class and its properties and methods and how to create and use an instance of that class. You also saw how to create and use collection classes. Finally, this chapter presented a few useful class examples for reading and writing text files and for manipulating data.

When deciding how to take advantage of VBA class modules, you are limited only by your imagination. Just keep the following tips in mind:

- Create one class for each "thing" you want to model.
- Use Property procedures when you need to control how property values are set and retrieved.
- Use pointers to other classes to represent relationships between objects.
- Implement collection classes to protect and extend VBA's Collection object.
- Define appropriate custom events that enable other parts of your application to respond to actions in a flexible fashion.

CHAPTER

FOUR

4

Database Design

- Database design and normalization theory
- Designing your databases: a practical, 20-step approach
- Normalizing a poorly designed database

Database design theory is a topic many people avoid learning; either they lack the time, or they give up because of the dry, academic treatment the topic is usually given. Unfortunately, building a database without a solid understanding of relational database design theory is like building a house on a cracked foundation.

This chapter begins with an introduction to relational database design theory, including a discussion of keys, relationships, integrity rules, and normal forms. We also present a practical, step-by-step approach to good database design and furnish an example that demonstrates how to normalize an existing, poorly designed database.

The Relational Model

The relational database model was conceived in 1969 by E.F. Codd, then a researcher at IBM. The model is based on mathematical theory—or, more specifically, on the disciplines of set theory and predicate logic. The basic idea behind the relational model is that a database consists of a series of unordered tables (or relations) that can be manipulated using nonprocedural operations that return tables. This model was in vast contrast to the more traditional database theories of the time, which were more complicated, less flexible, and dependent on the physical methods used to store the data.

NOTE

It is commonly thought that the word *relational* in the relational model comes from the fact that you *relate* tables to each other in a relational database. Although this is a convenient way to think of the term, it's not accurate. Instead, the word *relational* has its roots in the terminology Codd used to define the relational model. The table in Codd's writings was actually referred to as a relation (a related set of information). In fact, Codd (and other relational database theorists) use the terms *relations, attributes,* and *tuples* where most of us use the more common terms *tables, columns,* and *rows,* respectively (or the more physically oriented—and thus less preferable for discussions of database design theory—*files, fields,* and *records*).

The relational model can be applied to both databases and database management programs themselves. The *relational fidelity* of database programs can be compared using Codd's 12 rules (since Codd's seminal paper on the relational model, the number of rules has been expanded to more than 300) for determining how DBMS products conform to the relational model. When compared with other database management programs, Access fares quite well in terms of relational fidelity. Still, it has a way to go before it meets all 12 rules completely.

Fortunately, you don't have to wait until Access is fully relational before you can benefit from the relational model. The relational model can also be applied to the design of databases, which is the subject of the remainder of this chapter.

Relational Database Design

When designing a database, you have to make decisions regarding how best to take some system in the real world and model it in a database. This process consists of deciding which tables to create and which columns they will contain, as well as the relationships between the tables. While it would be nice if this process were totally intuitive and obvious or, even better, automated, this is simply not the case. A well-designed database takes time and effort to conceive, refine, and build.

The benefits of a database that has been designed according to the relational model are numerous, including the following:

- Data entry, updates, and deletions are efficient.
- Data retrieval, summarization, and reporting are efficient.
- Because the database follows a well-formulated model, it behaves predictably.
- Because much of the information is stored in the database rather than in the application, the database is somewhat self-documenting.
- Changes to the database schema (the definition of the tables) are easy to make.

The goal of this chapter is to explain the basic principles behind relational database design and demonstrate how to apply these principles when designing a database using Access. This chapter is by no means comprehensive, and it is certainly not definitive. Many books have been written on database design theory; in fact, many careers have been devoted to its study. Instead, this chapter is meant as an informal introduction to database design theory for the Access developer.

NOTE

For a more detailed discussion of database design, we suggest you read *An Introduction to Database Systems, Volume I*, by C.J. Date (Addison-Wesley); *SQL and Relational Basics* by Fabian Pascal (M&T Books); or *Database Processing: Fundamentals, Design, and Implementation* by David M. Kroenke (Macmillan). Or if you prefer a lighter, less academic approach, we suggest *Database Design for Mere Mortals* by Michael J. Hernandez (Addison-Wesley).

Tables, Uniqueness, and Keys

Tables in the relational model are used to represent "things" in the real world. Each table should represent a collection of one type of thing. These things (or *entities*) can be real-world objects or events. For example, a real-world object might be a customer, an inventory item, or an invoice. Examples of events include patient visits, orders, and telephone calls.

Tables are made up of rows and columns. The relational model dictates that each row in a table be unique. If you allow duplicate rows in a table, there's no way to uniquely address a given row programmatically. This creates all sorts of ambiguities and problems.

You guarantee uniqueness for a table by designating a *primary key*—a column or set of columns that contains unique values for a table. Each table can have only one primary key, even though several columns or combinations of columns may contain unique values. All columns (or combinations of columns) in a table with unique values are referred to as *candidate keys,* from which the primary key must be chosen. All other candidate key columns are referred to as *alternate keys.* Keys can be simple or composite. A *simple key* is a key made up of one column, whereas a *composite key* is made up of two or more columns.

The decision as to which candidate key is the primary one rests in your hands; there's no absolute rule as to which candidate key is best. Fabian Pascal, in his book *SQL and Relational Basics,* notes that the decision should be based on the principles of minimality (choose the fewest columns necessary), stability (choose a key that seldom changes), and simplicity/familiarity (choose a key that is both simple and familiar to users). For example, let's say a company has a table of customers called tblCustomer that looks like the one shown in Figure 4.1.

FIGURE 4.1:

The best choice for primary key for tblCustomer would be CustomerId.

tblCustomer : Table

CustomerId	LastName	FirstName	Address	City	State	ZipCode	Phone
1	Jones	Paul	1313 Mockingbird Lane	Seattle	WA	98117	2068886902
2	Nelson	Greg	45-39 173rd St	Redmond	WA	98119	2069809099
3	Madison	Ken	2345 16th NE	Kent	WA	98109	2067837890
4	Jones	Geoff	1313 Mockingbird Lane	Seattle	WA	98117	2068886902

Record: 1 of 4

Candidate keys for tblCustomer might include CustomerId, LastName + FirstName, Phone, Address + City + State, and Address + ZipCode. Following Pascal's guidelines, you would rule out the last three candidates because addresses and phone numbers can change fairly frequently. The choice between CustomerId and the name composite key is less obvious and would involve trade-offs. How likely is it that a customer's name will change (for example, because of marriage or divorce)? Will misspelling of names be common? How likely is it that two customers will have the same first and last names? How familiar will CustomerId be to users? There's no right answer, but most developers favor numeric primary keys because names do sometimes change and because, in Access (and most other databases), searches and sorts of numeric columns are more efficient than searches and sorts of text columns.

AutoNumber columns (referred to as counter columns prior to Access 95) make good primary keys, especially when you're having trouble coming up with good candidate keys and no existing arbitrary identification number is already in place. Don't use an AutoNumber column if you'll sometimes need to renumber the values or if you must have an automatically incrementing number with no gaps in the sequence of values.

Foreign Keys and Domains

Although primary keys are a function of individual tables, if you created databases that consisted only of independent and unrelated tables, you'd have little need for them. Primary keys become essential, however, when you start to create relationships that join multiple tables in a database. A *foreign key* is a column in one table that references the primary key of another table.

Determining Which Type of AutoNumber Column to Use

The AutoNumber datatype replaced the Counter datatype with the introduction of Access 95. In addition, Microsoft has added two new field properties to the AutoNumber properties collection: FieldSize and NewValues.

You can set FieldSize to either Long Integer or Replication ID, with the default being Long Integer. Unless you're using the replication facilities of Access, you should leave this set to the default. (See Chapter 10 of *Access 2000 Developer's Handbook, Volume II* for more details on replication.)

You can set the NewValues property to Increment or Random. Access 1.*x* and 2 supported only Increment. Increment is a good choice when you want an AutoNumber column that increases by one for each new record and you want the number to approximate the number of records in the table. We use the term *approximate* here because an incrementing AutoNumber column will invariably contain gaps of records that were undone or deleted. You can't reuse the numbers that fall into these gaps.

A NewValues property setting of Random might be a better choice when you want to have data entered at multiple sites and then want to merge the separate databases at some later time (whether or not you are using Access replication). In this situation, an incrementing AutoNumber column won't work, because each copy of the database would be assigning the same numbers. If you used a random AutoNumber column, however, there would be only a slight chance that each copy of the database would use the same number.

Continuing the example presented earlier, let's say you choose CustomerId as the primary key for tblCustomer. If you created a second table, tblOrder, you would likely include a copy of the CustomerId column in this table (see Figure 4.2). CustomerId is a foreign key in tblOrder because you can use it to refer to a row in the tblCustomer table.

It is important that both foreign keys and the primary keys they reference share a common meaning and derive their values from the same domain. *Domains* are simply pools of values from which columns are drawn. For example, CustomerId is a member of the domain of valid customer ID numbers, which might in this case be Long integers ranging between 1 and 50,000. Similarly, a column named Sex might be based on a one-letter domain made up of the letters *M* and *F*. You can think of domains as user-defined column types, the definition of which implies certain rules the columns must follow and certain operations you can perform on those columns.

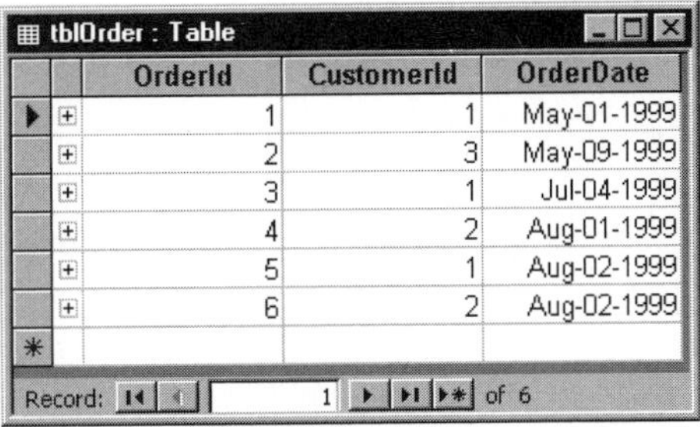

tblOrder : Table

OrderId	CustomerId	OrderDate
1	1	May-01-1999
2	3	May-09-1999
3	1	Jul-04-1999
4	2	Aug-01-1999
5	1	Aug-02-1999
6	2	Aug-02-1999

Record: 1 of 6

FIGURE 4.2:

CustomerId is a foreign key in tblOrder that you can use to reference a customer stored in tblCustomer.

Access supports domains only partially. For example, Access will prevent you from creating a relationship between two tables using columns of differing datatypes. On the other hand, Access will not prevent you from joining the Integer column EmployeeAge from one table to the Integer column YearsWorked from a second table, even though these two columns are obviously from different domains.

Relationships

You define foreign keys in a database to model relationships in the real world. Relationships between real-world entities can be quite complex, involving numerous entities, all having multiple relationships with each other. For example, a family has multiple relationships among multiple people—all at the same time. In a relational database such as Access, however, you can only consider relationships between two tables at a time. These pairs of tables can be related in one of three different ways: one-to-one, one-to-many, or many-to-many.

In Access, of course, you specify relationships using the Tools ➢ Relationships command.

One-to-One Relationships

Two tables are related in a *one-to-one* (1→1) relationship if, for each row in the first table, there is at most one row in the second table. True one-to-one relationships seldom occur in the real world. This type of relationship is often created to get around some limitation of the database management software rather than to model a real-world situation.

In Access, 1→1 relationships may be necessary in a database when you have to split a table into two or more tables because of security or performance concerns or because of the limit of 255 columns per table. For example, in a medical research database you might keep most patient information in tblPatient but put especially sensitive information (for example, patient name, social security number, and address) in tblPtConfidential (see Figure 4.3). Access to the information in tblPtConfidential could be more restricted than for tblPatient. Tables in a 1→1 relationship should always have the same primary key, which serves as the join column.

FIGURE 4.3:

The tblPatient and tblConfidential tables have a one-to-one relationship. The primary key of both tables is PatientId.

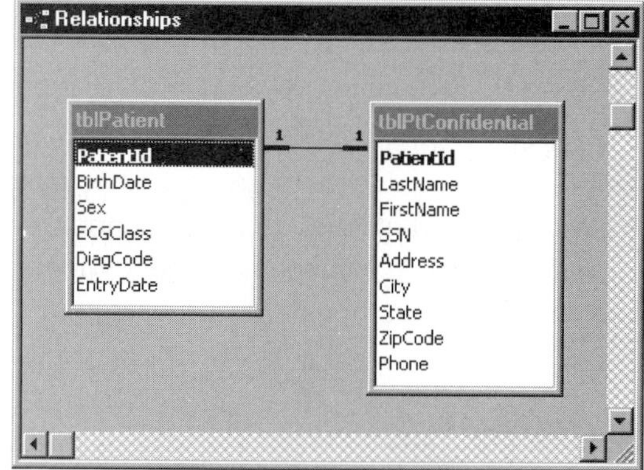

One-to-Many Relationships

Two tables are related in a *one-to-many* (1→M) relationship if, for each row in the first table, there can be zero, one, or many rows in the second table, but for each row in the second table, there is exactly one row in the first table. For example, for each order of a pizza delivery business, you can have multiple detail items. Therefore, tblOrder is related to tblOrderDetail in a 1→M relationship (see Figure 4.4).

FIGURE 4.4:

There can be many detail lines for each order in the pizza delivery business, but each detail line applies to only one order. tblOrder and tblOrderDetail are therefore related in a one-to-many relationship.

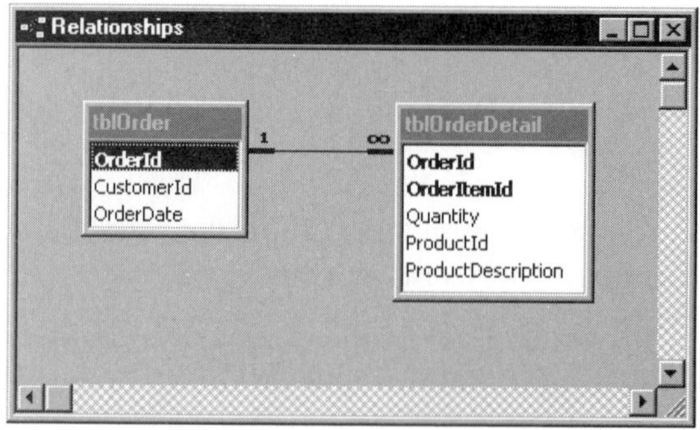

The 1→M relationship is also referred to as a *parent-child* or *master-detail* relationship. 1→M relationships are the most commonly modeled type of relationship. They are also used to link base tables to information stored in *lookup tables.* For example, in the example shown earlier in Figure 4.3, tblPatient has a numeric field, DiagCode, which serves as a foreign key to the tblDiagCode table where the actual diagnoses are stored. In this case, tblDiagCode is related to tblPatient in a 1→M relationship (that is, one row in the lookup table can be used in zero or more rows in the patient table).

Many-to-Many Relationships

Two tables have a *many-to-many* (M→M) relationship when, for each row in the first table, there can be many rows in the second table, *and* for each row in the second table, there can be many rows in the first table. M→M relationships can't be directly modeled in many relational database programs, including Access. These types of relationships must be broken into multiple 1→M relationships. For example, a patient may be covered by multiple insurance plans, and an insurance company covers multiple patients. Thus, the tblPatient table in a medical database would be related to the tblInsurer table using a M→M relationship. To model the relationship between these two tables, you would create a third table, a *linking table,* perhaps called tblPtInsurancePgm, that would contain a row for each insurance program under which a patient was covered (see Figure 4.5). Thus, the M→M relationship between tblPatient and tblInsurer could be represented by two 1→M relationships: tblPatient would be related to tblPtInsurancePgm in a 1→M relationship, and tblInsurer would be related to tblPtInsurancePgm in a second 1→M relationship.

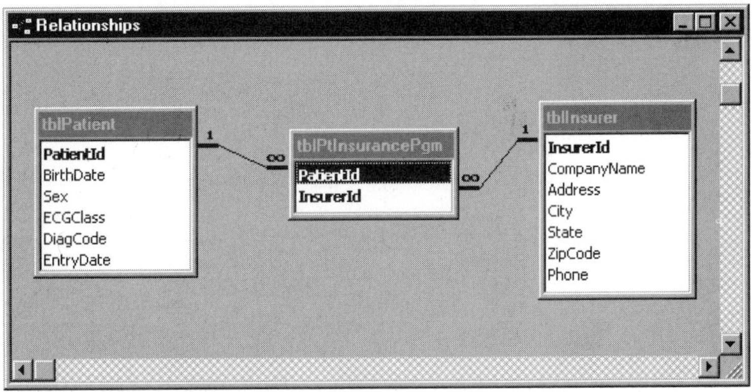

FIGURE 4.5:

A linking table, tblPtInsurancePgm, is used to model the many-to-many relationship between tblPatient and tblInsurer.

Normalizing a Set of Tables

As mentioned at the beginning of this chapter, when designing databases you are faced with a series of choices. How many tables will there be, and what will they represent? Which columns will go in which tables? What will be the relationships between the tables? The answer to each of these questions lies in something called *normalization*, the process of simplifying the design of a database so it achieves optimum structure.

Normalization theory gives us the concept of normal forms to assist in achieving the optimum structure. The *normal forms* are a progression of rules you apply to your database, with each higher normal form achieving a better, more efficient design. The normal forms are:

- First Normal Form
- Second Normal Form
- Third Normal Form
- Boyce/Codd Normal Form
- Fourth Normal Form
- Fifth Normal Form

In this chapter, we discuss normalization through Third Normal Form.

Before First Normal Form: Relations

The normal forms are based on *relations*, special types of tables that have the following attributes:

- They describe one entity.
- They have no duplicate rows; hence, there is always a primary key.
- The columns are unordered.
- The rows are unordered.

Access doesn't require you to define a primary key for every table, but it strongly recommends you do so; the relational model makes this an absolute requirement. In addition, tables in Access generally meet the third and fourth attributes listed above. That is, with a few exceptions, the manipulation of tables in Access doesn't depend on a specific ordering of columns or rows.

NOTE

For all practical purposes, the terms *table* and *relation* are interchangeable, and we use the term *table* in the remainder of this chapter. However, when we use this term, we actually mean a table that also meets the stricter definition of a relation.

First Normal Form

First Normal Form (1NF) says that all column values must be atomic. The word *atom* comes from the Latin *atomis,* meaning "indivisible" (or, literally, "not to cut"). 1NF dictates that for every row-by-column position, there exists only one value. The benefits of this rule should be fairly obvious. If lists of values are stored in a single column, there is no simple way to manipulate those values. Retrieval of data becomes much more laborious and less generalizable. For example, the table in Figure 4.6, tblOrder1, which is used to store order records for a hardware store, violates 1NF because the data contained in the Items field contains multiple values.

FIGURE 4.6:

tblOrder1 violates First Normal Form because the data stored in the Items column is not atomic.

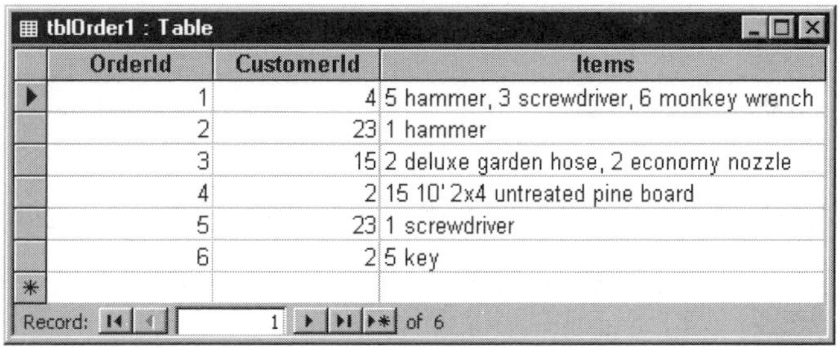

tblOrder1 : Table

OrderId	CustomerId	Items
1	4	5 hammer, 3 screwdriver, 6 monkey wrench
2	23	1 hammer
3	15	2 deluxe garden hose, 2 economy nozzle
4	2	15 10' 2x4 untreated pine board
5	23	1 screwdriver
6	2	5 key

Record: 1 of 6

You'd have a difficult time retrieving information from this table because too much information is stored in the Items column. Think how difficult it would be to create a report that summarized purchases by item.

1NF also prohibits the presence of *repeating groups* of information, even if they are stored in multiple columns. For example, you might improve upon tblOrder1 by replacing the single Items column with six columns: Quant1, Item1, Quant2, Item2, Quant3, Item3 (see Figure 4.7).

FIGURE 4.7:

A better, but still flawed, version of the Orders table, tblOrder2. The repeating groups of information violate First Normal Form.

tblOrder2 : Table

OrderId	CustomerId	Quant1	Item1	Quant2	Item2	Quant3	Item3
1	4	5	hammer	3	screwdriver	6	monkey wrench
2	23	1	hammer				
3	15	2	deluxe garden hose	2	economy nozzle		
4	2	15	10' 2x4 untreated pine				
5	23	1	phillips screwdriver				
6	2	5	key				

Record: 1 of 6

While this design has divided the information into several columns, it's still problematic. For example, how would you go about determining the quantity of hammers ordered by all customers during a particular month? Any query would have to search all three Item columns to determine whether a hammer was purchased and then sum over the three Quantity columns. Even worse, what if a customer ordered more than three items in a single order? You could always add more columns, but where would you stop—10 items, 20 items? Say you decided a customer would never order more than 25 items in any one order and designed the table accordingly. That means you would be using 50 columns to store the item and quantity information for each record, even for orders that involved only one or two items. Clearly, this is a waste of space. And someday, someone will want to order more than 25 items.

Tables in 1NF do not have the problems of tables containing repeating groups. The table in Figure 4.8, tblOrder3, is in 1NF, since each column contains one value and there are no repeating groups of columns. To attain 1NF, we have added a column, OrderItemId. The primary key of this table is a composite key made up of OrderId and OrderItemId.

You could now easily construct a query to calculate the number of hammers ordered. Figure 4.9 shows an example of such a query.

FIGURE 4.8:

The tblOrder3 table is in First Normal Form because all column values are atomic.

tblOrder3 : Table

OrderId	OrderItemId	CustomerId	Quantity	Item
1	1	4	5	hammer
1	2	4	3	screwdriver
1	3	4	6	monkey wrench
2	1	23	1	hammer
3	1	15	2	deluxe garden hose
3	2	15	2	ecomomy nozzle
4	1	2	15	10' 2x4 untreated pine board
5	1	23	1	screwdriver
6	1	2	5	key

Record: 1 of 9

FIGURE 4.9:

Because tblOrder3 is in First Normal Form, you can easily construct a totals query to determine the total number of hammers ordered by all customers.

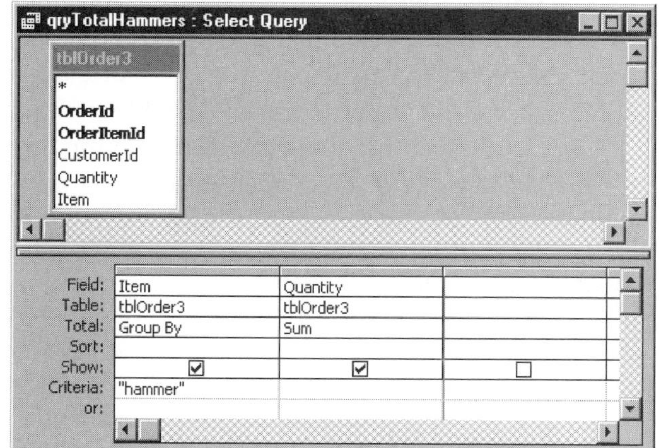

Second Normal Form

A table is said to be in Second Normal Form (2NF) if it is in 1NF and every nonkey column is fully dependent on the (entire) primary key. Put another way, tables should store data relating to only one "thing" (or entity), and that entity should be fully described by its primary key.

The table shown in Figure 4.10, tblOrder4, is a slightly modified version of tblOrder3. Like tblOrder3, tblOrder4 is in First Normal Form because each column is atomic, and there are no repeating groups.

FIGURE 4.10:

The tblOrder4 table is in First Normal Form. Its primary key is a composite of OrderId and OrderItemId.

tblOrder4 : Table

OrderId	OrderItemId	CustomerId	OrderDate	Quantity	ProductId	ProductDescription
1	1	4	May-01-1999	5	32	hammer
1	2	4	May-01-1999	3	2	screwdriver
1	3	4	May-01-1999	6	40	monkey wrench
2	1	23	May-09-1999	1	32	hammer
3	1	15	Jul-04-1999	2	113	deluxe garden hose
3	2	15	Jul-04-1999	2	121	ecomomy nozzle
4	1	2	Aug-01-1999	15	1024	10' 2x4 untreated pine boards
5	1	23	Aug-02-1999	1	2	screwdriver
6	1	2	Aug-02-1999	5	52	key

Record: 1 of 9

To determine whether tblOrder4 meets 2NF, you must first note its primary key. The primary key is a composite of OrderId and OrderItemId. Thus, in order to be 2NF, each nonkey column (that is, every column other than OrderId and OrderItemId) must be fully dependent on the primary key. In other words, does the value of OrderId and OrderItemId for a given record imply the value of every other column for that record? The answer is no. Given the value of OrderId, you know the customer and date of the order, *without* having to know the OrderItemId. Thus, these two columns are not dependent on the *entire* primary key, which is composed of both OrderId and OrderItemId. For this reason, tblOrder4 is not 2NF.

You can achieve Second Normal Form by breaking tblOrder4 into two tables. The process of breaking a non-normalized table into its normalized parts is called *decomposition.* Because tblOrder4 has a composite primary key, decomposition is simple: put everything that applies to each order in one table and everything that applies to each order item in a second table. The two decomposed tables, tblOrder and tblOrderDetail, are shown in Figure 4.11.

Two points are worth noting here:

- When normalizing, you don't throw away information. In fact, this form of decomposition is termed *nonloss* decomposition because no information is sacrificed to the normalization process.
- You decompose the tables in such a way as to allow them to be put back together using queries. Thus, it's important to make sure tblOrderDetail contains a foreign key to tblOrder. The foreign key in this case is OrderId, which appears in both tables.

FIGURE 4.11:

The tblOrder table (top) and tblOrderDetail table (bottom) satisfy Second Normal Form. OrderId is a foreign key in tblOrderDetail that you can use to rejoin the tables.

tblOrder : Table

OrderId	CustomerId	OrderDate
1	1	May-01-1999
2	3	May-09-1999
3	1	Jul-04-1999
4	2	Aug-01-1999
5	1	Aug-02-1999
6	2	Aug-02-1999

Record: 1 of 6

tblOrderDetail : Table

OrderId	OrderItemId	Quantity	ProductId	ProductDescription
1	1	5	32	hammer
1	2	3	2	screwdriver
1	3	6	40	monkey wrench
2	1	1	32	hammer
3	1	2	113	deluxe garden hose
3	2	2	121	ecomomy nozzle
4	1	15	1024	10' 2x4 untreated pine boards
5	1	1	2	screwdriver
6	1	5	52	key

Record: 1 of 9

Third Normal Form

A table is said to be in Third Normal Form (3NF) if it is in 2NF and if all nonkey columns are mutually independent. One example of a dependency is a calculated column. For example, if a table contains the columns Quantity and PerItemCost, you could opt to calculate and store in it a TotalCost column (which would be equal to Quantity * PerItemCost), but this table wouldn't be in 3NF. It's better to leave this column out of the table and make the calculation in a query or on a form or report instead. This saves room in the database and keeps you from having to update TotalCost every time Quantity or PerItemCost changes.

Dependencies that aren't the result of calculations can also exist in a table. The tblOrderDetail table in Figure 4.11, for example, is in 2NF because all its nonkey columns (Quantity, ProductId, and ProductDescription) are fully dependent on the primary key. (That is, given the values of OrderID and OrderItemId, you know the values of Quantity, ProductId, and ProductDescription.) Unfortunately, tblOrder-Detail also contains a dependency between two of its nonkey columns, ProductId and ProductDescription.

Dependencies cause problems when you add, update, or delete records. For example, say you need to add 100 detail records, each of which involves the purchase of screwdrivers. This means you will have to input a ProductId code of **2** *and* a ProductDescription of **screwdriver** for each of these 100 records. Clearly, this is redundant. And, if you decide to change the description of the item to **No. 2 Phillips-head screwdriver** at some later time, you will have to update all 100 records. As a further example, let's say you wish to delete all the 1999 screwdriver purchase records at the end of the year. Once all the records are deleted, you will no longer know what a ProductId of 2 is because you've deleted from the database both the history of purchases and the fact that ProductId 2 means "No. 2 Phillips-head screwdriver." You can remedy each of these anomalies by further normalizing the database to achieve Third Normal Form.

NOTE

An *anomaly* is an error or inconsistency in the database. A poorly designed database runs the risk of introducing numerous anomalies. There are three types of anomalies: insert, delete, and update. These anomalies occur during the insertion, deletion, and updating of rows, respectively. For example, an insert anomaly would occur if the insertion of a new row caused a calculated total field stored in another table to report the wrong total. If the deletion of a row in the database deleted more information than you intended, this would be a delete anomaly. Finally, if updating a description column for a single part in an inventory database required you to make a change to thousands of rows, this would be called an update anomaly.

You can further decompose the tblOrderDetail table to achieve 3NF by breaking out the ProductId-ProductDescription dependency out into a lookup table, as shown in Figure 4.12. This gives you a new detail table, tblOrderDetail1, and a lookup table, tblProduct. When decomposing tblOrderDetail, take care to put a copy of the linking column, in this case ProductId, in both tables. ProductId becomes the primary key of the new table, tblProduct, and becomes a foreign key column in tblOrderDetail1. This allows you to rejoin the two tables later using a query.

FIGURE 4.12:

The tblOrderDetail1 table (left) and tblProduct table (right) are in Third Normal Form. The ProductId column in tblOrderDetail is a foreign key referencing tblProduct.

tblOrderDetail1 : Table

OrderId	OrderItemId	Quantity	ProductId
1	1	5	32
1	2	3	2
1	3	6	40
2	1	1	32
3	1	2	113
3	2	2	121
4	1	15	1024
5	1	1	2
6	1	5	52

Record: 1 of 9

tblProduct : Table

ProductId	ProductDescription
2	screwdriver
32	hammer
40	monkey wrench
52	key
113	deluxe garden hose
121	ecomomy nozzle
1024	10' 2x4 untreated pine boards

Record: 1 of 7

Higher Normal Forms

After Codd defined the original set of normal forms, it was discovered that Third Normal Form, as originally defined, had certain inadequacies. This led to several higher normal forms, including the Boyce/Codd, Fourth, and Fifth Normal Forms. This book does not discuss these higher normal forms because the discussion would require the introduction of additional terminology and concepts and, more importantly, because all that extra effort would give you little added value over 3NF. Instead, we direct you to the books listed in the section "Relational Database Design" earlier in this chapter. Still, several points are worth noting here:

- Every higher normal form is a superset of all lower forms. Thus, if your design is in 3NF, by definition it is also in 1NF and 2NF.
- If you've normalized your database to 3NF, you've likely also achieved Boyce/Codd Normal Form (and maybe even 4NF or 5NF).
- To quote C.J. Date, the principles of database design are "nothing more than *formalized common sense.*"
- Database design is more art than science.

This last item needs to be emphasized. While it's relatively easy to work through the examples in this chapter, the process gets more difficult when you are presented with a business problem (or another scenario) that needs to be computerized (or downsized). We will outline one approach later in this chapter, but first we must introduce the subject of integrity rules.

Integrity Rules

The relational model defines several integrity rules that, while not part of the definition of the normal forms, are nonetheless a necessary part of any relational database. There are two types of integrity rules: general and database-specific.

General Integrity Rules

The relational model specifies two general integrity rules: entity integrity and referential integrity. They are referred to as general rules because they apply to all databases.

The *entity integrity rule* is very simple. It says that primary keys cannot contain null (missing) data. The reason for this rule should be obvious. You can't uniquely identify or reference a row in a table if the primary key of that table can be null. It's important to note that this rule applies to both simple and composite keys. For composite keys, none of the individual columns can be null. Fortunately, Access automatically enforces the entity integrity rule for you; no component of a primary key in Access can be null.

The *referential integrity rule* says that the database must not contain any unmatched foreign key values. This implies that

- A row may not be added to a table with a foreign key unless the referenced value exists in the referenced table.
- If the value in a table that's referenced by a foreign key is changed (or the entire row is deleted), the rows in the table with the foreign key must not be orphaned.

As defined by the relational model, three options are available when a referenced primary key value changes or a row is deleted:

Disallow The change is completely disallowed.

Cascade For updates, the change is cascaded to all dependent tables. For deletions, the rows in all dependent tables are deleted.

Nullify For deletions, the dependent foreign key values are set to null.

Access allows you to disallow or cascade referential integrity updates and deletions using the Edit Relationships dialog (see Figure 4.13). There is no Nullify option. In the example shown in Figure 4.13, any updates of CustomerId in tblCustomer will be cascaded to tblOrder. Since the Cascade Delete Related Records check box hasn't been checked, deletions of rows in tblCustomer will be disallowed if rows in tblOrder would be orphaned.

Database-Specific Integrity Rules

All integrity constraints that do not fall under entity integrity or referential integrity are termed *database-specific rules*, or *business rules*. This type of rule is specific to each database and comes from the rules of the business being modeled. Nonetheless, the enforcement of business rules is just as important as the enforcement of the general integrity rules discussed in the previous section.

FIGURE 4.13:

Specifying a relationship with referential integrity between the tblCustomer and tblOrder tables using the Tools ➢ Relationships command

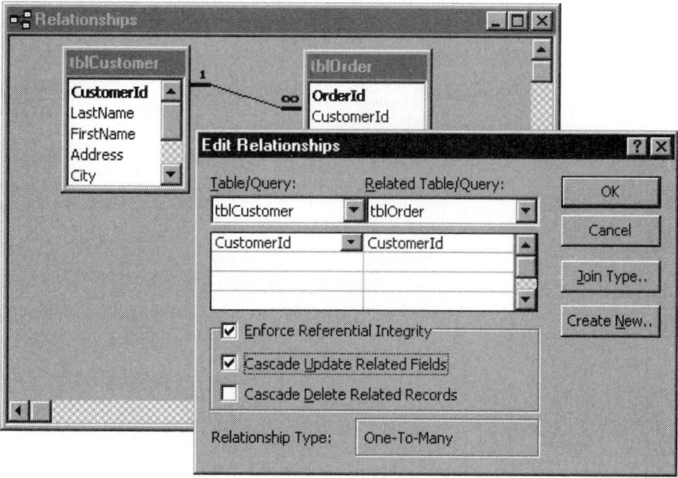

Without the specification and enforcement of business rules, bad data will get into the database. The old adage "garbage in, garbage out" applies aptly to the application (or lack of application) of business rules. For example, a pizza delivery business might have the following rules that need to be modeled in the database:

- The order date must always be greater than or equal to the date the business started and less than or equal to the current date.
- The order time and delivery time can occur only during business hours.
- The delivery date and time must be greater than or equal to the order date and time.
- New orders cannot be created for discontinued menu items.
- Customer zip codes must be within a certain range (the delivery area).
- The quantity ordered can never be fewer than 1 or greater than 50.
- Non-null discounts can never be smaller than 1 percent or greater than 30 percent.

Access supports the specification of validation rules for each column in a table. For example, the first business rule from the preceding list has been specified in Figure 4.14 by setting the ValidationRule and ValidationText properties for the OrderDate field.

FIGURE 4.14:

A column validation rule has been created to limit all order dates to sometime between the first operating day of the business (May 3, 1997) and the current date.

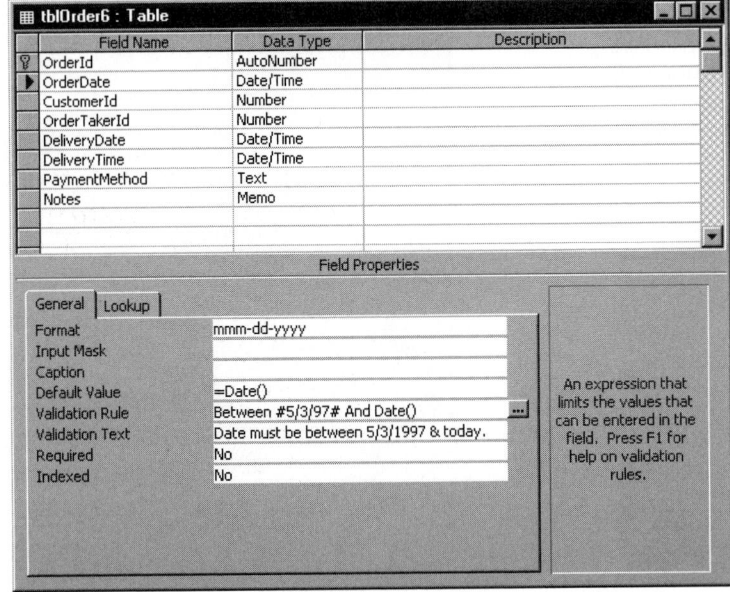

You can specify a global rule that applies to the entire table in Access using the Table Properties dialog. This is useful for creating rules that cross-reference columns, as the example in Figure 4.15 demonstrates. Unfortunately, you can create only one global rule for each table, which can make for some awful validation error messages (for example, "You have violated one of the following rules: 1. Delivery Date >= Order Date. 2. Delivery Time > Order Time. . .").

Although Access business rule support is better than most other desktop DBMS programs, it is still limited, so you will typically build additional business rule logic into applications, usually in the data entry forms. This logic should be layered on top of any table-based rules and can be built into the application using combo boxes, list boxes, and option groups that limit available choices; form-level and field-level validation rules; and event procedures.

TIP

Use application-based rules only when the table-based rules cannot do the job. The more you can build into the rules at the table level, the better, because these rules will always be enforced and will require less maintenance.

FIGURE 4.15:

A table validation rule that requires deliveries be made on or after the date the pizza was ordered.

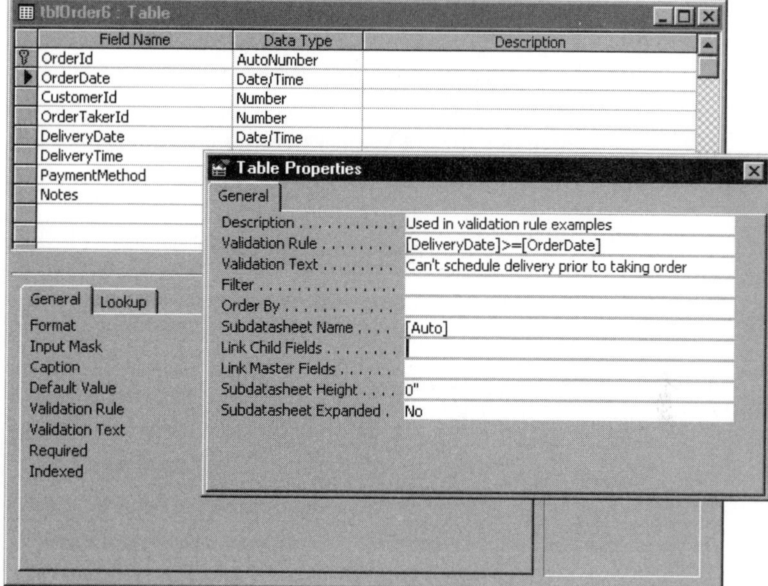

A Practical Approach to Database Design

As mentioned earlier in this chapter, database design is more art than science. While it's true that a properly designed database should follow the normal forms and the relational model, you still have to come up with a design that reflects the business you are trying to model. Relational database design theory can usually tell you what *not* to do, but it won't tell you where to start or how to manage your business. This is where it is essential to understand the business (or other scenario) you are trying to model. A well-designed database requires business insight, time, and experience. Above all, it shouldn't be rushed.

To assist you in the creation of databases, we've outlined the following 20-step approach to sound database design:

1. Take some time to learn the business (or other system) you are trying to model. This usually means meeting with the people who will be using the system and asking them lots of questions such as, "What's the nature of your business?" or "What do you sell?" or "What information is vital to your business?"

2. On paper, write out a basic mission statement for the system. For example, you might write something like, "This system will be used to take orders from customers and track orders for accounting and inventory purposes." In addition, list the requirements of the system. These requirements will guide you in creating the database schema (the definition of the tables) and business rules. Create a list that includes entries such as, "Must be able to track customer addresses for subsequent direct mail."
3. Turn off the computer and rough out on paper the data entry forms. That's right—there's no substitute for working with pencil and paper through the many iterations to make sure you get this part right. The specific approach you take will be guided by the state of any existing system:
   - If this system was never before computerized, take the existing paper-based system and rough out the table design based on these forms. It's very likely that these forms will be non-normalized.
   - If the database will be converted from an existing computerized system, use its tables as a starting point. Remember, however, that the existing schema will probably be non-normalized. It's much easier to normalize the database *now* rather than later. Print out the existing schema, table by table, and the existing data entry forms to use in the design process.
   - If you are starting from scratch (for example, for a brand-new business), rough out on paper the forms you envision using.
4. Based on the forms you created in step 3, rough out your tables on paper. (Yes, again on paper!) If normalization doesn't come naturally (or from experience), you can start by creating one huge, non-normalized table for each form you will later normalize. If you're comfortable with normalization theory, try to keep it in mind as you create your tables, remembering that each table should describe a single entity.
5. Look at your existing paper or computerized reports. (If you're starting from scratch, rough out the types of reports you'd like to see on paper.) For existing systems that aren't currently meeting user needs, it's likely that key reports are missing. Create them now on paper.
6. Take the roughed-out reports from step 5 and make sure the tables from step 4 include this data. If information is not being collected, add it to the appropriate tables or create new ones.
7. On paper, add several rows to each roughed-out table. Use real data if at all possible.

8. Start the normalization process. First, identify candidate keys for every table and, using the candidates, choose the primary key. Remember to choose a primary key that is minimal, stable, simple, and familiar. (See the section "Tables, Uniqueness, and Keys" earlier in this chapter.) *Every* table must have a primary key! Make sure the primary key will guard against all present *and* future duplicate entries.
9. Note foreign keys also, adding them if necessary to related tables. Draw relationships between the tables, noting whether they are 1→1 or 1→M. If they are M→M, create linking tables. (See the section "Relationships" earlier in this chapter.)
10. Determine whether the tables are in First Normal Form. Are all fields atomic? Are there any repeating groups? Decompose if necessary to meet 1NF.
11. Determine whether the tables are in Second Normal Form. Does each table describe a single entity? Are all nonkey columns fully dependent on the primary key? Put another way, does the primary key imply all other columns in each table? Decompose to meet 2NF. If the table has a composite primary key, you should, in general, decompose the table by breaking apart the key.
12. Determine whether the tables are in Third Normal Form. Are there any computed columns? Are there any mutually dependent nonkey columns? Remove computed columns. Eliminate mutually dependent columns by breaking out lookup tables.
13. Using the normalized tables from step 12, refine the relationships between the tables.
14. Create the tables using Access. Create the relationships between the tables using the Edit Relationships command. Add some sample data to the tables.
15. Create prototype queries, forms, and reports. While you are creating these objects, design deficiencies should become obvious. Refine the design as needed.
16. Bring the users back in. Have them evaluate your forms and reports. Are their needs met? If not, refine the design. Remember to renormalize if necessary (see steps 8–12).
17. Go back to the Table Design screen and add business rules.
18. Create the final forms, reports, and queries. Develop the application. Refine the design as necessary.
19. Have the users test the system. Refine the design as needed.
20. Deliver the final system.

This list doesn't cover every facet of the design process, but you may find it useful as a framework from which you can start. (This approach is based on the writings of Access developer and database design wizard Michael Hernandez.)

Normalizing a Database with Existing Data

From time to time, you may be faced with having to normalize a poorly designed database. You can usually accomplish this without loss of data by using a series of action queries. For example, you could normalize the version of the orders table (tblOrder4) shown earlier in Figure 4.10, taking it from 1NF to 3NF, by following these steps:

1. Make a copy of your table and work on the copy. For example, we made a copy of tblOrder4 and named it tblOrder5. At this time, it's also a good idea to make a backup copy of the database. Store it safely in case you make a mistake.
2. Break out the item-related columns that are dependent on both OrderId and OrderItemId from tblOrder5 using a make-table query. Include the following fields: OrderId, OrderItemId, Quantity, ProductId, and ProductDescription. This query, qmakOrderDetail5, will create tblOrderDetail5 and is shown in Design view in Figure 4.16. Don't delete any columns from tblOrder5 yet.

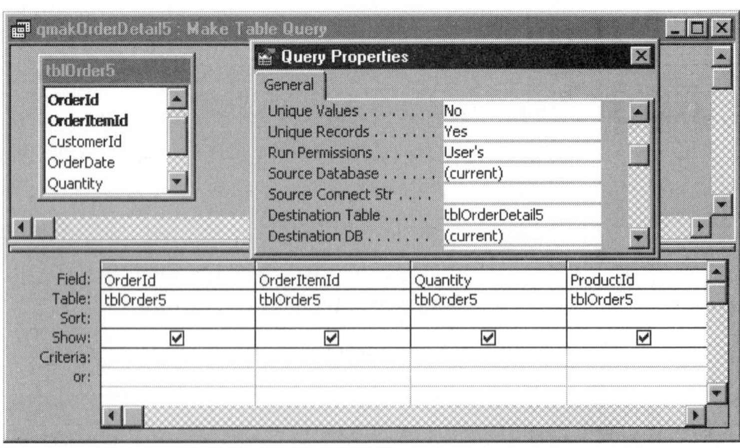

FIGURE 4.16: The qmakOrderDetail5 make-table query copies item-related data to a new table as part of the normalization process.

3. Move the product description information into a third table. Create this lookup table using a query based on tblOrderDetail5 with the UniqueValues property set to Yes. You use this type of query because you want only one record created for each instance of the ProductId code. Include the following fields: ProductId and ProductDescription. This query, qmakProduct5, is shown in Design view in Figure 4.17. It creates the tblProduct5 lookup table. Don't delete any columns from tblOrderDetail5 yet.

FIGURE 4.17:

The qmakProduct5 make-table query copies product-related data to a new lookup table as part of the normalization process.

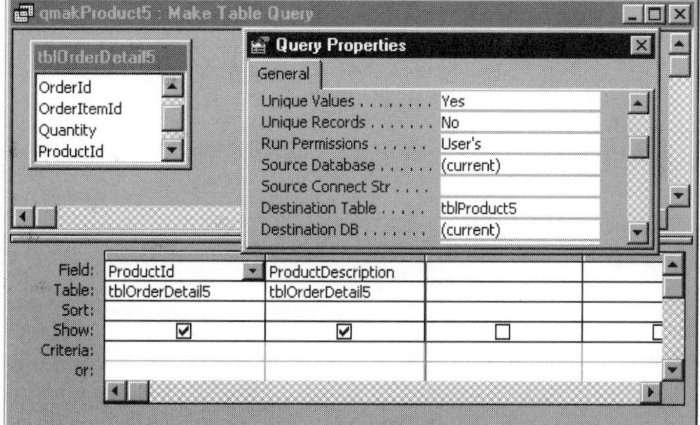

4. Open the tblOrderDetail5 and tblProduct5 tables in Datasheet view and make certain each contains the required information. Make sure that things look okay before you delete any columns from tblOrder5. (You should still see duplicate rows in tblOrder5; you'll fix this in the next step.) At this point, you may find it helpful to create a select query that rejoins the three tables to help you make certain all is well.

5. Create a third make-table query based on tblOrder5 to create the final orders table, tblOrder5a. In this query, include only columns that will be in the final orders table (OrderId, CustomerId, and OrderDate). Because tblOrder5 contains duplicate rows, you must set the UniqueValues property of the query to Yes. This query, qmakOrder5a, is shown in Design view in Figure 4.18.

6. Create one more make-table query to create the final normalized version of the order details table, tblOrderDetail5a. In this query, include only columns that should remain in the final order details table (OrderId, OrderItemId, Quantity, and ProductId). This query, based on tblOrderDetail5, is shown in Design view in Figure 4.19.

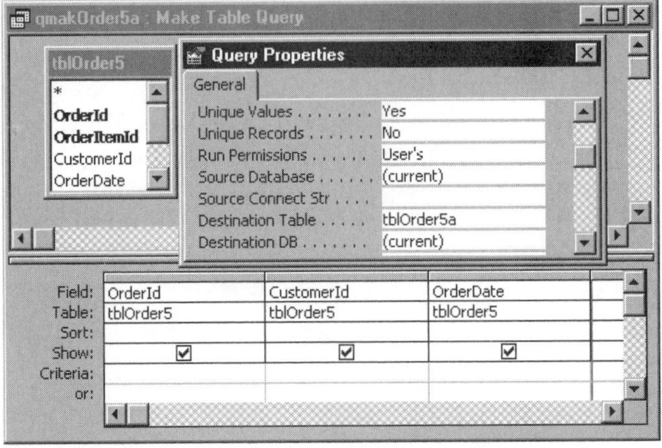

FIGURE 4.18:

The qmakOrder5a make-table query creates the normalized version of the orders table.

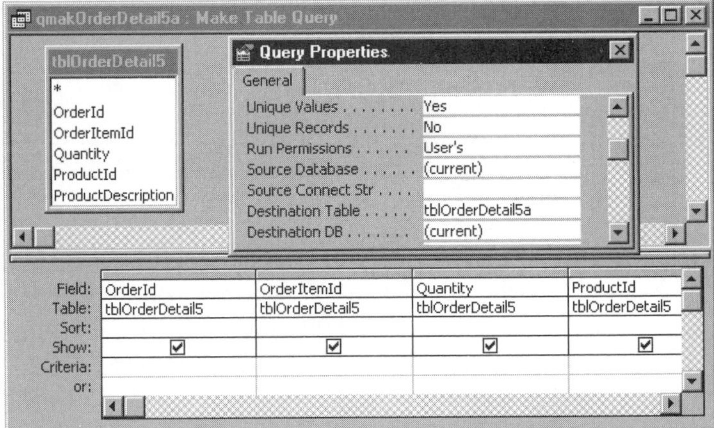

FIGURE 4.19:

The qmakOrderDetail5a make-table query creates the normalized version of the order details table.

7. Open tblOrder5a, tblOrderDetail5, and tblProduct5, in turn, in Design view and define the primary key columns for each (OrderId, OrderId + OrderItemId, and ProductId, respectively).

8. Create another select query that joins the three tables. If the datasheet looks okay, delete the original tables and rename the three new tables to their final names.

9. Create relationships between the tables using the Tools ➢ Relationships command. The screen in Figure 4.20 shows the relationships prior to renaming the tables.

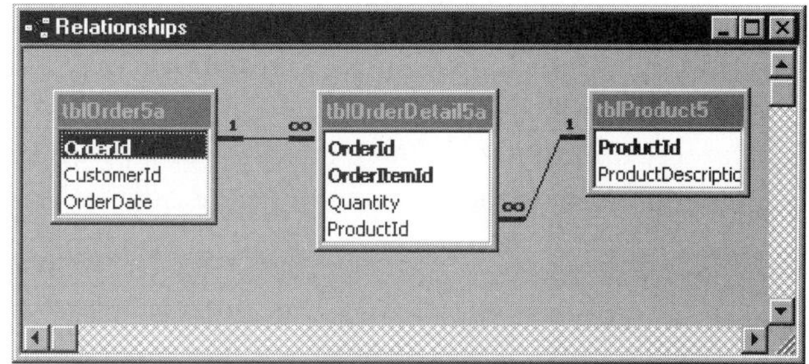

FIGURE 4.20: Relationships for the normalized tables, which are now in Third Normal Form

> **NOTE** Access ships with a Wizard called the Table Analyzer, but it's probably not worth using. You start the Table Analyzer by choosing the Tools ➢ Analyze ➢ Table command. If you run the Table Analyzer against tblOrder4 in automatic mode ("Yes, let the wizard decide."), you can see how it fares: not so well. The Wizard only knows how to break out lookup tables (taking you from 2NF to 3NF). If you use the Wizard in manual mode ("No, I want to decide.") against tblOrder4, you'll find you can use it to break out the product information, but you can't decompose tblOrder4 further into order and order detail components.

Breaking the Rules: When to Denormalize

Sometimes it's necessary to break the rules of normalization and create a database that is deliberately less normal than Third Normal Form. You'll usually do this for performance reasons or because the users of the database demand it. While this won't get you any points with database design purists, ultimately you have to deliver a solution that satisfies your users. If you do decide to break the rules and denormalize your database, however, it's important that you follow these guidelines:

- Break the rules deliberately; have a good reason for denormalizing.
- Be fully aware of the trade-offs this decision entails.
- Thoroughly document your decision.
- Create the necessary application adjustments to avoid anomalies.

This last point is worthy of elaboration. In most cases when you denormalize, you will be required to create additional application code to avoid insert, update, and deletion anomalies that a more normalized design would avoid. For example, if you decide to store a calculation in a table, you'll need to create extra event procedure code and attach it to the appropriate event properties of forms that are used to update the data on which the calculation is based.

If you're considering denormalizing for performance reasons, don't always assume the less normalized version of the database is the fastest—only benchmarking can tell you this for sure. We suggest you first fully normalize the database (to Third Normal Form or higher) and then denormalize only if it becomes necessary for performance reasons.

When to Break the Rules

Here are two scenarios where you might choose to break the rules of normalization:

- You decide to store an indexed computed column, Soundex, in tblCustomer to improve query performance, in violation of 3NF (because Soundex is dependent on LastName). The Soundex column contains the sound-alike code for the LastName column. It's an indexed column (with duplicates allowed), and it's calculated using a user-defined function. (If you're interested in such a function, see adhSoundex in the basSoundex module of CH04.MDB.) If you wish to perform searches on Soundex code with any but the smallest tables, you'll find a significant performance advantage in storing the Soundex column in the table and indexing this computed column. You'd likely use an event procedure attached to a form to perform the Soundex calculation and store the result in the Soundex column. To avoid update anomalies, you'll want to ensure that the user cannot update this column and that it is updated every time LastName changes.
- To improve report performance, you decide to create a column named TotalOrderCost that contains a sum of the cost of each order item in tblOrder. This violates 2NF because TotalOrderCost is not dependent on the primary key of the table. TotalOrderCost is calculated on a form by summing the column TotalCost for each item. Since you often create reports that need to include the total order cost but not the cost of individual items, you break 2NF to avoid having to join these two tables every time this report needs to be generated. As in the preceding example, you have to be careful to avoid update anomalies. Whenever a record in tblOrderDetail is inserted, updated, or deleted, you will need to update tblOrder, or the information stored there will be erroneous.

If you're considering denormalizing because your users think they need it, investigate the reason. Often they will be concerned about simplifying data entry, which you can usually accomplish by basing forms on queries while keeping your base tables fully normalized.

Summary

In this chapter, we covered the basics of database design in the context of Access. The main concepts we covered were

- The relational database model, created by E.F. Codd in 1969, is founded on set theory and predicate logic. A database designed according to the relational model will be efficient, predictable, self-documenting, and easy to modify.
- Every table must have a primary key that uniquely identifies each row.
- Foreign keys are columns used to reference a primary key in another table.
- You can establish three kinds of relationships between tables in a relational database: one-to-one, one-to-many, or many-to-many. Many-to-many relationships require a linking table.
- Normalization is the process of simplifying the design of a database so it achieves optimum structure.
- A well-designed database follows the Normal Forms: First Normal Form requires all column values to be atomic; Second Normal Form requires every nonkey column to be fully dependent on the table's primary key; Third Normal Form requires all nonkey columns to be mutually independent.
- The entity integrity rule forbids nulls in primary key columns.
- The referential integrity rule says the database must not contain any unmatched foreign key values.
- A well-designed database implements business rules (domain integrity) and requires business insight, time, and experience.
- You can normalize a poorly designed database using a series of action queries.
- Sometimes you may need to denormalize a database. Always have a good reason to do this, and fully normalize to Third Normal Form before denormalizing.

CHAPTER

FIVE

Access SQL

- Understanding Access SQL
- Learning the differences between Access SQL and ANSI SQL
- Using subqueries and union queries
- Creating SQL pass-through queries
- Using the new ANSI-92 Extensions to Jet SQL

Structured Query Language (or SQL, pronounced both as "ess-cue-ell" and "see-quel"; we prefer the latter pronunciation) is by far the most popular non-procedural data access language today on computers of all sizes. Access has always included very strong support for the SQL language.

This chapter attempts to cover Access SQL in its entirety. It should prove useful to both the SQL-fluent developer coming to Access from other SQL implementations *and* the SQL-naive developer looking to make sense of this strange new language. You'll find a detailed discussion of each of the SQL statements supported by Access.

NEW!

Access has been somewhat uneven in its support of the ANSI SQL standards, with the last few versions of Access supporting a flavor of SQL that was somewhat of a hybrid of SQL-89, SQL-92, and Access-specific extensions. For the most part, Access 2000's support for SQL remains virtually unchanged, but the Jet 4 engine—the database engine underlying Access 2000—supports a number of new ANSI SQL-92 extensions that are unavailable from the Access user interface. The new Jet 4 SQL-92 extensions are only available when executing SQL programmatically via ActiveX Data Objects (ADO) and the Jet OLE DB provider. The new extensions are *not* available from the Access query window or when using the older Data Access Objects (DAO) object model.

NOTE

So as not to confuse the reader, we have chosen to discuss the SQL that is supported by the Access user interface in the bulk of this chapter. We limit the discussion of the new Jet 4 SQL extensions to the section "Jet 4 ANSI SQL-92 Extensions" at the end of this chapter.

A Brief History of SQL

Like many database standards, including the relational model itself and query by example, SQL was invented at an IBM research laboratory in the early 1970s. SQL was first described in a research paper presented at an Association for Computing Machinery (ACM) meeting in 1974. Created to implement E.F. Codd's relational model (originally described in an ACM paper in 1970—see Chapter 4 for more information), it began life as SEQUEL (for Structured English Query Language), briefly becoming SEQUEL/2 and then simply SQL.

NOTE

Today, there are hundreds of databases on platforms ranging from billion-dollar supercomputers down to thousand-dollar personal computers supporting SQL. This makes it the de facto data access language standard, but at the same time, it's also an official standard. There are three American National Standards Institute (ANSI) SQL standards: SQL-86 (the most commonly implemented SQL today), SQL-89 (a minor revision), and the current SQL-92 (a major revision). Like the rest of this volume, in this chapter we'll focus on Access SQL in the context of Access databases (MDB files) and the Jet engine. You'll want to check out the SQL chapters in *Access 2000 Developer's Handbook, Volume II* if you're planning on creating an Access Project (ADP file) that stores its data in a Microsoft SQL Server or Microsoft Data Engine (MSDE) database. You may also find the section at the end of this chapter, "Differences between Access SQL, SQL-92, and T-SQL," of interest.

Where Can You Use Access SQL?

Unlike most other products that support SQL, Access has no SQL command line or similar facility into which you can directly enter SQL statements and press the Enter key or click a button to view the results. The closest thing to this in Access is the VBA Immediate window, but it doesn't allow you to directly enter SQL statements. Instead, you must enter SQL statements into the SQL view of the Access query facility and switch to Datasheet view to display the results.

Most of the time, you'll find Access' way of doing things preferable to a SQL command-line interface because Access formats the data in a fully forward and backward scrollable window. What's more, you can instantly switch between SQL view, where you enter the SQL statements; Query view, where you compose and view the equivalent query specification using QBE; and Datasheet view, where the results of the query are displayed.

If you find yourself still missing a SQL command-line type facility, you can always create your own using a simple form, such as the one shown in Figure 5.1. The main advantage of this type of SQL scratchpad facility is that you can view the SQL statement and its output simultaneously.

We created this scratchpad form using a text box, where the SQL statement is entered, and a list box control, where the results are displayed. A list-filling function is used to fill the list box with the results of the query. The form contains two additional text boxes that are used to display the total number of returned records and any error messages encountered when running the query.

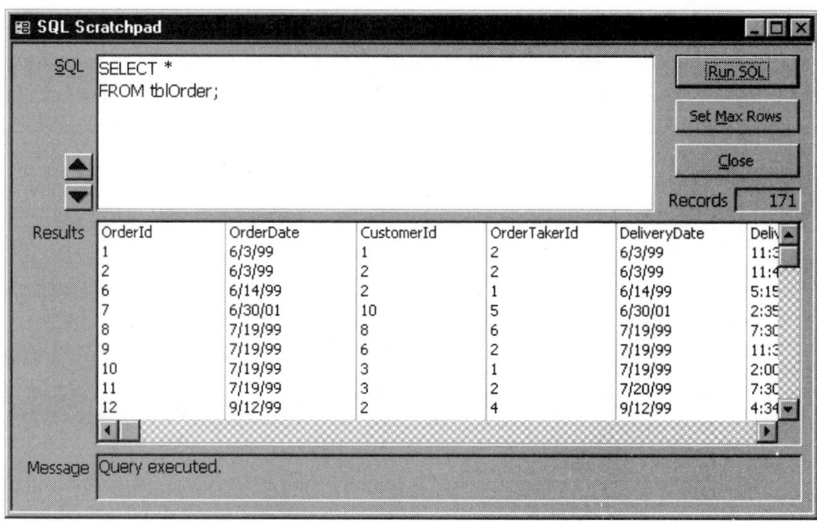

FIGURE 5.1:

Simple SQL scratchpad form for testing SQL statements

The form, frmSQLScratchpad, is included in the CH05.MDB database. To use the form in another database, import the frmSQLScratchpad form plus the ControlResize, FormResize, and SectionResize class modules. Many of the examples in this chapter areshown using this simple SQL scratchpad form.

NOTE

The SQL Scratchpad form and all of the tables and queries used in the examples in this chapter are included in the CH05.MDB database on the companion CD included with this book. In addition, we have created an add-in version of this form, SQLSCRAT.MDA, which you can also find on the CD. Once you install this add-in, you can call up the SQL Scratchpad form from any database using the Tools ➢ Add-ins command.

WARNING

The SQL Scratchpad form uses ADO and a list-filling function to return records. Thus, you are bound by the rules of ADO, which differ slightly from the rules for creating a query using the Access query designer. One big difference: the Access wildcard characters "*" and "?" do not work in the SQL Scratchpad form. You must use the ANSI "%" and wildcard characters instead.

In addition to SQL view, there are several other places in Access where you can use SQL statements. You can use SQL as the record source for a form or report or the row source for a combo box, list box, or embedded graph control. You can also use SQL to create and execute queries using ActiveX Data Objects (ADO) or Data Access Objects (DAO). As previously mentioned in this chapter, when using ADO, you are afforded additional ANSI SQL-92 functionality that is unavailable from the Access UI or DAO.

Learning Access SQL

Although SQL may at first seem daunting in its complexity, when it comes right down to it, it's a fairly straightforward language to learn and use.

SQL Syntax Conventions

This chapter uses the following conventions for the specification of SQL syntax:

Items in all UPPERCASE indicate keywords you must enter literally. Items in *italicized* lowercase indicate placeholders for specific values you enter.

If the placeholder includes the word *list* or *clause*, this indicates a simplification of a more detailed syntax that is discussed elsewhere in the chapter. For example, "WHERE *where-clause*" is the syntax for a simplified WHERE clause.

Square brackets ([item]) in the syntax diagrams in this chapter denote optional items. For example, "CONSTRAINT [UNIQUE] *index*" indicates that CONSTRAINT is required, that the keyword UNIQUE is optional, and that you must enter the name of an index in place of *index*.

Curly braces combined with vertical bars ({OPTION1 | OPTION2}) denote a choice. In this case, you can choose only OPTION1 *or* OPTION2.

An ellipsis (…) combined with the square brackets notation indicates a repeating sequence. For example, "*column1* [, *column2* [, …]]" indicates that you may include one or more columns.

You customarily start each clause of a SQL statement on a new line, but this is done only for the sake of clarity; you may break the lines wherever you please. Another custom is to enter keywords in all caps, but this is not required. We follow these customs throughout this chapter.

The SELECT Statement

The *SELECT statement* is the bread and butter of Access SQL, or any SQL, for that matter. If you learn the SELECT statement and all its clauses, you'll know most of what there is to know about SQL. Select queries *select* rows of data and return them as a recordset.

The basic syntax of the SELECT statement is

SELECT *column-list*

FROM *table-list*

[WHERE *where-clause*]

[ORDER BY *order-by-clause*];

SELECT statements *must* include SELECT and FROM clauses. The WHERE and ORDER BY clauses are optional.

The SELECT Clause

You use the *SELECT clause* to specify which columns to include in the resulting recordset. The column names are analogous to fields dropped onto the QBE grid with the Show box checked. The syntax of the SELECT clause is

SELECT {* | *expression1* [AS *alias1*] [, *expression2* [AS *alias2*] [, …]]]}

The expressions can be simple column names, computed columns, or SQL aggregate functions. Just as in QBE, you can use an asterisk (*) to indicate all fields from a table like this:

```
SELECT *
```

You indicate a single column—for example, LastName—like this:

```
SELECT LastName
```

You choose multiple columns—for example, Customer#, FirstName, and LastName—like this:

```
SELECT [Customer#], LastName, FirstName
```

In the preceding example, the Customer# column is enclosed in square brackets because its name contains a *nonalphanumeric* character. You need to use square brackets to delimit all column names that include these characters or spaces. (Don't confuse these *required* square brackets with the square brackets used in the syntax diagrams to indicate optional parameters.) At your discretion, you may also use brackets to enclose names that don't require brackets. For example, you could enter the preceding statement as:

```
SELECT [Customer#], [LastName], [FirstName]
```

You can change the name of output columns and create computed columns using SQL, just as you can in QBE. To create a computed column, enter an expression instead of a table-based column. To rename a column, add "AS *aliasname*" after the column or expression.

For example, to return Customer#, renamed as "ID", and the concatenation of first and last names, renamed as "Customer Name", you could enter the following:

```
SELECT [Customer#] AS ID, [FirstName] & " " & [LastName] AS
[Customer Name]
```

If you include multiple tables (or queries) in the SELECT statement (see the section "Joining Tables" later in this chapter), you will likely need to refer to a particular column that has the same name in more than one table included in the query. In this case, you must use the fully qualified version of the column name using this syntax:

table-or-query.column

For example, you could select the column OrderId from table tblOrderDetails using the following:

```
SELECT tblOrderDetails.OrderId
```

NOTE

Access QBE *always* generates SQL that uses fully qualified column names, even for single-table queries.

The FROM Clause

You use the *FROM clause* to specify the names of the tables or queries from which to select records. If you use more than one table, you must specify here how the tables are to be joined. See the section "Joining Tables" later in this chapter for more details on multitable queries. For now, here's the simplified single-table syntax:

FROM *table-or-query* [AS *alias*]

For example, you would enter the following SELECT statement to return all columns and all rows from table tblOrder. (This query was shown earlier in Figure 5.1.)

```
SELECT *
FROM tblOrder;
```

If you wished to return only the OrderId and OrderDate columns, you could enter the following SELECT statement:

```
SELECT OrderId, OrderDate
FROM tblOrder;
```

As with the SELECT clause, where you can alias (temporarily rename) columns, you can alias table names in the FROM clause. Include the alias, sometimes called a *correlation name,* immediately after the table name, along with the AS keyword. To expand on the last example, you could have renamed tblOrder as Orders Table using the following SELECT statement:

```
SELECT OrderId, OrderDate
FROM tblOrder AS [Orders Table];
```

Correlation names are often used for convenience (correlation names such as T1 and T2, where T1 stands for *table 1*, are often used to reduce typing) but *sometimes* they are required. You must use them for the specification of self joins (see the section "Self Joins" later in this chapter) and certain correlated subqueries (see the section "Subqueries" later in this chapter).

The WHERE Clause

You use the optional *WHERE clause* to restrict or filter the rows returned by a query. The WHERE clause corresponds to the Criteria and Or lines of QBE. Columns referenced in the WHERE clause needn't be included in the SELECT clause column list. (You can accomplish the same end in QBE by unchecking the Show box under a column used to set criteria.) A WHERE clause in Access SQL may contain up to 40 columns or expressions linked by the logical operator AND or OR. You may also use parentheses to group logical conditions.

The syntax of the WHERE clause is

WHERE *expression1* [{And | Or} *expression2* [...]]

For example, you could restrict the rows returned by the SQL statement presented earlier to only those orders in which OrderTakerId = 2 with the following SELECT statement:

```
SELECT OrderId, OrderDate
FROM tblOrder
WHERE OrderTakerId = 2;
```

Figure 5.2 shows the result of this query.

FIGURE 5.2:

Sample select query that displays OrderId and OrderDate for all orders taken by order taker

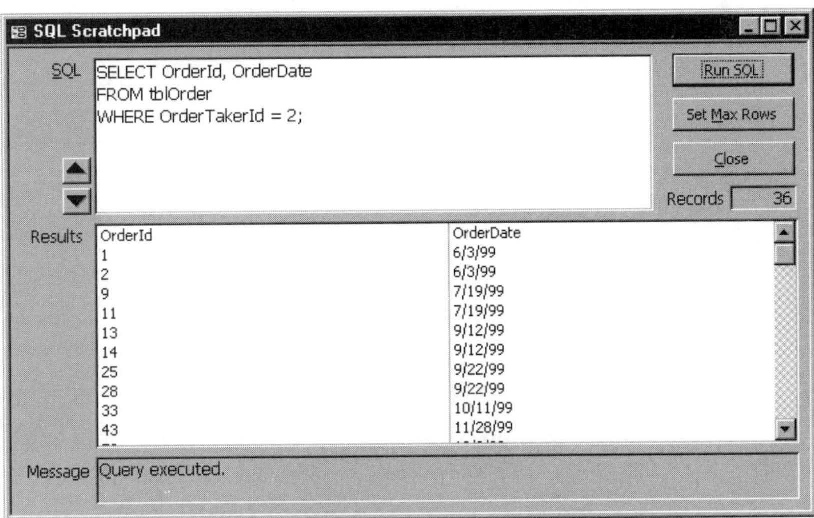

WHERE clause expressions take the same format as expressions in QBE. You may reference columns, built-in and user-defined functions, constants, and operators in each expression. Here are several examples of valid WHERE clauses:

```
WHERE CustomerId = 4
WHERE Sex = "Female" AND Age BETWEEN 21 AND 29
WHERE LastName IS NOT NULL OR (LastName IS NULL AND
 FirstName = "Joe")
WHERE OrderDate > DateAdd("yyyy", -1, Date())
```

Access SQL is less forgiving than Access QBE about the specification of criteria, so you need to keep the following rules in mind when entering expressions:

- Always enclose text strings in WHERE clauses in quotes; either single or double quotes are fine. For example:

```
WHERE LastName = "Jones"
```

- Enclose dates with the pound sign (#). For example:

```
WHERE OrderDate > #4/15/2000#
```

- Always use the keyword LIKE with wildcard characters when you wish to use inexact pattern-matching criteria. For example:

```
WHERE FirstName LIKE "P*"
```

NOTE ANSI SQL uses double quotes the same way Access uses square brackets. In ANSI SQL, you can use only single quotes for text strings.

The ORDER BY Clause

You use the optional *ORDER BY clause* to sort the rows returned by the query by one or more columns. You use the ASC or DESC keyword to specify ascending or descending order. Ascending is the default. The ORDER BY clause corresponds to the Sort line in QBE. As with QBE, precedence in sorting is left to right.

The sort order Access uses is specified at the time you create the database using the Tools ➢ Options ➢ General ➢ New Database Sort Order setting. By default, Access uses the General (U.S.) sort order, which you can change to some other sort order. Once a database is created, a change in sort order has no effect until you compact the database.

Just as with the WHERE clause, columns referenced in the ORDER BY clause needn't be included in the SELECT clause column list. You can sort text, numeric, and date/time columns, which will be sorted alphabetically, numerically, and chronologically, respectively, just as you'd expect. You can't sort on an OLE object field; however, new in Access 2000, you can sort on fields of Memo and Hyperlink data types. The ORDER BY syntax is as follows:

ORDER BY *column1* [{ASC | DESC}] [, *column2* [{ASC | DESC}] [, ...]]

For example, if you wanted to list your customers alphabetically by last and then first name, you could use the following SQL statement:

```
SELECT *
FROM tblCustomer
ORDER BY LastName, FirstName;
```

You can also use expressions in an ORDER BY clause. For example, you could achieve the same result with:

```
SELECT *
FROM tblCustomer
ORDER BY LastName & ", " & FirstName;
```

If you have a choice, however, it's best to sort on columns (especially those that are indexed) rather than expressions because sorting on expressions is much slower.

Joining Tables

If you've properly normalized your database (see Chapter 4), you'll undoubtedly need to create queries that draw data from more than one table. When you access multiple tables in SQL, just as in Access QBE, you must *join* the tables on one or more columns to produce meaningful results. If you don't join the tables, you'll produce a Cartesian product query, which is almost always undesired. (A *Cartesian product* is the arithmetic product of two or more input tables. For example, two 25-row tables joined this way result in a 625-row recordset.)

There are two ways to join tables in Access SQL (actually, three, if you include subselects, which are covered in the section "Subqueries" later in this chapter): in the FROM clause and in the WHERE clause. Joins in the WHERE clause have always been a part of SQL; joins in the FROM clause are a feature that was added to the ANSI standard in SQL-92.

Using the older SQL-89–compliant syntax, you join tables like this:

SELECT *column-list*

FROM table1, table2

WHERE table1.column1 = table2.column2;

Note that this syntax makes no provision for outer joins, although some vendors have suggested extensions to the standard.

In contrast, the SQL-92–compliant syntax looks like this:

SELECT *column-list*

FROM *table1* {INNER | LEFT [OUTER] | RIGHT [OUTER]} JOIN *table2*

ON *table1.column1* = *table2.column2;*

The keyword OUTER is optional.

Say you wished to select OrderId, OrderDate, and LastName for all orders occurring on or after June 1, 1999. Using the older SQL-89–compliant join syntax, you would enter the SQL statement shown in Figure 5.3. Using the newer syntax, you would enter the equivalent statement shown in Figure 5.4.

Although it's useful to be familiar with the SQL-89–style join syntax, you're better off using the SQL-92–compliant syntax for joining tables. It's more powerful, and it's consistent with the SQL generated by Access QBE. More important, recordsets produced using the SQL-89 syntax are not updateable.

Multiple Joins

As when using Access QBE, you can create SELECT statements that join more than two tables. A simplified syntax for specifying joins of multiple tables in the FROM clause is

FROM (… (*table1* JOIN *table2* ON *conditionA*) JOIN *table3* ON *conditionB*) JOIN …)

You may find this nested-style syntax a little confusing. It implies a set order in which the joins are performed—for example, "first join table1 to table2 and then join that result to table3 and then…." But the order of joins doesn't really matter in Access. No matter how you specify the order in the FROM clause, the Jet query processor decides on the optimum ordering of joins for the sake of efficiency. This is the way it *should* be in the relational model.

NOTE

To simplify the preceding syntax diagram, we've used the word *JOIN* to indicate *any* type of join. You would, of course, use one of the following instead: INNER JOIN, LEFT OUTER JOIN, or RIGHT OUTER JOIN.

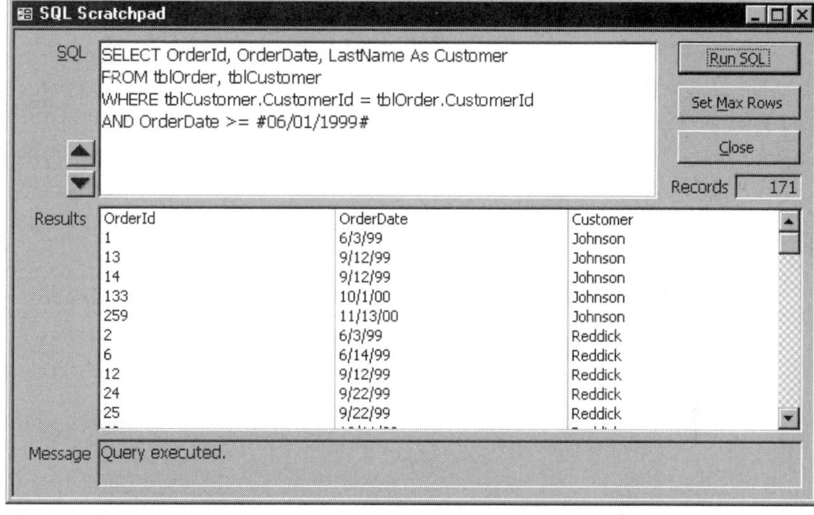

FIGURE 5.3:

SELECT statement that joins the tables tblOrder and tblCustomer using SQL-89–compliant join syntax. The results of this query will be read-only.

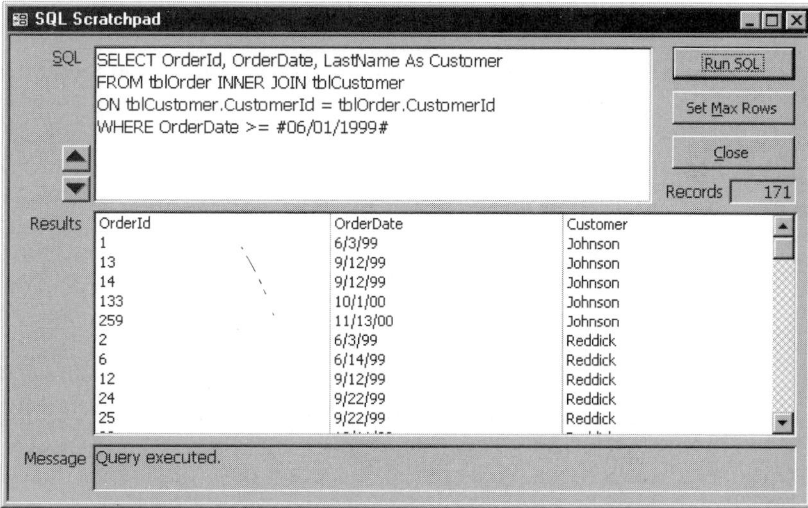

FIGURE 5.4:

SELECT statement that joins the tables tblOrder and tblCustomer using SQL-92–compliant join syntax. The results of this query will be fully updateable.

It would seem that this syntax is counter-intuitive. Alas, this type of syntax *is* necessary for the specification of outer joins in the ANSI SQL standard because order *does* matter with outer joins. But there's yet another twist: even though ANSI SQL supports the use of parentheses to allow you to arbitrarily combine outer and inner joins in any order, Access does not. This arises from the fact that the Jet query processor ignores the placement of parentheses when processing queries. Because of this, Access SQL has very specific rules on how outer joins can be combined with inner joins or other outer joins.

The Jet engine enforces the following rules when combining joins in a single query:

- The nonpreserved table in an outer join *cannot* participate in an inner join.
- The nonpreserved table in an outer join *cannot* be the nonpreserved table of another outer join.

TIP

In a left outer join, the unmatched rows in the table on the left side of the join are *preserved.* In a right outer join, the unmatched rows in the table on the right side of the join are preserved. As Access executes an outer join, it first looks at each row in the preserved table. If a row in the other (nonpreserved) table matches a row in the preserved table, Access creates a result row from the two. Otherwise, Access creates a result row from the columns in the preserved table and fills the columns from the other (nonpreserved) table with nulls. An outer join will always have as many rows as or more rows than the equivalent inner join.

These rules can also be expressed using QBE: a table with an arrow pointing toward it *can't* also be connected to either a line with no arrow or another arrow pointing toward it.

So, even though you must use the parentheses, for all practical purposes they are ignored as the Jet query engine processes your query. Instead, you must follow the preceding rules when combining outer joins. If you fail to, you will receive the "Query contains ambiguous outer joins" or "Join expression not supported" error message.

If you need to create a query that does not follow these rules, you can usually break it up into multiple stacked queries that Jet *can* handle. For example, say you wished to list all customers and the items they ordered but include customers who made no orders. To solve this problem, you might create a four-table, three-join query that looks like this:

```
SELECT LastName, OrderDate,
Quantity, MenuDescription
FROM ((tblOrder INNER JOIN tblOrderDetails
ON tblOrder.OrderId = tblOrderDetails.OrderId)
INNER JOIN tblMenu ON tblOrderDetails.MenuId = tblMenu.MenuId)
RIGHT JOIN tblCustomer ON tblOrder.CustomerId =
tblCustomer.CustomerId
ORDER BY LastName, OrderDate DESC;
```

Unfortunately, the preceding query will not work. If you attempt to execute it, you get the "Join expression not supported" error message. This is because the nonpreserved side of the outer join (in this case, a right outer join) is combined with several inner joins.

The solution to this dilemma is to create the query in two steps:

1. Create a query that joins the tables tblOrder, tblOrderDetails, and tblMenu using inner joins. Save the query, for example, as qryItems.
2. Create a second query that combines the result of qryItems with tblCustomer using an outer join.

The first query's SELECT statement (qryItems) would look like this:

```
SELECT CustomerId, OrderDate, Quantity, MenuDescription
FROM tblOrder INNER JOIN (tblMenu INNER JOIN tblOrderDetails
ON tblMenu.MenuId = tblOrderDetails.MenuId)
ON tblOrder.OrderId = tblOrderDetails.OrderId;
```

The second query would then look like this:

```
SELECT LastName, OrderDate,
Quantity, MenuDescription
FROM tblCustomer LEFT JOIN qryItems ON
tblCustomer.CustomerId = qryItems.CustomerId
ORDER BY LastName, OrderDate DESC;
```

You can use these two *stacked* queries, the datasheet for which is shown in Figure 5.5, to produce the correct answer.

FIGURE 5.5:

Customers and their orders, including rows where no orders were made (note the first row). This query, because it requires combining outer and inner joins with inner joins on the nonpreserved side of the outer join, must be created using two stacked queries.

qryCustomerItems : Select Query

LastName	OrderDate	Quantity	MenuDescription
Ayala			
Babitt	30-Jun-2001	45	Large Cheese Pizza
Babitt	30-Jan-2001	5	Small Sprite
Babitt	30-Jan-2001	1	Salad
Babitt	30-Jan-2001	6	Small Diet Coke
Babitt	30-Jan-2001	1	Large Sprite
Babitt	30-Jan-2001	1	Baked Ziti
Babitt	30-Jan-2001	6	Lasagna
Comstock	19-May-2001	6	Medium Cheese Pizza
Comstock	19-May-2001	3	Large Diet Coke
Comstock	19-May-2001	1	Spaghetti Plate
Comstock	19-May-2001	10	Large Diet Coke
Comstock	19-May-2001	1	Large Cheese Pizza
Comstock	19-May-2001	1	Large Coke
Comstock	19-May-2001	7	Lasagna

Record: 1 of 466

Self Joins

Self joins are useful for answering certain types of queries when you have recursive relationships or when you wish to pull together and "flatten" multiple rows from a table. For example, if you stored the ID number of supervisors in an employees table, you could join the employees table to itself to display employees and their supervisors on a single row of a report. And, in a database in which you stored multiple addresses of a customer in separate rows of an address table, you could use a self join to pull together into a single record both home and work addresses.

The trick to creating self joins in QBE is to alias the second copy of a table so that it is treated as though it were a separate table. You use this same trick to create self joins with SQL. For example, tblEmployee contains a column, SupervisorId, that is recursively related to EmployeeId (see Figure 5.6). Say you wished to view the names of all employees and their supervisors' names and include employees who lacked a supervisor. (This last requirement means you need to use an outer join to create the desired query.) The SELECT statement that accomplishes this is shown in Figure 5.7.

tblEmployee : Table

EmployeeId	LastName	FirstName	Address	City	State	ZipCode	SupervisorId
1	Jones	Peter	34 15th Ave West	Fall City	WA	98789	
2	Alabaster	Suzanne	3409 Red Street	Federal Way	WA	98009	1
3	McGahan	Karen	3 Maple NE	Kent	WA	98019	5
4	Ronald	Alan	624 NW 79th St	Seattle	WA	98117	5
5	Peters	Beth	89 NE 64th St	Seattle	WA	98109	1
6	Carey	Phil	37 West Government	Mountlake Terrace	WA	98789	1
7	Peters	Joe	2529 13th Ave East	New York	NY	11358	5

Record: 1 of 7

FIGURE 5.6:

The tblEmployee table was designed with a recursive relationship between EmployeeId and SupervisorId. This design allows you to store information about both employees and their supervisors in a single table.

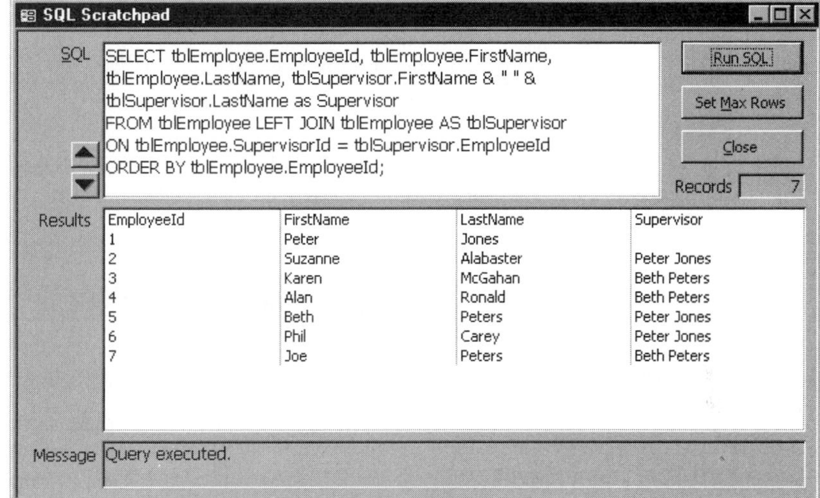

FIGURE 5.7:

This self-join query produces a list of all employees and their supervisors. By using an outer join, you can include the CEO, Peter Jones, even though he has no supervisor.

Non-Equi-Joins

All the joins discussed in this chapter so far have been *equi-joins*—joins based on one field being equal to another. You can also create *non-equi-joins* in Access using the operators >, >=, <, <=, <>, and Between. You'll probably use non-equi-joins far less frequently than the standard equi-join, but sometimes a non-equi-join is exactly what you need.

The CH05.MDB database includes a table called tblEvents that lists special sales events and the beginning and ending dates for each event (see Figure 5.8). Say that you'd like to create a query that lists information on each order from tblOrder linked to the special events table and limited to Visa sales on or after October of

1999. Because the events from tblEvents are listed as a range of dates, you can't use an equi-join to link this table to tblOrder. You can, however, join the two tables using the BETWEEN operator, like this:

```
ON (tblOrder.OrderDate BETWEEN tblEvents.BeginningDate AND
tblEvents.EndingDate)
```

FIGURE 5.8:

The tblEvents table tracks special events for a restaurant.

tblEvents : Table

EventId	Event	BeginningDate	EndingDate	Comments
1	Presidents' Day Sale 1999	01-Feb-1999	03-Feb-1999	a big flop
2	July 4th Two For One Sale 1999	01-Jul-1999	04-Jul-1999	50% increase in sales
3	Fall Clearance Sale 1999	01-Oct-1999	31-Oct-1999	better than last year
4	Say Goodbye to 1999 Sale	26-Dec-1999	31-Dec-1999	the turkey pizza didn't work
5	New Years Day Special 2000	01-Jan-2000	01-Jan-2000	good sales
(AutoNumber)				

Record: 1 of 5

The complete query is shown in Figure 5.9. We used a left outer join to include all orders, not just those occurring during special events.

FIGURE 5.9:

This query joins the tblOrder and tblEvents tables using the BETWEEN operator and a left outer join.

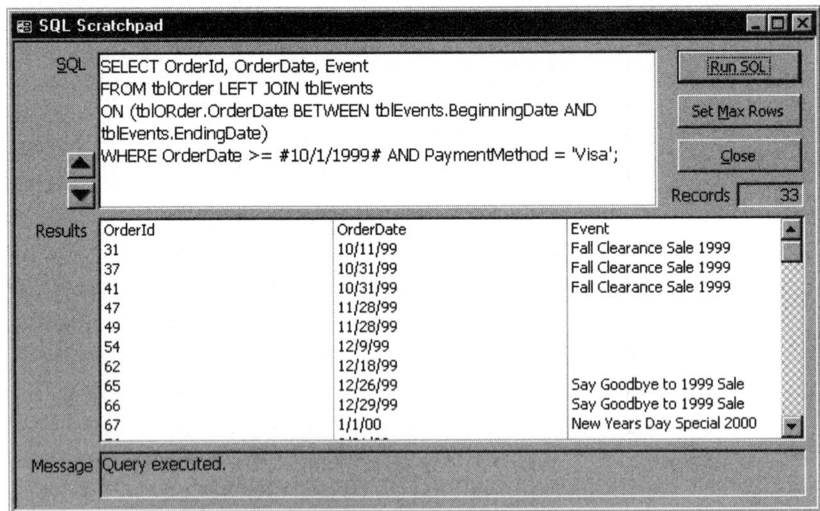

The ALL, DISTINCTROW, and DISTINCT Predicates

You can precede the SELECT clause column-name list with one of the mutually exclusive quantifier predicates: ALL, DISTINCTROW, or DISTINCT. (The

DISTINCTROW predicate is unique to Access SQL.) These quantifiers control how duplicate values and duplicate records are handled. Here's the basic syntax of the SELECT clause predicates:

SELECT [{ ALL | DISTINCT | DISTINCTROW }] *column-list*

If you use no keyword, ALL is assumed. ALL returns all rows that meet the specified criteria. No special processing of the rows is performed to ensure uniqueness. This is equivalent in QBE to setting both the UniqueValues and UniqueRecords properties to No.

NOTE

When you created a query using QBE in versions of Access prior to Access 97, Access set the UniqueRecords property to Yes by default, which is equivalent to using the DISTINCTROW predicate. In an effort to be more consistent with ANSI SQL, Access 97 and Access 2000 QBE set the UniqueRecords property to No by default, which is equivalent to using the ALL (or no) predicate.

If you use the keyword DISTINCT, Access eliminates any duplicate rows in the result set *based on the columns contained in the SELECT clause.* If more than one column is specified in the SELECT clause, Access discards duplicates based on the values of them all. When you use DISTINCT, the query's recordset is never updateable, and performance may be adversely affected. Thus, use DISTINCT only when necessary. Using the DISTINCT predicate in a SELECT statement is equivalent to setting the UniqueValues property to Yes in QBE.

If you use the keyword DISTINCTROW, Access eliminates any duplicate rows in the result set *based on all columns in the source tables.* DISTINCTROW has *no* effect when the query references only one table or returns at least one column from all included tables. In these cases, which include the vast majority of queries, using DISTINCTROW is equivalent to using ALL (or no predicate) and doesn't affect the performance of the query. The DISTINCTROW predicate corresponds to the UniqueRecords property in QBE. The DISTINCTROW predicate is unique to Access SQL.

It's worth noting that for most types of queries for which DISTINCTROW is applicable—queries with multiple tables *and* where at least one table is included in the FROM clause without a corresponding column in the SELECT clause (that is, a table is included without any output columns)—it produces the same result as the DISTINCT predicate, with one significant difference: the query's recordset is updateable.

For example, you might use the following query to list the descriptions of all menu items that have been ordered at least once since June of 2000:

```
SELECT ALL MenuDescription
FROM (tblMenu INNER JOIN tblOrderDetails ON tblMenu.MenuId =
tblOrderDetails.MenuId)
INNER JOIN tblOrder ON tblOrderDetails.OrderId =
tblOrder.OrderId
WHERE tblOrder.OrderDate > #6/1/2000#
ORDER BY MenuDescription;
```

With the ALL predicate, this query returns 260 rows—one row for each Order Detail item since 6/1/2000. Replacing ALL with DISTINCT returns 17 rows in a read-only recordset—one row for each distinct menu item ordered at least once since 6/1/2000. Replacing DISTINCT with DISTINCTROW returns the same 17 rows, but this time the query is updateable. The datasheets returned by the three queries, each using a different predicate, are contrasted in Figure 5.10.

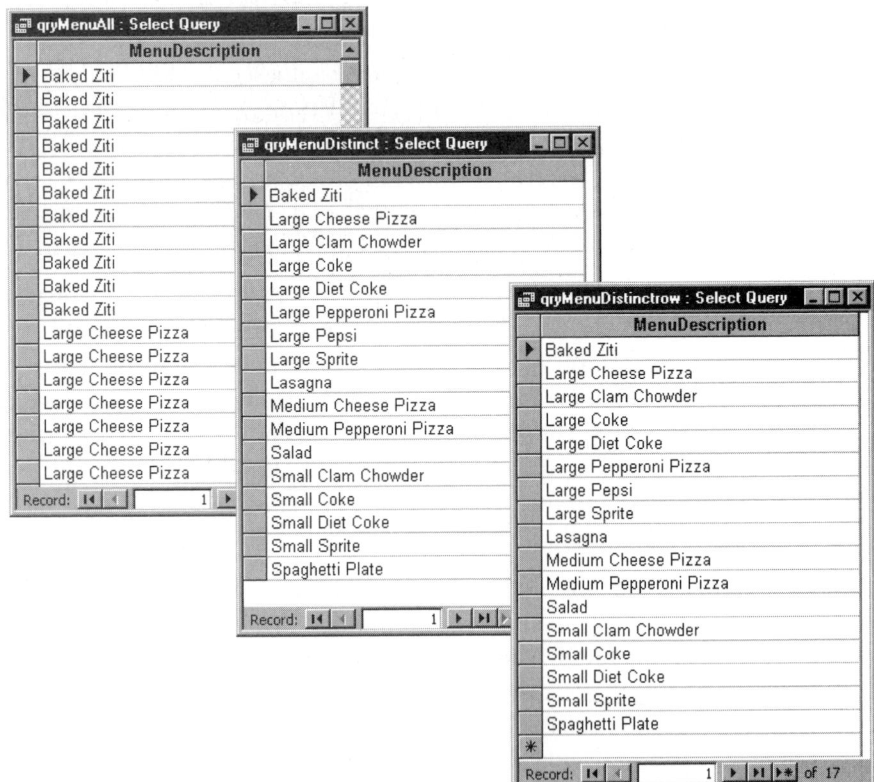

FIGURE 5.10:

Three queries of menu items sold since June 2000. The first query (top) uses the ALL predicate, which returns 260 rows, including duplicates. The second query (middle) uses DISTINCT and returns 17 rows, but the recordset is read-only. The third query (bottom) uses DISTINCTROW and returns 17 rows, but the recordset is updateable. (Note the new-row asterisk at the bottom of the datasheet.)

The TOP Predicate

You use the TOP predicate to return the top *n* rows or top *n* percent of rows from a recordset. This is useful when you wish to return only a select proportion of records meeting the query criteria. The TOP predicate is equivalent to using the TopValues property in QBE.

Unless you don't care which proportion of records you get, you should only use the TOP predicate with an ORDER BY clause. Otherwise, you get a more or less random assortment of records. If you use an ORDER BY clause with the ASC keyword (or no keyword), TOP returns the bottommost records. If you use an ORDER BY clause with the DESC keyword, TOP returns the topmost records.

TIP

The TOP predicate treats nulls as the smallest numeric value, earliest date, or first alphabetical text string. Thus, when you know in advance that the top column may contain nulls, you may wish to explicitly exclude nulls in the WHERE clause.

There are two forms of TOP: alone and with PERCENT. You can combine either form of TOP with the ALL, DISTINCT, or DISTINCTROW predicate. The syntax is as follows:

SELECT [{ ALL | DISTINCT | DISTINCTROW }] [TOP *n* [PERCENT]]
column-list

For example, to return the top seven most costly items ever ordered, where cost equals Quantity*Price*(1–Discount), you could use the SELECT statement shown in Figure 5.11.

Access processes the TOP predicate after all criteria, joins, sorts, grouping, and other predicates have been applied. Ties are treated like any other row, except when multiple rows qualify as the last selected row—for example, the seventh row for a Top 7 specification (see Figure 5.11). When there is a tie on the last selected row, Access returns *all* rows with equivalent values. With no ORDER BY clause, Access uses all the columns from the SELECT clause to decide on ties. Otherwise, Access uses only the columns contained in the ORDER BY clause to determine both the ordering of rows and the resolution of ties, even if some or all of the ORDER BY columns don't appear in the SELECT clause.

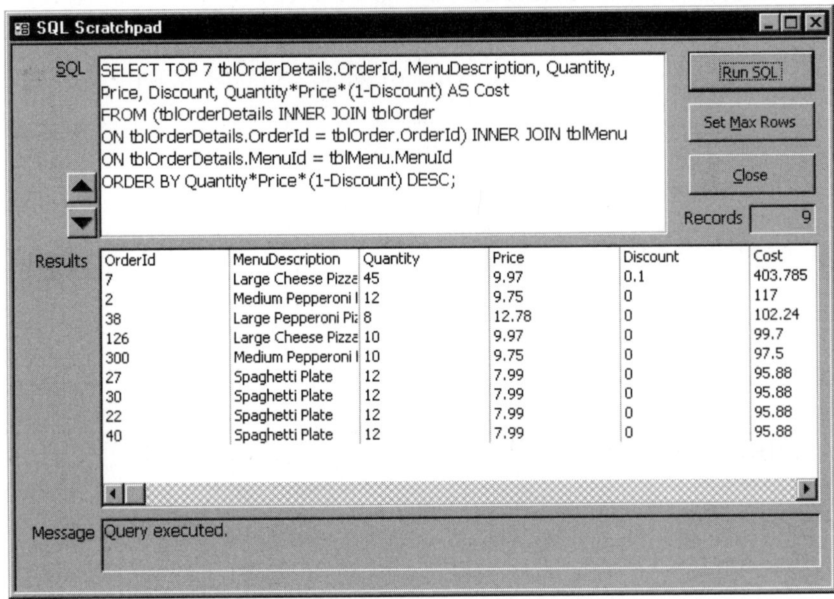

FIGURE 5.11:

This query returns the top seven largest item sales by using the TOP predicate and a descending ORDER BY clause. Note that more than seven rows are returned because of a tie for seventh place.

The WITH OWNERACCESS OPTION Declaration

You use the WITH OWNERACCESS OPTION declaration to allow users of a query you have created to inherit *your* security rights while running the query. This gives the users of a query you've created the ability to run the query, even if they don't have the necessary security permissions to one or more of the underlying tables. When you omit this declaration, the user without proper security clearance to the source tables does not inherit your security and thus cannot run the query. Using the declaration is equivalent to setting the RunPermissions property in QBE to Owner's. Omitting the declaration is equivalent to setting it to User's. The syntax for using the WITH OWNERACCESS OPTION declaration is as follows:

SELECT *column-list*

FROM *table-list*

[WHERE *where-clause*]

[ORDER BY *order-by-clause*]

[WITH OWNERACCESS OPTION];

WARNING The WITH OWNERACCESS OPTION declaration works only with saved queries; if you use it in a SQL statement that has not been saved as a query (for example, by directly entering a SQL statement in a form's RecordSource property), it has no effect.

Aggregating Data

Aggregate queries are useful for summarizing data, calculating statistics, spotting bad data, and looking for trends. These types of queries produce read-only recordsets.

You can construct three types of aggregate queries using Access SQL:

- Simple aggregate queries based on a SELECT statement *without* a GROUP BY clause
- GROUP BY queries using a SELECT statement *with* a GROUP BY clause
- Crosstab queries that use the TRANSFORM statement

All these queries have one thing in common: they use at least one aggregate function in the SELECT clause. The valid aggregate functions are detailed in Table 5.1.

TABLE 5.1: The SQL Aggregate Functions and Their Usage

Aggregate Function	Purpose	Includes Null values?
Avg([column[1]])	Mean or average.	No
Count([column])	Count of the number of nonnull values for a column.	No
Count(*)	Count of the total number of rows in the result set.	Yes
Sum([column])	Sum of the values for the column.	No
Min([column])	Smallest value for the column.	No
Max([column])	Largest value for the column.	No
First([column])	Value of the column in the first row of the result set.	Yes
Last([column])	Value of the column in the last row of the result set.	Yes

Continued on next page

TABLE 5.1 CONTINUED: The SQL Aggregate Functions and Their Usage

Aggregate Function	Purpose	Includes Null values?
StDev([column])	Sample standard deviation for the column. This is a measure of the dispersion of values[2].	No
StDevP([column])	Population standard deviation for the column. This is a measure of the dispersion of values[2].	No
Var([column])	Sample variance for the column. The square of the sample standard deviation[2].	No
VarP([column])	Population standard deviation for the column. The square of the population standard deviation[2].	No

1. Although [column] is used throughout the table, you can also use expressions instead of columns in each of the aggregate functions.

2. The sample standard deviation and variance use a denominator of (n–1), whereas the population aggregate functions use a denominator of (n), where n = the number of records in the result set. For most statistical analyses, the sample aggregate functions are preferable.

You can create expressions made up of a combination of aggregate functions combined mathematically. Aggregate functions can also reference expressions. For example, these aggregate expressions are all valid:

Aggregate Expression	Use
Sum(Abs(Discontinued))	Calculates the sum of the absolute value of the yes/no column Discontinued, which counts the number of Yes values
Sum(Abs(Discontinued+1))	Calculates the sum of the absolute value of the yes/no column Discontinued plus 1, which counts the number of No values (since Access stores Yes as –1 and No as 0)
Avg(DeliveryDate)–Avg(OrderDate)	Calculates the difference in the average delivery and order dates
Avg(Price*Quantity*(1–Discount))	Calculates the average cost of items

Aggregate Queries without a GROUP BY Clause

You can use an aggregate SELECT statement without a GROUP BY clause to calculate summary statistics on all rows meeting the WHERE clause criteria. This is useful for calculating grand totals for an entire table or a subset of a table. To create this type of aggregate SELECT, you must include aggregate functions and nothing *but* aggregate functions in the SELECT clause of a SELECT statement. (If you try to mix aggregate and nonaggregate expressions without a GROUP BY clause, you will get an error message.)

For example, say you wished to count the total number of orders in the tblOrder table and the earliest and latest times an order was taken. You could construct an aggregate query like the one shown in Figure 5.12.

FIGURE 5.12:

This simple aggregate query calculates the total number of orders and the earliest and latest delivery times.

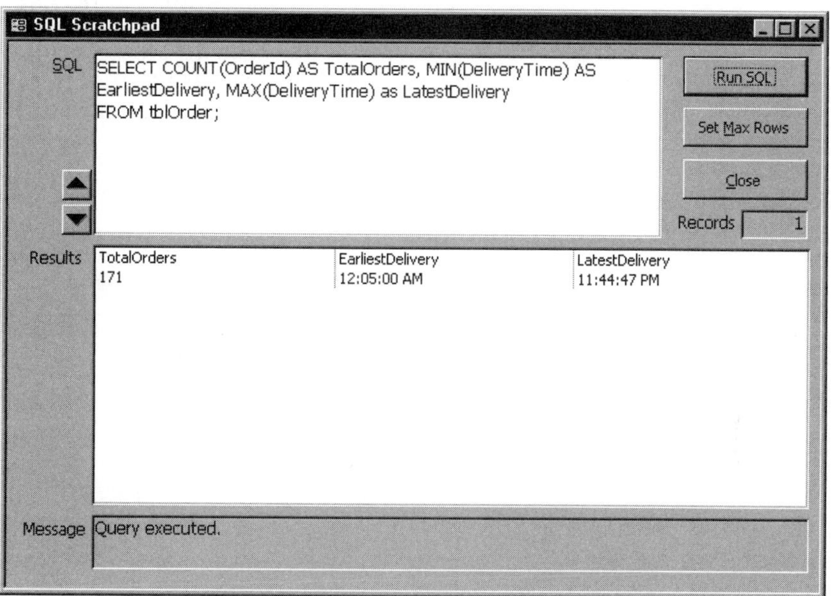

Using a GROUP BY Clause

You use a *GROUP BY clause* to define groups of rows for which you wish to calculate some aggregate function. Here's how the GROUP BY clause (and HAVING clause) fit into the overall SELECT statement syntax:

SELECT *column-list*

FROM *table-list*

[WHERE *where-clause*]

[GROUP BY *group-by-clause*]

[HAVING *having-clause*]

[ORDER BY *order-by-clause*];

The syntax of the GROUP BY clause is

GROUP BY *group-by-expression1* [, *group-by-expression2* [, …]]

Expressions in the GROUP BY clause can reference table columns, calculated fields, or constants. Calculations cannot include references to aggregate functions. The GROUP BY fields define the groups returned by the query. When you use a GROUP BY clause, all fields in the SELECT clause must be either arguments to an aggregate function or present in the GROUP BY clause. In other words, each column included in the resulting recordset must either define a group or compute some summary statistic for one of the groups. For example, the SQL statement in Figure 5.13 computes the number of orders by customer.

FIGURE 5.13:

This GROUP BY SELECT statement counts the number of orders each customer made.

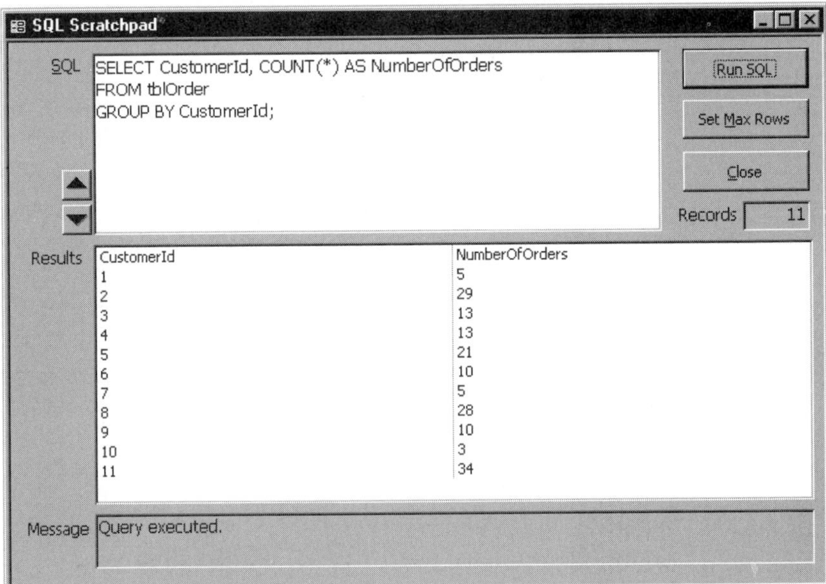

When you use multiple GROUP BY fields, the groups are defined from left to right, just as in an ORDER BY clause. The GROUP BY clause automatically orders values in ascending order without needing an ORDER BY clause (see Figure 5.13).

If, however, you wish the groups to be sorted in descending order, you can reference the same fields in an ORDER BY clause with the keyword DESC.

For example, say you wished to count the number of orders by menu item and date, with menu items sorted alphabetically and dates sorted in descending order to show the most recent orders first. This GROUP BY SELECT statement is shown in Figure 5.14.

FIGURE 5.14:

This SELECT statement groups alphabetically by MenuDescription and then in reverse date order to show the total number of orders taken each day for a particular menu item.

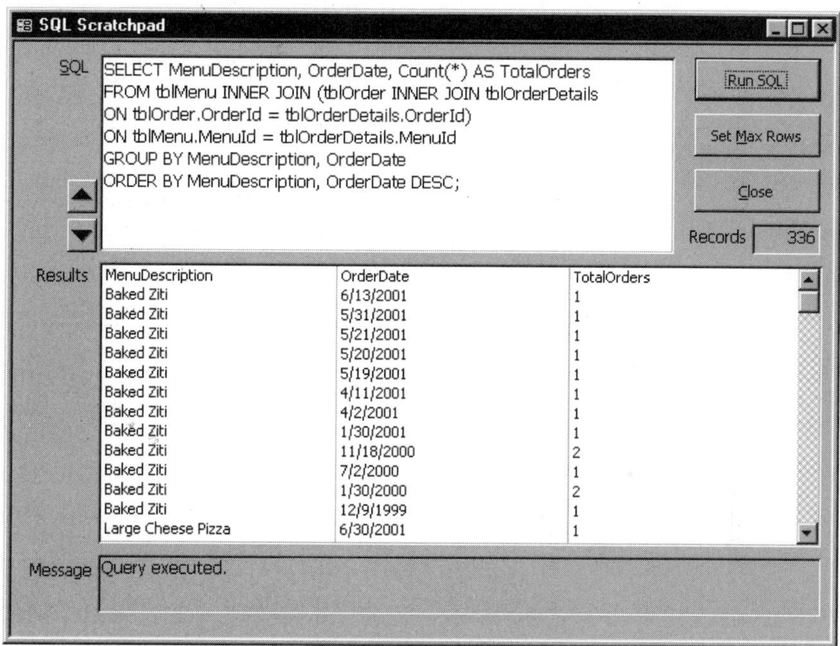

You may also find it useful to sort by one of the aggregate columns. For example, if you calculated total sales grouped by employee, you could sort by total sales in descending order rather than by employee. This would allow you to list the top performing employees first.

You can specify up to ten GROUP BY fields, but be careful about adding unnecessary fields to the GROUP BY clause, because each additional field requires additional processing.

Using the HAVING Clause

Aggregate select queries may contain a WHERE clause, a *HAVING clause,* or both. Any criteria contained in a WHERE clause are applied *before* the grouping of rows.

Thus, you can use WHERE clause criteria to exclude rows you don't want grouped. In contrast, any criteria contained in a HAVING clause is applied *after* grouping. This allows you to filter records based on the summary statistics calculated for each group. The syntax for the HAVING clause is similar to that for the WHERE clause:

HAVING *expression1* [{AND | OR} *expression2* [...]]

For example, say you wished to calculate the average quantity ordered for each menu item but exclude any individual order from the calculation if a quantity of five or fewer were ordered. Since this requires the rows with a quantity of five or fewer to be excluded prior to grouping, you would use a WHERE clause. The SELECT statement would be constructed as follows:

```
SELECT MenuDescription, Avg(Quantity)
AS AvgOrdered
FROM tblMenu INNER JOIN tblOrderDetails ON tblMenu.MenuId =
tblOrderDetails.MenuId
WHERE Quantity > 5
GROUP BY MenuDescription;
```

On the other hand, you might want to calculate the same query but eliminate a menu item from the recordset if, *on average,* fewer than six of the items were sold for each order. This type of query requires the criteria to be applied *after* the average quantity has been calculated for each group, so you would use a HAVING clause instead. The SQL statement and result of this query are shown in Figure 5.15.

FIGURE 5.15:

The criteria for this group needs to be applied after the grouping of data, so you use a HAVING clause.

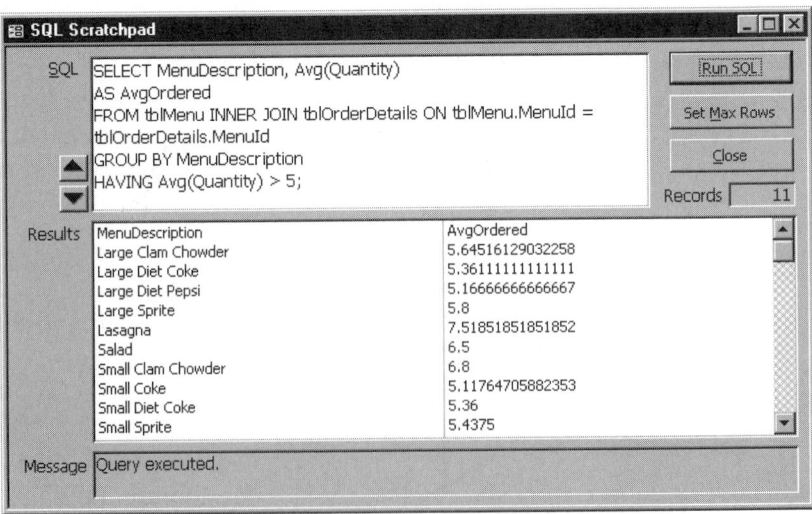

TIP

You can easily remember when WHERE and HAVING criteria are applied by looking at their placement in the SELECT statement. The WHERE clause comes before the GROUP BY clause, which corresponds with the fact that WHERE criteria are applied *before* grouping. The HAVING criteria come after the GROUP BY clause, which corresponds with the fact that HAVING criteria are applied *after* grouping.

Creating Crosstab Queries with the TRANSFORM Statement

You use the *TRANSFORM statement* in Access SQL to create crosstab queries. The basic syntax of the TRANSFORM statement is shown here:

TRANSFORM *aggregate-function*

select-statement

PIVOT *column-headings-field* [IN (*value1* [, *value2* [, ...]])];

The *aggregate-function* must be one of the SQL aggregate functions discussed earlier in this chapter. This aggregate function is used for the values of each cell of the crosstab table. The *select-statement* is a slightly modified GROUP BY SELECT statement. The *column-headings-field* is the field that is pivoted to become the column headings. The values in the optional IN clause specify fixed column headings.

Transforming a Group By Query into a Crosstab Query

The TRANSFORM statement is tricky to construct, especially because it is nonstandard SQL. An easy way to create a TRANSFORM statement is to start with an existing GROUP BY SELECT statement and transform it into a TRANSFORM statement.

Before you can hope to do this, however, you must have a suitable SELECT statement. It must have at least two GROUP BY fields and no HAVING clause. The TRANSFORM statement doesn't support the use of HAVING clauses. (You can work around this limitation by basing a crosstab query on the results of a totals query that has already applied the needed HAVING clause.) In addition, you'll want to make sure the column headings field won't have more than 254 values. (While this is the theoretical limit, in practice you'll find that crosstab queries are probably inappropriate where the column headings field contains more than 20 or so values.) As long as your SELECT statement meets these criteria, you can convert it into a TRANSFORM statement.

An example should help make this clearer. Say you wished to look at the total dinner sales for each dinner menu item by employee. You might start by constructing a GROUP BY query that joined the tables tblMenu, tblEmployee, tblOrder, and tblOrderDetails. The GROUP BY columns would be tblEmployee.LastName and tblMenu.MenuDescription. The query would look like this:

```
SELECT LastName AS Employee,
MenuDescription, Sum(Quantity*Price*(1-Discount))
AS Sales
FROM tblMenu INNER JOIN (tblEmployee INNER JOIN
(tblOrder INNER JOIN tblOrderDetails ON tblOrder.OrderId =
tblOrderDetails.OrderId) ON tblEmployee.EmployeeId =
tblOrder.OrderTakerId) ON tblMenu.MenuId =
tblOrderDetails.MenuId
WHERE Unit = "Dinner"
GROUP BY LastName, MenuDescription;
```

The datasheet for this query is shown in Figure 5.16.

FIGURE 5.16:

This GROUP BY query computes the total sales of each menu item by employee.

qtotEmployeeDinnerSales : Select ...

Employee	MenuDescription	Sales
Alabaster	Baked Ziti	70.5
Alabaster	Lasagna	391.05
Alabaster	Spaghetti Plate	631.21
Carey	Baked Ziti	51.7
Carey	Lasagna	49.5
Carey	Spaghetti Plate	95.88
Jones	Baked Ziti	89.3
Jones	Lasagna	94.05
Jones	Spaghetti Plate	63.92
McGahan	Baked Ziti	4.7
McGahan	Lasagna	29.7
McGahan	Spaghetti Plate	631.21
Peters	Baked Ziti	18.8
Peters	Lasagna	138.6
Peters	Spaghetti Plate	209.338
Ronald	Baked Ziti	65.8
Ronald	Lasagna	297
Ronald	Spaghetti Plate	287.64

Record: 1 of 18

Continuing with this example, say you wanted the result of this query displayed as a crosstab table instead. You could convert the SELECT statement into a TRANSFORM statement using the following steps:

1. Take the existing GROUP BY SELECT statement and plug it into the skeleton of a TRANSFORM statement. That is, insert a line with the word *TRANSFORM* before the SELECT statement and a line with the word *PIVOT* after it. This would give you the following:

```
TRANSFORM
SELECT LastName AS Employee,
MenuDescription, Sum(Quantity*Price*(1-Discount))
AS Sales
FROM tblMenu INNER JOIN (tblEmployee INNER JOIN
(tblOrder INNER JOIN tblOrderDetails ON tblOrder.OrderId =
tblOrderDetails.OrderId) ON tblEmployee.EmployeeId =
tblOrder.OrderTakerId) ON tblMenu.MenuId =
tblOrderDetails.MenuId
WHERE Unit = "Dinner"
GROUP BY LastName, MenuDescription;
PIVOT;
```

2. Move the aggregate function that will define the value of each crosstab cell from the SELECT clause into the TRANSFORM clause. In this example, you would move the expression that calculates sales. Thus, the SQL becomes:

```
TRANSFORM Sum(Quantity*Price*(1-Discount)) AS Sales
SELECT LastName AS Employee, MenuDescription
FROM tblMenu INNER JOIN (tblEmployee INNER JOIN
(tblOrder INNER JOIN tblOrderDetails ON tblOrder.OrderId =
tblOrderDetails.OrderId) ON tblEmployee.EmployeeId =
tblOrder.OrderTakerId) ON tblMenu.MenuId =
tblOrderDetails.MenuId
WHERE Unit = "Dinner"
GROUP BY LastName, MenuDescription;
PIVOT;
```

3. Move the field from the GROUP BY clause that will become the column headings to the PIVOT clause. Also, delete the reference to this field from the SELECT clause. Thus, you have:

```
TRANSFORM Sum(Quantity*Price*(1-Discount)) AS Sales
SELECT LastName AS Employee
FROM tblMenu INNER JOIN (tblEmployee INNER JOIN
(tblOrder INNER JOIN tblOrderDetails ON tblOrder.OrderId =
```

```
tblOrderDetails.OrderId) ON tblEmployee.EmployeeId =
tblOrder.OrderTakerId) ON tblMenu.MenuId =
tblOrderDetails.MenuId
WHERE Unit = "Dinner"
GROUP BY LastName
PIVOT MenuDescription;
```

That's it! The crosstab datasheet produced by the preceding TRANSFORM statement is shown in Figure 5.17.

FIGURE 5.17:

This crosstab query is equivalent to the totals query shown in Figure 5.16. Note that the crosstab statement produces a more compact, readable summarization of the data.

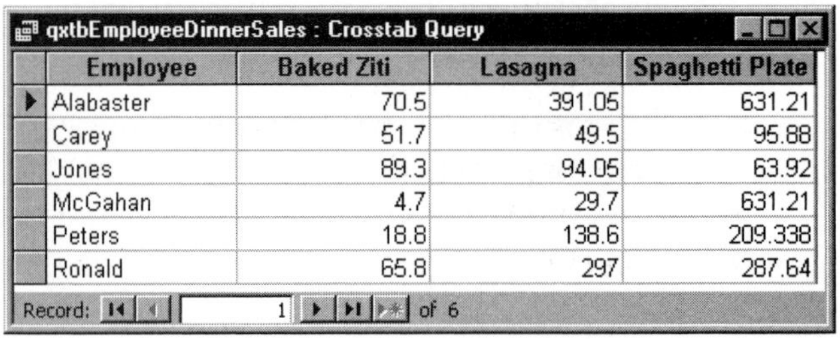

qxtbEmployeeDinnerSales : Crosstab Query

Employee	Baked Ziti	Lasagna	Spaghetti Plate
Alabaster	70.5	391.05	631.21
Carey	51.7	49.5	95.88
Jones	89.3	94.05	63.92
McGahan	4.7	29.7	631.21
Peters	18.8	138.6	209.338
Ronald	65.8	297	287.64

Record: 1 of 6

NOTE

The datasheets shown in Figures 5.16 and 5.17 lack any field formatting. We could have used the field property sheet in Design view to format the cell values as currency. Alternately, we could have used the Format function to format the calculations directly in the Select clause. You can't alter field properties from SQL view.

To recap the conversion process in more general terms, here are the steps for converting a SELECT statement into a TRANSFORM statement:

1. Ensure that the SELECT statement contains at least two GROUP BY fields, no HAVING clause, and a field suitable to become the column headings. Enclose the existing SELECT statement in a Transform shell like this:

   ```
   TRANSFORM
   select-statement
   PIVOT;
   ```

2. Move the aggregate function that will be used for the crosstab cell values from the SELECT clause into the TRANSFORM clause. The SQL should now look like this:

   ```
   TRANSFORM aggregate-function
   select-statement
   PIVOT;
   ```

3. Move one of the GROUP BY fields—the one that is to become the column headings—to the PIVOT clause. Delete the reference to this same field from the SELECT clause. The resulting TRANSFORM statement should now produce a crosstab query:

```
TRANSFORM aggregate-function
select-statement
PIVOT column-heading-field;
```

Multiple Row Headings

TRANSFORM statements can include multiple row headings. You create the additional row headings by adding another GROUP BY field to the embedded SELECT statement. For example, you might wish to break down sales additionally by PaymentMethod. The SQL statement that creates this additional row heading and its output are shown in Figure 5.18. Note that the only difference between the earlier SQL statement and this one is the addition of PaymentMethod to the SELECT and GROUP BY clauses of the embedded SELECT statement.

FIGURE 5.18:

This TRANSFORM statement produces a crosstab table that contains two row headings, Employee and PaymentMethod.

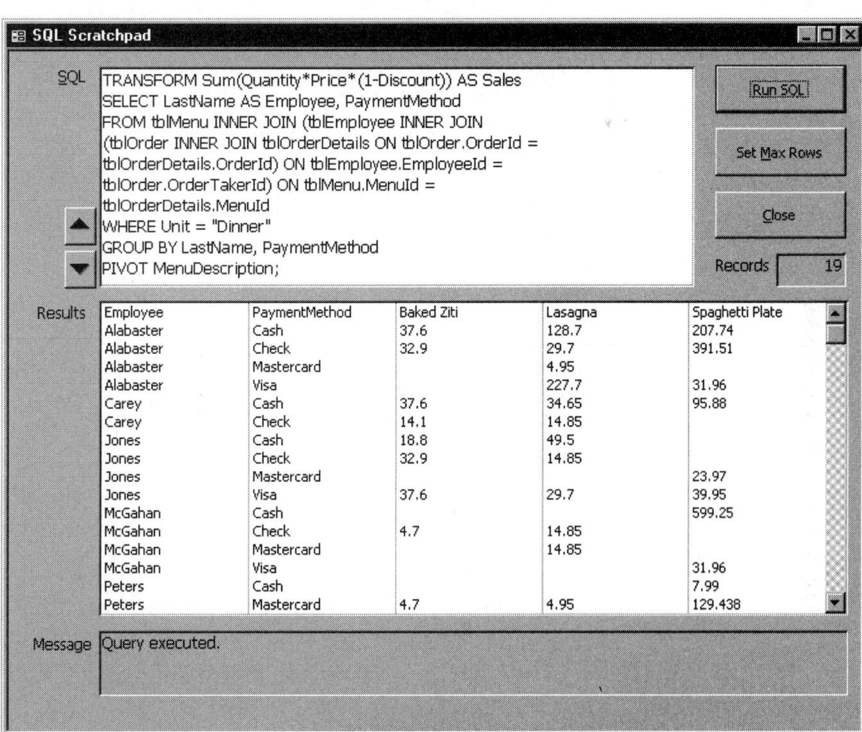

Creating a Totals Column

You can create an additional column to calculate row totals in a crosstab query by adding an additional aggregate field to the SELECT clause of the TRANSFORM statement. Don't include the additional aggregate function anywhere else in the TRANSFORM statement. Any aggregate functions you add to the TRANSFORM statement's SELECT clause will be added to the crosstab between the row headings field(s) and the column headings field. For example, the TRANSFORM statement shown in Figure 5.19 was created by adding a Sum aggregate function to the SELECT clause.

FIGURE 5.19:

By adding an aggregate function to the SELECT clause, you can create a column that totals the values for each row.

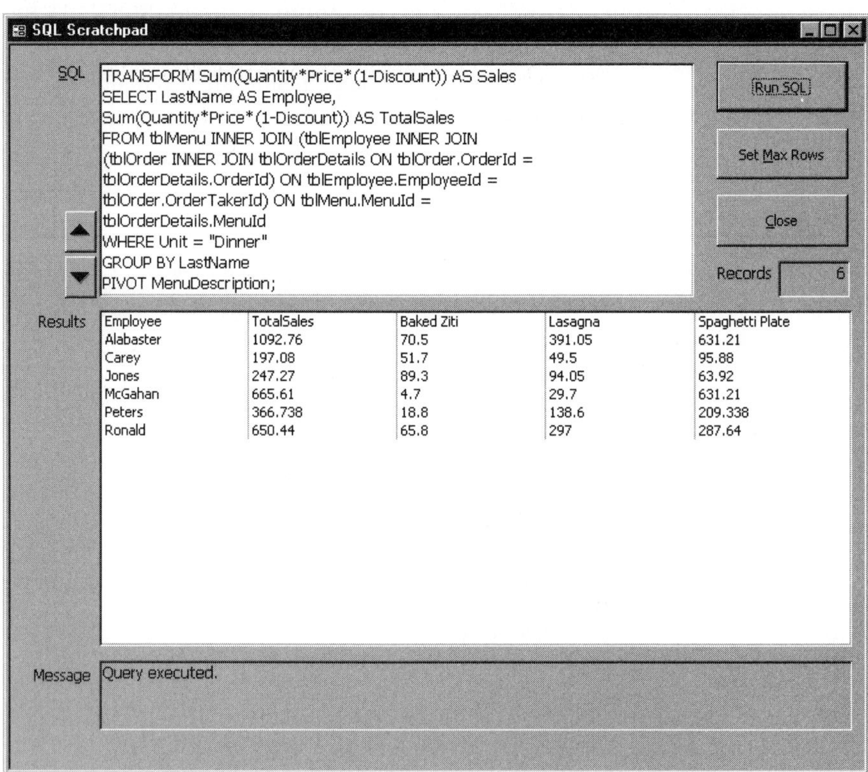
SQL Scratchpad
SQL
TRANSFORM Sum(Quantity*Price*(1-Discount)) AS Sales
SELECT LastName AS Employee,
Sum(Quantity*Price*(1-Discount)) AS TotalSales
FROM tblMenu INNER JOIN (tblEmployee INNER JOIN
(tblOrder INNER JOIN tblOrderDetails ON tblOrder.OrderId =
tblOrderDetails.OrderId) ON tblEmployee.EmployeeId =
tblOrder.OrderTakerId) ON tblMenu.MenuId =
tblOrderDetails.MenuId
WHERE Unit = "Dinner"
GROUP BY LastName
PIVOT MenuDescription;
Run SQL
Set Max Rows
Close
Records 6
Results
Message
Query executed.

Employee	TotalSales	Baked Ziti	Lasagna	Spaghetti Plate
Alabaster	1092.76	70.5	391.05	631.21
Carey	197.08	51.7	49.5	95.88
Jones	247.27	89.3	94.05	63.92
McGahan	665.61	4.7	29.7	631.21
Peters	366.738	18.8	138.6	209.338
Ronald	650.44	65.8	297	287.64

This additional aggregate function isn't limited to totaling the row values; you can use any valid SQL aggregate function here. For example, you could calculate the average sales per order. You could also include multiple aggregate functions in the SELECT clause; each would be displayed between the row headings and column headings fields.

Using the IN Clause to Create Fixed Columns

You can create fixed column headings by using the *IN clause.* This is equivalent to using the ColumnHeadings property in QBE. Place the optional IN clause immediately after the PIVOT clause in the TRANSFORM statement. The syntax is

PIVOT *column-headings-field* [IN *(value1* [, *value2* [, ...]])]

You can use the IN clause to order the values other than alphabetically (this is especially useful for alphanumeric date strings), exclude columns you don't wish to appear in the crosstab result, or include columns that may not exist in the recordset. For example, to create a crosstab table that excluded sales of spaghetti plate but included columns for baked ziti, lasagna, and dinner salad, even if there weren't any sales of these items, you would use the following PIVOT and IN clauses:

```
PIVOT MenuDescription IN ("Baked Ziti", "Lasagna","Dinner Salad")
```

Union Queries

You must use SQL to create a *union query* in Access; there is no equivalent QBE method for creating a union query. UNION is not a SQL statement or even a clause. Instead, it is an operator you use to vertically splice together two or more compatible queries. The basic syntax is

select-statement1

UNION [ALL]

select-statement2

[UNION [ALL]

select-statement3]

[...]

Union queries produce *read-only* recordsets.

Access matches columns from each SELECT statement by their position in the SELECT statement, *not* by their names. For example, say you wished to create a query that combined the names and addresses of both employees and customers for a mailing. You might create a union query like that shown in Figure 5.20.

FIGURE 5.20:

This union query combines the names and addresses from the tblEmployee and tblCustomer tables.

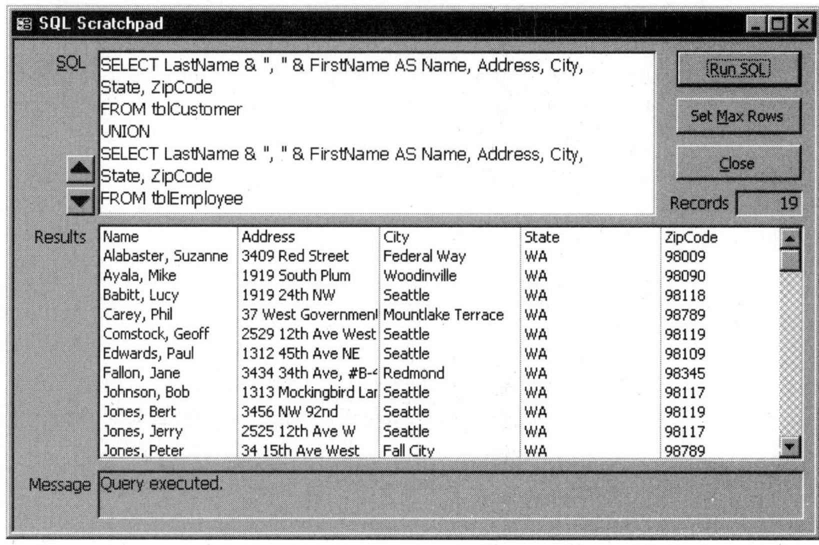

WARNING Although the Design view button is disabled when you create a SQL-specific (union, data definition, or SQL pass-through) query, you can always change the type of the query to a select or action query using the Query menu. Be careful, however, because when you change the query type of a SQL-specific query, your existing SQL statement is erased without so much as a confirming dialog.

Using the TABLE Option

You can use a shortcut syntax when you wish to include all the columns from a table or another query. This syntax employs the TABLE option and allows you to replace any of the SELECT statements with:

TABLE *table-or-query*

which is equivalent to the following SELECT statement:

SELECT * FROM *table-or-query*

For example, the following two union queries are equivalent:

```
SELECT * FROM tblCustomer
UNION
SELECT * FROM tblCustomerNew;
```

and

```
TABLE tblCustomer
UNION
TABLE tblCustomerNew;
```

The ALL Option

By default, Access eliminates duplicate records for union queries. You can force Access to include duplicates, however, by using the *ALL option* after the UNION operator. Using the ALL option speeds up the execution of union queries even if they don't have any duplicate records because Access can skip the extra comparison step, which can be significant with large recordsets.

Sorting the Results

You can use an ORDER BY clause in the *last* SELECT statement of a union query to order the resulting recordset. If some of the column names differ, you need to reference the name assigned to the column by the *first* SELECT statement. For example:

```
SELECT LastName FROM tblNames
UNION ALL
SELECT EmployeeName FROM tblContacts
ORDER BY LastName;
```

While each SELECT statement in a union query *can* have an ORDER BY clause, all but the last one are ignored.

Compatible Queries

You can string together as many select queries as you'd like in a union query; you're limited only by the fact that, as with all queries, the entire compiled query definition must fit into memory. The queries need to be compatible, however, which means they must have the same number of columns. Typically, the column names and data types of the unioned queries would be the same, but this isn't required. If they aren't the same, Access uses the following rules to combine them:

- For columns with *different names,* Access uses the column name from the first query.
- For columns with *different data types,* Access converts the columns to a single data type that is compatible with all the columns' data types. For example, Access uses the Long integer type when you combine an integer column with a long integer column. Similarly, text combined with a number produces a text column, date data combined with a yes/no column produces a text type, and so on.
- Access does not allow you to use OLE-object fields in a union query.

The union query shown in Figure 5.21 takes the union query rules to an extreme, combining the values from a text field with the values from a numeric field and a date/time field.

FIGURE 5.21:

This nonsensical but syntactically correct union query combines LastName from tblCustomer with MenuId from tblMenu and CustomerId from tblOrder. The data type of the output column is text.

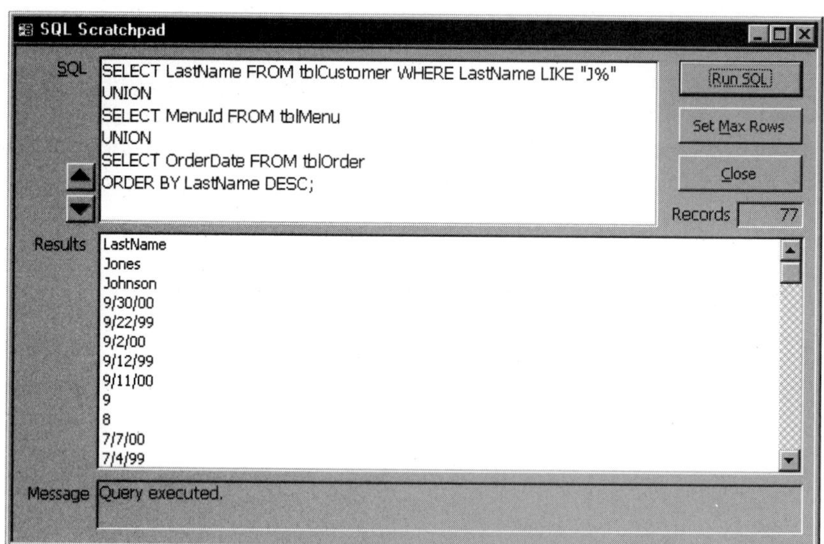

NOTE

New for Access 2000: you can now include Memo and Hyperlink fields in a union query.

Subqueries

Subqueries are a useful part of SQL that allow you to embed SELECT statements within other SELECT statements (or action SQL statements, which are covered later in this chapter in the section "Updating Data with SQL"). Typically, you use subqueries (which are also known as subselects) in the WHERE clause of a SQL statement to filter the query based on the values in another query (the subquery). There are three forms of syntax for subqueries:

- expression [NOT] IN (select-statement)
- comparison [{ANY | SOME | ALL}] (select-statement)
- [NOT] EXISTS (select-statement)

You may nest subqueries several levels deep; the actual limits on subquery nesting are undocumented. We discuss the use of each of the three types of subqueries in the next sections.

TIP

Most of the time you can use either a subquery or a join to create equivalent queries. You'll find a subquery is often easier to conceptualize than the same query that employs joins. On the other hand, a query containing a subquery usually executes more slowly than an equivalent query that uses joins. In terms of performance, neither type of query is necessarily faster than the other—sometimes the performance of the join version is faster, and other times the performance of the subquery version is faster.

NOTE

You can also use subqueries in Access QBE. Their use in QBE is analogous to their use in Access SQL. In QBE you can use subqueries in the Criteria or Field cell of a query.

Checking Values against a Lookup Table

Often, you'd like to be able to check the value of a column against some list of values in another table or query. For these situations, you use the IN form of a subquery. For example, say you wish to view the number, name, and price of all menu items that have ever been sold in quantities of ten or more. You could do this with the subquery shown in Figure 5.22. (Alternatively, this query could have been expressed using a join instead of a subquery. The equivalent join query is shown in Figure 5.23.)

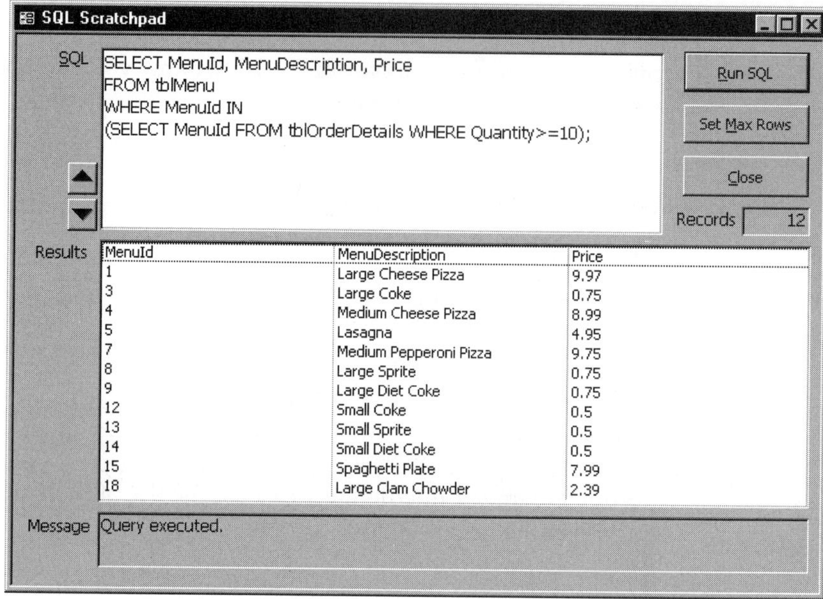

FIGURE 5.22:

This select query employs a subquery to find all menu items that have sold in quantities of ten or more.

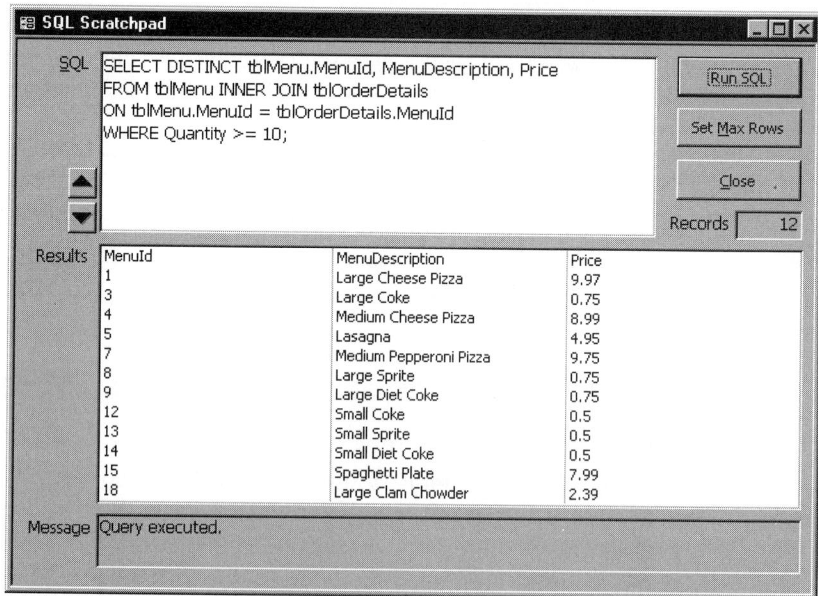

FIGURE 5.23:

This select query uses a join to find all menu items that have sold in quantities of ten or more. This query produces the same result as the query in Figure 5.22.

This form of subquery can return only a single column. If it returns more than one column, Access complains with an error message.

Using the NOT operator, you can also use this form of subquery to look for values that are *not* contained in the list.

Comparing Values against Other Values

Subqueries also come in handy when you wish to compare a value against rows in another query. You can do this using the second form of the subquery syntax. This form of subquery is also limited to returning a single column. For example, you could use the subquery in Figure 5.24 to list all menu items that are more expensive than baked ziti (which sells for $4.70).

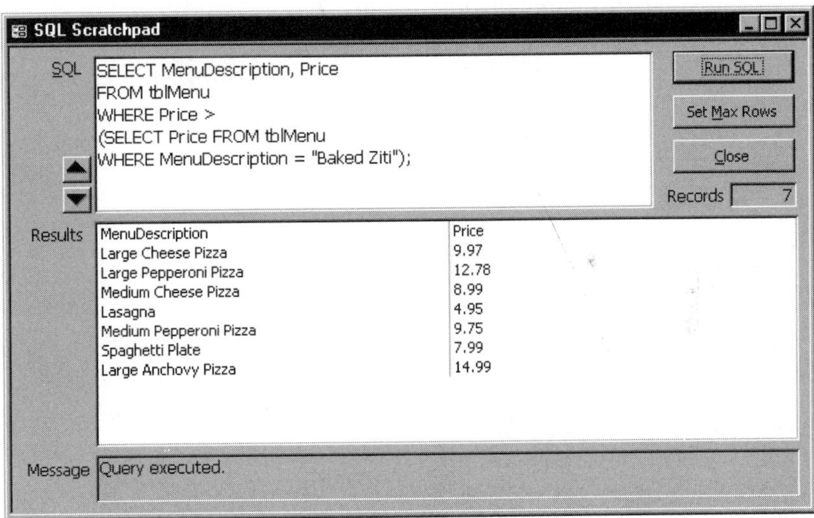

FIGURE 5.24:

This query lists all menu items for which the price is higher than the price of baked ziti ($4.70).

Note that the subquery in the query in Figure 5.24 returns one value, so you don't need to use a special predicate. If it had returned more than one row, it would have produced an error. When a subquery returns multiple rows, you must use one of the following predicates:

Predicate	Meaning
none	Makes a comparison with a single value

Predicate	Meaning
ANY or SOME	Is true if the comparison is true for any row returned by the subquery—in other words, if the comparison is true against the first row or the second row or the third row, and so on
ALL	Is true if the comparison is true for all rows returned by the subquery—in other words, if the comparison is true against the first row and the second row and the third row, and so on

If you don't use the ALL, SOME, or ANY predicate, you must guarantee that at most one value is returned. You can accomplish this by placing criteria on the subquery that selects a row by its primary key value. Alternately, you could use a SQL aggregate function or a Top 1 predicate in the subquery. For example, the following three comparisons might all be used to ensure that Age is less than the age of the oldest student (assuming, of course, you knew in advance that student number 35 was the oldest):

```
WHERE Age < (SELECT Age FROM tblStudent WHERE StudentId = 35)
WHERE Age < (SELECT MAX(Age) FROM tblStudent)
WHERE Age < (SELECT Top 1 Age FROM tblStudent ORDER BY Age DESC)
```

You can use the ANY or SOME predicate (the two are equivalent) to make a comparison against any of the rows returned or use the ALL predicate to make a comparison against all the rows returned by the subquery. For example, the following comparison would select rows in which Age was less than the age of *any* of the students—in other words, where age was *less than the oldest student*:

```
WHERE Age < ANY (SELECT Age FROM tblStudent)
```

On the other hand, you could use the following comparison to select rows in which Age was less than the age of *all* of the students—in other words, where Age was *less than the youngest student*:

```
WHERE Age < ALL (SELECT Age FROM tblStudent)
```

NOTE

The ANY, SOME, and ALL predicates will include rows with null values. This differs from the equivalent statements using the Min and Max aggregate functions, which exclude nulls.

Checking for Existence

The last form of a subquery comparison uses the EXISTS predicate to compare values against the existence of one or more rows in the subquery. If the subquery returns any rows, the comparison is True; if it returns no rows, the comparison is False. You can also use NOT EXISTS to get the opposite effect. Since you're checking only for the existence of rows, this form of subquery has no restriction on the number of columns or rows returned.

So far, all the subqueries presented in this chapter have been independent of the *outer* query (the query that contains the subquery). You can also create subqueries that are linked to the outer query. This type of subquery is termed a *correlated subquery* because it references the other query using its correlation name (discussed in the section "The FROM Clause" earlier in this chapter). The correlation name can be the same as the table name, or it can be a table's alias.

Each of the three types of subqueries can be correlated, but subqueries that use the EXISTS predicate are almost always correlated (otherwise, they wouldn't be very useful).

For example, you might want to find menu items that have never been ordered. You could accomplish this using the NOT EXISTS subquery shown in Figure 5.25. Running this query shows you that large anchovy pizzas have never been ordered.

FIGURE 5.25:

Using a NOT EXISTS correlated subquery, you can determine that no one has ever ordered a large anchovy pizza.

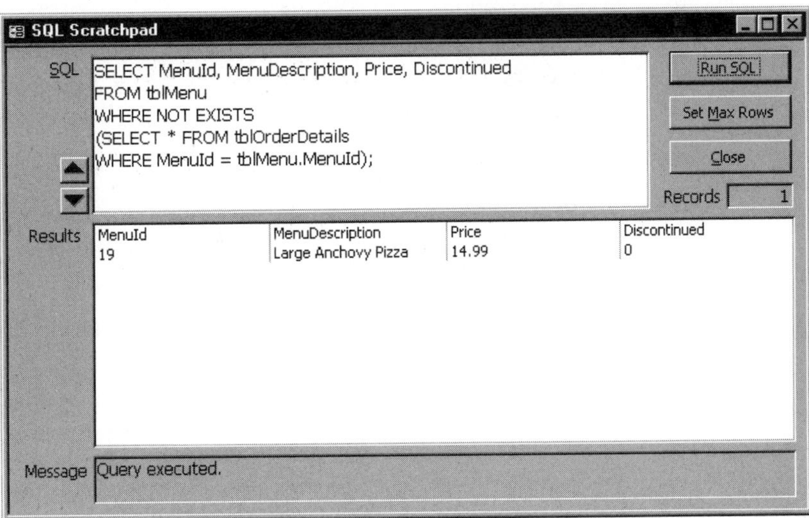

The subquery in Figure 5.25 is termed a correlated subquery because it references the data in the outer query—the data in tblMenu—in the WHERE clause of the subquery.

Using Subqueries in the SELECT Clause

Typically, you use subqueries in the WHERE clause of a query, but you may also find occasion to use a subquery that returns a single value in the SELECT clause. For example, say you wished to create a query similar to the one in Figure 5.25, but instead of listing only menu items that have never been ordered, you'd prefer to list all menu items with an additional field that indicates whether they've ever been ordered. You could accomplish this with the query shown in Figure 5.26. This query moves the subquery into the SELECT clause, gives it an alias, "Ever Ordered?", and formats it using the IIf function.

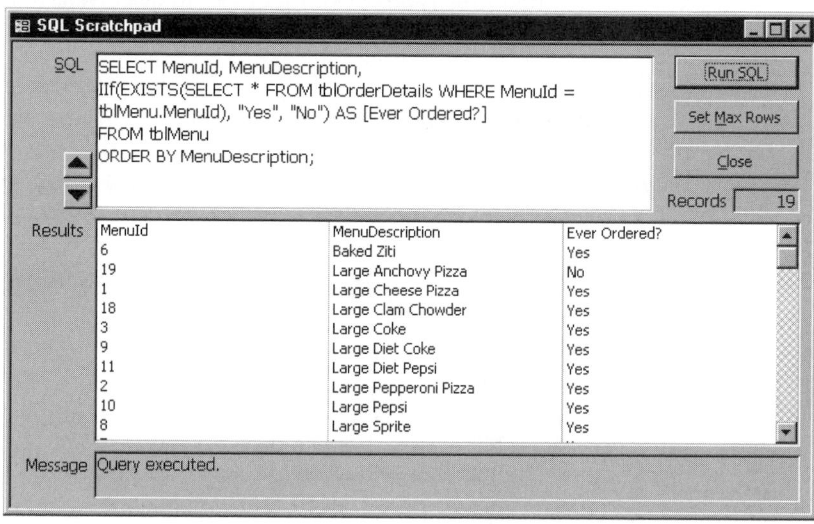

FIGURE 5.26:

This query lists each menu item and whether or not it has ever been ordered. It accomplishes this using a correlated subquery in the SELECT clause of a query.

You might also use a subquery in a SELECT clause to list a calculated constant that is used in selecting the rows. For example, you might want to list all menu items with prices higher than the average price, along with the average price as an output column. You could accomplish this with the following SELECT statement:

```
SELECT MenuId, MenuDescription, Price,
(SELECT Avg(Price) FROM tblMenu)
AS AveragePrice
FROM tblMenu
WHERE Price > (SELECT Avg(Price) FROM tblMenu);
```

Example: Using a Subquery to Find Duplicates

Say you have a table called tblImport that contains duplicate orders that prevent you from designating OrderId as the primary key for the table. You can eliminate the duplicates using the following correlated subquery:

```
SELECT *
FROM tblImport
WHERE OrderId In (SELECT OrderId FROM tblImport
GROUP BY OrderId HAVING Count(*)>1) ORDER BY OrderId;
```

This subquery produces a recordset with all the columns from tblImport but only the duplicate records. You can use this recordset to visually scan through each of the duplicate rows and prune out the true duplicates.

Subqueries have many more uses than the ones this chapter has presented. As mentioned previously, you can solve most queries as either subqueries or joined queries. Choose the method that makes the most sense for you.

Parameterized SQL

Just as in Access QBE, you can specify *parameters* to be resolved at run time using SQL. To do this, you use the PARAMETERS declaration. The syntax for its usage is

PARAMETERS *parameter1 datatype1* [,*parameter2 datatype2* [, …]];

sql-statement;

For example, if you want to list the date and employee number of all items for a particular order but have the user select the order when the query is run, you could construct a SELECT statement with a PARAMETERS declaration like this:

```
PARAMETERS [Enter Customer Number] Long;
SELECT OrderDate, OrderTakerId
FROM tblOrder
WHERE CustomerId=[Enter Customer Number]
ORDER BY OrderDate;
```

NOTE

The SQL Scratchpad form (frmSQLScratchpad) does not work with parameter queries. If you want to try out this example in the sample database, you'll need to use the SQL view of a query instead.

You must choose the data type for a parameter from the list of SQL data types in Table 5.2.

TABLE 5.2: SQL Data types and Their Counterparts in Table Design View

SQL Data type and Synonyms	Table Design Field Type
BIT, BOOLEAN, LOGICAL, LOGICAL1, YESNO	Yes/No
BYTE, INTEGER1	Number, FieldSize = Byte
COUNTER, AUTOINCREMENT	Autonumber, FieldSize = Long Integer
CURRENCY, MONEY	Currency
DATETIME, DATE, TIME	Date/Time
SHORT, INTEGER2, SMALLINT	Number, FieldSize = Integer
LONG, INT, INTEGER, INTEGER4	Number, FieldSize = Long
SINGLE, FLOAT4, IEEESINGLE, REAL	Number, FieldSize = Single
DOUBLE, FLOAT, FLOAT8, IEEEDOUBLE, NUMBER, NUMERIC	Number, FieldSize = Double
TEXT, ALPHANUMERIC, CHAR, CHARACTER, STRING, VARCHAR	Text
LONGTEXT, LONGCHAR, MEMO, NOTE	Memo
LONGBINARY, GENERAL, OLEOBJECT	OLE Object
GUID	Autonumber, FieldSize = Replication ID

Using External Data Sources

There are three ways to refer to data sources physically located outside an Access database in a SQL statement:

- Using linked tables
- Using the IN clause
- Using direct references to the external tables

Using Linked Tables

By far the easiest and most efficient way to reference external tables is to use linked tables. (Prior to Access 95, these were known as attached tables.) Once a table is linked to an Access database, you refer to it in SQL statements exactly as you would if it were a native Access table.

Although it is less efficient, you can also refer to nonlinked tables from a query using either the IN clause or the direct reference technique. These techniques are discussed in the next two sections.

Using the IN Clause

For nonlinked tables, you can use either the IN clause or the direct reference technique. To refer to one or more nonlinked tables located in the same Access database, the same ODBC database, or the same subdirectory for a given type of nonnative ISAM database, it's easiest to use the IN clause. The syntax you use depends on the type of table you are querying. Be aware that this is one place where Access is not very forgiving; if you misplace a semicolon, a quote, or even, in some cases, a space, the SQL statement will fail.

Access Databases

For Access databases, you use the following syntax:

FROM *tablelist* IN *"path-and-database"*

The following SQL statement selects fields from the tblOrder and tblCustomer tables located in another Access database:

```
SELECT OrderId, OrderDate, LastName AS Customer
FROM tblOrder INNER JOIN tblCustomer
ON tblOrder.CustomerId = tblCustomer.CustomerId
IN "d:\a2kdh\VolumeI-2370\ch04\ch04.mdb";
```

External ISAM Databases

For external ISAM databases you use either the following syntax:

FROM *tablelist* IN *"database" "product;"*

or this syntax:

FROM *tablelist* IN "" [*product*; DATABASE=*database*;]

NOTE

Unlike prior syntax statements in this chapter, the brackets in the preceding statement represent literal bracket characters.

Table 5.3 lists the syntax for the various ISAM format product, tablelist, and path values.

TABLE 5.3: External ISAM Product, Tablelist, and Database Choices

Product	Tablelist	Database
Access	Name of Access table	path and name of database
dBase III*	Name of dBase file	directory path
dBase IV*	Name of dBase file	directory path
dBase 5.0*	Name of dBase file	directory path
Excel 3.0	Name of worksheet or range	path and name of workbook file
Excel 4.0	Name of worksheet or range	path and name of workbook file
Excel 5.0	Name of worksheet or range	path and name of workbook file
Excel 8.0****	Name of worksheet or range	path and name of workbook file
Exchange 4.0	Name of Exchange folder	directory path** (and ";mapilevel=name_of_parent_folder|;")
HMTL Import	Name of HTML table or HTML file	path and name of HTML file
Lotus WJ2	Name of worksheet file	path and name of worksheet file
Lotus WJ3	Name of worksheet file	path and name of worksheet file
Lotus WK1	Name of worksheet file	path and name of worksheet file
Lotus WK3	Name of worksheet file	path and name of worksheet file
Lotus WK4	Name of worksheet file	path and name of worksheet file
Outlook 9.0	Name of Outlook folder	directory path** (and ";mapilevel=name_of_parent_folder|;")
Paradox 3X*	Name of Paradox table	directory path
Paradox 4.X*	Name of Paradox table	directory path

Continued on next page

TABLE 5.3 CONTINUED: External ISAM Product, Tablelist, and Database Choices

Product	tablelist	Database
Paradox 5.X*	Name of Paradox table	directory path
Paradox 7.X*	Name of Paradox table	directory path
Text	Name of text file***	directory path

* In order to update dBase and Paradox data, you must purchase the Borland Database Engine from Inprise.

** Exchange and Outlook require a default MAPI client installed on the desktop. You must set the database entry to point to the name of an existing subdirectory into which the engine will place a schema.ini file. You must also include a mapilevel entry set to the name of the parent folder of the folder you wish to access followed by a pipe character (|).

*** For text files, you must include the name of the file and its extension, replacing the period (.) with a pound sign (#).

**** Also works with Excel 9 (Excel 2000) files.

NOTE

Access 2000 no longer includes ISAM support for FoxPro. To use FoxPro data, you must now use the FoxPro ODBC driver.

The following SQL statement selects fields from the dbase III NewOrder and NewCust tables (files) using the first version of the syntax:

```
SELECT OrderId, OrderDate, LastName as Customer
FROM NewOrder INNER JOIN NewCust
ON NewOrder.CustomerId = NewCust.CustomerId
IN "D:\A2Kdh\VolumeI-2370\Ch05" "dbase III;";
```

The next SQL statement uses the alternate syntax to return the same data:

```
SELECT OrderId, OrderDate, LastName as Customer
FROM NewOrder INNER JOIN NewCust
ON NewOrder.CustomerId = NewCust.CustomerId
IN "" [dbase III;DATABASE=D:\A2Kdh\VolumeI-2370\Ch05;];
```

Here are a few additional examples of the proper syntax for HMTL, Text, Outlook, Exchange, Lotus, and Excel formats using the first form of the ISAM syntax:

```
SELECT *
FROM NWCustomers
IN "D:\A2Kdh\VolumeI-2370\Ch05\Customers.htm" "HTML Import;"

SELECT *
FROM tblMenu#txt
IN "D:\A2Kdh\VolumeI-2370\Ch05" "Text;"
```

```
SELECT [To], [From], [Subject], [Received]
FROM Inbox
IN "c:\temp" "Outlook 9.0;MAPILEVEL=Personal Folders|;"
WHERE [Received] >= #12/23/98#
ORDER BY [Received];

SELECT *
FROM Contacts
IN "c:\temp" "Exchange 4.0;mapilevel=personal folders|;"

SELECT *
FROM tblMenu
IN "D:\A2Kdh\VolumeI-2370\Ch05\tblMenu.wk3" "Lotus WK3;"

SELECT *
FROM Menu
IN "D:\A2Kdh\VolumeI-2370\Ch05\test5.xls" "Excel 5.0;"
```

NOTE

The path you provide for the Outlook or Exchange driver has nothing to do with where your Outlook or Exchange files are located. You provide this folder so the Outlook/Exchange ISAM driver has a place to save a temporary schema file.

Figure 5.27 shows the results of running a query that retrieves Inbox records using the Outlook ISAM driver.

FIGURE 5.27:

This query retrieves records from the Inbox folder of the user's default MAPI client, which in this case is Outlook 2000.

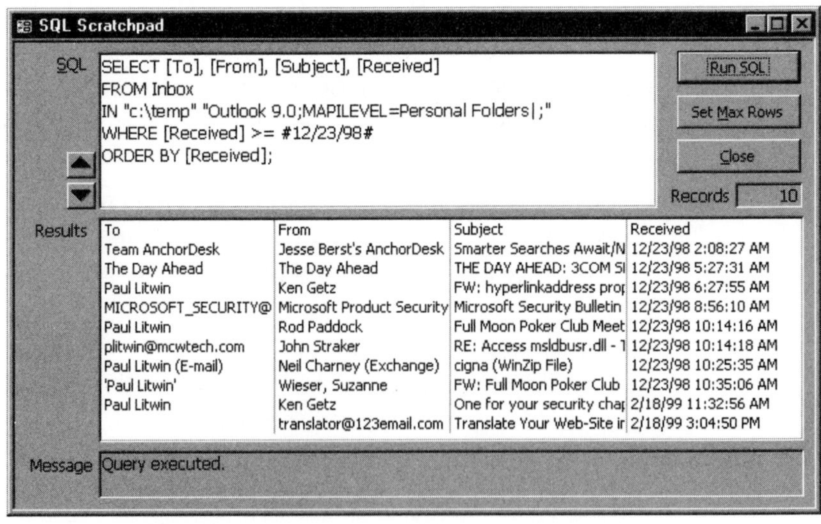

NOTE The Exchange/Outlook ISAM engines don't actually use Exchange or Outlook; rather, they use the default MAPI client you have installed on the desktop. The only difference is that the Exchange driver has a slightly different set of fields than the Outlook client. Both engines are very slow, so be patient.

Take care not to mix the two forms of the syntax for ISAM files. You must use one or the other; a hybrid will not work.

ODBC Databases

For ODBC data sources, you must use yet another syntax:

FROM *tablelist* IN "" [ODBC; *connect-string*;]

NOTE The brackets in the preceding statement represent literal bracket characters.

The exact connect string is dependent on the ODBC driver you use. Microsoft SQL Server uses a connect string like this:

DSN=*data-source*;UID=*user-id*;PWD=*password*;DATABASE=*database*

The *data-source* (DSN) is the name of the data source you have prespecified using the ODBC driver manager program. A DSN can refer to either a single database or multiple databases; if it refers to a single database, you don't need to use the DATABASE parameter. The UID and PWD parameters are optional. In a secured environment, however, you probably *won't* want to embed the password in the connect string. If you leave out these or any other parameters, you will be prompted for the missing parameters at run time.

The following SELECT statement selects data from two SQL Server tables that are part of the SQLPizza data source. This SELECT statement is analogous to those presented earlier in this chapter that used Access and FoxPro data sources.

```
SELECT OrderId, OrderDate, LastName AS Customer
FROM tblOrder INNER JOIN tblCustomer
ON tblOrder.CustomerId = tblCustomer.CustomerId
IN ""[ODBC;DSN=SQLPizza;UID=Bob;];
```

Anyone who executes this SQL statement will be prompted for Bob's password.

TIP When working with server data, it is more efficient to use linked tables, ADO, or an Access project than to use the techniques shown here.

Using Direct Table References

Sometimes you need to refer to multiple external data sources that are located either in different subdirectories/databases or in heterogeneous data sources. For example, you might want to join a table that's stored in dBASE format with a Paradox table. In these cases, the IN clause technique will not work, but Access provides another way to refer to these tables: the direct reference method. (This is our terminology, not Microsoft's.) The syntax for each different data source type is detailed in the following table.

Data Source Type	Direct Reference Syntax
Access	[*path-and-database*].tablename
External ISAM	[*product*;DATABASE=*path*;].*tablename*
ODBC	[ODBC; *connect-string*;].*tablename*

NOTE The brackets in the preceding statements represent literal bracket characters.

For example, the query shown in Figure 5.28 joins an external Paradox 5 table, Customer, to an external dBASE III table, NewOrder. Of course, this is only an example of what you *could* do, and an inefficient example at that. In general, it's best to design your database and queries so that you minimize the number of heterogeneous joins (joins across tables from different data sources). This is of special importance when one of the data sources comes from a client-server database. Since this will almost always force Access to perform the join locally, it should be avoided.

NOTE There doesn't appear to be any way to use a native OLE DB driver to retrieve records from a query. You can, of course, always use ADO to accomplish the same end result.

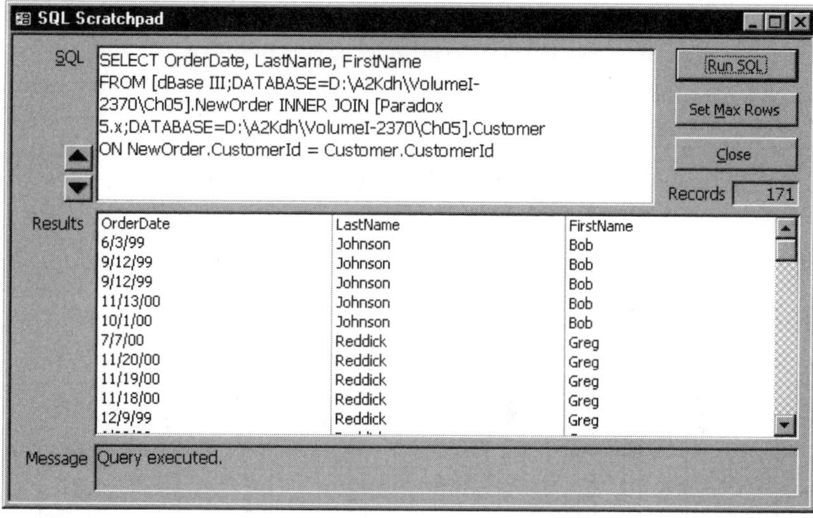

FIGURE 5.28:

This SELECT statement performs a heterogeneous join of two external tables.

Updating Data with SQL

In addition to querying data, you can use SQL to make changes to data. You can use Access SQL to update records, delete records, or copy records to another table. Access SQL has four statements for updating data, all of which have analogous counterparts in Access QBE:

SQL Statement	**QBE Query**
UPDATE	Update
DELETE	Delete
INSERT INTO	Append
SELECT INTO	Make-table

All but the last one, SELECT INTO, are part of the ANSI SQL standard. (The ANSI standard uses SELECT INTO in a very different way to move a single row of data into a list of variables. The two usages are not equivalent.)

Once you have learned the SELECT statement and all its predicates, declarations, and clauses, you'll find learning the action SQL statements relatively easy.

This is because each of these statements is similar syntactically to SELECT. Thus, even though each one includes WHERE clauses, for example, we will not repeat the discussion of WHERE clauses here. We will note, however, where there are differences between clauses in action SQL statements and the SELECT statement.

The UPDATE Statement

You use the *UPDATE statement* to change values in one or more columns in a table. The syntax is

UPDATE *table-or-query*

SET *column1* = *expression1* [,*column2* = *expression2*] [, ...]

[WHERE *criteria*];

You can update the values in either a table or a query, but if you use a query, it must be updateable. The expressions in the SET clause can be a constant or the result of a calculation. For example, to increase the price of all nonpizza menu items by 10 percent, you could use the following update query:

```
UPDATE tblMenu
SET tblMenu.Price = [Price]*1.1
WHERE MenuDescription Not Like "*Pizza*";
```

The ANSI standard supports the use of subqueries in the SET clause, while Access SQL does not. Fortunately, Access SQL supports the use of joins in the UPDATE clause (this is nonstandard SQL), which gives you almost equivalent functionality. The syntax used for joins in the UPDATE clause is the same as the join syntax used for SELECT statements in the FROM clause. For example, to change the phone numbers in the tblCustomer table to new phone numbers stored in another table, tblCustomerMods—which you might have imported from another copy of the database on another machine—you could use the following UPDATE statement:

```
UPDATE tblCustomerMods INNER JOIN tblCustomer ON
tblCustomerMods.CustomerId = tblCustomer.CustomerId
SET tblCustomer.Phone = tblCustomerMods.Phone
WHERE tblCustomer.Phone<>tblCustomerMods.Phone;
```

This UPDATE statement uses a WHERE clause to limit the updates only to records that need to be modified—those in which the phone numbers are different.

The DELETE Statement

You use the *DELETE statement* to delete rows from tables. Its syntax is

DELETE [*table*.*]

FROM *from-clause*

[WHERE *criteria*];

The use of *table*.* is optional for delete queries that refer to only a single table.

NOTE

Access also allows you to refer to a single column in the DELETE clause—for example, "DELETE tblOrder.OrderDate". In fact, Access QBE often generates DELETE statements in this misleading style, but don't let this confuse you; the entire record is deleted, not just the values in the column.

For single-table queries, the syntax can be simplified:

DELETE

FROM *table*

[WHERE *criteria*];

For example, to delete all discontinued items from tblMenu, you could use the following DELETE statement:

```
DELETE
FROM tblMenu
WHERE Discontinued = True;
```

You can create DELETE statements that reference multiple tables, but you must follow these rules:

- You can use the data in one table to decide which rows to delete from another related table. You can accomplish this by using a join in the FROM clause or by using a subquery in the WHERE clause. Tables can be related in either a one-to-one or a one-to-many relationship. (Note that you may be prevented from deleting rows from a table if referential integrity is turned on without cascaded updates.)

- You can delete rows from multiple tables in a single delete query if the tables are related in a one-to-one relationship.
- You can delete rows from multiple tables related in a one-to-many relationship with a series of DELETE queries.

For example, to delete all customers from tblCustomer who have not placed an order during the past year, you would create and execute the following DELETE statement, which uses a subquery to find the proper rows:

```
DELETE
FROM tblCustomer
WHERE tblCustomer.CustomerId NOT IN
(SELECT CustomerId FROM tblOrder WHERE OrderDate >
DateAdd('yyyy',-1,Date()));
```

Access SQL departs from the ANSI standard through its support for named tables in the DELETE clause and joins in the FROM clause.

TIP

You can use a single DELETE statement to delete the records in two tables related in a one-to-many relationship if you've defined a relationship between the two tables and have turned on the cascading deletes option. In this case, if you delete a row from the "one" side of a relationship, Access automatically deletes the related rows in the "many-sided" table.

The INSERT INTO Statement

You use the *INSERT INTO statement* to copy rows from one table (or query) into another table. You can also use it to add a single row of data to a table using a list of values. The syntax of the first form of the INSERT INTO statement is

INSERT INTO *target-table*

select-statement;

TIP

The *target-table* reference can refer to an external table using the IN predicate or a direct reference. (See the discussion in the section "Using External Data Sources" earlier in this chapter.)

In its simplest form, you can use this form of the INSERT INTO statement to copy the contents of one table to another. For example, to copy all the rows from tblCustomerNew to tblCustomer, you could use the following INSERT INTO statement:

```
INSERT INTO tblCustomer
SELECT * FROM tblCustomerNew;
```

You can use any valid SELECT statement that produces recordsets, including SELECT statements with GROUP BY clauses, joins, UNION operators, and sub-queries. This embedded SELECT statement can include references to one or more queries. For example, to append records from the GROUP BY SELECT statement presented earlier in the chapter in the section "Creating Crosstab Queries with the TRANSFORM Statement" to a table named tblEmployeeDinnerSales, you could use the following INSERT INTO statement:

```
INSERT INTO tblEmployeeDinnerSales
SELECT LastName, MenuDescription,
Sum(Quantity*Price*(1-Discount)) AS Sales
FROM tblMenu INNER JOIN (tblEmployee INNER JOIN
(tblOrder INNER JOIN tblOrderDetails ON tblOrder.OrderId =
tblOrderDetails.OrderId) ON tblEmployee.EmployeeId =
tblOrder.OrderTakerId) ON
tblMenu.MenuId = tblOrderDetails.MenuId
WHERE Unit="Dinner"
GROUP BY LastName, MenuDescription;
```

You use the second form of the INSERT INTO statement to add a single row to a table and populate it with values. Its syntax is

> INSERT INTO *target-table* [(*column1* [,*column2* [, …]])]
>
> VALUES (*value1* [,*value2* [, …]]);

If you omit the column references in the INSERT INTO clause, you must include a value for each column in the target table in the exact order in which the columns appear in the table definition. If you include the column references, you may omit columns (other than the primary key and other required columns) or change the order in which they appear in the table definition. For example, you could add a new row to tblMenu using the following INSERT INTO statement:

```
INSERT INTO tblMenu (MenuId, Price, MenuDescription)
VALUES (50, 29.99, "Family Platter");
```

The SELECT INTO Statement

You use the *SELECT INTO statement,* unique to Access SQL, to create a new table from the rows in another table or query. Its syntax is

SELECT *column1* [,*column2* [, …]] INTO *new-table*

FROM *table-list*

[WHERE *where-clause*]

[ORDER BY *order-by clause*];

For example, you could use the following SELECT INTO statement to copy all purchases made by CustomerId = 9 from tblOrder to a new table called tblJonesOrders:

```
SELECT OrderId, OrderDate, CustomerId, OrderTakerId,
DeliveryDate, DeliveryTime, PaymentMethod, Notes
INTO tblJonesOrders
FROM tblOrder
WHERE CustomerId=9;
```

Like the INSERT INTO statement, the SELECT INTO statement can include any valid SELECT statement that produces a recordset, including SELECT statements with GROUP BY clauses, joins, UNION operators, and subqueries.

NOTE Tables created by SELECT INTO statements will not contain primary keys, indexes, or any column or table properties other than the defaults assigned to any new table.

Data Definition with SQL

You can use two methods to programmatically create and manipulate table schemas in Access: ActiveX Data Objects Extensions for DDL and Security (ADOX) and Data Definition Language (DDL) queries. (Actually, there are three methods if you count the older Data Access Objects [DAO].) In this section, we discuss the use of DDL queries. Chapter 6 covers using ADOX to create and modify schemas.

As with union queries, you must enter DDL queries using SQL view; there's no QBE counterpart. You can also execute a DDL query by defining and executing a querydef created using VBA.

Access SQL supports four DDL statements:

DDL Statement	Purpose
CREATE TABLE	Creates a new table schema
ALTER TABLE	Modifies an existing table schema
CREATE INDEX	Creates a new index
DROP	Deletes a table schema or an index

In addition, you can use the CONSTRAINT clause in either a CREATE TABLE or ALTER TABLE statement to create constraints. (In Access' simplified support of CONSTRAINT, this means the creation of indexes.) The next few sections discuss each of these statements, as well as the CONSTRAINT clause.

NOTE The new Jet 4 SQL extensions provide additional DDL query functionality (both additional statements and increased functionality of existing statements) that is discussed later in this chapter in the section "Jet 4 ANSI SQL-92 Extensions."

The CREATE TABLE Statement

You use the *CREATE TABLE statement* to create a new table. Its syntax is

CREATE TABLE *table*

(*column1 type1* [(*size1*)] [CONSTRAINT *column-constraint1*]

[,*column2 type2* [(*size2*)] [CONSTRAINT *column-constraint2*]

[, ...]]

[CONSTRAINT *table-constraint1* [,*table-constraint2* [, ...]]]);

You specify the data type of a column using one of the Jet engine SQL data type identifiers or its synonyms, which were summarized earlier in Table 5.2.

WARNING The Jet engine SQL data types and their synonyms, which are derived from ANSI SQL data types, differ from the Access data types in several subtle ways. Use care when selecting the correct data type keyword. Most notably, using the SQL data type INTEGER produces a number column with Size = *Long* because INTEGER in ANSI SQL is a 4-byte integer value (which in Access is a Long integer).

You can use the optional *size* parameter to specify the length of a text column. If *size* is left blank, text columns are assigned a size of 255. Note that this differs from the default column size of 50 assigned when new tables are created with the user interface. Other data types do not use this option.

You can create two types of constraints using a CREATE TABLE statement: single-column indexes and multicolumn (or table) indexes. You specify both of these indexes using the CONSTRAINT clause, which is discussed in the next section.

For example, to create a table tblNewMenu to mimic the schema of the tblMenu table found in the CH05.MDB sample database, you would use the following CREATE TABLE statement:

```
CREATE TABLE tblNewMenu
(MenuId LONG, MenuDescription TEXT (50), Unit TEXT (50),
Price CURRENCY, Discontinued BIT);
```

The CONSTRAINT Clause

In the SQL-92 standard, constraints are used to restrict the values that can be added to a table. You can use constraints in SQL-92 to create primary and foreign keys, constrain columns to be UNIQUE or NOT NULL, and create validation rules (the CHECK constraint). Access SQL supports each of these uses except for the NOT NULL and CHECK constraints. Since the only constraints Access currently supports are ones requiring the definition of indexes, you might find it convenient to think of the Access CONSTRAINT clause as being used to create indexes.

NOTE The new Jet 4 SQL extensions provide additional check constraint functionality. See the section "Jet 4 ANSI SQL-92 Extensions" later in this chapter.

You use the CONSTRAINT clause in CREATE TABLE and ALTER TABLE statements. The CONSTRAINT syntax takes two forms. You use the first form for single-column constraints:

CONSTRAINT *name* {PRIMARY KEY | UNIQUE |

REFERENCES *foreign-table* [(*foreign-column*)]}

The multiple-column version of the CONSTRAINT clause is

CONSTRAINT *name*

{PRIMARY KEY (*column1* [, *column2* [, ...]])

| UNIQUE

| FOREIGN KEY (*column1* [, *column2* [, ...]]) REFERENCES

foreign-table [(*foreign-column1* [,*foreign-column2* [, ...]])]}

For example, you could use the following CREATE TABLE statement to create the tblNewMenu table and a unique index on the column MenuDescription:

```
CREATE TABLE tblNewMenu
(MenuId LONG, MenuDescription TEXT CONSTRAINT MenuDescription
UNIQUE, Unit TEXT, Price CURRENCY, Discontinued BIT);
```

TIP

Anytime you create an index in Access, even a single-column index, you must assign it a name. Since the Access UI assigns primary key indexes the name PrimaryKey and single-column indexes the same name as the column and there's no good reason to do otherwise, we recommend using the same naming conventions in DDL queries. Less clear is what to name foreign key indexes; we have chosen here to use the naming convention *referenced-tablename*FK. For example, a foreign key to tblCustomer would be tblCustomerFK. (The Access UI gives less descriptive names of the form *Reference, Reference1,* and so forth.)

As a second example, say you wished to create two tables, tblNewOrders and tblNewItems, and relate them in a one-to-many relationship. You need tblNewOrders to have the following columns: OrderId (the primary key), OrderDate, and CustomerId. Table tblNewItems should contain OrderId, ItemId, and ItemDescription. For tblNewItems, OrderId and ItemId will make up the primary key and OrderId will be a foreign key reference to the same-named column in tblNewOrders. You could use the following two CREATE TABLE statements, executed one after the other (you can't place multiple SQL statements in a DDL query), to create the two tables:

```
CREATE TABLE tblNewOrders
(OrderId LONG CONSTRAINT PrimaryKey PRIMARY KEY,
OrderDate DATETIME, CustomerId LONG );

CREATE TABLE tblNewItems
(OrderId LONG CONSTRAINT tblNewOrdersFK REFERENCES
tblNewOrders, ItemId LONG, ItemDescription TEXT (30),
CONSTRAINT PrimaryKey PRIMARY KEY (OrderId, ItemId) );
```

TIP

For foreign key references, you can omit the name of the foreign key column if it is the primary key in the referenced table.

Both forms of CONSTRAINT lack any way to create nonunique indexes within a CREATE TABLE or ALTER TABLE statement. This *is* consistent with the SQL-92 standard. Fortunately, you can use the CREATE INDEX statement, described in the next section, to create this type of index. A shortcoming of Access' CONSTRAINT clause is that there's no support for the specification of foreign key relationships with either cascading deletes or updates. (The new Jet 4 SQL extensions support this feature.)

The CREATE INDEX Statement

In addition to the CONSTRAINT clause of the CREATE TABLE and ALTER TABLE statements, you can use the *CREATE INDEX statement* to create an index on an existing table. (CREATE INDEX is not a part of the ANSI standard, but many vendors include support for it.) The syntax of the CREATE INDEX statement is

CREATE [UNIQUE] INDEX *index*

ON table (*column1* [,*column2* [, …]])

[WITH {PRIMARY | DISALLOW NULL | IGNORE NULL}];

If you include the UNIQUE keyword, the index disallows duplicate values. You must give a name to each index, even if it's a single-column index. See the preceding section for suggested index-naming conventions.

You can create a primary key index by using the PRIMARY option in the WITH clause. All primary key indexes are automatically unique indexes, so you needn't (but you can) use the UNIQUE keyword when you use the PRIMARY option.

You use the IGNORE NULL option to prevent Jet from creating index entries for null values. If the indexed column will contain nulls and there may be many nulls, you can improve the performance of searches on nonnull values by using this option. This is equivalent to using the IgnoreNulls property of the index in Table Design view.

You can use the DISALLOW NULL option to have the Jet engine prevent the user from entering null values in the column. This is similar to setting the Required property of a column in Table Design view to Yes. Choosing this option has the same effect, but this "hidden" feature is maintained by the index, not the column, and has no analogous property in the UI. If you use this option, you won't be able to turn it off through the user interface—the Required property of the underlying column will act independently—unless you delete the index.

You can create a multicolumn index by including more than one column name in the ON clause.

You can create only one index at a time with the CREATE INDEX statement. Also, there's no facility for creating descending-ordered indexes using the CREATE INDEX statement; you must use the UI or DAO to alter the sort order of any indexes created using DDL queries.

You could use the following CREATE INDEX statement to add a unique index that ignored nulls to the column Price in tblNewMenu:

```
CREATE UNIQUE INDEX Price
ON tblNewMenu (Price)
WITH IGNORE NULL;
```

The ALTER TABLE Statement

You can use the *ALTER TABLE statement* to alter the schema of an existing table. With it you can add a new column or constraint or delete a column or constraint. (You can't modify the definition of either.) You can operate on only one field or index with a single ALTER TABLE statement. The ALTER TABLE statement has four forms.

You use the first form to *add a column* to a table:

> ALTER TABLE *table* ADD [COLUMN] *column datatype* [(*size*)]
>
> [CONSTRAINT *single-column-constraint*];

The keyword COLUMN is optional. As in the CREATE TABLE statement, you specify the data type of the new column by using one of the Jet engine SQL data type identifiers or its synonyms (see Table 5.2 earlier in this chapter). You can use the optional SIZE parameter to specify the length of a text column. If *size* is left blank, text columns are assigned a size of 255. You can also specify an optional index for the column using the CONSTRAINT clause. (See the section "The CONSTRAINT Clause" earlier in this chapter.)

NOTE The new Jet 4 SQL extensions provide additional ALTER TABLE functionality that lets you alter the definition of a column. See the section "Jet 4 ANSI SQL-92 Extensions" later in this chapter.

For example, you could use the following ALTER TABLE statement to add the integer column Quantity to the tblNewItems table:

```
ALTER TABLE tblNewItems ADD Quantity SHORT;
```

You use the second form of ALTER TABLE to *add constraints* to a table:

> ALTER TABLE *table* ADD CONSTRAINT *constraint;*

For example, you could use the following ALTER TABLE statement to add an index to the new column:

```
ALTER TABLE tblNewItems ADD CONSTRAINT Quantity UNIQUE (Quantity);
```

As with the CREATE TABLE statement, you are limited to creating indexes that are unique or serve as primary or foreign keys.

You use the third form of ALTER TABLE to *remove a column* from a table (the COLUMN keyword is optional):

> ALTER TABLE *table* DROP [COLUMN] *column;*

For example, you could use the following ALTER TABLE statement to remove the ItemDescription column from tblNewItems:

```
ALTER TABLE tblNewItems DROP COLUMN ItemDescription;
```

NOTE You can't remove an indexed column from a table without first removing its index.

You use the final form of ALTER TABLE to *remove an index* from a table:

ALTER TABLE *table* DROP CONSTRAINT *index;*

You refer to an index by its name. For example, to remove the primary key from tblNewOrders, you would use the following ALTER TABLE statement:

```
ALTER TABLE tblNewOrders DROP CONSTRAINT PrimaryKey;
```

NOTE You can't delete an index that is involved in a relationship without first deleting all the relationships in which it participates.

The DROP Statement

You can use the *DROP statement* to remove tables or indexes. It has two forms.

You use the first to *remove a table* from a database:

DROP TABLE *table;*

For example, you could use the following DROP statement to remove the tblNewItems table from the current database:

```
DROP TABLE tblNewItems;
```

You use the second form of DROP to *remove an index* from a table:

DROP INDEX *index* ON *table;*

For example, to delete the index named Price from tblNewMenu, you could use the following DROP statement:

```
DROP INDEX Price ON tblNewMenu;
```

NOTE To drop an index from a table, you can use either the ALTER TABLE statement or the DROP statement. You must use caution when using DROP, because there is no confirming dialog when it is executed.

NOTE

The new Jet 4 SQL extensions provide four additional forms of the DROP statement for dropping views, procedures, users, and groups. See the section "Jet 4 ANSI SQL-92 Extensions" later in this chapter.

Creating SQL Pass-Through Queries

You can use SQL pass-through queries to send uninterpreted SQL statements to a server database. Pass-through queries can be used only with ODBC data sources; you can't use pass-through queries with ISAM or OLEDB data sources. Access performs no syntax checking, interpretation, or translation of the SQL in a pass-through query. It's entirely up to you to compose your query using the proper syntax of the server's dialect of SQL.

You create a SQL pass-through query by creating a new blank query and then choosing Query ➢ SQL Specific ➢ Pass-Through. It's important that you choose this command rather than just switch to SQL view. If you don't, Access will think you are creating a normal (non-pass-through) query.

TIP

You can convert a non-pass-through query entered into SQL view by choosing Query ➢ SQL Specific ➢ Pass-Through from within SQL view.

When you create a pass-through query, Access adds several new properties to the query's property sheet. These new properties are shown in Figure 5.29 and summarized in Table 5.4.

TABLE 5.4: Query Properties Unique to SQL Pass-Through Queries

Property	Description	Default Value
ODBCConnectStr	The ODBC connection string to be used when executing the pass-through query.	ODBC;
ReturnsRecords	Specifies whether the query returns any records.	Yes
LogMessages	Specifies whether Access logs warning and informational messages from the server to a local table. Messages are logged to a table the name of which is derived from the user name (for example, Mary-00, Mary-01, Mary-02, and so on). This does not include error messages.	No

FIGURE 5.29:

This pass-through query creates a table on the SQLPizza data source.

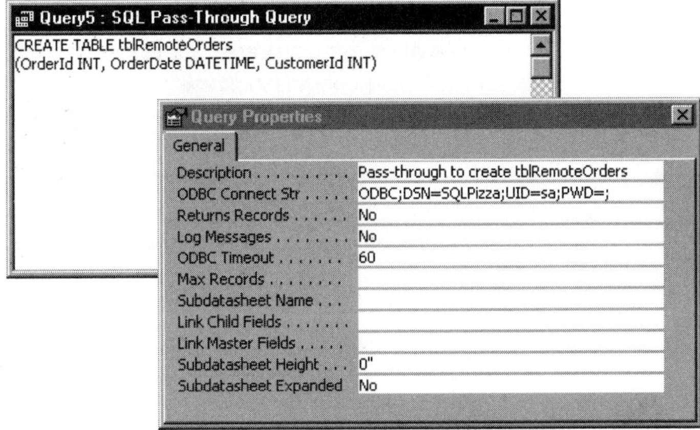

TIP

To create a pass-through query programmatically, set the Connect property of the querydef to a valid connect string.

SQL pass-through (SPT) queries are useful for

- Using server-specific SQL that's not supported by ODBC.
- Running SQL DDL (Data Definition Language) commands to create and modify the schema of server databases.
- Executing stored procedures on the server.
- Joining more than one database on the server. (If run as a normal query, Jet would have to join the databases locally.)
- Forcing a query to be fully executed on the server.

SQL pass-through queries have the following disadvantages:

- Any records returned in an SPT query are read-only.
- Jet will not check the syntax of SPT queries.
- You can't use Access' built-in or user-defined functions (although the server may have similar functions).
- You can't use an OLE DB driver in an SPT query.

NOTE

Access 2000 supports several other client-server technologies—ADO and Access projects—which in many cases are preferable to the use of SPT queries. See *Access 2000 Developer's Handbook, Volume II* for more details.

TIP

When creating queries that go against ODBC data sources (both pass-through and non-pass-through queries), you may wish to take advantage of the MaxRecords property. Use this property to set a maximum limit for the number of records returned from a query. For ODBC data sources, this property is more efficient than using the TopValues property.

There are two types of pass-through queries: those that return records and those that don't. Pass-through select queries and some stored procedures return records. DDL queries and server action queries, as well as many stored procedures, do not return records.

For example, a pass-through query that creates a three-column table, tblRemote-Orders, on a Microsoft SQL Server database was shown in Figure 5.29. Because this is a DDL query, its ReturnsRecords property is set to No. On the other hand, the pass-through query shown in Figure 5.30 returns a snapshot of records, so we have set its ReturnsRecords property to Yes.

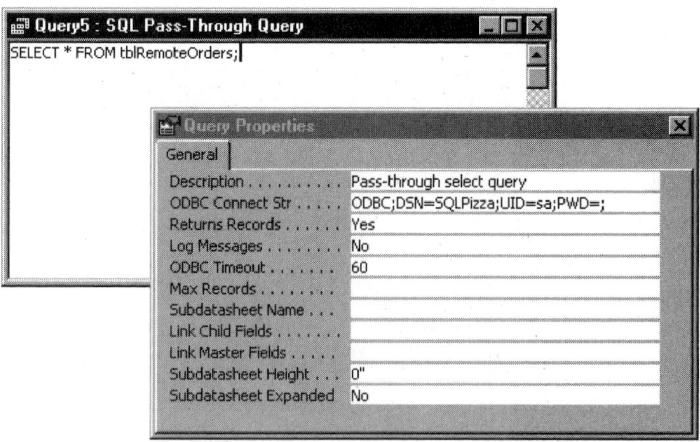

FIGURE 5.30:

This pass-through query executes a simple SELECT statement on the tblRemoteOrders table, returning a snapshot recordset to Access.

The pass-through query shown in Figure 5.31 executes a SQL Server system stored procedure, sp_rename, to rename the tblRemoteOrders table to tblOrders2.

FIGURE 5.31:

This pass-through query executes a stored procedure, sp_rename, to rename the tblRemoteOrders table to tblOrders2.

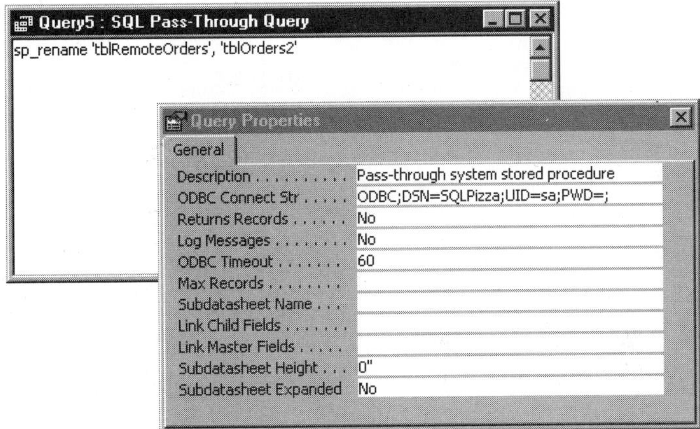

Jet 4 ANSI SQL-92 Extensions

Microsoft has made several changes to the version of the Jet database engine that ships with Access 2000—version 4—that significantly expands its support for the ANSI SQL-92 standard. You can take advantage of these new SQL-92 extensions when using ADO and the Jet OLE DB provider. Most of these SQL-92 extensions, however, are not available from the Access UI.

TIP The Jet OLE DB provider is automatically used when you create an ADO Connection object in an Access module and set it to CurrentProject.Connection.

In this section, we discuss the ANSI-92 extensions, highlighting the differences between standard Access SQL and the new Jet 4 extensions. The Jet 4 SQL-92 extensions are summarized in Table 5.5.

TABLE 5.5: Summary of Jet 4 SQL-92 Extensions

Category	Statement	Jet 4 Extension
Tables	ALTER TABLE	Added support for altering column definition
	CREATE TABLE	Added support for defaults, check constraints, cascading referential integrity, fast foreign keys, Unicode string compression, and custom AutoNumber seed and increment values
Views and Procedures	CREATE PROCEDURE	Creates a stored procedure
	CREATE VIEW	Creates a view
	DROP PROCEDURE	Deletes an existing procedure
	DROP VIEW	Deletes an existing view
	EXECUTE	Executes a procedure
Transactions	BEGIN TRANSACTION	Initiates a transaction
	COMMIT [TRANSACTION]	Commits a transaction
	ROLLBACK [TRANSACTION]	Rolls back a transaction
Security	ADD USER	Adds a user to a group
	ALTER DATABASE	Changes the database password
	ALTER USER	Changes a user's password
	CREATE GROUP	Adds a new group account to the workgroup
	CREATE USER	Adds a new user account to the workgroup
	DROP GROUP	Deletes a group account
	DROP USER	Deletes a user account or removes a user from a group
	GRANT	Grants privileges to a user or group
	REVOKE	Revokes privileges from a user or group

NOTE

If only it were so simple! Contrary to the Microsoft documentation, we have found that some of the Jet 4 ANSI-92 extensions *are* available from saved SQL queries. Which extensions are supported? None of the extensions in the areas of security, transactions, or views and procedures are supported by the Access UI. However, many (but not all) of the extensions to the ALTER TABLE and CREATE TABLE statements are available from the Access UI.

Jet 4 Table Extensions

The Jet 4 ANSI-92 extensions in the area of tables include several changes to the CREATE TABLE and ALTER TABLE statements.

CREATE TABLE

The Jet 4 ANSI-92 extensions add a number of new features to the CREATE TABLE statement. The extensions add support for defaults, check constraints, cascading referential integrity, fast foreign keys, Unicode string compression, and the ability to alter the AutoNumber seed and increment values.

Default You use the following syntax to create a default for a column:

DEFAULT (*value*)

For example, the following CREATE TABLE statement sets a default of 0 for the QOH column:

```
CREATE TABLE tblInventory (ItemId LONG CONSTRAINT
PrimaryKey PRIMARY KEY, QOH LONG DEFAULT 0);
```

Check Constraint Check constraints allow you to create business rules for a table. Check constraints serve the same purpose as Access column and table-level validation rules, but they are even more powerful because they can span multiple tables. In fact, you can use check constraints to perform much of the functionality of triggers—a feature that many high-end database servers, including SQL Server, support. Another advantage of check constraints is that they allow you to create multiple table-level validation rules—something the Access UI doesn't allow. On the other hand, unlike validation rules you can create via the Access UI, you can't specify a custom error message for a check constraint.

Here's the basic syntax for a check constraint:

> [CONSTRAINT [*name*]] CHECK (*search_condition*)

If you don't include a name for a constraint, Jet assigns one for you. Constraint names must be unique across the database.

For example, say you wished to create the tblInventory table with a check constraint that limits the QOH column to values between 0 and 10,000. You could use the following CREATE TABLE statement:

```
CREATE TABLE tblInventory (ItemId LONG CONSTRAINT PrimaryKey PRIMARY
KEY, QOH LONG, CONSTRAINT QOHLimit CHECK (QOH BETWEEN 0 AND 10000));
```

The following CREATE TABLE statement includes a check constraint that ensures the Quantity column is less than or equal to the value of QOH in tblInventory for the item:

```
CREATE TABLE tblNewOrder1 (OrderId AUTOINCREMENT,
ItemId LONG, Quantity LONG,
CONSTRAINT QuantityOnHand CHECK (Quantity <= (SELECT QOH
FROM tblInventory WHERE ItemId = tblNewOrder1.ItemId)))
```

Cascading Referential Integrity The Jet 4 SQL-92 extensions add support for the creation of cascading referential integrity constraints. This feature has been supported by the Access UI for some time but not via SQL DDL.

The syntax for the enhanced foreign key constraint is:

> CONSTRAINT *name* FOREIGN KEY (*column1* [, *column2* [, …]])
>
> REFERENCES *foreign-table* [(*foreign-column1* [, *foreign-column2*
>
> [, …]])] [ON UPDATE {NO ACTION | CASCADE}]
>
> [ON DELETE {NO ACTION | CASCADE}]

If you specify ON UPDATE NO ACTION or do not include the ON UPDATE keyword, you won't be able to change the value of a primary key if it's referenced by one or more records in the foreign table. If you specify CASCADE, however, the updated primary key value will be cascaded to any referenced records in the foreign table.

If you specify ON DELETE NO ACTION or do not include the ON DELETE keyword, you won't be able to delete a record from the primary table if it's referenced by one or more records in the foreign table. If you specify CASCADE, however, the referenced records in the foreign table will also be deleted.

For example, the foreign key created in the following CREATE TABLE statement will cascade deletions and updates:

```
CREATE TABLE tblNewItems2
(OrderId LONG, ItemId LONG, ItemDescription TEXT (30),
CONSTRAINT PrimaryKey PRIMARY KEY (OrderId, ItemId),
CONSTRAINT tblNewOrders1FK FOREIGN KEY (ItemId) REFERENCES
tblNewOrders1 ON UPDATE CASCADE ON DELETE CASCADE);
```

Fast Foreign Keys Jet normally indexes all foreign key columns, which is usually a good thing. However, these automatically created indexes can adversely affect performance and concurrency when the foreign key columns contain a large number of duplicated values. For example, a column such as gender, country, or city might contain a large number of duplicates. In these cases, you may wish to tell Jet to create a *fast foreign key*, that is, a key without an accompanying index.

The syntax for creating a fast foreign key is as follows:

CONSTRAINT *name* FOREIGN KEY NO INDEX (*column1* [, *column2* [, …]])

REFERENCES *foreign-table* [(*foreign-column1* [, *foreign-column2*

[, …]])] [ON UPDATE {NO ACTION | CASCADE}]

[ON DELETE {NO ACTION | CASCADE}]

Of course, if you leave out the NO INDEX keywords, Jet creates a normal foreign key column, that is, one with an index.

In the following example, we create two tables: tblGender and tblCustomer2. The second table, tblCustomer2, contains a fast foreign key for the Gender column:

```
CREATE TABLE tblGender
(Gender TEXT (1) CONSTRAINT PrimaryKey PRIMARY KEY);
CREATE TABLE tblCustomer2
(CustomerId INTEGER CONSTRAINT PrimaryKey PRIMARY KEY,
FirstName TEXT (50), LastName TEXT (50), Gender TEXT (1),
CONSTRAINT tblGenderFK FOREIGN KEY NO INDEX (Gender)
REFERENCES tblGender);
```

TIP Jet 4 SQL provides the only way to create fast foreign keys.

Unicode String Compression All character data in Jet 4 is now stored in the Unicode two-byte character representation format. Among other things, this means that string data now takes up twice as much space as it did before. To help alleviate the potential increase in database size, Microsoft has added the ability to automatically compress string columns. The Access table designer supports this feature through the Unicode Compression property. The Jet 4 SQL-92 extensions also add support for compressing string data via the WITH COMPRESSION keywords.

The syntax for creating a compressed string column is as follows:

column string_data_type [(*length*)] WITH COMPRESSION

where *string_data_type* is a synonym for any string data type including TEXT, MEMO, and any of the synonyms for these data types. Strings are stored uncompressed by default.

WARNING The Access query designer does not support the WITH COMPRESSION keywords.

AutoNumber Enhancements The Jet 4 SQL-92 extensions add support for customizing the seed and increment values of AutoNumber columns.

The syntax is as follows:

column AUTOINCREMENT (*seed*, *increment*)

You can also use the synonyms IDENTITY or COUNTER instead of AUTOINCREMENT.

TIP Jet 4 SQL provides the only way to alter the seed and increment values of AutoNumber fields. The Access UI and ADOX provide no mechanism for customizing AutoNumber seed or increment values.

For example, to create the OrderId AutoNumber column with a sequence that started at 1000 and was incremented by 10, you could use the following CREATE TABLE statement:

```
CREATE TABLE tblNewOrder2 (OrderId AUTOINCREMENT (1000, 10),
ItemId LONG, Quantity LONG)
```

You can also modify the seed and increment value for an existing AutoNumber column using the ALTER TABLE statement. For example:

```
ALTER TABLE tblOrder ALTER COLUMN OrderId COUNTER (2000, 50)
```

NOTE

Jet won't prevent you from altering AutoNumber seed and increment values that produce duplicate values. (However, if the AutoNumber column has been designated as the primary key or it contains a unique index, you will be prevented from saving rows with duplicates.)

The Jet 4 extensions also add support for querying for the last-assigned AutoNumber value using the same syntax as SQL Server:

```
SELECT @@IDENTITY
```

The ADO code from basAutoIncTest shown below illustrates how you might use the @@IDENTITY system variable:

```
Private Sub AutoIncTest()
    Dim cnn As ADODB.Connection
    Dim cmd As ADODB.Command
    Dim rst As ADODB.Recordset

    Set cnn = CurrentProject.Connection
    Set cmd = New ADODB.Command

    Set cmd.ActiveConnection = cnn
    cmd.CommandType = adCmdText
    cmd.CommandText = "INSERT INTO tblNewOrder2 " & _
     "(ItemId, Quantity) VALUES (1, 20)"

    cmd.Execute
    Set cmd = Nothing

    Set rst = New ADODB.Recordset
    rst.Open "SELECT @@IDENTITY AS LastOrderId", _
     cnn, Options:=adCmdText
    Debug.Print "OrderId for new record = " & _
     rst("LastOrderId")
    rst.Close
    Set rst = Nothing
End Sub
```

ALTER TABLE

The Jet 4 ALTER TABLE statement has been extended to include support for the ALTER COLUMN clause. In the past, there was no programmatic support for modifying the definition of a column, which meant that to change a column's definition was an arduous process of creating a new table, copying the old records into the new table, deleting the old table, and renaming the new table. Support for ALTER COLUMN makes a column change much simpler.

There are three forms of the ALTER COLUMN clause. The first form is used to change the definition of a column:

ALTER TABLE *table* ALTER [COLUMN] *column datatype* [(*size*)]

[DEFAULT default-value] [CONSTRAINT *single-column-constraint*];

For example, to change the data type of the ItemId column in the tblNewItems table from Long integer to integer (also known as "short"), you could use the following statement:

```
ALTER TABLE tblNewItems ALTER COLUMN ItemId SHORT;
```

The second form of the ALTER COLUMN clause is used to add a default for an existing column:

ALTER TABLE *table* ALTER [COLUMN] *column* SET DEFAULT default-value;

For example, to add a default of 1001 to the column definition of ItemId, you could use this statement:

```
ALTER TABLE tblNewItems ALTER ItemId SET DEFAULT "1001";
```

The third form of the ALTER COLUMN clause is used to remove a default for a column:

ALTER TABLE *table* ALTER [COLUMN] *column* DROP DEFAULT;

For example, to drop the default for ItemId, you might use the following statement:

```
ALTER TABLE tblNewItems ALTER COLUMN ItemId DROP DEFAULT;
```

Jet 4 View and Stored Procedure Extensions

In order to make Jet more compatible with SQL Server, Jet 4 has added support for views and stored procedures. Jet 4's views and stored procedures are not new Jet objects; instead they are Jet queries repackaged to work like ANSI-92 views and SQL Server stored procedures.

NOTE

Views and stored procedures are stored as queries, but these special queries are not visible in the Access database container.

Views

You use the CREATE VIEW statement to create a view using the following syntax:

CREATE VIEW *view* [(*field1* [, *field2* [, ...]])] AS *select-statement*;

The field names are optional; if you include them, Jet uses these names in lieu of the names of the fields from the underlying tables.

A view is very similar to a saved Access select query. You can use just about any SELECT statement in the view definition; however, don't include an ORDER BY clause.

For example, the following CREATE VIEW statement creates a view that joins the tblOrder and tblCustomer tables:

```
CREATE VIEW qryOrderCustomer AS
SELECT OrderId, LastName & ", " & FirstName AS Customer,
OrderDate
FROM tblOrder INNER JOIN tblCustomer
ON tblOrder.CustomerId = tblCustomer.CustomerId
```

Once created, you can use the view in the same places you can use an Access saved query.

To drop a view, you use the DROP VIEW statement using the following syntax:

DROP VIEW *view*;

For example:

```
DROP VIEW qryOrderCustomer;
```

Stored Procedures

You use the CREATE PROCEDURE statement to create a stored procedure using the following syntax:

CREATE PROC[EDURE] *procedure*

[(*param1 datatype1* [, *param2 datatype2* [, ...]])]

AS *sql-statement*;

The SQL statement can be just about any SELECT, action query, or DDL statement.

You use the EXECUTE statement to execute a stored procedure using the following syntax:

EXEC[UTE] *procedure*

[*param1* [, *param2* [, ...]]] ;

For example, you might create the following stored procedure that returns a single record from tblMenu:

```
CREATE PROCEDURE procGetMenu (lngItem LONG) AS
SELECT *
FROM tblMenu
WHERE MenuId = lngItem
```

You could then execute procGetMenu using the following EXECUTE statement:

```
EXECUTE procGetMenu 5
```

The following CREATE PROCEDURE statement inserts a record into tblMenu using an INSERT INTO statement:

```
CREATE PROC procAddMenu
(lngId LONG, strDescription TEXT, strUnits TEXT,
curPrice CURRENCY, blnDiscontinued BIT) AS
INSERT INTO tblMenu
VALUES (lngId, strDescription, strUnits,
curPrice, blnDiscontinued);
```

The following EXECUTE statement adds a row to tblMenu using the procAddMenu stored procedure:

```
EXECUTE procAddMenu 25, "Cherry Pie", "Slice", 3.50, False;
```

To drop a stored procedure, you use the DROP PROCEDURE statement using the following syntax:

DROP PROC[EDURE] *procedure;*

For example:

```
DROP PROC procAddMenu;
```

Jet 4 Transaction Extensions

The Jet 4 ANSI-92 extensions add support for managing transactions using SQL. This support doesn't replace the transaction support already supplied by ADO, it merely serves an alternative syntax for managing transactions. A transaction may span multiple operations over a single ADO connection.

To start a transaction, you use the following syntax:

BEGIN TRANSACTION

To commit a transaction, you use the following syntax:

COMMIT [TRANSACTION]

To cancel a transaction, you use the following syntax:

ROLLBACK [TRANSACTION]

The following subroutine from basTestSQLTrans illustrates how you might use the SQL transaction support:

```
Public Sub TestSQLTrans(fCommit As Boolean)
    Dim cnn As ADODB.Connection
    Dim cmd As ADODB.Command

    Set cnn = CurrentProject.Connection
    Set cmd = New ADODB.Command

    Set cmd.ActiveConnection = cnn
    cmd.CommandType = adCmdText
    cmd.CommandText = "BEGIN TRANSACTION"
    cmd.Execute

    cmd.CommandText = "DELETE FROM tblMenu WHERE MenuId > 5"
    cmd.Execute

    If fCommit Then
        cmd.CommandText = "COMMIT"
    Else
        cmd.CommandText = "ROLLBACK"
    End If
    cmd.Execute

    Set cmd = Nothing
End Sub
```

Jet 4 Security Extensions

The Jet 4 ANSI-92 security extensions provide a welcome alternative to the confusing security syntax employed by ADOX (and the older DAO). The Jet 4 security extensions support many of the Jet security features, although a few (for example, the ability to change object ownership) are not supported.

NOTE

See *Access 2000 Developer's Handbook, Volume II* for a general discussion of Jet security and information on how to use ADOX and DAO to manage Jet security.

Creating Accounts

You use the CREATE USER statement to create a new user account:

CREATE USER *user1 password1 pid1* [, *user2 password2 pid2*
[, ...]]

User is the user name used to log into the account. Password is a modifiable password that is also required at login time. Pid is a personal identifier that makes an account unique across security workgroups. Notice that you separate the user, password, and pid values for an account with spaces, not commas!

For example, to create two user accounts, Paul and Suzanne, you might use the following CREATE USER statement:

```
CREATE USER Suzanne squeaky SF67, Paul sparky NY58;
```

You use the CREATE GROUP statement to create a new group account:

CREATE GROUP *group1 pid1* [, *group2 pid2* [, ...]]

Group accounts don't have passwords because they are not login accounts. Group and user account names share the same "namespace," so you can't create a user and group account with the same name.

The following CREATE GROUP statement creates the Programmers group:

```
CREATE GROUP Programmers 89rootbeer;
```

Changing Passwords

You change a user account password using the ALTER USER statement:

ALTER USER *user* PASSWORD *new_password old_password*

For example, you might use the following ALTER USER statement to change Suzanne's login password from *plus* to *minus*:

```
ALTER USER Suzanne PASSWORD minus plus
```

You use the ALTER DATABASE statement to change the database password:

ALTER DATABASE PASSWORD *new_password old_password*

To change the database password from no password (Null) to *foo*, you'd use the following ALTER DATABASE statement:

```
ALTER DATABASE PASSWORD foo Null
```

Adding Users to Groups

You use the ADD USER statement to make a user account a member of a group. The syntax is as follows:

ADD USER *user1* [, *user2* [, ...]] TO *group*

For example, to add the Peter account to the Programmers group, you would use the following ADD USER statement:

```
ADD USER Peter TO Programmers
```

You would use the following ADD USER statement to add Paul and Suzanne to the built-in users group:

```
ADD USER Suzanne, Paul TO Users
```

WARNING You should add any new user account you create using the CREATE USER statement to the built-in Users group using the ADD USER statement. If you don't add a new user account to the Users group, then you won't be able to login using the new account!

Dropping Users and Groups

The DROP USER statement has two forms. You use the first form to delete a user account:

DROP USER *user1* [, *user2* [, ...]]

For example, to delete the Paul user account, you would use the following DROP USER statement:

```
DROP USER Paul
```

You use the second form of the DROP USER statement to remove a user from a group:

DROP USER *user1* [, *user2* [, ...]] FROM *group*

For example, you could use the following DROP USER statement to remove Suzanne from the Programmers group:

```
DROP USER Suzanne FROM Programmers
```

You use the DROP GROUP statement to delete a group account:

DROP GROUP *group1* [, *group2* [, ...]]

For example, you could use the following DROP GROUP statement to delete the Managers account:

```
DROP GROUP Managers
```

Granting and Revoking Permissions

You use the GRANT statement to assign security privileges for an object to an existing user or group account. The syntax of the GRANT statement is shown here:

GRANT *privilege1* [, *privilege2* [, ...]] ON

{TABLE *table* | OBJECT *object* | CONTAINER *container*}

TO *account1* [, *account2* [, ...]]

The privilege can be any of the following:

- SELECT
- DELETE
- INSERT
- UPDATE
- DROP

- SELECTSECURITY
- UPDATESECURITY
- DBPASSWORD
- UPDATEIDENTITY
- CREATE
- SELECTSCHEMA
- SCHEMA
- UPDATEOWNER

Table is the name of any table; object can be the name of any nontable object; container is the name of any object container. Valid object container names include:

- Tables
- Forms
- Reports
- Modules
- Scripts

The Tables container includes tables, queries, views, and procedures. The Scripts container contains Access macros.

For example, the following GRANT statement grants the Programmers group the ability to view, delete, add, and update rows from tblCustomer:

```
GRANT SELECT, DELETE, INSERT, UPDATE
ON TABLE tblCustomer
TO Programmers
```

You use the REVOKE statement to revoke security privileges for an object from an existing user or group account. The syntax of the REVOKE statement is shown here:

REVOKE *privilege1* [, *privilege2* [, ...]] ON

{TABLE *table* | OBJECT *object* | CONTAINER *container*}

FROM *account1* [, *account2* [, ...]]

For example, the following REVOKE statement revokes the DELETE privilege to tblCustomer from the Programmers group:

```
REVOKE DELETE
ON TABLE tblCustomer
FROM Programmers
```

NOTE

See *Access 2000 Developer's Handbook, Volume II* for more information on Jet security.

Differences between Access SQL, SQL-92, Jet SQL-92, and T-SQL

The SQL dialects are so varied that it's difficult to pin down all the differences between Access and the various flavors of SQL. Many of these differences have been noted throughout the chapter. Nonetheless, we have attempted to summarize the major differences between Access SQL, Access SQL with the Jet 4 ANSI SQL-92 extensions, SQL Server 7 T-SQL, and the ANSI SQL-92 standard in Table 5.6. This table is not meant to be comprehensive; it covers only the major differences.

TABLE 5.6: Major Differences between Access SQL, Access SQL with Jet 4 SQL-92 Extensions, SQL Server 7 T-SQL, and ANSI SQL-92

Feature	Supported by Access SQL	Supported by Access SQL with Jet SQL-92 Extensions	Supported by SQL Server 7 T-SQL	Supported by ANSI SQL-92
Security (GRANT, REVOKE, and so on)	No	Yes	Yes	Yes
Transaction support (COMMIT, ROLLBACK, and so on)	No	Yes	Yes	Yes
Views (CREATE VIEW statement)	No	Yes	Yes	Yes
Temporary tables	No	No	Yes	Yes

Continued on next page

TABLE 5.6 CONTINUED: Major Differences between Access SQL, Access SQL with Jet 4 SQL-92 Extensions, SQL Server 7 T-SQL, and ANSI SQL-92

Feature	Supported by Access SQL	Supported by Access SQL with Jet SQL-92 Extensions	Supported by SQL Server 7 T-SQL	Supported by ANSI SQL-92
Joins in FROM clause	Yes	Yes	Yes	Yes
Joins in UPDATE and DELETE statements	Yes	Yes	No	No
Support for FULL OUTER JOIN and UNION JOIN	No	No	Yes	Yes
Support for subqueries in the SET clause of UPDATE statements	No	No	Yes	Yes
Support for multiple tables in DELETE statements	Yes	Yes	No	No
SELECT DISTINCTROW	Yes	Yes	No	No
SELECT TOP	Yes	Yes	Yes	No
Cursors (DECLARE CURSOR, FETCH, and so on)	No	No	Yes	Yes
Domain support (CREATE DOMAIN, ALTER DOMAIN, and so on)	No	No	No	Yes
Support for check constraints	No	Yes	Yes	Yes
Assertions (CREATE ASSERTION, DROP ASSERTION, and so on)	No	No	No	Yes
Row value constructors	No	No	No	Yes
CASE expressions	No	No	Yes	Yes
Full referential integrity support in CREATE TABLE statement	No	No, but now supports CASCADE	No	Yes
Standardized system tables and error codes	No	No	No, but more completely than Access	Yes

Continued on next page

TABLE 5.6 CONTINUED: Major Differences between Access SQL, Access SQL with Jet 4 SQL-92 Extensions, SQL Server 7 T-SQL, and ANSI SQL-92

Feature	Supported by Access SQL	Supported by Access SQL with Jet SQL-92 Extensions	Supported by SQL Server 7 T-SQL	Supported by ANSI SQL-92
Standard data types	Yes	Yes	Yes	Yes
Standard string operators	No	No	Yes	Yes
Standard wildcard characters	No	Yes	Yes	Yes
Support for VBA functions	Yes	Yes	No	No
Additional aggregate functions	Yes	Yes	No	No
TRANSFORM statement	Yes	Yes	No	No
Parameters in queries or stored procedures	Yes	Yes	Yes	No
SELECT INTO statement	Yes	Yes	Yes	No

Summary

In this chapter, we covered all the components of Access SQL, including:

- The SELECT statement and all its clauses, predicates, and variations
- The various types of joins: inner, outer, self, and non-equi-joins
- The ALL, DISTINCT, and DISTINCTROW predicates
- The TOP predicate
- The WITH OWNERACCESS OPTION declaration
- Aggregate queries, including GROUP BY and TRANSFORM (crosstab) queries

- Union queries
- Subqueries and all their variations
- Parameterized SQL
- Using external data sources
- Action SQL: UPDATE, DELETE, INSERT INTO, and SELECT INTO
- Data Definition Language (DDL) SQL: CREATE TABLE, CONSTRAINT, CREATE INDEX, ALTER TABLE, and DROP
- SQL pass-through queries
- The Jet 4 ANSI SQL-92 extensions to Access SQL
- The differences between ANSI SQL and other dialects of SQL

CHAPTER

SIX

6

ActiveX Data Objects

- Handling ActiveX Data Objects programmatically
- Creating, deleting, and modifying database objects from VBA
- Working with recordsets
- Using the CurrentProject collections

No matter which program you're using as an interface to your data, at times you'll need programmatic access to your database's structure and its data. You might want to retrieve the schema of a table, create a new index, or walk through the data returned by a query, one row at a time. Perhaps you need to manipulate your application's security or find a particular row on a form. You can accomplish any of these tasks thanks to Access' use of ActiveX Data Objects (ADO) and ADO Extensions for DDL and Security (ADOX), a pair of COM libraries that are part of Microsoft's Universal Data Access strategy for retrieving and manipulating data. In this chapter, we'll cover the basics of ADO and present some useful examples along the way.

NOTE

One thing's for sure: ADO is a huge topic. All we can hope to do here is to get you started, show you the big picture, and fill in some of the important details. Full coverage of ADO can, and does, fill entire volumes, and our point here is not to cover every single issue, but to cover the points you're most likely to need as an Access developer.

ADO? What About DAO?

Previous versions of Access used a different library, named Data Access Objects (DAO), for programmatic access to data. DAO began life as an interface to the Jet database engine in Access 1 and grew in size and complexity through Access 97. Although DAO is still present in Access 2000, it's no longer the preferred method for retrieving data, and it's not the best library to learn for new applications. If you need to maintain an existing application that uses DAO, see Appendix C. This appendix is a reprint of a chapter from an earlier edition of this book that provides basic coverage of DAO, parallel to this chapter's coverage of ADO.

You'll still run into DAO within Access 2000 in several situations:

- If you retrieve the recordset of a form in an Access database, you'll get a DAO recordset, not an ADO recordset. (Forms in an Access project use ADO recordsets.) See Chapter 8 for more information on forms and recordsets.
- If you convert a database from a previous version of Access, it will use DAO by default. (If you create a new database in Access 2000, it will use ADO by default.)

NOTE

This chapter won't dwell on converting from DAO to ADO—there's simply too much new material on ADO for us to devote major portions of the chapter to DAO as well. Where appropriate, we've pointed out important issues you'll need to watch out for if you're converting applications from previous versions of Access.

Setting References

When you create a new Access database (an MDB file) or an Access data project (an ADP file) in Access, Access assumes that you'll want to work with ADO and sets a reference for you to the Microsoft ActiveX Data Objects 2.1 library. If you convert an existing Access application into Access 2000 format, Access updates your original reference (that is, to DAO) up to the current version of DAO and does not add a reference to ADO to your project.

Whether Access assigns DAO or ADO by default to your database, you can choose to use the other library, either in addition to or as a replacement for the default library. To do this, from the Visual Basic editor, choose Tools ➢ References. This will open the References dialog box, shown in Figure 6.1. This dialog box lists the available object libraries installed on your computer. You can use objects from any of the libraries to which you've set a reference by checking its name within your application.

FIGURE 6.1:

The References dialog box

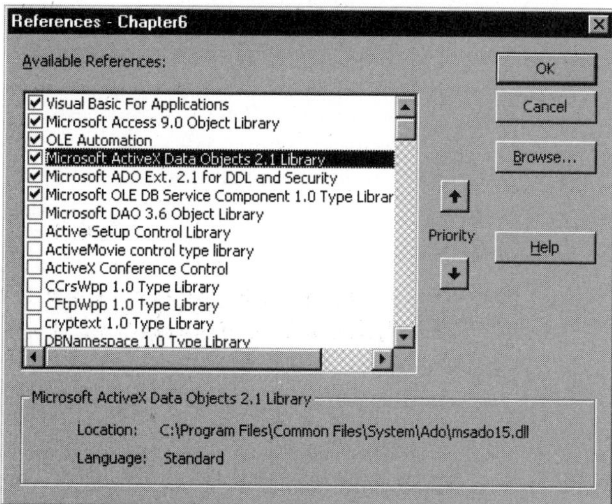

If you select Microsoft ActiveX Data Objects 2.1 Library, your application will use ADO. If you select Microsoft DAO 3.6 Object Library, your application will use DAO.

What happens if you select both libraries within a single application? The answer is that you can use both ADO and DAO within that application. However, you need to be aware of problems that can be caused by the fact that both libraries have some objects with the same name. For example, both ADO and DAO contain RECORDSET objects. In this case, a reference to the object refers to whichever library appears first in the References dialog box (you can use the Priority buttons in the dialog box to rearrange references). So, depending on the references, a line of code such as

```
Dim rst As Recordset
```

might refer to either a DAO or an ADO recordset. You can't tell which one you'll get without checking the References dialog to see which appears first in the list.

To solve this problem, you can disambiguate (yes, that's a real word) the reference by prepending the name of the library. Such disambiguated references specify both the object name and the library name. Thus, the following two lines of code refer to two different objects:

```
Dim rst1 As ADODB.Recordset
Dim rst2 As DAO.Recordset
```

In this book, we've tried to always use disambiguated object names. You may want to adopt the same convention.

NOTE

Note that the name of the library isn't necessarily what you think it is; the name of the ADO library in code is ADODB. You can determine the library name by looking at the list of available libraries in the Object Browser, which is displayed when you press F2 from the Visual Basic editor.

TIP

If you're an experienced DAO developer, you may also find the Microsoft white paper "Migrating from DAO to ADO" very helpful. You'll find this white paper on the book's accompanying CD.

Disambiguating Unleashed

Disambiguating references can never hurt. In addition, it can help make your code run a tiny bit faster. Because VBA doesn't need to peruse the entire list of libraries to determine which one contains the object you're programming, your code can run faster. Microsoft recommends that you disambiguate all references, and we do too. It's a difficult habit to get into, but it's worth it. You can carry it to extremes, if you like. That is, you could preface every VBA function call with the VBA library name. Because Access always places VBA at the top of the list of references and you can't move it lower, all VBA method references will be resolved quickly. On the other hand, if you add a reference to a COM library yourself, using the Tools ➢ References dialog box, you should consider always adding the library name to each reference you use.

Which Library to Use?

Given the dual data access libraries available with Access 2000, how do you choose which one to use for any particular application? Access 2000 allows you to create two different kinds of applications, natively. You can create an MDB file, or you can choose to create an ADP file (an Access Data Project): in both cases, for new applications, Access uses OLE DB (through ActiveX Data Objects, or ADO) to retrieve data. If your data is stored in SQL Server, MDB files can only link to the tables, using Jet to manage the data and its retrieval. For ADP files, however, the data comes directly from SQL Server, and Jet is never involved. If you want to work with SQL Server data, we think you'll find that ADP files give you the best development environment for your projects. If you don't need the power of SQL Server, or you need to distribute workgroup applications that don't require the overhead and maintenance of SQL Server, MDB files will work well for your applications. (For more information on the differences between MDB files and ADP files, see *Access 2000 Developer's Handbook, Volume II.*)

Even given the choice of project types you create, you can still choose whether you want to use ADO or DAO as the mechanism for working with data programmatically. How can you choose which is the right choice for you? Here are some guidelines:

- If you're working in an Access project (an ADP file, as opposed to an MDB file), you should definitely stick with ADO. This is the native data access library for projects, and using ADO will make it simpler to work with data already in the project.

- If you're importing data access code from an existing Access 95 or Access 97 application, that code is already using DAO. In this case, you'll need to set a reference to DAO and disambiguate object references in the existing code, at least until you can rewrite the code to use ADO.
- If you're working with an application that was converted from a previous version of Access and don't expect to make major enhancements, stick with DAO. It's not worth rewriting all of the code just to be modern. (If you convert an existing Access application from an earlier version, you won't need to change the references. Access will automatically set a reference to DAO 3.6 for you.)
- If you're building a new application in Access 2000, we recommend that you use ADO for your data access needs. If you're an experienced Access developer, learning the new material may initially be painful. But we think it's worth it in the long run, because DAO probably won't ever get the new functionality that's now being added to ADO.

Dueling Object Hierarchies

Although it can be confusing, before investigating ADO, you must realize that Access supports its own object hierarchy, in addition to that supplied by ADO. That is, Access provides a mechanism whereby you can gather information about any open page, form, report, or module; write to the Debug object; or retrieve information from the Screen object, for example. This application hierarchy is completely separate from the ADO hierarchy (see Figure 6.2).

NOTE

Although Access makes it possible to get to the Document Object Model (DOM), providing programmatic access to the design of data access pages, this isn't part of Access, nor is it part of ADO. We'll cover the DOM in *Access 2000 Developer's Handbook, Volume II*, Chapter 12.

FIGURE 6.2:

The Access object hierarchy

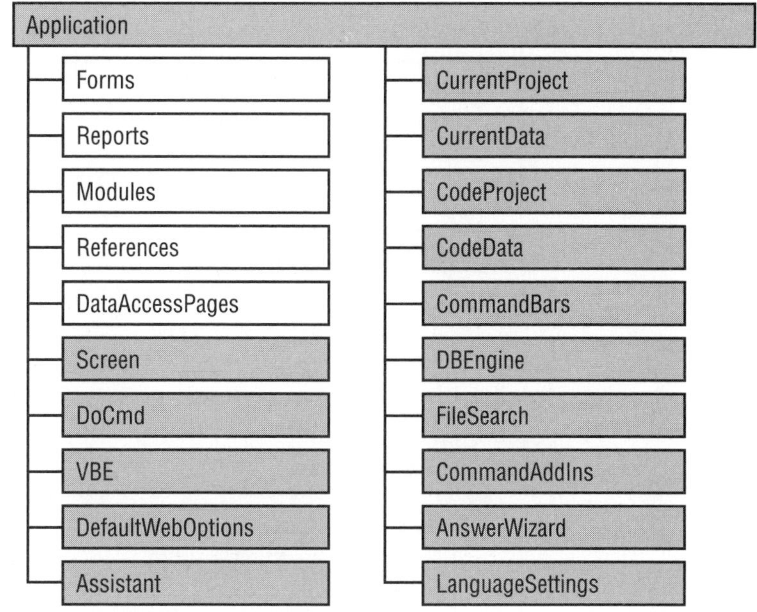

NOTE

Saying that Access supports two object hierarchies is somewhat misleading. Actually, Access supports an infinite number of object hierarchies. It handles ADO the same way it handles the object models for Word, Excel, the Office Assistant, or any other COM component. It's just that it's hard to use Access without encountering the ADO object model, and beginning developers tend to see Access as a single product. It's not; ADO is just another of the many components available to Windows developers. Of course, it's the most crucial component for Access developers.

The application hierarchy consists of the UI objects that Access itself maintains. These objects consist of all the open forms, reports, data access pages, and modules; the controls, sections, and class modules associated with those objects; and the Application, DoCmd, Screen, Err, and Debug objects. These objects will play only a peripheral part in this chapter because the focus is the ADO object hierarchy—the objects that can be used to manipulate the database engine, whether that engine is the Jet engine, the SQL Server, or MSDE (Microsoft Database Engine) engine. These objects are outlined in Figure 6.3.

FIGURE 6.3:

The ADO object hierarchy

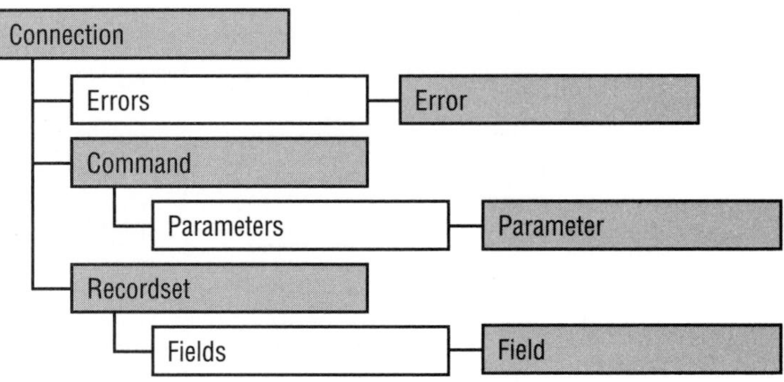

Each of the Connection, Command, Recordset, and Field objects also has a Properties collection.

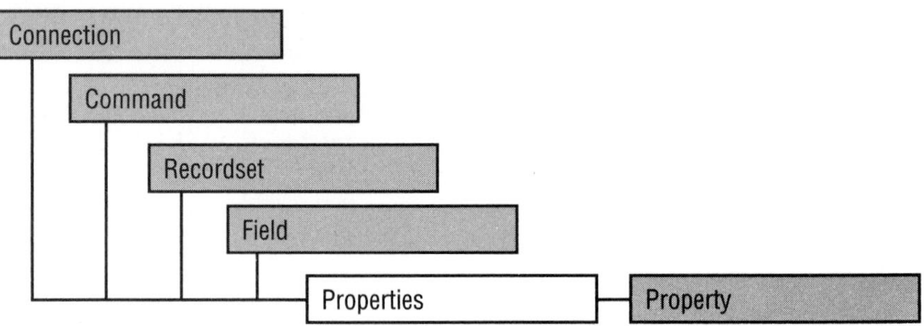

In this chapter, we'll concentrate on the use of the ADO object hierarchy to access data within Access databases—that is, databases that use the Jet database engine as opposed to Access projects, which use the newer SQL Server/MSDE engine. You'll find coverage of ADO in Access projects in Chapter 6 of *Access 2000 Developer's Handbook, Volume II.*

In addition to the Access and ADO object hierarchies, we'll use a third object hierarchy in this chapter as well: the ADO Extensions for DDL and Security, usually called ADOX. ADOX contains an extra set of objects that work together with the ADO objects to allow you to manipulate the structure of a database. Figure 6.4 shows the objects in the ADOX library.

NOTE

Although we won't cover it here, there's yet another ADO extension object model available as part of Access: JRO (Jet Replication Objects). The JRO library allows you to work programmatically with Jet replication. For more information on JRO, see Chapter 9 in *Access 2000 Developer's Handbook, Volume II*.

FIGURE 6.4:

The ADOX object hierarchy

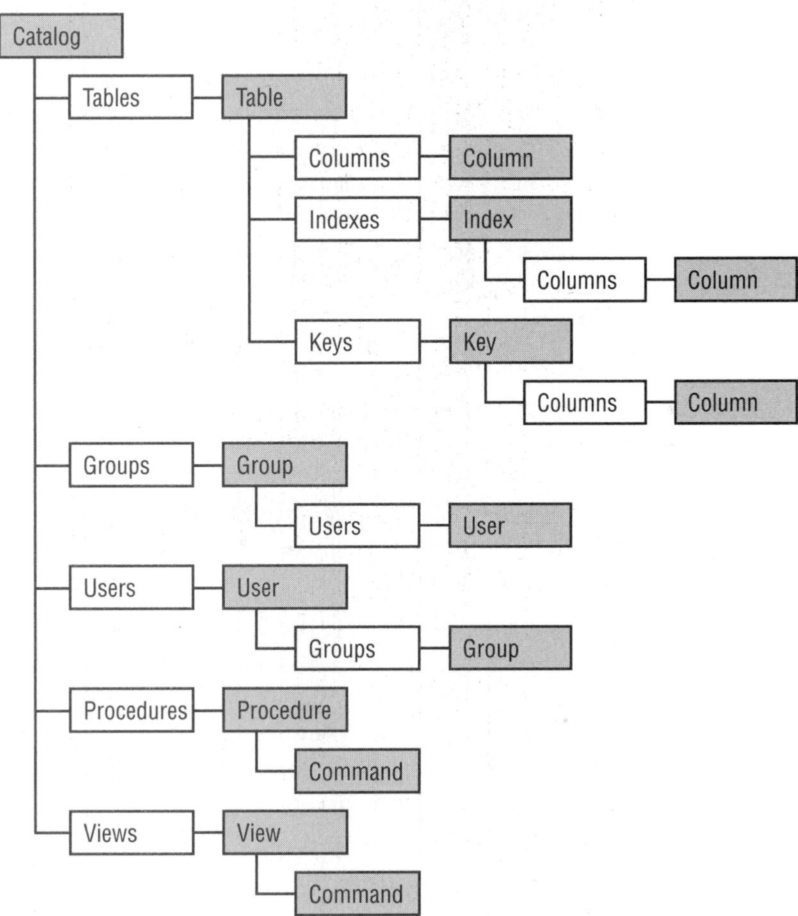

Each of the Table, Index, and Column objects also has a standard ADO Properties collection.

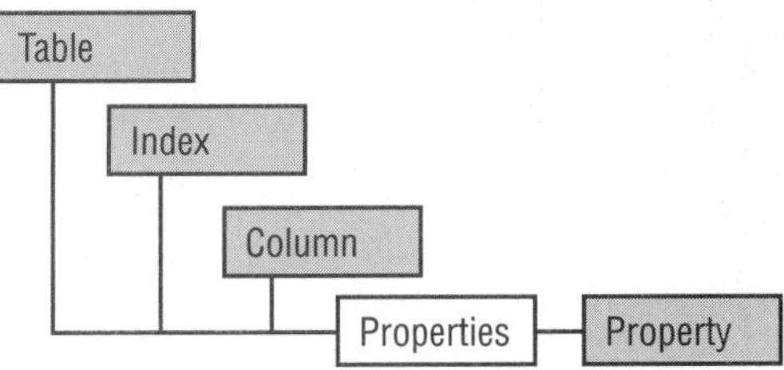

ADO, UDA, and OLE DB

The ADO object model is part of a wider Microsoft initiative, Universal Data Access (UDA). Older data access libraries such as DAO and Remote Data Objects (RDO) concentrated on retrieving data from databases containing sets of records in tables. However, Microsoft's data access designers recognized that much useful data resides in other types of storage, such as electronic mailboxes and files on disk. The idea of UDA is to use a single method to retrieve data from any data source whatsoever.

The low-level interfaces that enable this idea to work are collectively known as OLE DB. OLE DB is an extension to COM, the Component Object Model, which increasingly dictates how all applications under Microsoft Windows interact with one another. OLE DB views the world as composed of *data providers*, which are programs that can take data from a data source and make it available through the OLE DB interfaces, and *data consumers*, which can use the OLE DB interfaces to read data. Within some limits (not all OLE DB providers support all OLE DB interfaces), any data consumer can use data from any data provider.

The OLE DB interfaces are designed with a procedural programming model in mind. What ADO brings to the picture is an object model that sits on top of any OLE DB provider, allowing you to use object-oriented programming techniques to communicate with the ultimate data source. When you retrieve data in Access using OLE DB, your request flows from your application through ADO to the OLE DB provider to the data source.

Microsoft Access databases (and the bulk of the examples in this chapter) use the Microsoft Jet 4 OLE DB Provider. Microsoft Access projects (ADP files) use the Microsoft OLE DB Provider for SQL Server. However, for the most part, it doesn't matter to your ADO code which of these providers is supplying the data. In fact, you can use ADO with any OLE DB provider to manipulate data from a wide variety of data sources programmatically within an Access database (or any other VBA, Visual Basic, Java, or C++ application, for that matter).

TIP

For more information on Universal Data Access, ADO, and OLE DB, visit the Microsoft Universal Data Access Web site at `http://www.microsoft.com/data`.

Nuts and Bolts: Syntax Explained

To use ADO, you'll need to be able to refer to objects and use the correct syntax when building expressions. The next few sections discuss issues surrounding the various methods of using and referring to objects.

Properties and Methods

Objects have both properties and methods. *Properties* are attributes of objects that can normally be retrieved and (sometimes) set. For example, many objects expose a Name property, which returns the name of the object. You could use the following statement to retrieve the name of a Form object referred to by the variable frm:

```
strName = frm.Name
```

You can think of properties as the adjectives that describe objects.

Methods are actions that can be applied to objects. For example, RECORDSET objects provide the MoveNext method, which moves the current record pointer to the next record. You could use the following statement to move to the next record of the recordset referred to by the variable rst:

```
rst.MoveNext
```

You can think of methods as the verbs that act upon objects.

Using Object Variables

Through the course of this book, we make many assumptions about your knowledge of Access and VBA. This isn't a book on beginning VBA, nor on getting started with Access. We use standard variable types without explanation, assuming you'll understand statements like the following:

```
Dim intX as Integer
```

On the other hand, *object variables,* the basis of all your program code surrounding ADO, may be new to you.

When you create a normal variable, you're asking Access to reserve enough space to hold the information for which you've specified a data type. If you don't specify a data type, Access assumes the most space the variable might need and uses a Variant-type variable. When you create an object variable (a variable that will refer to either a user-interface object or a data access object), Access creates only a "pointer." That is, the variable it creates only *refers* to a real object; it's not a real object itself. It contains not the value of the object, but its memory address instead.

For example, when you write code like this:

```
Dim cnn As ADODB.Connection
Dim rst As ADODB.Recordset
Dim frm As Form
Dim ctl As Control
```

none of those variables actually hold any data, nor do they refer to any real objects at this point. Each variable can contain the address of some in-memory object, but doesn't at this point. To make an object variable actually refer to a real object, you must use the Set keyword. In every case, you use Set to point the variable either at a real object (which must already exist) or at an instance of the object created with the New keyword. For example, using the variables in the previous example, you might see code like this:

```
Set cnn = CurrentProject.Connection
Set rst = New ADODB.Recordset
Set frm = Forms("frmCustomers")
Set ctl = frm.Controls("txtCompanyName")
```

In each case, you've made the object variable refer to an actual object (that is, it contains the memory address of that particular object). Without this step, the object variables are just placeholders, waiting to actually refer to something.

If, in the course of your code, you point a data object variable (such as a command or recordset) at an actual object, Access will destroy the reference when the variable goes out of scope. If your variable is the only reference to the object in memory, the object in memory will automatically be destroyed (that is, removed from memory). If you have qualms about Access releasing the memory your object references use, you can explicitly delete the linkage by setting the variable equal to the predefined value Nothing:

```
Set rst = Nothing
```

In addition, if you created or opened an object as part of your assignment and want to be completely overt about your intentions, you should also use the Close method of the object to close it:

```
Set cnn = CurrentProject.Connection
rst.open "tblCustomers", cn
.
.
.
rst.Close
Set rst = Nothing
```

Although these steps aren't required, and we, too, tend to count on Access for these housekeeping details, you may want to consider these options.

WARNING It's important that you understand what happens when you set an object variable to Nothing. All this does is set the value of the object variable so that it no longer contains the address of a real object. This doesn't explicitly remove the object from memory. Under the covers, Access (using COM) removes the object from memory when no variable or internal reference to the object exists. Therefore, it's important that you do release the reference to the object when you're done with it. On the other hand, setting a variable to Nothing doesn't guarantee that the object will be removed from memory. It simply reduces the reference count by one. When the reference count is 0, the object gets removed from memory automatically.

Dimension and Set in One Statement?

If you read other developers' code, you'll often find that the code collapses the Dim and Set statements into a single statement, like this:

```
Dim rst As New ADODB.Recordset
```

instead of

```
Dim rst As ADODB.Recordset
Set rst = New ADODB.Recordset
```

In this case, VBA both creates a variable named rst and sets up internal code that will instantiate the object referred to by the variable when necessary. (That is, the code doesn't create the Recordset object in memory at this point—it waits until it actually needs the object in memory before creating it.) The problem with this technique is that it's not clear when your object gets initialized, especially if the object is public and might be referenced from within any module. To make it possible for VBA to instantiate the object at any time within the application and to determine if the object must be instantiated before executing the line of your code, VBA must insert internal code between each line of your code. This has, of course, detrimental effects on the speed of your running code.

We recommend that you never use the shortcut of skipping the explicit Set statement. Yes, you save a single line of code, but you pay for it with every other line of code running a tiny bit slower. Although there may be extenuating circumstances, where the single-line declaration works for you, we'd suggest you avoid it unless you have a specific reason to use it.

The Connection Object

The Connection object is the top-level object in the ADO library. To refer to any object in the ADO hierarchy, you must specify the Connection that will be used to retrieve the data. This Connection object corresponds to a single connection to an OLE DB data provider. You can either explicitly create the Connection object, or you can implicitly create it by supplying the connection information when you create a subsidiary object such as a recordset. You can think of a Connection object as providing a way for Access to find the data it needs. It includes information about the data source (is it an MDB file, a SQL Server database, or what?) and where that data is located (on a particular server, or in a particular path?).

If you're using ADO from outside Access, you have no choice: you must create a Connection object, either implicitly or explicitly. From within Access, you can and should use the CurrentProject object to obtain a reference to the current database's connection. This object is automatically created by Access when you open a database, and it has a Connection property that you can use to retrieve a reference to the ADO connection that Access itself is using. To reference objects that aren't part of the current database, however, you'll need to create a Connection object even from within Access.

NOTE

We could list, in this chapter, all the properties and methods of each object. However, this information is neatly encapsulated in ADO's online help. For each object type, search through online help and choose the object summary page for a complete list of the properties and methods each object exposes.

Connection Strings

The most important property of the Connection object is its ConnectionString property. The ConnectionString property contains all of the information that ADO uses to locate and configure the OLE DB provider that's being used to retrieve data. Here's a typical ConnectionString property for an Access database:

```
Provider=Microsoft.Jet.OLEDB.4.0;
User ID=Admin;
Data Source=C:\Sybex\Ch06.mdb;
Mode=Share Deny None;
Extended Properties="";
Locale Identifier=1033;
Persist Security Info=False;
Jet OLEDB:System database=C:\SYSTEM.MDW;
```

```
Jet OLEDB:Registry Path="";
Jet OLEDB:Database Password="";
Jet OLEDB:Engine Type=5;
Jet OLEDB:Database Locking Mode=1;
Jet OLEDB:Global Partial Bulk Ops=2;
Jet OLEDB:Global Bulk Transactions=1;
Jet OLEDB:New Database Password="";
Jet OLEDB:Create System Database=False;
Jet OLEDB:Encrypt Database=False;
Jet OLEDB:Don't Copy Locale on Compact=False;
Jet OLEDB:Compact Without Replica Repair=False;
Jet OLEDB:SFP=False
```

A connection string specifies three types of information:

- The name of the OLE DB provider to use (in this case, Microsoft.Jet.OLEDB.4.0, the version of the Jet provider that ships with Access 2000).
- Standard ADO Connection properties (in this case, all the lines from "User ID" to "Persist Security Info") that are applicable to all, or nearly all, OLE DB providers.
- Provider-specific Connection properties (in this case, all the lines that start with "Jet OLEDB") that are applicable only to the particular provider.

TIP

Almost anywhere that a Connection object is required in ADO, you can supply a ConnectionString instead to have the Connection object implicitly created. That is, generally, you needn't create an explicit Connection object. You can simply assign the ConnectionString property, which contains all the information ADO requires in order to create a Connection object for you.

If you're working within Access and are therefore reusing CurrentProject.Connection, you can safely ignore all the complexity of the connection string. If you're opening a connection to another database, though, or working in a non-Access VBA host, you may need to build your own connection strings. Fortunately, if you just want to retrieve data from an unsecured Access database, you can use a very simple connection string, as shown here (from basADO):

```
Public Sub Reconnect()
    Dim cnn As ADODB.Connection
```

```
    Set cnn = New ADODB.Connection
    cnn.ConnectionString = _
     "Provider=Microsoft.Jet.OLEDB.4.0;" & _
     "Data Source=" & _
      CurrentProject.Path & "\ConnectToMe.MDB"
    cnn.Open
    Debug.Print cnn.ConnectionString
    Set cnn = Nothing
End Sub
```

TIP

This example uses the CurrentProject.Path property to determine the path of the current database or project file. The example then uses this path to find another database, ConnectToMe.MDB, as the data source. You may want to use the current path or some other path as your own data source in a connection string.

This code creates an ADO Connection object, sets its ConnectionString property, and opens the connection. The code then verifies its success by printing the ConnectionString property to the Immediate window. As you can see, the only required portions of the ConnectionString property are the name of the OLE DB provider and the name of the database to open.

TIP

One of the great things about ADO is its flexibility. That is, you often have many choices you can make when writing code with ADO. For example, in the previous code fragment, we specified the ConnectionString property of the Connection object before calling its Open method. We could also have passed the same connection string as the first parameter of the Open method. As you read our code (and other developers' code), you'll see that everyone handles these issues a little differently, and often inconsistently, within an application. We've tried to mix and match here, so you'll see different ways to specify parameters, set properties, and call methods.

Inevitably, the time will come when you need to construct a more complex connection string. As you can see, the format of a connection string is simple: a set of property=value pairs, separated by semicolons. Table 6.1 shows the properties you're most likely to need to set in a connection string using the Jet OLE DB provider. The table indicates for each property whether it applies to all ADO connections or only to those made with the Jet OLE DB provider.

NOTE

For a complete list and discussion of the properties you can set in a connection string for the Jet Provider, see the white paper "ADO Provider Properties and Settings," which is included on the companion CD.

TABLE 6.1: Connection String Properties for the Jet OLE DB Provider

Property Name	Type	Explanation
Jet OLEDB: Database Locking Mode	Jet	0 for page-level locking, 1 for row-level locking.
Jet OLEDB:Database Password	Jet	Password to be used for a password-protected database. Don't confuse this with the user password for a secured database, which is set with the PASSWORD property.
Data Source	ADO	The full path and filename of the database to open.
Mode	ADO	One of the following intrinsic constants to indicate how the database should be opened: adModeRead (read-only), adModeWrite (write-only), adModeReadWrite (read/write), adModeShareDenyRead (prevents others from opening in read mode), adModeShareDenyWrite (prevents others from opening in write mode), or adModeShareDenyExclusive (prevents others from opening in any mode).
Password	ADO	Password to use when connecting to the data source. Don't confuse this with the password for a password-protected database, which is set with the Jet OLEDB:Database Password property.
Prompt	ADO	One of the following intrinsic constants that controls whether the user is prompted for connection information when the connection is initialized: adPromptAlways (always prompt, even if enough information is present), adPromptComplete (prompt only if more information, such as a password, is required to complete the connection), adPromptCompleteRequired (prompt for more information if necessary, but don't accept optional information), or adPromptNever (fail rather than prompting if not enough information is supplied in the connection string).
Jet OLEDB: System Database	Jet	Full path and filename of the system database to use when verifying user ID and password information.
User ID	ADO	User name to use when connecting to the data source.

Data Links

Rather than using CurrentProject.Connection or entering your own connection information, ADO also supports storing connection information in an external file, called a data link file (which normally has a UDL file extension). Data link files provide two important capabilities:

- They implement a graphical interface for constructing OLE DB connection strings.
- They offer a way to allow users to edit connection information, for example, by entering their own user name and password, without the necessity of writing code to capture this information.

To create a new data link file, right-click in Windows Explorer and choose New ➢ Microsoft Data Link. This will create a file named New Microsoft Data Link.UDL in the current folder. You can rename the file, but it's best to keep the UDL extension. After you've named the file, double-click it to edit the Data Link properties. Select the Provider tab in the Data Link Properties dialog and choose the Microsoft Jet 4.0 OLE DB Provider. Then select the Connection tab and fill in the database name and logon information, as shown in Figure 6.5. You can test the connection to verify that the information entered is correct, and then click OK to save the file.

FIGURE 6.5:

Setting the Connection properties for a Jet data link file

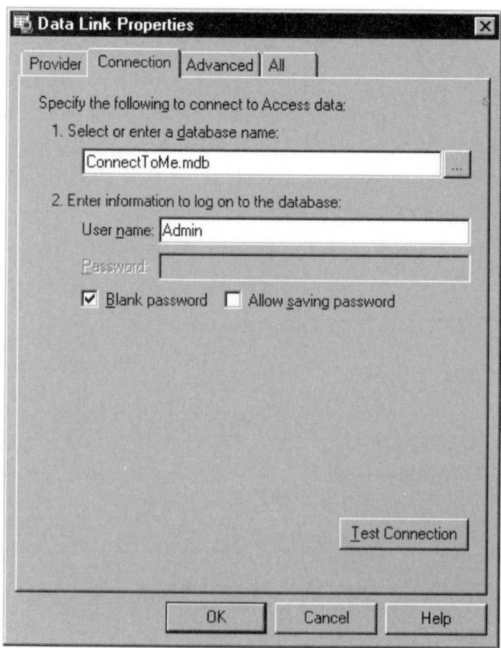

If you'd like to edit any of the provider-specific properties for this connection, use the All tab of the Data Link properties dialog.

Once you've created a data link file, you needn't supply any information when opening the connection in code other than the location of the UDL file. This makes it simple for you to manage changing data sources without having to modify any code. When you want to open a connection based on a UDL file, you simply specify

```
FileName="YourFileName.UDL"
```

as the ConnectionString property, or specify this when you call the Open method. This code sample (from basDataLink) shows how you can use a saved data link file to open an ADO connection to a database:

```
Public Sub TestDataLink()
    ' To set things up, run the
    ' ShowDataLink procedure before
    ' running this one.
    Dim cnn As ADODB.Connection
    Set cnn = New ADODB.Connection
    cnn.Open "File Name=" & _
     CurrentProject.Path & "\Ch06.UDL"
    Debug.Print cnn.ConnectionString
    Set cnn = Nothing
End Sub
```

WARNING If you're using a UDL file to refer to an Access database, you'll need to specify the path to the database file in the UDL file. In the example shown here, you'll need to modify the Ch06.UDL file, and set the path to the ConnectToMe.MDB file to refer to the path in which you've installed this file. Otherwise, ADO looks in the current path for the MDB file.

Programming Data Links

You can also use the Data Link interface from code in your database. To do this, you need to set a reference to the Microsoft OLE DB Service Component 1.0 Type Library (use the Tools ➢ References menu item to do this; it's already done for you in the sample database), which implements a DataLinks object, using the MSDASC type library. You can create a new DataLinks object, assign default properties to the connection, and then present those properties to the user to edit in the Data Link Properties dialog. Listing 6.1 shows code that does this, from basDataLink in CH06.MDB.

TIP

Don't look for online help for objects within the MSDASC type library. It's just not there. This type library ships without a help file.

Listing 6.1

```
Public Sub ShowDataLink()
    Dim cnn As ADODB.Connection
    Dim dlk As MSDASC.DataLinks

    Set cnn = New ADODB.Connection
    Set dlk = New MSDASC.DataLinks
    ' Set default properties for the connection
    cnn.Provider = "Microsoft.Jet.OLEDB.4.0"
    cnn.Properties("Data Source") = _
     CurrentProject.Path & "\ConnectToMe.MDB"
    ' Tell the Data Link Properties dialog which
    ' window will be its parent
    dlk.Hwnd = Application.hWndAccessApp
    ' Prompt the user for information
    If dlk.PromptEdit(cnn) Then
        cnn.Open
    End If
    Set cnn = Nothing
    Set dlk = Nothing
End Sub
```

Referring to Objects

Referring to objects within a hierarchy follows a specific pattern. You can see this most clearly when using the ADOX library, which has a deeper hierarchy than the ADO library. You refer to ADOX objects by following the hierarchy presented earlier in Figure 6.4. Start with a Catalog object and work your way down. The general format for referring to objects is

Catalog.*ParentCollectionItem.ChildCollection("ChildObject")*

where it may take several iterations through parent collections before you get to the child collection you're interested in.

Before you can use the Catalog object, you must instantiate it and connect it to the database you're interested in. Typically, you'll be working with the current user database. In this case, you can use the CurrentProject.Connection property that we've already discussed, as in this code fragment:

```
Dim cat As ADOX.Catalog
Set cat = New ADOX.Catalog
cat.ActiveConnection = CurrentProject.Connection
Debug.Print cat.Tables(0).Name
```

To refer to any member of any collection, you can use one of four syntactical constructs. Table 6.2 lists the four available methods. (In each example, you're attempting to refer to the field named Street Number in a table named tblCustomers, starting with a Catalog variable named cat.)

TABLE 6.2: Methods for Referring to Objects

Syntax	Details	Example
collection("name")		cat.Tables("tblCustomers").Fields ("Street Number")
collection(*var*)	Where *var* is a string or variant variable	strTable = "tblCustomers" strField = "Street Number" cat.Tables(strTable).Fields(strField)
collection(*ordinal position*)	Where *ordinal position* is the object's position within its collection	cat.Tables(0).Fields(0)
collection!*name* collection![*name*]	Brackets are necessary if *name* contains a nonstandard character, such as a space	cat.Tables("tblCustomers").Fields! [Street Number]

WARNING Access and ADO number all built-in collections with ordinal values beginning with 0. Almost all other components in the Microsoft world number their collections starting with 1, and user-defined collections within Access are also numbered starting with 1. This is a point about which you'll want to be very careful.

TIP

ADOX objects provide information on the *design* of objects, but that's all they provide. That is, you won't be able to use ADOX to retrieve information on data stored within a table or retrieved by a query. Think of it this way: ADOX provides information on Access objects, and ADODB provides data. If you want to retrieve information about the controls on Access forms or reports, however, neither library provides that information. You'll need to open the object within Access and use Access' Forms, Reports, or DataAccessPages collection to retrieve information about an open form, report, or data access page.

All ADOX objects except the Catalog object have an associated collection that contains all the objects of the given type. For example, the Tables collection contains a Table object for each table saved in the database. Collections make it easy to "visit" all the objects of a specific type, looping through all the items in the collection. Because you can refer to all the items in a collection either by name or by position, you have the best of both worlds. If you know the specific object's name, you can find it by name, as in the following code fragment:

```
Debug.Print cat.Tables("tblCompanies").DateCreated
```

If you want to refer to an object by number, you can do that, too:

```
Debug.Print cat.Tables(0).DateCreated
```

If you're working with objects deep within a hierarchy, you can create references in one long string. For example, the following statement will retrieve the name of a column in an index in a table in the specified catalog:

```
Debug.Print cat.Tables("tblCustomers"). _
 Indexes(0).Columns(0).Name
```

As this statement demonstrates, you're also free to mix references by name and by ordinal position within a single statement.

Bang (!) versus Dot (.) versus Quotes (" ")

The bang ("!") and dot (".") identifier operators help describe the relationships among collections, objects, and properties in an expression. They indicate that one part of an expression belongs to another.

In general, you follow the bang with the name of something you created: a form, report, or control. The bang also indicates that the item to follow is an element of a collection. You'll usually follow the dot with a property, collection, or method name. Actually, under the covers, the bang separator really says, "retrieve the following object from the default collection of the parent object." (See the section "Using

Default Collections" later in this chapter.) For example, when working with forms, you can refer to a control on a form like this:

```
Set ctl = Forms("frmTest").Controls("txtName")
```

or, because Controls is the default collection of a form, you can abbreviate that as either of the following:

```
Set ctl = Forms("frmTest")("txtName")
Set ctl = Forms("frmTest")!txtName
```

You can also think of the uses of these operators this way: a bang (or parentheses and quotes) separates an object from the collection it's in (a field in a table, a form in the Forms collection, a control on a form), while a dot separates an object from a property, method, or collection of that object.

If you refer back to Table 6.2, you'll see that there's always an alternative to using the bang operator: you can use the parentheses and quotes syntax. For example, these two statements refer to exactly the same property:

```
cat.Tables!tblCustomers.Columns!Address.Type
cat.Tables("tblCustomers").Columns("Address").Type
```

It turns out that, behind the scenes, the former style of dot-and-bang reference is translated to the latter style of parentheses-and-quotes reference when you execute such a statement. This means that, although using the bang operator will save you a bit of typing, you'll pay for it in a speed penalty. Our recommendation, and the style we've followed throughout this book, is to always use the parentheses and quotes format for referring to a member of a collection unless it's absolutely necessary to use the bang operator. In addition, if the object to which you're referring contains spaces (or other nonstandard characters), you'll have to treat these names specially when using the bang syntax—you'll need to surround the name in square brackets. If you use the parentheses/quotes syntax, all names are treated equally.

WARNING

One place where the bang operator is necessary is in query parameters that refer to form fields. That is, you cannot avoid the Forms!FormName!ControlName syntax in this case.

TIP

It's a hard habit to break—we've been using "!" since Access 1. But the fact is, except in a very few places (query parameters is the one that comes to mind) you needn't ever use a bang and should probably think about weaning yourself from this syntax if you currently use it. It's important that you understand what it's doing and what it means when you see it, but we suggest you not use it in your VBA code.

Finally, one more reason to use "("")" rather than "!" in your code: when you use parentheses/quotes, you're using a string expression to identify an object. If you're using a string expression, you can just as easily use a string variable. Using this technique makes it possible to identify the object you want to work with at runtime, using a variable. This can be a useful technique, and we'll employ it throughout this book.

Ordinal Positions

As you've seen, you can refer to an object using the ordinal position within its collection. The database engine assigns and maintains these ordinal positions, and they always start with position number 0. For example, if you open a Recordset variable and inspect its collection of Field objects, the first one will have the ordinal of zero.

An object's ordinal position is dependent on the order in which it was added to its collection. If you're creating a recordset by appending fields, the first field you append will have a lower ordinal than the later fields. As you create and delete objects, an object's ordinal position changes within its collection. For this reason, it is not a good idea to refer to a specific object using its ordinal position. You should use the ordinal position of objects only as loop indexes for iterating through all the objects in a collection.

NOTE

Using an object's ordinal position has become less important with the addition of the For Each...Next construct a few versions back. There are times, however, when you must loop through the entries in a collection. If your action changes the number of elements in the collection, using For Each...Next will, in general, fail. In cases when you're closing objects or deleting them from their collection, use a For...Next loop, using the objects' ordinal position to refer to them. Also, For Each...Next can only visit items in a collection from front to back. If you need to iterate through items in any other order (from back to front, for example), you'll need to use a normal For...Next loop instead.

Using Default Collections

You can see from previous examples that a simple object reference can result in a long line of code. Fortunately, ADO provides default collections for some object types: if you don't specify a collection, Access assumes you're referring to the default collection for the parent object. You can use the default collection behavior of objects to make your code more compact (but somewhat less readable). Table 6.3 lists the default collection within each object type.

TABLE 6.3: Default Collections for ADO and ADOX Objects

Object	Default Collection
Connection	(none)
Command	Parameters
Recordset	Fields
Error	(none)
Parameter	(none)
Field	(none)
Property	(none)
Catalog	Tables
Table	Columns
Index	(none)
Key	(none)
Group	(none)
User	(none)
Procedure	(none)
View	(none)

Using default collections, you can shorten this expression:

```
Recordset.Fields(0)
```

to

```
Recordset(0)
```

This expression means, "Refer to the first field within the recordset" because the default collection for the Recordset object is the Fields collection.

You can use similar contractions on both Fields and Parameters to simplify your code. Be aware, though, that using default collections to reduce your code also makes it less readable: whoever is reading the code will have to understand the meaning of the expression without any visual clues. In addition, it doesn't make your code run any faster—it's simply a way to make it easier for you to type the code.

Enumerating Objects in Collections

Because you can access any object in any collection by its position in the collection, you can use a loop to look at or modify any object in the collection. Use the Count property of a collection to determine the size of the collection. Remember that the ordinal position of objects within an ADO collection starts at 0; if a collection contains three elements, they'll be numbered 0 through 2.

For example, you could use code like this (from basADO) to print out the names of all the Fields in a Recordset:

```
Public Sub ListFields()
    Dim rst As ADODB.Recordset
    Dim fld As ADODB.Field
    Dim intI As Integer

    Set rst = New ADODB.Recordset
    rst.Open "tblCustomers", CurrentProject.Connection
    For intI = 0 To rst.Fields.Count - 1
        Set fld = rst.Fields(intI)
        Debug.Print fld.Name
    Next intI
    rst.Close
    Set fld = Nothing
    Set rst = Nothing
End Sub
```

The simplest way to loop through any collection, however, is to use the For Each...Next syntax. This syntax requires you to create a variable that can refer to the object type in the collection you're looping through and then use code like this to do the work:

```
Public Sub ListFieldsForEach()
    Dim rst As ADODB.Recordset
    Dim fld As ADODB.Field

    Set rst = New ADODB.Recordset
    rst.Open "tblCustomers", CurrentProject.Connection
    For Each fld In rst.Fields
        Debug.Print fld.Name
    Next fld
    rst.Close
    Set rst = Nothing
End Sub
```

In this case, For Each...Next does the "Set" operation for you. That is, it iterates through each item in the collection, uses an implicit Set to point to the object variable you've supplied at each object in the collection, in turn, and allows you to work with that object variable. When you ask it to move on, it resets the pointer to refer to the next object for you.

Working with Properties

If you have worked with forms, reports, and controls, you are already familiar with referencing properties. (See Chapters 7 through 9 for more information on user-interface objects.) However, the interaction between the Jet engine and Microsoft Access introduces new subtleties when you are working with properties.

Properties for ADO objects behave somewhat differently from Microsoft Access properties. As you saw earlier in this chapter, every object has a collection of properties.

Types of Properties

ADO properties can be either built-in or dynamic.

Built-in properties always exist for an object. They define the basic characteristics of an object and are available to any application that uses the object via ADO or ADOX. For example, for Field objects *Name* and *Type* are built-in properties. They define the basic characteristics of a field. You can refer to these properties using the dot syntax, for example, fld.Name. However, these properties are *not* a part of the Properties collection of the object and cannot be retrieved from that collection. Attempting to do so will generate runtime error 3265, "ADO could not find the object in the collection corresponding to the name or ordinal reference requested by the application."

Dynamic properties are defined by the OLE DB provider that supplies the object. These properties do not necessarily exist for every instance of an object, though they will be the same for all objects of a specific type from a specific provider. You can refer to these properties using the Properties collection only. Attempting to use the dot syntax will result in uncompilable code.

Dynamic properties have four (and only four) properties of their own:

- Name, a string that identifies the property
- Type, an integer specifying the property data type

- Value, the current value of the property
- Attributes, a Long integer carrying provider-specific information

Listing 6.2 (from ShowProperties in basObjects) demonstrates the difference between built-in and dynamic properties.

Listing 6.2

```
Dim rst As ADODB.Recordset
Dim fld As ADODB.Field

Set rst = New ADODB.Recordset
rst.Open "tblCustomers", _
 CurrentProject.Connection, _
 adOpenKeyset, adLockOptimistic

Set fld = rst.Fields(0)
' Return the built-in name property
Debug.Print fld.Name

' Return the dynamic BASECOLUMNNAME property
Debug.Print fld.Properties("BASECOLUMNNAME")

' Attempt to retrieve a built-in property from
' the properties collection gives error 3265
Debug.Print fld.Properties("Name")

' BASECOLUMNNAME is a dynamic property. The
' next line won't even compile
' Debug.Print fld.BASECOLUMNNAME
```

WARNING

The DAO library supported a third class of properties, *user-defined properties*, that could be added to the Properties collection of an object. These properties could be added either by Microsoft Access as a client of the Jet engine or by you as an application developer. ADO version 2.1, as used in Office 2000, does not support user-defined properties. If you have a need to use such properties, you'll need to use the DAO library. Although ADO doesn't directly support user-defined properties, Access supplies the AccessObjectProperties collection, to which you can add your own properties for forms, reports, or any other Access object. However, this subject is beyond the scope of this chapter; see online help for more information on using the AccessObjectProperties collections.

Enumerating the Properties

Listing 6.3 shows code you could use to print out all the dynamic properties of any table:

Listing 6.3

```
Public Sub ListProperties(strTable As String)
    Dim cat As ADOX.Catalog
    Dim tbl As ADOX.Table
    Dim prp As ADOX.Property

    Set cat = New Catalog
    cat.ActiveConnection = CurrentProject.Connection
    ' You could use the following expression:
    ' Set tbl = cat.Tables(strTable)
    ' but the Tables collection is the default
    ' collection for the Catalog object, so its use
    ' is unnecessary in the expression
    Set tbl = cat(strTable)

    For Each prp In tbl.Properties
        Debug.Print prp.Name, prp.Value
    Next prp
    Set cat = Nothing
    Set tbl = Nothing
End Sub
```

You'll find ListProperties in basProperties (in CH06.MDB). The output from the preceding code might look something like the output shown in Figure 6.6.

FIGURE 6.6:

Sample property listing for tblCustomers

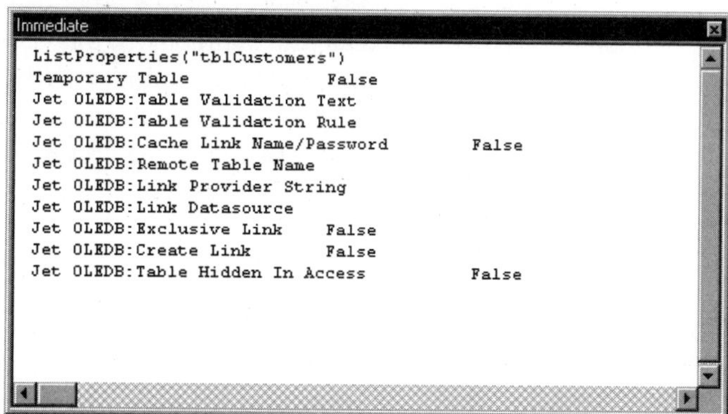

WARNING

Note that the built-in properties of the table, such as its Name and Type, do not appear in the enumeration. Unfortunately, ADO does not provide a way to enumerate built-in properties. If you need to see all of the properties of an ADO or ADOX object, you'll need to use a tool such as the Object Browser to see what the built-in properties are.

Data Definition Using ADOX

The previous sections used ADO to refer to existing objects and their properties. However, you can also programmatically create and manipulate objects. To do this, you'll need to set a reference to the Microsoft ADO Extensions for DDL and Security (ADOX). This library contains additional objects that work with the core ADO objects to let you manipulate the schema of your database.

Creating Objects

To create a new object, follow these four steps:

1. Open a Catalog object corresponding to your database.
2. Create the new object by instantiating an object variable to refer to it.
3. Define the new object's characteristics by setting its properties.
4. Append the object to its collection to make it a permanent part of your database.

In cases where the new object contains other objects (a table contains fields, for instance), you must create the main object, then create the subordinate objects, append them to the appropriate collection, and then append the main object to its collection. You can use this same technique when creating a new table, index, or relation programmatically. The following sections demonstrate how to create these complex objects.

Creating a New Table

The following example creates a new table called tblOrders and adds two fields to it. You'll find the complete function in basCreateTable:

```
Public Sub CreateOrdersTable()
    Dim cat As ADOX.Catalog
    Dim tblOrders As ADOX.Table
    Dim col1 As ADOX.Column
    Dim col2 As ADOX.Column

    Set cat = New ADOX.Catalog
    cat.ActiveConnection = CurrentProject.Connection

    ' Delete the table, if it exists.
    On Error Resume Next
    cat.Tables.Delete "tblOrders1"

    Set tblOrders = New ADOX.Table
    tblOrders.Name = "tblOrders1"

    Set col1 = New ADOX.Column
    col1.Name = "OrderID"
    col1.Type = adInteger
    Set col2 = New ADOX.Column
    col2.Name = "CustomerName"
    col2.Type = adVarWChar
    col2.DefinedSize = 30
    ' Code continues...
```

At this point, the new table and its two fields exist only in memory. To make the new objects a permanent part of the database, you must use the Append method. If you do not append a new object to a collection, it will not be saved as an object in the database.

WARNING

Creating objects and giving them properties is not enough. You must take the step of appending them to the correct collection, or Access will never know of their existence. If your program exits before you've used the Append method to add your objects to a collection, they will be discarded.

NOTE

ADOX is meant to work with any database engine. As a consequence of this, it uses the object name "Column" for what Access generally calls a "Field," at least in reference to table design. In recordsets, however, they're still called Fields.

The next lines save the new objects to the database:

```
With tblOrders.Columns
    .Append col1
    .Append col2
End With

With cat.Tables
    .Append tblOrders
    .Refresh
End With
' Code continues...
```

Finally, you can refresh the TableDefs collection to ensure that the new objects are included in it. In a multiuser environment, the new table may not be immediately available to other users unless you refresh the collection. The following line refreshes the TableDefs collection:

```
cat.Tables.Refresh
```

Even using the Refresh method, Access won't update the database window itself until it must. It will only show the new table you've created once you move to a different collection and then back to the list of tables. To solve this problem, Access 97 added the RefreshDatabaseWindow method of the Application object. Adding this line of code will refresh the database window's display:

```
Application.RefreshDatabaseWindow
```

When you're creating new columns using ADOX, you need to know which ADOX data type to use for each field. Table 6.4 shows the mapping between the ADOX Column object's Type property and the data type you'll see if you inspect the resulting table in the Access table designer.

TABLE 6.4: ADOX Column Data Types

ADOX Type	Access Data Type
adBinary	Binary
adBoolean	Boolean

Continued on next page

TABLE 6.4 CONTINUED: ADOX Column Data Types

ADOX Type	Access Data Type
adUnsignedTinyInt	Byte
adCurrency	Currency
adDate	Date
adNumeric	Decimal
adDouble	Double
adGUID	GUID
adSmallInt	Integer
adInteger	Long
adVarWChar	Text
adSingle	Single
adLongVarWChar	Memo

ADOX will allow you to combine creating and appending objects into a single step. For example, you can call the Append method of the Table object to both create and append a column. Using this approach allows you to dispense with variables to refer to columns.

For example, you could rewrite the preceding function as shown in Listing 6.4.

Listing 6.4

```
Public Sub CreateOrdersTable2()
    Dim cat As ADOX.Catalog
    Dim tblOrders As ADOX.Table

    Set tblOrders = New ADOX.Table
    Set cat = New ADOX.Catalog
    cat.ActiveConnection = CurrentProject.Connection

    ' Delete the table, if it exists.
    On Error Resume Next
    cat.Tables.Delete "tblOrders2"
```

```
    ' The table object is already created, so
    ' just assign its properties
    tblOrders.Name = "tblOrders2"

    ' Create the columns by appending them
    With tblOrders.Columns
        .Append "OrderID", adInteger
        .Append "CustomerName", adVarWChar, 30
    End With

    With cat.Tables
        .Append tblOrders
        .Refresh
    End With

    Application.RefreshDatabaseWindow
    Set cat = Nothing
    Set tblOrders = Nothing
End Sub
```

Creating an Index

As part of your applications, you may need to create an index programmatically. Follow these steps to create a new index:

1. Create an Index object and set its Name property.
2. Assign values to the new index's properties, as appropriate. All the properties are read/write for an index object that hasn't yet been appended to the Indexes collection but are read-only once that has occurred. The ones you'll most likely be interested in are the Name, PrimaryKey, Unique, and IndexNulls properties.
3. Create a Column object for each field that makes up part of the index, and append each to the index's Columns collection. This collection of fields indicates to the index the fields for which it must maintain values in order to keep itself current.
4. Use the Append method of the original Table object to append the index object to its Indexes collection.

NOTE

Because all the properties of an index object are read-only once the object has been appended to its collection, if you need to modify a property of an index once it's been created, you must delete the object and then create a new one. You should also investigate the SQL ALTER TABLE statement, covered in Chapter 3.

TIP

In Access, using ADOX, you can name your indexes any way you wish. If you have code you're using, however, that counts on your primary key being named PrimaryKey, you must ensure that your primary keys are named with the standard value, PrimaryKey. Otherwise, existing code might break.

The adhCreatePrimaryKey function in Listing 6.5 creates the primary key for any specified table. You pass to this function the name of the table, the name of the primary key, and one or more field names to use as part of the primary key. Along the way, adhCreatePrimaryKey calls the FindPrimaryKey function, which returns the name of the primary key if it exists or Null if it doesn't. If a primary key already exists, adhCreatePrimaryKey deletes the primary key so it can create a new one. We've also included a test procedure, TestCreatePK, to test the functionality. You'll find all these examples in the module basPK in CH06.MDB.

Listing 6.5

```
Public Function adhCreatePrimaryKey( _
 strTableName As String, _
 strKeyName As String, _
 ParamArray varColumns() As Variant) _
 As Boolean

    Dim cat As ADOX.Catalog
    Dim idx As ADOX.Index
    Dim tbl As ADOX.Table
    Dim varPK As Variant
    Dim varIdx As Variant
    Dim idxs As ADOX.Indexes

    On Error GoTo HandleErrors

    Set cat = New ADOX.Catalog
    cat.ActiveConnection = _
     CurrentProject.Connection
```

```
    Set tbl = cat.Tables(strTableName)
    Set idxs = tbl.Indexes

    ' Find out if the table currently has a primary key.
    ' If so, delete it now.
    varPK = FindPrimaryKey(tbl)
    If Not IsNull(varPK) Then
        idxs.Delete varPK
    End If
    ' Create the new index object
    Set idx = New ADOX.Index
    idx.Name = strKeyName

    ' Set up the new index as the primary key
    ' This will also set
    '    IndexNulls to adIndexNullsDisallow
    idx.PrimaryKey = True
    idx.Unique = True

    ' Now create the columns that make up the index,
    ' and append each to the collection of columns
    For Each varIdx In varColumns
        AddColumn idx, varIdx
    Next varIdx

    ' Now append the index to the Table's
    ' indexes colletion
    idxs.Append idx
    adhCreatePrimaryKey = True

ExitHere:
    Set cat = Nothing
    Set idx = Nothing
    Set tbl = Nothing
    Set idxs = Nothing
    Exit Function

HandleErrors:
    MsgBox "Error: " & _
     Err.Description & " (" & Err.Number & ")"
    adhCreatePrimaryKey = False
    Resume ExitHere
End Function
```

```
Private Function FindPrimaryKey( _
 tbl As ADOX.Table) As Variant

    ' Given a particular table, find the primary
    ' key name, if it exists.

    ' Returns the name of the primary key's index, if
    ' it exists, or Null if there wasn't a primary key.

    Dim idx As ADOX.Index

    For Each idx In tbl.Indexes
        If idx.PrimaryKey Then
            FindPrimaryKey = idx.Name
            Exit Function
        End If
    Next idx
    FindPrimaryKey = Null
End Function

Private Function AddColumn( _
 idx As ADOX.Index, _
 varIdx As Variant) As Boolean
    ' Given an index object, and a column name, add
    ' the column to the index.
    ' Returns True on success, False otherwise.

    Dim col As ADOX.Column

    On Error GoTo HandleErrors

    If Len(varIdx & "") > 0 Then
        Set col = New ADOX.Column
        col.Name = varIdx
        idx.Columns.Append col
    End If
    AddColumn = True

ExitHere:
    Set col = Nothing
    Exit Function
```

```
HandleErrors:
    AddColumn = False
    Resume ExitHere
End Function

Public Sub TestCreatePK()
    Debug.Print adhCreatePrimaryKey("tblCustomerItems", _
     "PrimaryKey", "CustomerID", "ItemID")
End Sub
```

TIP

You may have never used the ParamArray modifier, as we did in adhCreatePrimaryKey. Using this modifier, callers of your procedure can pass as many parameters as they like in that position. On the receiving side (in your code), you see all the parameters in that "slot" as a single array. Using ParamArray has some limitations, so you'll want to check out this interesting VBA feature in the online help.

Although the method shown above works for any index, ADOX provides shortcuts for creating primary and foreign key fields. When you create an index and set its PrimaryKey property to True, you're automatically creating a new Key in the Table's Keys collection as well. Similarly, if you create a relationship in the Access user interface, the foreign key field will automatically be indexed and a Key will be added to the Keys collection behind the scenes. You can reverse this process if you like by creating Keys directly. If you follow this procedure, Access will automatically create the corresponding indexes for you.

The adhCreatePrimaryKey2 function in Listing 6.6 demonstrates this alternative.

Listing 6.6

```
Public Function adhCreatePrimaryKey2( _
 strTableName As String, _
 strKeyName As String, _
 ParamArray varColumns() As Variant) _
 As Boolean

    Dim cat As ADOX.Catalog
    Dim pk As ADOX.key
    Dim tbl As ADOX.Table
    Dim varPK As Variant
    Dim varIdx As Variant
    Dim keys As ADOX.keys
```

```
    On Error GoTo HandleErrors

    Set cat = New ADOX.Catalog
    cat.ActiveConnection = CurrentProject.Connection
    Set tbl = cat.Tables(strTableName)
    Set keys = tbl.keys

    ' Find out if the table currently has a primary key.
    ' If so, delete it now.
    varPK = FindPrimaryKey2(tbl)
    If Not IsNull(varPK) Then
        keys.Delete varPK
    End If
    ' Create the new key object
    Set pk = New ADOX.key
    pk.Name = strKeyName

    ' Set up the new key as the primary key
    pk.Type = adKeyPrimary

    ' Now create the columns that make up the key,
    ' and append each to the collection of columns
    For Each varIdx In varColumns
        AddColumn2 pk, varIdx
    Next varIdx

    ' Now append the key to the Table's
    ' keys colletion
    keys.Append pk
    adhCreatePrimaryKey2 = True

ExitHere:
    Set cat = Nothing
    Set pk = Nothing
    Set tbl = Nothing
    Exit Function

HandleErrors:
    MsgBox "Error: " & _
     Err.Description & " (" & Err.Number & ")"
    adhCreatePrimaryKey2 = False
    Resume ExitHere
End Function
```

```
Private Function FindPrimaryKey2( _
 tbl As ADOX.Table) As Variant

    ' Given a particular table, find the primary
    ' key name, if it exists.

    ' Returns the name of the primary key, if
    ' it exists, or Null if there wasn't a primary key.

    Dim key As ADOX.key

    For Each key In tbl.keys
        If key.Type = adKeyPrimary Then
            FindPrimaryKey2 = key.Name
            Exit Function
        End If
    Next key
    FindPrimaryKey2 = Null
End Function

Private Function AddColumn2( _
 key As ADOX.key, _
 varIdx As Variant) As Boolean
    ' Given a key object, and a column name, add
    ' the column to the key.
    ' Returns True on success, False otherwise.

    Dim col As ADOX.Column

    On Error GoTo HandleErrors

    If Len(varIdx & "") > 0 Then
        Set col = New ADOX.Column
        col.Name = varIdx
        key.Columns.Append col
    End If
    AddColumn2 = True

ExitHere:
    Set col = Nothing
    Exit Function
```

```
HandleErrors:
    AddColumn2 = False
    Resume ExitHere
End Function

Public Sub TestCreatePK2()
    Debug.Print adhCreatePrimaryKey2("tblCustomerItems", _
     "PrimaryKey", "CustomerID", "ItemID")
End Sub
```

Creating Relationships

Follow these steps to create a new relationship:

1. Open the catalog that will be the basis for your relation.
2. Verify that the referenced table (the primary table in the relation) has a primary key in place.
3. Create a Key object to represent the foreign key (the many side of the relation). Append columns to this key.
4. For each column object in the foreign key, supply the RelatedColumn property, which corresponds to the name of the matching key field in the primary table.
5. Use the Append method to append the new key object to the table's keys collection.

To specify cascading updates or cascading deletes, you set properties of the new foreign key object. To enforce cascading updates, set the key's UpdateRule property to the constant adRICascade. To enforce cascading deletes, set the key's DeleteRule property to the constant adRICascade, as well.

Listing 6.7 demonstrates, in the simplest case, the steps involved in creating a relationship. This function (from basRelations in CH06.MDB) creates a one-to-many relationship between tblCustomers and tblCustomerItems and enables cascading updates. Just to make sure the function succeeds, if it finds that the relation already exists, it deletes that relation and recreates it.

Listing 6.7

```
Const adhcErrObjectExists = -2147467259

Public Function CreateRelationship() As Boolean
    ' Create a relationship between tblCustomers
    ' and tblCustomerItems.
    ' The relation will have cascading deletes
    ' enabled.

    Dim cat As ADOX.Catalog
    Dim fk As ADOX.key
    Dim tbl As ADOX.Table
    Dim keys As ADOX.keys

    On Error GoTo HandleErrors

    ' Get the catalog for the current database
    Set cat = New ADOX.Catalog
    cat.ActiveConnection = CurrentProject.Connection

    ' Get the keys collection for the many-side table
    Set tbl = cat.Tables("tblCustomerItems")
    Set keys = tbl.keys

    ' Create the foreign key
    Set fk = New ADOX.key
    fk.Name = "CustomerItemsCustomers"
    fk.Type = adKeyForeign
    fk.RelatedTable = "tblCustomers"

    ' Specify cascading deletes
    fk.DeleteRule = adRICascade
    ' Append a column to the key
    fk.Columns.Append "CustomerID"
    ' Set the related column name
    fk.Columns("CustomerID").RelatedColumn = _
     "CustomerID"
    ' Append the key object to save it
    tbl.keys.Append fk
    CreateRelationship = True
```

```
ExitHere:
    Set fk = Nothing
    Set keys = Nothing
    Set tbl = Nothing
    Set cat = Nothing
    Exit Function

HandleErrors:
    Select Case Err.Number
        Case adhcErrObjectExists
            ' If the relationship exists,
            ' just delete it and try again
            tbl.keys.Delete fk.Name
            Resume
        Case Else
            MsgBox "Error: " & Err.Description & _
             " (" & Err.Number & ")"
            CreateRelationship = False
            Resume ExitHere
    End Select
End Function
```

Working with Recordsets

In almost any Access application, sooner or later you'll need to manipulate data from within VBA. ADO provides a rich set of data access objects to allow you to view, edit, add, and delete fields, rows, and tables. In addition, ADO allows you to specify a number of properties that control the behavior of recordsets, including cursor type, lock type, cursor location, and recordset options. The following sections discuss these issues.

NOTE ADO uses the term *cursor* to refer to the behavior of the record pointer that specifies the current row in a recordset.

Meet the Cursors

A cursor, in ADO, is the underlying object that makes it possible for you to move around within the set of rows returned by a recordset. The cursor manages movement, updatability, and currency of the rows you've requested. In DAO, you'll find three simple cursor types: table, dynaset, and snapshot. ADO's cursor options are a bit more flexible and are perhaps more complex.

Although ADO provides four types of recordset cursors, the one you use in any given situation depends on the source of the data being referenced and the methods you need to use to access the data. Table 6.5 lists each cursor type, along with its benefits and drawbacks.

TABLE 6.5: Cursor Types and Their Benefits/Drawbacks

Cursor Type	Description	Benefits	Drawbacks
Dynamic	Set of records in a table or other data source in a database	Shows all record changes by other users.	Allows bookmarks only if the provider supports them. Not supported by the Jet OLE DB provider in this manner. Jet uses this cursor type to provide best performance for cursors based on SQL strings.
Keyset	Set of pointers (bookmarks) referring to data in tables or queries in a database	Shows data changes by other users. Always supports bookmarks.	Does not show new records added by other users. Prevents access to records deleted by other users.
Static	Copy of a set of records as it exists at the time the recordset is created	Always supports bookmarks. The only type of recordset allowed by client-side cursors.	Doesn't reflect changes to data made in a multiuser environment.
Forward-only	Copy of a set of records as it exists at the time the recordset is created	Faster than a static cursor.	Only allows scrolling forward through records.

WARNING Don't be fooled by the name "static." Static recordsets contain a fixed set of records, but these records may or may not be editable depending on the lock type of the recordset.

Creating a Recordset

You use code like the following to create a recordset:

```
Dim rst As ADODB.Recordset
Set rst = New ADODB.Recordset
rst.Open Source, Connection, CursorType, LockType, Options
```

All of the parameters are optional. Additionally, ADO lets you specify parameters before you open the recordset. Therefore, either of these code snippets has the same effect:

```
Set rst.ActiveConnection = CurrentProject.Connection
rst.CursorType = adopenStatic
rst.LockType = adLockOptimistic
rst.Open "Customers"
```

or

```
rst.open "Customers", CurrentProject.Connection, _
 adOpenStatic, adLockOptimistic
```

NOTE Throughout this chapter, and throughout the book, we'll interchange the use of the different ways you can open a recordset. Sometimes, we'll set the properties first and then call the Open method. Other times, we'll pass all the values in the Open method call itself. The point here is that it doesn't matter which way you do it—it's up to you. In addition, we'll often use named parameters; that is, supplying a *ParameterName:=Value* pair for parameters. This makes your code easier to read, we think, when you have multiple parameters to send to a procedure.

The *Source* parameter indicates where the data will come from and must be one of the following:

- Name of an existing table
- Name of an existing query or stored procedure that returns rows
- A SQL statement that returns rows
- An existing Command object variable name
- The file name of a persisted recordset

The *CursorType* parameter specifies the type of cursor that ADO will use to move through the recordset. It should be one of the following built-in constant values:

- adOpenDynamic, to open a dynamic recordset
- adOpenKeyset, to open a keyset recordset
- adOpenStatic, to open a static recordset
- adOpenForwardOnly, to open a forward-only recordset

If you don't specify a cursor type, ADO defaults to the fastest type, which is a forward-only recordset.

The *LockType* parameter specifies the record-locking behavior that will be used for editing operations in this recordset. It should be one of the following built-in constant values:

- adLockReadOnly, for recordsets that cannot be edited
- adLockPessimistic, for recordsets that use pessimistic locking
- adLockOptimistic, for recordsets that use optimistic locking
- adLockBatchOptimistic, for recordsets that will use the UpdateBatch method to update multiple records in a single operation

If you don't specify a lock type, ADO defaults to the fastest type, which is a read-only recordset.

WARNING

The default recordset in ADO is forward-only and read-only. This means that if you simply open a recordset, you won't be able to do much with it. If you want to move through records at random or edit records, you must specify the cursor type and lock type to use!

The Options parameter tells ADO how to evaluate the Source parameter. It can be one of the values listed in Table 6.6.

TABLE 6.6: Options for Recordsets

Constant	Description
adCmdText	Tells the provider to evaluate the source as a SQL statement.
adCmdTable	Tells ADO to generate a SQL query to retrieve all rows from the table or query whose name is specified as the source.
adCmdTableDirect	Tells the provider to return all records from the table or query whose name is specified as the source.
adCmdStoredProc	Tells the provider to evaluate the source as the name of a stored procedure or query.
adCmdUnknown	Tells ADO to query the provider to determine whether the source is a stored procedure, table name, or SQL statement.
adCmdFile	Tells ADO that the source parameter is the name of a file containing a persisted recordset.

If you don't specify any options, ADO defaults to adCmdUnknown. This will cause slightly slower performance, since ADO needs to query the system tables from the OLE DB provider to determine what type of object the recordset is to be based on.

NOTE You can also open a recordset by calling the Execute method of a Command object or a Connection object. However, a recordset opened with the Execute method is always forward-only, read-only. For flexibility, you'll want to stick to the Open method of the Recordset object.

Direct Table Access

By default, recordsets are based on SQL statements that retrieve rows from the specified data source. Even if you specify the name of a table as the Source parameter to the recordset's Open method, ADO will translate this into the SQL statement

```
SELECT * FROM Source
```

and send that statement to the OLE DB provider to be evaluated.

Using SQL statements to retrieve records allows ADO to work with the most general OLE DB providers. However, with some providers (including the Jet and SQL Server OLE DB providers), you can bypass building a SQL statement when your data source is an actual table in the database. To do this, you specify adCmdTableDirect as the Options parameter to the Open method of the recordset.

If you want your code to be as general as possible for use against any OLE DB provider, you should avoid the adCmdTableDirect option. However, some operations (such as using the Seek method to locate a record using an index) can only be performed if you use adCmdTableDirect.

Consistent versus Inconsistent Updates

When you create a recordset object based on more than one table, Jet allows you to make changes only to the "many" side of a join, by default. This is known as a *consistent update.* At times, you may want to update both sides of a join. To do this, you need to tell ADO that you wish to make *inconsistent updates*. This allows you to update fields in both sides of the join. Note that this may violate the relationships between tables that your application needs. It is up to you to provide the necessary code to ensure that any "implied" referential integrity is maintained.

If you've turned on referential integrity for a relationship and enabled cascading updates, the inconsistent and consistent updates will cause identical behavior. In this case, the referential integrity takes control, and the cascading updates will update the many side of the relationship when you update the "one" side.

Most OLE DB providers do not support inconsistent updates, so this is not something that's part of the default ADO object model. Jet, however, does support this behavior. When you open a recordset using the Jet provider, the provider adds a dynamic property to the recordset object that lets you use inconsistent updates if you choose. To do so, you must first set the connection for the recordset, then set the value of the property, and then open the recordset, as shown in Listing 6.8 (from basRecordset).

Listing 6.8

```
Public Sub OpenInconsistent()
    Dim rst As ADODB.Recordset

    Set rst = New ADODB.Recordset
    rst.ActiveConnection = CurrentProject.Connection
    rst.Properties("Jet OLEDB:Inconsistent") = True
```

```
    rst.Open _
     Source:="SELECT * FROM tblCustomers" & _
     " INNER JOIN tblOrders " & _
     " ON tblCustomers.CustomerID = tblOrders.CustomerID", _
     Options:=adCmdText
    Debug.Print rst.RecordCount
    Set rst = Nothing
End Sub
```

Cursor Locations

If you've worked with DAO previously, you know that you never have to be concerned with where Jet places the cursor. As a matter of fact, this isn't an issue that even comes up using DAO. A *cursor* is the cached rows, or row pointers, provided by the database engine when you open a recordset. ADO supports two cursor locations: client-side and server-side. A client-side cursor is created on the same machine as the client (that's you), and a server-side cursor is created on the same machine as the server (that might be on your machine, or it might be on some server machine. If you're using Jet, this is always your machine, because Jet always runs on your machine.) To choose between the two, you set the CursorLocation property of the Recordset object to one of two intrinsic constants before opening the recordset:

- adUseServer (the default) specifies that ADO should use server-side cursors
- adUseClient specifies that ADO should use client-side cursors

When you specify client-side cursors, ADO passes your request to the Microsoft Cursor Service for OLE DB. This component is designed to enhance the functionality of recordsets retrieved from any OLE DB provider. The Cursor Service first requests all the data from the OLE DB provider using a forward-only, read-only recordset. Then it caches this data locally and presents it to the application as a static recordset.

In most cases, using client-side cursors with an Access database only adds overhead to data access, because data is being cached twice on the same machine: once in the Jet database engine and once in the Cursor Service. However, you must use client-side cursors for some advanced functionality. In particular, client-side cursors are necessary if you want to call the Sort method on a recordset, or if you want to create a disconnected recordset that will later reconnect to the database and update multiple records in a batch.

In general, you should use the default server-side cursors unless you discover that the additional functionality of client-side cursors is necessary for your application.

TIP

When using Jet to provide your data (as opposed to using SQL Server/MSDE or some other OLE DB provider), you'll want to use a server-side cursor whenever possible. You'll get better performance, and you won't have an extra layer of ADO (the client-side cursor is provided by ADO) between you and Jet. On the other hand, there are some things you simply cannot do with a server-side cursor. The Sort method, for example, only works with client-side cursors. Still, whenever possible, use the default, server-side cursor when working with Jet data.

Recordset Property Interactions

With two cursor locations, four cursor types, and four lock types, there are theoretically 32 variations of recordsets (not counting the fine details such as direct table access or inconsistent updates). ADO is designed to be very forgiving on this count. You can request any combination of location, cursor type, and lock type, and ADO will open a recordset without error. However, it may not open precisely what you request. For combinations that aren't supported, ADO will change one or more options to get a recordset type that it's able to deliver.

Table 6.7 shows the mapping between what you ask for and what you get in server-side recordsets. Table 6.8 shows the same mapping for client-side recordsets. If you'd like to investigate this behavior yourself, the tables were generated from information gathered by the SeeCursorInfo function in basRecordset (see Listing 6.9).

TABLE 6.7: Server-Side Recordset Properties

Requested	Delivered
Forward-only, read-only	Forward-only, read-only
Forward-only, pessimistic	Keyset, batch optimistic
Forward-only, optimistic	Keyset, optimistic
Forward-only, batch optimistic	Keyset, batch optimistic
Keyset, read-only	Keyset, read-only

Continued on next page

TABLE 6.7 CONTINUED: Server-Side Recordset Properties

Requested	Delivered
Keyset, pessimistic	Keyset, batch optimistic
Keyset, optimistic	Keyset, optimistic
Keyset, batch optimistic	Keyset, batch optimistic
Dynamic, read-only	Static, read-only
Dynamic, pessimistic	Keyset, batch optimistic
Dynamic, optimistic	Keyset, optimistic
Dynamic, batch optimistic	Keyset, batch optimistic
Static, read-only	Static, read-only
Static, pessimistic	Keyset, batch optimistic
Static, optimistic	Keyset, optimistic
Static, batch optimistic	Keyset, batch optimistic

TABLE 6.8: Client-Side Recordset Properties

Requested	Delivered
Forward-only, read-only	Static, read-only
Forward-only, pessimistic	Static, batch optimistic
Forward-only, optimistic	Static, optimistic
Forward-only, batch optimistic	Static, batch optimistic
Keyset, read-only	Static, read-only
Keyset, pessimistic	Static, batch optimistic
Keyset, optimistic	Static, optimistic
Keyset, batch optimistic	Static, batch optimistic
Dynamic, read-only	Static, read-only
Dynamic, pessimistic	Static, batch optimistic

Continued on next page

TABLE 6.8 CONTINUED: Client-Side Recordset Properties

Requested	Delivered
Dynamic, optimistic	Static, optimistic
Dynamic, batch optimistic	Static, batch optimistic
Static, read-only	Static, read-only
Static, pessimistic	Static, batch optimistic
Static, optimistic	Static, optimistic
Static, batch optimistic	Static, batch optimistic

Note that these tables only apply to recordsets opened on native Jet data sources. The recordsets delivered by ADO depend both on the capabilities of ADO itself and the capabilities of the underlying OLE DB provider. So, for example, although Jet doesn't ever deliver Dynamic recordsets, some other data source used from an Access database (such as a SQL Server table) might.

Listing 6.9

```
Public Sub SeeCursorInfo()
    Dim rst As ADODB.Recordset
    Dim lngLocation As Long
    Dim lngCursorType As Long
    Dim lngLockType As Long

    On Error GoTo HandleErr

    Set rst = New ADODB.Recordset
    For lngLocation = 2 To 3
        For lngCursorType = 0 To 3
            For lngLockType = 1 To 4
                Debug.Print "Requesting " & _
                 GetLocation(lngLocation) & ", " & _
                 GetCursorType(lngCursorType) & ", " & _
                 GetLockType(lngLockType)

                rst.CursorLocation = lngLocation
                Set rst.ActiveConnection = _
                 CurrentProject.Connection
```

```
                rst.Open "tblCustomers", _
                 CursorType:=lngCursorType, _
                 LockType:=lngLockType

                Debug.Print "       Got " & _
                 GetLocation(rst.CursorLocation) & ", " & _
                 GetCursorType(rst.CursorType) & ", " & _
                 GetLockType(rst.LockType)
NextType:
                If Not rst Is Nothing Then
                    rst.Close
                End If
            Next lngLockType
        Next lngCursorType
    Next lngLocation

ExitHere:
    On Error Resume Next
    rst.Close
    Set rst = Nothing
    Exit Sub

HandleErr:
    Debug.Print "  Error : " & _
     Err.Description & " (" & Err.Number & ")"
    Resume NextType
End Sub

Private Function GetLocation( _
 lngLocation As ADODB.CursorLocationEnum) As String
    Select Case lngLocation
        Case adUseServer
            GetLocation = "Server side"
        Case adUseClient
            GetLocation = "Client side"
    End Select
End Function

Private Function GetLockType( _
 lngLockType As ADODB.LockTypeEnum) As String
    Select Case lngLockType
        Case adLockReadOnly
            GetLockType = "Read only"
```

```
        Case adLockPessimistic
            GetLockType = "Pessimistic"
        Case adLockOptimistic
            GetLockType = "Optimistic"
        Case adLockBatchOptimistic
            GetLockType = "Batch optimistic"
    End Select
End Function

Private Function GetCursorType( _
 lngCursorType As ADODB.CursorTypeEnum) As String
    Select Case lngCursorType
        Case adOpenForwardOnly
            GetCursorType = "Forward-only"
        Case adOpenKeyset
            GetCursorType = "Keyset"
        Case adOpenDynamic
            GetCursorType = "Dynamic"
        Case adOpenStatic
            GetCursorType = "Static"
    End Select
End Function
```

The Supports Method

As you'll see throughout this chapter, not all recordsets are created equal. When you take into account the different ways that you can open recordsets; the various permutations of the CursorLocation, CursorType, LockType, and Options properties; and the different potential OLE DB providers that can be supplying the data, it can be difficult to be sure just which methods will work on which recordsets. If you're trying to write general-purpose code to manipulate any recordset, this can be a real problem. Fortunately, ADO provides the Supports method, which allows you to query a recordset as to the functionality that it supports.

The Supports method returns True or False for specific options:

```
fReturn = rst.Supports(Option)
```

Where Option is one of the intrinsic constants shown in Table 6.9.

TABLE 6.9: Constants for the Supports Method

Option	Returns True If...
adAddNew	You can use the AddNew method to add records to this recordset.
adApproxPosition	You can use the AbsolutePosition and AbsolutePage properties with this recordset.
adBookmark	You can use the Bookmark property with this recordset.
adDelete	You can use the Delete method to delete records from this recordset.
adFind	You can use the Find method to find records in this recordset.
adHoldRecords	You can change the recordset position without committing changes to the current record.
adIndex	You can use the Index property to set an index for this recordset.
adMovePrevious	You can use MoveFirst and MovePrevious or the Move method to move backwards in this recordset.
adResync	You can use the Resync method to resynchronize this recordset with the underlying data.
adSeek	You can use the Seek method to find records in this recordset.
adUpdate	You can use the Update method to modify records in this recordset.
adUpdateBatch	You can use the UpdateBatch and CancelBatch methods on this recordset.

Listing 6.10 shows how you can use the Supports method in your code to check the functionality of a recordset. You'll find both the RecordsetSupport function and the TestRecordsets function in basRecordset.

Listing 6.10

```
Private Sub RecordsetSupport(rst As ADODB.Recordset)
    If rst.Supports(adAddNew) Then
        Debug.Print "Supports AddNew"
    Else
        Debug.Print "Doesn't support AddNew"
    End If
    If rst.Supports(adApproxPosition) Then
        Debug.Print "Supports AbsolutePosition"
    Else
```

```
    Debug.Print "Doesn't support AbsolutePosition"
End If
If rst.Supports(adBookmark) Then
    Debug.Print "Supports bookmarks"
Else
    Debug.Print "Doesn't support bookmarks"
End If
If rst.Supports(adDelete) Then
    Debug.Print "Supports Delete"
Else
    Debug.Print "Doesn't support Delete"
End If
If rst.Supports(adFind) Then
    Debug.Print "Supports Find"
Else
    Debug.Print "Doesn't support Find"
End If
If rst.Supports(adHoldRecords) Then
    Debug.Print "Supports move without save"
Else
    Debug.Print "Doesn't support move without save"
End If
If rst.Supports(adIndex) Then
    Debug.Print "Supports Index"
Else
    Debug.Print "Doesn't support Index"
End If
If rst.Supports(adMovePrevious) Then
    Debug.Print "Supports MovePrevious"
Else
    Debug.Print "Doesn't support MovePrevious"
End If
If rst.Supports(adResync) Then
    Debug.Print "Supports Resync"
Else
    Debug.Print "Doesn't support Resync"
End If
If rst.Supports(adSeek) Then
    Debug.Print "Supports Seek"
Else
    Debug.Print "Doesn't support Seek"
End If
```

```
    If rst.Supports(adUpdate) Then
        Debug.Print "Supports Update"
    Else
        Debug.Print "Doesn't support Update"
    End If
    If rst.Supports(adUpdateBatch) Then
        Debug.Print "Supports UpdateBatch"
    Else
        Debug.Print "Doesn't support UpdateBatch"
    End If
End Sub

Public Sub TestRecordsets()
    Dim rst As ADODB.Recordset

    Set rst = New ADODB.Recordset
    rst.Open "tblCustomers", CurrentProject.Connection
    Debug.Print "Default recordset:"
    Debug.Print "=================="
    RecordsetSupport rst
    rst.Close
    Debug.Print

    rst.Open "tblCustomers", _
     CurrentProject.Connection, adOpenKeyset, _
     adLockOptimistic, adCmdTableDirect
    Debug.Print "Direct table recordset:"
    Debug.Print "======================="
    RecordsetSupport rst
    rst.Close
    rst.CursorLocation = adUseClient
    Debug.Print

    rst.Open "tblCustomers", _
     CurrentProject.Connection, adOpenKeyset, _
     adLockOptimistic
    Debug.Print "Client-side recordset:"
    Debug.Print "======================"
    RecordsetSupport rst
    rst.Close
    Set rst = Nothing
End Sub
```

Creating Recordset Objects

One of the wonderful things about ADO is that it's so flexible. This flexibility is also the curse of ADO, because there are so many ways you can write the same code, and no two programmers' code will look the same. For instance, the following examples show a number of ways you can create Recordset objects. This list isn't exhaustive, but it does show some representative cases.

- To create a recordset based on a table or a saved query:

```
' This will create a forward-only,
' read only recordset
Set rst = New ADODB.Recordset
rst.Open "Customers", CurrentProject.Connection

' Another forward-only, read only
' recordset
rst.Open "qryCustOrders", CurrentProject.Connection
```

- To create an editable recordset that supports full navigation and sorting based on a SQL string:

```
' Client side recordset that can be sorted
rst.CursorLocation = adUseClient
rst.Open "SELECT * FROM Customers", _
 CurrentProject.Connection, _
 adOpenKeyset, adLockOptimistic
```

- To create a recordset that supports using the Seek method:

```
' This recordset supports Seek
rst.CursorLocation = adUseServer
rst.Open "Customers", _
 CurrentProject.Connection, adOpenKeyset, _
 adLockOptimistic, adCmdTableDirect
```

TIP

Not all recordsets are created equally. To find out what features any given recordset supports, you can use the Supports method of the Recordset object. See the section "The Supports Method" earlier in this chapter for more information.

Moving through a Recordset

Once you've created a recordset, ADO provides a variety of methods for navigating through the rows: MoveFirst, MoveLast, MovePrevious, and MoveNext. Each of these works in the manner you would expect based on the name. In addition, ADO provides the Move method, which can move a specified number of rows forward or backward, either from the current row or from a stored bookmark (if the recordset in question supports bookmarks). Recordsets also support the AbsolutePosition property, which allows you to read and write the current position within the recordset, based on the data in the current set of rows. The AbsolutePosition property returns a number from 1 to the total number of records in the recordset, or one of three intrinsic constants:

- adPosUnknown, if the recordset is empty or the provider doesn't support the property
- adPosBOF, if the BOF property is true (the cursor is before the first record in the recordset)
- adPosEOF, if the EOF property is true (the cursor is beyond the final record in the recordset)

The procedure in Listing 6.11, from basRecordset, demonstrates how the AbsolutePosition property works.

Listing 6.11

```
Public Sub ShowAbsolutePosition()
    Dim rst As ADODB.Recordset

    Set rst = New ADODB.Recordset
    rst.Open "tblCustomers", _
     CurrentProject.Connection, adOpenKeyset

    Debug.Print rst.Fields(0).Value
    ' Move approximately halfway
    rst.AbsolutePosition = 0.5 * rst.RecordCount
    Debug.Print rst.Fields(0).Value
    ' Move to the 35th row
    rst.AbsolutePosition = 35
    Debug.Print rst.Fields(0).Value
    rst.Close
    Set rst = Nothing
End Sub
```

Using the Move Method

Although the actions of the other Move methods are obvious, based on their names, the Move method is a bit more ambiguous. The Move method of a recordset accepts one or two parameters:

rst.Move *numrecords* [,*start*]

The *numrecords* parameter indicates the number of rows to move (greater than 0 for forward, less than 0 for negative), and the optional *start* parameter can contain a saved bookmark. If you supply the value for the bookmark, ADO starts there and moves the appropriate number of rows from that spot. If you don't specify the start location, ADO assumes you want to start moving from the current row. See the section "Adding New Rows to a Recordset" later in this chapter for an example of using the Move method.

TIP

See the section "Using Bookmarks" later in the chapter for more information on retrieving a bookmark and saving its value.

The Move method won't generate an error even if you try to move by too many records (for example, moving forward 100 records in a recordset containing only 50 records). In such a case, the record pointer stops at BOF or EOF, depending on the direction of the move.

NOTE

When working with a forward-only recordset, the *rows* parameter can be either positive or negative. However, an error results if you attempt to move backwards before the first record in the current record cache. You can set the number of records in the cache with the CacheSize property.

Using the AbsolutePosition Property

You can set the value of the AbsolutePosition property to move to a specific row in the recordset. If you wanted to move to the row approximately 50 percent of the way through your rows, you could use code like this:

```
rst.AbsolutePosition = .5 * rst.RecordCount
```

To move to the 35th row within the rows currently in the recordset, given the current filtering and sorting, you could use code like this:

```
rst.AbsolutePosition = 35
```

You can also use this property to find out where you are in the recordset—that is, to find out the current position, by number.

WARNING

The AbsolutePosition property is *not* a record number and should not be thought of as such. It simply returns the current row's position within the current set of rows, and it will change as you modify the filter or the sort order of the rows. To be able to find a row, no matter how you've modified the sorting or filtering, you'll need to use a bookmark (see the section "Using Bookmarks" later in this chapter) or store the primary key for later retrieval.

Finding the Number of Rows in a Recordset

You use the RecordCount property of a recordset to find the number of rows contained in the recordset. If ADO can't determine the number of rows, or if the type of cursor you've chosen (forward-only, for example) doesn't support finding the number of rows, the property returns –1.

In a single-user environment, the RecordCount property always correctly returns the number of rows in the recordset. If you delete a row, either interactively or programmatically, the RecordCount property stays in sync. In a multi-user environment, things are a bit more complex. If you're sharing data with another user and you both have a recordset open that's based on the same data, the issues are more complex. See Chapter 2 in *Access 2000 Developer's Handbook, Volume II* for more information on sharing data with multiple users.

TIP

If a recordset supports approximate positioning or bookmarks (see the section "The Supports Method," earlier in the chapter, to see how to find out if the recordset supports these features), ADO can retrieve the RecordCount property with minimal overhead. On the other hand, if the recordset doesn't support approximate positioning, ADO must actually populate the recordset to find out the record count, and this can be an expensive proposition—that is, it might cause a significant delay in your application. Be wary of using the RecordCount property, unless you've used the Supports method to verify that doing so won't take a long time.

Testing for Boundaries

Every recordset supports two properties, BOF and EOF, that indicate whether the current row is currently at the end of the recordset (EOF) or at the beginning of the recordset (BOF).

- If you use MovePrevious while the first row is current, BOF becomes True and there is no current row.
- If you use MovePrevious again, BOF stays True but a runtime error (3021) occurs.
- If you use MoveNext while the last row is current, EOF becomes True and there is no current row.
- If you use MoveNext again, EOF stays True but a runtime error (3021) occurs.

Testing for an Empty Recordset

Often when you create a recordset, you want to know immediately whether that recordset actually contains any rows. It's quite possible to create a recordset that doesn't return any rows, and you might need to take different steps based on whether the result contained any rows.

You can test for an empty recordset in a number of ways, but the two methods that follow ought to serve your needs. The following expression:

```
rst.Open "qryCust", CurrentProject.Connection
If Not rst.BOF And Not rst.EOF Then
    ' You'll only be in here if there are some rows.
End If
```

checks to see whether both the BOF and the EOF properties for the recordset are True. If so, there must *not* be any rows because that's the only way the current position could be at both the beginning and the end of the recordset. In addition, you often will want to loop through the rows of your recordset. In that case, you needn't check; just write the loop so that it won't start if there are no rows:

```
rst.Open "qryCust", CurrentProject.Connection
Do Until rst.EOF
    ' Process rows in here
Loop
```

You can also check the RecordCount property of a recordset: if it's 0, you know there aren't any records in the recordset. For example, you might use code like this:

```
rst.Open "qryCust", CurrentProject.Connection
If rst.RecordCount > 0 Then
    ' You'll only be in here if there are some rows.
End If
```

You may find this technique easier to use. However, this technique will not work on all recordsets, due to the behavior of the RecordCount property. For example, it will fail on forward-only recordsets, where the RecordCount is –1. We recommend that you use the first technique, rather than relying on the RecordCount property.

Looping through All the Rows

Although you're likely to have less reason than you'd think to loop through all the rows of a recordset (that's what action queries are for), the syntax is quite simple. The code in Listing 6.12 walks through a recordset backwards, from the end to the beginning and, if there are any records to be had, prints out one of the fields in the underlying data. (Look for ListNames in basRecordset.)

Listing 6.12

```
Public Sub ListNames()
    Dim rst As ADODB.Recordset

    Set rst = New ADODB.Recordset
    With rst
        Set .ActiveConnection = CurrentProject.Connection
        .CursorType = adOpenKeyset
        .Open "tblCustomers", Options:=adCmdTableDirect
        If .RecordCount > 0 Then
            ' Move to the end
            .MoveLast
            ' Loop back towards the beginning
            Do Until .BOF
                Debug.Print .Fields("ContactName")
                .MovePrevious
            Loop
        End If
```

```
        .Close
    End With
    Set rst = Nothing
End Sub
```

Using Arrays to Hold Recordset Data

You can use the GetRows method of any recordset to copy its data into a Variant variable. Access will create a two-dimensional array with enough space to hold the data:

```
varData = rst.GetRows(intRowsToGrab, varStart, astrFields)
```

You don't have to set the size of the array; Access will do that for you. Because arrays give you random access to any row or column within the array, you may find it more convenient to work with arrays than with the recordset itself. For example, if you want the fastest access to data that you don't need to write to, you might want to use a forward-only recordset. But using this type of recordset limits your movement in the data. If you create a forward-only recordset and copy its data to an array, you've got the best of both worlds: fast access *and* random access.

The GetRows method takes three parameters, all optional. The first indicates the number of rows to move to the array; it defaults to moving all rows. The second is a bookmark indicating the record to start with; the default is to start with the current record. The third is an array of field names or ordinal positions indicating which fields in the recordset should be copied to the array. If you don't specify this parameter, you'll get all the fields.

If you ask for more rows than exist, ADO returns as many as there are. Use the UBound function to find out how many rows were actually returned:

```
intRows = UBound(varData, 2) + 1
```

The ", 2" tells UBound to find the number of rows (the second dimension of the array); then you must add 1 to the result because the array is zero-based.

TIP

Be careful when creating your recordset before calling the GetRows method. Because Access will copy all the columns, including memos and long binary fields, you may want to exclude large fields from the recordset before you create the array; they can consume large amounts of memory and can be slow to load. You can also use the Fields parameter to specify exactly which fields to copy to the array.

The code in Listing 6.13 (from basRecordset) fills an array with data and then prints it out, in reverse order.

Listing 6.13

```
Public Sub TryGetRecords()
    ' Use an array to process data in a recordset

    Dim rst As ADODB.Recordset
    Dim varData As Variant
    Dim intCount As Integer
    Dim intI As Integer

    Set rst = New ADODB.Recordset
    ' Note that we can't move backwards through
    ' this recordset.
    Set rst.ActiveConnection = CurrentProject.Connection
    rst.CursorType = adOpenForwardOnly
    rst.LockType = adLockReadOnly
    rst.Open "tblCustomers"

    ' Get all the rows, but only the CompanyName
    ' and ContactName fields.
    varData = rst.GetRows( _
     Fields:=Array("CompanyName", "ContactName"))
    rst.Close
    Set rst = Nothing

    ' How many rows did it actually send back?
    intCount = UBound(varData, 2) + 1
    ' Loop through all the rows, printing out the
    ' data
    For intI = intCount - 1 To 0 Step -1
        Debug.Print varData(0, intI), varData(1, intI)
    Next intI
End Sub
```

TIP

Another way to enable movement in reverse, when you have an OLE DB provider that only supplies forward-only recordsets, is to set the CursorLocation property of the recordset to adUseClient. As we discussed earlier in the chapter, this technique is most useful with providers other than Jet.

Creating a Recordset Based on a Command Object

If you need to create a recordset based on any select query (about which you might know nothing at all until your program is running), you must be prepared to supply the recordset with all the parameters the query requires. Without ADO, doing so requires knowing in advance what the parameters are and supplying their values in your code. Using ADO, you can loop through all the parameters of your query and evaluate the necessary parameters. Command objects provide a useful Parameters collection, each element of which represents a single query parameter.

When you open a form based on a query that requires parameters, Access does the work of resolving all the parameter values for you. When you do the same thing in code, however, Access cannot fill in the parameter values for you, even if the parameter values are available to Access. It's up to you to supply those values for the Command object before you attempt to create the recordset.

TIP

Your query won't be able to run at all unless all the necessary parameter values are available. If your query uses form objects as parameters, for example, you need to make sure the appropriate form is open and running, with appropriate values filled in, before you attempt to run a query based on those parameters.

Code like that shown in Listing 6.14 (from basRecordset) will work with any Command object that represents a select query, as long as its parameters pull their values from controls on forms and the necessary forms are open when you run this code.

Listing 6.14

```
Public Sub DemoParameters()

    ' Done without using ADOX
    Dim cmd As ADODB.Command
    Dim rst As ADODB.Recordset
    Dim prm As ADODB.Parameter

    ' Before running this procedure, open
    ' frmInfo and enter a value, like "Berlin",
    ' into the City text box, then tab off
    ' of the text box.
    ' You must move the focus out of the
    ' City text box in order for this to work.
```

```
    Set cmd = New ADODB.Command
    Set cmd.ActiveConnection = _
       CurrentProject.Connection
    cmd.CommandText = "qryCustCity"
    ' If you use adCmdStoredProc,
    ' this won't work.
    cmd.CommandType = adCmdTable

    ' This next statement is actually optional.
    ' If you leave it out, ADO does it anyway.
    cmd.Parameters.Refresh
    ' Loop through the parameters
    For Each prm In cmd.Parameters
       prm.Value = Eval(prm.Name)
    Next prm

    ' And populate the recordset
    Set rst = cmd.Execute
    Do Until rst.EOF
       Debug.Print rst.Fields(0).Value
       rst.MoveNext
    Loop
    rst.Close
    Set rst = Nothing
    Set cmd = Nothing
End Sub
```

The code loops through all the parameters of the object (and there may be none, in which case the loop won't ever execute), pointing a Parameter variable at each of the parameters for the command, one at a time. For each parameter, the code evaluates the Name property using the Eval function and assigns the return value to the Value property of the parameter. This retrieves the value of each parameter without your having to know in advance where the parameter is getting its value.

For example, if your query has a single parameter on the City field:

```
Forms!frmInfo!CityField
```

the command contains a single parameter object, for which the Name property is Forms!frmInfo!CityField. Through the use of the Eval function, the code in the example retrieves the value stored in that field and assigns it to the *Value* property of the specific parameter object. This satisfies the needs of the Command object, and you'll be able to create the recordset you need, based on that Command. The Incremental Search example in Chapter 7 uses this mechanism to allow the underlying code to create a recordset on almost any select query, whether or not it requires parameter values

Finding Specific Records

You handle the task of finding specific data in a recordset in different ways, depending on the type of the recordset. Recordsets using the adCmdTableDirect option can use an indexed search to find data, but other recordsets cannot.

Finding Data in a Direct Table Recordset

If you've created a direct table access recordset object, you can use the fast Seek method to locate specific rows. (Attempting to use the Seek method with any other recordset results in a runtime error.) You must take two specific steps to use the Seek method to find data:

1. Set the recordset's Index property. This tells Access through which index you'd like it to search. If you want to use the primary key for searching, you must know the name of the primary key. (It's usually PrimaryKey, unless your application has changed it.)
2. Use the Seek method to find the value you want, given a seek option and one or more values to search for. The search operator must be one of the intrinsic constants shown in Table 6.10. To indicate to Access what it needs to find, you supply one or more values corresponding to the keys in the index you selected. If you based your index on one field, you need to supply only one value here. If you want to seek using an index that includes multiple columns, you can seek on just the first column using a single value. To seek on multiple columns, supply the values as an array (perhaps using the Array function to create the array).

WARNING

Seek only works with recordsets whose CursorLocation property is set to something besides adUseClient. Because adUseServer is the default cursor location, this isn't normally a problem, but be aware that this won't work for client-side cursors.

TABLE 6.10: Seek Options

Seek Option	Meaning
adSeekAfterEq	Seek the key equal to the value supplied, or if there is no such key, the first key after the point where the match would have occurred
adSeekAfter	Seek the first key after the point where a match occurs or would occur
adSeekBeforeEq	Seek the key equal to the value supplied, or if there is no such key, the first key before the point where the match would have occurred
adSeekBefore	Seek the first key before the point where a match occurs or would occur
adSeekFirstEq	Seek the first key equal to the value supplied
adSeekLastEq	Seek the last key equal to the value supplied

If you want to seek using an index that includes multiple columns, you can seek on just the first column using a single value. To seek on multiple columns, supply the values as an array (perhaps using the Array function to create the array).

For example, if your database contained an index named PrimaryKey (the default name that Access assigns to primary key indexes), and you wanted to find the first customer with a primary key value greater than or equal to "BBBBB", the following fragment could get you to the correct row:

```
rst.Index = "PrimaryKey"
rst.Seek "BBBBB", adSeekAfterEq
```

The values you send to the Seek method must match the data types of the values in the index. In this case, the value is a string. Had it been numeric or a date, you would have needed to use matching data types in the call to the Seek method.

Once you've used the Seek method to find a row, you must, *without fail,* use the recordset's EOF property to check that you actually found a row. The following code expands on the previous fragment, handling the success or failure of the seek (see SeekExample in basRecordset for the full procedure):

```
Set rst.ActiveConnection = CurrentProject.Connection
rst.CursorType = adOpenKeyset
rst.LockType = adLockOptimistic
rst.Open "tblCustomers", Options:=adCmdTableDirect
rst.Index = "PrimaryKey"
rst.Seek "BBBBB", adSeekAfterEq
```

```
If rst.EOF Then
    MsgBox "Unable to find a match!"
Else
    MsgBox "The customer name is: " & rst("CompanyName")
End If
```

TIP

The Seek method always starts at the beginning of the recordset when it searches. Therefore, using Seek inside a loop, searching for subsequent rows that match the criteria, is generally fruitless. Unless you modify the value once you find it so that further searches no longer find a match on that row, your loop will continually find the same row.

Finding Data Using the Find Method

Most recordsets cannot use the Seek method for finding data. Because these recordsets might well be based on ordered subsets of the original data or supplied by providers that don't support indexed recordsets, ADO can't always use an index to speed up the search. Therefore, a search involving a recordset might be a linear search, visiting every row in the recordset until it finds a match. ADO will use an index if it can.

On a bright note, however, ADO provides greater flexibility in general recordset searches than it does when using the Seek method. The flexibility of the Find method allows you to optimize the search so it has to look through the smallest number of rows to find the data it needs. Because you can use Find to continue searching with the record following the previous match, you won't need to start back at the beginning of the recordset to find subsequent matches. In addition, you can use loops to walk your way through the records because you can restart the search without going back to the first row.

WARNING

If you're moving to ADO from DAO, you'll notice the absence of all the various Find methods: FindFirst, FindNext, FindPrevious, and FindLast. These are all rolled up into the single Find method, but replacing all those methods requires careful use of the Find method's parameters. Specifically, the SearchDirection and Start parameters indicate in which direction to search and where to start.

If Find succeeds, the found row will be the current row. If it fails, the recordset's EOF property is true—that is, you're moved to the end of the recordset.

The syntax for the Find method is:

Recordset.Find *criteria, SkipRows, SearchDirection, Start*

All but the first parameter are optional. The four possible parameters are:

- *Criteria* is a WHERE clause formatted as though in a SQL expression, without the word *WHERE.* For example, "OrderId = 5". This can only consist of a single field name, a comparison operator, and a value. Find does not handle complex WHERE clause values. String literals must be surrounded with single quotes, and dates must be surrounded with "#" characters. You can also use the Like operator, with the wildcard character "*".
- *SkipRows* specifies the offset from the current row where the search should begin. It defaults to starting with the current row.
- *SearchDirection* can be adSearchForward (the default) or adSearchBackward.
- *Start* is an optional bookmark where the search should begin. The default is to begin with the current row. (See the section "Using Bookmarks" later in the chapter for more information.)

For example, the following fragment searches for a contact title of "Owner," looking forward from the current row.

```
rst.Find "ContactTitle = 'Owner'"
```

Just as with the Seek method, you must follow every call to a Find method with a check of the recordset's EOF property (or BOF property, if SearchDirection is adSearchBackward). If that property is True, there is no current row, and the search has failed. Often, when performing some operation that requires looping through all the rows that match some criteria, you can use code like that in Listing 6.15 (from basRecordset).

Listing 6.15

```
Public Sub FindExample()
    Dim rst As ADODB.Recordset
    Dim strCriteria As String

    Set rst = New ADODB.Recordset
    strCriteria = "ContactTitle = 'Owner'"

    rst.Open "tblCustomers", CurrentProject.Connection, _
```

```
        adOpenKeyset, adLockOptimistic, adCmdTable
    With rst
        .Find strCriteria
        Do While Not .EOF
            ' There's a matching row,
            ' do something with it
            Debug.Print .Fields("CompanyName")
            ' Skip the current record
            ' and continue searching
            .Find strCriteria, 1
        Loop
    End With
    rst.Close
    Set rst = Nothing
End Sub
```

Of course, many such loops can be replaced with action queries, which are almost always a better solution to the given programming problem.

WARNING

Find criteria treat Null differently from the way that Access does. Because the ADO Find method does not understand the IsNull() function, the correct way to search for a Null using the Find method is with an expression such as "FieldName = Null" or "FieldName <> Null." This goes against all normal Access handling of Null (where Null doesn't equal anything, not even itself), but it's the only way to make Find work with Null values.

Using Variables in Strings

In building criteria for Find methods and in several other places in VBA (when calling domain functions and when creating SQL strings, for example), you often need to embed variable values into a string. Because ADO (and Jet, for that matter) has no way of finding the value of VBA variables, you need to supply their values before you ask it to do any work for you. This can cause trouble, because Access requires delimiters (quotes for strings, # for dates) around those values, but they aren't part of the variables themselves. This causes many Access developers, experts and neophytes alike, a great deal of anguish.

Numeric values require no delimiters at all, and you can simply represent a string variable using an expression like this:

```
"[NumericField] = " & intNumber
```

Date variables need to be delimited with # in an expression. The general solution for the date problem would be

```
"[DateField] = #" & varDate & "#"
```

That's not so bad!

The difficulty arises when you attempt to embed a variable containing a string value inside a string. For example, imagine you have a variable named strName that contains the name you'd like to match in your call to the Find method (for the sake of simplicity here, "Smith"). You need to build a string that represents the required WHERE clause:

```
[LastName] = 'Smith'
```

As a first attempt, you might try this:

```
strCriteria = "[LastName] = strName"
```

When you attempt to run the search, Access complains with a runtime error. The problem is that the expression in strCriteria was this:

```
[LastName] = strName
```

Most likely, no one in your table has that particular last name.

As a second attempt, you might try a new approach:

```
strCriteria = "[LastName] = " & strName
```

When you attempt to run the search this time, Access again complains with a runtime error. In this case, it was using the value

```
[LastName] = Smith
```

which won't work because ADO expects string values to be enclosed in apostrophes.

It should be clear by now that you need to get the apostrophes into that string. ADO provides a solution to this problem.

All the solutions need to arrive at a value for strCriteria that looks like this:

```
[LastName] = 'Smith'
```

WARNING

With the old DAO FindFirst method, you had several other alternatives to solving this problem, based on the fact that DAO would accept double-quote characters to delimit a string in a FindFirst criterion. However, ADO requires single quotes in this context.

The solution involves including the apostrophes in the string. You can think of this as a three-step process:

```
[LastName] = 'Smith'
```

becomes the string

```
"[LastName] = 'Smith'"
```

which can be broken up into several strings

```
"[LastName] = '" & "Smith" & "'"
```

which becomes (finally)

```
"[LastName] = '" & strName & "'"
```

The main problem with this solution (which many developers use) is that the value stored in strName cannot contain an apostrophe. If it did, you'd end up with an apostrophe embedded within a string that's enclosed in apostrophes. That's not allowed in ADO syntax. Therefore, you can use this method only when strName contains a value that could never contain an apostrophe.

A General Solution for Strings (Well, Almost)

So what can you do when your string contains an apostrophe? As you've just seen, this won't work:

```
strCriteria = "[CompanyName] = '" & strName & "'"
```

because the string might contain an apostrophe, too.

It turns out that embedded apostrophes are not really a problem. Because ADO interprets two apostrophes inside a string as a single apostrophe, and VBA accepts this as well, you can just double the delimiter to "escape" it and turn it into a single delimiter within the string. In this case, you can modify strName by doubling any apostrophes in it.

To do this, you'll need a function that accepts a string value and the delimiter character as parameters and returns the string with any occurrences of the delimiter inside it "doubled up." You'll find that function, adhHandleQuotes, in basHandleQuotes in CH06.MDB. It can solve the previous problem:

```
strCriteria = "[CompanyName] = " & _
 adhHandleQuotes(strName, "'")
```

The adhHandleQuotes function looks for all the delimiter characters inside strName, doubles them, and returns the string, surrounded with the delimiter character. If you're interested in seeing how adhHandleQuotes works, look in basHandleQuotes; the code uses simple string manipulations. If you want to use this technique in your own applications, just import the basHandleQuotes module and call adhHandleQuotes yourself.

Unfortunately, this still isn't the end of the story. Although ADO allows doubling an apostrophe to escape it within a string, it only allows this *once per string*. So, you can't use the adhHandleQuotes function to manage a search for a company with this name:

```
StrName = "Ed's And Mary's Cafe'"
```

There's a solution to this problem, too. Although it's undocumented, you can use # as a character to quote a string that has multiple apostrophes embedded in it. In this case, you can build your criteria string like this:

```
strCriteria = "[CompanyName] = " & _
  "#" & strName & "#"
```

So, does that solve the general problem? No! Apparently no one at Microsoft considered the problem of strings containing both multiple apostrophes and pound signs. It's unlikely that this will be your search string

```
StrName = "Joe's #9 Winner's Grill"
```

but if it is, give up. You can't quote that string with apostrophes, because it has two apostrophes in it. You can't quote it with pound signs because it has a pound sign in it. If you need to be able to handle absolutely any search string, your best bet may be to use the undocumented pound-sign quoting and just hope that you don't get a string containing pound signs to search for.

To test out all these options, try out the FindWithVariables procedure (from basRecordset), shown in Listing 6.16.

Listing 6.16

```
Public Sub FindWithVariables()
    Dim rst As ADODB.Recordset
    Dim strCriteria As String
    Dim strName As String

    Set rst = New ADODB.Recordset
    strName = "Alfreds Futterkiste"

    ' This will give error 3001:
    ' strCriteria = "[CompanyName] = strName"
    ' So will this:
    ' strCriteria = "[CompanyName] = " & strName
    ' This worked in DAO, but doesn't in ADO, because ADO
    ' doesn't allow double-quotes for quoting
    ' strCriteria = "[CompanyName] =""" & strName & """"
    ' This works -- unless your string contains
    ' an apostrophe!
    strCriteria = "[CompanyName]='" & strName & "'"

    rst.Open "tblCustomers", CurrentProject.Connection, _
     adOpenKeyset, adLockOptimistic, adCmdTable
    rst.Find strCriteria
    If Not rst.EOF Then
        Debug.Print rst.Fields("CustomerID")
    End If

    ' Now let's try an apostrophe:
    strName = "La corne d'abondance"

    ' The previous solution gives error 3001 again,
    ' because of the embedded apostrophe
    ' strCriteria = "[CompanyName]='" & strName & "'"
    ' But we can double the embedded apostrophe:
    strCriteria = "[CompanyName]=" & _
     adhHandleQuotes(strName)
```

```
    rst.Find strCriteria
    If Not rst.EOF Then
        Debug.Print rst.Fields("CustomerID")
    End If

    ' What about two apostrophes?
    strName = "Joe's and Ed's Grocery"

    ' This gives error 3001...ADO only understands
    ' ONE doubled apostrophe
    strCriteria = "[CompanyName]=" & adhHandleQuotes(strName)
    rst.Find strCriteria

    ' This is undocumented, but it works:
    strCriteria = "[CompanyName]=#" & strName & "#"

    rst.Find strCriteria
    If Not rst.EOF Then
        Debug.Print rst.Fields("CustomerID")
    End If

    ' But what about this one...
    strCriteria = "Joe's #9 Winner's Grill"
    ' You're sunk! There's no way to delimit this variable
    ' so that ADO can find it. More than one apostrophe, or
    ' any "#" within the string makes it impossible
    ' for ADO to find this string.
    rst.Close
    Set rst = Nothing
End Sub
```

Using Bookmarks

One of the primary functions needed in any database product is the ability to move quickly to a specified row. ADO provides a number of ways to move about in recordsets, as seen in the section "Moving through a Recordset" earlier in this chapter. In addition to the methods presented there, ADO provides the Bookmark property, which allows you to quickly preserve and restore the current location within a recordset.

What Is a Bookmark?

Every active recordset maintains a single current row. To retrieve a reference to that row, you can store the Bookmark property of the recordset, representing the current row, into a Variant variable. The bookmark itself is a 4-byte–Long integer, the exact value of which is of no particular importance to you. ADO uses the value, but you won't ever look at, or care about, the particular value. You can perform three basic operations with bookmarks:

- Retrieve the value of the bookmark, in order to store it for later retrieval
- Set the value of the bookmark to a previously stored value, effectively setting the current row to be the row where you were when you originally saved the bookmark
- Compare two bookmarks, in order to determine their relative positions within the recordset

You can retrieve and store as many bookmarks for a given recordset as you wish to maintain, but at any given moment, the recordset's Bookmark property always represents the current row. Manipulating bookmarks in ADO is the fastest way to maneuver through rows. For example, if you need to move from the current row and then move back to it, you can use one of two methods:

- Store the primary key value: Move from the row and use the Seek or Find method to move back to the original row, using the saved primary key value to find the row.
- Store the bookmark: Move from the row and then use the bookmark to move back to the original row.

The second method, using the bookmark, is generally much faster than the first. The code to do this might look something like the following example:

```
Dim varBookmark as Variant

varBookmark = rst.Bookmark
' Move to the first row.
rst.MoveFirst
'
' Now do whatever you moved from the current row to do.
'
' Then move back to the original row.
rst.Bookmark = varBookmark
```

NOTE

You might wonder why a bookmark must be stored in a Variant and not a Long integer. A bookmark really is a Long integer, but it's a special kind of Long integer: an *unsigned* Long integer. That is, the value of a bookmark can vary between 0 and 4294967295. VBA's Long integer values are always signed and can store values between -2,147,483,648 and 2,147,483,647. As you can see, attempting to store a bookmark value in a Long integer type would sometimes fail. Storing the value in a Variant, however, avoids this problem.

Bookmarks and Record Numbers

If you're moving to Access from an Xbase environment, you might be tempted to think of bookmarks as a replacement for record numbers. In reality, that's not the case. Because Access is set-based, row numbers really have no validity here. Access neither stores nor maintains a record number in its data, and you can't count on a bookmark to act as a permanent locator for any given row. Once you close a recordset, the bookmark value is no longer valid. In addition, you cannot use bookmarks as locators across different recordsets, even though the recordsets might be based on the same data and might contain the same rows in the same order. On the other hand, as stated in the preceding section, bookmarks provide an excellent means of moving about in an open recordset.

To Bookmark or Not to Bookmark

Not all ADO recordsets support the Bookmark property. Some data sources make it impossible for ADO to maintain bookmarks, so it is your responsibility as a developer to check whether a recordset supports bookmarks before attempting to use bookmarks with that recordset. To do this, you can use the Supports method, discussed earlier in this chapter.

Also, be aware that there is no valid bookmark when you've positioned the current row to be the "new" row in a recordset. That is, the following code (from basRecordset) will trigger runtime error -2147217887, "Errors occurred":

```
Public Sub BookmarkError()
    Dim rst As ADODB.Recordset
    Dim varBookmark As Variant

    Set rst = New ADODB.Recordset
    rst.Open "tblCustomers", _
     CurrentProject.Connection, _
     adOpenKeyset, adLockOptimistic
```

```
    rst.AddNew
    varBookmark = rst.Bookmark
    rst.Close
    Set rst = Nothing
End Sub
```

NOTE

Many ADO error conditions raise the all-purpose "Errors occurred" error. Good luck figuring out what this means. We haven't found any way to determine the actual error when we get this error value.

Comparing Bookmarks

You may occasionally want to know the relative position of one bookmarked record in relation to another bookmarked record. Because bookmarks are, as far as we're concerned, arbitrary values, you cannot reliably use standard comparison operators for this task. Instead, ADO supplies a CompareBookmarks method of a Recordset object. Given two bookmarks stored away for rows in the same recordset, the CompareBookmarks method returns one of the following values:

adCompareLessThan The first bookmark is before the second.

adCompareEqual The bookmarks are equal.

adCompareGreaterThan The first bookmark is after the second.

adCompareNotEqual The bookmarks are not equal and not ordered.

adCompareNotComparable The bookmarks cannot be compared.

You might use the CompareBookmarks method like this:

```
Select Case rst.CompareBookmarks(varBM1, varBM2)
    Case adCompareLessThan
        ' The first row is earlier than the second
    Case adCompareEqual
        ' Both bookmarks point to the same record
    Case adCompareGreaterThan
        ' The second row is earlier than the first
    Case adCompareNotEqual
        ' The records are not the same
    Case adCompareNotComparable
        ' The bookmarks are not from the same recordset
End Select
```

The Clone Method

Every open recordset supports only a single current row. For bookmarkable recordsets, you can use the Bookmark property to set and retrieve a value corresponding to that current row. If you need to refer to the same recordset in two different ways with two different current rows, you can use the Clone method to create a clone of a recordset. (To retrieve a clone of a form's recordset, use either the form's RecordsetClone or Recordset property instead of the Clone method. See Chapter 8 for more information.) With a clone of the original recordset, you can effectively maintain two separate current rows. This way, you can compare the values in two of the rows in the recordset, for example.

You might be tempted to ask, "Why use the Clone method instead of just creating a new recordset based on the same source?" The answer is clear: creating a recordset clone is faster, in most cases, than creating a new Recordset object. When the source of the data is a query, the difference can be measurable. Rather than reexecuting the entire query to produce the new recordset, the Clone method just points a separate object variable at the original set of rows. This effectively gives you two current rows and two bookmarks, based on the same data. You can also assign the bookmark from one recordset to its clone, because they really are the same recordset.

Be aware of these issues:

- You can only clone a recordset that supports bookmarks.
- A recordset created with the Clone method has its first record as the current record.
- To set a specific row as the current row, use any of the Find or Move methods (Find, MoveFirst, and so on) or set the recordset's Bookmark property with a value retrieved from the original recordset. Remember that bookmark assignments work only when applied to identical recordsets (as are the original and its clone).
- Using the Close method on either the original recordset or its clone doesn't affect the other recordset.
- Changes you make to one clone are immediately reflected in all other clones of the same recordset. However, if you execute the Requery method on a recordset, it will no longer be synchronized with its clones.

The Clone method takes one optional parameter, which indicates the type of locking you desire for the new recordset:

```
Set rstNew = rstOriginal.Clone(LockType)
```

The LockType parameter can be one of two intrinsic constants:

- adLockUnspecified, the default, means that the clone inherits the locking behavior of the original recordset.
- adLockReadOnly creates the clone as read-only, regardless of the original recordset's locking.

Sorting Recordsets

When using recordsets as part of your applications, you'll often need to present the rows in a specific order. ADO treats direct table recordsets differently from other recordsets. For all objects, however, remember that if you want a particular sort order, you must specify it yourself.

Sorting Direct Table Recordsets

For table-type recordsets, you can specify the ordering by setting the Index property. (Access does not allow you to set the Index property of any other type of recordset. Attempting to do so will only get you runtime error 3251, "The operation requested by the application is not supported by the provider.") As soon as you set that property, the rows appear in their new ordering.

Listing 6.17 shows a function that lists the fields in the index, in index order, for each index in a specified table. ListIndexFields does its work by looping through the ADOX Table object's collection of indexes. For each index in the collection, it gathers up the index name and the column names and uses them to set the index and print out the value of each field for each row in the recordset. To test ListIndexFields, you might want to create a table with just a few rows and create an index for a few of the columns. Then, in the Immediate window, enter:

```
? ListIndexFields("YourTableName")
```

replacing *YourTableName* with the name of your table. This should show all the indexes in your table, with the first indexed field in indexed order. (Look for ListIndexFields in basRecordset in CH06.MDB.)

Listing 6.17

```
Public Sub ListIndexFields( _
 strTableName As String)
    Dim rst As ADODB.Recordset
    Dim cat As ADOX.Catalog
    Dim idx As ADOX.Index
    Dim tbl As ADOX.Table
    Dim col As ADOX.Column
    Dim strField As String

    Set rst = New ADODB.Recordset
    Set cat = New ADOX.Catalog

    cat.ActiveConnection = CurrentProject.Connection
    Set tbl = cat.Tables(strTableName)
    rst.Open strTableName, _
     CurrentProject.Connection, adOpenKeyset, _
     adLockOptimistic, adCmdTableDirect

    ' List values for each index in the collection
    For Each idx In tbl.Indexes
        ' Set the index to use in the recordset
        rst.Index = idx.Name
        ' The index object contains a collection of columns,
        ' one for each column the index contains
        Debug.Print
        Debug.Print "Index: " & rst.Index
        Debug.Print "=============================="
        ' Move through the whole recordset, in index order,
        ' printing out the index fields, separated with tabs
        rst.MoveFirst
        Do While Not rst.EOF
            For Each col In idx.Columns
                strField = strField & vbTab & rst(col.Name)
            Next col
            If Len(strField) > 0 Then
                strField = Mid$(strField, 2)
            End If
            Debug.Print strField
            strField = ""
            rst.MoveNext
```

```
        Loop
    Next idx
    rst.Close
    Set tbl = Nothing
    Set rst = Nothing
    Set cat = Nothing
End Sub
```

Sorting Other Recordsets

Just as with direct table recordsets, unless you specify a sorting order for other recordsets, the rows will show up in an indeterminate order. The natural order for these derived recordsets is a bit more complex because it might depend on more than one table and on the OLE DB provider that's supplying the original data. In any case, if you need a specific ordering, you must set up that ordering yourself.

To create sorted recordsets, you have two choices, described in the next two sections.

Using a SQL ORDER BY Clause

You can create a Recordset object using a SQL statement including an ORDER BY clause. To do so, specify the SQL expression as the row source for the recordset's Open method. For example, the procedure in Listing 6.18 (from basRecordset) creates a recordset based on tblCustomers, including all the columns, sorted by the ContactName column:

Listing 6.18

```
Public Sub TestOrderBy()
    Dim rstSorted As ADODB.Recordset

    Set rstSorted = New ADODB.Recordset

    rstSorted.Open _
     "SELECT * FROM tblCustomers ORDER BY [ContactName];", _
     CurrentProject.Connection
    Do Until rstSorted.EOF
        Debug.Print rstSorted("ContactName")
        rstSorted.MoveNext
    Loop
```

```
    rstSorted.Close
    Set rstSorted = Nothing
End Sub
```

Using the Sort Property

You can also set the Sort property of any recordset to change its sort order. The Sort property must be a string in the same style as the ORDER BY clause of a SQL expression (that is, a comma-separated list of field names, optionally with ASC or DESC to indicate ascending or descending sorts). You must specify the column on which to sort and, optionally, the ordering. The following fragments show how to set the Sort property:

```
rst.Sort = "LastName"        ' Defaults to ascending
rst.Sort = "LastName ASC"    ' Ascending sort
rst.Sort = "LastName DESC"   ' Descending sort
' Sort on two fields, LastName in ascending order, and
' FirstName in descending order.
rst.Sort = "LastName ASC, FirstName DESC"
```

Here are some items to remember when using the Sort property:

- The new sort order takes effect immediately when you change the property.
- Because the Jet provider doesn't support the necessary OLE DB interfaces for sorting, you must set the CursorLocation property of the recordset to adUseClient in order to use the Sort property. This isn't necessarily true for other providers, but it does limit the usefulness of this property for Jet recordsets.
- It might be faster to open a new recordset based on a SQL expression than to use the Sort property.

The procedure in Listing 6.19, from basRecordset, opens a recordset and sorts it in two different ways, printing out the primary key value from the first row each time.

Listing 6.19

```
Public Sub TestSort()
    Dim rst As ADODB.Recordset

    Set rst = New ADODB.Recordset
```

```
    ' MUST use client-side cursors for sorting, for Jet.
    ' SQL Server supports the Sort method on server-side
    ' cursors, as well.
    rst.CursorLocation = adUseClient
    rst.Open "tblCustomers", _
     CurrentProject.Connection, adOpenKeyset, _
     adLockOptimistic
    ' You'll see different CustomerID values,
    ' because the sort order will have changed.
    rst.Sort = "CompanyName"
    Debug.Print rst("CustomerID")
    rst.Sort = "City"
    Debug.Print rst("CustomerID")
    rst.Close
    Set rst = Nothing
End Sub
```

Filtering Recordsets

Just as with sorting a recordset, you have two choices if you want to create a filtered subset of rows. These choices are outlined in the next two sections. You'll need to decide which method to use based on the circumstances of your application.

Using a SQL WHERE Clause

You can create a recordset by using a SQL statement including a WHERE clause. To do so, specify the SQL expression as the row source for the recordset's Open method. For example, this fragment:

```
rstFiltered.Open _
 "SELECT * FROM tblCustomers WHERE [ZipCode] = '90210'"), _
 CurrentProject.Connection
```

creates a recordset based on all the columns in tblCustomers, including only the rows where the ZipCode field is "90210".

Using the Filter Property

You can also set the Filter property of any recordset to change the set of rows it contains. The Filter property must be a string in the same style as the WHERE clause of a SQL expression. The filtering takes effect immediately. For example, you generally use the Filter property like this:

```
' rst is an existing recordset.
rst.Filter = "[Age] > 35"
' Now rst contains all the rows from rst that
' have an [Age] field greater than 35.
```

Here are some items to remember when using the Filter property:

- The new filtering takes effect immediately.
- It might be faster to open a new recordset based on a SQL expression than to use the Filter property.
- All the issues described in the section "Using Variables with Strings" apply here, because you're likely to want to build your filter string programmatically from variables.
- The new filtering will never retrieve additional rows from the original source tables. It will filter only rows that are already in the recordset.

In addition to a WHERE clause, you can use two other types of information for a filter:

- You can supply an array of bookmarks that are valid in the current recordset to filter the recordset to show only those records.
- You can supply one of the intrinsic constants listed in Table 6.11.

For example, to remove any existing filter from a recordset you can use this code fragment:

```
rst.Filter = adFilterNone
```

TABLE 6.11: Filter Constants

Constant	Meaning
adFilterNone	Remove any existing filter, showing all records in the original recordset.
adFilterPendingRecords	Filter the recordset to contain only records that have been changed but not yet saved.
adFilterAffectedRecords	Filter the recordset to contain only records that were affected by the last Delete, Resync, UpdateBatch, or CancelBatch method.

Continued on next page

TABLE 6.11 CONTINUED: Filter Constants

Constant	Meaning
adFilterFetchedRecords	Filter the recordset to only show the records most recently fetched to the local cache.
adFilterConflictingRecords	Filter the recordset to contain only the records that failed to commit during a batch update operation.

Refreshing Recordsets

Most ADO recordsets you create will only contain your own changes to the data in the recordset. But because Access is a multiuser database and other users can add, edit, and delete records, your copy of a recordset can get increasingly out of synch with what's actually stored in the database. ADO provides two methods to allow you to update your recordset to match what's actually in the database: Requery and Resync.

The Requery method is roughly the equivalent of calling the recordset's Close method and then calling its Open method again with the original arguments. This method causes the underlying OLE DB provider to carry out the steps that it originally used to retrieve the data all over again. Note that if you need to change any of the properties that govern the behavior of the recordset (CursorLocation, CursorType, or LockType), you can't use the Requery method. Instead, you'll need to explicitly close the recordset, change the properties, and then call the Open method to repopulate the recordset.

The Resync method resynchronizes the records in your recordset with the underlying database. Thus, calling the Resync method on a recordset won't show you records added by other users. It will, however, pick up any changes other users have made and make any deleted records invalid in your recordset. Because it doesn't have to execute the original query all over again, Resync is faster than Requery.

WARNING Not all recordsets support the Resync method. You may want to call the Supports method (see the section "The Supports Method" earlier in this chapter for more information) using the adResync constant to verify that this method will work before using it.

Editing Data in a Recordset Object

Of course, almost any database application needs to be able to add, update, and delete data. ADO provides methods for accomplishing each of these tasks. The next few sections discuss the various data-manipulation methods that ADO supports.

When Is a Recordset Modifiable?

When you open a recordset, it may only be possible to retrieve the data for viewing. If so, your attempts to modify the data will result in a runtime trappable error. You can edit direct table recordsets, unless someone else has placed a lock on that table (opened it exclusively or created a recordset based on it with an option that precludes others from changing its data). You can edit other recordsets unless locks have been placed by other users. In addition, join rules may prevent editing of certain fields. Of course, read-only recordsets are never modifiable.

Changing Data in a Recordset

To programmatically change the data in any recordset (assuming the recordset is updatable), take the following steps:

1. Move to the desired row.
2. Make changes.
3. Optionally, use the Update method to save the edits.

Calling the Update method of the recordset is generally not necessary, but we highly recommend that you don't skip this step. If you modify a row and then leave that row, ADO automatically updates the row for you. If you modify a row and then attempt to close the recordset without explicitly updating the row's data, however, ADO will trigger a runtime error. Therefore, we recommend that you always call the Update method. This not only makes your code more explicit (that is, it's obvious from reading the code what it's doing), but it means you needn't worry about whether the row got committed or not, before you attempt to close the recordset.

If ADO automatically commits a row when you leave that row, how can you leave a row and discard the changes? To do that, call the recordset's CancelUpdate method. This method tosses out any changes you've made to the current row.

The code in Listing 6.20 (from basRecordset) finds the first row in a recordset in which the ContactTitle field contains "Owner" and changes it to "Manager".

Listing 6.20

```
Public Sub ModifyRow()
    ' Demonstrate how you modify data.

    Dim rst As ADODB.Recordset

    Set rst = New ADODB.Recordset
    Set rst.ActiveConnection = CurrentProject.Connection
    rst.CursorType = adOpenKeyset
    rst.LockType = adLockOptimistic
    rst.Source = "tblCustomers"
    rst.Open Options:=adCmdTable
    With rst
        .Find "[ContactTitle] = 'Owner'"
        If .EOF Then
            MsgBox "No Match was Found!"
        Else
            .Fields("ContactTitle") = "Manager"
            .Update
        End If
    End With
    rst.Close
    Set rst = Nothing
End Sub
```

WARNING

If you're a DAO programmer, note the serious differences between DAO and ADO on the issue of updating data. First of all, DAO requires you to call the Edit method of the recordset before you start making changes. ADO doesn't require this and doesn't even provide an Edit method. In DAO, if you leave a row without calling the Update method of the recordset, your changes are automatically discarded. In ADO, if you leave a row without calling the Update method, your changes are automatically *saved* (unless you call the CancelUpdate method to cancel your updates). These two changes will challenge every Access developer moving code from DAO to ADO. Be wary of these differences!

Batch Updates

If you use the client-side cursor library with a keyset or static cursor, you can also take advantage of ADO's ability to perform batch updates. That is, you can edit multiple records in a database and then send all of the updates to the underlying OLE DB provider to be stored in a single operation. The code in Listing 6.21 (from BulkUpdate in basRecordset) finds all records where the contact title is "Owner," changes the title to "Partner," and then sends all of the changes back to the database in a single operation.

Listing 6.21

```
Public Sub BulkUpdate()
    ' Demonstrate the BatchUpdate method.
    ' Note that this requires both a client-side
    ' cursor, and a LockType property of
    ' adLockBatchOptimistic.
    Dim rst As ADODB.Recordset
    Dim strCriteria As String

    Set rst = New ADODB.Recordset
    strCriteria = "[ContactTitle] = 'Owner'"

    With rst
        Set .ActiveConnection = CurrentProject.Connection
        .Source = "tblCustomers"
        .CursorLocation = adUseClient
        .LockType = adLockBatchOptimistic
        .CursorType = adOpenKeyset
        .Open

        .Find strCriteria
        Do While Not .EOF
            ' There's a matching row,
            ' so change the title
            .Fields("ContactTitle") = "Partner"
            ' Skip past the current record
            ' and continue searching
            .Find strCriteria, 1
        Loop
        ' Commit all the changes
        .UpdateBatch
```

```
    End With
    rst.Close
    Set rst = Nothing
End Sub
```

If any of your changes can't be saved (for example, because another user has deleted the record), a runtime error occurs. In this case, you can use the Filter property with the adFilterAffectedRecords constant to filter the recordset down to only those records that had problems.

Adding New Rows to a Recordset

To programmatically add new rows to a recordset (assuming neither updatability nor security keeps you from doing so), follow these steps:

1. Use the AddNew method to add a new row. All fields will be set to their default values.
2. Fill in fields as needed.
3. Optionally (but suggested), use the Update method to save the new row. If you don't call the Update method but you leave the row, ADO will save it automatically. If you attempt to close the recordset with an update pending but haven't explicitly saved the row, you'll get a runtime error.

NOTE The new record becomes the current row as soon as you call the Update method.

The following example adds a new row to the recordset and fills in a few of the fields. Once it's done, it makes the new row the current row:

```
With rst
    .AddNew
        .Fields("LastName") = "Smith"
        .Fields("FirstName") = "Tommy"
    .Update
End With
```

TIP We like to indent the lines of code between the calls to the AddNew method and the Update method. This makes it clear, when reading code, that you're working with a pending update. This isn't required, but it's a nice touch.

Deleting Data from a Recordset

To delete a row from a recordset, follow these steps:

1. Move to the desired row.
2. Use the Delete method to delete it.

TIP

You don't need to use the Update methods when deleting a row. Once you delete it, it's gone—unless, of course, you wrapped the entire thing in a transaction. In that case, you can roll back the transaction to retrieve the deleted row. (See Chapter 2 in *Access 2000 Developer's Handbook, Volume II* for more information on using transactions.)

TIP

After you delete a record, it's still the current record. The previous row is still the previous row, and the next row is still the next row. Use MoveNext to move to the next row, if that's where you'd like to be. If you attempt to do anything with the row you've just deleted, you'll receive a runtime error.

The code in Listing 6.22 deletes all the rows from a table, although it is not necessarily the best way to solve the problem. In reality, you'd use a Delete query to do the work. To try this function out, check in basRecordset in CH06.MDB.

Listing 6.22

```
Public Sub ZapTable(strTable As String)
    Dim rst As ADODB.Recordset

    Set rst = New ADODB.Recordset
    rst.Open strTable, CurrentProject.Connection, _
     adOpenStatic, adLockOptimistic
    With rst
        If .RecordCount > 0 Then
            .MoveFirst
            Do
                .Delete
                ' Without this MoveNext, ADO would
                ' continually try to delete the
```

```
                    ' same row, the first one.
                    .MoveNext
                Loop Until .EOF
            End If
        End With
        rst.Close
        Set rst = Nothing
    End Sub
```

Persisting Recordsets

In previous data access libraries, recordsets have been completely ephemeral. They existed only when opened in memory, and, if you shut down your application, they were automatically destroyed. ADO adds the ability to persist a recordset to a file on disk. In fact, you can persist a recordset, later reopen it, edit it, reconnect it to the original data source, and save changes.

To persist a recordset to disk for later use, you call its Save method:

```
rst.Save Filename, Format
```

The Filename parameter is the full path and filename to the file that you wish to use to hold the contents of this recordset. The Format parameter can be one of two intrinsic constants:

- **adPersistADTG** (default) saves the recordset in the Microsoft proprietary Advanced Data Tablegram format.
- **adPersistXML** saves the recordset as XML. If you save the recordset in XML format, you can easily use the saved XML file as a data source for another application or control that understands XML (an emerging Internet standard for transferring data).

ADTG files are smaller than XML files, so unless you need the ability to distribute data in XML format, stick to ADTG.

The code in Listing 6.23, from basPersist in CH06.MDB, opens the customers table and then saves the resulting recordset to a disk file in the same folder as the Access database itself.

Listing 6.23

```
Public Sub SaveRecordset()
    Dim rst As ADODB.Recordset
    Dim strFile As String

    Set rst = New ADODB.Recordset

    ' Open the recordset from the database
    rst.Open "tblCustomers", CurrentProject.Connection, _
     adOpenStatic, adLockOptimistic

    ' Construct a file name to use
    strFile = CurrentProject.Path & "\Customers.adtg"

    ' Destroy any existing file
    On Error Resume Next
    Kill strFile
    Err.Clear

    ' Now save the recordset to disk
    rst.Save strFile, adPersistADTG
    ' Close the recordset in memory
    rst.Close
End Sub
```

TIP

Calling the Save method will fail if the specified file already exists. The example procedure deletes the file before it attempts to write out a new one. You may want to do this in your own code, as well.

If you apply a filter to a recordset and then save it, only the filtered rows are saved. If you save a recordset and continue to work with it, updating records, your changes are written to the disk file whenever you call the Update method until you call the recordset's Close method. When the Save method is invoked, the current record is reset to the first record in the recordset.

Although the Jet OLE DB provider supplies all of the functionality necessary to save recordsets, this is not true of all providers. If you're using data from another source and want to be sure you can save a recordset, set the CursorLocation property to adUseClient to create a client-side cursor.

To retrieve a saved recordset, you use the Open method of the recordset object. As the Source parameter, you supply the name of the disk file that contains the previously saved recordset. You should not specify a Connection when you reopen the recordset. The procedure in Listing 6.24, from basPersist, demonstrates how you can open a persisted recordset.

NOTE

Although we've managed to save and open persisted XML recordsets, we haven't managed to update them. Perhaps this limitation will be corrected by the time you read this, but as we were writing, we were unable to successfully update recordsets saved in XML format.

Listing 6.24

```
Public Sub RetrieveRecordset()
    Dim rst As ADODB.Recordset
    Dim strFile As String

    Set rst = New ADODB.Recordset

    ' Construct a file name to use
    strFile = CurrentProject.Path & "\Customers.adtg"

    ' Make sure the file exists
    If Len(Dir(strFile)) > 0 Then
        ' Open the recordset from the file
        rst.Open strFile, , adOpenStatic, adLockOptimistic
        ' Show that we've got data
        Debug.Print rst.Fields("ContactTitle")
        ' Reconnect the recordset to the database
        rst.ActiveConnection = CurrentProject.Connection
        ' Make a change and save it
        rst.Fields("ContactTitle") = "Sales Rep"
        rst.Update
    End If
    rst.Close
    Set rst = Nothing
End Sub
```

As you can see in the previous code, to reconnect a recordset to a database, you set the recordset's ActiveConnection property to a valid Connection property for the database. Once you've done this, you can update the recordset just like any other recordset.

WARNING

Cursor options are not persisted as part of a saved recordset. Be sure to specify the cursor type and locking type when you reopen a saved recordset. Otherwise, you'll get a default forward-only, read-only recordset.

TIP

You can change the ActiveConnection property for any recordset, not just for one retrieved from a disk file. If you open a recordset from a connection to a database named Nwind.MDB, change the connection to use a database named NwindBAK.MDB, and then make changes, your changes will be saved to NwindBAK.MDB.

Using Recordsets in Place of Arrays

For a long time, Access developers have had to choose whether to use recordsets or arrays for temporary data storage. Arrays could be easily created and destroyed in memory, whereas recordsets required tables to store their data. Using recordsets, on the other hand, meant you could use familiar operations such as Find and Sort to manipulate the temporary data. You could also refer to values using their field names in a recordset.

With ADO, you no longer have to make the tradeoff. ADO allows you to create recordsets in memory, not connected to any table or query, and add data to them. You'll find an example in the RecordsetArray function in basArray. This function starts by declaring a recordset variable, but instead of opening the recordset, it appends two fields to the Fields collection:

```
Dim rst As ADODB.Recordset
Dim intI As Integer

' Instantiate the recordset.
Set rst = New ADODB.Recordset

' Append two fields
rst.Fields.Append "ColorID", adSmallInt
rst.Fields.Append "ColorName", adVarChar, 10
```

When you append a field to a new recordset, ADO creates the recordset object in memory and leaves it up to you to specify the structure of the recordset. The Append method for the Fields collection of a recordset works just like the Append method that we covered earlier in the chapter in the section "Creating a New Table" for the Fields collection of a table. In this example, we've created one integer field and one text field and assigned names to both of them.

After you're done appending fields, you can open the recordset and work with it just like any other recordset. You don't need to supply any arguments to the Open method, but you do need to call it. For example, here's the remaining code from the RecordsetArray function. As you can see, there's no difference in manipulating this created recordset compared to any other recordset.

```
' Put some data in the recordset
rst.Open
rst.AddNew _
 Array("ColorID", "ColorName"), _
 Array(1, "Red")
rst.AddNew _
 Array("ColorID", "ColorName"), _
 Array(2, "Orange")
rst.AddNew _
 Array("ColorID", "ColorName"), _
 Array(3, "Yellow")
rst.AddNew _
 Array("ColorID", "ColorName"), _
 Array(4, "Green")
rst.AddNew _
 Array("ColorID", "ColorName"), _
 Array(5, "Blue")
rst.AddNew _
 Array("ColorID", "ColorName"), _
 Array(6, "Indigo")
rst.AddNew _
 Array("ColorID", "ColorName"), _
 Array(7, "Violet")

' Save the data. This isn't required,
' because ADO will do it for you.
rst.UpdateBatch
```

```
' Dump the recordset to the Immediate Window
rst.MoveFirst
Do Until rst.EOF
    Debug.Print rst("ColorID"), rst("ColorName")
    rst.MoveNext
Loop
```

TIP

This example also demonstrates a shortcut for the AddNew method. You can pass the method two arrays, one containing field names and the other containing the data for those fields, to both create the new record and populate it within a single operation. Sometimes, you may find this shortcut method simpler than calling the AddNew method and setting field values individually. You can use the same shortcut with the Update method, if you're changing values in a recordset.

Using Command Objects for Bulk Operations

You've already seen that you can use a Command object as the source for a recordset. You can also use a Command object to execute bulk SQL operations. These operations (the equivalent of Update, Append, and Delete queries in the Access user interface) use the SQL UPDATE, INSERT INTO, or DELETE commands to quickly modify sets of records.

To execute bulk SQL operations, you use the Execute method of the Command object, as in the code from basCommand, in Listing 6.25:

Listing 6.25

```
Public Sub ExecuteCommand()
    Dim cmd As ADODB.Command
    Dim lngAffected As Integer

    Set cmd = New ADODB.Command

    ' Set the connection to use for this command
    cmd.ActiveConnection = CurrentProject.Connection
    ' Set the properties of the command
```

```
    cmd.CommandType = adCmdText
    cmd.CommandText = _
     "UPDATE tblOrders " & _
     "SET ShipCountry = 'United States' " & _
     "WHERE ShipCountry = 'USA'"

    ' And execute it
    cmd.Execute lngAffected
    Debug.Print lngAffected & " Records modified"
    Set cmd = Nothing
End Sub
```

TIP

Note the first parameter passed to the Execute method: this parameter gets filled in by ADO, so that you can tell how many rows were affected by the Command. Pass a Long integer in this parameter and, after the call to the Execute method, you can use this value to determine what happened while the Command was executing.

You can also specify the adExecuteNoRecords argument, to indicate to ADO that the command does not return any data. You can execute bulk update SQL perfectly well without supplying this argument; however, supplying it does speed up the execution of the command. If the command requires parameters, you can supply them as the second argument to the Execute method. You can also use the same technique to execute a saved action query in your database, as shown in the procedure from basCommand in Listing 6.26:

Listing 6.26

```
Public Sub ExecuteCommand2()
    Dim cmd As ADODB.Command
    Dim lngAffected As Long

    Set cmd = New ADODB.Command

    ' Set the connection to use for this command
    cmd.ActiveConnection = CurrentProject.Connection

    ' Set the properties of the command
```

```
    cmd.CommandType = adCmdStoredProc
    cmd.CommandText = "qupdCountry"

    ' And execute it
    cmd.Execute lngAffected, , adExecuteNoRecords
    Debug.Print lngAffected & " Records modified"
    Set cmd = Nothing
End Sub
```

NOTE Note that even though Jet doesn't support stored procedures, you set the CommandType property of the Command object to adCmdStoredProc when you want to run a query that doesn't return any rows.

Finally, if your bulk SQL command does not require any parameters, you can execute it without explicitly creating a Command object. You do this by using the Execute method of the Connection object, which implicitly creates and then executes a Command object. This technique allows you to simplify the code greatly, in this case, from basCommand:

```
Public Sub ExecuteDirect()
    Dim lngAffected As Long

    CurrentProject.Connection.Execute "qupdCountry", _
     lngAffected, adExecuteNoRecords
    Debug.Print lngAffected & " Records modified"
End Sub
```

Schema Recordsets

In addition to recordsets containing data from the tables in your database, ADO allows you to open recordsets containing information about the database itself, called *schema recordsets*. For example, you can open a recordset that contains a list of all of the tables in your database, with their descriptions, creation date, and other information. While much of this information is available through ADOX, there are some pieces of information that are most readily retrieved from a schema recordset.

To open a schema recordset, you use the OpenSchema method of the Connection object:

```
Connection.OpenSchema QueryType, Criteria, SchemaID
```

- **QueryType** is one of the intrinsic constants listed in Table 6.12. This tells the method what type of information you'd like.
- **Criteria** is an optional parameter that lets you filter the resulting recordset. For example, you could filter a recordset of tables to retrieve information on only a particular table.
- **SchemaID** is a required parameter only when the QueryType is adSchemaProviderSpecific, in which case it is a GUID (a Globally Unique Identifier: a 16-byte value, as is used by Windows to manage installed applications in the Registry) that identifies a schema supported only by one provider.

Table 6.12 shows the available QueryType constants you can use with the OpenSchema method.

TABLE 6.12: Types of Schema Recordsets

QueryType	Returns
adSchemaAsserts	Recordset of constraints in the database. Not supported by the Jet Provider.
adSchemaCatalogs	Recordset of all available databases. Not supported by the Jet Provider.
adSchemaCharacterSets	Recordset of all character sets supported by the database engine. Not supported by the Jet Provider.
adSchemaCheckConstraints	Recordset of validation rules.
adSchemaCollations	Recordset of sort orders supported by the database engine. Not supported by the Jet Provider.
adSchemaColumnPrivileges	Recordset of column-level security information. Not supported by the Jet Provider.
adSchemaColumns	Recordset of information on all fields in all tables.
adSchemaColumnsDomainUsage	Recordset of columns dependent on a particular domain. Not supported by the Jet Provider.
adSchemaConstraintColumnUsage	Recordset identifying fields used by validation rules and keys.

Continued on next page

TABLE 6.12 CONTINUED: Types of Schema Recordsets

QueryType	Returns
adSchemaConstraintTableUsage	Recordset of information about table-level constraints. Not supported by the Jet Provider.
adSchemaCubes	Recordset of information about multidimensional data available from the database. Not supported by the Jet Provider.
adSchemaDBInfoKeywords	Recordset of reserved words.
adSchemaDBInfoLiterals	Recordset of quoting and escape characters.
adSchemaDimensions	Recordset of cube dimensions. Not supported by the Jet Provider.
adSchemaForeignKeys	Recordset of foreign key information.
adSchemaHierarchies	Recordset of cube hierarchies. Not supported by the Jet Provider.
adSchemaIndexes	Recordset of all indexes in the database.
adSchemaKeyColumnUsage	Recordset of fields that are contained in any primary or foreign key.
adSchemaLevels	Recordset of levels within a cube hierarchy. Not supported by the Jet Provider.
adSchemaMeasures	Recordset of cube measures. Not supported by the Jet Provider.
adSchemaMembers	Recordset of cube members. Not supported by the Jet Provider.
adSchemaPrimaryKeys	Recordset of all primary keys in the database.
adSchemaProcedureColumns	Recordset of columns in all stored procedures in the database. Not supported by the Jet Provider.
adSchemaProcedureParameters	Recordset of parameters to all stored procedures in the database. Not supported by the Jet Provider.
adSchemaProcedures	Recordset of stored procedures. Not supported by the Jet Provider.
adSchemaProperties	Recordset of database properties. Not supported by the Jet Provider.
adSchemaProviderSpecific	Schema information from a particular OLE DB Provider. You must supply the QueryID value for a particular schema to use this constant.

Continued on next page

TABLE 6.12 CONTINUED: Types of Schema Recordsets

QueryType	Returns
adSchemaProviderTypes	Recordset of data types supported by the provider.
adSchemaReferentialConstraints	Recordset of relationships.
adSchemaSchemata	Recordset of schemas. Not supported by the Jet Provider.
adSchemaSQLLanguages	Recordset of information on ANSI SQL support. Not supported by the Jet Provider.
adSchemaStatistics	Recordset of the cardinality (number of rows) in every table in the database.
adSchemaTableConstraints	Recordset of table-level validation rules.
adSchemaTablePrivileges	Recordset of table-level security information. Not supported by the Jet Provider.
adSchemaTables	Recordset of tables.
adSchemaTranslations	Recordset of defined character translations. Not supported by the Jet Provider.
adSchemaTrustees	Recordset of users.
adSchemaUsagePrivileges	Recordset of security information. Not supported by the Jet Provider.
adSchemaViewColumnUsage	Recordset of fields in views. Not supported by the Jet Provider.
adSchemaViews	Recordset of queries.
adSchemaViewTableUsage	Recordset of tables in views. Not supported by the Jet Provider.

For example, you can use the code in Listing 6.27 (from basSchema) to list all of the tables in your database to the Immediate Window.

Listing 6.27

```
Public Sub ShowTableSchema()
    Dim rst As ADODB.Recordset
    Dim fld As ADODB.Field

    Set rst = CurrentProject.Connection. _
     OpenSchema(adSchemaTables)
    For Each fld In rst.Fields
        Debug.Print fld.Name & vbTab;
```

```
        Next fld
        Debug.Print
        Debug.Print String(130, "-")
        Do Until rst.EOF
            For Each fld In rst.Fields
                If Not IsNull(fld.Value) Then
                    Debug.Print fld.Value & vbTab;
                Else
                    Debug.Print "(null)" & vbTab;
                End If
            Next fld
            Debug.Print
            rst.MoveNext
        Loop
        rst.Close
        Set rst = Nothing
        Set fld = Nothing
    End Sub
```

The Jet Provider also defines four provider-specific schema recordsets:

- A recordset of current users of the database
- A recordset of query performance information
- A recordset of partial replica filters
- A recordset of replica conflict tables

We've included the GUIDs for these recordsets in basSchema so that you can use them in your own code. As an example, the code in Listing 6.28 retrieves the current list of users of the current database. For each user, it shows the user name, the name of the computer at which they're logged in, and whether they've left the database in a suspect (needing repair) state. This sort of information can be very useful if you're trying to determine who's leaving a database open in a multiuser situation.

Listing 6.28

```
Const JET_SCHEMA_USERROSTER = _
 "{947bb102-5d43-11d1-bdbf-00c04fb92675}"

Public Sub ShowUserRoster()
```

```
    Dim rst As ADODB.Recordset
    Dim fld As ADODB.Field

    Set rst = CurrentProject.Connection.OpenSchema( _
     adSchemaProviderSpecific, , JET_SCHEMA_USERROSTER)
    For Each fld In rst.Fields
        Debug.Print fld.Name & vbTab;
    Next fld
    Debug.Print
    Debug.Print String(80, "-")
    Do Until rst.EOF
        For Each fld In rst.Fields
            If Not IsNull(fld.Value) Then
                Debug.Print fld.Value & vbTab;
            Else
                Debug.Print "(null)" & vbTab;
            End If
        Next fld
        Debug.Print
        rst.MoveNext
    Loop
    rst.Close
    Set rst = Nothing
    Set fld = Nothing
End Sub
```

NOTE

You'll see other examples of using Schema recordsets in Chapter 17 of this volume as well as in *Access 2000 Developer's Handbook, Volume II*.

Using the CurrentProject and CurrentData Collections

When you're developing applications, you'll often need to present users with a list of database objects. You might, for example, want to enumerate all of the reports in your database in a list box, so that the user can select a report to execute. Although this information is all available in the Database window, allowing users unfettered access to this window is dangerous because they can then open and alter objects without constraint. In professional applications, you'll normally want to hide the Database window and use your own interface to let users manipulate only the objects that you want them to use.

Because ADO is a general-purpose interface, it doesn't know about Access objects such as Forms, Reports, Macros, Modules, and Data Access Pages. In order to get around this limitation, the Access designers supplied a number of useful collections as properties of the CurrentProject and CurrentData objects. The CurrentProject object represents all of the user interface (nondata-bearing) objects in your Access database. The CurrentData object represents all of the data-bearing objects in your Access database. Table 6.13 lists these collections.

TABLE 6.13: Database Object Collections

Collection	Parent	Useful in MDB?
AllDataAccessPages	CurrentProject	Yes
AllDatabaseDiagrams	CurrentData	No
AllForms	CurrentProject	Yes
AllMacros	CurrentProject	Yes
AllModules	CurrentProject	Yes
AllQueries	CurrentData	Yes
AllReports	CurrentProject	Yes
AllStoredProcedures	CurrentData	No
AllTables	CurrentData	Yes
AllViews	CurrentData	No

You'll see that some of these collections are not useful in an Access database. They're intended for use in Access projects using SQL Server or the MSDE engine, which expose some different objects. You'll learn more about these collections in *Access 2000 Developer's Handbook, Volume II.*

WARNING

Don't confuse the AllForms and AllReports collections with the Forms and Reports collections supplied by Access. The former contain all of the forms and reports in your database, while the latter contain only the forms and reports currently open in the user interface.

Each of these collections is a collection of AccessObject objects. An AccessObject has the following properties:

Name The name of the object as it appears in the Database window.

FullName The filename, including path, of a Data Access Page. This property is an empty string for other types of object.

IsLoaded True if the object is currently open in the user interface, and False otherwise.

Type An intrinsic constant indicating the type of the AccessObject. It will contain one of acDataAccessPage, acDiagram, acForm, acMacro, acModule, acQuery, acReport, acServerView, acStoredProcedure, or acTable.

Parent A reference to the containing collection.

In addition, an AccessObject has a Properties collection containing user-defined properties, if any have been added to the object.

Listing 6.29 (from basListObjects) shows how you can use these collections to list all of the objects in an Access database to the Immediate window.

Listing 6.29

```
Public Sub ListObjects()
    Dim aob As AccessObject
    With CurrentData
        Debug.Print "Tables"
        For Each aob In .AllTables
            Debug.Print "  " & aob.Name
        Next aob
        Debug.Print "Queries"
        For Each aob In .AllQueries
            Debug.Print "  " & aob.Name
        Next aob
    End With
```

```
    With CurrentProject
        Debug.Print "Forms"
        For Each aob In .AllForms
            Debug.Print "    " & aob.Name
        Next aob
        Debug.Print "Reports"
        For Each aob In .AllReports
            Debug.Print "    " & aob.Name
        Next aob
        Debug.Print "Pages"
        For Each aob In .AllDataAccessPages
            Debug.Print "    " & aob.Name
        Next aob
        Debug.Print "Macros"
        For Each aob In .AllMacros
            Debug.Print "    " & aob.Name
        Next aob
        Debug.Print "Modules"
        For Each aob In .AllModules
            Debug.Print "    " & aob.Name
        Next aob
    End With
End Sub
```

A Case Study: Using the Collections

As an example of using the CurrentProject and CurrentData collections as part of an application, we've provided a simple replacement for the database window (see Figure 6.7) that you can import into any application. You can use it directly as is, or you can modify it to add new functionality. You might want to remove some of the objects for your own applications. For example, you might like to provide users with a list of only certain tables and queries. Perhaps you don't want to show your users a list of macros or modules. Given frmDBC as a starting place, you can make as many changes as you wish to fit your own needs. The point of the sample is to demonstrate the use of the objects we've discussed in this chapter to handle the objects in a database. In the interest of simplicity, we've modeled this form on the Access 97 database container. If your users are familiar with that interface, they'll be happy with this look. If not, you can certainly use one of the many custom controls available and have Access display this information in a different format. (For a different approach to this problem, see Chapter 17.)

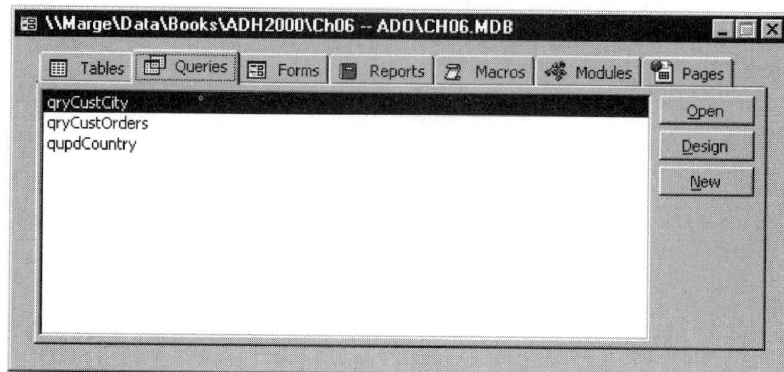

FIGURE 6.7:

The sample database container is simpler than the one you'll find in Access, but it provides many of the same features.

Designing frmDBC

The design considerations for frmDBC were to

- Provide a list of all the tables, queries, forms, reports, pages, macros, and modules in the current database
- Keep the interface as simple as possible
- Allow for customization

The following sections discuss the form itself and how it does its work.

Choosing an Object Type and an Action

When you click one of the tabs in the Tab control (tabObjects), the code attached to the control's Change event refills the list box (lstObjects) that displays the list of objects. The particular list that lstObjects displays depends, of course, on the selected tab.

TIP

To make the code as simple as possible, we've used the intrinsic constants acTable, acQuery, acForm, acReport, acDataAccessPage, acMacro, and acModule wherever possible. Whenever possible, use the Access-defined constants in your code.

Once you've chosen an object type (and forced the list box to refill itself) and selected an object from the list, you can select one of the action buttons at the top of the form (New, Open, or Design). Depending on the circumstances, one or more of those buttons might have a different caption and might be disabled.

Displaying the Object List

To make the form work as simply as possible, frmDBC fills the list box (lstObjects) by providing a semicolon-delimited list of names as the RowSource property for the list box. This requires that the list box's RowSourceType property be set to Value List, and the form's Open event procedure handles that chore. We could have used a list-filling callback function or an ActiveX control to fill the list box, but we decided on this simpler method instead. (See Chapter 7 for more information on list-filling callback functions or using an ActiveX control in place of Access' native list box control.) Because the RowSource property is limited to 2048 characters, the number of objects you can display in this sample form will be artificially constrained. The longer your object names, the fewer you'll be able to display in the list box. (Remember that every entry in the list will have an extra character, its trailing semicolon.) If you can accept that limitation, you may find this example a good starting place.

Filling the Object List

The GetObjectList function is the heart of this entire form. Given the object type to enumerate, it creates a semicolon-delimited list of object names and returns that string. Listing 6.30 shows the entire function, and the following sections go through the code, one bit at time.

Listing 6.30

```
Private Function GetObjectList( _
 ByVal lngType as AcObjecType) As String
    Dim intI As Integer
    Dim fSystemObj As Boolean
    Dim strName As String
    Dim fShowHidden As Boolean
```

```
Dim fIsHidden As Boolean
Dim strOutput As String
Dim fShowSystem As Boolean
Dim objCollection As Object
Dim aob As AccessObject

On Error GoTo HandleErrors
DoCmd.Hourglass True

' Are you supposed to show hidden/system objects?
fShowHidden = _
 Application.GetOption("Show Hidden Objects")
fShowSystem = _
 Application.GetOption("Show System Objects")

Select Case lngType
    Case acTable
        Set objCollection = CurrentData.AllTables
    Case acQuery
        Set objCollection = CurrentData.AllQueries
    Case acForm
        Set objCollection = CurrentProject.AllForms
    Case acReport
        Set objCollection = CurrentProject.AllReports
    Case acDataAccessPage
        Set objCollection = _
         CurrentProject.AllDataAccessPages
    Case acMacro
        Set objCollection = CurrentProject.AllMacros
    Case acModule
        Set objCollection = CurrentProject.AllModules
End Select

For Each aob In objCollection
    fIsHidden = IsHidden(aob)
    strName = aob.Name
    fSystemObj = IsSystemObject(aob)
    ' Unless this is a system object and
    ' you're not showing system objects...
    If (fSystemObj Imp fShowSystem) Then
        ' If the object isn't deleted and its hidden
        ' characteristics match those you're
        ' looking for...
```

```
                If Not isDeleted(strName) And _
                 (fIsHidden Imp fShowHidden) Then
                    ' If this isn't a form, just add it to
                    ' the list. If it is, one more check:
                    ' is this the CURRENT form? If so, and if
                    ' the flag isn't set to include the current
                    ' form, then skip it.
                    Select Case intType
                        Case acForm
                            If Not (adhcSkipThisForm And _
                             (strName = Me.Name)) Then
                                strOutput = _
                                strOutput & ";" & strName
                            End If
                        Case Else
                            strOutput = _
                             strOutput & ";" & strName
                    End Select
                End If
            End If
        Next aob
        strOutput = Mid$(strOutput, 2)

ExitHere:
        DoCmd.Hourglass False
        GetObjectList = strOutput
        Exit Function

HandleErrors:
        HandleErrors Err.Number, "GetObjectList"
        Resume ExitHere
End Function
```

The main body of GetObjectList, once it's initialized local variables and set up the environment by turning on the hourglass cursor, consists of a Select Case statement with one case for each of the possible object types. For each type of object, the code uses the CurrentProject or CurrentData collections to iterate through the different objects.

Gathering Options

To emulate the built-in database window, frmDBC must know whether you've elected to display hidden and/or system objects. To gather this information, the GetObjectList function uses the Application.GetOption method. Based on the return values, the function sets the fShowHidden and fShowSystem variables; the function uses these variables to determine whether to include hidden and system objects in the output string. For more information on using Application.GetOption, see Appendix B.

Gathering Lists of Objects

In previous editions of this book, we used markedly different code to list the Jet objects (tables and queries) and the Access objects (in previous versions of Access, forms, reports, macros, and modules). From the users' point of view, there's no difference between Jet objects and Access objects, but from the developer's point of view, they're really separate types of objects. In this new version of the code, though, we can completely ignore these differences. That's because the CurrentProject and CurrentData collections bundle up all of these objects for you in identical ways.

Finding a Container

When you ask GetObjectList to produce a list of objects, you'll be looping through one of seven different collections. Although these collections each have a different object type, they each have identical methods and properties. Because of this, one of these collections can be treated like any other. Your first step then is to create a variable of type Object to refer to the correct collection. Following is the code from GetObjectList that performs this task:

```
Dim objCollection As Object
.
.
.
Select Case lngType
    Case acTable
        Set objCollection = CurrentData.AllTables
    Case acQuery
        Set objCollection = CurrentData.AllQueries
    Case acForm
        Set objCollection = CurrentProject.AllForms
    Case acReport
        Set objCollection = CurrentProject.AllReports
```

```
        Case acDataAccessPage
            Set objCollection = _
             CurrentProject.AllDataAccessPages
        Case acMacro
            Set objCollection = CurrentProject.AllMacros
        Case acModule
            Set objCollection = CurrentProject.AllModules
    End Select
```

Looping through the Collection

Once you've pointed the variable objCollection at a particular container, the code to loop through all the elements of the collection should look very familiar. It's a basic For...Each loop:

```
For Each aob In objCollection
    ...
Next aob
```

The code within the loop has to make decisions based on four factors:

- Is the object a system object?
- Is the object a hidden object?
- Is the object the current form?
- Is the object deleted?

Deciding Whether to Add an Object

For each particular object, you may or may not want to add it to the output string. If you have not requested that the function include system objects and the current object is a system object, you'll want to skip it. The same reasoning applies to hidden objects: you only want to show hidden objects if you've requested them.

```
fIsHidden = IsHidden(aob)
strName = aob.Name
fSystemObj = IsSystemObject(aob)
' Unless this is a system object and
' you're not showing system objects...
If (fSystemObj Imp fShowSystem) Then
' If the object isn't deleted and its hidden
' characteristics match those you're
' looking for...
```

```
        If Not isDeleted(strName) And _
         (fIsHidden Imp fShowHidden) Then
            ' later in the code:
            strOutput & ";" & strName
        End If
    End If
```

Checking for System Objects

The first step in the preceding code was to determine whether or not the current table is a system object. To determine this you can call the IsSystemObject function:

```
Private Function IsSystemObject(aob As AccessObject) _
 As Boolean

    ' Determine whether or not the specified object is
    ' an Access system object or not.

    Const conSystemObject = &H80000000
    Const conSystemObject2 = &H2

    If (Left$(aob.Name, 4) = "USys") Or _
     Left$(aob.Name, 4) = "~sq_" Then
        IsSystemObject = True
    Else
        If (aob.Attributes And conSystemObject) = _
         conSystemObject Then
            IsSystemObject = True
        Else
            If (aob.Attributes And conSystemObject2) = _
             conSystemObject2 Then
                IsSystemObject = True
            End If
        End If
    End If
End Function
```

The current object should be treated as a system object in three instances:

- If the name of the object is Usys followed by any text. This naming convention allows the user to create objects that Access will display, in the database container, only when the Show System Objects option is set to Yes.

- If the object is a query, built by Access for its own internal use with a name starting with "~sq_".
- If the object has particular bits in its Attribute property set.

The last test brings us into the murky waters of undocumented Access. We have no guarantee that our code for determining system objecthood from the Attributes property works. The Attributes property of the AccessObject object is hidden and undocumented. Presumably, it exists for the convenience of the Access designers, perhaps to help in implementing Wizards. It seems reasonable to assume that, like other Attributes properties elsewhere in the object models for Access, it consists of a series of bit constants. Exploring the Attributes properties for the default system tables, we found that MSysAccessObjects has an Attributes value of &H2, and the other system tables have an Attributes property of &H80000000. Why are there two different values? We don't know. We only know that Access treats all of these tables as system tables and that we need to do the same.

TIP

To discover hidden properties, you can open the object browser, right-click in it, and choose Show Hidden Members. This will reveal many methods, properties, and even whole objects that aren't documented. Of course, you use any of these at your own risk!

Checking for Hidden Objects

The code to check for hidden objects is similar to the code that checks for system objects, but it's simpler because there are no special cases, just a call to the Get-HiddenAttribute method of the Application object:

```
Private Function IsHidden( _
 aob As AccessObject) As Boolean

    ' Determine whether or not the specified object is
    ' hidden in the Access database window

    If Application.GetHiddenAttribute( _
     aob.Type, aob.Name) Then
        IsHidden = True
    End If
End Function
```

NOTE

One has to wonder about the GetHiddenAttribute (and corresponding SetHidden-Attribute) method. Why isn't Hidden a property of each AccessObject? We don't know—most likely, this was a feature added after the design review was done for the properties and methods of an AccessObject. In any case, this sort of non-conformist way of solving a problem should be a good lesson for you if you're creating your own objects with properties and methods—think hard about what properties your objects need before finalizing the design. This one was clearly tacked on after the fact and, because of that, feels rather odd.

Checking for Inclusion

You'll want to include the object in your list unless one of the following situations exists:

- You've asked not to include hidden objects, and this object is hidden.
- You've asked not to include system objects, and this object is a system object.

Let's consider the case of system objects first. You need to check whether to include an object, based on the fShowSystem setting and whether this particular object is a system object. These two conditions give you four possible outcomes, as shown in Table 6.14.

TABLE 6.14: Decision Table for System Object Inclusion

System Object?	Include System Objects?	Include This Object?
Yes	Yes	Yes
Yes	No	No
No	Yes	Yes
No	No	Yes

As you can see in Table 6.14, you'll want to include the current object in the output string unless the current object is a system object and you've elected not to include system objects. You could build a complex logical expression to indicate this information to Access, but Access makes this a bit simpler by providing a single logical operator that works exactly as you need.

The IMP (implication) operator takes two values and returns a True value *unless* the first operand is True and the second is False. This exactly matches the truth table shown in Table 6.14. Given that the variable fSystemObj indicates whether or not the current table is a system object and the variable fShowSystem indicates whether or not you want to include system objects, you can use the expression

```
fSystemObj Imp fShowSystem
```

to know whether to exclude the table based on whether or not it's a system table. Therefore, to check both criteria for inclusion, you can use the following expression (which also checks for hidden objects in the same manner):

```
If (fSystemObj Imp fShowSystem) And _
 And (fIsHidden Imp fShowHidden) Then
```

This expression returns a True value if all subexpressions return a True value.

The Current Form and Deleted Objects

Once you've determined that the current object matches the caller's interest in system and hidden objects, you have two new problems to handle:

- If this object is a form, should you list the current form?
- Is this object deleted? Access doesn't immediately remove deleted objects from the containers, and you won't want to display these objects in the list.

Set the constant adhcSkipThisForm in the module's declarations area to indicate whether you want to exclude the current form from the list. The following code fragment adds the current object name to the output string, depending on whether the item is deleted or hidden and if it's the current form:

```
If Not isDeleted(strName) And _
 (fIsHidden Imp fShowHidden) Then
    ' If this isn't a form, just add it to
    ' the list. If it is, one more check:
    ' is this the CURRENT form? If so, and if
    ' the flag isn't set to include the current
    ' form, then skip it.
    Select Case lngType
        Case acForm
            If Not (adhcSkipThisForm And _
             (strName = Me.Name)) Then
                strOutput = _
                strOutput & ";" & strName
            End If
        Case Else
```

```
                strOutput = _
                 strOutput & ";" & strName
        End Select
    End If
```

The isDeleted function takes a very low-tech approach to checking for deleted objects:

```
    Private Function IsDeleted( _
     ByVal strName As String) As Boolean
        IsDeleted = (Left(strName, 7) = "~TMPCLP")
    End Function
```

The function looks for object names that start with ~TMPCLP, which is how Access renames deleted objects.

Adding the Object

Once you've decided that a particular object is to be added to the list of tables, you'll want to place the Name property of the current object in the output string:

```
    strOutput = strOutput & ";" & aob.Name
```

When the loop is done, the output string, strOutput, will contain one item for each acceptable object in the database.

Finishing It Up

Finally, once you've created a string containing all the object names for the selected type, GetObjectList returns the string to the calling procedure. The calling function, ListObjects, uses that string to fill the list box's RowSource property.

Using frmDBC in Your Own Applications

To use frmDBC in your own applications, just import it. Because all the code it requires to run is encapsulated in its module, you need nothing else. However, you might want to consider making various alterations to it. For example, you might want to add some columns or remove some of the tabs that appear as part of the tab control. In any case, we left the sample form simple so that you can modify it for your own needs.

TIP

You may want to allow the user to resize this form and resize or move all the controls on the form to match the current size. For more information on resizing objects on forms to match the current size of the form, see Chapter 8.

Summary

This chapter presented a broad introduction to programming data access using ADO. We've made attempts to bring our personal perspectives into this chapter, but a full understanding of this material requires far more depth than we can cover here. Because of the similarities between the object models in Access, Visual Basic, and the rest of Microsoft Office, you would be well served to spend as much time as possible digging in to this material: This is clearly the way future Microsoft products will be going.

This chapter covered these major topics:

- Access' support for ADO with Jet
- Objects provided by ADO and ADOX
- Referring to objects
- Iterating through collections
- Using properties
- Jet data definition using ADO
- Working with ADO recordsets
- Schema recordsets
- Persisting recordsets
- Using Command objects
- Using collections supplied by CurrentData and CurrentProject

We purposefully neglected some key areas of ADO programming, mostly due to lack of space. Two major areas are:

- Events raised by ADO objects
- Handling disconnected, optimistic batch updates, including all the errors that can occur when you use this technique

For coverage of these and many other ADO-specific topics, you'll need to research books and articles specifically about ADO.

There's much, much more to know. As a start, Chapter 8 works extensively with forms and their recordsets. In addition, many of the chapters in *Access 2000 Developer's Handbook, Volume II* cover the use of ADO in file-server and client/server situations.

CHAPTER

SEVEN

7

Controlling Controls

- Using form and report controls
- Understanding control events and properties
- Using the Tag property in a standardized way
- Combining controls to work together
- Creating forms and controls programmatically

In this chapter, you'll learn about some of the different Access controls and find some hints on deciding which control is best for a given data type or situation, along with examples of many of the control types. In addition, you'll find a number of reusable solutions to common challenges you'll confront when designing your user interfaces.

Controls and Their Uses

Controls are the workhorses of Access applications. You can use them for inputting and outputting data, as well as for displaying static information. In addition, you can use controls as global variables, to calculate intermediate values, or to add aesthetic interest to your forms. Forms and reports share the same controls. (You can put a button on a report, for example, but it doesn't really make much sense to do so.) The focus of this chapter is on controls for forms.

Think of controls in Access as being windows, just as all the other elements of a Windows application are windows. As with any window, a control can receive information from the user only when it has input focus. To allow a user to be able to enter text into a text box or to check an item in a check box, that control must first have been selected, either by the user or under your program's control.

Some controls have *values,* supplied by you at design time, by the data from which the control is being fed, or by the user at runtime. The value of the control is the value you see displayed in that control. For a text box, the value is obviously the text displayed inside the box. For a list box, the value of the control is the chosen item (or Null, if no item is chosen).

Controls also have *properties* that your application can set and change. This chapter touches on the useful, pertinent, and difficult properties throughout its discussion of the various controls. If you're upgrading to Access 2000 from an earlier version, you'll find some new properties, although changes from Access 97 are minimal.

TIP

Access 2000 is fussier about the data types you assign to properties than any previous version of Access before Access 97. For example, the ControlSource property of a text box previously accepted a string expression or a null value (indicating an empty ControlSource). No longer. You must assign the correct data type—String, in this particular case—to all properties. This change will be most evident when you attempt to convert existing applications from Access 95 or earlier to Access 2000. Code that worked fine in earlier versions may fail to run correctly now, if you were using Null to set property values that now require explicit types. VBA cannot catch most of these errors at compile time, so if you were in the habit of assigning null values to properties that should have been strings, you'll need to test existing converted code carefully. In addition, code that tested these property values to see if they were Null won't work any more—you'll need to check for an empty string instead. These issues also applied to Access 97, so if you have your application running there, you should be all set. But if you're upgrading from an earlier version, beware of these differences in property types.

Code Associated with Forms: Class Modules

In Access, every form and report can carry its own module with it. In Access 2 and Access 95, all forms and reports maintained a module; in Access 97 and Access 2000, forms and reports are "born" without a module. You can cause Access to create a module by adding any VBA code to the object, and you can remove the module by setting the object's HasModule property to False. The code in this module is sometimes referred to as *Code-Behind-Forms* (CBF), and it's in this module that you'll usually attach code to any event property for any control. The module itself is called the form or report's Class module. (It's called a class module because the code associated with a form or report defines a class, just as any other class module. See Chapter 3 for more information on creating and using standalone class modules.) Chapter 8 discusses this feature in greater depth, but be aware that when this chapter refers to attaching code to a given control or to a property of a control, it is talking about creating event procedures that are stored with the form itself. You can gain access to the Class Module by clicking the Build button next to the specific event property in the Property window and choosing Code Builder from the Choose Builder dialog box. Note that you can also reverse the order. If you choose [Event Procedure] from the row's drop-down list, you can then click the Build button, and Access will take you directly to the class module for the form. You can also choose the Code button on the toolbar to access this code. The property sheet (with a builder button) is shown here.

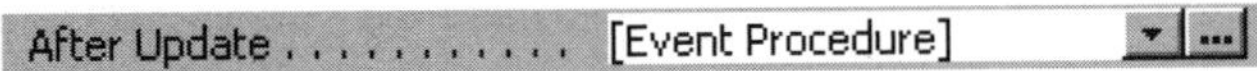

Figure 7.1 shows the dialog box.

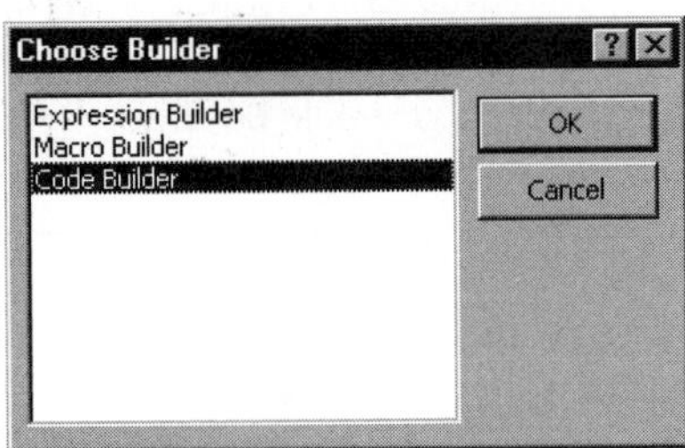

FIGURE 7.1:

Choose the Code Builder item to edit code attached to the chosen event.

TIP

In response to suggestions from many Access users, Microsoft added a feature allowing you to bypass the dialog you normally see when you click the Build button, which asks whether you'd like to create an event procedure, create a macro, or use the Expression Builder. If you normally want to react to events using VBA code (and if you're reading this book, we hope you will), choose the Tools ➢ Options menu, select the Forms/Reports tab, and make sure the Always Use Event Procedures check box is set. This way, you can bypass a mouse click every time you create an event procedure.

Working with Groups of Controls

Access 2000 adds a new feature that makes working with groups of controls much simpler—the ability to group controls and treat them as a group. If you've ever fought with selecting a group of controls and attempting to move them as a group, and later tried to move the group again, you'll appreciate this new feature.

To group the controls, select the controls you want grouped (using Shift+click, or by clicking and dragging the mouse pointer to bound the controls, or by whatever means you like). Then, select the Format ➢ Group menu item. The individual selection handles disappear, and you see a rectangle bounding all the selected controls. Figure 7.2 shows frmMultiPik (more on frmMultiPik later in the chapter) with several of its controls grouped together.

FIGURE 7.2:

After grouping controls, they move as a single unit.

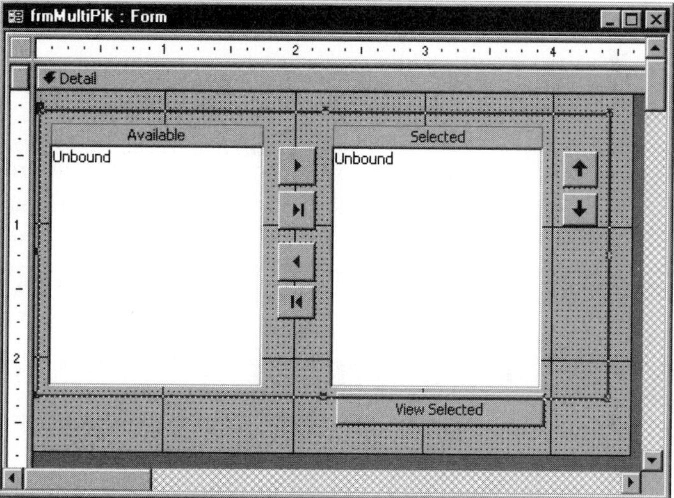

If you later want to ungroup your controls, you can use the Format ➢ Ungroup menu item to return the controls to their individually selected state. If you want to work with an individual control within the group, simply select that control as usual and move or size it as necessary. If you move a grouped control outside group's borders, the group will expand to include the control.

TIP

If you want to remove a control from a group, you can't simply slide it outside the group—Access will expand the group to include that moved control. To remove a control from a group, you'll need to either ungroup and then regroup without the control, or cut the control to the clipboard and then paste the control back onto the form.

WARNING

You may want to group controls programmatically if you're writing an application that creates forms for users (a Wizard of some sort, for example). To group the controls, you would look for a constant to be used with the DoCmd.RunCommand method—that's the way you execute menu items from code. Unfortunately, Microsoft neglected to include RunCommand constants for the Group and Ungroup menu items. Therefore, if you want to group controls from within code, you'll need to use the SendKeys procedure. This isn't the preferred method, but it's all there is at this point.

Some Standard Control Properties

Before launching into a discussion of all the different controls and their various properties and events, this seems like a good time to discuss some of the standard properties and events that most controls share. Later in this chapter, we'll discuss individual controls with their unique properties and events.

Using the Tag Property to Create Your Own Properties

Access provides the general-purpose Tag property, which allows you to specify and store up to 2048 characters of information attached to any control. Access never uses what's stored in this property, so it makes a perfect place to store information about a control that is pertinent to your application. In an example later in this chapter, you'll need to store the old default value for a control so that you can restore it later. Controls don't supply an "OldDefaultValue" property, but you can store the data in the Tag property of the control while the form is running so that you can retrieve it later.

You might find it tempting to place arbitrary values in this unused slot, but it's a good idea to avoid this urge. If you adopt a standard method of storing values in the Tag property, you can actually create your own user-defined properties for controls. In previous editions of this book, we proposed a standard that has gained acceptance within the Access development community for formatting this information.

We suggest using the following format for enabling the Tag property to contain user-defined information:

Name1=Value1; Name2=Value2; Name3=Value3;

This format guarantees that various pieces of your application won't overwrite information stored in the Tag property of a given control. If all access to the Tag property goes through a set of functions that set and get the specific values by their names, you have an ordered and safe way to store and retrieve values. Using this technique allows you to store multiple bits of information about a control and retrieve those bits when necessary.

To implement this functionality, we've provided two classes that you can include in any of your applications. (To use these classes, import both the TaggedValue and TaggedValues classes from the sample database.) We'll use the functions in these classes throughout this book, not only to work with the Tag property, but anyplace we need to store more than one item in a single string. These classes make it simple for you to set and retrieve any single tagged value from a string of tag/value pairs and to set and retrieve the entire set of values.

NOTE For more information on creating and using class modules in order to create your own object types, see Chapter 3.

In addition, to make this interface as simple as possible, we've made the rules describing the structure of the tagged values string a bit stringent. In particular, the syntax for the tagged values string is as follows:

Name1=Value1; Name2=Value2;…; NameN=ValueN;

To use the TaggedValues class, follow these rules:

- Separate each item name and value pair with an equal sign (=).
- Follow each pair with a semicolon (;), although you can change this particular separator by modifying the Separator property.
- Do not include the separator character (;) within the tag value itself.

If you use the provided classes to place values into the Tag property, these rules won't be a concern, because the code will follow them. The only problem occurs when you place values into the Tag property at design time. In that case, be careful to follow the rules exactly, because the provided functions may not work otherwise.

Table 7.1 lists the properties and methods of the TaggedValues class. (The TaggedValue class exists only for data storage, and provides two string properties: Name and Value.)

TABLE 7.1: Properties and Methods of the TaggedValues Class

Name	Type	Data Type	Description
Count	Property	Long	Returns the number of tagged value pairs in the Text property.
Exists	Property	Boolean	Given a tag name, returns True if the name=value pair exists in the Text property; otherwise, False.
Separator	Property	String	Sets or retrieves the separator to be used between name=value pairs. By default, this is a semi-colon (";").
Text	Property	String	Sets or retrieves the full set of name=value pairs.
Add	Method	TaggedValue	Given a name and a value, adds the pair to the Text property and returns the TaggedValue item that was added.
Item	Method	String	Given a Name value, returns the associated value (or an empty string, if the name doesn't exist).
Remove	Method		Given a Name value, removes the name=value pair from the Text property.

To use the TaggedValues class, you must follow these steps:

1. Declare a TaggedValues variable and instantiate it.
2. Assign text into the Text property of your TaggedValues objects.
3. Set or retrieve values, as necessary.

For example, Listing 7.1 shows a test procedure (from basTestTaggedValues) that exercises the properties and methods of the TaggedValues class. Figure 7.3 shows the output from running the test procedure.

Listing 7.1

```
Public Sub TestTaggedValues()

    ' Test out the TaggedValues class.
```

```
    Dim tv As TaggedValues
    Set tv = New TaggedValues

    tv.Add "OldState", "TX"
    tv.Add "NewState", "CA"
    tv.Add "Phone", "3335551212"

    Debug.Print tv.Count
    Debug.Print tv.Text

    Debug.Print tv.Item("Phone")
    Debug.Print tv.Exists("OldState")
    tv.Remove "NewState"
    tv.Separator = "[-]"
    Debug.Print tv.Text

    Set tv = Nothing
End Sub
```

FIGURE 7.3:

Running TestTaggedValues results in this output.

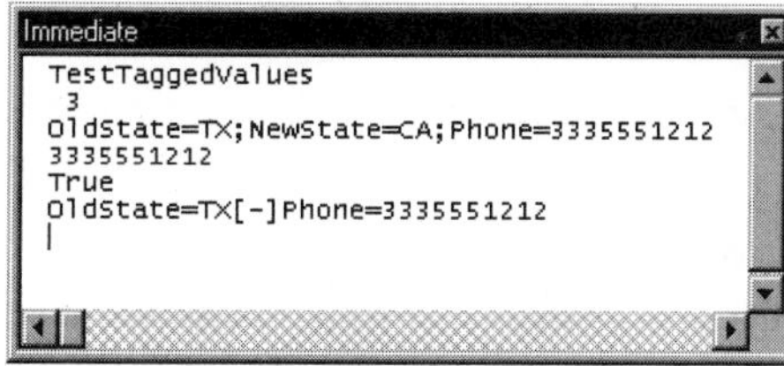

To use the TaggedValues class with the Tag property of a control, you'll want to take the Tag property, assign it to the Text property of a TaggedValues object, do your work with the TaggedValues object, and then store the Text property back into the Tag property of the control. Your code might look something like this:

```
Dim tv As TaggedValues
Set tv = New TaggedValues

' Get the current Tag property value.
tv.Text = Me.txtName.Tag

' Add and remove items as necessary...
tv.Add "Name1", "Value1"
```

```
' Put the data back into the Tag property.
Me.txtName.Tag = tv.Text
Set tv = Nothing
```

TIP

To include the functionality described here in your own applications, import the TaggedValue and TaggedValues class modules from the sample database.

NOTE

Access 2000 has the ability to persist property changes made at runtime. Although this is, perhaps, not generally a great idea, it doesn't help at all, in this case. Access never records any property changes your running application makes while a form is in Form view, only those made by the user. Just as with any other property changed programmatically, changes made to the Tag property with the TaggedValues class will not appear in the property sheet. If you want to make persistent changes to any property, you need to make them when your form is in Design view.

TIP

The TaggedValues/TaggedValue pair of class modules works with any name=value pairs, not just with the Tag property. You'll find these classes useful in many circumstances, and we'll take advantage of them when necessary throughout the book.

The ControlType Property

You may need to determine what type of control you're working with from within your applications. That is, if you visit each control on a form programmatically and want to take some action based on the current type of control, you need to be able to determine the control's type. One alternative is to use the (somewhat laborious) *If TypeOf* construct, like this:

```
Dim ctl as Control
For Each ctl In Me.Controls
    If TypeOf ctl is TextBox Then
        ' Do something with text box
    Else If TypeOf ctl Is ListBox Then
        ' Do something with list box
    ' and so on
    End If
Next ctl
```

An easier way to do this is to query the ControlType property of a control directly and get an integer that indicates the control type. Table 7.2 lists the different control types, along with their ControlType values and the Access constants that represent them.

TABLE 7.2: ControlType Property Values

Control	Integer	Constant
Bound object frame	108	acBoundObjectFrame
Check box	106	acCheckBox
Combo box	111	acComboBox
Command button	104	acCommandButton
Custom control	119	acCustomControl
Image	103	acImage
Label	100	acLabel
Line	102	acLine
List box	110	acListBox
Option button	105	acOptionButton
Option group	107	acOptionGroup
Page	124	acPage
Page break	118	acPageBreak
Rectangle	101	acRectangle
Subform/subreport	112	acSubform
Tab control	123	acTabCtl
Text box	109	acTextBox
Toggle button	122	acToggleButton
Unbound object frame	114	acObjectFrame

In addition, the ControlType property is read/write in Design view. (You can't change a control's type while a form is running in Form view.) This makes it possible to write tools that directly manipulate the control's type (and this is just how the Format ➢ Change To menu item works).

TIP

The Object Browser provides the easiest way for you to investigate enumerated values like the ones shown in Table 7.2. To open the Object Browser, press F2 from within any module. In the Search Text combo box (the second combo box from the top, on the left) enter the name of any constant (or other object) you'd like to investigate. Using this technique, you can retrieve lists of all the enumerated values provided by any application. Once you have the list displayed, you can select an item, press F1, and get help on that item.

The ControlTipText and ShortCutMenuBar Properties

Access allows you to create *control tips* (those little boxes describing controls you see when you leave your mouse over a control for a short period of time) and *context-sensitive menus* (the menus you get when you right-click an object) for any control. The ControlTipText property can contain up to 255 characters of text, and you can modify this property at runtime if you need to. Although you may not, in general, supply control tips for controls other than command buttons, they can be handy in other circumstances, as well. For example, frmFillTest, shown in Figure 7.4, allows you to fill a list with different items. (You'll see how frmFillTest fills its lists in the section "Changing the RowSource Property" later in this chapter.) Depending on which items you're displaying, you may want a different control tip for the text box on the form. The fragment of the code that does the work, from the SetListBox-Contents procedure in the form's module, sets the ControlTipText property of the selected text box when you choose one of the command buttons.

```
Select Case st
    Case ShowProducts
        strField = "Products"
        strTable = "tblProducts"
        txtSelected.ControlTipText = "Selected product"
    Case ShowLocations
        strField = "Locations"
        strTable = "tblLocations"
        txtSelected.ControlTipText = "Selected location"
    Case Else
        Exit Function
End Select
```

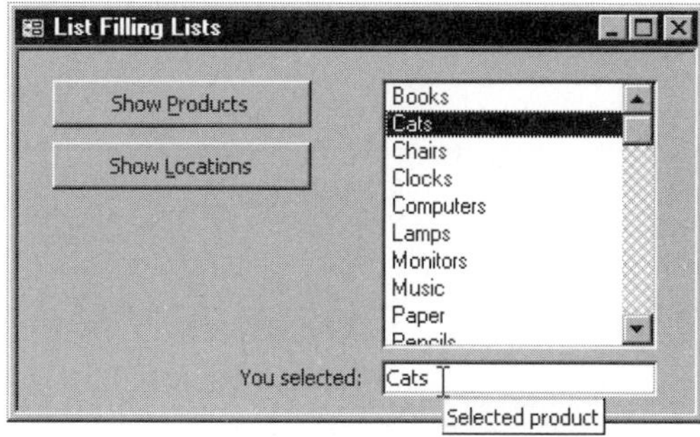

FIGURE 7.4:

Attach tool tips to controls with the ControlTipText property.

> **WARNING** At the time of this writing, control tips for list boxes simply didn't work. All other controls we tested worked fine, but the ControlTipText property for a list box was completely disabled. This may be fixed by the time you read this, but don't be alarmed if you attempt to display a control tip while hovering over a list box and you don't see anything at all.

To supply a context-sensitive menu for a control, create a shortcut command bar and choose that command bar name for the ShortCutMenuBar property of the control. The sample form frmFillTest uses this technique on the list box, as shown in Figure 7.5.

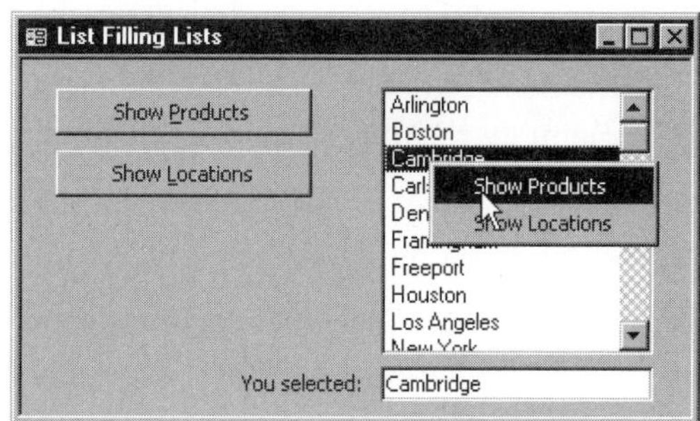

FIGURE 7.5:

Attach a context-sensitive menu to a control using the ShortCutMenuBar property.

Creating Shortcut Menus

Because Access uses command bar objects supplied by Office to create its menus, you'll use these command bars to create your shortcut menus. In addition, due to vagaries in the user interface Access supplies for creating menus and toolbars, it's not obvious what's going on as you create your shortcut menus. (For more information on working with command bars and their object models, see Chapter 11.)

TIP

If you want to convert existing shortcut menus (created with macros in earlier versions of Access), first select your menu macro (not a macro containing the AddMenu actions, but one that contains the menu items themselves) and then select the Tools ➢ Macro ➢ Create Shortcut Menu from Macro menu item. This will create a new pop-up menu (stored as a command bar) for you.

Take the following steps to create a shortcut menu from scratch. (We'll use the example shown in Figure 7.5.)

1. Select the View ➢ Toolbars ➢ Customize menu item to start the process. Make sure to select the Toolbars tab on the dialog box Access displays.
2. Click the New button on the Customize dialog to create the new, empty menu.
3. Supply a value for the name of the new menu. You'll now see a small, empty menu bar awaiting your commands.
4. Select the Commands tab on the Customize dialog so you can set the new menu's commands.
5. Click and drag the Custom command from the right-hand column. (You'll do this once for each menu item you want to create.)
6. Once you see Custom on the new menu, right-click to set the properties of the item. Fill in at least the Name property (which sets the caption for the menu item). You can also set the image for the item here.
7. Click the Properties item at the bottom of the menu, and you'll see yet another dialog. This one allows you to enter properties of the menu control.
8. Select a value for the OnAction property. This tells Access what you want to do when someone selects the menu item. You can choose an existing macro name from the drop-down list. You can also choose a public function in a standard module using the =FunctionName() syntax.
9. When you're done working with the properties of your menu control, close the dialog.

10. Up to this point, everything you've done applies to normal menus, as well as to shortcut menus. To convert this menu into a shortcut menu, select the Properties button on the Customize dialog. Once you're on the Toolbar Properties dialog, change the Type property to Pop-up. (You'll see an alert at this point, which is explained in the following paragraph.)

Access has no way, in its Toolbar customization user interface, to display shortcut menus. To work around this, all your shortcut menus appear under the Custom item on the Shortcut Menus toolbar. To edit your shortcut menu once you've set its Type property to Pop-up, follow these steps:

1. Select the View ➢ Toolbars ➢ Customize menu item to start the process.
2. Select the Shortcut Menus item from the list of available toolbars.
3. Click the Custom item at the far right of the Shortcut Menu tree. Your shortcut menu should appear as one of the items on this list.
4. Edit your items just as you would any other menu.

NOTE

Chapter 11 covers how to manipulate the CommandBar object model programmatically. Most likely, you won't need that information to create and use your forms' shortcut menus. For more information on programmatic control over menus and toolbars, see Chapter 11.

Once you've created your shortcut menu, attach it to the appropriate control, selecting it from the list of available shortcut menus in the control's ShortCutMenuBar property. The sample form, frmFillList, has a pop-up menu associated with the list box on the form, as shown in Figure 7.5.

The TabStop and TabIndex Properties

The TabIndex property allows you to control the order in which users will arrive at controls as they use the Tab or Enter key to move from control to control on your form. The TabIndex property lets you assign an ordinal value (zero-based) to each control on your form, specifying how you want the user to move between controls. Access maintains the list, ensuring that no value is used twice. You can also use the View ➢ Tab Order menu item to edit the TabStop properties in a more visual environment.

The TabStop property (Boolean) can remove a control from the form's tab list. Normally, if you press the Tab key to move from control to control on a form, the focus moves in tab order through the controls. If you set a control's TabStop property to No, Access skips that particular control. Controls that have their TabStop property set to No will still appear in the View ➢ Tab Order dialog box, however.

You can use the TabStop and TabIndex properties to gain complete control over the flow of your application's forms. You could, for example, change the tab order of fields based on a choice the user made. The example form, frmTabOrder, changes the tab order from row-first to column-first, based on a choice the user made.

The code required to change the tab order at runtime is simple. The following example was attached to the AfterUpdate event of the chkTabOrder control. All it needs to do is check the state of the check box and set the tab order accordingly.

```
Private Sub chkTabOrder_AfterUpdate()
    If chkTabOrder Then
        ' Use a column-wise ordering
        txtFirstName.TabIndex = 1
        txtLastName.TabIndex = 2
        txtMiddleInitial.TabIndex = 3
        txtAddress.TabIndex = 4
        txtCity.TabIndex = 5
        txtState.TabIndex = 6
        txtHomePhone.TabIndex = 7
        txtWorkPhone.TabIndex = 8
        txtFax.TabIndex = 9
    Else
        ' Use the AutoOrder ordering.
        txtFirstName.TabIndex = 1
        txtAddress.TabIndex = 2
        txtHomePhone.TabIndex = 3
        txtLastName.TabIndex = 4
        txtCity.TabIndex = 5
        txtWorkPhone.TabIndex = 6
        txtMiddleInitial.TabIndex = 7
        txtState.TabIndex = 8
        txtFax.TabIndex = 9
    End If
End Sub
```

The DisplayWhen Property

On forms, you can influence when Access will display a control with the DisplayWhen property. (Report controls don't include the DisplayWhen property but must use the Visible setting instead.) If you want the control to appear only when you print the form, set the DisplayWhen property to Print Only (1). To make the control appear at all times, select Always (0), and to make it display only on-screen and not at print time, choose Screen Only (2). Set the DisplayWhen property to Screen Only for all the controls you want displayed only when you're looking at the form on screen.

TIP

Access provides the IsVisible property for report controls, which are available only at print time. Using this property, you can find out whether a control has been hidden because you've turned on the HideDuplicates property and, for the current row, whether the value is the same as that in the previous row. See Chapter 9 for more information.

Controlling Text Layout

Access 2000 adds three new properties (actually, six new properties, but we're treating four of them as a single property) for labels and text boxes that control the way text is displayed and entered. These new properties are

LineSpacing Allows you to control the space between lines, in twips.

Vertical If True, displays text starting at the upper right-hand corner to the lower left-hand corner. (Text normally displays starting at the upper left-hand corner down to the lower right-hand corner.)

LeftMargin, RightMargin, TopMargin, and BottomMargin Controls the placement of text. Each of these properties allows you to specify a value, in twips, indicating the amount of white space you want around your text on each side.

To demonstrate these properties, try out frmTestMargins, shown in Figure 7.6. This sample form allows you to set the Vertical and LineSpacing properties, along with the four margin properties individually, to see their effects on text in a label control.

FIGURE 7.6:

Use the Vertical, LineSpacing, LeftMargin (and its friends) properties to control the text layout in a text box or label.

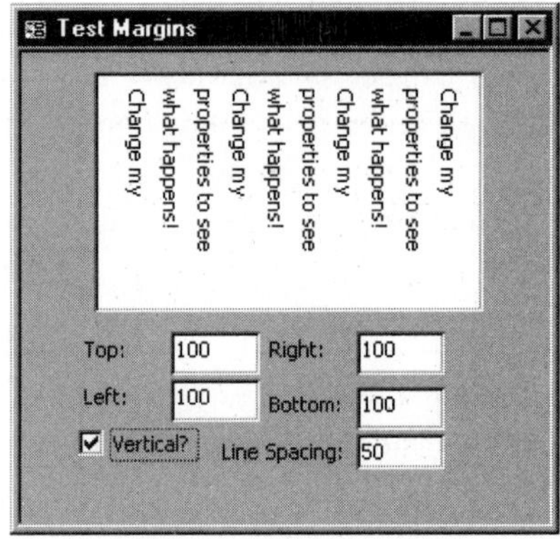

Using Labels

Labels are the simplest of all nongraphic Access controls. A label presents *static* text on a form or report. That is, the text doesn't change as you move from record to record. Labels can never receive input focus and, thus, can never be used to input data. The form's tab order skips over them. Labels, then, are best for displaying information on forms you never want your users to be able to change, such as data-gathering instructions or your company's name. Generally, you also use labels to display the field names for bound controls. Unless told otherwise, Access creates a label control to accompany any bound control you create, including the field name and a colon.

TIP

If you want to change the way Access creates labels for your bound fields, edit the default text box properties (and those of other controls you use). If you select the text box button in the toolbox, the property sheet heading should be Default Textbox. Modify the AutoLabel and AddColon properties to match your preferences. In addition, you can set the LabelX and LabelY properties to control the offset of the label from the text box to which it's attached.

NOTE You cannot create a label without text. That sounds obvious, but it's very disconcerting when you accidentally try to do it. If you size a label just right but then click some other control before entering a caption value, Access removes the label as though you had never created it. You can, however, enter a single space character, if you like, to create a label without visible text.

You can change the color, font name, font size, and text alignment for text in a label. You can also change the Color and SpecialEffect properties of the label itself. It's best to standardize the appearance of the field labels in your application, and you'll find that the control default properties can help you out. (See the section "Using Default Control Properties to Your Advantage" later in this chapter for more information.)

Once you've changed the font (name or size) for a particular label, you may find the text no longer fits inside the label. Double-clicking any of the control *handles* (the little black boxes that surround the control frame) causes Access to resize the control for best fit—that is, Access resizes the control so it's just big enough for your text. This is equivalent to choosing the Format ➢ Size ➢ To Fit menu item and can be useful if you're trying out different font sizes. You can emulate this in your code using the SizeToFit method in Design view, as well.

The Parent Property

Although you won't find it on the property sheet, labels expose a Parent property, which returns to you the control that is the parent for the label. Other control types return the logical value for their Parent property: items in option groups return the option group as their parent, and all other controls return the form as their parent. (For more information on option groups, see the section "Using Option Groups—Controls inside Controls" later in this chapter.)

For example, imagine you have a label named lblOption1 that's attached to a check box, chkOption1, which resides inside the option group grpCheckBoxes on frmOptionGroups. The Immediate window session shown in Figure 7.7 demonstrates the relationships between controls and their parents. (You can try this out yourself by opening frmOptionGroups and the Immediate window at the same time.)

FIGURE 7.7:

The Parent property allows you to walk up the hierarchy of controls on a form.

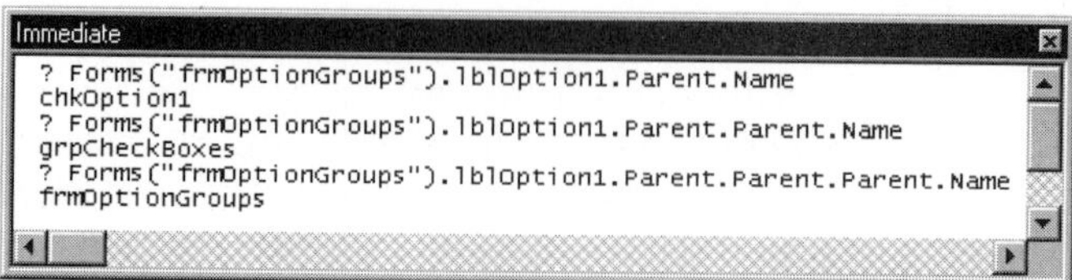

Immediate
? Forms("frmOptionGroups").lblOption1.Parent.Name
chkOption1
? Forms("frmOptionGroups").lblOption1.Parent.Parent.Name
grpCheckBoxes
? Forms("frmOptionGroups").lblOption1.Parent.Parent.Parent.Name
frmOptionGroups

TIP

Just as you can use the Parent property of a label to find the control to which it's attached, you can use the Controls collection of any control to find the label attached to it (or any other controls the control contains). See the section "Using Controls' Controls Collection" later in the chapter for more information.

Using Text Boxes

Although labels may be the simplest of all Access controls, text boxes are the most common. You can use text boxes to display data, as well as to capture it. They can contain single or multiple lines. They can display scroll bars if you wish. Text boxes can contain any amount of textual information (sure, there's a limit, but you're not likely to hit it).

You can think of a text box as a mini-notepad that allows you to enter free-form text. If you think your data entry will require more than one line or if you are using a text box to display information from a memo field, your best bet is to enable scroll bars. (Set the ScrollBars property to Vertical rather than None. Unfortunately, there is no way to have scroll bars appear only if you need them. They're either on or off.)

TIP

As is the Windows standard, the Enter key causes Access not to insert a carriage return/line feed in your text box, but rather to move to the next control. To move to a new line, you must press Ctrl+Enter. To make the Enter key insert a carriage return/line feed, set the EnterKeyBehavior property of the text box to New Line in Field. This makes the text box work more as you might expect but less like the rest of Windows.

NOTE

Access text boxes can support only a single font and a single text attribute (bold, italic, or underline). Unless you care to embed an object (either the RTF text ActiveX control, available with Visual Basic and the Microsoft Office Developer, or a Microsoft Word document), you will need to forego multiple fonts and formatting within text boxes.

Carrying Values Forward into New Records

In some instances, your application may require the ability to carry forward existing field values into the new row when your user adds a new row using a form. Access does not provide this ability on its own, but it's not difficult to implement it in Basic. This functionality requires modifying the DefaultValue property of your controls, storing away field values. Then, when you add a new row, those default values will be placed into the controls for you.

This is a perfect situation in which you can make good use of the Tag property, as described in the section "Using the Tag Property to Create Your Own Properties" earlier in this chapter. For each control, you can use the Tag property to store the original DefaultValue property, so if you decide to stop carrying values forward for a specific text box, you can reset the original default value.

In addition, the example form, frmCarryTest, shown in Figure 7.8, allows you to interactively decide which fields will be carried. The form includes toggle buttons next to the fields you're likely to want to carry into a new row. Each of these toggle buttons includes, in its Tag property, a string indicating which bound control it's to be associated with.

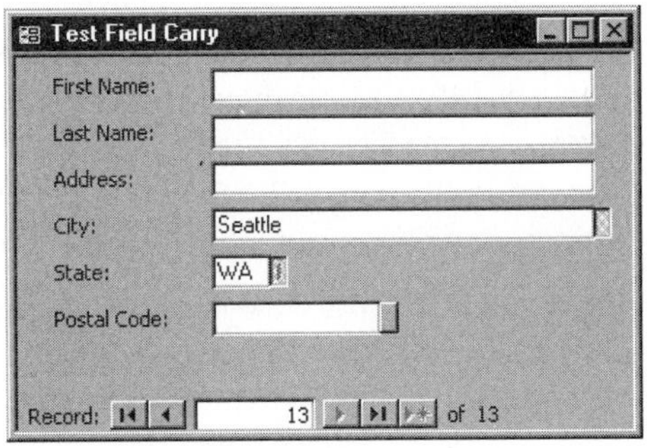

FIGURE 7.8:

The sample form, frmCarry-Test, allows you to selectively carry values forward into a new row.

How Does It Work?

Each of the toggle buttons on the sample form includes, in its Tag property, a string that associates the button with a bound control on the form. For example, the toggle button next to the City field contains this string in its Tag property:

```
Ctl=txtCity
```

If you want to use this same technique, and need to store your own information in the Tag property as well, separate the name=value pairs with semicolons.

The code called when you click the toggle button will use the Ctl tagged value to find out which control it needs to modify. Each of the toggle buttons calls, from its AfterUpdate event, a common procedure:

```
=HandleCarry([Form],[Screen].[ActiveControl])
```

This common function, HandleCarry (in basCarry), handles all the details. Listing 7.2 shows the entire procedure.

TIP

You might be tempted to count on the ActiveForm, ActiveControl, and Previous-Control properties of the screen object, which allow you to write generic functions to be called from forms. For the most part, you're better off passing the Form property (from the property sheet) or the Me property (from a form's class module) down to functions called in standard modules. The main problem is that often in the Access environment there is no current form or control. Attempting to access one of these properties at those times causes a runtime error. This makes it particularly difficult to debug code that contains these objects. There is, however, no simple replacement for Screen.ActiveControl, which is what we've used in this example.

Calling Procedures from Events

If you want to run code when a control event occurs, you have three options. You can

- Call an event procedure in the form's class module and place [Event Procedure] in the associated event property in the Properties window.
- Call a macro and place the name of the macro in the associated event property. We don't recommend this technique, primarily because Access cannot pass to the macro important information about the event (the key that was pressed, the mouse button that was clicked, and so on).

Continued on next page

- Call a public function (not a sub) in a standard module. To do this, place =FunctionName() in the associated event property (you can pass parameters to the function, as well).

We've elected to use the third option in this example, even though this isn't the way you'll normally handle events. In this case, it's likely you'll use this carrying technique in a form that doesn't otherwise have any code associated with it, and adding a module for just these procedure calls seemed like more trouble than it was worth. In addition, because the property value is the same for all the controls, it's easy to set the value for all of them in one step. Simply select them all and enter the same value for each, all at once, in the Properties window.

You'll need to decide for yourself which of the three techniques you'll use when reacting to events on forms or reports, but we'll almost always use the first—writing VBA code in the class module of the form or report. However, rules are meant to be broken.

Listing 7.2

```
Public Function HandleCarry _
 (frm As Form, ctlToggle As Control) As Boolean

    ' This constant must match the Tag value you
    ' used when creating the toggle buttons on the form.
    Const adhcCtlID As String = "Ctl"
    Const adhcDV As String = "DefaultValue"

    Const adhcQuote As String = """"

    Dim ctlCarry As Control
    Dim strOldDV As String
    Dim tv As TaggedValues
    Dim strName As String

    On Error GoTo HandleErrors

    ' Get the associated control
    ' name for the toggle button.
    Set tv = New TaggedValues
    tv.Text = ctlToggle.Tag
    strName = tv.Item(adhcCtlID)
```

```
' Now that you've got the associated control
' name, get its Tag property value and
' set the new DefaultValue property.
If Len(strName) > 0 Then
    ' Get a reference to the control containing
    ' the data.
    Set ctlCarry = frm(strName)
    If ctlToggle.Value Then
        ' The button is depressed, so set up associated
        ' control to carry forward.
        ' First, store away the current DefaultValue
        ' property, so it's there when you "untoggle".
        ' This'll put a string like:
        '   DefaultValue="Old Default Value"
        ' in the control's Tag property.

        ' Parse the current Tag property.
        tv.Text = ctlCarry.Tag
        ' Add the new default value to the
        ' tagged values.
        tv.Add adhcDV, ctlCarry.DefaultValue
        ' Store the new tagged/value list
        ' to the Tag property of the text box.
        ctlCarry.Tag = tv.Text

        ' Set the control's DefaultValue to be what
        ' you got from the Tag property,
        ' surrounded with quotes. Make sure
        ' and double up quotes inside the text
        ' so that you can use quotes in the
        ' default value.
        ctlCarry.DefaultValue = _
         adhcQuote & _
         Replace(ctlCarry.Value, adhcQuote, _
          adhcQuote & adhcQuote) & _
         adhcQuote

    Else
        ' The button is cleared, so reset the default
        ' value to its previous value.

        ' Parse the Tag property in tv.
```

```
            tv.Text = ctlCarry.Tag
            ' Set the default value back
            ' to the stored default value.
            ctlCarry.DefaultValue = tv.Item(adhcDV)
        End If
    End If
    HandleCarry = True

ExitHere:
    On Error Resume Next
    Set tv = Nothing
    Exit Function

HandleErrors:
    HandleCarry = False
    Select Case Err.Number
        Case Else
            MsgBox "Error: " & Err.Description & _
             " (" & Err.Number & ")"
    End Select
    Resume ExitHere
End Function
```

To use this function, pass to it a reference to the current form (in the example, by sending the form's Form property in the function call) and a reference to the current control—the toggle button that triggered the event procedure (using Screen.ActiveControl in the sample form). The function first attempts to retrieve, from the current control, the name of the bound control with which it's associated (adhcCtlID contains the value Ctl—the tag used on the form to designate the control whose value should be carried").

```
Set tv = New TaggedValues
tv.Text = ctlToggle.Tag
strName = tv.Item(adhcCtlID)
```

If strName contains text, the code sets a variable to refer to the bound control and then decides what to do based on the value of the toggle button. If the toggle button is depressed, the code follows these four steps:

1. It retrieves the text box's current Tag property and assigns it into a TaggedValues object.

2. It adds a tag/value pair for the current DefaultValue property of the text box.
3. It replaces the text box's Tag property with a new value, including the control's original DefaultValue property.
4. It sets the DefaultValue property of the text box to be the value that's to be carried over to new rows.

In the following code fragment, ctlCarry is a reference to the control whose value is being carried forward. (In this fragment, the constant adhcDV contains the text to be used as the tag name, DefaultValue.)

```
tv.Text = ctlCarry.Tag
tv.Add adhcDV, ctlCarry.DefaultValue
ctlCarry.Tag = tv.Text
ctlCarry.DefaultValue = _
 adhcQuote & _
 Replace(ctlCarry.Value, _
  adhcQuote, adhcQuote & adhcQuote) & _
  adhcQuote
```

If the button is raised, the code resets the bound control's DefaultValue property to the value retrieved from the control's Tag property.

```
tv.Text = ctlCarry.Tag
' Set the default value back
' to the stored default value.
ctlCarry.DefaultValue = tv.Item(adhcDV)
```

NOTE

The DefaultValue property must be a string, and it must be enclosed in quotes. That explains why the code must wrap ctlCarry.Value in quotes (using the adhcQuote constant) before assigning it to ctlCarry.DefaultValue. In addition, if the property value contains a quote itself, this code would fail. Therefore, the code also calls the VBA Replace function, replacing a single quote with two quotes. This allows VBA to parse the expression containing quotes within a quoted string.

Carrying Values in Your Own Forms

To use this technique in your own applications, follow these steps:

1. Import the basCarry, TaggedValue, and TaggedValues modules into your application.

2. Create your bound form, or use an existing bound form.
3. Add toggle buttons next to controls bound to fields that you might like to carry forward as you add new rows to the form.
4. For each toggle button, set the Tag property to indicate which bound control it is to be associated with, as discussed above.
5. Select all the toggle buttons and call the HandleCarry function from the AfterUpdate event, as discussed above.

That's all there is to it. When you run your form and select one of the toggle buttons, HandleCarry will set the DefaultValue for the selected control to be the current value of the control. When you go to the new row, Access will supply the default value for you.

The ControlSource Property and Calculated Controls

Access developers often use text boxes to display calculated values. Figure 7.9 shows the sample form, frmControlSource, with a DueDate field that draws its data from a table and two text boxes that display the number of days overdue for this payment. To create a calculated control, you have two choices:

- Use an expression
- Use a user-defined function

FIGURE 7.9:

Using calculated controls on a form. Note that both methods (using an expression and using a function) return the same value.

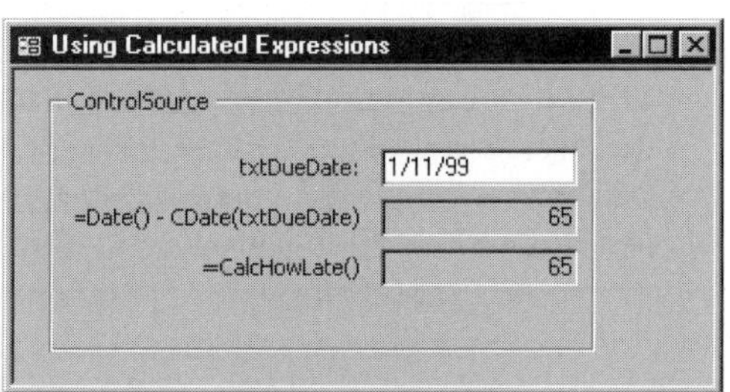

The second and third text boxes on the sample form use one of the preceding methods for calculating the number of days late.

In either case, you must precede the value in the property sheet with an equal sign (=), which indicates to Access that it must include what follows.

To create an expression that will be evaluated when the control is recalculated—for example, to calculate the past due amount—use the expression

```
=Date() - CDate([txtDueDate])
```

This simple expression calculates the number of days since the due date and displays it. Figure 7.9 shows this example in action.

Your other option is to create a function that places a value in the text box.

NOTE

In general, if you want a specific event to place a value into a control on a form, it is not enough to specify a function call in the property sheet. Your function must explicitly place its value into the control. In most properties, Access completely disregards the return value from the function. Combined with the fact that Access can call only functions (which must return values), not subroutines (which do not return values), from the property sheet, it's easy to get confused. On top of that, Access is inconsistent as to how it treats function calls from the property sheet. The DefaultValue and ControlSource properties, for example, pass the return value from a function call on to the text box. All event properties disregard the return value.

Using the same example as above, you could create a function:

```
Function CalcHowLate()
    CalcHowLate = Date() - CDate(txtDueDate)
End Function
```

To use a function to supply the ControlSource value, precede its name with an equal (=) sign. That is, in the above example, you would use =CalcHowLate().

NOTE

The expression in the previous example uses the CDate function to convert the value in the text box into a date. Because all control values are stored internally as variants but this calculation requires a date value, the CDate function ensures that Access understands what it is the expression needs to do.

Using Two-State Controls (the Yes/No Crowd)

All the controls described in the following sections (toggle button, option button, and check box) can represent data that has two states when used outside an option group on a form. (When grouped in an option group, they can represent more information.) Therefore, they all represent reasonable ways to present the user with yes/no data for acceptance. Each represents its two states differently, and you can use these differences to your advantage.

If you also need to represent a third state in which you don't yet know the value for the control, Access provides the TripleState property for toggle buttons, option buttons, and check boxes, as long as they're not embedded in an option group.

The Toggle Button

In an option group, the toggle button has two states: up and down. Its up state represents the False/No condition (unselected), and its down state represents the True/Yes condition (selected). It can display either text or a picture (but, unfortunately, not both). Access creates a dithered version of the picture on the button for its depressed state, relieving you from having to supply two separate bitmaps, one for the up state and one for the down state. Outside an option group, you can set the TripleState property to allow the button to also show a null value.

TIP

If you require a button that includes both text and a picture, you can create a bitmap in a graphics program, like Microsoft PaintBrush, that includes both and use that bitmap as the image for your button. From the user's perspective, it will look right, even though it's just a bitmap. You can even include a hot key: in your bitmap, underline the character you'd like to have activate the button, and include in the button's Caption property a string with that specific character preceded by an ampersand (&) (&A, for example, to make Alt+A trigger your button).

Using toggle buttons to represent yes/no information to the user can make your forms more visually appealing than using simple check boxes, but they make sense in only a limited number of situations. If your user is inputting information that answers a simple yes/no question, toggle buttons aren't as clear as check boxes. On the other hand, if you are gathering other two-state information (alive or deceased, U.S. citizen or not), toggle buttons often are quite useful. Here's the real test: if you're tempted to use a toggle button alone on a form with a text description, use a check box instead. If you need a group of check boxes or if you can use a picture instead of text, consider using toggle buttons.

The Option Button

Option buttons do represent two states, but common usage suggests you use them most often in option groups to allow selection of a single item from the group. In that situation, the two states can be thought of as selected and not selected. For that reason, programmers often refer to option buttons as *radio buttons,* harking back to the automobile radios of yesteryear with mechanical buttons used to select stations. You could depress only one button at a time, and pressing one unpressed the rest.

When representing yes/no data, the option button displays a filled circle when it's in the True/Yes state. When representing the False/No state, it displays just an empty circle.

Although you can use option buttons alone on a form and can use the TripleState property in that situation, avoid using single option buttons on forms. You should limit their usage to the radio button metaphor in option groups. If you need a single option button, use a check box instead.

The Check Box

The check box is the standard two-state control. When in the Yes (True) state, the control displays a check mark inside a box. When in the No (False) state, it displays an empty box. Check boxes commonly stand alone or are used in groups to select multiple options. You can use check boxes in option groups, but common usage suggests you avoid this situation. Using check boxes in an option group allows you to choose only a single value, and this spoils the point of using check boxes, which is to allow multiple choices. If you want to make a group of check boxes *look* like an option group, you can enclose them within a rectangle. Figure 7.10 shows all the combinations of these two-state controls.

TIP

At some point, you may want to change the size of a check box or the character displayed within the check box. You can't. If you want to do either of these things, you'll need to create your own hybrid control that looks like a check box and acts like a check box but can be sized and change characters. You can do this, with enough effort, by grouping other controls in a way that looks like a check box. You'll need to write all the supporting code yourself, of course.

FIGURE 7.10:

All the two-state controls (in rectangles, not option groups, so they can be null)

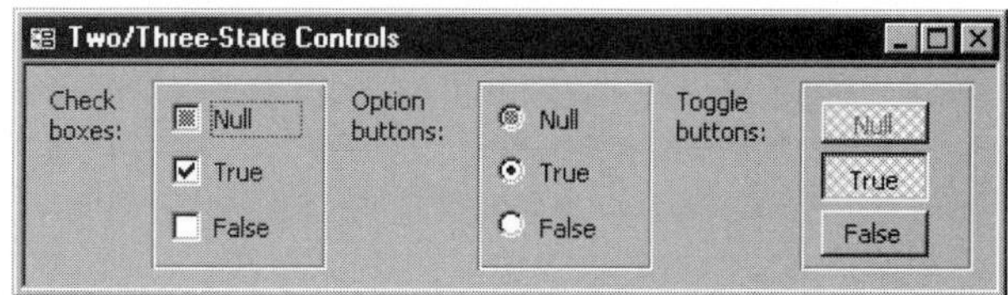

Using Option Groups—Controls inside Controls

The option group allows you to group multiple controls (toggle buttons, option buttons, or check boxes) for the purpose of choosing a single value. Each subcontrol has its own value (set in its OptionValue property) and, when it's chosen, it assigns that value to the option group. Usually an option group consists of multiples of a single type of control. Figure 7.11 shows the sample form frmOptionGroups with three different option groups, one for each type of subcontrol. In addition, this figure includes an option group composed of various subcontrols. Although there's no reason not to create an option group combining different subcontrols, it's a good idea to avoid doing so since it's confusing and serves no real purpose.

TIP

You can only place option buttons, toggle buttons, and check box controls inside an option group control. Other controls can be placed in the same real estate as the option group, but the option group won't contain them.

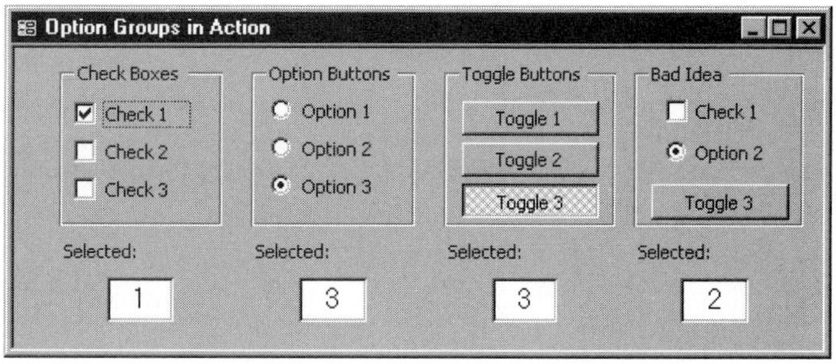

FIGURE 7.11:

Four option group examples. We don't recommend creating option groups composed of different subcontrols.

TIP

Don't be shy about using the Control Wizards to help you build option groups. The Option Group Control Wizard can save you some steps, and you'll find it a useful tool. Don't believe anyone who tells you that real programmers don't use Wizards! Real programmers do anything that will save them time, and the Control Wizards do.

There's nothing keeping you from assigning the same OptionValue property to multiple subcontrols. In fact, if you copy a control within an option group, Access assigns the new control the same option value as the original control. This can be confusing because choosing one subcontrol will simultaneously select all subcontrols with the same OptionValue property. On the other hand, there's nothing keeping you from skipping option values. They need not be contiguous. The only limitation is that they must be Long integer values.

TIP

In the interest of preserving screen real estate and simplifying your input forms, consider using a combo box if you find your option group includes more than five items. Option groups take up a great deal of space on the screen, and, with more than five subcontrols in the group, it becomes difficult to choose the correct item.

The value of an option group can be only a single whole number, no matter how much you'd like an option group to return a string or any other data type. This means the option value of each internal subcontrol is also limited to being a whole number. If you must use text values, for example, you can create an array of strings in your application and use the value returned from the option group as an index into your array. (See the section "Returning 'Real' Information from Option Groups" later in this chapter for information on returning string values.)

TIP

Because option groups can return only a single value, you are limited to making only one choice from the group of subcontrols inside it. This design indicates you would be better off using only toggle buttons or option buttons in an option group, because each of those is suited for making a single choice. If you need an option group that contains check boxes, allowing you to choose several items, consider creating a "faux" option group. To do this, enclose your check boxes within a rectangle (rather than within an option group). This way, they'll look as though they are part of an option group, but they will allow multiple selections. Note, though, that you will have to examine each check box separately to find which ones you have selected. If you have controls inside an option group, you don't need to examine each separately, because all you care about is the single control you've selected, and Access assigns that value to the option group.

TIP

Another alternative to the option group control is to use a tab control. The tab control can contain almost any other control type (option groups can contain only the three types of controls shown in Figure 7.11), and it grants you some of the benefits of an option group without its limitation of one selected control. See the section "Using the Tab Control as a Container" later in this chapter for more information.

Access treats the option group, once it's populated with subcontrols, as a single control; when you select the container and move it, all the internal controls move, too. When you delete the container, Access deletes all the internal controls. Unless you're aware that this will happen, it can cause havoc in your development. Make sure you really intend to delete all the internal controls before you delete an option group!

Moving Controls to a New Neighborhood

You'll find that moving a currently existing control into an option group does not work. Although the subcontrol will appear to be inside the option group, the two will not function together. (This same problem occurs with pages of a tab control, and you can use the same solutions.) To add items to an option group, use either of the following two methods:

Create a new control Select the option group and then choose your subcontrol from the toolbar and place it in the option group. Note that when you move the cursor to drop a subcontrol, the option group becomes highlighted as you pass the cursor over it. This visual prompt indicates that the option group is ready to receive a subcontrol.

Cut and paste an existing control Once you've used the Edit ➢ Cut menu item to cut the control, select the option group. With the option group selected, choose Edit ➢ Paste. Access places the control inside the option group as a real, active subcontrol.

NOTE

Controls in an option group lose their properties that deal with the underlying data, such as the ControlSource, TripleState, and ValidationRule properties, because they are no longer independent representations of data from the underlying record source. On the other hand, they gain the OptionValue property, because you must assign each a unique value. This is the value the control will return to the option group once you've made a choice. Therefore, you'll note that the properties for an independent control are a bit different from the properties for an identical control in an option group.

Assigning and Retrieving Values

Because the option group's value is the value of the chosen subcontrol, you can assign a value to the option group by making an assignment to the option group name. For example, the following code assigns the value 3 to the option group grpTestGroup:

```
grpTestGroup = 3
```

This would cause Access to select the subcontrol in grpTestGroup that had the OptionValue of 3.

Likewise, you can retrieve the value of the option group just by referencing its name. The expression

```
varNewValue = grpTestGroup
```

assigns the value chosen in grpTestGroup to the Variant variable varNewValue.

The reason the previous assignment works is that you're actually assigning the Value property of grpTestGroup to varNewValue. Because the Value property of a control is its default property, Access knows that's what you meant when you've specified no property at all.

NOTE The option group's value is Null when there are no items chosen. Therefore, just as with any other form control, consider retrieving its value into a variant-type variable that can handle the possible null return value.

Returning "Real" Information from Option Groups

Although option groups can return only integral values, you can work around this problem if you want an option group to gather and show information from a text field that has only a limited number of possible values. It may be that you're sharing data with other applications or that you just aren't able to change the field format to meet Access' requirements. In that case, you'll need a few tricks to use option groups to represent textual information.

TIP

If at all possible, try to reorganize your tables in such a way that limited-option fields can be stored as whole numbers. Not only does this make it simple to use an option group to show the data, it cuts down on memory usage. Imagine you have 1000 records with one of the following in the Delivery field: Overnight, 2nd Day Air, or Ground. Not only is this field prone to data entry problems, it uses a lot more disk/memory space than necessary. If you were to create a small table with those three values and an integer attached to each, you could just store the integers in your main table. Data entry would be simpler, you'd be using less memory, and everyone involved would be happier.

To bind the option group to text values rather than integer values, create an extra text box on your form. Normally, you would make this text box invisible (set its Visible property to No), but for this example, it will stay visible. Figure 7.12 shows the finished form frmDelivery. For the purposes of this example, the option group's name is grpDelivery and the text box's name is txtDelivery. The text box is bound to the field containing the text, and the option group is unbound; the text box is the control that will send and receive data to and from the underlying table, and the option group will be used only to collect and display that data.

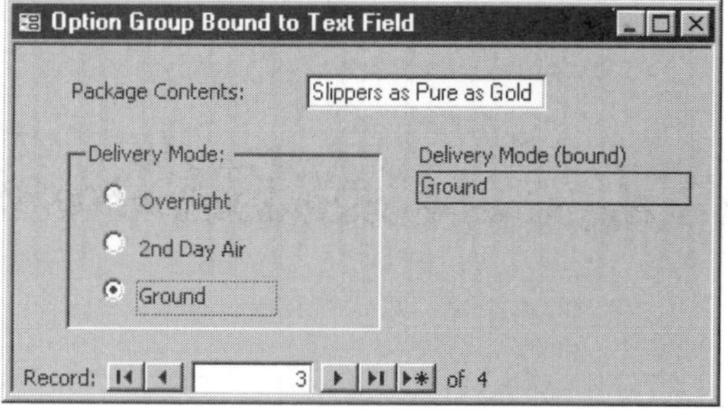

FIGURE 7.12: Binding an option group to a text value. Note the bound text box, which normally would be invisible.

Once you have the bound text box on the form, you need to solve two problems:

- As you move from record to record, how do you get the right option in the option group to be chosen?
- As you make a choice in the option group, how do you get its value written out to the underlying data, if it's not bound?

To answer the first question, you need to attach code to the form's Current event. Access raises this event each time it makes a record current and allows you to set the value of the option group for each record. For this simple case, you can use the Switch function, which returns the value corresponding to the first True statement it finds in its parameters.

```
grpDelivery = Switch( _
 txtDelivery = "Overnight", 1, _
 txtDelivery = "2nd Day Air", 2, _
 txtDelivery = "Ground", 3, _
 True, Null)
```

Using the Switch Function

You can use Switch to take the place of nested If...Then...Else...End If statements. Its general syntax is

retval = Switch(*expr1*, *var1* [,*expr2*, *var2*([,*exprN*, *varN*]])

where *expr1* through *exprN* are expressions that return either True or False and *var1* through *varN* are the values to be returned if the corresponding expression is True. Switch returns the value corresponding to the first expression it finds in its list that returns True.

For example, the Switch function call in the previous example:

```
grpDelivery = Switch( _
 txtDelivery = "Overnight", 1, _
 txtDelivery = "2nd Day Air", 2, _
 txtDelivery = "Ground", 3, _
 True, Null)
```

could have been written as

```
If txtDelivery = "Overnight" Then
    grpDelivery = 1
ElseIf txtDelivery = "2nd Day Air" Then
    grpDelivery = 2
ElseIf txtDelivery = "Ground" Then
    grpDelivery = 3
Else
    grpDelivery = Null
End If
```

Be aware of a few issues that arise when you use Switch:

- In early versions of Access, you were limited to seven pairs of expressions. Now, the list is basically unlimited. Common sense would indicate that you should limit your list to a reasonable, understandable number of entries.
- Switch returns Null if either none of the expressions return a True value, or if the value associated with the first True expression is Null.
- Although only one of the expressions may be True, Access will evaluate every one of them. This can lead to undesirable side effects. For example, if you try the following code, you will inevitably end up with an Overflow error because, if either x or y is 0, you end up dividing by 0, even though it appears that you've checked for that in the first expression:

  ```
  varValue = Switch(x = 0 Or y = 0, 0, _
   x >= y, x/y, _
   x < y, y/x)
  ```

To answer the second question, you need to attach code to the AfterUpdate event of the option group. This code will place the correct value into the bound txtDelivery text box, which will, in turn, send it to the underlying data source. For this example, you should use code like this:

```
txtDelivery = Choose(grpDelivery, _
 "Overnight", _
 "2nd Day Air", _
 "Ground")
```

Using the Choose Function

Like the Switch function, the Choose function is yet another replacement for nested If...Then...Else...End If statements. It takes an integer as its first parameter and then a list of parameters from which to choose. Access returns the value corresponding, in position, to the index you passed as the first parameter. Its general syntax is

Choose(intIndex, *expr1* [,*expr2*]...)

Be aware of the following issues that arise when you use Choose:

- In early versions of Access, you were limited to 13 possible values in the expression list. Now you can use a seemingly unlimited number of elements.

Of course, if the list becomes too long, your execution speed and code maintainability will suffer.

- The index value can only be a value between 1 and the number of expressions you've provided, inclusive. If you pass a floating-point value, Access converts it to an integer following the same rules it does for the Fix function.
- Although Choose returns only one of the values, it evaluates them all. Beware of possible side effects. If you call a function in one or more expressions, each of those functions will be called. For example, if each of your expressions called the InputBox function, each and every one of the expressions would get evaluated, causing the InputBox dialog box to pop up multiple times as Access evaluated the list of expressions.

Using Controls' Controls Collection

In early versions of Access before Access 97, it was impossible to tell, given a reference to an option group, which controls were inside it. It was impossible to tell, programmatically, which label control on a form was attached to which text box. These problems, and others, were resolved with the addition of the Controls collection of most control types.

For example, the Controls collection of an option group contains references to all the controls placed inside the option group. This seems so obvious that you have to wonder why it wasn't in the product from the very beginning. The following fragment (from the EnableAll procedure in the class module of frmControlsProperty) enables/disables all the option buttons in the option group:

```
Private Sub EnableAll( _
 ctlMain As Control, fEnable As Boolean)
    ' Given a control, enable/disable all the
    ' option button controls it contains.

    Dim ctl As Control

    For Each ctl In ctlMain.Controls
        If ctl.ControlType = acOptionButton Then
            ctl.Enabled = fEnable
        End If
    Next ctl
End Sub
```

In versions of Access before Access 97, this process would have required looping through all the controls on the form, checking the Parent property of each control, and, for those option buttons in the right option group, setting the Enabled property. That could take a lot more time and effort.

Another useful artifact of the Controls collection is that you can now find out the label control attached to another control. For example, perhaps you want to set the foreground color of the label attached to a check box if that check box is selected. In versions of Access before Access 97, you'd have to use some artificial naming convention, storing the attached control's name in the Tag property, or use some other workaround to find out which label was attached to the check box. Now, you can use the Controls collection. The label control will be the only control in the collection, for most control types; therefore, its ordinal position in the collection of controls will always be 0. The following code fragment, from frmControlsProperty, sets the foreground color of the label attached to a check box to either black or red, depending on whether you've checked or unchecked the control.

```
Private Sub ColorLabel(ctl As Control)
    ' Depending on the value of ctl,
    ' set the label to be black or red.
    With ctl.Controls(0)
        If ctl Then
            .ForeColor = vbRed
        Else
            .ForeColor = vbBlack
        End If
    End With
End Sub
```

It couldn't be much simpler than that!

In addition to the uses shown here, the Controls collection of various objects can aid you in many situations. For example, if you want to work with all the controls in the Header section of a form, you can enumerate all the controls in that one section. In previous versions of Access, you had to work through all the controls on the form and, for each control, check its Section property. That is, instead of writing code like this:

```
Dim ctl As Control
For Each ctl in Me.Controls
    If ctl.Section = acHeader Then
        ' Use this control
    End If
Next ctl
```

you can write the same fragment this way:

```
Dim ctl As Control
For Each ctl In Me.Sections(acHeader).Controls
    ' Use this control
Next ctl
```

The same technique applies to working with controls inside a page of a tab control. Use the Controls collection of the Page object to manipulate each of the controls on the page.

Using List and Combo Boxes

List boxes and combo boxes share many similar properties and uses. Combo boxes combine a text box and a list box in one control. Both list and combo boxes present a list of values, allowing you to choose a single item. They can present multiple columns of data, and you can use them as full data structures with hidden columns that can contain data.

Differences between List and Combo Boxes

Although list and combo boxes share many of the same properties, events, and uses, several of their specific details are unique to their particular control type. Table 7.3 lists those idiosyncrasies.

TABLE 7.3: Differences between List and Combo Boxes

Item	List Box	Combo Box
Item choices	Allows you to choose only from the items already in the list.	Allows you either to choose from the values in the list or to add new ones. This actually depends on the LimitToList property and on which column is bound to the underlying field (for more information, see the section "The LimitToList Problem" later in this chapter.)
Screen real estate	Takes up as much space as you assign it. Works best when as many items as possible are immediately visible.	Takes up the space of a single text box when it doesn't have the input focus and as many lines as you specify (in the ListRows property) when it has the focus.

Continued on next page

TABLE 7.3 CONTINUED: Differences between List and Combo Boxes

Item	List Box	Combo Box
Keyboard handling	Matches only the first character of items in its list against letters you press. Pressing **M** matches the first item that starts with M. Pressing it again finds the next, and so on. Pressing a different letter finds the first item that starts with that letter.	Performs an incremental search as you type. That is, if you press **M**, it scrolls to find the first item that begins with M. If you then press **i**, it finds the first item that begins with Mi and scrolls to that item. Pressing Backspace returns the selection to the previous item you chose. In addition, if you've set the AutoExpand property to Yes, as you type, Access automatically finds and displays the first underlying data element that matches the number of characters you've typed so far. This auto-fill feature, similar to that found in several popular financial packages, is useful, especially when combined with the LimitToList property. On the other hand, it does slow down data entry somewhat.
Selected Items	List boxes can be configured to allow multiple selections. Once you set the MultiSelect property appropriately, you can choose one or more contiguous or noncontiguous items.	Combo boxes can never select more than a single item.

Important Properties of List and Combo Boxes

Access' Control Wizards can perform most of the work of creating list and combo boxes on your forms. At times, though, you might want to create the combo or list box from scratch if you find you don't get the flexibility you need when using the Wizard. List and combo boxes provide great flexibility in how they allow you, as a programmer, to display information to the user while controlling the input. Unfortunately, with this degree of flexibility, the large number of options can be daunting. Many of the properties are interrelated and collectively affect how the control operates. The following sections detail some of the properties you need to understand to get the full benefit of these controls.

The Name Property

The Name property specifies the internal reference name for the control. The actual value of this property has no real significance, except as a convenience for the programmer.

TIP

Many beginning Access programmers confuse the Name property with the Control-Source property. The control name specifies only the name by which you, the programmer, will refer to the control. It has nothing to do with the underlying data, while the control source is actually linked with the data.

The ControlSource Property

The ControlSource property links the control with the underlying data. Specifying a field name tells Access where to retrieve the value of the control and where to place the value returned from the control once you select an item. The control returns the value from the column set in the BoundColumn property. With other controls, you can enter an expression preceded by an equal (=) sign for the Control-Source property. With list and combo boxes, this option succeeds only in making the control read-only.

The RowSourceType Property

The RowSourceType property specifies where to retrieve the rows of data the control displays. The options are

Table/Query The data comes from a table or query or from a SQL expression. In any case, the RowSource property specifies the table/query name or the SQL expression that will retrieve the dataset.

Value List The data comes from a list you specify explicitly in the Row-Source property.

Field List The data will consist of a list of fields from the table or query specified in the RowSource property.

(User-Defined) If you specify a function name with no equal sign and no trailing parentheses, Access calls it to fill the list or combo box. (See the section "Filling a List or Combo Box Programmatically" later in this chapter for more information.)

The RowSource Property

The RowSource property specifies which data to retrieve for presentation in the list or combo box. Its syntax depends on the RowSourceType property. Figure 7.13 (frmLists from the sample database) demonstrates some of the methods of filling a list box via the property sheet. The following sections detail the information you need to supply for the RowSource property, based on your choice in the RowSourceType property.

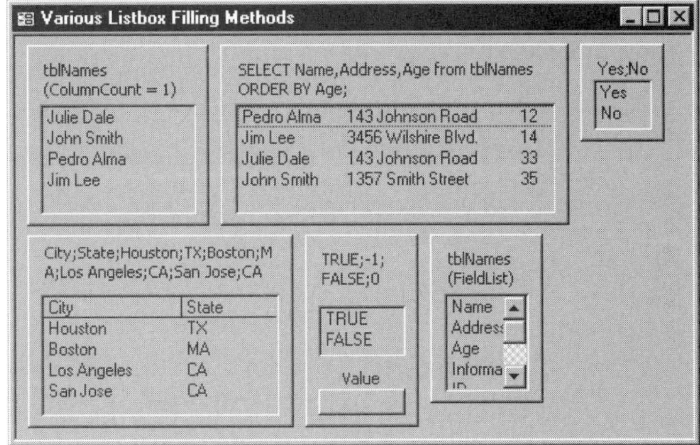

FIGURE 7.13:

One form showing some of the various methods of filling a list or combo box via the property sheet

Table/Query Enter the name of a table, query, or SQL expression that will retrieve the data you wish to display. Here are some examples:

tblNames Retrieves as many columns from the table named tblNames as the ColumnCount property specifies.

SELECT Name, Address, Age FROM tblNames ORDER BY Age Retrieves a maximum of three columns from tblNames, ordered by age. If the number in the ColumnCount property is less than the requested number of columns in the RowSource, the ColumnCount property controls the number of columns Access displays.

WARNING If you use a table name as the RowSource, you must be aware of changes to the table. For example, making a database replicable will add new columns to the front of every table and will therefore break such combo boxes.

Value List Enter a list of values, separated by semicolons, one row at a time (up to 2048 characters). If the ColumnHeads property is Yes, the first row of data will go into the column headings in the control. If you set the ColumnCount property incorrectly, the data will not go into the columns and rows as you had planned. Here are some examples:

Yes;No Displays only the two values Yes and No. Note that the display is also tied to the ColumnCount property. If the ColumnCount is 1, Yes and No each appear in their own row. If the ColumnCount is 2 or higher, Yes and No both appear on the first row of the control.

City;State;Houston;TX;Boston;MA;Los Angeles;CA;San Jose;CA Displays a two-column list with four rows of data, assuming these properties:

ColumnCount = 2

ColumnHeads = Yes

True;–1;False;0 Displays only the two values True and False and stores a yes/no value back to the underlying field, given these properties:

ColumnCount = 2

ColumnWidths = ;0

BoundColumn = 2

ControlSource = a Yes/No field from the underlying data source

Figure 7.13 shows these examples, and more, in action.

Field List Enter the name of a table or query from the form's record source. The fields will be listed in their physical order in the table or in the order in which they were placed into the query. There is no way to alphabetize the list using this option.

The ColumnCount Property

The ColumnCount property controls the number of columns of data Access will place into the control's data storage. The actual number of displayed columns can be no more than the number specified in this property, but it might be less, depending on the contents of the ColumnWidths property. Even if you render some of the data invisible (by using a ColumnWidth setting of 0), it's still loaded into the control, and you can retrieve it using the Column property.

Set the ColumnCount property with a number or a numeric value. Access rounds nonintegral values to the nearest whole number.

The ColumnWidths Property

The ColumnWidths property sets the widths of the columns in the control and should be filled with a semicolon-delimited list of numbers, one per column. The default width is approximately 1 inch or 3 centimeters, depending on the unit of measurement. Leaving a value out of the list accepts the default width. A setting of 0 hides a column. If the physical area dedicated to the control is not wide enough to display all the columns, Access truncates the right-most column, and the control displays horizontal scroll bars. Note that a single-column control will never have horizontal scroll bars, no matter how wide that single column is.

For each of the examples, the control contains four columns and is 5 inches wide. All measurements are in inches:

2;2;2;2 Each column is 2 inches wide. Because the total requested size is 3 inches wider than the control, Access provides horizontal scroll bars.

2 The first column is 2 inches wide, and the rest assume the default width (1 inch).

2;0;3;0 The first and third columns are displayed. The second and fourth are hidden.

(Blank) All four columns are evenly spaced over the width of the control, because the control is wider than the sum of the default widths. If it were narrower than the total widths, the first three columns would each be 1 inch wide (the default width) and the last column would use the rest of the space (2 inches).

Figure 7.14 shows these example list boxes, from frmListWidths.

FIGURE 7.14: Various ColumnWidths settings

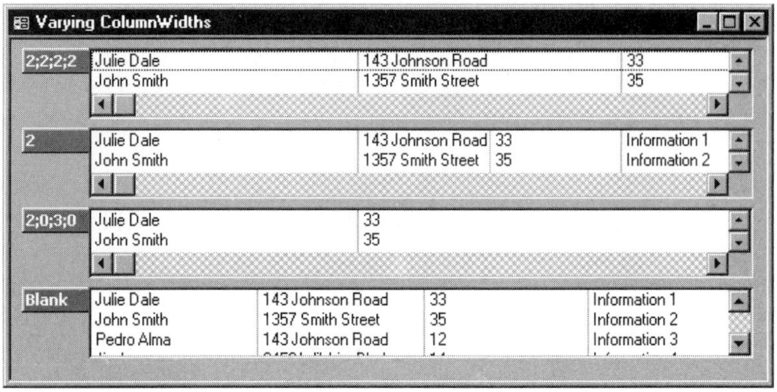

The ColumnHeads Property

The ColumnHeads property indicates whether Access should display a single row of column headings at the top of the control. (For combo boxes, Access displays this heading row only when you've asked it to expose the drop-down list.) When the RowSourceType property is ValueList, the first row of data goes into the header. If the RowSourceType is FieldList, the first field in the list goes into the header row. You should therefore not use the FieldList row source type when displaying column headers. If you do, Access displays field names in the header row.

TIP

It's best to avoid setting the ColumnHeads property to True for a combo box. Not only is it somewhat odd to open the combo box and find a row of column heads there in the drop-down portion, but there are subtle errors in the way Access handles rows of data in the combo box if you've set this property on. Just avoid the issue: only use this property in list boxes.

The BoundColumn Property

The BoundColumn property indicates which of the columns in the control will actually be returned when you've made a selection from the list. This means the control returns the value from this column when you assign its value to a variable, for example.

Normal Operation You must set the BoundColumn property as an integer between 0 and the number stored in the ColumnCount property. To retrieve the value from the control, use an expression like this:

```
varMyVariable = cboTestCombo
```

The variable varMyVariable receives the value from the chosen row in cboTestCombo, from the column specified in its BoundColumn property.

To set the value of the control, use an expression like this:

```
cboTestCombo = varMyVariable
```

This code selects the first row in cboTestCombo in which the value in the column specified in the BoundColumn property matches the value stored in varMyVariable. If Access can't find a match, the control value will be Null.

The Special Case If you set the BoundColumn property to 0, Access returns the selected row number in the control; the value of the control will be the row number of the selected row. Although this isn't very useful for bound controls—the chosen row number won't mean much when stored in a database—it can be very useful if you need to select a particular row in the control.

Suppose, for example, you want to make sure you've selected the first row of an unbound list box for each record, before the user even gets a chance to make a choice. Normally, to specify the row of the control you want selected, you would just assign a value to the control.

Unfortunately, in some cases (for example, when the RowSource of the control is a SQL query), you don't know the value of the bound field in the first row. To get around this problem, you can set the BoundColumn property to 0. Once you've done this, you can assign the control the value 0, which will select the first row. (The row values are zero-based.) To retrieve values from a control with the BoundColumn set to 0, use the Column property, discussed in the next section. For an example of setting the BoundColumn property to 0, see the section "Making Multiple Selections in a List Box" later in this chapter.

There are alternatives, of course. The ItemData method of a list or combo box returns the data from the bound column in any row you want. For example, rather than set the BoundColumn property to 0 in order to initialize a list box to the first row, you can set the default value to this expression instead:

```
=cboExample.ItemData(0)
```

The Column Property

The Column property of list and combo boxes is not available at design time but figures prominently at runtime. It allows you access to data in any of the columns of any row of the control. The general syntax looks like this:

value = ListOrCombo.Column(column[,row])

In a fit of nonstandardization, Access uses zero-based numbers for the column and row numbers: when you set the BoundColumn property to 1, you use Column(0) to retrieve the value stored there.

For example, to retrieve the data stored in the second column of the chosen row of cboTestCombo, use

```
varTestVariable = cboTestCombo.Column(1)
```

To retrieve the value in the third column of the fourth row of cboTestCombo, use

```
varTestVariable = cboTestCombo(2, 3)
```

Present a Name, Store an ID

It's easy to create a list or combo box that displays user-friendly information (such as a name) but stores information the user doesn't normally care to see (such as a counter value), given these facts:

- A list/combo box can contain more than one column (ColumnCount > 0).
- The first visible column is the one Access displays in the text box portion of the combo box.
- Any column in the list/combo box can be bound to the underlying data (BoundColumn).
- You can set the width of any column to 0, rendering it invisible (ColumnWidths).
- List/combo boxes have their own separate source of data (RowSource).

Figure 7.15 (frmTextToID) shows such a combo box in action. In this example, you're filling in a shipping form and want to choose the delivery method from a combo box. The delivery method is stored as an integer, but you can't expect users to remember the integer associated with each carrier. Therefore, you can use a query (qryDeliveryMethod) to feed the data for the combo's RowSource property. The second column in the combo has been made invisible (ColumnWidths set to ";0"), and the combo box will store the chosen value in its second column, the ID, to the underlying data (BoundColumn = 2, ControlSource = *DeliveryMethod*). You should be able to apply this same method to any situation where you want to present the user with one piece of information but store a different, related piece of information.

FIGURE 7.15:

Display text, but store an ID to the underlying data.

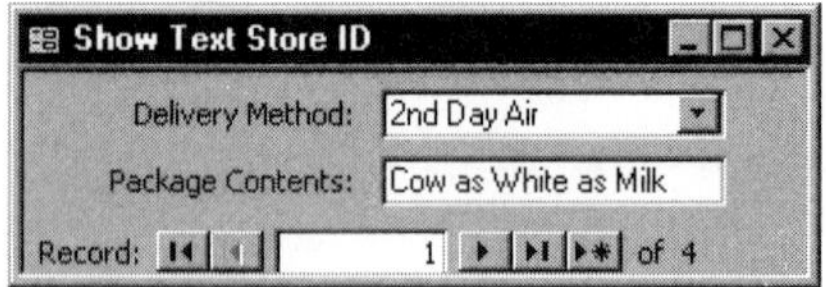

TIP

When your combo is bound to a numeric field (as it is in the previous example), you need to set the TextAlign property yourself. Because Access thinks you're really displaying a numeric value, it aligns the text to the right (which is how it treats numeric values). Set the TextAlign property manually to display the text the way you want it aligned.

Present a Calculated Value, List Individual Fields

Combo boxes can display only a single value in their text box portions, and it's always the value from the first visible column of the selected row in the control's drop-down list. What if you want to display a number of pieces of information in the text box portion but present discrete fields to the user in the drop-down list? Figure 7.16 shows such a scenario (frmHiddenColumn): the control displays a concatenated company, contact, and title in the text box portion but individual fields in the drop-down list.

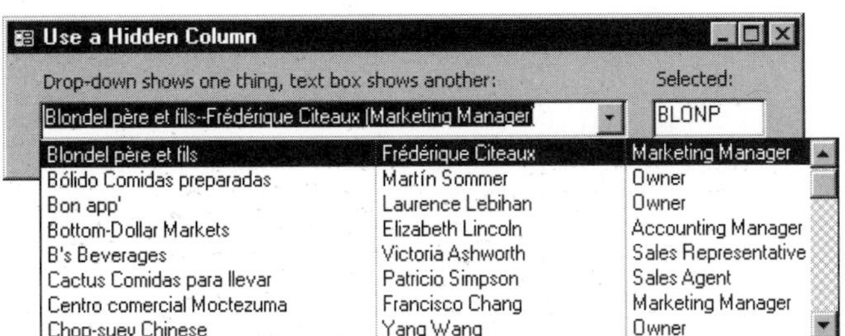

FIGURE 7.16: You can display a calculated field in the combo but display separate fields in the list.

How can you make this happen? It's simple, once you know the trick. It counts on the fact that Access displays in the text box the data from the first visible column in the control's drop-down list. In addition, the combo box can't physically display any column with a width set to less than 1/100 inch. Therefore, you fill the combo with a query that performs the calculation you need and put that value in the first column of the combo. Figure 7.17 shows the query filling the example combo box. The first column creates a calculated field. The second becomes a hidden column containing the primary key, and the other columns make up the list portion of the control.

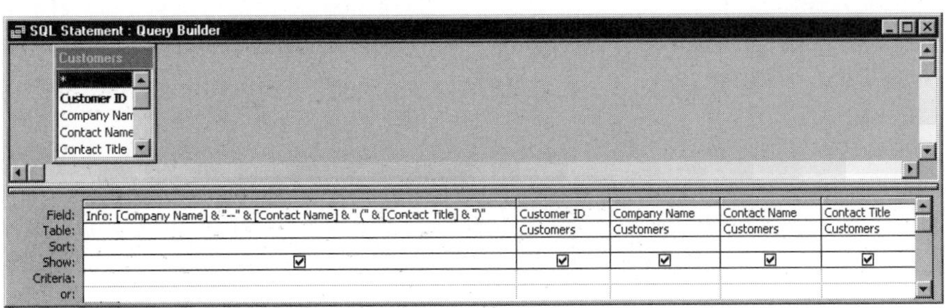

FIGURE 7.17: Count on Access' treatment of combo box columns to hide or display data.

In the ColumnWidths property, set the width of the first column to 0.001 or so. (Depending on your screen resolution, Access may alter the value after you've entered it. The widths of the other columns are up to you.) Be sure to set the ColumnCount property to accurately match the number of columns you want to pull in from your query, and Access will do the rest. In this example, the ColumnWidths property is set to 0.001";0";2";1.5";1"; the ColumnCount property is set to 5; and the BoundColumn property is set to 2.

Multiselect List Boxes

In many applications, you want to allow users to select multiple items from a list box. Access makes this possible and provides the MultiSelect property for the ListBox control. This property allows you to control exactly how users select items in your list box:

Setting	Description	Value
None	Single selection only (default).	0
Simple	The user selects or deselects multiple items by choosing them with the mouse or pressing the spacebar.	1
Extended	Shift+click or Shift+arrow key extends the selection from the previously selected item to the current item. Ctrl+click selects or deselects an item.	2

By choosing Extended or Simple, you can choose one or more items from the list box.

NOTE

The MultiSelect property is read-only at runtime. You won't be able to switch selection types while your form is in use; you can do so only at design time.

Once the user has selected one or more items, how can you tell which items are selected? There are two methods, and they're both read/write. That is, you can both retrieve the selected list and select items programmatically. Figure 7.18 shows a list box (frmMultiSelect) with its MultiSelect property set to Extended. As you select each item, code attached to the list box's AfterUpdate event updates the text box to its right.

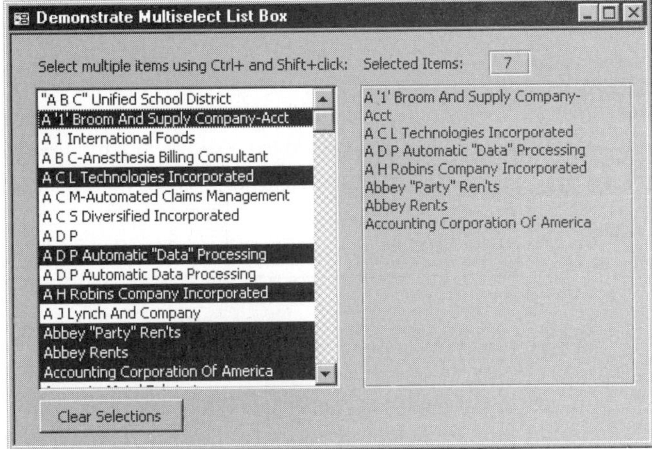

FIGURE 7.18:

The multiselect list box on frmMultiSelect allows you to use Shift+click and Ctrl+click to select multiple items.

The Selected Property

The Selected property of a list box returns an array of Boolean values, one for each row of data in the list box. If there are 100 items in the list box, the Selected property will return an array of 100 True or False values. Each value in the array indicates whether the corresponding item in the list is selected. You can check to see whether the first item is selected

```
If lstCompanies.Selected(0) Then
    MsgBox "You've selected the first item!"
End If
```

or you can set the first four items as selected (as long as you've set the MultiSelect property to something other than None—this code will fail with a runtime error, otherwise):

```
With lstCompanies
    For intI = 0 To 3
        .Selected(intI) = True
    Next intI
End With
```

You cannot use the Selected array with a single-select list box during the list box's AfterUpdate event, because it hasn't yet been updated at that point. After that event, it's current, but it will always have only one item that's True; the rest will always be False (because you can select only one item in the list box). This limits the Selected array's usefulness for single-select list boxes.

WARNING

When writing code that will work when the MultiSelect property is set to any of its three values, you'll need to be aware that the Selected property and its cousin, the ItemsSelected property, work slightly differently depending on the value in the MultiSelect property. The examples in this chapter check this property's value when necessary.

The ItemsSelected Property

If you want to do something with every selected item in a multiselect list box, you could use the Selected property to return an array of items and walk the array looking for rows in which the Selected array holds a True value. That is, you could use code such as this to list out the selected items:

```
Dim intI As Integer
With lstCompanies
    For intI = 0 To .ListCount - 1
        If .Selected(intI) Then
            Debug.Print .ItemData(intI)
        End If
    Next intI
End With
```

TIP

The ListCount property of a list box is zero-based. This means that you'll need to loop from 0 to ListCount–1 if you need to visit each item in the list box.

This requires Access to loop through every single row of the Selected array, which takes a long time. To make this simpler, Access supplies the ItemsSelected property, which returns a collection of selected row numbers. To do something with each selected item, just walk this collection, working with each item in the collection, as in this fragment from frmMultiSelect (Figure 7.18):

```
With lstCompanies
    If .MultiSelect = 0 Then
        txtSelected = .Value
```

```
        Else
            ' varItem returns a row number.
            ' It's up to you to retrieve the
            ' data you want from that row
            ' in the list box.
            For Each varItem In .ItemsSelected
                strList = strList & .Column(0, varItem) & vbCrLf
            Next varItem
            txtSelected = strList
        End If
    End With
```

This example also uses the ability of the Column property of a list box to return data from any column of any row. In this case, you want the data from the first column (column number 0) in the row specified by varItem.

Like any other collection, the ItemsSelected collection provides a Count property that tells you how many items are currently selected. In frmMultiSelect, the text box showing the number of selected items has this expression as its ControlSource:

```
=lstCompanies.ItemsSelected.Count
```

The LimitToList Problem

The LimitToList property indicates to Access whether it should allow you to enter new values into a combo box. Setting this property to No allows you to disregard the current list of values and enter a new one, and setting it to Yes forces you to choose a value from the current list. If you set your combo box's BoundColumn property to any column aside from the first visible column, Access will (and must) set the LimitToList property to Yes.

At first thought, you may not agree with this design decision. Imagine for a moment what's really going on here, however. Access displays and lets you enter values for the first visible column in the combo box. Therefore, if the control's BoundColumn property is set to 1, Access can take whatever it is you type and store it in the underlying data, even if it's not currently in the list. On the other hand, if the BoundColumn property is greater than 1 and you enter a value that's not already part of the list, Access needs to be able to store a value it doesn't have. Therefore, Access has no choice but to disallow new entries into combo boxes where the first column isn't displaying the bound field. Figure 7.19 shows, in pictorial form, why Access must make this limitation.

FIGURE 7.19:

LimitToList must be set to Yes if you've bound your combo box to a column other than the first column.

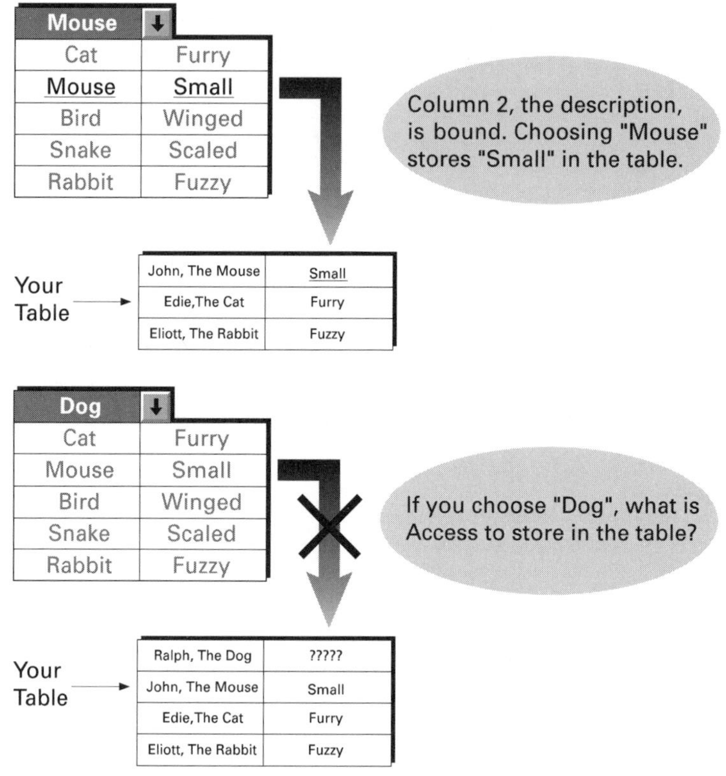

Combo boxes don't always do exactly what you might expect in terms of string matching. For example, if the LimitToList property is set to Yes, you might think that typing enough characters to find a match at all would be sufficient for Access to accept the selected value. That is not the case. You must type enough characters to indicate a *unique* match before Access will accept your value and let you leave the field. This can be frustrating for users who will type some characters, see the match in the combo box, and attempt to accept that value by pressing Enter. Unless the characters they've typed so far constitute a unique match, they'll need to keep typing. Combining the LimitToList property with the AutoExpand property, though, will make many users happy. If you set both LimitToList and AutoExpand to Yes, your users can leave the combo box as soon as Access has found any matching value in the list. This will, however, add some serious processing overhead. Although combo box performance in Access has greatly improved over earlier versions, if you find the performance still doesn't meet your needs, turn off the AutoExpand property.

In addition, null values are always a problem. If the LimitToList property is Yes and you type a value into a combo box and then delete it by backspacing over all the characters, the value now will not match any value in your list (unless you happen to have an empty value in the list). Prior to Access 95, you were not able to leave the combo box in this situation. Now, LimitToList accepts null values, so you can just delete the value and exit. Another easy way out is to press the Esc key, which undoes your change and lets you leave the control.

Taming the NotInList Event

When a user attempts to enter an item into a combo box (whose LimitToList property is set to Yes) that doesn't match one of the existing items in the list, Access raises the NotInList event for the combo box. The event procedure declaration looks like this:

```
Private Sub cboNotInList_NotInList( _
 NewData As String, Response As Integer)

End Sub
```

Access passes two parameters to your event procedure:

NewData Contains the text that triggered the event (that is, the text that's not already in the list).

Response Allows you to control what happens after your event procedure has completed its work.

If you have an event procedure reacting to that event, you can take one of three actions, depending on how you fill in the Response argument that Access passes to the event procedure:

- If you place the value acDataErrDisplay in Response, Access displays its standard error message.
- If you place acDataErrContinue in Response, Access doesn't display its error message, giving you the chance to display your own. If you use this option, make sure you really do display your own error message. Otherwise, users will be confused.
- If you place acDataErrAdded in Response, you must add the item to the underlying record source, and then Access requeries the combo box for you, effectively adding it to the list.

Because the third option is the most interesting, it is the focus of the following discussion.

ADO or DAO?

This is a tricky question. Many of the examples in this chapter need to work programmatically with data, and we simply couldn't predict whether readers would want to use ADO or DAO when accessing the data. (For more information on ADO, see Chapter 6. For more information on DAO, see Appendix C.) To satisfy everyone, we voted to do it both ways—each of the examples in this chapter that requires data access includes code for both ADO and DAO. In each case, the modules contain a compile-time constant, USEDAO, which has been set to True. If you want to use ADO instead, simply change the value of this constant to be False. In the code, look for compile-time conditionals, like this:

```
#If USEDAO Then
    ' This code uses DAO.
#Else
    ' This code uses ADO.
#End If
```

The simple case shown in Listing 7.3 from frmNotInList asks the user whether to add the new item to the list (we show only the DAO path through the code—the ADO version is similar):

Listing 7.3

```
Private Sub cboNotInList_NotInList( _
 NewData As String, Response As Integer)
    Dim strMsg As String
    Dim rst As DAO.Recordset
    Dim db As DAO.Database

    strMsg = "'" & NewData & "' is not in the list.  "
    strMsg = strMsg & "Would you like to add it?"
    If vbNo = MsgBox(strMsg, vbYesNo + vbQuestion, _
     "New Company") Then
        Response = acDataErrDisplay
    Else
        Set db = CurrentDb()
        Set rst = db.OpenRecordset("tblCompanies")
        rst.AddNew
            rst("Company") = NewData
        rst.Update
```

```
            Response = acDataErrAdded
            rst.Close
        End If
    End Sub
```

The code first pops up a message box asking you whether to add the new value. If you consent, the procedure runs code to add the new value. By passing back acDataErrAdded in the Response parameter, you're telling Access it should requery the combo and then try again to verify that the item exists in the list. If the item still isn't in the list for some reason (the sample code doesn't deal with errors, and it ought to), you'll still see the default error message from Access.

In general, your situations won't be this simple. Most likely, you'll need to gather some information from the user before adding a new row to the table. In that case, you'll probably want to pop up a form (using the acDialog WindowMode option), gather the information, add it to the table, and then send the acDataErrAdded back to Access to indicate that you've added the new row.

To see this solution, try out frmNotInListWithForm, shown in Figure 7.20. In this example, if you enter a name that's not already in the combo box, the code pops up a form that allows you to enter all the data besides the data you've already entered. Listing 7.4 shows the entire event procedure that does the work in this example.

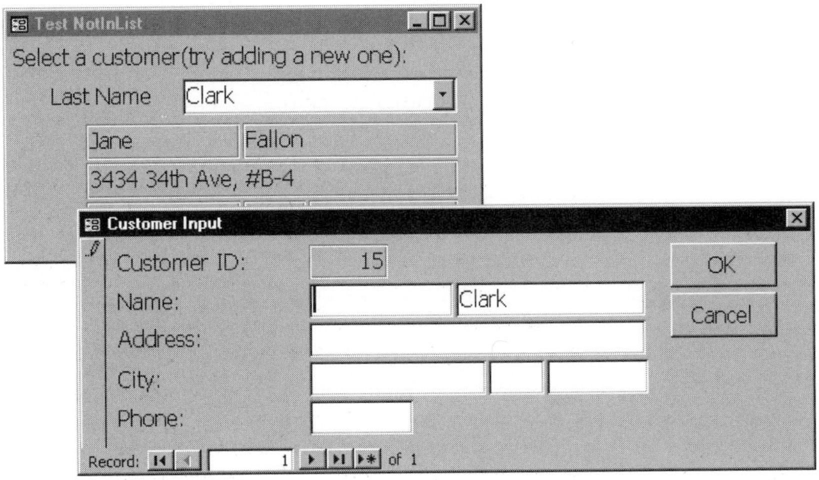

FIGURE 7.20:

Normally, you'll want to gather data from the user if the combo box raises its NotInList event.

Listing 7.4

```
Private Function IsLoaded(strName As String, _
 Optional lngType As AcObjectType = acForm) As Boolean
    IsLoaded = (SysCmd(acSysCmdGetObjectState, _
     lngType, strName) <> 0)
End Function

Private Sub cboCustomer_NotInList( _
 NewData As String, Response As Integer)
    Dim mbrResponse As VbMsgBoxResult
    Dim strMsg As String

    strMsg = NewData & _
     " isn't an existing customer. " & _
     "Add a new customer?"
    mbrResponse = MsgBox(strMsg, _
     vbYesNo + vbQuestion, "Invalid Customer")
    Select Case mbrResponse
        Case vbYes
            DoCmd.OpenForm "frmCustomer", _
             DataMode:=acFormAdd, _
             WindowMode:=acDialog, _
             OpenArgs:=NewData

            ' Stop here and wait until the form
            ' goes away.
            If IsLoaded("frmCustomer") Then
                Response = acDataErrAdded
                DoCmd.Close acForm, "frmCustomer"
            Else
                Response = acDataErrContinue
            End If
        Case vbNo
            Response = acDataErrContinue
    End Select
End Sub
```

When the combo box's NotInList event occurs, Access runs the event procedure code. It first asks the user to confirm adding a new customer. Then, if requested, the code displays frmCustomer using the acDialog WindowMode parameter and the acFormAdd DataMode parameter. Opening the form using the acDialog option causes the form to be displayed as a dialog box, and all subsequent code in the calling procedure stops and waits for the form to be either hidden or closed before continuing. (See "Creating Pop-up Forms" in Chapter 8 for more information on this technique.)

Listing 7.5 shows all the code associated with the pop-up form. This code includes support for three event procedures:

Form_Load When the form loads, this code takes the value sent to the form in its OpenArgs parameter and copies it into the LastName text box on the form.

cmdOK_Click Indicates that the user has completed filling in the fields on the form. You want the calling code to be able to retrieve these values, so don't close the form—just hide it.

cmdCancel_Click In this case, you do want to completely unload the form, so the calling code knows that you don't want to save any changes. Because the form was loaded in add mode, you must also undo any changes made on the form.

Listing 7.5

```
Private Sub cmdCancel_Click()
    Me.Undo
    DoCmd.Close acForm, Me.Name
End Sub

Private Sub cmdOK_Click()
    Me.Visible = False
End Sub

Private Sub Form_Load()
    If Len(Me.OpenArgs) > 0 Then
        Me.LastName = Me.OpenArgs
    End If
End Sub
```

Once the form is either closed or hidden, the code in Listing 7.4 continues and uses the IsLoaded function (also in Listing 7.4) to determine whether the user pressed OK or Cancel on the pop-up form. If the form is still loaded (the user pressed OK), the code sets the Response parameter to be acDataErrAdded and closes the form. If the form isn't still loaded (the user pressed Cancel), the code sets the Response parameter to be acDataErrContinue so Access knows that it must handle the issue itself.

Auto-Drop Combo Boxes

In some situations, you may want to have a combo box drop down automatically when you enter it. Access provides the DropDown method for combo boxes, which forces a combo box to open.

The simplest solution is to add code to your combo box's GotFocus event:

```
Sub cboOpenSesame_GotFocus()
    cboOpenSesame.DropDown
End Sub
```

That way, anytime you enter this combo box, it'll drop its list. (If the control doesn't have the focus, however, calling the DropDown method will trigger an error. Either call this only when you're sure the control has the focus—the GotFocus event is one such place—or add error handling to your code to manage the possible run-time error.)

The BeforeUpdate and AfterUpdate Events

As with the other controls, for list and combo boxes Access raises the Before-Update event just before it attempts to update the underlying record set, and the AfterUpdate event occurs just after. You can attach code to either of these events to trap the selection event in either a list or combo box.

Even more interesting is the ability to trap *movement* in a list box. Access triggers both the BeforeUpdate and AfterUpdate events every time you move the selection bar in a list box. Access must do this because, were you to leave the list box with a Tab or Shift+Tab key at any point, the currently selected item would become the value of the control. This doesn't occur in a combo box, though, because Access won't write any value to the recordset until you've made a selection by clicking, pressing Enter, or leaving the combo. Because you can attach code to the Before/AfterUpdate events in a list box, you can make changes to other controls on your form based on the current value in the list box. Thus, you have the choice of using a push method for filling unbound controls on your form (that is, you *push* values into them) in addition to the simpler pull method, where the controls use expressions to *pull* in their values from other sources.

Using Combo and List Boxes to Fill In Other Controls

Access provides several methods by which you can choose a value and have the corresponding data from other fields filled in for you on a form. The method you choose depends on whether the controls to be filled in are bound and how many controls you want filled in.

Data Filled In for Free: Using AutoLookup AutoLookup is a misunderstood and underutilized feature. It comes into play anytime you have a one-to-many join, your form's RecordsetType property is set to Dynaset (or you're working with a raw query datasheet instead of a form), and you make a change to the joining field on the many side of the one-to-many relationship. If the field you change on the many side is the linking value between the two tables, Access knows only one set of data will match that value and fills in all the new data based on the changed value. AutoLookup is really of value only when you're looking up some information for part of a larger form, such as information in an address on a shipping form, since the lookup must take place in a one-to-many relationship.

To see AutoLookup in action, open frmAutoLookupDemo. This form, shown in Figure 7.21, draws its data from qryRowFixup, and this query gets its data from the Customers and Orders tables. The important issue is that the combo box on frmAutoLookupDemo is bound to the Customer ID field from the Orders table. It's crucial in this situation that you take the linking field from the *many* side of the relationship. When you make a choice in the combo box, Access automatically looks up the values in the one side of the relationship, and those values are the ones you see in the etched read-only text boxes on the form.

FIGURE 7.21:

AutoLookup makes it easy to look up values, but only in a one-to-many relationship.

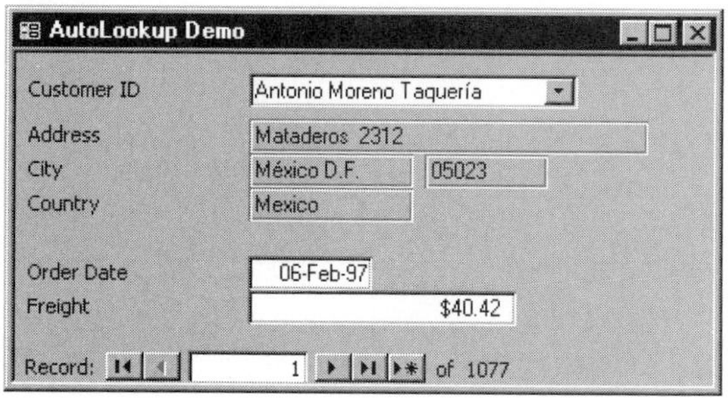

Pulling versus Pushing Data into Controls Imagine you want to provide a combo box from which you can choose a value. Once a value has been chosen, you want to fill in various other controls on the form with data found in the row that corresponds to the value the user just chose. The methods for doing this differ, depending on whether those other fields are bound. If the other controls are bound, you must push data into them; otherwise, they can pull the new data in themselves. You might think of the pull method as being *passive,* since the data just flows in, and the push method as being *active,* since you must provide code to copy the data from the list or combo box. For examples of each type of mechanism, you can investigate frmPullTest and frmPushTest. Figure 7.22 shows frmPullTest in action, and Figure 7.23 shows frmPushTest.

FIGURE 7.22:

frmPullTest uses the Column property in each of its text boxes to retrieve the values from the current row.

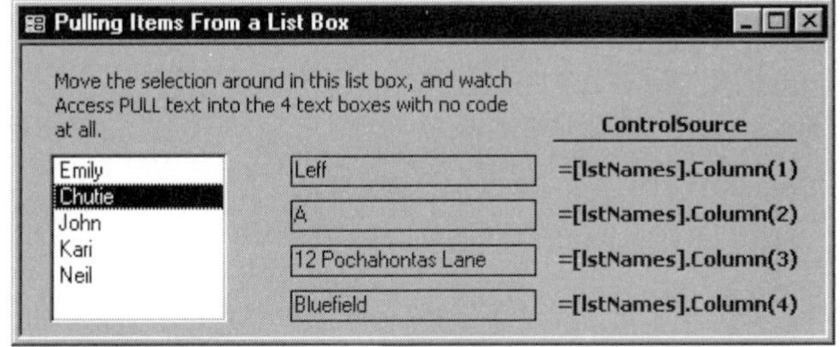

FIGURE 7.23:

frmPushTest uses a small function to copy values from 1stNames to each of the text boxes.

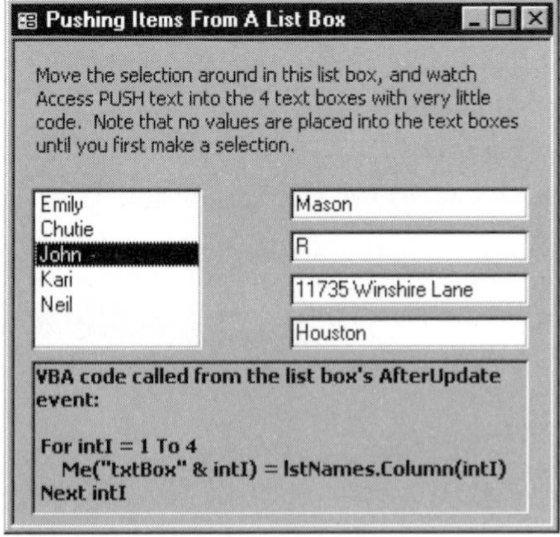

Pulling Data into Unbound Controls If the controls to be filled in are unbound, it means their ControlSource property is otherwise empty, and you can use an expression to pull in data from the combo box where the user just made a choice. All references in this example work equally well for list boxes and combo boxes.

To pull in data from the combo box, follow these steps:

1. Fill the combo: Create a query (or use an existing table) that contains the data you want to present, plus any other fields you want filled in automatically once the user makes a choice. Later steps will be simpler if you make sure the value to be displayed in the combo is the first field in the table or query, but that isn't imperative.

2. Prepare the combo: Set the ColumnWidths property so that the correct column is visible and the other columns are invisible. If the first column is the one you want displayed and you have five columns total, your ColumnWidths setting would be

   ;0;0;0;0

   This tells Access to use the default width for the first column and 0 width (hidden) for the next four columns.

3. Prepare the other controls: Set the ControlSource property for each of the controls into which you want data pulled. In each case, set the ControlSource property to

   =*YourCombo*.Column(*n*)

   where *YourCombo* is the ControlName property of the combo and *n* is the column number (starting at 0) you want pulled into the control.

Once you've set up the form, Access takes care of the rest. Anytime the combo box changes, the other controls on the form will recalculate and pull the value they need from the combo box. If you're pulling information from a list box, the information will be updated each time you move the selection bar in the list box. This is a convenient way for users to browse items as they move through the list box using the arrow keys. It takes absolutely no programming to accomplish a great deal!

NOTE

Although the method described above is very simple, it exacts a heavy price in performance. Because Access recalculates all dependencies on the form anytime you change a value on the form, you may find that pulling in data from a combo or list box is somewhat slow if the control contains a large number of rows. If you implement the pull method demonstrated here and your form slows down, you'll want to switch to the push method described in the next section.

TIP

Because the controls must have a calculated ControlSource for the method described above to work (and are therefore read-only), you might find it useful to also set the Locked property to Yes and the Enabled property to No. This way the control will appear normal, but your user won't be able to make changes.

Pushing Data into Bound Controls If you need to fill in controls that are bound, it means their ControlSource property is not empty, and you can't use the pull method described in the previous section. Instead, you'll need to push data into the controls once you've made a choice from the combo or list box. This is also simple, but it requires a bit of code.

The steps you follow to implement this method are the same as they were for the pull method. In this case, though, you need to leave the ControlSource property of the text boxes alone. The assumption is that you're using this method because those controls are bound to data fields. To apply the push method, you attach code to the AfterUpdate event of the combo or list box, which will fill the appropriate controls. In the example form, frmPushText, the code just loops through all the columns and sends out data to each of the four conveniently named text boxes:

```
Dim intI As Integer
For intI = 1 To 4
    Me("txtBox" & intI) = lstNames.Column(intI)
Next intI
```

Filling a List or Combo Box Programmatically

Access provides you with many ways to get data into a list box without programming at all. You can supply a table or query name, a list of items, or a SQL string.

Sometimes, however, you'll need to fill a list or combo box with data that doesn't come from one of the "approved" sources. You may want to fill a list with all the files in a folder. You may want to provide a sorted list of field names. Or, perhaps, you want to allow the user to specify items to be added to a list or combo box. In these cases, you'll need to write code in order to fill the control.

It's the RowSourceType property of the control that indicates how you'll get data into the control. You've already seen discussion of the Table/Query and Field List options, in the earlier section, "The RowSourceType Property." If you specify Value List for the property, you must supply a semicolon-delimited list of values. If you specify a function name, Access uses that function, in a very special way, to fill the list.

There is at least one particular case in which you'll need to write code to fill a list box: if you need to fill the list box with values from an array, you must write code to do it. We suggest two such methods, but creative programmers can probably come up with others. You can either manipulate the RowSource property directly, providing a semicolon-delimited list of values, or write a callback function to provide Access with the needed values.

In this section, we'll also take a look at using controls provided for MS Forms (the forms used as part of the VBA package, but not normally used in Access). These ActiveX controls require a bit more effort to use on forms than built-in Access controls, but they do add flexibility when filling list and combo boxes. (See Chapter 12 for more information on using ActiveX controls on Access forms.)

If you're coming to Access from other environments, you may be surprised to find out that you can't call a method of the control to clear its list and then call a method to add each individual item to the list. Access list and combo boxes don't work that way—they're geared towards displaying bound data and really weren't designed for random access or adding items under programmatic control. That's not to say that it isn't possible, it just takes some effort.

Changing the RowSource Property

Imagine a situation in which you have two buttons on your form. Choosing one of those buttons fills a list box with values from one specific list, and choosing the other fills the list box with values from a different list. Figure 7.24 shows a form like this in action (frmFillTest in the sample database). (In this example, the form is pulling data from two different fields and could easily have simply changed the RowSource to be one table or the other. But in some cases, you will need to fill the controls from a delimited list of values.)

FIGURE 7.24:

Click the Show Locations button to see a list of locations or the Show Products button to see a list of products.

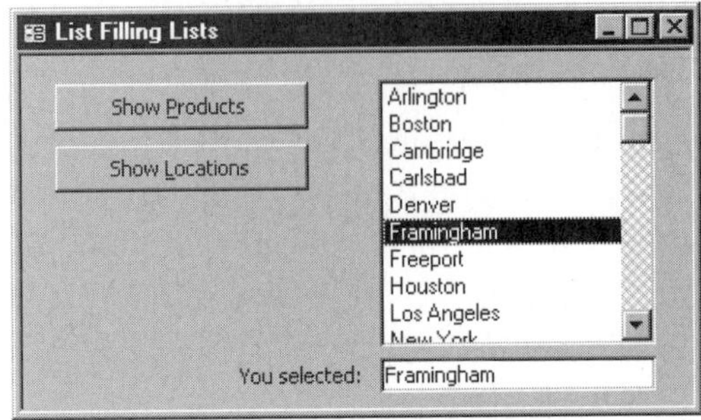

Although there may have been uses for this technique in previous versions, one glaring lack in Access' design makes this feature even more useful: there's no way to assign an open recordset into a list or combo box. That is, if you have a recordset (either ADO or DAO) open, and you want to display data from that recordset in a list or combo box, you must write code to make that happen. This example emulates that situation.

If you're using ADO, you can use the GetString method of the ADO recordset object to quickly create the semicolon-delimited string required by the RowSource property of the control. If you're using a DAO recordset, you'll need to do the work yourself, starting with the GetRows method of the recordset. (For more information on working with recordsets, see Chapter 6.)

Listing 7.6 shows the pertinent part of the SetListBoxContents procedure (called from the two command buttons on the sample form). Whether you choose to use DAO or ADO, the steps are the same. The code creates the appropriate SQL string, opens the recordset, and places a semicolon-delimited list of values into strFill. The code then sets the RowSource property of the list box to be the string containing information from the recordset. (See the sidebar "ADO or DAO?" for information on the use of compile-time constants in this example.)

Listing 7.6

```
    strSQL = "SELECT [" & strField & "] FROM " _
     & strTable & " ORDER BY [" & strField & "]"

#If USEDAO Then
    Dim db As DAO.Database
    Dim rst As DAO.Recordset
```

```
    Set db = CurrentDb()
    Set rst = db.OpenRecordset(strSQL, dbOpenDynaset)
    strFill = GetString(rst)
#Else
    Dim rst As ADODB.Recordset
    Set rst = New ADODB.Recordset

    rst.Open _
     Source:=strSQL, _
     ActiveConnection:=CurrentProject.Connection, _
     CursorType:=adOpenStatic, _
     Options:=adCmdText

    ' ADO provides a neat method for
    ' retrieving all the necessary data.
    strFill = rst.GetString(adClipString, _
     ColumnDelimeter:=";", RowDelimeter:=";")
#End If
    lstShowList.RowSource = strFill
    rst.Close
```

WARNING

The RowSource property can contain only 2048 characters. You're limited to small recordsets when you use this technique for filling a list.

Listing 7.7 shows the GetString function, called only if you're using DAO to create your recordset. This procedure isn't necessary when using ADO, because ADO provides its own GetString function that does almost the same thing. This function uses the GetRows method of a recordset. In order to use this method, you must supply the number of rows you want to retrieve. (In ADO, if you don't supply the number of rows to its parallel method, it retrieves all the rows. Too bad DAO doesn't work the same way.) The code requests 65000 rows—if the recordset doesn't contain that many rows, it will simply return the number of rows that it does contain, in a two-dimensional array. Because the GetString function doesn't know how many rows or columns to expect, it loops through both dimensions using the LBound and UBound functions to determine the endpoints. For each item, it adds the text to a semicolon-delimited output string and returns the string when it's done.

In ADO, this is all a lot simpler. Using ADO, you can call the GetString method of a Recordset object, specifying the string format (only adClipString is allowed at this time, but you must specify this value as if there were other options), and, optionally, the number of rows to return, the string to use for delimiting columns, the string to use for delimiting rows, and the string to use to replace Null values. The function returns the data from the requested rows, delimited as you've requested.

WARNING At the time of this writing, the help topic for the ADO GetString function was incorrect in three places. The help indicates that you need to use the Set keyword to assign the value returned by GetString. However, it's a string, not an object, so no Set is required. The help also misspells two of the parameters. (Actually, the developer misspelled them, but no one caught that. They're spelled correctly as far as the English language goes, but if you attempt to use that spelling in a method called as named parameters, as does the example in Listing 7.6, your code will mysteriously not compile. (You must spell the parameters incorrectly [ColumnDelimeter and RowDelimeter] in order for the code to work right.)

Listing 7.7

```
Private Function GetString( _
 rst As DAO.Recordset) As String
    Dim strOut As String
    Dim varItems As Variant
    Dim i As Integer
    Dim j As Integer

    ' NOTE: This procedure leaves the current
    ' row at the end of the recordset.
    rst.MoveFirst

    ' If you want more than 65000 rows, you'll need to
    ' change this!
    varItems = rst.GetRows(65000)
    For i = LBound(varItems, 2) To UBound(varItems, 2)
        For j = LBound(varItems, 1) To UBound(varItems, 1)
            strOut = strOut & varItems(j, i) & ";"
        Next j
    Next i
    GetString = strOut
End Function
```

Interestingly, we performed some simple timing tests. Compared to the more obvious method, which is to set the RowSourceType to Table/Query and the RowSource to a SQL string describing the list, this method performed favorably for small lists. For larger lists, you'll have to try both and convince yourself.

Using a Callback Function to Fill the List Box

To fill a list or combo box with an array of values or display information from an internal Access data structure, your best alternative is to use a list-filling callback function. Access allows you to supply a function that tells it all about the list or combo box you want displayed. You tell Access the number of columns, the number of rows, the formatting for individual elements, and the actual data elements. This is the only case in which Access directly calls a user-created function and uses the information it receives back from that function. This is, in effect, what makes your function a *callback* function—you are supplying information Access needs to do its job. This technique requires more effort than does providing a semicolon-delimited list, but it has none of the limitations of the simpler technique. Most importantly, you aren't limited to only supplying 2048 bytes for the list.

All this flexibility comes at a price, however. For Access to be able to communicate with your function, it needs to have a very specific interface, and that interface must respond in specific ways when Access requests information from it. Access calls your function at various times as it's filling the list box and indicates to your function exactly which piece of information it requires at that moment by providing an action code as one of the parameters. Metaphorically, every time Access calls this function, it's asking a question. It's up to your function to supply the answer. The question might be, "How many columns are there?" or "What value do you want displayed in row 1, column 2?" In any case, Access supplies all the information you need to retrieve or calculate the necessary answer. The return value from the function returns the question's answer to Access.

To attach your function to the list/combo box on a form, type its name (*without* a leading equal sign and *without* trailing parentheses) in the RowSourceType on the property sheet. This break in the normal syntax for the property sheet tells Access you're specifying a callback function. This is the property sheet set up to use a callback function:

Control Source	
Row Source Type	FillTableOrQueryList
Row Source	

Setting Up Your Callback Function

Any function that will be used as a list-filling callback function must accept exactly five parameters, the first declared As Control and the rest using simple data types. The following table lists the various parameters (the names used for them by convention; feel free to choose your own) and their descriptions:

Parameter	Description
ctl	Control-type variable that refers to the list box or combo box being filled.
varID	Unique value that identifies the control being filled; you may find it more useful to check ctl.Name if you need to differentiate between controls using this code.
lngRow	Row being filled in (zero-based).
lngCol	Column being filled in (zero-based).
intCode	The question Access is asking your function; its value indicates what action your function should take.

A typical function declaration looks like this:

```
Function FillList(ctl as Control, varID as Variant, _
 lngRow as Long, lngCol as Long, intCode as Integer) _
 As Variant
' See Listing 7.8 for the full procedure.
```

Your function reacts to each of the values in intCode, returning the information Access requests. Table 7.4 lists the possible values for intCode, their constant names as defined by Access, and the information Access is requesting when it sends you each of the constants.

TABLE 7.4: The acLB… Constants and Their Uses in Filling a List or Combo Box Programmatically

intCode	Constant	Meaning	Return Value
0	acLBInitialize	Initialize	Nonzero if your function can successfully fill the list; 0 or Null otherwise.
1	acLBOpen	Open	Nonzero ID value if the function can successfully fill the list; 0 or Null otherwise. Many functions use the return value from the Timer function to get a unique value.

Continued on next page

TABLE 7.4 CONTINUED: The acLB... Constants and Their Uses in Filling a List or Combo Box Programmatically

intCode	Constant	Meaning	Return Value
2	Not used		Not used, although Access does call the function with this value. Its use is not documented.
3	acLBGetRowCount	Number of rows	Number of rows in the list (can be 0); –1 if unknown. If you specify –1, Access calls the function to retrieve values (acLBGetValue) until you return a null value.
4	acLGGetColumnCount	Number of columns	Number of columns in the list (can't be 0); should match the value in the property sheet. You can, of course, just pass back ctlField.ColumnCount or skip this option altogether.
5	acLBGetColumnWidth	Column width	Width of the column specified in the varCol parameter (can be 0), measured in twips (inch). Specify –1 to use the property sheet values, or just skip this option.
6	acLBGetValue	Value	Value to be displayed at row lngRow and column lngCol.
7	acLBGetFormat	Format string	Format string to be used in displaying the value at row lngRow and column lngCol. Specify –1 to use the default format, or skip this option.
8	acLBClose	Not used	Not used, so no return value. Access does call your function with this value, though. Its use is not documented.
9	acLBEnd	End	Returns nothing. Used when you close the form or requery the control. Use this portion of your function to release memory or clean up as necessary.

When Access requests values for the list (acLBGetValue), it supplies a row and a column number in the lngRow and lngCol parameters, implying that you need to have random access to your data. Filling a list box from a recordset, then, is a tricky issue, because you don't really have random access to all Recordset objects in Access. (You can use the AbsolutePosition property to set the position directly for all but table-type recordsets.) You can emulate random access, however, using the Move method for Recordset objects. We present both methods of solving this problem. The first solution here suggests copying data from your recordset into an array, so you actually *can* access specific rows at will, but this method becomes quite slow when your datasets are large. The second solution uses the Move method to get to the exact record you need, based on the most recent record you were on and the new row number you need to get to. This method starts up more quickly because it's not copying data into an array, but it's slower in execution since it must refer to actual data on disk to display its contents.

In general, your callback function will probably look something like the example code in Listing 7.8. It needn't be terribly complex, and once you've written a few of these functions, you should be able to cut-and-paste a new one in seconds.

Listing 7.8

```
Function FillList(ctl As Control, varId As Variant, _
 lngRow As Long, lngCol As Long, intCode As Integer) _
 As Variant

    Dim varRetval as Variant
    Dim intRows as Integer
    Dim intCols as Integer
    Static aData() as Variant

    Select Case intCode
        Case acLBInitialize
            ' Initialization code
            ' Figure out how many rows and columns there are
            ' to be, and ReDim the array to hold them.
            ReDim aData(intRows, intCols)
            ' Code to fill the array would go here.
            varRetval = True

        Case acLBOpen
            ' Return a Unique ID code. The built-in Timer
            ' function works well.
            varRetval = Timer

        Case acLBGetRowCount
            ' Return number of rows
            varRetval = intRows
```

```
        Case acLBGetColumnCount
            ' Return number of columns
            varRetval = intCols

        Case acLBGetColumnWidth
            ' Return the column widths. If you return -1
            ' from this call, Access will use the default
            ' width for the specific column. That way,
            ' you can use the property sheet to supply the
            ' column widths.
            Select Case lngCol
                Case 0
                    ' Handle the first column
                    varRetval = 1440
                Case 1
                    ' Handle the second column
                    ' and so on.
                    varRetval = -1
            End Select

        Case acLBGetValue
            ' Return actual data.
            ' This example returns an element of the
            ' array filled in case acLBInitialize
            varRetval = aData(lngRow, lngCol)

        Case acLBGetFormat
            ' Return the formatting info for a given row
            ' and column.
            Select Case lngCol
                Case 0
                    ' Handle each column, setting the format.
                    varRetval = "ddd"
            End Select

        Case acLBEnd
            ' Clean up
            Erase aData
    End Select
    FillList = varRetval
End Function
```

Using Your Callback Function

The task of displaying a list of table and/or query names provides a good reason to use a callback function. Because you can retrieve such a list only by enumerating Access objects, the callback function provides the most reasonable way to get the values into a list box. This example makes heavy use of DAO (or ADO) to do its work. (See Chapter 6 for more information on the object collections.) Figure 7.25 shows the example form (frmListTables) in use. Open the form's module to follow the description of the code.

FIGURE 7.25:

Choose Tables, Queries, or Both to display a list of the selected items.

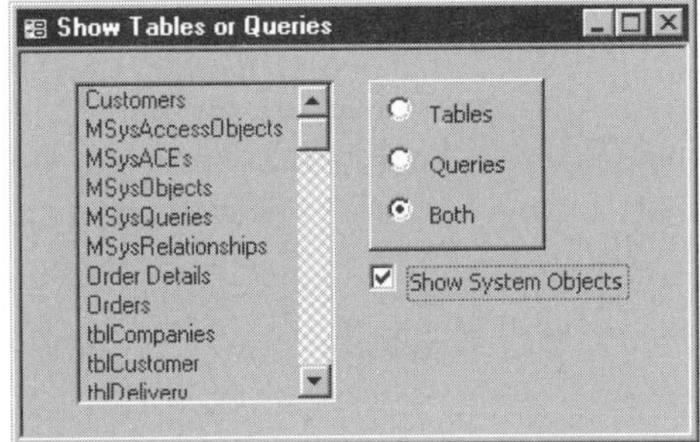

NOTE Again, this example supplies code for both ADO and DAO. The two versions of the code are slightly different, but the concepts are the same in both cases. Here in the book, you'll see the ADO version of the code. If you're interested in making this work using DAO, check out the sample form's module.

Listing 7.9 shows the entire list-filling function. This procedure has only a few lines of code—most of the code is in other procedures. From this listing, it should be clear what's going on: the procedure must fill an array with a list of tables, queries, or both, and must supply each name, when asked.

Listing 7.9

```
Private Function FillTableOrQueryList( _
 ctl As Control, varID As Variant, lngRow As Long, _
 lngCol As Long, intCode As Integer) As Variant
    ' Fill a combo or list box with a list of
    ' tables or queries.
```

```
    ' These variables "hang around" between
    ' calls to this function.
    Static sastrNames() As String
    Static sintItems As Integer

    Dim varRetval As Variant

    varRetval = Null
    Select Case intCode
        ' Initialize
        Case acLBInitialize
            sastrNames = InitArray()

            ' Set up variable to hold the number of names.
            sintItems = FillArray(sastrNames)

            ' Tell Access that the list box is OK, so far.
            varRetval = (sintItems > 0)

        Case acLBOpen
            ' Get a unique ID number for control.
            varRetval = Timer

        Case acLBGetRowCount
            ' Get the number of rows.
            varRetval = sintItems

        Case acLBGetValue
            ' Get the actual data for the row.
            varRetval = sastrNames(lngRow)

        Case acLBEnd
            ' Clean up (release memory)
            Erase sastrNames
    End Select

    FillTableOrQueryList = varRetval
End Function
```

In the acLBInitialize case, the code must set up the array to be used for later retrieval in the acLBGetValue case. In this example, the code needs to find out how many tables and queries there are and store that value away. If there are no tables or queries (an unlikely event, since every database has at least the system tables), the function returns a False value, telling Access that the function is unable to initialize the list box:

```
sastrNames = InitArray()

' Set up variable to hold the number of names.
sintItems = FillArray(sastrNames)

' Tell Access that the list box is OK, so far.
varRetval = (sintItems > 0)
```

The InitArray function (Listing 7.10) uses the AllTables and AllQueries collections. It sets up its return value, the array in which to place all the names, large enough to contain all the information. (The DAO version of the same procedure uses the TableDefs and QueryDefs collections in order to calculate the same value.)

Listing 7.10

```
Private Function InitArray() As String()
    Dim astrItems() As String
    Dim intCount As Integer

    With Application.CurrentData
        intCount = .AllTables.Count + .AllQueries.Count
    End With
    If intCount > 0 Then
        ' Set up the array to hold names.
        ReDim astrItems(0 To intCount - 1)
    End If
    InitArray = astrItems
End Function
```

Once you've found there are some tables or queries to display, your next step in the initialization case is to build up the array you will send to Access in the acLBGetValue case. Based on choices you've made on the form, the function will pull in different items for the list. Listing 7.11 shows the FillArray function, which fills in the array it's passed with all the table and/or query names. It also shows the AddTables function. The AddTables function and its parallel, the AddQueries function, loop through the appropriate collections, adding text items to the array. (If you're interested in how those procedures work, check out the form's class module. IsSystem, IsTemp, and ShowSys are all functions defined in the form's module.)

Listing 7.11

```
Private Function FillArray(astrNames() As String) As Integer
    ' If the "Show Tables" or "Show Both" option button
    ' is selected, gather up table names.
    Dim intItems As Integer

    intItems = 0
    If ShowTables() Then
        intItems = AddTables(astrNames, intItems)
    End If
    ' If the "Show Queries" or "Show Both" option button
    ' is selected, gather up query names.
    If ShowQueries() Then
        intItems = AddQueries(astrNames, intItems)
    End If
    ReDim Preserve astrNames(0 To intItems - 1)
    FillArray = intItems
End Function

Private Function AddTables(varItems As Variant, intStart As Integer) _
As Long
    ' Add all the available tables to varItems (an array)
    ' and return the next available position within the array.

    Dim tdf As AccessObject
    Dim intPos As Integer

    intPos = intStart
    For Each tdf In CurrentData.AllTables
        ' The Imp operator returns TRUE except when the
        ' first condition is True and the second is False.
        ' That is, it will return True unless this is
        ' a system table and system tables are not
        ' being shown.
        If IsSystem(tdf) Imp ShowSys() Then
            varItems(intPos) = tdf.Name
            intPos = intPos + 1
        End If
    Next tdf
    AddTables = intPos
End Function
```

Referring back to the callback function (Listing 7.9), the variable intItems will indicate the number of elements in the list box once you've finished all the looping, and this is the value you pass back to Access in the acLBGetRowCount case.

The rest of the code closely follows the skeleton example. It uses the default column widths and doesn't even bother dealing with the acLBGetFormat case, because it's just using the default formats. When asked to supply a value (in the acLBGetValue case), it just returns the value for the given row from the array it built in the acLBInitialize case. Finally, when Access shuts down the list box, the acLBEnd case uses the Erase command to release the memory the array uses.

To include this form in your own application, follow these steps:

1. Import the form frmListTables into your application.
2. Modify the AfterUpdate event of the list box lstTables to *do* something with the user's choice. Perhaps you'll want to place it into a global variable for later use.

The Simple Solution

There's an easier way to list-fill, but it's not built into Access. If you can handle the extra overhead of using an ActiveX control, you can make list filling simple. The ActiveX controls that are part of the Microsoft Forms package (the forms package that's part of the VBA environment) include a list box and a combo box control that are simple to use and easy to fill. If you insert a Microsoft Forms ListBox or ComboBox control onto your form, you can fill it simply, using its AddItem and Clear methods. Try out frmListTablesMSForms, which looks the same as the previous example but uses a different list box to do its work.

The Microsoft Forms controls look like built-in Access controls, for the most part, but provide different (sometimes better, sometimes worse) functionality than the built-in Access controls. None of the Microsoft Forms controls can be bound to Access data, for example, so you won't use them if you're building bound forms. On the other hand, the MS Forms controls make list filling easy and provide useful controls that Access doesn't, such as scroll bars and spin buttons.

To insert a Microsoft Forms list box control, first bring up a form in Design view. Then select the Insert ➢ ActiveX Control menu item and select Microsoft Forms 2.0 ListBox from the list of available controls. Figure 7.26 shows the dialog and the choice you should make. Once you've inserted the control on your form, you're ready to use it like any other control. (For more information on getting started with ActiveX controls on Access forms, see Chapter 12.)

FIGURE 7.26:

Use the Insert ActiveX Control dialog box to insert the Microsoft Forms 2.0 ListBox control.

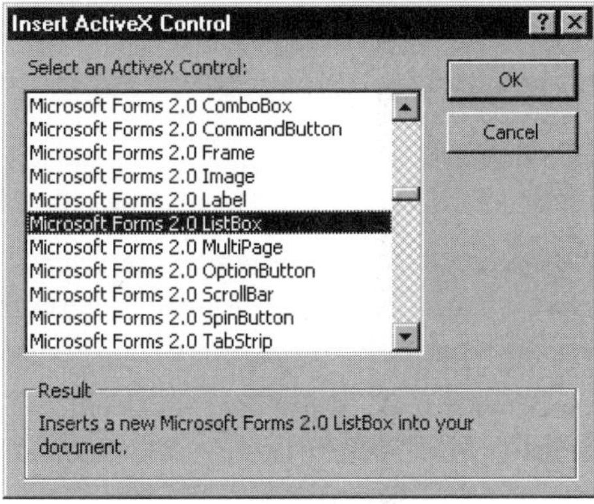

You'll want to study all the methods, properties, and events provided by this new control, but for now, there are two methods you'll need to know about: AddItem and Clear. The Clear method removes all items from the list box, and the AddItem method allows you to add a new item to the list. (The AddItem method also allows you to specify where in the list the item should be inserted, but that's not an issue in this example.)

Using this control, you needn't worry about a list-filling function. You needn't create an array in which to store the object names. You just need to loop through the appropriate collection and call the AddItem method for each table or query you find. Listing 7.12 shows the AddTables procedure from frmListTablesMS-Forms. As you can see, the code is simpler in this case, because it doesn't need to fill an array of items.

Listing 7.12

```
Private Sub AddTables()
    Dim tdf As AccessObject

    For Each tdf In CurrentData.AllTables
        ' The Imp operator returns TRUE except when the
        ' first condition is True and the second is False.
        ' That is, it will return True unless this is
        ' a system table and system tables are not
        ' being shown.
        If IsSystem(tdf) Imp ShowSys() Then
            lst.AddItem tdf.Name
```

```
        End If
    Next tdf
End Sub
```

If you check out the code in frmListTablesMSForms, you'll see how much simpler it is not to use a list-filling callback function. In fact, after years of using these convoluted, difficult-to-debug, complex procedures, we've declared independence. In this version of Access, you can be guaranteed that anyone running your application will definitely have a copy of the Microsoft Forms controls, so you needn't even bother worrying about distributing these controls separately, as you might have to for most ActiveX controls. If you need to be able to fill a list or combo box programmatically, consider using the Microsoft Forms controls.

Setting Up the ActiveX Control

Because of the way Access hosts ActiveX controls, the best use of them in code requires an extra step or two. Unless you take these extra steps, you'll only be able to refer to the control as the object contained within the ActiveX container on your forms. That is, if you place an ActiveX control named lstTables on a form, you're actually placing a container for a control on the form. To refer to the container, use the name lstTables (if you want to affect the positioning or the visibility of the ActiveX control, work with the container directly.) If you want to programmatically control the actual control, however, you must refer to the Object property of the control. That is, you must use code like this:

```
lstTables.Object.AddItem "Item1"
```

There's two problems here: you must remember to use the .Object in the code, and you don't get help from VBA's IntelliSense features as you type. There's a solution, however: in the module's Declarations area, declare your own variable that will refer to this control:

```
Private lst As MSForms.ListBox
```

Then, in the Open event of the form, set your variable to refer to the real control:

```
Set lst = lstTables.Object
```

From now on, everywhere in your form's module, you can refer to `lst` as if it were the actual control. If you want to react to events of the control, you can use the WithEvents keyword in your definition as well. (We use the WithEvents keyword in several examples in this chapter, so the code can react to events of the object the variable refers to. In this example, there was no need.) For more information on using WithEvents and reacting to events of other objects, see Chapter 12.

Emulating a Permanently Open Combo Box

Access does not supply a drop-down list box control, and there will be times when you must have the list portion of a combo-like control permanently open. You can emulate this arrangement, however, with the pairing of a list box and a text box. The issue, of course, is performing the incremental search and finding the matching elements of the list box as you type into the text box. Because Access provides the Change event for the text box, you can attach code to this event property that finds the first entry in the list box that matches the text you currently have in the text box. This functionality looks and feels comfortable for many users and should fit well into many applications. Figure 7.27 shows a sample form, frmTestIncSrch, in action.

FIGURE 7.27:

Typing into the text box will find the first matching value in the list box.

The drawbacks to this pairing, however, are somewhat serious. Because Access must do a lookup in the underlying data source for every change the user makes in the text box, response time can be slow in certain cases. On the other hand, if you can bind the list box to a table (and guarantee the use of an index for lookups), the speed is quite reasonable, even for large lists.

This example, which can be easily reused in any application that requires this behavior, relies on the IncrementalSearch class (in the sample database) to do its work. Again, because we've attempted to include code for both ADO and DAO, the class module appears more complex than it would have had we included code for only one data access technology. The IncrementalSearch class is, once you pull out the duplicate code, quite small. Table 7.5 lists the properties of the class. (The class exposes no public methods.)

TABLE 7.5: Properties of the IncrementalSearch Class

Property	Data Type	Description
BoundField	String	Name of the field to which the list box has been bound. That is, if the IncrementalSearch object needs to assign a value to the list box, this field name specifies which field's data the class should retrieve and assign as the value of the list box. In many cases, this will be the same as the DisplayField property, and if you don't assign this property a value, the class will assume it's the same as the DisplayField property.
DisplayField	String	Name of the field that's displayed in the list box. Unless you're displaying a field that's different than the bound field for the list box, this will be the same as the BoundField property.
Index	String	Name of the index to be used for searches, if possible. If your list box is based on a table, the IncrementalSearch class will most likely be able to use an index to speed up searching. For large tables, an index can help a great deal. If you're using the primary key index, and haven't explicitly changed its name, the name is PrimaryKey.
ListBox	ListBox	A reference to the ListBox control that's displaying the list of data to be searched.
TextBox	TextBox	A reference to the TextBox control in which you type the search text.

To use the IncrementalSearch class, you must create a new instance of the class and specify a few properties, as shown in Listing 7.13 (from frmTestIncSrch).

Listing 7.13

```
Private mis As IncrementalSearch

Private Sub Form_Load()
    Set mis = New IncrementalSearch
    mis.DisplayField = "Company"

    ' BoundField and Index
    ' are optional. Index will only
    ' have an effect if the application
    ' can make use of it (if you ask
    ' to read data from a table directly).
    ' Use "PrimaryKey" if you want to specify
    ' the primary key index, and you've never
```

```
    ' changed its name.
    ' BoundField allows you to
    ' have a field to which the list box
    ' is bound, but isn't the display field.
    ' The BoundField property must match the
    ' field indexed in the Index property.

    ' You should set these properties
    ' before you set the ListBox property,
    ' which hooks up all the data.
    mis.BoundField = "Company"
    mis.Index = "Company"

    Set mis.ListBox = lstIncSrch
    Set mis.TextBox = txtIncSrch

End Sub
```

That's all there is to it. From then on, if you type into the text box specified in the TextBox property, code in the IncrementalSearch class will find the first row matching the text you've typed in the text box and will display it in the list box.

What kind of magic is going on here? How is it that just setting a few properties enables a class to react to the Change event of a text box (the only logical place to hook the code)? We'll use this technique several times in this chapter and the next, so if you're interested in how this mechanism works, here's your chance to learn.

Using WithEvents to React to Events

The problem is easily described: you have a class module that needs to react to events raised by a control placed on a form. But wait: isn't that the way it always works? Don't you always place a control on a form and then write code to react to its events? Sure, if you place the event code in the class module associated with the form containing the control, everything works as it always has. No problem there. But what if you want to react to the event in a *different* class module?

VBA makes this easy, although not as easy as the first case. If you want to react to events of an object from a class module other than the form or report module where the control is placed, you must declare a reference to that object using the WithEvents keyword. (For more information on using WithEvents, see Chapter 12.) That is, you must declare a variable like this:

```
Private WithEvents mtxt As TextBox
```

Note that this variable must be a module-level variable, and it can only exist in a class module. (Why only in a class module? That seems like a complex restriction. It makes sense, however—you're going to use this variable in order to react to events, and the only place in VBA that you can write event procedures is in a class module.)

Declaring the variable isn't enough. If you want to use it, you must also make the variable point at some object. In the IncrementalSearch class, that happens in the TextBox and ListBox Property Set procedures, like this:

```
Public Property Set TextBox(txt As TextBox)
    Set mtxt = txt
End Property
```

From that point on, you can treat mtxt as if it actually were a live text box and react to its events in your code. In fact, you'll now find mtxt on the drop-down list of objects in the VBA editor and, once you choose it, you'll find all its events in the drop-down list of events. Perhaps you're seeing the similarities here to what happens when you place a control on an Access form? In that case, Access does the WithEvents hookup for you. It creates a module-level variable with the same name as the control's container and points that variable at the control. You don't have to write the code—Access does it for you under the covers. When you want to react to events of the control from outside the form's module, however, you must hook up the WithEvents connection yourself.

Now, once you've created the variable and hooked it up to refer to the real control, your class module (in this case, the IncrementalSearch class module) can react to any event of the control. In the IncrementalSearch class, you'll find event procedures for the Change and LostFocus events. (During the change event, the class looks up the matching item in the list box and highlights it. In the LostFocus event, the class copies whatever's currently selected in the list box into the text box.)

You can use WithEvents with any object that raises events. Almost all controls do, and using a class module like IncrementalSearch allows you to hide all the code that implements functionality for the controls in one place. With just a few lines of code in any form, you can hook up an instance of the IncrementalSearch class (or any class like it that uses WithEvents connections to objects), and you don't have to add any event procedures to your form to implement the behavior you need. This is a great way to encapsulate code, and it makes it easy to distribute and share modules. (That's why we've chosen to implement a good number of classes in this way for this book. You simply import the class, add a few lines of code to your application, and it works.)

Events Don't Happen on Their Own

If you look carefully at the code in the IncrementalSearch class module, you'll note that the Property Set procedure for the TextBox and ListBox properties is somewhat more complex than you saw previously. It turns out that Access makes an optimization, in order to speed its own processing, that causes you a bit more work, as a developer.

Simply put, unless Access finds the words [Event Procedure] in an event property for an object, Access doesn't raise the event. That means that even though you've set up your WithEvents variable and pointed it at the object, none of your code will ever run unless you've also set the corresponding property of the object correctly. We could have told you to go to each object with which you want to use the classes provided here and set all the appropriate event properties to be [Event Procedure], but that spoils the point of drop-in code. Therefore, in each class that uses this WithEvents technology, you'll see property procedures that allow you to set up the controls the class should operate on and, in those procedures, code that sets up the necessary events. For example, in the IncrementalSearch class, the complete Property Set procedure for the TextBox property looks like this:

```
Public Property Set TextBox(txt As TextBox)
    Set mtxt = txt
    mtxt.OnChange = "[Event Procedure]"
    mtxt.OnLostFocus = "[Event Procedure]"
End Property
```

Although the changes to the OnChange and OnLostFocus event properties are made only at runtime, that's enough. Access sees the text in the property and knows that it must raise the event. If you ever decide to emulate this technique in your own classes, it's almost assured that you'll someday write your own class, hook up the WithEvents variables, and have no event code run. If that happens, you'll know (after reading this) that you must also hook up the events themselves, one at a time, with code like the TextBox Property Set procedure.

How Does It Work?

Once you've set up the two control properties of the IncrementalSearch class, you're ready to go. Under the covers, however, when you set the ListBox property, the class opens a recordset (either an ADO or a DAO recordset, depending on the value of the USEDAO compile-time constant in the class) and uses that for searching the Change event of the text box. The SetupRstADO (or SetRstDAO, if you're using DAO) procedure takes the RowSource property of the list box (that is, the table, query, or SQL string that's providing the list of data displayed in the list box) and opens a recordset based on that property value. In both ADO and DAO, you can search more effectively if you open data that's based closely on a table and provide the name of an index on which to search. Therefore, the SetupRstADO (or DAO) procedure attempts to first open a recordset in which it can use an index and the Seek method for searches. If that fails (if the RowSource is a query, for example), it drops down to a normal recordset, which may or may not use an index for its searches. (In DAO, this is a dynaset-type recordset. There's no corresponding name in ADO.) In this case, the ADO code uses the Filter property of the recordset to find the first row that's greater than or equal to what you've typed. The DAO code uses the FindFirst method of the recordset. In either case, if it's possible to use an index, you'll normally get better performance using one.

If you're interested in the gory details of setting up the recordset used by the IncrementalSearch class, study the SetupRstDAO and SetupRstADO procedures in the class module. Both are somewhat ugly so that they can be as flexible as possible.

WARNING

One small problem: Access and ADO don't always agree on the use of wildcard characters in SQL strings. If you have a query that uses a LIKE clause, with a "*" or "?" wildcard, Access correctly converts these into the "%" and "_" that ADO wants to see. If you do the same thing directly in the RowSource property of a list box, however, ADO will treat those characters as literals, and the whole thing won't work correctly. Yes, we could have written the code to handle this case, but it would have more than doubled the size of the class. You're welcome to add this code, if you like—it's a matter of parsing the SQL string, looking for the WHERE clause, and replacing "*" with "%" and "?" with "_". On the other hand, it's simple enough to say, "We only handle wildcards in queries, not in the RowSource property," and let it go at that.

Dealing with Parameters

As you probably know, queries can have parameters that must be resolved at runtime. Often, those parameters are form-based—that is, the query retrieves one or more values from a form and then returns rows based on the value(s). But you've also noticed (and if you haven't, see Chapter 6 for a more complete explanation) that you cannot programmatically create recordsets based on a query if that query contains parameters, unless you satisfy the parameter values in your code. We've tried to make the IncrementalSearch class capable of handling the simplest type of query parameters. That is, if you have a parameter in your query like this, the class should be able to handle it:

```
Like [Forms]![FormName]![ControlName] & "*"
```

When your query contains a parameter like this, ADO (or DAO) adds it to the Command (or QueryDef) object's Parameters collection. The Parameters collection consists of Parameter objects, each of which has a Name and a Value property. All the code needs to do is loop through all the parameters and attempt to set the Value property of each to be the correct value. If the parameters are all based on control values, you can use the Eval function in Access to do the work. As long as the associated form is already open, Eval can take a control reference as a string and evaluate that string to retrieve its value. Listing 7.14 shows the HandleParametersADO function (you'll also find a similar HandleParametersDAO function in the class module, which takes care of resolving the parameter values and then executes the Command object to retrieve the recordset. In HandleParametersDAO, the module uses the OpenRecordset method of a QueryDef object once it's satisfied all the parameters, rather than the Execute method of a Command object.) Note that this function returns the new recordset and also sets a module-level variable indicating that this is a dynaset-like recordset, not a table-like recordset.

NOTE

Although you can use a dot to separate a form reference from a control on that form when writing VBA code, that syntax will not work when designing queries. You can also use ("") around control names when working in VBA, but you cannot use it when working with queries. The only way to refer to control references from within queries is to use Forms!FormName!ControlName.

Listing 7.14

```
Private Function HandleParametersADO( _
 Optional ct As CommandTypeEnum = adCmdTableDirect) _
 As ADODB.Recordset
    Dim cmd As ADODB.Command
    Dim intCount As Integer
    Dim prm As ADODB.Parameter

    On Error GoTo HandleErrors

    ' Open a new Command object.
    Set cmd = New ADODB.Command
    Set cmd.ActiveConnection = CurrentProject.Connection
    cmd.CommandText = "(" & mlst.RowSource & ")"
    cmd.CommandType = ct
    intCount = cmd.Parameters.Count
```

```
    ' If there are any parameters,
    ' evaluate them now.
    If intCount > 0 Then
        For Each prm In cmd.Parameters
            prm.Value = Eval(prm.Name)
        Next prm
        ' If you've set up a Command
        ' object like this, you cannot
        ' use the Index, or the Seek method later.
        ' Indicate that this is a dynaset-like
        ' thing.
        mot = otDynaset
    End If
    Set HandleParametersADO = cmd.Execute

' Error handling removed

End Function
```

Searching for Text

Doing the search work is quite simple. If the list box is bound to a table, the function uses the Seek method to find the first value greater than or equal to the value in the text box. If the list box is bound to a row source in which you can't use an index, the function builds a string expression to be used as the criteria for either the Filter (ADO) or the FindFirst (DAO) method and uses it to search for the first match.

The DAO code that performs the search (from the mtxt_Change event procedure) looks like this:

```
Case otDynaset
    strFilter = DisplayField & _
     " >= " & FixQuotes(mtxt.Text)
    mrst.FindFirst strFilter
Case otTable
    ' If there is an index set,
    ' you can use Seek.
    mrst.Seek ">=", mtxt.Text
```

If the class has opened a dynaset-type recordset (although ADO doesn't support dynaset-type recordsets, its recordsets do support similar behavior), the code sets up a string to be used with the FindFirst method. If the class has opened a table-type recordset, it uses the Seek method instead. Note that the first case calls the

FixQuotes function, shown in Listing 7.15. The FindFirst method (and its ADO parallel, the Filter method) require you to specify a string containing the search criteria. That string must be delimited (ADO requires apostrophes, DAO accepts apostrophes or quotes). Chapter 6 discusses this problem in detail, but in short, if the string you are seeking contains the delimiter character, you must have some way to indicate that the character is part of the string and is not itself a delimiter. Both ADO and DAO allow you to double up the delimiter character when it appears within the string. That is, if ADO or DAO encounters two apostrophes within an apostrophe-delimited string, the two characters are treated as a single character. The FixQuotes function accepts a string as input, and returns that same string, surrounded with the requested delimiter, with all internal instances of the delimiter doubled.

Listing 7.15

```
Private Function FixQuotes(strValue As String, _
 Optional strDelimiter As String = "'") As String

    FixQuotes = _
     strDelimiter & _
     Replace(strValue, strDelimiter, strDelimiter & strDelimiter) & _
     strDelimiter
End Function
```

WARNING

One small problem (there's always one small problem): At this time, ADO has a problem parsing strings that include more than one doubled delimiter. It's just a bug. It may be fixed by the time you read this, but at the time of this writing, it was there and unlikely to be fixed in the immediate future. Someone at Microsoft must have known about this before we brought it to their attention, because they dug up an undocumented delimiter: "#". That is, you can use "#" to delimit strings, and, even if the string includes apostrophes, ADO will be able to parse the string. So, you think, the problem is solved? Not so. What if your search criteria includes a "#" within it? You'd think you could simply double up the "#", right? Wrong. It doesn't work. Although they allow you to delimit strings with quotes in them, they didn't allow that "##" to be treated as "#" within the string. Therefore, there's simply no completely bullet-proof method for supplying a search criterion in ADO. The IncrementalSearch class attempts to first search for an apostrophe-delimited string. If that fails, because of the bug mentioned earlier, the code then tries to delimit the string with "#". But this also may fail, if there's both multiple apostrophes and one or more "#" signs in your text. If this happens, you'll see an alert from IncrementalSearch. On the other hand, the likelihood of this happening is quite small.

You might also notice that we've included code to fill in the text box with the currently selected value from the list box if you either click in the list box or leave the text box at any point. This seems like reasonable and helpful behavior, similar to the way the AutoExpand property for combo boxes works.

In summary, the issues surrounding the use of this code are as follows:

- The list box's RowSource must be either a table, a query, or a SQL string with no wildcards.
- If the RowSource is a table, the field you display can be different from the bound field, but if the fields are different, you must specify both the BoundField and DisplayField properties. (If they're the same, you only need specify the DisplayField property.)
- Using a query or a SQL string as the RowSource may be more flexible, but it might be slower than using a table. This issue is less important on small datasets.
- Because IncrementalSearch encapsulates all its own code, you can instantiate as many copies of the object as you need. You will need one object for each text box/list box pair on your form, however.

To include this functionality in your own application, follow these steps:

1. Import the IncrementalSearch class module from the sample database.
2. Create the text box and the list box.
3. Add code to your form's module, like the code shown in Listing 7.13. Replace the example control names with your own. The code that's not bold in Listing 7.13 is optional and depends on your situation. It's imperative that you get all the details right—that is, specify the correct DisplayField, BoundField, and Index property values. If these are wrong, you'll see a number of cryptic error messages.
4. In the IncrementalSearch class module, set the USEDAO constant to reflect your own preferences. If you want to use ADO in your project, set the constant to be False. (If you're using IncrementalSearch in a new Access 2000 database or project, the reference to DAO won't be set for you, so you'll most likely want to set this constant to be False.)

Making Multiple Selections in a List Box

Access list boxes allow multiple selections, as you saw in the section "MultiSelect List Boxes" earlier in this chapter. One problem with using multiple-select list boxes is that it's difficult for users to see which items they've selected if the list is too long to fit on the screen. In addition, there's really no way, using a single list box, to change the ordering of the choices.

Fortunately, you can code around these problems by showing the user two list boxes, one representing available items and the other representing selected items. By moving items from one list to the other, your users can select a group of items on which to work. We've provided three different solutions to this problem in this chapter:

- Using the MultiPik class module with Access list boxes
- Using the MultiPikMSForms class module with Microsoft Forms list boxes
- Use bound list boxes, pulling data directly from a table into Access list boxes

Figure 7.28 shows a sample multipick list box, frmMultiPik, in action. Both list boxes on frmMultiPik allow multiple selections, so you can select as many items as you wish in either list box and move them all to the other list box. In addition, the arrow buttons to the right of the Selected list box allow users to reorder their chosen items.

FIGURE 7.28:

By clicking the buttons (or double-clicking the list boxes), the user can select a group of items.

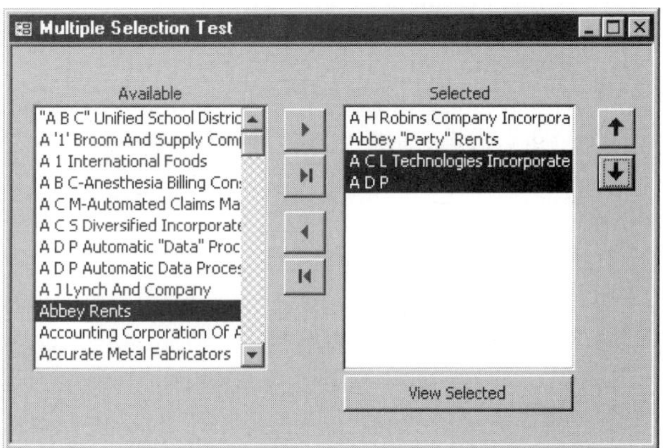

NOTE

Because of the way Access handles multiselect list boxes, it's not possible to alter the position of items in the list box if the MultiSelect property is set to Extended. We're not sure why this doesn't work, but the code exhibits different behavior when the MultiSelect property has been set to Extended. Therefore, the right-hand list box has its MultiSelect property set to Simple. If you don't intend to allow users to alter the ordering of items in the list, or if you must use Extended multiselect (in which case you cannot alter positions), modify the MultiSelect property yourself.

VBA provides several ways to accomplish this goal, and we've chosen a method that allows you some flexibility. By using the code presented here, you'll be able to base your multiple-pick hybrid control either on a recordset (either a table or a query), or on two arrays or collections of values, one representing the available list and one representing the selected list. You might want to open frmMultiPik and experiment a bit while reading the following sections.

Using MultiPik

Because we've encapsulated all the code for providing users with the familiar set of list boxes and buttons in a single class module, it's easy for you to use in your own applications. Not only is the class itself useful, but the technique you use to hook it up to your forms is interesting and useful itself. (The MultiPik, MultiPikMSForms, and MultiPikTable classes all use a technique similar to the one described in the previous example—hooking events of controls using the WithEvents keyword and then placing all the event code in the class module, not in the form's module.)

The MultiPik class exposes a group of properties and methods. Table 7.6 lists the public elements of the class.

TABLE 7.6: Members of the MultiPik Class

Member	Type	Data Type	Description
AddAllCmd	Property	CommandButton	Sets or retrieves the button on your form that acts as an Add All button.
AddOneCmd	Property	CommandButton	Sets or retrieves the button on your form that acts as an Add One button.

Continued on next page

TABLE 7.6 CONTINUED: Members of the MultiPik Class

Member	Type	Data Type	Description
AvailableItems	Property	Variant()	Returns array of variants containing all the selected items. (Read-only. To set this value, call the SetArrays method.)
AvailableLst	Property	ListBox	Sets or retrieves the list box on your form that displays the list of available items.
BumpDownCmd	Property	CommandButton	Sets or retrieves the command button that moves items down in the selected list.
BumpUpCmd	Property	CommandButton	Sets or retrieves the command button that moves items up in the selected list.
DelAllCmd	Property	CommandButton	Sets or retrieves the button on your form that acts as a Delete All button.
DelOneCmd	Property	CommandButton	Sets or retrieves the button on your form that acts as a Delete One button.
Field	Property	String	Retrieves the name of the field that's displayed in the list boxes. (Read-only. Use the SetData method to modify the value.)
RecordSource	Property	String	Retrieves the name of the table or query that's filling the list boxes. (Read-only. Use the SetData method to modify the value.)
SelectedItems	Property	Variant()	Returns array of variants containing all the available items. (Read-only. To set this value, call the SetArrays method.)
SelectedLst	Property	ListBox	Sets or retrieves the list box on your form that displays the list of selected items.
FillLists	Method		List-filling callback function called by a stub for the function within your form. Your form cannot call a list-filling function in a class directly, so you must call a local function that, in turn, calls this method. See frmMultiPik for an example.

Continued on next page

TABLE 7.6 CONTINUED: Members of the MultiPik Class

Member	Type	Data Type	Description
RegisterControls	Method		Allows you to specify to the MultiPik object which controls on your form have specific actions associated with them. Pass this method two list box controls (the Available and Selected lists), four command button controls (the Add One, Add All, Delete One, and Delete All buttons), and two more optional command buttons (Bump Up and Bump Down). This method sets up the WithEvents links to the controls, so the MultiPik class can handle the events of these controls for you.
SetArrays	Method		Allows you to specify two arrays containing items for the Selected and Available lists. Both are optional (although you ought to supply items in at least one list). Use the SetArrays, SetCollections, or SetData method to indicate where MultiPik should get the data for its lists.
SetCollections	Method		Allows you to specify two collections containing items for the Selected and Available lists. Both are optional (although you ought to supply items in at least one list). Use the SetArrays, SetCollections, or SetData method to indicate where MultiPik should get the data for its lists.
SetData	Method		Allows you to specify a data source (a table, query, or SQL string) and a field name within that data source. The class uses these two items in order to fill the Available list box (the Selected list box is always empty at first when using this method). Note that this method includes no provision for satisfying parameters in a query or SQL string.

Just as with any other class you want to use in your applications, you must start by declaring and instantiating a MultiPik object (the code examples are from frmMultiPik's module):

```
Private mmp As MultiPik
Private Sub Form_Open(Cancel As Integer)

    Set mmp = New MultiPik

    ' Code removed here...
End Sub
```

Next, as with other classes that use WithEvents to trap events of controls on your forms, you must indicate to the class which controls to "hook." The MultiPik class lets you do this in two ways: you can specify each control individually, using the AddOneCmd, AddAllCmd, DelOneCmd, DelAllCmd, AvailableLst, SelectedLst, BumpUpCmd, and BumpDownCmd properties, or you can do all this at once using the RegisterControls method. (The BumpUp and BumpDown parameters are optional. If you don't specify values for these properties, you won't be able to move items up and down in the list.) The sample form uses the RegisterControls method, but you can set individual controls if you'd rather:

```
mmp.RegisterControls _
 lstAvailable, lstSelected, _
 cmdAddOne, cmdAddAll, _
 cmdDeleteOne, cmdDeleteAll, _
 cmdUp, cmdDown
```

Because using MultiPik isn't very interesting without some data to display, you should add items to one or both of the two list boxes. You have three methods you can call to do this:

SetData Specify a table name, query name, or SQL string to use as the data source, and a field name within that data source to be displayed. The SetData method will never put any items in the Selected list.

SetArrays Specify an array of available items, an array of selected items, or both. MultiPik uses this method to fill one or both list boxes on your form with the data in the array(s).

SetCollections Specify a collection of available items, a collection of selected items, or both. MultiPik uses this method to fill one or both list boxes on your form with the data in the collection(s).

Choose one of these three methods to supply data to MultiPik. The sample form uses code like this:

```
mmp.SetData "tblCompanies", "Company"
```

Either at design time or at runtime, you must instruct the two list boxes on your form to get their data by calling the FillLists function, which you must add to your form yourself. You can set the RowSourceType property in your form's Open event, or you can do it when you're designing your form. (The sample form does it programmatically from the Open event.) Your FillLists function should call the FillLists method of the MultiPik object you're using. Access will see that the list boxes use a function named FillLists to retrieve their data and will call the FillLists function in your form. It, in turn, calls the FillLists method of the MultiPik object, passing in the five parameters it received. This way, you needn't duplicate the code for the FillLists function in every form that uses this technology. All you need to supply is the little stub shown in Listing 7.16. This code contains everything you'll need to do in any form on which you'd like to hook MultiPik.

Listing 7.16

```
Private mmp As MultiPik

Private Function FillLists(ctl As Control, _
 varID As Variant, lngRow As Long, lngCol As Long, _
 intCode As Integer) As Variant

    If Not mmp Is Nothing Then
        FillLists = mmp.FillLists( _
         ctl, varID, lngRow, lngCol, intCode)
    End If
End Function

Private Sub Form_Open(Cancel As Integer)
    Set mmp = New MultiPik

    mmp.RegisterControls _
     lstAvailable, lstSelected, _
     cmdAddOne, cmdAddAll, _
     cmdDeleteOne, cmdDeleteAll, _
     cmdUp, cmdDown
    ' Specify a recordsource (table
    ' or query name) and a field to display.
```

```
        mmp.SetData "tblCompanies", "Company"

        lstAvailable.RowSourceType = "FillLists"
        lstSelected.RowSourceType = "FillLists"

    End Sub
```

If you want to retrieve the list of available or selected items at any time, you might write code that uses the AvailableItems or SelectedItems properties, like the following example (from frmMultiPik), which loops through the selected items and displays them using MsgBox:

```
Private Sub cmdChosen_Click()
    Dim aSelected() As Variant
    Dim strShowIt As String
    Dim varItem As Variant

    ' Get an array filled with the selected items.
    aSelected = mmp.SelectedItems
    For Each varItem In aSelected
        strShowIt = strShowIt & varItem & vbCrLf
    Next varItem
    MsgBox strShowIt, , "Multiple Pick Test"
End Sub
```

How Does It Work?

Under the covers, our implementation of the MultiPik class uses an array and two collections; the array holds the actual data and the selection status of the items. The two collections keep pointers to the rows in the master array that are available and those that are selected. The array (aFullArray in the code) is based on this structure:

```
Type DataRow
    varData As Variant
    fSelected As Integer
End Type
```

The two collections (mcolAvailable and mcolSelected) do no more than store the index numbers of the available and selected items. When the code needs to fill in the Available or Selected list, it uses list-filling callback functions. (See the section "Using a Callback Function to Fill the List Box" earlier in this chapter.) In each case, the callback function walks through each element of the available or selected collection and fills the appropriate list box with the data from the master array. Given that varRow represents an index in the Selected list box, the item displayed in the list box will be

```
aFullArray(mcolSelected.Item(varRow + 1)).varData
```

Like many other examples in this chapter, multiple-pick lists can be easily incorporated into your own applications. Rather than dissecting the full code for multiple-pick lists here, we refer you to the MultiPik class module. There are some points worth discussing here, though, covered in the next few sections.

Filling the Two List Boxes Unlike most other examples in this book, the two list boxes in this example have their BoundColumn property set to 0. As mentioned in the section "The Special Case" earlier in this chapter, setting the BoundColumn property to 0 effectively binds the list box to the selected row number, starting with 0. If the list boxes had a ControlSource (these don't), you'd end up storing the chosen row number in the underlying data. In this case, setting the BoundColumn property to 0 makes it easier to programmatically specify the particular row to select.

In addition, these list boxes contain two columns. The first column (which is visible) contains the data from the master array. The second column (which is hidden) contains the master array index from which this particular piece of data came. Therefore, it takes two passes through the callback function to fill both columns. In one call to the function, when varCol is 0, Access retrieves the value for the first column. Access retrieves the value for the second column in a second call to the list-filling function:

```
Case acLBGetValue
    ' Get the data for each of the two columns.
    varValue = mcolAvailable.Item(lngRow + 1)
    If lngCol = 0 Then
        varRetval = aFullArray(varValue).varData
    Else
        varRetval = varValue
    End If
```

One Callback or Two? It's true that Access does pass your callback function a unique identifier for each control that calls into that function; it also passes a handle to the control being filled. Given that information, it would seem that you could write a single function to fill the two list boxes used in this example. Actually, it turns out that combining these two functions, FillSelected and FillAvailable, into one function is more work than it's worth. The problem, we found, is that the two list boxes get filled in bits and pieces, overlapping in time. Although they could physically be combined, the resulting code would be so convoluted and difficult to maintain that it made more sense to separate them.

To simplify matters a little, the MultiPik class module provides its FillLists method. You call this method only from the list-filling function on your form. This method acts as a single procedure that calls both of the list-filling functions that do the work. That is, in your form, you'll set the RowSourceType property of your list boxes to be FillLists and add code like this:

```
Private Function FillLists(ctl As Control, _
 varID As Variant, lngRow As Long, lngCol As Long, _
 intCode As Integer) As Variant

    If Not mmp Is Nothing Then
        FillLists = mmp.FillLists( _
         ctl, varID, lngRow, lngCol, intCode)
    End If
End Function
```

Then, in the MultiPik class, you'll find the FillLists method, which determines which internal list-filling function to call, passing all the parameters on through:

```
Public Function FillLists( _
 ctl As Control, varID As Variant, _
 lngRow As Long, lngCol As Long, _
 intCode As Integer) As Variant
    Select Case ctl.Name
        Case mlstAvailable.Name
            FillLists = FillAvailable( _
             ctl, varID, lngRow, lngCol, intCode)
        Case mlstSelected.Name
            FillLists = FillSelected( _
             ctl, varID, lngRow, lngCol, intCode)
        Case Else
            ' Do nothing at all.
    End Select
End Function
```

Retrieving the Selected List This hybrid control, the pairing of two different list boxes, wouldn't do you much good if you couldn't easily find out which items the user had selected. Therefore, the MultiPik class includes a property your application can call to retrieve an array containing the list of selected items. The sample form (frmMultiPik) displays the list in a message box when you click the View Selected button. To retrieve the list for your own use, use the Selected-Items or AvailableItems property to retrieve the list you need. For example, in the sample form, the Click event of the View Selected button executes this code:

```
Private Sub cmdChosen_Click()
    Dim aSelected() As Variant
    Dim strShowIt As String
    Dim varItem As Variant

    ' Get an array filled with the selected items.
    aSelected = mmp.SelectedItems
    For Each varItem In aSelected
        strShowIt = strShowIt & varItem & vbCrLf
    Next varItem
    MsgBox strShowIt, , "Multiple Pick Test"
End Sub
```

Issues to Consider

You should be aware of several issues before you attempt to use this hybrid control in your own applications:

- The data must come from a table, query, a pair of arrays, or a pair of collections. To use an open recordset variable to fill the list of available items, you need to create arrays and fill them with the appropriate data before setting up your controls.
- Think twice before using this method with large lists (more than 1000 data elements or so). It can take a long time to fill the collections when you have many elements.
- Multiple-pick lists make sense only when the data elements you present to the user are unique. You may need to concatenate multiple fields in a query, creating a list of unique values. Once you have that unique list, you can present it to the user.

To include multiple-pick lists in your own applications, follow these steps:

1. Import the class module named MultiPik from the sample database.

2. Create your form, including two list boxes and four data movement buttons. If you want to include the buttons to move selected data up and down, you can add those buttons, as well. You may find it easiest to just copy the eight controls from frmMultiPik in the sample database by importing frmMultiPik, selecting the group of controls, copying and pasting the group to your new form, and then deleting frmMultiPik from your database.

3. If you want, set the AutoRepeat properties of all the command buttons to Yes.

4. Copy code from frmMultiPik, or add the following code, to the new form's module. Modify the call to SetData and the control names to match your own form's needs. (The lines marked in bold are the ones you'll want to modify.)

```
Private mmp As MultiPik

Private Function FillLists(ctl As Control, _
 varID As Variant, lngRow As Long, lngCol As Long, _
 intCode As Integer) As Variant

    If Not mmp Is Nothing Then
        FillLists = mmp.FillLists( _
         ctl, varID, lngRow, lngCol, intCode)
    End If
End Function

Private Sub Form_Open(Cancel As Integer)
    Set mmp = New MultiPik

    mmp.RegisterControls _
     lstAvailable, lstSelected, _
     cmdAddOne, cmdAddAll, _
     cmdDeleteOne, cmdDeleteAll, _
     cmdUp, cmdDown
    ' Modify the following line to
    ' match your own needs.
    ' Specify a recordsource (table
    ' or query name) and a field to display.
    mmp.SetData "tblCompanies", "Company"

    lstAvailable.RowSourceType = "FillLists"
    lstSelected.RowSourceType = "FillLists"

End Sub
```

5. If you've created new controls, you must set the properties correctly. Set the ColumnCount to 2, the ColumnWidths to ;0", and the BoundColumn to 0.

6. In the Form_Open event, you need to call one of three methods. You can call the MultiSetArrays method, passing to it the two arrays you want displayed:

   ```
   Call mmp.SetArrays(varAvailable, varSelected)
   ```

   or the SetData method, passing to it the name of the field to display and the table from which to retrieve it:

   ```
   Call mmp.SetData("tblCompanies", "Company")
   ```

   or the SetCollections method, passing to it the name of two collections.

7. In the call to the RegisterControls method, change the control names, if necessary, to match the names of the appropriate controls on your form.

8. If you're filling your list boxes from arrays, you'll need to fill those arrays from your form's Open event before you call the SetArrays method.

Other Areas of Interest

If you're interested in studying user-defined collections, MultiPik's source code is a good place to start. It uses all the methods of collections (Add, Remove, Item) and exercises all the mechanisms for working with multiselect list boxes, as well. You'll find the methods that move selected items up and down the list (BumpUp and BumpDown) of particular interest, because these use many advanced features of collections.

The code that copies data from your table into aFullArray is interesting, as well. It uses the GetRows method of a recordset to return all the rows you care about in one single statement. Rather than looping through the rows of data one by one, this method returns all the rows you request into a variant array. In the sample case, because you need the data in an array of user-defined types, the code still has to walk the entire set of data. But the loop now is all in memory instead of looping through rows on the disk, one by one. The following code fragment is from RetrieveData, in the MultiPik class module:

```
' Get all the data.
intCount = rst.RecordCount
ReDim aFullArray(1 To intCount)

' Get all the rows of data in one fell swoop.
varData = rst.GetRows(intCount)
```

```
' Now copy that data into the array of
' total items, avarItemsToFill.
' The array returned by GetRows is 0-based.
Set mcolSelected = New Collection
Set mcolAvailable = New Collection
For intLoop = LBound(aFullArray) To UBound(aFullArray)
    ' aFullArray is 1-based, but the array from GetRows
    ' is 0-based. Therefore, the "intLoop - 1" in the
    ' next line.
    aFullArray(intLoop).varData = varData(0, intLoop - 1)
    aFullArray(intLoop).fSelected = False
    Call AddItem(mcolAvailable, intLoop)
Next intLoop
```

Isn't There a Better Way?

This really seems like a lot of code to do something that ought to be easy. Isn't there a better way? Of course. You can implement this same sort of functionality very easily, with a lot less code. The form frmMultiPikTable implements this technique. It works by using the MultiPikTables class to do the work and Yes/No column named Selected in your table that keeps track of which rows are selected. The code reacts to clicks of the selection buttons by setting the Selected field in the underlying table to either True or False and then refilling the list boxes with the appropriate (selected or not) subset of the data. Experiment with frmMultiPikTable to get a feel for how this works.

You may find this simple technique satisfies your needs, but you may also find some drawbacks that make it unsuitable:

- Because the code writes directly to the table, you'd have to take extra steps to make this work in a multiuser environment. One solution is to create a new table that works in parallel with the main table in a one-to-one relationship that's kept locally. This table could keep track of the selected items.
- The code fills the lists directly from the table. If you wanted to control the order of the selected list, you'd need to add another field to keep track of the order in which they were selected. Again, there are multiuser concerns involved.

On the other hand, this technique is quite fast: all it does is write directly to the table, setting the Selected field and then requerying the two list boxes. Investigate the MultiPikTable class and its properties and methods, if you're interested.

TIP

The sample database includes yet a third class for working with pairs of list boxes, MultiPikMSForms. This class assumes you're using list box controls from the Microsoft Forms set of controls. These controls make it easy to add and remove items programmatically, so the code is significantly less difficult. On the other hand, using this class requires working with external controls. If you're interested, dig into MultiPikMSForms and its demonstration form, frmMultiPikMSForms, to see how these controls can make the code simpler.

How and When to Use Subforms

To display data from more than one table in any but a one-to-one relationship (you can use subforms in a one-to-one case, but they are not required, and a single form based on a query will handle a simple one-to-one case), you need to investigate subforms. A subform is nothing more than a related form displayed within a form; it can be displayed in Datasheet or Form view, and it can, in turn, contain another subform. Access allows nesting subforms two deep so you can display data in a one-to-many-to-many relationship. In addition, subforms have a bit of an identity crisis: from their own point of view, they're forms. From the point of view of their parent form, they're controls, just like any other control.

Creating a Subform

You first need to create the form you wish to use as a subform. It needs no special handling and can be any form you happen to have created. You'll need to set the form's properties so that it appears as you want it to appear on the parent form. The DefaultView, ViewsAllowed, and ScrollBars properties are important to consider when designing your subforms. If you save the form that will become the subform without scroll bars and in a particular view, that's how Access will display it on the main form.

Drag-and-Drop That Form

The easiest way to create a subform is to select and drag an existing form from the database window to your main form. Access will understand that you intend to create a subform and do the work for you. In addition, if you have created any default relationships between the tables on which you've based the form and subform, Access will fill in the LinkChildFields and LinkMasterFields properties for you. Note that this subform is not a copy of the original form, just a reference to it. That is, if you make changes to the original form that is now a subform, closing and reopening the main form will update all the information stored in the main form, and the subform will reflect any changes you've made. After you've dragged the form to be displayed as a subform to the parent form, Access will display the subform Wizard, allowing you to specify how the two forms should be related.

NOTE

If your main form has its DefaultView property set to Continuous Forms and you place a new subform control on that form, Access displays a dialog box warning you that it will change the form to single-form mode. Access cannot display subforms on continuous forms.

TIP

You can drag a table or a query directly to a form, as well. When you drop the object onto the form, Access will create a simple form for you and continue as if you'd dragged a form onto the parent form.

Choosing a Control from the Toolbox

You can create a subform by choosing the Subform control from the toolbox. Once you place your control on the form, you can specify the source object, which tells Access where to retrieve the form at display time. Access provides you with a list of possible objects, which, in this case, will be a list of the currently defined forms in your database or a list of tables and queries. If you choose to use a table or query, you can choose any fields from any tables you need. In addition, you can change the SourceObject property while your form is in use. That is, when you change the SourceObject property for the subform control, Access pulls in different forms as you make the change.

TIP

In previous versions of Access, parent forms displayed subform controls as white rectangles. In Access 2000, subforms in Design view appear as if they, too, were in Design view. Figure 7.29 shows the sample form, frmNestedOrders, showing a main form and a subform in Design view. Note that Access displays the subform completely, not as a white rectangle. In theory, this should be useful. But if your subform isn't very tall, like this one, it's almost impossible to do any work with the subform because the ruler and border take up too much space. And, to make it even worse, there's no way to open the subform as a second form designer once it's been opened this way. To solve this problem, if you know you're going to want to work with a subform and its parent form, open the subform first. In this case, Access will display the subform as a white rectangle, as in previous versions, and you'll be able to edit both easily.

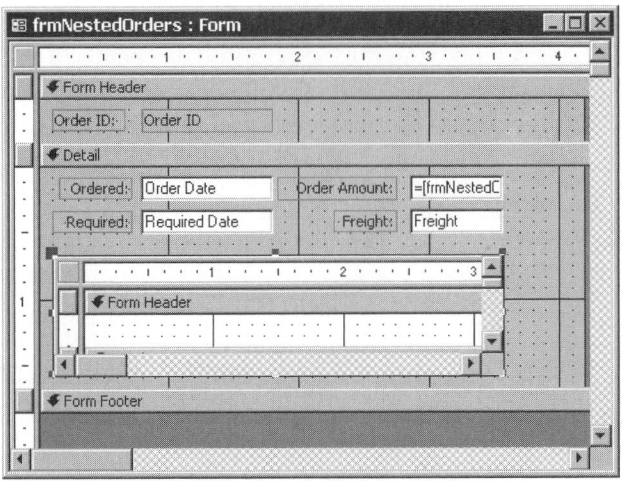

FIGURE 7.29:

It may be difficult to edit subforms, because they're displayed completely in Design view.

Relating the Parent to the Child

The LinkChildFields and LinkMasterFields properties control how the main form and the subform relate and interact. Once you have properly set these properties, record pointer movement in the master form will trigger appropriate movement in the child form. This way, the records displaying in the child form should always match the record displaying in the master form.

Allowable Settings

The LinkChildFields property applies to the subform, and the LinkMasterFields property applies to the main form. In each case, you can enter one of the following:

- A field name from the underlying recordset (a table or query), identified in the RecordSource property
- A list of fields, separated by semicolons

The number of fields you enter must match exactly in both property settings. Although the field names can match, there is no reason why they must. As long as the data types match and the data is related, this connection should work.

Setting the Values Automatically

Under either of the following two conditions, Access fills in the LinkChildFields and LinkMasterFields properties automatically:

- Both forms are based on tables, and the Tools ➢ Relationships menu item has been used to create default relationships between the two tables.
- Both forms contain fields of the same name and data type, and the field on the main form is the primary key of the underlying table.

Always check the validity of the supplied links, because Access might make some incorrect assumptions. Unless one of the preceding conditions is true, Access cannot make a determination of how to link the forms and therefore leaves the properties empty.

Retrieving Calculated Values from Subforms

You may find it useful to employ subforms to display detail records and report on the total of some value displayed there on the main form. This is one of the questions most commonly asked by Access developers: how do you retrieve values from subforms back to the main form?

The complete syntax is rather complex and not at all obvious:

Forms(*"Your Form Name")("SubForm Control Name")*.Form.Controls(*"Your Control Name")*

The important issue here is that you must use the Form property of the subform control to find the form contained within it and the Controls collection of that form to refer to controls on the form. To explore this syntax, you might take a look at the properties available when you have selected your subform in Design view. You'll notice that none of the actual form properties are available at this point. Therefore, were you to use the syntax

Forms(*"Your Form Name")("SubForm Control Name")*

you'd have access only to those properties that you see in the property sheet. For example, you could set the Visible property of the subform:

Forms(*"Your Form Name")("SubForm Control Name")*.Visible = True

Luckily, you don't have to worry about any of these details. The default property of a subform control is its Form property. The default collection for a Form object is its Controls collection. Therefore, if you just use something like this:

```
Debug.Print Me.fsubOrder.Form.Controls("txtTotal")
' equivalent to:
Debug.Print Me.fsubOrder("txtTotal")
```

Access will know to look at the fsubOrder subform on the current form and then, on that form, to find the txtTotal text box and retrieve its value.

TIP

When creating references to subforms and the forms and controls they contain, remember that the only place you need to be concerned with the name of the form filling the subform control is in the control's SourceObject property. None of your code will care about, and none of your references will include, the actual name of the form. What your code needs is the name of the subform *control*, which will often be different than the name of the form contained in the subform control.

Syntax is Tricky

It's very tempting to try to use dots (".") to separate the pieces of the subform syntax, but it doesn't work. This is all terribly confusing, but it boils down to this: Access forms make a special case for controls on the form and exposes them as properties of the form itself. You can't delve deeper into the object hierarchy from controls referenced as properties. You can only retrieve and set properties of that control.

You can never use a dot to separate a collection of objects from an object within that collection. (It works for controls on forms only because of Access' special casing.) Therefore, you can use code like this to reference a control:

```
Forms!frmNestedOrders.frmNestedOrderDetail
' or
Forms("frmNestedOrders").frmNestedOrderDetail
```

but you cannot use a dot to reference a form within the Forms collection. This will fail, for example:

```
Forms.frmNestedOrders.frmNestedOrderDetails
```

Continued on next page

The same problem applies when attempting to refer to controls within a subform—you're not actually dealing with a property of the subform, so you can't use a dot. For example, the following code will fail:

```
Forms!frmNestedOrders!frmNestedOrderDetail.txtOrderAmount
```

but the following code works fine:

```
Forms!frmNestedOrders!frmNestedOrderDetail!txtOrderAmount
```

as does this:

```
Forms!frmNestedOrders.frmNestedOrderDetail!txtOrderAmount
```

(This works because frmNestedOrderDetail is a control on frmNestedOrders, and is therefore handled as a property of the form.)

Just remember these rules:

- Dots (".") can only be used to preface properties or methods, not objects within collections. Access makes a special case for controls on forms (and reports), so you can use a dot to preface these objects. This can make your code run a bit faster, if it references these objects.
- Bang ("!") turns into parentheses/quotes around an object internally, so there's little reason to use it. In any case, you use bang or parentheses/quotes to separate an object from the collection containing that object.

Going All the Way

Access allows you to nest subforms two deep. That is, you can place a form that itself contains a subform as a subform on a form. This ability can be useful if you want to represent a one-to-many-to-many relationship on a form. For example, your client, a law office, might need to display information about each lawyer, the lawyer's clients, and billing information for each client. By nesting subforms, you could create a form that allowed your client to page through each lawyer and, for each, view each client. For each client, a third form could display the billable events for that client. Figure 7.30 shows a very simple form, frmNested, with two nested subforms.

NOTE

Since most of the interesting things you can do with subforms involve their acting as real forms, we cover subforms in more detail in Chapter 8.

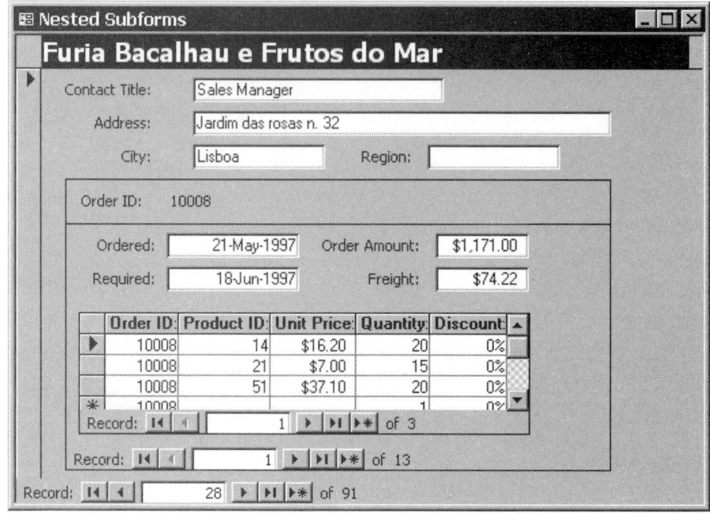

FIGURE 7.30:

The main form represents a customer, the first subform represents one of the customer's orders, and the second subform represents the order items for that particular order.

Using Command Buttons

Command buttons are most often associated with actions. Their most common use is with a macro or Basic code attached to their Click event. They have several interesting and useful properties and events, as described in the following sections.

Macros to Buttons, Automagically

Knowing that many people are likely to create macros and then assign them to command buttons on forms, Access allows you to select a macro name in the database window and drag it onto a form. Doing this creates a command button for you, with the Caption property set to be the name of the macro. This feature is of limited value if you store more than one macro in a given macro group, but if you store one macro for each group, it's a nice feature. As a developer, you're more likely to be writing code in modules than writing macros, so there's not much point in dwelling on this feature.

Command Button Properties

Some of the properties associated with command buttons are different from those for all other controls, so it's worth a moment to go over the unique properties here.

The Picture Property

Unlike other controls, a command button can display either a bitmapped image or a text caption on its surface. (It would be nice if you could mix both on the button, but that option is not currently available. You can, however, use a graphics editor to create a bitmap image that includes text.) You can specify either a bitmap or an icon file to be placed on the surface of the button. Access displays your chosen picture centered and clipped on the button. In addition, Access attempts to display the *center* of your image in the center of the button; this way, if you shrink the button size so that it's smaller than the picture, the center of the picture will still show.

TIP

Access previously stored only the bitmap image, not a pathname reference to that image, in the button's properties. If you changed your mind about the image or just wanted to find out which file was currently being displayed in the button's picture, you were out of luck. Starting with Access 95, however, Access stores the full path to the image in the Picture property if you use your own image (as opposed to one retrieved from the Command Button Wizard). In addition, the PictureData property can return the bit-level image of the picture. You can also use the PictureData property to set the picture on a button. The simplest use for this is to copy a picture from one button to another by assigning a PictureData property from one to the other. See Chapter 17 for more information on using the PictureData property.

The Transparent Property

The command button's Transparent property turns off all display attributes but leaves the button active. This property allows you to overlay a button on another control that might not normally be able to receive focus or raise events. For example, you could place a transparent command button on top of a line and assign an action to its Click event. To the user, it would appear as though the line were reacting to the mouse click! You can also overlay transparent command buttons on bitmaps on forms, allowing various pieces of the bitmap to react to mouse clicks. Imagine a bitmap of the United States, with each state's name printed on the state. With a transparent button overlaid on the state's name, you could allow users to click the image of the state and have Access react to the click.

NOTE

Do not confuse the Transparent property with the Visible property. When you set a control's Visible property to No, you completely disable that control. Not only is it invisible, Access removes it from the form's tab order, and it can never receive focus or trigger an event. When the Transparent property is Yes, Access turns off only the display attributes for the button. All the other attributes still apply. You can reach it by tabbing to it or clicking it. All its events are active.

The Default/Cancel Properties

Every form can have exactly one button that acts as the default button (its Click event gets triggered when you press Enter on the form) and exactly one button that acts as the Cancel button (its Click event gets raised when you press Esc on the form). A button with its Default property set to Yes acts as the form's default, and a button with its Cancel property set to Yes acts as the form's cancel button. Note that each form can have at most one of each of these, and setting a button's Default or Cancel property to Yes sets any other button's matching property to No.

You might think, as do many developers, that setting a button's Cancel property actually causes something to happen, perhaps closing the form. This is simply not true. All that happens as a result of a button's Default or Cancel property being set to Yes is that that button receives focus and Access raises its Click event when you press the correct key.

Give the assignment of Default and Cancel properties some serious thought. For situations in which something destructive might happen at the click of a button, make the Cancel button the default button. To do so, set both the Default and Cancel properties to Yes.

The Visible Property

Unlike the Transparent property, setting the Visible property to No for a button both hides and disables the button completely. This is the same behavior as with other controls, but it can be confusing for command buttons, which also support the Transparent property.

The DisplayWhen Property

If you are inclined to print single records from your form, you will find the DisplayWhen property indispensable. Since you probably will not wish to print the buttons on the form with the data, set the DisplayWhen property for the buttons to

Screen Only (2) (the other options are Always [0], and Print Only [1]). This way, when you print the form, the buttons won't print along with the data.

The Enabled Property

In modern, user-driven applications, it's important to make sure users can't make choices that shouldn't be available. In the past, it may have been reasonable for a user to click a button and be confronted only with a dialog box that shouted, "This option is not currently available!" However, the correct way to handle this situation is for you to disable the button when the option isn't available so the user can't click it in the first place. Set the Enabled property to No when you want the button to be unavailable. Set it to Yes when you want the user to be able to click the button. You may be tempted to make unavailable buttons invisible, but many people find this distracting, since they tend to think, "I saw that option a minute ago; where did it go?"

The AutoRepeat Property

The AutoRepeat property determines whether Access will repeat the code attached to the Click event for a button while you hold down the button. Access fixes the initial repeat to be 0.5 seconds after the first repetition. Subsequent repeats occur each 0.25 seconds or at the duration of the macro, whichever is longer.

NOTE

The AutoRepeat property has no effect if the code attached to the button causes record movement on the form. Moving from row to row cancels any automatic repetitions.

One use for the AutoRepeat property is to simulate a spin-button control. In this sort of arrangement, you create a text box and two little buttons, usually one with an up arrow and one with a down arrow. As you press the up arrow button, some value in the text box increases; as you press the down arrow button, the value decreases. One issue to consider when doing this, though, is that Access performs the repeat without consideration for Windows' screen-painting needs. Therefore, your code will probably get far ahead of Windows' ability to repaint the text box. Anytime you cause screen activity using an auto-repeat button, you need to use the Repaint method of the form.

Why bother creating your own spin buttons when there are ActiveX controls that perform this same function? First of all, most of the spin-button controls we've seen are unattractive. If you create your own, you control how they look.

Also, ActiveX controls still exact a somewhat hefty overhead in terms of resources, speed, and application size. Because spin buttons are so easy to create using Access built-in controls, it seems like overkill to use an ActiveX control for this. In addition, because you're writing the code here, you can control the behavior. For example, the spin buttons we'll create here allow you to limit the range and, possibly, cycle back to the beginning or end once you reach an endpoint.

Example: Simulating Spin-Button Controls

Spin buttons provide one way to both control the values your users input and make it simpler for them to change numeric and date values. The basic concept should be familiar—it includes two buttons, one pointing up and the other pointing down, attached to a text box. Pressing the up button increments the value in the text box and pressing the down button decrements the value. Although you could theoretically use this mechanism for text values, it's not often used that way. For the most part, spin buttons are restricted to date and integer entry.

We've provided a class, SpinButtons, which makes using the two buttons/text box combination simple. Once you create an instance of the class and set a few properties, it's ready to go. To see the SpinButtons class in action, see frmSpin-Test, shown in Figure 7.31. This form uses all the properties of the SpinButtons class, and Table 7.7 lists all the properties and methods of the class.

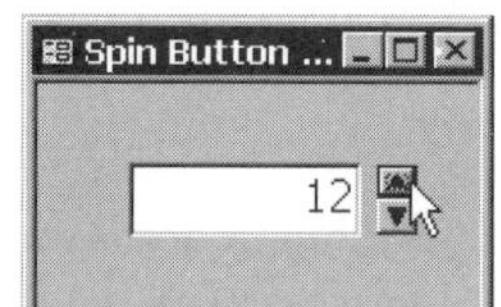

FIGURE 7.31: The SpinButtons class makes it easy to use the spin button functionality on any form.

TABLE 7.7: Properties and Methods of the SpinButtons Class

Member	Type	Data Type	Description
AllowKeys	Property	Boolean	If True, allows the plus and minus keys to increment and decrement the value of the text box, respectively. If False, you must use the up and down buttons to increment the value of the text box.

Continued on next page

TABLE 7.7 CONTINUED: Properties and Methods of the SpinButtons Class

Member	Type	Data Type	Description
AllowWrap	Property	Boolean	If True, causes the changing value to reset to the lowest value when spinning up, and the value becomes the Max property value; or it will reset to the highest value when spinning down, and the value becomes the Min property value. If either of the Min and Max properties haven't been specified, AllowWrap has no effect—wrapping will not occur.
Control	Property	TextBox	Reference to the text box to be used to display the changing value. This property is not optional.
Delay	Property	Long	If set to a nonzero value, forces the spinning to delay the specified number of milliseconds between each value. Because Access, by default, can cause the values to go by too fast, you may want to set this value to 100 or more to slow down the changes.
DownButton	Property	CommandButton	Reference to the command button that causes the value of the text box to decrement. This property is optional, but you won't be able to use the mouse to decrement the value in the text box unless you specify a command button for this property.
Interval	Property	Long	Sets or retrieves the amount to increment and decrement on each click of the up and down buttons. The default value is 1.
Max	Property	Variant	If AllowWrapping is True, specifies the maximum value the text box can reach before wrapping back to the Min value. Unless both Min and Max have been set and AllowWrap is True, this property has no effect.
Min	Property	Variant	If AllowWrapping is True, specifies the minimum value the text box can reach before wrapping back to the Max value. Unless both Min and Max have been set, and AllowWrap is True, this property has no effect.
UpButton	Property	CommandButton	Reference to the command button that causes the value of the text box to increment. This property is optional, but you won't be able to use the mouse to increment the value in the text box unless you specify a command button for this property.

Continued on next page

TABLE 7.7 CONTINUED: Properties and Methods of the SpinButtons Class

Member	Type	Data Type	Description
Value	Property	Variant	Sets and retrieves the value of the text box associated with the SpinButtons class. Although you could retrieve the value yourself from the form, this property helps encapsulate the class so you needn't worry about the name of the control if you don't want to.
Init	Method		Rather than setting the properties individually, you can call the Init method, passing in the properties you want to set. This method accepts as its parameters each of the possible class properties. For more information, see the Parameter Tip.
SpinDown	Event		Raised when the value of the text box is about to be decremented. The event passes to you the current value and a Boolean Cancel parameter. Set the parameter to True if you want to cancel the change. See the sample form for an example.
SpinUp	Event		Raised when the value of the text box is about to be incremented. The event passes to you the current value and a Boolean Cancel parameter. Set the parameter to True if you want to cancel the change. See the sample form for an example.
Change	Event		Raised when the value of the text box has been changed. If you don't care whether the value is going up or down, and you care only that the value has changed, use this event. By the time this event is raised, the value has already changed, and it's too late to cancel the change. The event passes to you the current value of the text box, which has already been changed.

Using SpinButtons

In order to use the SpinButtons class, you'll need to import the class module into your project. In addition, you'll need a form that contains at least the controls necessary for the spin buttons: a text box and two command buttons. (You can copy and paste the control group we've created on frmSpinTest, if you like. If you do that, you'll probably want to adjust the size of the text box and its font.) If you create the buttons yourself, you'll want to set their AutoRepeat property to Yes so that holding the buttons down will repeat the change to the value.

Once you have the form set up, you'll need to write code to instantiate the SpinButtons object and hook it up with the form. To do that, add code like this to your form (of course, replace the sample control names with your actual control names, if you've created new ones yourself):

```
Private sb As SpinButtons

Private Sub Form_Load()
    Set sb = New SpinButtons

    ' Set the required properties individually.
    Set sb.Control = txtValue
    Set sb.DownButton = cmdDown
    Set sb.UpButton = cmdUp
End Sub

Private Sub Form_Unload(Cancel As Integer)
    Set sb = Nothing
End Sub
```

If you like, you can set all those properties at once, using the Init method:

```
sb.Init _
 Control:=txtValue, _
 UpButton:=cmdUp, _
 DownButton:=cmdDown
```

Here are some suggestions about using SpinButtons and their properties:

- If you want to limit the range of the spin buttons, set the Min and Max properties.
- If you want to both limit the range and wrap around from top to bottom and vice versa, set the Min, Max, and AllowWrap properties.
- If you want to allow users to press the "+" and "-" keys to spin up and down, respectively, set the AllowKeys property to True.
- If you don't like the speed at which the changes occur, set the Delay property to the number of milliseconds you'd like to delay between changes. (You can't make the changing faster, only slower, by inserting a delay.)
- You can either set each property individually, or use the Init method to set any or all the properties at once.

- If you want to react to events of the SpinButtons class in a class module, add WithEvents to the declaration of the SpinButtons object. Once you've done that, you can add event procedure code for the SpinUp, SpinDown, and Change events. You can cancel the SpinUp and SpinDown events by setting the Cancel parameter sent to the event procedures to True. (See the frmSpinTest example for code that demonstrates this technique.)
- SpinButtons work both with dates and with numbers. If you enter a date in the text box, the buttons will raise and lower the date. If you enter a number, the buttons raise and lower the number.

How Does It Work?

Like several other classes we've presented in this chapter, the SpinButtons class does its work by grabbing WithEvents connections to controls on your form. Rather than forcing you to write event procedure code for each of the command buttons, you simply specify the control references, and the SpinButtons class does the rest of the work.

When you set the Control, UpButton, and DownButton properties of the form, the SpinButtons class stores away the reference in variables that use the With-Events keyword and sets the appropriate event properties to be [Event Procedure]. For example, Listing 7.17 shows the Property Set procedure for the UpButton property.

Listing 7.17

```
Private WithEvents mcmdUp As CommandButton

Public Property Set UpButton(cmd As CommandButton)
    On Error GoTo HandleErrors
    Set mcmdUp = cmd
    mcmdUp.OnClick = "[Event Procedure]"
    mcmdUp.OnKeyPress = "[Event Procedure]"

ExitHere:
    Exit Property

HandleErrors:
    Select Case Err.Number
        Case Else
            Err.Raise Err.Number, _
```

```
            "SpinButtons.UpButton", Err.Description
    End Select
    Resume ExitHere
End Property
```

Once you've set the control properties, the SpinButtons class can react to the Click and KeyPress events of the command buttons and can change the value of the associated text box.

Raising Events

To make the group of controls act more like a real ActiveX control, the SpinButtons class raises three events as you work with it: SpinUp, SpinDown, and Change. The SpinButtons class raises the SpinUp and SpinDown events before it changes the text in the text box control and allows you to cancel the change. It raises the Change event after changing the value.

To raise events from a class, you must first declare the events, like this:

```
Public Event Change(Value As Variant)
Public Event SpinUp(Value As Variant, Cancel As Boolean)
Public Event SpinDown(Value As Variant, Cancel As Boolean)
```

Then, at the moment you want to raise the events, use the RaiseEvent statement. For example, the SpinButtons class uses the following code fragment, from its private Spin procedure, to raise the SpinUp and SpinDown events:

```
Select Case Sgn(intInterval)
    Case 1
        RaiseEvent SpinUp(varData, fCancel)
    Case -1
        RaiseEvent SpinDown(varData, fCancel)
    Case 0
        ' Do nothing at all.
End Select
If fCancel Then
    GoTo ExitHere
End If
```

This code first determines the sign of the interval (+1 or –1), and raises the SpinUp or SpinDown event, accordingly.

In your form, using SpinButtons allows you to add event procedures for any of the SpinUp, SpinDown, and Change events. For example, the sample form reacts to the SpinDown event and cancels the event if the value of the text box control is less than or equal to 10:

```
Private Sub sb_SpinDown( _
 Value As Variant, Cancel As Boolean)
    ' Sample SpinDown event procedure.
    ' You wont', in general, use this code.

    If Value <= 10 Then
        Cancel = True
    End If
End Sub
```

Command Button Events

Command buttons provide the same events as other controls, but you're likely to use just one of them, the Click event. You might be tempted to assign different actions to the Click and DblClick events. Don't bother. Access can't differentiate between the two events and will always attempt to raise the Click event before the DblClick event. This functionality can be useful to you at times, though. When you want the DblClick event to add to the Click event, it works to your advantage. In general, if you want to attach code to both events, make sure the code attached to the DblClick event extends the action done in the Click event. In actuality, you won't want to use the DblClick event for buttons very often.

The Tab Control

The tab control allows developers to create standard tabbed dialogs that match the Windows "look." Figure 7.32 shows a simple example (frmTabSimple) using the tab control.

FIGURE 7.32:

The tab control makes it simple to create multipage, standard tabbed dialogs.

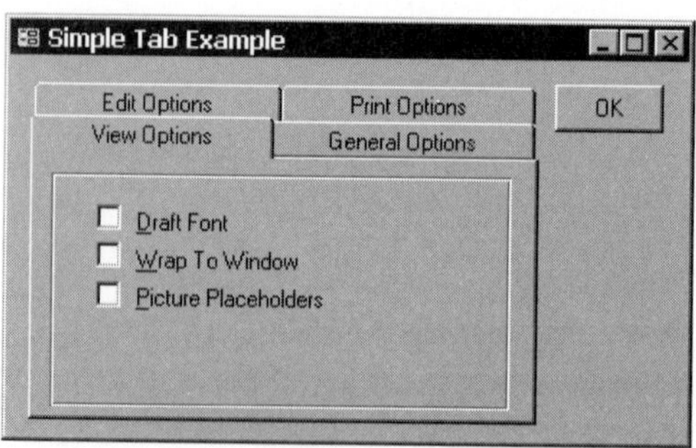

What Works and What Doesn't

Although the built-in tab control is missing some useful functionality (you can't place the tabs anywhere except on the top edge of the control, and you can't change the color of individual tabs, for example), its simplicity and programmability far outweigh any perceived disadvantages. The following lists point out some of the features (and nonfeatures) of the built-in tab control.

You can

Display multiple rows of tabs Set the MultiRow property to match your preference.

Place icons on the tabs Each page on the tab supports a Picture property, and you can display both a picture and text on the tab. If you must have colored tabs, this is the way to get them—create a bitmap that displays the text you want in the color you want, and use that bitmap. Be careful, however—you must supply a caption, or Access will display its internal caption. Use a space character, if you want to supply the caption in your bitmap.

Hide the tabs altogether You can set the Style property to Tabs, Buttons, or None. Setting it to None provides a neat way to create multipage forms, just as Access has always been able to do, without most of the effort.

Place ActiveX controls on the pages No problem! Each page can contain its own set of controls, any of which can be ActiveX controls.

Float a control above the tab If you have a control you want to display at the same place on all pages, just place it on the form and then position it on top of the tab control. The sample form frmTabSimple uses this technique to display the etched rectangle.

Hide/move pages at runtime If you need to change the number of pages, or rearrange them, at runtime, you can do it. Each Page object supports a Visible property that you can set to be True or False. Each Page object also supports a PageIndex property, which is read/write both when designing and displaying the form, that allows you to set the order of the pages as they're displayed by the tab control.

You cannot

Nest tab controls Although you can float a tab control on top of another (so that the smaller control appears on every page of the larger control), you cannot place a tab control on a page of a tab control.

Provide transition effects Some ActiveX tab controls provide ways to show effects as you change from one page to another (page turning, slides, and so on). The Access tab control does not provide any such mechanisms.

Change orientation of the tabs With the Access tab control, you can have any text orientation you like, as long as it's horizontal, on the top of the control.

Drag-and-drop controls between pages Page controls work very much like option groups. To place a control on either control, you must either create it fresh or copy/cut/paste it from another location.

Create or delete pages at runtime You can add to or delete from the Pages collection only in Design view. If you want to be able to control the number of pages at runtime, you'll need to create as many pages as you think you might need at design time and then use the Visible property of the pages to display them when your form is opened. (The sample from, frmTabCustomers, uses this technique.)

TIP

Although you can't place a tab control inside another tab control, you can work around this limitation by placing a tab control on a form and embedding this second form inside a page of your main tab control.

NOTE

As mentioned above, the PageIndex property of a Page object determines its position within the tab control. This is the only place we know of in Access where you can set the position of an item within its collection without removing it first. In addition, it's the only place where an object's position within its collection is linked to the display of the object. There's no visible link between the position of a control within the Controls collection and its position on the screen, for example.

How the Tab Control Works

You can think of the tab control as a container for Page controls, each of which is a container for other controls. Only one Page object is visible at a time, and the tabs allow you to switch from displaying one page to another.

The tab control provides a Pages collection that includes all the Page objects. You could, for example, write code like this to list out the Caption property for all the pages in a tab control:

```
Dim pge As Page
For Each pge In tabItems.Pages
    Debug.Print pge.Caption
Next pge
```

Each Page object is also a member of the form's Controls collection. (For more information on forms and their Controls collection, see Chapter 8.)

Just as with any other collection (see Chapter 6 for more information on collections and referencing items in them), you can use several methods for referring to a Page object. For example, if the first page in a tab control were named Page1, you could use any of the following methods to retrieve a reference to that page:

```
Dim pge As Page
Set pge = tabItems.Pages(0)
' or
Set pge = tabItems!Page1
' or
Set pge = tabItems("Page1")
```

Each Page object provides a Controls collection, allowing you to programmatically visit every control within a specific page. For example, the following code fragment would change the ForeColor property of every control on a specific page to red:

```
Dim ctl As Control

' Disregard errors: Some controls don't support the
' ForeColor property.
On Error Resume Next
For Each ctl In tabItems.Pages(0).Controls
    ctl.ForeColor = 255
Next ctl
```

In addition, Access makes all the Page objects, and all the controls on those pages, elements of the Controls collection of the form itself. Think of it this way: all the controls (the tab control itself, pages, and controls on each page) are elements of the form's Controls collection. Access just neatly "corrals" them into the Pages collection of the tab, and the Controls collection of each Page object, to make it easier for you to work with them.

TIP

When you first start working with tab controls, you may have a hard time selecting the entire control, as opposed to a specific page within the control. With the property sheet open, it's easy to tell which has been selected: just look at the title of the window. If you want to select a page, click the tab for that page. If you want to select the entire tab control, click the edge of the control—in other words, clicking on the right or bottom black border edge never fails.

Where Am I?

At any time, if you want to know what page is the current page, use the Value property of the Tab control. For example, you could use an expression like this:

```
Debug.Print tabTest.Value
```

to print the current page number to the Immediate window. If you want to know the caption of the selected page, you can use the Pages property, like this:

```
intPage = tabTest.Value
Debug.Print tabTest.Pages(intPage).Caption
' or
Debug.Print tabTest.Pages(tabTest.Value).Caption
```

An Advanced Example Using the Tab Control

As an example of the kinds of things you can do with a tab control, frmTab-Customers (see Figure 7.33) provides a tab for each different country in the Customers table. If you run the form, you'll see that it displays a single tab for each different country in the table, and once you select a tab, the form displays rows only for the selected country.

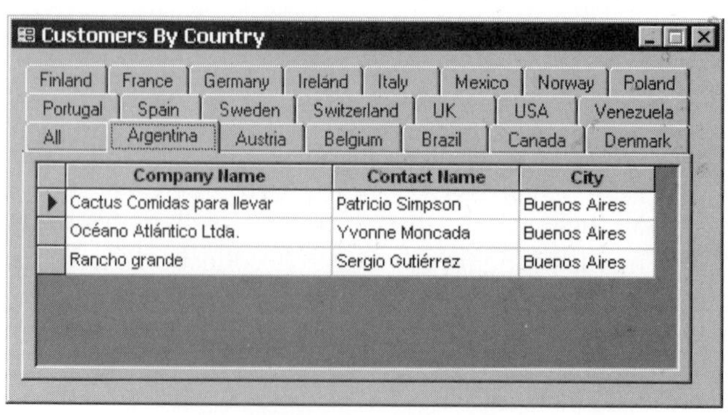

FIGURE 7.33: The sample form, frmTab-Customers, modifies the tab captions as it loads.

The mechanics of loading the tab labels is somewhat complex, mostly because you cannot add or delete pages at runtime. This means that for an interface like this, you must create as many tabs as you'll ever need in Design view and then hide the extra tabs as you load the form. This means, of course, that this technique isn't as general purpose as it might be, but really, how many pages can a given tab control support, anyway? If your tab control has more than 30 pages or so, it's too complex. Even the example shown here is pushing it.

Creating the Tab Control

Adding a page or two to a tab control isn't a problem, but adding 10 or 20 can become a chore. To simplify the task, you can use the PrepareTab procedure (in basTabSetup). This subroutine accepts two parameters: a reference to a tab control and the number of tabs you'd like that control to have. When the code runs, it either removes pages or adds them to get the page count to the value you request. The code, shown in Listing 7.18, does its work by sheer brute force.

Listing 7.18

```
Public Sub PrepareTab(ctl As TabControl, _
 ByVal intPages As Integer)

    Dim pge As Page
    Dim intI As Integer
    Dim pges As Pages

    On Error GoTo HandleErrors

    Set pges = ctl.Pages
    If intPages < 1 Then
        Exit Sub
    Else
        If intPages < pges.Count Then
            For intI = pges.Count - 1 To intPages Step -1
                pges.Remove intI
            Next intI
        Else
            For intI = 1 To intPages - pges.Count
                pges.Add
            Next intI
            ctl.MultiRow = True
```

```
            End If
        End If

    ExitHere:
        Exit Sub

    HandleErrors:
        Select Case Err.Number
            Case Else
                MsgBox "Error: " & Err.Description & _
                 " (" & Err.Number & ")"
        End Select
        Resume ExitHere
    End Sub
```

In this example, if the number of pages in the Pages collection is greater than the number you've requested, the code walks backward through the collection, using the Remove method to delete pages until the number of pages is correct. If there are fewer than you require, the code uses the Add method to add as many pages as necessary.

To create the sample control on frmTabCustomers (with 30 pages), add a tab control to the form, set its name (tabCustomers in this example), and then call PrepareTab like this, from the Immediate window:

```
Call PrepareTab(Forms("frmTabCustomers").tabCustomers, 30)
```

Modifying Tabs at Runtime

Once you've created a control that contains enough pages, modifying it at runtime is simple: you simply set the Caption and Visible properties of each page you want shown and set the Visible property for those you want hidden. In the example, code called from the form's Load event takes these steps:

1. Creates a distinct list of country names from the Customers table.
2. Sets the caption for the first page (page number 0) to All.
3. Loops through the rest of the pages, copying country names to each page's caption and setting the Visible property to True. Stops when there are no more pages or no more countries.

4. If there are still pages (that is, there were fewer countries than pages), loops through the rest of the pages, setting the Visible property to False.
5. Finally, because the number of tabs affects the height of the display area for the pages, set the size of the display subform to match the size of the first page. If there are only two countries, the display area will be larger than if there are 30 countries.

See Listing 7.19 for the entire procedure.

TIP

If you're going to be working with page captions programmatically, you may find it useful to disable form updates until you're finished. That way, you can avoid the flashing that occurs as Access updates the display of the tab control. To do this, use the Painting property of the form: set the property to False when you start, and set it to True when you're done.

NOTE

The sample form, frmTabCustomers, allows you to use either ADO or DAO to retrieve the data from the Customers table. By default, the code uses DAO. You can use ADO instead by setting the USEDAO compile-time constant to be False. If you use ADO, you'll need a reference to ADO. If you use DAO, you'll need to make sure you've set a reference to DAO. (Use the Tools ➢ References menu to set a reference to the correct data access library.)

Listing 7.19

```
Private Sub Form_Load()
    Dim intI As Integer
    Dim strSQL As String
    Dim sfm As SubForm

    ' Fill the existing tabs on a Tab control with the
    ' values from the selected field
    On Error GoTo HandleErrors

    Me.Painting = False
    strSQL = "SELECT DISTINCT " & adhcFieldName & _
     " FROM " & adhcTable
```

```
#If USEDAO Then
    ' Open a DAO Recordset.
    Dim rst As DAO.Recordset
    Dim db As DAO.Database

    Set db = CurrentDb()
    Set rst = db.OpenRecordset(strSQL)
#Else
    ' Open an ADO recordset.
    Dim rst As ADODB.Recordset
    Set rst = New ADODB.Recordset
    rst.Open Source:=strSQL, _
     ActiveConnection:=CurrentProject.Connection, _
     CursorType:=adOpenForwardOnly, _
     LockType:=adLockReadOnly, _
     Options:=adCmdText
#End If

    ' Set up all the object variables.
    Set sfm = Me(adhcSubForm)
    Set mfrm = sfm.Form
    Set mtbc = Me(adhcTabs)
    ' Make sure you hook up any other event
    ' properties for events you want to sink.
    mtbc.OnChange = "[Event Procedure]"

    mfrm.Filter = ""

    intI = 0
    ' Work with the Pages collection.
    ' Note that adhcTabs is NOT the
    ' name of the control -- it's
    ' a constant containing a string
    ' (the name of the tab control).
    With mtbc
        With .Pages
            With .Item(0)
                ' Set the first tab
                ' page's caption to be
                ' "All"
                .Caption = adhcShowAll
                .Visible = True
```

```
            End With
            ' Loop through all rest of the pages. Once
            ' you run out of pages, you have to stop!
            ' If you hit the end of the records,
            ' jump out and make all the
            ' rest of the pages invisible.
            For intI = 1 To .Count - 1
                If rst.EOF Then
                    Exit For
                End If
                With .Item(intI)
                    .Caption = rst(adhcFieldName)
                    .Visible = True
                End With
                rst.MoveNext
            Next intI
            ' Loop through any unused tabs, making
            ' them invisible.
            Do While intI < .Count
                .Item(intI).Visible = False
                intI = intI + 1
            Loop
        End With
        ' Set the list box to fit into the page, no matter
        ' how many rows of tabs are showing.
        With .Pages(0)
            sfm.Top = .Top
            sfm.Height = .Height
            sfm.Left = .Left
            sfm.Width = .Width
        End With
    End With
    mfrm.FilterOn = True

ExitHere:
    On Error Resume Next
    rst.Close
    Me.Painting = True
    Exit Sub

HandleErrors:
    Select Case Err.Number
```

```
            Case Else
                MsgBox "Error: " & Err.Description & _
                 " (" & Err.Number & ")"
        End Select
        Resume ExitHere
    End Sub
```

Reacting to Page Changes

If you need to do something every time a different page is displayed on the tab, you can write code that reacts to the control's Change event. In the example, the control must apply a different filter to the subform every time a different country is selected. (See Chapter 8 for more information on using the Filter and FilterOn properties.)

To make this possible, use the Value property of the tab control. This property contains the PageIndex property of the selected page. The sample code uses this property to retrieve the caption for the selected page:

```
With mtbc
    strValue = .Pages(.Value).Caption
    ' code removed here.
End With
```

Once the code knows the caption of the selected page, it builds a SQL WHERE clause and filters the subform accordingly. The code in Listing 7.20, called from the tab control's Change event, does the work.

Listing 7.20

```
Private Sub mtbc_Change()
    ' This code is called by Access when
    ' the tab control's page changes.

    Dim strWhere As String
    Dim strValue As String

    On Error GoTo HandleErrors

    With mtbc
        strValue = .Pages(.Value).Caption
        If strValue = adhcShowAll Then
            strWhere = ""
```

```
        Else
            strWhere = _
             adhcFieldName & " = " & FixQuotes(strValue)
        End If
    End With

    With mfrm
        .Filter = strWhere
        .FilterOn = True
    End With

ExitHere:
    Exit Sub

HandleErrors:
    Select Case Err.Number
        Case Else
            MsgBox "Error: " & Err.Description & _
             " (" & Err.Number & ")"
    End Select
    Resume ExitHere
End Sub
```

Using This Technique in Your Own Applications

It's simple to use this sample technique in your own applications. To do so, follow these steps:

1. Create the subform that will display the data. Include the fields you want displayed and set the DefaultView property to Datasheet.
2. Import frmTabCustomers into your own application and rename it appropriately.
3. If you will need substantially more or fewer than the 30 pages currently displayed on the form, use the PrepareTab procedure, as discussed in the earlier section "Creating the Tab Control," to set the number of pages. (The form must be opened in Design view in order for PrepareTab to work.)
4. Modify the SourceObject property of the subform control on frmTab-Customers so that it will load your new subform.

5. Modify the constants adhcTable and adhcFieldName in the class module for frmTabCustomers. The first constant should be the name of the table filling your subform, and the second should be the name of the field you want to group on (Country, in this example). If you've changed the name of the tab control or the subform controls, modify the adhcTabs and/or adhcSubForm constants, as well.

That's all it takes. Remember, this technique won't be effective with more than 20–30 unique items, but it works well with dynamic sets of data up to that size.

NOTE

In this code, you're using the name of the tab control to refer to it, yet the code is reacting to events of that control. As you know, you must hard-code the name of objects to which you're sinking events in the class module associated with the form. (That is, if the tab control's name is tabCustomers, then Access expects to find a procedure named tabCustomers_Change in the class module.) To make it possible for you to change the tab control name without having to modify the code at all, we've used a WithEvents reference to the tab control. That way, the code can base its event procedures off the mtbc variable, instead of the specific tab control itself. You'll find mtbc_Change as an event procedure, and this procedure sinks the event from whatever tab control you've specified. The form's Load event sets up the link between the WithEvents variable and the real control. (See the middle of Listing 7.19, where the code sets the mtbc variable.)

Using the Tab Control as a Container

Although it may not be an obvious use, you can also turn off a tab control's labels (set the Style property to None) and use the control as a container for other controls. (If you also want to hide the border, set the BackStyle property to Transparent.) But why would you want to do that? Read on.

Replacing Multipage Forms

The tab control makes a great replacement for Access' multipage forms. Rather than fighting with the 22-inch limit and working with forms that won't fit on your screen, you can place a tab control on your form and let its multiple pages handle the job a single multipage form used to handle it. If you want to allow users to change from page to page, you can either react to the PgUp and PgDn keys or supply navigation buttons. In either case, set the Value property of the tab control to display a new page.

Augmenting Rectangles and Option Groups

The tab control is the only control (aside from the option group) that can contain other controls. But an option group can only contain option buttons, check boxes, and toggle buttons. What if you want a logical grouping of controls that contains controls other than the blessed three?

One solution is to surround a group of controls with a rectangle control, but that doesn't connect them in any way. When you use a tab control, the internal controls are logically grouped. When you move a tab control, all the contained controls move with it. You can cut and paste the entire group of controls to a different form by selecting just the container. You can also iterate the Controls collection of the container to take some action on each of the contained controls. (Try doing that for a group of controls surrounded by a rectangle!)

You can create a tab control with a single page, set the Style property to None (and the BackStyle to Transparent, if you don't want the border displayed), and then place controls inside it. You can place any control except another tab control inside a page, unlike an option group. You can also place a number of check boxes on a page and allow multiple selections, which doesn't work with an option group.

Using Default Control Properties to Your Advantage

Access stores default settings for each type of control with each form. To describe the settings for individual controls on the form, Access stores just the settings that *differ* from the default settings. Therefore, if a control has the same settings as the form defaults, Access won't need to store settings for that control. This affects only the stored image of the form; the comparison to the default values is only a save/load issue. All settings for all controls are available once Access loads the form (so there's no actual runtime memory savings).

You can change the default settings for a specific control in two ways. The first involves setting the properties before you actually create the control. The second lets you create the control, specify all its settings, and then tell Access to make those settings the default settings for that type of control.

Either way, when you specify the default settings, other controls of that type you create will inherit the default settings. Previously created controls won't be affected by changes to the default settings.

To set the default settings for a specific type of control before creating one, click that control in the toolbox. Notice that the title for the property sheet has changed to indicate that you're now setting properties for the *default* version of the control. Make whatever changes you want.

To set the default settings based on a specific control you've already created, create your control and set the properties you want. Once you're satisfied, choose the Format ➢ Set Control Defaults menu option. This stores the settings used in the selected control in the form's default settings for that type of control.

Either way you do it, once you've set the default properties, any controls of that type that you create from then on, on the current form, will inherit those properties. When you save the form, for each control, Access will save only the properties that differ from the default values. Judicious use of default properties can speed up your development time, as well as make forms smaller and therefore speed their load time.

Using the DefaultControl Method to Set Up Default Properties

What if you want to control properties for the default version of a control programmatically? You can use the DefaultControl method of a form or report to retrieve a reference to the default control of any given type. Once you have that reference, you can set the properties of the default control, and any controls you create from then on will inherit those settings. This has two effects:

- You'll save steps, both in code and in the user interface. Controls you create will inherit the settings you want from the default controls.
- You'll save time and space. Because Access stores only control properties that differ from the default properties for that control type, if you've set the defaults for the control type and used those for most of your controls, you won't have to save most properties for most controls.

The syntax for calling DefaultControl looks like this:

Set *control* = *object*.DefaultControl(*controlType*)

where *control* is an object variable of type Control, *object* is a form or report reference, and *controlType* is one of the ac... constants that refer to controls (see Table 7.2 for a complete listing).

The control reference returned from a call to the DefaultControl method doesn't refer to a real control on the form or report, but rather to the internal representation of the default for that control type. Setting properties of this control won't make any changes to existing controls or to the form or report on screen. On the other hand, once you've set the default properties for various control types, subsequent controls you create will use these new settings. Of course, the DefaultControl method works only when the form or report is in Design view.

For example, the following code fragment sets the default font name and size for all text boxes you create after calling this code:

```
With Me.DefaultControl(acTextBox)
    .FontName = "Tahoma"
    .FontSize = 10
End With
```

TIP

Default control settings are associated with a form or report. Settings you make on one form or report will not affect any other form or report. If you want to make global default settings, you'll need to create a form or report template. See Chapter 8 for more information on creating templates.

WARNING

Note that we use the DefaultControl property directly—we didn't create an object variable to refer to the control and then work with that object variable. If you do create an object variable and use that when setting the DefaultControl properties, you'll need to set it to Nothing when you're done with it. If you don't, you may receive a mysterious runtime error later, when you're working with the form and its controls programmatically.

Creating Controls Programmatically

Access provides functions to create forms and reports, and the controls on these objects programmatically. This is, of course, how the Access Form and Report Wizards work. They gather information from you about how you want the form or report to look, and then they go through their code and create the requested form or report. Chapter 18 covers in detail how you can create your own Wizards, but there are other uses for those functions. Specifically, if you want to create a form or report with many similar controls that can be easily described programmatically, you may be able to use one or more of these functions.

Functions That Create Forms and Controls

CreateForm and CreateReport create a form or report and return that object as the return value of the function:

Set *newForm* = CreateForm([*database* [,*formtemplate*]])

Set *newReport* = CreateReport([*database* [,*reporttemplate*]])

The form or report these functions create is lightweight. (That is, it doesn't contain a module—its HasModule property is set to False—until you add some code.) The following table describes the parameters for these two functions:

Argument	Description
database	String expression representing the database in which to look for the template form. To look in the current database, omit this argument.
template	String expression representing the form or report template to use in creating the new form or report. Use the word Normal to use the standard template. To use the template specified in the Tools ➢ Options menu, omit this argument.

The following fragment will create a new form, with the caption "My New Form":

```
Dim frm As Form
Set frm = CreateForm()
frm.Caption = "My New Form"
```

Use CreateControl and CreateReportControl to create new controls on forms and reports, respectively. The following fragment details the parameters you use when calling CreateControl and CreateReportControl:

```
CreateControl(formname As String, controltype As Integer _
 [, sectionnumber As Integer [, parent As String _
 [, fieldname As String _
 [, left As Integer [, top As Integer _
 [, width As Integer [, height As Integer]]]]]]] )

CreateReportControl(reportname As String, _
 controltype As Integer[, section as Integer _
 [, parent As String[, columnname As String _
 [, left As Integer[, top As Integer _
 [, width As Integer[, height As Integer]]]]]]])
```

Table 7.8 lists the parameters for the two functions, along with the possible values for those parameters.

TABLE 7.8: Parameters for CreateControl and CreateReportControl

Argument	Description	
formname, reportname	String expression identifying the name of the open form or report on which you want to create the control. If you've just created a form using CreateForm and have assigned the return value of that function to a variable (frmNewForm, for example), you can reference that form's FormName property here (frmNewForm.FormName).	
controltype	Constant identifying the type of control you want to create:	
	Constant	**Control Type**
	acLabel	Label
	acRectangle	Rectangle
	acLine	Line
	acImage	Image
	acCommandButton	Command button
	acOptionButton	Option button
	acCheckBox	Check box
	acOptionGroup	Option group
	acBoundObjectFrame	Bound object frame
	acTextBox	Text box
	acListBox	List box

Continued on next page

TABLE 7.8 CONTINUED: Parameters for CreateControl and CreateReportControl

Argument	Description	
controltype	**Constant**	**Control Type**
	acComboBox	Combo box
	acSubform	Subform/subreport
	acObjectFrame	Unbound object frame
	acPage	Page
	acPageBreak	Page break
	acCustomControl	Custom Control
	acToggleButton	Toggle button
	acTabCtl	Tab control
section	Constant identifying the section that will contain the new control:	
	Constant	**Section**
	acDetail	(Default) Detail section
	acHeader	Form or report header section
	acFooter	Form or report footer section
	acPageHeader	Form or report page header section
	acPageFooter	Form or report page footer section
	acGroupLevel1Header	Group-level 1 header section (reports only)
	acGroupLevel1Footer	Group-level 1 footer section (reports only)
	acGroupLevel2Header	Group-level 2 header section (reports only)
	acGroupLevel2Footer	Group-level 2 footer section (reports only)
	If a report has additional group-level sections, the header/footer pairs are numbered consecutively beginning with 9.	
parent	String expression identifying the name of the parent control. If you don't wish to specify the parent control, use " ".	
bound FieldName	String expression identifying the name of the field to which the new control should be bound. If you specify the boundFieldName, not only does it fill in the ControlSource property, it inherits the table properties, such as the Format and ValidationRule properties.	
left	Top, Integer expressions indicating the coordinates for the upper-left corner of the control, in twips.	
width	Height, Integer expressions indicating the width and height of the control, in twips.	

An Example Using CreateForm and CreateControl

As part of a project, imagine that you need to create a form with 42 similar command buttons, numbered 1 through 42, in six rows of seven buttons each. You could do this by hand, spending a while getting all the controls just right. You could also do this with the CreateForm and CreateControl functions. Listing 7.21 contains the entire function you can use to create the form, as shown in Figure 7.34.

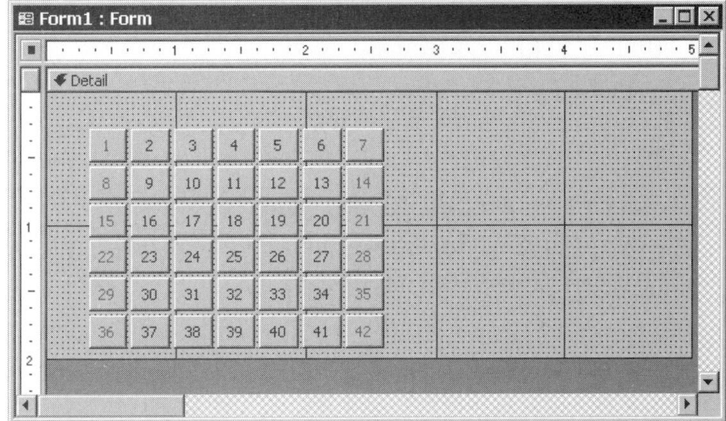

FIGURE 7.34: The Calendar form in Design view, after the CreateCalendar function has created all the buttons.

CreateCalendar creates the form by calling the CreateForm function. Since it specifies neither the database nor the template, it will use the template specified in the Tools ➢ Options settings:

```
Set frm = CreateForm()
frm.Caption = "Calendar"
```

All measurements specified for CreateControl must be in twips (1/1440 of an inch), so you need to convert all your values into twips before calling the function. These controls are to be 0.25 inch in height and 0.30 inch in width, with a 0.03-inch gap between them:

```
intHeight = 0.25 * adhcTwipsPerInch
intWidth = 0.3 * adhcTwipsPerInch
intGap = 0.03 * adhcTwipsPerInch
```

CreateCalendar loops through six rows of seven command buttons, creating each control with a call to CreateControl. It uses the width and height values to figure where to place the buttons and then sets the Width, Height, and Caption properties of the button it has just created. Note that this call to CreateControl uses the FormName property of the newly created form to reference the form, creates a control of type acCommandButton in the Detail section, and specifies no parent or bound field name.

Listing 7.21

```
Public Sub CreateCalendar()

    Const adhcTwipsPerInch As Long = 1440

    Dim frm As Form

    Dim intI As Integer
    Dim intJ As Integer

    Dim intHeight As Integer
    Dim intWidth As Integer
    Dim intGap As Integer
    Dim intCount As Integer

    ' You can specify the database in which
    ' to create your form, and the template
    ' to use for the form -- this can
    ' be the name of any other form you have
    ' in the current database.
    Set frm = CreateForm()
    frm.Caption = "Calendar"

    ' Measurement properties are specified in twips in
    ' VBA. So we need to convert all values from
    ' inches to twips, by multiplying by 1440.
    intHeight = 0.25 * adhcTwipsPerInch
    intWidth = 0.3 * adhcTwipsPerInch
    intGap = 0.03 * adhcTwipsPerInch

    ' Set some default control properties,
    ' so you needn't set them for each and
    ' every command button.
    With frm.DefaultControl(acCommandButton)
        .Width = intWidth
        .Height = intHeight
    End With

    For intI = 1 To 6
```

```
            For intJ = 1 To 7
                intCount = intCount + 1
                With CreateControl( _
                 FormName:=frm.Name, _
                 ControlType:=acCommandButton, _
                 Section:=acDetail, _
                 Left:=intJ * (intWidth + intGap), _
                 Top:=intI * (intHeight + intGap))
                    ' Set the name to be something
                    ' like "cmd0203", indicating the row
                    ' and column in the name.
                    .Name = "cmd" & _
                     Format(intI, "00") & Format(intJ, "00")

                    ' Set the caption, as well.
                    .Caption = intCount

                    ' Set the color for weekend
                    ' days to be red. You'll need
                    ' to change the logic if your
                    ' calendar doesn't start on Sunday.
                    If intJ = 1 Or intJ = 7 Then
                        .ForeColor = vbRed
                    End If
                End With
            Next intJ
        Next intI
    End Sub
```

TIP

To create a control within a page of a tab control, specify the name of the page on which you want the control to appear as the Parent parameter. Coordinates you specify for the new control will be in relation to the upper-left corner of the page object, not the main form.

What Are These Controls, Anyway?

Those readers moving to Access from Visual Basic may be surprised to find out that the controls you see on forms in Access are not actual windows. (That is, they don't have window handles and don't respond to Windows messages.) The Access controls are just "paint on the screen," at least until each becomes the active control. Access uses this technique to conserve resources: because you may have 200, 300, or more controls on a single form, it's important that you not run out of window handles, graphics resources, and so on. (Yes, it's still possible to run out of resources under 32-bit Windows. It's difficult, but possible—and it's a lot harder to do with Windows NT or Windows 2000 than it is with Windows 95/98.)

But Visual Basic programmers are used to being able to manipulate controls as windows. You want to be able to use the SendMessage API function to control your controls. The fact is, this just isn't possible, in general, in Access. There are two important reasons why this won't work:

- The control becomes active at different times, depending on whether you enter it with the mouse or from the keyboard. Because you can't count on either the Enter or GotFocus event to magically transform a painted control into a real window, it's nearly impossible to find an event that will, in general, serve your purposes.
- The controls are subclassed versions of the Windows standard controls. They just don't react to many of the normal Windows messages, if any. Even if you manage to find a control when it's active, it will most likely ignore any message you send to it with SendMessage.

Using SendMessage to Limit Input Characters

You can't count on using the SendMessage API function to manipulate any Access controls. On the other hand, it just so happens that by mistake, chance, or fate, Access text boxes do respond to at least one message: EM_SETLIMITTEXT. You can use the SendMessage Windows API function to limit the number of characters users can type into a text box. This can be useful if your text box is bound to a memo field and you want to allow users to enter, for example, no more than 1000 characters.

NOTE

You may wonder why you can't use the Change event and limit the number of characters there? The problem with the Change event is that you can't cancel it. By the time the code runs, the character has already been added to the text box. You could try using the KeyDown or KeyPress events, but they, too, have their limitations. Sending a message to the text box is the simplest way we can think of to limit its text.

The sample form, frmLimitChars, allows you to specify the character limit and then calls the SendMessage API function to tell the text box the maximum number of characters it should accept. Figure 7.35 shows the form in use. Listing 7.22 shows all the code the form uses to limit the characters in the text box.

FIGURE 7.35:

frmLimitChars shows how you can limit the number of characters typed into a text box.

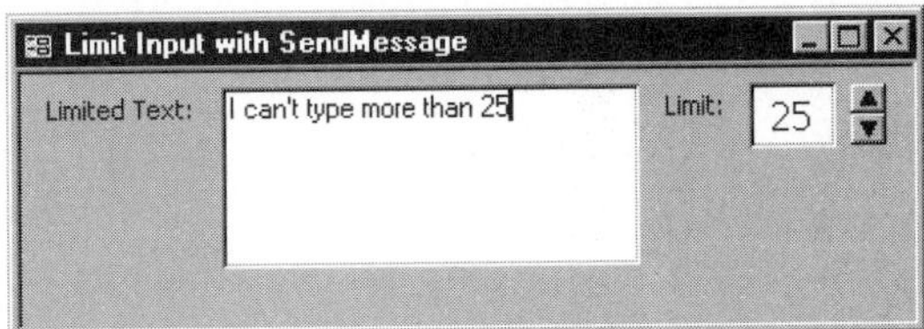

The one limitation on this technique is that you can't count on the control being a real window in either the Enter or GotFocus event, as mentioned above. One point at which you're guaranteed that this control is a real window is in its Change event, so that's where we have hooked the code. This means, of course, that the code calls the SendMessage API every time you type a character. Since this API call incurs so little overhead compared to the speed at which you can type, the extra work just didn't seem to matter in this case.

The code first gets the window handle for the current window, using the GetFocus API call:

```
' Get the window handle for the current window.
hWnd = GetFocus()
```

It then plays some tricks to make sure that, if you've set the maximum number of characters to less than the number of characters already in there, it will readjust the allowable number of characters to be the actual number of characters. (Otherwise, the text box wouldn't even let you delete one character at a time. If you have too many characters in a text box, Windows allows you to delete only the entire entry.) Each time you type a character, the code calls SendMessage again, so as you delete characters, the code continually resets the maximum size as necessary:

```
lngNewMax = Len(txt.Text)
If lngNewMax < lngLimit Then
    lngNewMax = lngLimit
End If
```

Finally, the code calls the SendMessage API function, which sends a message to the window identified by the supplied window handle:

```
SendMessage hWnd, EM_SETLIMITTEXT, lngNewMax, 0
```

Experimentation has shown that although there are many EM_* messages that normal text boxes understand, Access text boxes respond to very few, if any, of these messages. You may find it interesting to dig through a Windows API reference, trying out various EM_* messages, as we've done here. Be warned: most won't work or will possibly crash Access. The technique we've shown here works not by design, but by chance. Therefore, although it's a useful technique, it may not work in future versions of Access.

Listing 7.22

```
Private Declare Function SendMessageLong _
 Lib "user32" Alias "SendMessageA" _
 (ByVal hWnd As Long, ByVal wMsg As Long, _
 ByVal wParam As Long, lngValue As Long) As Long

Private Declare Function GetFocus _
 Lib "user32" () As Long

Private Const EM_SETLIMITTEXT As Long = &HC5

Public Sub adhLimitChars(txt As TextBox, lngLimit As Long)
    ' You actually CAN use SendMessage with
    ' Access controls, but you must remember that
    ' the changes you make are only active
    ' as long as this control has the focus.
    ' Therefore, if you want to limit the text in a text
    ' box, you MUST do it each time you enter the
    ' control. To be safe, the only place you can really
    ' do this is in reaction to the Change, BeforeUpdate
    ' or AfterUpdate events.

    Dim hWnd As Long
    Dim lngResult As Long
    Dim lngNewMax As Long

    ' Get the window handle for the current window.
    hWnd = GetFocus()

    ' Hey, what if there's ALREADY too much text in
    ' there?  Limiting the text would make it
    ' impossible to type in there at all.  You want
    ' to set the limit to be the max of the amount
```

```
    ' you want and the amount that's in there!
    lngNewMax = Len(txt.Text)
    If lngNewMax < lngLimit Then
        lngNewMax = lngLimit
    End If

    ' Send the message to the current text box
    ' to limit itself to lngNewMax characters.
    SendMessageLong hWnd, EM_SETLIMITTEXT, lngNewMax, 0
End Sub
```

Summary

This chapter introduced most of the built-in Access control types. We attempted to cover the nonintuitive properties and events and suggested solutions to some common Access problems. In general, we covered the following topics:

- Working with Access controls and their properties, events, and methods that make up the bulk of your user interface
- Using VBA and the Tag property to emulate the creation of user-defined control properties
- Using VBA in combination with controls to emulate several hybrid controls that are not intrinsic to Access
- Using a control's default properties to ease the development burden
- Creating controls and forms programmatically, leading to a more uniform layout
- Working with the tab control and its pages
- For the adventurous, using the SendMessage API call to control Access controls, but only in a severely limited fashion

8

CHAPTER

EIGHT

Topics in Form Design and Usage

- Understanding the appearance and operation of forms
- Retrieving information about forms
- Resizing forms to match screen resolution
- Building form-based encapsulated tools
- Working with forms' recordsets

If your applications are like many of the Access applications in use, a large majority of their functionality is centered around forms. Most likely, from the user's perspective, your application *is* just a set of forms. In this chapter, you'll find insights into using and creating forms in ways you might not otherwise have considered. This chapter doesn't attempt to show you how to create or design forms, but rather how to use the forms that you've created, in original and interesting ways.

NOTE

Although you won't find a complete discussion of using the Windows API (Application Programming Interface) until Chapter 16, some of the examples in this chapter rely heavily on API calls. If you find yourself buried too deeply in the details, you may want to skip ahead to Chapter 16 and peruse the information there concurrently with this chapter.

TIP

Several examples in this chapter use data, stored in an MDB file, as part of the demonstration. As you'll see later in the chapter, although Microsoft Access 2000 and this book focus on ADO as the preferred data access object model, this particular chapter focuses on DAO. Why? When you work with a form's recordset in an MDB file, you're always using a DAO recordset, even if you're using ADO everywhere else in your application. If you're new to DAO, you may want to peruse Appendix C for information on working with DAO and Chapter 6 for information comparing ADO and DAO.

Introduction to Class Modules in Forms

Access allows you to store program code and a form (or report) in one neat package. Each form and report can carry its own module with it (although new forms and reports are "born" without a module—you have to add code before Access creates the module for you), and, unless you specify otherwise, every procedure and variable in that module is private. This means that, as in Visual Basic, choosing an event from the property list takes you directly to a subroutine that is tied to that particular event. The event procedures are subroutines named

```
Private Sub controlName_eventName(parameters)
```

and their scope is, by default, private to the form. In several cases, Access passes parameters to these procedures that provide information about the circumstances of the particular event. For example, mouse events receive information about the mouse location and clicked buttons, and key events receive information about the particular key that was pressed. This encapsulation makes it very easy to create forms that perform a single purpose, which you can reuse in various applications.

NOTE

Controls can contain spaces in their Name properties, but event procedures, being standard VBA code, cannot have spaces in their names. To solve this problem, Access must do some work on the names of controls that include illegal procedure name characters before it can name the event procedure. If you need to programmatically retrieve the event procedure name that corresponds to a control, check the EventProcPrefix property of any control on a form or report. This property, which doesn't appear on the property sheet, returns the modified name Access uses in its event procedures. If you're writing an application that creates event procedures, this property is essential.

To get to a form's module, you have several choices:

- From the database container window, once you see the list of forms, you can click the Code button on the toolbar. (This opens the form in Design view as well.)
- In Form Design view, click the same toolbar button.
- From the form's property sheet, for any event property, you can click the … button, which takes you to the particular event procedure for this control.
- In Form Design view, right-click any control and choose the Build Event menu item.

TIP

A form's module is just a class module, the same as any other class module. For more information on working with class modules in general, see Chapter 3.

A common misconception about controls and their attached event procedures causes new Access programmers a great deal of trouble. Most beginners assume that copying a control from one form to another also copies the control's event procedures to the new form. But this is not so, unfortunately. Copying a control copies only the control and its properties. You must manually copy its event procedures from one form's module to the other's.

Many of the forms demonstrated in this chapter rely heavily on form class modules to maintain their reusability. By keeping all their code in their own class module, these forms become encapsulated entities that you can import directly into your own applications. In 16-bit versions of Access, searching through source code using Access' Find/Replace options skipped over code in form or report (class) modules. Happily, Access' Find dialog box includes an option to search through all the modules in the database, including form/report modules. Finding procedures hidden away in form (or report) class modules is no longer an onerous chore.

In addition, you may find that in our attempt to modularize the examples in this chapter, some procedures occur in multiple forms' class modules. If you import more than one of the forms from this chapter into your own applications, you might want to take a few minutes and peruse the imported forms' class modules. You will probably find some general-purpose procedures duplicated. We've attempted to point these out to you along the way. Moving those routines to standard modules can save you some memory overhead.

The next sections suggest solutions to some common form-related problems.

Events and Forms

How is it that code in a form's class module can react to events that occur on the form? Perhaps you've wondered about this and thought that there was some "magic" behind the scenes. The fact is, any class module, whether it's attached to a form or not, can react to events of other objects. This is the basis of many of the examples in this book, where we create a class module, associate it with an object that raises events, and sink (react to) the events in the class module. In the examples we've provided, we must use the WithEvents keyword to link our object reference to the object that's raising events. (See the FormResize class module and fsubNavigation's class module for examples that use WithEvents to sink events.)

For controls on forms, however, this WithEvents linkage happens automatically. That is, when you place a control on a form in Access, the form automatically creates a variable with the same name as the control, under the covers. In addition, this under–the-covers variable has been declared with the WithEvents keyword. Therefore, without you having to create this linkage yourself, you can react to events raised by the control on your form, in the form's class module. Think of the alternative: if Access didn't do this for you, you would have to declare a variable corresponding to each control on the form, using the WithEvents keyword. Then, you'd have to react to events of your own variable, as opposed to reacting to events of the variable "mirroring" the control itself. It's a lot easier to let Access do that linkage for you.

Controlled Closing

You can disable or remove the standard Close button and provide your own Close button in an attempt to control the way users close your forms, but there is still at least one more way to close the form: users can use the Ctrl+W or Ctrl+F4 key (for normal forms) or the Alt+F4 key (for pop-up forms) to bypass your own form-closing mechanism. If you want complete control over your forms, you need to plug this one last hole.

To close this final loophole allowing users to close your forms behind your back, you must restrict the use of the Ctrl+W, Alt+F4, and Ctrl+F4 keys. Fortunately, you can accomplish this without having to check whether the user pressed Ctrl+W, Alt+F4, or Ctrl+F4 to close your form. For this method to work, your form must include some method of allowing the user to close it, usually using a command button. It involves these four simple steps:

1. Set the CloseButton property of the form to No, which removes the "x" in the upper-right corner of the form and disables the Close item on the form's system menu. (You can also set the form's ControlBox property to No, if you like. That completely removes both the "x" button and the system menu from the form.)
2. In your form's class module, in the declarations area, define a public Boolean variable (OKToClose, for this example):

```
Public OKToClose As Boolean
```

3. In your form's Open or Load event, set the value of OKToClose to False:

```
Private Sub Form_Load()
    OKToClose = False
End Sub
```

4. In the code attached to the Click event of the button used to close your form, set OKToClose to True, and call the Close method of the DoCmd object (calling the Close method will trigger the Unload event of the form):

```
Private Sub cmdClose_Click()
    OKToClose = True
    DoCmd.Close
End Sub
```

5. In your form's Unload event (triggered by the call to the DoCmd.Close method), check the value of OKToClose. If it's False, set the Cancel parameter to True, halting the form's closing.

```
Private Sub Form_Unload(Cancel As Integer)
    Cancel = Not OKToClose
End Sub
```

That's all there is to it. Unless your user clicks your button, there's no way this form is going to close. Listing 8.1 shows the minimal code your form might contain to implement this method. You can investigate frmCloseTest to see it in action.

Listing 8.1

```
Public OKToClose As Boolean

Private Sub Form_Load()
    ' Set the trap, so no one can close
    ' the form without clicking the
    ' Close button.
    OKToClose = False
End Sub

Private Sub cmdClose_Click()
    ' If you click the Close button, set
    ' the variable so the Unload event
    ' will let you out.
    OKToClose = True

    ' Now that you've cleared the way,
    ' close the form.
    DoCmd.Close
End Sub

Private Sub Form_Unload(Cancel As Integer)
    Cancel = Not OKToClose
End Sub
```

Why use a public variable for OKToClose? By making this value a public variable, VBA exposes it as a property of the form. (See the section "Creating User-Defined Properties" later in this chapter for more information.) Because other parts of the application see the form's OKToClose property, you can set that property from any other place within your application. Users won't be able to close the form without your permission, but you'll be able to provide that permission from any place within your application.

Which Form Is This?

If you write Visual Basic code attached to controls or sections on a form, you'll often need to pass to that code an object that refers to the current form. Many beginning developers count on the Screen.ActiveForm object to get this information. However, you should avoid this method if at all possible, because Screen.ActiveForm often returns a reference to a different form from the one you intended.

Access provides a simple solution to this problem. From anywhere on the form's design surface, you can retrieve and pass to Visual Basic code any of the form's properties. One of these properties is the form's Form property, which is a reference to the form itself. You can pass this property as a parameter to any function (and only functions work—you cannot call a sub from the Properties window directly) you call from the property sheet so the function can identify the form with which it should be concerned. For example, if your form calls a function named FormOnCurrent from its Current event, you could place this expression:

```
=FormOnCurrent(Form)
```

in the property sheet to pass a reference to the current form to the function. The function declaration would be something like this:

```
Function FormOnCurrent(frm as Form)
```

On the other hand, if your code exists in the form's class module, you can use the object reference returned in the Me property to refer to the current form. (The Me property is only available from within the form's class module—you cannot use it when calling a function directly from the Properties window.) That is, in the external function declared above, you could retrieve the form's caption with this expression:

```
strCaption = frm.Caption
```

but in a form's class module, you could use this expression:

```
strCaption = Me.Caption
```

If you need to create global procedures that can be called from multiple forms, you can still call these from a form's class module. Just pass Me to those functions as a parameter from the form's event procedure. For example, to call the previously mentioned FormOnCurrent function from a form's module, use this:

```
Call FormOnCurrent(Me)
```

Does a Specific Form Exist?

You may need to determine if a particular form exists in the current database. To make this easy, Access provides the AllForms collection, a property of the CurrentProject object. You can check this collection to see if the form exists as part of the collection. If you're going to go to this effort, however, it makes sense to work a little harder and create a function that can determine if any object, of any type, exists. Listing 8.2 shows the adhExists function (from basObjectExists). This function allows you to specify the name of an object and its type. The adhExists function returns a Boolean value, indicating the existence of the specified object. (The object type parameter is optional, with a default value of acForm. Therefore, if you don't specify the object type, the function assumes you're interested in a form.)

Listing 8.2

```
Public Function adhExists( _
 strName As String, _
 Optional lngType As AcObjectType = acForm) As Boolean
    Dim aob As AccessObject

    On Error Resume Next
    Select Case lngType
        Case acDataAccessPage
            Set aob = _
             CurrentProject.AllDataAccessPages(strName)
        Case acForm
            Set aob = CurrentProject.AllForms(strName)
        Case acMacro
            Set aob = CurrentProject.AllMacros(strName)
        Case acModule
            Set aob = CurrentProject.AllModules(strName)
        Case acReport
            Set aob = CurrentProject.AllReports(strName)
        Case acStoredProcedure
            Set aob = _
             CurrentData.AllStoredProcedures(strName)
        Case acDiagram
            Set aob = _
             CurrentData.AllDatabaseDiagrams(strName)
        Case acServerView
```

```
            Set aob = CurrentData.AllViews(strName)
        Case acQuery
            Set aob = CurrentData.AllQueries(strName)
        Case acTable
            Set aob = CurrentData.AllTables(strName)
        Case Else
            ' Just raise some error, so later code
            ' will know something went wrong.
            Err.Raise 1
    End Select
    adhExists = (Err.Number = 0)
    Err.Clear
End Function
```

To call this function, you might write a fragment like this:

```
If adhExists("tblCustomers", acTable) Then
    ' You know tblCustomers exists.
End If
If adhExists("frmCustomers") Then
    ' You know frmCustomers exists. You didn't
    ' have to specify acForm, because that's the default.
End If
```

The adhExists function uses the All… collections, which are either properties of the CurrentProject object (referring to all the Access user-interface objects), or the CurrentData object (referring to all the Access data objects). The code disables error handling (using On Error Resume Next) and then attempts to set an object variable to refer to the specified object. If the object doesn't exist, attempting to retrieve the object will trigger an error and Err.Number will be something besides 0. The code, therefore, compares the Err.Number value to 0, and returns the value of the comparison as the return value of the function:

```
adhExists = (Err.Number = 0)
```

TIP To use adhExists in your own applications, import the basObjectExists module.

Is a Specific Form Loaded?

If you want to find out if a specific form is currently open, Access 2000 provides a simple solution—the IsLoaded property of each member of the AllForms collection. Each member of the AllForms collection is an AccessObject object and has an IsLoaded property. The IsLoaded property returns True if the object is open, either in Design or Run view. You can, therefore, write a function like adhIsFormOpen (from basIsFormOpen), shown in Listing 8.3. As you can see in the code, the AllForms collection (and its cousins, the AllReports, AllModules, and so on) is a property of the CurrentProject object. (See Chapter 6 for more information on the All… collections.)

Listing 8.3

```
Public Function adhIsFormOpen( _
 strName As String) As Boolean
    On Error Resume Next
    Dim fIsOpen As Boolean
    fIsOpen = _
     CurrentProject.AllForms(strName).IsLoaded
    adhIsFormOpen = (Err.Number = 0) And fIsOpen
    Err.Clear
End Function
```

Although using the IsLoaded property makes sense, it's not a perfect solution. Specifically:

- If the form is new and open but hasn't yet been saved, it won't be in the AllForms collection, so the adhIsFormOpen function will return False.
- If you want to extend the function to work with any type of Access object, you'll need to create a new function for each different object type. You can pass as a parameter the specific object type (use a parameter of type AcObjectType), but inside the procedure you'll need a large Select Case statement, using a different All… collection for each different object type. See the adhExists function, earlier in the chapter, for an example that uses this technique.
- If the object you're checking on doesn't exist at all, the All… collection triggers a runtime error when you attempt to retrieve the object's IsLoaded property. You must remember to handle this error in your code.
- If you need to determine whether the object is open in Design or Run view, or if you need to know whether the object's design has been changed, the IsLoaded property can't help you.

NOTE The IsLoaded property returns False if the form has been opened as a subform, whether it's open in Design or Run view.

The alternative, which handles all these issues, is to use the SysCmd function. The SysCmd function returns information about any object, of any type. If you call SysCmd, passing to it the constant acSysCmdGetObjectState—along with the name of your object and a constant indicating the object type (acForm, acReport, and so on)—it returns a value indicating the current state of that object. The return value can be one or more of these values (or 0, indicating that the object isn't open).

Constant	Description	Value
(no constant)	The object is not open.	0
acObjStateOpen	The object is open, but neither new nor changed.	1
acObjStateDirty	The object's design is changed and not yet saved.	2
acObjStateNew	The object is new and not yet saved. There have been no changes to its design.	4

SysCmd returns a value which is either 0 (meaning that the object isn't open), or one or more of the constants listed here, combined with the Or operator. To determine whether the object is in the state in which you're interested, you have two choices. You can compare the return value to 0 to see if the object is open or not. Or, you can compare the return value to a specific constant to check its exact open state.

TIP The acObjStateDirty flag doesn't return the information that many developers assume it does. The SysCmd function never returns information about the dirty state of data displayed by a form—it provides information only about the state of the form itself. That is, SysCmd returns acObjStateDirty only if a form is open in Design view and its design has been changed and not saved.

In the case of the adhIsOpen function, shown in Listing 8.4, all you care about is whether the object is open. Therefore, the code compares the return value from SysCmd to 0. As long as the return value is nonzero, you know the object is open. Because the lngObjectType parameter is optional (and defaults to acForm), if you pass the isOpen function just an object name, it assumes you want to know about a form. If you pass it both an object name and an object type, it will look for open objects of the specified type.

Listing 8.4

```
Public Function adhIsOpen( _
 strName As String, _
 Optional lngObjectType As AcObjectType = acForm)
    ' Returns True if strName is open, False otherwise.
    ' Assume the caller wants to know about a form.
    adhIsOpen = (SysCmd(acSysCmdGetObjectState, _
     lngObjectType, strName) <> 0)
End Function
```

NOTE

SysCmd doesn't raise an error if the object whose name you've specified doesn't exist—it simply returns 0 (meaning that the object isn't currently open).

TIP

The adhIsOpen function uses an interesting technique, which makes it easier for you to call the function from your own code. It specifies the second parameter as being of type AcObjectType. This isn't a new data type, it's simply the name of the built-in enumeration (see online help for the Enum statement to see how to do this yourself) that supplies the various constants representing Access object types. By using this name here when you attempt to call this function, you'll get an IntelliSense drop-down containing all the possible values.

Although the IsLoaded property of an AccessObject object provides a simple way to determine if a given object is open, it's not particularly flexible. We continue to use the SysCmd function (which has existed, providing this same functionality, since before Access 2) because it's easier to use in the long run, and it's more flexible.

NOTE

Several forms in the sample database use a copy of the adhIsOpen function. Rather than require you to import the basIsOpen module in addition to the form so you can use it in your own applications, we've provided this simple procedure in each module that requires it.

Creating Pop-up Forms

If you write many applications, you will begin to notice a class of tools that is needed over and over—for example, pop-up calendars to select dates or pop-up calculators to calculate values. Once you create these items, you'd like to be able to use them in multiple applications. To see this pop-up behavior in action, try out frmTestPopup in the sample database.

The technique for providing a pop-up tool that returns a value is really simple in Access:

1. Open the form using the DoCmd.OpenForm method, using the acDialog flag for the WindowMode parameter. This forces all VBA code that follows the OpenForm method to pause, waiting for the form to be either closed or hidden.

TIP

It's not enough for you to use the Pop-up and/or Modal properties of the form to accomplish the goal of creating a pop-up form. You'll get a form that's modal and/or pop-up, but opening it won't cause the code to pause and wait for you to dismiss the form. To do that, you must use the acDialog WindowMode value. Opening the form using the acDialog flag, however, means that you cannot set properties, from the calling code, of the form once it's been opened—the code has stopped running. For a solution to this problem, see the section "Using Multiple Instances for Pop-up Forms" later in the chapter.

2. Pass parameters, as necessary, to the form in the OpenArgs parameter.

TIP

You're likely to want to pass multiple parameters to a form in its OpenArgs parameter. You're allowed to pass only a single string value, however. To work around this problem, you can use the TaggedValue and TaggedValues classes, discussed in Chapter 7.

3. In the form's Open event procedure, retrieve items from the OpenArgs property, as necessary. Use these values to initialize the form. (Remember, you can't modify the form's appearance or behavior from the calling code, because that code isn't running while the form is open.)

4. On the form itself, provide OK and Cancel buttons (or their equivalents). The OK button should set the form's Visible property to False, and the Cancel button should actually close the form (using DoCmd.Close).
5. Once back in your original procedure, you know that the form has been either closed or hidden. To check which, use a function such as IsLoaded, as in the section "Is a Specific Form Loaded?" earlier in this chapter, to check whether the form is still open. If it is, you know the user clicked OK and wants to use the data from the form. If the form is not loaded, you know the user clicked Cancel and you should disregard anything the user did with the form open.
6. If the form is still loaded, retrieve the value(s) as necessary from the form (which is currently invisible), and then close the form.

NOTE

You don't actually have to close the form once you're done with it. If you want to leave it open but hidden, the next time you open the form Access will just make it visible, and it will still show the state in which the user last left it. Unfortunately, Access will not send the OpenArgs property unless it actually opens the form, so this technique will work only if you are not sending any parameters to the form.

Using Pop-up Tools

We've provided two pop-up tools, a calendar and a calculator, which fit into your application in the manner described in the previous section. In both cases, you make a single function call that returns to your application the value returned from the pop-up form. In the case of the calendar, the return value will be the chosen date (or Null, if none was chosen). For the calculator, the function will return the result of the user's calculations. The inner workings of these tools aren't the issue here, but rather their interface to your application. Once you see how these forms work, you should be able to use the techniques from the previous section to create your own pop-up tools.

To test out the calendar and calculator forms, open frmTestPopup. This form demonstrates the use of both forms, calling the appropriate wrapper function for each.

NOTE

Using forms this way, as encapsulated tools, is really taking advantage of the fact that every form carries with it its own class module. You can accomplish this same sort of task using class modules on their own, as long as you don't need any user interface. For more information on building objects using class modules, see Chapter 3.

TIP

To use frmCalendar or frmCalc in your own applications, import both the form you need and the corresponding standard module (basCalendar or basCalc) into your application. Then, from your code, call adhDoCalendar or adhDoCalculator, as necessary. See frmTestPopup for an example of calling each form.

How Do the Sample Forms Work?

Both the calendar and calculator pop-up forms use the same technique, Property Let/Get/Set procedures, to set and retrieve user-defined properties of forms. (See the section "Using Property Let/Set/Get Procedures" later in this chapter for more information. Chapter 3 also contains information on this technique.) In this simple case, adhDoCalc retrieves the Value property of the pop-up form to return the result of the calculation.

Here is the code for the adhDoCalc function:

```
Private Const adhcCalcForm As String = "frmCalc"

Public Function adhDoCalc() As Variant

    DoCmd.OpenForm _
     FormName:=adhcCalcForm, _
     WindowMode:=acDialog

    ' Stop here and wait.

    If IsOpen(adhcCalcForm) Then
        ' Retrieve the return value,
        ' then close the form.
        adhDoCalc = Forms(adhcCalcForm).Value
        DoCmd.Close acForm, adhcCalcForm
    Else
        adhDoCalc = Null
    End If
End Function
```

NOTE

So that you needn't import any more modules than necessary, the adhDoCalc and adoDoCalendar functions call private copies of the adhIsOpen function (named simply IsOpen), contained in the same module as the calling code.

The code used to pop up the calendar is very similar to that used for the calculator. Again, you'll check the Value property of the Calendar form (supplied by a Property Get procedure in the Calendar form) to see what date the user chose:

```
Private Const adhcCalendarForm As String = "frmCalendar"

Public Function adhDoCalendar( _
 Optional ByVal varStartDate As Variant) As Variant
    '
    Dim dtmStartDate As Date

    ' If they passed a value at all, attempt to
    ' use it as the start date.
    If IsMissing(varStartDate) Then
        dtmStartDate = Date
    Else
        If IsDate(varStartDate) Then
            dtmStartDate = varStartDate
        Else
            ' OK, so they passed a value that
            ' wasn't a date.
            ' Just use today's date in that case, too.
            dtmStartDate = Date
        End If
    End If
    DoCmd.OpenForm FormName:=adhcCalendarForm, _
     WindowMode:=acDialog, _
     OpenArgs:=dtmStartDate

    ' Stop here and wait.

    '
    ' If the form is still loaded, then get the
    ' final chosen date from the form.  If it isn't,
    ' return Null.
    If IsOpen(adhcCalendarForm) Then
```

```
        adhDoCalendar = Forms(adhcCalendarForm).Value
        DoCmd.Close acForm, adhcCalendarForm
    Else
        adhDoCalendar = Null
    End If
End Function
```

NOTE

If you don't want to display the OK and Cancel buttons at the bottom of the calendar, open the frmCalendar module and set the adhcShowCancelOK constant to be False. If frmCalendar is loaded as a subform, those buttons are always hidden. If you use the form as a standard pop-up form, however, you can control their visibility.

In this case, you can pass to the function the date you want to have displayed on the calendar when it first appears. You can also pass a null value to have it use the current date, or you can just leave the parameter out. (It's optional, so you don't have to supply a value at all.)

TIP

If you include more than one module from this book in your own application, you may find duplicated private functions or subroutines. Because we can't know which combinations of modules and forms you'll want to include in your own applications, we've placed these small helper functions in the particular modules where they're needed. You may want to remove the Private keyword from one such instance, move it to a stand-alone module, and delete the other local instances; there's no need to carry around multiple copies of the same function.

Using the Sample Forms

You can easily include the pop-up calendar (Figure 8.1), the calculator (Figure 8.2), or both in your own applications. Follow these steps to include one or both:

1. From the sample database, import the module basCalc or basCalendar.
2. Import the corresponding form, frmCalc or frmCalendar.
3. When you want to pop up the calendar, call it with code like this, where varStartDate is either null or a specific date/time value. The function returns the date the user selected by either double-clicking or pressing Enter:

   ```
   varDate = adhDoCalendar(varStartDate)
   ```

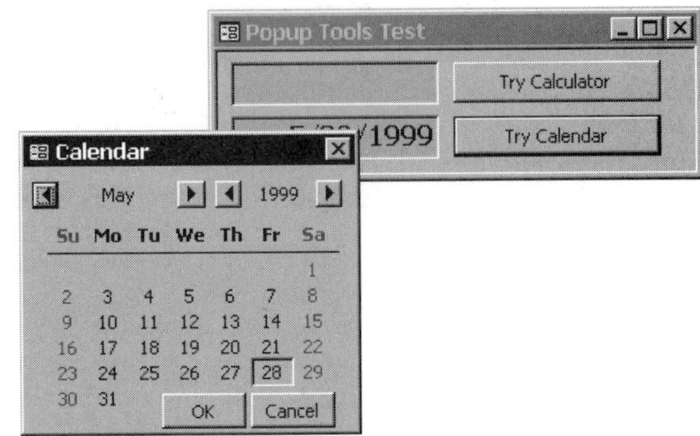

FIGURE 8.1:

Calendar (frmCalendar, called from frmTestPopup)

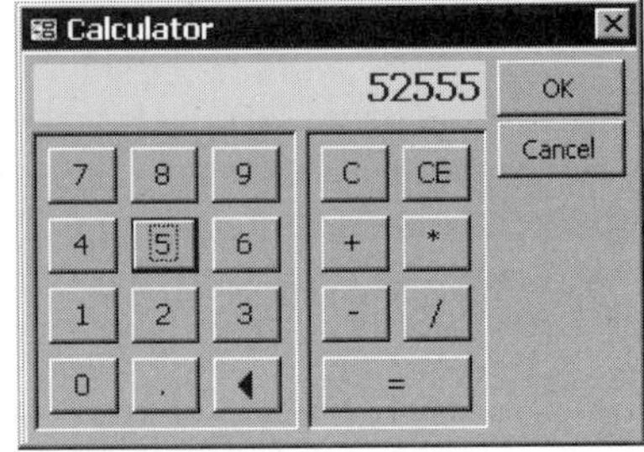

FIGURE 8.2:

Pop-up calculator (frmCalc) in action

4. When you want to pop up the calculator, call it with code like this, which returns the result of the user's calculations:

```
varValue = adhDoCalc()
```

TIP

We suggest that you provide the values you need to retrieve from a pop-up form as properties of that form. In the case of the calendar pop-up form (see Figure 8.1), the Value property of the form returns or sets the selected date. In the calculator pop-up form (see Figure 8.2), the Value property returns the result of the calculation. You can, if you must, retrieve values directly from the form, but doing so requires the calling code to know the names of specific controls on the form—that is, the caller must know too much about the pop-up form's design. Using a user-defined property of the form, the "outside world" need know nothing about how the form supplies the property's value. We believe this is the right way to use forms as components.

Creating User-Defined Properties

In Access, you can create properties and methods of forms from outside the form that feel just like built-in properties and methods. These properties and methods correspond directly to the user-defined properties and methods of class modules, as described in Chapter 3. The next few sections explain how you can create and use your own form properties and methods. You'll use the Calendar form, as an example.

Using a Public Form Variable

If the property you'd like to expose equates directly with a public module-level variable in the form's module, then there's no problem: just refer to the variable as though it were a property of the form. For example:

```
' In the module's declarations area
Public Value As Variant
' somewhere in your code
Forms("YourForm").Value = 5
```

will set the form's Value property to 5.

Using Property Let/Set/Get Procedures

If, on the other hand, you want to provide a property that requires some code to set or retrieve, you'll need to use VBA's Property Let/Set/Get procedures. Property Get procedures retrieve the value of a form property. Property Set procedures set the value of an object property of a form, and Property Let procedures allow you to set the value of a simple (nonobject) form property. These names, of course, correspond to the VBA Set and (seldom-used) Let keywords. (For example, for a form, you might want to create a ParentForm property that refers to the form that was active when you loaded the current form. That way you'd know which form to make current when you closed the current form again.) These procedures allow you to do any necessary work to set or retrieve information about the form. For example, in the calendar, this code allows you to set the FirstDay property:

```
Public Property Let FirstDay( _
 intNewStartDay As Integer)
    ' Set the first day of the week.
```

```
    ' Fix up errant values.
    If intNewStartDay < 1 Or _
     intNewStartDay > 7 Then
        intNewStartDay = 1
    End If
    mintFirstDay = intNewStartDay
    RedisplayCalendar
End Property
```

You don't actually call Property Let procedures. Instead, you set the value of the property as though it were a built-in property. Given the code in the previous example, setting the form's FirstDay property looks like this:

```
Forms("frmCalendar").FirstDay = 2
```

If you want to try this, load frmCalendar in Form view. In the Immediate window, type the previous line (setting the FirstDay property to 2). The Calendar form will immediately redisplay itself with Monday as the first day of the week.

You can supply either the Property Let or Get procedure or both, but if you do supply both, the input data type to the Let routine must match the output type for the Get routine. For example, the Calendar form supplies Let and Get procedures for the form's Value property:

```
Public Property Let Value(dtmNewDate As Date)
    mdtmStartDate = dtmNewDate
    RedisplayCalendar
End Property

Public Property Get Value() As Date
    Value = DateSerial( _
     Me.Year, Me.Month, Me.Day)
End Property
```

To test this out, with frmCalendar open, enter the following statement in the Immediate window:

```
Forms("frmCalendar").Value = #5/16/1956#
```

This moves the calendar so that it has the specific date selected. To use the Property Get procedure, use standard property retrieval syntax:

```
Debug.Print Forms("frmCalendar").Value
```

The following table lists all the properties exposed by frmCalendar:

Property	Description
Day	Gets or sets the selected day of the month
FirstDay	Gets or sets the first day of the week (1=Sunday, 2=Monday, and so on)
Month	Gets or sets the selected month
ShowOKCancel	Shows the OK and Cancel buttons
Value	Gets or sets the selected date
Year	Gets or sets the selected year

Using Form Procedures as Methods

VBA allows Access to expose any public function or subroutine in a form's module as a method of that form. Using the Public keyword, you can create methods any other object can use to manipulate the form. The Calendar form does this, making it a completely reusable, embeddable "object."

If you use form procedures as methods, no object outside the form needs to know anything about the form except its exposed methods and properties. For example, the Calendar form exposes the methods shown in Table 8.1. When your code calls these methods (for example):

```
Forms("frmCalendar").PreviousMonth
```

the Calendar form knows what to do and reacts by moving to the previous month.

TABLE 8.1: Methods Exposed by frmCalendar

Method	Description
NextDay	Moves selection to the next day
NextWeek	Moves selection to the next week

Continued on next page

TABLE 8.1 CONTINUED: Methods Exposed by frmCalendar

Method	Description
NextMonth	Moves selection to the next month
NextYear	Moves selection to the next year
PreviousDay	Moves selection to the previous day
PreviousWeek	Moves selection to the previous week
PreviousMonth	Moves selection to the previous month
PreviousYear	Moves selection to the previous year
Today	Moves selection to the current date

If you create reusable objects so that they expose as many properties and methods as you need, you should be able to pick them up and move them from application to application with no rewriting at all.

To create a method for a form, all you need to do is add the Public keyword in front of the subroutine or function definition. Because the procedure is public, you can call it from anywhere else as a method of the form. For example, the code for the form's NextMonth method looks like this:

```
Public Sub NextMonth()
    ChangeDate _
     adhcMonthStr, dtMoveForward
End Sub
```

To test this from the Immediate window, open frmCalendar in Form view, and type

```
Forms("frmCalendar").NextMonth
```

This moves the calendar to the next month after the one it's currently displaying.

To test this functionality, check out frmCalendarTest, shown in Figure 8.3. Clicking any of the buttons calls one of the exposed methods for the subform. For example, clicking the Next Month button calls this code:

```
Private Sub cmdNextMonth_Click()
    ' Make sure the screen repaints so
    ' the user sees the cursor move.
    Calendar.Form.NextMonth
    Me.Repaint
End Sub
```

In this example, the name of the subform control is Calendar. To interact with the methods of the form embedded within the subform control, you must use methods and properties of the Form property of the subform control. Because of this, you must use expressions like Calendar.Form.NextMonth in order to programmatically control the form embedded within a subform control.

FIGURE 8.3:

Because frmCalendar exposes methods and properties, you can embed it and use it as a single entity.

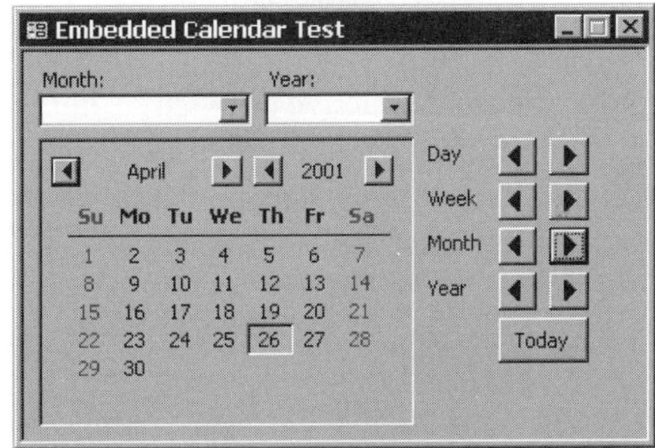

Filtering Data

As part of many applications, you'll be called upon to allow your users to choose a subset of rows and perhaps supply their own ordering from a table or query. Access provides two visual ways to filter data: Filter by (or Excluding) Selection and Filter by Form (often called Query By Form, or QBF). The next few sections discuss these features and the form methods and properties that are associated with them. These include the Filter and FilterOn properties and the Filter and ApplyFilter events. Along the way, you'll also need to investigate the FilterLookup property for controls, because this property allows you to fine-tune the performance of your QBF forms.

The Filter Property

Forms and reports provide a Filter property, which contains the current or last applied filter for the form. The Filter property takes the form of a SQL WHERE clause, such as

```
[LastName] = "Smith" And [City] Like "S*"
```

A filter can be either active or inactive, depending on the state of the FilterOn Property. (See the section "The FilterOn Property" a little later in this chapter for more information.) Filter By (or Excluding) Selection, Filter by Form, Advanced Filter/Sort, the ApplyFilter method, or direct manipulation via code or macro will update the Filter property. The results of these actions might be different, but they all do their work by modifying the Filter property.

Forms begin life with a Filter property that's an empty string. Any of the actions listed above will insert a string into the Filter property, and the resulting filter can be either active or inactive, depending on the state of the FilterOn property. Subsequent uses of the actions mentioned above will either replace or add on to the existing Filter property, depending on the specific action and whether or not the filter was active when you took the action.

Filter by Selection

Filter by Selection allows you to create a filter by pointing to the values by which you'd like to filter. For example, selecting the value *Peter* in the FirstName field and then clicking the Filter By Selection toolbar button places

```
[FirstName] = "Peter"
```

in the form's Filter property. Selecting just the *P* in the FirstName field places

```
[FirstName] Like "P*"
```

in the Filter property, and selecting the *t* places

```
[FirstName] Like "*t*"
```

in the property.

If there was an existing value in the Filter property before you used Filter by Selection, Access' behavior depends on the setting of the FilterOn property. If the filter was active (the FilterOn property was set to True), using Filter by Selection will be cumulative: Access will place an And operator between the existing Filter property and the new expression generated by your activity in the Filter by Selection mode. Subsequent uses of Filter by Selection will continue to add to your criteria, using the And operator. If the filter was not active when you started your Filter by Selection session, Access replaces the Filter property value with the new criteria rather than adding on to it. When you close your form, Access will save the current Filter property along with the form.

WARNING Access does not check the validity of your criteria. Because of the additive property of filters when you use Filter by Selection, you may end up with useless criteria. There's nothing Access can really do about this, so it's just a matter of being aware that it's possible to paint yourself into a corner when you use Filter by Selection.

Filter by Form

When you start a Filter by Form session, all the existing filter criteria are parsed into the current form's controls. When you leave Filter by Form mode, Access recreates the filter from the criteria specified in each control. If the form's Filter property references fields that don't exist as controls on the form, then when you leave Filter by Form mode, Access drops the errant criteria from the Filter expression.

In any case, Filter by Form results always replace the current Filter property. Every time you use Filter by Form, Access parses the existing filter, allows you to change it, and then creates a new filter based on your selections in Filter by Form. (See the section "Fine-Tuning Filter by Form" later in the chapter for a few more details on Filter by Form.) When you close the form, Access saves the current Filter property with the form.

Advanced Filter/Sort

The Advanced Filter/Sort mechanism, left over from Access 2, allows you to create any type of filtering/sorting criteria you wish. In all cases, when you change the Filter property using Advanced Filter/Sort, Access completely replaces the value, regardless of whether it was active.

The ApplyFilter Method

Access allows you to apply a filter to a form, using the ApplyFilter method of the DoCmd object. You can specify a WHERE clause, a query, or both from which to extract the filter criteria. If you specify either a WHERE clause or a query name, Access places the appropriate criteria in the form's Filter property. That is (assuming the WHERE clause on qrySimple is "ID = 5"), the following two statements will have the same effect: the Filter property of frmSimple will contain the expression "ID = 5".

```
DoCmd.ApplyFilter FilterName:="qrySimple"
' or:
DoCmd.ApplyFilter WhereCondition:="ID = 5"
```

If you use both arguments, Access applies the WHERE clause to the results of the query you specify. In other words, it combines the two WHERE clauses, using the And operator.

Whether you supply one or both parameters to ApplyFilter, Access replaces the existing Filter property for the form with the new criteria specified by your parameters.

What Happens When You Change the Filter Property?

Any of the above actions (using Filter by Selection, Filter by Form, Advanced Filter/Sort, or the ApplyFilter action) will

1. Change the form's Filter property
2. Filter the form accordingly
3. Set the form's FilterOn property to True
4. Requery the underlying recordset
5. Set the "(Filtered)" description next to the form's navigation buttons
6. Put "FLTR" in the Access status bar

Changing the Filter Property Programmatically

When you change the Filter property programmatically (using VBA or macros), the result depends on whether or not the filter was active previously. If filtering is active when you change the Filter property programmatically, the new filter takes effect immediately. If filtering is inactive when you change the Filter property, it remains inactive, but the Filter property accepts the new value. The next time you work with the Filter property (either by setting the FilterOn property to True or by entering Filter by Form mode), Access will use your new filter. If you set the Filter property programmatically, Access will not automatically save the new Filter property when you close the form.

Removing the Filter

Access provides several methods you can use to remove the current filter from a form. If you use the ShowAllRecords method of the DoCmd object or click the Remove Filter toolbar button, Access leaves the current filter intact but sets the FilterOn property to False for you. If you change the form's record source or set the Filter property to an empty string, you'll actually remove the Filter property's value.

The first methods leave the Filter property intact but make it inactive. Using the second set of methods actually removes the Filter property value altogether.

Saving the Filter Property

If you change the Filter property because of Access user interface operations (Filter by Form, Filter by Selection, or Advanced Filter/Sort), Access saves the new Filter property when you close the form, regardless of whether you specifically ask for the form to be saved. When you open a form with a Filter property set, Access will not automatically make the filter active; you'll need to set the FilterOn property to True for the filter to take effect. If you change the Filter property programmatically at any time while a form is open, Access will not save the Filter property when you close the form.

The FilterOn Property

When you open a form that has a nonempty Filter property, Access doesn't filter the data automatically. To cause Access to make the filtering active, set the FilterOn property of the form to True. This read/write property allows you to both set the filtering to be active or not and find out whether filtering is active. (Remember, changing the filter via the user interface might set this property without your knowing about it.) For example, you could use code like this:

```
' Make a label on the form visible if filtering is active
lblWarning.Visible = Me.FilterOn
' or
' Force filtering to be inactive.
Me.FilterOn = False
```

When you set the FilterOn property to True, Access applies the existing filter; it works the same as clicking the Apply Filter toolbar button. (As a matter of fact, if you set the FilterOn property for a form to True, Access will also select the Apply Filter toolbar button for you.) Setting the FilterOn property to False, if it's currently True, is the same as deselecting the Apply Filter toolbar button.

If you set the FilterOn property to True for a form with no Filter property, Access does not complain. The FilterOn property will be True; there just won't be any active filter. If you then subsequently set the Filter property, that filter will take effect immediately (because the FilterOn property is already set to True).

The Filter Event

Access triggers a form's Filter event whenever you select Filter by Form or Advanced Filter/Sort but it does this before it actually goes into the filtering user interface mode. Access passes two parameters to your event procedure: Cancel, which you can set to True to cause Access to cancel the filter activity that triggered the Filter event, and FilterType, which will be either 0 (acFilterByForm) for Filter by Form, 1 (acFilterAdvanced) for Advanced Filter/Sort, or 2 (acServerFilterByForm).

NOTE

When you're working with an Access data project, you can work with filters on the server so that your form won't need to retrieve all the rows from the server to display filtered data. Set the ServerFilterByForm and ServerFilter properties to manage these settings. *Access 2000 Developer's Handbook, Volume II* includes more information on creating data projects and working with server data.

You can use the Filter event to control what happens before a filtering session gets started. You could

- Make certain controls on the form invisible or disabled. If you do disable or hide controls, you'll want to reset them in the ApplyFilter event procedure. (See the next section for more details.)
- Clear out a previous Filter property so the filter starts "clean" every time. (Of course, changing the Filter property programmatically will prohibit its being saved with the form when you next close the form.)
- Cancel the event completely (set the Cancel parameter to True) or replace the standard Access interfaces with your own.

The sample form, frmQBFDemo, uses the first technique to hide the button on the form that starts the Filter by Form session. The button, cmdQBF, uses the RunCommand method to switch into Filter by Form mode. When you're in Filter by Form mode, Access disables all buttons but doesn't change their appearance. To make the current mode clearer, the example hides the button, as well. It also disables the Address field, just to show that it's possible. This is the code attached to the form's OnFilter event property; it reacts only to requests to start a Filter by Form session:

```
Private Sub Form_Filter( _
 Cancel As Integer, _
 FilterType As Integer)
```

```
    On Error Resume Next
    If FilterType = acFilterByForm Then
        txtCustomerId.SetFocus
        txtAddress.Enabled = False
        cmdQBF.Visible = False
    End If
End Sub
```

The ApplyFilter Event

Once you've created your filter and applied it to your form, Access triggers the ApplyFilter event. Access calls this event procedure for all user-initiated filtering (Filter by Form, Filter by Selection, Filter Excluding Selection, Advanced Filter/Sort) and most program-initiated filtering.

Access calls the ApplyFilter event procedure at different points, depending on the filtering action you've taken. The event is always triggered before Access modifies the Filter property, and it is a cancelable event. Using this event, you could

- Trap attempts to remove a filter, or set a new one, and request confirmation.
- Modify the filter expression manually, before Access applies it. (Modifying the filter in code prohibits Access from saving the new filter with the form when you close the form.)
- Reset the display of the form, putting things back the way they were before you modified them in the Filter event.
- Change or update the display of the form before Access applies the filter.

Again, Access allows you to cancel the ApplyFilter event by setting the Cancel parameter it sends to your event procedure to True. In addition, Access sends you the ApplyType parameter, indicating the action you took that triggered the event:

Constant	Value	Description
acShowAllRecords	0	Removed the filter
acApplyFilter	1	Applied the filter
acCloseFilterWindow	2	Closed the filter window without applying a filter
acApplyServerFilter	3	Applied a server filter
acCloseServerFilterWindow	4	Closed the server filter window without applying a filter

The example form, frmQBFDemo, uses this event to reset the form to its previous state and to confirm changes. The event procedure, shown below, first makes the command button visible again and enables the Address field. Then, if you are attempting to set a new filter and that filter isn't empty, the form displays the filter string to be applied and requests confirmation. If you're trying to show all records or the filter you're applying is empty, the form requests confirmation to show all the rows:

```
Private Sub Form_ApplyFilter( _
 Cancel As Integer, ApplyType As Integer)
    Dim strMsg As String
    Dim strFilter As String
    ' Put things back the way they were before the Filter event
    ' changed them.
    cmdQBF.Visible = True
    txtAddress.Enabled = True

    strFilter = Me.Filter
    If (ApplyType = acApplyFilter Or _
     ApplyType = acApplyServerFilter) _
     And Len(strFilter) > 0 Then
        strMsg = "You've asked to filter the form " & _
         "given the condition:"
        strMsg = strMsg & vbCrLf & vbCrLf & strFilter
        strMsg = strMsg & vbCrLf & vbCrLf & "Continue?"
        If MsgBox(strMsg, vbYesNo Or vbQuestion, _
         "Apply Filter") = vbNo Then
            Cancel = True
        End If
    ElseIf ApplyType = acShowAllRecords Or _
     Len(strFilter) = 0 Then
        strMsg = "You've asked to show all records."
        strMsg = strMsg & vbCrLf & vbCrLf & "Continue?"
        If MsgBox(strMsg, vbYesNo Or vbQuestion, _
         "Apply Filter") = vbNo Then
            Cancel = True
        End If
    End If
End Sub
```

TIP

Because the ApplyFilter event can be canceled, you must place error handling around calls to the ShowAllRecords and ApplyFilter actions when called from VBA. If you don't handle the error, Access will trigger a runtime error if you cancel the filter, and your code will halt. This is similar to the way the Print action has always worked in Access: if you don't handle errors and the user clicks the Cancel button while printing, your code halts with a runtime error.

Fine-Tuning Filter by Form

When you enter Filter by Form mode, Access attempts to convert every text box on your form into a drop-down list, showing each unique item already in that field. In general, this is very useful, but with large datasets it can be inordinately slow. You can control whether Access fills those lists with values in two ways:

- Find the text box in the Tools ➢ Option ➢ Edit/Find dialog that's labeled, "Don't display lists where more than this number of records read:". You can set that value to any number between 0 and 32766. Once you set the value, Access will read rows to fill your lists only until it reaches that number of rows. Once it has run out of rows, it knows not to display the list of values, and instead supplies only Is Null and Is Not Null as choices in the drop-down list. In other words, you're telling Access: "If you can't get all the unique values by reading fewer than this many rows, then just stop trying."
- You can also set the FilterLookup property for each control on your form. This property has three possible values: Never, if you never want Access to supply a list of values; Database Default, if you want to use the maximum number of rows described in the previous bullet point; or Always, if you always want Access to create the list, even if Access will have to read more rows than specified in the Options dialog.

The only remaining issue, then, is how many rows Access actually reads. The answer to this question is related to whether the field in question is indexed. If it is indexed, Access needs to read only unique values, so there's a much better chance you'll find all the unique values within the specified number of rows to be read. If the field is not indexed, Access has to look at every single row in order to create a unique list of values. Because Access will stop reading when it has reached the number of rows you specified in the Options dialog, you'll need to plan ahead before specifying that value. If you want Access to always pull up a list of unique values, set the option value to be at least as large as the number of rows in any nonindexed field in the underlying table. If, however, Access manages to build the full list of unique values before reaching the maximum number of rows to be read, it always displays unique values, regardless of whether the field was indexed.

Ordering Your Rows

Just as with the Filter property, you can specify an OrderBy property for a form, report, query, or table and then make that order active by setting the OrderByOn property to True. This functionality corresponds to the quick-sort toolbar buttons: if you open frmQBFDemo, choose the City field, and then click the Sort Ascending or Sort Descending toolbar button, you're actually setting the form's OrderBy property. To see this, check it out in the Immediate window.

```
? Forms("frmQBFExample").OrderBy
```

will show you the current OrderBy value.

Just as it does the Filter property, Access saves the OrderBy property of the form when you close the form. If you want to make the sort order active, set the OrderByOn property to True.

If you want to sort on multiple fields, set the property to be the names of the fields, separated with commas:

```
Forms("frmQBFExample").OrderBy = "Country,City"
```

To make one or more of the fields sort in descending order, append DESC to the field name (just as you would in a SQL string, which is, of course, where this all comes from—you're just building the SQL ORDER BY clause):

```
Forms("frmQBFExample").OrderBy = "Country,City DESC"
```

When you open a form, Access does apply the OrderBy setting automatically (as opposed to the Filter property, which you must apply manually). Regardless of whether the OrderBy setting is active, it's stored with the form, and you can activate and deactivate it with the form's OrderByOn property.

Working with Forms' Data

Most of the forms you create in Access will be bound forms—that is, they'll display data pulled directly from some data source. Although Access provides many tools to help you work with these forms, you may need some information that isn't readily available. For example, you may want to know what the current row is or whether the user has moved to the new row. You'll find the solutions to these and other problems in the sections that follow.

At the New Record?

It is sometimes vitally important for your application to be able to sense whether your user has moved to the "new" record (the extra record at the end of editable recordsets). Access provides a simple way for you to know whether or not users have positioned themselves on the new record: the NewRecord property. This property returns True if the form is displaying the new row and False otherwise. The sample form, frmCategories, includes a single line of code that will make a label visible if you're on the new row. Figure 8.4 shows this form, with the new row current. To set the visibility of the label, the form calls the following line from its Current event:

```
lblNew.Visible = Me.NewRecord
```

That is, if the NewRecord property returns a True value, it sets the label to be visible and sets it to be invisible otherwise.

FIGURE 8.4:

Use the NewRecord property to tell whether or not you're on the new row.

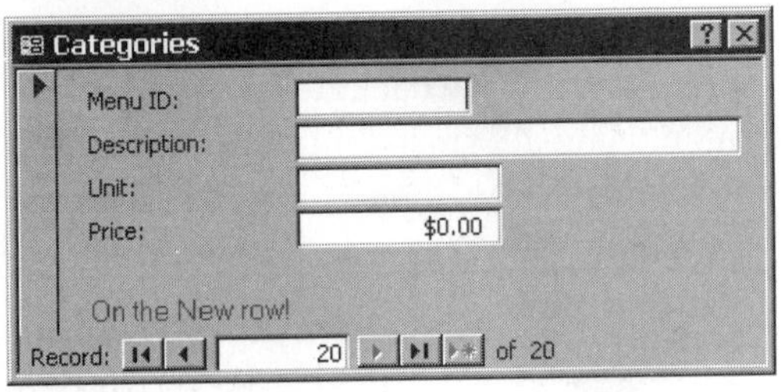

What's the Current Row, and How Many Rows Are There, Anyway?

For some applications, you may not want to use the default navigation buttons on your forms. You can turn them off, but you can't modify the default behavior or appearance. In addition, if you turn off the navigation buttons, you lose the display of the current row and the total number of rows. Access makes it easy to find out what row you're on, however, by supplying the CurrentRecord property. Every bound form provides this read-only property, allowing you to display the current row number.

The sample form frmNavigate, shown in Figure 8.5, includes a subform that recreates the current row and total rows display that Access normally provides. (The section "Creating Self-Disabling Navigation Buttons" later in this chapter discusses how to create the navigation controls on the subform.) Handling the current row is simple: in the main form's Current event, the following statement updates the txtCurrRec text box in the subform:

```
txtCurrRec = frmMain.CurrentRecord
```

As for determining the total number of rows, you have to work a bit harder; this information isn't available from the form itself, but rather from the recordset that's filling the form. The recordset's RecordCount property ostensibly returns the number of rows that have, so far, been loaded. Common knowledge says you must use the MoveLast method to move to the end of the recordset before you can know the number of rows in the recordset. And this is true for DAO recordsets if you want to know the record count immediately on opening the recordset. Experience shows that this isn't really necessary for some types of recordsets: if you just wait long enough, Access will actually update the RecordCount value, loading rows in the background until they've all been visited. (For more information on using a form's data programmatically, see the section "Using the Recordset and RecordsetClone Properties" later in the chapter.)

FIGURE 8.5:

Use form properties to determine the current row and the total number of rows.

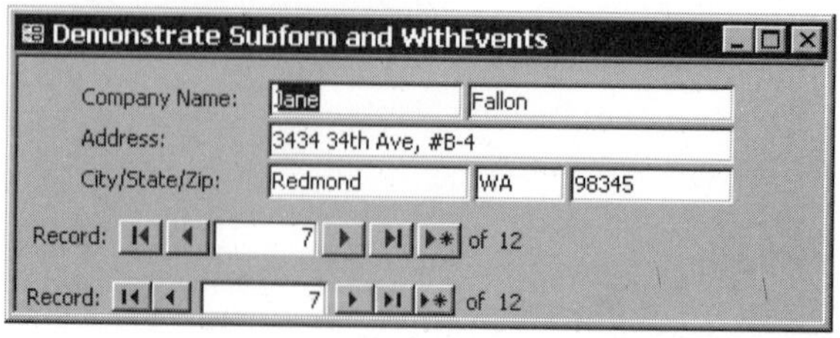

The subform counts on this behavior, although it would be simple to change. This is the code that does the work, pulled from code called by the main form's Current event:

```
Set rst = frmMain.RecordsetClone

' Sooner or later, Access will figure out
' how many rows there really are!
txtTotalRecs = rst.RecordCount + _
 IIf(frmMain.NewRecord, 1, 0)
```

The code displays the current value in the recordset's RecordCount property, assuming that sooner or later it will be correct. For small recordsets, it's correct as soon as you move to a row other than the first row. For large recordsets, it may take a few seconds or longer to know the total number of rows. Every time you move from row to row and trigger the Current event, the sample form calls this code, which updates the display on the form itself.

If this updating display for large recordsets bothers you, there are a few alternatives:

- In the subform's Open event, force the recordset to move to the last row (rst.MoveLast) and then back to the beginning (rst.MoveFirst) so it knows immediately how many rows there are. However, this can be slow for large recordsets.
- In the subform's Timer event, call code that uses a static variable to hold the RecordCount from the last time you called the routine. If the current value equals the previous value, you know the value has "settled," and you can change the Visible property of txtTotalRecs from False to True. You'll also want to disable the timer at that point (by setting the form's TimerInterval property to 0).

No matter how you solve this problem, you'll still want to update the text box during the form's Current event so it always reflects the actual number of rows.

TIP

If you use Access' built-in navigation buttons, the total number of rows increases by one when you're on the new row. That is, if there are eight rows in the table, when you're on the new row, Access displays "Record: 9 of 9." To emulate that, the example code adds one to the RecordCount property if it detects that you're on the new row.

Has the Form's Data Been Changed?

Access always knows if the data on the current form has been changed: if you have the form's RecordSelectors property set to True, you'll see the little pencil icon in the record selector when the data is dirty. Access also makes this information available to you through the form's Dirty property and Dirty event.

Basically, it's simple: when the form first becomes dirty—that is, the data on the form gets changed for the first time within the current row—Access raises the Dirty event for the form. At this point, you can react to the event in the form's Dirty event procedure. Perhaps you'll want to log the information or provide some visual indication that the form's data has been changed.

A form's Dirty property returns True when the little pencil would be visible on the record selector (regardless of whether you're actually displaying the record selector). You can use this property to provide your own indicator when the data has been changed or to cause your code to take action, depending on whether or not the data has been changed.

Only one problem: although the Dirty event is raised whenever the form's data first becomes dirty, there's no corresponding event that occurs if you press Escape (or use the menus) to undo your changes. That is, if you need to know that any change has been made to the data, the Dirty event is useful. If you need to know whether the current set of data is different from the saved set of data, and you care if the user has undone changes, the Dirty event won't really help.

NOTE

Access doesn't trigger the form's Before/AfterUpdate events unless the data has been changed, so there's no point in checking the value of this property in those events. You wouldn't be there at all if the data weren't dirty.

The sample form, frmCategories, makes a label visible when you dirty the data on the form (see Figure 8.6). The form's Dirty event procedure looks like this:

```
Private Sub Form_Dirty(Cancel As Integer)
    lblDirty.Visible = True
End Sub
```

As mentioned earlier, the problem here is that the label won't ever disappear using this technique, until you move to a new row—even if you undo your changes (the form's Current includes code to hide the label every time you move a new row.) We've provided a solution for this issue, as well, using the Timer event in frmCategories. Every 250 milliseconds (1/4 second, an arbitrary interval), Access calls the Timer event procedure, which checks the state of the Dirty property of the form and makes lblDirty visible if the form is dirty:

```
Private Sub Form_Timer()
    Dim fDirty As Boolean
    fDirty = Me.Dirty
    If Not (fDirty Eqv lblDirty.Visible) Then
        lblDirty.Visible = fDirty
    End If
End Sub
```

FIGURE 8.6:

You can display a message on your forms indicating that the current row has been changed.

The Elusive Eqv Operator

Although you can use the equals operator ("=") to compare two logical values, the correct operator to use is Eqv. Here's why: in VBA, an expression whose value is 0 is treated as being False. An expression whose value is anything besides 0 is treated as being True. If you compare the actual value of two expressions using "=", it's possible that two True expressions will return a False comparison. (That is, both the values 3 and 5 are treated as True, if you're using an If...Then statement, but certainly 3 does not equal 5). If you're interested in the equivalence of two logical values, Eqv handles these differences. Although comparing the values 3 and 5 returns False, using Eqv to compare the values returns True. That is, because both expressions are True, they're logically equivalent.

To try this out, compare the results of typing the two following expressions in the Immediate window:

```
? CBool(3 = 5)
? CBool(3 Eqv 5)
```

In addition, the Dirty property is read/write. You can set the Dirty property to False, and if it's currently True, you'll force Access to save the current row, triggering the BeforeUpdate and AfterUpdate events. To test this, load frmCategories, dirty the form (change a field on it), and then, from the Immediate window, type

```
Forms("frmCategories").Dirty = False
```

This writes the data to disk and forces the dirty label to become invisible again.

NOTE

When writing the code for this example, we were tempted to set the Visible property of lblDirty to be the same as the Dirty property of the form—that is, if the form was dirty, make the label visible, and vice versa. The problem with this is that if you set the Visible property of a control every 250 milliseconds, you're tying up a major portion of your application's processing power in this tiny feature. To avoid that problem, the sample code sets the Visible property only if it's not currently equivalent to the form's Dirty flag. If the form is dirty and the label isn't visible, the code makes the label visible. If the form isn't dirty but the label is visible (which can happen if you change the data and then undo your change), the code makes the label invisible. With this technique, you avoid spending any more processing power on this feature than necessary.

Which Rows Are Selected?

If you need to know which rows the user has selected on a datasheet or continuous form, Access makes the information available to you, although it's not obvious how to retrieve the information. Using the SelLeft, SelTop, SelWidth, and SelHeight properties, you can tell exactly which cells the user has selected.

WARNING

In previous versions of Access, these properties have worked as advertised. In Access 2000, however, forms displayed in Datasheet view have values for their SelLeft property which are off by one. That is, the SelLeft property often, but not always, returns a value that is one larger than the actual value. We've included a sample form, frmSelTest, that you can use in order to test these properties. If you're working with a datasheet, however (the situation we think is most likely, when using these properties), beware that the value of the SelLeft property may be incorrect.

Using the Recordset and RecordsetClone Properties

Although you can go far in Access by simply using bound forms, sooner or later you'll need to work with the data displayed in a form programmatically. Access 2000 provides two ways of getting to a form's displayed data: the form's RecordsetClone property and its Recordset property. The next few sections discuss each, show examples, and discuss why you'd choose one or the other.

TIP

The next few sections rely on your understanding both ADO and DAO, the two data access methods supported by Access 2000. Chapter 6 covers ADO in detail, and Appendix C covers DAO. If you're completely new to programming in Access, we suggest you at least work through the beginning sections of each of these before digging into the following sections. The background you'll find there will make the information shown here flow smoother for you.

The RecordsetClone Property

You use a bound form's RecordsetClone property to retrieve a reference to a form's recordset. Any bound form maintains its own recordset, the set of rows onto which the form provides a window. You'll often need to manipulate that set of rows without showing your work on the visible form. To do this, you create a copy of the form's recordset and do your manipulations there. The RecordsetClone property of a form creates that copy for you and hands back a reference to that copy. The recordset you get back has its own current row and its own bookmark, and any repositioning you do in the recordset you retrieve will be invisible, as far as the form is concerned. (The form maintains a separate current row and a separate bookmark from the copy you've retrieved.)

For example, the code in Listing 8.5, called from the AfterUpdate event of a combo box, searches for a specific company name on a form and sets the form to show the correct row once it finds a match. (The code uses the recordset and the form's Bookmark property. By setting the form's Bookmark to be the same as the recordset's bookmark, Access will make the form have, as its current row, the same row that's current in the recordset.) To see this form in action, try out frmLookup in the sample project. Figure 8.7 shows this form in use. (The form includes some unusual company names, testing the code that manages embedded quotes and apostrophes in strings.)

TIP

It's useful to note that normally, if you have two separate recordsets that provide bookmarks, the bookmark value from one recordset can't be equated with the bookmark value from the other. That is, their bookmarks are "incompatible." Unlike creating a clone of a recordset (see Chapter 6 for more information), using the RecordsetClone property of a form retrieves a *copy* of the form's recordset, but this copy provides a bookmark compatible with the original recordset. Therefore, you can perform useful tricks (as we'll do in the example for this section) such as assigning the Bookmark property of the form to be the same as the Bookmark property of the recordset you've retrieved from the form. Using this technique, you can use the RecordsetClone property to retrieve an invisible recordset, move around in that recordset, and then, when you're ready, make the form display the same row as the "hidden" recordset you've been manipulating.

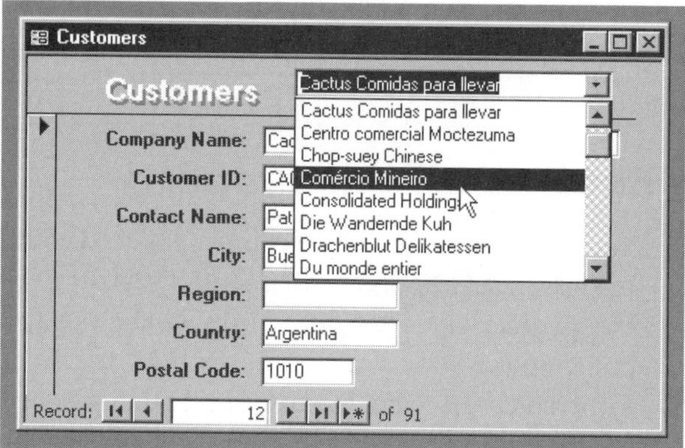

FIGURE 8.7: Choosing a name from the combo box forces the code in Listing 8.5 to locate the correct row.

TIP

The RecordsetClone property of a form returns a recordset based on the form's bound recordset. In an MDB file, the RecordsetClone will be a DAO recordset. In an ADP file, it will be an ADO recordset. This ADO vs. DAO thing gets very complicated when you start thinking about bound forms. See the sidebar "ADO vs. DAO" for more information.

Listing 8.5

```
Private Const adhcQuote = """"

Private Sub cboCompany_AfterUpdate()
    Dim rst As DAO.Recordset
```

```
    Set rst = Me.RecordsetClone
    rst.FindFirst "[CompanyName] = " & _
     adhHandleQuotes(Me!cboCompany, adhcQuote)

    If rst.NoMatch Then
        MsgBox "No match was found. Something is wrong!"
    Else
        Me.Bookmark = rst.Bookmark
    End If
    rst.Close
Set rst = Nothing
End Sub
```

NOTE

Assigning a recordset variable using the RecordsetClone property is the only time you set a DAO recordset object without using the standard syntax starting with a database object. Because you're retrieving a special kind of recordset, Access treats this case a bit differently. The results are almost the same, though: you end up with a Recordset object variable referring to the set of rows filling the form. The recordset you're pointing to, however, doesn't support all the same properties as a real recordset. You can't set a form recordset's Filter or Sort property, for example. Because you're not creating a new recordset but obtaining a reference to an existing one, the current row is undefined once you return the reference.

Handling quotes when using the DAO FindFirst method can be somewhat tricky. (It's tricky in ADO, too—see Chapter 6 for more information.) Generally, in VBA, if the string you're working with contains quote characters, you have to find some way to explain to VBA exactly what you want, since the string is delimited with quotes as well. In some situations, it's acceptable to simply "double up" the quotes inside the string, indicating that VBA should interpret two quotes inside a string as a single quote when evaluating the string.

Unfortunately, this won't work when calling the FindFirst method. All attempts we've made at this solution fail, when called from our sample form. Therefore, you'll need to use a function like adhHandleQuotes, which makes an ugly transformation of the input string before calling the FindFirst method: the adhHandleQuotes function replaces quotes inside a quoted string with " & Chr$(34) & ", which effectively splits the string into multiple "chunks," using VBA's Chr$ function to insert a character representing a quote into the string. This technique works well, and Listing 8.6 contains the entire adhHandleQuotes function (from basHandleQuotes). This function replaces all occurrences of the delimiter (a quote character, by default) with the appropriate string, so that DAO will be able to interpret the string even if it contains quote characters.

TIP

The adhHandleQuotes function accepts an optional second parameter, indicating the delimiter to use. For DAO, that should always be a quote character, and that's why it's optional. To indicate that the value of the optional parameter is a quote character, the code uses four quotes in a row. This looks confusing to us, but it's clear to VBA—the two outer quotes delimit a string, and the two inner quotes are seen by VBA as a single quote character. It's too bad that the DAO FindFirst method doesn't handle quotes the same way. If it did, the adhHandleQuotes procedure would be much simpler—it would just need to replace a single delimiter with two. Alas, that doesn't work.

Listing 8.6

```
Public Function adhHandleQuotes(strValue As String, _
 Optional strDelimiter As String = """") As String
    Dim strInsert As String
    strInsert = "Chr$(" & Asc(strDelimiter) & ")"

    adhHandleQuotes = _
     strDelimiter & _
     Replace(strValue, strDelimiter, _
      strDelimiter & " & " & strInsert & " & " _
      & strDelimiter) & _
      strDelimiter
End Function
```

ADO vs. DAO

When we first started working on this book, we planned to create a new version of Chapter 6, covering ADO (Active Data Objects) and never even mentioning DAO (Data Access Objects) except in passing. Late in the cycle, however, it became clear that DAO wasn't going away; at least, not with this version. (For information on what these acronyms mean, and how they affect you, see Chapter 6.)

Continued on next page

We wish this was simple, but it's not. ADO is the future of data access, as far as Microsoft is concerned, and so is the "premiere" data access technology in Access 2000. But DAO (a programmatic layer originally included in Access as a way to work with the Jet database engine) just hasn't completely gone away. Chapter 6 focuses on the details of manipulating data programmatically using ADO, because we think you need to know ADO, and that's the default data access object model you get when you create a new MDB or ADP file in Access 2000. Unfortunately, if you create a bound form in an MDB file, the form's recordset is still going to be a DAO recordset. The Access team simply couldn't rearchitect Access forms in an MDB file to use an ADO recordset and still ship the product on time. If you're new to Access, therefore, it won't be enough to simply learn ADO—you'll also need to know a little about DAO, in order to program form's recordsets when working in an MDB file. Appendix C is an introduction to DAO (it repeats many of the sections in Chapter 6 from a DAO point of view), and you may want to peruse this appendix if you're new to DAO.

Because form data manipulation in an MDB file will require DAO knowledge in Access 2000 (and we think that's the only place in Access 2000 that you're required to use DAO), we've used DAO for many of the examples in this chapter. Perhaps in the next edition, we'll be able to convert all these examples to ADO exclusively; in this version we cannot. Therefore, if you haven't worked with DAO previously, you may want to work through Appendix C before progressing through the rest of this chapter.

The RecordsetClone Dilemma

Say, for the moment, that you're an experienced Access 97 programmer. You've used forms and their RecordsetClone property for years. Now, you come to Access 2000, and you figure that you can take advantage of your previous experience and get rolling immediately. You create a new Access database (not a project, but an old-style MDB file), just like you did in Access 97. You create a table and then base a form on that table. You want to use the form's recordset, so you add this code to some event of the form:

```
Dim rst As Recordset
Set rst = Me.RecordsetClone
```

and then other code that uses the recordset. You run your project; Access hits the Set statement in the code shown above, and you get a runtime error: Type Mismatch. What's wrong? This code certainly worked in Access 97!

The problem is that for new databases, Access provides only a reference to ADO. That is, it assumes that for new development, you want to use ADO and its recordsets, commands, and connections, in your code. Because you wrote

```
Dim rst As Recordset
```

ADO provided a recordset. Then, when you tried to execute the code

```
Set rst = Me.RecordsetClone
```

Access tried to oblige—it returned a recordset, all right, but it was a DAO recordset. And, as you've found out, you can't assign a DAO recordset into an ADO recordset variable.

We guess that this will hit a large number of Access 97 developers, and we're expecting a mass wailing and gnashing of teeth over this. The solution? If you want to work with a form's RecordsetClone property in an MDB file in Access 2000, you must do two things:

1. Open a module, use the Tools ➢ References dialog, and add a reference to Microsoft DAO 3.6 Object Library.
2. Modify your code to disambiguate the reference. That is, change the declaration so that it looks like this:

   ```
   Dim rst As DAO.Recordset
   ```

Following these two steps will guarantee you a DAO recordset and will allow you to write code just as you would have in Access 97. We certainly wish that this problem wasn't there, but it is, and unless you're prepared, it will hit you, too.

Using a Form's Recordset Property

As you saw earlier, you can use a form's RecordsetClone property to retrieve a copy of the form's recordset with its own current row and separate bookmark. New in Access 2000, you can also retrieve a form's Recordset property and assign it to a Recordset variable. Using the Recordset property, you don't get a copy of the recordset—you get the actual recordset itself. This means that any changes you make to the recordset are visible immediately on the form, and any movement you make in the recordset cause the form to change rows, as well.

If you wanted to display two views of the same data in Access 97 and keep the current row on both views in synch, you would have had to do some amount of programming, in Access 97. In Access 2000, however, this is simple. Figure 8.8 shows a sample form (frmSynchRecordset) containing two subforms. The first subform displays tabular data, and the second displays details pertaining to the selected row in the top subform. As you move from row to row in either subform, the other subform tracks to the same row. In Access 97, this would have required writing code reacting to the Current event of both subforms, and each subform's code would have had to have been aware of the other subform.

FIGURE 8.8:

It's easy to synchronize two separate subforms, using the forms' Recordset property.

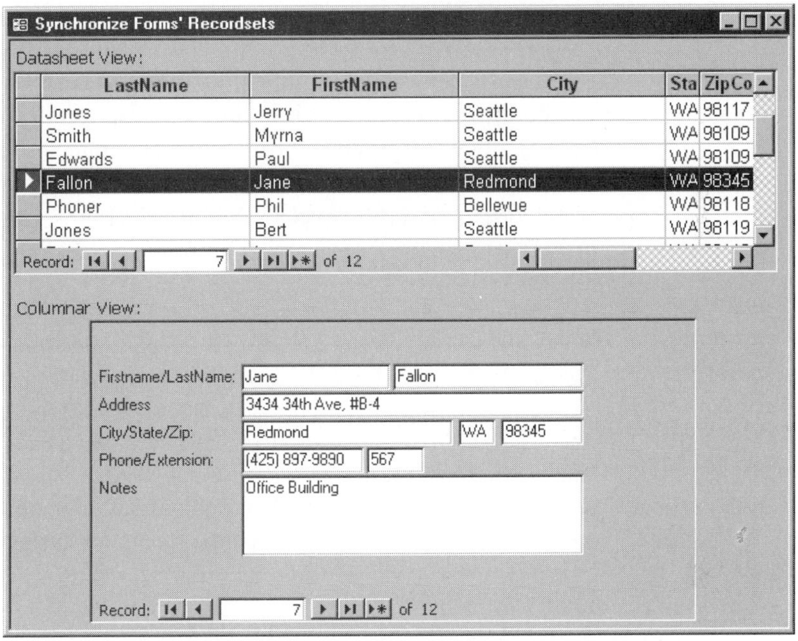

In Access 2000, creating this form is simple. All we did was create two subforms (fsubTabular and fsubColumnar, in this case), based on the same data. One form displays data in single form view, and the other displays it in datasheet view. We embedded both, as subforms, on a main form. Finally, we added a single line of code to the main form's Load event procedure:

```
Private Sub Form_Load()
    ' Make both subforms share the same recordset.
    Set subColumnar.Form.Recordset = _
     subTabular.Form.Recordset
End Sub
```

(We named the subform controls subColumnar and subTabular—different names than their constituent forms—to make it clear that the code is referring to the subform controls, not the forms stored in the database.) This code sets the Recordset property of one subform to be the same as the Recordset property of the other subform. With that one line of code, you have two forms linked, sharing the same recordset. Record movement in one form shows up instantly in the other. Data changes made in one are visible in the other.

As you can see, assigning a recordset into a form is easy: simply use the Set statement to place an existing recordset into the form's Recordset property. In this case, the recordset is coming from another form, but it doesn't have to work this way. You could use DAO code (or ADO, if working in an Access ADP project file) to create a recordset programmatically, filter and sort it the way you'd like, and then assign the open recordset into the Recordset property of a form. The example shown in Listing 8.7 (from basFormRecordset), creates a recordset and then assigns it into an open form. If you examine the code, you'll see that the code in Listing 8.7 opens a recordset based on qryCustomerOrderItems, retrieving only the rows where the customer ordered more than five of a particular item, sorted by the quantity.

TIP

To run the code in Listing 8.7, you can simply open the module, place your cursor within the procedure, and press F5. Because this procedure accepts no parameters, you can run it directly by pressing F5. If it had parameters, or if you would rather, you could call it from the Immediate window. In addition, you can use this technique to single-step through procedures. Just place your cursor inside the procedure and press F8 to begin stepping through the code one line at a time.

Listing 8.7

```
Public Sub TestRecordsetToForm()
    Dim db As DAO.Database
    Dim rst As DAO.Recordset

    ' Get your recordset ready.
    Set db = CurrentDb()
    Set rst = db.OpenRecordset( _
     "SELECT * FROM qryCustomerOrderItems " & _
     "WHERE Quantity > 5 " & _
     "ORDER BY Quantity")

    ' Open the form hidden. Set its Recordset property,
    ' and then make it visible.
    DoCmd.OpenForm "frmConditionalFormatting", _
     WindowMode:=acHidden
```

```
    With Forms("frmConditionalFormatting")
        Set .Recordset = rst
        .Visible = True
    End With

    ' Don't close the recordset, because that will also
    ' close the recordset used by the form!
    Set rst = Nothing
    Set db = Nothing
End Sub
```

TIP

Although this example uses a DAO recordset in an MDB file, you could accomplish the same goal using an ADO recordset in an Access project (ADP) file.

Recordset vs. RecordsetClone

These two properties seem suspiciously similar. How are you, as a developer, to know which one to use, and when? Hopefully, this section will help clear up the similarities and the differences between these two properties.

What You Get

When you retrieve a form's RecordsetClone property, Access creates a copy of the recordset filling the form and returns a reference to that copy back to you. You don't get a full-featured recordset—you can't use the Filter or Sort properties of this recordset, for example. This recordset has its own distinct current row (and Bookmark property), and you can move around in this recordset independently from the associated form. That is, if you use the MovePrevious method of your recordset, the form's current row, and its bookmark, won't have changed.

When you retrieve a form's Recordset property, Access returns a reference to the exact recordset that's providing data for the form. The recordset you now have a reference to, and the form itself, share the same bookmark and the same current row. If you move the record pointer in one, it changes in both.

For both the RecordsetClone property and the Recordset property, retrieving the property will return a DAO recordset in an MDB file and an ADO recordset in an ADP file. In addition, the recordset you retrieve using either the RecordsetClone or Recordset property won't support the Seek method.

What You Can Do

Using the RecordsetClone property of a form, you can retrieve a recordset that corresponds to the one that the form shows on the screen. The property is read-only, so you can only retrieve, not set, this property. When you retrieve the property, the current row is not necessarily the same as the current row on the form, so you'll need to either set the Bookmark property of the new recordset, or use one of the Move… or Find… methods.

When you retrieve the Recordset property of a form, the current row of the recordset you retrieve is the same as the form's. In addition, if you change the current row in either, the current row in the other changes to match. One exciting new feature is the ability to assign an open recordset to the Recordset property of a form (see the section "Using a Form's Recordset Property" earlier in the chapter).

Another important feature to note is that because you can assign a recordset directly to the Recordset property of a form, you can now control transactions on forms. For a single form, being able to roll back changes isn't all that exciting—you could do that in Access 97 using the Undo method of the form. The real interest comes when you find that you can use this technique with subforms, as well. Although the technique isn't as simple as it ought to be, and it requires a good deal of code, it can be done. (See the section "Subforms and Transactions" later in this chapter.)

You can only set a form's Recordset property to a recordset based on Jet or SQL Server data, using an ADO or DAO recordset. In addition, the read/write behavior of the data on the form will change, depending on what type of recordset you choose. The following chart describes the options you have when assigning a recordset to the Recordset property of a form.

Recordset Type	Based on SQL Data	Based on Jet Data
ADO	Read/Write	Read-Only
DAO	N/A	Read/Write

In addition, in order to set a form's Recordset property to a read/write SQL Server recordset, the recordset's CursorLocation property must be set to adUseClient, and the UniqueTable property must be set to the "one" table in a one-to-many join. This property is available in ADP files on the property sheet, but it is not available for MDB files. In MDB files, you must set the property from within VBA code. (See *Access 2000 Developer's Handbook, Volume II* for more information on working with forms and their recordsets in ADP files.)

NOTE Although we'll mention it again later, it's important to note that you cannot change the Recordset property of a form while in a transaction. This one limitation, in fact, made it impossible for us to devise a generalized mechanism whereby you could buffer up a large number of form transactions (across several rows of data, for example) with subform-related data and roll back all the changes at will.

Conditional Formatting

Since Access 1 shipped, developers have been asking for some way to have rows on continuous forms show formatting depending on the values of individual fields. And, since Access 1, developers have been finding hacks and workarounds to this problem, because Access has always viewed each instance of a given control on a continuous form as a single control—any property changes you make to any instance of the control applied to all instances. Finally, in Access 2000, Microsoft has provided a solution, and it works well. By applying formatting rules to text box and combo box controls on your forms, you can cause Access to format the data for you.

You can manipulate formatting conditions both at design time and at runtime; at design time, you use the dialog box shown in Figure 8.9. At runtime, you use the FormatConditions collection.

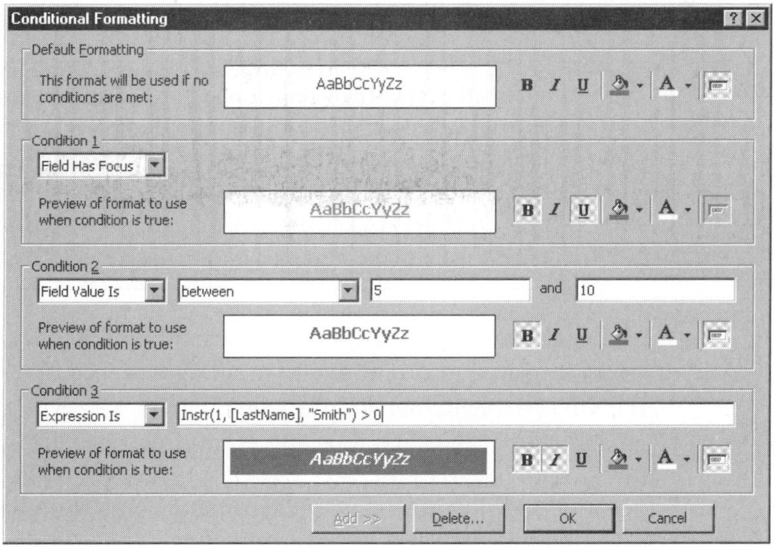

FIGURE 8.9:

Use the Format ➢ Conditional Formatting menu item to set control formatting based on field values.

NOTE

Yes, you can accomplish a very limited form of this technique in previous versions of Access. In the past, Access allowed you to provide a value for the Format property, including three or four colors (depending on the version), for values less than zero, equal to zero, greater than zero, or Null. But this technique was cumbersome, worked only for numeric values, and didn't help where it was needed most—with continuous forms.

Working with Conditions

Whether you're working at design time or at runtime, Access' support for conditional formatting has clearly defined limits. Specifically:

- You can add no more than three conditions for any control.
- You can set conditional formatting only for a text box or a combo box control.
- You can test for only three situations: the control has received the focus; the value of the control is equal to, greater than, or less than some specific value, or is within (or isn't within) some specific range; or some expression is true.
- You can modify the bold, italic, or underlined state of the text; the color of the background and/or the foreground of the text; and the enabled state of the control.

TIP

Although the new conditional formatting tools are most useful with continuous forms and datasheets, they're not limited to being used there. The same conditional formatting works whether you've displayed your form in continuous forms, datasheet, or single form view. Note, however, that because this formatting applies to combo box and text box controls, it has no effect on tables and queries displayed in datasheet view directly. You must use a form to get this functionality.

To demonstrate the conditional formatting functionality, we've provided a sample form, frmConditionalFormatting (see Figure 8.10). This form includes conditions that demonstrate all the different ways you can use conditional formatting, both at design time and at runtime. Specifically:

- The LastName field displays orange, underlined, bold text when it gets the focus.

- The FirstName field displays orange, underlined, bold text when it gets the focus and displays blue, underlined, bold text when the value of the field is *Greg*.
- The MenuDescription field displays brown, underlined, bold text if it contains the word *Coke*.

FIGURE 8.10:

This sample form demonstrates all the possibilities—design time and runtime conditional formatting.

Last Name	First Name	Order Date	Quantity	Menu Description
Thomas	Bob	01-Oct-2000	1	Medium Cheese Pizza
Thomas	Bob	01-Oct-2000	10	Large Diet Coke
Thomas	Bob	13-Nov-2000	4	Spaghetti Plate
Thomas	Bob	13-Nov-2000	10	Small Sprite
Reddick	Greg	03-Jun-1999	5	Large Cheese Pizzas
Reddick	Greg	03-Jun-1999	10	Lasagna
Reddick	Greg	03-Jun-1999	12	Medium Pepperoni Pizza
Reddick	Greg	03-Jun-1999	3	Large Pepsi
Reddick	Greg	14-Jun-1999	12	Large Diet Coke

Demonstrate Conditional Formatting — Record: 13 of 465

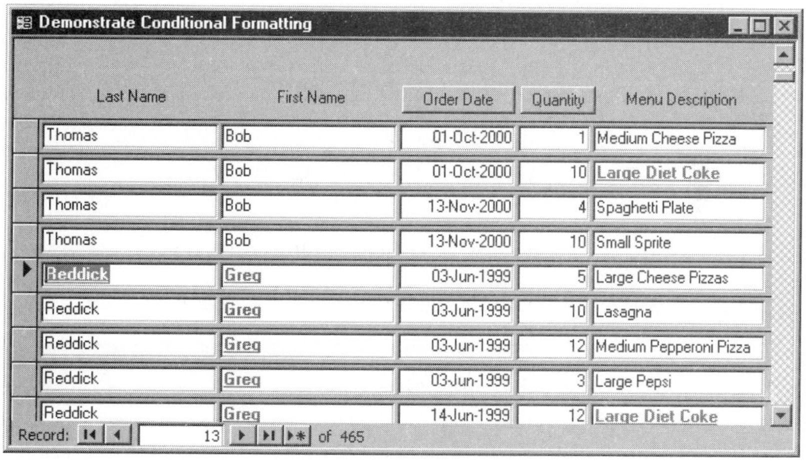

In addition, if you select either the Order Date or Quantity button above the associated field, the form displays input controls so that you may add simple conditional formatting for the Order Date or Quantity text boxes. Figure 8.11 shows formatting applied to the Order Date text box. These buttons use the FormatConditions collection to programmatically set conditions on the Order Date or Quantity text boxes.

FIGURE 8.11:

The sample form also allows you to programmatically control conditional formatting. Here, specific order dates are displayed in red text and underlined.

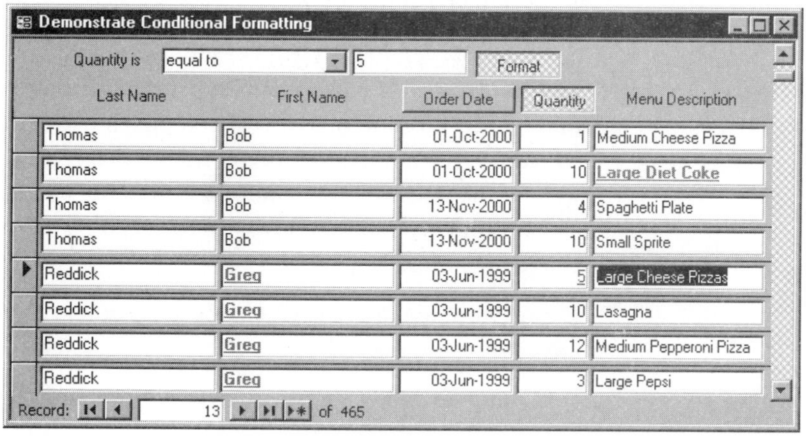

Demonstrate Conditional Formatting — Quantity is: equal to 5 — Format

Last Name	First Name	Order Date	Quantity	Menu Description
Thomas	Bob	01-Oct-2000	1	Medium Cheese Pizza
Thomas	Bob	01-Oct-2000	10	Large Diet Coke
Thomas	Bob	13-Nov-2000	4	Spaghetti Plate
Thomas	Bob	13-Nov-2000	10	Small Sprite
Reddick	Greg	03-Jun-1999	5	Large Cheese Pizzas
Reddick	Greg	03-Jun-1999	10	Lasagna
Reddick	Greg	03-Jun-1999	12	Medium Pepperoni Pizza
Reddick	Greg	03-Jun-1999	3	Large Pepsi

Record: 13 of 465

Working with Conditional Formatting at Design Time

If you'd like to apply conditional formatting to text box or combo box controls on a form, you can select the control on the form and then use the Format ➢ Conditional Formatting menu item to set up formatting rules. When you first display the dialog box, it looks like Figure 8.12. That is, it shows how the control will be formatted if none of the conditions you supply are met, and it then allows you to specify a condition. You add conditions one at a time, specifying criteria and formatting information for each rule.

TIP

If you have the form's Allow Design Changes property set to Design View Only, you'll need to be in Design view to use the Conditional Formatting dialog box. If you've allowed design changes in any view, you can use the Conditional Formatting dialog at any time.

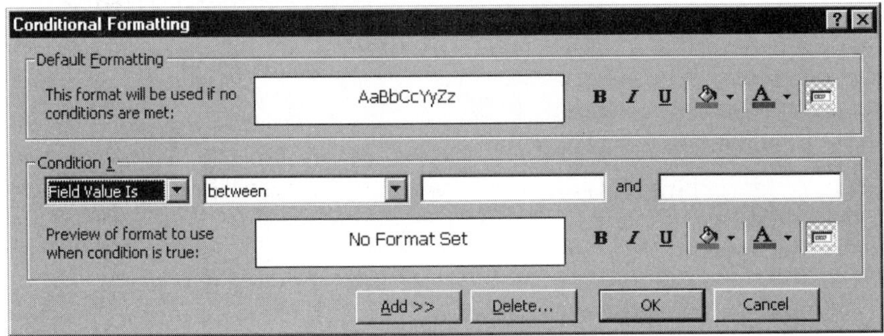

FIGURE 8.12: You can add conditional formatting, one rule at a time.

To specify a condition, start by selecting a condition type from the first combo box in the dialog box. You can choose one of the following items:

Field Value Is If you specify this item, the dialog box will display a second combo box and one or two text boxes. The second combo box contains the comparison operators between, not between, equal to, not equal to, greater than, less than, greater than or equal to, and less than or equal to. The text box (or boxes) allow you to specify a value or endpoints for a range of values.

Expression Is If you specify this item, you must supply a valid expression that evaluates to be either True or False. The dialog box performs no parsing on this condition, so it's up to you to enter some valid Boolean expression. For example, you might type something like this, to display text a specific way if the address field is longer than 15 characters:

```
Len([Address]) > 15
```

Field Has Focus In this case, the dialog box doesn't require any more input. You've specified that when the control gets the focus, Access should use the specified formatting to display the control.

For this condition, you can specify how you want the control to be displayed. That is, you can specify any combination of the following attributes:

- Bold text
- Italic text
- Underlined text
- Fill/Back color
- Font/Fore color
- Enabled

Once you close the dialog box, Access will apply your condition(s) against the text it finds in the control and will format it accordingly.

Although conditional formatting is a powerful feature, and it's a highly requested addition to the product, it's not perfect. Some issues you should be aware of include:

- You can have, at most, three conditions. We assume this restriction is performance-based (that is, each additional condition adds to the processing overhead, so the designers limited you to three conditions).
- If you want to have a condition based on the field having the focus, it must be the first condition. A Field Has Focus condition can't be second or third.
- Conditions are examined in the order they're added. That is, if you have conflicting conditions, Access will find the first true condition and not even examine the rest. Say, for example, you have conditions that set a numeric field to be red if it's exactly 5, and then blue if it's between 1 and 10. For a value of 1, you'll see blue text. For 5, you'll see red text—Access didn't even look at the second condition, because the first was satisfied.

- Access doesn't supply a way to control the visibility of a control using conditional formatting, nor does it supply a way to change the frame type (or any other attribute).

Also, make sure you understand how Expression Is conditions work. Using this type of condition, you must supply a valid expression, possibly using built-in or user-defined VBA functions, that returns True or False. You must include an entire expression, including the name of any field (or fields), that you'd like to have manage the formatting of your control.

TIP

Just as when creating expressions in queries, you must remember to surround field or control names in the Conditional Formatting dialog box in square brackets ([]). If you neglect to add these brackets, the dialog box will interpret your field or control name as a literal string. That is, it will automatically place quotes around the name. In that case, the expression will not perform as you expect.

To delete one or more conditions, select the Delete button on the Conditional Formatting dialog box. When you do, you'll see the dialog box shown in Figure 8.13. This dialog box allows you to delete one or all the conditions you've created.

FIGURE 8.13:

Use this dialog box to delete one or more conditions that you've created.

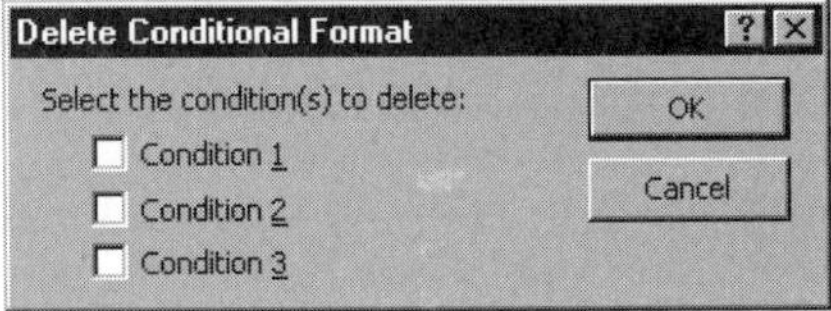

Working with Conditional Formatting at Runtime

To make it possible for you to control conditional formatting programmatically, Access provides a FormatConditions collection for text box and combo box controls. Using this collection of FormatCondition objects, you can do anything using code that the Conditional Formatting dialog box accomplishes in the Access user interface. (This is one of the few places in Access where the user interface and the programmatic interface meet up almost 100 percent—enjoy it!)

In order to work with conditional formatting programmatically, you'll use the FormatConditions collection of a control. This collection contains up to three FormatCondition objects, each of which describes one condition/formatting pair for the control. Just as with the user interface dialog box, the order in which you add the conditions plays a part in how the affected control behaves, so be aware of the order in which you programmatically create or delete conditions.

Each text or combo box control provides a FormatConditions property that returns a FormatConditions collection, and this collection provides the properties and methods you'd expect from a collection, plus a few extra:

Application Returns a reference to the parent application (in this case, the instance of Access you're running). Most Access objects provide this property, and it's there solely for your convenience.

Count Returns the number of FormatCondition objects in the collection. This value can only be 0, 1, 2, or 3, in this case.

Item (the default property) Returns a particular FormatCondition object by zero-based number within the collection. That is, you could use code like this to retrieve the third condition (note that the item number is zero-based):

```
Dim fcd As FormatCondition
Set fcd = txtName.FormatConditions.Item(2)
' Or, because Item is the default property:
Set fcd = txtName.FormatConditions(2)
```

Parent Returns a reference to the parent form (not the parent control). Like Application, this property has been provided only for your convenience.

Add Allows you to add a new FormatCondition object to the collection. See the next section for complete details.

Delete Deletes all the FormatCondition objects. Each individual object has its own Delete method, but using the collection's Delete method removes all the FormatCondition objects and effectively resets the collection. (Perhaps DeleteAll would have been a better name for this method?) To delete all the FormatCondition objects for a specific control, you might write code like this:

```
txtOrderDate.FormatConditions.Delete
```

To use the FormatConditions collection, you needn't do anything special—just call the Add method to add FormatCondition objects as necessary.

Working with the FormatCondition Object

Whether you add new format conditions or modify existing ones, you'll work with the properties and methods of the FormatCondition object. Table 8.2 describes the properties and methods of the FormatCondition object. The formatting properties of the object (FontBold, FontItalic, Enabled, and so on) apply to the control if its condition is met for a particular row.

TABLE 8.2: Properties and Methods of the FormatCondition Object

Member	Data Type	Description
BackColor	Long	Background color to be used for the control if this condition is met.
Enabled	Boolean	Determines whether the control should be enabled or disabled if this condition is met.
Expression1	String	(Read-only) Contains the text of the first expression for this condition.
Expression2	String	(Read-only) Contains the text for the second expression for this condition.
FontBold	Boolean	Determines whether the control's text should be bold if this condition is met.
FontItalic	Boolean	Determines whether the control's text should be italicized if this condition is met.
FontUnderline	Boolean	Determines whether the control's text should be underlined if this condition is met.
FontColor	Long	Specifies the font color to be used if this condition is met.
Operator	AcFormatConditionOperator	(Read-only) Contains the operator used for this condition. See the section "Adding New FormatCondition Objects" for more information.
Type	AcFormatConditionType	(Read-only) Contains the type of condition to be used. See the section "Adding New FormatCondition Objects" for more information.
Delete	(Method)	Deletes this FormatCondition object from the FormatConditions collection.
Modify	(Method)	Allows you to modify an existing FormatCondition object. See the section "Adding New FormatCondition Objects" for information on the (identical) parameters for this method.

For example, if you wanted to change the font color for an existing Format-Condition object, you might write code like this:

```
txtOrderDate.FormatConditions(1).FontColor = vbBlue
```

Once you've done that, if the condition contained in FormatConditions(1) is met, the text will be displayed in blue.

To delete a specific FormatCondition object, you can use its Delete method, like this:

```
txtOrderDate.FormatConditions(1).Delete
```

Note that you can only change properties that affect the formatting of the control (FontColor, BackColor, FontBold, and so on). You can only change properties that are associated with the condition (Type, Operator, Expression1, Expression2) using the Modify method, described in the section "Modifying Existing FormatCondition Objects."

Adding New FormatCondition Objects

To create a new FormatCondition (and the corresponding conditional formatting, on the form), use the Add method of a control's FormatConditions collection. This method accepts up to four parameters; the number depends on the type of condition you're creating. Specifically, the method accepts these parameters:

Type One of the following enumerated values (corresponding to the three types of conditions, in the user interface), indicating which type of condition you're creating:

- acExpression
- acFieldHasFocus
- acFieldValue

Operator One of the following enumerated values (corresponding to the operator choices in the user interface), indicating which type of operator you need. This parameter is optional, and acBetween is the default:

- acBetween (default)
- acEqual
- acGreaterThan

- acGreaterThanOrEqual
- acLessThan
- acLessThanOrEqual
- acNotBetween
- acNotEqual

Expression1 String expression containing the first value to compare against. Note that this value (and Expression2) are both strings, not variants or any other data type. If you want to send date values, for example, you'll need to enclose them yourself in "#" characters (see the sample form's code).

Expression2 String expression containing the second value to compare against. Unless the Operator is acBetween or acNotBetween, Access ignores this parameter.

You might write code like Listing 8.8 to create a new condition that checks to see if a txtOrderDates's value is between the current date and one month prior to the current date. This code first deletes any existing FormatCondition objects, and then creates a new one. Finally, the code sets the BackColor property of the FormatCondition object to be red. That is, if the value in the text box falls into the selected date range, Access will display it with a red background.

Listing 8.8

```
Dim fcd As FormatCondition

With txtOrderDate
    With .FormatConditions
        .Delete
        Set fcd = .Add(acFieldValue, acBetween, _
         "#" & Format(DateAdd("m", -1, Date), _
          "mm-dd-yyyy") & "#", _
         "#" & Format(Date, "mm-dd-yyyy") & "#")
        fcd.BackColor = vbRed
    End With
End With
```

TIP

Note the formatting applied to the dates in Listing 8.8. Just as in many other places throughout Access (basically, any place working with dates and Jet), you must format dates into the U.S. format (mm-dd-yyyy, or some variation on that). In addition, all literal dates must be enclosed in "#" characters. Although Access won't complain if you get this wrong, it also won't display the data as you've requested. When working with a FormatCondition object, you must set up dates using "#" characters delimiting the date values and a U.S. date format within the string.

Modifying Existing FormatCondition Objects

To modify an existing FormatCondition object, changing the criteria on which it's displaying data, you must use the Modify method of the object. (You can change the display characteristics using properties of the object, but you must call the Modify method to change the operator, type of criteria, or the two expressions.)

Use the Modify method just as you would the Add method of the FormatConditions collection. The parameters are the same, the issues are the same (see the previous section and its discussion of date issues), and the code is similar. Access provides both the FormatConditions.Add and FormatCondition.Modify methods so that you needn't delete a condition and re-add it to modify its behavior. Doing so would modify the order of the conditions (remember, conditions are numbered by the order in which you add them to the FormatConditions collection, and the order matters when Access processes the conditions). Using the Modify method allows you to keep a particular condition at a particular order within the collection and still change its properties.

The Sample Form

Most of the code associated with frmConditionalFormat (Figure 8.10) handles the user interface for the form, not the conditional formatting issues. The important code, shown in Listing 8.9, runs when you click the Format button on the form. Depending on the choices you've made in other controls, this code adds a new FormatCondition object to the FormatConditions collection for the txtOrderDate or txtQuantity text box.

The code starts by filling in two values, strValue1 and strValue2, with the two string values to use as criteria for the condition. If you've selected anything besides acBetween or acNotBetween for the type of condition, strValue2 won't contain real data, and Access won't even look at it. No matter which text box you're working with, the code first calls the Delete method of the FormatConditions collection for the other control (deleting all existing conditions, just to make the user interface cleaner):

```
Select Case fraCondition
    Case ctOrderDate
        Set txt = txtOrderDate
        txtQuantity.FormatConditions.Delete
        strValue1 = _
         "#" & Format(txtValue1, "mm-dd-yyyy") & "#"
        strValue2 = _
         "#" & Format(txtValue2, "mm-dd-yyyy") & "#"
    Case cttxtQuantity
        Set txt = txtQuantity
        txtOrderDate.FormatConditions.Delete
        strValue1 = txtValue1 & ""
        strValue2 = txtValue2 & ""
End Select
```

Once the code has set up the string values and set the txt variable to refer to the correct text box, the following code deletes existing conditions for the selected control, and, if you've depressed the Format toggle button, creates a new FormatCondition object, and sets its properties:

```
With txt.FormatConditions
    ' Delete the conditions, no matter what.
    ' Only create a new condition if you've selected
    ' the toggle button.
    .Delete
    If tglFormat Then
        Set fcd = .Add(acFieldValue, _
         cboConditions, strValue1, strValue2)
        fcd.ForeColor = vbRed
        fcd.FontUnderline = True
        fcd.Enabled = True
    End If
End With
```

Listing 8.9

```
Private Sub tglFormat_Click()
    Dim fcd As FormatCondition
    Dim txt As TextBox
```

```
    Dim strValue1 As String
    Dim strValue2 As String

    Select Case fraCondition
        Case ctOrderDate
            Set txt = txtOrderDate
            txtQuantity.FormatConditions.Delete
            strValue1 = _
             "#" & Format(txtValue1, "mm-dd-yyyy") & "#"
            strValue2 = _
             "#" & Format(txtValue2, "mm-dd-yyyy") & "#"
        Case cttxtQuantity
            Set txt = txtQuantity
            txtOrderDate.FormatConditions.Delete
            strValue1 = txtValue1 & ""
            strValue2 = txtValue2 & ""
    End Select
    With txt.FormatConditions
        ' Delete the conditions, no matter what.
        ' Only create a new condition if you've selected
        ' the toggle button.
        .Delete
        If tglFormat Then
            Set fcd = .Add(acFieldValue, _
             cboConditions, strValue1, strValue2)
            fcd.ForeColor = vbRed
            fcd.FontUnderline = True
        End If
    End With
End Sub
```

Form-Level Error Handling

Many errors can occur while your form is active. Some of these are standard runtime errors: perhaps a file is missing, a query your form expects to find isn't actually there, or the user does something you hadn't expected. Other errors are errors in the Access engine itself, and they can't be caught with normal error trapping. (For information on handling runtime errors, see Chapter 14.) You may find that you want to replace the standard Access behavior when these engine errors occur with behavior that is a little friendlier toward the user.

Access provides a form event to handle these errors. If you attach code to the Error event of a form, your procedure will be called whenever a trappable error occurs while the form is running. If you place your code in the form's class module (and you should, in this case), Access sends you two parameters. The syntax for the call is

```
Sub Form_Error (DataErr As Integer, Response As Integer)
```

The value *DataErr* will contain the error number for the error that just occurred, and *Response* allows you to specify how you want Access to handle the error. If your code handles the error to your satisfaction and you don't want Access to intervene or display its own message, place the value acDataErrContinue in *Response*. If you want Access to display its own error message, place acDataErrDisplay in *Response*.

The sample Form_Error subroutine shown in Listing 8.10 traps four errors that might pop up. In each case, the procedure replaces the standard Access error message with its own. If an error occurs that it hadn't planned on, the subroutine just passes the responsibility back to Access. The form frmErrorSample in CH08.MDB includes this particular error handler. In this example, the following special conditions occur:

- The State field has a table-level validation rule (only "TX" will be allowed as the state).
- The Age field is set up to accept numeric input only, between 0 and 255 (that is, it's a Byte field).
- The LastName field is set up as the primary key field, implying that a given last name can be used only once, and each row must contain a non-null value for this field.

The error-handling procedure reacts to any of the following events:

- The user enters a state other than "TX" in the State field.
- The user enters a non-numeric value in the Age field or a value out of range.
- The user creates or modifies a record such that the LastName field is empty.
- The user creates or modifies a record such that the LastName field (the primary key) is not unique.

In any of these cases, the error-handling procedure takes over and displays the prepared message. If any other engine-level error occurs, Access' own error handling prevails.

TIP

Access behaves badly if your Form_Error event procedure contains a compile-time error. It won't compile this code for you when you run the form, only when it hits the error situation. At that time it complains of the compile error and then has Access handle the error. Make sure you compile your code before running your form.

Chances are you'll find a number of uses for form-level error handling. You could replace the error handling for these and other engine errors with your own, more personal, error handler. In Access 2, the Error event was not as powerful as it might have been in that it did not, in general, allow you to handle multiuser errors. Access now handles these errors correctly. (For more information on trapping multiuser errors with the Form Error event, see Chapter 2 in *Access 2000 Developer's Handbook, Volume II.*)

NOTE

The form error handler will not trap VBA runtime errors. If your code causes an error to occur or if the user is executing your code when an error occurs, your code should deal with those errors. The form-level error handler is meant to deal with errors that occur while the form has control and you're just waiting for the user to choose some action that will place your code into action again.

Listing 8.10

```
Private Sub Form_Error( _
 DataErr As Integer, Response As Integer)

    Const adhcErrDataValidation = 3317
    Const adhcErrDataType = 2113
    Const adhcErrDuplicateKey = 3022
    Const adhcErrNullKey = 3058

    Dim strMsg As String
    Select Case DataErr
        Case adhcErrDataValidation, adhcErrDataType
            strMsg = "The data you entered does not " & _
             "fit the requirements for this field."
            strMsg = strMsg & vbCrLf & "Please try again, " & _
             "or press Escape to undo your entry."
            MsgBox strMsg, vbExclamation
            Response = acDataErrContinue
```

```
        Case adhcErrDuplicateKey
            strMsg = "You've attempted to add a record " & _
             "that duplicates an existing key value."
            strMsg = strMsg & vbCrLf & "Please try again, " & _
             "or press Escape to undo your entry."
            MsgBox strMsg, vbExclamation
            Response = acDataErrContinue

        Case adhcErrNullKey
            strMsg = "You've attempted to add a new " & _
             "record with an empty key value."
            strMsg = strMsg & vbCrLf & "Please supply " & _
             "a key value, or press Escape to undo your entry."
            MsgBox strMsg, vbExclamation
            Response = acDataErrContinue
            ' You can even place them on the right field!
            txtLastName.SetFocus

        Case Else
            ' It's an unexpected error.  Let Access handle it.
            Response = acDataErrDisplay
    End Select
End Sub
```

Controlling the Pesky Users

Much of your development time will be spent in limiting the actions users can take while your applications are running. That is, your application must be able to react to anything your users do, any key they press, any mouse button they click. The next few sections will discuss some ways you can take control over the actions users can make while running your application.

Using the Cycle Property

In 16-bit versions of Access, as you moved past the last field on a bound form, Access automatically moved to the next row of data. Moving backward (Shift+Tab) past the first control moved you to the previous row. You could work around this through a bit of work, using hidden controls and a little bit of code, but it wasn't simple, and you had to do it on each and every form for which you wanted to restrict row movement.

You can now more easily restrict movement to the current row. The Cycle property of a form allows you to cause the cursor to wrap around the current form or the current page of the form. The options for the Cycle property are listed in the following table:

Setting	Description	Value
All Records	Pressing Tab on the last control or Shift+Tab in the first control in the tab order moves to the next or previous row in the underlying data	0
Current Record	Wraps around to the first control on the form after pressing Tab on the last control, or to the last control after pressing Shift+Tab on the first control	1
Current Page	Wraps around to the first control on the page after pressing Tab on the last control, or to the last control after pressing Shift+Tab on the first control	2

Setting the Cycle property to 1 (Current Record) will handle the most common case: you'd like Access not to change the current row unless you tell it to. The sample form, frmCustomers in CH08.MDB, has its Cycle property set this way. Load it and give it a try. You'll see that you can't move to a new row using the Tab or Shift+Tab keys—you must use the navigation buttons or the PgUp or PgDn key. (If you wish to disable the PgUp and PgDn keys as well, see the next section, "Trapping Keys Globally: The KeyPreview Property.") (For multipage forms, you'll always want to set the Cycle property to 2 [Current Page]. In this situation, having the user move from page to page inadvertently using the Tab or Shift+Tab keys can ruin the look of your form.)

Trapping Keys Globally: The KeyPreview Property

There are probably many situations in which you'd like to be able to trap keystrokes before Access sends them on to the controls on the form and perhaps reacts to them on a form-wide basis—for example, disabling the PgUp and PgDn keys. Without some global key-trapping mechanism, you'd have to attach code to the KeyDown event of each and every control on the form, watching for those particular keystrokes.

Access provides a mechanism to allow you to trap keystrokes before it sends them to controls on the form: the KeyPreview property of a form routes all keys you press while that form is active to the form's key-handling events before the active control's events get them. This way, you can react to, alter, or discard the keypresses at the form level.

Keep Users on a Single Row

Imagine you've set the form's Cycle property to 1 (Current Form) and you'd also like to make sure the user can't move from row to row by pressing the PgUp or PgDn key. In Access 2, this would have been inordinately difficult, requiring you to attach code to each control's KeyDown event. Now, you can set the form's KeyPreview property to Yes and attach code like this to the form's KeyDown event:

```
Private Sub Form_KeyDown(KeyCode As Integer, _
 Shift As Integer)
    If KeyCode = vbKeyPageDown Or KeyCode = vbKeyPageUp Then
        KeyCode = 0
    End If
End Sub
```

By setting the value of KeyCode to 0, you're telling Access to disregard the keystroke altogether. The sample form frmCustomers is set up this way. The only way to move from row to row on that form is to use the built-in navigation buttons. The sample form, frmCustomers, includes the code shown above. Try opening that form and pressing the PageUp or PageDown keys. You'll see that the form simply disregards either key.

Navigate Continuous Forms as Spreadsheets

Perhaps you'd like to make your continuous forms navigable as though they were spreadsheets. Out of the box, Access treats the right-arrow and down-arrow keys the same way on a continuous form if an entire field is selected: it moves the highlight to the next field on the row or to the first field on the next row if you're on the last field of the current row. However, you might want the down-arrow key to move you to the current field in the next row, instead.

The KeyPreview property makes this possible. Once you've set the KeyPreview property to Yes, Access routes all keystrokes to the form's Key events first. Using a KeyDown event procedure such as the following causes Access to move to the previous row when you press the up-arrow key or the next row if you press the down-arrow key. In either case, the code sets the value of KeyCode to 0 once it's done, so Access doesn't try to handle the keypress itself once this procedure has done its work.

```
Private Const adhcErrInvalidRow = 2105

Private Sub Form_KeyDown( _
 KeyCode As Integer, Shift As Integer)
    ' Code removed here...

    ' Of course, pressing up or down could cause an
    ' error, when you get to the top or bottom of the
    ' set.  Make sure and trap for errors, to avoid
    ' unsightly error alerts!
    On Error GoTo HandleErrors
    Select Case KeyCode
        Case vbKeyDown
            DoCmd.GoToRecord Record:=acNext
            KeyCode = 0
        Case vbKeyUp
            DoCmd.GoToRecord Record:=acPrevious
            KeyCode = 0
        Case Else
            ' Do nothing at all!
    End Select

ExitHere:
    Exit Sub

HandleErrors:
    Select Case Err.Number
        Case adhcErrInvalidRow
```

```
            KeyCode = 0
        Case Else
            MsgBox "Error: " & Err.Description & _
             " (" & Err.Number & ")"
    End Select
    Resume ExitHere
End Sub
```

To see this procedure in action, take a look at frmCustomersTabular, shown in Figure 8.14. This form allows you to toggle the key handling on and off so you can see how it feels both ways.

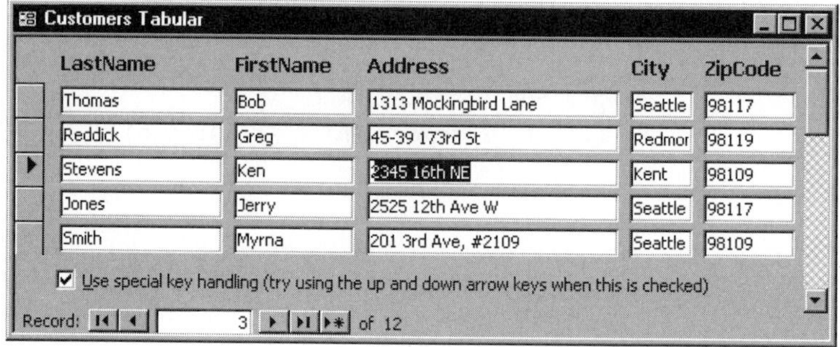

FIGURE 8.14:

Use the form's KeyPreview property to handle keystrokes on a form-wide basis.

TIP

Access includes intrinsic constants representing most of the keystrokes you'd ever want to use in your applications. (CH08.MDB uses these constants in several of its examples, including frmCustomersTabular, frmCalendar, and frmCalc.) To see the list yourself, open the Object Browser window (press F2 from the module editor), and then browse down the list of items until you find the objects starting with *ac*. These objects are the enumerations for all the Access constants. The Object Browser will show, in its right-hand window (see Figure 8.15), a list of all the constants for each enumeration Access provides. You'll also find a list of all the constants provided by VBA, including the useful keycode names (under the KeyCodeConstants enumeration). Those are the key constants you'll use in your key-handling event procedures.

FIGURE 8.15:

The Object Browser allows you to find a list of all the key constants.

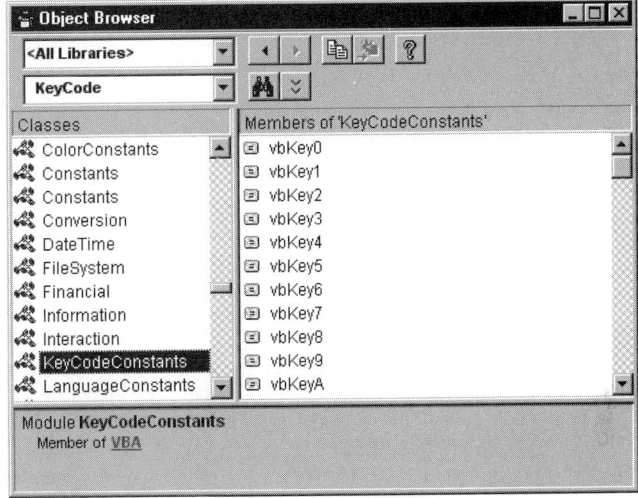

Displaying Multiple Instances of Forms

In Access 2, if you wanted to display a form more than once in a given session, you needed to create as many physical copies of the actual form as you wanted to display. Starting in Access 97, you can open multiple instances of the same form (or report—the mechanism works the same for either) without making physical copies. There is no user interface for this functionality. If you want to display multiple instances, you'll need to write VBA code to make it happen. This whole concept is nothing other than the same issues discussed in Chapter 3. Under the covers, a form is really a class module with a user interface attached and, just as you can create multiple instances of a class, you can create multiple instances of a form.

NOTE

We could just as easily have placed this section of this chapter in Chapter 9, which discusses reports, but we feel you're more likely to need multiple instances of forms than reports, so we decided to place it here.

Although you can create multiple instances of a master form, the original form is the only one for which you can permanently alter properties. Access will not save any changes you make to the instances of the original form, although you are allowed to make programmatic changes to the properties of any instance. You won't be able to switch the form instances into Design view, so any changes you wish to make to the instances will be through code, and they'll be temporary.

What Happens When You Create a New Instance?

When you create multiple instances of forms or reports, each new instance has its own set of properties, its own current row (if it's bound), and its own window. All instances of the same form or report share the same *name*, however, and this is a concept that takes some getting used to. Any place in VBA that requires you to supply a form or report name, therefore, will be generally useless when you are working with multiple instances. A side issue here is that because all the instances share the same name, you won't be able to use syntax like this:

```
Debug.Print Forms("frmCustomer").Caption
```

and expect to find any of the extra instances of frmCustomer. (On the other hand, Access does add an item to the Forms collection for each form instance you create, and you can always refer to these items by number. See Chapter 6 for information on the different ways you can refer to objects in collections.) Although Access does not create a named element of the Forms or Reports collection for each instance, it does add a reference in the collection, so this code will still work, even if several instances of forms are open:

```
For Each frm In Forms
    Debug.Print frm.Caption
Next frm
```

Because each form instance can (and should) have a unique caption, the previous example can actually be useful if you want a list of all the open forms, regardless of whether they're "real" forms or instances of real forms.

How Do You Create a New Instance?

Creating a new instance is simple: just declare a form variable and set it equal to a new form:

```
Dim frm As Form_frmCustomers
Set frm = New Form_frmCustomers
```

The "Form_" syntax indicates to Access that you want a new member of the form class that's named frmCustomers. The name of the form after the "Form_" must be a real, existing form, and by using the New keyword, you are asking Access to create a new instance for you. As soon as the variable referring to the new form goes out of scope, Access destroys the new form instance. What's more, using the New keyword creates the new form with its Visible property set to False; if you want to actually *see* the form, you'll need to set its Visible property to True.

TIP

You'll get slightly better performance if you dimension the variable as the specific form class ("As Form_frmCustomers", for example, rather than "As Form"). On the other hand, if you want your variable to be able to refer to multiple different classes of forms, you can use "As Form" to declare the variable.

NOTE

Creating multiple instances of forms is really no different than creating multiple instances of any class. Chapter 3 contains more information on creating multiple class instances, and all the concepts apply here, as well. The only difference is that when you want to instantiate a form class, you must provide its name as "Form_" before the real class name. In addition, when you create an instance of a form, you can set its Visible property to True and see the object on screen. Try that with a normal class module!

It should be pretty clear, at this point, that if you write a procedure like this one:

```
Sub BadIdea()
    Dim frm As Form_frmCustomers
    Set frm = New Form_frmCustomers
    frm.Visible = True
End Sub
```

you're never going to actually see that new form. Because Access will destroy the form when the reference to it goes out of scope as soon as this procedure is complete, the form you created in it is history. What's the solution, then? You need to find some place to store that form reference until you're finished with it.

A simple solution is to make frm a static, module, or public variable. That way it simply will never go out of scope. If you want to close it manually, you can always use code like this:

```
frm.SetFocus
DoCmd.Close
Set frm = Nothing
```

which sets focus to the form, closes it, and then releases the connection between the form variable and the object it was referring to. (Remember, you can't use the name of the object to close it. The DoCmd.Close method requires you to specify a form's name if you attempt to close any form besides the current form, so you'll first have to make your form the current form and then close it.)

A Better Solution

If you're going to be working with more than one extra instance of a form, you'll need a better way to manage the references to those new instances. One solution is to store the form references in a user-defined collection. (See Chapter 3 for more information on user-defined collections.)

For example, try out frmCustomers in CH08.MDB. Open the form itself, and then click the New Instance button a few times. Each time you click the button, you're running code that's creating a new form instance and placing a reference to it in a user-defined collection. If you want a list of all the extra instances, click the List Instances button on any of the forms, which will write a list of instance captions to the Immediate window. Figure 8.16 shows what such a test might look like.

FIGURE 8.16:

Use the New Instance button to create multiple instances of the main form.

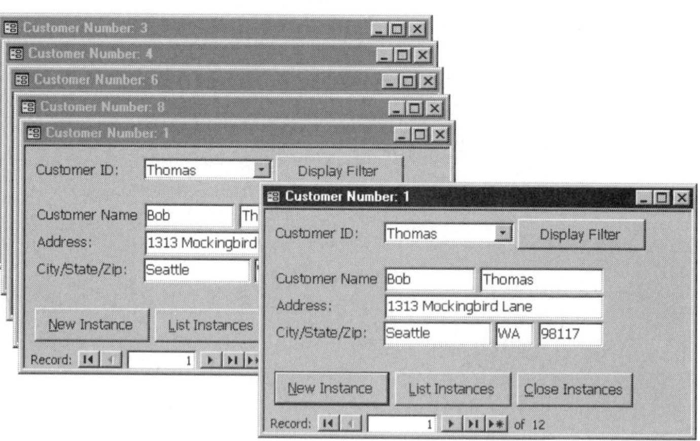

Every time you click the New Instance button, you're calling the New-CustomerForm procedure (in basFormInstance), which creates a new instance for frmCustomers and adds that new form reference to colForms, the collection of form instances:

```
Dim colForms As New Collection
Private mintI As Integer
```

```
Public Sub NewCustomerForm(frmOld As Form_frmCustomers)
    Dim frm As Form_frmCustomers

    Set frm = New Form_frmCustomers
    mintI = mintI + 1
    ' The Key value must be a string, so tack on a
    ' null string to force the conversion. You'll
    ' use the hWnd later when you try and
    ' remove the window from the collection of windows.
    colForms.Add Item:=frm, Key:=frm.hWnd & ""
    frm.Caption = "Customers " & mintI
    DoCmd.MoveSize (mintI + 1) * 80, (mintI + 1) * 350

    ' Pass along the filter information.
    frm.Filter = frmOld.Filter
    frm.FilterOn = frmOld.FilterOn
    frm.Visible = True
End Sub
```

NewCustomerForm increments a global variable, mintI, to keep track of which instance is the newest. That integer becomes part of the new instance's caption. When NewCustomerForm adds the new form reference to colForms, it stores the form reference itself, along with the hWnd (the window handle, guaranteed to be unique) as the key for the item. That way, later code can retrieve an item from the collection, given its window handle. (Remember, each form instance you create has the same name, so you can't refer to any instance individually by name.) The procedure also places the new form at a convenient location, sets its Filter and FilterOn properties to match the original form's, and then makes the new form visible.

Now that you've created these new form instances, you have a collection (colForms) that contains a reference to each of the forms. You can iterate through that collection (as you'll do when you attempt to close them all) or refer to a single form, given its hWnd.

Closing a Form Instance

If you close one of the form instances, you'll want to make sure the collection of form references is up to date. To make that happen, we've attached code to the form's Close event that removes the particular form from the collection:

```
Public Sub RemoveInstance(frm As Form_frmCustomers)
    ' Each form calls this code when it closes itself.
```

```
        ' This is also hooked to the main
        ' form's Close event, so skip over the
        ' error that occurs when you try to close the
        ' main form (which doesn't have an entry in the
        ' collection!)
        On Error Resume Next
        colForms.Remove frm.hWnd & ""
    End Sub
```

Each form calls the following code in its Close event procedure:

```
Call RemoveInstance(Me)
```

That way, the collection of instances always accurately reflects the current group of form instances.

NOTE

The original form isn't in the collection of form instances—it never added itself, only the new instances did that. On the other hand, it has the call to RemoveInstance in its Close event, and its form reference is not in the collection. To avoid the error that would occur when trying to remove the form itself from the collection of instances, we just set up RemoveInstance so it doesn't complain about errors.

Closing All the Instances

If you want to close all the instances of the main form, you have a few choices. Here are two options:

- Remove each form reference from the collection. This forces each one to go out of scope and thus will close the instances.
- Set the focus to each instance in turn and then explicitly close each form.

We chose the second method, for a very specific reason. (The first method works fine in this simple example, and the code to do it appears in the CloseInstances procedure, although it's commented out.) If your forms were complex and perhaps had validation rules that had to be met, it's possible that the form wouldn't be allowed to close. Imagine, for example, that you hadn't fulfilled a validation rule. The second method, closing each form explicitly, guarantees that Access doesn't close the form before removing its form reference from the user-defined collection. It's just a cleaner way to close the forms, even though it does require physically setting the focus to each form in turn.

The code that's called from the Close Instances button, therefore, is quite simple (it's mostly comments):

```
Public Sub CloseInstances()
    Dim frm As Form_frmCustomers
    ' The user may have closed some or all of the
    ' forms by hand.  Skip any errors that
    ' occur because the collection count
    ' doesn't match reality.
    On Error GoTo HandleErrors
    For Each frm In colForms
        ' Go to the form, and then close it.
        ' You can't close it given the name, because
        ' all the form instances have the same name.
        frm.SetFocus
        DoCmd.Close
        ' You could also use
        '   colForms.Remove 1
        ' to remove the first element
        ' of the collection, over and over,
        ' but what happens if you can't close
        ' the form for some reason (Key violation,
        ' for example)? Explicitly closing
        ' the form is safer.

    Next frm
    mintI = 0

ExitHere:
    Exit Sub

HandleErrors:
    Resume ExitHere
End Sub
```

All the example code for this simple test case is in basFormInstance. You'll need to modify it for any example in which you use it (because it requires the actual name of the form you're working with as part of its code), but the example ought to at least get you started.

NOTE

In this example, one form was different from all the rest: the original form. This needn't be the case. That is, you don't have to actually open the "seed" form in order to make instances of it. The form you refer to when you create the new instance can be closed, and as long as it's in the current database, Access can find it and create a new instance of that class of form. If you follow this technique, all open forms with the same name are equivalent—they're clones of the master.

Using Multiple Instances for Pop-up Forms

Earlier in the chapter, in the "Creating Pop-up Forms" section, you learned how to use the acDialog WindowMode value to open the form as a pop-up form. That is, while that form is open and visible, code stops running, and you can't work with any other part of the Access user interface. One problem with that technique is that there's no way to modify any of the form's properties before you display it. There's just no way to open a form invisibly, set some properties, and then have it displayed in such a way that code will stop running.

Using the techniques discussed in this section, however, you can work around this limitation. All you need to do is find some way to pause execution of code while your form is visible and determine how the form was dismissed once your code starts running again. To make this possible, we've added code to the basCalendar module discussed previously in the chapter. Now, rather than calling adhDoCalendar to display the calendar and wait until it's been dismissed, you can call adhDoCalendarLoop. This procedure opens a new instance of the form invisibly, allows you to modify properties of the form, and then calls the ShowFormAndWait procedure (in the same module) to display the form and wait. This procedure returns True if the form was dismissed by its OK button and False if it was dismissed by its Cancel button.

Listing 8.11 shows the adhDoCalendarLoop function. (Although you have no reason to call this procedure rather than the previously discussed adhDoCalendar, it demonstrates how you might use this technique.) The procedure declares a variable, frm, that will refer to the form instance. Then, after manipulating the input values, it creates a new instance of the calendar form, allows you to modify properties of that form, and calls the ShowFormAndWait function. If this procedure returns True, adhDoCalendarLoop returns the selected date and closes the form. Otherwise, it simply returns Null.

Listing 8.11

```
Public Function adhDoCalendarLoop( _
 Optional ByVal varStartDate As Variant) As Variant
    Dim dtmStartDate As Date
    Dim frm As Form_frmCalendar

    If IsMissing(varStartDate) Then
        dtmStartDate = Date
    Else
        If IsDate(varStartDate) Then
            dtmStartDate = varStartDate
        Else
            ' OK, so they passed a value that
            ' wasn't a date.
            ' Just use today's date in that case, too.
            dtmStartDate = Date
        End If
    End If

    ' Open the form module (effectively, loading an
    ' instance of the form, as well). Then, set
    ' properties of that form.
    Set frm = New Form_frmCalendar
    frm.ShowOKCancel = False
    frm.Value = dtmStartDate

    ' Call the ShowFormAndWait procedure. This
    ' returns True if the form is still loaded,
    ' but invisible, or False if it's been unloaded.
    If ShowFormAndWait(frm) Then
        ' If the form is still loaded, then get the
        ' final chosen date from the form.  If it isn't,
        ' return Null.
        adhDoCalendarLoop = frm.Value
        DoCmd.Close acForm, adhcCalendarForm
    Else
        adhDoCalendarLoop = Null
    End If
End Function
```

The ShowFormAndWait procedure (also in basCalendar), shown in Listing 8.12, loops infinitely until you close or hide the form. It takes, as its only parameter, a reference to an opened form. (Note that it accepts a value declared "As Form", so that it can work with any form. This procedure can manage any form you have opened, but be aware that it cannot work if you've opened multiple instances of the form. Because it must use the form's name in order to determine if the form's open or not, and all form instances have the same name, this code will fail for forms with multiple instances.)

ShowFormAndWait sets its form's Visible property to True and goes into an infinite loop. Each time through the loop, the code checks to see whether the form is still loaded and whether it's still visible. If either one of these checks fails, the code exits with the appropriate value. You might note the use of the DoEvents statement and the counter value in the procedure, as well. Because all those checks to see if the form's loaded can be expensive (taking processor cycles away from your foreground task), we've modified the code so that it checks the form's condition only every 1000 times through the loop. (That number worked well for us—you may want to increase or decrease that value.)

Listing 8.12

```
Public Function ShowFormAndWait(frm As Form) As Boolean
    Dim blnCancelled As Boolean
    Dim lngLoop As Long
    Dim strName As String

    Const adhcInterval As Long = 1000

    strName = frm.Name
    frm.Visible = True

    Do
        If lngLoop Mod adhcInterval Then
            DoEvents
            ' Is the form still open?
            If Not IsOpen(strName) Then
                blnCancelled = True
                Exit Do
            End If
            ' OK, it's still open. Is it visible?
            If Not frm.Visible Then
```

```
                blnCancelled = False
                Exit Do
            End If
            lngLoop = 0
        End If
        lngLoop = lngLoop + 1
    Loop
    ShowFormAndWait = Not blnCancelled
End Function
```

You can use this technique whenever you have the need to open a form invisibly, set one or more properties of the form, and make the form visible and modal. It's definitely not the most attractive possible solution, but it works well and is easily transportable from one application to another.

NOTE

This example shows one huge difference between Access forms and Visual Basic and VBA forms. In both those other forms packages, you can load a form, set its properties, and then display it modally (to halt the running code in the calling module). In Access, the technique in this section is the only way we know to accomplish that same goal. Perhaps one day all Microsoft products will share a common forms package. For now, you need to know the tricks of each different forms package that you use.

Using Subforms in Your Applications

Subforms are most useful for displaying data from one-to-many relationships. In previous versions of Access, they were often used as a means of grouping controls on forms. You may find that the tab control, however, does a better job of grouping controls, for the most part. (See Chapter 7 for more information on using the tab control.) The next few sections deal with areas of subform use that may be giving you difficulty.

TIP

New in Access 2000, you can display a table or query, in datasheet view, in a subform control. Set the SourceObject property to be Table.TableName or Query.QueryName, and you've got a simple form/subform arrangement. In this section, we'll only be discussing using forms as the source object for a subform control.

Nested Subforms versus Separate, Synchronized Subforms

As long as you're interested in displaying one-to-many relationships, you'll find it easy to drag-and-drop a form onto another form. If you've defined relationships for the tables involved, it becomes even easier, because Access fills in the LinkChildFields and LinkMasterFields properties for you.

This method has its good and bad sides. If you nest subforms, you're limited to having at most three levels of data: the main form plus two levels of nested subforms. On the other hand, forms involving nested subforms are simple to set up. Figure 8.17 shows an example from CH08.MDB, frmNested, which includes frmNestedOrders, which in turn includes frmNestedOrderDetail. The two inner forms are linked on OrderId, and the two outer forms are linked on CustomerID. This example requires absolutely no macros or VBA code.

FIGURE 8.17:

Access makes it easy to create a form with two nested subforms, as long as you need only three levels and don't need to display any but the lowest-level forms in Form view.

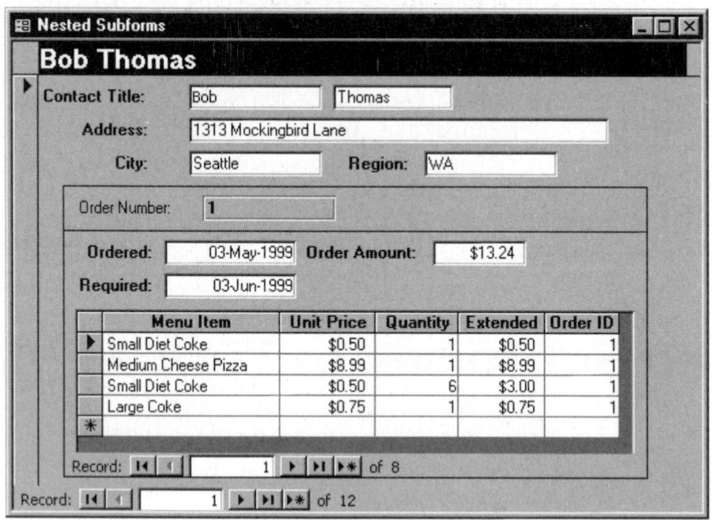

Although you'll find it easy to create examples like frmNested, you'll also run into some limitations if you want the form to look much different from the example. You can't, for example, make any form except the lowest-level form appear in Datasheet or Continuous Forms view, and you can't use more than two subforms. If you want any of the intermediate forms to appear in Datasheet or Continuous

Forms view or if you need more than three levels of data displayed, you'll have to consider some other method.

The syntax for referring to objects on subforms, in its most complete form, can be daunting. For example, to retrieve a value from txtName on the subform for which the ControlName property is frmSub1, which lives on frmMain, you could use the syntax

```
varName = Forms("frmMain").Controls("frmSub1"). _
  Form.Controls("txtName")
```

The reference to frmSub1 takes you to the control that contains the subform. The ".Form" gets you to the actual form property of that control, from which you can access any control on the form through the Controls collection.

Referencing controls on nested subforms follows the same pattern. To reference a check box named chkAlive on frmSub2, which is a control on frmSub1, which is a control on frmMain, you'd use the syntax

```
fAlive = Forms("frmMain").Controls("frmSub1"). _
  Form.Controls("frmSub2").Form.Controls("chkAlive")
```

Fortunately, Access makes this all a lot easier. The Controls collection is the default collection of a Form object, so referencing it is optional. In addition, the Form property is the default property of a subform control, so the ".Form" is optional. Therefore, you can refer to objects on subforms with a simple syntax. For example, the previous reference to a control on a subsubform could be condensed to:

```
fAlive = Forms("frmMain")("frmSub1")("frmSub2")("chkAlive")
```

Yes, it's true: if you've struggled with subform references in Access 2, you can disregard all you've learned. The Form property is now the default property for the subform control, and the default collection for a form object is the Controls collection. Both references are therefore optional.

One more concern: the expression might be able to be abbreviated, depending on the current scope when you need to retrieve the value. For example, if you were trying to retrieve the value on frmSub2 as part of the ControlSource expression for a text box on frmSub1, you'd only need to refer to:

```
frmSub2("chkAlive")
```

because you're already on the form contained in frmSub1.

TIP

Although we mentioned this in Chapter 7, it can't hurt to reiterate. This issue hits so many Access developers, we thought we'd mention it again here: when referring to controls within a subform, use the name of the subform *control*, not the form contained in the subform control, in any references. From your form's point of view, the name of the contained form is irrelevant once that form's been loaded into memory. It's the name of the subform control that determines how you access items within that subform.

Using Synchronized Subforms

To avoid the limitations mentioned earlier, when you need to display multiple concurrent subforms, we suggest that you investigate using synchronized subforms, as opposed to using nested subforms. Figure 8.18 shows frmSubformSynch with its included subforms, frmSubformSynchOrders and frmNestedOrderDetail. Instead of nesting the two subforms, frmSubformSynch synchronizes the two subforms individually. The mechanism is simple: in the "primary" subform's Current event, the example fills in a (normally) hidden text box. The code might look something like this:

```
Private Sub Form_Current()
    ' Disregard errors that would occur if you
    ' opened this subform as a normal form, without
    ' a parent property or without a textbox
    ' named txtLink.
    On Error Resume Next

    ' Using the Parent property allows this form to
    ' be used as a subform on any form which happens
    ' to use a textbox named txtLink to link it with
    ' other subforms.
    Me.Parent("txtLink") = [OrderId]
End Sub
```

TIP

You needn't actually use the LinkChildFields and LinkMasterFields properties if you don't want to use them. The section "Managing Linking Yourself," later in the chapter, shows how you can manage all the issues yourself. Doing this work yourself can give you greater flexibility than using the built-in linking mechanism.

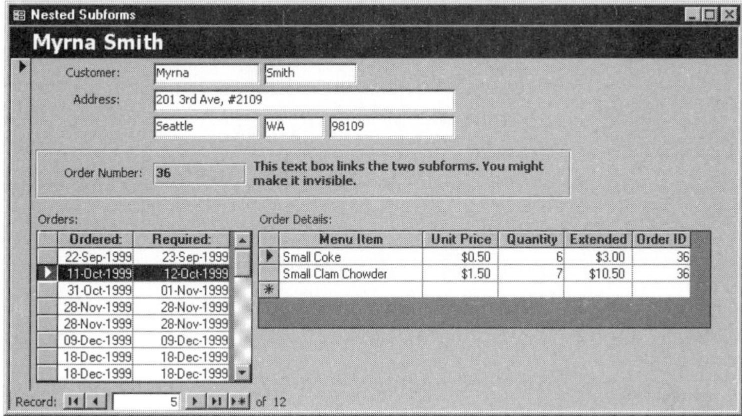

FIGURE 8.18:

frmSyncMain with its included subforms

The error handler takes care of the case in which you might try to open the form on its own (without its being a subform of a form that contains a linking text box named txtLink).

The "secondary" subform's LinkMasterFields property is set to that same text box, with its LinkChildFields property set to the control name of the text box (OrderID in this example). Therefore, as the user moves from row to row in frmSubformSynchOrders, frmNestedOrderDetail will show only the orders with the same OrderID field as the chosen row in frmSubformSynchOrders. This concept could be extended even further. If there were a one-to-many relationship starting from frmNestedOrderDetail, its Current event could fill in a text box to which yet another form could be linked with its LinkMasterFields property.

Is It Loaded as a Subform?

You may have instances in which you'll want a form to work a certain way if loaded as a subform but a different way when loaded as a stand-alone form. For example, you may want to hide certain controls if the form is currently a subform.

There's no built-in function or property to get this information for you, but it's easy to write one yourself. The trick is that subforms always have a Parent property that refers to a real form, and stand-alone forms do not. Attempting to retrieve the Parent property of the form when it's not being used as a subform will always trigger a runtime error, and you can count on this error as you perform your test.

NOTE

You could also take advantage of the fact that forms opened as subforms aren't members of the Forms collection. Therefore, you could investigate the Forms collection and check for the existence of your form to determine if the form has been opened as a subform. We've selected a different technique, but either works effectively.

The following function, IsSubForm, from basIsSubform, returns True if the form you inquire about is currently loaded as a subform and False if it's a stand-alone form. It does its work by attempting to retrieve the Name property of its parent. If that triggers a runtime error, you can be assured the form is not a subform.

```
Public Function adhIsSubForm(frm As Form) As Boolean
    ' Is the form referenced in the
    ' parameter currently loaded as a subform?
    ' Check its Parent property to find out.

    Dim strName As String
    On Error Resume Next
    strName = frm.Parent.Name
    adhIsSubForm = (Err.Number = 0)
    Err.Clear
End Function
```

To call the function, you could use code like this in your form's event procedures:

```
If adhIsSubform(Me) Then
    ' It's a subform.
Else
    ' You know it's not a subform.
End If
```

TIP

The FormInfo class, discussed later in the chapter, includes a version of this procedure as a property of the class. If you're using that class as part of an application, you won't need a separate copy of this code. In addition, many of the self-contained classes include a local copy of this or a similar procedure. Normally, you won't need to import basIsSubForm unless you're creating new code that doesn't already include this functionality.

Managing Linking Yourself

You needn't actually use the LinkChildFields and LinkMasterFields properties of the subform control in order to use the subform control in a parent/child relationship. Setting these properties causes Access to do these three things:

- Filter the subform to show only records where the child fields matches the master field values.
- Fill in the values from the master fields to the child fields when adding a new record to the subform.
- Requery the subform when the master field values change. (You might, for example, use a combo box on the main form as a mechanism for choosing the master field—a CustomerID value, for example. In that case, you need both the main form to redisplay the correct data and the subform to redisplay, as well.)

If you want to have a subform work as if these properties were set, you can easily write the code necessary to emulate this behavior. This way, you can extend and enhance the normal form/subform interactions. In the sample project, the pair of forms frmSubformLinks and frmSubformLinksSub demonstrates this behavior. If you want to manage the linkage between a form and its subform yourself, you can follow these steps:

1. Create a query containing all the fields you'll need for your subform. Set the criterion on the query to filter based on the LinkMasterFields values you would have used in the main form. As an example, see qrySubformLinks in the sample project. The SQL expression there is as follows:

```
SELECT [OrderId], [OrderDate], [CustomerId], [OrderTakerId],
 [DeliveryDate], [DeliveryTime], [PaymentMethod]
FROM tblOrder
WHERE
 (((CustomerId)=[Forms]![frmSubformLinks]![CustomerID]));
```

2. In the form you'd like to use as a subform, add code that fills in the fields you would have used as the LinkChildFields, so that if you add a new row, the values are pulled from the parent form. You'll want to call the IsSubForm function from the previous section, so you don't attempt to call this code when the form is loaded normally. The sample form, frmSubformLinksSub, includes this code:

```
Private Sub Form_BeforeUpdate(Cancel As Integer)
```

```
        If IsSubForm(Me) Then
            If IsNull(Me.CustomerId) Then
                Me.CustomerId = Me.Parent.CustomerId
            End If
        End If
    End Sub
```

3. If you have a situation where you can select the LinkMasterFields without moving to a new row on the main form (a combo box, perhaps), you'll need to add code to the AfterUpdate event of the control that makes the selection, forcing the subform to requery. The sample forms don't need this extra code.

Once you've got this groundwork laid out, you can control exactly how you display hierarchical data in Access. Don't get fooled into thinking you must use the LinkMasterFields/LinkChildField pair of properties—it's not required.

Creating Self-Disabling Navigation Buttons

Access provides several methods for your users to move from one row of data on a form to another. You can use the standard form navigation buttons, but they provide no flexibility to you as a developer. You can also use the Button Wizard to create the navigation buttons on your form. In each case, the solutions lack one feature that many clients request: buttons that don't do anything to be disabled. That is, if users are already at the last row in the recordset, the button that takes them to the last row ought to be disabled. If they're on the new row, the button that takes them there ought not be available. Few things are more frustrating to the end user than clicking a button and having nothing happen or, worse, clicking a button and finding out the action isn't available.

FIGURE 8.19:

fsubNavigation doesn't do much on its own—it needs to be used as a subform in order to be useful.

To make it easy for you to turn off the built-in navigation buttons and create your own replacements, we've supplied the form fsubNavigation (see Figure 8.19). On its own, this form doesn't do anything. When embedded as a subform on a bound form, however, fsubNavigation automatically hooks itself up to the parent form and reacts to and raises the necessary events, so that it works as a custom set of navigation buttons. Figure 8.20 shows the sample form, frmNavigate, which includes both the built-in navigation buttons and the subform, fsubNavigation, embedded. (We've left the standard Access navigation buttons enabled for this sample form so you can compare the two sets. Of course, on a real form, you'd set the NavigationButtons property to No if you were going to use fsubNavigation.)

FIGURE 8.20:

Once you embed fsubNavigation on another bound form, it comes to life.

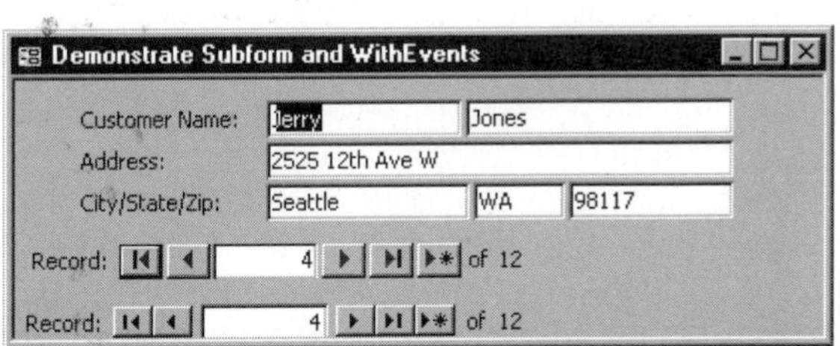

Because fsubNavigation is used as a subform, you gain some useful capabilities:

- You can easily include it on as many forms as you need within your application without having to cut and paste or copy code. When you embed the subform on a main form, all the code comes with it.
- If you want to modify all the navigation controls for all your forms (perhaps to remove the New button, or change the bitmaps), you only need to make changes in one location.
- If you want several different looks for your navigation controls, you can simply make multiple copies of fsubNavigation and embed the different versions on different forms.
- There's only one copy of the navigation code. If you need to make a change, it affects all the forms that have the subform embedded.

The next few sections describe the details involved in how fsubNavigation does its job. You may want to open fsubNavigation in Design view and display its class module, so you can follow along with the discussion.

WARNING

The demo form, fsubNavigation, uses WithEvents to grab onto events of the main form and react to them. For this to work, the main form must have a module. If your main form doesn't already have a module associated with it, you can simply set the HasModule property of the form to be Yes, in Design view. This is true of any situation where you want to react to a form's events from a different class—the form must have its own module, or Access simply doesn't raise any events for the form.

Understanding the HasModule Property

When you load a form, Access must also load the module attached to that form. If there's no module, the form loads more quickly. (Sure, it's more complex than that, but at least you get the idea.) If you're working with forms that contain no code, you'll want to be sure to set their HasModule property to False, guaranteeing the fastest possible load time for the form. On the other hand, if you're using a WithEvents variable to react to events of the form (as we do often, throughout this book), the form must have an associated module. That is, if the HasModule property is False (or No), Access doesn't even bother raising events for the form, so any code outside the form expecting to react to the form's events will not get called by Access.

Forms and Their Data

As mentioned in the earlier section, "Using the Recordset and RecordsetClone Properties," every bound form acts as a moving "window" for the form's underlying data. At any given time, your form can display one or more rows from that dataset, and your VBA code can also manipulate that dataset. You can create a Recordset variable and assign to it the value of the form's RecordsetClone property. In this manner, Access allows you to view and modify the same set of data that the user sees on the form. Because Access maintains separate record pointers for the form and for its underlying recordset, you can move around freely in the recordset, while the form's displayed record doesn't change at all.

In addition, when Access loads the data in a recordset, it creates a unique bookmark value for each row of data. You can read the Bookmark property of the form or of the underlying recordset. In either case, you're retrieving the bookmark associated with the current row. You can set the Bookmark property, as well. This allows you to save and retrieve the form's bookmark independently of the form's recordset bookmark.

When you first retrieve a copy of the form's recordset (using the RecordsetClone property), your position in the recordset is officially undefined, and you'll need to position yourself on a particular row. You can use any of the Move… (MoveFirst, MoveLast, MoveNext, MovePrevious) methods to position the record pointer, or you can equate the recordset and the form's Bookmark properties.

Doing so sets the current row in your recordset to be the same as the row currently shown on the form. Code to do this might look like the following:

```
Dim rst as DAO.RecordSet
Set rst = frmMain.RecordSetClone
rst.Bookmark = frmMain.Bookmark
```

Hooking Up the Subform

In the subform's Load event procedure, you'll find code, shown in Listing 8.13, that links the subform with the main form. The subform's Declarations area contains a WithEvents reference to the main form, frmMain. If the subform's Load event procedure determines that it's been loaded as a subform, it sets up a hook to the parent form, so it can react to events of its parent:

```
mfIsSubform = IsSubForm(Me)
If mfIsSubform Then
    Set frmMain = Me.Parent
    ' code removed
End If
```

Next, the Load event procedure sets up properties of the parent form, so the subform can do its job. (Note that none of the changes is permanent—they're all only effective while the form is open. When it's closed, all these changes are lost.) The code ensures that the necessary event properties include the text "[Event Procedure]" as the property setting. (Access doesn't bother raising the event for outside objects to sink unless it thinks it must. Therefore, you must make sure that all events you want to trap include the text "[Event Procedure]" in the associated property.)

```
' Code won't run unless the words
' "[Event Procedure]" show up in the
' main form's event properties.
frmMain.OnCurrent = "[Event Procedure]"
frmMain.OnDirty = "[Event Procedure]"
```

Finally, if you left the adhcCalcTotalRecs constant with the default (True) value, the code will calculate the total number of records available on the form and display that information immediately. If your form is bound to a large recordset, however, you may want to set this value to be False. It might take some measurable time to perform the calculation, but most people expect this value to be immediately available:

```
' Calculate the total number of records?
If adhcCalcTotalRecs Then
    Dim rst As DAO.Recordset
    Set rst = frmMain.RecordsetClone
```

```
    rst.MoveFirst
    rst.MoveLast
    txtTotalRecs = rst.RecordCount
    Set rst = Nothing
End If
```

Listing 8.13 contains the entire procedure.

Listing 8.13

```
Private WithEvents frmMain As Form

Private Sub Form_Load()
    mfIsSubform = IsSubForm(Me)
    If mfIsSubform Then
        Set frmMain = Me.Parent


        ' Code won't run unless the words
        ' "[Event Procedure]" show up in the
        ' main form's event properties.
        frmMain.OnCurrent = "[Event Procedure]"
        frmMain.OnDirty = "[Event Procedure]"

        ' Calculate the total number of records?
        If adhcCalcTotalRecs Then
            Dim rst As DAO.Recordset
            Set rst = frmMain.RecordsetClone
            rst.MoveFirst
            rst.MoveLast
            txtTotalRecs = rst.RecordCount
            Set rst = Nothing
        End If
    End If


ExitHere:
    Exit Sub

HandleErrors:
    Select Case Err.Number
        Case Else
            MsgBox "Error: " & _
```

```
            Err.Description & _
            " (" & Err.Number & ")"
    End Select
    Resume ExitHere
End Sub
```

Once you've hooked up the subform with its parent, you can sink events of the parent form from within the subform's class module. In this example, the subform provides code for the main form's Current and KeyDown events.

Controlling Row Movement

Two issues are involved in controlling the row movement programmatically:

- Moving from row to row
- Disabling the correct buttons at the correct time

The issues involved in moving from row to row are simple. Each button calls, from its Click event, a distinct procedure in the form's module. Each of these event procedures calls into a common private procedure NavMove, which performs the action. For example, the First button calls this procedure:

```
Private Sub cmdFirst_Click()
    ' Move to the first row on a form.
    Call NavMove(acFirst)
End Sub
```

(The constants acLast, acPrevious, acNewRec, acNext, and acLast are all defined by Access as part of the AcRecord enumeration.) NavMove (Listing 8.14) uses the Move… methods of the form's recordset to move about, rather than using the GotoRecord method, because you can control the movement with more precision, trapping errors as necessary, if you move in the form's recordset first and then make the form display the new record once you've found it in the recordset.

Listing 8.14

```
Private Sub NavMove(lngWhere As AcRecord)
    '
    ' Move to the correct row in the form's recordset,
    ' depending on which button was pushed.  This code doesn't
```

```
    ' really need to check for errors, since the buttons
    ' that would cause errors have been disabled already.
    '
    Dim rst As DAO.Recordset
    Dim fAtNew As Boolean

    Const adhcErrNoCurrentRow = 3021

    On Error GoTo HandleErrors
    If lngWhere = acNewRec Then
        DoCmd.GoToRecord _
         acForm, frmMain.Name, Record:=acNewRec
    Else
        fAtNew = frmMain.NewRecord
        Set rst = frmMain.RecordsetClone
        rst.Bookmark = frmMain.Bookmark
        Select Case lngWhere
            Case acFirst
                rst.MoveFirst
            Case acPrevious
                If fAtNew Then
                    rst.MoveLast
                Else
                    rst.MovePrevious
                End If
            Case acNext
                rst.MoveNext
            Case acLast
                rst.MoveLast
        End Select
        frmMain.Bookmark = rst.Bookmark
    End If

ExitHere:
    Me.Repaint
    Exit Sub

HandleErrors:
    If Err.Number = adhcErrNoCurrentRow And _
     frmMain.NewRecord Then
        Resume Next
    Else
        MsgBox Err.Description & " (" & Err.Number & ")"
```

```
        End If
        Resume ExitHere
    End Sub
```

In theory, this code should be all you need to move around in your recordset. There are two problems, though. This code won't handle the disabling of unavailable buttons. It also causes an error condition (3021, "No Current Record") when you try to move past the last row or before the first row.

Disabling Buttons

To correctly enable and disable navigation buttons, you need to be able to retrieve the current row location. That is, if you're currently on the first row, you need to know that fact as soon as you get there so the appropriate buttons (Previous and First) can be disabled. If you're on the last row, you'll want the Next and Last buttons to be disabled. If you're on the new row, you'll want the New, Next, and Last buttons disabled (see Figure 8.21).

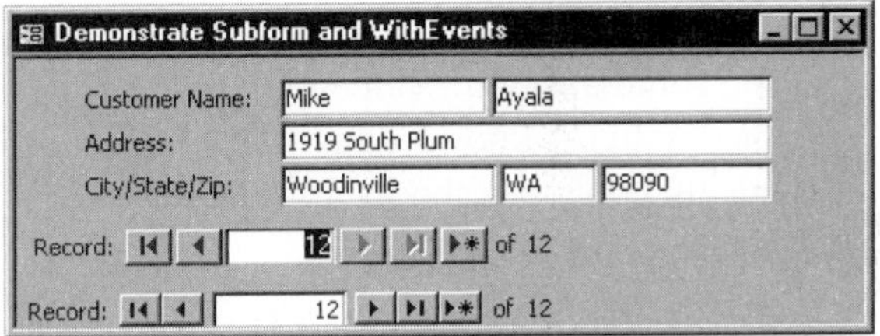

FIGURE 8.21: Because the current row is the last row in the recordset, the Next and Last buttons are disabled.

Checking the Current Location You can use the form's recordset and the Bookmark property to check the current row's location within its recordset. For example, you could take these steps to check whether the currently displayed row in the form was the first row:

1. Retrieve a reference to the form's recordset using the RecordsetClone property. (You don't want to use the Recordset property here, because the record pointer in the recordset needs to move. If you used the Recordset property, the form's current row would change, as well!)
2. Set the location in the recordset to be the same as that displayed on the form, using the Bookmark property.

3. In the recordset, move to the previous record, using the MovePrevious method. If the recordset's BOF property is now True, you must have been on the first row.

If you want to write a function that just checks to see whether you're on the first row for any form, here's one way to do it:

```
Private Function AtFirstRow(frm As Form) As Boolean
    ' Return True if at first row, False otherwise.
    Dim rst As DAO.Recordset

    On Error Resume Next

    Set rst = frm.RecordsetClone
    rst.Bookmark = frm.Bookmark
    rst.MovePrevious
    AtFirstRow = rst.BOF

    Set rst = Nothing
    Err.Clear
End Function
```

You could apply the same logic to check whether you were at the last row. Armed with the knowledge assembled here, you should now be able to write a single function that checks all these states and disables the correct buttons.

There's one more issue, though. Some forms are not updatable at all. If they're based on nonupdatable queries or tables, if you've set the RecordsetType property for the form to Snapshot, or if you've set the AllowAdditions property for the form to No, you can't add a new row. In this case, you also need to disable the New button.

The function you want should execute the following steps to determine which buttons are available as you move from row to row on the form:

1. Check the updatability of the form and its recordset, and set the New button's availability based on that information. Also, if you're on the new row, disable the button, since you can't go there if you're already there.
2. If you're on the new row already, enable the First and Previous buttons if there's any data in the recordset (disable them otherwise), and disable the Next and Last buttons.
3. If you're not on the new row, check for the beginning and end of recordset cases, as discussed above.

You'll find the procedure you need in Listing 8.15. This procedure, run in reaction to the Current event of the parent form, contains all the code necessary to enable and disable the appropriate buttons on the subform.

NOTE The procedure shown in Listing 8.15 runs in reaction to the main form's Current event. Because the subform has a WithEvents connection to the main form, it can react to any event of the parent form. Note that the code in the subform will always run after any corresponding event code in the main form. That is, if you have a Form_Current event procedure in the main form, the frmMain_Current event procedure, in the subform's module, would run after the main form's event procedure code had run.

Listing 8.15

```
Private Sub frmMain_Current()
    ' Called from the the main form's Current event.
    '
    ' This function enables and disables buttons as
    ' necessary, depending on the current
    ' record on the main form.
    '
    ' This code will run after any code associated
    ' with the main form's Current event.

    Dim rst As DAO.Recordset
    Dim fAtNew As Integer
    Dim fUpdatable As Integer

    If Not mfIsSubform Then
        Exit Sub
    End If

    On Error GoTo HandleErrors
    txtCurrRec = frmMain.CurrentRecord
    Set rst = frmMain.RecordsetClone

    ' Sooner or later, Access will figure out
    ' how many rows there really are!
    txtTotalRecs = rst.RecordCount + _
     IIf(frmMain.NewRecord, 1, 0)
```

```
    ' Check to see whether or not you're on the new record.
    fAtNew = frmMain.NewRecord

    ' If the form isn't updatable, then you sure
    ' can't go to the new record!  If it is, then
    ' the button should be enabled unless you're already
    ' on the new record.
    fUpdatable = rst.Updatable And frmMain.AllowAdditions
    If fUpdatable Then
        cmdNew.Enabled = Not fAtNew
    Else
        cmdNew.Enabled = False
    End If

    If fAtNew Then
        cmdNext.Enabled = False
        cmdLast.Enabled = True
        cmdFirst.Enabled = (rst.RecordCount > 0)
        cmdPrev.Enabled = (rst.RecordCount > 0)
    Else
        ' Sync the recordset's bookmark with
        ' the form's bookmark.
        rst.Bookmark = frmMain.Bookmark

        ' Move backwards to check for BOF.
        rst.MovePrevious
        cmdFirst.Enabled = Not rst.BOF
        cmdPrev.Enabled = Not rst.BOF

        ' Get back to where you started.
        rst.Bookmark = frmMain.Bookmark

        ' Move forward to check for EOF.
        rst.MoveNext
        cmdNext.Enabled = Not (rst.EOF Or fAtNew)
        cmdLast.Enabled = Not (rst.EOF Or fAtNew)
    End If

ExitHere:
    Me.Repaint
    Exit Sub
```

```
HandleErrors:
    Select Case Err.Number
        Case adhcCantDisableFocus
            txtCurrRec.SetFocus
            Resume
        Case Else
            MsgBox "Error: " & _
             Err.Description & " (" & Err.Number & ")"
    End Select
    Resume ExitHere
End Sub
```

Doing Time on the New Row While you're on the new row, you might enter data, finish the entry, and then want to move immediately to a *new* new row so you can add another record. The problem is that we've disabled cmdNew for as long as you're on the new row. To get around this problem, you can call code to reenable cmdNew as soon as the form becomes dirty. To make that happen, you'd follow these steps:

1. Set the main form's OnDirty property to be "[Event Procedure]". (The form fsubNavigation does this in its Load event procedure.)
2. React to the main form's Dirty event by enabling cmdNew.

Therefore, the subform contains code like this:

```
Private Sub frmMain_Dirty(Cancel As Integer)
    cmdNew.Enabled = True
End Sub
```

Specifying a Row Number Just as with Access' own navigation buttons, this subform allows you to type a row number into the text box, and once you leave that text box, the code will take you to the selected row. This code (called from the AfterUpdate event of the text box, shown in Listing 8.16) does its work by setting the form's Recordset property's AbsolutePosition property to match the value entered by the user:

```
' Move to the correct row. Note that
' the form's CurrentRecord property is
' READ-ONLY, so you have to go around
' the back, using the form's Recordset property's
' AbsolutePosition property.
frmMain.Recordset.AbsolutePosition = lngRec - 1
```

NOTE

This one was tricky. There were other, more complicated ways to force a form to display a specific row by number, but this is surely the simplest. The problem is that although the form provides an AbsolutePosition property, it's read-only. To work around this, the code sets the AbsolutePosition property of the recordset provided by the form. Note that the AbsolutePosition property is zero-based, and lngRec is 1-based, so the code must subtract 1 to get the correct row position.

Listing 8.16 shows the entire AfterUpdate event procedure. Most of the code, as you can see, ensures that the value entered by the user makes sense (that it isn't too large or too small, that is).

Listing 8.16

```
Private Sub txtCurrRec_AfterUpdate()
    Dim lngRec As Long
    Dim lngTotalRecs As Long

    ' Move to a specified row.

    On Error GoTo HandleErrors

    lngTotalRecs = txtTotalRecs

    ' If they entered a non-numeric value,
    ' just put the old position back.
    If Not IsNumeric(txtCurrRec) Then
        txtCurrRec = frmMain.CurrentRecord
        Exit Sub
    End If
    ' Get the current value, and make sure
    ' it's a long integer
    lngRec = CLng(txtCurrRec)
    If Err.Number <> 0 Then
        txtCurrRec = frmMain.CurrentRecord
        Exit Sub
    End If

    ' If they put in 0 or a negative number,
    ' put 1 in instead.
    If lngRec < 1 Then
```

```
        lngRec = 1
    ElseIf lngRec > lngTotalRecs Then
        lngRec = lngTotalRecs
    End If

    ' Move to the correct row. Note that
    ' the form's CurrentRecord property is
    ' READ-ONLY, so you have to go around
    ' the back, using the form's Recordset property's
    ' AbsolutePosition property.
    frmMain.Recordset.AbsolutePosition = lngRec - 1
    txtCurrRec = lngRec

ExitHere:
    Exit Sub

HandleErrors:
    Select Case Err.Number
        Case Else
            MsgBox "Error: " & _
             Err.Description & " (" & Err.Number & ")"
    End Select
    Resume ExitHere
End Sub
```

Creating Your Own Navigation Buttons You can easily create your own navigation buttons for use on your own forms. To do so, just follow these steps:

1. Import the form fsubNavigate from CH08.MDB.
2. Open the form on which you'd like to add the navigation buttons in Design view and drag fsubNavigate from the Database window onto your form. You'll most likely want to remove the label Access attaches to the subform control. Place the subform where you'd like it.
3. Make sure that the main form's HasModule property is set to True.
4. If you like, set the main form's NavigationButtons property to No, so that you'll see only the user-defined buttons, not the built-in ones.

Once you've set up the subform, you should be able to open the form in Form view and use the navigation buttons to move about in your form's data.

TIP

Because all the forms in your project on which you place a copy of fsubNavigation share the same subform, if you make changes to the subform, all the "parent" forms will see the changes immediately. If, for example, you decide that you want different bitmaps on all your navigation buttons, open fsubNavigation in Design view, change the bitmaps, and you're all set. Next time you open any form that uses this subform, you'll see your changed bitmaps. On the other hand, this may be a limitation for you. If you want a different look for different forms' navigation buttons, you'll need to make multiple copies of fsubNavigation, give each a unique name, and set the properties of each differently.

Subforms and Transactions

Once you've set up your form and subform so that it doesn't require using the LinkMasterFields/LinkChildFields properties, you can take advantage of another new feature in Access 2000—that is, that ability to wrap changes to the subform's data in a transaction for a given row on the main form.

Here's the problem: your form is displaying customer information on the main form and order information on a subform. You make changes to the customer information and, if you want to undo your changes, you simply use the menu item or add a command button that calls the Undo method of the form.

What if you want to be able to undo both the changes to the main form and any changes you've made to the data in the subform, as well? The Undo method of the main form doesn't roll back changes you've made on the subform at all, and all the Undo method of the form displayed in the subform can do is undo a single row's changes, at most. In order to "batch up" a number of changes to multiple rows, you need to take advantage of transactions. (See Chapter 2 in *Access 2000 Developer's Handbook, Volume II* for more information on using transactions.)

NOTE

In a nutshell, a transaction is a group of changes to data, managed by the database engine. You use the BeginTrans method of a Workspace object to begin a transaction, and until you call the CommitTrans method of the Workspace object, none of your changes to any recordset opened within the workspace will be stored. If you explicitly call the Rollback method of the Workspace object, all changes since you began the transaction will be discarded.

Although this technique would be somewhat tricky to generalize, we've created a simple form (frmSubformTransactions, shown in Figure 8.22) that demonstrates the subform rollback capability. You're welcome to study, copy, and modify the code associated with this form and its subform, frmSubformTransactionsSub.

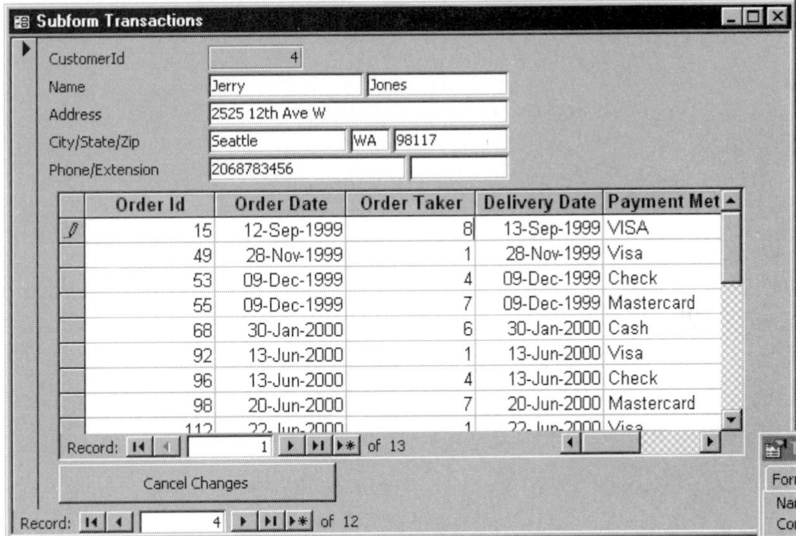

FIGURE 8.22: You can use DAO transactions to roll back or commit changes made on a form/subform.

How It Works

If you want to use transactions to allow rollback of changes to subform data, you'll find that you cannot rely on the LinkChildFields and LinkMasterFields properties to link the two forms. Using transactions requires setting the Recordset property of the subform, and the Recordset property has no knowledge of the LinkChild/LinkMasterFields properties. Depending on those properties, you'll end up with all rows showing in the subform, not just the appropriately filtered rows.

Therefore, the first step in creating a form/subform combination that allows rollback is to follow the steps in the earlier section, "Managing Linking Yourself," so that you needn't rely on the properties to link. In our sample, we've created a query named qrySubformTransactions that fills the subform with its data, based on the selected row in the parent form. We also added the code for the BeforeUpdate event of the subform's form, so that it fills in the CustomerID field on the subform, if it's currently empty, based on the parent form's CustomerID value. These steps simply get you to the same place as you might have in the previous section.

You'll need to place a command button on the main form or provide some other mechanism for undoing all the changes to the subform. In the example form, we've created a command button named cmdRollbackSubform. In the Current event of the main form, code sets the Enabled property of this button to be False—that is, for each parent row you visit, there's nothing to undo until you make changes to the subform's data. To enable the button, you'll find code in the Dirty event procedure for both the parent form and the child form, enabling the command button. Here's the code from the subform form's event procedure (you'll find similar code in the main form's Dirty event procedure, as well):

```
Private Sub Form_Dirty(Cancel As Integer)
    If IsSubForm(Me) Then
        Me.Parent.cmdRollbackSubform.Enabled = True
    End If
End Sub
```

(You would need to modify this code, of course, if your button had a different name.) That's all you need to do to the subform's form. Listing 8.17 contains all the code for the subform's form.

Listing 8.17

```
Private Sub Form_BeforeUpdate(Cancel As Integer)
    If IsSubForm(Me) Then
        If IsNull(Me.CustomerId) Then
            Me.CustomerId = Me.Parent.CustomerId
        End If
    End If
End Sub

Private Sub Form_Dirty(Cancel As Integer)
    If IsSubForm(Me) Then
        Me.Parent.cmdRollbackSubform.Enabled = True
    End If
End Sub

Function IsSubForm(frm As Form) As Boolean
    ' Is the form referenced in the
    ' parameter currently loaded as a subform?
    ' Check its Parent property to find out.

    Dim strName As String
    On Error Resume Next
    strName = frm.Parent.Name
    IsSubForm = (Err.Number = 0)
    Err.Clear
End Function
```

TIP

The following section takes advantage of DAO Workspace, Database, QueryDef, Recordset, and Parameter objects. If you're unfamiliar with the DAO object model, you might want to take the time to review these objects and their usage in Appendix C.

In the main form's module, you'll find code that does most of the work. In the Declarations area, you'll find the workspace variable (mwks) to be used by the code in beginning, committing, and rolling back transactions. You'll also find a Boolean value (mfIntrans), which keeps track of whether the code is currently in a transaction. Finally, you'll find a constant that contains the name of the data source, used simply to make the code a bit easier to move from one form to another:

```
Private mwks As DAO.Workspace
Private mfInTrans As Boolean

Private Const adhcSource _
 As String = "qrySubformTransactions"
```

In the form's Unload event procedure, it's possible that you might have made changes to data in the subform, and you might already be in a transaction. In that case, the code, shown below, commits the transaction and resets the reference to the Workspace object. (You might, if you like, modify this code to ask the user whether the changes should be saved or rolled back. We opted for the behavior Access shows—all data is saved unless explicitly undone.)

```
Private Sub Form_Unload(Cancel As Integer)
    If mfInTrans Then
        mwks.CommitTrans
    End If
    Set mwks = Nothing
End Sub
```

The most important procedure, ResetData (see Listing 8.18), handles most of the work. It starts by declaring DAO variables it will need. (Note the use of disambiguation, with the "DAO." prefix on the variables. See the section "ADO? What about DAO?" in Chapter 6 for more information on disambiguating variables):

```
Dim db As DAO.Database
Dim qdf As DAO.QueryDef
Dim rst As DAO.Recordset
Dim prm As DAO.Parameter
Dim strSource As String
```

The code then commits the current transaction, if one has already been started:

```
If mfInTrans Then
    mwks.CommitTrans
End If
```

The next three lines of code are the trickiest:

```
' Create and assign filtered recordset for subform.
Set mwks = DBEngine.CreateWorkspace("mwks", "Admin", "")
Set db = mwks.OpenDatabase(CurrentDb.Name)
Set qdf = db.QueryDefs(mstrSource)
```

The first line creates a new DAO Workspace object. When you open a database in the Access user interface, Access always creates a default workspace for you. In this case, this form is creating a new workspace, so you can manage transactions individually for each form that uses this same code. You'll use the BeginTrans, CommitTrans, and Rollback methods of this object to manage the transactions. The second line uses the OpenDatabase method of the Workspace object to open a reference to the current database. (Why not simply use the CurrentDb() function to retrieve a reference to the current database? The problem is that CurrentDb() returns a reference to the database open in the default workspace. You're working in a separate workspace, so you must use that workspace to open a new reference to the database for you.) Finally, the third line retrieves a reference to the querydef that's filling the subform's form. (Note that this code won't work unless you're filling the subform from a query. You may be able to modify it to work with a SQL string, but we haven't attempted that.)

Because your query has at least one parameter, pulling its criteria from data on the main form, you must supply a value for each parameter before you can open the recordset. (See Appendix C for more information on working with Parameter objects.) This code loops through the Parameters collection of the QueryDef object and uses the Eval function to satisfy the value of each parameter.

```
For Each prm In qdf.Parameters
    prm.Value = Eval(prm.Name)
Next prm
```

The next block of code turns off painting for the main form (keeping things clean on screen); retrieves the recordset it needs based on the querydef, in order to fill the subform's data; sets the LockEdits property to False, so that the form will use optimistic locking; sets the Recordset property of the subform control's form; and turns screen painting back on:

```
Me.Painting = False
Set rst = qdf.OpenRecordset
```

```
rst.LockEdits = False
Set subOrders.Form.Recordset = rst
Me.Painting = True
```

Finally, the code begins a transaction (so that your changes can be rolled back later); sets the mfInTrans variable to True, so other code can tell that the transaction has started; and enables the Cancel Changes button on the main form.

```
'Start a new subform transaction
mwks.BeginTrans
mfInTrans = True
cmdRollbackSubform.Enabled = False
```

Listing 8.18

```
Private Sub ResetData()
    Dim db As DAO.Database
    Dim qdf As DAO.QueryDef
    Dim rst As DAO.Recordset
    Dim prm As DAO.Parameter
    Dim strSource As String

    ' Note the intentional lack of error handling.
    ' This one's just an example.

    ' Assume user wants to commit changes in subform,
    '  if they haven't canceled them.
    If mfInTrans Then
        mwks.CommitTrans
    End If

    ' Create and assign filtered recordset for subform.
    Set mwks = DBEngine.CreateWorkspace("mwks", "Admin", "")
    Set db = mwks.OpenDatabase(CurrentDb.Name)
    Set qdf = db.QueryDefs(mstrSource)

    ' This will fail if the query has any parameters
    ' that aren't based on form values that it can resolve.
    For Each prm In qdf.Parameters
        prm.Value = Eval(prm.Name)
    Next prm

    Me.Painting = False
    Set rst = qdf.OpenRecordset
```

```
        rst.LockEdits = False
        Set subOrders.Form.Recordset = rst
        Me.Painting = True

        'Start a new subform transaction
        mwks.BeginTrans
        mfInTrans = True
        cmdRollbackSubform.Enabled = False
    End Sub
```

Every time you move from one row to another on the main form, you need to call the ResetData procedure. Therefore, the Current event procedure for the form does that for you:

```
Private Sub Form_Current()
    Call ResetData
End Sub
```

Finally, the moment you've been waiting for: what happens when you click the Cancel Changes button? This code, shown in Listing 8.19, first calls the Undo method of the main form to undo changes there. (You might want to remove this line of code and the code in the Dirty event procedure of the main form if you want to only undo changes on the subform.) Next, the code checks to see if it's in a transaction—a sanity check only, since the button shouldn't be enabled unless you're in a transaction—then rolls back the transaction, moves the focus to a different location on the form, and disables the command button. Finally, the code calls the ResetData procedure, to reset the data in the subform for more changes.

Listing 8.19

```
Private Sub cmdRollbackSubform_Click()
    Me.Undo
    If mfInTrans Then
        mwks.Rollback
        mfInTrans = False

        'Shift focus, so button can be disabled
        txtFirstName.SetFocus

        Call ResetData
    End If
End Sub
```

Using Subform Transactions in Your Own Applications

We tried to generalize the use of subform transactions so that we could provide a "plug and play" solution to the problem of being able to roll back subform changes. To do it right, however, would have been a monumental effort that would have worked only in a small subset of all possible cases, so we chose the "low road"—we've provided an example you can study and modify for your own needs.

Certainly, to make this work, you'll need to follow the issues mentioned in the previous section and modify your form/subform combination to match. You may have other issues to work through, too, as our example was somewhat simple. We suggest that you start with a working form/subform combination using the LinkChild/LinkMasterFields properties, work through the steps to remove the dependency on those properties, and add in the support for transactions.

Windows Handles, Classes, Access Forms, and MDI

Much of the remainder of this chapter works with Access forms as windows. That is, the issues discussed here work with Access forms without paying much attention to Access and its data. To make the best use of the different types of forms in Access, you must first have a basic understanding of Windows handles, classes, and parent-child relationships. These concepts will play a large part in your understanding the different form types in Access.

The Windows Handle (or hWnd)

Just as in Access, in Windows, almost every object you see on the screen is an object with properties and events. Every button, scroll bar, dialog box, and status bar is a window. To keep all these windows straight, Windows assigns to each a unique window handle—a unique Long integer—through which it can refer to the specific window. This window handle is generally referred to as the window's *hWnd* (*h*andle to a *w*indow). Access makes this value available to you, for every form, in that form's hWnd property. (Like many other properties, the hWnd property is available only at runtime and therefore can't be found in the form's property sheet.)

Window Classes

In addition, every window in Windows is a member of a window *class*. Window classes share events and code, so windows of the same class can react the same way to outside stimuli. For example, all scroll bars are either part of the class SCROLLBAR or part of a class derived from the SCROLLBAR class. (Actually, not all scroll bars are necessarily based on this class, because a programmer can create a scroll bar from scratch. It's just a combination of bitmaps and code. But almost no one does it that way, because Windows provides this standard class that requires little effort on your part.) Every window type in Access has its own class name. You'll find some of these classes listed in Table 8.3, along with the parent for each window type (which will be important in the next section's coverage of the Multiple Document Interface used in Access). Figure 8.23 shows a simple class hierarchy diagram for these Access window classes.

FIGURE 8.23:

Small sample of the Access window class hierarchy

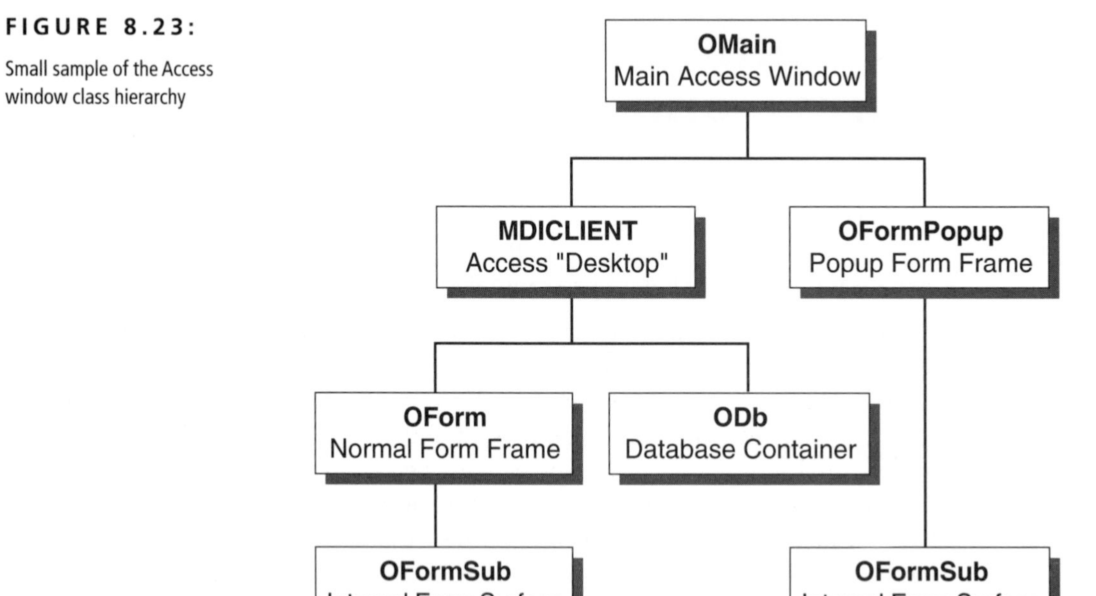

NOTE

Unlike in Visual Basic, controls in Access are not individual windows and don't supply an hWnd property. A control in Access is simply "paint on the screen" until it receives the focus, when it becomes a real window. See Chapter 7 for more information on working with controls as windows.

TABLE 8.3: Sample Access Window Classes and Their Parents

Class Name	Description	Parent
OMain	Main Access window	
MDICLIENT	Access desktop	Main Access window
ODb	Database container	MDIClient window
OForm	Normal form frame	MDIClient window
OFormPopup	Pop-up form frame	Main Access window
OFormSub	Access form (the area that contains other controls)	Any normal or pop-up form window

Multiple Document Interface (MDI)

The Multiple Document Interface (MDI) presents a standard way of writing applications for Windows in which one main window can contain many subordinate, or child, windows. Access is such an application, as is Excel, among many others. In MDI applications, the child windows minimize within the bounds of the parent window and show a tray within the parent when minimized. You can't size or drag child windows beyond the borders of their parent. The hierarchical organization of every MDI application is basically the same: you have a main window containing a special window—the MDI client—and within that window you have multiple child windows. In Access, the MDI client window's class is MDICLIENT and the main Access window's class is OMain. As you'll note in Table 8.3, the MDI client's parent is the main Access window, for which the window class is OMain. It is actually the window that's situated within the Access main window; it contains all the other Access windows, including the design surfaces and running applications. This window normally extends from the bottom of the docked toolbars to the top of the status bar and from the left to the right of the main Access window.

Manipulating Forms

Although Access forms work well when working with data, they fall short when you attempt to position a form at some specific location on the screen, or if you need to determine where the form currently is located. Basically, the only control over form positioning and appearance Access provides are the properties on the Format tab of the Properties window and the MoveSize method of the DoCmd object. If you want more control over where you place your forms and how the forms appear, you need to take matters into your own hands.

To make this necessary functionality available, we've provided the FormInfo class. This class allows you to precisely control placement and appearance of forms. In addition, this class contains many properties and methods that you may find useful in your applications, all dealing with the manipulation of the physical form itself. (None of the members of this class work with data—they all focus on the appearance and position of the form.)

The following sections provide an overview of the functionality provided by the FormInfo class and how you might use it. Table 8.4 lists all the members of the FormInfo class.

FIGURE 8.24:

The sample form demonstrates most of the features of the FormInfo class.

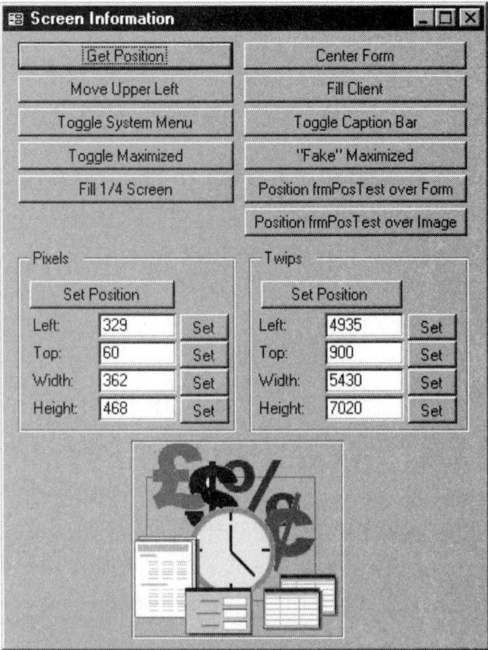

Demonstrating the FormInfo Features

To show off most of what the FormInfo class can do for you, we've provided the sample form, frmPosition. This form, shown in Figure 8.24, demonstrates most of the interesting features of the FormInfo class. Open frmPosition and give it a try, working through the following explanations of the various buttons:

Get Position—Retrieves the current position of the form (using the GetSize method of the FormInfo class) and displays the coordinates, both in twips and in pixels, in the eight text boxes in the middle of the form. Try moving the form around on the screen and then clicking this button to verify the coordinates.

Center Form—Centers the form within the Access client area, using the Center method of the FormInfo class. (If the form had its Popup property set to True, this method would center the form on the screen, rather than within the Access client window.)

Move Upper Left—Moves the form to the upper-left corner of the Access client area using the SetSize method of the FormInfo class. (If the form had its Popup property set to True, this method would set the coordinates in relation to the upper-left corner of the screen.)

Fill Client—Positions and sizes the form so that it covers the entire Access client area window, using the FillClientArea method of the FormInfo class.

Toggle System Menu—Removes or replaces the form's system menu using the ShowSystemMenu property of the FormInfo class.

Toggle Caption Bar—Removes or replaces the form's caption bar using the ShowCaptionBar property of the FormInfo class.

Toggle Maximized—Maximizes or restores the form, using the IsMaximized property of the FormInfo class. (The class also includes a read/write IsMinimized property.)

"Fake" Maximized—Many Access developers have requested a simple way to make a form look maximized but not to have the Minimize/Maximize/Close buttons available for the form. Normally in Access, this isn't possible. Using the ShowCaptionBar property and the FillClientArea method of the FormInfo class, it's easy to hide the caption bar and make the form fill the entire client area. (To close the form after running this test, use the Toggle Caption Bar button to display the caption bar, and then click the Close button.)

Fill 1/4 Screen—Make the form half as wide and half as tall as the Access client area, and then center the form in the client area. This example uses the PercentWidth and PercentHeight properties and the Center method of the FormInfo class.

Position frmPosTest Over Form—Loads and positions frmPosTest directly on top of the current form. This example uses the Left and Top properties and the SetSize method to position the form.

Position frmPosTest Over Image—Loads and positions frmPosTest directly on top of the image control on the sample form. This example uses the LeftInTwips, TopInTwips, ClientOffsetXInTwips, ClientOffsetYInTwips properties and the SetSize method to position the form.

Set Position (Pixels) and **Set Position** (Twips)—Positions the form at the coordinates specified in the four text boxes in the corresponding frame on the form, using the SetSize method. The four individual Set buttons in each frame move the form to the specified coordinate, using the individual Top, Left, Width, and Height properties of the FormInfo class.

Try out the various features of this sample form and see how they affect the behavior and positioning of the form. The next section describes each of the properties and methods in some detail and includes code samples showing how to use each.

Members of the FormInfo Class

This section works through each of the members of the FormInfo class, starting with the most important: the Form property. Table 8.4 lists the properties of the FormInfo class that describe the status of the selected form.

TABLE 8.4: FormInfo Properties/Methods Pertaining to the Status of the Selected Form

Member	Data Type	Description
Form	Form	Sets or retrieves the form associated with the FormInfo object.

Continued on next page

TABLE 8.4 CONTINUED: FormInfo Properties/Methods Pertaining to the Status of the Selected Form

Member	Data Type	Description
IsMaximized	Boolean	Sets or retrieves the maximized state of the form. If True, the form is maximized. If False, the form is returned to the normal state (that is, neither maximized nor minimized).
IsMinimized	Boolean	Sets or retrieves the minimized states of the form. If True, the form is minimized. If the property is set to False, the form is returned to the normal state (that is, neither maximized nor minimized).
IsPopup	Boolean	(Read-only) Returns True if the form is opened as a pop-up form. This can happen either by setting the Popup property of the form to True, or by using the acDialog WindowMode option with the OpenForm method of the DoCmd object.
IsSubForm	Boolean	(Read-only) Returns True if the form is open as a subform within another form.
WindowState	WindowState (wsNormal (0), wsMinimized (1), wsMaximized (2))	Sets or retrieves the window state. Rather than using the IsMaximized or IsMinimized properties individually, if you want to know or set the current window state, you can set this property to be one of wsNormal (0), wsMinimized (1), or wsMaximized (2) (the property returns one of those values, as well). This property is included as a convenience to you, making it easier to find the current window state.
ScreenX	Long	(Read-only) Width of the screen, in pixels, taking into account any docked Windows toolbars.
ScreenY	Long	(Read-only) Height of the screen, in pixels, taking into account any docked Windows toolbars.
ScreenXInTwips	Long	(Read-only) Width of the screen, in twips, taking into account any docked Windows toolbars.
ScreenYInTwips	Long	(Read-only) Height of the screen, in twips, taking into account any docked Windows toolbars.
TwipsPerPixelX	Long	(Read-only) Returns the number of twips (a logical measurement) per pixel (a physical measurement) in the horizontal direction, given the current screen driver. Although the sample form doesn't use this property, it can be useful if you need to convert from Access coordinates, in twips, to Windows API coordinates, in pixels.
TwipsPerPixelY	Long	(Read-only) Returns the number of twips per pixel in the vertical direction.

In order to use the FormInfo class, you must declare and instantiate it, just as you would any other class. You must also set the object's Form property, indicating on which form you want it to operate. Without setting this single property, none of the other properties will work.

To get started, you'll need to write code like the following from frmPosition, the sample form demonstrated in the previous section (the ShowCoords procedure is part of the sample form, and updates the display of the form's coordinates):

```
Private mfi As FormInfo

Private Sub Form_Load()
    Set mfi = New FormInfo
    Set mfi.Form = Me
    Call ShowCoords
End Sub
```

As you can see, you must assign a reference to a form that's already open to the Form property of the FormInfo object. In this case, the example used Me, a reference to the current form.

TIP There's no reason that the Form property of the FormInfo class must be tied to the current form. You can use the Forms("FormName") syntax to set a reference to any form, if you like.

Once you've set the Form property, you can use any of the other properties and methods of the FormInfo class. For example, the Toggle Maximized button on the sample form uses this code to do its work:

```
Private Sub cmdToggleMax_Click()
    mfi.IsMaximized = Not mfi.IsMaximized
    Call ShowCoords
End Sub
```

Table 8.5 lists the members of the FormInfo class that control the behavior of the status bar and the system menu.

TABLE 8.5: Properties That Control the Status Bar and System Menu of a Form

Member	Data Type	Description
ShowCaptionBar	Boolean	If True, the form displays its caption bar. If False, the form displays no caption bar.

Continued on next page

TABLE 8.5 CONTINUED: Properties That Control the Status Bar and System Menu of a Form

Member	Data Type	Description
ShowSystemMenu	Boolean	If True, the form displays its Windows system menu. If False, the form displays no system menu. (Removing the system menu removes the minimize, maximize, restore, and "what's this" help buttons, as well.)

The sample form's Toggle Caption Bar button uses the following code to display or hide the form's caption bar:

```
Private Sub cmdToggleCaptionBar_Click()
    mfi.ShowCaptionBar = Not mfi.ShowCaptionBar
    Call ShowCoords
End Sub
```

For another example using the same property, try out the form frmNoCaptionBar, in the sample project. This form, shown in Figure 8.25, hides its caption bar in the form's Load event, using the following code:

```
Private Sub Form_Load()
    Dim fi As FormInfo
    Set fi = New FormInfo
    Set fi.Form = Me
    fi.ShowCaptionBar = False
    Set fi = Nothing
End Sub
```

FIGURE 8.25:

You can remove the caption bar from any form during the form's Load event procedure.

NOTE

If you try the Toggle Caption Bar button on frmPosition, you'll note that the form seems to move up and down as you toggle the caption bar. If you remove the caption bar without moving the form itself, you'll see a "hole" where the caption bar was. To avoid this problem, the code in the FormInfo class moves the form up to fill the space left by the caption bar.

As you might expect, the code to toggle the system menu, in frmPosition, looks very similar to the code used for toggling the caption bar:

```
Private Sub cmdToggleSystemMenu_Click()
    mfi.ShowSystemMenu = Not mfi.ShowSystemMenu
    Call ShowCoords
End Sub
```

The bulk of the properties and methods in the FormInfo class manage the positioning of the form assigned to the FormInfo object's Form property. Table 8.6 lists the remainder of the FormInfo class' properties, and Table 8.7 lists the methods of the FormInfo class.

NOTE

Yes, you could easily use the TwipsPerPixelX and TwipsPerPixelY properties of the FormInfo class to convert from twips to pixels, and the LeftInTwips property is perhaps redundant—you could calculate it from the Left property. Sometimes, it makes sense to add separate properties for calculated values, like these. It may save you time and effort in your own code, for little overhead.

TABLE 8.6: Most of the FormInfo Class Properties Manage the Location and Size of the Associated Form

Member	Data Type	Description
Left	Long	Sets or retrieves the horizontal position of the form, in pixels.
Top	Long	Sets or retrieves the vertical position of the form, in pixels.
Width	Long	Sets or retrieves the outside width of the form, in pixels.
Height	Long	Sets or retrieves the outside height of the form, in pixels.
LeftInTwips	Long	Sets or retrieves the horizontal position of the form, in twips.
TopInTwips	Long	Sets or retrieves the vertical position of the form, in twips.
WidthInTwips	Long	Sets or retrieves the outside width of the form, in twips.
HeightInTwips	Long	Sets or retrieves the outside height of the form, in twips.
PercentWidth	Double	Sets or retrieves the width of the form, as a percentage of the parent width. If this is a pop-up form, the parent is the full screen. If not, the parent is the Access client window—that is, the area not including the menus, toolbars, and so on.
PercentHeight	Double	Sets or retrieves the height of the form, as a percentage of the parent height.

Continued on next page

TABLE 8.6 CONTINUED: Most of the FormInfo Class Properties Manage the Location and Size of the Associated Form

Member	Data Type	Description
ClientOffsetX	Long	Returns the horizontal offset of the Access MDI client area from the left edge of the main Access window. Some coordinates measure from the edge of the Access window (the SetSize method of the FormInfo object, for example), and others measure from the edge of the MDI client window (the Left property of the FormInfo object, for example). This property allows you to convert from one coordinate system to the other.
ClientOffsetY	Long	Returns the vertical offset of the Access MDI client area from the top edge of the main Access window. See the ClientOffsetX property for more information.
ClientOffsetXInTwips	Long	Returns the horizontal offset of the form's internal area from the left edge of the form window, in twips. Effectively, this is the width of the vertical form border.
ClientOffsetYInTwips	Long	Returns the vertical offset of the form's internal area from the top edge of the form window, in twips. Effectively, this is the height of the top form border.

TABLE 8.7: Methods of the FormInfo Class

Member	Description
Center	Centers the form within the confines of the MDI parent window. If the form is a pop-up form, then centers on the screen.
GetSize	Retrieves any or all of the Left, Top, Width, and Height properties of the form referred to by the FormInfo class. All the parameters are optional (specify just the dimensions you care about). If you want to retrieve more than one coordinate for the form, calling this method will be faster than querying the individual properties. Pass True in the final parameter (InTwips) if you want to retrieve the coordinates measured in twips. By default, the coordinates are measured in pixels.
SetSize	Sets any or all of the Left, Top, Width, and Height properties of the form referred to by the FormInfo class. All the parameters are optional (specify just the dimensions you care about). If you want to set more than one coordinate for the form, calling this method will be faster than setting the individual properties. Pass True in the final parameter (InTwips) if you want to specify the coordinates measured in twips. By default, the coordinates are measured in pixels.
FillClientArea	Moves a form so that it fills the entire MDI Client area in Access. This allows you to remove the Close button (or the entire caption bar, if you like) and appear to "maximize" the form without Access adding those pesky buttons back.

Continued on next page

TABLE 8.7 CONTINUED: Methods of the FormInfo Class

Member	Description
SaveCoords	Given an application name (of your choosing), saves coordinates for this form (based on its Name property) in the Windows Registry (you can retrieve the coordinates later using the RetrieveCoords method).
RetrieveCoords	Given an application name (of your choosing), retrieves coordinates for this form (based on its Name property) previously saved in the Windows Registry (using the SaveCoords method).

On the sample form, the ShowCoords procedure (called from the Get Position button, and, after the form has been moved or sized, from all of the other buttons) uses the GetSize method to retrieve all four coordinates at once. As you can see from the example in Listing 8.20, the ShowCoords procedure retrieves the four coordinates and places them into four text boxes on the form. It repeats the same steps with the coordinates in twips.

Listing 8.20

```
Private Sub ShowCoords()
    Dim lngLeft As Long
    Dim lngTop As Long
    Dim lngWidth As Long
    Dim lngHeight As Long

    Call mfi.GetSize( _
     lngLeft, lngTop, lngWidth, lngHeight)
    txtLeft = lngLeft
    txtTop = lngTop
    txtWidth = lngWidth
    txtHeight = lngHeight

    Call mfi.GetSize( _
     lngLeft, lngTop, lngWidth, lngHeight, InTwips:=True)
    txtLeftInTwips = lngLeft
    txtTopInTwips = lngTop
    txtWidthInTwips = lngWidth
    txtHeightInTwips = lngHeight
End Sub
```

To center the form, the Center button on the sample form calls the following code:

```
Private Sub cmdCenter_Click()
    mfi.Center
    Call ShowCoords
End Sub
```

TIP

If you've set a form's Popup property to True or you've used the acDialog flag when opening the form, the Center method will center the form on the screen. For normal forms, the Center method places the form in the center of the Access MDI client window.

To move the form to the upper-left corner of the Access MDI client window (or of the screen, for a pop-up form), the sample form's Move Upper Left button uses the following code, calling the SetSize method. (You should notice that this example only passes the Left and Top parameters. They're all optional, and you can specify just the ones you need. You can also specifically set the Left and Top properties individually—using the SetSize method is a bit simpler):

```
Private Sub cmdMoveUpperLeft_Click()
    mfi.SetSize 0, 0
    Call ShowCoords
End Sub
```

NOTE

You might wonder why you would ever use the SetSize method, as opposed to the built-in MoveSize method. For one thing, MoveSize can only work with the current form, whereas you can use the FormInfo class (and its SetSize method) with any form. In addition, if you're doing other work with forms, using the FormInfo class, you can use pixels (the native unit of the class) instead of converting coordinates to twips. The MoveSize method requires coordinates measured in twips and, therefore, requires a conversion from the native FormInfo coordinates. The SetSize method doesn't require this conversion.

The Toggle System Menu button on the sample form uses the following code to toggle the display of the system menu. The Toggle Caption Bar button does the same work, using the ShowCaptionBar property, as does the Toggle Maximized button:

```
Private Sub cmdToggleSystemMenu_Click()
    mfi.ShowSystemMenu = Not mfi.ShowSystemMenu
End Sub
```

The "fake" Maximized button solves a problem faced by many Access developers: you want to remove the Minimize and Maximize buttons from the caption bar, and you also want the form maximized. If you've tried this, you've noticed that no matter how the form properties are set, Windows always displays the Minimize and Maximize buttons when you've maximized a form. Using the FormInfo class, you can remove the caption bar totally, and then force the form to fill the entire Access MDI client window, like this:

```
Private Sub cmdFakeMaximized_Click()
    mfi.ShowCaptionBar = False
    mfi.FillClientArea
    Call ShowCoords
End Sub
```

TIP

If you want to use this technique in an application, you should make sure your form's BorderStyle property has been set to something besides Sizable. Using a sizable border makes it possible for your users to resize the form once you've "maximized" it. Each of the other options makes this impossible.

The Position frmPosTest Over Form button simply opens a second form and sets the coordinates of the second form to cover the current form exactly:

```
Private Sub cmdCoverForm_Click()
    Dim fi As FormInfo

    Set fi = New FormInfo
    DoCmd.OpenForm "frmPosTest", WindowMode:=acHidden

    Set fi.Form = Forms("frmPosTest")
    fi.SetSize mfi.Left, mfi.Top, mfi.Width, mfi.Height

    ' Make the form visible.
    fi.Form.Visible = True
End Sub
```

The Position frmPosTest Over Image button provides the most complex code in the sample form (see Listing 8.21). This code first opens frmPosTest hidden, turns off its caption, and then positions it immediately above the Image control on the sample form.

This tricky line of code does most of the work:

```
fi.SetSize _
 Left:=mfi.LeftInTwips + _
```

```
    mfi.ClientOffsetXinTwips + ctl.Left, _
   Top:=mfi.TopInTwips + _
    mfi.ClientOffsetYinTwips + ctl.Top, _
   Width:=ctl.Width, _
   Height:=ctl.Height, _
   InTwips:=True
```

TIP

We've used named parameters in the call to the SetSize method in this example. We didn't use them in the previous example, because the code was self-evident by inspection. In this case, however, it's not completely clear what each parameter contains, and named parameters make the code easier to read, in the long run.

This code calculates the horizontal and vertical coordinates for the form by taking the LeftInTwips property of the sample form and adding to that the ClientOffsetX-InTwips property (the width of the form's border) and the Left coordinate of the Image control. The code repeats these steps for the Top coordinate, adding together the TopInTwips property of the form and the ClientOfficeYInTwips property to add in the height of the form's caption bar. Figure 8.26 demonstrates the geometry graphically.

FIGURE 8.26:

Add together the necessary coordinates to calculate the location for placing the second form.

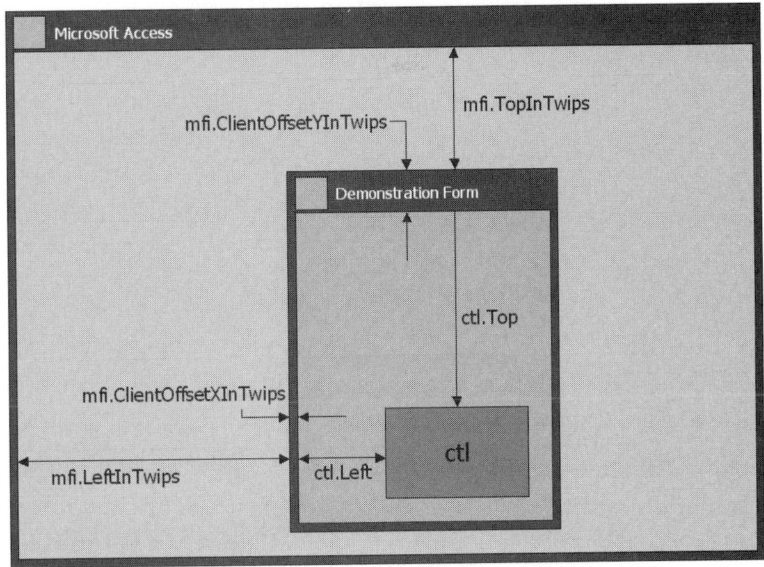

Listing 8.21

```
Private Sub cmdSetFormPos_Click()
    Dim fi As FormInfo
    Dim ctl As Control

    ' Position a form (frmPosTest) on top of a control.
    ' This code won't work for popup forms (the positions
    ' are off) unless BOTH forms are POPUP forms. That way,
    ' both forms are using the same coordinate system.

    Set ctl = Me.imgTest

    Set fi = New FormInfo
    DoCmd.OpenForm "frmPosTest", WindowMode:=acHidden

    ' Place the form frmPosTest right
    ' on top of imgTest.
    Set fi.Form = Forms("frmPosTest")
    fi.ShowCaptionBar = False

    ' The border adds one extra pixel, so add that in, too.
    ' You would need to modify this for various
    ' border types.
    fi.SetSize _
     Left:=mfi.LeftInTwips + _
      mfi.ClientOffsetXinTwips + ctl.Left, _
     Top:=mfi.TopInTwips + _
      mfi.ClientOffsetYinTwips + ctl.Top, _
     Width:=ctl.Width, _
     Height:=ctl.Height, _
     InTwips:=True

    ' Make the form visible.
    fi.Form.Visible = True
End Sub
```

Save and Retrieve Form Coordinates

Many Windows applications save information about the size and location of their forms (or windows) from one invocation to the next. That way, when the user starts the program, the application is laid out just as it was when it was last used.

The SaveCoords and RetrieveCoords methods of the FormInfo class make this operation simple. To demonstrate this functionality, load frmSaveCoords in the sample project. Move the form, resize it, and then close it. Open it again, and it should be right where it was when you closed it.

To save a form's coordinates, add code to the form's Close event procedure, like this:

```
Const adhcAppName = "SaveSizeTest"

Private Sub Form_Close()
    Dim fi As FormInfo
    Set fi = New FormInfo
    Set fi.Form = Me
    fi.SaveCoords adhcAppName
    Set fi = Nothing
End Sub
```

If you're in a rush, you can condense the code like this:

```
Private Sub Form_Close()
    Dim fi As New FormInfo
    Set fi.Form = Me
    fi.SaveCoords adhcAppName
End Sub
```

We don't normally recommend that you use the shortened syntax, which combines the Dim and New keywords:

```
Dim fi As New FormInfo
```

but in this case, because the variable is local, and because it's only going to be around for such a short time, it's not so bad. In addition, although we normally recommend that you set all your object references to Nothing when you're done with them, in this case, you can be assured that when you leave the procedure and fi goes out of scope, the object will be removed from memory.

To restore the coordinates when you open the form, you can add code like this to the form's Open event procedure:

```
Private Sub Form_Open(Cancel As Integer)
    Dim fi As FormInfo
    Set fi = New FormInfo
    Set fi.Form = Me
    fi.RestoreCoords adhcAppName
    Set fi = Nothing
End Sub
```

Again, you could condense the code, if you felt the need.

Because you're likely to want to save and restore coordinates for all the forms in your application, we've provided a simple interface to this code, in the basSaveSize module. You can use the adhSaveCoords and adhGetCoords procedures to do all the work. (These procedures simply call the code shown previously in this section, hiding all the details of instantiating and working with the FormInfo objects.) Listing 8.22 contains the code for the two procedures in basSaveSize.

Listing 8.22

```
Public Sub adhGetCoords(strApp As String, _
 frm As Form)

    On Error GoTo HandleErrors

    Dim fi As FormInfo

    Set fi = New FormInfo
    Set fi.Form = frm
    fi.RetrieveCoords strApp

ExitHere:
    Set fi = Nothing
    Exit Sub

HandleErrors:
    MsgBox "Unable to retrieve all coordinates.", _
     vbInformation, "Get Coords"
    Resume ExitHere
End Sub

Public Function adhSaveCoords(strApp As String, _
 frm As Form)

    Dim fi As FormInfo

    On Error GoTo HandleErrors

    Set fi = New FormInfo
    Set fi.Form = frm
    fi.SaveCoords strApp
```

```
ExitHere:
    Set fi = Nothing
    Exit Function

HandleErrors:
    MsgBox "Unable to save all coordinates.", _
     vbInformation, "Save Coords"
    Resume ExitHere
End Function
```

TIP

To use the adhGetCoords and adhSaveCoords procedures, you'll need to import both the basSaveSize module and the FormInfo class module into your application.

How Does It Work?

Much of the functionality for the FormInfo class is based on Windows API calls. Some of these API calls are beyond the scope of this book, but we will explain, in the following sections, how much of the code in the FormInfo class works. If you're interested, you can open the class, follow along with the discussion here, and peruse the code we bypass at your leisure.

Setting up the Form Property

As mentioned earlier, before you can use the FormInfo class, you must "bind" it to an open form. You do that by setting the Form property of your FormInfo object:

```
Dim fi As FormInfo
Set fi = New FormInfo
Set fi.Form = Forms("SampleForm")
```

Internally, the code causes Access to call the Form Property Set procedure:

```
' From the FormInfo class module
Public Property Set Form(Value As Form)
    On Error GoTo HandleErrors
    Set frm = Value
    Call GetScreenInfo
    Call GetClientOffsets
    mfIsPopup = GetIsPopup()
    mfIsSubform = GetIsSubform()
```

```
ExitHere:
    Exit Property

HandleErrors:
    Select Case Err.Number
        Case Else
            Call HandleError("FormInfo.Form", _
             Err.Number, Err.Description)
    End Select
    Resume ExitHere
End Property
```

NOTE

You can find the HandleError procedure in the FormInfo class module. It simply displays a message box with the current error information. The code is surrounded with compile-time directives that normally cause the code to be "compiled out." If you want to debug any sort of odd behaviors, you may want to set the #DEBUGGING constant at the top of the module to be True.

As you can see, the Form Property Set procedure not only stores away a reference to the form you've passed in, it also performs some one-time information gathering. The GetScreenInfo procedure (also in the FormInfo class module) is the most interesting, and we'll focus on that specific procedure.

Retrieving Information about the Screen

The GetScreenInfo procedure retrieves several values that are required if you're going to programmatically work with the screen in Access. This procedure retrieves two pairs of values:

The screen horizontal and vertical size, in pixels These values are exposed through the ScreenX, ScreenY, ScreenXInTwips, and ScreenYInTwips properties of the class.

The ratio between twips and pixels, for both the horizontal and vertical dimensions This ratio is crucial, because it allows the code to convert from pixels (all the API calls use pixels) to twips (Access uses twips for its own measurements).

The GetScreenInfo procedure, shown in Listing 8.23, uses four API functions to do its job:

GetDC, ReleaseDC A DC, or "device context," allows Windows to communicate with a specific device. You can retrieve a device context for the screen device using the window handle for the Windows desktop. Once you have the device context for the screen, you can retrieve information about the screen. After using GetDC to retrieve a device context, you should use ReleaseDC to release it, when you're done.

```
Const HWND_DESKTOP = 0

lngDC = GetDC(HWND_DESKTOP)

' If the call to GetDC didn't fail (and it had
' better not, or things are really busted),
' then get the info.

If lngDC <> 0 Then
    ' Code removed here...
    Call ReleaseDC(HWND_DESKTOP, lngDC)
End If
```

GetSystemMetrics Allows you to retrieve various bits of information about your system. You specify which "bit" you need, and the function returns what you've requested. In this case, the code requests the width and height of the full screen, passing the SM_CXFULLSCREEN and SM_CYFULLSCREEN constants to the function.

```
mptCurrentScreen.x = GetSystemMetrics(SM_CXFULLSCREEN)
mptCurrentScreen.y = GetSystemMetrics(SM_CYFULLSCREEN)
```

GetDeviceCaps Retrieves specific device capabilities. In this case, the code needs to retrieve, from the screen driver, the logical pixels per inch in both the horizontal and vertical directions. Once it has those values, the code divides the number of twips per inch (the constant value, 1440) by the number of pixels per inch to retrieve the twips per pixel in each direction:

```
ptCurrentDPI.x = GetDeviceCaps(lngDC, LOGPIXELSX)
ptCurrentDPI.y = GetDeviceCaps(lngDC, LOGPIXELSY)

mptTwipsPerPixel.x = adhcTwipsPerInch / ptCurrentDPI.x
mptTwipsPerPixel.y = adhcTwipsPerInch / ptCurrentDPI.y
```

Listing 8.23

```
Private Sub GetScreenInfo()
    On Error GoTo HandleErrors
    Dim lngDC As Long
    Dim ptCurrentDPI As POINTAPI
    Const HWND_DESKTOP = 0

    lngDC = GetDC(HWND_DESKTOP)

    ' If the call to GetDC didn't fail (and it had
    ' better not, or things are really busted),
    ' then get the info.

    If lngDC <> 0 Then
        ' Find the number of pixels in both directions
        ' on the screen, (640x480, 800x600, 1024x768,
        ' 1280x1024?). This also takes into account
        ' the size of the task bar, whereever it is.
        mptCurrentScreen.x = _
         GetSystemMetrics(SM_CXFULLSCREEN)
        mptCurrentScreen.y = _
         GetSystemMetrics(SM_CYFULLSCREEN)

        ' Get the pixels/inch ratio, as well.
        ptCurrentDPI.x = GetDeviceCaps(lngDC, LOGPIXELSX)
        ptCurrentDPI.y = GetDeviceCaps(lngDC, LOGPIXELSY)

        mptTwipsPerPixel.x = _
         adhcTwipsPerInch / ptCurrentDPI.x
        mptTwipsPerPixel.y = _
         adhcTwipsPerInch / ptCurrentDPI.y

        ' Release the information context.
        Call ReleaseDC(HWND_DESKTOP, lngDC)
    End If

ExitHere:
    Exit Sub

HandleErrors:
```

```
    Select Case Err.Number
        Case Else
            Call HandleError("FormInfo.GetScreenInfo", _
             Err.Number, Err.Description)
    End Select
    Resume ExitHere
End Sub
```

Retrieving Border Information

After calling GetScreenInfo, the Form Property Set procedure next calls the GetClientOffsets procedure (in the FormInfo class module). Because you may want to relate screen coordinates to coordinates of controls on forms, you need some way to factor in the width of the top and left borders of a form. Figure 8.26 (shown earlier) demonstrates why the class needs to determine this information: Access provides coordinates of controls on forms relative to the inside border of the form's client area, so you'll need the sizes of the top and left borders of a form to be able to relate screen and form coordinates.

The GetClientOffsets procedure does this work for you, in a somewhat roundabout way. The code uses two Windows API functions to fill in the mptClientOffset module-level variable:

ClientToScreen Takes in a POINTAPI structure and a window handle. The window handle indicates which window you're interested in (here, it's the hWnd property of the form). The POINTAPI structure contains the coordinate of the point, in relation to the window, that you'd like converted to screen coordinates. In our case, that's (0, 0). On return from the ClientToScreen procedure, the POINTAPI structure contains the coordinates for the same point, but now in terms of the screen (not the form). In this way, you can find the screen coordinates of a point for which you don't know the absolute location.

GetWindowRect Given a window handle (the form, again) and a RECT structure, the API procedure fills in the RECT structure with the screen coordinates of the bounding rectangle of the selected window.

Given these two sets of coordinates, the code in GetClientOffsets can subtract the outside coordinate (retrieved using GetWindowRect) from the inside (further towards the bottom-right corner, and therefore larger) coordinate (retrieved using ClientToScreen), to determine the width of the form border. Listing 8.24 contains the full procedure.

Listing 8.24

```
Private Sub GetClientOffsets()
    Dim p As POINTAPI
    Dim rct As RECT

    ' Convert 0, 0 within the form's client area to
    ' absolute screen coordinates.
    p.x = 0
    p.y = 0
    Call ClientToScreen(frm.hWnd, p)
    Call GetWindowRect(frm.hWnd, rct)

    mptClientOffset.x = p.x - rct.Left
    mptClientOffset.y = p.y - rct.Top
End Sub
```

Although the FormInfo class uses these API calls in other ways, once you've seen how these procedures work, the rest should be easier to understand. The following sections discuss the details of specific properties and methods of the FormInfo class.

Removing a Form's Caption Bar

As part of an application, you may need to remove a form's caption bar. Although Access allows you to remove the entire border, this may not be what you need for a particular look. Removing the control menu and the Minimize/Maximize buttons and setting the form's caption to a single space will almost work, but it still leaves the thick bar above the form.

Removing the form's caption bar relies on changes to the form's window style. When any application creates a new window, it sets up some information about the style of that window. The Windows API provides functions to retrieve and set the style information, and you can change many of the window styles even after the window has been created. The presence or absence of the caption bar is one of those modifiable styles, and the code in Listing 8.25 (the ShowCaptionBar Property Let procedure) works by changing the form's window style when called from the form's Open event.

Changing the Window Style

To change the window's style, follow these steps:

1. Retrieve the current window style (a Long integer).
2. Turn off the particular bit in the value that controls whether the window has a caption bar.
3. Set the style for the window with the newly altered style value.

To retrieve and set the style value, you can call the Windows API functions GetWindowLong and SetWindowLong. In each case, you tell Windows which particular value you're getting or setting by passing the constant GWL_STYLE.

To tell Windows to turn off the caption bar, you need to change the value returned from the call to GetWindowLong. Windows treats the 32-bit value as a set of 32 binary flags, each controlling one attribute of the window, where each can have a value of 0 (False) or 1 (True). For example, the window style value contains a bit controlling the display of the caption bar, the Minimize and Maximize buttons, and the control menu. The only one of these Access doesn't give you control over is the display of the caption bar.

To change one of the settings, you use either the And or the Or bitwise operator. The And operator takes any two values and returns 1 in any of the positions that was nonzero in both values and 0 in any of the positions where either or both were 0. The Or operator sets any position to 1 if either of the corresponding positions is 1, and 0 otherwise.

Therefore, to force a specific bit to be on, you use the Or operator with a number that has all zeros except in the particular bit you care about, where you have a 1. (This works because any value Ored with 0 isn't changed, but any value Ored with 1 is set to 1.) Figure 8.27 shows how using the Or operator with the WS_CAPTION constant would force a single bit to be on.

To force a bit to be off, you use the And operator with 1s in all the bits except the one you care about, where you have a 0. (This works because any value Anded with 1 isn't changed, but any value Anded with 0 is set to 0.) To control whether you're turning bits on or off, you can use the Not logical operator, which flips all the bits of a value from 0 to 1 or from 1 to 0. Figure 8.28 shows how using the And operator with the WS_CAPTION constant would force a single bit to be off.

FIGURE 8.27:

Use the Or operator to force a single bit to be on.

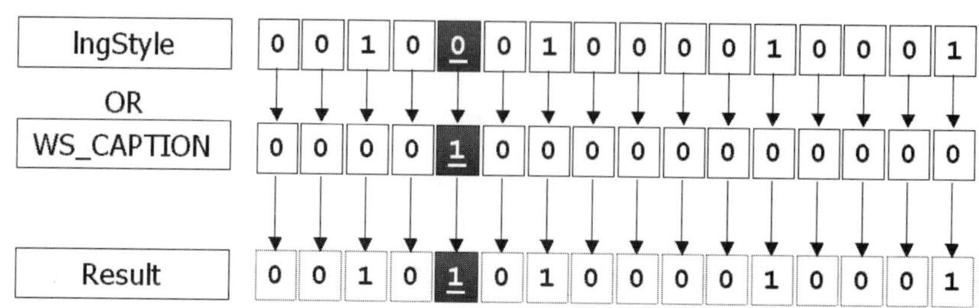

FIGURE 8.28:

Use the And operator (along with the Not operator) to force a single bit to be off.

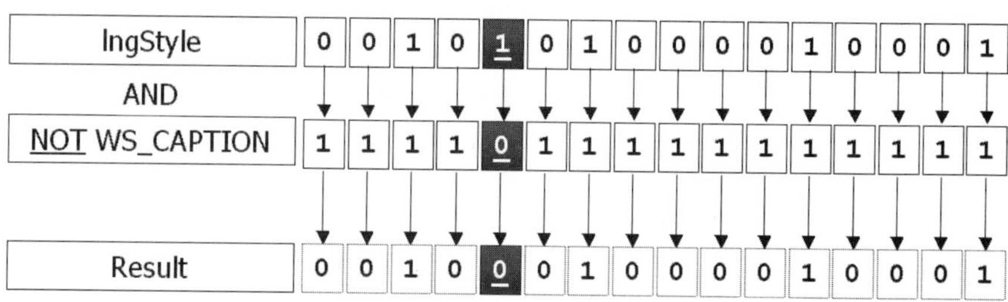

Therefore, given that the constant WS_CAPTION contains the correct bit settings to turn on the display of the caption bar, you could Or it with the value returned from GetWindowLong to force the display on. To turn it off, you And it with NOT WS_CAPTION. This leaves all the bits alone except the one controlling the caption bar display, which is set to 0. When you make this change and call SetWindowLong, Windows redisplays the window without the caption bar.

The following lines of code execute the steps necessary to retrieve and set the window style value:

```
' Get the current window style of the form.
lngOldStyle = GetWindowLong(frm.hWnd, GWL_STYLE)

If ShowIt Then
    ' Turn off the bit that enables the caption.
    lngNewStyle = lngOldStyle Or WS_CAPTION
Else
```

```
        ' Turn off the bit that enables the caption.
        lngNewStyle = lngOldStyle And Not WS_CAPTION
    End If

    ' Set the new window style.
    lngOldStyle = SetWindowLong(frm.hWnd, _
     GWL_STYLE, lngNewStyle)
```

Resizing the Window

Unless you do a little more work, the form will look rather odd at this point. Because you haven't told Windows to redraw the form, Access becomes confused: If you're turning off the caption bar, the caption will still show, but Windows won't know it's there. You must resize the form without the caption bar.

This section of code requires three Windows API functions:

GetWindowRect Fills a user-defined datatype—a variable of type RECT—with the current coordinates of the form.

GetSystemMetrics Tells you the height of the caption bar that was just removed. When you pass in the SM_CYCAPTION constant, Windows returns to you the height of the caption bar.

MoveWindow Moves the window. (Actually, it won't be moved; you'll just call MoveWindow to resize it. Other Windows API functions are available to resize windows, but this one is the easiest to call, given the coordinate information you'll know at this point.)

This code requires some brute-force calculations: figuring out the height of the old caption and subtracting that from the current height of the window. Subtracting the height of the caption bar from the current height of the form should leave you with a form that's the correct height. See Listing 8.25 for the details. (The GetCoords function, used in the procedure, calculates the coordinates of the form, using API calls discussed already.)

Listing 8.25

```
Private Type COORDS
    Left As Long
    Top As Long
    Width As Long
    Height As Long
    State As WindowState
End Type
```

```
Private mCoords As COORDS

Public Property Let ShowCaptionBar(ShowIt As Boolean)
    On Error GoTo HandleErrors

    Dim lngOldStyle As Long
    Dim lngNewStyle As Long
    Dim rct As RECT
    Dim intDiff As Integer

    ' If there is nothing to do, get out.
    If Me.ShowCaptionBar = ShowIt Then
        Goto ExitHere
    End If

    Call GetCoords(frm.hWnd, mCoords)

    ' Get the current window style of the form.
    lngOldStyle = GetWindowLong(frm.hWnd, GWL_STYLE)

    If ShowIt Then
        ' Turn off the bit that enables the caption.
        lngNewStyle = lngOldStyle Or WS_CAPTION
    Else
        ' Turn off the bit that enables the caption.
        lngNewStyle = lngOldStyle And Not WS_CAPTION
    End If

    ' Set the new window style.
    lngOldStyle = SetWindowLong(frm.hWnd, _
     GWL_STYLE, lngNewStyle)

    ' How much room does that caption take up?
    intDiff = GetSystemMetrics(SM_CYCAPTION)

    ' Calculate the new height.
    If ShowIt Then
        mCoords.Height = mCoords.Height + intDiff
    Else
        mCoords.Height = mCoords.Height - intDiff
    End If

    ' Move the window to the same left and top,
    ' but with new width and height.
```

```
        ' This will make the new form appear
        ' a little shorter or a little taller.
        With mCoords
            Call MoveWindow(frm.hWnd, _
             .Left, .Top, .Width, .Height, 1)
        End With
        Call GetClientOffsets

    ExitHere:
        Exit Property

    HandleErrors:
        Select Case Err.Number
            Case Else
                Call HandleError("FormInfo.ShowCaptionBar", _
                 Err.Number, Err.Description)
        End Select
        Resume ExitHere
    End Property
```

Showing and Hiding the System Menu

For all intents and purposes, this code is almost exactly the same as the code that shows and hides the caption bar. There's one big difference, however: when you hide the system menu, Access doesn't necessarily know that it needs to repaint the border of the form. You need to tell it that the form's border requires repainting, and you can do that by sending a message to the form. The SendMessage API function allows you to send messages to any particular window, given its window handle, and if you send a form the WM_NCPAINT message, the window will repaint its border for you.

Listing 8.26 shows the entire ShowSystemMenu Property Let procedure, and its workings should be familiar, based on the previous section's discussion. Look for the call to SendMessage, near the end of the procedure, which forces the window to repaint. (Try commenting out that line of code to see what happens if you don't call it!)

```
Public Property Let ShowSystemMenu(ShowIt As Boolean)
    On Error GoTo HandleErrors
    Dim lngOldStyle As Long
    Dim lngNewStyle As Long

    ' If there is nothing to do, get out.
```

```
        If Me.ShowSystemMenu = ShowIt Then
            Exit Property
        End If

        ' Get the current window style of the form.
        lngOldStyle = GetWindowLong(frm.hWnd, GWL_STYLE)

        If ShowIt Then
            ' Turn on the bit that enables system menu.
            lngNewStyle = lngOldStyle Or WS_SYSMENU
        Else
            ' Turn off the bit that shows the system menu.
            lngNewStyle = lngOldStyle And Not WS_SYSMENU
        End If

        ' Set the new window style.
        Call SetWindowLong(frm.hWnd, GWL_STYLE, lngNewStyle)

        ' The 1 as the third parameter tells
        ' the window to repaint its entire border.
        Call SendMessage(frm.hWnd, WM_NCPAINT, 1, 0)

ExitHere:
    Exit Property

HandleErrors:
    Select Case Err.Number
        Case Else
            Call HandleError("FormInfo.ShowSystemMenu", _
             Err.Number, Err.Description)
    End Select
    Resume ExitHere
End Property
```

Saving and Restoring Form Locations

The SaveCoords and RetrieveCoords methods of the FormInfo class allow you to save and restore form coordinates to the Windows Registry. VBA provides four procedures that make it possible to read and write values to a specific location in the Registry:

Procedure	Description
SaveSetting	Saves a single item and value to the Registry

Procedure	Description
GetSetting	Gets the value of a single item in a subkey
GetAllSettings	Gets a list of settings and their respective values from a key in the Registry
DeleteSetting	Deletes a section or setting from the Registry

These procedures are extremely limited. They can work only with subkeys under this particular subkey:

```
HKEY_CURRENT_USER\Software\VB and VBA Programs
```

(If you want to dig in, Chapters 16 and 17 cover different ways to work with the Registry.)

Using SaveSetting and GetSetting

SaveSetting allows you either to write to an existing subkey or to create a new one and write data there. The general syntax is this:

```
SaveSetting(appname, section, key, setting)
```

Use its parameters as described in the following table:

Parameter	Description	Example
appname	Name of the project or application	SaveSizeTest
section	Name of the item within the project	frmSaveCoords
key	Name of the key for which you'd like to set the value	Bottom
setting	Value for the specified key	409

GetSetting works just about the same way. Here is its syntax:

```
GetSetting(appname, section, key[, default])
```

Use its parameters as described in the following table:

Parameter	Description	Example
Appname	Name of the project or application.	SaveSizeTest
Section	Name of the item within the project.	frmSaveCoords
key	Name of the key whose value you'd like to retrieve.	Bottom

Parameter	Description	Example
Default	Value to use if the key isn't found. If you don't specify a value, Access will use an empty string ("").	0

Wrapping up the Registry Functions

Once you know how to read and write information in the Registry, you can follow the RetrieveCoords and SaveCoords methods of the FormInfo class. The SaveCoords method is straightforward: it simply calls the SaveSetting sub for each of the values the procedure needs to save, passing the AppName that you've supplied, the name of the form, a constant representing the coordinate to be saved, and the current value of the coordinate. Listing 8.26 shows the entire procedure.

Listing 8.26

```
Private Const adhcTop = "Top"
Private Const adhcLeft = "Left"
Private Const adhcRight = "Right"
Private Const adhcBottom = "Bottom"
Private Const adhcWidth = "Width"
Private Const adhcHeight = "Height"
Private Const adhcState = "State"

Public Sub SaveCoords(AppName As String)

    Dim strName As String

    On Error GoTo HandleErrors

    strName = frm.Name

    ' Use the name of the application as the highest
    ' level, and the form's name as the next level.
    ' This way, you could have multiple forms in the same
    ' app use this code.

    Call SaveSetting( _
     AppName, strName, adhcState, WindowState)
    Call SaveSetting( _
     AppName, strName, adhcTop, Top)
    Call SaveSetting( _
```

```
         AppName, strName, adhcLeft, Left)
        Call SaveSetting( _
         AppName, strName, adhcWidth, Width)
        Call SaveSetting( _
         AppName, strName, adhcHeight, Height)

ExitHere:
    Exit Sub

HandleErrors:
    Select Case Err.Number
        Case Else
            Call HandleError("FormInfo.SaveCoords", _
             Err.Number, Err.Description)
    End Select
    Resume ExitHere
End Sub
```

The RetrieveCoords procedure does the same sort of work, but instead of calling the SaveSetting procedure, it calls GetSetting instead. In this case, the code doesn't do anything if the form was maximized or minimized when its coordinates were saved. If you're interested, look at the RetrieveCoords procedure in the FormInfo class module.

What's Left?

By now, you've seen what's in the FormInfo class module and how to use the methods and properties it contains. You've seen how many of the procedures work, although we haven't discussed every single line of code. You may find it interesting to study the GetCoords and GetParentCoords procedures, private to the class. These procedures calculate the coordinates of windows and the coordinates of windows' parents. You may also want to investigate the Center method, which uses the GetCoords and GetParentCoords procedures to calculate the coordinates at which to place a centered form.

Whether or not you study the source code in the FormInfo class module, you will most likely find the functionality it provides useful in your Access applications. Because Access gives you so little information about the size and location of its forms, you're sure to find many uses for the class and its properties and methods.

TIP

Although not directly related to forms, we've taken the FormInfo class and created a similar AccessInfo class. This class allows you to manipulate the main Access window in much the same way as you might manipulate a form. If you need to position the main Access window, or you want to remove the Access caption bar, check out the AccessInfo class in the sample project. In addition, the form frmSystemMenu demonstrates using the AccessInfo class.

Automatically Resizing Forms

When you set up Windows to run on your computer, you must choose a screen driver for use with your hardware. Your choice of screen driver allows your monitor to display a specific screen resolution, usually 640×480 (standard VGA), 800×600 (Super VGA), 1024×768 (XGA, Super VGA, or 8514/a), or 1280×1024. These numbers refer to the number of picture elements (*pixels*) in the horizontal and vertical directions.

If you create forms that look fine on your screen running at 1024×768, those same forms may be too large to be displayed by a user who's working at 640×480. Similarly, if you create forms at 640×480, someone working at 1280×1024 will see them as very small forms. (A full-screen form created at 640×480 takes up about a quarter of the screen at 1280×1024—although this is not necessarily something your users will want to change. Many people who use large displays and high-resolution adapters appreciate the fact that they can see not only a full-screen form, but other Access objects at the same time.)

One unattractive solution to this problem is to create multiple versions of your forms, one for each screen resolution you wish to support. This, of course, requires maintaining each of those forms individually. The following sections deal directly with the resolution issue. We present a class module you can use to scale your forms as they load, allowing them to look reasonable at almost any screen resolution. In addition, once you've solved the original problem, it's not difficult to extend this so the code allows users to resize a form and all its controls at runtime.

The sample form, frmScaleTest, demonstrates the technique of resizing a form to fit your screen resolution at load time. It also allows you to resize all the controls on the form as you resize the form. To try this out, load the form and try it out.

Figure 8.29 shows a "mocked-up" image, containing the same form displayed at two different sizes at once. If you want to see now what's involved in making this happen, open frmScaleTest in Design view and check out the code in its module. Most of what you find there is comments—it takes very little effort on your part to get forms to scale. Basically, you must instantiate an object, set a property or two, and it works.

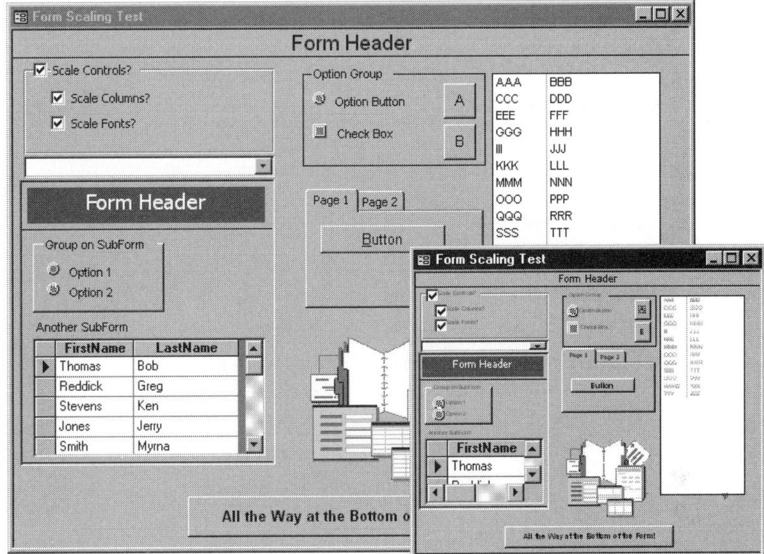

FIGURE 8.29:

Two instances of the same form, one at full size and the other scaled to a smaller size

Understanding Screen Resolutions

Before you can understand the solution to the screen resolution issue, you must understand the problem. Figure 8.30 shows a scale image of the four standard Windows screen resolutions, superimposed. As you can see, a form that appears full screen at 640×480 will take up only a small portion of a 1280×1024 screen, and a full-screen form at 1024×768 will be too large for a screen at 800×600.

FIGURE 8.30:

All four standard screen resolutions, superimposed

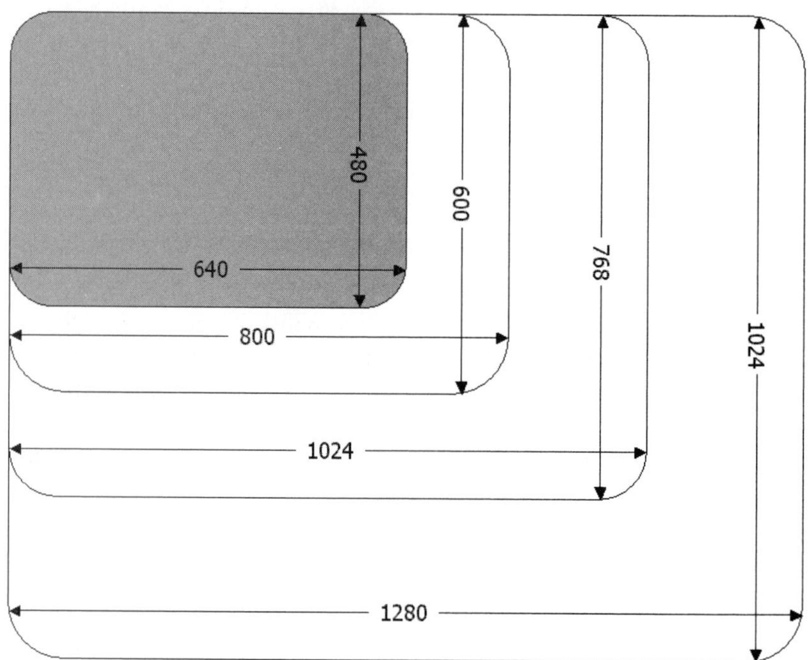

The difference in the number of pixels is only one of two issues you need to consider in scaling forms. You must also think about the size of the pixels—the number of pixels per logical inch of screen space. Each screen driver individually controls how large each pixel is in relation to what Windows thinks an "inch" is. Windows provides API calls to gather all this information, which we'll need later in this section. For now, the information of concern is the number of twips per pixel. (A *twip* is equivalent to 1/1440 inch.) Practical experience shows that screens at 640×480 use 15 twips per pixel, and all other VGA screen resolutions use 12 twips per pixel (although this isn't a requirement, nor is it always true). This means that at low-resolution VGA, 100 pixels take up 1500 twips (a little more than one logical inch), while at higher resolutions, 100 pixels take up 1200 twips (a little less than one logical inch). Therefore, to correctly scale your forms for different resolutions, you need to take both ratios into account. You need to compare, for both the screen on which the form was prepared and the screen on which it will be displayed, the pixels used and the twips-per-pixel value. The ratios of these values control how you scale the form.

The class module FormResize (and its helper classes, ControlResize and SectionResize) includes the code necessary to scale your forms at load time and to allow resizing by users at runtime. This code makes extensive use of Windows API calls to retrieve information about the current display and the sizes of forms. (For more information about the Windows API and calling DLLs, see Chapter 16.)

Scaling Forms as They Load

To solve the problem of displaying forms so that they take up the same proportion of the screen real estate on different screen resolutions, it would seem that all you need to do is calculate the ratio of the original screen dimensions to the current screen dimensions and scale the form accordingly. Unfortunately, the calculation is further complicated by the twips-per-pixel issue. Because different screen resolutions use a different number of twips for each pixel, you must also take this into account when calculating the new size for the form. The x-axis sizing ratio, when moving from 640×480 to 1024×768, is not just 1024/640. You must multiply that value by the ratio of the twips-per-pixel values. (Think of it this way: as far as Windows is concerned, pixels are "bigger" at 640×480. At higher resolutions, a pixel takes up fewer twips.) Figure 8.31 shows a single form, 320×240 pixels, created in 640×480 resolution, as it would display on a screen in 1024×768 resolution. The first example shows it unscaled, and the second example shows it scaled.

FIGURE 8.31:

Scaling a form causes it to appear approximately the same on screens with different resolutions.

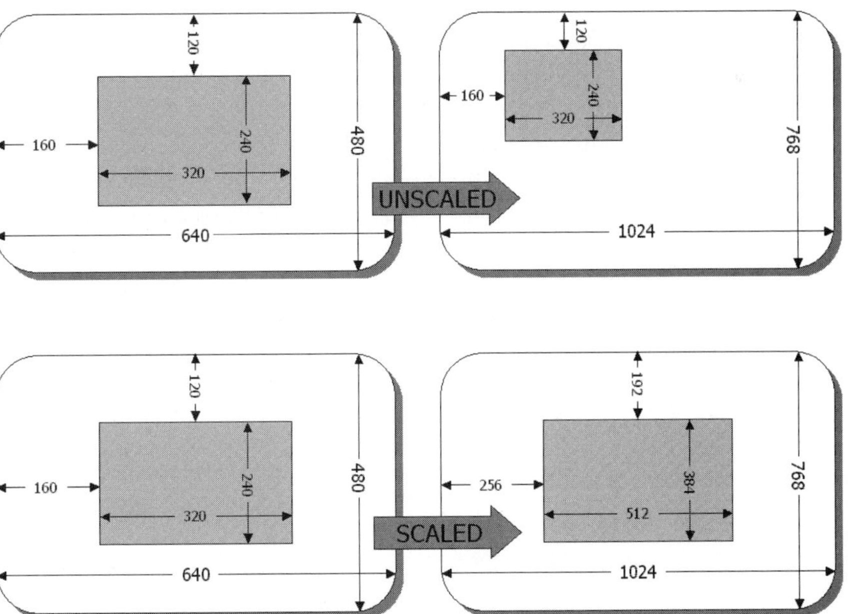

Necessary Information

To correctly scale your form, the code needs to know the screen resolution at which you created your form (so it can calculate the ratios between the screen widths and heights). It also needs to know the logical dots-per-inch values for the vertical and horizontal dimensions of the screen where you created the form. You may know offhand the screen resolution you use on your development machine, but you're unlikely to know the logical dots-per-inch values. Therefore, we've provided the frmScreenInfo form, shown in Figure 8.32. This form has one purpose in life: it provides information about your current screen settings so you can correctly call the SetDesignCoords method described below.

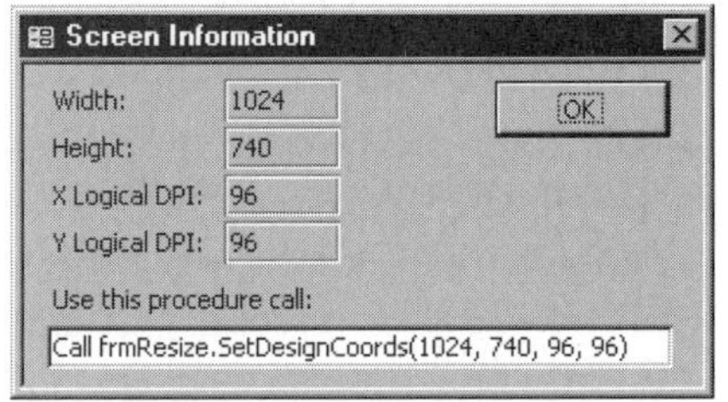

FIGURE 8.32: Use frmScreenInfo to calculate necessary screen coordinate information.

The code in this form's class module calculates the current size of the screen, taking into account the area chewed up by taskbars docked to the edges of your screen. It also calculates the logical dots-per-inch values and formats the method call as you'll need for your form. Once you've run this form, cut the value in the text box to the clipboard and paste it into your form's Open event procedure code. (The frmScreenInfo form does assume that you've named your FormResize variable as frmResize. If you change that name, you'll need to modify the method call, as well.)

TIP

The information form, frmScreenInfo, takes taskbars into account when it calculates the screen resolution. If your users don't display their taskbars, you might want to set all taskbars on your system to be hidden when not in use. (Usually, this is the AutoHide property for the application.) That way, at worst, your form will scale too small (if you don't show taskbars but users do).

Using FormResize

From your application's perspective, the FormResize class manages all the scaling of your form and its controls. Once you've set up a connection between your form and its "shadow" FormResize object, the code in the class module handles all the work for you.

In order to hook up your form, you'll need to add a little code to the form's module. You must, at least, follow these steps:

1. To the form module's Declarations area, add a variable declaration for the FormResize object. Most likely, you'll want it to be Private:

   ```
   Private frmResize As FormResize
   ```

2. In the form's Open event procedure, you must instantiate the FormResize object, and tell the object which form to shadow:

   ```
   Private Sub Form_Open()
       Set frmResize = New FormResize
       Set frmResize.Form = Me
   End Sub
   ```

If you go no further than that, your form:

- Will *not* perform scaling at load time. That is, it will not redimension itself to fit a changed screen resolution. (See the ScaleForm property in Table 8.8.)
- Will resize all its controls in reaction to the user resizing the form's border. (See the ScaleControls property in Table 8.8.)
- Will scale fonts for text box, combo box, list box, label, command button, toggle button, and tab controls so that they'll appear correctly in resized controls. (See the ScaleFonts property in Table 8.8.)
- Will scale columns in multicolumned list and combo box controls. (See the ScaleColumns property in Table 8.8.)

If you want to allow the form to scale its size, position, and contents at load time, based on its original design-time dimensions, you need to take one extra step: you must call the SetDesignCoords method of the FormResize object, indicating the screen size and dots/inch ratios on your design machine. As discussed in the "Necessary Information" section above, you can use the sample form frmScreenInfo to retrieve information about your screen, as you create your form. With this step added, your Open event procedure might look like this:

```
Private Sub Form_Open()
    Set frmResize = New FormResize
```

```
    Set frmResize.Form = Me
    Call frmResize.SetDesignCoords(1280, 1024, 96, 96)
End Sub
```

TIP

One of the benefits of using a class module to contain all this code (besides the fact that it allows the code to react to events of your form) is that you can attach the FormResize class to as many forms as you like, open them all at once, and have each form scale and resize individually. Although VBA loads multiple copies of the data—that is, each instance of the FormResize class in memory has its own property values—it only loads a single copy of the code. Using this technique is efficient and makes coding easier.

Working with FormResize Properties

Once you've set up the code, as in the previous section, you can programmatically control the behavior of the FormResize object. By setting various properties of the object, you can retrieve information about the form, make the form resize in just the way you want, or control the state of the form. Table 8.8 lists all the properties of the FormResize object, and Table 8.9 lists the public methods of the object. Some of these properties are somewhat subtle. For example:

- The Controls property returns a collection of ControlResize objects. Each of these objects has a Control property, which returns a reference to the control being shadowed. Although you can work through the FormSize's Controls collection to get to a particular control on your form, you're better off using the form's Controls collection instead. You'll generally touch only three properties of a ControlResize object: ScaleIt, FloatIt, and SizeIt, described in the next section.
- The four Scale… properties (ScaleColumns, ScaleControls, ScaleFonts, ScaleForm) allow you to control various behaviors of the form's resizing. All these properties are Boolean values except the ScaleControls property, which has three possible values: scYes, scNo, and scAtLoad. Choosing scAtLoad tells the FormResize class to scale controls at load time only, and then never again. This option is useful if you want to make sure your form displays correctly at load time, resizing the form and its controls based on the screen resolution, but from then on, you want to keep the controls the size they were at load time.

- The MaxWidth, MaxHeight, MinWidth, and MinHeight properties allow you to set minimum and maximum sizes for the form. Using these properties (all measured in twips), you can specify the range of sizes for your form. In addition, if you specify values less than 1 (that is, fractional values) the code interprets these as indicating fractions of the available space. That is, if you specify a MinWidth property of 0.25, the form will never be allowed to be narrower than one-fourth of the client area (or the screen, if it's a pop-up form). (If you need to convert from twips to pixels, or back, you can use the TwipsPerPixelX and TwipsPerPixelY properties.)

The following sample code, from frmScaleTest, sets up many of the form FormResize properties (some of these are redundant—they're setting values to match the defaults):

```
Private Sub Form_Open(Cancel As Integer)
    Set frmResize = New FormResize
    Set frmResize.Form = Me
    Call frmResize.SetDesignCoords(991, 721, 96, 96)
    frmResize.ScaleFonts = True
    frmResize.ScaleForm = True
    frmResize.ScaleColumns = True
    frmResize.ScaleControls = scYes
    frmResize.MinWidth = 0.1
    frmResize.MaxWidth = 0.9
    frmResize.MinHeight = 0.1
    frmResize.MaxHeight = 0.9
End Sub
```

TABLE 8.8: FormResize Properties

Property	Type	Description
Controls	Collection	(Read-only) Collection of ControlResize objects contained within the FormResize object. Generally, you won't need to work with this collection, but it's available for your convenience. Under no circumstances should you add or delete anything from this collection in your code.
Form	Form	Sets or retrieves the reference to the real form that the FormResize class is associated with. No other properties or methods will work correctly until you've set this property.
HeightInTwips	Long	(Read-only) Returns the current height, in twips, of the associated form.

Continued on next page

TABLE 8.8 CONTINUED: FormResize Properties

Property	Type	Description
IsMaximized	Boolean	Sets or retrieves the maximized state of the associated form. Set the property to True in order to programmatically maximize the form.
IsMinimized	Boolean	Sets or retrieves the minimized state of the associated form. Set the property to True in order to programmatically minimize the form.
MaxHeight	Single	Sets or retrieves the maximum height of the associated form. If greater than 1, specifies the maximum height in twips. If less than or equal to 1, specifies the percentage of the available space to fill (the MDI client for normal forms, the screen for pop-up forms).
MaxWidth	Single	Sets or retrieves the maximum width of the associated form. If greater than 1, specifies the maximum width in twips. If less than or equal to 1, specifies the percentage of the available space to fill (the MDI client for normal forms, the screen for pop-up forms)
MinHeight	Single	Sets or retrieves the minimum height of the associated form. If greater than 1, specifies the minimum height in twips. If less than or equal to 1, specifies the percentage of the available space to fill (the MDI client for normal forms, the screen for pop-up forms).
MinWidth	Single	Sets or retrieves the minimum width of the associated form. If greater than 1, specifies the minimum width in twips. If less than or equal to 1, specifies the percentage of the available space to fill (the MDI client for normal forms, the screen for pop-up forms).
ScaleColumns	Boolean	Set to False to disable scaling of column widths within combo and list boxes (the default value is True).
ScaleControls	ScaleControlsWhen	Set to scNo (0) to disable scaling of controls on the form. Set to scAtLoad (1) to cause controls to be scaled when you first load the form, and then never again. Set to scYes (-1) (the default) to always scale controls in relation to the shape of the form.
ScaleFonts	Boolean	Set to False to disable scaling of fonts on the screen (the default value is True).
TwipsPerPixelX	Long	(Read-only) Returns the ratio between twips and pixels in the horizontal direction for the current screen driver. Can be used to convert from twips to pixels, when necessary.
TwipsPerPixelY	Long	(Read-only) Returns the ratio between twips and pixels in the vertical direction for the current screen driver. Can be used to convert from twips to pixels, when necessary.
ScaleForm	Boolean	Set to False to disable scaling of the form to match its original screen size. This doesn't disable scaling of controls when you resize the form at runtime, only the automatic scaling of the form to match its original shape.
WidthInTwips	Long	(Read-only) Returns the current width, in twips, of the associated form.

TABLE 8.9: FormResize Methods

Method	Parameters	Description
RescaleForm		Forces a recalculation of control and font sizes. If you change a property manually (ScaleFonts or ScaleColumns, for example), you'll want to call this method to force a recalc of the form's display.
SetDesignCoords	Width, Height, DPIX, DPIY	Optionally, call this method to indicate the original, design-time screen coordinates. If you don't call this method, FormResize will assume that the design-time coordinates match the runtime coordinates, and no automatic scaling at load time will occur. Use frmScreenInfo to gather the necessary information for this method call at design time. (Width and Height represent coordinates of the screen, and DPIX and DPIY represent the dots/inch in the horizontal and vertical directions.)

Managing Features on a Control-by-Control Basis

In some cases, you won't want to scale each and every control on a form. You may want to scale some controls but leave others the same size they were when you created them, no matter how the end-user mangles your form's shape. In order to "turn off" scaling, you have several options:

- You can set the FormResize object's ScaleControls property to scNo at design time. No controls will ever scale.
- You can set the FormResize object's ScaleControls property to scNo at any time while the form is running. Doing this will temporarily turn off scaling of the controls on the form, as the user resizes the form. (Change the property back to scYes when you want scaling to start again.)
- You can leave the ScaleControls property alone but modify properties of each individual control for which you'd like to disable scaling.

This section provides the details for taking the third option and adds some new functionality along the way, as well.

Properties of the ControlResize Object

In order to do its work, the FormResize object keeps track of information about each control on the form with which it's associated. To manage the information, it uses the ControlResize class to create a ControlResize object corresponding to each control. This object keeps track of items such as the control's name, its coordinates, and its parent (a FormResize object). Most of the object's public methods and properties are public only so that they can be used from the parent object, but it does include some properties that you'll find useful. Table 8.10 describes each of the properties of the ControlResize object that you're likely to use.

TABLE 8.10: Useful Properties of the ControlResize Object

Property	Data Type	Description
FloatIt	ControlFloat: cfRight, cfBottom, cfBoth, ***cfNone****	As you resize the form, the code can float the control towards the right, bottom, or both. (The size won't change.) The distance between the upper-left corner of the control and the specified edge of the form will remain constant.
ScaleIt	ControlScale: csYes, csNo, ***csDefault***	As you resize the form, the code can both float and size the control based on the size of the form (this is the standard rescaling behavior). You can control this on a control-by-control basis, using this property. If you specify csDefault, the control will resize based on the settings you've made for the entire form. Otherwise, you can disable or enable scaling for each particular control.
SizeIt	ControlSize: czRight, czBottom, czBoth, ***czNone***	As you resize the form, the code can size the control towards the right, bottom, or both (the upper-left corner of the control won't move). The distance between the upper-left corner of the control and the specified edge of the form will remain constant.

*Default values marked in bold. All values are members of Enums, in ControlResize's class module.

As you can see from Table 8.10, you have more flexibility than simply controlling which controls scale. If you want to control the scalability of individual controls, you can set the ScaleIt property of any control, like this:

```
' mfr is a FormResize object, previously
' instantiated.
mfr.Controls("cmdCancel").ScaleIt = csNo
```

NOTE

If you want to programmatically control scaling, sizing, or floating, you must use the Controls collection of the FormResize object, not the form itself. Controls in the form's Controls collection don't have ScaleIt, SizeIt, and FloatIt properties—only objects based on the ControlResize class have those properties. Members of the FormResize's Controls collection are based on the ControlResize class, so you'll need to use that Controls collection instead.

Using code as in the previous fragment, you'll be able to manage, on a control-by-control basis, whether any specific control should scale to match the size of the form.

TIP

The ControlResize ScaleIt property always overrides the FormResize object's ScaleControls property. Even if you've set the ScaleControls property to False, setting an individual ControlResize object's ScaleIt property to scYes will cause that control to be scaled.

In addition to the ScaleIt property, the ControlResize class also provides two other useful properties that aren't really linked to scaling at all. Using the FloatIt and SizeIt properties, you can control the positioning and sizing of controls in relation to the lower right-hand corner of the form.

For example, Figure 8.33 shows two instances of the same sample form (frmFloatAndSize, from the sample project). As the form grew larger, the controls didn't scale—they actually moved, or resized, to fit the larger space. What's the difference between scaling, floating, and sizing?

- When scaling, the controls' left and top coordinates change, and normally, fonts change size, as well. (You can control this using the FormResize object's ScaleFonts property.) You can control when scaling occurs: always, never, or only when the form first loads.
- When sizing, the controls' left and top coordinates stay fixed, but the width and height change to maintain a constant offset from the bottom and right edge of the form. You can control the direction of the sizing towards the bottom, towards the right, neither, or both.

- When floating, the controls' top and left coordinates change to maintain a constant offset from the bottom and right edge of the form, but the width and height of the controls remain fixed. You can control the direction of the floating towards the bottom, towards the right, neither, or both.

In Figure 8.33, all the controls include one or more of these settings. The form's Load event includes the following code, which sets up all the values (mfr is the module-level variable that refers to the FormResize object):

```
mfr.Controls("txtMain").SizeIt = czBoth
mfr.Controls("cmdTest").FloatIt = cfBoth
mfr.Controls("cmdOK").FloatIt = cfRight
mfr.Controls("cmdCancel").FloatIt = cfRight
With mfr.Controls("lblStatus")
    .FloatIt = cfBottom
    .SizeIt = czRight
End With
```

FIGURE 8.33:

Using the FloatIt and SizeIt properties, you can cause controls to float and size in relation to the lower-right corner of the form.

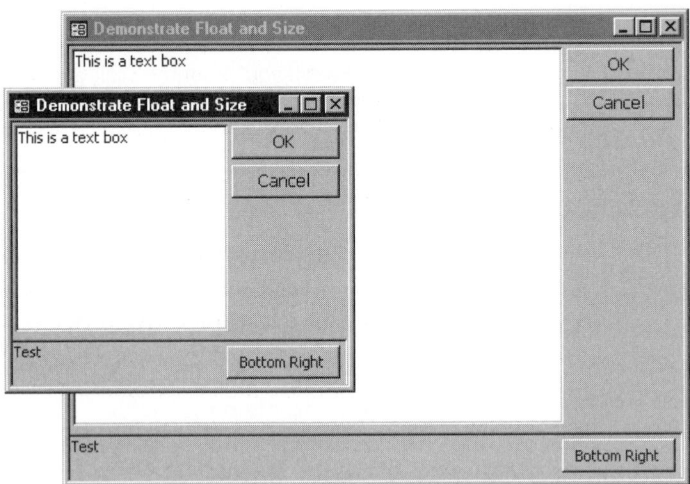

Looking carefully at the property settings, you can work through the details:

- The form sets the ScaleControls property for the associated FormResize object to be scNo, so the controls don't scale to fit the sized form. The ScaleForm property is set to False, as well, so the form doesn't attempt to scale to fit the current screen resolution at load time.

- The text box (txtMain) sizes in both directions as you resize the form. Its upper-left corner doesn't move, but its width and height change.
- The Bottom Right command button (cmdTest) floats in both directions. Its upper-left corner moves to the right and down, as you resize the form. Its width and height never change.
- The two command buttons (cmdOK and cmdCancel) float only to the right. This means that their Left properties change but not their Top properties. Because they're floating, their width and height never change.
- The sunken label (lblStatus) at the bottom of the form floats with the bottom of the form (that is, its Top property changes, but not its Left property). In addition, it floats with the right edge of the form (that is, its Width property changes, but not its Height).

As you might guess, using these control-level properties gives you immense flexibility in the way you create forms. Even if you use none of the scaling features provided by the FormResize class, being able to float and size controls based on the changes made to the size of the form can make your life as a programmer simpler.

Using the Tag Property to Manage Scaling

Because you're most likely to want to set the FloatIt, SizeIt, and ScaleIt properties for your controls once and never modify them again, you may want a way to set these properties at design time. That way, you needn't write any code to set the properties at runtime. Unfortunately, controls don't normally have FloatIt, SizeIt, or ScaleIt properties. To work around this problem, we've set up the ControlResize class module so that you can specify these properties as part of the Tag property of each control. If you follow the rules for supplying tag/value pairs, as discussed in the section "Using the Tag Property to Create Your Own Properties" in Chapter 7, you can easily set the properties you need at design time.

The ControlResize class (the class that manages the scaling of each individual control) includes code that checks the Tag property of each control as it's initializing information about the form and keeps track of the values it finds there. Using the standard technique described in Chapter 7, the code looks for portions of the Tag property containing text like this:

```
ScaleIt=Yes;FloatIt=Yes
```

That is, the code looks for a property name, an equal sign, and a value for the property. If you set up the Tag property for each affected control this way, you needn't write any code in the form's Load event procedure, as shown in the previous section. The sample form, frmFloatAndSizeTag, uses this technique to produce the same results as the sample shown in the previous section. For a complete list of tag names and possible values, see Table 8.11.

TABLE 8.11: Possible Tag Names and Values for Sizing, Scaling, and Floating Individual Controls

Tag Name	Possible Tag Values	Description
FloatIt	Right, Bottom, Both, ***None****	As you resize the form, the code can float the control towards the right, bottom, or both. (The size won't change.) The distance between the upper-left corner of the control and the specified edge of the form will remain constant.
SizeIt	Right, Bottom, Both, ***None***	As you resize the form, the code can size the control towards the right, bottom, or both (the upper-left corner of the control won't move). The distance between the upper-left corner of the control and the specified edge of the form will remain constant.
ScaleIt	Yes, True, On, No, False, Off, ***Default***	As you resize the form, the code can both float and size the control based on the size of the form (this is the standard rescaling behavior). You can control this on a control-by-control basis using this tag value. If you specify Default, the control will resize based on the settings you've made for the entire form. Otherwise, you can disable or enable scaling for each particular control.

*Default values marked in bold.

If you decide to initialize the individual control properties using the Tag property technique, you'll need to add two more class modules to your application: TaggedValues and TaggedValue. Therefore, if you weren't already using those classes for some other reason, you might want to consider carefully whether you want to set those properties. If you set the properties at runtime using code, you don't need the two extra classes. On the other hand, this means you have to write the code to set the properties yourself. If you set the properties at design time, you have to write less code, but you must include the two extra classes.

WARNING

If you do decide to write code, setting the various control properties at runtime, and you leave the TaggedValues/TaggedValue classes out of your project, you may get a compile error when you compile your code. The ControlResize class includes code that references the extra two classes. If you decide to not use the TaggedValues pair of classes, make sure you set the READTAGS conditional compile constant in the ControlResize class to be False. The constant is True by default, and you'll need to change it manually if you decide to not include the two extra classes.

Steps to Successful Scaling

If you're upgrading to the current version of this technology from a previous version of this book, you'll find that the resizing algorithm used in this book works much better than it did in previous versions. We no longer see the troublesome round-off errors when resizing fonts that plagued previous versions of the code.

Even though the code works better in this version, there are still some rules you must follow to make it possible for this code to work:

- Use TrueType fonts for each control you will scale. This code will scale only the fonts in text box, combo box, list box, label, command button, toggle button, and tab controls. Unfortunately, the default font used in all controls is not scalable. You must either modify your form defaults or select all the controls and change the font once you're finished designing. On the other hand, beware of using fonts that won't be available on your users' machines. All copies of Windows 95 and NT ship with Arial and Times Roman fonts; choosing one of these for your buttons and labels and list, combo, and text boxes guarantees a certain level of success. Of course, all the Office applications use the Tahoma font, and you may wish to use this font in order to "blend in" with the rest of Office.
- Do not design forms at 1280×1024 and expect them to look good at 640×480. By the time forms get scaled that far down, they're very hard to read. Using 800×600 or 1024×768 for development should provide forms that look reasonable at all resolutions.
- The current implementation of this code cannot resize subforms shown as datasheets. We tried vainly to accomplish this—there's simply too much information we need that isn't available about the row and column sizes to make this possible. You should be aware that the contents of datasheets will not scale, although their physical size will.

- Do not attempt to mix the AutoCenter property with the ScaleForm property of a FormResize object set to True. The AutoCenter property will attempt to center the form before it's scaled and will cause Access to place the form somewhere you don't expect it to be.
- Make labels and text boxes a bit wider than you think you actually need. Windows doesn't always provide the exact font size the code requests, so you're better off erring on the generous side when you size your controls.

Scaling Your Own Forms

To include this functionality in your own applications, follow these steps:

1. Import the class modules FormResize, ControlResize, and SectionResize from CH08.MDB into your own application. If you intend to use the Tag property of controls to manage their behaviors, you'll also need to import the TaggedValues and TaggedValue class modules. (If you do this, make sure the READTAGS compile-time constant in the ControlResize class module is set appropriately. If you include TaggedValues/TaggedValue, set it to True. If you don't, set the constant to be False.)
2. Ensure that all the fonts on your form are scalable. (Use TrueType fonts if possible, since they're all scalable.)
3. In the Declarations area of the form module for each form you'd like to scale, declare an object variable to refer to the FormResize object that will mirror your form (the actual name doesn't matter, of course):

   ```
   Private frmResize As FormResize
   ```

4. In the form's Open event procedure, instantiate your object variable and set its Form property to be the current form. If you intend to scale the form so that it appears proportional to the screen, as it did when you designed it, you must also call the SetDesignCoords method. Pass to the method the x- and y-resolutions of the screen for which it was designed, along with the logical dots-per-inch values for the horizontal and vertical dimensions of your screen. (Use frmScreenInfo to generate this line of code.)

   ```
   Private Sub Form_Open(Cancel As Integer)
       ' Instantiate the class to handle all resizing.
       Set frmResize = New FormResize
   ```

```
        ' Tell the new object what form you want
        ' it to work with.
        Set frmResize.Form = Me

        ' Tell the object the size of the screen
        ' on which you designed the form, and the
        ' dots/inch in that screen resolution.
        ' Replace these four integers with your own
        ' values. Use frmScreenInfo to calculate
        ' these for you.
        ' If you don't call this method at all,
        ' the code will display the form as you
        ' originally designed it, with no scaling
        ' at load time.
        Call frmResize.SetDesignCoords(1024, 740, 96, 96)
    End Sub
```

5. If you'd like, set any/all of the optional FormResize properties, such as ScaleControls, ScaleForm, ScaleFonts, or ScaleColumns. (See Table 8.8.)

6. If you want to control floating, scaling, or sizing of individual controls, either set their Tag properties appropriately, or write code in the form's Load event to handle these individual properties. (See the sample forms, frmFloatAndSize, and frmFloatAndSizeTag.)

WARNING Code in the FormResize class sets the OnResize and OnLoad event properties of your form to be "[Event Procedure]". If you have other values in those properties already, they will be overwritten at runtime. That is, if you're calling a macro or a function from those properties, the macro or function won't be called. Instead, the code in the FormResize class will run. If you're already calling an event procedure from the Resize or Load event (that is, you've set the OnLoad and OnResize properties to be "[Event Procedure]", your code will run first, and then the code in the FormResize class will run.

Reacting to Form Events

The FormResize object has event procedures that run in reaction to your form's Load and Resize events. Because of this, if you look in the FormResize class module, you'll find frm_Load and frm_Resize event procedures. And these event procedures actually do run, in reaction to your forms' events. How does this happen?

Continued on next page

Look carefully at the Declarations area in the FormResize class module, and you'll find the following declaration:

```
Private WithEvents frm As Form
```

When you set the Form property of the FormResize object, code within the Property Set procedure makes frm refer to your form. The WithEvents keyword adds an extra feature: when events occur in your form, event procedures in the associated class module (FormResize, in this case) are run. Inside a form's own class module, this all happens without the WithEvents reference, but it works in exactly the same way. That is, the class module associated with a form is given preferred treatment—you needn't declare or set up that reference to the form yourself, but under the covers, that's what's going on.

We've used this "ghosting" technique several times throughout this book, most notably in Chapters 7, 8, and 17. It's a great way to provide classes that hook up to events of an object you've created, without you, as the developer, having to modify your own objects to set up event procedures.

Some issues to consider:

- If you have your own event procedures, their code will run before the "ghosted" procedures in the class modules. Specifically, code in your form's Resize event procedure will run before the matched code in the FormResize class module.
- In an attempt to optimize form and report behaviors, these objects don't even raise their events so other classes can synch with them unless you've placed the text "[Event Procedure]" in the associated event property. That's why you'll find code like the following fragment in classes that use this technique. This code makes sure that the necessary event properties have the correct values:

```
If Len(frm.OnResize) = 0 Then
    frm.OnResize = "[Event Procedure]"
End If
If Len(frm.OnLoad) = 0 Then
    frm.OnLoad = "[Event Procedure]"
End If
```

How It Works

Although you can use the FormResize class without understanding how it works at all, you may be interested in delving into the workings of the class. It's not as complex as you might think, once you get past the mountain of API calls required to do the work.

When you first set the Form property of the FormResize object, the Property Set procedure calls the GetScreenInfo procedure within the class. This procedure is almost identical to the similar procedure in the FormInfo class discussed earlier in the chapter. For a discussion about retrieving screen information, see the previous section, "Retrieving Information about the Screen."

When your form raises its Load event, the associated event procedure in the FormResize object starts the scaling process (unless you've set the ScaleForm property to be False). The event procedure calls the ScaleFormSize procedure, which includes the following code:

```
Call GetScreenScale(decFactorX, decFactorY)

If (decFactorX <> 1) Or (decFactorY <> 1) Then

    Call ScaleFormContents(decFactorX, decFactorY)
    Call MoveForm(decFactorX, decFactorY)

End If
```

The GetScreenScale procedure fills in the two parameters, decFactorX and decFactorY, with the scaling factors in the two directions. It fills these values based on comparing the current screen resolution and the original, design-time resolution. Basically, the GetScreenScale procedure boils down to these two lines of code:

```
decFactorX = CDec(mptCurrentScreen.x / mptDesignScreen.x) _
 * (mptDesignDPI.x / mptCurrentDPI.x)
decFactorY = CDec(mptCurrentScreen.y / mptDesignScreen.y) _
 * (mptDesignDPI.y / mptCurrentDPI.y)
```

These lines calculate the ratio of the current screen resolution to the resolution that was active when the form was created. The original values have already been stored into the mptDesignScreen POINTAPI value, and the current screen resolution values have already been placed into mptCurrentScreen. (The POINTAPI data type, defined in the FormResize class, contains two Long integers, x and y.) Starting on this fresh, you might be tempted to write this code simply, like this:

```
decFactorX = mptCurrentScreen.x / mptDesignScreen.x
decFactorY = mptCurrentScreen.y / mptDesignScreen.y
```

and it would, in general, work. There are two issues still left to be resolved:

- The code needs to take into account the differences in the number of twips per pixel between different display adapters.

- Division of Long integers will result in an unknown data type. It might be a Long integer, or it might be a Double. Rather than leaving this to fate, the code needs to convert the result to a known data type that won't have any round-off errors.

To solve the first issue, the code multiplies the scaling factors by the ratio of the twips-per-pixel value for the original display, as compared to the value for the current display:

```
decFactorX = mptCurrentScreen.x / mptDesignScreen.x _
 * (mptDesignDPI.x / mptCurrentDPI.x)
decFactorY = mptCurrentScreen.y / mptDesignScreen.y _
 * (mptDesignDPI.y / mptCurrentDPI.y)
```

Finally, to convert the results to a specific data type, we decided to use the barely supported Decimal type. This subtype of the variant provides for less round-off errors than does the Double data type and requires no more space in memory. Unfortunately, you can't define a variable "As Decimal"—you must declare it "As Variant" and use the CDec function to assign a Decimal value into the variable. Therefore, the code uses this function to convert output value into a Decimal:

```
decFactorX = CDec(mptCurrentScreen.x / mptDesignScreen.x) _
 * (mptDesignDPI.x / mptCurrentDPI.x)
decFactorY = CDec(mptCurrentScreen.y / mptDesignScreen.y) _
 * (mptDesignDPI.y / mptCurrentDPI.y)
```

Armed with the values for decFactorX and decFactorY, ScaleFormSize has the information it needs to correctly scale the form as you open it in the new display resolution. The code should be able to multiply the form's width, height, and position of the upper-left corner by that scaling factor and end up with the form in a relative position on the screen with the new width and height.

Scaling the Form's Contents

Scaling the form is only part of the problem, however. Just changing the size of the container won't help much if you can't see all the controls inside it. Therefore, you need a way to change the size of all the controls inside the form as well. The ScaleFormContents procedure does this work for you, and the code resizes each control, in turn, to maintain its proportions based on the new screen resolution. In addition, the same code gets called when you resize the form and scale all the controls to fit the new form size. This can be a striking feature, allowing the user to make a form take up less screen real estate but still be available for use.

To accomplish this visual feat, the FormResize class reacts to the Resize event of your form, calls the ScaleFormContents procedure (just as the code in the form's Load event procedure did, if necessary), and loops through all the controls on the form, scaling them by the ratio between the original size of the form and the current size of the form. Note that in this situation you don't care about any screen resolution issues; you're just comparing the current size of the form to its original load size to find the sizing ratio.

TIP

If you switch a form from Design view to Form view and the form will shrink at runtime (it was designed at a higher screen resolution than the current resolution), Access will not repaint the screen correctly. We recommend that in this situation, you close the form and open it again in Form view, rather than switching directly between views.

Scaling the Controls

In theory, ScaleFormContents does nothing more than loop through all the controls on the form, scaling their locations and sizes by the scaling factors calculated in the calling function. In practice, there are a number of details that aren't, at first, obvious. These are some of the issues:

- The order of events is important. If your form is growing, you must expand the section heights before you allow the controls to expand. Otherwise, the expanding controls will push out the boundaries of the sections and make the scaling invalid. The opposite holds true if your form is shrinking. In that case, you cannot shrink the section heights until after you've sized all the controls. Otherwise, you risk artificially compressing the control locations.
- You must deal carefully with controls that contain other controls. The code handles these as "groups"—that is, a group of controls contained within a container control. A group can contain toggle buttons, option buttons, and check boxes. A subform or a tab control can contain any control and possibly yet another subform (nested, at most, two levels deep). To maintain the correct scaling, you need to walk through all the controls on the form, build an array containing information about all the container controls, scale all the controls on the form, and then scale the containers. In addition, if you run across a subform, you must recursively call the function again, scaling all the controls on that subform. If that subform contains a subform, you must

call the function once more to handle that final subform. Once the function has handled all the controls on the form, it loops through the array of containers and scales them correctly.

- Some controls don't need their height or font scaled. For example, you can't really change the height of a check box. Several controls don't even expose a FontName property. The code calls the ChangeHeight and ChangeFont functions to find out whether it should bother trying to change the particular property at all.
- You want to *move* forms only when they're first loaded. After that, moving forms should be up to the user. Therefore, the code that positions the form itself should be called only if the subroutine was called from the form's Open event procedure.

Using Collections of Objects

Under the covers, the FormResize class contains a collection of ControlResize objects, each one of which corresponds to a control on the form. When you set the Form property of the FormResize object, the code builds the Controls collection and uses that collection when it works with the controls on the form. (The code can't use the built-in Controls collection because it must store more information than is normally available for any given control.) Each ControlResize object maintains a reference (a pointer or a memory address) referring to its parallel control. There's one problem: if you resize the form so small that a subform control can't be displayed, Access destroys the control and later recreates it when you resize the form larger again. This isn't a problem for Access, but it caused us immense problems as we tried to architect this class. If you dig carefully through the code in FormResize, you'll find several procedures devoted to catching this problem and recreating the Controls collection when necessary. Access' optimization attempt (that is, destroying and recreating subforms) certainly didn't make this entire process simple for us.

The rest of the gory details concerning how the individual controls are resized is, well, no fun. If you're interested in modifying the code to meet your own needs, work your way down through the code, starting at the frm_Resize or frm_Load. There are some interesting procedures you may want to look into:

- The RescaleForm procedure is called from the form's Resize event procedure and can be called from your own code as well (that is, it's a public method of the FormResize class). This procedure is the top-level procedure that handles all the work of scaling the form's contents. From here, the code calls CheckAndFixCoords, a procedure that sets the new form size according to the Min/MaxWidth and Min/MaxHeight properties, and then calculates the ratio between the current form size and the original form size. Finally, this procedure calls the ScaleFormContents procedure, which does all the work.

- The ScaleFormContents procedure performs the actual work of changing the size of controls on the form. This procedure is the "heart" of the resizing and scaling operation: it ends up looping through each control on the form and may call itself recursively if the code runs across a subform control.

There's a great deal of code you can work through, if you like. We've attempted to document all the intricacies of this class (which is, most likely, the most complex code you'll find in this book) in the code itself. Even if you never dig through the code to see how it works, you should be able to take advantage of the FormResize class in your own applications, simply by following the instructions provided in the previous sections.

TIP

As you're working through the code, you may want to jump to the definition of a procedure while the cursor is sitting on a call to that procedure. The simplest way to do that is to press the Shift+F2 key. You'll be magically transported to the definition of the procedure, so you can work through its code. To get back to where you were before pressing Shift+F2, press Ctrl+Shift+F2.

```
Private Sub Form_Resize()
    Dim lngWidth As Long
    Dim lngHeight As Long

    ' Get the current coordinates
    lngWidth = Me.InsideWidth
    lngHeight = Me.InsideHeight

    ' Set the detail section height
    Me.Section(acDetail).Height = lngHeight

    ' Set the coordinates of the button so that
    ' it's centered.
    With cmdCentered
        .Width = lngWidth \ 2
        .Height = lngHeight \ 2
```

```
            .Left = (lngWidth - .Width) \ 2
            .Top = (lngHeight - .Height) \ 2
        End With
    End Sub
```

Retrieving and Using the Interior Coordinates of a Form

Aside from issues of screen resolution, you might want to move or resize controls on your form based on the form's size. For example, check out frmCentered, which contains a single button. Code in the form's Resize event procedure keeps the button centered, half the width and half the height of the form, no matter how you change the size of the form.

The InsideWidth and InsideHeight properties of the form make this operation easy. These properties tell you the width and height of the inside area of a form window. (You can't use the Detail section's width to gather this information, because the Detail section's width may be different from the visible window width.) To size a control proportionally, all you need to do is retrieve the InsideWidth and InsideHeight properties of the form, place the control accordingly, and set the height of the Detail section as well. The following fragment shows the code attached to the Resize event of the sample form (frmCentered). Note that this example uses integer division (\) rather than normal division (/) to center the control; this makes the form work more smoothly, because it has no need for the fractional parts of the measurements and can use integer math throughout.

Summary

This chapter focused on many different types of form issues, including working with the form's data and managing the display and location of forms using the Windows API. Through the use of Windows API calls and VBA code, you can exact a great deal of control over the appearance and actions of your forms. In particular, you can control

- The border controls, individually or collectively
- The modality of the form

- When or whether your form gets closed
- The size and position of forms from one Access session to the next
- Form-level error handling

You learned to create various Access tools, including

- Pop-up utilities
- Auto-sizing forms
- Self-disabling navigation buttons

You seen some useful techniques, including

- Working with multiple instances of forms
- Controlling form filtering

And finally, along the way, you encountered some useful tidbits, such as

- Reading and writing items in the System Registry
- Using the Recordset, RecordsetClone and Bookmark properties of forms
- Determining whether a specific form is loaded
- Detecting record position states
- Moving and sizing windows
- Resizing forms for various screen resolutions
- Using the Cycle and KeyPreview properties to control form behavior

Finally, this chapter also provided a number of reusable tools, either as class modules or stand-alone forms. For example, frmCalendar and frmCalc provide simple pop-up forms you can easily import into your own applications. The FormResize class makes it simple for you to control sizing and scaling of your forms, and the FormInfo class makes it simple to manage the positioning and appearance of your forms.

CHAPTER

NINE

9

Topics in Report Design

- Using report and section events and properties
- Controlling sorting and grouping programmatically
- Altering a report layout programmatically

Designing reports ought to be a simple task. In theory, you never have to worry about data input, validation, movement from field to field, or capturing an endless number of different fields on the same form. On the other hand, designing a report that is both functional and aesthetically pleasing can be difficult. You may be attempting to simulate an existing report that exists on paper or is in some other database system, or you may be designing your own reports. In this chapter, we cover some of the basics involved in designing creative reports, focusing on the issues that elude or confuse many developers: report and section events and sorting and grouping. Unlike in many other chapters, you won't find any Windows API calls in this one, since API calls won't help much when you're creating reports. Access gives you all the flexibility you need.

Learning to harness that flexibility is the challenge you face when you create reports. This chapter assumes you've already managed to create simple reports and now need to work with the various events and properties to add functionality. In addition, this chapter covers some common problem areas and suggests interesting solutions to those problems. To get started, you'll take a look at filtering reports to get only the data you need.

WARNING Some of the later examples in this chapter depend on the Snapshot Viewer Control being installed on your machine. If you haven't installed this control (and it's not installed by default), it's likely that the code in this chapter won't compile or run. To fix this problem, you must run the Office 2000 setup program and change the setting for this control to be Run from My Machine instead of the default Install on First Use.

Report versus Forms

As you have most likely discovered, designing effective reports is a very different task than designing forms. A given form may contain various sections, like a report, but unlike reports, most forms are not geared toward repetitive, front-to-back processing. Forms are most often oriented toward presenting and retrieving information from the user in an interactive environment, while reports generally leave the user out of the process. As a matter of fact, your entire mind-set must be different when preparing reports and when dealing with report events, properties, and methods. You might imagine the Access formatting engine walking forward through your report design, formatting sections, pulling

Continued on next page

in data, formatting the data, and retreating as it discovers that the section won't fit on a page, always moving on a forward roll. Sometimes the engine makes two passes through a report (if the report requires a total page count, for example), but in general the Access reporting engine makes a single pass, almost straight through the report's data source. It's this forward motion that propels the Access report engine: there's no going back as Access lays out and prints your reports.

Although you won't be concerned with user input on reports, you will be concerned with undoing actions taken by the steamroller-like reporting engine. When creating a form, you might have placed some initialization code in the form's Open event. This won't work for reports, as you'll see, because the user might open the report in Preview mode and want to restart the report several times, moving back to the first page. Because you haven't reopened the report, the code in the report's Open event won't run again. Understanding the conglomerate of report and section methods, events, and properties and how these differ from the corresponding elements of forms, then, will allow you to tame the Access report engine.

Filtering Your Reports

The Filter, FilterOn, OrderBy, and OrderByOn properties work for reports in very much the same way that they work for forms. That is, you can use these properties to set a filter and turn it on and off and to set a sort order and turn it on and off. To see these properties in action, take a look at frmFilterCustomers. This form allows you to filter your data any way you wish (using the standard Access Filter by Selection, Filter by Form, or Advanced Filter/Sort menu options). Once you're ready, click the Preview Report button to display a report showing just the filtered data. The Preview Report button's Click event executes the code shown in Listing 9.1.

Listing 9.1

```
Sub cmdPreview_Click()
    On Error GoTo HandleErrors

    ' There are three possible scenarios:
    ' 1. No filter
    ' 2. Filter, but not applied
    ' 3. Filter, applied
```

```
        ' The following statement
        ' works for all three cases.
        ' If there's no filter, or
        ' it's not on, strFilter will
        ' be an empty string.
        Dim strFilter As String
        If Me.FilterOn Then
            strFilter = Me.Filter
        End If

        DoCmd.OpenReport ReportName:="rptPhoneBook", _
         View:=acPreview, _
         WhereCondition:=strFilter

    ExitHere:
        Exit Sub

    HandleErrors:
        Select Case Err.Number
            Case 2501
                MsgBox "There are no rows to display!"
            Case Else
                MsgBox Err.Description
        End Select
        Resume ExitHere
    End Sub
```

This code checks the form's Filter and FilterOn properties and opens the report with either the form's current filter or no filter at all. The WhereCondition parameter in the OpenReport method call will contain either a string representing a valid filter, or an empty string (in which case the report will show all its rows). Figure 9.1 shows the form/report pair in action. For more information on using the Filter property, see Chapter 8.

TIP

The sample report, rptPhoneBook, has code in its NoData event that cancels the report if it has not sent any rows to display (see the section "Avoiding Empty Reports—Using the NoData Event," for more information). In that case, the report raises error 2501, indicating that the report's Open event was canceled. You'll need to trap for this error anytime you count on a report's NoData event procedure to cancel a report.

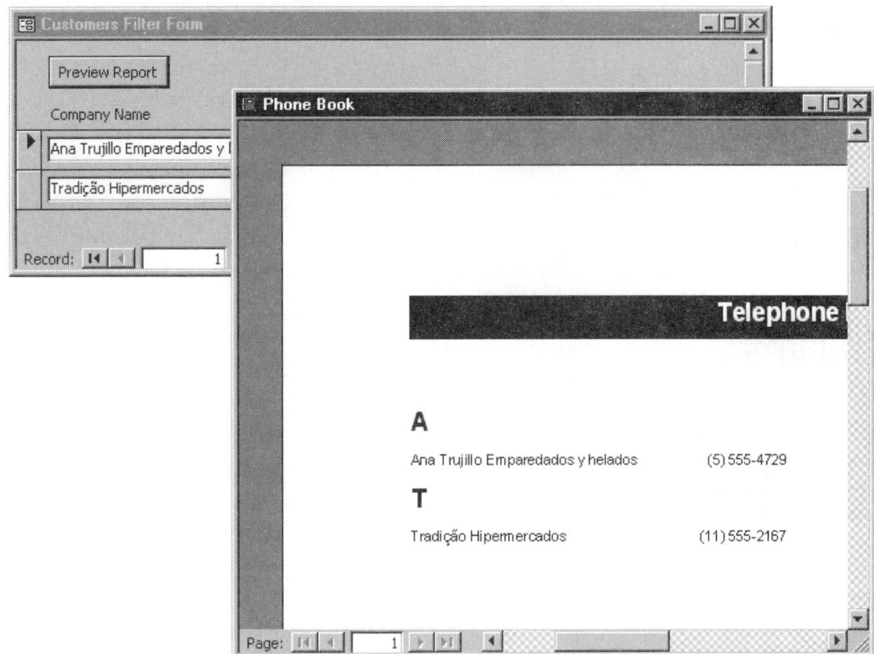

FIGURE 9.1: With the sample form filtered to only display companies where the contact name begins with "Ana," the report shows only the two filtered rows.

To see the OrderBy property at work, open frmOrderByProperty. (Opening this form opens rptOrderByProperty for you.) The form allows you to choose the sort field and sort order—it supplies toggle buttons for Company Name and Sales and a check box for ascending or descending sort. When you make a choice, code attached to the AfterUpdate event of the option group on the form sets the OrderBy property of the report by calling the SortReport procedure in the form's module:

```
Private Const adhcReportName = "rptOrderByProperty"

Private Sub SortReport()
    On Error Resume Next
    Dim strOrderBy As String

    With Reports(adhcReportName)
        strOrderBy = Choose(grpSort, _
         "Company Name", "Sales")
        If chkDescending Then
            strOrderBy = strOrderBy & " DESC"
        End If
```

```
            .OrderBy = strOrderBy
            .OrderOn = True
        End With
    End Sub
```

The OrderBy property becomes the highest-level sort, added on to the normal sorting applied in the Grouping/Sorting dialog box. You'll find you cannot override the sorting that's been done at design time, so you'll have the best luck using this property with reports that aren't currently sorted. Figure 9.2 shows the form and report working together to set the sort order.

FIGURE 9.2:

You can set a report's OrderBy and OrderOn properties programmatically, controlling the sort order. Be careful: the report's native sort order(s) come first, and the OrderBy property then adds on to that sort.

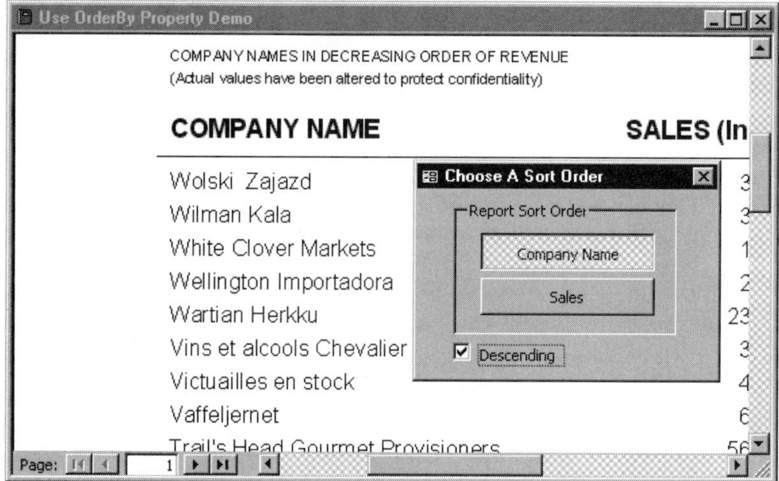

WARNING

Setting the OrderBy property for a report triggers that report's Close and Open events. If you have code attached to either of those events, be aware that changing the sort order for the report will run those event procedures as though you closed and then reopened the report.

To set the ordering based on multiple fields, separate their names with commas. To force one or more of the fields to sort descending, append DESC to the field name. For example, to sort on LastName and FirstName, with FirstName in descending order for each last name, you might create a string for the OrderBy property like this:

```
strOrderBy = "LastName, FirstName DESC"
```

The OrderBy expression works in addition to (that is, *after*) any sorting applied by the report's internal sorting. (See the section "Controlling Sorting and Grouping" later in this chapter for detailed information on controlling the report's internal sorting and grouping from your applications.)

Controlling Sorting and Grouping

After layout of the controls on the report, the highest-level control you have over the results from a report is the sorting/groupings. It's impossible to completely separate these two issues, because grouping is so dependent on the sort order. Figure 9.3 shows a typical report layout, with groups set up based on the OrderDate and LastName fields. If you've created any reports up to this point, you're probably well aware of the possibilities involved with using group headers and footers. What you might not have noticed is that group headers and footers, as well as every other section on the report, supply event hooks; you can use the break in the processing as a signal to your program code, which might need to react to the new group that is about to be printed or has just been printed. (We discuss report and section events throughout this chapter.)

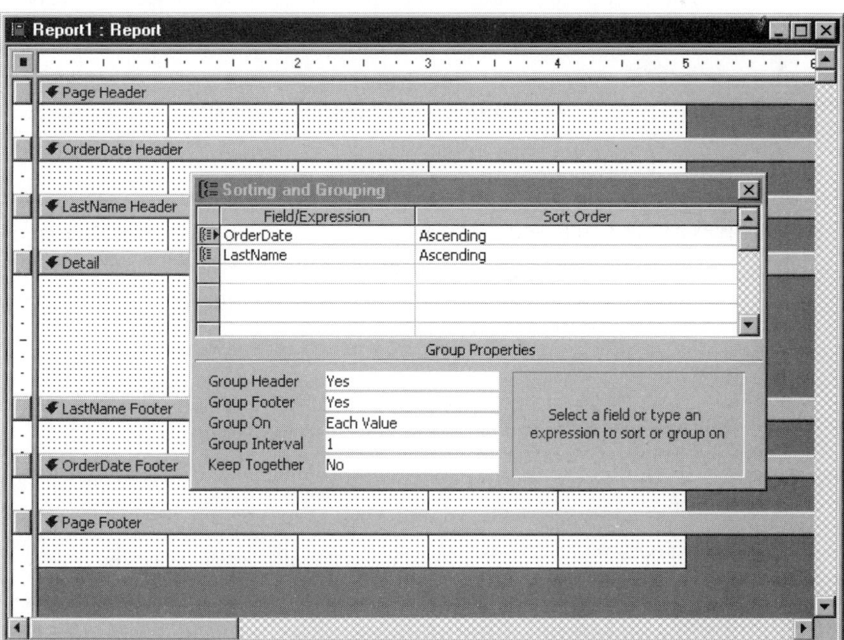

FIGURE 9.3: The sample report is grouped on the OrderDate and LastName fields.

You also may be unaware that you can control the sorting and grouping properties of reports programmatically. You can create new reports or modify existing ones, creating new sections as necessary, and you can modify the built-in sort information as well. The next few sections suggest methods for controlling the sorting and grouping characteristics of reports from your VBA code.

The Section Property

Forms, reports, and all controls expose a Section property. For controls, the Section property is an indication of which section of the parent form or report the control appears on, but this isn't the issue here (although the value returned from a control's Section property corresponds with the numbers used in specifying a form or report's section). For forms and reports, the Section property provides an array of all the sections contained in the given object, referred to by number, as shown in Table 9.1. To refer to any specific section, you treat it as an element from an array of sections, as in the following:

```
Reports("rptExample").Section(1).Visible = False
' or, because Access defines the constant acHeader to be 1:
Reports("rptExample").Section(acHeader).Visible = False
```

Each of these statements makes the Report Header section invisible for rptExample. (As you'll see later in the chapter, a Section object, like any other object, has its own share of properties, methods, and events.)

TABLE 9.1: Section Numbers and Their Descriptions

Setting	Description	VBA Constant
0	Detail section	acDetail
1	Form or Report Header section	acHeader
2	Form or Report Footer section	acFooter
3	Form or Report Page Header section	acPageHeader
4	Form or Report Page Footer section	acPageFooter
5	Group-level 1 Header section (reports only)	
6	Group-level 1 Footer section (reports only)	
7	Group-level 2 Header section (reports only)	
8	Group-level 2 Footer section (reports only)	
9–25	Group-level 3 through 10 Header and Footer sections	

Here are two more items to remember about sections:

- Group-level section headers and footers are numbered consecutively, starting with 5.
- Forms never contain more than five sections (numbered 0 through 4).

There's not much you can do with the Section property on its own; anytime you deal with the Section property, you'll be interested in the properties and events of that particular section. Unlike other property arrays in Access (the Column property, for example, which returns a variant), the Section property does not ever return a value on its own—it just returns a reference to the section in question.

Referring to Sections by Name

Access allows you to refer to form and report sections by name, as well as by number. For example, if you create a new report, the Name property of its Detail section will be Detail, and you can use that name in expressions:

```
Debug.Print Reports("rptSample").Detail.Height
```

That is, Access exposes a property of the report that matches the name of the section, through which you can access any property of that section. The name you type in your expression must match the name of the section, exactly as Access sees it in the property sheet for that section. Names of sections are unique and depend on the order in which the sections were created. To use the name in this context, you'll need to look in the property sheet to find the name of the section and then use that name (or change the name to one of your choosing) to refer to the section.

NOTE

In previous versions of Access, the default names for the Page Header and Page Footer sections were PageHeader and PageFooter, respectively. Reports already expose PageHeader and PageFooter properties, so these names conflicted with the built-in property names, and there was no way to refer to these sections by name—you had to use the section number or constant. To get around this, Access now names these two sections as PageHeaderSection and PageFooterSection, respectively, avoiding the naming conflict.

Working with the Section Property

Once you know how to retrieve a reference to a particular section, you may want to work with that section. For example, you may want to determine if a particular section exists. You may want to change the height of a section or its visibility. Perhaps you need to know how many sections there are. The following paragraphs detail how to accomplish all these tasks.

Determining Whether a Particular Section Exists

Your code may need to take one action if a section exists and a different action if the section hasn't been created. Access provides no simple way of determining whether a given section has been created on a form or report. The following function (from basSections, shown in Listing 9.2) demonstrates one method: it attempts to retrieve the height of the section in question. If this attempt doesn't trigger a runtime error, the section must have existed. Just pass it a reference to the form or report you're interested in, along with a number or constant representing the section on which you need to check. The function returns True if the section exists, and False otherwise:

Listing 9.2

```
Public Function adhIsSection(obj As Object, _
 intSection As AcSection) As Boolean
    ' Returns TRUE if the specified section exists
    ' on the form/report, FALSE otherwise.
    ' Call as:
    ' If adhIsSection(Reports("Report1"), acFooter) Then...
    ' to see if Report1 includes a footer section.

    Dim lngTemp As Variant
    On Error Resume Next

    If TypeOf obj Is Form Or TypeOf obj Is Report Then
        lngTemp = obj.Section(intSection).Height
        adhIsSection = (Err.Number = 0)
    Else
        adhIsSection = False
    End If
End Function
```

This function uses a few interesting techniques:

- It accepts, as its first parameter, a variable of type Object. Because you might want to call this function for a form or a report, it must use a generic object type as a parameter. Later in the function, however, you don't want to check for sections if the object isn't a form or report. To check for this, the code uses the If TypeOf construct:

```
If TypeOf obj Is Form Or TypeOf obj Is Report Then
```

- It accepts, as its second parameter, a variable of type AcSection. This enumerated type includes all the constants representing the various sections (acHeader, acFooter, and so on—check the Object Browser for a full list). By specifying that the parameter is of type AcSection, you'll get IntelliSense—a drop-down list of options—when you write code to call the function. Figure 9.4 shows the drop-down list when calling adhIsSection from the Immediate Window. On the other hand, you needn't choose an option from the list. If you want to check on section 23, you can simply bypass all the values in the list and enter that number as the parameter.
- To determine if the specific section exists or not, the code attempts to retrieve the Height property of the section. If the section doesn't exist, Access will trigger a runtime error, and the code checks for that. If Err.Number is 0, the code returns True; otherwise, it returns False.

```
lngTemp = obj.Section(intSection).Height
IsSection = (Err.Number = 0)
```

FIGURE 9.4:

By specifying the parameter as being of type AcSection, you'll get IntelliSense support when you call the function in code.

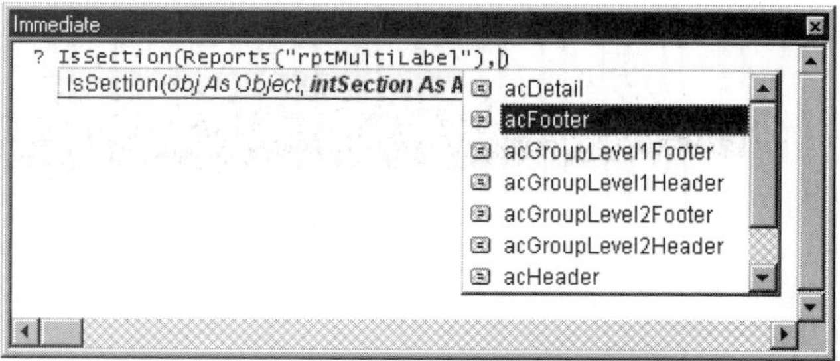

TIP

If you want a section to be as short as possible (just tall enough to include the controls inside it, with no extra vertical space), set the height to 0. A section can never obscure controls it contains, and setting its height to 0 is the quick and easy way to make the section just big enough. Of course, you may want to set it to 0, then retrieve its height (which will be just tall enough for the controls in the section), and then set it a bit taller, so there's some extra "breathing space" around your controls.

Determining How Many Sections Exist

Forms are guaranteed to have no more than 5 sections but may have fewer. Reports may have up to 25 sections (5 standard, plus up to 10 groups, each with both a header and a footer). Access provides no built-in way to determine how many sections an object contains, and you may need to know this information. The function in Listing 9.3 demonstrates one solution to this problem: loop through the report, retrieving section heights and counting all the sections for which you don't trigger a runtime error. Because no report can contain more than 25 sections, that's as far as you need to look.

NOTE

It was tempting, when trying to optimize this function, to make assumptions about the existence of sections. Unfortunately, all the sections aside from the paired page header/footer and report header/footer are individually selectable. This means you really do need to check out every section from 0 through 24.

Listing 9.3

```
Private Const adhcStandardGroups = 5
Private Const adhcMaxGroups = 10

' There are 5 fixed sections,
' plus a possible 10*2 for groupings.
Private Const adhcMaxSections = _
 adhcMaxGroups * 2 + adhcStandardGroups

Public Function adhCountSections(rpt As Report) As Integer
    ' Count the number of sections in a report.

    Dim intCount As Integer
    Dim i As Long

    On Error Resume Next
    intCount = 0

    ' Loop through all the sections,
    ' counting up the ones that exist.
    For i = 0 To adhcMaxSections - 1
        If adhIsSection(rpt, i) Then
            intCount = intCount + 1
```

```
        End If
    Next i
    adhCountSections = intCount
End Function
```

Creating New Report Sections

You can only create new sections on your reports while your report is open in Design view. If you must create a section on-the-fly, you must first open the report in Design view, make your change programmatically, and then open the report in Run view.

To create Page or Report Header or Footer sections, use the DoCmd.RunCommand method, like this:

```
DoCmd.RunCommand acCmdReportHdrFtr
DoCmd.RunCommand acCmdPageHdrFtr
```

For creating group headers and footers, Access provides the CreateGroupLevel function. Because sections beyond the Detail section and the page and report headers and footers are all manifestations of groupings, this function allows you to create all sections except the standard five (Detail, Report Header, Report Footer, Page Header, and Page Footer). This function takes four parameters:

intLevel = CreateGroupLevel(*strReport*, *strExpr*, *fHeader*, *fFooter*)

The following list describes the parameters:

- *strReport* is a string expression containing the name of the report on which to create the group.
- *strExpr* is the expression to use as the group-level expression.
- *fHeader* and *fFooter* are Boolean values that indicate whether to create sections for the header and/or footer. Use True to create the section, False otherwise.

The function returns an index into the array of group levels on your report. (See the next section for more information.) Access supports no more than 10 group levels: Access returns runtime error 2153, "You can't specify more than 10 group levels," if you attempt to create more groups than that.

Listing 9.4 shows a sample procedure, from basSections, that opens a simple report in Design view, adds report header and footer sections, and creates a group based on the OrderDate field. Once it's done, it opens the report in Run mode. If you run this procedure and then attempt to close the report, Access will ask if you want to save your changes. In this case, you'll probably want to choose No.

Listing 9.4

```
Public Sub TestAddGroupLevel()

    ' Open a report in design view, add
    ' report header/footer, and a grouping.

    Const adhcReport = "rptAddGroupLevel"

    On Error GoTo HandleErrors
    DoCmd.Echo False
    DoCmd.OpenReport adhcReport, View:=acViewDesign

    DoCmd.RunCommand acCmdReportHdrFtr
    Call CreateGroupLevel( _
     ReportName:=adhcReport, _
     Expression:="OrderDate", _
     Header:=True, Footer:=True)

    DoCmd.OpenReport adhcReport, View:=acViewPreview

ExitHere:
    DoCmd.Echo True
    Exit Sub

HandleErrors:
    MsgBox Err.Number & Err.Description
    Resume ExitHere
End Sub
```

NOTE

This procedure turns off screen updates before doing its work and turns screen updates back on when it's done. This doesn't guarantee a "clean" screen, however—any subsidiary design windows that were open when you last worked on the report (the Field List window, for example) will still display briefly. This behavior has persisted through four versions of Access. You'd think they would have gotten this one right, by now.

Accessing Group Levels

Access treats group levels in the same manner as sections. It maintains an array of group levels, which you access like this:

```
intOrder = Reports("Report1").GroupLevel(0).SortOrder
```

Just as with a Section object, the GroupLevel object does not provide a default property; rather, you must explicitly access one of its properties. The expression

```
varTemp = Reports("Report1").GroupLevel(0)
```

generates runtime error 438, "Object doesn't support this method or property," because you haven't specified a property or method, and the GroupLevel object can't guess what you're requesting. Just as with sections, Access externalizes no information about the number of group levels.

Although you can't access any properties of GroupLevel or Section objects, you may want to declare an object variable to refer to one and use that object variable in further references (just as you can with any other object type). For example, you can use code like this:

```
Dim glv As GroupLevel
Set glv = Reports("Report1").GroupLevel(0)
Debug.Print "Sort Order: "; glv.SortOrder
Debug.Print "Group Header: "; glv.GroupHeader
Debug.Print "Group Footer: "; glv.GroupFooter
```

to list information about a specific group level. (The next few sections provide details about various GroupLevel properties.)

Because a GroupLevel is an object, you can also use the With...End With construct. The previous code fragment could be rewritten like this:

```
With Reports("Report1").GroupLevel(0)
    Debug.Print "Sort Order: "; .SortOrder
    Debug.Print "Group Header: "; .GroupHeader
    Debug.Print "Group Footer: "; .GroupFooter
End With
```

To enumerate the group levels in a report, you need a function similar to that found in Listing 9.3 that will count or traverse the array of GroupLevels. See Listing 9.5 for such a function. Note that this function is much simpler than the similar one in Listing 9.3, because groups must be consecutively numbered. Removing a group level bumps up the list all the group levels that follow it, so there are never any missing levels, numerically. The adhCountGroups function does its work by attempting to retrieve the SortOrder property for every group. As long as it can continue without generating a runtime error, it keeps looping through groups. As soon as it can no longer retrieve the property, the code halts and returns the number of groups it worked through. You can find the functions presented in Listing 9.3, 9.4, and 9.5 in basSections.

Listing 9.5

```
Private Const adhcMaxGroups = 10

Public Function adhCountGroups(rpt As Report) As Integer
    ' Count the number of groups in a report.

    Dim intI As Integer
    Dim intOrder As Integer

    On Error Resume Next
    For intI = 0 To adhcMaxGroups - 1
        intOrder = rpt.GroupLevel(intI).SortOrder
        If Err.Number <> 0 Then
            Exit For
        End If
    Next intI
    adhCountGroups = intI
    Err.Clear
End Function
```

GroupLevel Properties

The GroupLevel object exposes the following interesting properties: GroupFooter, GroupHeader, GroupInterval, GroupOn, KeepTogether, SortOrder, and ControlSource. The following sections describe each of these properties and its use.

GroupHeader and GroupFooter Properties

The GroupHeader and GroupFooter properties tell you whether a specific group level shows a Header and/or Footer section. These properties are each read-only, so you can't use them to create new Header/Footer sections: you must use the CreateGroupLevel function mentioned earlier in this chapter to do that.

This code fragment determines whether there is a group header for group 0:

```
If Reports("rptTest1").GroupLevel(0).GroupHeader Then
    ' Do something, perhaps change the ControlSource
    ' property for the group level.
End If
```

The ControlSource and SortOrder Properties

The ControlSource property specifies the field or expression on which the group is to be grouped and/or sorted. By default, the ControlSource property matches the value you used to create the group level and should be identical to the second parameter you passed to the CreateGroupLevel function. Although you cannot use CreateGroupLevel to alter the field on which a group is based, you can change the group's ControlSource property. Like all the rest of the GroupLevel properties, you change the ControlSource and SortOrder properties only when the report is in Design view or in the report's Open event.

TIP

You might be tempted to try and change a GroupLevel object's ControlSource property after the report's open, but you won't be able to. If you want to modify the sorting or grouping from a report's module, the only place you can do so is from the report's Open event procedure. In addition, you cannot create new group levels from the report at all—that must be done in Design view, when the report's code isn't running.

Use the SortOrder property to set the sorting order of rows in the Detail section of a group level. Table 9.2 shows the possible values for the SortOrder property. You use this property in combination with the ControlSource property to define the sorting characteristics of the group.

TABLE 9.2: Possible Values for the GroupLevel's SortOrder Property

Setting	Value	Description
Ascending	False	Sorts values in ascending order (0–9, A–Z) (default)
Descending	True	Sorts values in descending order (9–0, Z–A)

TIP

Although it seems somewhat backward, a GroupLevel object's SortOrder property is True if the sorting is descending.

To demonstrate these properties, open frmSortOrder (which opens rptPhoneBookOpenEvent for you). The sample form, shown in Figure 9.5, allows you to specify a grouping and a sort order. When you select the Open the Report button, the report opens in Preview mode. In the report's Open event procedure, you'll find the code shown in Listing 9.6. If the selection form isn't already open, this code opens the form and waits for you to close or hide it. Once that happens, if the form is still open, the report retrieves the user-defined SortField and SortOrder properties from the form and applies them to ControlSource and SortOrder properties of the two grouping levels.

Listing 9.6

```
Private Sub Report_Open(Cancel As Integer)
    ' This is the only event where you can work
    ' with GroupLevel properties at run-time
    ' (that is, without opening the report in Design view).

    Dim strField As String
    Dim frm As Form

    ' Open the selection form (frmSortOrder), and get
    ' information from it.
    If Not IsOpen(adhcSortOrderForm) Then
        DoCmd.OpenForm adhcSortOrderForm, _
         WindowMode:=acDialog, OpenArgs:=Me.Name
    End If

    ' Is it still open? If so, set things up here.
    If IsOpen(adhcSortOrderForm) Then
        Set frm = Forms(adhcSortOrderForm)
        strField = frm.SortField
        txtName.ControlSource = strField
        txtLetter.ControlSource = _
         "=Left$([" & strField & "], 1)"
        Me.GroupLevel(0).ControlSource = strField
        Me.GroupLevel(1).ControlSource = strField
        Me.GroupLevel(0).SortOrder = frm.SortOrder
        Me.GroupLevel(1).SortOrder = frm.SortOrder
        DoCmd.Close acForm, adhcSortOrderForm
    End If

End Sub
```

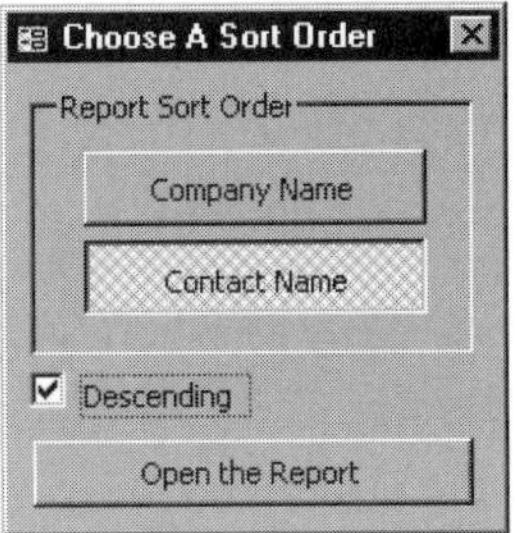

FIGURE 9.5:

You can use a form, like this one, to determine a report's grouping and sort order.

The GroupOn Property

The GroupOn property specifies how data is to be grouped in a grouping level. The values for the property depend on the datatype of the field or expression on which the GroupLevel is grouped. None of the settings except 0 (Each Value) is meaningful unless you have a group header or group footer selected for the group.

Table 9.3 displays all the possible values for the GroupOn property.

TABLE 9.3: Possible Values for the GroupLevel's GroupOn Property

Data Type	Setting	Value
Text or Number	Each Value	0
Text	Prefix Characters	1
Date/Time	Year	2
Date/Time	Qtr	3
Date/Time	Month	4
Date/Time	Week	5
Date/Time	Day	6
Date/Time	Hour	7
Date/Time	Minute	8
Number	Interval	9 (see the GroupInterval property)

TIP

Just as with the SortOrder and ControlSource properties, you can set the GroupOn and GroupInterval properties from a report's Open event procedure.

The GroupInterval Property

The GroupInterval property defines an interval that is valid for the field or expression on which you're grouping. You can set the property only when the report is in Design view, and Access' interpretation of its value is dependent on the value of the GroupOn property. As with the GroupOn property, the Access documentation states that you must have created a group header or footer before setting the value of this property to anything other than its default value (1). Actually, you can change it if you wish, but unless you have a group header or footer created, it won't have any effect. If the GroupOn value is 0 (Each Value), the GroupInterval property is treated as though it were 1, no matter what its value.

Set the GroupInterval property to a value that makes sense for the field or expression on which you're grouping. If you're grouping on text, the GroupInterval property defines the number of characters on which to group. If you're grouping on dates and you set the GroupOn property to 5 (Grouping on Weeks), setting the GroupInterval property specifies how many weeks to group together.

The following example (not in the sample database) creates a group, grouping on the time stored in a date/time field and breaking into groups of five minutes:

```
Dim intLevel As Integer

intLevel = CreateGroupLevel("rptTest", "DateField", _
 Header:=True, Footer:=False)
With Reports("rptTest").GroupLevel(intLevel)
    .GroupOn = 8
    .GroupInterval = 5
End With
```

TIP

Although you'll almost always set the GroupOn and GroupInterval properties when you're creating a report (either manually or programmatically), you can also set these properties from the report's Open event. You cannot create a group level except in Design view (using the CreateGroupLevel function), but you can set properties for existing group levels from the report's Open event.

The KeepTogether Property

The GroupLevel object's KeepTogether property specifies whether Access should make an attempt to keep the data in the group level together with the group level header when printed. (Note that report sections also have a KeepTogether property. That's a different property, and that property keeps track of whether you want Access to attempt to print the entire section's data together on one page.) You can set the GroupLevel object's KeepTogether property only when the report is in Design view or, as with the GroupOn/GroupInterval properties, from the report's Open event. The possible values for the KeepTogether property are shown in Table 9.4.

TABLE 9.4: Possible Values for the GroupLevel's KeepTogether Property

Setting	Value	Description
No	0	Makes no attempt to keep the header, detail, and footer on the same page
Whole Group	1	Attempts to print the header, detail, and footer all on same page
With First Detail	2	Attempts to print the header and the first detail row on the same page

Under some circumstances, Access is forced to ignore this setting. For example, if you've specified Whole Group (1), Access attempts to print the Group Header, Detail, and Footer sections on the same page. If that combination will not fit on a single page, Access is forced to ignore the setting and print it as best it can. The same concept can hold true if you've chosen With First Detail (2). In that case, Access attempts to place the group header and the first detail row on the same page. If the combination of the two is larger than a single page, all bets are off and Access prints as best it can.

As with all the rest of the GroupLevel properties, you set KeepTogether as a property of an individual GroupLevel object. For example, the following code fragment asks Access to attempt to print all of GroupLevel 0 on the same page:

```
Reports("rptTest").GroupLevel(0).KeepTogether = 2
```

Section Design-Time Properties

A GroupLevel object defines logically how data is to be grouped and sorted on your reports, but that data is actually displayed using Section objects. Table 9.5 lists the interesting properties of a Section object, and the following sections discuss the properties and give examples and hints for their use in designing your reports.

NOTE

Each of the properties in Table 9.5 applies to all form and report sections except the page header and footer sections.

TABLE 9.5: Report Section Properties

Property	Description	Settings
CanGrow	Determines whether the size of a section will increase vertically so Access can print all its data	True (–1); False (0)
CanShrink	Determines whether the size of a section will shrink vertically to avoid wasting space if there is no more data to print	True (–1); False (0)
NewRowOrCol	Specifies whether Access always starts printing a section in a multicolumn layout at the start of a new row (Horizontal layout) or column (Vertical layout)	None (0); Before Section (1); After Section (2); Before & After (3)
ForceNewPage	Determines whether Access prints a section on the current page or at the top of a new page	None (0); Before Section (1); After Section (2); Before & After (3)
KeepTogether	Determines whether Access attempts to print an entire section on a single page	True (–1); False (0)
RepeatSection (Group Header sections only)	Specifies whether Access repeats a group header on the next page or column when a group spans more than one page or column	True (–1); False (0)

Keeping Groups Together across Columns—the GrpKeepTogether Property

In early versions of Access, there really was no reasonable way to ensure that your sections didn't break across columns if you created a multicolumn report. You can now use the Report object's GrpKeepTogether property, which allows you to specify that you want to group data for which you've specified either Whole Group or With First Detail together in a single column (Per Column) or on the whole page (Per Page).

To see this property in action, take a look at rptPhoneBook. This report prints in a phone book–type layout and is the subject of several examples in this chapter. The report's Grp-KeepTogether property is set to Per Column so that groups aren't broken across columns. Try it out this way, and then change the setting to Per Page to see the difference it makes in the printout.

The CanGrow/CanShrink Properties

Setting either the CanGrow or CanShrink property causes other controls on the report to move vertically to adjust for changes in the sections' heights. Sections can grow or shrink only across their whole widths, so they must account for the maximum size needed within them. If you have a text box horizontally aligned with an object frame that cannot shrink, the section will not shrink, no matter how little text is in the text box.

TIP

If you set a control's CanGrow property to Yes, Access sets the CanGrow property for the control's section to Yes, also. You can override this setting by changing the section's CanGrow property back to No if you need to. On the other hand, setting a control's CanShrink property to Yes will not set its section's CanShrink property to Yes, and the default for a section's CanShrink property is No. You'll need to manually set sections' CanShrink properties the way you want them.

Why CanShrink Doesn't and CanGrow Won't

CanGrow and CanShrink properties might not always do what you think they ought. Here are some reasons why these properties may not perform as expected:

- Overlapping controls will not shrink, even when you've set the CanShrink property to Yes. If two controls touch at all, even by the smallest amount, they won't grow or shrink correctly.
- Controls shrink line by line (vertically). This means, for example, that if a group of controls is placed on the left side of a page and a large control (for example, a vertical line control) is on the right side of the page, the controls on the left side will not shrink.
- The CanShrink or CanGrow property does not affect space between controls.
- Controls located in the page header or page footer will grow to, at most, the height of the section. Neither the Page Header nor the Page Footer section itself can grow or shrink.
- Sometimes (and we haven't been able to prove or reproduce this) controls simply decide that they're not going to grow or shrink for you. If you've verified that there's no control in the same horizontal space as your control and your control isn't touching any other control, yet it still won't grow or shrink correctly, you may want to consider deleting and recreating the control. It sounds a bit overzealous, but this approach has worked in the past.

Note that although Form sections also support the CanShrink and CanGrow properties, these properties only have an effect when you're printing the form. These properties never have any effect for a form shown in Run view, only when printing.

Solving a Common CanShrink Issue

Access does a great job creating and managing mailing lists, and many people use it to create mailing labels. The Mailing Label Wizard makes simple work of creating labels, and they usually work. Because of the way the CanShrink property works, however, many developers get stuck trying to create real labels that don't contain blank lines.

The problem is that if there's any control in the same horizontal space as the control that needs to shrink because it doesn't contain any data, Access simply won't shrink the control. For example, check out rptSuppliersLabelBad. This simple mailing label report contains the standard mailing label fields but also includes a vertical line control to the left of the text boxes on the label. If any row of data is missing fields that leave a text box empty (as is the case for New Orleans Cajun Delights, on the second page of labels), you see a blank line. Access is not capable of fixing this problem without some extra help. Figure 9.6 shows the report running, and Figure 9.7 shows the report in Design view.

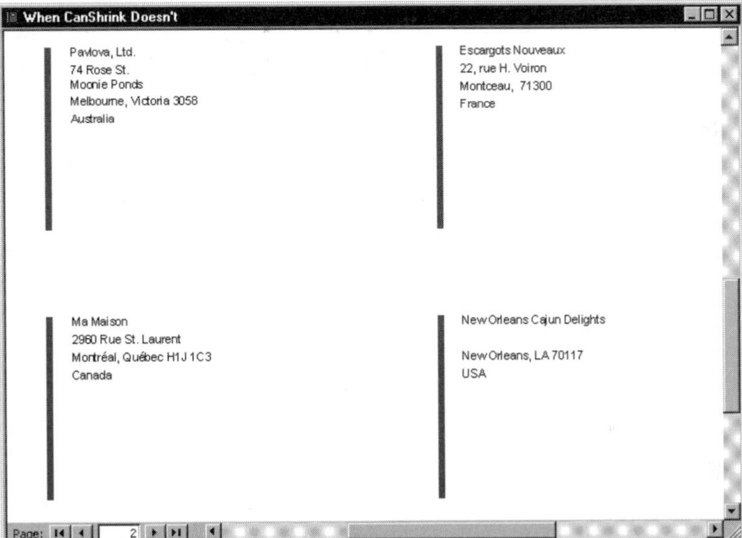

FIGURE 9.6: When running, this report may not be able to shrink empty controls correctly.

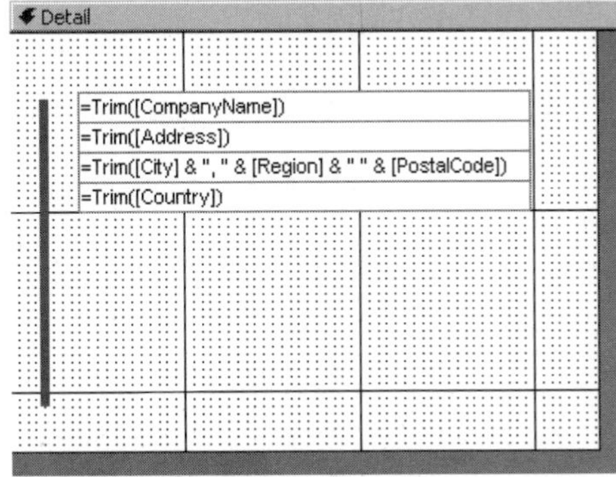

FIGURE 9.7: Because there's a control to the left of the controls you want to shrink, Access can't shrink controls when necessary.

A workable, but not perfect, solution is to redesign the label control. If you run rptSuppliersLabelsGood, you'll see that the problem with New Orleans Cajun Delights has been fixed. The solution? Rather than using individual text boxes for each line of data, use a single text box, and take care of the missing data yourself. Figure 9.8 shows the fixed report running, and Figure 9.9 shows the fixed report in Design view.

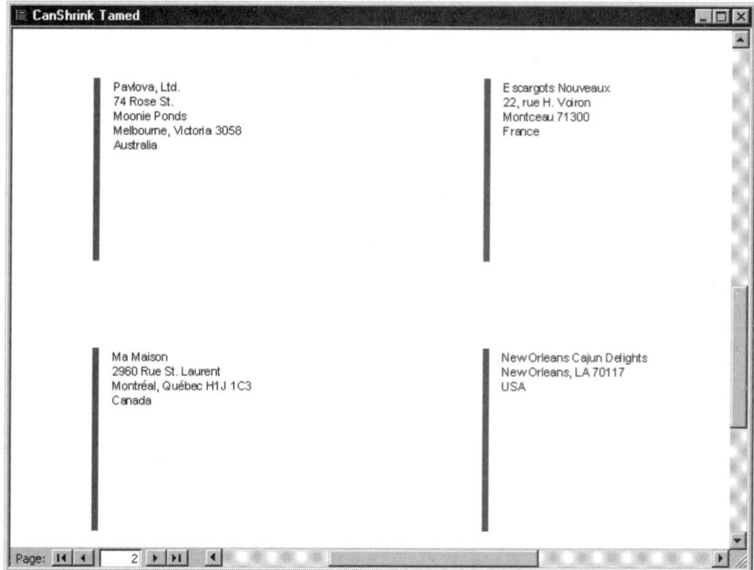

FIGURE 9.8:

When running, this report appears to shrink empty controls correctly.

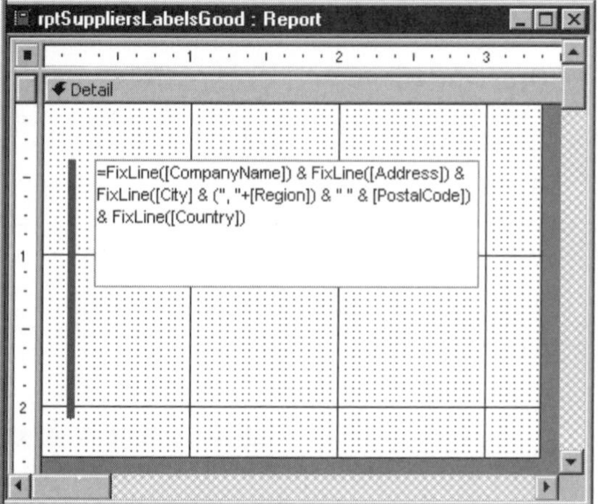

FIGURE 9.9:

Because all the data is displayed in a single text box, there's no need to shrink any controls.

If you take the expression from the ControlSource property in the "fixed" example and format it neatly, it looks like this:

```
=FixLine([CompanyName]) & _
 FixLine([Address]) & _
 FixLine([City] & (", " + [Region]) & " " & [PostalCode]) & _
 FixLine([Country])
```

Based on this, it looks like the FixLine function does all the work, and so it does. This little function, in the module for rptSuppliersLabelsGood, doesn't do much, but what it does do is important:

```
Private Function FixLine(varValue As Variant) As Variant
    ' If varValue is Null, FixLine returns Null.
    ' Otherwise, it returns the field value passed in
    ' with a Cr/Lf on the end.
    FixLine = varValue + vbCrLf
End Function
```

The point of this function is to take in a variant value (which may be Null, in which case you want to shrink away the line) and return either a Null value back, or the input text with a carriage return/line feed added. Although there are many ways to accomplish this, the simplest is to count on the fact that using a plus sign ("+") with a Null value will always result in a Null return value. (This is called *Null propagation*.) Therefore, if the input to this function is Null, the output will be Null. Otherwise, the output will be the original text with a vbCrLf value added. Using this function, the text box does all its own shrinking, and the vertical line to the left of the text box causes no trouble.

If you look carefully, you'll note that the expression uses another "+" sign in the third line of the label:

```
FixLine([City] & (", " + [Region]) & " " & [PostalCode]) & _
```

In this case, if the [Region] field is Null, you don't want that extra comma. Combining the comma and the [Region] field with a "+" sign makes the whole thing disappear if the [Region] field is Null. Yes, you can accomplish the same goal with a bunch of calls to the IsNull function, but this is much simpler.

You may want to use this technique whenever you want to make sure shrinking of Null fields takes place and you can't guarantee that Access will do it for you.

Using Null Propagation

Using a "+" sign to force Null propogation can be useful in many circumstances. If you have, for example, FirstName, MiddleInitial (with no period), and LastName fields, and you want to concatenate them, adding a period if necessary, you could use the IIf and IsNull functions to do your work, like this:

```
=[FirstName] & _
IIf (IsNull([MiddleInitial]), "", (" " & [MiddleInitial] & ".")) & _
" " & [LastName]
```

Or, in the interest of making things simpler, you could use an expression like this:

```
=[FirstName] & _
(" " + [MiddleInitial] + ".") & _
" " & [LastName]
```

With that sort of expression, if [MiddleInitial] is Null, the entire middle portion of the expression just goes away—its value is Null, and using the "&" operator to concatenate strings disregards Null values. Think about using this technique before trotting out the IIf and IsNull functions to do your work.

The NewRowOrCol Property

The NewRowOrCol property applies only when your report uses multiple columns for its display. When you choose to use multiple columns in the Page Setup dialog (by selecting the Columns tab), you can select either a horizontal or a vertical layout for your items. Choosing Vertical prints items down the first column, then down the second, and so on. Choosing Horizontal prints across the first row in the first column, the second column, and so on, and then goes on to the second row, printing in each column. You might use the Vertical layout for printing phone book listings and the Horizontal layout for printing mailing labels.

The NewRowOrCol property allows you to maintain fine control over how the Detail section of your report prints when it's using multiple columns. Table 9.6 describes each of the property's possible settings and how you can use it to control the layout of your report.

TABLE 9.6: NewRowOrCol Property Settings

Setting	Value	Description
None	0	Row and column breaks occur naturally, based on the settings in the Page Setup dialog and on the layout of the current page so far (default).
Before Section	1	The current section is printed in a new row or column. The next section is printed in the same row or column.
After Section	2	The current section is printed in the same row or column as the previous section. The next section is printed in a new row or column.
Before & After	3	The current section is printed in a new row or column. The next section is also printed starting in a new row or column.

You'll want to experiment with the NewRowOrCol property if you're working with multicolumn reports. You can find an example of its use in the section "Companies, Contacts, and Hardware" later in this chapter. You might want to compare the layouts of rptPhoneBook and rptPhoneBookHorizontal, as well. In the first report, items are printed down, then across. In the second, they're printed across, then down. To make the horizontal layout look better, the CompanyName Header section has its NewRowOrCol property set to 3 (Before & After). Figure 9.10 shows a little of each of the two reports.

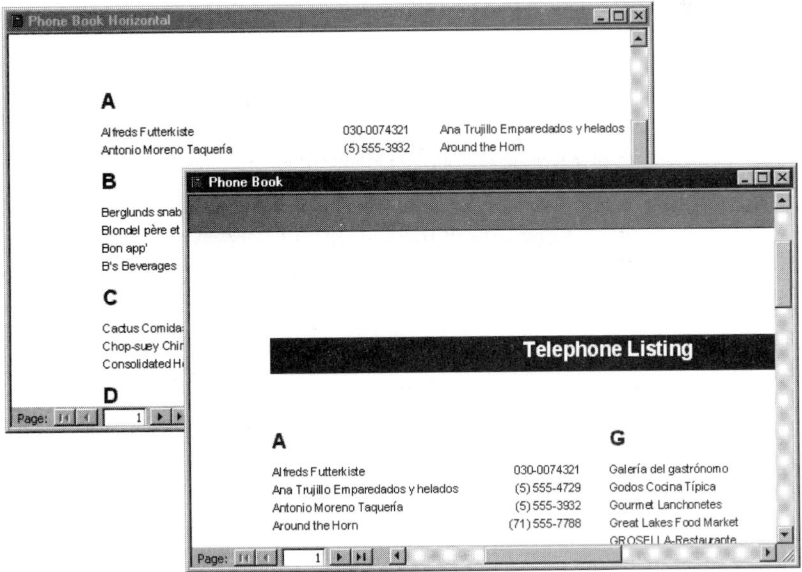

FIGURE 9.10: Use the NewRowOrCol property to force a new row or column before and/or after any section.

The ForceNewPage Property

The ForceNewPage property allows you to control page breaks in relation to your report sections. Table 9.7 details the four options that are available for this property. Because you can control this option while the report is printing, you can, based on a piece of data in a particular row, decide to start the section printing on a new page. You can accomplish the same effect, although not quite as elegantly, by including a page break control on your report and setting its Visible property to Yes or No, depending on the data in the current row.

TABLE 9.7: ForceNewPage Property Settings

Setting	Value	Description
None	0	Access starts printing the current section on the current page (default)
Before Section	1	Access starts printing the current section at the top of a new page
After Section	2	Access starts printing the next section at the top of a new page
Before & After	3	Access starts printing the current section at the top of a new page and prints the next section starting on a new page, too

The KeepTogether Property

Setting a Section object's KeepTogether property to True instructs Access to attempt to print a given section all on one page. If it can't fit on the current page, Access starts a new page and tries printing it there. Of course, if it can't fit on one page at this point, Access must continue printing on the next page, no matter how the property is set.

The KeepTogether property for sections is simpler than the KeepTogether property for groups. The Section property doesn't attempt to keep multiple sections together, as does the GroupLevel property. For sections, the KeepTogether property just attempts to have Access print the entire section on a single page, if possible.

The RepeatSection Property

Often, when you print a group on your report, Access has to start a new page or column in the middle of the group. In that case, you may decide you'd like Access to reprint the group header for you on the new page or column. The RepeatSection property for group headers controls whether Access repeats the group header at the top of the new page or column. The sample report, rptPhoneBook, uses this property to force Access to reprint the group header at the top of the column if a group has been broken across a column. (To see this property in action, change the report's GrpKeepTogether from Per Column to Per Page, and you'll probably see a group header repeated when the group repeats over two columns or two pages.)

Repeating Heads in Subreports

The RepeatSection property is available only for group headers, not the report header. For report headers you don't really need this functionality—you can just use a page header instead. If you're printing a subreport, however, and you'd like to emulate this behavior for the subreport's ReportHeader section, you can fake it:

- In the subreport, create a group that's grouped on the string expression =1. This creates a static grouping that won't change from row to row of data.
- Use this group header as the report header. (That is, don't show the Report Header section; use this group header instead, since it won't change throughout the report.) Because it's a group header, it will have a RepeatSection property, and Access will repeat it at the top of a new page.

Events of Reports and Their Sections

As in all the other areas of Access, it's the events that drive the application when you're working with reports. As users interact with Access' user interface, it's up to your application to react to the events Access fires off. Reports themselves support only a few events (Error, NoData, and Page) besides the standard load/unload events (Open, Activate, Close, Deactivate, and Error), but their sections react to events that occur as Access prints each row of data.

Report Events

Table 9.8 lists the events raised by reports. As indicated in the table, when you open a report, Access raises the Open and then the Activate event. When you close the report, Access raises the Close and then the Deactivate event.

TABLE 9.8: Report Events

Event	Raised When
Open	You open a report but before the report starts printing or becomes visible (before the Activate event).
Close	You close the report (before the Deactivate event).
Error	A database engine error occurs while the report is printing. (This event does not trap runtime errors in your VBA code, just errors that occur in the database engine while processing the data.)
Activate	The report becomes the active window or starts printing (after the Open event).
Deactivate	You move to another Access window or close the report (after the Close event).
NoData	You attempt to open a report for printing or previewing, and its underlying record source provides no rows.
Page	The current page has been formatted but hasn't yet been printed.

Activation versus Deactivation

When you switch from one report to another (in Preview view), the report you're switching away from executes its Deactivate event before the new report executes its Activate event. If you switch to any other Access window from a report, the report's Deactivate event still executes. If you switch to a different application or to a pop-up window within Access, the Deactivate event does not fire; that is, the Deactivate event fires off only when you switch to another window for which the parent is also the Access MDI Client window. (See Chapter 8 for more information on the MDI client window.)

Using the Open and Activate Events

When Access first opens the report, it runs the code attached to the report's Open event before it runs the query that supplies the data for the report. Given this fact, you can supply parameters to that query from the report's Open event. You might, for example, pop up a form that requests starting and ending dates or any other information your query might need. To see this in action, open rptPhoneBook-Param. This report opens frmParam from its Open event, and the form requests you to specify a starting letter (or letters). The report then uses the letter(s) you've typed to filter the query that's filling the report. (See Figure 9.11, although this figure is somewhat misleading—the form and the report would never actually be visible at the same time.)

FIGURE 9.11:

The report's Open event loads the parameter-gathering form, which, in turn, provides a parameter for the report's underlying query.

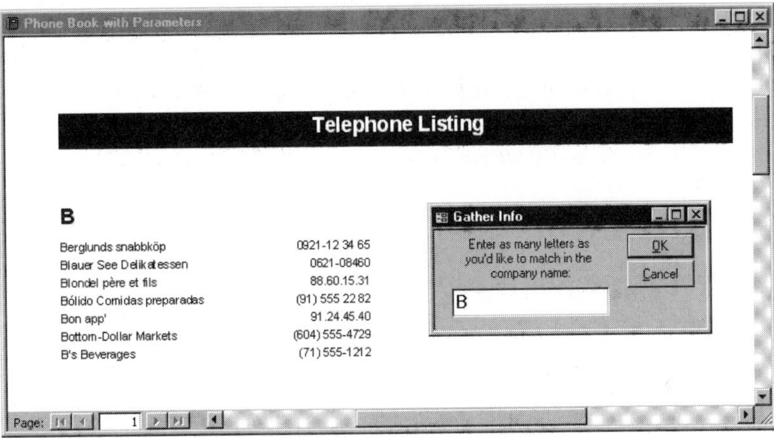

In this example, rptPhoneBookParam's Open event executes the code found in Listing 9.7.

Listing 9.7

```
Private Sub Report_Open(Cancel As Integer)

    ' Perhaps you opened the form first?
    If Not IsOpen(adhcParamForm) Then
        DoCmd.OpenForm _
         FormName:=adhcParamForm, _
         WindowMode:=acDialog
    End If

    ' Set the Cancel flag if the form isn't still open.
    ' That would mean the user pressed the Cancel button.
    Cancel = Not IsOpen(adhcParamForm)
End Sub
```

This code first opens frmParam modally so that code execution halts until you either hide or close the form. Just as described in Chapter 8, the OK button hides the form and the Cancel button closes the form altogether. On return from the OpenForm action, the code checks to see whether the form is still open, using a call to the IsOpen function (which uses the SysCmd function to determine if the form is still open). If not, the report sets the Cancel parameter to True, to indicate that Access should abort the attempt to load the report.

Once Access has executed the Open event, it can go ahead and load the data that's going to populate the report. Because Access wouldn't be at this point at all for this report unless the parameter-providing form were still open (but hidden), you're assured that Access will be able to find the form it needs in order to supply the parameter for qryCustomerNameParam. The query uses the following expression to fill its rows:

```
Like Forms!frmParam!txtName & "*"
```

Avoiding Empty Reports—Using the NoData Event

In the previous example, there's nothing stopping you from choosing a filter for the report that returns no rows at all. In this case, the report prints #Error in the Detail section. If you want to avoid this problem, you can add code to the NoData event of your report that reacts to this exact situation and cancels the report if there's no data to be printed. If there aren't any rows and you want to cancel the report, you can use code like this, from rptPhoneBookParam:

```
Private Sub Report_NoData(Cancel As Integer)
    MsgBox "There aren't any rows to display!"
    ' Close the parameter form, as well.
    DoCmd.Close acForm, adhcParamForm
    ' Tell Access to just skip it.
   Cancel = True
End Sub
```

To test this code, try entering a value that is guaranteed to return no rows, such as **ZZ**, when rptPhoneBookParam requests a value from you.

NOTE

Unsurprisingly, Access doesn't even bother with the NoData event for unbound reports. Finding out that an unbound report's recordset (which doesn't exist) doesn't contain any rows wouldn't be very useful information.

TIP

If you cancel a report (that is, set the Cancel parameter to True in the Open or NoData event procedures), Access triggers a runtime error in the code that's called the DoCmd.OpenReport method. You'll generally want to put error-handling code in the calling procedure so that your users aren't bothered with this error.

Using the Report's Error Event

Access triggers a report's Error event when an error occurs in the database engine (normally, the Jet database engine) while the report is either formatting or printing. Although this eventuality is less likely with a report than it might be for a form, it can still occur. For example, if a table is opened exclusively by some user or a report is bound to a recordset that doesn't exist, Access triggers this error.

Although you could handle this event by calling a macro, you're better off using the report's class module to handle the Error event. In this case, Access provides two parameters to your event handler, allowing you some functionality you'd be missing if you called a macro or an external routine to handle this event. By using the class module, you can control how Access handles the error once you've investigated it.

Listing 9.8 shows a simple error handling routine (from rptPhoneBookParam in the sample database). Although this example does little more than display a message box in response to the error that can occur when a user has removed the query or table to which a report has been bound, it should provide a starting place for your own error handlers.

NOTE Because of the separation of VBA, the Access report engine, and Jet, you can't use the Err.Description property to return information on Jet errors. In this case, you'll need to use the AccessError method of the Access Application object. This is just one of the many ways Access changed due to the addition of the VBA-shared component back in Access 95.

Listing 9.8

```
Private Sub Report_Error(DataErr As Integer, _
 Response As Integer)
    Const adhcErrNoRecordSource = 2580

    Select Case DataErr
        Case adhcErrNoRecordSource
            MsgBox "This report is bound to a table " & _
             "or query that doesn't exist: '" & _
            Me.RecordSource & "'", vbExclamation
        Case Else
            MsgBox AccessError(DataErr)
```

```
        End Select
        DoCmd.Close acForm, adhcParamForm
        Response = acDataErrContinue
    End Sub
```

The Page Event

You'll find there are some actions that you can't take at any time except when Access has finished formatting a page but before it actually prints the page. You can most easily draw a border around the page, for example, right before Access prints the page. The Page event gives you the flexibility you need to make any last-minute changes just before Access sends the formatted page to the printer.

The following code, from the Page event of rptBankInfo, draws a rectangle surrounding the entire printed page once Access has formatted the page (see Figure 9.12):

```
Private Sub Report_Page()
    Me.Line (0, 0)-(Me.ScaleWidth, Me.ScaleHeight), , B
End Sub
```

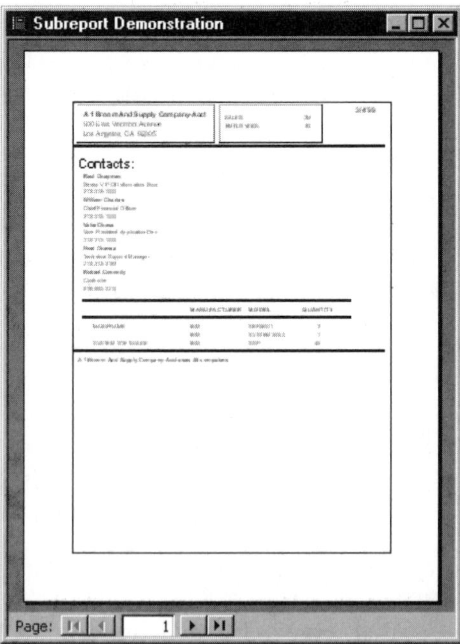

FIGURE 9.12: Use the Page event to draw on the report page once all the data for the page has been placed on the page.

NOTE

You may find that printing a border around the printable region causes the border to extend past the printable region on your printer. In that case, you may need to experiment with subtracting a few twips from Me.ScaleHeight or Me.ScaleWidth until the entire border prints.

Section Events

Just as report events focus mainly on loading and unloading the report itself and setting up the overall data that will populate the report, section events deal with the actual formatting and printing of that data. Table 9.9 lists the three events that apply to report sections.

TABLE 9.9: Section Events

Event	Raised When
Format	Access has selected the data to go in this section but before it formats or prints the data
Print	Access has formatted the data for printing (or previewing) but before it prints or shows the data
Retreat	Access needs to move to a previous section while formatting the report

The Format Event

Access raises its Format event once it has selected the data to be printed in the section but before it actually prints it. This allows you to alter the layout of the report or to perform calculations based on the data in the section at this particular time.

For a report's Detail section, Access calls your code just before it actually lays out the data to be printed. Your code has access to the data in the current row and can react to that data, perhaps making certain controls visible or invisible. (See the example in the section "Altering Your Report's Layout Programmatically" later in this chapter for more information on this technique.)

For group headers, the Format event occurs for each new group. Within the event procedure, your code has access to data in the group header and in the first row of data in the group. For group footers, the event occurs for each new group, and your code has access to data in the group footer and in the last row of data in the group. (For an example of using this information, see the section "The Sales Report" later in this chapter.)

For actions that don't affect the page layout or for calculations that absolutely must not occur until the section is printed, use the Print event. For example, if you're calculating a running total, place the calculation in the Print event because doing so avoids any ambiguities about when or whether the section actually printed.

If you've placed code for the Format event in the report's class module, Access passes you two parameters: FormatCount and Cancel. The FormatCount value corresponds to the section's FormatCount property. The Cancel parameter allows you to cancel the formatting of the current section and move on to the next by setting its value to True. This parameter corresponds to using

```
DoCmd.CancelEvent
```

from within your code.

To see an example that uses the Format event (there are several), in the sample database, open rptPhoneBook in Preview mode. Zoom the report so you can see the entire page at once and move from page to page. Note that the footer information is right-aligned on the first page and left-aligned on the second. If you intend to print a report back-to-back, it's standard to print footer information away from the bound edge. That is, on the right on odd pages and on the left on even pages. The code in the Page Footer section's Format event handles this for you. See the section "Handling Odd and Even Pages" later in the chapter for a complete explanation.

The Print Event

Access raises a section's Print event once it has formatted the data to be printed in the section but before it actually prints it. For a report's Detail section, Access calls your code just before it prints the data. Your code has access to the data in the current row. For group headers, the Print event occurs for each new group. Within the event procedure, your code has access to data in the group header and in the first row of data in the group. For group footers, the event occurs for each new group, and your code has access to data in the group footer and in the last row of data in the group.

Just as it does for the Format event, Access passes two parameters to your code for the Print event if you place your code in the report's class module. The PrintCount parameter corresponds to the section's PrintCount property. The Cancel parameter allows you to cancel the printing of the current section and move on to the next by setting its value to True.

The Print event provides a good place to calculate sums or count things, because you know this code won't run unless the section is actually about to be printed. (That is, there's no chance the code will run and then Access will decide that it can't print this section.) To see this in use, try out rptSales and look for the page total at the bottom of each page. Code in the Print event of the Detail section calculates this page total. For more information, see the section "Step 2: Adding Page Totals" later in the chapter.

The Retreat Event

Sometimes Access needs to move back to a previous section while it's formatting your report. For example, if your group level's KeepTogether property is set to With First Detail Row, Access formats the group header and then the first row and checks to make sure they'll both fit in the space available on the current page. Once it has formatted the two, it retreats from those two sections, executing the Retreat event for each. Then it again formats the sections and finally prints them.

If you've made any changes during the Format event, you may wish to undo them during the Retreat event. Because you really can't know during the Retreat event whether the current section will actually be printed on the current page, you should use this event as a chance to undo any layout changes made during the Format event.

Counting rows from the Format event makes a very simple example. If you include code attached to a section's Format event procedure that increments a counter for each row, include code in the Retreat event that decrements the counter. Otherwise the Format event may be fired multiple times for a given row, and the count will be incorrect. (Of course, there are several other ways to take care of this problem, including checking the FormatCount property. This example is intended only to explain why you might need to use the Retreat event.)

TIP

Access triggers the Retreat event in two very predictable places, among others. If you've created a group and set its KeepTogether property to With First Detail, Access triggers the Format event, then the Retreat event, and then the Format and Print events for the first row in the group as it attempts to fit the header and the first row on the same page. The same concept applies to groups in which you've set the KeepTogether property to All Rows, in which case Access formats each row, retreats from each row, and then formats the ones that will fit on the current page. Although there are many other circumstances in which Access will fire off the Retreat event, you can be assured that setting the group's KeepTogether property will force it.

Section Runtime Properties

Because there are some properties of sections that can't be available until your report is printing, Access provides a group of properties that you can use only at runtime. (That is, you won't see these properties on a property sheet.) Table 9.10 lists these runtime properties, and the following sections present more information and suggestions for their effective use.

TABLE 9.10: Section Runtime Properties

Property	Description	Settings
MoveLayout	Specifies whether Access should move to the next printing location on the page	True (–1): the section's Left and Top properties are advanced to the next print location; False (0): the Left and Top properties are unchanged
NextRecord	Specifies whether a section should advance to the next record	True: advance to the next record; False: stay on the same record
PrintSection	Specifies whether a section should be printed	True: the section is printed; False: the section isn't printed
FormatCount	Indicates the number of times the Format event has occurred for the current section	Read-only while the report is being formatted; not available in Design view
PrintCount	Indicates the number of times the Print event has occurred for the current section	Read-only while the report is printing; not available in Design view
HasContinued	Indicates whether the current section has been continued from the previous page	True or False: available in the section's Format event
WillContinue	Indicates whether the current section will continue on the next page	True or False: available in the section's Print event

The MoveLayout, NextRecord, and PrintSection Properties

The MoveLayout, NextRecord, and PrintSection properties, when combined, control exactly how Access moves from row to row in the underlying data and whether the current row will be printed. Table 9.11 presents all the possible combinations of these three properties and how they interact. By combining these three layout properties, you'll have a great deal of flexibility in how you lay out your reports. The examples in the sections "Printing Multiple Labels," "Printing Mailing Labels Starting at a Specific Location," and "Inserting Blank Lines" later in this chapter demonstrate the use of these properties.

TABLE 9.11: Section Runtime Properties and Their Interactions

MoveLayout	NextRecord	PrintSection	Results
True	True	True	Moves to the next print location, moves to the next row, and then prints the row (default).
True	True	False	Moves to a new row and moves to the next print location, but doesn't print the row (it leaves a blank space where the row would have printed).
True	False	True	Moves to the next print location, stays on the same row, and prints the data.
True	False	False	Moves to the next print location but doesn't skip a row and doesn't print any data. This effectively leaves a blank space on the paper without moving to a new row in the data.
False	True	True	Doesn't move the print location but prints the next row right on top of the previous one. This allows you to overlay one row of data on another.
False	True	False	Doesn't move the print location and doesn't print anything, but skips a row in the data. This allows you to skip a row without leaving any blank space on the page.
False	False	True	Not allowed.
False	False	False	Not allowed.

The FormatCount Property

Access increments a section's FormatCount property each time it executes the Format event for that section. Once it moves to the next section, it resets the FormatCount property to 0.

In some circumstances, Access must format a section more than once. For example, as Access reaches the end of a page, it's possible that the current section won't fit. Access attempts to format the section and, if it doesn't fit, formats it again on the next page. It calls the Format event code twice, first with a FormatCount value of 1 and then with a FormatCount value of 2.

If you're performing some calculation or action from your Format event code, pay careful attention to the FormatCount value. For example, perhaps you want to increment counters only if the FormatCount value is 1. If you normally take an action in the Format event code, you must skip the action if the FormatCount value is greater than 1.

The PrintCount Property

Access increments a section's PrintCount property each time it executes the Print event for that section. Once it moves on the next section, it resets the PrintCount property to 0.

Access attempts to print a section more than once when a specific section spans more than one page. For example, if a section requires more than a single page for its output, Access calls the Print event code once for each page, incrementing the PrintCount property. If you're attempting to maintain running totals, adding in an amount each time a report section prints, you need to check the PrintCount property and add in the value only once. The following code might be used in a section's Print event code. (If you place the code in the report's class module, Access passes the PrintCount property to the code as a parameter. If not, you need to refer to the PrintCount property using the standard syntax.)

```
If PrintCount = 1 Then
    lngRunningTotal = lngRunningTotal + OrderAmount
End If
```

The WillContinue/HasContinued Properties

The pair of section properties WillContinue and HasContinued are intended to allow code in your event procedures to react to the fact that a given section has continued from the previous page or will continue on the next page. These are both properties of sections, and they return either True or False. Each works a bit differently, and the following sections explain the details of using them. Unfortunately, they're both constructed in such a way that we were unable to find a use for either in any but the most trivial situations or by employing some difficult workarounds. For the sake of completeness, however, the next few sections explain how they work.

The WillContinue Property

Access sets the WillContinue property during a section's Print event, and the property returns True if any portion of the current section will print on the next page. Therein lies the problem: Access' trigger is wound a bit too tightly. Access doesn't distinguish between white space and controls when setting this property, so it sets the WillContinue property to True for almost every page. All you care about is whether text has been printed on one page and continued on the next, not whether white space from the next row to be printed has touched the current page, but Access can't discern between these two situations.

Once Access has set the property to True for a given section, it remains True until the same section's next Print event (PrintCount > 1, on the next page). Therefore, you can use the value of the section's WillContinue property from the Format or Print event procedures of any section that will print before Access prints the rest of your section. (For Detail sections, this means you could check in the current page's Page Footer section or the next page's Page Header section, for example.)

The HasContinued Property

Access sets a section's HasContinued property during the section's Format event, and it sets the property to True only if the FormatCount property is greater than 1 (which is, of course, exactly what it should do). As a matter of fact, our experiments found that Access always sets the HasContinued property correctly, even when it has incorrectly set the WillContinue property on the previous page.

The problem with the HasContinued property is that you can't check it from the location where it would be the most useful—when you're printing the page header. At that point, Access hasn't yet set the FormatCount property for the section to a number greater than 1, so the HasContinued property will still be False if you examine the Detail section's properties from the page header. By the time you start printing the second portion of the Detail section (with its FormatCount property now set to 2), it's too late to do anything useful with the HasContinued property.

Of course, even though you can't set the visibility of a control based on the HasContinued property, you can use the report's Print method to write text directly onto the report if you find the Detail section's HasContinued property is True. You may find this useful, but in our testing it appeared to be more work than it was worth.

Perhaps you can tell from our tone that we're still a bit disappointed in the functionality these properties provide (after a version or two of uselessness). They *sound* good, but they just don't provide the right results in the cases where they'd be most useful. We hope the properties will work correctly, or at least better, in future releases of the product.

One Simple Solution

If your goal is to print a Continued label in a group header section if that section is continued from the previous page, there's a simple solution:

- If you've set the RepeatSection property of the GroupHeader section to be Yes so that the group header will print at the top of the second page for the group

and

- If you can determine one field that's unique for each group (generally, the field or expression that you're grouping on)

and

- If, in the GroupHeader section's Print event, you compare the current value for that field with the last one you printed, you'll know whether you need to display the Continued label.

The sample report, rptContinuedLabel, demonstrates this technique. After setting the RepeatSection property for the SupplierID header to be Yes, the code shown below will handle showing and hiding lblContinued as necessary.

```
Private Sub GroupHeader0_Print( _
 Cancel As Integer, PrintCount As Integer)
    ' Only show the Continued label if the
    ' CompanyName field hasn't changed since
    ' the last time you printed it.
    Static strCompany As String

    lblContinued.Visible = _
     (CompanyName = strCompany)

    ' Store away the company name you just printed.
    strCompany = CompanyName
End Sub
```

This procedure, called every time the report prints the group header, compares the current company name to the one that printed last. (The variable, strCompany, is declared using the Static keyword, so that it maintains its value between calls to the procedure.) Finally, the procedure stores away the current CompanyName field for the next pass-through.

Try out rptContinuedLabel, and you'll see that the Continued label only shows up when a section is continued from the previous page. The code is simple and accomplishes what the HasContinued property should do for you.

Examples Using Report and Section Events and Properties

The following sections contain examples and solutions to some common problems. Each example refers to a specific report or form in the sample database. In each case, you might find it useful to open the specific report in Design view and follow along with the description you find here. Change properties and see what happens. Experimentation is the best way to find out how each of the report and section properties affects the printed output.

Printing Multiple Labels

Printing multiple labels based on a count stored with the label data makes a perfect example of the use of the MoveLayout, NextRecord, and PrintSection properties. In this example, the user has stored, in the LabelCount column of a table, the number of copies of the row to be printed. Listing 9.9, which would be called from the Print event of the Detail section containing the label, shows the code necessary to print the correct number of labels. (See rptMultiLabel to test this example.) Given the data shown in Figure 9.13, the design surface shown in Figure 9.14 creates the labels shown in Figure 9.15.

FIGURE 9.13:

Each row in the table contains a column indicating the number of labels to be printed.

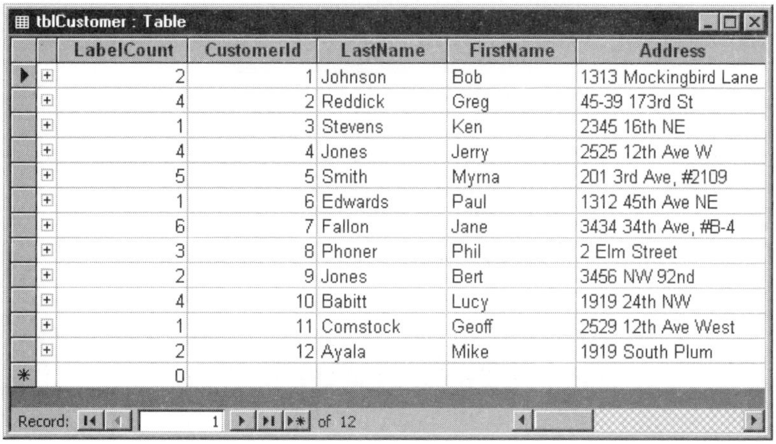

tblCustomer : Table

LabelCount	CustomerId	LastName	FirstName	Address
2	1	Johnson	Bob	1313 Mockingbird Lane
4	2	Reddick	Greg	45-39 173rd St
1	3	Stevens	Ken	2345 16th NE
4	4	Jones	Jerry	2525 12th Ave W
5	5	Smith	Myrna	201 3rd Ave, #2109
1	6	Edwards	Paul	1312 45th Ave NE
6	7	Fallon	Jane	3434 34th Ave, #B-4
3	8	Phoner	Phil	2 Elm Street
2	9	Jones	Bert	3456 NW 92nd
4	10	Babitt	Lucy	1919 24th NW
1	11	Comstock	Geoff	2529 12th Ave West
2	12	Ayala	Mike	1919 South Plum
0				

Record: 1 of 12

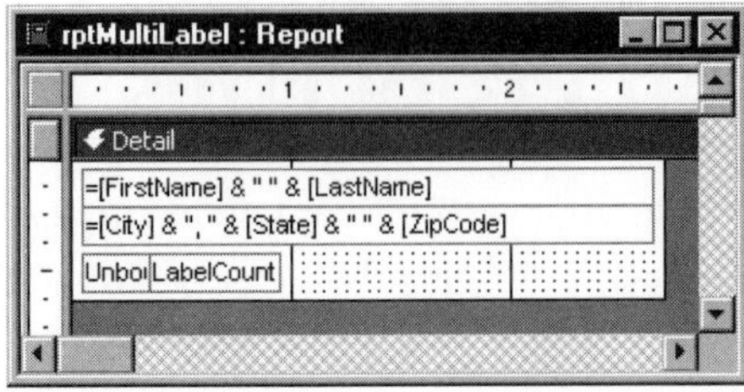

FIGURE 9.14: The report design includes a visible control containing the LabelCount column. In your labels, this could be made invisible.

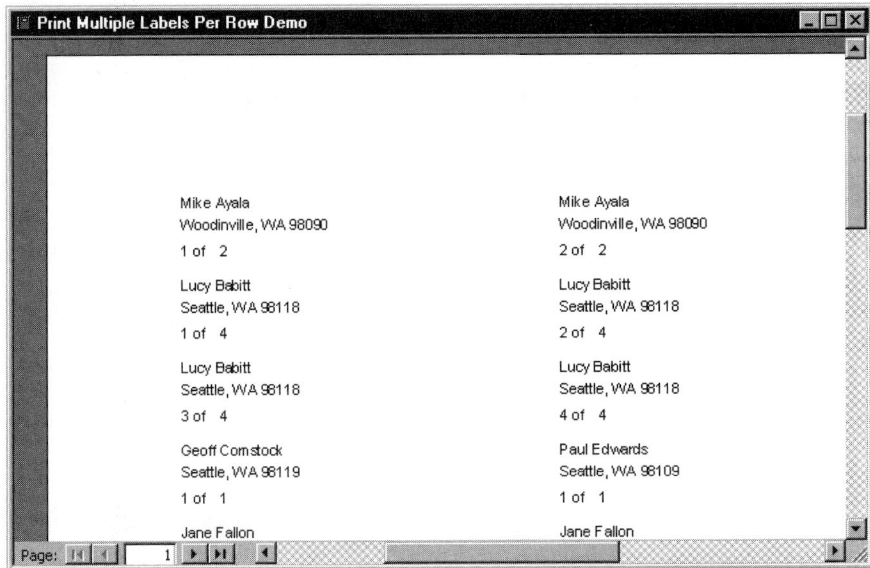

FIGURE 9.15: The labels will contain as many multiples as you requested in your table.

Listing 9.9

```
Private Sub Detail1_Print( _
 Cancel As Integer, PrintCount As Integer)
    txtLabel = PrintCount & " of "
    If txtLabelCount = 0 Then
        Me.NextRecord = True
        Me.MoveLayout = False
```

```
        Me.PrintSection = False
    Else
        If PrintCount < txtLabelCount Then
            Me.NextRecord = False
        End If
    End If
End Sub
```

To make this technique work, you must create a text box on your report for the field that contains the count. You can make it invisible, but it has to be on the report for the code to be able to get to it. (In this example, the text box control is named txtLabelCount.) Unlike forms, reports must contain a control bound to any column they reference. Forms can reference any column in the underlying data without actually having to contain a control bound to that field.

This example does its work quite simply. If the user has requested no labels at all for the particular row, the code tells Access to move to the next record (NextRecord = True) but not to move to the next print position (MoveLayout = False) and not to print anything at all (PrintSection = False). Otherwise, if the PrintCount value is less than the number of labels to be printed (txtLabelCount), don't move to the next record (NextRecord = False), but use the default value for the other properties. This causes Access to print the data from the current row and move to the next print location.

Although you might be tempted to attach this code to the Format event, it won't work correctly. Because Access must decide at format time how to lay out the labels on the page, the FormatCount value to which the Format event has access won't always be correct, especially when you've filled a page without completing the run of a particular row.

NOTE

Although this particular example displays n of m where n is the current label and m is the total to be printed for each row of data, you needn't do this. You can set the Visible property for txtLabelCount to False and not display it at all. We've chosen to display it in this example to prove that the code is indeed working.

TIP

If you want to print a full page of labels for a particular row, simply change the line of code that compares the current PrintCount value to txtLabelCount. Replace txt-LabelCount with the total number of labels on a page, and you'll get one page of labels for each row of data.

Printing Mailing Labels Starting at a Specific Location

If you print mailing labels on full sheets of paper (as do most people with laser printers), you've probably needed, at one point or another, to start a printout at the first unused label on the page rather than on the first label. The technique to make this happen is very simple and uses the same properties used in the previous example: NextRecord and PrintSection. If you want to try out this technique, open rptSkipLabels in Preview view. This causes frmSelectLabel to pop up, requesting that you choose the first label on which to print (see Figure 9.16). Once you've made a selection, the form disappears and the report prints, starting on the label you chose (see Figure 9.17).

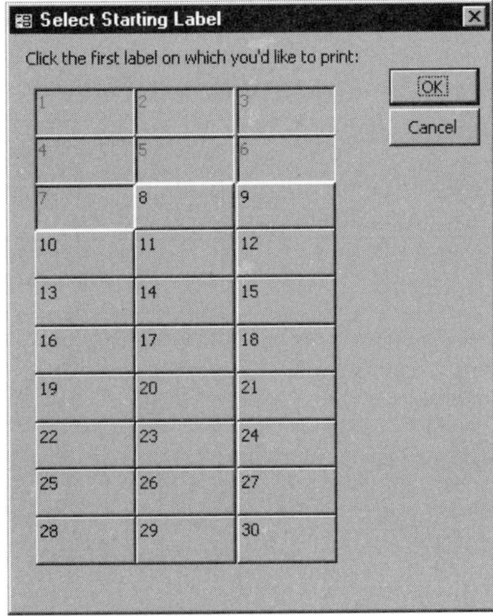

FIGURE 9.16:

Choose a label from frm-SelectLabel on which to start printing.

FIGURE 9.17:

Once you've selected a starting label, the report will skip labels up to that label number.

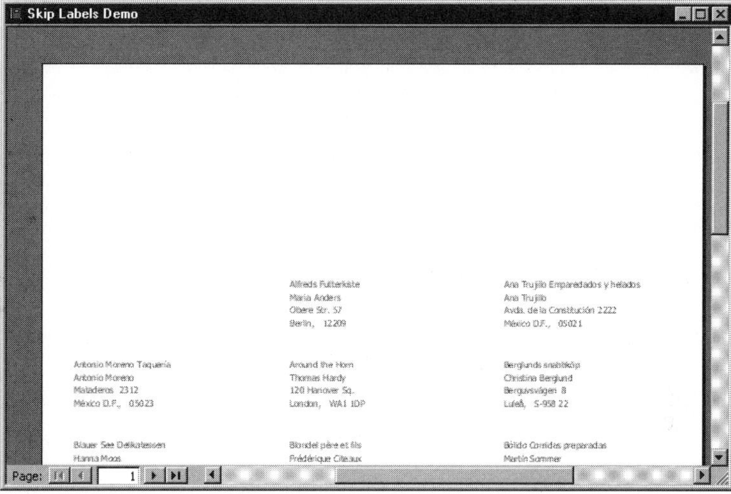

How Does It Work?

The functionality demonstrated in this example is encapsulated in a class module, SkipLabels. From your report's Open event procedure, you can add code like this to instantiate the class and have it figure out how many labels to skip:

```
Private msl As SkipLabels

Private Sub Report_Open(Cancel As Integer)
    Set msl = New SkipLabels
    msl.Cols = 3
    msl.Rows = 10
    Set msl.Report = Me
If msl.Cancel Then
     Cancel = msl.Cancel
     Set msl = Nothing
End If
End Sub
```

You'll need to set properties of the class indicating how you want the form to look—it should match the layout of the report. Table 9.12 lists the properties of the SkipLabels class and describes each.

TABLE 9.12: Properties of the SkipLabels Class

Property	Data Type	Default Value	Description
Cancel	Boolean	False	Read-only. Indicates whether the user canceled the pop-up form requesting the starting label. Normally, you'll want to cancel the report in its Open event if this property is True.
Cols*	Integer	3	Sets or retrieves the number of columns to display on the pop-up form. Maximum value is 5.
FormName*	String	frmSelectLabel	Name of the form to be used to request a starting label.
PrintAcross*	Boolean	True	True if your report is set to print across then down. False if your report is set to print down then across.
Report	Report		Set this property to be the report you're printing. Normally, set this to be Me in the report's Open event.
Rows*	Integer	10	Sets or retrieves the number of rows to display on the pop-up form. Maximum value is 10.
StartLabel*	Integer	1	Sets or retrieves the label at which to default starting. If you set this to a value besides 1, the pop-up form will open with the specified number of labels already selected.

* Read/write until you've set the Report property. Read-only after that.

That's it! That's all the code you need to write to have this happen. How can that be? What makes the labels skip down to the correct location? When you set the Report property of the SkipLabels object, you need to set up a WithEvents connection to the detail section of the report you're running. This allows the class to react to the Format event of the section and use runtime properties of the section to control the label's layout on the page. (For more information on using the WithEvents keyword, see Chapter 3.) An interesting problem, however: Access doesn't provide a specific report Section object, only a generic Section object that appears both in forms and reports.

Why do you care? Because if you want to trap the Format event for the Detail section of the report that's open in the SkipLabels class, you have to have a reference to an object that exposes such an event. And the Section object does not. (Don't believe us? Go look in the Object Browser. Find the Section object and check out its events. No Format, Print, or Retreat events in there.) But this class does manage to trap the events. How? We used a trick. Figuring that there had to be a public object that exposed these three events, we did what any VBA developer who's desperate would do: we right-clicked in the Object Browser and turned on the display of hidden members. Once we did that, we found the _SectionInReport object, which does raise the three events you'd expect to find. (Note that _SectionReport is an invalid name in VBA, so you must surround it with square brackets in order to use it in code.) Listing 9.10 shows the pertinent code from the SkipLabels class.

Listing 9.10

```
Private WithEvents mrpt As Report
Private WithEvents msec As [_SectionInReport]

Public Property Set Report(Value As Report)
    Set mrpt = Value
    Set msec = mrpt.Detail

    ' If the event property isn't
    ' set to "[Event Procedure]", you won't
    ' be able to trap its events.
    msec.OnFormat = "[Event Procedure]"
    mrpt.OnPage = "[Event Procedure]"

    ' Call the procedure that pops
    ' up the form, and gets the number
    ' of labels to skip.
    mintSkipped = 0
    mintToSkip = GetLabelsToSkip()
End Property
```

This procedure receives a reference to the report that's being printed and stores that in mrpt. Then, it stores a reference to the Detail section in msec, a variable declared using the WithEvents keyword, so that later code can react to events of that section. Then, in the Format event procedure for the section the code is monitoring, you'll find code like this:

```
Private Sub msec_Format( _
 Cancel As Integer, FormatCount As Integer)
    ' If the report hasn't skipped enough
    ' labels yet, move on to the next label.
    ' This only applies on the first printed
    ' page.
    If mrpt.Page = 1 Then
        If mintSkipped < mintToSkip Then
            mrpt.NextRecord = False
            mrpt.PrintSection = False
            mintSkipped = mintSkipped + 1
        End If
    End If
End Sub
```

From the Format event of the Detail section, the code keeps track of how many labels it has skipped. Once it reaches the value in mintToSkip, it actually starts printing labels. Up to that point, however, it sets the NextRecord and PrintSection properties to False, stalling until it reaches the right label.

The GetLabelsToSkip function, shown in Listing 9.11, does most of the work in the class. This procedure first passes the layout properties (Rows, Cols, StartLabel, PrintAcross) to the form in its OpenArgs property and then opens the form using the acDialog WindowMode option. (Code in the form parses that information and adjusts the layout of buttons on the form to match. For more information on passing multiple parameters in a single string, see Chapter 7.) The user interacts with the form and chooses the OK or Cancel button. If the user presses OK, the form remains loaded in memory, and the GetLabelsToSkip function can call the IsLoaded function (also in Listing 9.11) to determine if the form's still in memory. If so, the code retrieves the LabelsToSkip property of the form and then closes it. (For more information on creating pop-up forms that return values, see the section "Using Pop-up Tools" in Chapter 8.)

Listing 9.11

```
Private Function GetLabelsToSkip() As Integer
    On Error GoTo HandleErrors
    ' Pop up a form, requesting the StartLabeling label.
```

```
    ' First, open the label-choosing form.
    Dim strOpenArgs As String
    strOpenArgs = Join( _
     Array( _
     "Rows=" & Rows, _
     "Cols=" & Cols, _
     "StartLabel=" & StartLabel, _
     "Across=" & PrintAcross), ";")

    DoCmd.OpenForm FormName:=FormName, _
     WindowMode:=acDialog, _
     OpenArgs:=strOpenArgs

    ' If the form's still loaded, the user selected a value.
    If IsLoaded(FormName) Then
        GetLabelsToSkip = Forms(FormName).LabelsToSkip
        DoCmd.Close acForm, FormName
    Else
        mfCancelled = True
        GetLabelsToSkip = 0
    End If
    ' Give Windows time to actually close the
    ' form before you go on about your business.
    DoEvents

ExitHere:
    Exit Function

HandleErrors:
    Select Case Err
        Case Else
            MsgBox "Error: " & Err.Description & _
             " (" & Err.Number & ")"
    End Select
    Resume ExitHere
End Function
```

TIP

To use this technique in your own applications, import frmSelectLabel and the three class modules: SkipLabels, TaggedValues, and TaggedValue, from the sample database. Copy the code from rptSkipLabels into your own report's module and modify the property settings to reflect your report's layout. When you open your report, it will pop up the form and request a starting label.

Inserting Blank Lines

If your report consists of a long list of values, you may wish to insert a blank line at regular intervals. Figure 9.18 shows such a report, with a blank line inserted after each group of three rows.

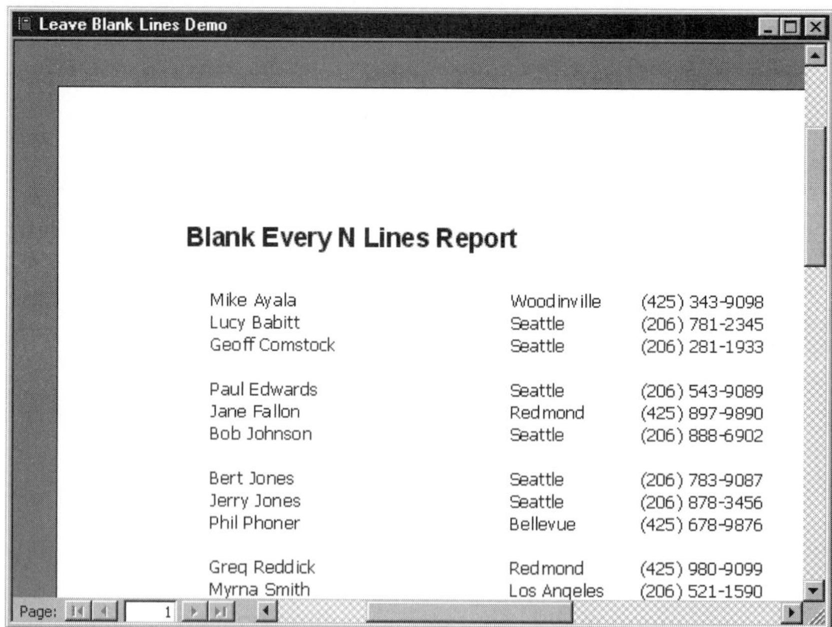

FIGURE 9.18: Insert a blank line to separate large groups into readable chunks.

This technique again involves the NextRecord and PrintSection properties. The code in Listing 9.12 (from rptBlankEveryNLines), called from a Detail section's Print event procedure, does the work for you, and you can copy it into any of your own report's modules. The code does its work by counting up the lines that have been printed so far on each page; when the number is an even multiple of the group size plus one (that is, if you're breaking after every three lines, you'll be looking for line numbers that are a multiple of four), the report skips to the next print location (MoveLayout = True) but does not move to the next record (Next-Record = False) and doesn't print anything (PrintSection = False). This inserts a blank row.

Listing 9.12 shows the HandleLine procedure.

Listing 9.12

```
Dim mintLineCount As Integer

Private Sub Detail1_Print( _
 Cancel As Integer, PrintCount As Integer)
     Call HandleLine
End Sub

Private Sub HandleLine()
    Dim fHideLine As Boolean

    ' Break every 3 lines.
    Const adhcBreakCount = 3

    fHideLine = _
     ((mintLineCount Mod (adhcBreakCount + 1)) = 0)
    If fHideLine Then
        ' If you're not showing the current
        ' row, then don't move to the next record,
        ' and don't print the section.
        Me.NextRecord = False
        Me.PrintSection = False
        Me.MoveLayout = True
        mintLineCount = 0
    End If
    mintLineCount = mintLineCount + 1
End Sub
```

If you want to reset the group count at the start of a new group, a new page, or at the start of the report, add code to set mintLineCount to 0 in the Format event procedure of the appropriate section. The sample report includes all three—most likely, you'll need to decide for yourself at which points you want to reset the group counter and reset the value to 0 only at that point.

TIP

If you just want to insert a blank line between your groups and don't care about breaking them into specific-sized groups, you can set up a group footer that's blank (with its CanShrink property set to No). Then, when the group breaks, Access inserts a blank space between groups.

As you can see from the previous three examples, you can use the MoveLayout, PrintSection, and NextRecord properties to create reports that would be difficult to generate by any other means. Don't be put off by their apparent complexity; once you get the hang of it, you can make them do exactly what you need.

Handling Odd and Even Pages

Perhaps you print your reports double-sided (either on a duplex printer or by using a printing utility that handles this task for you). In general, given that the first page of a document prints on the front of a piece of paper, odd-numbered pages appear on the right, and even-numbered pages appear on the left when you bind the document. Quite often, in published documents, you'll want the page numbers to appear flush right on odd-numbered pages and flush left on even-numbered pages. Although Access doesn't provide a built-in method to accomplish this, it's easy to do. (See rptPhoneBook or rptPhoneBookParam for this example. On those reports, as you move from page to page, the footer information alternates being left-aligned and right-aligned.)

To control left and right alignment for alternating pages, take these two steps:

1. Create your page footer control so that it spans the entire width of your report (see Figure 9.19). Enter the ControlSource value you'd like.
2. Attach the code in Listing 9.13 to the Format event of the Page Footer section. This handles setting the TextAlign property for the Footer section as each page gets printed. For every page, the code calls the IsEven function, which uses the MOD operator to evaluate the page number and determine if it's even. The event procedure then sets the TextAlign property to acAlignRight for odd pages and acAlignLeft for even pages.

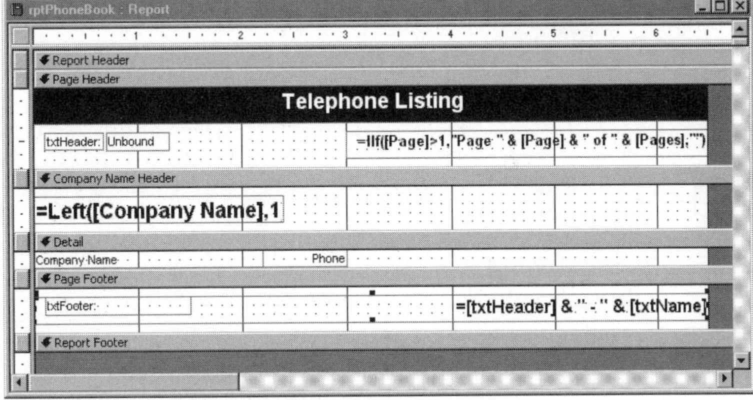

FIGURE 9.19:

Your footer can alternate alignments easily if it spans the entire page.

The IsEven function uses the MOD operator to determine if a value is even. If you haven't used the MOD operator, this might appear confusing. Basically, the MOD operator returns the remainder you get when you divide the first operand by the second. That is, if you have

```
? 5 MOD 2
```

the result would be 1 because the remainder when you divide 5 by 2 is 1. The MOD operator is most useful for determining whether one number is a multiple of another since, if it is, the result will be 0. To tell whether a number is even, you can use the expression

```
If x MOD 2 = 0 Then ...
```

Listing 9.13

```
Private Function IsEven(intValue As Integer) As Boolean
    ' Is intValue even, or not?
    IsEven = (intValue Mod 2 = 0)
End Function

Private Sub PageFooter2_Format( _
 Cancel As Integer, FormatCount As Integer)

    ' Constants Access should supply.
    Const acAlignLeft = 1
    Const acAlignRight = 3
```

```
    txtFooter.TextAlign = IIf(IsEven(Me.Page), _
     acAlignLeft, acAlignRight)
End Sub
```

Controlling the Starting Page Number

Every report supports the Page property: a read/write property that indicates and/or sets the current page number. By inspecting the Page property of the current report, you can determine which page is currently active. You can also set the Page property, effectively resetting Access' understanding of the current page number. You could, if you had a reason to, set the Page property to 1 in the page header's Format event. Then, every time Access formatted a page header (once per page), it would reset the report's Page property to 1.

TIP If you're printing a report that consists of invoices, for example, you could reset the Page property to 1 in the page header's Format event procedure. That way, each invoice you printed, as part of this report, would effectively start on page 1.

A more useful trick involving the Page property is the ability to set the starting page number to some value other than 1. This is especially useful if you need to chain reports or number chapters with a page number including the chapter number, with each chapter starting at page 1. The only tricky issue here is deciding when to reset the page number. If you want to print an entire report, starting at a particular page number, set the Page property in the report header's Format event. If you need to set the Page property based on data that could occur at the top of any given page, set the value in the page header's Format event.

For an example, see rptSales. This report sets the first page number to 6 in the report header's Format event, as if this was the sixth page of a longer document. Numbers increase consecutively from there. The code to make this change is minimal, of course:

```
Sub ReportHeader0_Format( _
 Cancel As Integer, FormatCount As Integer)
    Me.Page = 6
End Sub
```

Because the report's Open event occurs before any of the formatting events, you could also use that hook to retrieve the starting page number, store it in a variable, and then assign the value of that variable to the Page property in the report header's Format event. (We discuss the other interesting features of this report, including the alternate gray bars, in the section "The Sales Report" later in this chapter.)

Numbering Items on a Report

Access makes it simple to number rows on a report (and this technique requires no coding at all). By changing two properties of a text box, you can create a row counter that will number rows either over the total report or just within a group. The sample report, rptNumberRows, demonstrates both types of row counters, as you can see in Figure 9.20.

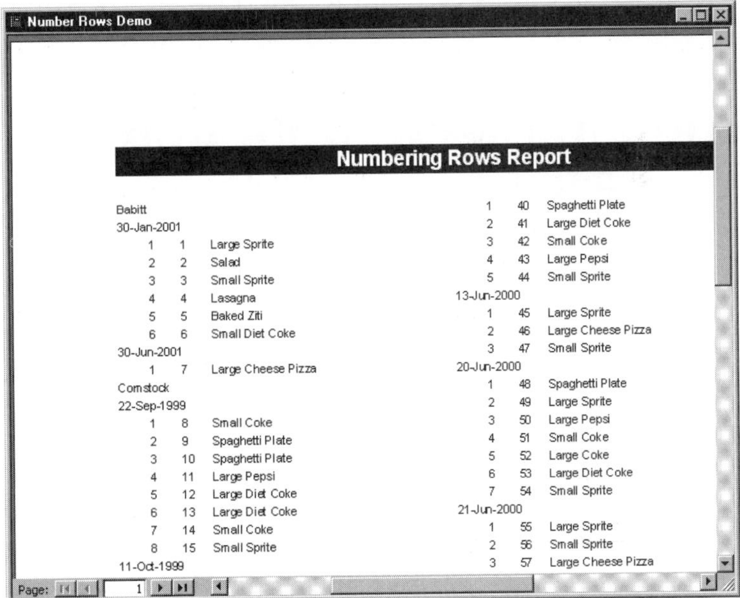

FIGURE 9.20:

Use the RunningSum property to create a row counter in a report.

To create a row counter on a report, set a text box's properties as follows:

Property	Setting
RunningSum	Over Group (1) or Over All (2)
ControlSource	=1

This technique takes advantage of the fact that setting the RunningSum property causes the current row's value to be the sum of all the previous rows' values plus the current row's value. Because the current row's value in this case is always 1, the running sum just increments by 1. You could, of course, place some other value in the ControlSource property to force it to increment by a different value.

You can examine rptNumberRows to see how it works, but the most important setting is that for the RunningSum property of the text boxes. If you set the RunningSum property to Over Group, the report sums only over the current group. Every time Access starts a new group, its value gets reset to 0. If you set the RunningSum property to Over All, the Access resets the value only at the beginning of the report and continues to increment for the rest of the report.

Some Simple Sample Reports

The following reports show off some of the effects various properties and event procedures can make on the printed output of an Access report. Each was designed to show off specific techniques:

- Sales report: Alternating gray bars, displaying report properties on the report, creating page totals
- Telephone book: Using multiple columns with full-page-width title, section titles, and footer page-range listing
- Companies, contacts, and hardware: Using multiple subreports and report properties to link separate reports

The Sales Report

The sales report (see Figure 9.21) lists companies in reverse order of sales and, within sets of equal sales, in alphabetical order by company name. For visibility, every other line is printed in gray, and each page contains a total sales amount for the companies printed on that page.

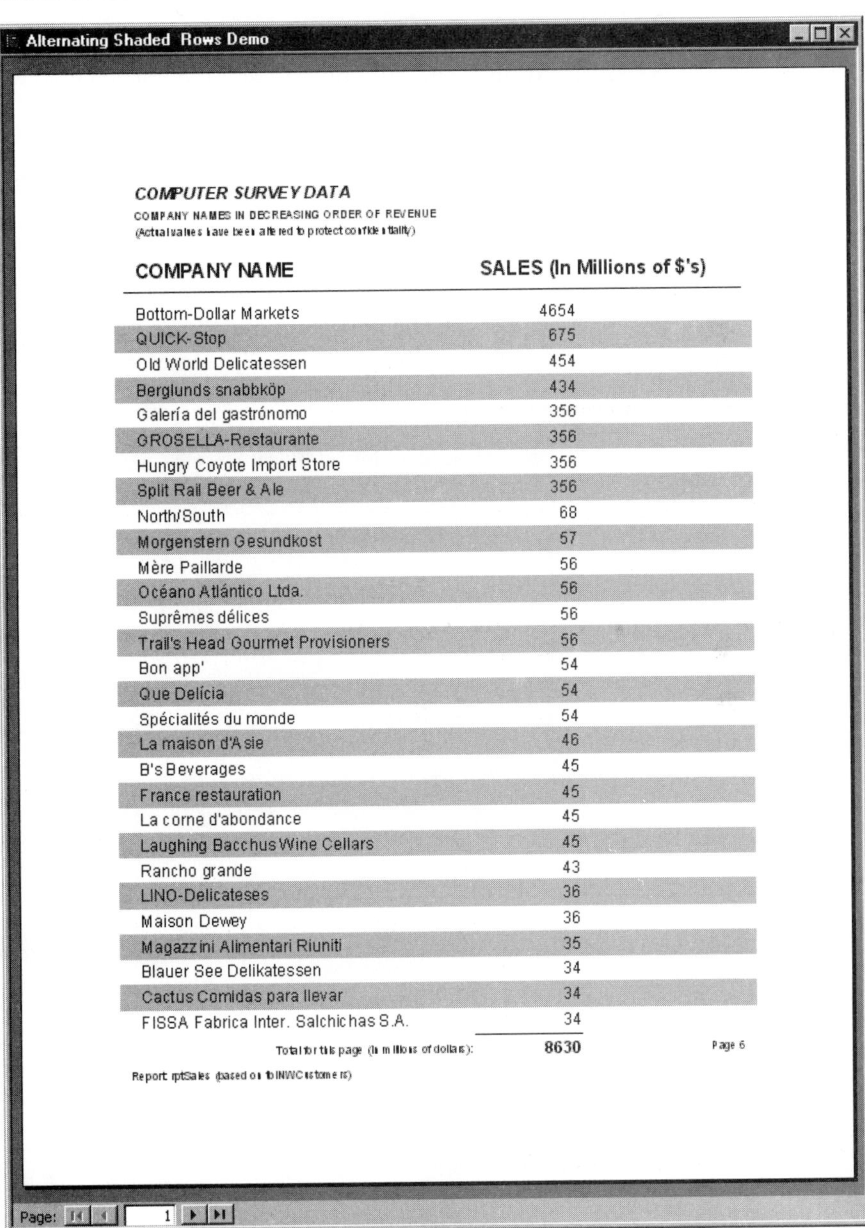

COMPUTER SURVEY DATA

COMPANY NAMES IN DECREASING ORDER OF REVENUE

(Actual values have been altered to protect confidentiality)

COMPANY NAME	SALES (In Millions of $'s)
Bottom-Dollar Markets	4654
QUICK-Stop	675
Old World Delicatessen	454
Berglunds snabbköp	434
Galería del gastrónomo	356
GROSELLA-Restaurante	356
Hungry Coyote Import Store	356
Split Rail Beer & Ale	356
North/South	68
Morgenstern Gesundkost	57
Mère Paillarde	56
Océano Atlántico Ltda.	56
Suprêmes délices	56
Trail's Head Gourmet Provisioners	56
Bon app'	54
Que Delícia	54
Spécialités du monde	54
La maison d'Asie	46
B's Beverages	45
France restauration	45
La corne d'abondance	45
Laughing Bacchus Wine Cellars	45
Rancho grande	43
LINO-Delicateses	36
Maison Dewey	36
Magazzini Alimentari Riuniti	35
Blauer See Delikatessen	34
Cactus Comidas para llevar	34
FISSA Fabrica Inter. Salchichas S.A.	34
Total for this page (In millions of dollars):	**8630**

Page 6

Report rptSales (based on tblNWCustomers)

FIGURE 9.21: Company names in decreasing order of sales, with added alternate gray bars

We'll take this in steps:

1. Create the basic report, with no gray and no totals.
2. Add the page total (using the Print event).
3. Add the alternate gray lines (using the Format event).

Step 1: Creating the Basic Report—No Gray, No Totals

Figure 9.22 shows the design surface for the basic, no-frills sales report. The sorting and grouping have already been performed, using the setup shown in Figure 9.23. For this report, Access prints information from the Report Header section once, on the first page. It prints the information in the Page Header and Page Footer sections once on each page and prints the Detail section once for each row of data.

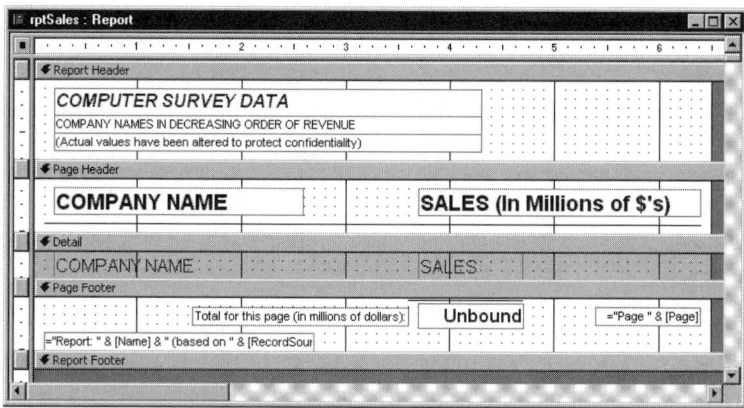

FIGURE 9.22:

Plain sales report's design surface

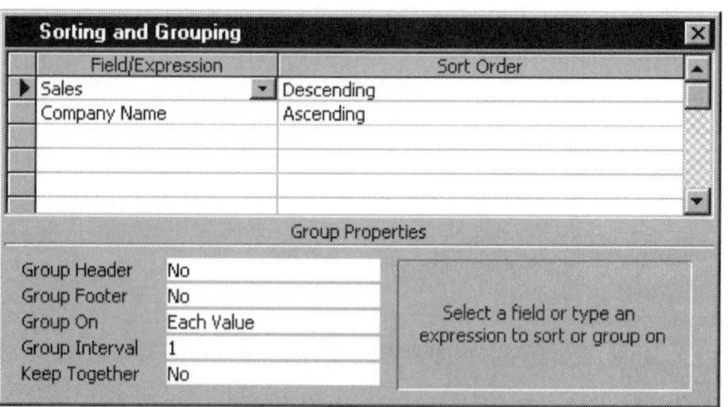

FIGURE 9.23:

Sorting and Grouping dialog for the sales report

TIP

If you're using a calculated expression as the ControlSource property for a text box on a report, make sure its Name property does not match one of the fields in your expression. If the Name property is the same as one of the fields used to fill the control, Access can't know whether you want it to get the value from the field or from the control with that particular name. Confused, Access will place #Error into the text box when you run the report. This is a common occurrence when you create reports using the Report Wizards and then customize them. The Wizards use the field name as the Name property for each control, which can lead to just this sort of problem.

Using Report Properties

If you look carefully at the Page Footer section of the report, you'll notice that it's using some of the report's properties—Name, RecordSource, and Page—as values that are shown on the report. You can use any of the report's properties as built-in variables on the report printout. This same feature applies to forms, although it's not as useful in that context because form properties aren't nearly as interesting as report properties while the object's being viewed. (Forms don't support the Page property except when printing, for example.)

Step 2: Adding Page Totals

Unlike the Report and Group Header/Footer sections, Page Header/Footer sections don't support aggregate functions (like Sum, for example), so you have to "fake out" Access in order to create page totals. Our solution (only one of many possible solutions) has two parts:

- As each page header is printed, reset the running total to 0 in preparation for accumulating the value for the current page.
- As each row is printed, accumulate the running total in a control in the page footer.

Each of these refers to a control in the page footer, necessary for accumulating the running total. In this sample report (rptSales), that text box is named txtPageTotal (the control with Unbound in it in Figure 9.22).

Because you surely do not want a value added into the running total unless that particular row has been slated to be printed on the current page, you should attach the code that updates the totals to the section's Print event. (If you insisted on using the Format event, you would need to add code to the matching Retreat event that would back out of the addition if the row were not to be printed.) In this simple example, there's no chance that the Print and Format events will be fired off independently (since there's only one printed row per row in the data), but you need to think about the differences between the Print and Format events when deciding how to attach actions to events. Access raises the Format event when it's formatting a section but isn't yet sure whether it will get printed. It raises the Print event only when it's about to actually print the row.

Resetting the Total for Each Page

In the Page Header's Format event (which occurs only as each page starts its formatting process), call the following code:

```
txtPageTotal = 0
```

This resets the text box in the page footer that will accumulate the total for each page.

Accumulating the Sales as You Go

In the Detail section's Print event, call the following code:

```
txtPageTotal = txtPageTotal + Nz(txtSales)
```

This code adds the current row's sales value to the current page total. Remember that the Print event handler is the only event procedure that can access each and every row's data, once you're sure the data is to be printed on the current page. It's here that you need to place any code that must react to each row as it gets printed. When each page is finally pushed out of the printer, this total will be correct, because you've been maintaining it while Access has printed each row.

Step 3: Alternating White and Gray Bars

If you want to display alternate shaded rows on your report, you have two options:

- You can make the controls in the Detail section transparent and shade just the Detail section's background

or

- You can shade each control in the Detail section individually.

The first technique is simpler—it requires only a change of one property, the Detail section's BackColor property. The second technique requires more work, but it will make it possible for you to export your reports to HTML or other output formats and retain the background coloring.

The rptSales example report includes code to do the work the simple way, and rptSales2 is set up to use the more flexible solution. To work through the simple solution, look at rptSales. You can find the procedure AlternateGray (Listing 9.14) in the module for rptSales. Because Access now allows text boxes to be transparent, showing the background color through them, the exercise is trivial: for every alternate row, change the background color of the section. The controls are transparent, and the background color for the section will be the background color for the row.

The routine uses a module-global variable, mfGray, to keep track of which color to use for printing the current row. The procedure switches the variable between True and False:

```
mfGray = Not mfGray
```

If you want to ensure that the first row on each page is printed in white, set the value of mfGray to False in the page header's Format event code. (Note that AlternateGray uses the built-in system color constant, vbMenuBar, to assign the gray color. You can choose any color you like, for your reports.)

Listing 9.14

```
Private Sub AlternateGray()

    ' If the current section is to be printed in gray,
    ' then set the BackColor property for the section.
    ' This works only because the controls on the section
    ' are all set to be transparent.
    Me.Section(acDetail).BackColor = _
     IIf(mfGray, vbMenuBar, vbWhite)

    ' Next time, do it the opposite of the way
    ' you did it this time.
    mfGray = Not mfGray
End Sub
```

TIP

To include this functionality in your own reports, copy the subroutine named AlternateGray from rptSales to your own report, declare the mfGray Boolean variable in the declarations area in the report's class module, and add the necessary call to AlternateGray to the Format event of the Detail section. You might also set the value of mfGray to False (or True) in the page header's Format event handler (to reset the first row on each page to a known color). Make sure the BackStyle property for each control in the Detail section of your report has been set to Transparent.

To do the work the hard (but more flexible) way, follow these steps:

1. Make sure the controls in your Detail section fill the entire space of the Detail section. There shouldn't be any background peeking through. If you're not sure, set the Detail section's BackColor property to some specific color and check to see if any of that color is visible. If you have extra space, place empty text box controls.
2. Make sure the BackStyle property of each control in the detail section has been set to Normal.
3. Add code to the Detail section's Format event to set the color for each control. The sample report, rptSales2, includes the procedure shown in Listing 9.15. You'll need to make sure that you include each control in the section, including empty controls added to fill the space.

Listing 9.15

```
Private Sub AlternateGrayTheHardway()
    Dim lngColor As Long

    lngColor = IIf(mfGray, vbMenuBar, vbWhite)
    txtCompany.BackColor = lngColor
    txtSales.BackColor = lngColor
    txtFiller.BackColor = lngColor

    ' Next time, do it the opposite of the way
    ' you did it this time.
    mfGray = Not mfGray
End Sub
```

Now, if you run either rptSales or rptSales2, you'll see alternating rows of shading, page totals, and property reports showing as data on the report.

The Phone Book

Many people use Access to maintain their phone books and address lists. The report you'll see in this section creates a phone book–like listing of names and telephone numbers and adds a few twists. It incorporates large group separators, prints in two vertical columns, and puts a "names on this page" indicator at the bottom of the page. Figure 9.24 shows the layout of the first page of rptPhoneBook.

FIGURE 9.24:

Multicolumn, grouped by company name

Telephone Listing

A

Alfreds Futterkiste	030-0074321
Ana Trujillo Emparedados y helados	(5) 555-4729
Antonio Moreno Taquería	(5) 555-3932
Around the Hom	(71) 555-7788

B

Berglunds snabbköp	0921-12 34 65
Blauer See Delikatessen	0621-08460
Blondel père et fils	88.60.15.31
Bólido Comidas preparadas	(91) 555 22 82
Bon app'	91.24.45.40
Bottom-Dollar Markets	(604) 555-4729
B's Beverages	(71) 555-1212

C

Cactus Comidas para llevar	(1) 135-5555
Centro comercial Moctezuma	(5) 555-3392
Chop-suey Chinese	0452-076545
Comércio Mineiro	(11) 555-7647
Consolidated Holdings	(71) 555-2282

D

Die Wandemde Kuh	0711-020361
Drachenblut Delikatessen	0241-039123
Du monde entier	40.67.88.88

E

Eastem Connection	(71) 555-0297
Emst Handel	7675-3425

F

Familia Arquibaldo	(11) 555-9857
FISSA Fabrica Inter. Salchichas S.A.	(91) 555 94 44
Folies gourmandes	20.16.10.16
Folk och fä HB	0695-34 67 21
France restauration	40.32.21.21
Franchi S.p.A.	011-4988260
Furia Bacalhau e Frutos do Mar	(1) 354-2534

G

Galería del gastrónomo	(93) 203 4560
Godos Cocina Típica	(95) 555 82 82
Gourmet Lanchonetes	(11) 555-9482
Great Lakes Food Market	(503) 555-7555
GROSELLA-Restaurante	(2) 283-2951

H

Hanari Cames	(21) 555-0091
HILARIÓN-Abastos	(5) 555-1340
Hungry Coyote Import Store	(503) 555-6874
Hungry Owl All-Night Grocers	2967 542

I

Island Trading	(24) 555-8888

K

Königlich Essen	0555-09876

L

La come d'abondance	30.59.84.10
La maison d'Asie	61.77.61.10
Laughing Bacchus Wine Cellars	(604) 555-3392
Lazy K Kountry Store	(509) 555-7969
Lehmanns Marktstand	069-0245984
Let's Stop N Shop	(415) 555-5938
LILA-Supermercado	(9) 331-6954
LINO-Delicateses	(8) 34-56-12
Lonesome Pine Restaurant	(503) 555-9573

M

Magazzini Alimentari Riuniti	035-640230
Maison Dewey	(02) 201 24 67
Mère Paillarde	(514) 555-8054
Morgenstem Gesundkost	0342-023176

N

North/South	(71) 555-7733

O

Océano Atlántico Ltda.	(1) 135-5333
Old World Delicatessen	(907) 555-7584
Ottilies Käseladen	0221-0644327

Alfreds Futterkiste - Ottilies Käseladen

Again, we'll take this in steps:

1. Create a basic list, sorted and grouped on Company Name, with a page number on each page.
2. Print the list in two columns, with a full-span page header and page footer.
3. Add the "names on this page" indicator with alternating alignment, and hide the page number on the first page.

Step 1: Creating the Basic List

Because reports do their own sorting, based on the choices made in the Sorting and Grouping dialog box, this report is based on a table rather than on a query. (There would be no point in basing this report on a query: if the query sorted the data, the report would then just sort it again!) If you look at the report design (Figure 9.25), you'll notice that the list is grouped on Company Name (Prefix Characters:1), which means Access will start a new group every time the first letter of the last name changes. When that happens, it prints out the current value's group footer and the next value's group header. To get Access to sort the companies within the group, you must add Company Name to the Sorting and Grouping dialog again.

FIGURE 9.25:

Phone book's design surface

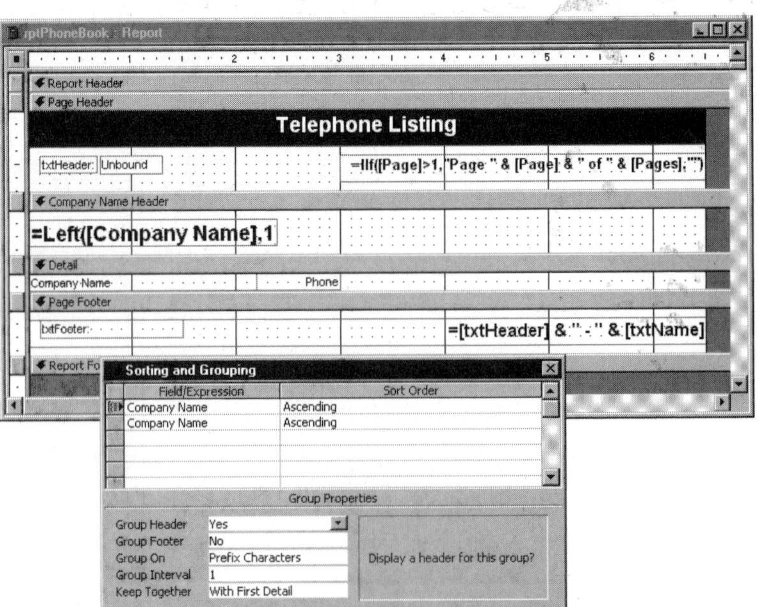

Each time Access starts a new group, it prints out the Company Name Header section, which consists of a large copy of the first letter of the company name at that moment. (Remember that the group header has access to the data from the first row of its section and the group footer has access to the last row of data in the section.)

Step 2: Printing the Multicolumn Report

Setting up reports to print in multiple columns requires digging around in a dialog box buried in the Page Setup dialog. Choose the Columns tab to find the options that control the number and type of columns you use in your report. Figure 9.26 shows the Page Setup dialog. Table 9.13 shows the items you'll be concerned with when creating a multicolumn report.

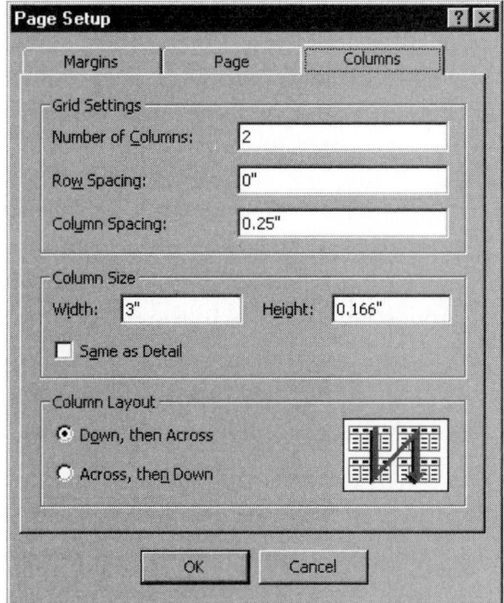

FIGURE 9.26: Choose the Columns tab in the Page Setup dialog to control the column settings for your report.

TABLE 9.13: Multicolumn Report Option Settings

Item	Setting for the Phone Book	Description
Items Across	2	Number of columns
Same as Detail	No (unchecked)	Determines whether each column is the same width as the Detail section in the report design

Contimued on next page

TABLE 9.13 CONTINUED: Multicolumn Report Option Settings

Item	Setting for the Phone Book	Description
Width	3	Width of each column
Layout Items	Down, then Across	Determines whether your columns will go across (Across, then Down) or up and down (Down, then Across)

Making the changes outlined in the table should transform your report from a one-column list to a phone book–style layout.

One important point: if you want the header and footer to span the entire report (as you do in this case), you must set the report design surface width to the width of the entire report. Then, place controls in the Detail section (and its Header/Footer sections) only as wide as your columns will be. Finally, make sure the Same as Detail option is unchecked, with the Width option set to the width each column will fill. This way the report's width determines the width of the Report Header and Footer sections, but the Width setting in the Page Setup dialog controls the width of each column.

You might also find it interesting to try setting the Item Layout property to print horizontally rather than vertically. In that case, Access prints each row and then moves horizontally to the next print location. When all the columns are full across the page, it moves to the next row. You'll most likely want to try setting the NewRowOrColumn property for the group header to Before & After Section. This places each section header on a new row, by itself, with the data beginning on the following row. Figure 9.27 shows the horizontally arranged phone book.

Step 3: Indicating the Group Names and Hiding the First-Page Page Number

You have two final challenges in creating this report:

- Provide an indication of the group of names that are shown on the current page.
- Hide the page number on the first page. (Okay, Access will do this for you if you choose the Insert ➢ Page Number command, but it's worth understanding the details.)

FIGURE 9.27:

Setting the Item Layout property to Horizontal changes the look of the phone book.

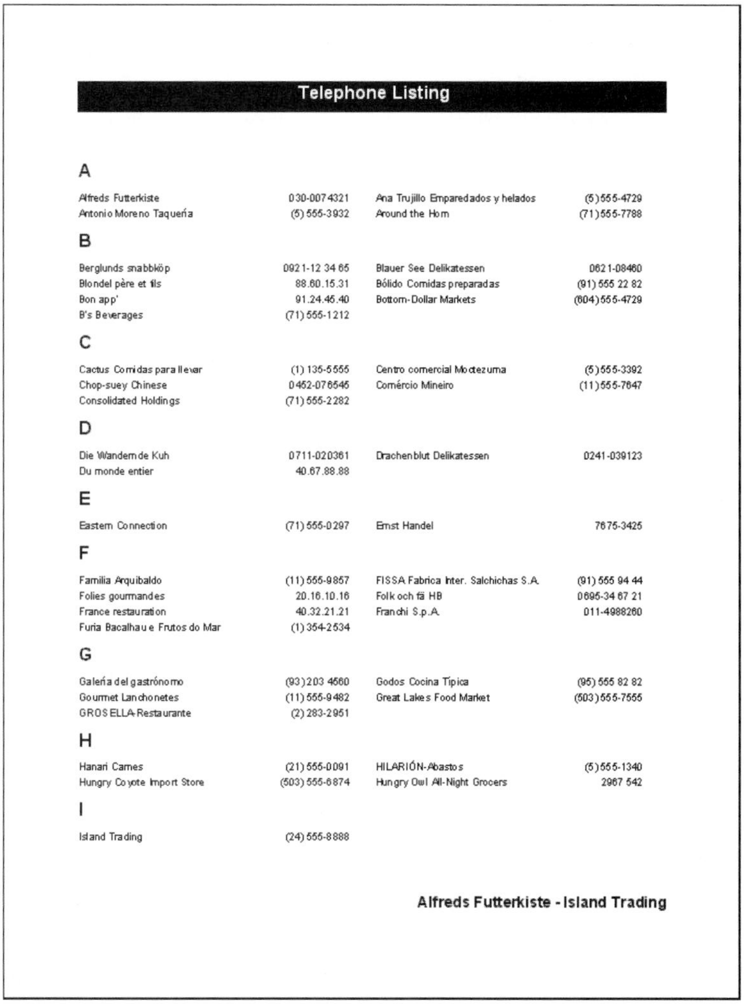

Telephone Listing

A

Alfreds Futterkiste	030-0074321	Ana Trujillo Emparedados y helados	(5)555-4729
Antonio Moreno Taquería	(5) 555-3932	Around the Horn	(71)555-7788

B

Berglunds snabbköp	0921-12 34 65	Blauer See Delikatessen	0621-08460
Blondel père et fils	88.60.15.31	Bólido Comidas preparadas	(91) 555 22 82
Bon app'	91.24.45.40	Bottom-Dollar Markets	(604)555-4729
B's Beverages	(71) 555-1212		

C

Cactus Comidas para llevar	(1) 135-5555	Centro comercial Moctezuma	(5)555-3392
Chop-suey Chinese	0452-076545	Comércio Mineiro	(11)555-7647
Consolidated Holdings	(71) 555-2282		

D

Die Wandernde Kuh	0711-020361	Drachenblut Delikatessen	0241-039123
Du monde entier	40.67.88.88		

E

Eastern Connection	(71) 555-0297	Ernst Handel	7675-3425

F

Familia Arquibaldo	(11) 555-9857	FISSA Fabrica Inter. Salchichas S.A.	(91) 555 94 44
Folies gourmandes	20.16.10.16	Folk och fä HB	0695-34 67 21
France restauration	40.32.21.21	Franchi S.p.A.	011-4988260
Furia Bacalhau e Frutos do Mar	(1) 354-2534		

G

Galería del gastrónomo	(93)203 4560	Godos Cocina Típica	(95) 555 82 82
Gourmet Lanchonetes	(11) 555-9482	Great Lakes Food Market	(503)555-7555
GROSELLA-Restaurante	(2) 283-2951		

H

Hanari Carnes	(21) 555-0091	HILARIÓN-Abastos	(5)555-1340
Hungry Coyote Import Store	(503) 555-6874	Hungry Owl All-Night Grocers	2967 542

I

Island Trading	(24) 555-8888		

Alfreds Futterkiste - Island Trading

Gathering Information, but Only in the Footer

To create a text box that displays the range of names on the current page, you need a bit more trickery. By the time Access formats the page footer, it has access to only the current row, which is the last row to be printed on the page. But you need to know the *first* name on the page, as well. The trick here is to store away the first name when you can get it—when Access is formatting the page header.

The easiest way to use it is to place it in a hidden text box in the report's page header during the page header's Format event. Then, as the control source for a text box on the page footer, you can retrieve the first name on the page from its storage place and concatenate it to the current (final) name. This works fine, except for one small problem: it can work only from the page footer. Because Access formats the page in a linear fashion (from the top section to the bottom), your names will be off by one page, one way or another, if you try this in any other sequence.

Therefore, in the Format event of the report's Page Header section, call the following code. In this example, the text box named txtName contains the current row's Company Name field, and txtHeader is the text box in the page header that's used for storage:

```
txtHeader = txtName
```

Then, as the ControlSource for a control in the page footer, use this expression:

```
=[txtHeader] & " - " & [txtName]
```

This concatenates the stored first name and current final name in the control.

Hiding the Page Number

Hiding the page number on the first page requires a single step: set the ControlSource property of the text box such that it prints an empty string on the first page and the page number on all the rest:

```
=IIf([Page]>1, "Page " & [Page] & " of " & [Pages], "")
```

That is, all reports support the Page and Pages properties (available only at runtime), and you can use them directly on your reports, as you can from your event procedures. (See the section "Controlling the Starting Page Number" earlier in this chapter.) In this case, if the current page number is larger than 1, display the current page number along with the total number of pages; otherwise, display nothing.

TIP

Be aware that if you use the Pages property anywhere on your report, you're forcing Access to run your report twice—once to count the pages and once again to print it. Likewise, if you ask Access to calculate percentages of totals in the body of your report, it will have to make a first pass to calculate the totals and then another to print the report. If you're printing a long report, this extra overhead may be noticeable. If you can avoid using the Pages property for long reports, you may be able to run the reports more quickly.

Keeping Things Together

In earlier versions of Access, it was difficult to ensure that groups didn't break across columns, leaving *widows*—headers with no matching detail rows in the same column. Now, it's simple: use the report's GrpKeepTogether property (set to Per Column) to have your groups' settings take effect over columns. (How you set your groups' Keep-Together property will be affected either by page breaks—Per Page—or by column breaks—Per Column.) It is confusing that this is a *report* property, not a group property, but because it applies to all groups, it therefore must be a global property.

To review, you'll find three report properties that affect how groups break:

- A GroupLevel object's KeepTogether property controls whether the group level header prints alone, with at least one row of the detail section, or with all the rows of the detail section.
- A Section object's KeepTogether property controls whether Access attempts to print the entire section on a single page.
- A Report object's GrpKeepTogether property controls whether to treat the other KeepTogether properties across columns, or just for entire pages.

Companies, Contacts, and Hardware

Sometimes you'll find that one complex report really requires several smaller, linked reports. Or, perhaps, you need to have sections of your report that, as a whole, can grow or shrink, depending on the amount of data you've got. The report in Figure 9.28 is one such report. It shows a single company site, the listed contacts for that site, and the computer hardware and software the company uses at that site. The data comes from three different tables:

- A list of companies' sites (with SiteID as the primary key)
- A list of names, with each row also containing a SiteID field—a foreign key from the site table
- A list of hardware and software items, one row per item, again with a SiteID field as a foreign key from the site table

The solution? The subreport control makes it possible to embed one report within another. Figure 9.28 shows the required output, created with almost no code at all.

FIGURE 9.28:

Subreports make this complex report possible.

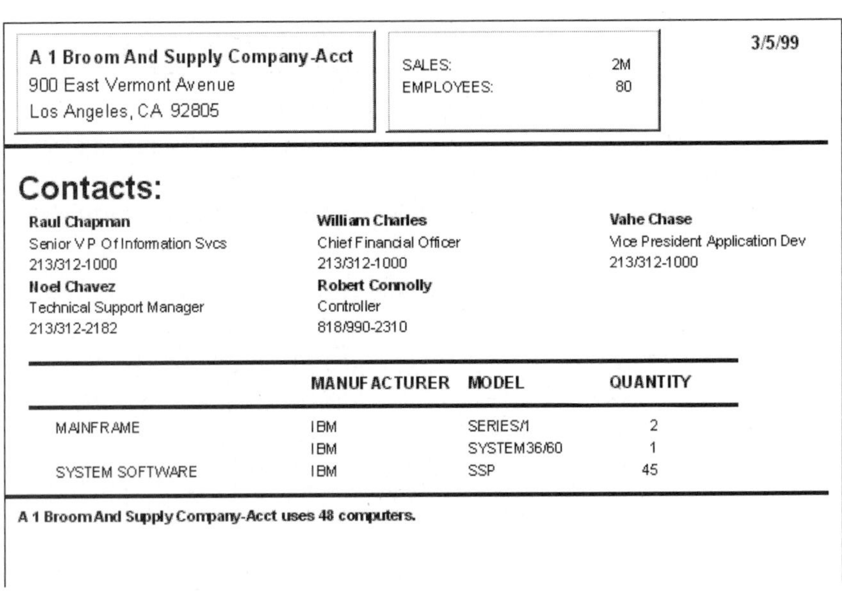

Designing the Report

Looking at the report, you see three distinct sections: the site information, the contact information, and the hardware/software list. Because there isn't any way to create those three different sections within the confines of a single report, this situation is a perfect candidate for using subreports. You create this report in three steps, by creating three separate reports and then combining them:

1. Contact Information
2. Hardware/Software List
3. Site Information (the main report)

The main report will contain the site information, and its SiteID will link it with the two subreports. As the report prints, moving from SiteID to SiteID, Access will display only the contacts and hardware/software for the specific SiteID. You should be able to create each of the subreports independently, as long as you plan ahead and include the linking field, SiteID, somewhere on the report surface (and it can be invisible, of course). Although the final report is rather complex, each piece is simple.

The Multicolumn Contact List

After building the phone book list in the previous example, creating the multicolumn contact list should be easy. The only differences in this case are that the items are to increment horizontally rather than vertically and that each item is in a vertical clump of data rather than a horizontal one. Figure 9.29 shows the design surface for this report (rptBankInfoSub1).

FIGURE 9.29:

Design surface for the three-column contact list

Pertinent Properties

To get the report just right, set the properties for the Header section as follows:

Property	Value
NewRowOrCol	After Section
ForceNewPage	Before Section (necessary only when the report is not used as a subform)

Set the Sorting and Grouping dialog so that the report is sorted/grouped on Company, then Last, and then First, with the properties on the first grouping as shown here:

Property	Value
GroupHeader	Yes
GroupFooter	No
GroupOn	Each Value
GroupInterval	1

Finally, open the Page Setup dialog and set the properties there, as shown in the following table, so the report will print in three columns:

Property	Value
Number of Columns	3
Same As Detail	No (unchecked)
Column Layout	Across, then Down
Width	2

As you set these properties, try variations and run the report. The best way to learn what each property does is to experiment with an existing report, changing properties and seeing how the output changes. Use Print Preview, of course, to save a few trees.

Hardware/Software List

The hardware/software report should seem simple compared with the other reports you've been creating. Figure 9.30 shows the design surface for this simple report (rptBankInfoSub2).

FIGURE 9.30:

Design surface for the simple list of hardware and software

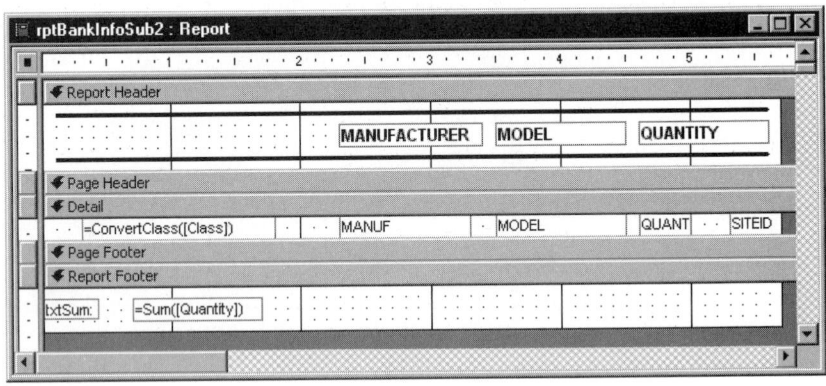

The only interesting feature of this report is its use of a simple function to convert the code representing the class type into an English word for that class of hardware. You can call any function to provide the contents of a report control: just assign the function you want placed in the control as the return value from the function. In the property sheet entry for the ControlSource property, enter:

```
=ConvertClass([Class])
```

Access calls the ConvertClass function shown in Listing 9.16 and places the return value from the function in the text box. The function itself can reside in either the report's module or a standalone module.

Listing 9.16

```
Private Function ConvertClass(varClass As Variant)
    ' Convert from the data field as stored
    ' into reasonable data.
    Select Case varClass
        Case "CPU"
            ConvertClass = "MAINFRAME"
        Case "OPR"
            ConvertClass = "SYSTEM SOFTWARE"
        Case "PRG"
            ConvertClass = "APPLICATION SOFTWARE"
        Case Else
            ConvertClass = "UNKNOWN"
    End Select
End Function
```

TIP

To avoid the display of consecutive items with the same class name, you can set the HideDuplicates property of the txtClass text box to Yes. In that case, Access won't display the class name if it matches the one used in the previous row.

TIP

Access provides the IsVisible property for controls on reports, which you can check from a section's Print event. You can use this property to detect whether a particular control has been hidden because you've set the HideDuplicates property to True and, for the current row, the value displayed in your control is in fact a duplicate of the previous row. During the Print event of the section, each hidden control's IsVisible property will be False, indicating that the control has been hidden because it's a duplicate of the value from the previous row. (Don't confuse this property with your controls' Visible property, which you manage yourself, either at design or runtime.)

The Main Report

The main report consists of little more than a few fields showing information about the particular site and the two subreports you just created (rptBankInfo). Figure 9.31 shows the design surface for the main report.

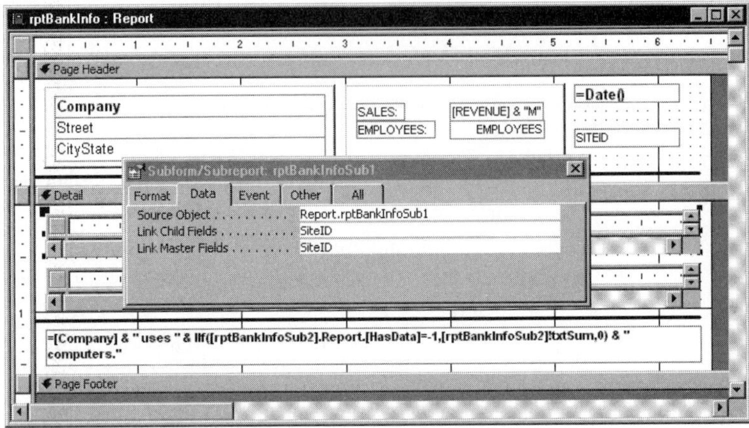

FIGURE 9.31:

Design surface for the main report

TIP

The simplest way to create a report with subreports is to make the main report design surface and the database window visible at the same time. Then, drag the subreport from the database window directly onto the report. In this case, you'll want to remove the labels Access attaches to the subreports.

Linking It All Up

Once you've created the main report, the only job left is to link it all up. To do this, you set some properties for the newly created subreports. From the main report's point of view (and that's where you are now—on the main report), these subreports are just controls, like any other report control. They have properties just like all other controls. In Figure 9.31 you can see the property sheet for the first subform, showing just the data properties for the subform.

To link the master and child reports, Access uses the LinkMasterFields and LinkChildFields properties in the subreport control. The LinkMasterFields property tells Access the name of the field(s) from the main report that must match the value(s) of the field(s) specified in the LinkChildFields property. In this case, as the report moves from SiteID to SiteID, you want to display just the rows in the two subreports for which the SiteID fields match the current siteID on the main report. It's important to remember that Access needs the actual name of the field, not the name of the control that displays that field, in the LinkChildFields property. Control names are acceptable in the LinkMasterFields property. (For more information on subforms and subreports and how Access links them with their parents, see the section "How and When to Use Subforms" in Chapter 7.)

Other Important Properties

Before leaving this report, you need to concern yourself with a few other properties, as described in the following sections.

The CanGrow Property

In this example, there's no way to know ahead of time how much vertical space the two subreports will require. Access provides the CanGrow property so you can decide whether to allow the subreport control to grow as necessary. Sometimes you'll want a fixed-size subreport. Here, though, you set the CanGrow property to Yes so all the information will be visible.

CanShrink Property

Some of the sites might not list any contacts. In that case, you'll want the contacts subreport to take up no space at all. To make that happen, you set the CanShrink property for the subreport control to Yes. (For details about when Access restricts the functionality of the CanShrink and CanGrow properties, see the section "Why CanShrink Doesn't and CanGrow Won't" earlier in this chapter.)

TIP

Just as with forms, reports load more quickly if they don't have a class module attached—that is, if they're lightweight. When you first create a report, Access sets its HasModule property to No because it doesn't have a module attached. If you ever enter any code for the report, however, Access creates a module at that time and sets the HasModule property to Yes. If you later delete the code, Access doesn't delete the module for you. To ensure that your lightweight reports are as lightweight as possible, check the HasModule property yourself. If your report has no code attached, setting this property back to No will visibly improve the load time for the report.

Avoiding #Error: Using the HasData Property

At times you need to know, after the report has opened, whether the report is showing any rows. Knowing this can be useful when you still want to view the report (or subreport) even if there are no rows, but you want to keep #Error? from displaying on your reports in places where you were performing calculations based on rows in the report. This is especially important for subreports, which don't raise the NoData event if you attempt to load a subreport based on an empty recordset.

The HasData property of a report, available only at runtime, returns one of three possible values:

Value	Description
–1	Bound report with records
0	Bound report with no records
1	Unbound report

The sample report, rptBankInfo, uses this property to avoid showing incorrect summary data if rptBankInfoSub2 doesn't contain any rows. The subreport contains a list of all the computers in use at the company, and it includes a total value in its footer. The main report extracts that value and displays it in the text box, txtSummary. If there are no rows in rptBankInfoSub2, however, you don't want an error message in txtSummary. To avoid this problem, txtSummary's ControlSource is

```
=[Company] & " uses " & _
 IIf([rptBankInfoSub2].[Report].[HasData]=-1, _
 [rptBankInfoSub2].[Report]![txtSum], 0) & " computers."
```

In other words, if the company's list of computers includes some items, the control will indicate that. If not, it just indicates that the company uses 0 computers.

Altering Your Report's Layout Programmatically

In some instances you may need to alter the complete layout of the Report Detail section on a row-by-row basis. Imagine, for example, you're printing a questionnaire and each question can be a yes/no, multiple-choice, write-in, or 1-through-10 type question. Your table containing the questions includes a column that indicates which question type to use on the report. RptQuestions is such a report; it makes different controls visible, depending on which question type is currently being printed. Figure 9.32 shows the printed report.

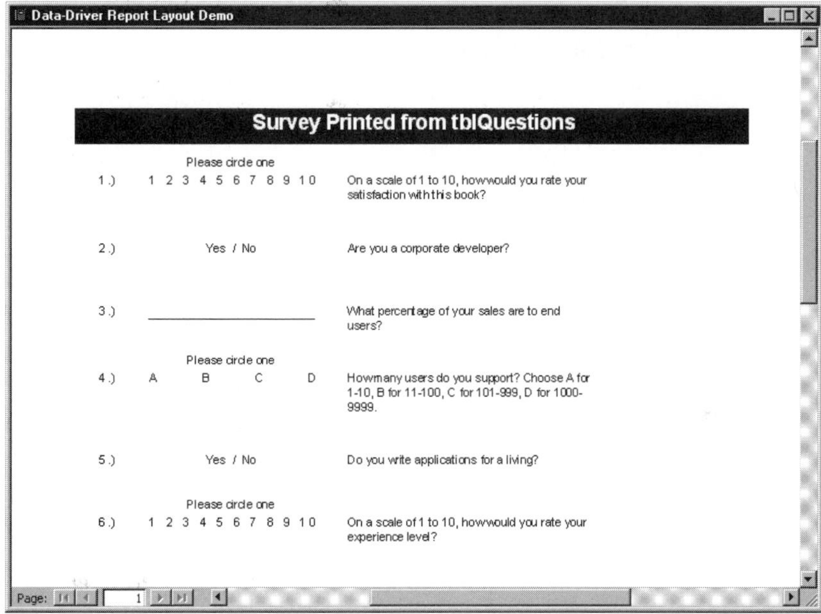

FIGURE 9.32:

The printed survey shows different controls, depending on the question type.

The concept here is simple. The report has several controls that always show up: dsptxtQuestion, dsptxtCount, and dsplblCount. (We're using the dsp prefix to indicate that these controls display for each row.) In addition, it contains five controls (four text boxes and a line) that Access displays or hides, depending on the question type. Figure 9.33 shows the design surface, with the controls spread out. Normally, all the user-response controls overlay one another. To make them easier to see, we've spread them out vertically.

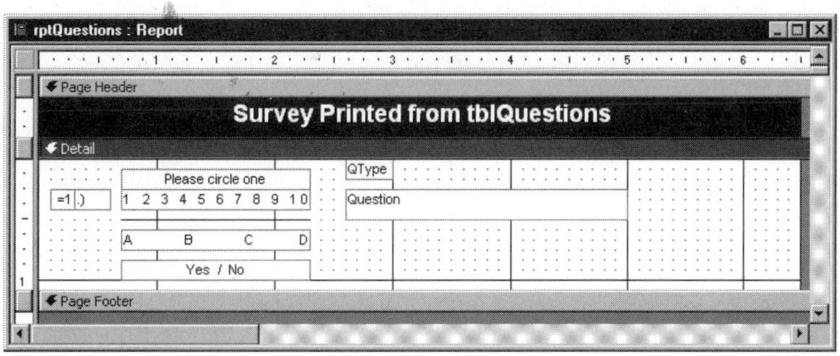

FIGURE 9.33:

The design surface with the controls spread out vertically

Listing 9.17 contains the code that controls which of the user-response controls are visible in each printed row. Because Access calls this code for each row in the Detail section, it must first hide all the user-response controls and then enable the ones that apply to this particular row. Once it has hidden all the nonessential controls, it shows the controls that are necessary for this particular question type.

Listing 9.17

```
' NOTE: These values must match the
' QType column in tblQuestions.
Private Enum QType
    qtFillIn = 1
    qt1To10 = 2
    qtABCD = 3
    qtYesNo = 4
End Enum

Private Sub Detail0_Format(Cancel As Integer, FormatCount As Integer)

    Dim intI As Integer
    Dim ctl As Control

    ' Turn off all the controls in the detail section,
    ' except the question and its counter, which never go away.
    For Each ctl In Me.Detail0.Controls
        If Left(ctl.Name, 3) <> "dsp" Then
            If ctl.Visible Then
                ctl.Visible = False
            End If
        End If
    Next ctl

    Select Case txtQType
        Case qt1To10
            lbl1To10.Visible = True
            lblCircleOne.Visible = True

        Case qtABCD
            lblABCD.Visible = True
            lblCircleOne.Visible = True

        Case qtYesNo
```

```
            lblYesNo.Visible = True

        Case qtFillIn
            linFillIn.Visible = True

        Case Else
            ' Do nothing.
    End Select
End Sub
```

Of course, this isn't the only solution to this problem. If you knew the user-response controls could all be labels, you could just as easily change the Caption property of the labels, based on the question type. In this case, though, because one of the controls is a line, that method isn't workable.

If you expand on the questionnaire method, you can create very complex reports that, in Design view, take up just a very small amount of space. This can be particularly useful when you remember that your reports are limited to 22 inches of design space! Rather than iterate through your questions by hand, create a report to create the questionnaire for you.

Creating a Report Based on a Crosstab Query

Crosstab queries are great for summarizing data in two dimensions, but creating a report based on a crosstab query has one serious technical challenge: There's no way, in general, for you to know ahead of time what the column names will be, nor how many there will be. It would appear that it's impossible to base a report on a crosstab query, if for no other reason than you can't specify the column names at design time.

If your report can live with the assumption that it can display no more than some arbitrary fixed maximum number of columns, you can make this work. The sample query, qryItemsByCityCrossTab, summarizes data from qryCustomerOrders, showing sales of particular items by city, as shown in Figure 9.34. In this query, the variable column names end up being the cities from which this store has taken orders, and there's no way to predict what these will be, nor how many there will be.

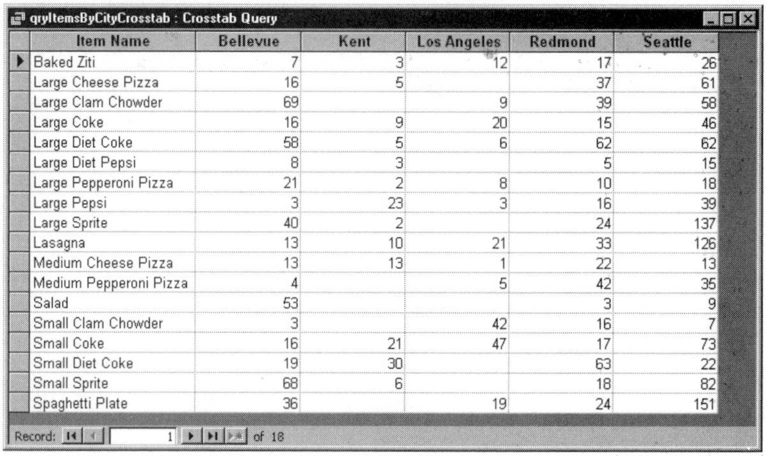

FIGURE 9.34:

In a crosstab query, you can't predict the number of columns, nor their names.

qryItemsByCityCrosstab : Crosstab Query

Item Name	Bellevue	Kent	Los Angeles	Redmond	Seattle
Baked Ziti	7	3	12	17	26
Large Cheese Pizza	16	5		37	61
Large Clam Chowder	69		9	39	58
Large Coke	16	9	20	15	46
Large Diet Coke	58	5	6	62	62
Large Diet Pepsi	8	3		5	15
Large Pepperoni Pizza	21	2	8	10	18
Large Pepsi	3	23	3	16	39
Large Sprite	40	2		24	137
Lasagna	13	10	21	33	126
Medium Cheese Pizza	13	13	1	22	13
Medium Pepperoni Pizza	4		5	42	35
Salad	53			3	9
Small Clam Chowder	3		42	16	7
Small Coke	16	21	47	17	73
Small Diet Coke	19	30		63	22
Small Sprite	68	6		18	82
Spaghetti Plate	36		19	24	151

Record: 1 of 18

If you run rptSalesCrossTab, the output looks like Figure 9.35—that is, a reasonable report. On the other hand, it wouldn't be reasonable to hard-code the field names (Bellevue, Kent, Los Angeles, and so on) at design time. You need some way to set up the report so that you can decide, when you load the report, what the field names are, and how many there are. Figure 9.36 shows the same report in Design view.

To solve this problem, you'll need to follow some sort of standard when creating your report, and you'll need a bit of code. In this example (see Figure 9.36), you'll find three sets of controls: 10 labels (named lblHeader1 through lblHeader10), 10 unbound text boxes in the Detail section (named txtData1 through txtData10), and 9 unbound text boxes in the Report Footer section (named txtSum2 through txtSum10—there's no txtSum1 because there's nothing to sum in that column). This is one instance where Access developers can drool over Visual Basic's control arrays—having control arrays in Access would make this example much simpler.

You only get one chance, as you load a report, to modify the ControlSource property of text boxes on the report, and that's in the report's Open event procedure. Listing 9.18 shows the entire procedure. The following paragraphs will describe how this procedure works.

FIGURE 9.35:

The sample report, based on a crosstab query, manages to dynamically fix up its Caption and ControlSource properties.

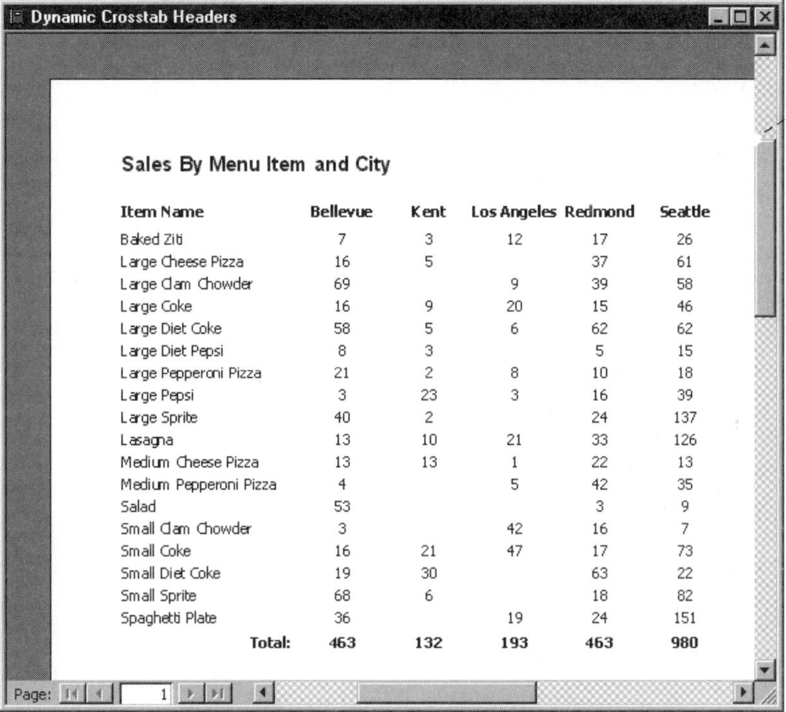

Sales By Menu Item and City

Item Name	Bellevue	Kent	Los Angeles	Redmond	Seattle
Baked Ziti	7	3	12	17	26
Large Cheese Pizza	16	5		37	61
Large Clam Chowder	69		9	39	58
Large Coke	16	9	20	15	46
Large Diet Coke	58	5	6	62	62
Large Diet Pepsi	8	3		5	15
Large Pepperoni Pizza	21	2	8	10	18
Large Pepsi	3	23	3	16	39
Large Sprite	40	2		24	137
Lasagna	13	10	21	33	126
Medium Cheese Pizza	13	13	1	22	13
Medium Pepperoni Pizza	4		5	42	35
Salad	53			3	9
Small Clam Chowder	3		42	16	7
Small Coke	16	21	47	17	73
Small Diet Coke	19	30		63	22
Small Sprite	68	6		18	82
Spaghetti Plate	36		19	24	151
Total:	**463**	**132**	**193**	**463**	**980**

FIGURE 9.36:

In Design view, you can see that the text boxes on the report must be unbound.

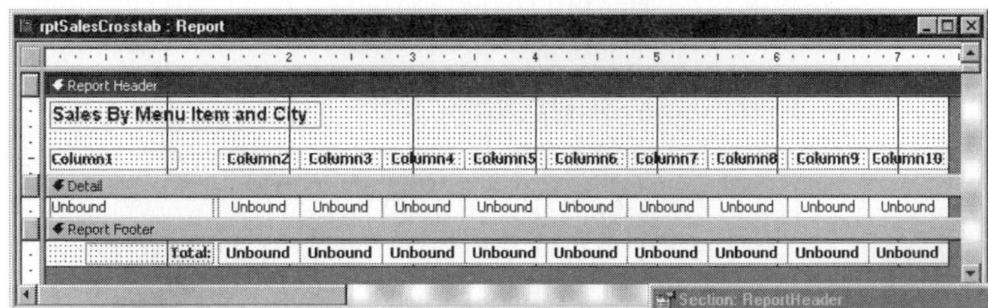

Listing 9.18

```
Private Sub Report_Open(Cancel As Integer)
    ' You didn't know how many columns, or what
    ' their names would be, until now.
    ' Fill in the label captions,
    ' and control ControlSources.
```

```
    Dim intColCount As Integer
    Dim intControlCount As Integer
    Dim i As Integer
    Dim strName As String

    On Error Resume Next

    Dim rst As ADODB.Recordset

    Set rst = New ADODB.Recordset
    rst.Open _
     Source:=Me.RecordSource, _
     ActiveConnection:=CurrentProject.Connection, _
     Options:=adCmdTable

    intColCount = rst.Fields.Count
    intControlCount = Me.Detail.Controls.Count

    If intControlCount < intColCount Then
        intColCount = intControlCount
    End If

    ' Fill in information for the necessary controls.
    For i = 1 To intColCount
        strName = rst.Fields(i - 1).Name
        Me.Controls("lblHeader" & i).Caption = strName
        Me.Controls("txtData" & i).ControlSource = strName
        Me.Controls("txtSum" & i).ControlSource = _
         "=Sum([" & strName & "])"
    Next i

    ' Hide the extra controls.
    For i = intColCount + 1 To intControlCount
        Me.Controls("txtData" & i).Visible = False
        Me.Controls("lblHeader" & i).Visible = False
        Me.Controls("txtSum" & i).Visible = False
    Next i

    ' Close the recordset.
    rst.Close
End Sub
```

Retrieving the Real Field Names

In order to retrieve the real field names, you must open a recordset based on the same RecordSource property that supplies the report with its data. If a report had a Recordset property (as does a form), you wouldn't have to do this. Because there's no way to retrieve a recordset based on a report's recordset, you'll need to do this manually.

This example uses a simple ADO recordset, based on the table or query that's specified in the report's RecordSource property. (If you want to have this work with SQL strings as well, you'll either need to let ADO guess what type of data source you're supplying, or modify the call to the Open method of the recordset, specifying the adCmdText constant instead.)

```
Set rst = New ADODB.Recordset
rst.Open _
 Source:=Me.RecordSource, _
 ActiveConnection:=CurrentProject.Connection, _
 Options:=adCmdTable
```

Calculating the Number of Fields to Display

With the recordset open, the code can calculate how many fields and controls to display. The report is set up to display a maximum of 10 fields, and you really can't change that without opening the report in Design view. Therefore, the code compares the number of controls in the Detail section with the number of fields to display and takes the minimum of those two values:

```
intColCount = rst.Fields.Count
intControlCount = Me.Detail.Controls.Count

If intControlCount < intColCount Then
    intColCount = intControlCount
End If
```

Fixing up Caption and ControlSource Properties

Now that the code knows how many fields to display, it loops through that many fields from the query and sets the Caption property for the labels and the Control-Source property for the text boxes. Note that for aggregate fields using the Sum function, fields that have illegal characters in them (as does the Los Angeles field, for example) require square brackets around the name. When setting the Control-Source property, the brackets aren't required, and the report doesn't use them. This code, then, loops through all the fields to be displayed and sets the Caption and ControlSource properties as necessary. Of course, if your crosstab returns more columns than you've prepared your report to display, they simply won't display on the report.

```
For i = 1 To intColCount
    strName = rst.Fields(i - 1).Name
    Me.Controls("lblHeader" & i).Caption = strName
    Me.Controls("txtData" & i).ControlSource = strName
    Me.Controls("txtSum" & i).ControlSource = _
     "=Sum([" & strName & "])"
Next I
```

Cleaning Up

Once the report has filled in all the useful properties, it must loop through the rest of the controls, make them invisible, and close the recordset. The following code finishes up the Open event procedure for the sample report:

```
' Hide the extra controls.
For i = intColCount + 1 To intControlCount
    Me.Controls("txtData" & i).Visible = False
    Me.Controls("lblHeader" & i).Visible = False
    Me.Controls("txtSum" & i).Visible = False
Next i

' Close the recordset.
rst.Close
```

Some Final Issues

If you're going to use this technique in your own applications, you shouldn't need to modify the code very much. You will need to follow these steps:

1. Create your report, laying out as many labels and text boxes as you think you'll need. Name the labels lblHeader1 through lblHeaderN (where N is the number of fields you're displaying). Name the text boxes txtData1 through txtDataN. If you want summary data, name those text boxes txtSum1 through txtSumN.
2. Set the RecordSource property of the report to reflect your data source.
3. Copy the code from rptSalesCrossTab into your own report. Modify the code, if necessary. (If you've used different control names, you're not displaying summary data, or you want some aggregate function besides Sum, you'll need to change the code.)

That's all there is to it. It seems complex, and, to be honest, it is a great deal more work than displaying data from a normal query, but this technique can work for you with a little effort on your part.

Distributing Access Reports

As much as Microsoft would like it to be so, not everyone who needs to look at the output of your reports actually has a copy of Access on a local machine. If you want to distribute Access reports to any user, post them on a Web site, or provide a report server on your network so that users can download just the reports while leaving the data on the server to reduce network traffic, you may be interested in looking at report snapshots.

NOTE

Data Access Pages provide another alternative for distributing reports. You can easily provide read-only, hierarchical HTML-based reports for display in a browser using this new Access feature. See in *Access 2000 Developer's Handbook, Volume II* for more information on creating and using Data Access Pages.

A report snapshot is just what it sounds like: it's a snapshot of your report at one particular moment in time. Once you've created a snapshot file (normally with an SNP extension), your snapshot contains the bytes that make up the image of your report, but it's no longer connected to any data. As long as your users have the Report Snapshot Viewer executable program, they can view your reports, whether or not they own a copy of Access.

If your users have a copy of Office 2000 installed, then they have access to the Report Snapshot Viewer program. If not, you can distribute the Snapshot Viewer ActiveX control in applications that need this functionality (this means you can use your reports on Web sites, as well). In other words, anyone running a 32-bit version of Windows can view your reports, by one means or another.

WARNING

Even if you have the Snapshot Viewer Control installed on your own machine, your code won't compile and run on your users' machines if they don't have it installed. This is a constant and serious problem that occurs in Access applications that take advantage of ActiveX controls. We've included some discussion, in Chapter 12, on fixing up references for missing ActiveX components at runtime, but the best bet is to make sure that your users have the control installed on their machines.

If you want to distribute a report snapshot, you must first create the snapshot file. To do this manually, select a report, right-click and choose Export (or use the File ➢ Export menu item), and scroll the Files of Type list until you find Snapshot Format (*.snp) at the bottom of the list. Select a location, then click the Save button. Access will, effectively, "print" your report to the selected file. It will prompt you for any necessary parameters—because your users don't have any data, all interactions with data must happen at the time you create the snapshot file—and then run the entire report. Once Access has exported your report, it will start up the Snapshot Viewer executable (SnapView.EXE), and display your report snapshot for you. This looks, basically, like the print preview mode within Access and allows users to scroll through pages, zoom, and print (see Figure 9.37).

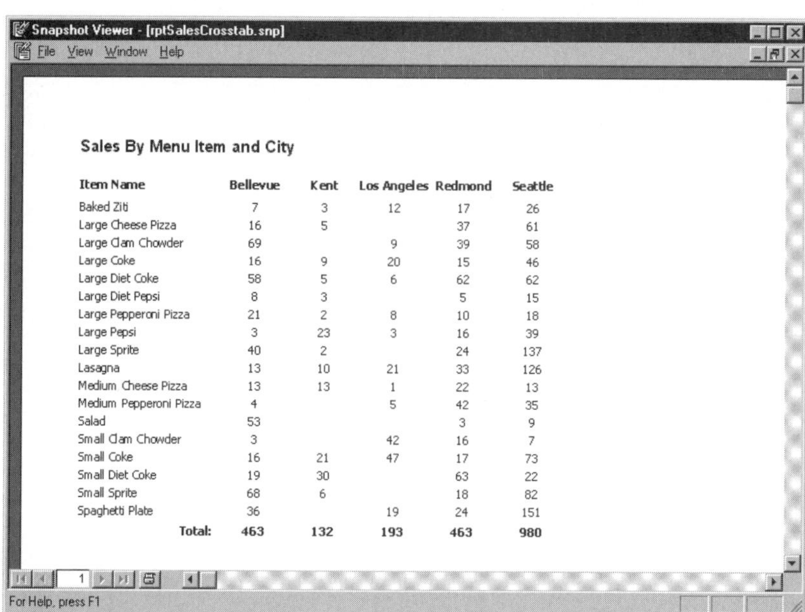

Sales By Menu Item and City

Item Name	Bellevue	Kent	Los Angeles	Redmond	Seattle
Baked Ziti	7	3	12	17	26
Large Cheese Pizza	16	5		37	61
Large Clam Chowder	69		9	39	58
Large Coke	16	9	20	15	46
Large Diet Coke	58	5	6	62	62
Large Diet Pepsi	8	3		5	15
Large Pepperoni Pizza	21	2	8	10	18
Large Pepsi	3	23	3	16	39
Large Sprite	40	2		24	137
Lasagna	13	10	21	33	126
Medium Cheese Pizza	13	13	1	22	13
Medium Pepperoni Pizza	4		5	42	35
Salad	53			3	9
Small Clam Chowder	3		42	16	7
Small Coke	16	21	47	17	73
Small Diet Coke	19	30		63	22
Small Sprite	68	6		18	82
Spaghetti Plate	36		19	24	151
Total:	**463**	**132**	**193**	**463**	**980**

FIGURE 9.37:

Use the Report Snapshot Viewer executable to view saved report snapshot (*.snp) files.

You can create report snapshots using two techniques from within your applications. You can use the OutputTo method or the SendObject method, of the DoCmd object. The OutputTo method allows you to save the report snapshot to disk (or directly to a Web site). The SendObject method allows you to e-mail a report to someone. To use OutputTo, you might write code like this:

```
DoCmd.OutputTo ObjectType:=acOutputReport, _
 ObjectName:="rptMultiLabel", _
```

```
OutputFormat:=acFormatSNP, _
OutputFile:="C:\Temp\rptMultiLabel.snp", _
AutoStart:=True
```

This example would export rptMultiLabel to a snapshot file in C:\TEMP and start the Snapshot Viewer immediately. To use SendObject, you might write code like this:

```
DoCmd.SendObject _
 ObjectType:=acSendReport, _
 ObjectName:=adhcReportName, _
 OutputFormat:=acFormatSNP, _
 To:="info@youraddress.com", _
 Subject:="Report Snapshot", _
MessageText:="Here's your report!", _
 EditMessage:=False
```

This example would create the snapshot, embed it in an e-mail message, add the appropriate address, subject, and text, and send it on without requiring you to edit the message at all. If you leave out parameters, Access will prompt you for them. (To see the SendObject method in action, try frmEmailSnapshot in the sample database.)

If you want to allow users who don't own a copy of Office 2000 to view your report snapshots, you can distribute applications that use the Snapshot Viewer ActiveX control, either written in Visual Basic, or any other environment that supports ActiveX controls. To demonstrate the use of the control, we've created frmReportSnapshot, shown in Figure 9.38. (Although you're unlikely to use this control in an Access application, it does work, as you can see. You're more likely to use the control in a Visual Basic application, or in a Web page. But at least with this Access demonstration, you can test it out in your native environment!)

To use this control, you'll need to add it to your environment (in Access, choose the Insert ➢ ActiveX Control menu item and select the Snapshot Viewer Control 9.0). To see a report, you'll need to set at least the SnapshotPath property—you can do this from either the Properties window or in code.

If you're interested in using the Snapshot Viewer ActiveX control, you'll want to investigate all its properties, events, and methods. (The sample form demonstrates the use of many of these.) Although you'll need to do some experimentation to see all the ways you can use this control, Table 9.14 lists all the properties, methods, and events, and includes descriptions of each. Table 9.15 lists the values that could be returned from the Error property of the control. Table 9.16 lists the possible values for the Zoom property of the control.

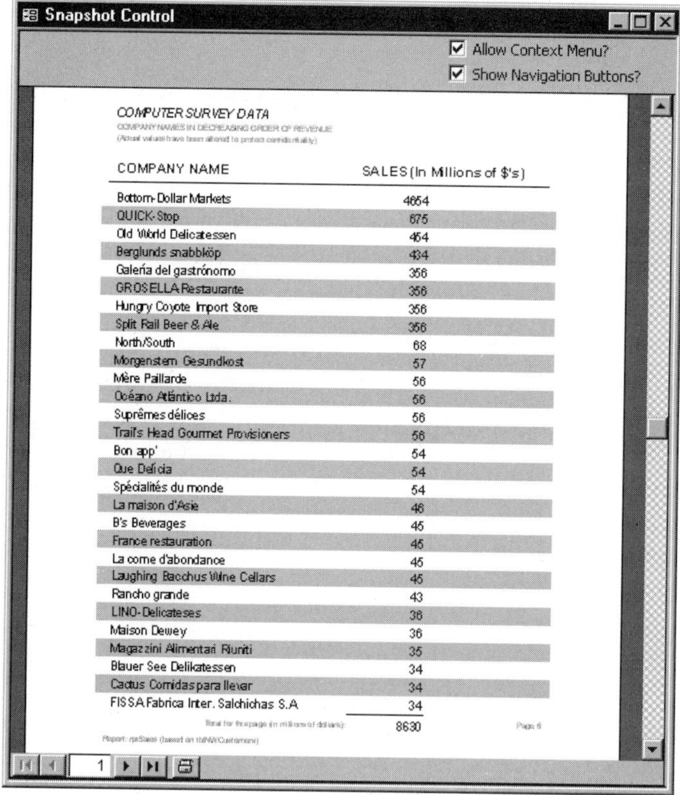

FIGURE 9.38: You can use the Snapshot Viewer ActiveX control for users that don't own a copy of Office 2000.

TABLE 9.14: Properties, Methods, and Events of the Snapshot Viewer Control

Member	Type	Data Type	Description
AllowContextMenu	Property	Boolean	Enables or disables the context menu for the control. If enabled, this menu includes options to navigate from page to page and to zoom the image.
CurrentPage	Property	Long	Returns or sets the current visible page of the report. Attempting to set this value outside the valid range results in runtime error 2501 ("Invalid page").
Error	Property	Long	Returns the error that occurred when loading or viewing the report. Table 9.15 lists all the possible error values.

Continued on next page

TABLE 9.14 CONTINUED: Properties, Methods, and Events of the Snapshot Viewer Control

Member	Type	Data Type	Description
PageCount	Property	Long	Returns the total number of pages in the report.
ReadyState	Property	Long	Returns a value indicating the state of the control. The possible values are: 0 (the control has not been initialized); 1 (the control is loading); 2 (the control is loaded, but the file is downloading from its remote location (either an HTTP or FTP site); 4 (the control has finished downloading the file—this is the only value you'll get if the file is local).
ShowNavigationButtons	Property	Boolean	Enables or disables the built-in navigation/printing buttons at the bottom of the control. If you disable these, you should create and enable your own controls that use the various methods of the Snapshot Viewer control to navigate through the report.
SnapshotPath	Property	String	Sets or returns the path for the current snapshot file. This can be a file path, or an HTTP or FTP site.
Zoom	Property	Long	Sets or returns the current zoom amount. Can be one of the values listed in Table 9.16.
AboutBox	Method		Displays the control's About box.
FirstPage	Method		Navigates to the report's first page.
LastPage	Method		Navigates to the report's last page.
NextPage	Method		Navigates to the report's next page.
PreviousPage	Method		Navigates to the report's previous page.
PrintSnapshot	Method		Prints the report, displaying the standard Print dialog box.
PrintSnapshotDirect	Method		Prints the report directly to an output device, given a device, a port, and a driver name. For more information on using these printer options, see Chapter 10.

Continued on next page

TABLE 9.14 CONTINUED: Properties, Methods, and Events of the Snapshot Viewer Control

Member	Type	Data Type	Description
FirstPage	Event		Raised when the current page has been changed to the first page (not raised when you call the FirstPage method, nor if you move to the first page by the PageUp keystroke, which does move the report to the first page if you're on the second page).
LastPage	Event		Raised when the current page has been changed to the last page (not raised when you call the LastPage method).
NextPage	Event		Raised when the current page has been changed to the next page (not raised when you call the NextPage method).
PrevPage	Event		Raised when the current page has been changed to the previous page (not raised when you call the PreviousPage method, nor when you use the PageUp key to move to the previous page).
Progress	Event		If downloading the control from a remote site, indicates the current progress in downloading (passes to your code the current percentage finished). Never raised for a local snapshot file.
ReadyStateChange	Event		Raised when the ReadyState property changes its value. Never raised for a local snapshot file.

TABLE 9.15: Possible Errors Raised by the Snapshot Viewer Control

Error	Description
2500	Invalid value.
2501	Invalid page.
2502	Missing or invalid snapshot file.
2503	Property is read-only.

Continued on next page

TABLE 9.15 CONTINUED: Possible Errors Raised by the Snapshot Viewer Control

Error	Description
2504	Operation canceled by user.
2505	You need a newer version of the Snapshot Viewer control to view this snapshot file.
2506	An error occurred while printing.
2507	An error occurred while opening a snapshot file.
2508	Out of memory.
2509	An error occurred writing to a temporary file while opening a snapshot file.
2510	You have no printer installed, or no printer has been selected as the default.

TABLE 9.16: Values for the Zoom Property of the Snapshot Viewer Control

Constant	Value	Description
snapZoomToFit	0	(Default) Zooms to a full-page display.
snapZoomToFill	1	Zooms the page to fill the available space in the control.
snapZoom200Percent	2	Zooms the page by a factor of 200 percent.
snapZoom150Percent	3	Zooms the page by a factor of 150 percent.
snapZoom100Percent	4	Zooms the page by a factor of 100 percent.
snapZoom75Percent	5	Zooms the page by a factor of 75 percent.
snapZoom50Percent	6	Zooms the page by a factor of 50 percent.
snapZoom25Percent	7	Zooms the page by a factor of 25 percent.
snapZoom10Percent	8	Zooms the page by a factor of 10 percent.

Summary

In this chapter, we took a look at reports from several angles. We covered these issues:

- Programmatically controlling sorting and grouping
- Report events and properties
- Section events and properties
- A series of tricky report issues
- A group of sample reports, using events, properties, and methods
- Using report snapshots to distribute your reports

We've worked through some problematic issues in report design, but we've barely scratched the surface. Once you get deeply into it, you'll find that report design can be even more complex, challenging, and rewarding than form design. As long as you keep forward motion of the report engine in mind, you can learn to control the flow of events on your reports.

CHAPTER

TEN

10

Controlling Your Printer

- Retrieving information about your printer
- Creating a list of available output devices
- Changing print destinations programmatically
- Using the Windows printing mechanisms to control printed output
- Using the PrinterCapabilities class to easily retrieve information about a printer's capabilities

Although Access provides a standardized Print Setup dialog box, you'll find it difficult to programmatically control printing options using the standard means. You might be tempted to try using SendKeys to control the print settings, but you'll quickly run into obstacles when you try to control specific printer settings, such as paper size, for which each printer driver provides a list. Even worse, every printer's Options dialog box is different, making the control of that portion impossible with SendKeys.

In this chapter, you'll find six class modules (Device and Devices, DevMode, DevNames, PrinterCapabilities, and PrintLayout) that make it relatively simple for you to tackle one of the most complex jobs in Access: handling printed output programmatically. This chapter explains how to use the mysterious PrtDevMode, PrtDevNames, and PrtMip properties and works through how you can use the wrapper classes to make these properties simple to manage. In addition, we've provided an explanation about and support for two other common Access printing issues: how to select an output device programmatically given a list of available printers and how to determine the capabilities of any of the installed printers.

NOTE

The main job of a visual development tool such as Access is to shield you from the details of the operating system. In a perfect world, it would be impossible to do anything from VBA that could cause you to halt Access or Windows or that could cause any sort of data loss. In general, that's true. Access usually buries most of the workings of Windows under a thick layer of protective wrapping. The properties we're discussing in this chapter, however, (PrtDevMode, PrtDevNames, and PrtMip) are extremely "raw." That is, there's almost no protective layer between you and the operating system when you're modifying Access' PrtDevMode or PrtDevNames property. If you set the values incorrectly or place an inappropriate value into one of the properties, you're likely to cause Access to crash. The classes we've provided here make the use of these properties as painless as possible, but be aware that there's not much of a net underneath you when you're working this close to the surface.

Introducing the PrtDevMode Property

The PrtDevMode property of a form or report contains information about the printing device you've selected for printing the object. It contains, among other things, the name of the device, information about the driver, the number of copies to print, the orientation of the printout, the paper tray to use when printing, and the print quality to use. All this information corresponds directly with Windows'

DEVMODE structure, used by just about every Windows program that ever intends to do any printing.

To modify the PrtDevMode property of a form or report, you must set specific printer settings for the object. To set these options, open the object in Design view, and select the File ➢ Page Setup menu item. Select the Page tab on the dialog box, choose the Use Specific Printer option, and click the Printer button. On the Printer's Page Setup dialog box, choose the Properties command button. The dialog you'll see next is printer-dependent, and Figure 10.1 shows the dialog box provided by the HP LaserJet 5P driver. You can use this dialog box to set various print settings, such as paper size, orientation, paper source, and so on. All these values are stored together in the form or report's PrtDevMode property.

FIGURE 10.1:

Use the Printer's Properties dialog box to set a form or report's PrtDevMode property.

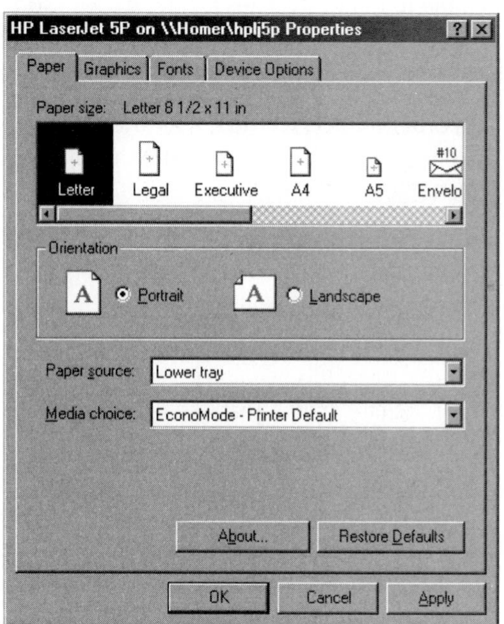

TIP

If you never set these properties with the user interface, the form or report's PrtDev-Mode property will be Null. In that case, when it comes time to print the object, Access uses the default information stored in the printer driver for the selected printer, instead of information in the form or report that's being printed. The code in this chapter does the same thing: if the PrtDevMode property for an object is Null, the code retrieves the corresponding information directly from the printer.

Windows provides a user-defined type, named DEVMODE, which contains all the information about characteristics of the output device. The PrtDevMode property of forms and reports in Access is a direct copy of that internal data structure. As a matter of fact, the PrtDevMode property is a byte-for-byte copy of the same structure that's used internally in Windows.

Although Access makes all this information available to you so you can programmatically retrieve and set print properties for reports and forms, it doesn't make it easy. Because the PrtDevMode property is nothing more than an array of bytes with all the information from the DEVMODE structure strung together, it's up to your code to pick apart the array, make changes as necessary, and reassign the property. And unlike almost every other property in Access, the PrtDevMode property is only read/write when the report or form is in Design view. You won't be able to make changes to the PrtDevMode property while running a report—which makes sense, because you really can't be changing such things as the printer name or margins while printing the report.

In order for you to work with the PrtDevMode property programmatically, we've supplied a DevMode class in the sample project. This class exposes properties that match the various bits of information stored in the PrtDevMode property of a form or report, and working with the class is a lot simpler than working with the property directly. We'll show you how to retrieve and modify the PrtDevMode property in the next sections. For now, here are some ideas to keep in mind as you work through the next few sections:

- Not all forms or reports will necessarily have a non-Null PrtDevMode property. Any code that works with the property should be able to handle this situation. If you've never touched the printer settings for a form or report, PrtDevMode will be Null. In that case, you'll need some way to retrieve the DEVMODE information for the default printer, and the sample project includes code to do this.
- Before providing your user with a list of choices (paper sizes, TrueType options, and so on), check the capabilities of the current device and limit your choices to options the device supports. Although Access does not provide this capability, you can use the Windows API to retrieve the information. We cover this functionality (using the PrinterCapabilities class) in the section "Retrieving Printer Capabilities" later in this chapter.
- Many printer drivers store additional information immediately following the DEVMODE structure. Therefore, when retrieving and setting the PrtDevMode property, be aware that most often it will require more than the documented size. Plan on 2048 bytes or more, and you must check the intDriverSize and

intExtraSize fields when manipulating the values. (The code in our examples does all this for you.)

- Text values retrieved using the PrtDevMode property (or any of the properties discussed in this chapter) are always ANSI values (that is, one byte per character). VBA strings, on the other hand, are always Unicode values (two bytes per character). If you assign a value into a String variable, VBA politely converts it to Unicode for you, thereby making the string useless in your work here. You'll see that our code is very careful to either use arrays of bytes, or variants, to handle the text values in these properties. If you use a string data type with LSet, however, you won't have this problem (and we use strings for this purpose). See the section titled "Using LSet to Replace the Data" later in this chapter for more information.

Device Information

Generally, a printer device is defined by three characteristics: device name, driver name, and output port. Many of the classes provided in this chapter rely on this information to allow you to select a specific printer and to keep track of that printer. To make this simpler for you, we've provided a Device class, used in conjunction with almost all of the other classes in the chapter. This class provides five properties, allowing you to work programmatically with a printer. Table 10.1 lists the properties of the Device class, along with a description of each.

TABLE 10.1: Properties of the Device Class

Property	Data Type	Description
Default	Boolean	When used in conjunction with a DevNames object, keeps track of whether the selected printer was the default printer at the time the PrtDevNames property was set. When used in conjunction with a form or report, indicates whether the object has been set up to print to the default output device.
DeviceName	String	The name of the device, assigned when you installed the printer. For example, HP LaserJet 5P.
DriverName	String	The name of the printer driver. For example, HPPCL5MS.
Port	String	The output port. Might be LPT1: for a local printer or a share name for a shared printer (e.g., \\homer\hplj5p).
PrintInfo	String (read-only)	A formatted string displaying DeviceName and Port, like this: HP LaserJet 5P on LPT1:. This property is used for displaying lists of available printers.

Although you can declare and instantiate a Device object yourself and then supply all its properties manually, you generally won't. Most often, you will declare a Device variable and point it at a specific device provided by another class, the Devices class. The Devices class provides a collection of Device objects, one for each installed printer device. When you instantiate a Devices object, code inside the class creates an internal collection of Device objects. You can then set a Device object to point to a specific printer and work from there. Table 10.2 lists the properties of the Devices class, along with a description of each.

TABLE 10.2: Properties of the Devices Class

Property	Data Type	Description
Count	Long	Number of installed printer devices.
CurrentDevice	Device	Reference to the current printer device. Set an existing Device object to point to this property to retrieve information.
Item	Device	Pass a DeviceName, or an index number, and retrieve a Device object with information about that specific printer.

To use the Devices class, you might write code like this (from basHowDoI in the sample project):

```
Public Sub ListPrinters1()
    Dim devs As Devices
    Dim i As Integer

    Set devs = New Devices
    For i = 1 To devs.Count
        Debug.Print devs.Item(i).PrintInfo
    Next i
    Set devs = Nothing
End Sub
```

If you want to retrieve information about the default printer device, you could write code like this (also from basHowDoI):

```
Public Sub ShowCurrentPrinter()
    Dim devs As Devices
    Set devs = New Devices
    With devs.CurrentDevice
        Debug.Print .DeviceName
```

```
        Debug.Print .DriverName
        Debug.Print .Port
        Debug.Print .PrintInfo
    End With
    Set devs = Nothing
End Sub
```

This example instantiates a new Devices object and then uses the CurrentDevice property of the class to retrieve the necessary information. You could also rewrite this code as follows (not in the sample project):

```
Public Sub ShowCurrentPrinter()
    Dim devs As Devices
    Dim dev As Device

    Set devs = New Devices
    Set dev = devs.CurrentDevice

    Debug.Print dev.DeviceName
    Debug.Print dev.DriverName
    Debug.Print dev.Port
    Debug.Print dev.PrintInfo

    Set devs = Nothing
    Set dev = Nothing
End Sub
```

This version works the same as the original, except that it creates a Device object to refer to the current device, as opposed to working with that device directly. (Note that you needn't use the New keyword with the Device object here, because you're pointing it at an existing Device object created by the Devices object.)

If you're interested, you can dig into how the Devices object does its work. In general, it reads information from WIN.INI. (Yes, unbelievably, this is still the place where most applications retrieve information about installed printers, and it is the recommended solution for code that must run both on Windows 95/98 and on Windows NT/2000.) The Devices class creates an internal collection of Device objects and allows you to retrieve any of those Device objects using the Item property of the class. You can also use the CurrentDevice property to retrieve a Device object that contains information about the current device.

Making a Collection Class More Collection-Like

When you create a class in VBA that wraps up a private collection, you'd like it to work as much as possible like a real collection. The Devices class is such a class, and it looks to the developer as if it was a built-in collection (like the Fields collection in a recordset, or the Forms collection in Access). Unfortunately, creating such a class in VBA generally makes it impossible to provide two standard collection-like properties: using Item as the default member of the class and using a For Each...Next loop to iterate through the elements of the collection. Standard collections can do these things, but your collection class wrappers cannot. It is possible to fake VBA into providing this functionality, although it does require exporting the class module, editing it by hand, and them re-importing it. (For more information, see Chapter 3.) We've done that work already for the Devices class, and you can therefore both take advantage of the default Item method and use a For Each...Next loop. That is, you could rewrite the previous code example as:

```
Public Sub ListPrinters()
    Dim devs As Devices
    Dim dev As Device

    Set devs = New Devices
    For Each dev In devs
        Debug.Print dev.PrintInfo
    Next dev
    Set devs = Nothing
End Sub
```

The upshot of this is that if you want to move the Devices class into another project, you must do it from within VBA, not from Access. Use the File ➢ Export File menu item to save the class, and then import it (using the File ➢ Import File menu item) into the new project.

TIP

To use the Devices class in your own projects, you'll need to import both the Devices and the Device classes. Also, make sure you move the Devices class from project to project using the VBA File menu options (or, you can use the Multicode Import/Export add-in, if you have Microsoft Office Developer). That is, move this class only when in the Microsoft Visual Basic environment. Do not use Access to import and export this module, or you'll lose important functionality. (This is the only module in this chapter that includes this limitation.)

Demonstrating the Device and Devices Classes

The sample form, frmPrinterList, demonstrates the use of the Devices and Device classes. The form, shown in Figure 10.2, provides a combo box filled with a list of available printers. Select a value from the list, and code in the form's module sets the active printer to be the selection you made.

FIGURE 10.2: Use frmPrinterList to test out the Device and Devices classes.

The combo box (cboPrinters) has its RowSourceType property set to adhFill-DeviceList. This function, in basDeviceList, can be used to fill any list or combo box with a list of all the available printers. You can peruse it, if you like, but it does its work by creating a static Devices object (it's static so that it maintains its value between calls to the function) and then providing information about each of the items in its internal collection when requested. The bound column (column 0) of the combo box contains text in the format provided by the PrintInfo property of a Device object (DeviceName on Port). The function places the DriverName property into column 1, the DeviceName property into column 2, and the Port property into column 3.

In the Load event procedure of frmPrinterList, the code instantiates a module-level Devices object and attempts to set the combo box to select the current default printer, using the following code:

```
Private mdevs As Devices

Private Sub Form_Load()
    On Error Resume Next
    Set mdevs = New Devices
    cboPrinters = mdevs.CurrentDevice.PrintInfo
End Sub
```

Note the use of On Error Resume Next. Because there may be no current device (and the CurrentDevice property will be Nothing in that case), it's important to either check for that case, or handle the error that occurs.

Once you make a selection in the combo box, the control's AfterUpdate event procedure saves the information from the selected row in the control into a new

Device object. When the code sets the CurrentDevice property of the Devices object to refer to that new Device object, code in the Devices class updates WIN.INI and broadcasts the change to all running Windows applications. Therefore, the code shown in Listing 10.1 changes the current Windows printer to match the selection you made in the combo box on the form.

Listing 10.1

```
Private Sub cboPrinters_AfterUpdate()
    ' After you make a selection, go write
    ' the string out to WIN.INI.

    Dim dev As Device
    Set dev = New Device

    ' Retrieve the pieces needed by dr from
    ' the combo box.
    With cboPrinters
        dev.DriverName = .Column(1)
        dev.DeviceName = .Column(2)
        dev.Port = .Column(3)
    End With
    Set mdevs.CurrentDevice = dev
    Set dev = Nothing
End Sub
```

NOTE

The Devices class contains a great deal of code that reads information from WIN.INI and parses out the various bits of information about the available print devices. If you're interested in working with INI files, you might take a look at the code in the Devices class to see how it works. For the most part, you won't have many reasons to retrieve information from INI files, so we haven't discussed the workings of this class here.

Using the DevMode Class

The DevMode class makes it simple for you to work with printer-specific properties of objects in Access (that is, it hides the complexities of working with the PrtDevMode property). The class provides a group of properties that map directly to elements of the Windows API DEVMODE structure and to the PrtDevMode property of forms and reports.

Table 10.3 lists the properties of the DevMode class, each property's data type, and a short description of each. Some of the properties return enumerated data, and the choices for those items are listed in Tables 10.2 through 10.6.

TABLE 10.3: Members of the DevMode Object

Member	Type	Read/Write?	Description
Bytes	Byte()	Yes	Array of bytes representing the PrtDev-Mode property of the object referred to by the Object property. You'll generally only retrieve this property, not set it.
Collate	dmCollate	Yes	Specifies whether multiple-copy output should be collated or not. Possible values are DMCOLLATE_TRUE (1) and DM-COLLATE_FALSE (0). Access doesn't seem to honor this setting and generally disregards it. It's here, therefore, only because it's part of the DEVMODE data structure. If you want to collate output, use the Print-Out method and specify the Collate parameter for that method.
Color	dmColor	Yes	If the device supports color printing, allows you to set or retrieve whether to print in monochrome: DMCOLOR_MONOCHROME (1) or in color: DMCOLOR_COLOR (2).
Copies	Integer	Yes	Sets or retrieves the number of copies to be printed.
DefaultSource	dmDefaultSource	Yes	Sets or retrieves the default location for paper (such as an upper bin, lower bin, envelope tray, and so on). Table 10.4 lists the possible constants that you can use for this property.
DeviceName	String	No	Read-only name of the current device corresponding to this object (like HP LaserJet 5P).
DriverVersion	Integer	No	Read-only version number of the printer driver. Assigned by the developer of the driver.

Continued on next page

TABLE 10.3 CONTINUED: Members of the DevMode Object

Memberr	Type	Read/Write?	Description
Duplex	dmDuplex	Yes	Selects duplex or double-sided printing for printers capable of duplex printing. The possible values are DMDUP_SIMPLEX (1), DMDUP_HORIZONTAL (2), and DMDUP_VERTICAL (3).
ExtraSize	Integer	No	Read-only size of the extra buffer at the end of the data structure. Set by the developer who created the driver.
Object	Object	Yes	Sets or retrieves the form or report whose PrtDevMode property this object mirrors. You can set this property to be a Device, Form, or Report object. If you specify a Device object, the code retrieves the default DEVMODE information for that device. If you specify a form or report, the code retrieves the PrtDevMode property for that object. You can use the Bytes property to retrieve this value back.
Orientation	dmOrientation	Yes	Sets or retrieves the orientation for printing on this device. Can be one of DMORIENT_PORTRAIT (1) or DMORIENT_LANDSCAPE (2).
PaperLength	Integer	Yes	Overrides the length of the paper specified in the PaperSize property, either for custom paper sizes or for printers that can print on a page of arbitrary length (such as dot-matrix printers). Measured in tenths of millimeters (see the PaperSize property for more information).
PaperSize	dmPaperSize	Yes	Sets or retrieves the size of paper to print on. Can be set to DMPAPER_USER (256), if you want to use the PaperLength and PaperWidth values to set the page size. (Not all printers support custom paper sizes.) Although the number of defined paper sizes grows continually, Table 10.5 contains a list of the most common paper sizes. You may find more documentation in MSDN or other sources, allowing you to expand this list yourself, in the future.

Continued on next page

TABLE 10.3 CONTINUED: Members of the DevMode Object

Memberr	Type	Read/Write?	Description
PaperWidth	Integer	Yes	Overrides the length of the paper specified in the PaperSize property, either for custom paper sizes or for printers that can print on a page of arbitrary length (such as dot-matrix printers). Measured in tenths of millimeters (see the PaperSize property for more information).
PrintQuality	dmPrintQuality	Yes	Sets or retrieves the printer resolution. The possible values are DMRES_HIGH (-4), DMRES_MEDIUM (-3), DMRES_LOW (-2), or DMRES_DRAFT (-1). If you specify a positive value, it's treated as the x-resolution, in dots per inch (DPI) and is device dependent. In this case, the YResolution property must contain the y-resolution in DPI.
SaveImmediately	Boolean	Yes	Sets or retrieves the save behavior for the class. If set to True (the default value), each change you make to the object is saved automatically. If set to False, you must explicitly call the Save method to save your changes.
ScaleAmount	Integer	Yes	Factor by which the printed output is to be scaled. The apparent page size is scaled from the physical page size by a factor of ScaleAmount/100. Has an effect only if your printer supports scaling.
Size	Integer	No	(Read-only) Retrieves the size of the DEVMODE structure for the specified object. This value, added to the ExtraSize property, provides the full number of bytes used by the data structure.
SpecVersion	Integer	No	(Read-only) Retrieves the version number of the corresponding DEVMODE structure in the Windows SDK.
TrueTypeOption	dmTrueType	Yes	Specifies how TrueType fonts should be printed. Possible values are listed in Table 10.6.

Continued on next page

TABLE 10.3 CONTINUED: Members of the DevMode Object

Memberr	Type	Read/Write?	Description
YResolution	Integer	Yes	Specifies the y-resolution for the printer in dots per inch (DPI). If this value is specified, you must also specify the x-resolution in the PrintQuality property. These values are device-specific.
Save		(Method)	This method allows you to explicitly save changes to the object's PrtDevMode property at any time. It's only necessary to call this method if you've set the Save-Immediately property to be False.

TABLE 10.4: Values for the DefaultSource Property of the DevMode Object

Constant	Paper Source
DMBIN_UPPER	Upper bin.
DMBIN_ONLYONE	Only one bin exists, so use it. Internally, the same value as DMBIN_UPPER.
DMBIN_LOWER	Lower bin.
DMBIN_MIDDLE	Middle bin.
DMBIN_MANUAL	Manual bin.
DMBIN_ENVELOPE	Envelope bin.
DMBIN_ENVMANUAL	Envelope manual bin.
DMBIN_AUTO	Automatic bin (the printer will use the first available bin).
DMBIN_TRACTOR	Tractor bin.
DMBIN_SMALLFMT	Small-format bin.
DMBIN_LARGEFMT	Large-format bin.
DMBIN_LARGECAPACITY	Large-capacity bin.
DMBIN_CASSETTE	Cassette bin.
DMBIN_USER	Device-specific bins start here. Using this value or any higher value will require studying the Windows API reference for the DEVMODE data type.

TABLE 10.5: Some of the Available DevMode PaperSize Property Values

Constant	Paper Size
DMPAPER_LETTER	Letter $8^1/_2 \times 11$ in
DMPAPER_LETTERSMALL	Letter Small $8^1/_2 \times 11$ in
DMPAPER_TABLOID	Tabloid 11×17 in
DMPAPER_LEDGER	Ledger 17×11 in
DMPAPER_LEGAL	Legal $8^1/_2 \times 14$ in
DMPAPER_STATEMENT	Statement $5^1/_2 \times 8^1/_2$ in
DMPAPER_EXECUTIVE	Executive $7^1/_4 \times 10^1/_2$ in
DMPAPER_A3	A3 297×420 mm
DMPAPER_A4	A4 210×297 mm
DMPAPER_A4SMALL	A4 Small 210×297 mm
DMPAPER_A5	A5 148×210 mm
DMPAPER_B4	B4 (JIS) 250×354
DMPAPER_B5	B5 (JIS) 182×257 mm
DMPAPER_FOLIO	Folio $8^1/_2 \times 13$ in
DMPAPER_QUARTO	Quarto 215×275 mm
DMPAPER_10X14	10×14 in
DMPAPER_11X17	11×17 in
DMPAPER_NOTE	Note $8^1/_2 \times 11$ in
DMPAPER_ENV_9	Envelope #9 $3^7/_8 \times 8^7/_8$
DMPAPER_ENV_10	Envelope #10 $4^1/_8 \times 9^1/_2$
DMPAPER_ENV_11	Envelope #11 $4^1/_2 \times 10^3/_8$
DMPAPER_ENV_12	Envelope #12 $4^3/_4 \times 11$
DMPAPER_ENV_14	Envelope #14 $5 \times 11^1/_2$
DMPAPER_CSHEET	C size sheet
DMPAPER_DSHEET	D size sheet
DMPAPER_ESHEET	E size sheet
DMPAPER_ENV_DL	Envelope DL 110×220mm

Continued on next page

TABLE 10.5 CONTINUED: Some of the Available DevMode PaperSize Property Values

Constant	Paper Size
DMPAPER_ENV_C5	Envelope C5 162 × 229 mm
DMPAPER_ENV_C3	Envelope C3 324 × 458 mm
DMPAPER_ENV_C4	Envelope C4 229 × 324 mm
DMPAPER_ENV_C6	Envelope C6 114 × 162 mm
DMPAPER_ENV_C65	Envelope C65 114 × 229 mm
DMPAPER_ENV_B4	Envelope B4 250 × 353 mm
DMPAPER_ENV_B5	Envelope B5 176 × 250 mm
DMPAPER_ENV_B6	Envelope B6 176 × 125 mm
DMPAPER_ENV_ITALY	Envelope 110 × 230 mm
DMPAPER_ENV_MONARCH	Envelope Monarch $3\frac{7}{8} \times 7\frac{1}{2}$ in
DMPAPER_ENV_PERSONAL	$6\frac{3}{4}$ Envelope $3\frac{5}{8} \times 6\frac{1}{2}$ in
DMPAPER_FANFOLD_US	US Std Fanfold $14\frac{7}{8} \times 11$ in
DMPAPER_FANFOLD_STD_GERMAN	German Std Fanfold $8\frac{1}{2} \times 12$ in
DMPAPER_FANFOLD_LGL_GERMAN	German Legal Fanfold $8\frac{1}{2} \times 13$ in
DMPAPER_USER	User-defined size (specify the size in the PaperLength and PaperWidth properties)

TABLE 10.6: Values for the TrueTypeOption Property of the DevMode Object

Value	True Type Option
DMTT_BITMAP	Prints TrueType fonts as graphics. This is the default for dot-matrix printers.
DM_TTDOWNLOAD	Downloads TrueType fonts as soft fonts. This is the default for Hewlett-Packard printers that use Printer Control Language (PCL).
DMTT_SUBDEV	Substitutes device fonts for TrueType fonts. This is the default for PostScript printers.
DMTT_DOWNLOAD_OUTLINE	Downloads TrueType fonts as outline soft fonts.

To use the DevMode class, you should follow these steps:

1. Declare a Devmode variable.
2. Instantiate the variable.

If you want to work with the PrtDevMode property of an existing form or report:

1. Set the DevMode object's Object property to refer to a form or report, open in Design view.
2. Modify properties of the DevMode object. Each change you make gets written immediately back to the form or report's PrtDevMode property.

If you want to retrieve the DEVMODE information for a specific printer in the Devices collection and perhaps assign that to the PrtDevMode property of a form or report (you'll need this technique later in the chapter, if you intend to change the output device for a form or report):

1. Set the DevMode object's Object property to refer to a specific Device object retrieved from the Devices object.
2. Copy the Bytes property of the DevMode object into the PrtDevMode property of a form or report open in Design view.

The code in Listing 10.2 demonstrates how you might use the DevMode object. This example (from basTestDevMode) allows you to pass in a reference to an open report and the number of copies it should print. See the example in the code for help on calling the procedure.

Listing 10.2

```
Public Sub SetCopies(obj As Object, intCopies As Integer)

    ' This simple function would require
    ' error checking for real use.  In addition,
    ' it requires that the object in question be
    ' already open in design mode (you can't set the
    ' prtDevMode property except in design mode).
```

```
    ' For example:
    ' Call SetCopies(Reports("rptCompany"), 3)

    ' WARNING: Not all drivers support changing this property.
    ' For example, the HP Deskjet 890C just totally
    ' disregards this value. HPLJ6P works fine, however.

    Dim dm As DevMode
    Set dm = New DevMode

    Set dm.Object = obj
    dm.Copies = intCopies
    Set dm = Nothing
End Sub
```

TIP

For more examples of using the DevMode class, see the "How Do I..." section at the end of this chapter and the basTestDevMode module.

Using the DevMode Class in Your Applications

If you want to use the DevMode class in your own applications, you must import the following class modules: DevMode, Device, and Devices. In addition, you must import the basPrtGlobal module. Once you have those modules in your application, you should be able to use the objects and properties you need to manipulate the PrtDevMode property of forms and reports effectively. And, using the supplied classes, you never really need to worry about moving the bytes around, as we'll discuss in the next few sections.

How Does It Work?

In this section, we'll spend a little time explaining exactly how the DevMode class interacts with the PrtDevMode property of a form or report. If you're happy simply using the DevMode class, you may want to skip over this section, which is admittedly complex. If you're interested in more detail about the inner workings of the class, or are interested in modifying it, read on.

Actually retrieving the PrtDevMode information is, of course, simple. Because PrtDevMode is a property of forms and reports, you can retrieve the information by simply copying it from the object into a Variant or a byte array. Once it's there, though, you must somehow get it into a structure with the appropriate fields set up for you. The Windows API DEVMODE structure (named adhDevMode in the DevMode class module) is where you want the data to go. The portion of the adhDevMode structure shown here demonstrates how the raw property overlays the user-defined structure:

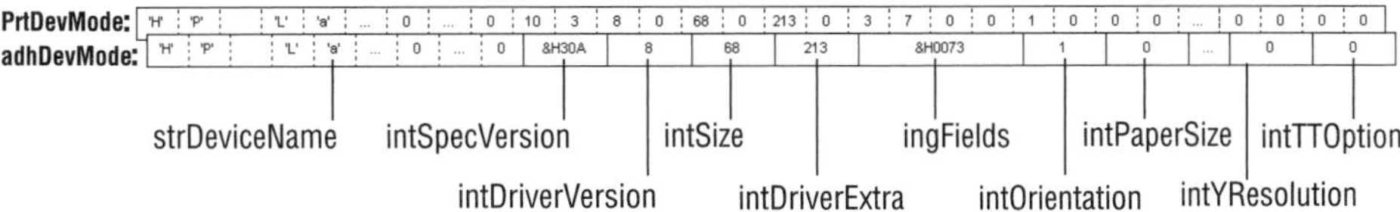

However, you also need a method for getting the bytes you've read directly from the object's property into the structure. The answer is VBA's LSet statement.

LSet allows you to copy bytes of data from one variable to another, even if they are of different data types. Normally, VBA allows you to copy information between two variables of compatible data types. In this case, you need to copy data from a byte array to a variable of type adhDevMode. The value returned by the PrtDevMode property is laid out perfectly, so performing a byte-by-byte copy into the adhDevMode structure fills in all the fields correctly. The previous graphic shows this "overlay" in progress. In the graphic, the top row represents the PrtDevMode bytes, and the bottom row represents the variable of type adhDevMode into which you've copied that data. The LSet command makes it easy to perform this operation, although there are a few issues you need to understand first, as described in the following sections.

Using LSet to Copy Unformatted Data

The LSet command has two variations. In the first variant, LSet allows you to left-align text within a string variable type, padding the extra room with spaces. In the second variant, LSet overlays the data stored in one user-defined type into a variable of a different user-defined type. This is the functionality you'll need. Note, however, the use of the term *user-defined.* Both variables must be of a user-defined type. Because your goal here is to move data from a byte array (the data retrieved directly from the object's PrtDevMode property) into a user-defined variable, you must first take one intermediate step: place the data into a user-defined type that is nothing more than a fixed-length string, like the type declared here:

```
' This is an arbitrary value. Based on experience,
' it ought to be large enough.
Private Const adhcExtraSize = 2048

' This is the number of bytes in the fixed portion of
' the DEVMODE structure.  We've just broken the
' two sizes into two separate values in
' case the fixed portion of the structure changes.
Private Const adhcDevModeSize = 148
Private Const adhcDevModeMaxSize = _
 adhcDevModeSize + adhcExtraSize

' Temp structure for prtDevMode info.
Private Type adhDevModeStr
    strDevMode As String * adhcDevModeMaxSize
End Type
```

Given a type declaration for such a datatype, you could retrieve the PrtDevMode property and assign it to a variable of type adhDevMode, as in the following code fragment:

```
Dim dm as adhDevMode
Dim dmStr as adhDevModeStr

dmStr.strDevMode = Reports("rptPhoneBook").PrtDevMode
LSet dm = dmStr
```

That code overlays the value retrieved from the PrtDevMode property of rptPhoneBook into the adhDevMode variable, dm. You should now be able to access any member of dm, just as you would with any other user-defined type. For example,

```
Debug.Print StrConv(dm.strDeviceName, vbUnicode)
```

should print the name of the printer assigned to print this particular report. (See the sidebar "ANSI versus Unicode" in this section for information on converting from ANSI to Unicode.)

ANSI versus Unicode

The 32-bit versions of Windows support two separate character sets: ANSI, in which each character takes 1 byte of storage and there are only 256 different possible characters; and Unicode, in which each character takes up 2 bytes of storage and there are 65,536 different possible characters. VBA, Access' programming language, supports Unicode only. In general, this works in your favor, allowing support for many languages, including those that use character sets different from the English ones.

There's one area of Access in which the Unicode support in VBA causes trouble: the PrtDevMode and PrtDevNames properties return the character strings in their values in ANSI format. This means that if you attempt to view the pieces of those properties directly, you'll see unreadable characters, because VBA is attempting to convert them to Unicode as it displays them.

This is why you'll find the StrConv function used in the DevMode and DevNames classes. This function allows you to convert back and forth between ANSI and Unicode. You shouldn't need this particular conversion anywhere in Access aside from working with PrtDevMode and PrtDevNames (and some Windows API functions), but it's important that you understand its purpose, should you ever want to write your own functions to handle these properties.

Using LSet to Replace the Data

With the data copied into the appropriate adhDevMode structure, it's simple for the properties in the DevMode class to read and write specific values in the structure. Although it's all hidden away in the class module, each of the properties in the class work with the associated members of the adhDevMode structure.

Once you've made the necessary changes to the data in the adhDevMode structure, you'll want to replace the value of the PrtDevMode property of a form or report. To do so, the code uses the LSet command again. If you were to write the code yourself, it might look like this:

```
Dim dm as adhDevMode
Dim dmStr as adhDevModeStr

dmStr.strDevMode = Reports("rptPhoneBook").PrtDevMode
```

```
LSet dm = dmStr
'
' Do work here, manipulating dm.
'
LSet dmStr = dm
Reports("rptPhoneBook").PrtDevMode = dmStr.strDevMode
```

The DevMode class provides two private functions, BytesToDevMode and DevModeToBytes, that handle these conversions in both directions. Both functions count on the VBA behavior that allows you to copy a byte array into a string and to return an array as the return value of a function. Listing 10.3 contains both functions.

Listing 10.3

```
Private Function DevModeToBytes(dm As adhDevMode) As Byte()
    ' Convert from an adhDevMode structure back into
    ' an array of bytes (that's what the prtDevMode
    ' property wants to receive).

    ' Take the adhDevMode structure, and use LSet to
    ' copy it, byte for byte, into an adhDevModeStr
    ' structure. This new structure contains only a single
    ' string (you can only LSet from one UDT into another).
    ' Then, return that string, converted into an
    ' array of bytes, as the return value.

    Dim dmStr As adhDevModeStr
    Dim abytTemp() As Byte

    On Error GoTo HandleErrors

    LSet dmStr = dm
    ' Trim off any extra stuff.
    abytTemp = LeftB(dmStr.strDevMode, _
     dm.intSize + dm.intDriverExtra)
    DevModeToBytes = abytTemp

ExitHere:
    Exit Function

HandleErrors:
    Select Case Err.Number
```

```
        Case Else
            Err.Raise Err.Number, Err.Source, _
             Err.Description, Err.HelpFile, Err.HelpContext
    End Select
End Function

Private Function BytesToDevMode(varBytes() As Byte) _
 As adhDevMode
    ' Convert from an array of bytes into a real
    ' adhDevMode structure. An object's prtDevMode property
    ' comes in as an array of bytes, but to work with this
    ' string of bytes, you need to copy it into a structure.

    Dim dmStr As adhDevModeStr
    Dim dm As adhDevMode

    On Error GoTo HandleErrors

    ' Take the array of bytes, and copy it into
    ' the adhDevModeStr structure, which contains only a
    ' single string element. (VBA allows you to copy
    ' directly from an array of bytes into a string.
    ' How convenient!) Then, slap those bytes
    ' on top of an adhDevMode structure, overlaying each
    ' byte into the correct fields. Finally, return
    ' that newly filled-in adhDevMode structure.

    dmStr.strDevMode = varBytes
    LSet dm = dmStr
    BytesToDevMode = dm

ExitHere:
    Exit Function

HandleErrors:
    Select Case Err.Number
        Case Else
            Err.Raise Err.Number, Err.Source, _
             Err.Description, Err.HelpFile, Err.HelpContext
    End Select
End Function
```

Modifying Printer Settings

You can change as many fields in the adhDevMode structure as you like, but Windows won't notice your changes unless you instruct it to do so. The adhDevMode structure includes a field named lngFields that is an indicator to Windows of which fields within the structure have been initialized. If you change a value in the structure, you must also include information in the lngFields member, indicating that you've modified the field.

The lngFields member is a Long integer, containing 32 bits. Each of those bits represents one possible setting within the adhDevMode structure. If the bit is on (contains a 1), then Windows knows that it should pay attention to the associated value. If the bit is off, Windows knows it can disregard the value in the corresponding field. This technique, using a series of bits to represent individual Boolean values (rather than a complete long integer) is called a *bitmap*.

To set any of the bits individually, you must tell VBA which bit you're referring to. In order to make that simpler, the Windows API provides a series of constants (see the dmFields Enum in the DevMode class module), which are basically a set of 32 bits with one bit set. For example, to indicate that you've modified the TrueTypeOption property, you'd need to use the DM_TTOPTION constant, which contains &H4000. In binary, that's equivalent to

```
0100 0000 0000 0000 0000 0000 0000 0000
```

If you use the Or operator to combine this flag with the value that's already in the lngFlags member, you'll turn on the bit associated with the TrueTypeOption value. (This may be more bit manipulation than you care to face. If so, simply take it at face value that each flag represents one possible field, and you must tell Windows which fields you've changed.)

Each Property Let procedure in the DevMode class stores a value into a module-level adhDevMode structure and then modifies the value in the structure's lngFields member. If the SaveImmediately property is True, then the code also copies the entire structure back out to the associated form or report's PrtDevMode property at that time.

For example, the following sample Property Let procedure handles the PaperLength property of the DevMode class:

```
Public Property Let PaperLength(Value As Integer)
    mdm.intPaperLength = Value
    mdm.lngFields = mdm.lngFields Or DM_PAPERLENGTH
    If SaveImmediately Then Save
End Property
```

An Important Reminder

Remember, all the properties mentioned in this section (PrtDevMode, PrtDev-Names, and PrtMip) are available only in *Design view*. You must make sure your report or form is open in Design view before attempting to set any of these properties. (You can *retrieve* the properties, of course, no matter what the mode.)

Controlling Print Layout Information

Access makes the print layout information for a given report or form available to you through the object's PrtMip property. This information includes margin settings, number of columns, spacing between columns, and the layout (horizontal or vertical) of those columns. Just as with the PrtDevMode property, Access provides this information as a single string value, which you must pick apart in code.

Just as we did with the DevMode class wrapping up the PrtDevMode property, we've also supplied a class that wraps up the PrtMip property. The PrintLayout class, in the sample project, provides all of the same functionality as the PrtMip property but makes it simple for you to manipulate the various pieces of the property.

Table 10.7 shows the properties of the PrintLayout object and their possible values. You can use these properties to manipulate the PrtMip property of a form or report open in Design view.

TABLE 10.7: PrintLayout Class Members

Member	Data Type	Description	Possible Values
Bottom	Long	Bottom margin, in twips.	Limited logically by the paper dimensions
Bytes	Byte()	Array of bytes representing the PrtDevMode property of the object referred to by the Object property. You'll generally only retrieve this property, not set it.	
ColumnSpacing	Long	Space between detail columns, in twips.	Limited logically by the paper dimensions

Continued on next page

TABLE 10.7 CONTINUED: PrintLayout Class Members

Member	Data Type	Description	Possible Values
DataOnly	Boolean	Prints only the data, without gridlines, borders, or graphics.	True (–1) or False (0)
DefaultSize	mipDefaultSize	Specifies whether each column should be the same size as the Detail section or use the Width and Height settings.	mdsUseDetail (1), or mdsUseWidthAndHeight (0)
FastPrinting	Long	Unused (reserved) in this version.	
Height	Long	Height, in twips, for each column.	Limited logically by the paper dimensions
ItemLayout	mipLayout	Specifies vertical or horizontal layout.	mloHorizontal (1953) or mloVertical (1954)
ItemsAcross	Long	Number of columns across for multicolumn reports or forms.	Limited logically by the paper dimensions
Left	Long	Left margin, in twips.	Limited logically by the paper dimensions
Object	Object	Sets or retrieves the form or report whose PrtMip property this object mirrors. You can set this property to be a Form or Report object. The code retrieves the PrtMip property for that object. You can use the Bytes property to retrieve this value back.	
PrintHeadings	Boolean	Unused (reserved) in this version.	
Right	Long	Right margin, in twips.	Limited logically by the paper dimensions
RowSpacing	Long	Space between detail rows, in twips.	Limited logically by the paper dimensions

Continued on next page

TABLE 10.7 CONTINUED: PrintLayout Class Members

Member	Data Type	Description	Possible Values
SaveImmediately	Boolean	Sets or retrieves the save behavior for the class. If set to True (the default value), each change you make to the object is saved automatically. If set to False, you must explicitly call the Save method in order to save your changes.	
Top	Long	Top margin, in twips.	Limited logically by the paper dimensions
Width	Long	Width, in twips, for each column.	Limited logically by the paper dimensions
Save	(Method)	This method allows you to explicitly save changes to the object's PrtMip property at any time. It's only necessary to call this method if you've set the SaveImmediately property to be False.	

To use the PrintLayout class, you should follow these steps:

1. Declare a PrintLayout variable.
2. Instantiate the variable.
3. Set the PrintLayout object's Object property to refer to a form or report, open in Design view.
4. Modify properties of the PrintLayout object. Each change you make is written immediately back to the form or report's PrtMip property.

The code in Listing 10.4 demonstrates how you might use the PrtMip object. This example (from basTestPrintLayout) assumes you've opened some report in Design view and want to set the number and width of columns to be printed. See the example in the code for help on calling the procedure.

Listing 10.4

```
Private Const adhcTwipsPerInch = 1440

Public Sub SetColumns(rpt As Report, _
 intCols As Integer, sglWidth As Single)
    ' For example,
    ' Call SetColumns (Reports("rptPhoneBook"), 3, 2.25)
    Dim pl As PrintLayout
    Set pl = New PrintLayout

    Set pl.Object = rpt
    pl.ItemsAcross = intCols
    pl.Width = adhcTwipsPerInch * sglWidth
    pl.ItemLayout = mloVertical
    pl.DefaultSize = mdsUseDetail
    Set pl = Nothing
End Sub
```

Using PrintLayout in Your Own Applications

To retrieve or modify settings in an object's PrtMip property, you need to import the PrintLayout class module from the sample project. Once you have that code in your application, you should be able to use the functions there to manipulate all the margin settings you need.

NOTE

The PrintLayout class works in a manner similar to the DevMode class. That is, it retrieves a string of information from a property, splits it up into a user-defined type, and then allows you to work with properties of the PrintLayout object. Changes you make to properties are written back out to the PrtMip property of the original object. The code uses the LSet statement, just as the DevMode object did. If you're interested in the details, check out the code in the PrintLayout class.

Introducing the PrtDevNames Property

Both reports and forms support a property that contains information about the current output device associated with that form or report. That is, if you use the

Print Setup menu option to select a specific printer for a form or report, that information is stored with the object. When you print the form or report, Access attempts to send the printout to the specified device based on what it finds in the PrtDevNames property of the object. To momentarily change the output device (to send the report to the fax instead of to the printer, for example), you need to retrieve the PrtDevNames property, set it to the fax device, print the document, and then set it back.

The PrtDevNames property stores three pieces of information about the specific output device in a manner that's convenient for programmers working in C or C++ (the standard Windows programming languages) but not as convenient for Access programmers. The property itself is an exact copy of the DEVNAMES structure that's used as part of the Windows SDK. The DEVNAMES structure, as defined by the Windows API, contains four integers: offsets within the text that follows the data structure. Each of the first three integers contains the offset of one of the three strings that follow, and the fourth contains a 0 or a 1, depending on whether the object has been set up to print to a specific device (0) or to the default printer (1). The text following the structure contains the device name, the driver, and the output port in a variable-length string, with each piece of information followed by a null character (CHR$(0)). The order of the three strings in the structure is not important, as long as the offsets are consistent with that ordering.

If you remember from earlier in the chapter, the three pieces of information the PrtDevNames property provides are the same three pieces of information stored in the Device object. This parallel information makes it easy to move data from a selected Device object in the Devices collection of installed printers into the PrtDevNames property of a form or report. The DevNames class takes care of this for you when you set the Object property of a DevNames object.

Using the DevNames Class

The DevNames class (provided in the sample project) makes it simple for you to retrieve and set the PrtDevNames information for a form or report open in Design view. Using this class, you'll never need to worry about the specific information in the PrtDevNames property. You simply work with the DevNames class and its properties, and the work's done for you.

The only reason you'll use the DevNames class, actually, is to send a document to a different output device than you'd originally planned. You can, of course, simply set your report or form to print to the default device and then use the Devices class to reset the default printer. This accomplishes the same goal, but modifying the default printer on your computer affects all applications, not just Access. On the other hand, using the DevNames class to modify the specific printer device for a specific form or report has no repercussions on any other application.

The drawbacks? First of all, the object must be open in Design view in order to be able to change its PrtDevNames property (or the PrtDevMode or PrtMip properties, as well). It's easy to open forms invisibly (check out the OpenForm method), but it's not easy to open reports invisibly. To do this, you must use the Echo method of the DoCmd object, and turn off the screen display. You open the report, do your work, print it, and then turn on screen display again. In addition, you cannot open a form or report in Design view if you're using an MDE (that is, if you've used the Make MDE File menu item). In that case, you cannot open any object in Design view. There is no way to make this technique work in an MDE.

WARNING No matter how much you'd like this to work, you will not be able to make design-time changes to forms or reports if your application is running as an MDE file.

Table 10.8 lists the properties of the DevNames object.

TABLE 10.8: PrtDevNames Fields and Their Contents

Item	Type	Description
Bytes	Byte()	Array of bytes representing the PrtDevNames property of the object referred to by the Object property. You'll generally only retrieve this property, not set it.
Default	Boolean	Specifies whether the strings specified in the DEVNAMES structure identify the default printer. Before you display the dialog box to select a printer, if Default is set to 1 and all of the values in the DEVNAMES structure match the current default printer, the selected printer is set to the default printer. Default is set to 1 if the current default printer has been selected.
Device	Device	Specifies the Device object representing the specific output device. Once you set the Object property, you can retrieve this property. If you set this property, you can then retrieve the Bytes property and assign it into an object's PrtDevNames property.
DeviceName	String	Device name for the output device.
DriverName	String	Driver name for the output device.

Continued on next page

TABLE 10.8 CONTINUED: PrtDevNames Fields and Their Contents

Item	Type	Description
Object	Object	Sets or retrieves the form or report whose PrtDevNames property this object mirrors. You can set this property to be a Form or Report object. The code retrieves the PrtDevNames property for that object. You can use the Bytes property to retrieve this value back.
Port	String	Output port for the output device (for example, LPT1:).

Actually making use of the DevNames class is a bit more complex than the previous classes, because it requires you to handle a few more issues. Generally, you'll want to use the DevNames class to select a new output device, perhaps by name. To do that, you'll need the Devices class, which provides a Device object matching each installed printer device. In addition (and this is a crucial step), if you modify an object's PrtDevNames property, you must modify its PrtDevMode property to match. Neglecting to keep these two properties in synch is like asking for your system to crash.

Therefore, assuming that your intent when using the DevNames class is to change the output device for a form or report, you'll need to follow these steps to effect the change:

1. Open the form or report in Design view.
2. Declare and instantiate new DevMode and DevNames objects.
3. Set the Object property of the DevMode and DevNames objects to be the device to which you'd like to print. In the example shown in Listing 10.5, the code uses one of the Device objects in the Devices collection of installed printer devices. Doing this fills in the Bytes property of both the DevMode and DevNames objects. In each case, the Bytes property will contain the information you need to fill in the PrtDevNames or PrtDevMode property of the object you're printing.
4. Set the PrtDevNames and PrtDevMode properties of the form or report by copying the Bytes property of the DevMode and DevNames objects into the appropriate property.
5. Print the form or report, using the PrintOut method of the DoCmd object.
6. Close the form or report and destroy the DevMode and DevNames objects.

Listing 10.5

```
Public Sub ChangeDevNames()
    ' Open rptPhoneBook in Design view,
    ' change its prtDevNames property
    ' to print to a specific printer,
    ' and then close the report.

    ' NOTE: It's imperative that if you
    ' change the PrtDevnames property,
    ' you change the PrtDevMode property
    ' to match.

    Dim rpt As Report
    Dim devs As Devices
    Dim dev As Device
    Dim dn As DevNames
    Dim dm As DevMode

    Const conReport As String = "rptPhoneBook"

    ' Whenever you use DoCmd.Echo,
    ' you need error handling.
    On Error GoTo HandleErrors

    ' Turn off screen updating, because
    ' you're opening a report in design view.
    ' Otherwise, it will be visible.
    ' Step 1:
    DoCmd.Echo False
    DoCmd.OpenReport conReport, acViewDesign
    Set rpt = Reports(conReport)

    ' Create new DevNames and DevMode objects.
    ' Step 2:
    Set dn = New DevNames
    Set dm = New DevMode

    ' Set the open report's PrtDevNames and
    ' PrtDevMode properties the appropriate
    ' values. Note that if you change
    ' an object's PrtDevNames property,
```

```
    ' you must also set its PrtDevMode
    ' property.

    ' Retrieve installed printer information.
    Set devs = New Devices
    Set dev = devs.Item("HP DeskJet 890c")

    ' Step 3:
    Set dn.Object = dev
    Set dm.Object = dev

    ' Step 4:
    rpt.PrtDevNames = dn.Bytes
    rpt.PrtDevMode = dm.Bytes

    ' Step 5:
    DoCmd.PrintOut

    ' If you don't want to close the report,
    ' but want to do other things with it, make
    ' sure you save away the original
    ' PrtDevMode and PrtDevNames properties,
    ' and restore them now.

ExitHere:
    ' Step 6:
    On Error Resume Next
    Set dn = Nothing
    Set dm = Nothing
    Set devs = Nothing
    Set dev = Nothing
    Set rpt = Nothing
    DoCmd.Close acReport, conReport, acSaveNo
    DoCmd.Echo True
    Exit Sub

HandleErrors:
    ' Rudimentary error handling...
    MsgBox "Error: " & Err.Description & _
     " (" & Err.Number & ")"
    Resume ExitHere
End Sub
```

Using the DevNames Class in Your Applications

If you want to the DevNames class in your own applications, you must import the following class modules: DevNames, DevMode, Device, and Devices. In addition, you must import the basPrtGlobal module. Once you have those modules in your application, you should be able to use the objects and properties you need in order to manipulate the PrtDevNames property of forms and reports effectively.

How Does It Work?

In this section, we'll spend a little time explaining exactly how the DevNames class interacts with the PrtDevNames property of a form or report. If you don't care how the class works, then skip on to the next section (or jump right to the "How Do I..." section at the end of the chapter).

To use the PrtDevNames property, you must be able to perform two basic manipulations: break apart the array of bytes containing offsets and values and put it back together. In order to follow the discussion here, you'll need some idea of what the structure looks like. Here is an example PrtDevNames string, using the Generic/Text Only driver:

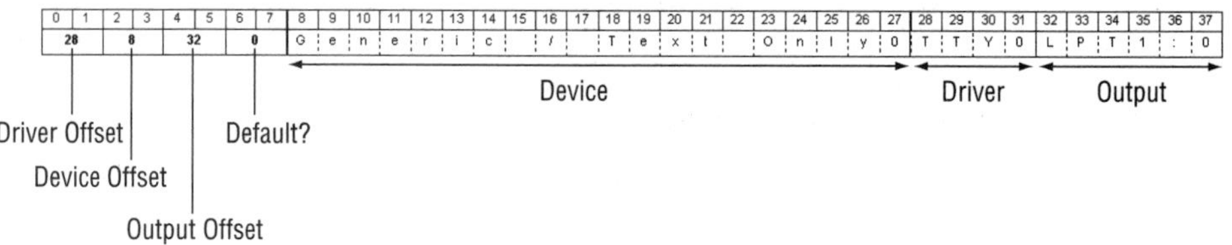

The DevNames class contains, basically, a data structure for maintaining the offsets of the three pieces of information and the three string variables themselves, stored in a Device object:

```
Private Type DevNamesOffsets
    intDriverPos As Integer
    intDevicePos As Integer
    intOutputPos As Integer
    intDefault As Integer
End Type
Private mdev As Device
```

Just as when working with the DevMode class, the code must be able to overlay the bytes in an object's PrtDevNames property with this data structure. To do that, the class provides a user-defined type (the four integers in DevNamesOffsets each take up two bytes, adding up to eight bytes total. Because strings are declared as Unicode, but treated as an array of bytes in the user-defined type, the DevNamesOffsetStr declares a string with four characters, taking up eight bytes, as it needs):

```
Private Const adhcDevNamesFixed = 8
Private Const adhcFixedChars = adhcDevNamesFixed / 2

Private Type DevNamesOffsetStr
    strDevInfo As String * adhcFixedChars
End Type
```

The DevNames class centers around four issues:

- Converting from raw bytes into a PrtDevNames property value
- Converting from PrtDevNames into a Device structure
- Converting from a Device structure back to PrtDevNames
- Getting the Object property set

The first procedure, BytesToDevNames, takes in a PrtDevNames property value and converts it into a DevNamesOffset structure, passing through a DevNamesOffsetStr type (remember, Lset can only copy bytes between two user-defined types, so the class requires that intermediate data structure, containing only a single string). This procedure copies only the offset information, not the actual string values. (Note the use of the LeftB$ function, which takes the specified number of bytes, not characters, from the input value.) Listing 10.6 contains the BytesToDevNames function.

Listing 10.6

```
Private Function BytesToDevNames( _
 varDevNames As Variant) As DevNamesOffsets
    Dim dn As DevNamesOffsets
    Dim doTemp As DevNamesOffsetStr

    On Error GoTo HandleErrors

    ' To use LSet, both sides must be user-defined types.
    ' Therefore, copy the string into a temporary
    ' structure, so you can LSet it into dn.
```

```
        doTemp.strDevInfo = LeftB$( _
         varDevNames, adhcDevNamesFixed)
        LSet dn = doTemp

ExitHere:
        BytesToDevNames = dn
        Exit Function

HandleErrors:
        Select Case Err.Number
            Case Else
                Err.Raise Err.Number, Err.Source, _
                 Err.Description, Err.HelpFile, Err.HelpContext
        End Select
End Function
```

Given the BytesToDevNames function (which provides the offsets for all the pieces of text within the PrtDevNames property), the BytesToDevice function can take a PrtDevNames property value and strip out the various bits of device information it needs. It fills in a Device object and returns that object. Note the use of three support functions:

- MidB$, which returns bytes (not characters), starting at the specified location to the end of the string. The code wants to retrieve bytes because the input value is an ANSI string, not a Unicode string as VBA would expect.
- ANSIToUni, a wrapper around the StrConv function. This function converts text from ANSI to Unicode and simply makes the BytesToDevice function clearer, as you read it.
- adhTrimNull, a Public function in basPrtGlobal, used in many of our chapters, which trims a string at its first null character (Chr$(0)). Because you know that all the pieces of text within the PrtDevNames property end with a Chr$(0), you can use the adhTrimNull function to chop off any extra text after that character.

Once the BytesToDevice function has completed, it returns a Device object with the various properties (DeviceName, DriverName, Port, and Default) filled in. Listing 10.7 contains the BytesToDevice function.

Listing 10.7

```
Private Function ANSIToUni(varAnsi() As Byte) As String
    ' Convert an ANSI string to Unicode.
    ANSIToUni = StrConv(varAnsi, vbUnicode)
End Function

Private Function BytesToDevice( _
 varDevNames As Variant) As Device

    ' Given the varDevNames string, this function
    ' fills in the appropriate fields in the output Device.
    '
    Dim dev As Device
    Dim dn As DevNamesOffsets

    On Error GoTo HandleErrors

    Set dev = New Device
    dn = BytesToDevNames(varDevNames)

    dev.DriverName = adhTrimNull(ANSIToUni( _
        MidB$(varDevNames, dn.intDriverPos + 1)))
    dev.DeviceName = adhTrimNull(ANSIToUni( _
        MidB$(varDevNames, dn.intDevicePos + 1)))
    dev.Port = adhTrimNull(ANSIToUni( _
        MidB$(varDevNames, dn.intOutputPos + 1)))
    dev.Default = CBool(dn.intDefault)

ExitHere:
    Set BytesToDevice = dev
    Exit Function

HandleErrors:
    Select Case Err.Number
        Case Else
            Err.Raise Err.Number, Err.Source, _
             Err.Description, Err.HelpFile, Err.HelpContext
    End Select
End Function
```

On the other side, the DevNames object must be able to take a Device object and output the bytes necessary to fill in an object's PrtDevNames property. This requires filling in the offsets in the DevNamesOffsets structure and converting those values into the first part of byte array. Then, the code must tack onto that the actual device information at the offsets stored in the first portion of the byte array. Finally, the function must return the byte array so other code can assign it into an object's PrtDevNames property. Listing 10.8 contains the DeviceToBytes function.

NOTE

The DeviceToBytes function takes advantage of another interesting feature in VBA—you can store bytes into a variant and coerce the variant into a Byte array when necessary. Because other functions expect to work with an array of bytes, the DeviceToBytes function must return an array of bytes. Working with an array of bytes, concatenating together bits of text, is difficult, however. Therefore, the DeviceToBytes function works with a variant, concatenating the various strings it needs, up until the time it returns a value. At that time, because it's declared as returning an array of bytes, VBA converts the variant into an array of bytes automatically, and that's what any caller sees as the return value. It's sure simpler than doing all the byte manipulations by hand!

Some interesting things to note about the DeviceToBytes function:

- The function must set the intDefault member of the DevNamesOffsets data structure. To do that, it must compare the DeviceName, DriverName, and Port values from the Device object it received as input to the settings for the current Windows default printer. It uses the Devices class to do its job.
- Just as with the other classes in this chapter, the DeviceToBytes function uses LSet to copy data from one type of data structure to another.
- The output value must contain null characters between each of the pieces of text, but inserting Chr$(0) would insert a Unicode character, which is two bytes. Because you must insert only a single null character, the code uses the ChrB$ function instead, which provides only a single byte.

Listing 10.8

```
Private Function DeviceToBytes(dev As Device) As Byte()

    ' Given the printer's device name, driver name,
    ' and port, create an appropriate prtDevNames
    ' structure.
```

```
Dim dn As DevNamesOffsets
Dim devStr As DevNamesOffsetStr
Dim varTemp As Variant
Dim devs As Devices

On Error GoTo HandleErrors

' Check for maximum length for the device name
' (leaving room for the null terminator)
If Len(dev.DeviceName) > adhcMaxDevice - 1 Then
    dev.DeviceName = _
     Left$(dev.DeviceName, adhcMaxDevice - 1)
End If

' The first offset is always offset 8
dn.intDriverPos = adhcDevNamesFixed
dn.intDevicePos = dn.intDriverPos + _
 Len(dev.DriverName) + 1
dn.intOutputPos = dn.intDevicePos + _
 Len(dev.DeviceName) + 1

' Because you're forcing a new printer setting, assume
' that it's not the default printer.
dn.intDefault = 0

' If all the information in dev matches the current
' default printer, then set Default to be 1.
Set devs = New Devices
With devs.CurrentDevice
    If .DeviceName = dev.DeviceName And _
     .DriverName = dev.DriverName And _
     .Port = dev.Port Then
        dn.intDefault = 1
    End If
End With
Set devs = Nothing

' Both sides of the LSet need to be user-defined types,
' so use devStr (of type DevNamesOffsetStr) instead of
' just a plain ol' string.
LSet devStr = dn
```

```
        ' Copy array to a variant, so it's easy to
        ' concatenate into output string.
        varTemp = devStr.strDevInfo

        ' The prtDevNames property is ANSI, so we've got
        ' to now convert these three strings BACK from
        ' Unicode to ANSI.
        varTemp = varTemp & _
         UniToAnsi(dev.DriverName) & ChrB$(0) & _
         UniToAnsi(dev.DeviceName) & ChrB$(0) & _
         UniToAnsi(dev.Port) & ChrB$(0)

    ExitHere:
        DeviceToBytes = varTemp
        Exit Function

    HandleErrors:
        Select Case Err.Number
            Case Else
                Err.Raise Err.Number, Err.Source, _
                 Err.Description, Err.HelpFile, Err.HelpContext
        End Select
    End Function
```

Finally, the DevNames class must be able to accept its Object property and, given that information, store away a Device object. It also stores away an array of bytes representing the associated PrtDevNames property value. Because you can assign either a Device object or a form or report object to the Object property, the code must handle two different cases:

- If you supply a Device object, the code retains the Device object and calls the DeviceToBytes function to create the associated PrtDevNames bytes.
- If you supply a form or report, either the input object has a non-Null PrtDevNames property, or it doesn't. If you've never set any specific printer settings, the value is Null. In that case, the code retrieves information about the default Windows printer. If the PrtDevNames property is not Null, the code retrieves the PrtDevNames property, stores it into its local array of bytes, and then calls the BytesToDevice function to extract the Device object it needs. If the original PrtDevNames property was Null, the code uses the

CurrentDevice property of a Devices object to retrieve the current printer device and calls the DeviceToBytes function to retrieve the associated PrtDevNames bytes.

Listing 10.9 contains the Property Set procedure for the Object property.

Listing 10.9

```
Public Property Set Object(Value As Object)
    ' The Object property can be either a Device
    ' object (in which case the code sets up
    ' a valid DevNamesOffsets structure for the
    ' device) or a form/report.

    On Error GoTo HandleErrors
    Dim devs As Devices

    If TypeOf Value Is Device Then
        ' We've got a Device, so fill in the array
        ' of bytes.
        Set mdev = Value
        maBytes = DeviceToBytes(mdev)
    ElseIf (TypeOf Value Is Form) Or _
     (TypeOf Value Is Report) Then
        ' We've got a form/report, so fill
        ' in the Device.
        If Len(Value.PrtDevNames & "") > 0 Then
            maBytes = Value.PrtDevNames
            Set mdev = BytesToDevice(maBytes)
        Else
            ' This object has never had its print settings
            ' touched. Get the default printer settings,
            ' so at least there's SOMETHING in there.
            Set devs = New Devices
            Set mdev = devs.CurrentDevice
            Set devs = Nothing
            maBytes = DeviceToBytes(mdev)
        End If
    Else
        Err.Raise 5      ' Invalid parameter.
    End If
```

```
ExitHere:
    Exit Property

HandleErrors:
    Select Case Err.Number
        Case Else
            Err.Raise Err.Number, Err.Source, _
             Err.Description, Err.HelpFile, Err.HelpContext
    End Select
End Property
```

Using the DevNames class is simple, as you've seen previously. Writing it, however, took some serious thought and digging into the workings of the Windows API's DEVNAMES structure. Luckily, this is the beauty of working with class modules. You write the code once, and from then on you simply work with the properties and methods of the objects you create. It's a great way to work!

Controlling Your Destination

Windows allows you to print a document to any of the installed printer devices just by changing the current printer selection, using the Page Setup dialog. You can install a fax printer driver that will intercept your printing and send your document out the fax modem, for example, or just have multiple printer choices installed for various printing jobs.

The Page Setup dialog box works fine in an interactive environment. Under program control, however, you must find some other way to specify a list of possible devices and provide a method for the user to choose a new output destination. Then, once you've changed the document's destination and told your application to send the document to that device, you need to set things back the way they were.

You've seen all the pieces necessary to make this happen. To put it all together, this section discusses the sample form, frmSetPrintDestination. This form allows you to select an existing form or report and displays its current print destination. A combo box on the form displays a list of all the installed output devices and allows you to select an output device. Clicking the Print to Chosen Destination button prints the selected object on the selected device. Figure 10.3 shows the form in action.

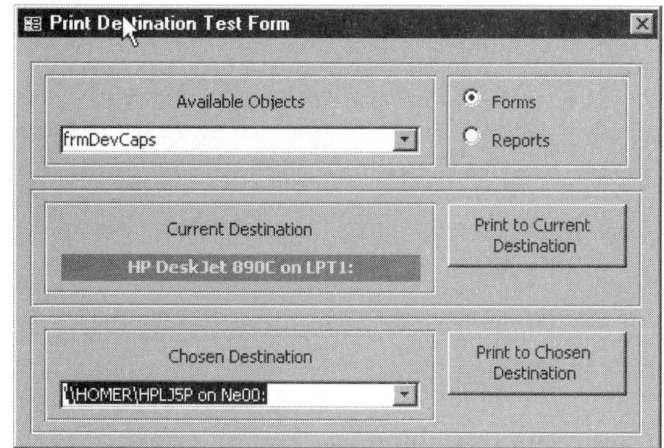

FIGURE 10.3: The sample form, frmSetPrintDestination, alters an object's PrtDevNames (and PrtDevMode) property.

WARNING If you want to write your own code that accomplishes the goal of switching output devices with the PrtDevNames property, it is imperative that you set the PrtDevMode property at the same time you set the PrtDevNames property. Changing just the PrtDevNames property will cause Access to crash unless you happen to be lucky: the PrtDevNames and PrtDevMode properties of an object must each refer to the same printing device. In the code that follows, you'll see that before you change the PrtDevNames property, you should request the DevMode information from the new printer, and that before changing the PrtDevNames property, you should set the object's PrtDevMode property. Failure to follow these steps will, sooner or later, cause Access to crash.

There are two problems in providing your users with a means of selecting a specific output device and sending the current document to that device. First of all, you must be able to build a list of all the installed output devices. Then, once your user has chosen a device from the provided list, you must be able to use the PrtDevNames property to control the destination of the particular document. Neither of these steps is terribly difficult, because the classes provided in this chapter make it easy.

Saving, Printing, and Restoring

Because you have the capabilities of the DevNames, DevMode, and Devices classes in your project, tackling the task of saving the current printer settings, modifying the PrtDevNames and PrtDevMode properties of an object, printing the object, and then restoring those settings is simple. To do the work, the cmdChosen_Click event procedure in frmSetPrintDestination follows these steps:

1. Store away the original PrtDevNames and PrtDevMode property values. If you're not intending to restore these later (i.e., you're just going to close the object after printing), there's no point doing this.
2. Set the new DevNames and DevMode objects to refer to the selected output device.
3. Copy any old print setup values to the new print setup.
4. Put the new DevMode and DevNames properties into the object to be printed.
5. Print the thing.
6. If you now want to print to the original location, put the original settings back.

Look at the code in the cmdChosen_Click event procedure for the full story, but the following paragraphs detail each of the six steps.

Step 1: Store Away Existing Prt... settings

The code first declares and instantiates two DevNames and two DevMode objects, one each for the old and new versions of these settings. Then, the code sets the Object property of the "old" DevNames and DevMode objects to refer to the selected form or report (referred to by the obj variable). Once this is done, the dmOld and dnOld objects contain the original PrtDevMode and PrtDevNames properties of the object.

```
Dim dnOld As DevNames
Dim dmOld As DevMode
Dim dnNew As DevNames
Dim dmNew As DevMode

Set dnOld = New DevNames
Set dnNew = New DevNames
Set dmOld = New DevMode
Set dmNew = New DevMode

' Get the DevNames and DevMode objects
' to retrieve information from the selected
' object (form or report).
Set dnOld.Object = obj
Set dmOld.Object = obj
```

Step 2: Set the "New" DevMode and DevNames Objects

The event procedure next calls the adhGetDevice function (in basDeviceList), passing in a combo box that must have been filled using the adhFillDeviceList function. This simple function retrieves a Device object based on the selected item in the combo box. If you're not using a combo box or list box to supply a list of output devices, it's up to you to provide a Device object representing the selected output device. The code sets the Object property of the new DevMode and DevNames objects to refer to the output device. (This effectively sets up PrtDevMode and PrtDevNames properties representing the new output device. Later, code will assign these to the object that's to be printed.)

```
' GetDevice is a function which gets
' the selected device info from the form.
' If you're doing this some other way, you just need
' to supply a Device object filled in with data
' about the selected output device.
Set dev = adhGetDevice(cboDestination)
Set dnNew.Object = dev
Set dmNew.Object = dev
```

Step 3: Copy Over Existing Print Settings

When you reset the print device, you lose printer settings. That is, when the code in Step 2 set the Object property of the dmNew object, for example, it received the default settings for the selected printer. If you had already set up other settings in your report or form, you'll want to copy those over to the new objects, as well. The example simply sets the number of copies, but you could manually copy over any of the DevMode properties:

```
dmNew.Copies = dmOld.Copies
```

Step 4: Put the New Properties into the Object to be Printed

Now that you have DevMode and DevNames objects corresponding to the selected output device, you must set up your form or report so that its PrtDevMode and PrtDevNames properties refer to that new output device. To do that, you must copy the Bytes property of the DevMode and DevNames objects into the parallel properties of the form or report:

```
obj.PrtDevMode = dmNew.Bytes
obj.PrtDevNames = dnNew.Bytes
```

Step 5: Print the Object

The sample code calls a user-defined procedure, DoPrint, which handles all the issues involved with printing the form or report, and then closes it if requested. Check out the DoPrint function in the sample form, if you're interested:

```
' This function leaves the object in design mode.
' Again, this is just meant to generalize the printing
' process so it works for both forms and reports.  Don't
' bother using this in your own apps.
Set obj = DoPrint(CloseIt:=False)
```

NOTE At the beginning of this procedure, the code stored away a reference to the form or report being printed in Design view, in the variable named obj. The DoPrint procedure opens the object in Run view, in order to print it. Doing so makes the original value of obj invalid. In order to allow the original procedure to continue using that same variable, DoPrint reopens the objects in Design view (if the CloseIt parameter is False) and returns a reference to the newly reopened object. This is why the line of code in the previous example sets obj equal to the return value of the DoPrint procedure.

Step 6: Reset the Properties

If you need to continue using the form or report without closing it, you must set the properties back to the way they were originally. If you're simply going to close the object without saving, then you needn't worry about this step at all: closing the object will throw away any changes to it.

```
obj.PrtDevMode = dmOld.Bytes
obj.PrtDevNames = dnOld.Bytes
```

At this point, the example code calls the DoClose procedure, which handles cleaning up all the various user interface elements and closes the form or report without saving changes.

The Whole Procedure

Listing 10.10 contains the entire cmdChosen_Click event procedure. The procedure uses several procedures and controls specific to this form:

- cboObjects is the combo box containing available forms or reports.
- cboDestination is the combo box containing a list of available printers.

- OpenSelectedObject is a function that opens the selected form or report and returns a reference to that object.
- adhGetDevice is a function that takes information from the supplied control (which must have been filled with the adhFillDeviceList function—both are in basDeviceList)
- DoPrint is a function that prints the selected object and, optionally, closes it. If it leaves the object open, it returns a reference to the object. It must return a new reference because it opened the object again, in Design view, and so destroyed any references to the original object.
- DoClose is a procedure that closes the selected object and cleans up the form's user interface.

Listing 10.10

```
Private Sub cmdChosen_Click()
    ' Print the object to the selected
    ' output device.

    Dim ctl As Control
    Dim dev As Device
    Dim obj As Object

    Dim dnOld As DevNames
    Dim dmOld As DevMode
    Dim dnNew As DevNames
    Dim dmNew As DevMode

    ' This will return the row number from the combo.
    ' From this, you can get the driver information.
    ' This works only because cboDestination's
    ' Bound Column is 0.
    Set ctl = cboDestination

    On Error GoTo HandleErrors
    If IsNull(cboObjects) Then
        GoTo ExitHere
    End If
    If Len(cboDestination & "") = 0 Then
        MsgBox "You must specify an output destination!", _
         vbCritical, "Print Selected Object"
```

```
    GoTo ExitHere
End If
Set obj = OpenSelectedObject()

' These calls are the "guts" of this routine.
'    1.) Store away the original prtDevNames and
'        prtDevMode property values. If you're
'        not intending to restore these later
'        (you're just going to close the object
'        after printing) there's no point doing
'        this.
'    2.) Set the new DevNames and DevMode objects
'        to refer to the selected output device.
'    3.) Copy any old print setup values to the
'        new print setup.
'    4.) Put the new DevMode and DevNames properties
'        into the object to be printed.
'    5.) Print the thing.
'    6.) If you now want to print to the original
'        location, put the original settings back.

' =========================
' 1.) Set up DevMode and DevNames structures.
'     If you're just going to close the object, and
'     don't care about resetting the values, then
'     there's no point storing away the old values.

Set dnOld = New DevNames
Set dnNew = New DevNames
Set dmOld = New DevMode
Set dmNew = New DevMode

' Get the DevNames and DevMode objects
' to retrieve information from the selected
' object (form or report).
Set dnOld.Object = obj
Set dmOld.Object = obj

' 2.) Set the new DevNames and DevMode objects to
'     refer to the selected output device.

' GetDevice is a function which gets
' the selected device info from the form.
```

```
    ' If you're doing this some other way, you just need
    ' to supply a Device object filled in with data
    ' about the selected output device.
    Set dev = adhGetDevice(cboDestination)
    Set dnNew.Object = dev
    Set dmNew.Object = dev

    ' 3.) Copy any old print setup values to the new
    '     print setup. When you change printers, you
    '     lose the DevMode settings (such as copies,
    '     orientation, and so on). If you want to
    '     copy those over, do it here. For example:
    dmNew.Copies = dmOld.Copies

    ' 4.) Put the new DevMode and DevNames properties
    '     into the object to be printed.
    obj.PrtDevMode = dmNew.Bytes
    obj.PrtDevNames = dnNew.Bytes

    ' 5.) Now print the thing.
    ' This function leaves the object in design mode.
    ' Again, this is just meant to generalize the printing
    ' process so it works for both forms and reports.  Don't
    ' bother using this in your own apps.
    Set obj = DoPrint(CloseIt:=False)

    ' 6.) If you want, put things back the way they were.
    obj.PrtDevMode = dmOld.Bytes
    obj.PrtDevNames = dnOld.Bytes

    ' Close up and clean up. This example doesn't
    ' save changes to the form or report, but it could.
    Call DoClose

ExitHere:
    Exit Sub

HandleErrors:
    MsgBox "Error: " & Error & " (" & Err & ")", _
     vbCritical, "Print Selected Object"
    Resume ExitHere
End Sub
```

Changing the Default Printer

You can accomplish the same goal—that is, sending a form or report to a specific printer—without having to open the object in Design view. If you specify that the object should print to the default Windows printer, you can simply change the Windows default printer, print, and then set the printer back the way it was. Although this technique modifies a global setting (the default printer), if you're working on a single-user machine, it shouldn't matter much as long as you reset the value when you're done. If you're distributing your application in MDE file format, you have no choice—you won't be able to open a form or report in Design view. The sample form, frmSetDefaultPrinter, looks and acts the same as frmSetPrintDestination, but it does its work by changing the default Windows printer. If you look at the cmdChosen_Click event procedure, you'll find the following code:

```
' 1.) Instantiate a Devices object.
Set devs = New Devices

' 2.) Get the current default printer.
Set devOld = devs.CurrentDevice

' 3.) Set the new default printer.
' GetDevice retrieves information about the
' selected device from the form.
Set devNew = adhGetDevice(cboDestination)
Set devs.CurrentDevice = devNew

' 4.) Now print the thing.
Call DoPrint(CloseIt:=False)

' 5.) Put things back.
Set devs.CurrentDevice = devOld

' Close up and clean up.
Call DoClose
```

This code is simpler than code working with DevMode and DevNames objects and would seem preferable. Remember, however, that you're better off not manipulating shared resources, such as the Windows default printer, if you can avoid it.

Retrieving Printer Capabilities

To use the DevMode object to its fullest, you'll want to provide a means of allowing your users to make choices about their printed output. You might want to allow them to programmatically choose a particular page size, the number of copies, or the paper source. Access, though, does not provide a means of determining your printer's capabilities. Windows, of course, does provide such a mechanism, but using this mechanism from within Access requires a bit of effort.

When Access (or any other Windows application) presents you with a Print dialog box, it has requested information from the printer driver to know which options to make available to you (available paper sizes, for example). Windows exposes this information directly from the printer driver, using the DeviceCapabilities API function. You can call this function from your own applications, retrieving information about which features the printer supports.

Doing this work yourself, however, requires a great deal of effort and a lot of code. We've wrapped all the details up in the PrinterCapabilities class, and the class is simple for you to incorporate and use in your own applications. The inner workings of the PrinterCapabilities class aren't the point here—if you're interested in digging into complicated API calls, feel free. In this book, however, we'll discuss only how you can use this class. By wrapping up the API calls in a class module, you needn't dig into how the code works, unless you care to. If you just need to use the class, you can instantiate a PrinterCapabilities class and use its properties. Table 10.9 includes a list of all the properties of the PrinterCapabilities class.

TABLE 10.9: Properties of the PrinterCapabilities Class

Property	Type	Description
BinNames	String()	Returns an array of strings, each one of which is the name of one of the printer's paper bins.
BinValues	Integer()	Returns an array of integers, each one of which is the ID of the bin. Each bin has an ID number associated with it, and this array contains an ID for each of the bins.
Device	Device	Sets or retrieves the printer device whose information you are retrieving. Normally, set to be one of the Device objects returned from the Devices collection.

Continued on next page

TABLE 10.9 CONTINUED: Properties of the PrinterCapabilities Class

Property	Type	Description
DevModeSize	Long	Returns the size of the DevMode structure associated with this printer.
DriverVersion	Long	Returns the driver version number.
ExtraSize	Long	Returns the number of bytes required for the device-specific portion of the DevMode structure for the printer driver.
FileDependencies	String()	Returns an array of strings, each of which contains the name of one of the additional files that must be loaded when the printer driver is installed. (In practice, we haven't found a driver that supplies these values.)
InitializedFields	Long	Returns a bitmap containing information about which fields within the internal DevMode structure have been initialized. Indicates both which properties in the DevMode structure that this printer supports, and which are set as defaults. For example, if the bit corresponding to the PaperSize property is set, and the bits for PaperLength and PaperWidth aren't set, this indicates that the default page size for the printer is a standard page size. Use the dmFields values in the DevMode class to figure out which bits are set. See the sample form frmDevCaps for examples of using these constants.
MaxCopies	Long	Returns the number of copies of each page the printer can print in one print job.
MaxExtent	PointAPI	Returns a PointAPI structure (with x and y properties) containing the maximum sized page the printer can print on. Measurements are in tenths of millimeters.
MinExtent	PointAPI	Returns a PointAPI structure (with x and y properties) containing the minimum sized page the printer can print on. Measurements are in tenths of millimeters.
Orientation	Long	Returns the relationship between portrait and landscape orientations for a device, in terms of the number of degrees that portrait orientation is rotated. The values can be 0 (no landscape), 90, or 270.
PaperNames	String()	Returns an array of strings, each of which contains the name of a supported paper size (for example, Letter $8^1/_2 \times 11$ in). The arrays for the PaperNames, Papers, and PaperSizes properties are parallel.

Continued on next page

TABLE 10.9 CONTINUED: Properties of the PrinterCapabilities Class

Property	Type	Description
Papers	Integer()	Returns an array of integers, each of which contains an ID corresponding to a supported paper size. Each paper size is provided an ID value by Windows. The arrays for the PaperNames, Papers, and PaperSizes properties are parallel.
PaperSizes	PointAPI()	Returns an array of PointAPI structures (with x and y properties) containing the sizes of each of the supported papers, in tenths of millimeters. The arrays for the Paper-Names, Papers, and PaperSizes properties are parallel.
Resolutions	PointAPI()	Returns an array of PointAPI structures (with x and y properties) each of which contains an available resolution for the printer, in dots per inch (DPI).
SpecVersion	Long	Returns the driver specification version to which the driver conforms.
SupportsDuplex	Boolean	Returns True if the printer supports duplex printing, False otherwise.
TrueType	Long	Retrieves the abilities of the printer to use TrueType fonts. The return value can be one or more values, combined into a bitmap. Although you can use this property directly, you're more likely to use the four individual properties, all starting with TTFonts.
TTFontsAsBitmap	Boolean	True if the device can print TrueType fonts as graphics, False otherwise.
TTFontsDownload	Boolean	True if the device can download TrueType fonts, False otherwise.
TTFontsReplace	Boolean	True if the device can replace TrueType fonts with device fonts, False otherwise.
TTFontsDownloadOutline	Boolean	True if the device can download outline TrueType fonts, False otherwise.

As you can see in Table 10.9, some of the properties of the PrinterCapabilities class return single values, and others return arrays. Some return simple data types, and others use the PointAPI user-defined type. You'll need to be careful when retrieving properties of this class to make sure you're expecting the correct return type.

Using the PrinterCapabilities Class

To use the PrinterCapabilities class, simply declare and instantiate an object of that type. Then, set the Device property to refer to an existing printer, like this:

```
Dim pc As PrinterCapabilities
Dim devs As Devices

Set devs = New Devices
Set pc = New PrinterCapabilities
Set pc.Device = devs.CurrentDevice
```

Once you've done that, you can use any of the properties of the object. For example, to display the maximum number of copies you can print on the current printer, you might write code like this (from basHowDoI):

```
Sub GetMaxCopies()
    Dim pc As PrinterCapabilities
    Dim devs As Devices

    Set devs = New Devices
    Set pc = New PrinterCapabilities
    Set pc.Device = devs.CurrentDevice
    Set devs = Nothing

    Debug.Print pc.MaxCopies
    ' Code removed...

    Set pc = Nothing
End Sub
```

To work with a property that's an array, you might use code like this, once you have all the references set up:

```
Dim i As Integer
Dim astrNames() As String

astrNames = pc.PaperNames
For i = LBound(astrNames) To UBound(astrNames)
    Debug.Print astrNames(i)
Next I
```

NOTE

When you're working with properties of the PrinterCapabilities class that return an array, you have two choices as to how you iterate through all the items in the array. You can declare a dynamic array of the correct type and assign the property into that array (as shown in the previous fragment). Then, when you need to iterate through the items in the array, use an integer variable, looping from LBound to UBound for the array. You cannot use a For...Next loop directly on the property itself—that code won't compile. An alternative is to use a For Each...Next loop to iterate through the array. This is simpler for you to type, but may be somewhat less efficient. Of course, given that you won't ever perform these loops many times, the efficiency may not matter. The following code example demonstrates how you might write that code:

```
Dim varItem As Variant
For Each varItem In pc.PaperNames
    Debug.Print varItem
Next varItem
```

Using For Each...Next won't work with properties that return an array of PointAPI structures (Resolutions and PaperSizes, for example), but it will work with properties that return an array of strings or numbers.

TIP

For more examples, see the section "How Do I..." later in the chapter.

Using the PrinterCapabilities Class

To see an example of all this technology in action, check out frmDevCaps (see Figure 10.4). This form provides a list of installed printer devices, allows you to select a device, and then displays all the information it can retrieve from the printer driver about the selected device. The code you'll find in the form module deals mostly with displaying the information, but in it you'll find lots of calls to the properties of the PrinterCapabilities object. Although it's doubtful you'll need all this information in any of your applications, you may well need one or more of the items from frmDevCaps when you present lists of formatting options to your users.

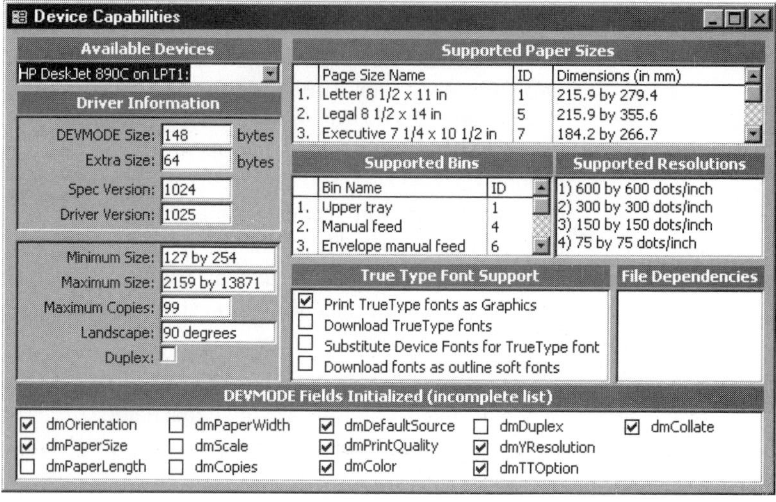

FIGURE 10.4:

The form frmDevCaps demonstrates all the properties available in the PrinterCapabilities class.

How Do I...

The material in this chapter is complex, no doubt about it. Most of that complexity is buried deep with the safe confines of class modules, so you needn't dig into the gory details unless you enjoy that sort of thing. On the other hand, this chapter provides so many capabilities, we thought it might be useful to include a section that summarizes all the information and shows how you might take on some common tasks, all in one place. If you don't care about how all this stuff works, skip the rest of the chapter, and just read through this section instead. If, on the other hand, you care about how these classes do their work, you might want to read the chapter straight through.

Figure Out All These Classes?

The sample project for this chapter includes six class modules that are meant to ease your development efforts when working with printers and print properties. Most of the classes involve a great deal of code, and this chapter doesn't intend to try to cover how that code works. The intent is to provide useful tools and an understanding of how those tools work.

WARNING None of the code or classes in this chapter will work correctly unless you have selected a default Windows printer. (To be honest, Access itself is very unhappy if you don't have a default printer installed.) If there is no default printer, the CurrentDevice property of the Devices class will return Nothing. You can use this behavior to verify that your users actually do have a default printer device installed before attempting to run your applications. This can save you from handling a lot of strange behavior that would occur if your applications attempted to run on a system with no default printer.

Table 10.10 lists the classes provided in this chapter and describes their uses. To use any of these classes, you'll need to both declare a variable of the specific type and instantiate that variable (that is, use the New keyword to create a new instance).

TIP For more information on creating and using classes, see Chapter 3, "Creating and Using Class Modules."

TABLE 10.10: Classes Provided in the Sample Project

Class	Description	Import These Modules as Well
Device	Information about a specific printer device. Includes properties such as DeviceName (e.g., HP LaserJet 6P), DriverName (e.g., HPPCL5MS), and Port (e.g., LPT1:).	Devices class
Devices	A collection of all the installed printer devices. Each item in the collection is a Device object, and the CurrentDevice property returns a Device object containing information about the currently selected Windows printer.	Device Class
DevMode	Information about a printer device, including number of copies, paper source, paper size, color, and duplex. This object maintains and provides its data so that it can work in conjunction with the PrtDevMode property of a form or report.	Device, Devices classes, basPrtGlobal module

Continued on next page

TABLE 10.10 CONTINUED: Classes Provided in the Sample Project

Class	Description	Import These Modules as Well
DevNames	Information about printer location. That is, this object contains the same information as a Device object, but it's formatted in such as way that it can be saved and restored from the PrtDev-Names property of a form or report.	Device, Devices, DevMode classes, basPrtGlobal module
PrinterCapabilities	Information about the capabilities of a specific printer device. Not correlated to any Access property, but you can use this object to find out what a printer can do. For example, if you need to supply a list of paper bins so that a user can supply a value for a DevMode object, use this object to supply that list.	Device and Devices classes, basPrtGlobal module
PrintLayout	Information about the layout of a form or report. This information corresponds to what you'll find on the Page Setup dialog in Access. It's set up so that it can work in conjunction with the PrtMip property of a form or report.	(None other required)

Fill a List or Combo Box with a List of Installed Printers?

The Devices class does most of the work for you. All you need to do is take the collection of printers it supplies and write a procedure to fill a list or combo box. To make it simple, we've provided that function for you. The basDeviceList contains the list-filling callback function, adhFillDeviceList, which does the job. You simply set the RowSourceType of a list or combo box control to be the text adhFillDeviceList, and you're all set.

Once you've called this function to fill your control, the control will contain four columns of information. You can use the Column property of the control to retrieve various bits of information about each of the available devices. The following chart lists the values contained in the columns:

Column	Contains	For Example
0	Device.PrintInfo	HP DeskJet 890C on LPT1:
1	Device.DriverName	PCL5MS

Column	Contains	For Example
2	Device.DeviceName	HP DeskJet 890C
3	Device.Port	LPT1:

To see this in action, check out the sample forms frmPrinterList, frmSetDefault-Printer and frmSetPrintDestination.

Usually, once you've selected an item from the control containing the list of printers, you'll want to take some action, using the suggestions later in this section, with the selected printer. In order to do that, you'll need to have a Device object that corresponds to the selected printer. Both frmSetDefaultPrint and frm-SetPrintDestination call the adhGetDevice procedure (from basDeviceList), shown in Listing 10.11, to take the data from the control and return a filled-in Device object.

Listing 10.11

```
Public Function adhGetDevice(ctl As Control) As Device
    ' Get the info about the selected printer into
    ' a Device object.

    ' This procedure only works if the control
    ' is a list box or combo box filled by
    ' the adhFillDeviceList list-filling function.

    Dim dev As Device
    Set dev = New Device

    On Error Resume Next
    dev.DriverName = ctl.Column(1)
    dev.DeviceName = ctl.Column(2)
    dev.Port = ctl.Column(3)
    Set adhGetDevice = dev
End Function
```

Programmatically Iterate through the List of Installed Printers?

If you want to peruse the list of available printers but not display them in a list or combo box, you'll need to take a different approach. You can use the Devices class to retrieve a collection containing information about all the installed printers. Once you have the collection, you can visit each item in the collection, as shown in Listing 10.12.

Listing 10.12

```
Sub ListPrinters()
    Dim devs As Devices
    Dim dev As Device

    Set devs = New Devices
    For Each dev In devs
        Debug.Print dev.PrintInfo
    Next dev
    Set devs = Nothing
End Sub
```

Determine the Default Printer?

You may need to find out the name, or other characteristics, of the current Windows default printer. To make this easy, the Devices class has a CurrentDevice property, which returns a Device object. To retrieve this information, you might write code like this (from basHowDoI):

```
Sub ShowCurrentPrinter()
    Dim devs As Devices
    Set devs = New Devices
    With devs.CurrentDevice
        Debug.Print .DeviceName
        Debug.Print .DriverName
        Debug.Print .Port
        Debug.Print .PrintInfo
    End With
    Set devs = Nothing
End Sub
```

The ShowCurrentPrinter procedure instantiates a new Devices object, then retrieves the object's CurrentDevice property, which is itself a Device object. The procedure displays various properties of the current printer device to the Immediate window.

Relying on Undocumented Behaviors

The For Each...Next loop demonstrated in Listing 10.12 relies on undocumented behavior. That is, in order to provide for a For Each...Next loop, VBA actually ends up calling a collection object's undocumented _NewEnum method. In order to provide your own For Each...Next loop for a user-defined class, you must supply your own replacement for this method. In addition, you must set the procedure attribute to be –4, indicating to VBA that this procedure is a replacement for a collection's For Each enumerator function. Normally, there's no way to set this procedure attribute from within VBA, but you can fake it by setting procedure attributes outside of VBA. We've done this for you. Be careful if you import and export this class into other applications—you must work through the VBA editor's Import/Export mechanism, not through Access'. The same issue applies to the fact that the Item method is the default method of the class—this, too, requires some undocumented attributes to be set in the class module.

If you're uncomfortable with this fragility, then don't use the mechanism: pretend you don't have this capability, and simply use the slower, more labor-intensive solution. That is, to replace Listing 10.12, you'd write code like this:

```
Sub ListPrinters1()
    Dim devs As Devices
    Dim i As Integer

    Set devs = New Devices
    For I = 1 To devs.Count
        Debug.Print devs.Item(i).PrintInfo
    Next i
    Set devs = Nothing
End Sub
```

This code provides the same output, but it requires a bit more effort to type and runs a bit slower.

Change the Default Printer?

If you want to change the default printer, you can set the CurrentDevice property of a Devices collection to be a specific Device object. For example, if you know the DeviceName property for a specific printer device (and you'll need to know either its name or its position within the collection of devices provides in a Devices collection), you can set the default device with code like this:

```
Sub SetDefaultPrinter()
    Dim devs As Devices

    Set devs = New Devices
    Set devs.CurrentDevice = devs("HP LaserJet 5P")
    Set devs = Nothing
End Sub
```

NOTE The device names used in this section are specific to the authors' environment. You'll need to change the code to use your specific printer devices in order for it to work.

The first line instantiates the collection of Device objects and fills it with a list of all the installed printing devices. The second line sets the CurrentDevice property of the Devices collection to be a specific item within the collection. Finally, the third line releases memory used by the Devices object.

If you want to change the default printer, print something, and restore it once you're done, you'll need to take a few more steps. Listing 10.13 demonstrates how you might do that.

TIP Although this technique works well, it only works if you've set up your reports (or forms) to print to the default printer device. Then, when you switch the default device and print, your printed object respects the default settings. If you need to change output devices from within an application distributed as an MDE, this is the only option you have. Because you cannot open the report or form in design mode to change its PrtDevNames property directly, you can only change the default printer and send the report or form to that device.

Listing 10.13

```
Sub ChangeDefaultPrinterAndPrint()
    Dim devs As Devices
    Dim dev As Device

    ' Set up the collection of devices.
    Set devs = New Devices
```

```
    ' Store away the current default printer.
    Set dev = devs.CurrentDevice

    ' Change the printer, and print.
    ' This will only work if your report
    ' is set up to print to the default printer.
    Set devs.CurrentDevice = devs("HP DeskJet 890C")
    DoCmd.OpenReport "rptPhoneBook"

    ' Set the default printer back the way it was.
    ' Destroy the Devices object.
    Set devs.CurrentDevice = dev
    Set devs = Nothing
    Set dev = Nothing
End Sub
```

Change a Report's Output Device?

Although you can change the system default printer, it's generally not a wise idea. Because the default printer is a shared resource, any other print requests that occur while you've modified the default device will also use that same changed printer. A better alternative, if you have the option, may be to programmatically change the output device associated with the particular form or report.

In order to change an object's output device, you must modify its PrtDevNames property, and you can only do this if the object is open in Design view. The DevNames object, provided in the sample project, does all the work for you. This object allows you to set its Object property to either a form or report, or to a Device object (normally, one of the items in the Devices collection). Once you do that, the code in the DevNames class works with the properties of the selected object so you can set or retrieve any of the particular pieces of information about the selected output device.

It's important to remember that if you change the PrtDevNames property for a given report or form, you must also change its PrtDevMode property to match. These properties must be in synch, and the code shown in Listing 10.14 demonstrates this issue.

To do this work yourself, follow these steps:

1. Open the form or report in Design view.
2. Declare and instantiate new DevMode and DevNames objects.

3. Set the Object property of the DevMode and DevNames objects to be the device to which you'd like to print. In the example shown in Listing 10.14, the code uses one of the Device objects in the Devices collection of installed printer devices. You might, at this point, also copy over specific printer settings you made in the original object (number of copies to print, for example). Otherwise, these settings will be lost.
4. Set the PrtDevNames and PrtDevMode properties of the form or report by copying the Bytes property of the DevMode and DevNames objects into the appropriate property.
5. Print the form or report, using the PrintOut method of the DoCmd object.
6. Close the form or report, and destroy the DevMode and DevNames objects.

Listing 10.14, repeated from Listing 10.5, works through each of these steps, allowing you to send a report formatted for one printer to a different device.

Listing 10.14

```
Public Sub ChangeDevNames()
    ' Open rptPhoneBook in Design view,
    ' change its prtDevNames property
    ' to print to a specific printer,
    ' and then close the report.

    ' NOTE: It's imperative that if you
    ' change the PrtDevNames property,
    ' you change the PrtDevMode property
    ' to match.

    Dim rpt As Report
    Dim devs As Devices
    Dim dev As Device
    Dim dn As DevNames
    Dim dm As DevMode

    Const conReport As String = "rptPhoneBook"

    ' Whenever you use DoCmd.Echo,
    ' you need error handling.
    On Error GoTo HandleErrors
```

```
' Turn off screen updating, because
' you're opening a report in design view.
' Otherwise, it will be visible.
' Step 1:
DoCmd.Echo False
DoCmd.OpenReport conReport, acViewDesign
Set rpt = Reports(conReport)

' Create new DevNames and DevMode objects.
' Step 2:
Set dn = New DevNames
Set dm = New DevMode

' Set the open report's PrtDevNames and
' PrtDevMode properties the appropriate
' values. Note that if you change
' an object's PrtDevNames property,
' you must also set its PrtDevMode
' property.

' Retrieve installed printer information.
Set devs = New Devices
Set dev = devs.Item("HP DeskJet 890c")

' Step 3:
Set dn.Object = dev
Set dm.Object = dev

' Step 4:
rpt.PrtDevNames = dn.Bytes
rpt.PrtDevMode = dm.Bytes

' Step 5:
DoCmd.PrintOut

' If you don't want to close the report,
' but want to do other things with it, make
' sure you save away the original
' PrtDevMode and PrtDevNames properties,
' and restore them now.
```

```
ExitHere:
    ' Step 6:
    On Error Resume Next
    Set dn = Nothing
    Set dm = Nothing
    Set devs = Nothing
    Set dev = Nothing
    Set rpt = Nothing
    DoCmd.Close acReport, conReport, acSaveNo
    DoCmd.Echo True
    Exit Sub

HandleErrors:
    ' Rudimentary error handling...
    MsgBox "Error: " & Err.Description & _
     " (" & Err.Number & ")"
    Resume ExitHere
End Sub
```

Modify Printer Characteristics for a Form or Report?

If you want to modify paper size, paper bin, orientation, number of copies, or print quality (among other settings), you'll need to modify the PrtDevMode property of a form or report. The simplest way to do this is to use a DevMode object, and its properties, to make the changes for you.

To make the changes you want, follow these steps:

1. Open the form or report in Design view.
2. Declare and instantiate a new DevMode object.
3. Set the Object property of the DevMode object to be the report or form you've opened in Design view.
4. Modify properties of the DevMode object. This will write changes back to the PrtDevMode property of the form or report.
5. Print the form or report, using the PrintOut method of the DoCmd object.
6. Close the form or report, and destroy the DevMode object.

Listing 10.15 demonstrates each of these steps.

Listing 10.15

```
Public Sub ChangePrinterSettings()
    ' Open rptPhoneBook in Design view,
    ' change its PrtDevMode property,
    ' print the report,
    ' and then close the report.

    Dim rpt As Report
    Dim dm As DevMode

    Const conReport = "rptPhoneBook"

    ' Whenever you use DoCmd.Echo,
    ' you need error handling.
    On Error GoTo HandleErrors

    ' Turn off screen updating, because
    ' you're opening a report in design view.
    ' Otherwise, it will be visible.
    DoCmd.Echo False
    DoCmd.OpenReport conReport, acViewDesign
    Set rpt = Reports(conReport)

    ' Create a new DevMode object.
    Set dm = New DevMode
    Set dm.Object = rpt

    ' Force the printer to look to the
    ' upper bin for paper, print on
    ' Monarch-size envelopes, and
    ' print two copies.
    dm.DefaultSource = DMBIN_UPPER
    dm.PaperSize = DMPAPER_ENV_MONARCH

    ' You could also set this value when
    ' you call the PrintOut method.
    dm.Copies = 2

    DoCmd.PrintOut
```

```
ExitHere:
    On Error Resume Next
    Set dm = Nothing
    Set rpt = Nothing
    DoCmd.Close acReport, conReport, acSaveNo
    DoCmd.Echo True
    Exit Sub

HandleErrors:
    ' Rudimentary error handling...
    MsgBox "Error: " & Err.Description & _
     " (" & Err.Number & ")"
    Resume ExitHere
End Sub
```

Modify Layout Characteristics for a Form or Report?

If you want to change the number of columns, margin settings, or print data only (for working with preprinted pages) you'll need to work with the PrintLayout object provided in this chapter. This object acts as a wrapper around the PrtMip property of a form or report. Using this technique, you can manipulate properties of an object to affect changes to the print layout characteristics.

To make the changes you want, follow these steps:

1. Open the form or report in Design view.
2. Declare and instantiate a new PrintLayout object.
3. Set the Object property of the PrintLayout object to be the report or form you've opened in Design view.
4. Modify properties of the PrintLayout object. This will write changes back to the PrtMip property of the form or report.
5. Print the form or report, using the PrintOut method of the DoCmd object.
6. Close the form or report, and destroy the PrintLayout object.

Listing 10.16 demonstrates each of these steps.

Listing 10.16

```
Public Sub ChangePrintLayout()
    ' Open rptPhoneBook in Design view,
    ' change its PrtDevMode property,
    ' print the report,
    ' and then close the report.

    Dim rpt As Report
    Dim pl As PrintLayout

    Const conReport As String = "rptPhoneBook"
    Const conTwipsPerInch As Long = 1440

    ' Whenever you use DoCmd.Echo,
    ' you need error handling.
    On Error GoTo HandleErrors

    ' Turn off screen updating, because
    ' you're opening a report in design view.
    ' Otherwise, it will be visible.
    DoCmd.Echo False
    DoCmd.OpenReport conReport, acViewDesign
    Set rpt = Reports(conReport)

    ' Create a new DevMode object.
    Set pl = New PrintLayout
    Set pl.Object = rpt

    ' Modify layout information.
    ' Set up margins, columns, and
    ' print only data.
    pl.Left = 0.5 * conTwipsPerInch
    pl.Right = 0.5 * conTwipsPerInch
    pl.ItemsAcross = 2
    pl.ItemLayout = mloHorizontal
    pl.DefaultSize = mdsUseWidthAndHeight
    pl.Width = 3 * conTwipsPerInch
    pl.DataOnly = True
    DoCmd.PrintOut
```

```
ExitHere:
    On Error Resume Next
    Set pl = Nothing
    Set rpt = Nothing
    DoCmd.Close acReport, conReport, acSaveNo
    DoCmd.Echo True
    Exit Sub

HandleErrors:
    ' Rudimentary error handling...
    MsgBox "Error: " & Err.Description & _
     " (" & Err.Number & ")"
    Resume ExitHere
End Sub
```

Find Out the Capabilities of a Printer?

As described earlier in the section "Retrieving Printer Capabilities," the project for this chapter includes a class, PrinterCapabilities, which you can use to determine the exact capabilities of a printer. If you need to retrieve a list of paper sizes or the resolutions supported by the printer, or find out whether a printer can print duplex, the PrinterCapabilities object can do the job for you.

In order to use the PrinterCapabilities object, you'll need to study the list of properties shown in Table 10.9. For each different property, you may need to assign the return value into a specific data type. For example, the BinNames property returns an array of strings, so you must assign the property's return value into an array of strings. For the Resolutions property, which returns an array of PointAPI types, you must assign the property to an array of PointAPI types.

In general, to use the PrinterCapabilities class, follow these steps:

1. Declare and create a new instance of the PrinterCapabilities class.
2. Set the Device property of the PrinterCapabilities object to be an existing device. In the example (Listing 10.17), we used the CurrentDevice property of a Devices object to get a Device object representing the current printer.
3. Retrieve properties, as necessary. In the example (Listing 10.17), we've used the PaperNames and BinNames properties (arrays of strings), Resolutions (array of PointAPI structures), and MaxCopies (Long). Other properties

return other data types, and you'll need to deal with each different type a little differently.

Listing 10.17 demonstrates a few of the concepts involved in using the Printer-Capabilities class. Also, see frmDevCaps in the sample project for a more complete example.

Listing 10.17

```
Public Sub GetPaperNameList()
    Dim intI As Integer
    Dim dev As Device
    Dim devs As Devices
    Dim pc As PrinterCapabilities
    Dim astr() As String
    Dim apt() As PointAPI

    ' Print out selected properties of
    ' a specific printer device.

    ' Set up the device.
    Set devs = New Devices
    Set pc = New PrinterCapabilities
    Set pc.Device = devs.CurrentDevice

    astr = pc.PaperNames

    Debug.Print "Paper Names:"
    For intI = LBound(astr) To UBound(astr)
        Debug.Print astr(intI)
    Next intI

    apt = pc.Resolutions

    Debug.Print "Print Resolutions:"
    For intI = LBound(apt) To UBound(apt)
        Debug.Print apt(intI).x & " by " & apt(intI).y
    Next intI

    astr = pc.BinNames
    Debug.Print "Bin Names:"
    For intI = LBound(astr) To UBound(astr)
```

```
        Debug.Print astr(intI)
    Next intI

    Debug.Print "MaxCopies: " & pc.MaxCopies

    Set pc = Nothing
    Set devs = Nothing
    Set dev = Nothing
End Sub
```

NOTE If you look carefully, you'll notice that the BinNames and PaperNames properties (among others) rely on a new feature in VBA 6. That is, you can now return a typed array (an array of strings or of PointAPI types) as the return type of a function. Therefore, you can assign the return value of the BinNames property directly to a dynamic array you've already declared. This makes it simple to have properties that return an array of values.

Summary

In this chapter, we took a look at printing issues from several angles. We covered these issues:

- Using the PrtDevMode property of objects to control printing details (managed using the DevMode class)
- Using the PrtMip property to control margins, columns, and so on (managed using the PrintLayout class)
- Using the PrtDevNames property to control the output device (managed using the DevNames class)
- Retrieving printer capabilities using the DeviceCapability Windows API function (managed using the PrinterCapability class)
- Retrieving a list of available printers and setting or retrieving the current default printer (managed using the Device and Devices classes)

Although the information presented here is relevant to all of Windows, Access is alone in the manner in which it presents this information (unlike Word, Excel, or any of the other Microsoft products). Getting at and changing printer characteristics isn't easy with Access, but you have enough generic classes available to at least make it possible. You should be able to use the PrtDevMode, PrtDevNames, and PrtMip properties in your own applications, given the sample classes in this chapter.

Table 10.11 summarizes the features of this chapter by functionality.

TABLE 10.11: Use This List to Help Figure out Which Modules to Import

If You Want To:	You Need This:
Present a list of available printers in a list box or combo box	Device, Devices
Retrieve or modify the current Windows printer	Device, Devices
Modify or retrieve print layout information for a form or report (open in Design view), such as number of columns, margins, and flow of columnar data	PrintLayout
Retrieve information about the capabilities of an installed printer	PrintCapabilities, basPrtGlobal, Device
Retrieve or modify printer settings for a form or report (open in Design view), such as the number of copies to print, orientation, paper size	DevMode, basPrtGlobal, Device, Devices
Retrieve or change the printer destination for form or report (open in Design view)	DevNames, basPrtGlobal, Device, Devices, DevMode

CHAPTER

ELEVEN

11

Shared Office Programmability

- Using the FileSearch object to find files
- Manipulating menus and toolbars using the CommandBars object model
- Animating applications using the Office Assistant

As Microsoft Office matures, more and more of the components of the individual applications are being shared between multiple Office applications. Office also provides a group of internal components, including the Office Assistant, command bars, and the FileSearch object, to each application. Each of these objects provides a rich programming model, making it possible for you to use them in your own applications. This chapter discusses each of these components in some depth, focusing on methods you can use to incorporate their functionality into solutions that you write.

NOTE

The shared components mentioned in this chapter aren't the only shared Office components. Scripts, HTMLProjectItems, Data Access Pages, DHTML support, and Scripting are a few others. *Access Developer's Handbook, Volume II* discusses several of these features, focusing on enterprise development.

References Are Everything

To use any of the shared Office components programmatically, your application will need to include a reference to the Office 9 type library. Adding this type library reference to your project allows you to use early binding (declaring objects of variable types unknown to the host application), use the Object Browser to view the exposed Automation structure of the object, and use the online help files associated with the object.

TIP

Access is the only Office application that doesn't include this reference to the Office 9 type library by default. In all other Office applications, you don't have to take these steps to use all the features discussed here. Actually, you don't even need to set the reference—Access properties of the Application object get you the items you need. The only time you'll need to set the reference is when you want to use an enumerated value (a constant) provided by Office.

To add the necessary reference to your project, follow these steps:

1. Open any module in Design view.
2. Choose the Tools ➢ References menu item.
3. From the list of installed type libraries, choose Microsoft Office 9.0 Object Library.
4. If this item doesn't appear on your list, click the Browse button and search for MSO9.DLL (although this item should appear on your list if you've installed Office correctly).
5. Click the OK button, and you're ready to go.

The FileSearch Object Model

If you've ever used the Office File Open dialog (and it's hard to imagine that you haven't), you've undoubtedly noticed the rich set of search capabilities it provides. You can search for files by name, date, author, or many other characteristics. If you want to provide that same type of searching functionality in your own applications, with or without a user interface, you can. Office's FileSearch object provides a rich object model for finding single or multiple files. Your Access applications (actually, applications written in any Office component that supports VBA) can take advantage of the object model and provide full-featured searching for files across local, network, and remote drives.

You can use the dialog itself in its simple mode (see Figure 11.1) or choose the Tools ➢ Find menu on the dialog to use its advanced mode (see Figure 11.2). The FileSearch object also supports two modes. Using the simple mode, you can search with simple criteria; advanced mode allows you to specify a collection of PropertyTest objects that correspond to multiple search criteria. In addition, if you've enabled Microsoft's Fast Find feature (installed for you by default in your Startup group when you install Microsoft Office), the FileSearch object will use the indexes the program creates, providing extremely quick searches. The following sections and tables document how you can make use of this useful technology to find documents.

FIGURE 11.1:

The simple Open dialog allows you to search on a few criteria.

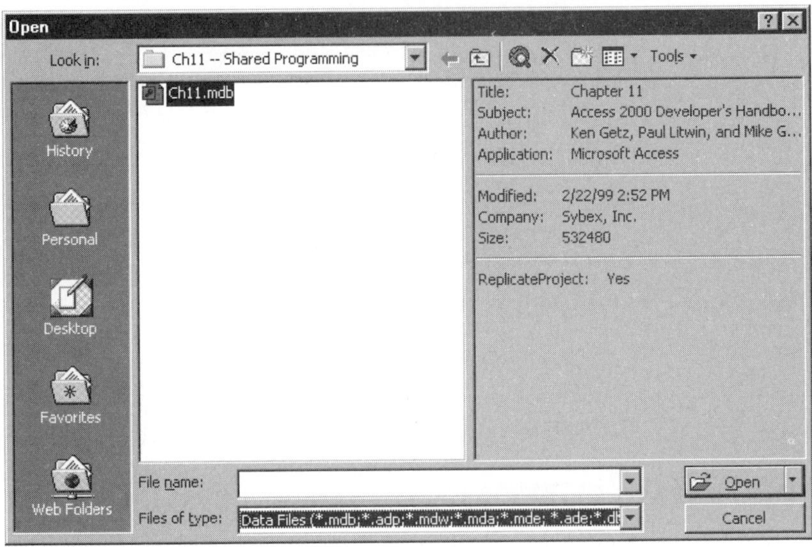

FIGURE 11.2:

The Advanced Find dialog allows you to search for specific values in multiple properties, combined in complex Boolean searches.

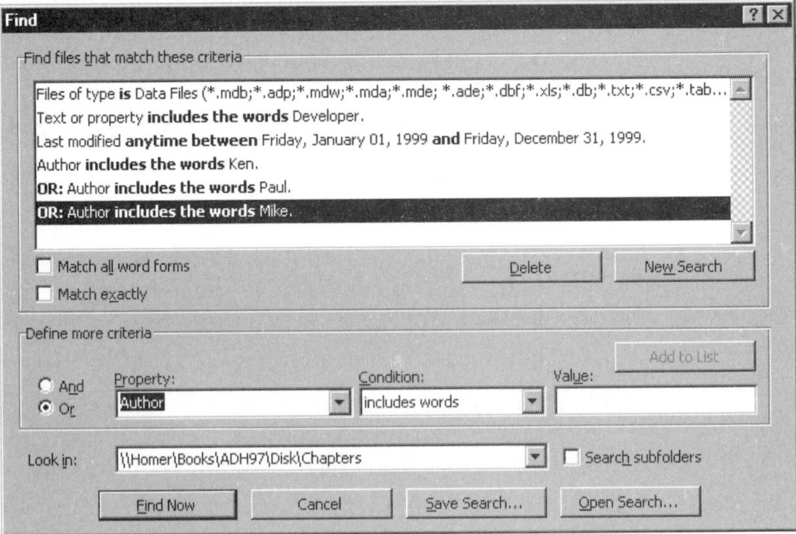

How Does It Work?

The Office programmability layer exposes only a single FileSearch object. That is, there's no collection of these objects, and the single object is precreated for you. You needn't use the New keyword when working with the FileSearch object. You can use either of the two techniques shown below to work with it:

```
Dim fs As FileSearch
Set fs = Application.FileSearch
With fs
...
End With
```

or

```
With Application.FileSearch
...
End With
```

NOTE Because Automation always takes the current context into account, you needn't explicitly reference the Application object in code that handles the FileSearch object. We've gotten into the habit of using the explicit specification because it makes it clear, from reading the code, that FileSearch isn't a user-defined object.

In its simplest mode you'll use the FileSearch object like this:

1. Supply a criterion on which to search (a file name or a file type, perhaps), using the FileName or TextOrProperty property.
2. Use the Execute method of the FileSearch object to start the search.
3. The Execute method returns the number of matching files it found. You can check that value to see whether the search was successful.
4. Loop through the FilesFound collection, each element of which is a string containing the path of a found file, performing whatever action you need to on each file.

For example, you might write a simple routine like the one shown in Listing 11.1, taken from basFileSearch in CH11.MDB. This procedure searches through the Windows directory for all files with INI as the file extension. If it finds any matches, it displays the list in the Immediate window.

Listing 11.1

```
Sub SimpleSearch()
    ' Perform simple search using the FileSearch object.
    Dim varItem As Variant
    With Application.FileSearch
        .NewSearch
        .FileName = "*.ini"
        .LookIn = "C:\WINDOWS"
        .Execute
        For Each varItem In .FoundFiles
            Debug.Print varItem
        Next varItem
    End With
End Sub
```

To perform more complex searches, you can replace the first step with a series of additions (using the Add method) to the PropertyTests collection. Once you've set up the PropertyTests collection, the rest of the steps are identical. (See the section "Using Advanced Search Techniques" later in this chapter for more information.)

To clear out your settings and start a new search, you can use the NewSearch method of the FileSearch object. This method only resets all the properties—it doesn't actually perform a search.

TIP

Don't forget to use the NewSearch method of the FileSearch object before each new search. Otherwise, you're likely to end up with criteria specified from an earlier search affecting the outcome of your latest search.

Getting Started with Searches

The following sections describe the properties you'll use when creating simple searches.

Specifying What to Look for and Where

Use the LookIn property (a string) to specify the drive and/or path in which to search. Specify the FileName property to indicate the name (or file specification) of the files to search for. This can be a specific file name or a file specification (using the DOS wildcard symbols "*" and "?").

WARNING If you specify an invalid location, after FileSearch has successfully found files in another folder, it appears that FileSearch simply uses the last valid location. That is, search for "*.ini" in C:\Windows and you will get found files. Then change C:\Windows to C:\Windowsxxxxx"and you will still find the files from the Windows directory. Even if you call the NewSearch method, you will find this behavior.

For example, the following code fragment searches for all text files in the root directory of the C: drive:

```
With Application.FileSearch
    .NewSearch
    .LookIn = "C:\"
    .FileName = "*.txt"
    .SearchSubFolders = False
    .Execute
End With
```

Specifying How to Look for Files

You can use any of the following properties to help narrow down the search or to provide more information for the search engine when locating your files. By using these options you can place fine control over the files you need to find.

TextOrProperty Use this string expression to specify text to search for in either the body or the properties of the document. There's no way to specify that the search should look only at one or the other. This option corresponds to choosing Text or Property from the Property combo box shown in Figure 11.2.

MatchAllWordForms Set this property to True to find matches on all word forms of the word entered in the TextOrProperty property. If you specify *talk* in the TextOrProperty property, setting this property to True will cause the search to find matches against *talk*, *talks*, *talking*, and *talked*. This option corresponds to the Match All Word Forms check box in Figure 11.2.

NOTE The MatchAllWordForms property will have an effect only if you've installed and registered mswds_en.lex. (The name will be different for various localized versions.) You may need to rerun the Office setup to install this feature.

MatchTextExactly If set to True, this property limits the search to an exact match on the text entered in the TextOrProperty property. This option corresponds to the Match Exactly check box in Figure 11.2. The default value is True.

SearchSubFolders If you set this property to True, the search will include not only the path specified in the LookIn property, but any folders contained within the specified folder. This option corresponds to the Search subfolders check box in Figure 11.2. The default value is False.

FileType This property allows you to specify the file type to search for. You can specify one of the following values: msoFileTypeAllFiles, msoFileTypeBinders, msoFileTypeDatabases, msoFileTypeExcelWorkbooks, msoFileTypeOfficeFiles, msoFileTypePowerPointPresentations, msoFileTypeTemplates, or msoFileTypeWordDocuments. This option corresponds to the Files of Type drop-down list in Figure 11.1. The default for this property is msoFileTypeOfficeFiles, so unless you specify a file type or file specification in the FileName property, you'll get Microsoft Office files.

LastModified Set this property to any one of the following constants, indicating a range for the last modification date: msoLastModifiedAnyTime, msoLastModifiedLastMonth, msoLastModifiedLastWeek, msoLastModifiedThisMonth, msoLastModifiedThisWeek, msoLastModifiedToday, or msoLastModifiedYesterday. The default value is msoLastModifiedAnyTime.

TIP

We've found FileSearch to be somewhat finicky if you supply a FileName property that's a file specification. The problem appears to be with the mismatch between the FileName property and the FileType property. To avoid trouble, unless you're searching for Office files, make sure you set the FileType property to be msoFileTypeAllFiles.

Executing the Search

To run a search, use the Execute method of the FileSearch object. The Execute method accepts three parameters, all of which are optional:

```
With Application.FileSearch
    intFilesFound = .Execute(SortBy, _
     SortOrder, AlwaysAccurate)
End With
```

The method returns the number of matching files it located.

These are the optional parameters:

SortBy Indicates the attribute on which to sort the returned collection of file names. Use one of the following constants: msoSortbyFileName (the default value), msoSortbyFileType, msoSortbyLastModified, or msoSortbySize.

SortOrder Indicates the sorting order. Use one of the following two constants: msoSortOrderAscending (the default value) or msoSortOrderDescending.

AlwaysAccurate Ordinarily, the search uses only the saved indexes (if you're using the Fast Find program) to perform its search. If you want the search to also look on your disks so that the returned list is accurate (even if the saved indexes are not), set this parameter to be True (the default value). It may be faster to choose False, but you may not find files that have been added or changed since the index file was last updated.

For example, the following fragment runs the specified search, returning values sorted by the last-modified date, in descending order, finding all matches regardless of whether they're in the Fast Find index:

```
With Application.FileSearch
    intFilesFound = .Execute _
     (msoSortByLastModified, msoSortOrderDescending, True)
End With
```

WARNING

If you are searching for a file for which there is also a .lnk file in the Windows\Recent directory, the FileSearch object will return two hits for the single file. For example, if you have MyDoc.doc in c:\my documents and there is also a MyDoc.lnk file in the Recent dir, then the Execute method will return two found files, even though there is really only one matching file. Beware of this odd behavior.

Using All the Simple Features

To test out all the features mentioned in the preceding paragraphs, try out frmTestSimpleSearch in the sample database (see Figure 11.3). This form allows you to try out all the simple properties (and the parameters to the Execute method) on your own files, to see how they work. Listing 11.2 shows the code that executes when you click the Search button on the form.

TIP

To make it simple to display an unbound list of data, we've chosen to use the Microsoft Forms 2.0 ListBox on this form. This control supports the simple AddItem method, making it easy to add individual items to the control. See Chapter 7 for more information on using the MSForms controls.

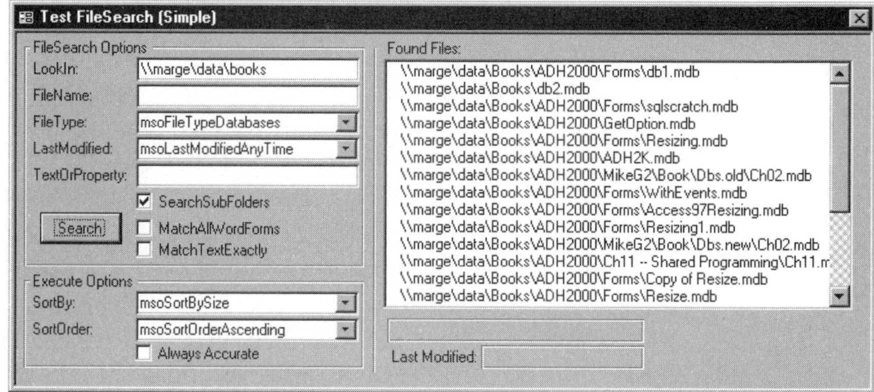

FIGURE 11.3: Use all the simple search properties on this sample form.

Listing 11.2

```
Private Sub cmdSearch_Click()
    Dim varItem As Variant

    With Application.FileSearch
        .NewSearch
        If Not IsNull(txtLookIn) Then
            .LookIn = txtLookIn
        End If
        If Not IsNull(txtFileName) Then
            .FileName = txtFileName
        End If
        If Not IsNull(cboFileType) Then
            .FileType = cboFileType
        End If
        If Not IsNull(cboLastModified) Then
            .LastModified = cboLastModified
        End If
```

```
        If Not IsNull(txtTextOrProperty) Then
            .TextOrProperty = txtTextOrProperty
        End If
        .MatchAllWordForms = chkMatchAllWordForms
        .MatchTextExactly = chkMatchTextExactly
        .SearchSubFolders = chkSearchSubFolders
        Call .Execute _
         (cboSortBy, cboSortOrder, chkAlwaysAccurate)
        For Each varItem In .FoundFiles
            mlstFoundFiles.AddItem varItem
        Next varItem
    End With
End Sub
```

Using Advanced Search Techniques

The FileSearch object also allows you to create a collection of properties and values for those properties specifying the files to find. As shown earlier in Figure 11.2, you can create a collection of PropertyTest objects, each containing a property name, a condition, and a value or two to check for. The following sections explain how to use the PropertyTests collection to create specific searches.

The PropertyTests Collection

The PropertyTests collection of the FileSearch object allows you to specify exactly the properties, and the values of those properties, you'd like to find as you search for files. When you run its Execute method, the FileSearch object will apply all the tests contained in its PropertyTests collection to each file that meets the location criteria (LookIn and SearchSubFolders properties). You can mix the simple File-Search properties mentioned earlier in this chapter with the more complex Property-Tests items, although the behavior is undefined if you overlap conditions. (In our tests, it appears that specifying a FileName property takes priority over using the File Name PropertyTest item. This isn't documented, however, and you'd do best not to count on the behavior.)

Adding Items to the PropertyTests Collection To add items to the Property-Tests collection, use the Add method of the collection. This method accepts up to five parameters, but only the first two (Name and Condition) are required. The allowed values for the properties are interrelated, and Tables 11.1 and 11.2 list the possible values for each. The general syntax for the Add method is:

FileSearch.PropertyTests.Add(*Name, Condition, Value, SecondValue, Connector*)

The following list discusses each of the parameters and their values:

Name A string value corresponding to one of the built-in properties shown in Table 11.1, or a user-defined property name. Table 11.1 also indicates which values from Table 11.2 are available for a given property name.

Condition A numeric constant value from Table 11.2, indicating the condition applied to the property supplied in the Name parameter. Some conditions require no parameters, others a single value (supplied in the Value parameter), and others two parameters (supplied in the Value and SecondValue parameters). Table 11.2 indicates how many parameters each condition requires.

Value A variant supplying the required value (if necessary) for the condition specified in the Condition parameter.

SecondValue A variant supplying the second parameter (if necessary) for the selected condition.

Connector A numeric value, either msoConnectorAnd or msoConnectorOr, indicating how the current member of the PropertyTests collection connects with other members that are modifying the same property Name. For example, in Figure 11.2, the two conditions applied to the Author parameter would use the msoConnectorOr value for this parameter in the second and third Author elements of the collection.

TABLE 11.1: Built-In Office Document Properties and Their Associated Conditions

Property Name	Available Conditions, from Table 11.2
Application name	Group 1
Author	Group 1
Category	Group 1
Comments	Group 1
Company	Group 1
Contents	Group 2

Continued on next page

TABLE 11.1 CONTINUED: Built-In Office Document Properties and Their Associated Conditions

Property Name	Available Conditions, from Table 11.2
Creation date	Group 3
File name	Group 4
Files of type	Group 5
Format	Group 1
Hyperlink base	Group 1
Keywords	Group 1
Last modified	Group 3
Last printed	Group 3
Last saved by	Group 1
Manager	Group 1
Number of characters	Group 6
Number of characters + spaces	Group 6
Number of hidden slides	Group 6
Number of lines	Group 6
Number of multimedia clips	Group 6
Number of notes	Group 6
Number of pages	Group 6
Number of paragraphs	Group 6
Number of slides	Group 6
Number of words	Group 6
Revision	Group 1
Size	Group 6
Subject	Group 1
Template	Group 1
Text or property	Group 1
Title	Group 1
Total editing time	Group 6
[User-defined Property]	Any constant, plus Group 7

TABLE 11.2: msoCondition Constants, Grouped by Functionality

Group 1		
Condition Constant	**UI Equivalent**	**Parameters Required***
msoConditionIncludes	includes words	1
msoConditionIncludesPhrase	includes phrase	1
msoConditionBeginsWith	begins with phrase	1
msoConditionEndsWith	ends with phrase	1
msoConditionIncludesNearEachOther	includes near each other	1
msoConditionIsExactly	is (exactly)	1
msoConditionIsNot	is not	1
Group 2		
Condition Constant	**UI Equivalent**	**Parameters Required***
msoConditionIncludes	includes words	1
msoConditionIncludesPhrase	includes phrase	1
msoConditionIncludesNearEachOther	includes near each other	1
Group 3		
Condition Constant	**UI Equivalent**	**Parameters Required***
msoConditionYesterday	yesterday	0
msoConditionToday	today	0
msoConditionLastWeek	last week	0
msoConditionThisWeek	this week	0
msoConditionLastMonth	last month	0
msoConditionThisMonth	this month	0
msoConditionAnytime	anytime	0
msoConditionAnytimeBetween	anytime between	2
msoConditionOn	on	1
msoConditionOnOrAfter	on or after	1

Continued on next page

TABLE 11.2 CONTINUED: msoCondition Constants, Grouped by Functionality

Group 3		
Condition Constant	**UI Equivalent**	**Parameters Required***
msoConditionOnOrBefore	on or before	1
msoConditionInTheLast	in the last	1
Group 4		
Condition Constant	**UI Equivalent**	**Parameters Required***
msoConditionIncludes	includes	1
msoConditionBeginsWith	begins with	1
msoConditionEndsWith	ends with	1
Group 5		
Condition Constant	**UI Equivalent**	**Parameters Required***
msoConditionFileTypeAllFiles		0
msoConditionFileTypeBinders		0
msoConditionFileTypeDatabases		0
msoConditionFileTypeExcelWorkbooks		0
msoConditionFileTypeOfficeFiles		0
msoConditionFileTypePowerPointPresentations		0
msoConditionFileTypeTemplates		0
msoConditionFileTypeWordDocuments		0
Group 6		
Condition Constant	**UI Equivalent**	**Parameters Required***
msoConditionEquals	equals	1
msoConditionDoesNotEqual	does not equal	1
msoConditionAnyNumberBetween	any number between	2

Continued on next page

TABLE 11.2 CONTINUED: msoCondition Constants, Grouped by Functionality

Group 6		
Condition Constant	**UI Equivalent**	**Parameters Required***
msoConditionAtMost	at most	1
msoConditionAtLeast	at least	1
msoConditionMoreThan	more than	1
msoConditionLessThan	less than	1

Group 7		
Condition Constant	**UI Equivalent**	**Parameters Required***
msoConditionTomorrow	tomorrow	0
msoConditionNextWeek	next week	0
msoConditionNextMonth	next month	0
msoConditionIsYes	is yes	0
msoConditionIsNo	is no	0
msoConditionInTheNext	in the next	1

*If 1, use the Value parameter. If 2, use both the Value and the SecondValue parameters.

Using the PropertyTests Collection The example shown in Figure 11.2 provides a perfect test case for the PropertyTests collection. To produce the same search from code, you might run a procedure like the one shown in Listing 11.3, taken from basFileSearch. (You'll need to change the specified path to run the example in your own environment.)

Listing 11.3

```
Sub ComplexSearch()
    ' Perform complex search using the FileSearch object and
    ' its PropertyTests collection.
    Dim varFile As Variant
    With Application.FileSearch
        .NewSearch
        ' Choose your own path here, of course!
        .LookIn = "\\MARGE\DATA\BOOKS\ADH2000"
```

```
            .SearchSubFolders = True
            .FileType = msoFileTypeOfficeFiles
            .TextOrProperty = "Developer"
            With .PropertyTests
                .Add "Last Modified", _
                 msoConditionAnytimeBetween, _
                 #1/1/1999#, #12/31/1999#
                .Add "Author", msoConditionIncludes, "Ken"
                .Add "Author", msoConditionIncludes, _
                 "Paul", msoConnectorOr
                .Add "Author", msoConditionIncludes, _
                 "Mike", msoConnectorOr
            End With
            .Execute
            If .FoundFiles.Count > 0 Then
                For Each varFile In .FoundFiles
                    Debug.Print varFile
                Next varFile
            End If
        End With
    End Sub
```

Given all this flexibility, you should be able to find any file, local or remote, given any simple or complex set of criteria. Remember that using the Microsoft Fast Find indexing program will speed up your searches, but you don't need to use it to take advantage of the FileSearch object.

Working with Command Bars

Microsoft Office provides a shared mechanism for creating menus and toolbars in all its products. Access takes advantage of this technology, and all its menus and toolbars get their functionality from shared Office code. To provide a unified object model for toolbars and menu bars, the Office team has provided the new CommandBar object hierarchy. A CommandBar object can appear in three guises:

- A standard menu
- A toolbar
- A shortcut menu

Although the menu bar incarnation of a CommandBar resembles a standard Windows menu, it is actually a very different beast. If you were thinking about using the Windows API and its many menu-handling functions to manipulate Access (or Office) menus, give it up. These API calls will not work with CommandBars. On the other hand, the CommandBar object model is full-featured and supplies most of the functionality you would want when working with menus.

The following sections discuss techniques you can use in applications to manipulate the new CommandBar object model. Along the way, you'll find techniques for solving typical programming problems involving menus.

In order to provide coverage of the CommandBar object model, we have made these assumptions:

- You've worked with Access' toolbars and menus.
- You've created and modified toolbars and menus from the user interface.
- You already have an understanding of objects, properties, and methods. (For more information on these topics, see Chapters 3 and 6.)
- In any application where you want to programmatically control the CommandBar object model, you've set up a reference to the Microsoft Office 9 Object Library.

In other words, this section is not about creating command bars using the user interface, nor about how to attach those command bars to forms. Access' online help covers these topics in good detail, and that's not our point. This section focuses on controlling and creating command bars programmatically at runtime from within your applications.

TIP

When you load Access, all built-in CommandBar objects contain all the items they're ever going to contain (unless you modify them by adding or removing items, of course). Access simply hides and shows the various items as necessary. You need to be acutely aware of this fact as you work with the CommandBar object model, because you cannot take what you see at face value. Always inspect the Visible property of any built-in object you work with, and be aware that the count of visible menu items is almost always different from the Count property of the corresponding object. Examples throughout the following sections take this discrepancy into account.

Adaptive Menus—Who Needs Them?

To be honest, we're not fans of the new adaptive menus used in Office 2000. If you feel the same way, you may want to turn them off. You can search for an option in the Tools ➢ Options menu that handles this, but you won't find one. The setting is buried in the Tools ➢ Customize ➢ Options dialog box, as the Menus Show Recently Used Commands First option.

If you want a quick, simple way to toggle this behavior off (and perhaps, someday, back on again), use this code:

```
Commandbars.AdaptiveMenus = False
```

For more properties dealing with adaptive menus, see the Priority and IsPriorityDropped properties discussed in Table 11.7.

NOTE The CommandBar object model is just too large to be able to discuss fully in this limited space. The following sections provide suggestions on ways to use command bars and work through some sample code. In addition, this chapter will focus on menus, rather than trying to manage both menus and toolbars. The only differences, of course, are how they're displayed, so all the techniques shown here should work for both. Use this discussion to get started with this complex technology, and then dig in through the Object Browser and the online help topics if you need to.

Where Are CommandBars Stored?

When you alter a built-in CommandBar object, Access stores that CommandBar information in the Registry, on a per-user, per-machine basis. That way, changes to built-in CommandBars will affect all databases you (or any other user on your machine) open. If you create new menus or toolbars, however, Access stores the information with the current database. The menus and toolbars move around with the database in which they were created. On the other hand, some information about custom menus and toolbars is stored in the Registry, on a per-user, per-machine basis. Access stores information about the positions and visibility of the user-defined toolbars in the Registry, so people with different toolbar preferences can use the same database.

What's the Difference between Menus and Toolbars?

There's really not much difference between menus and toolbars. They're both stored the same way. The big difference is how they're displayed. A menu bar contains only text items, although the drop-down menus that hang off menu bars can contain text and graphics items. A toolbar, on the other hand, normally contains just graphics elements, with little or no text. The line can blur, of course, as you mix the text and graphics elements on a given command bar. The following sections focus mainly on the menu bar side of things because you're most likely to want to programmatically control the menus in your application. You can, of course, apply everything discussed here to either menus or toolbars—they "program" just the same. Although a given application can only have a single active menu bar, you can display any menu bar and as many toolbars as your screen can contain. You control whether an object displays as a menu bar or as a toolbar, where it appears, whether it's docked, and which items on the menu bar/toolbar are visible and enabled.

If you intend to distribute an application, make sure you test it on a "clean" machine (that is, a machine on which your menus and toolbars have never been used), emulating the end users' machines. That way you'll be able to see exactly what users will see when they attempt to use built-in and application-defined command bars. Remember that any specific settings about your application-defined command bars are stored in the Registry, and those Registry settings won't be distributed with your application. You'll need to programmatically set up the command bars the way you want them the first time a user runs your application.

NOTE

If you've used macros to create menus (which was the only way to create menus before Access 97), the SetMenuItem method of the DoCmd object will continue to work with those menus. You won't need to change code that uses this method, although it will work only with menus you've created with macros. If you use the Tools ➢ Macros ➢ Create Menu from Macro (or the other two similar items) menu item to convert your macro-type menus to CommandBars, SetMenuItem will no longer work. It never worked with built-in menus, and it won't work on menus you create as CommandBars, either.

NOTE

If you think you can use the Windows API to manipulate a form's system menu (the menu hanging off the control box), you're out of luck—there's just no way it's going to work. Because those menus are CommandBar objects, the API can't even retrieve a handle for the system menu. And because there's no exposed way to retrieve information about that menu from Access (unlike the rich CommandBar object model for menus and toolbars), there's just no reasonable way to work with these menus.

What Kinds of Objects Are There?

As you can see in Figure 11.4, there really are only two types of objects in the CommandBar object hierarchy: CommandBar objects and CommandBarControl objects. Each CommandBar object contains a collection of CommandBarControl objects. The interesting part is that the CommandBarControl object can be one of several types, as shown in Table 11.3.

TABLE 11.3: Base and Derived Classes for Command Bars

Object	Description
CommandBarControl	Base class for all the command bar controls. In addition to the three types listed below, you can create a simple edit box control, using the Add method of the CommandBarControls collection of a CommandBar.
CommandBarButton	Derived type for command bar buttons. May look like a typical menu bar item or like a toolbar button.
CommandBarComboBox	Derived type for various drop-down/combo box lists, like Access' list of controls when in Form Design view.
CommandBarPopup	Derived type for a menu bar item that contains another menu bar. Use the CommandBar property of an item of this class to obtain a reference to the CommandBar object it contains.

NOTE

Of course, things aren't this simple. Built-in CommandBar objects can contain control types other than the ones shown in Table 11.3. This table lists the control types *you* can create on command bars. As usual, what you can do programmatically is a version or so behind what the Microsoft programmers can do with the same objects. In a future version of Access, you may be able to create drop-down grids and use all the other interesting command bar widgets that Access itself uses, but not now.

FIGURE 11.4: The CommandBar object model is quite simple. Working with it is not.

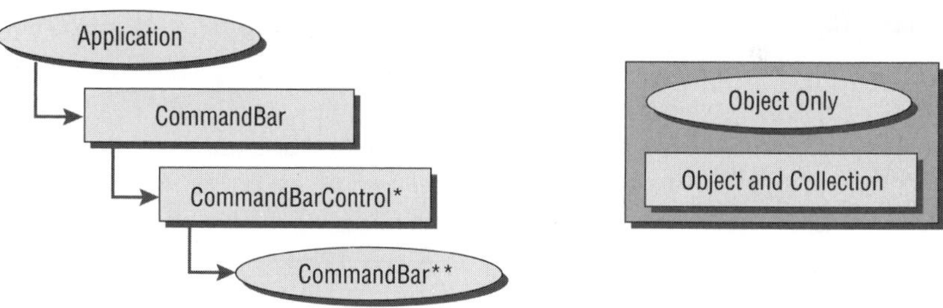

* Can be one of the CommandBarControlButton, CommandBarControlComboBox, CommandBarControlPopup subclasses. Each of the different classes adds its own set of properties and methods.

** Appears only if parent's Type is CommandBarControlPopup

Microsoft Office supplies many properties and methods for the CommandBar family of objects, and Tables 11.4 through 11.9 introduce the most useful properties and methods of each of the objects. The sections that follow demonstrate the use of many of these methods and properties. The tables do not attempt to be definitive; we have included them here only to allow you to easily peruse the options available to you. (In these tables, if the Returns column includes an enumerated type, such as msoMenuAnimation, check the Object Browser for the complete list of values.)

TABLE 11.4: A Subset of the Methods, Properties, and Events of the CommandBars Collection

Name	Type	Returns	Read-Only?	Description
ActionControl	Property	CommandBarControl	Yes	In the code called from a control's OnAction property, returns a reference to the calling control. This allows your code to react differently depending on which button was selected.
ActiveMenuBar	Property	CommandBar	Yes	Returns a reference to the active menu bar. (There can be only one single active menu bar at any time.)
AdaptiveMenus	Property	Boolean	No	Indicates whether command bars hide less-used menu items until they're used (that is, whether Office uses adaptive menus). Its effect is Office-wide.

Continued on next page

TABLE 11.4 CONTINUED: A Subset of the Methods, Properties, and Events of the CommandBars Collection

Name	Type	Returns	Read-Only?	Description
Count	Property	Long	Yes	Returns the number of command bars in the collection.
DisplayFonts	Property	Boolean	No	Determines whether font names in the font drop-down list are displayed in the actual font. Its effect is Office-wide.
DisplayKeysInToolTips	Property	Boolean	No	Determines whether shortcut keys are shown in ToolTips. Its effect is Office-wide.
DisplayToolTips	Property	Boolean	No	Determines whether ToolTips are displayed for command bar controls. Its effect is Office-wide.
LargeButtons	Property	Boolean	No	Controls whether command bars are using large or small buttons. Its effect is Office-wide.
MenuAnimationStyle	Property	msoMenuAnimation	No	Controls the current menu animation style. Its effect is Office-wide.
Add	Method	CommandBar		Adds a new, empty, initially hidden CommandBar to the CommandBars collection.
FindControl	Method	CommandBarControl		Finds a specific control in the CommandBars collection. (See online help and the section "Referring to Items Other Than Top-Level CommandBars" in this chapter for more information on the parameters the method uses.)
FindControls	Method	CommandBarControls		Working similarly to the FindCommand method, this method returns a collection of controls that meet the specified criteria.
ReleaseFocus	Method			Releases the focus from the CommandBar objects in the UI. Even if a nested control has the focus, the focus is released completely (not just one level).
OnUpdate	Event			Occurs when a change is made to any command bar. Use WithEvents in code to trap events of command bars. This event should generally be trapped only to find out when a COM Add-in makes a change to a command bar.

TABLE 11.5: A Subset of the Methods and Properties of a CommandBar Object

Name	Type	Returns	Read-Only?	Description
AdaptiveMenus	Property	Boolean	No	Indicates whether this particular command bar displays personalized (adaptive) menus.
Built-In	Property	Boolean	Yes	Indicates whether the CommandBar object is built-in.
Controls	Property	CommandBarControls	Yes	Returns a reference to the collection of controls contained in this command bar.
Enabled	Property	Boolean	No	Indicates the enabled state of the CommandBar. For built-in CommandBars, setting the Enabled property to True simply allows Access to control the state (that is, you cannot enable a built-in command bar that Access intends to be disabled. All you can do is allow Access to control its state by setting the Enabled property to True.)
Height	Property	Long	No	Returns the current height of the CommandBar (not counting the frame) in pixels. If you set the property, the height will be snapped to the closest valid value. Attempting to set this property will fail if the command bar is not in a sizable state (docked or protected).
Left	Property	Long	No	Returns the X coordinate of the bar, in pixels. If floating, the value indicates screen coordinates. If not, the value is with respect to the docking area. If set, the value will be snapped to the nearest valid value and will fail if the bar isn't movable.
Name	Property	String	No	Returns the name of the bar. For built-in bars, this is the English name of the CommandBar object, and it is read-only. Setting this property will fail with a run-time error if the name already exists in the CommandBars collection.
NameLocal	Property	String	No	Returns the localized name for the CommandBar.
Parent	Property	Object	Yes	Returns a reference to the parent of the CommandBar. If the CommandBar is a pop-up menu, its parent is the Command-BarPopup control to which it's attached.

Continued on next page

TABLE 11.5 CONTINUED: A Subset of the Methods and Properties of a CommandBar Object

Name	Type	Returns	Read-Only?	Description
Position	Property	msoBarPosition	No	Indicates the current bar position. Setting this property to msoBarFloating returns the bar to its last floating position. You cannot set a bar's Position property to msoBar-Popup; that value is available only to pop-up bars, and that setting is determined when you create the CommandBar object. You cannot set a toolbar's position to be msoBarMenuBar—that's reserved for the main menu bar.
Protection	Property	msoBarProtection	No	Indicates the bar's protection from various actions in the UI. You can combine the msoBarProtection values with the Or operator. For example, setting the property to be msoBarNoHorizontalDock Or mso-BarNoResize will make it impossible for the bar to be docked horizontally, and it won't be able to be resized.
RowIndex	Property	Long	No	Indicates the logical row used by the bar when it docks. Set to a positive integer, or one of msoBarRowFirst (0) and msoBar-RowLast (–1).
Top	Property	Long	No	Returns the y coordinate of the bar, in pixels. If floating, the value indicates screen coordinates. If not, the value is with respect to the docking area. If set, the value will be snapped to the nearest valid value and setting the property will fail if the bar isn't movable.
Type	Property	msoBarType	Yes	Indicates the command bar type (top-level toolbar, menu bar, or pop-up menu).
Visible	Property	Boolean	No	Indicates whether a CommandBar is currently visible. Cannot be set for pop-up menus, but it can be read. If you want to make a pop-up menu visible, use the Execute method of the parent control instead. Setting this property to True will fail with a runtime error if the CommandBar isn't currently enabled.

Continued on next page

TABLE 11.5 CONTINUED: A Subset of the Methods and Properties of a CommandBar Object

Name	Type	Returns	Read-Only?	Description
Width	Property	Long	No	Returns the width of the bar, in pixels. If floating, the value indicates screen coordinates. If not, the value is with respect to the docking area. If set, the value will be snapped to the nearest valid value and setting the property will fail if the bar isn't movable.
Delete	Method			Deletes the CommandBar from the UI. Fails for built-in CommandBar objects.
FindControl	Method	CommandBarControl		Finds a specific control on this CommandBar only. To search all CommandBars, see the FindControl method of the CommandBars collection.
Reset	Method			Resets a built-in CommandBar to its default state. Fails for user-defined CommandBars.
ShowPopup	Method			Shows a pop-up menu at a specified location. Allows you to create your own pop-up menus anywhere on the screen. In order for this to work, you must have converted the command bar into a shortcut menu, using the user interface.

TABLE 11.6: A Subset of the Methods and Properties of the CommandBarControls Collection

Name	Type	Returns	Read-Only?	Description
Count	Property	Long	Yes	Returns the number of controls in the collection, not including gaps (toolbars) and separators (menus).
Item	Property	CommandBarControl	Yes	Returns a reference to a particular CommandBarControl object. This is the default property, so you can normally leave out the .Item in a reference to a particular control.
Add	Method	CommandBarControl		Adds a control to the collection and returns a reference to the newly added CommandBarControl object. See online help for complete details.

TABLE 11.7: A Subset of the Methods and Properties of a CommandBarControl Object

Name	Type	Returns	Read-Only?	Description
BeginGroup	Property	Boolean	No	Indicates that the control starts a group. On toolbars, the start of the new group appears as a gap. On menus, it appears as a divider line above the control.
BuiltIn	Property	Boolean	Yes	Indicates whether the control is built-in. Assigning a value to a control's OnAction property causes this value to be set to False, and removing the property value causes this value to revert to its original setting (for built-in controls only).
Caption	Property	String	No	Returns or sets the caption text. Use an ampersand (&) to include a keyboard mnemonic.
Enabled	Property	Boolean	No	Indicates whether the control is enabled. For a built-in control, Access maintains the enabled state. You can disable any built-in control, but you cannot enable a control that Access deems disabled. For nonbuilt-in controls, this property is used without interpretation.
Height	Property	Long	No	Returns the current height of the control, in pixels. If you set the property, the height will be snapped to the closest valid value. Set to 0 to use the default height. For menu bars, you can specify any reasonable value.
Id	Property	Long	Yes	Specifies the action associated with a built-in control. Every built-in command bar control has an associated Id value that indicates what that control does. All custom items have an Id value of 1.
IsPriorityDropped	Property	Boolean	Yes	Indicates whether the control has been dropped from the menu because of infrequent use. This is different from the Visible property, which indicates whether the item is visible at all. This property indicates whether you must scroll to the bottom of the menu to see this particular item. See online help for complete details on how to predict when a control will be dropped from the adaptive menus. See the AdaptiveMenus property for information on turning off this feature altogether.

Continued on next page

TABLE 11.7 CONTINUED: A Subset of the Methods and Properties of a CommandBarControl Object

Name	Type	Returns	Read-Only?	Description
Left	Property	Long	Yes	Returns the current x coordinate of the control, in pixels, from the left edge of the screen.
OnAction	Property	String	No	Indicates the action to take for a nonbuilt-in control. Use the name of a macro, or a function in the form =*FunctionName*(), or just *FunctionName*. Due to limitations in the design, you can't call functions in form or report class modules. Instead, call functions in standard modules. In addition, to call a COM add-in from a command bar control, use the special syntax "!<AddInName>".
Parameter	Property	String	No	Allows you to specify a user-defined string identifying this particular control. In the function called by the OnAction property, you can retrieve this property and take action based on its value. Basically, acts as a second Tag property.
Priority	Property	Long	No	Specifies the priority of a command bar control, in terms of deleting controls from the command bar if all the controls can't be displayed, because there's not enough room on the screen. All values besides 1 (indicating never to delete) are ignored. Values from 0 to 7 are allowed. Access uses 3 for all built-in controls, and the property is generally unused.
Tag	Property	String	No	Can be used to store any user-defined data. Useful when searching for a control.
ToolTipText	Property	String	No	Returns the text displayed in the control's ToolTip.
Top	Property	Long	Yes	Returns the y coordinate of the top of the control, in pixels, from the top of the screen.
Type	Property	msoControlType	Yes	Returns the type of the control, as specified in the list of controls in msoControlType.
Visible	Property	Boolean	No	Indicates the visibility of the control. Setting this property to True allows Access to control the visibility.

Continued on next page

TABLE 11.7 CONTINUED: A Subset of the Methods and Properties of a CommandBarControl Object

Name	Type	Returns	Read-Only?	Description
Width	Property	Long	No	Indicates the width of a control, in pixels. Not all controls can have their width changed.
Copy	Method	CommandBarControl		Copies the current control onto a specified CommandBar at a specified location.
Delete	Method			Deletes a control (temporarily, if requested).
Execute	Method			Executes the action associated with the control. If the control has a drop-down menu hanging off it, this will make that menu visible.
Move	Method	CommandBarControl		Moves a control to a specified Command-Bar at a specified location.
Reset	Method			Resets a control to its default state (only valid for built-in controls).
SetFocus	Method			Moves the keyboard focus to the control. This will fail if the control isn't visible and enabled.

TABLE 11.8: Additional Items for the CommandBarButton Object*

Name	Type	Returns	Read-Only?	Description
BuiltInFace	Property	Boolean	No	Indicates whether the button is displaying the built-in face. Setting this property to True forces the button to use the built-in face.
FaceId	Property	Long	No	Indicates the ID of the icon shown on the button. This value will be 0 if the button is showing a custom face. For built-in controls, the FaceId and the Id property will generally be the same. The FaceId and Id properties don't have to be the same—you can easily modify the FaceId property of any command bar control to differ from its default and from its Id property.

Continued on next page

TABLE 11.8 CONTINUED: Additional Items for the CommandBarButton Object*

Name	Type	Returns	Read-Only?	Description
HyperlinkType	Property	msoCommandBar-ButtonHyperlinkType	No	If you want a command bar button to act as a hyperlink, set this property to be something besides its default (that is, no hyperlink). If you do set this property, use the ToolTipText property to indicate the URL to which to link.
ShortcutText	Property	String	No	Indicates the shortcut key text (Ctrl+O, for example) that displays in a menu. This doesn't cause the application to map the keystroke to an action, however. Your application must supply the necessary bindings to make this happen (perhaps using an AutoKeys macro). You can apply this property only to buttons that have an OnAction property value.
State	Property	msoButtonState	No	Indicates the state of a button (up, down, or mixed). You can set this property only for buttons that have an OnAction property setting. If a button is on a menu and has no image, setting this property to msoButtonDown causes the item to have a check mark in front of it. Setting it to msoButtonUp removes the check.
Style	Property	msoButtonStyle	No	Controls how the button displays its icon and/or caption. For example, to show both an icon and a caption below the icon, select msoButtonIconAndCaptionBelow.
CopyFace	Method			Copies the control's icon to the clipboard.
PasteFace	Method			Pastes the icon on the clipboard onto the button.
Click	Event			Event that occurs when a user clicks on a command bar button. In your code, use the WithEvents keyword to trap this event. Use the CancelDefault parameter to indicate that you want the default action for this button to be skipped.

*Not including those it inherits from also being a command bar control

TABLE 11.9: Additional Items for the CommandBarComboBox Object*

Name	Type	Returns	Read-Only?	Description
DropDownLines	Property	Long	No	Specifies the number of lines in the drop-down list. Set to 0 to have Access compute this for you. This property can be changed only for nonbuilt-in controls.
DropDownWidth	Property	Long	No	Specifies the width, in pixels, of the drop-down list. Set to 0 to use the width of the control. Set to –1 to use the longest item in the list. You can change this property only for nonbuilt-in controls.
List	Property	String	No	Returns an array (indexed starting with 1) allowing you to set or retrieve the text of any item in the list. Read-only for built-in combo box controls.
ListCount	Property	Long	Yes	Returns the number of items in the list
ListHeaderCount	Property	Long	No	Indicates the number of items drawn above the separator line, commonly used as a most-frequently-used list (see frmCustomers in the sample database). Set to –1 (the default) to have no separator. Set to 0 to indicate an empty list. You can set this property only for non–built-in controls.
ListIndex	Property	Long	No	Returns the index (starting with 1) of the selected item in the list. Returns 0 if nothing is selected.
Style	Property	msoComboStyle	No	Specifies the display style for the combo box. Choose to include a label (msoComboLabel) or not (msoComboNormal).
Text	Property	String	No	Returns the text displayed in the edit area of the control.
AddItem	Method			Adds an item to the combo box. Fails for built-in controls.
Clear	Method			Removes all items from the list. Fails for built-in controls.
RemoveItem	Method			Removes the specified item from the list. Fails for built-in controls.
Change	Event			Occurs when you change the selection in a command bar combo box control.

*Not including those it inherits from also being a command bar control

CommandBars and CommandBarControls

Although the object model for CommandBars is simple, there are so many options and variations that the actual work becomes quite complex. Because there are so few object types and the objects all contain other objects, the recursion can get tricky. On the other hand, the basics of command bars can be boiled down to a few statements:

- Each CommandBar object contains a collection of CommandBarControl objects (its Controls collection).
- Each CommandBarControl object within the collection of controls can be a CommandBarComboBox, a CommandBarButton, or a CommandBarPopup control.
- If a control is a CommandBarComboBox or CommandBarButton, it has its own set of properties and methods, but it cannot contain other controls.
- If the control is a CommandBarPopup, then it has a CommandBar property that refers to the CommandBar object it contains. The menus hanging off CommandBarPopup controls are called pop-up menus, and their Type property indicates that they're not menu bars.

Examples in the sections that follow demonstrate how to enumerate, modify, and create objects within these collections.

TIP

Because there is so little documentation on CommandBars and their subsidiary objects, you'll want to spend a lot of time in the Object Browser. Start with the top-level object you're interested in and work your way down through the objects and their properties until you find the item you need. For example, to investigate the various control types you might find on a built-in menu bar, start with the CommandBarControl object on the left side of the Browser. On the right, find the Type property. In the bottom pane, you'll see Property Type as MsoControlType. Click MsoControlType, and the Browser takes you to a list of the different control types. Make use of the Go Back and Go Forward buttons at the top of the Browser, as well, to move back to a previous location or forward to the next.

Working with the CommandBar Collections

CommandBar collections work just like collections of any other type of object. The only difficult issue is that a CommandBar object can contain a collection of

CommandBarControl objects, each of which might contain a single CommandBar object itself, accessed through the CommandBar property of the control. The simple procedure in Listing 11.4, from basEnumerate, lists all the members of the CommandBars collection to the Immediate window. You'll see right away that very few of the available CommandBar objects are actually visible. (Imagine the chaos that would ensue if all command bars were visible all the time!) Most likely, only the menu bar and one or two other CommandBar objects are visible when you run this code. Any CommandBar object with its Visible property set to True will be visible in Access.

Listing 11.4

```
Sub ListAllCBRs()
    Dim cbr As CommandBar
    For Each cbr In CommandBars
        Debug.Print cbr.Name, cbr.Visible
    Next cbr
End Sub
```

Perusing Controls on a CommandBar

Each CommandBar object contains a collection of controls, and you can enumerate the elements of this collection, as well. The example in Listing 11.5 prints a list of all the CommandBar objects, as well as the caption and type of each of the controls on each command bar.

To make the output from the procedure a bit more useful, it accepts an optional Boolean parameter. This parameter allows you to control whether the procedure displays all command bars or just the visible ones. If you want to see the list of visible command bars, either call it with no parameter or send it a True value (the default). If you want to see them all, pass a False value for the parameter.

Figure 11.5 shows the output from DumpCBRs (Listing 11.5, in basEnumerate). If you study the output, you'll see that most of the items on the Visual Basic command bar are type 1 (msoControlButton), although the first item is type 14 (msoControlSplitButtonMRUPopup). You can create your own items of type 1, but you won't be able to create your own type 14s (at least, not in this version of Access). Also, note that all the items on the CommandBar that are displayed as a menu are type 10 (msoControlPopup), as they should be. This is the type you'll find for all pop-up menus.

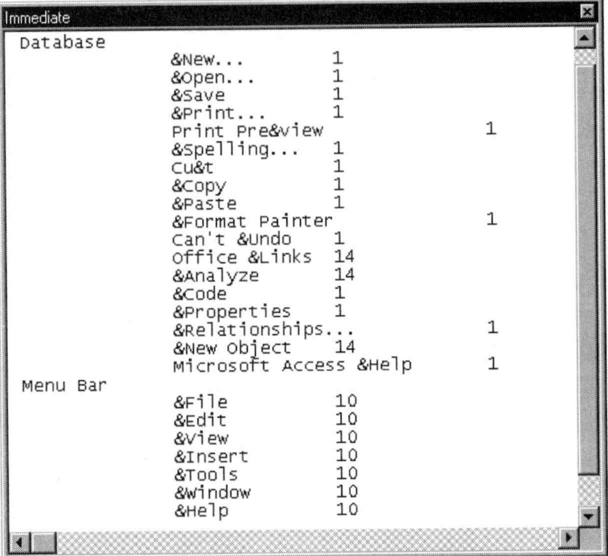

FIGURE 11.5: DumpCBRs provides a list of menu items and their types.

TIP

You can use any datatype for an optional parameter in VBA. The IsMissing function, however, works only with variants. If you want to pass a nonvariant optional parameter, don't count on using IsMissing to check for its existence. Instead, supply a default value directly in the procedure's formal declaration. This is how the DumpCBRs procedure works.

Listing 11.5

```
Public Sub DumpCBRs(Optional VisibleOnly As Boolean = True)
    Dim cbr As CommandBar
    Dim cbc As CommandBarControl

    For Each cbr In CommandBars
        If VisibleOnly Imp cbr.Visible Then
            Debug.Print cbr.Name
            For Each cbc In cbr.Controls
                If VisibleOnly Imp cbc.Visible Then
                    Debug.Print , cbc.Caption, cbc.Type
                End If
```

```
            Next cbc
        End If
    Next cbr
End Sub
```

NOTE

The Imp operator is an odd one—it's a seldom-used logical operator that returns a True value in all cases *except* when the first parameter is True and the second is False. In this case, you want to display all command bars except when the VisibleOnly flag is True and the object's Visible property is set to False. You want to hide the object from the output only in that single case. You could get the same effect with a more complex logical expression, but the Imp operator is elegant and does exactly what you need in this example.

Looking at All Menu Items

The final example procedure in this section, DumpAllMenus (Listing 11.6, from basEnumerate), prints a list of all the items on the Access menus or on a specific pop-up menu. It displays each item's caption and its menu ID. DumpAllMenus calls the DumpMenu procedure to list items on a particular pop-up menu. That procedure calls itself recursively if it finds a control for which the type is CommandBarPopup on the current pop-up menu. (None of the Access menus are nested more than two levels deep, but you could nest your own menus more deeply than that and this procedure would still work correctly.)

You can call DumpAllMenus a number of ways. You can pass it no parameters, and it lists all the items on all the top-level pop-up menus and their nested menus. You can also pass the name of a top-level submenu (File, Edit, Help, and so on), and DumpAllMenus will list all the items on that particular pop-up menu.

NOTE

Because this procedure uses the particular pop-up menu name to obtain a reference to the menu, it will work only with the English-language version of Access. Access maintains English and localized versions for the names of all the built-in command bars themselves, but not for all the controls on those menus. If you look in the Object Browser, you'll see that CommandBar objects expose both a Name and a NameLocal property, but these are the only objects that include both names. For the most part, you cannot refer to CommandBar subobjects by name. Instead, you need to use the FindControl method, discussed in the section "Referring to Items Other Than Top-Level CommandBars" a little later in this chapter.

Listing 11.6

```
PublicSub DumpAllMenus(Optional TopMenu As String = "Menu Bar")
    Dim cbr As CommandBar
    Dim cbp As CommandBarPopup

    Set cbr = CommandBars("Menu Bar")
    If TopMenu <> "Menu Bar" Then
        Set cbp = cbr.Controls(TopMenu)
        Call DumpMenu(cbp, 1)
    Else
        For Each cbp In cbr.Controls
            Debug.Print cbp.Caption
            Call DumpMenu(cbp, 1)
        Next cbp
    End If
End Sub

PrivateSub DumpMenu(cbp As CommandBarPopup, intLevel As Integer)
    Dim cbc As CommandBarControl
    Dim intI As Integer

    For Each cbc In cbp.CommandBar.Controls
        ' Insert enough spaces to indent according to the
        ' level of recursion.
        For intI = 0 To intLevel
            Debug.Print "    ";
        Next intI
        Debug.Print cbc.Caption, cbc.Id
        If cbc.Type = msoControlPopup Then
            ' Call this routine recursively, to document
            ' the next-lower level.
            Call DumpMenu(cbc.Control, intLevel + 1)
        End If
    Next cbc
End Sub
```

NOTE

Because DumpAllMenus is only a diagnostic tool, it includes no error handling. In a real application, this sort of routine would need to trap for the error that would occur if the caller supplied an invalid menu name.

TIP

In the basDumpIDs module in the sample database, you'll find a procedure (DumpIDs) that fills the contents of the tblControlID table in the database with a list of all the built-in menu items and the Id property of each. You'll need this information later if you want to programmatically control any of the built-in menu items. Run this procedure once (you can just place the cursor inside the procedure, and then press F5 to run it) to fill the table and then use it to find the ID you need.

Referring to CommandBars and Their Items

Because there's no simple way for you to know which items exist in any given CommandBar's collection of items, you'll need to take some special steps to obtain a reference to a specific object within Access' hierarchy of CommandBars. The following sections discuss the various techniques you can use to point at the object you need.

Referring to CommandBars

To make it easy for you to retrieve a reference to a specific top-level CommandBar object, you can refer to the object by its English name. Even though your application may be translated into a local language other than English, the English references will work (just as they do for the GetOption and SetOption methods, which require string parameters). That is, the following code will work in any localized version of Access:

```
Dim cbr As CommandBar
Set cbr = CommandBars("Menu Bar")
```

On the other hand, it won't be very useful when working with CommandBars and their objects to attempt to use syntax like this:

```
Set cbr = CommandBars(0)
```

unless your intent is to iterate through all the CommandBars. Although you can refer to an element of the CommandBars collection by its ordinal position in the collection, you won't want to, for the most part. When you start Access (or any Office application), the CommandBars collection contains all the built-in items, and the application hides and shows them as necessary. Therefore, you can't figure out an item's index by looking at a menu or toolbar; all the hidden items take up an index "slot," as well. Instead, you'll most often refer to elements at the CommandBar level by name and, at lower levels, using the techniques shown in the next section.

Referring to Items Other Than Top-Level CommandBars

Unfortunately, objects other than top-level CommandBar objects expose only their local name, not their English name, so you'll need to take extra steps to find a particular object within a command bar. If you attempt to refer to items on a command bar by their English names, your code won't work in any other localized version of Access. If you don't care about this issue, you can build long strings of references, working your way through the collections. For example, to obtain a reference to the Tools ➢ Analyze ➢ Table menu item, you could use code like this:

```
Dim cbc As CommandBarControl
Set cbc = CommandBars("Menu Bar"). _
 Controls("Tools").CommandBar.Controls("Analyze"). _
 CommandBar.Controls("Table")
```

On the other hand, if you need to be able to find a specific control in any localized version of Access, you'll use the FindControl method. This method, of either the CommandBars collection or of a specific CommandBar object, makes it possible to find the exact CommandBarControl object you need.

The syntax for the FindControl method looks like this:

object.FindControl(*Type*, *Id*, *Tag*, *Visible*, *Recursive*)

For this method, all the arguments are optional, but you must at least supply one of Type, Id, and Tag. Table 11.10 describes each of the parameters.

Why is the FindControl method available to the entire CommandBars collection and to specific CommandBar objects as well? If you need to find a control and you don't know on which command bar the user has placed it, code like this will search all CommandBar objects until it finds a match:

```
Set cbc = CommandBars.FindControl(Id:=123, Recursive:=True)
```

WARNING Be careful how you specify the parameters for the FindControl method, if you're searching the entire CommandBars collection. Be sure to *completely* identify the control for which you're searching.

If you want to search just a particular CommandBar object, you'll want to use code like this:

```
Dim cbrMenu as CommandBar
Dim cbcDebug as CommandBarControl
Set cbrMenu = CommandBars("Menu Bar")
' Find the "Hide the Office Assistant" menu item.
Set cbcDebug = cbrMenu.FindControl(Id:=1004, _
 Recursive:=True)
```

TIP

Although using the ID of a menu command is the only way to search for and find a specific built-in menu item, it's not a worry-free technique. Because you have no guarantee that a given menu's Id property won't change from version to version, you're leaving yourself open to maintainability problems if you use the ID directly. Unfortunately, you have no other choice if you want to find and modify an existing menu item. For menu items you create, you'll use the value you've set in the Tag property instead, so there will be no issues of upgradability. Of course, you can set the Tag property of a built-in menu item using the Access user interface (right-click on the item in Customize mode and choose the Properties item from the menu), but that doesn't help if you want to write an application to work on many users' machines.

TABLE 11.10: Parameters for the FindControl Method*

Parameter	Description
Type	The type of control to be searched for. Must be one of the items from the mso-ControlType enumeration list from the Object Browser. Supply the constant value indicating for which control type you're searching.
Id	The identifier of the control you're searching for. This is useful only if you're searching for a built-in control. Use the values from tblControlID. (Create this table by running DumpIDs in basDumpIDs in the sample database.)
Tag	The tag value of the control you're searching for. You're most likely to use this parameter if you're searching for a control your code created (and you set the Tag property when you created it).
Visible	Set to True to search only for visible controls. The default value is False.
Recursive	Set to True to include the selected object and all its subcommand bars in the search. The default is False.

*Applies both to the CommandBars collection or a specific CommandBar object

Tips to Get You Started

If you've made it this far, you at least have a basic concept of what a CommandBar object is and how menu items hang off a CommandBar. The following sections contain a number of small tidbits, some with longer explanations, to help you further in your exploration of CommandBars. Using CommandBars is such a large topic, and it is so rich with possibilities, there's no way we can cover all the options here. But these sections contain all the information you need to get started, and studying the examples is a great way to begin on your own CommandBar projects.

Referring to CommandBarControl Captions

You can use item names without the ampersand (&) (indicating the position of the hot key), and the names are not case-sensitive. In addition, the trailing "..." included on some menu items is significant: if it's on the menu, you must include it in your object reference. (This tip really applies only if you're searching for the menu control by name. That's not a good idea if your intent is to write an application that will work in multiple localized languages.)

Everything's a Control

The objects on a given CommandBar are all controls. Whether you're displaying the command bar as a toolbar or a menu bar, most elements are command buttons. (The difference between a toolbar and a menu is how the button is displayed.) Toolbars can also display controls besides command buttons (drop-down lists, for example); menus cannot.

Divide and Conquer

Divider lines in menus and spaces in toolbars aren't counted as controls. To indicate to the CommandBar that you want a divider line before a control, set the control's BeginGroup property to True. The divider/space has no effect on any item counts, nor does it affect indexes within collections.

For example, in Listing 11.7 (from basCommandBars) a divider line is inserted before the third item ("Get External Data") on the command bar referred to by cbrPopup (the pop-up menu hanging off the first control on the main menu bar, the File menu). This example also demonstrates three different techniques you can use to refer to items on a command bar. Make sure to single-step through this procedure, and look at the menus in Access (not in the VBA development environment) during the procedure to see what's going on.

TIP

To single-step through a procedure, place your cursor somewhere inside the procedure and press F8 to execute each line of code. This technique works only when the procedure doesn't expect any parameters.

Listing 11.7

```
Public Sub StartGroup()
    ' Start a new group by setting the BeginGroup
    ' property.
    Dim cbrMain As CommandBar
    Dim cbrPopup As CommandBar
    Set cbrMain = CommandBars("Menu Bar")
    Set cbrPopup = cbrMain.Controls("File").CommandBar
    cbrPopup.Controls("Get External Data").BeginGroup = True

    ' or

    With CommandBars("Menu Bar")
        With .Controls("File").CommandBar
            .Controls("Get External Data").BeginGroup = True
        End With
    End With

    ' or

    ' Turn it off now.
    CommandBars("Menu Bar"). _
     Controls("File").CommandBar. _
     Controls("Get External Data").BeginGroup = False
End Sub
```

Roll Your Own? We Think Not

The controls used on command bars are specific to their implementation and aren't ActiveX controls, intrinsic Access controls, or Office forms controls. You cannot create your own control types, nor can you add to the list of controls that you can place on Access' command bars. You can add buttons and edit controls, drop-down lists, combo boxes, and pop-up menus. That's it.

Head Them Off at the Pass

Once you've set up command bars in your applications, you may not want to allow users to modify them. There's no simple way to accomplish this, because there are several ways for them to get there. Users can

- Choose the Tools ➢ Customize menu item
- Right-click on an existing command bar and choose Customize
- Choose the View ➢ Toolbars ➢ Customize menu item

To completely turn off the capability of customizing command bars, you'll have to remove all three opportunities.

The first step should be easy: simply disable the Tools ➢ Customize menu item. If you're only working in English language versions of Access, it *is* easy. You can use code like this:

```
CommandBars("Menu Bar"). _
 Controls("Tools").CommandBar. _
 Controls("Customize...").Enabled = False
```

If you're concerned about having your code work in any version of Access, however, you'll need to use the FindControl method mentioned in the section "Referring to Items Other Than Top-Level CommandBars," earlier in this chapter. In this case, it's even more complicated by the fact that the Customize menu item, with the same Id value, appears in several locations on various command bars. You want to disable the particular one that's hanging on the Tools menu. Therefore, you cannot simply start at the top-level menu bar and recursively search menus until you find the item you need. You must start at the Tools pop-up menu and look through only its items, like this:

```
Dim cbc As CommandBarControl

' 797 is the ID of the Tools|Customize menu item.
' Find the "Customize..." item on the Tools menu.
Set cbc = CommandBars("Menu Bar"). _
 Controls("Tools").CommandBar. _
 FindControl(ID:=797, Recursive:=False)
If Not cbc Is Nothing Then
    cbc.Enabled = False
End If
```

What about the right-click menu on any command bar? That's a bit trickier, as it's not obvious what to disable to make that go away. It turns out that there's a command bar named Toolbar List which is what you see when you right-click on a command bar. If you disable that particular command bar, right-clicking on a command bar does nothing at all. Therefore, to turn off the right-click capability, you could write code like this:

```
CommandBars("Toolbar List").Enabled = False
```

And what about the third option, the View ➢ Toolbars menu item? Disabling the Toolbar List command bar disables this menu item, as well, so you're all done.

TIP

Don't go looking for the Toolbar List command bar in the list of available CommandBar objects, because it won't be there. The Toolbar List command bar is created dynamically for you, so you'll never find it there, except from within a running application's code.

To make it easy for you, we've provided, in basCommandBars, a procedure that takes care of all this. Listing 11.8 shows the HandleCustomizations procedure—if you pass it False or no parameter at all, it disables the three items you need to disable to disallow customizations. If you pass it True, it re-enables those items.

Listing 11.8

```
Public Sub HandleCustomizations( _
 Optional EnableIt As Boolean = False)
    Dim cbr As CommandBar
    Dim cbc As CommandBarControl

    ' 797 is the ID of the Tools|Customize menu item,
    ' but that ID is used in several places. You can't
    ' simply start at the Menu Bar and search from there.
    ' You must start at the Tools menu explicitly.

    ' Find the "Customize..." item on the Tools menu.
    Set cbc = CommandBars("Menu Bar"). _
     Controls("Tools").CommandBar. _
     FindControl(ID:=797, Recursive:=False)
    If Not cbc Is Nothing Then
        cbc.Enabled = EnableIt
    End If
    CommandBars("Toolbar List").Enabled = EnableIt
End Sub
```

IDs and Actions

A built-in CommandBar item's Id property indicates the action that control will take when it's selected, and it also indicates the image that appears on the built-in item by default. In addition, you can use the FaceId property to set just the image displayed on a control without affecting the action it takes. Finally, the OnAction property allows you to override the built-in action for any control that can take an action. The following list details the interactions between the three properties:

- You can use the Add method of a CommandBar's Controls collection, setting the Id parameter to match the ID of a built-in control to indicate that your control should match the appearance and action of the built-in control. This property is read-only once you've added the control to its collection. See DumpIDs in basDumpIDs to create a complete list of controls' Id values.
- You can use the FaceId property of a control to set its appearance to match one of the built-in controls. If you want to look at various FaceIds and their icons, run the ShowFaceIds procedure in basShowFaceIds. This procedure creates opens the command bar named Demo FaceIDs (it creates the command bar for you if you haven't run this procedure already). The code adds buttons to the command bar and sets the FaceId property of each to be a specific FaceId. Office includes several thousand FaceIds you could use, so be prepared to wait if you want to see them all.
- You can use the OnAction property of a control to specify an action that can override the action provided by the Id property for the control. See the next section for more information on using the OnAction property. If you want to take an action, you'll need to set the OnAction property to call a macro or a function that performs the action.

To make it easier for you to work with menu ID values, we've included the DumpIDs procedure, in basDumpIDs. This procedure writes all the Id property values to tblControlID, allowing you to find the exact ID value you need.

Using the OnAction Property

Use the OnAction property of CommandBarControl objects to execute an action when you select the item. The property can contain a string expression resolving to either the name of a macro (supply just the macro name, as a string) or a function call, in the form

```
=FunctionName()
```

(You can also just enter the function name without the leading "=" and the trailing "()".)

To cause a menu item to be checked, or to create a two-state button, the control must have its OnAction property set to call something. (To see two-state buttons in action, check out the View menu when the database window is selected; the Large Icons, Small Icons, List, and Details items all use a two-state button to indicate the current setting.)

See the next section for an example using the OnAction property.

Creating Your Own Menu Items

To create your own item on a menu (or toolbar), you use the Add method of a CommandBar object, which returns to you a reference to the new CommandBar-Control object. Once you've created the new CommandBarControl object, you need to set its properties so it does what you need. You must at least set the Caption property so the control displays a caption. You should also set either the Id property so the control emulates one of the built-in controls, set the OnAction property so the item does something when you select it, or use a WithEvents reference to the control so you can react to its Change or Click event. You can also set any or all of the other CommandBarControl properties described in the Object Browser and online help.

For example, the code in Listing 11.9 (from basCustomItem) adds a menu item with the caption "Minimize Window" to the File menu, right before the Save item. The menu item will call the MinimizeIt function when it's selected. The code also sets the item's Tag property to match its caption so you'll be able to use the FindControl method later if you need to find the menu item again. To show that this works, the code also adds a Maximize Window menu item, using the FindControl method to find the previously added control and adding the new item right above it.

Listing 11.9

```
PublicSub AddMinimize()

    ' Demonstrate creating a new menu item.

    Dim cbr As CommandBar
    Dim cbc As CommandBarControl
```

```
Dim cbcFile As CommandBarControl
Dim cbcSave As CommandBarControl
Dim cbcMinimize As CommandBarControl

Set cbr = CommandBars("Menu Bar")

' Search for the top-level File menu.
Set cbcFile = cbr.FindControl(ID:=30002, Recursive:=False)

' Search for the "Save" item on the File menu.
Set cbcSave = cbr.FindControl(ID:=3, Recursive:=True)

If Not cbcFile Is Nothing Then
    If cbcSave Is Nothing Then
        ' Add the item to the end of the menu.
        ' This shouldn't happen, but it never
        ' hurts to add "sanity checking" code.
        Set cbc = cbcFile.CommandBar.Controls.Add( _
         msoControlButton)
    Else
        ' Add the item before the Save item.
        Set cbc = cbcFile.CommandBar.Controls.Add( _
         msoControlButton, Before:=cbcSave.Index)
    End If
    With cbc
        .Caption = "Minimize Window"
        .OnAction = "MinimizeIt"
        ' Set the Tag property, so you can
        ' get back to this item later using FindControl.
        .Tag = "Minimize Window"
    End With
End If
' Now, find the item you just added, and add a
' new item below it. Of course, you don't really have to
' search for the control here - you've already got it
' referred to in the cbc variable. Just trying to
' prove a point here.
Set cbcMinimize = cbr.FindControl( _
 Tag:="Minimize Window", Recursive:=True)
If Not cbcMinimize Is Nothing Then
    Set cbc = cbcFile.CommandBar.Controls.Add( _
     msoControlButton, Before:=cbcMinimize.Index)
```

```
            With cbc
                .Caption = "Maximize Window"
                .OnAction = "MaximizeIt"
                ' Set the Tag property, so you can
                ' get back to this item later using FindControl.
                .Tag = "Maximize Window"
            End With
        End If
    End Sub

    Public Sub ResetMenus()
        ' Use this procedure to reset your menus.
        CommandBars("Menu Bar").Reset
    End Sub
```

TIP

When working with CommandBars, you'll often want to reset the main menu bar. To do so, include a subroutine like the ResetMenus procedure in Listing 11.9. That way, all you need to do is place your cursor in the routine and press F5 to run it; your menu bars will be reset to their "factory" state. You can get the same effect from the user interface, but in this case, code is simpler.

Reacting to Command Bar Control Events

Although you can set the OnAction property of a command bar control to be the name of a macro or a function, this gives you little flexibility. What if you want to pass some information to that function? The OnAction property makes that difficult.

A better alternative may be to react to the Click event of a CommandBarButton control or the Change event of the CommandBarComboBox control. Just like normal controls, these controls raise these specific events at the appropriate times.

The issue, then, is to find a way to allow your code to react to the events these controls raise. Unlike normal controls, these have no event properties on the Property window, and they don't show up in the list of objects (the left-hand combo box in the VBA editor). To react to the events of these controls, you'll need to use the WithEvents keyword when you define the variable that refers to the control. If you look in the class module attached to frmCustomer, you'll see the following declaration at the top:

```
Private WithEvents cboNames As CommandBarComboBox
```

Once you've entered a reference like this, your code can react to events of the object you've referred to using WithEvents. In this example, when the control's Change event occurs, its event procedure calls the FindRowFromEvent procedure, passing a reference to the control itself, like this:

```
Private Sub cboNames_Change( _
 ByVal Ctrl As CommandBarComboBox)
    Call FindRowFromEvent(Ctrl)
End Sub
```

The only step left is to attach the cboNames variable to the actual control. In the example, when the code creates the combo box on the command bar, it assigns the reference to the control it created into cboNames. From then on, any time you refer to cboNames, you're actually working with the combo box on the command bar.

At this point, whenever anyone changes the value of the combo box on the command bar, the control's Change event will be raised, and its Change event procedure will be run, locating the row corresponding to the selected customer.

TIP

WithEvents, and sinking events raised by objects, works only in class modules (and therefore, form modules). If you want to use this technique, the WithEvents variable and its event procedure(s) must exist within a class module of some sort.

Working with Other CommandBarControl Objects

Although most of the controls you'll use on command bars will be command buttons, you may want to place an edit box or a combo box on a command bar. Each control has its own set of properties and methods, but the combo box control is interesting and useful.

The sample form, frmCustomers, creates a new command bar with a few normal command button controls (Print, Filter By Form, Filter By Selection, Apply Filter), and a combo box control as well. The combo box (actually, a drop-down list, which acts like a combo box but doesn't allow you to add new items) lists all the last names for all the rows displayed in the form's recordset and allows you to select a row to view. Listing 11.10 contains the code used to create the CommandBar and its controls. Note that this example uses WithEvents to react to the Change event of the combo box. In the Change event procedure, the code calls the FindRowFromEvent procedure. Listing 11.11 contains the code for that function, found in the basCallback module.

TIP

Take some time to investigate the properties of the CommandBarComboBox control; it works more like the Visual Basic combo box than any Access control. In addition, it includes some new properties, such as the Style property, that control how it appears on the command bar. (Although we've used the msoControlDropDown constant when creating this control, it's still a CommandBarComboBox control.)

Listing 11.10

```
Private WithEvents cboNames As CommandBarComboBox

Private Sub cboNames_Change(ByVal Ctrl As CommandBarComboBox)
    Call FindRowFromEvent(Ctrl)
End Sub

Private Sub Form_Load()
    Dim cbr As CommandBar
    Dim ctl As CommandBarControl

    ' Note that a form's recordset
    ' is a DAO recordset, in an MDB.
    Dim rst As DAO.Recordset

    ' Create the new commandbar.
    Set cbr = CommandBars.Add("Customers", _
     Position:=msoBarTop, Temporary:=True)

    ' Copy items from the Form View commandbar
    ' to the new commandbar.
    With CommandBars("Form View").Controls
        .Item("Print...").Copy cbr
        .Item("Filter By Selection").Copy cbr
        .Item("Filter By Form").Copy cbr
        .Item("Toggle Filter").Copy cbr
    End With

    Set cboNames = cbr.Controls.Add( _
     Type:=msoControlDropdown, Before:=1)

    With cboNames
```

```
            .Tag = "CustomerID"
            .Caption = "Select Customer &Lastname:"
            .Style = msoComboLabel
            ' Use the default width for the dropdown.
            .DropDownWidth = -1

            Set rst = Me.RecordsetClone
            Do While Not rst.EOF
                .AddItem rst!LastName
                rst.MoveNext
            Loop
            ' Although you could specify
            ' the OnAction property here,
            ' you can use WithEvents to
            ' trap the events of the combo box
            ' instead. This allows you more
            ' flexibility.
            ' .OnAction = "FindRowInActiveControl"
        End With
        Me.Toolbar = "Customers"
    End Sub
```

Listing 11.11

```
Public Function FindRowFromEvent( _
 cbc As CommandBarComboBox)
    ' Function called from the Change event
    ' of the frmCustomers commandbar control.

    ' Recordsets behind forms in MDB files
    ' must be DAO recordsets, not ADO.
    Dim rst As DAO.Recordset
    Dim strID As String

    strID = cbc.Text
    If Len(strID) > 0 Then
        With Screen.ActiveForm
            Set rst = .RecordsetClone
            rst.FindFirst "LastName = " & FixQuotes(strID)
            If Not rst.NoMatch Then
```

```
                .Bookmark = rst.Bookmark
                Call AddToListHeader(cbc)
            End If
            ' Reset the control to have
            ' no item selected.
            cbc.ListIndex = 0
        End With
    End If
End Function

Private Function FixQuotes(varValue As Variant)
    ' Double any quotes inside varValue, and
    ' surround it with quotes.
    FixQuotes = """" & _
     Replace(varValue & "", """", """""") & """"
End Function
```

In Listing 11.10, the following code creates the new command bar object, sets it to appear docked at the top, and marks it as temporary:

```
Set cbr = CommandBars.Add("Customers", _
 Position:=msoBarTop, Temporary:=True)
```

The code then copies command bar controls from the Form View command bar to the new command bar. Notice that the syntax for the Copy method is somewhat odd—you call the Copy method of the control you're copying from and pass as a parameter the CommandBar object you're copying to:

```
With CommandBars("Form View").Controls
    .Item("Print...").Copy cbr
    .Item("Filter By Selection").Copy cbr
    .Item("Filter By Form").Copy cbr
    .Item("Toggle Filter").Copy cbr
End With
```

Next, the code creates a new CommandBarControl object, the drop-down list of last names. The code places the new control before the first control, thereby placing it at the beginning of the new command bar:

```
Set cboNames = cbr.Controls.Add( _
 Type:=msoControlDropdown, Before:=1)
```

The code sets properties of the new control, and adds all the data to its list:

```
With cboNames
    .Tag = "CustomerID"
    .Caption = "Select Customer &Lastname:"
    .Style = msoComboLabel
    ' Use the default width for the dropdown.
    .DropDownWidth = -1

    Set rst = Me.RecordsetClone
    Do While Not rst.EOF
        .AddItem rst!LastName
        rst.MoveNext
    Loop
End With
```

Finally, the code sets the form's Toolbar property to refer to the new CommandBar object, so that it will appear in place of the Form View command bar:

```
Me.Toolbar = "Customers"
```

In addition, to make this example a bit more interesting, the FindRowFromEvent function creates a collection of most recently used key values in the combo box. The CommandBarComboBox control allows you to create a dividing line in the list of items in the control. You can place items above the line or below it. In this case, once you've selected a key value, the code in AddToListHeader (see Listing 11.12) adds the selected item to the top of the list. Like many solutions, this one assumes that if you once wanted to find a particular row, you're likely to want to find that row again. By creating a most recently used list, you can quickly return to any of the rows you've already visited.

Listing 11.12

```
Private mcolFound As Collection

Private Function AddToListHeader( _
 cbc As CommandBarComboBox) As Boolean

    ' Add item to the header of the list if it's
    ' not already there, and return True if the
    ' item got added.
```

```
    On Error Resume Next
    Dim strID As String

    ' If this is the first time through here,
    ' you'll need to instantiate this Collection object.
    If mcolFound Is Nothing Then
        Set mcolFound = New Collection
    End If

    ' Get the selected text and
    ' add it to the internal collection of values.
    ' If it's already in the list, Err.Number
    ' will be non-zero.
    strID = cbc.Text
    mcolFound.Add strID, Key:=strID

    ' Yes, this code should be smarter about errors.
    ' It's only example code!
    If Err.Number <> 0 Then
        AddToListHeader = False
    Else
        ' Add the ID to the combo box on the command bar.
        ' Always add it at the top of the list.
        Call cbc.AddItem(strID, 1)

        ' The ListHeaderCount will be -1 the first time
        ' you come through here, indicating no divider
        ' line at all. If ListHeaderCount is 0, you
        ' have a divider line with nothing above it.
        ' This code either increments the value of the
        ' property, or sets it to be 1 in the first place.
        If cbc.ListHeaderCount > 0 Then
            cbc.ListHeaderCount = cbc.ListHeaderCount + 1
        Else
            cbc.ListHeaderCount = 1
        End If
        AddToListHeader = True
    End If
End Function
```

Making Things Happen

What if you want to execute the code associated with an item on a command bar without actually clicking on it? To cause a CommandBarControl object to execute its action, you can use the object's Execute method. For example, the following fragment will run the Table Analyzer Wizard:

```
CommandBars("Menu Bar").Controls("Tools"). _
 CommandBar.Controls("Analyze"). _
 CommandBar.Controls("Table").Execute
```

There are some problems here, however:

- Do you really want to type in and debug a command like this to simply execute a menu command?
- What about applications that must run in various localized versions of Access? In German, you won't find a Tools menu, so you'll need to use the FindControl method mentioned earlier in the chapter.
- What if the user has removed the menu item you're trying to execute? There's nothing, in general, keeping a user from removing any item from any command bar by using the user interface. If you attempt to use the Execute method of a command bar control that doesn't exist, you'll only trigger a runtime error.

To avoid these issues, Access provides the RunCommand method of the DoCmd object. To use RunCommand, you find the acCmd… constant corresponding to the menu item you'd like to execute, and use that instead. For example, the previous example turns into the following line of code:

```
DoCmd.RunCommand acCmdAnalyzeTable
```

No matter what language you're working with, no matter what the user has done to the command bars, this code will work as if the user had selected the corresponding menu item.

So what's wrong with RunCommand? (By now, you know that almost every alternative in Access has at least a minor down side.) Using RunCommand requires you to know the corresponding acCmd… constant. At this point, there's no simple way to find, for a given CommandBarControl, the associated RunCommand constant. Not only is this difficult programmatically, it's difficult manually, as well. Microsoft doesn't provide a reasonable mapping of menu items to RunCommand options, so you're guessing until testing. In addition, if your code is handed a

CommandBarControl object, there's no simple way to map that control to its equivalent RunCommand constant.

Given all these issues, the Execute method will come in handy if you've got a reference to the CommandBarControl and you want to "make it happen." You can also use this technique if you need to take an action that isn't normally available in the current context. The Execute method doesn't take the context into account, so you must take extra care when using it.

TIP

Be aware that you give up some readability and maintainability if you use this technique rather than the RunCommand method. That is, using the specific acCmd... constant in your code will make it explicitly clear what that code will do. Using the Execute method of a CommandBarControl object implicitly specifies the action, but you'll need to include a comment indicating what's actually going on.

For example, the code in Listing 11.13 (from basCommandBars) displays the Properties window, but only if the menu item is currently visible. This is one case in which it makes sense to use the Execute method; you have to get to the menu item to check its visibility anyway, so once there, you can just perform its Execute method. Listing 11.13 demonstrates this technique for finding a particular built-in menu item and executing its action. (You could, of course, just use RunCommand to accomplish the same task. If you use that technique, however, you can't check the visibility of the menu item first.)

To test this procedure, first select the Database window, then run ShowPropertiesWindow. Because the menu item isn't visible when you've selected the Database window, the code won't do anything. Open a form in Design view, make sure the Properties window is closed, and then repeat the code. This time, because the menu item is visible, running the code makes the Properties window visible by calling the Execute method of the menu item.

Listing 11.13

```
Public Sub ShowPropertiesWindow()
    ' Show the Properties Window, but only if the menu
    ' item is visible.
    Dim cbcProperties As CommandBarControl

    With CommandBars("Menu Bar")
        ' Find the Properties Window menu item.
```

```
            Set cbcProperties = .FindControl(ID:=222, _
             Recursive:=True)
        End With
        If cbcProperties Is Nothing Then
            MsgBox "Unable to find the requested menu item!"
        Else
            With cbcProperties
                ' If the menu item is visible, execute
                ' its action (that is, display the
                ' Properties Window).
                If .Visible Then
                    .Execute
                End If
            End With
        End If
    End Sub
```

Handling Missing RunCommand Constants

We count on the Microsoft developers to provide a RunCommand constant for each and every menu item that they add to the product. Because there's no one-to-one mapping available, it's hard to prove that they've done this correctly. While writing this chapter, we noticed that there's at least one constant missing: there's no adCmd… constant corresponding to the File ➢ Print Relationships menu item. (Yes, we're happy that you can print relationships in this version—too bad you can't do it programmatically!)

What's the solution then? If you have an application that needs to print relationships from within the application, you can't simply use the Execute method of the control, even if you use the FindControl method to find it. Because a user may have removed that menu item from the user interface, calling its Execute method will fail if it's not there. (Note that using the RunCommand method will work, even if the user has removed the control from the command bar.)

We don't have a perfect solution, but here's a suggestion: attempt to use the Execute method. If that fails, you'll need to add the menu item back to the command bar, perhaps hidden, so you can execute it. It's ugly, but it should work. (If you want to do this, you'll need to use the Id value of the built-in menu item, which is 3840. We found this using the DumpCBIds procedure and looking in tblControlID.)

Continued on next page

The following procedure (from basCommandBars) demonstrates how you can call a menu item for which you can't find a RunCommand constant, using the Execute method of the command bar control:

```
Public Sub CallPrintRelationShips()
    Dim cbc As CommandBarControl
    Dim cbrMain As CommandBar
    Dim cbr As CommandBar

    On Error Resume Next
    Set cbrMain = CommandBars("Menu Bar")

    ' Attempt to find the Print Relationships menu item.
    Set cbc = cbrMain.FindControl(ID:=3840, Recursive:=True)

    ' If someone removed it, cbc is Nothing.
    ' In that case, attempt to add it back,
    ' temporarily, hidden.
    If cbc Is Nothing Then
        Set cbr = cbrMain.Controls("File").CommandBar
        Set cbc = cbr.Controls.Add( _
         msoControlButton, ID:=3840, Temporary:=True)
    End If
    ' If cbc is STILL Nothing, there's not much
    ' left you can do. Just error out. Otherwise,
    ' use its Execute method.
    If cbc Is Nothing Then
        MsgBox "Unable to print relationships!"
    Else
        cbc.Execute
    End If
End Sub
```

Actually, you don't need to do all this work for this one particular instance. The Print Relationships code exists in an Access Wizard, written in VBA. Because of that, you can call it directly, using Application.Run. In this case, call this code to run the Wizard:

```
Application.Run acwzlib.pr_entry
```

Although this shortcut solves the problem of the missing constant for this one item, if you run across other constants that are missing, you'll need to use the Execute method as shown above, instead.

Where Am I?

From within the code called by the string in the OnAction property, you can use the ActionControl property of the CommandBars collection to retrieve a reference to the control that called the code. This makes it possible to take different actions, depending on the menu or toolbar item that was just selected. If you've placed information in the control's Tag property, you can also use that in your code, once you've used the ActionControl property to find out just which control called the code. The example in the section "Checking/Unchecking a Menu Item" later in this chapter that shows how you can group menu items that use this property in order to know which item was just selected.

The demo form, frmCustomer, can use this property if you set the OnAction property of the CommandBarComboBox control (rather than reacting to its Change event directly). If you remove the WithEvents keyword from the definition of cboNames, look in the Form_Load event procedure for the form, and uncomment the line of code that sets the OnAction property, you'll end up calling the FindRowInActiveControl procedure when you select a name.

The FindRowInActiveControl procedure, in basCallback, does the same work as the code shown in Listing 11.11, except this procedure doesn't receive a parameter containing the control that triggered the event—it must use the CommandBars.ActionControl to get that information. The following two lines, in FindRowInActiveControl, show the only real differences between the two techniques:

```
Dim cbc As CommandBarComboBox

Set cbc = CommandBars.ActionControl
' Continue with code to find the correct row...
```

Doing Things the CommandBar Way

Once you've got the hang of working with CommandBars, you'll want to start using some advanced techniques to really get them to do what you need. It's not always obvious how to do that, however. The following sections provide some tips, hints, and suggestions on working with CommandBars programmatically in your applications.

Avoid Dots

As you work with CommandBar objects, you'll find that you're using very long strings of objects, connected with dots, to get to the object you care about. Because each dot takes some time to resolve, you'd do better to avoid using all those dots in your references. A better alternative is to either use the With...End With statement, or set an object variable to refer to the lowest object you can in the hierarchy.

To use an existing CommandBar object (for example, the menu hanging off the View ➢ Database Objects menu item), use code like this (in the English-language version of Access):

```
Dim cbr As CommandBar
Set cbr = CommandBars("Menu Bar").Controls("View"). _
 CommandBar.Controls("Database Objects").CommandBar
' Or, because popup menus are handled as command bars,
' you can also simply say:
Set cbr = CommandBars("Database Objects")
```

If you want to write code that will work in any localized version, you'll need to use the FindControl method of the CommandBar object:

```
Dim cbr As CommandBar
  ' Find the Database Objects popup menu.
Set cbr = CommandBars("Menu Bar").FindControl( _
 Id:=30107, Recursive:=True).CommandBar
```

This technique counts on your knowing the ID for each built-in menu item. Use the code in basDumpIDs to create tblControlID, a list of all the built-in ID values. Of course, as mentioned previously, you can use the Tag property to find a menu item you've created, as long as you set the Tag property when you create the item (or at least before you need to find the item).

Retrieving the Number of Items in a Menu

Your application may need to know the number of items on a menu. If you try writing simple code that retrieves the Count property of a given CommandBar, you'll get some odd results. This doesn't work because the Count property also includes all the items that aren't visible in the current context. You might use something like the function in Listing 11.14, from basCountItems, to retrieve the number of visible items on any command bar. (The TestCount procedure, shown in Listing 11.14 as well, demonstrates the use of GetMenuItemCount.)

WARNING

The meaning of the word *visible*, as it applies to command bar controls, can be misleading. Because of the new adaptive menu technology, the code in Listing 11.14 will count menu items that would appear if the menu were fully displayed (that is, expanded). Therefore, it's possible that the function will return item counts that differ from what you see, because adaptive menus have hidden items which are, for all other intents and purposes, visible.

Listing 11.14

```
PublicFunction GetMenuItemCount( _
 Optional cbr As CommandBar = Nothing, _
 Optional ByVal CountAll As Boolean = False) _
 As Integer

    Dim cbc As CommandBarControl
    Dim intCount As Integer

    ' If you've not specified the menu bar
    ' assume you want the top-level
    ' Menu Bar.
    If cbr Is Nothing Then
        Set cbr = CommandBars("Menu Bar")
    End If
    For Each cbc In cbr.Controls
        ' Increment the count if either
        ' you're counting all, or this item
        ' actually is visible.
        If CountAll Or cbc.Visible Then
            intCount = intCount + 1
        End If
    Next cbc
    GetMenuItemCount = intCount
End Function

PrivateSub TestCount()
    Debug.Print "Menu Bar     : "

    Debug.Print "   Visible   : " & _
     GetMenuItemCount(CommandBars("Menu Bar"))
    Debug.Print "       All   : " & _
     GetMenuItemCount(CommandBars("Menu Bar"), True)
    Debug.Print
    Debug.Print "File Menu    : "
    Debug.Print "   Visible   : " & _
     GetMenuItemCount(CommandBars("Menu Bar"). _
     Controls("File").CommandBar)
    Debug.Print "       All   : " & _
     GetMenuItemCount(CommandBars("Menu Bar"). _
     Controls("File").CommandBar, True)
End Sub
```

Disabling/Enabling a Menu Item

Disabling and enabling a menu item is as simple as changing the Enabled property of a control. Once you have a reference to the item you want to enable or disable, just set the value of its Enabled property, and you're all done.

To disable the Edit ➢ Undo Typing menu item programmatically, you might write code like the following. (Note that all the items that appear in the Undo slot share the same ID—Access simply changes the caption as necessary.)

```
Dim cbc As CommandBarControl
Set cbc = CommandBars("Menu Bar").FindControl _
 (Id:=128, Recursive:=True)
cbc.Enabled = False
```

Attempting to enable a menu item that Access wants disabled is a fruitless exercise. You're welcome to programmatically disable an enabled menu item, such as Edit ➢ Undo Typing, and Access will respect your changes. On the other hand, if you attempt to enable a menu item that Access thinks should be disabled, your change will be discarded without triggering an error. For example, attempting to enable the Edit ➢ Can't Undo menu item will have no effect as long as Access thinks it ought to be disabled. The same issues apply when you attempt to make a command bar visible; if Access doesn't want that item to be shown, nothing you can do will cause it to be displayed.

To try this out, open frmCustomer and note that the first item on the Edit menu (Can't Undo) is disabled. Click the Re-Enable Undo Command button on the form, and then check the menu item again—it's not enabled, is it? By setting the command bar control's Enabled property to be True, all you've done is told Access that it's welcome to handle the Enabled property itself. Type some text into a text box on the form and then check the menu item. Now it should be enabled. Click the Disable Undo Command button and check out the menu—now it's disabled. By setting its Enabled property to False, you've told Access that you want the menu item to be disabled. Click the Re-Enable Undo Command button, and the menu item will be enabled again.

Checking/Unchecking a Menu Item

From a CommandBarControl's point of view, the checked state of a menu item is the same as the selected state for a two-state toolbar button. For example, in Form Design view, the Align Left, Center, and Align Right toolbar buttons could also be represented on a menu, with one of the three items being checked. You won't find a Checked property in the Object Browser or online help, because it doesn't exist. Instead, you'll use the State property of a CommandBarControl object to control the checked condition. To work with the checked state, your selected control must follow some rules. It must

- Either have no specific value set for its Id property or have a value set that doesn't insert a picture to the left of the menu item. (You can also set the Style property so that the control doesn't display the associated image.)
- Not be a built-in control.
- Call a macro or function from its OnAction property.

So, when can you control the State property of a CommandBarControl? If you've created the item, set it up to call a macro or function when selected, and haven't set an image or explicitly hidden the image, you will be able to set its State property. If you attempt to set the State property for a built-in control, all you'll get for your efforts is a runtime error.

For example, the code in Listing 11.15 (from basCreateColors) creates a new menu containing five colors. Each item on the menu calls the HandleColors function when you select it, and that function places a check mark next to the selected item and clears the check for all other items. (Of course, in real life, you'd want the HandleColors routine to also perform some action in response to the menu selection.)

TIP

There's no simple way to implement an option group on a menu. As you can see in the HandleColors procedure, the only suggestion we have is to loop through all the items in the group (and you might use the Tag property of the grouped controls to indicate to you, in code, which ones are part of the group), and check and uncheck items as necessary.

Listing 11.15

```
Public Sub CreateColors()
    ' Create checked menus.
    Dim cbp As CommandBarPopup
    Dim varColors As Variant
    Dim intI As Integer

    ' Set up the array of colors.
    varColors = Array("Blue", "Green", "Pink", _
```

```
     "Yellow", "White")

    ' Create the top-level menu.
    Set cbp = CommandBars("Menu Bar").Controls.Add( _
    msoControlPopup, Temporary:=True)
    cbp.Caption = "&Color"

    ' Loop through the array, adding one menu item for
    ' each element of the array.
    With cbp.CommandBar.Controls
        For intI = LBound(varColors) To UBound(varColors)
            With .Add(msoControlButton)
                .Caption = varColors(intI)
                .OnAction = "HandleColors"
            End With
        Next intI
    End With
End Sub

Public Function HandleColors()
    ' Function called from OnAction property.
    Dim strCaption As String
    Dim cbc As CommandBarControl
    Dim cbcItem As CommandBarControl

    ' Get the selected control, and store its caption.
    Set cbc = CommandBars.ActionControl
    strCaption = cbc.Caption

    ' Loop through all the controls in the CommandBar
    ' object that's the parent of the selected control.
    For Each cbcItem In cbc.Parent.Controls
        With cbcItem
            ' Check the selected item, uncheck all the rest.
            If .Caption = cbc.Caption Then
                cbcItem.State = msoButtonDown
            Else
                cbcItem.State = msoButtonUp
            End If
        End With
    Next cbcItem
End Function
```

Changing the Text of a Menu Item

Using the CommandBar object model, you easily change the Caption property (and perhaps the ToolTipText, ShortCutText, and DescriptionText properties as well) of any control.

For example, to modify the text of the Edit ➢ Delete menu item, you could write code like this:

```
With CommandBars("Menu Bar"). _
 Controls("Edit").CommandBar.Controls("Delete")
    .Caption = "Remove"
    .ToolTipText = "Remove the selected item"
End With
```

Deleting a Menu Item

To delete a menu item, use the Delete method of a CommandBarControl—even a control on the main menu bar. (If the control is a CommandBarPopup control and has a menu hanging off it, the Delete method for the item will delete its child menu as well.)

Take note of these items:

- Think twice before deleting a menu item. It's easier in the long run to set a control's Visible property to False instead. That way, if you need to show the item again, you don't need to recreate it. If your intent is to delete it from one place and insert it in another, consider the Move method instead.
- If you delete a built-in item by mistake, you can use the Reset method of a CommandBar object to set the menus back the way Access created them.

Displaying a Pop-up Menu

Access makes it easy to assign a shortcut menu to any control or form, but what if you want to pop up a menu at any location, at any time? Command bars make displaying a pop-up menu simple. You can use the ShowPopup method of a pop-up CommandBar object—that is, a CommandBar object whose Style property has been set to msoBarTypePopup (2)—and specify the location, if you like. If you don't specify the location, the menu will appear at the current mouse location.

The code in Listing 11.16, from basPopup, uses the ShowPopup method of a CommandBar object to display the pop-up menu at either the current location or at a specified location. This example provides two optional parameters for the coordinates. They're both assumed to be –1 (an invalid value) if you don't supply them, and the code makes assumptions based on checking for that value in both coordinates.

Listing 11.16

```
Public Function TrackPopupMenu(cbr As CommandBar, _
 Optional X As Long = -1, Optional Y As Long = -1)
    ' Display a popup menu at a specified location.
    ' Assume that -1 is an invalid location.
    If cbr.Type = msoBarTypePopup Then
        If X = -1 And Y > -1 Then
            cbr.ShowPopup , Y
        ElseIf X > -1 And Y = -1 Then
            cbr.ShowPopup X
        ElseIf X = -1 And Y = -1 Then
            cbr.ShowPopup
        Else
            cbr.ShowPopup X, Y
        End If
    End If
End Function
```

To pop up the Database Background menu at the current vertical position but at the left edge of the screen, you could call code like this:

```
TrackPopupMenu CommandBars("Database Background"), 0
```

Working with Pop-up Menus

Access' user interface for creating shortcut menus is anything but intuitive. The trick you must understand is that Access groups all shortcut menus together underneath the Shortcut Menus menu bar. Any shortcut menu you create will appear under the Custom tab on this toolbar.

To create a new shortcut menu, follow these steps:

1. Start as if you were creating a normal menu. Choose View ➢ Toolbars ➢ Customize and click the New button.

Continued on next page

2. Enter the name for your new shortcut menu.
3. Click the Properties button on the Customize dialog, make sure that your new menu bar is selected (choose it from the drop down on the Toolbar Properties dialog, if it's not already selected), and, from the Type drop-down list, select Popup.
4. Access will warn you with a dialog box that it's moving the menu bar to the Shortcut Menus menu bar. Close the Toolbar Properties dialog.
5. Select the Shortcut Menus menu bar, which will make the Shortcut Menus menu appear. From the Custom list (far right side), select your new menu bar, to which you can add new items.

If you want to delete a shortcut menu that you've created, good luck! There's no obvious way to do this. Before you can delete a shortcut menu, you'll need to convert it back into a standard menu bar. To do that, follow these steps:

1. Again, display the ShortCut Menus menu bar.
2. Click the properties button on the Customize dialog.
3. Select your shortcut menu from the drop-down list of toolbars.
4. Change the Type from Popup back to Toolbar.
5. Finally, delete the toolbar from the list of toolbars.

Some Final Thoughts

The preceding sections have touched but a tiny portion of the functionality provided by the CommandBar object model. If you want to work with Office menus, take the time to dig through the online help topics and the lists of properties and methods in the Object Browser. You'll find a great deal of flexibility (perhaps too much). It may take some time to work through all the details and possibilities, but you should be able to accomplish almost any menu task you need using the CommandBar object model.

The Office Assistant

The Office Assistant is a third shared component provided by Microsoft Office. Its intent is to help users feel comfortable with all the Office applications and to provide suggestions that will help them make better use of the products. However you personally feel about the Assistant's usefulness, it's hard to discount the fact that the Assistant is just plain fun. The following sections explain what you can do with the Assistant in applications and how to take advantage of this technology to make your users more productive.

In Office 2000, the Assistant no longer appears in a window, as it did in Office 97. Now, the Assistant shows up floating above your applications and looks more like part of them, as opposed to a separate window sharing the screen. It can easily move around and point out interesting features.

Office 2000's Assistant is based on technology used in Microsoft's Agent ActiveX control. It acts as a "wrapper" around the more full-featured Agent control, which provides you with animated characters that can do everything the Office Assistant can do, and more. On the other hand, the Office Assistant has some properties and methods that are tied in directly with Office technology (such as the Answer Wizard), and it works closely with Office to allow you to create seamless applications.

Using Microsoft Agent

There are circumstances in which you'll need to use the Agent ActiveX control in your applications rather than using the Office Assistant. Specifically:

- You need to use the Assistant in an Access runtime application on a machine that doesn't have Office installed. In this environment, the Assistant isn't available. You'll need to use the Agent instead.
- You want to have your Assistant speak, verbally. The Office Assistant can't do this, but the Agent can. (It can listen and respond to commands, as well!)

For more information on using the Agent, visit `http://msdn.microsoft.com/msagent/default.asp`

Using the Assistant: Advantages and Limitations

If you're like most developers we know, the first thing you'll want to do with the Assistant is turn it *off*! For developers, it's a cute little oddity that quickly wears thin. No matter what you want to do or need to know, if you've been developing applications with Access for a while, you can get the job done more quickly without the Assistant.

TIP

Unlike in Office 97, you actually can turn off the Assistant. That is, if you press F1 for help, the Assistant will not magically appear, as in the previous version. To do this, right-click on the Assistant, choose Options, and uncheck the Use the Office Assistant check box. To do this programmatically, you'll need to set the On property of the Assistant object to False. (See Table 11.11 for more information.)

On the other hand, end users and beginners may find this addition to Office products a welcome helper. All Office applications use the Assistant to provide help, tips, and guides as users work with the products. Because users can choose their own "character" with its own personality (see the section "Personality and Neighborhood" a little later in this chapter), many end users will find this seemingly simple yet quite complex technology a worthwhile addition to the product.

You can use the Assistant in your own applications to do the same sorts of things it does for the standard Office applications:

- Provide context-sensitive help
- Show specific animations, based on options the user has chosen, steps the user has taken, or any other whim of your imagination
- Use the Assistant's Balloon object to provide a powerful replacement for Access' MsgBox

The following sections examine the second and third of these options.

NOTE

The Assistant is available only to users who own a copy of Microsoft Office. If you're a Word or Excel developer, this isn't an issue, because anyone using your add-in or product will, of course, own the product. If you're an Access or VB developer, however, this complicates issues. Applications distributed with the runtime version of Access or as VB executables don't have the legal rights to distribute the Office DLLs and character files that would be necessary to make the Assistant available to your application. Of course, if those users also have a copy of Office installed, they can run applications that use the Assistant. From VB, you simply set a reference to an Office application's Type Library (from the Project ➢ Reference menu) and then use that application (Access.Application.Assistant, for example) to get to the Assistant.

The Assistant Object Model

The Assistant object model is simple, and Figure 11.6 shows it in its entirety. Note that a Balloon object can contain a collection of up to five BalloonCheckBox objects (in the CheckBoxes collection) and up to five BalloonLabel objects (in the Labels collection), but you're not likely to use both of these object types at the same time.

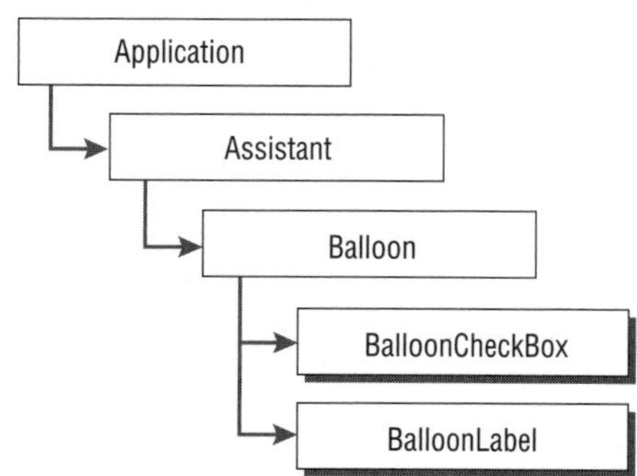

FIGURE 11.6:

The Assistant object model. Boxes with a shadow represent objects and collections; those without represent single objects.

As you can see from Figure 11.6, the Assistant object can own a single Balloon object (that's the area with buttons, labels, and icons that looks like a cartoon balloon). The balloon can contain up to five check boxes or up to five *labels* (the little blue "lights" on balloons that you can click). In addition, if you specify text for the Labels collection (the collection of BalloonLabel objects) you can display the text with blue lights, numbers, or bullets, depending on the BalloonType property.

NOTE

Attempting to use more than five labels or check boxes on a balloon will trigger a runtime error.

Working with the Assistant

What can you do with the Assistant? Even if you don't work with Balloon objects (discussed later in this chapter), you can make many choices about the activities and display of the Assistant. The following sections detail some of the properties and methods of the Assistant you'll be able to take advantage of in your own applications.

Being a Good Neighbor

There's only one Assistant, and its properties are global throughout all the Office applications. If your application comes along and changes the behavior, the visibility, or the character used by the Assistant, it will affect all other Office applications as well.

In order to maintain the current settings of the Assistant when you're done with it, you should always save and restore the Assistant settings around your use of it. To make that simple, we've provided the SaveAssistantSettings and RestoreAssistantSettings functions, in basSaveSettings. You should always call these procedures when working with the Assistant.

If you look at the code in these procedures, you'll see that all they do is store (or restore) settings in private variables. The code is simple, but it's crucial when using the Assistant if you want to be a good Office neighbor.

Personality and Neighborhood

The most important characteristic of the Assistant is its character. The specific animations and sounds associated with a given character are stored in files with the extension ACS, normally in a folder inside the folder where you installed Office. You'll use the FileName property to retrieve and set the file name for the character you want displayed. Once you've selected a character, the Name property returns a user-friendly name for the character (this is the name you see when you right-click the character and open the Choose Assistant dialog).

Where Are Those Characters?

If you want to supply users with a list of installed characters, you can use a technique like that used in frmAnimations, shown in Figure 11.7. This form gathers a list of all the installed actors and provides that list to the user. The form also demonstrates all available animations and some other visible option settings. The following sections discuss other features demonstrated by this form.

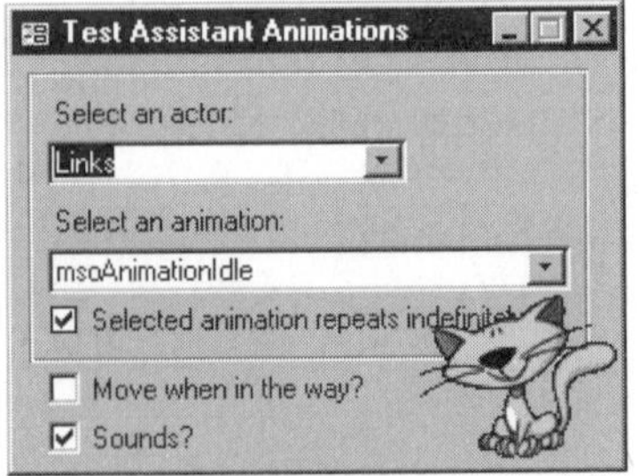

FIGURE 11.7:

frmAnimations allows you to select actors and specific animations.

The code in frmAnimations retrieves the path for all the actor files from the Registry, using the GetActorPath function. If you're interested in learning how to retrieve arbitrary values from the Registry, you might take a peek at that function. Once the code knows where the files live (*.ACS), it uses the File Server object in the GatherList procedure to loop through all the files in the directory, setting the Assistant's FileName property to each file, in turn. While each actor is loaded, the code retrieves the Name property as well and then moves on to the next file. As the code works, it builds up a semicolon-delimited list of file names and actor names and stuffs that string into the RowSource property of the combo box on the form. Listing 11.17 shows the code from frmAnimations.

Listing 11.17

```
Private Sub GatherList(strPath As String)
    ' Add all the actor file names and friendly names
    ' to the collection.
    Dim strOut As String
    Dim varFile As Variant
    Dim strOldFile As String

    With Assistant
        strOldFile = .FileName
        .Visible = False
        .On = True

        With Application.FileSearch
            .LookIn = strPath
            .FileName = "*.acs"
            .Execute
        End With
        For Each varFile In FileSearch.FoundFiles
            varFile = GetFileName(varFile & "")
            .FileName = varFile
            strOut = strOut & ";" & varFile & ";" & .Name
        Next varFile

        ' Put the file name back the way it was, and then
        ' force the Assistant to be visible.
        .FileName = strOldFile
        If Len(strOut) > 0 Then
            cboActors.RowSource = Mid$(strOut, 2)
        End If
```

```
        .Visible = True
    End With
End Sub

Private Function GetFileName(strName As String) As String
    ' Given a full path,
    ' retrieve just the file name portion.
    ' If you get only a file name,
    ' (that is, no "\") return
    ' the full name.

    Dim intPos As Integer

    intPos = InStrRev(strName, "\")
    If intPos > 0 Then
        GetFileName = Mid$(strName, intPos + 1)
    Else
        GetFileName = strName
    End If
End Function
```

Along with the Name and FileName properties, you can set other properties that affect the location and display of the Assistant. Table 11.11 describes these properties.

TABLE 11.11: Properties Controlling the Display of the Assistant

Property	Description
FileName	Specifies the file containing the animations and information for the actor. Actor files have an ACS extension.
Name	Contains the user-friendly name for the actor. Read-only.
Top	Specifies the upper coordinate of the Assistant, in pixels.
Left	Specifies the left coordinate of the Assistant, in pixels.
On	Specifies whether the Assistant is available at all. If False, Visible is also False, and you cannot display the Assistant. If True, Visible can be True or False, hiding and displaying the Assistant.
Visible	Specifies the visibility of the Assistant. Set to True or False to control whether the Assistant is visible on-screen.

Animations 'R' Us

The Assistant provides the Animation property, which allows you to control which animation the character displays at any time. You can choose only from the supplied animations, and not all characters respond to all the animations. For a list of possible values for the Animation property, see the Object Browser (msoAnimationType), or check out tblAnimations in the sample database. The sample form, frmAnimations, allows you to try out all the settings with each actor.

NOTE

Some animation settings (msoAnimationGreeting, for example) contain more than one possible display. When you select a particular Animation property setting, there's no way for you to control exactly which of the possible animations you'll get; it's a random choice. You just have to give up a little control once in a while!

I'm Dancing as Fast as I Can!

No matter how hard you try, you cannot convince the Assistant to display a series of animations strung together. Because the actor will "act" only during your computer's idle time to keep it from getting in the way of real work, there's no way for it to take over and perform animations serially. If you supply a list of actions, one after the other, you'll most likely see only the final animation in the list. You may be able to work around this by adding timing loops to your code, but don't. It's just not the point.

Try out the DanceTwerpDance procedure in basAssistant, shown in Listing 11.18. You'll see that although the code requests a series of animations, only one of them will be visible, most likely the final one.

Listing 11.18

```
Sub DanceTwerpDance()
    ' Note that the Assistant can handle animation only
    ' in "down time". In this case only the final animation
    ' will have any visible effect.
    With Assistant
        .On = True
        .Visible = True
        .Animation = msoAnimationGestureLeft
        .Animation = msoAnimationGestureRight
        .Animation = msoAnimationGestureUp
```

```
            .Animation = msoAnimationGestureDown
            .Animation = msoAnimationCharacterSuccessMajor
        End With
    End Sub
```

TIP

If you do want to string together a series of actions and have them all visible, you'll need to cause the Assistant to wait between actions. You can use the Sleep API function, declared in basAssistant, to do this. Try DanceTwerpDanceSlower (in basAssistant), and you'll see how it works out. This version of the routine has calls to the Sleep API function between each action. Even this may not look good, depending on which character you've chosen.

Handling All the Options

Many of the Assistant's properties correspond one-to-one with options available in its Options dialog (right-click on the Assistant and choose Options). All the options shown in Table 11.12 contain Boolean values and are read/write.

TABLE 11.12: Assistant Properties Corresponding to the Options Dialog

Property	Corresponding Item
AssistWithAlerts	Display alerts
AssistWithHelp	Respond to F1 key
AssistWithWizards	Help with Wizards
FeatureTips	Using features more effectively
GuessHelp	Guess help topics
HighPriorityTips	Only show high-priority tips
KeyboardShortcutTips	Keyboard shortcuts
MouseTips	Using the mouse more effectively
MoveWhenInTheWay	Move when in the way
SearchWhenProgramming	Search for both product and programming help when programming
Sounds	Make sounds
TipOfDay	Show the Tip of the Day at startup

Assistant Methods

The Assistant object supplies three additional methods:

Help The Help method pops up a balloon filled with its guesses as to what you're trying to do, with jumps to the appropriate help topics.

Move The Move method allows you to move the Assistant to any location on the screen. For example,

```
Assistant.Move 0, 0
```

moves the Assistant to the upper-left corner. (Unlike other location values, these values must be supplied in *pixels*, not twips.)

ResetTips The ResetTips method resets the display of built-in tips back to the first item so users can see tips they've seen before.

TIP

Even though the Assistant, in Office 2000, doesn't display itself inside a window, it's still bounded by an invisible rectangle. If you ask the Assistant to move to the upper-left corner of the screen (using the Move method and 0, 0 as the coordinates), it may not quite move there. You may need to experiment to get the character positioned exactly where you want it.

Creating a New Balloon

A silent Assistant wouldn't do you much good, so Access allows you to create Balloon objects that display text from the Assistant. (No, the Assistant still can't talk. If you want sounds, use the Microsoft Agent instead. See the sidebar "Using Microsoft Agent," earlier in this chapter.) To create a balloon, you'll usually follow these steps:

1. Use the NewBalloon method of the Assistant object to create the new balloon. This balloon will be blank and invisible.
2. Set the Heading property to assign a heading.
3. Set the Text property to assign some text to the body of the balloon.
4. Specify text for controls (labels or check boxes) as needed.
5. Use the Show method to display the balloon.

6. If you're using a modeless balloon (see later sections for more information), use the Close method to dismiss the balloon.

The Assistant can display only a single balloon object at a time, and it has no mechanism for internally maintaining a collection of Balloon objects. If you want to create multiple balloons and have them ready for use, you'll need to write code to manage these yourself, perhaps in your own Collection object. You use the NewBalloon method of the Assistant to return a reference to a new Balloon object, and you can use this Balloon object to display text, labels, check boxes, and so on, to the user.

For example, Listing 11.19 (from basAssistant) creates and displays a very simple balloon. Figure 11.8 shows the output of running this code. (The next section of this chapter offers more information about creating and using balloons and their text.)

FIGURE 11.8:

The simple balloon contains a heading, text, and an OK button, and it's modal.

Listing 11.19

```
Sub SimpleBalloon()
    Dim bln As Balloon
    Set bln = Assistant.NewBalloon
    With bln
        .Heading = "The Simplest Balloon!"
        .Text = "This is the simplest balloon ever!"
        .Show
    End With
End Sub
```

Working with Balloons

Balloon objects allow you to display text, request information, and interact in many ways with your applications' users. The following sections discuss the properties and methods of Balloon objects that allow you to create useful dialogs.

What Can You Put on a Balloon?

A Balloon object can contain any or all of the following items:

- A heading (using the Heading property)
- A section of text (using the Text property)
- Up to five labels, buttons, or numbered items (using the predefined Labels collection)
- Up to five check boxes (using the predefined CheckBoxes collection)
- A group of command buttons (using the Button property)
- A graphic inserted into any text element

The example in Listing 11.20 shows how to create the Balloon object and assign its Heading and Text properties. Examples in the following sections show how to use the other Balloon object properties.

Showing a Balloon

Once you've set up your Balloon object as you want it to appear, use the Show method to make it visible. See the example in Listing 11.19, which sets up the Heading and Text properties and then displays the balloon.

Inserting a Bitmap

You can insert a bitmap at any point in the text of a balloon. To do so, place a brace-delimited string indicating the image type ("bmp" for a bitmap) and the path to the bitmap directly into your text. For example, to place the Windows CIRCLES.BMP file into the header of your balloon, you could use code like the code in Listing 11.20.

Listing 11.20

```
Public Sub ShowBitmap()
    ' Display a balloon that contains a bitmap.
    With Assistant.NewBalloon
        .Heading = "This is a picture " & _
         "{bmp C:\WINDOWS\CIRCLES.BMP} of circles."
        .Show
    End With
End Sub
```

You cannot, however, replace the numbers, bullets, or blue lights of the balloons with your own bitmaps.

To specify the graphic type, use one of the following text strings preceding the file name:

String	Meaning
bmp	Insert a Windows bitmap
wmf	Insert a Windows metafile
pict	Insert a Macintosh picture

Inserting Colors and Underline

To show various colors and underline attributes in the text on a balloon, you'll need to insert formatting characters in the text you send to the various properties of the balloon. The following list shows the text you must insert to control the color and underline attributes:

Insert	To do this
{ul 1}	Turn on underlining
{ul 0}	Turn off underlining
{cf n}	Change text to a specific color, where n can be any value from Table 11.13

TABLE 11.13: Allowed Color Values in a Balloon

Value	Color
0	Black
1	Dark red
2	Dark green
3	Dark yellow
4	Dark blue
5	Dark magenta
6	Dark cyan
7	Light gray
248	Medium gray
249	Red
250	Green
251	Yellow
252	Blue
253	Magenta
254	Cyan
255	White

As an example, try out the SimpleColor procedure, from basAssistant, shown in Listing 11.21. Figure 11.9 shows the output from running this procedure.

FIGURE 11.9: The SimpleColor procedure creates a balloon with underlining and multiple text colors.

Listing 11.21

```
Public Sub SimpleColor()
    ' Display a simple balloon.
    Dim bln As Balloon

    Call SaveAssistantSettings
    Assistant.On = True
    Assistant.Visible = True
    Set bln = Assistant.NewBalloon
    With bln
        .Heading = "The Simplest Balloon!"
        .Text = "This {ul 1}isn't{ul 0} the " & _
         "{cf 248}simplest{cf 0} balloon ever!"
        .Show
    End With
    Call RestoreAssistantSettings
End Sub
```

If you want to see all the possible effects in one garish balloon, run the Colors-AndUnderline procedure, in basAssistant. This procedure creates a single balloon, showing one line of text in each possible text attribute.

Getting Modal

You can display a Balloon object in one of three modalities: Modal, Modeless, or AutoDown. Table 11.14 lists the available settings and outlines the issues involved with each.

TABLE 11.14: Available Settings for a Balloon's Mode Property

Modality	Constant	Description	Issues
Modal	msoModeModal	The balloon maintains the focus until you click on a label (if the BalloonType property is set to msoBalloonTypeBullets) or on a button, at which point it disappears (this is the default value of the Mode property).	Use the return value of the Show method to find out exactly which label or button the user has selected.

Continued on next page

TABLE 11.14 CONTINUED: Available Settings for a Balloon's Mode Property

Modality	Constant	Description	Issues
Modeless	msoModeModeless	The balloon stays visible until you dismiss it with code.	You must supply a callback function to react to clicks on the balloon. You can use the Close method only with a modeless balloon.
AutoDown	msoModeAutoDown	The balloon disappears as soon as you click anywhere outside it.	If your balloon includes buttons, the balloon will disappear once you click outside the balloon, regardless of whether you've clicked one of the buttons. This may be confusing to users of your applications.

Using the Button Property to Handle Dismissals

Use the Button property of the Balloon object to indicate which combination of command buttons you'd like to see on the balloon. Table 11.15 lists the possible combinations. (See the msoButtonSetType enumeration in the Object Browser for complete details.)

TABLE 11.15: Possible Button Combinations for Balloon Objects

msoButtonSetType Value	Buttons Displayed
msoButtonSetAbortRetryIgnore	Abort, Retry, and Ignore
msoButtonSetBackClose	Back and Close
msoButtonSetBackNextClose	Back, Next, and Close
msoButtonSetBackNextSnooze	Back, Next, and Snooze
msoButtonSetCancel	Cancel
msoButtonSetNextClose	Next and Close
msoButtonSetNone	No buttons at all
msoButtonSetOK	OK

Continued on next page

TABLE 11.15 CONTINUED: Possible Button Combinations for Balloon Objects

msoButtonSetType Value	Buttons Displayed
msoButtonSetOkCancel	OK and Cancel
msoButtonSetRetryCancel	Retry and Cancel
msoButtonSetSearchClose	Search and Close
msoButtonSetTipsOptionsClose	Tips, Options, and Close
msoButtonSetYesAllNoCancel	Yes, Yes to All, No, and Cancel
msoButtonSetYesNo	Yes and No
msoButtonSetYesNoCancel	Yes, No, and Cancel

Just as with the MsgBox function in VBA, the buttons don't actually do anything. When you select one of the buttons, the balloon either disappears or calls a function, depending on the Mode property. If the balloon is opened with the msoMode-Modeless setting, clicking a button calls the function specified in the CallBack property. If it's set to msoModeModal, clicking a button closes the balloon, and the return value of the Show method indicates which button you clicked. For example, running the code in Listing 11.22 results in the display shown in Figure 11.10.

FIGURE 11.10: Use the Button property of the Balloon object to control which buttons the Balloon displays.

Listing 11.22

```
Public Sub SimpleBalloonButtons()
    ' Display a simple balloon.
    Dim bln As Balloon

    Call SaveAssistantSettings
```

```
    Assistant.On = True
    Assistant.Visible = True
    Set bln = Assistant.NewBalloon
    With bln
        .Heading = "The Simplest Balloon!"
        .Text = "This balloon has some buttons!"
        .Button = msoButtonSetTipsOptionsClose
        .Show
    End With
    Call RestoreAssistantSettings
End Sub
```

Table 11.16 lists the possible return values from the Show method. Note that if you've set the BalloonType property for the balloon to msoBalloonTypeButtons and you've supplied text for one or more of the Labels collection items (see the next section for more details), the Show method will return a number between 1 and 5, indicating which label was selected.

TABLE 11.16: Possible Return Values from the Show Method of a Balloon

msoBalloonButtonType Value	Button Selected
msoBalloonButtonAbort	Abort
msoBalloonButtonBack	Back
msoBalloonButtonCancel	Cancel
msoBalloonButtonClose	Close
msoBalloonButtonIgnore	Ignore
msoBalloonButtonNext	Next
msoBalloonButtonNo	No
msoBalloonButtonNull	No button was selected
msoBalloonButtonOK	OK
msoBalloonButtonOptions	Options
msoBalloonButtonRetry	Retry
msoBalloonButtonSearch	Search

Continued on next page

TABLE 11.16 CONTINUED: Possible Return Values from the Show Method of a Balloon

msoBalloonButtonType Value	Button Selected
msoBalloonButtonSnooze	Snooze
msoBalloonButtonTips	Tips
msoBalloonButtonYes	Yes
msoBalloonButtonYesToAll	Yes to All
Values: 1 through 5	If the BalloonType property is set to msoBalloon-TypeButtons, indicates which label was selected

The procedure in Listing 11.23, from basAssistant, demonstrates the use of buttons and checking their value. Figures 11.11 and 11.12 demonstrate how running this code might look.

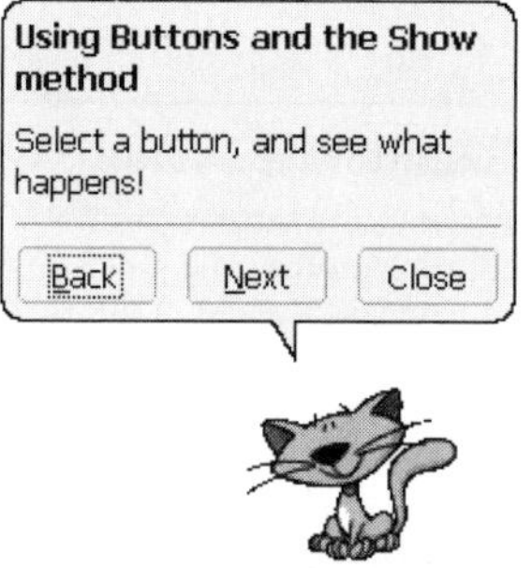

FIGURE 11.11: If the balloon is modal, clicking on a button returns a value indicating which button you selected and closes the balloon.

FIGURE 11.12: Because you clicked the Back button, the code can react to the return value and decide the path to take next.

Listing 11.23

```
Public Sub TestShow()
    ' Demonstrate the Show method.
    Dim intRetval As Integer
    Dim strText As String

    Call SaveAssistantSettings
    With Assistant
        .On = True
        .Visible = True

        With .NewBalloon
            .Heading = "Using Buttons and the Show method"
            .Text = "Select a button, and see what happens!"
            .Button = msoButtonSetBackNextClose
            .Mode = msoModeModal
            intRetval = .Show
            Select Case intRetval
                Case msoBalloonButtonBack
                    strText = "You chose Back!"
                Case msoBalloonButtonNext
                    strText = "You chose Next!"
                Case msoBalloonButtonClose
                    strText = "You chose Close!"
            End Select
        End With
        ' Now create a new balloon, with the new text.
        ' Make this balloon go away as soon as you click
        ' anywhere outside the balloon.
        With .NewBalloon
            .Heading = "What Did You Choose?"
            .Text = strText
            .Mode = msoModeAutoDown
            .Show
        End With
    End With
    Call RestoreAssistantSettings
End Sub
```

WARNING Balloon objects require a dismissal method. If there's no way to make the balloon go away, Access won't display it in the first place. If you display the Labels collection as bullet items, for example, and don't otherwise provide some means for getting rid of the balloon, you'll never see the balloon.

Using the Labels Collection

You can add up to five short paragraphs of text to a Balloon object, in the Labels collection. Depending on the value in the BalloonType property, the paragraphs will appear as numbered items, bulleted items, or as items in an option group. (You can select one, and only one, of the items in the collection.) Table 11.17 lists the possible values for the BalloonType property. (See msoBalloonType in the Object Browser.)

TABLE 11.17: Possible Values for the BalloonType Property

BalloonType Value	Description
msoBalloonTypeBullets	Shows Labels collection as bullets
msoBalloonTypeButtons	Shows Labels collection as selectable options
msoBalloonTypeNumbers	Shows Labels collection as numbered items

The example shown in Listing 11.24, from basAssistant, creates a simple set of labels from which the user can choose a value. Call the TestGetLevel procedure from the Immediate window to test it out. Figure 11.13 shows the balloon in action.

FIGURE 11.13: Testing out the Labels collection

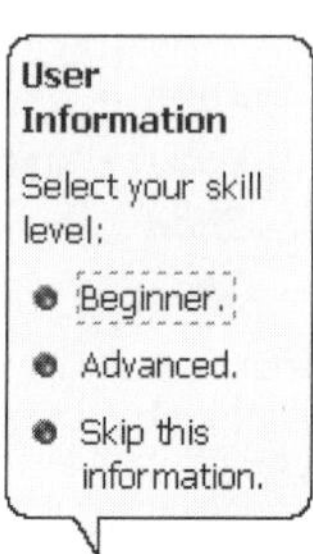

Listing 11.24

```
Public Function GetLevel()
    ' Call a modal balloon and return the value of the selected
    ' label on the balloon.
    Dim bln As Balloon

    Call SaveAssistantSettings
    Assistant.On = True
    Assistant.Visible = True

    Set bln = Assistant.NewBalloon
    With bln
        .Heading = "User Information"
        .Text = "Select your skill level:"
        .Labels(1).Text = "Beginner."
        .Labels(2).Text = "Advanced."
        .Labels(3).Text = "Skip this information."
        .Mode = msoModeModal
        .BalloonType = msoBalloonTypeButtons
        .Button = msoButtonSetNone
        GetLevel = .Show
    End With
    Call RestoreAssistantSettings
End Function

Public Sub TestGetLevel()
    ' Test the GetLevel function.
    Select Case GetLevel()
        Case 1
            Debug.Print "A beginner!"
        Case 2
            Debug.Print "An advanced user!"
        Case 3
            Debug.Print "Who knows?"
        Case Else
            Debug.Print "Invalid data!"
    End Select
End Sub
```

Controlling the Icon

You can control the icon displayed on your balloon. Set the Icon property to one of the constants listed in Table 11.18. (See the msoIconType enumeration in the Object Browser for more details.)

TABLE 11.18: Icon Constants for Assistant Balloons

msoIconType Value	Description
msoIconAlert	Displays an alert icon
msoIconAlertCritical	Displays the MsgBox Critical icon
msoIconAlertInfo	Displays the MsgBox Information icon
msoIconAlertQuery	Displays the MsgBox Question icon
msoIconAlertWarning	Displays the MsgBox Exclamation icon
msoIconNone	Displays no icon at all (the default)
msoIconTip	Displays the tip icon (a light bulb)

The example shown in Listing 11.25, from basAssistant, shows a balloon that uses an icon. Figure 11.14 shows the example as it's running.

FIGURE 11.14: The wrong animation, the wrong icon, and disasters don't mix.

Listing 11.25

```
Public Sub BadThing()
    ' This whole example is a bad idea.

    Call SaveAssistantSettings

    With Assistant
        .On = True
        .Visible = True

        .Animation = msoAnimationCharacterSuccessMajor
        With .NewBalloon
            .Heading = "Terrible Disaster!"
            .Icon = msoIconTip
            .Text = "I need to format your hard drive."
            .Button = msoButtonSetOkCancel
            If .Show = msoBalloonButtonCancel Then
                MsgBox "Sorry, it's too late for that!", _
                 vbExclamation, "Your Drive is Toast!"
            End If
        End With
    End With

    Call RestoreAssistantSettings
End Sub
```

Using the CheckBoxes Collection

Just as you can place up to five text paragraphs in the Labels collection, you can place up to five check boxes on a balloon, as well. (Normally, you'll use either labels or check boxes, but not both.)

To set a check box's caption, set its Text property. To determine whether it's been selected, look at its Checked property.

The example in Listing 11.26 demonstrates the simple use of the CheckBoxes collection, from basAssistant. It doesn't, however, allow you to find out which checks the user selected; that requires a modeless balloon and a callback function. See the next section for more information on providing callback functions and reacting to users' choices. Figure 11.15 shows this procedure running.

FIGURE 11.15:

Using check boxes on a simple balloon

Listing 11.26

```
Public Sub ShowChecks()
    ' Simple example with checks.
    With Assistant.NewBalloon
        .Heading = "Your Menu"
        .Text = "Choose the items you'd like " & _
         "included in your meal:"
        .Checkboxes(1).Text = "Appetizer"
        .Checkboxes(2).Text = "Salad"
        .Checkboxes(3).Text = "Soup"
        .Checkboxes(4).Text = "Main Course"
        .Checkboxes(5).Text = "Dessert"
        .Show
    End With
End Sub
```

Supplying a Callback Function

If you create a modeless balloon, you'll need to supply a macro or function that Access will call when you click any label or button. This function (and, although you can use a macro for this, you should not, because you won't get the information Access passes to the function) will, at least, need to dismiss the balloon. In addition, it can determine which check boxes, if your balloon displays check boxes, the user has selected.

To supply the name of your callback function, set the Callback property value to be a string containing the name of the function or macro. In the function, you can make decisions based on the check boxes on the balloon, and you can use the Close method to close the balloon. Access passes to your function three parameters:

- A reference to the balloon object
- An integer indicating which button, label, or check box was selected
- An integer representing the balloon's Private property, which can contain information indicating exactly which balloon, if you're using more than one with the same callback function, caused you to be in the function

You can use these parameters to determine what action your callback function must take. Listing 11.27 demonstrates a simple example using check boxes and a callback function. To try it, run the GetStatistics procedure in basAssistant. The GetStatistics procedure pops up a balloon with four check boxes on it and waits for the user to respond. Note that it's modeless (its Mode property is set to msoModeModeless), so you can do other work in the application while this balloon is visible. Once you press the OK button, the balloon calls the function specified in its Callback property: CountChecks.

The CountChecks procedure looks at the check boxes, counts how many were selected, and makes a decision about what to do based on that value. It closes the original balloon (passed as a parameter to the procedure) and then opens a new balloon with more information.

Listing 11.27

```
Public Sub GetStatistics()
    ' Use a modeless balloon with check boxes and
    ' a simple callback function.

    Call SaveAssistantSettings
    Assistant.On = True
    Assistant.Visible = True

    With Assistant.NewBalloon
        .Heading = "Check your Statistics."
```

```
        .Checkboxes(1).Text = "Over 30."
        .Checkboxes(2).Text = "Smoker."
        .Checkboxes(3).Text = "Drinker."
        .Checkboxes(4).Text = _
          "Greater than 40 pounds overweight."
        .Text = "Which of the following " _
           & .Checkboxes.Count & " choices apply to you?"
        .Mode = msoModeModeless
        .Callback = "CountChecks"
        .Button = msoButtonSetOK
        .Show
    End With

End Sub

Public Function CountChecks(bln As Balloon, _
 intButton As Integer, intPrivate As Integer)
    ' Callback function from GetStatistics example.
    Dim intI As Integer
    Dim intCount As Integer
    Dim strText As String

    With bln
        For intI = 1 To 5
            If .Checkboxes(intI).Checked Then
                intCount = intCount + 1
            End If
        Next intI
        .Animation = msoAnimationGestureDown
        Select Case intCount
            Case 0
                strText = "No risk! Don't you have a life?"
            Case 1
                strText = "Only one risk category. " & _
                 "You'll probably make it to 50."
            Case 2
                strText = "Things are looking grim!"
            Case 3
                strText = "Better think about " & _
                 "life insurance."
            Case 4
                strText = "Who's your next of kin?"
        End Select
```

```
        ' Close the original balloon.
        .Close
    End With
    With Assistant.NewBalloon
        .Heading = strText
        .Show
    End With
    Call RestoreAssistantSettings
End Function
```

TIP

You can't call RestoreAssistantSettings while you're displaying a modeless balloon—what if the Assistant was invisible before you displayed the balloon? Because the balloon is modeless, the Assistant just disappears again, as RestoreAssistantSettings puts it back the way you found it. In this example, we worked around the problem by calling RestoreAssistantSettings from the callback function. That is, once the callback was done doing its thing, it put the Assistant back the way you found it.

Using Multiple Balloons in a Session

The Assistant supports only a single visible Balloon object at any time. You can, however, use the Assistant.NewBalloon method repeatedly, creating all the balloon objects you need. Then, when you want to show one balloon or another, set its Visible property to True.

TIP

Because the Assistant supports only a single balloon at a time, if you use the Show method on one balloon, make sure you use the Close method on the one that was previously visible. If you don't, the Assistant gets confused.

If you're going to use multiple balloons in a given session, you'll often want to use modeless balloons. If you use modeless balloons, you'll want to use callback functions for those balloons, allowing you to take action based on the button clicked or the label selected.

Using a Callback with Multiple Balloons

If you intend to use a single callback function with multiple balloons, you have to find some way to differentiate the balloons. You can set the value of your balloons'

Private property. This property is simply a Long integer that you can use for your own needs—Access never uses or modifies its value. When it calls your callback function, it passes the Private property for your balloon in the function's third parameter. You can then base decisions in the callback function on that value. The example shown in Listing 11.28, from basAssistant, takes advantage of this technique. It uses the value passed from the Private property in the third parameter in order to know which balloon is visible. Note that the example uses the callback function's second parameter to know which button was selected and then takes appropriate action.

TIP

The example uses two Balloon variables. If you're preparing a real application that uses many balloons, you'll probably want to prepare some data structure for managing the balloons—either a collection or an array. In any case, you could create all the balloons at your application's startup, add them to the data structure, and use them as needed later on in your application.

Listing 11.28

```
Private mbln1 As Balloon
Private mbln2 As Balloon

Public Sub MultipleBalloonsModeless()
    ' This example can't save/restore settings,
    ' because you show the Assistant non-modally, and
    ' restoring settings at the end would hide the
    ' Assistant again (if it was hidden to begin with).

    Assistant.On = True
    Assistant.Visible = True

    Set mbln1 = Assistant.NewBalloon
    Set mbln2 = Assistant.NewBalloon
    With mbln1
        .Heading = "This is balloon 1. " & _
         vbCrLf & _
         "Go work with the application while I'm visible."
        .Private = 1
        .Mode = msoModeModeless
        .Callback = "MultipleBalloonCallback"
        .Button = msoButtonSetNextClose
    End With
```

```
    With mbln2
        .Heading = "This is balloon 2. " & _
         vbCrLf & _
         "You can still work in the real application."
        .Private = 2
        .Mode = msoModeModeless
        .Callback = "MultipleBalloonCallback"
        .Button = msoButtonSetBackClose
    End With
    mbln1.Show
End Sub

Public Function MultipleBalloonCallback(bln As Balloon, _
 intButton As Integer, intPrivate As Integer)

    ' Callback for MultipleBalloonsModeless procedure.
    Select Case intButton
        ' No matter which balloon, the Close
        ' button closes both.
        Case msoBalloonButtonClose
            mbln1.Close
            mbln2.Close
        Case Else
            Select Case intPrivate
                Case 1
                    Select Case intButton
                        Case msoBalloonButtonNext
                            mbln1.Close
                            mbln2.Show
                        Case Else
                            ' No other buttons, right?
                    End Select
                Case 2
                    Select Case intButton
                        Case msoBalloonButtonBack
                            mbln1.Show
                            mbln2.Close
                        Case Else
                            ' No other buttons, right?
                    End Select
            End Select
    End Select
End Function
```

TIP

If you want the callback function to do anything with a balloon other than the current one, make sure the reference to the balloon is scoped so your function can "see" it. In most cases, you'll want to declare a variable that refers to the Balloon object at the module level so any procedure in the module can work with it. Of course, Access passes your callback function a reference to the current balloon, so that's not an issue. But all other balloons are invisible to your callback unless they're referred to by accessible variables. In the example, they're stored in module-level variables.

Handling Balloon Errors

It's possible that you'll create a Balloon object and ask it to do something it can't or set its options in such a way that it can't be displayed. Anytime you use a Balloon object in a real application, you should check the Assistant's BalloonError property once it has been dismissed. That way, your application can know if something went wrong while the balloon was in use. For a complete listing of BalloonError property values, check the Object Browser (msoBalloonErrorType) and online help.

For example, in Listing 11.29, from basAssistant, the code attempts to create a modeless balloon with no buttons. Because Access won't allow you to create a modeless balloon that doesn't also supply a way to get rid of the balloon, you'll never see this balloon.

Listing 11.29

```
Public Sub NoButtonsNoBalloon()
    ' Demonstrate the BalloonError property.
    Call SaveAssistantSettings

    With Assistant
        .On = True
        .Visible = True
        With .NewBalloon
            .Heading = "This will never show."
            .Text = "Imagine a balloon here."
            .Button = msoButtonSetNone
            .Mode = msoModeModal
            .Show
```

```
        End With
        If .BalloonError = _
         msoBalloonErrorButtonlessModal Then
            MsgBox "You need a button to " & _
             "dismiss the balloon."
        End If
        .Visible = True
    End With

    Call RestoreAssistantSettings
End Sub
```

Finishing Touches

Here are some additional thoughts on using balloons:

Plan carefully Plan your use of balloons wisely before beginning to add them to your application. Because of the limitation on the number of checks and labels you can use, you'll need to design them very carefully.

One Assistant, many balloons If you want to use multiple balloons in a session, make sure the Assistant is visible first. Otherwise, you may see the Assistant appear and disappear for each balloon.

Respect the users' configurations If you use the Assistant, be sure to reset its visibility when you're done. Most of the examples in this portion of the chapter follow this suggestion. You can call the SaveAssistantSettings and RestoreAssistantSettings procedures, provided in basSaveSettings.

No runtime distribution allowed Remember that runtime applications cannot use this functionality unless the intended user already has a copy of Office installed. If you plan on shipping an application to a mixed group of end users (some using the retail version and others using only the runtime version), you'll need to provide forms or MsgBox calls to replace the balloons for runtime users. Or, you can use the Microsoft Agent ActiveX control instead. Any of these options will require considerable modification to existing Assistant code, so make sure you understand the limitations before you begin your application.

Is There More?

This rounds out the introduction to the three shared Office components you can use in Access. Are there more? Of course! Almost all Office components can be controlled via Automation, and they expose rich object models to allow you to control them. Other, smaller features of Office allow you to control them programmatically, as well. Once you've set up the appropriate reference to the type library using the Tools ➢ References menu, you can program to your heart's content. The best documentation you'll find on these object models is the Office Object Model Guide that's part of Microsoft Office 2000 Developer. You can also visit Microsoft's Web site (`http://www.microsoft.com/officedev`) for more information. As time goes on, more and more of the shared components will become documented, and the Web site is the place to look for the new information.

Summary

In this chapter, we covered the three object models supplied by MSO9.DLL. We discussed finding Files with the FileSearch object, including:

- Using properties to provide a simple search
- Using the PropertyTests collection to provide complex searches

We examined the subject of programming command bars, including:

- Perusing the CommandBars collection
- Creating new CommandBar objects
- Working with CommandBarControl objects
- Adding objects to command bars
- Using the OnAction property to take an action when an object is selected
- Reacting to events of CommandBarControl objects, using WithEvents

We also took a look at controlling the Office Assistant, including:

- Using properties to control the Assistant
- Creating balloons
- Using Balloon properties to control a balloon's activities
- Using check boxes and labels on balloons
- Using callback functions to react to actions on modeless balloons

Office supplies a major increment in the number of Automation servers it provides, and the three covered here are just the tip of the iceberg. For more information, see Chapters 12 and 13, which deal directly with Access as an Automation controller and server.

CHAPTER

TWELVE

12

Using Access As an Automation Client

- Understanding how Automation works
- Writing simple Automation code
- Creating integrated solutions using Microsoft Office 2000
- Using Automation to manipulate ActiveX controls
- Creating event sinks to monitor other applications

The term *Automation* refers to a technology that allows two separate application components to communicate with each other. Communication can take the form of data exchanges or commands issued by one component for another to carry out. The driving force behind the creation and exploitation of this technology is the desire to combine numerous independent software components into a single integrated solution. For several versions, Microsoft Access has supported the programming interfaces that make Automation possible. In this chapter, we explain the basics of Automation and explore ways to use it to create integrated solutions using applications like those found in Microsoft Office. We also look at using Automation techniques with ActiveX controls, the bright star in the galaxy of reusable software components. After reading this chapter, you should have an understanding of how the pieces of the Automation puzzle fit together and how you can use them to your advantage.

Automation Basics

Under the covers, Automation is a fairly complex technology that involves numerous programming interfaces. Fortunately, VBA has encapsulated those interfaces and made Automation relatively simple to implement. Its greatest strength is that it lets you work with objects from other applications using the same techniques you use now with Access objects. Before beginning to write integrated solutions using Automation, you should be familiar with the basics. In this section, we explain the terminology we'll be using, where Automation information is stored, and how to examine an Automation component's objects, properties, and methods.

Terminology

There have been some changes in Automation terminology since we began discussing it in earlier editions of this book. In addition, some of the terms used in this book have meanings that differ when taken outside the context of Automation. In both cases, it's important that you understand the specific meanings of these terms.

Changes in Terminology

In the beginning, Microsoft created Object Linking and Embedding and it saw that it was good. But the masses cried, "That's too much to remember! Give us a three letter acronym!" So Microsoft decried that Object Linking and Embedding would be henceforth known as OLE and it saw that that was also good. And OLE grew and prospered and before long it encompassed much and so Microsoft created ActiveX, which it said was OLE but with much greatness. And the customers rejoiced, yea the programmers were confused. And then there came the Internet with much promise and mystery. So Microsoft created COM and proclaimed that COM was supreme and forever and that Object Linking and Embedding, and OLE, and ActiveX had never been. And Microsoft rejoiced, yea the customers and programmers were confused.

Well, if there's one thing Microsoft can't be accused of, it's letting its names for technology get stale. Over the past decade, we've seen a number of technologies designed to enable software to work better together. As this book was being written, the *nom du jour* was COM, short for Component Object Model. (And COM+ is right around the corner!) COM is the all-encompassing term for everything we once knew as Object Linking and Embedding, OLE, and ActiveX. (Despite this, the term ActiveX is still used for some subset technologies.) The following list provides both the old and new terms for some of the technologies involved.

- OLE automation is now COM Automation or simply Automation.
- OLE automation components are now COM components.
- OLE custom controls or OLE controls are now ActiveX controls.
- OLE document objects are now ActiveX documents.

Terminology Used in This Chapter

Now, let's clarify some common terms used in this chapter.

Automation requires a client (sometimes called a *controller*) and a server. The *server* is the application or component that provides services to the client. It may exhibit behaviors independently of the client, but, for the most part, it depends on the client's giving it commands to do things. The *client*, on the other hand, is the application that uses the services of an Automation server. In a narrow context, a client application is one that implements a development language that allows you to write code that controls a server. Access is an obvious example of an Automation client. Other Automation clients include Microsoft Visual Basic, Excel, Word, PowerPoint, and Outlook. In fact, any application that supports VBA has Automation client capabilities. An Automation client need not be a development tool, but development tools such as Access are the ones of most interest here.

In addition to understanding clients and servers, you should be familiar with the difference between object classes and objects. *Object classes* are the types of objects that an Automation server makes available for you to control. Object classes have a defined set of properties, methods and, in some cases, events that dictate how instances of that object class look and act. When you write Automation code, you manipulate *objects*—particular instances of object classes. The same holds true for VBA class modules and the instances you create and manipulate. (For more information on class modules, see Chapter 3.) You can think of objects and object classes as being similar to variables and data types. VBA supports a fixed set of data types, but you can declare and use as many variables of a single type as you wish. In this chapter, when we discuss a server application's *object model,* we are talking about its set of object classes. When you write VBA code, you're using instances of those classes, which are called objects.

What's the Value of Automation?

Automation's biggest benefit is its capacity to let you use prebuilt, robust, and debugged software components in your applications. Just imagine having to build your own spreadsheet module instead of using Microsoft Excel. Obviously, for simple tasks, you may decide to "roll your own," but as the complexity of a component increases, the benefits of using off-the-shelf software increase as well. Automation takes component reuse one step further by allowing you to control objects using your own code, extending whatever built-in intelligence the objects may have. Finally, the architecture of Automation lets you do this unobtrusively. That is, you control objects using Automation the same way you control them in Access, by using sets of properties, methods, and events. With a few extensions to your current understanding of Access and its objects, you can start controlling other applications' objects, such as those found in Microsoft Office (Excel, Word, PowerPoint, FrontPage, and Outlook) and ActiveX controls.

Object Classes

Before you can start controlling objects, you need to understand which objects are available to you. As you install applications and ActiveX controls, these components will make entries in the Windows Registry that mark them to Windows as controllable. (Technically speaking, Automation servers are those applications that support the IDispatch programming interface.) Because each application may make more than one object class available to Automation clients, you need to know not only the application name, but the object type as well. This information is encapsulated in the program identifier, or ProgID, for the particular object class. ProgIDs are expressed as follows:

ApplicationName.ObjectClass

For example, Microsoft Excel exports a controllable Chart class that has an associated ProgID of "Excel.Chart." Furthermore, this convention lets you append a version number to the ProgID to restrict manipulation of the object to a particular version of the software. "Excel.Chart.5" refers to a Chart object that is manipulated by Excel version 5. Most applications register a pointer to the latest version installed on your computer, so leaving off the version number will force VBA to use the latest version.

WARNING

As software versions are released at an ever-increasing pace, it occasionally becomes necessary to have multiple versions of a particular program installed on your computer. Furthermore, sometimes you will install an older version of a program on a computer that already has a newer version installed. When this happens with an Automation component, the older version sometimes overwrites the Registry information so that an unqualified ProgID (one with no version number appended) will point to the older version. Automation clients that use this ProgID and depend on features that exist only in the newer version will no longer work. When this happens, you should reinstall the newer version. This should restore the Registry settings. As a precaution, however, you can use qualified ProgIDs if you depend on certain features that aren't available in all versions.

While it is not always the case, most applications that feature a user interface (as opposed to "UI-less" servers, which operate transparently behind the scenes) register an Application class. Normally, this object represents the highest-level object in the application's object model, and from it you can derive most other object types. As we discuss the examples in this chapter, the use of ProgIDs should become clear.

Type Libraries: The Key to Classes

These days, almost all COM components implement *type libraries*. Type libraries are databases that list the objects, methods, properties, and events offered by a server application. Automation clients such as VBA can use the information stored in a library to "learn" about another application. Type libraries offer a number of benefits:

- VBA does not actually have to run the server application to interrogate its object model.
- The VBA editor and interpreter can use type libraries to perform syntax checking on your Automation code.
- You can obtain context-sensitive help for another application's keywords.

Type libraries can exist as separate files or be implemented as part of an application EXE or DLL. Most components' type libraries that exist as separate files have a TLB or OLB (for object library) file extension, and you use them in your VBA project by adding them to the list of references in the References dialog. Most well behaved components make the proper Registry entries to make this happen automatically. Occasionally, however, you must add it to the references list yourself. To do this, follow these steps:

1. Open the Visual Basic Editor.
2. Select Tools ➢ References. You should see a list of references similar to the ones shown in Figure 12.1.
3. Check the box next to the reference you want to add.
4. If the reference is not listed, click the Browse button and locate the type library or executable file of the component you want to use.

FIGURE 12.1:

References dialog showing loaded and available references

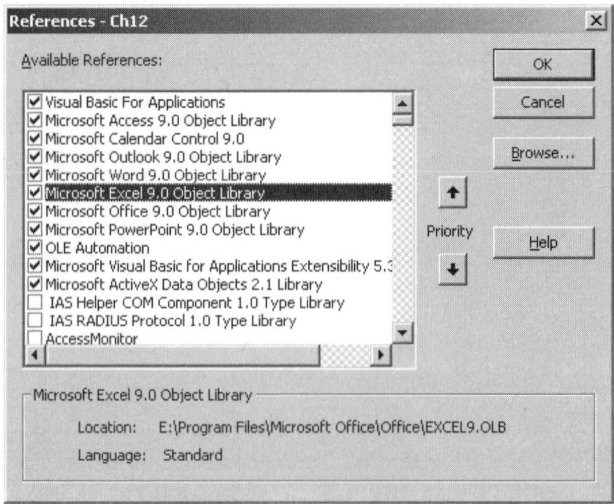

Once you've loaded a type library, you can use the objects, properties, and methods in your VBA code. VBA will be able to correctly verify syntax, as well as provide context-sensitive help for the server component's keywords. One important issue is that the complete path to the type library is stored with your VBA project. If you move the type library or install your application on another computer, you will need to reestablish the link to the type library.

NOTE

Type libraries are also essential to *early binding*, the preferred approach to Automation, described in the following sections.

Type Libraries, References, and Broken Apps

In the many years we've been writing, teaching, and speaking on Automation, a few issues regarding server applications and references have been raised again and again. A common one is, "If I use Automation to control Application X, do my users need Application X in order to run my solution?" The answer, of course, is yes. Automation does not magically compile a server application's functionality into your program; it merely controls the application at runtime. The server application must be installed in order for your program to work.

Another common question is, "What happens if the application isn't installed and a user tries to run my program?" The answer depends on whether you've used a type library reference or not. If not, then the first time you try to start an Automation session, VBA will raise a runtime error that you can trap and handle as you see fit. If you have used a type library, however, it's a bit trickier, since VBA tries to resolve type library references prior to executing code. In this case, however, you can be proactive and run code to validate references.

To do this, you must completely separate the code that uses Automation servers from the code that checks for valid references in different code modules. This is necessary because of VBA's demand load behavior. VBA loads and compiles modules only as needed but will preload modules when they contain procedures referenced by a loaded module. (This, of course, is necessary to compile the requested module completely.) By having a completely separate module that runs a startup procedure to check references, you have the opportunity to find missing type library references before getting a compile error.

To check references, use the References collection of Access' Application object. Use a For Each… loop to iterate through each Reference object, inspecting its IsBroken property. If this returns True, then any code that uses the reference will not work and you should disable this functionality in your application. Reference issues are covered in more detail in Chapter 18.

Browsing Objects with Object Browser

Once you've added references to an Automation component's type library, you can use the VBA Object Browser to view a list of the component's classes, properties, methods, and events. To make Object Browser available, open the Visual Basic Editor and press the F2 key, click the Object Browser toolbar button, or select the View ➢ Object Browser menu command. Figure 12.2 shows Object Browser open to the Application class of Microsoft Excel's type library.

FIGURE 12.2:

Object Browser showing details on Excel's Application object

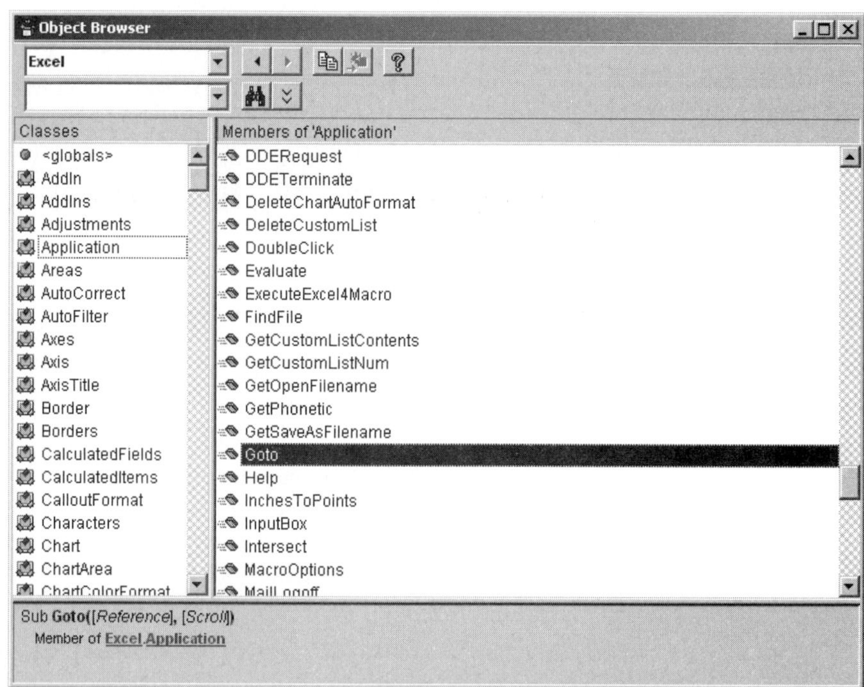

When Object Browser first opens, it displays a list of all the classes exposed by every referenced Automation component, including the current VBA project. You can use the Project/Library drop-down list at the top left of the screen to select a single component, thus making the list of classes a bit more manageable. Object Browser changes the contents of the Classes and Members lists to reflect the change. The Classes list shows all the object classes available from the Automation component. Selecting any one of them causes Object Browser to display the methods and properties for that class in the right-hand list. Icons denote various elements of the type library, such as constants, classes, properties, and methods.

Note that collections are also shown in the left-hand (object) list. When you select a collection, usually denoted as the plural form of the object class name, Object Browser displays the methods and properties for the collection, not the object.

If you're not sure of the exact name of a property or method, you can use Object Browser's search engine. Enter a text string in the text box just below the list of libraries and click the Find button (the one with binoculars on it). After searching the selected type libraries, Object Browser opens the Search Results pane, as shown in Figure 12.3. You can collapse the pane by clicking the button with the up arrows.

FIGURE 12.3: Object Browser displaying search results

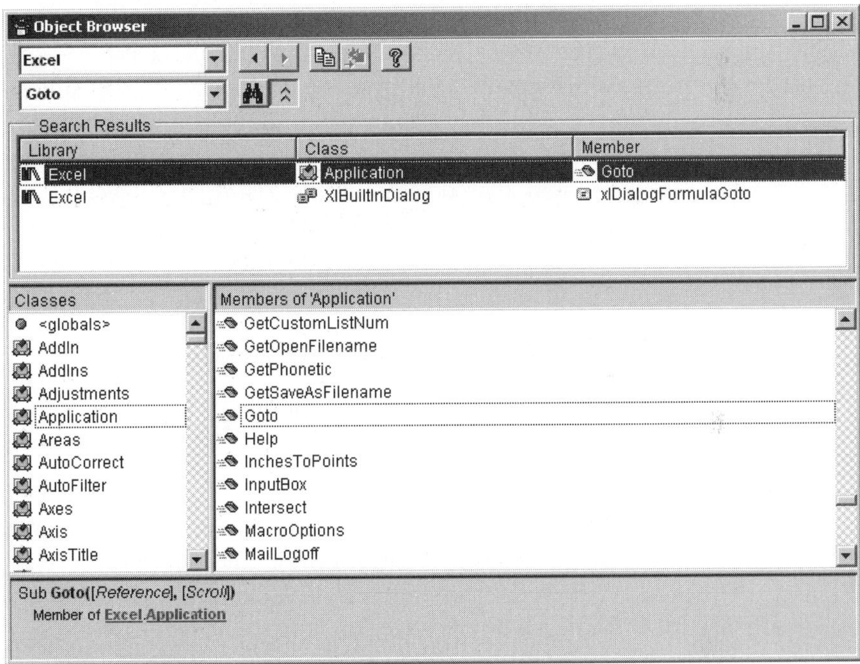

Figures 12.2 and 12.3 also show the Application object's Goto method highlighted in the right-hand list. Note the syntax example at the bottom of the dialog. Object Browser shows you the calling syntax of the property or method, including any arguments. You can highlight any portion of the syntax and use the Copy button to copy the highlighted portion to the clipboard for subsequent pasting into a module. If you don't highlight any of the syntax, the Copy button simply copies the method or property name to the clipboard. If the type library being viewed supports a help file, pressing the Help button (the one with a question mark) or pressing F1 opens that file to the proper page for the displayed property or method.

Object Browser can be especially helpful when you're using an Automation component for the first time. It gives you a class-by-class overview of the object model, allowing you to browse the individual classes and their properties and methods. As you become more familiar with a component, you'll be able to write Automation code from memory, but until then, Object Browser is a good place to start learning about what's available and how to use it.

Creating Object Instances

All Automation sessions begin with the client application creating an instance of a server object. By *creating* an object instance, we mean establishing a conversation with the server application and telling it which of its objects you wish to control. The result of this creation process is a pointer to an instance of the server's object stored in an object variable. Using this object variable, you can control the server application's object using the same techniques you use to control Access objects—by manipulating their methods and properties.

Early Binding and Late Binding

There are two approaches to creating instances of Automation component objects: early binding and late binding. Each approach has its own pros and cons.

With *early binding*, you add a reference to a component's type library at design time to inform VBA about the Automation server and its objects. This technique is called early binding because VBA knows which object classes the component supports (along with all their properties and methods) before you execute your code.

Late binding, on the other hand, does not require a reference to a type library. Instead you instantiate objects at runtime. This approach is known as late binding because VBA has no way of knowing what type of object will be created until runtime.

Most Automation components support early binding, and you should use early binding whenever possible. Early binding offers several benefits:

Speed Because you tell VBA about a component in advance, it does not need to worry that a particular property or method might not be supported. With late binding, extra communication takes place to determine whether the server supports a given property or method *with each line of code!* This decreases performance.

VBA editor support When you use early binding, VBA can perform syntax checking on your source code and provide developer IntelliSense features like statement completion.

Online help Early binding gives you context-sensitive help for components that have help files. Just highlight any member name and press F1.

Early binding has a drawback, however. Since you must use a reference to a type library, if the type library or application is not installed on a user's workstation your solution will not compile or run. Late binding, at least, lets your code compile and run because it does not require a reference in the first place. (Statements that reference the Automation server's objects, properties, and methods will still fail, however.) In general, you should use late binding only when an Automation component does not support early binding.

A Simple Early Binding Example

Controlling Automation components using early binding is extremely simple and very similar to the way you work with built-in Access components and custom classes constructed using VBA class modules. To demonstrate early binding, we've created a simple example that uses Microsoft Excel as an Automation server. If you already know everything there is to know about early binding, you can skip to the next section. Otherwise, start up Access and follow these steps:

1. Create a new database.
2. Open the Visual Basic Editor by pressing Alt+F11.
3. Add a new module to the project.
4. Open the References dialog by selecting the Tools ➢ References menu command.
5. Locate Microsoft Excel 9.0 Object Library in the list and mark the check box. Click OK to close the dialog.
6. Enter the VBA code shown in Listing 12.1 in the new module.
7. Highlight any line of code in the TestXL procedure and press F8 to step through the code.

Listing 12.1

```
Sub TestXL
    Dim objXL As Excel.Application

    ' Create a new instance of Excel
    Set objXL  = New Excel.Application

    ' Reference a few properties
    MsgBox objXL.Name & " " & objXL.Version
    objXL.Visible= True
    objXL.Quit
    Set objXL = Nothing
End Sub
```

NOTE

Notice that we prefaced the object class, Application, with the name of the server, Excel. You must qualify the object class with the server name whenever the object class is ambiguous. (Access also has an Application object.) If you're unsure of the server name to use, look at the list of libraries in Object Browser. Object Browser uses the name of each component, which is what you should use to qualify objects exported by that component.

As you step through the code, you'll notice several things happen. First, you'll observe a slight delay and some disk activity as you execute the New statement. This is because a new instance of Excel is being launched. After the new instance loads, VBA continues executing code and displays the dialog announcing Excel's name and version.

At this point, a new copy of Excel will be running, but you won't be able see it. That's because when Excel is launched in response to a request from an Automation client, it makes its main window invisible. This behavior is application-specific. For more information on how the other Microsoft Office applications react, see the section "Differences in Application Behavior" later in this chapter.

To make Excel's main window visible, execute the next statement. Excel's Application object has a Visible property that controls this behavior. Changing the property to True displays Excel's main window.

Executing the next statement (objXL.Quit) terminates Excel. You'll notice another slight delay as Excel shuts down. The final statement, which sets the object variable to the intrinsic constant Nothing, is a housekeeping task that frees any memory VBA was using to manage the Automation session.

When to Instantiate

In the previous example, you saw how a new instance of Excel was created when you executed a New statement. This forced VBA to create a new instance of Excel explicitly. As an alternative (and just like VBA class modules), if you *declare* an object variable using the New keyword, the object is instantiated the first time you reference one of its properties or methods. For instance, you could modify the example as shown in Listing 12.2.

Listing 12.2

```
Sub TestXLDelayed()
    Dim objXL As New Excel.Application

    ' Excel is started on the next line automatically
    MsgBox objXL.Name & " " & objXL.Version
    objXL.Visible= True
    objXL.Quit
    Set objXL = Nothing
End Sub
```

In this case, Excel will be launched automatically the first time VBA references a property or method that is in the MsgBox statement. In general, however, we don't recommend this technique, even though it saves you typing one line of code. The reason is that in a complex application it may not be obvious (as it is here) when the object becomes instantiated. This can make debugging Automation problems more difficult. Therefore, you should always use explicit instantiation.

NOTE

You cannot use a specific Automation server version (e.g., "Excel.Application.9") with the New keyword. If you need access to version-specific objects, you must use the CreateObject or GetObject functions described in the next section.

CreateObject and GetObject

CreateObject and GetObject are VBA functions (as opposed to a keyword like New) used to instantiate Automation component objects. Both return pointers to an instantiated object that you must store in an object variable. You can declare a variable using the generic Object datatype, or you can use a server-specific datatype if you have added a reference to the server's type library to your VBA project. For example:

```
' If you don't want to use the type library, do this:
Dim objExcel As Object

' If you are using the type library you can do this:
Dim objExcel As Excel.Application
```

Both CreateObject and GetObject are essential to working with late-bound Automation servers (those that don't use a type library) but can also be used with early binding.

Using CreateObject

CreateObject accepts a string containing a component object's ProgID, as described in the section "Object Classes" earlier in this chapter. When you call CreateObject, VBA attempts to create an object of the type specified using the application specified. If it cannot create the object, perhaps because the application is not installed or does not support the object type, it fails with a runtime error.

If you want to try a simple example of late-bound Automation using CreateObject, create the procedure shown in Listing 12.3 and step through it.

Listing 12.3

```
Sub TestXLLateBound()
    Dim objXL As Object

    ' This creates a new instance
    Set objXL = CreateObject("Excel.Application.9")

    ' The rest is pretty much the same as before
    MsgBox objXL.Name & " " & objXL.Version
    objXL.Visible = True
    objXL.Quit
    Set objXL = Nothing
End Sub
```

You'll notice that this is almost the same code as in the prior examples, except that we've used a generic Object variable to store the pointer to Excel's Application object. If you don't include a reference to a component's type library, you must use the Object data type. We've also used CreateObject to instantiate the object variable rather than the New keyword. Note that the ProgID, "Excel.Application.9", is passed as text. We could have stored this in a variable that VBA could evaluate at runtime. This is something that is not possible if you use the New keyword, because the ProgID must be hard coded as part of the New statement.

Using GetObject

GetObject is similar to CreateObject, but instead of accepting a single argument, it allows for two optional arguments, a document name and/or a ProgID. The general form of a GetObject statement is

Set *objectvariable* = GetObject([*docname*], [*ProgID*])

Note that both arguments are optional, but you must supply at least one of them. GetObject is a more flexible function that you can use to create an object from an application's document (an Excel workbook file, for example) or from an existing instance of an application. The flexibility of GetObject is revealed by the combination of arguments used. Table 12.1 explains the results of these combinations.

TABLE 12.1: Various Uses of the GetObject Function

Combination	Example	Results
Document name only	Set objAny = GetObject ("C:\BOOK1.XLS")	The application associated with the document type is launched and used to open the specified document. If the application supports it, an existing instance will be used, and if the document is already open, the object pointer will refer to that instance.
Object class only	Set objAny = GetObject (, "Excel.Application")	If the server application is running, an object pointer is created for the running instance; otherwise, GetObject returns a runtime error.
Object class and empty document name	Set objAny = GetObject ("", "Excel.Application")	Same behavior as CreateObject. Opens a new instance of the application.
Both document name and object class	Set objAny = GetObject ("C:\BOOK1.XLS","Excel. Application")	Same behavior as passing only the document name, except that you can pass document names that aren't normally associated with the server (as determined by the file extension).

As you can see, GetObject is more complex than CreateObject, although it does offer the benefit of using running instances of applications rather than launching new copies each time your Automation code runs. This is especially critical on low-memory computers. In fact, the sample code we've created for this chapter uses GetObject by default, assuming it's better to reuse running instances of applications than starting new ones.

Understanding Class Instancing

In the preceding examples using the Application class, a new copy of Microsoft Excel is launched each time VBA requests a new instance of the class. This is because the Application class is, by default, a single-use class. Automation server classes fall into two broad categories: single-use and multiple-use.

Single-Use Classes

Single-use classes cause a new instance of the application to launch when a client application instantiates them. We've illustrated this in Figure 12.4. Each instance of the Application class created by client applications references an Application object created by a separate copy of Excel.

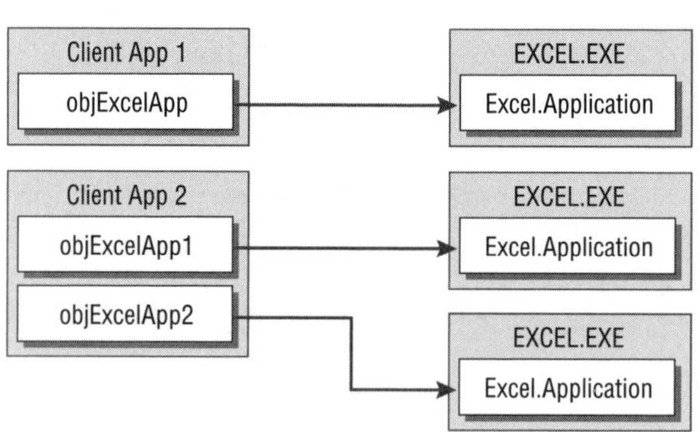

FIGURE 12.4: Single-use classes are each hosted by a different copy of the application.

Multiple-Use Classes

Multiple-use classes, on the other hand, allow multiple Automation client applications to share the *same instance* of the class. An example of a multiple-use class is

Microsoft Outlook's Application class. Only one instance of the class can exist at any given time. Figure 12.5 illustrates this type of class. Even though client applications might instantiate the class using the New keyword or CreateObject, all references point to the same instance in the server application. Applications that expose multiple-use classes are typically those that allow you to launch only one instance from the Windows shell.

FIGURE 12.5:

Multiple-use classes are all hosted by a single copy of the application.

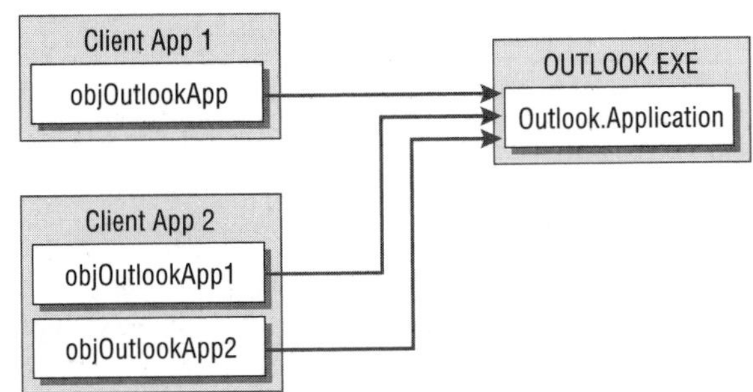

What's more, classes that are single-use by default can sometimes be used like a multiple-use class, as illustrated in Figure 12.6. For example, you can use Excel's Application class as though it were a multiple-use class, even though it is single-use by default. To accomplish this, you must first ensure that a copy of the application is already running. Then, instead of using the New keyword or CreateObject function to instantiate an object, use a normal Set statement or the GetObject function. Code in Listing 12.4 demonstrates this.

FIGURE 12.6:

Using a single-use class as though it were multiple-use

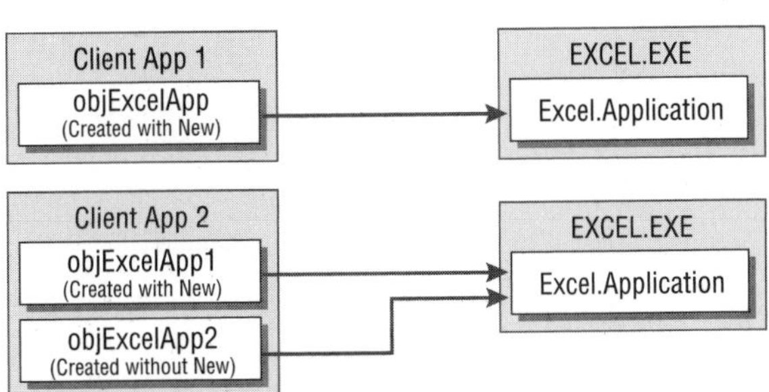

While you can use most single-use classes in the multiple-use role, the converse is not true. Each time you request a new instance of a multiple-use class, you receive a new reference to a preexisting instance if one exists. Only the first request results in a copy of the application being launched.

Listing 12.4

```
Sub TestXLExisting()
    Dim objXL As Excel.Application

    ' Use an existing instance (this will fail
    ' if Excel isn't running!)
    Set objXL = GetObject( ,"Excel.Application.9")

    ' The rest is the same
    MsgBox objXL.Name & " " & objXL.Version
    objXL.Visible = True
    objXL.Quit
    Set objXL = Nothing
End Sub
```

Table 12.2 lists the programs in Microsoft Office 2000 and indicates whether they are single-use or multiple-use by default.

TABLE 12.2: Single-Use and Multiple-Use Office 2000 Applications

Application	Default Behavior	Multiple-Use?
Access	Single-use	Yes
Excel	Single-use	Yes
FrontPage	Multiple-use	N/A
Outlook	Multiple-use	N/A
Publisher	N/A	N/A
PowerPoint	Multiple-use	N/A
Word	Single-use	Yes

Reference Counting and Server Termination

When working with multiple references to object instances, you need to be aware of *reference counting* by the server application. Every time you ask a server application for an object instance using New, CreateObject, or GetObject, the server application increments an internal counter. Conversely, when you destroy an object reference by setting it equal to Nothing (or when the object variable goes out of scope), the server decrements the counter. With multiple-use classes, this can lead to problems if you're not careful.

Most Automation servers terminate automatically when the internal reference count reaches zero. Furthermore, some will not terminate unless the count is zero. For this reason, you should take care when creating multiple references in your program to a single Automation class. If you must do this for whatever reason, be sure to destroy all references to the server when your application terminates. There is no way to determine a server's internal reference count using VBA code.

Some applications will not terminate automatically when the reference count reaches zero if you've done something that enabled the user to interact with the application. For example, displaying Excel's main window will prevent Excel from terminating if the user creates a new workbook.

Controlling Other Applications

Now that you understand the basics of Automation, you're ready to start writing code to control Automation components, be they mega-applications such as Microsoft Excel and Word, or smaller elements such as ActiveX controls. The rest of this chapter explains how you can write code like this, using the other applications in Microsoft Office to illustrate.

Learning an Application's Object Model

The techniques involved in using another component's objects through Automation are the same as those for manipulating Access objects; the only difference is the set of objects themselves. Before beginning to write Automation client code, you must familiarize yourself with the server component's object model.

Unfortunately, the availability and quality of documentation vary enormously, even among Microsoft products. As a general rule, those applications that have their own development language (such as VBA in Microsoft Excel, Outlook, Word, FrontPage, and PowerPoint) have better documentation than those that don't (for example, MapPoint). Resources are available that you can use to learn another application's object model. Some of them are listed here:

- The *Microsoft Office 2000/Visual Basic Programmer's Guide* is included with Microsoft Office 2000 Developer (also available separately from Microsoft Press) and contains information on creating integrated solutions with Microsoft Office, including object model descriptions.
- The *Microsoft Developer Network Library* is an online and CD-ROM resource for those developing solutions with any type of Microsoft technology. You can access a portion of the library (as well as sign up for a paid membership that includes quarterly CD mailings) at `http://msdn.microsoft.com/`.

As mentioned earlier, you can also use Object Browser to interrogate a component's object model. Even with online help, though, this tends to be a trial-and-error method that does not offer the supplementary information that other documentation sources do.

Perhaps one of the most productive ways to get an overview of an object model is by inspecting a graphical view of the relationships between objects. Office 2000 includes help files for each application that include a diagram like the one shown in Figure 12.7. Finding the diagram can be tricky, however.

First, you need to make sure you've installed the VBA help files (they're an optional component of the standard install). Then, the easiest way to locate the diagrams is to:

1. Start Access and open the VBA editor.
2. Set a reference to an application's type library.
3. Open the object browser and select the application's type library from the drop-down list.
4. Click the Help button.

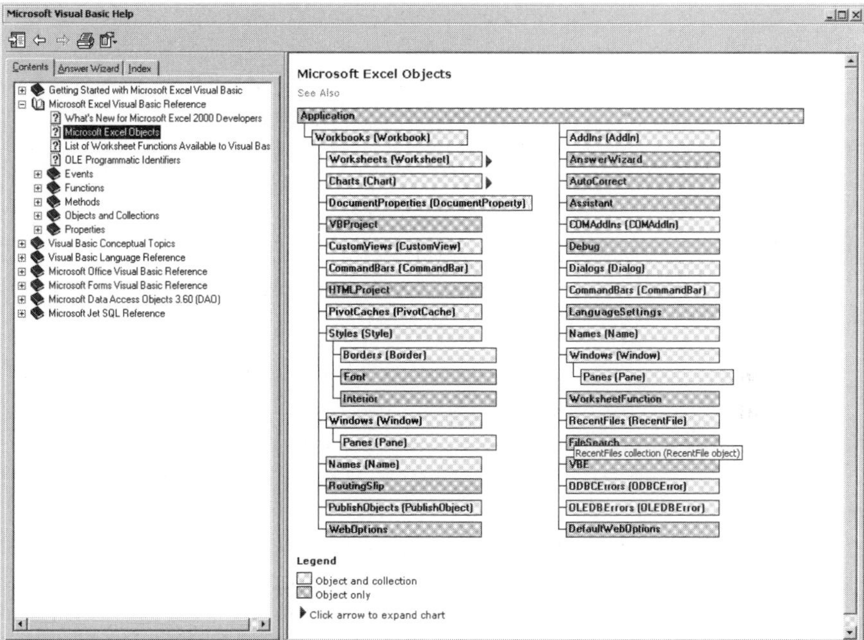

FIGURE 12.7: Office 2000 includes help files with object model diagrams.

The application's object model diagram should appear as the default help topic. If you don't see it, you should be able to select it from the help browser's topic list. It would be nice if it were easier than this but, alas, the perky Office Assistant seems woefully unaware of object models.

Differences in Application Behavior

When creating Automation objects, be aware that component applications exhibit unique behavior when used as Automation servers. Differences in an application's behavior will dictate how you use it in your Automation client code. Table 12.3 lists differences in behavior of the Application object among the programs that make up Microsoft Office 2000. The table explains four facets of Office application behavior:

- Does the application open as a hidden window when launched through Automation?
- Does the application include a Visible property for toggling the visible state of the main window?

- Does the application terminate automatically when its internal reference count equals zero?
- Does the application have a UserControl property to indicate that the user has interacted with the application?

As you use other Automation components, you may want to note how they behave in respect to the list provided.

TABLE 12.3: Differences in Behavior among Microsoft Office 2000 Applications

Application	Opens Hidden?	Visible Property?	Terminates When Ref Count = 0?[1]	UserControl Property?
Access	Yes	Yes[2]	Yes	Yes
Excel	Yes	Yes	Yes	Yes
PowerPoint	Yes	Yes	No	No
Outlook	Yes	No[3]	No	No
Word	Yes	Yes	No	Yes

1. Assumes user has not interacted with the application.

2. Exhibits inconsistent behavior. See Chapter 13 for more information.

3. You must use the Windows API ShowWindow function to change the visible state.

Memory and Resource Issues

One very important piece of information to keep in mind when creating integrated solutions using Automation is how controlling multiple applications at the same time will affect the overall performance of a user's system. Large server applications such as Excel and Word consume a lot of memory. While it is now more difficult to produce the dreaded "Out of System Resources" error, thanks to better memory management in Windows 9*x* and NT, RAM is still an issue. Computers with fewer than 32 megabytes of RAM may perform poorly when many large applications are running, due to disk swapping. If low memory is a problem, you may want to consider closing each server after using it.

The other side of the coin is the time it takes to start and stop large applications. If you frequently use large applications as Automation servers, you may want to leave them open despite the effect this will have on memory consumption. In other words, you will likely have to experiment to get the right mix of performance and memory utilization.

Creating Automation Solutions with Microsoft Office

Statistically speaking, if you are reading this book you already own a copy of Microsoft Office. Since most copies of Access are sold as part of Office, if you're developing Access applications, chances are your users own a copy of Office as well. This gives you an opportunity to leverage the vast functionality in those applications by creating integrated solutions based on Automation. To get you started, we'll spend a good portion of this chapter demonstrating several sample applications that use Office components. You'll be able to see examples of how each can be controlled from Access. We'll also point out some of the minor differences and idiosyncrasies that still exist in this supposedly integrated suite of products.

Specifically, we'll show you how to accomplish four sets of tasks:

- Creating and manipulating documents and tables using Microsoft Word
- Sending and processing e-mail using Microsoft Outlook
- Producing custom presentations using Microsoft PowerPoint
- Charting Access data using Microsoft Excel

Each of these examples will highlight a slightly different aspect of using Automation. First off, the Word application demonstrates the basics of controlling an Automation component and shows how to work with a document-oriented server. Our Outlook example explores the unique aspects of this all-in-one organizer, which relies on the Exchange messaging system. The PowerPoint example highlights the challenges involved in creating completely free-form documents (PowerPoint slides). Finally, the Excel example shows how to use existing documents as the target of Automation commands. We've taken care to utilize features that apply to both Office 97 and Office 2000. While we assume that if you're reading this book you're developing solutions with Access 2000, we know that you may deploy solutions (especially using the Access runtime) to desktops with older versions of Office.

The Office Object Models

While we don't have nearly enough room in this chapter to fully explain the object models of Office applications, we can describe some of their more significant aspects. This will provide a good basis for explaining the sample applications in the rest of the chapter. We've included diagrams from the Office help files that illustrate abridged versions of the object models. They include just a few of the applications' classes. Table 12.4 lists the classes that are exposed to Automation clients. All the other classes implemented by the applications are available through collections, methods, and properties of the exposed classes.

TABLE 12.4: Object Classes Exposed by Microsoft Office 2000 Applications

Server Name	Class Name	Description
Access	Application	Pointer to an instance of Microsoft Access.
Excel	Application	Pointer to an instance of Microsoft Excel.
	Chart	Pointer to a new Chart object. Launches Excel and opens a new workbook if necessary.
	Sheet	Pointer to a new Worksheet object. Launches Excel and opens a new workbook if necessary.
FrontPage	Application	Pointer to an instance of Microsoft FrontPage.
Outlook	Application	Pointer to an instance of Microsoft Outlook.
PowerPoint	Application	Pointer to an instance of Microsoft PowerPoint.
Word	Application	Pointer to an instance of Microsoft Word.
	Document	Pointer to a new Document object. Launches Word if necessary.

Excel

Excel has what might be described as the "granddaddy" of Office object models. It was the first application to integrate VBA (with version 5 in 1993), and with that came a very rich object model that allowed developers complete control over Excel worksheet-based applications. Figure 12.8 illustrates a small portion of the object model.

FIGURE 12.8:

A very small portion of the Excel object model

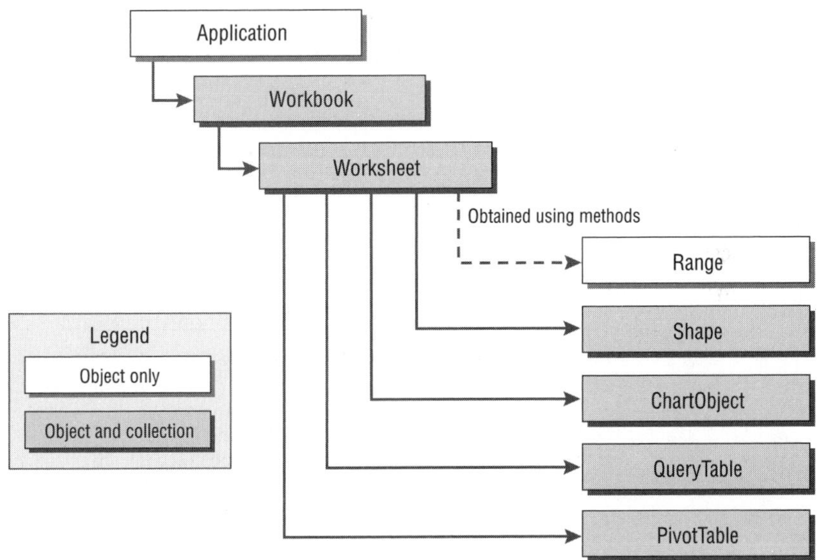

As you can see in Figure 12.8, Excel's object model follows its user interface design very closely. Its top-level class, Application, represents the main Excel application. Descending from that is a Workbooks collection representing all open workbooks (XLS files), and contained within each workbook is a collection of worksheets.

Within each worksheet are collections of objects representing embedded charts, lines, pictures, and so on. What you won't see is any collection symbolizing data in individual cells. This is because implementing a Cells collection, for example, would require managing 16,777,216 objects (because an Excel worksheet is 256 columns wide by 65,536 rows deep)! Instead, you use methods to return references to data. These references are stored using a generic Range object. A range can be a single cell, a block of cells, a discontinuous group of cells, or an entire row or column. You'll find numerous methods designed to return Range objects—for example, Cells, Range, Column, Row, Union, and Intersect. Once you have a valid Range object, you can use some of its more than 160 properties and methods to manipulate data, change formats, and evaluate results.

Word

Word 97 was the first version of Microsoft's flagship word processor to have an exposed object model. While it has been an Automation component since version 2, prior versions have exposed only a single class, Word.Basic, representing Word's macro interpreter. You used this class to execute WordBasic commands against the current instance of Word. Without a rich object model, writing Automation code was cumbersome. WordBasic macros operate only on the currently selected text or object, so it took a great deal of code to ensure that the proper element was selected before you could execute a command that modified it.

Fortunately, this limitation became history with Word 97, and Microsoft has extended the object model in Word 2000. Figure 12.9 illustrates a small portion of Word's object model.

FIGURE 12.9:

Highlights of Word's object model

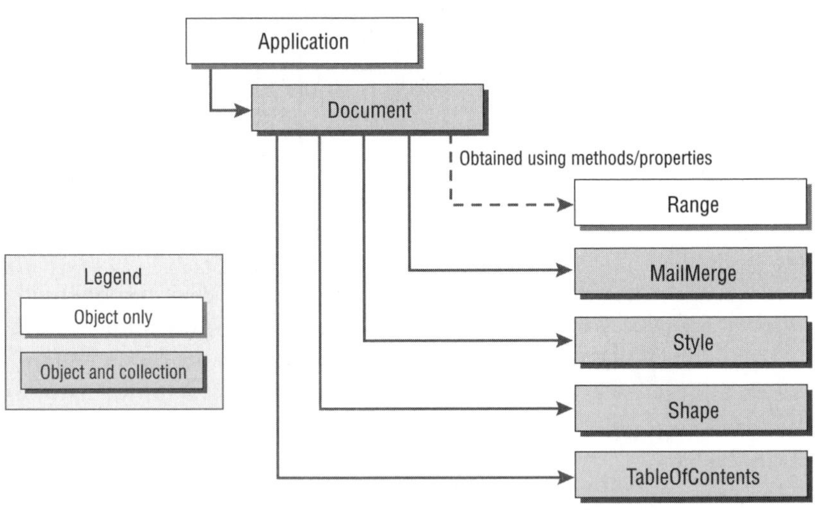

Word's object model shares a number of similarities with that of Excel. At its root is the Application object, which contains a collection of Document objects, one for each open document. Each Document object has several properties that allow you to manipulate text, including Sections, Paragraphs, Sentences, and Words. Each property returns a pointer to a Range object. Word Range objects are similar in concept to those in Excel in that they give you access to the contents and formatting of blocks of text.

PowerPoint

While PowerPoint has had an object model since PowerPoint 95, it wasn't until Microsoft integrated the VBA development environment in PowerPoint 97 that developers really began taking advantage of its functionality. PowerPoint has a rich object model that, like Excel and Word, is aimed at managing the contents of documents. (In Excel, workbooks are the "documents.") PowerPoint's document paradigm, however, deals with presentations and slides. Figure 12.10 shows a portion of the PowerPoint object model, which should look familiar to you by now. It features the requisite Application object and Presentations and Slides collections.

FIGURE 12.10:

PowerPoint's object model deals with Presentation and Slide objects.

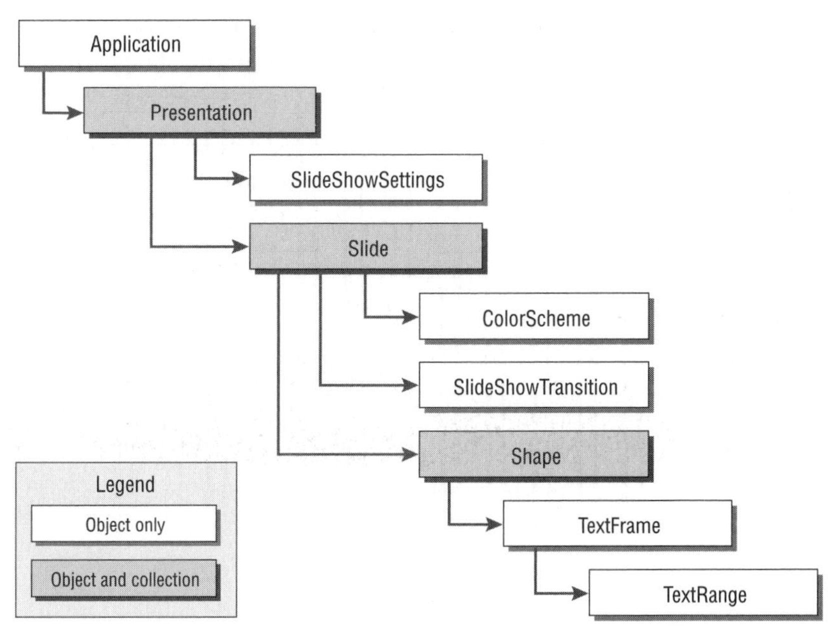

Manipulating textual information in PowerPoint is a bit more convoluted than in Word or Excel because of the unstructured, free-form nature of PowerPoint slides. Each Slide object has a collection of Shapes representing the various graphical components placed on the slide. For those shapes that can contain text, there is a TextFrame object, which controls how contained text is displayed (margins, orientation, and so on). Finally, the TextFrame object contains a TextRange object with text and formatting properties and methods.

Outlook

Microsoft added an object model to Outlook in its first release, Outlook 97, and made minor enhancements in Outlook 98, an interim release. With Outlook 2000, Microsoft has added new members to the object model as well as greatly expanding Outlook's support of events. Outlook's object model is unlike any of the other Office products, however, primarily because it does not follow the same document-centric metaphor. The data it manipulates is far less structured and, like its predecessor Schedule+, the object model can be difficult to learn and use. Furthermore, Outlook is designed to be an integral part of your electronic messaging system and, as such, must cope with various service providers, addressing schemes, storage mechanisms, and electronic mail functions.

Figure 12.11 illustrates the Outlook object model, which may at first appear less complex than that of the other applications. It has an Application class at its root, but that's where similarities end.

FIGURE 12.11:

Outlook's object model is quite different from other Office applications.

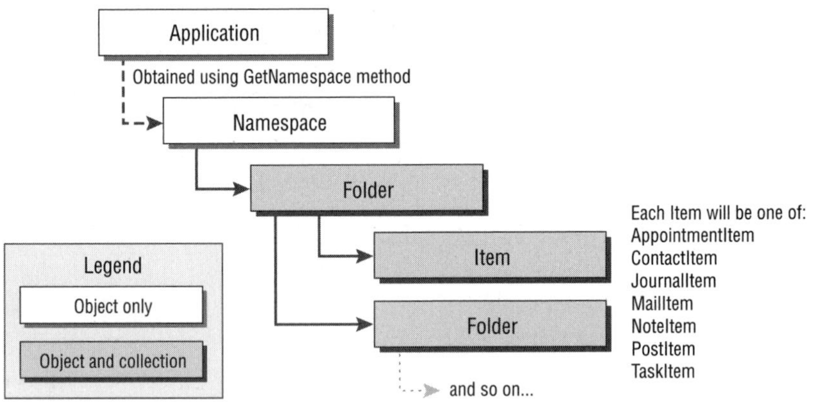

First, Outlook requires that you create a reference to what it calls a Namespace class. This represents one of the messaging service provider layers that Outlook depends on for data storage (although MAPI is the only type of namespace Outlook supports). MAPI (Messaging Application Programming Interface) implements persistent data storage using a hierarchical folder metaphor similar to disk subdirectories. Outlook's Namespace class contains a Folders collection representing the top-level folder of each installed storage system. Each of these, in turn, contains a Folders collection with members for each subfolder (Inbox, Outbox, and so on). Every folder object has a Folders collection, allowing for infinite nesting of data storage.

Data in folders is represented by an Items collection. Each element of this collection can be one of a variety of object classes that represent such things as mail messages, appointments, journal entries, contacts, and tasks. It is this uncertainty about what a folder contains that makes programming with Outlook challenging.

Office Objects

Finally, Microsoft Office implements a set of objects that individual programs share. These include the Office Binder, Office Assistant, command bars, a file search tool, PhotoDraw, and Microsoft Graph. You'll find information about some of these objects elsewhere in this book. For the others, consult Object Browser or online help.

Example: Word As a Report Writer

It might seem odd to suggest using Word as a report writer in a book on Access but using Automation to produce Word documents does have its advantages. Word documents are often more flexible and certainly more powerful than Access reports, since a user can take the output and further modify it. They are also more portable (Access report snapshots notwithstanding) and produce richer HTML output for Web applications. For this reason (and because it's a great demonstration of basic Word Automation techniques), we've chosen to create a sample that accomplishes the following tasks:

1. Launches Microsoft Word if it is not already running
2. Creates a new Invoice document based on a Word template with several bookmarks defined
3. Copies customer and order data from an Access form to the invoice header in Word
4. Copies line item data from an ADO recordset to a Word table
5. Previews the document using Word's print preview mode

To run this sample, you'll need to have Word installed on your computer and have the sample template INVOICE.DOT in the same directory as the sample database.

Creating the Word Template

The sample application included in CH12.MDB relies on the existence of a Microsoft Word template file with predefined bookmarks. Figure 12.12 shows the template open in Microsoft Word. The vertical gray bars on the left side of the document are Word bookmarks. The sample uses the bookmarks to denote where to insert text from an Access form. Consider creating Word templates containing static elements and bookmarks for your applications rather than creating entire documents from scratch.

FIGURE 12.12:

The sample invoice template uses bookmarks to define data insertion points.

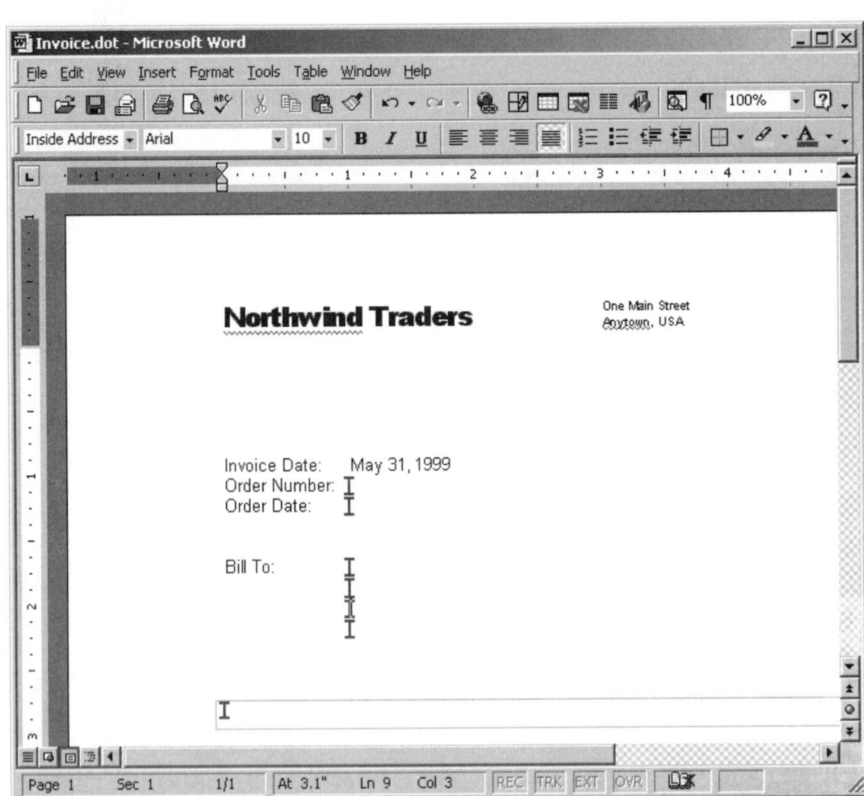

You define a bookmark by setting the insertion point at the spot in the document where you want to create the bookmark and then choosing the Insert ➢ Bookmark command. Figure 12.13 shows the dialog that appears. It lists any existing bookmarks, and you can click the Go To button to go to the point in the document marked by the bookmark. To create a new bookmark or redefine an existing one, enter the name of the bookmark in the text box and click the Add button.

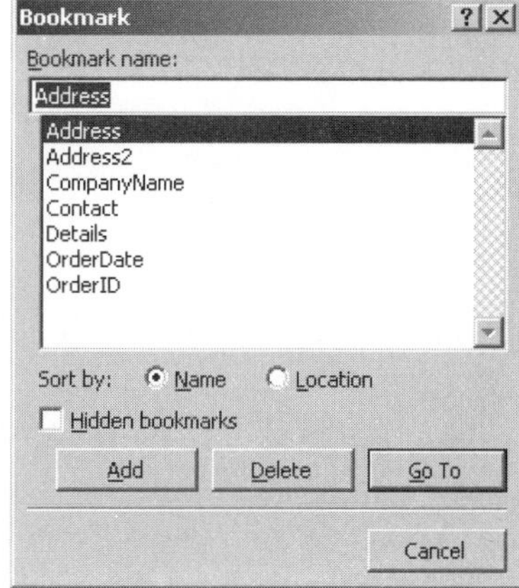

FIGURE 12.13:

Word's Bookmark dialog, showing bookmarks defined in the sample template

You can see in Figure 12.13 that our sample template has a number of bookmarks already defined. We'll use these bookmarks to drive the data transfer process.

Building the Invoice

Once you've installed the invoice template, you can test our application by opening the Orders form in CH12.MDB (see Figure 12.14). (Remember: make sure INVOICE.DOT is in the same directory as CH12.MDB). We've copied the Orders form from NORTHWIND.MDB and modified the Print Invoice button to call a procedure that uses Automation to control Word. The procedure, PrintInvoice-WithWord, is contained in basWord in CH12.MDB, and it creates the invoice in three steps:

- Loads the template in Word
- Adds header information
- Builds the details table

NOTE

We've included the code for PrintInvoiceWithWord in several chunks in the next few sections. For a complete listing, open the procedure yourself in CH12.MDB.

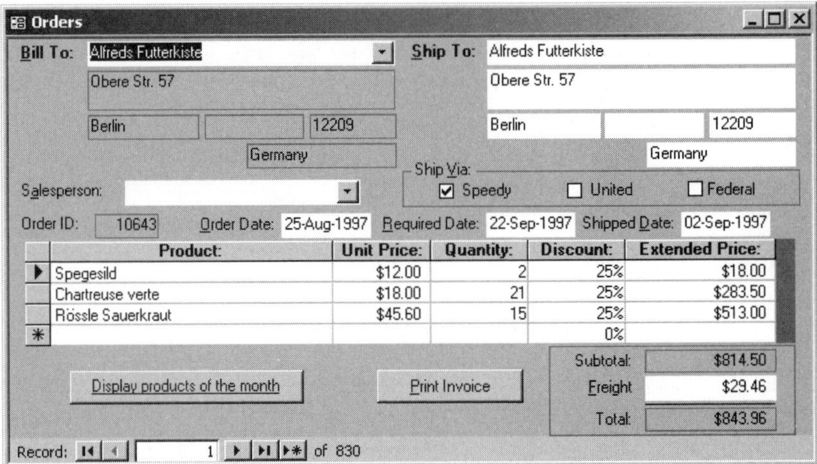

FIGURE 12.14: This modified version of Northwind's Orders form prints invoices using Microsoft Word.

Loading the Template in Word

The first step is to launch Microsoft Word and load a new document based on the invoice template. Word implements a Documents collection representing all open documents, and you create new ones by calling the collection's Add method. Here's the code that does it (objWord is declared as a Word Application object):

```
' Launch Word and load the invoice template
Set objWord = New Word.Application
objWord.Documents.Add _
 Application.CurrentProject.Path & "\Invoice.dot"
objWord.Visible = True
```

The Add method accepts as its first argument the name of a document template on which to base the new document. You can see we've provided a complete path to INVOICE.DOT contained in the same folder as the sample database. If you omit the path, Word looks in the standard Office template folders. You can also omit the template entirely, in which case Word will base the new document on the default template, NORMAL.DOT.

Adding Header Information

Once Word creates the new document, you can begin adding text to it. Our sample procedure uses bookmarks to control the location of inserted text. While you can insert text at any point in a document using objects and collections like Paragraphs, Sentences, Words, and Characters, you'll find it much easier to use predefined bookmarks. Bookmarks retain the same relative location in a document as additional content is added or removed. The aforementioned collections change, and this often makes it hard to position text at a precise location. Listing 12.5 shows the Automation code that copies the invoice header from the Orders form to the Word document.

Listing 12.5

```
' Add header information using predefined bookmarks
With objWord.ActiveDocument.Bookmarks
    .Item("OrderID").Range.Text = frmOrder.OrderID
    .Item("OrderDate").Range.Text = frmOrder.OrderDate
    .Item("CompanyName").Range.Text = frmOrder.CompanyName
    .Item("Address").Range.Text = frmOrder.Address
    .Item("Address2").Range.Text = frmOrder.City & ", " & _
     frmOrder.Region & " " & frmOrder.Country & " " & _
     frmOrder.PostalCode
End With
```

The code in Listing 12.5 shows how to reference individual bookmarks using the Document's Bookmarks collection. Bookmark objects implement a Range method that returns a reference to a text range enclosed by the bookmark. In our example, this is a simple insertion point, but bookmarks can span blocks of text and other objects.

Once the procedure has a reference to a bookmark's Range object, it's a simple matter to set the Text property to a value from the Orders form. A form variable passed into the procedure (frmOrder) provides easy access to fields on the form.

Building the Details Table

The final stage in the process is to add invoice details based on the currently selected order. This involves querying the database for the required information, transferring the data to Word, and building and formatting a Word table. Listing 12.6 shows the code that accomplishes these tasks.

Listing 12.6

```
' Build SQL string for details
strSQL = "SELECT [Product Name], [Unit Price], Quantity, " & _
 "Disc, Extended FROM [Order Details Formatted] " & _
 "WHERE OrderID = " & frmOrder.OrderID

' Get details from database and create a table
' in the document
Set rst = New Recordset
rst.Open strSQL, CurrentProject.Connection
With CreateTableFromRecordset( _
 objWord.ActiveDocument.Bookmarks("Details").Range, rst, True)

    ' Add rows for subtotal, freight, total
    With .Rows.Add
        .Cells(1).Range.Text = "Subtotal"
        .Cells(5).Range.Text = _
         FormatCurrency(frmOrder.Subtotal)
    End With
    With .Rows.Add
        .Cells(1).Range.Text = "Freight"
        .Cells(5).Range.Text = _
         FormatCurrency(frmOrder.Freight)
    End With
    With .Rows.Add
        .Cells(1).Range.Text = "Total"
        .Cells(5).Range.Text = _
         FormatCurrency(frmOrder.Total)
    End With

    ' Apply formatting
    .AutoFormat wdTableFormatProfessional
    .AutoFitBehavior wdAutoFitContent

    ' Fix up paragraph alignment
    .Range.ParagraphFormat.Alignment = wdAlignParagraphRight
    .Columns(1).Select
    objWord.Selection.ParagraphFormat.Alignment = wdAlignParagraphLeft
    objWord.Selection.MoveDown
End With
```

Getting the data is pretty straightforward—we simply use a predefined query, Order Details Formatted, to create an ADO Recordset. You may wonder, however, why we didn't use the recordset associated with the Order Details subform embedded on the Orders form. We chose not to do this for three reasons that were driven by how we'll use the recordset. First, the recordset contained more fields than we needed, and the field names were abbreviated. Second, the numeric values in the recordset are not formatted for currency values (even though they appear as such on the form.) Last, and most important, our sample application requires an ADO Recordset object, and the recordset associated with the subform is based on DAO since it's linked to a Jet database. If you're using this technique with ADP files, you can use form recordsets directly.

After creating the recordset, our procedure calls a custom function called CreateTableFromRecordset (see Listing 12.7). CreateTableFromRecordset is a very useful generic function that builds a table in a Word document given an ADO Recordset. PrintInvoiceWithWord takes the table returned by CreateTableFromRecordset and adds rows for subtotal, freight, and total information, applies some formatting, and then fixes up paragraph alignment of the columns containing numeric data—it's a pretty simple task.

Listing 12.7

```
Function CreateTableFromRecordset( _
 rngAny As Word.Range, _
 rstAny As ADODB.Recordset, _
 Optional fIncludeFieldNames As Boolean = False) _
 As Word.Table

    Dim objTable As Word.Table
    Dim fldAny As ADODB.Field
    Dim varData As Variant
    Dim strBookmark As String
    Dim cField As Long

    ' Get the data from the Recordset
    varData = rstAny.GetString()

    ' Create the table
    With rngAny

        ' Creating the basic table is easy,
        ' just insert the tab-delimted text
```

```
            ' add convert it to a table
            .InsertAfter varData
            Set objTable = .ConvertToTable()

            ' Field names are more work since
            ' you must do them one at a time
            If fIncludeFieldNames Then
                With objTable

                    ' Add a new row on top and make it a heading
                    .Rows.Add(.Rows(1)).HeadingFormat = True

                    ' Iterate through the fields and add their
                    ' names to the heading row
                    For Each fldAny In rstAny.Fields
                        cField = cField + 1
                        .Cell(1, cField).Range.Text = fldAny.Name
                    Next
                End With
            End If
        End With
        Set CreateTableFromRecordset = objTable
    End Function
```

CreateTableFromRecordset works like this: First it calls the recordset's GetString method, which returns the recordset's data as a tab and carriage return–delimited string. This is why we needed to use an ADO Recordset—DAO Recordsets do not support GetString. Once we have the data, we copy it to the Word document using the InsertAfter method of the Word Range object passed to the procedure. The Range object indicates where in the document you want to create the table. Next, the procedure calls the Range object's ConvertToTable method to morph the newly inserted text into a table. This technique of creating a table from delimited text is the fastest way to create tables in Word using Automation—far faster than copying data one row and column at a time.

From here, it's relatively simple to add field names to the table by inserting a new row in the table and iterating through recordset fields, copying their names to each newly added cell. Once the process is complete, the function returns a pointer to the newly created table.

Figure 12.15 shows the completed document. Even though this was a relatively simple example, it illustrated two techniques for automating Word, manipulating bookmarks and tables, that you will find useful in your applications.

FIGURE 12.15:

A completed invoice created using Automation to control Microsoft Word

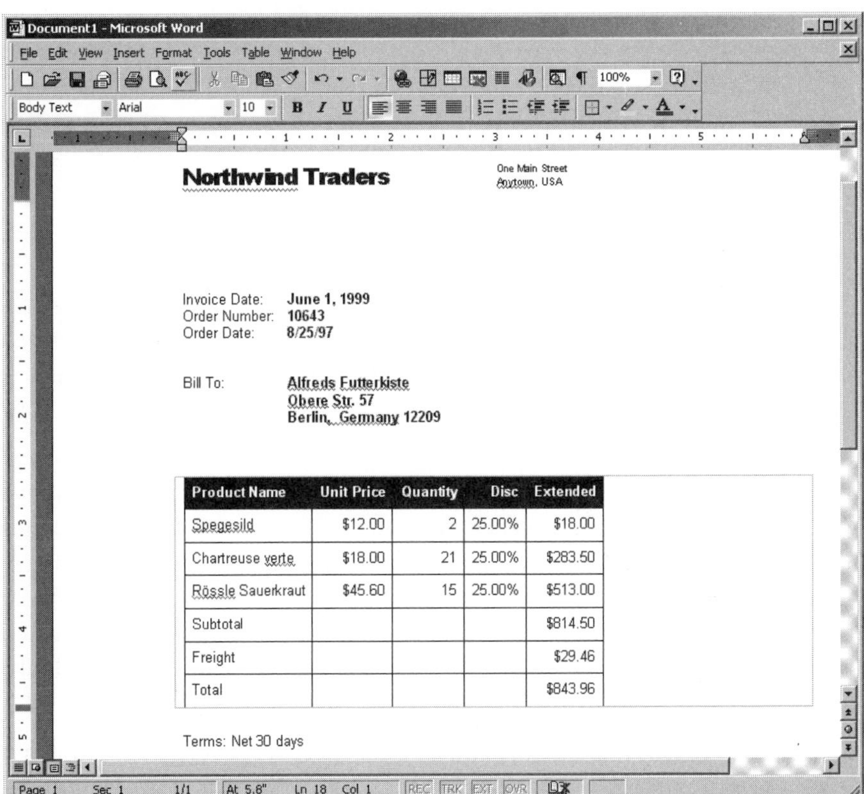

Northwind Traders

One Main Street
Anytown, USA

Invoice Date: **June 1, 1999**
Order Number: **10643**
Order Date: **8/25/97**

Bill To: **Alfreds Futterkiste**
Obere Str. 57
Berlin, Germany 12209

Product Name	Unit Price	Quantity	Disc	Extended
Spegesild	$12.00	2	25.00%	$18.00
Chartreuse verte	$18.00	21	25.00%	$283.50
Rössle Sauerkraut	$45.60	15	25.00%	$513.00
Subtotal				$814.50
Freight				$29.46
Total				$843.96

Terms: Net 30 days

Example: Outlook Time Reporting

If you polled Office users to see which Office application they used most, it would probably be Outlook. As a premier e-mail client, most users have it running all day, every day, to tackle e-mail, scheduling, and contacts. For this reason, it makes a great component of a solution created using Automation. To demonstrate just a portion of Outlook's power, we've created a simple time-reporting application using the Outlook journal. The application allows you to create journal entries in Outlook and then load that schedule information back into an Access database. The application is a simple time-reporting system that tracks the length of time spent on various tasks using the Outlook journal.

To test this application, you'll need a copy of Outlook installed on your computer. To get the maximum benefit, you'll also need to create some journal entries. You can do this by using the first component of this sample project or Outlook itself.

Outlook and Exchange

Even if you don't use Outlook to send and receive e-mail, you're still using Exchange, Microsoft's messaging product, to some degree. This is because Outlook relies on Exchange, or more specifically MAPI (Messaging Application Programming Interface), for data storage. MAPI uses a hierarchical collection of folders for data storage. Every folder can have subfolders, ad infinitum. Individual folder items are just blobs of data. It's up to the applications that use them to make sense of the bits and bytes.

At a minimum, to use Outlook you'll need to create a set of *personal folders* on your hard drive. Outlook stores these in a PST (personal message store) file. When you create your PST file, your set of personal folders will contain subfolders for electronic messaging (Inbox, Outbox, Sent Items, and Deleted Items). Outlook will create additional folders for its use (Calendar, Contacts, Journal, Notes, and Tasks). Part of creating Automation solutions with Outlook is navigating this folder hierarchy.

Finally, to access any of the folders managed by Outlook, you'll need to tell Outlook what messaging system, known as a *namespace,* to use. You do this by calling the GetNamespace method of Outlook's Application object. Currently only one namespace, MAPI, is supported, but this method allows for future extensibility.

Conversing with Outlook

Beginning an Automation session with Outlook involves creating a new instance of the Application class, specifying a namespace to use, and logging on to the messaging system. We've wrapped these steps inside a function in basOutlook called GetOutlook, shown in Listing 12.8, that returns a pointer to the MAPI namespace after logging in.

Listing 12.8

```
Function GetOutlook() As Outlook.NameSpace
    Dim objOutlook As New Outlook.Application
    Dim objNamespace As Outlook.NameSpace
    Dim frmLogon As Form_frmChooseProfile
    Dim strProfile As String
    Dim strPassword As String

    Const conLogonForm = "frmChooseProfile"

    ' Open the logon form
    DoCmd.OpenForm FormName:=conLogonForm, _
     windowmode:=acDialog

    ' If the user didn't cancel, continue
    If Application.CurrentProject.AllForms( _
     conLogonForm).IsLoaded Then

        ' Set a reference to the form
        Set frmLogon = Forms(conLogonForm)

        ' Get the profile and password to use
        strProfile = frmLogon.Profile
        strPassword = frmLogon.Password
        frmLogon.CloseForm

        ' Get a reference to the MAPI workspace
        Set objNamespace = objOutlook.GetNamespace("MAPI")

        ' Log on, creating a new MAPI session,
        ' using the profile and password
        Call objNamespace.Logon(strProfile, _
         strPassword, False, True)

        ' Return a reference to the namespace
        Set GetOutlook = objNamespace
    End If
End Function
```

We begin by opening a dialog, shown in Figure 12.16, that prompts the user for an Exchange profile and the password associated with it. Exchange profiles are used to define combinations of data storage and electronic messaging systems for use during an Exchange session. Once the user has made a selection, the GetOutlook function calls GetNamespace, passing "MAPI" as the namespace type, and then calls the namespace's Logon method. Logon takes four arguments:

- The name of an Exchange profile
- The password associated with that profile
- A True/False value that determines whether a logon dialog is displayed
- A True/False value that determines whether a new Exchange session is created

FIGURE 12.16:

Selecting an Exchange profile prior to working with Outlook

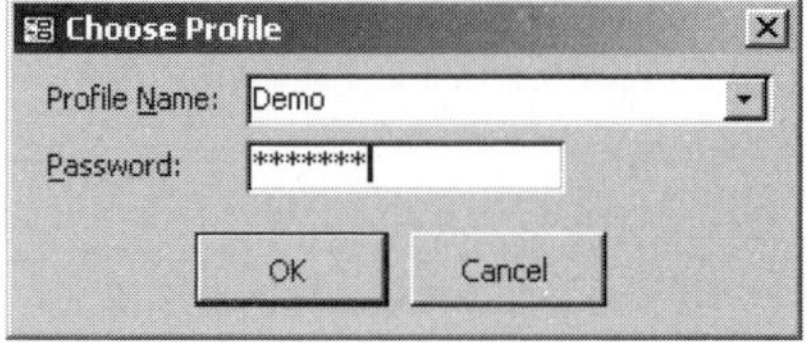

WARNING

The logon form calls a function in basOutlook, GetProfileList, which reads a list of Exchange profiles from the Windows Registry. It appears that the location of this information changes between versions of Outlook and Windows (NT vs. 9*x*). You may need to update the constant in GetProfileList that stores the name of the Registry key.

Creating New Journal Entries

GetOutlook is used to begin an Automation session by the two forms that make up the sample application. The frmOutlookWriteJournal form, shown in Figure 12.17, lets you create journal entries by selecting a date on the calendar ActiveX control, entering subject, start time, and end time information, and clicking the Log button.

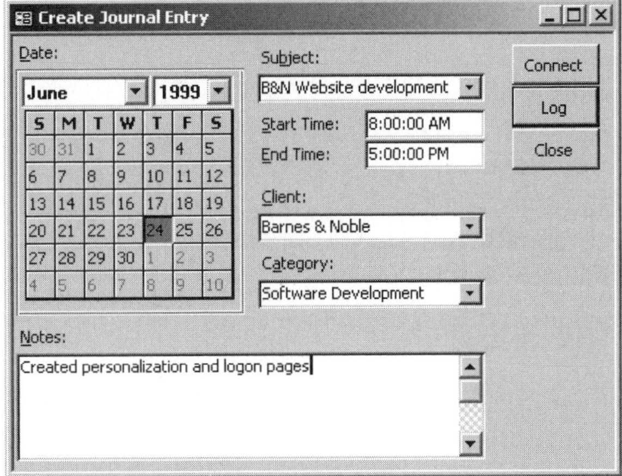

FIGURE 12.17: The frmOutlookWriteJournal form lets you create new journal entries.

Before you click the Log button, however, you must click the Connect button to begin the Automation session. Code behind this button calls GetOutlook and stores the resultant Namespace object in a module-level variable. It does this so you can use the same namespace to create multiple journal entries without repeatedly starting and stopping Outlook. After you connect to Outlook, the button becomes disabled.

Code behind the Log button, shown in Listing 12.9, uses the Namespace object to create a new journal entry by first obtaining a reference to the Journal folder. It does this by calling the namespace's GetDefaultFolder method with the olFolderJournal constant. While you could use the Folders collection to navigate the hierarchy manually, using GetDefaultFolder is easier when you need to access any of the messaging or Outlook folders.

Listing 12.9

```
Private Sub cmdLog_Click()
    Dim objOLJournal As Outlook.MAPIFolder

    ' Make sure we have a valid reference
    If mobjOLNamespace Is Nothing Then
        Me.cmdConnect.Enabled = True
        Me.cmdConnect.SetFocus
        Me.cmdLog.Enabled = False
```

```
        Else
            ' Get a reference to the "Journal" folder
            Set objOLJournal = mobjOLNamespace. _
             GetDefaultFolder(olFolderJournal)

            ' Create a new journal item, set it's
            ' properties, and save it
            With objOLJournal.Items.Add(olJournalItem)
                .Start = CVDate(Me.calMain.Value & _
                 " " & Me.txtStart)
                .End = CVDate(Me.calMain.Value & _
                 " " & Me.txtEnd)
                .Subject = Me.cboSubject
                .Categories = Me.cboCategory
                .Companies = Me.cboClients
                .Body = Me.txtNotes
                .Type = "Task"
                .Save
            End With
        End If
    End Sub
```

Once a reference to the Journal folder has been obtained, the procedure calls the Add method of the folder's Items collection. This creates a new journal entry. The procedure uses a With block to set various properties before calling the new object's Save method.

Loading Journal Information

Once you've created a few journal entries, you can use the frmOutlookReadJournal form shown in Figure 12.18 to load them into an Access table. The contents of this table, tblJournalEntries in the sample database, are displayed on the form as well as summarized on a report, rptTime. You can open the report by clicking the Report button.

Reading journal entries from Outlook is quite similar to creating them. First, the application calls GetOutlook, then creates a reference to the Journal folder, and finally, uses a For Each… loop to iterate through each item in the folder. Listing 12.10 shows a portion of the code that accomplishes this. The rstJournal variable in the listing refers to an ADO recordset based on the tblJournalEntries table, and obj-FilteredItems is declared as an Outlook.Items variable.

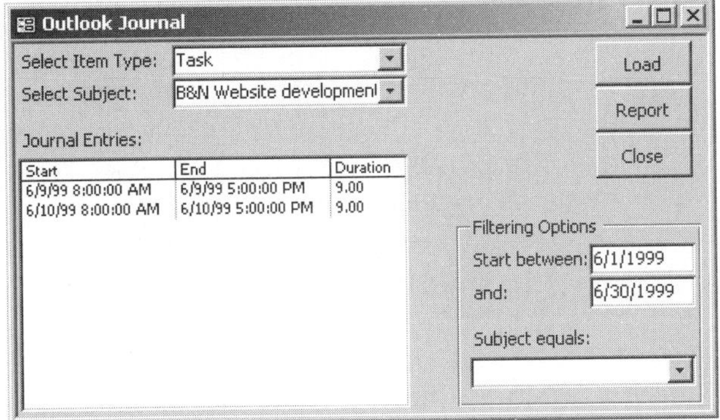

FIGURE 12.18:

The frmOutlookReadJournal form loads and displays journal entries.

Listing 12.10

```
' Get a reference to the "Journal" folder
Set objOLJournal = objOLNamespace. _
 GetDefaultFolder(olFolderJournal)

' Filter the items in the folder
Set objFilteredItems = _
 FilterOutlookItems (objOLJournal.Items)

' Process the items in the folder, adding them
' to the journal entries table
With rstJournal
    For Each outItem In objFilteredItems
        .AddNew
        !EntryID = outItem.EntryID
        !Type = outItem.Type
        !Subject = outItem.Subject
        !Start = outItem.Start
        !End = outItem.End
        .Update
    Next
End With
```

In addition to simply reading the items from the folder, we optionally apply a filter to them using the Items collection's Restrict method. Listing 12.11 shows the FilterOutlookItems function that accomplishes this. It builds a filter string based on controls on the form. Applying the Restrict method does not change the existing Items collection but instead returns a new Items collection representing items that match the filter expression. It is this new collection that is returned as a result of calling FilterOutlookItems.

Listing 12.11

```
Private Function FilterOutlookItems (objItemsToFilter As _
 Outlook.Items) As Outlook.Items

    Dim strFilter As String
    Dim strQuote As String * 1

    ' Get a double quote for delimiters
    strQuote = Chr$(34)

    ' First check date range
    If IsDate(Me!txtFilterStart1) And _
     IsDate(Me!txtFilterStart2) Then

        strFilter = "[Start] >= " & strQuote & _
         Me!txtFilterStart1 & strQuote & " AND " & _
         "[Start] <= " & strQuote & _
         Me!txtFilterStart2 & strQuote
    End If

    ' Then check Subject
    If Not IsNull(Me!cboFilterSubject) Then
        If Len(strFilter) Then
            strFilter = strFilter & " AND "
        End If
        strFilter = "[Subject] = " & strQuote & _
         Me!cboFilterSubject & strQuote
    End If

    ' If we have a filter, apply it to the Items collection,
    ' otherwise just return the original collection
    If Len(strFilter) Then
        Set FilterOutlookItems= objItemsToFilter. _
         Restrict(strFilter)
    Else
        Set FilterOutlookItems= objItemsToFilter
    End If
End Function
```

The Restrict method (and its relative, the Find method) is useful when you have many items in a particular folder. Reading each item one at a time to locate specific ones can take a lot of time. Filter expressions used with the Restrict and Find methods must obey these rules:

- You can use any property name (for example, Subject), as long as it is enclosed in square brackets.
- You can use only property names and literal values.
- You can use only the =, >, <, >=, <=, and <> operators.
- You can combine individual expressions using the And, Or, and Not operators.
- Each individual expression must evaluate to True or False.

Example: Creating a PowerPoint Presentation

Our third sample Automation application uses Microsoft PowerPoint to create a slide presentation based on the data in tblJournalEntries. It demonstrates how to work with PowerPoint's somewhat cumbersome object model to create simple slide presentations, complete with transition effects and timings. While PowerPoint is a document-based application like Word and Excel, the documents (specifically, slides) are much less structured, containing various elements such as text, graphics, sound, and video clips. Creating complex presentations requires a bit of hard work, but once you've familiarized yourself with the basic structure of a PowerPoint slide, you should be able to accomplish this without much trouble.

Understanding PowerPoint Slides

On the surface, PowerPoint's object model is very similar to those of Word and Excel. At its root is the Application class, which contains a collection of Presentation objects. Each Presentation object, in turn, contains a collection of Slide objects. You add new slides to a presentation using the Add method of the Presentations collection. Add accepts two arguments: the position in the presentation where the new slide is to appear and a constant representing the slide layout. Layout options include blank, title and subtitle, title only, title and text, and so on. Layout options correspond to those shown in PowerPoint's Add Slide dialog.

From here, the object model diverges greatly from its counterparts. The contents of a slide fall into the general category of Shapes. A shape could be a line, rectangle, text box, chart, picture, or one of a variety of other objects. You create new shapes by calling one of the methods listed in Table 12.5. Each method returns a pointer to a Shape object that you can manipulate using its properties and methods.

TABLE 12.5: Methods for Creating PowerPoint Shapes

Method	Shape Created
AddCallout	Callout with arrow
AddComment	Slide comment
AddConnector	Shape connector
AddCurve	Curved line
AddLabel	Text label
AddLine	Straight line
AddMediaObject	Media object (AVI, WAV, etc.)
AddOLEObject	Other embedded object
AddPicture	Graphical image based on a file
AddPlaceholder	Placeholder (a preset shape from the slide's original layout)
AddPolyline	Multisegmented line
AddShape	Predefined shape (rectangle, circle, star, etc.)
AddTable	PowerPoint table
AddTextbox	Text box
AddTextEffect	WordArt image
AddTitle	Title placeholder
BuildFreeForm	FreeForm drawing object

Depending on the style of slide you create, you may already have several shapes on the slide. For example, the ppLayoutText style (the traditional bullet point with title slide) has two Shape objects, one for the title and one for the bulleted text. In addition to the methods listed in Table 12.5, the Shapes collection has two useful properties, HasTitle and Title. HasTitle is a Boolean property that determines whether the slide has a shape designated as the title. If so, it will be the first Shape object in the Shapes collection, and you can use the Title property to return a pointer to it.

We've created a wrapper function for adding new slides to a presentation that handles the task of designating a layout style and setting title text, if applicable. The function, AddNewSlide, is shown in Listing 12.12 and included in the sample database's basPowerPoint module. You will notice that we've used optional arguments to provide sensible default values for various slide properties.

Listing 12.12

```
Function AddNewSlide(objPres As PowerPoint.Presentation, _
 Optional intStyle As Integer = ppLayoutText, _
 Optional strTitle As String = "", _
 Optional intIndex As Integer = 0) _
 As PowerPoint.Slide

    Dim objSlide As PowerPoint.Slide

    ' Use the passed Presentation
    With objPres

        ' Find out where to put the slide
        If intIndex = 0 Or intIndex > .Slides.Count + 1 Then
            intIndex = .Slides.Count + 1
        End If

        ' Create new slide
        Set objSlide = .Slides.Add(intIndex, intStyle)

        ' If the slide has a title, set it
        With objSlide.Shapes
            If .HasTitle Then
                .Title.TextFrame.TextRange.Text = strTitle
            End If
        End With
```

```
        ' Return pointer to the slide
        Set AddNewSlide = objSlide
    End With
End Function
```

After creating the new slide, AddNewSlide returns a pointer to it that the calling procedure can use to set slide properties. The code that sets the slide's title text requires a bit of explanation. For that, we'll have to delve more deeply into the structure of PowerPoint Shape objects.

Working with PowerPoint Shapes

PowerPoint shapes are rather complex objects. A shape has properties that control its appearance, contained text, animation settings, and actions during a slide show. Of most interest to us are those that control the text contained in the shape. Other appearance properties, such as Fill, Rotation, and Shadow, should be fairly self-explanatory.

You cannot access contained text directly. Instead, you must first reference a shape's TextFrame property, which returns a pointer to a TextFrame object. A TextFrame object is the rectangular region in which PowerPoint draws text. It has properties that control overall text margins, anchor points, and orientation. It also has a Ruler property that returns a pointer to a Ruler object. Using the Ruler object, you can set indentation levels and tab stops.

To actually manipulate text inside a shape, you use the TextFrame's TextRange property. TextRange returns a pointer to an object of the same name. TextRange objects are similar to Range objects in Word and Excel in that they contain actual data that you can manipulate. The default property of a TextRange object is Text, which returns the actual characters. You can also use properties such as Font and ParagraphFormat to control the text's appearance. The TextRange class also has a variety of methods for dissecting text, such as Paragraphs, Sentences, Words, and Characters, and others for editing text, such as Cut, Copy, Paste, InsertAfter, and InsertBefore.

We touch on only a few of these in our sample application. If you're serious about using PowerPoint as an Automation component, spend an afternoon using Object Browser and online help to explore its extremely rich object model.

Creating a Simple Presentation

Our sample application uses the data in tblJournalEntries, described earlier in this chapter, to create a slide presentation that details total time spent on various tasks. The process is initiated from the frmCreatePPT form shown in Figure 12.19. The form lets you specify text for a title slide, as well as options for a slide show that you can run after the presentation has been created.

FIGURE 12.19:

Use the frmCreatePPT form to create a new presentation.

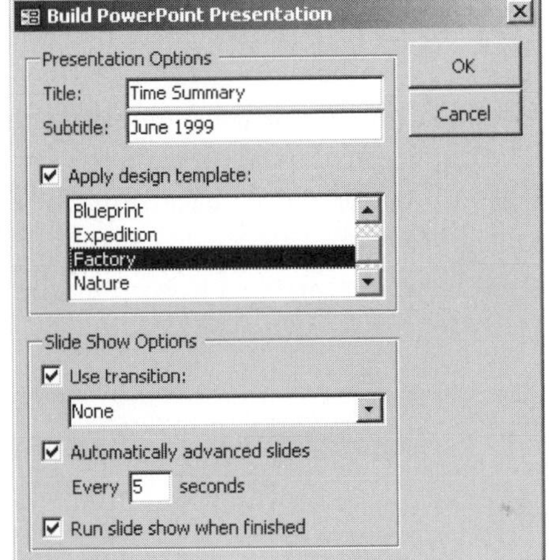

Code behind the OK button creates the new presentation. Listing 12.13 shows a portion of the code. (For a complete listing, refer to the form in CH12.MDB.) You'll notice that the procedure uses the AddNewSlide function mentioned earlier in this chapter.

Listing 12.13

```
Dim objPPApp As New PowerPoint.Application
Dim objPPPres As PowerPoint.Presentation
Dim objPPSlide As PowerPoint.Slide

' Create a new presentation
Set objPPPres = objPPApp.Presentations.Add

' If user wants a design template, apply it
If Me!chkTemplate Then
```

```
        objPPPres.ApplyTemplate mstrTemplatePath & _
         "\" & Me!lstTemplates & ".pot"
    End If

    ' Add a new title slide
    Set objPPSlide = AddNewSlide(objPPPres, _
     ppLayoutTitle, Nz(Me!txtTitle))
    objPPSlide.Shapes(2).TextFrame.TextRange.Text = _
     Nz(Me!txtSubtitle)
    Call adhSetSlideShowOptions(objPPSlide)
```

After creating a new presentation using the Add method of the Presentations collection, the procedure optionally applies a design template based on the user's selection. Design templates supply colors, fonts, and other aspects of a presentation. The procedure then adds a title slide using the ppLayoutTitle constant and the text from the form. At this point, the new presentation contains a single slide. Figure 12.20 shows an example of what it might look like.

FIGURE 12.20:

Title slide from a newly created presentation

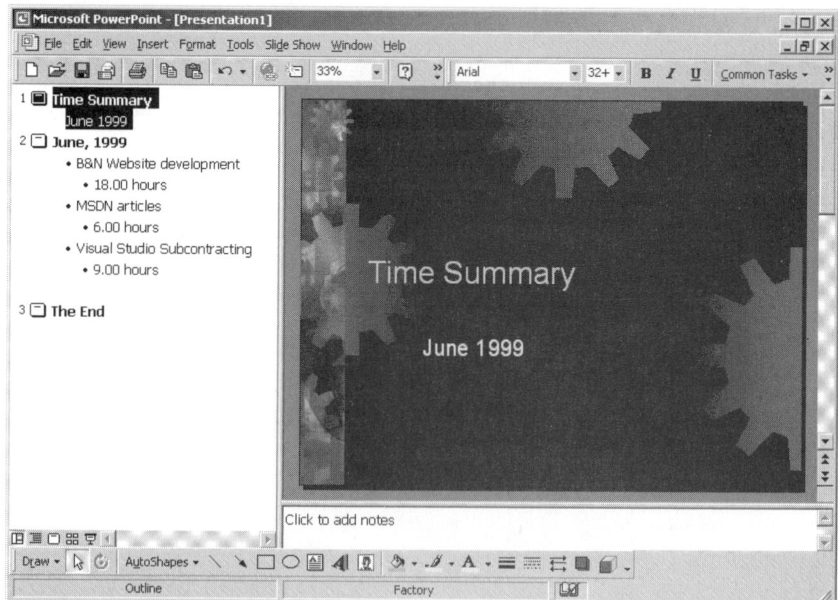

Additional slides are created inside a Do loop that iterates through data summarized from tblJournalEntries. A new slide is created for every month that appears in the summarized data. The code shown in Listing 12.14 enters details on tasks and times on the slide. (Note that we've left out some of the code to keep the listing short.)

Listing 12.14

```
' Add a new slide
Set objPPSlide = AddNewSlide(objPPPres, , _
 rstPeriods!MonthYear)
Call adhSetSlideShowOptions(objPPSlide)

' Insert the main bullet point (Subject)
With objPPSlide.Shapes(2).TextFrame. _
 TextRange.InsertAfter

    .IndentLevel = 1
    .Text = rstTime!Subject & vbCrLf

    ' Insert the sub head (Duration)
    With .InsertAfter
        .IndentLevel = 2
        .Text = Format(rstTime!Duration, _
         "0.00 hours") & vbCrLf
    End With
End With
```

You can see how we use the TextFrame and TextRange properties of Shape(2) (the bulleted text frame on the slide). We also make heavy use of the InsertAfter method. When called with a String argument, InsertAfter inserts the text after any existing text and returns a TextRange object that points to the newly inserted text. When called with no arguments, it returns a pointer to an empty TextRange object at the end of the current text stream. Once we have this in a With block, we can set its IndentLevel and Text properties. Figure 12.21 illustrates what one of the slides created using this code looks like.

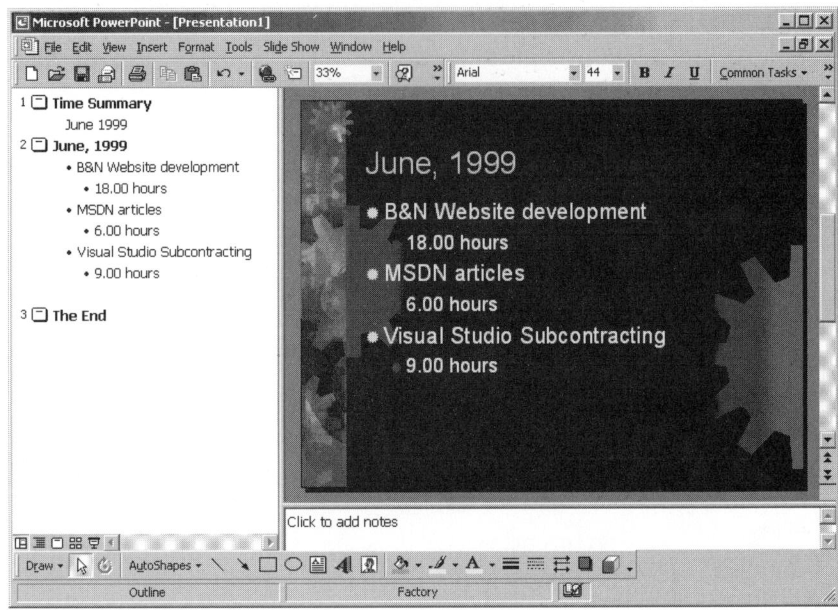

FIGURE 12.21: PowerPoint slide with detail information from an Access table

Apply Slide Show Effects

frmCreatePPT also contains controls for setting slide show options. Specifically, you can select a transition to use between slides, the amount of time before advancing to the next slide, and whether to start the slide show automatically after creating the presentation. The SetSlideShowOptions procedure shown in Listing 12.15 applies these choices.

Listing 12.15

```
Private Sub SetSlideShowOptions(objSlide _
 As PowerPoint.Slide)

    With objSlide.SlideShowTransition
        If Me!chkTransition Then
            .EntryEffect = CInt(Me!cboTransitions)
        End If
        If Me!chkAdvance Then
            .AdvanceOnTime = msoTrue
```

```
            .AdvanceTime = CSng(Me!txtSeconds)
        End If
    End With
End Sub
```

The procedure operates on the slide's SlideShowTransition object, setting the EntryEffect, AdvanceOnTime, and AdvanceTime properties. Calling the Run method of the presentation's SlideShowSettings object in the event procedure for the OK button actually starts the slide show. As you can imagine, there is a host of other properties and methods of these objects. Once again, use Object Browser to your advantage when exploring PowerPoint's object model.

Example: Populating an Excel Worksheet

Microsoft Excel is probably one of the most satisfying Automation servers you can work with. It has a rich, well-documented object model that lets you control just about every element of an Excel worksheet, right down to individual character formatting within a cell. In this section, we show you how to update a simple worksheet and chart with data in an Access database. We've already discussed most of what you need to know about using Automation servers, so we'll keep this section brief.

Using an Existing File

One thing we haven't yet discussed is using an Automation server to manipulate an existing document. Manipulating existing documents is a technique that becomes critical when you need to retrieve data from a file that was edited by another process or even a (gasp!) human being. Because you don't have complete control over it, you must be careful when altering and saving it to make sure you don't inadvertently overwrite another person's changes. Using existing files is also a good compromise between completely manual and completely automated creation of documents. For example, the VBA code required to create a complex Excel chart can be quite long. It is often better to use an existing chart and modify only a few properties.

From a programming standpoint, you can approach this problem in one of two ways. You can either create an instance of Excel's Application object and use it to open an existing file, or you can use the GetObject function, which will return a reference directly to the workbook. In this example, we've used GetObject to demonstrate how to use it with existing documents. GetObject lets you specify a document name and path instead of a ProgID. As long as the file type is correctly registered, Windows will start the appropriate Automation component application (if it's not already running) and load the specified file.

Our Scenario

The scenario for our sample Excel application involves a fictitious airline. CH12.MDB contains a table of airport codes (tblAirports) and a table filled with randomly generated lost-luggage rates (tblLostCount) for each North American airport for the month of January 1999. In our example, we've also created an Excel workbook called STATREQ.XLS that allows users to request data on any given airport. You might think of it as a query form a user could fill out and send to someone else for processing. The workbook contains two worksheets. The Query worksheet, shown in Figure 12.22, lets the user fill in an airport code (the standard, three-character code assigned by the International Air Transport Association) in a cell. Our Access application will query the database and, based on the current date, return information on month-to-date lost-luggage rates. The second worksheet in STATREQ.XLS, Results, provides a table of data and a chart. In our example, we show you how to perform the following steps using Automation to control Excel:

1. Open the workbook.
2. Retrieve the airport code from the Query worksheet.
3. Query the Access database.
4. Return the results to the worksheet.
5. Redefine the data range the chart uses to reflect new data.

Creating an Object from an Existing Document

There is no user interface for our simple example function. Rather, we've created one procedure, called UpdateAirportStats, in basExcel, which handles all the processing. The module basExcel, in CH12.MDB on the companion CD, shows the entire subroutine. If you view the module in Design view, you can see from the variable declarations that we use quite a few Excel object variables in the procedure.

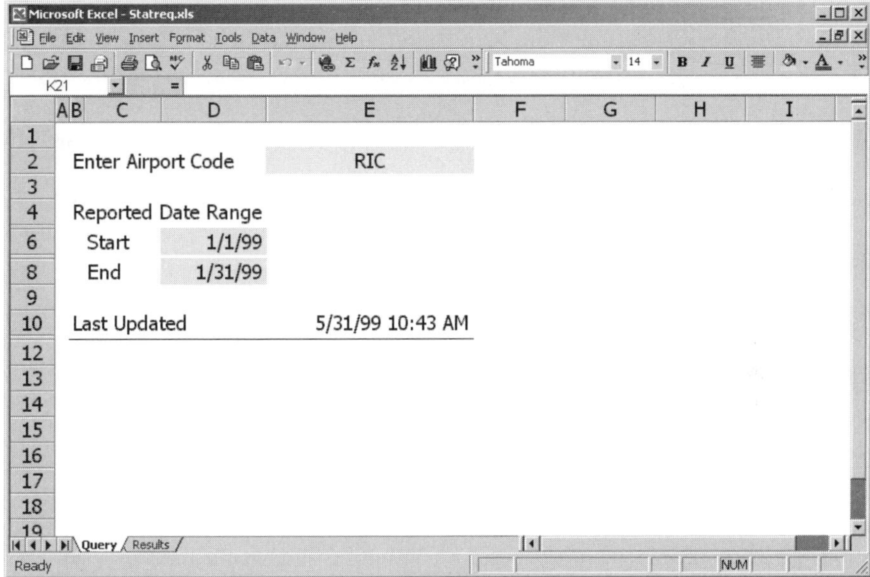

FIGURE 12.22: Query worksheet in STATREQ.XLS

The first thing the procedure does is call GetObject, passing it the path to the STATREQ.XLS file. As long as Excel is installed correctly and the path is valid, GetObject should return a reference to an Excel workbook. This differs from the other examples we've discussed so far, which used the Application object of each Automation server. Keep this in mind as you create object references to documents. The object you create will be somewhere in the middle of the object hierarchy, not at the top, as is the case with Application objects.

Because we will want to manipulate Excel's Application object in addition to a Workbook object, we need a way to create a reference to it. Fortunately, rather than using another call to GetObject or CreateObject, we can use the Parent property of Excel objects to return a reference to the object immediately above the current object in the object hierarchy. Using the Parent property, we can create references to the Application object using the following code:

```
Set objXLApp = objXLBook.Parent
```

WARNING

With Excel 97 and 2000, Microsoft has made a change to the way an XLS file is referenced using GetObject. Passing an XLS file now returns a Workbook object. In Excel 95 and earlier, GetObject returned a Worksheet object representing the first worksheet in the XLS file. This will undoubtedly break some existing applications. If you have existing VBA code that uses GetObject in this fashion, be sure to take note of this change in behavior.

Updating the Worksheets and Chart

The bulk of the processing in UpdateAirportStats involves running a query against the tblLostCount table and poking the results into the Results worksheet in STATREQ.XLS. We do this by first querying the data and placing the results in a Variant array using the GetRows method of the Recordset object:

```
' Run our query (note that it has
' parameters we need to set)
strSQL = "SELECT tblLostCount.DateLost," _
 & " tblLostCount.LostCount" _
 & " FROM tblLostCount" _
 & " WHERE (((tblLostCount.DateLost)" _
 & " Between [pStart] And [pEnd]) AND ((" _
 & " tblLostCount.IATACode)=[pIATACode]))"

Set cmdLost = New Command
With cmdLost
    .ActiveConnection = _
     Application.CurrentProject.Connection
    .CommandText = strSQL
    .Prepared = True

    .Parameters("[pIATACode]") = varIATACode
    .Parameters("[pStart]") = varStart
    .Parameters("[pEnd]") = varEnd

    Set rstLost = .Execute()
End With

' Snag all the results into an array using GetRows
' and large (2 ^ 15) row count to get all rows
varResults = rstLost.GetRows(2 ^ 15)
rstLost.Close
```

We then clear any existing data using the Clear method of a Range object corresponding to the data shown in Figure 12.23. This figure also shows the Chart object, which we will update once all the data has been copied.

The code that clears the existing data is shown below. Notice that we use the worksheet's Range method with a named cell range.

```
objResultsSheet.Range("rngDataAll").Clear
```

FIGURE 12.23:

Results worksheet showing a data table and chart

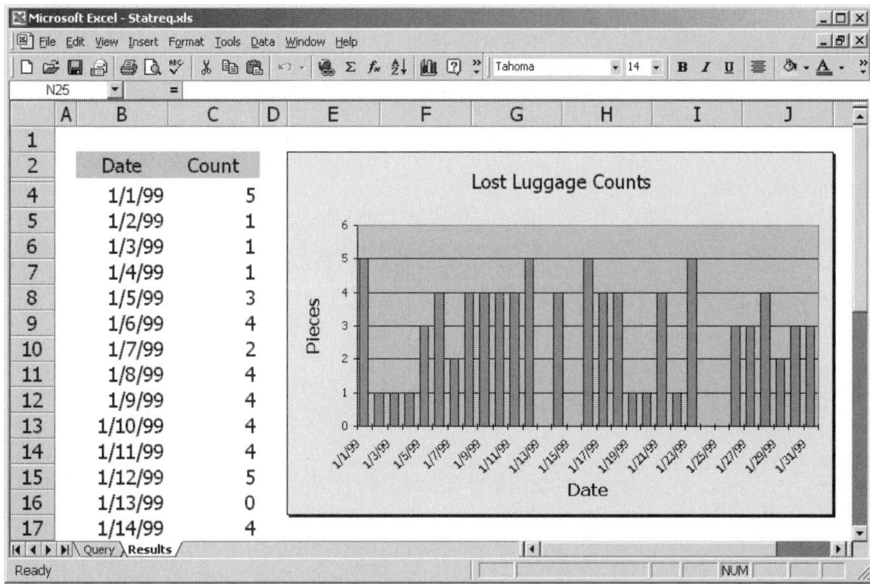

We can now copy the results of our query into the Excel worksheet. The simplest and fastest way to do this is to construct a Range object that refers to the block of cells where the data belongs and set its FormulaArray property equal to the query results stored in our Variant array. The other alternative, iterating through each cell in the range, is extremely slow because Excel is running as an out-of-process server. (If you want to know more, see the sidebar "In-Process versus Out-of-Process Servers" later in the chapter.) The following code demonstrates how to use the FormulaArray property. Note that we need to use Excel's Transpose function because the array returned by GetRows is not oriented correctly.

```
Set objXLRange = objResultsSheet. _
 Range("B4:C" & 4 + UBound(varResults, 2))

objXLRange.FormulaArray = _
 objXLApp.Transpose(varResults)
```

The last task remaining once the data is on the worksheet is to redefine the source for the chart to reflect the current amount of data. We use Excel's Union method (a method of the Application object) to combine the data range computed in the prior step with cells B2 and C2, which contain the headings for the data and chart. We use this with the ChartWizard method of the Chart object on the Results worksheet to set the new data source equal to the existing data set:

```
objResultsSheet.ChartObjects(1). _
 Chart.ChartWizard Source:=objXLApp. _
 Union(objResultsSheet.Range("B2:C2"), _
 objXLRange)
```

To test UpdateAirportStats, you'll need to copy STATREQ.XLS to a directory on your hard disk and make sure it's in the same directory as CH12.MDB. Then run UpdateAirportStats from the VBA Immediate window. UpdateAirportStats should work regardless of whether Excel is currently running or STATREQ.XLS is currently loaded.

In-Process versus Out-of-Process Servers

Automation components can be grouped into two categories that describe how the operating system treats their program code. *In-process* servers are loaded into the same memory address space (or *process space*) as the client application. ADO is an example of an in-process server, as are ActiveX controls. When you reference an ADO object, for example, you're communicating with an instance of ADO loaded into Access' process space using Automation. You can also create your own in-process servers using Visual Basic, where they are called COM DLLs.

Out-of-process servers, on the other hand, are loaded into their own address space. All the Microsoft Office applications, as well as normal Automation servers you create in Visual Basic, are out-of-process servers.

From a practical standpoint, the biggest difference between the two types of servers is the rate at which communication takes place between them and your client application. In-process servers are, as a rule, much faster than out-of-process. This is because Windows does not need to manage data and communications between two separate processes and address spaces.

While you can't control what type of server an Automation server is, you can modify your code when using out-of-process servers. Try to avoid repeated references to objects, properties, and methods. In our example, we've taken advantage of the fact that you can insert several cells' worth of data into an Excel worksheet with a single statement. We avoided referencing individual cells one at a time.

Using ActiveX Controls

Access 2 was the first application to support ActiveX controls, then called OLE custom controls. ActiveX controls, or *OCXs,* as they are sometimes called because of their file extension, are the successors to VBX controls, the modular components that helped make Visual Basic such a success. ActiveX controls encapsulate a certain degree of functionality that you can integrate into your application simply by placing one on your Access form. Access 2000 integrates ActiveX controls much better than Access 2 but, in most respects, controls are used in the same way.

In addition to being self-contained chunks of functionality, you can control ActiveX controls the same way you control other applications using Automation. ActiveX controls implement their own objects, properties, methods, and events. In this section, we show you how to control the calendar control that ships with Access 2000.

ActiveX Control Registration

Before you can use an ActiveX control, you must make sure it is properly registered. By this, we mean that the correct entries are made in the Windows Registry to enable the control's functionality. If you purchase a development tool that includes ActiveX controls, such as Microsoft Visual Basic or the Office 2000 Developer, the installation program usually installs and registers the controls for you. If you acquire controls separately or are installing controls on your users' computers to support your application, you will have to register the controls yourself.

To register controls, you can use either the ActiveX Controls dialog in Microsoft Access or the REGSVR32.EXE program that ships with Visual Basic. Figure 12.24 shows the Access 2000 ActiveX Controls dialog. You display the dialog by selecting Tools ➢ ActiveX Controls. As you can see, the dialog lists the controls that are currently registered and features buttons for registering and unregistering controls. The unregistering feature is useful for deleting Registry entries for controls you no longer plan to use.

To register a new control, click the Register button and select the control from the file dialog that appears. To unregister a control, simply select it from the list and click the Unregister button.

FIGURE 12.24:

Access 2000 ActiveX Controls dialog

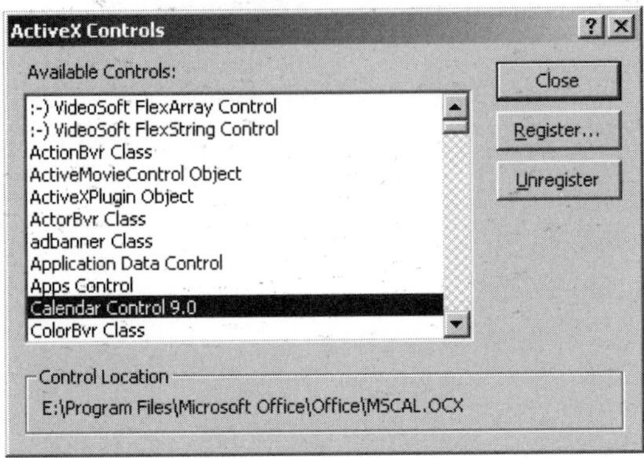

If you are distributing your application to others whom you do not want messing with the ActiveX Controls dialog, you can register controls using a small program, REGSVR32.EXE. The syntax of REGSVR32.EXE is shown here:

REGSVR32.EXE [/u] *filename*.ocx

You run REGSVR32.EXE using the path to the ActiveX control you wish to register. The program uses information in the OCX file to create the proper Registry entries. You can use the /u switch to unregister a control.

If you're using the Setup Wizard that comes with the Office 2000 Developer, you can include any ActiveX controls your application uses as part of the installation file list. The installation program that installs your application will register the controls for you automatically.

Inserting ActiveX Controls

You place ActiveX controls on forms by selecting Insert ➢ ActiveX Control while in Form Design view. This action displays the Insert ActiveX Controls dialog, as shown in Figure 12.25.

The dialog's list box displays the controls that have been registered on your computer and are available to you. To insert the control, select the control name from the list and click the OK button. Access inserts the control on your form. You can then size it to meet your needs.

FIGURE 12.25:

The Insert ActiveX Control dialog listing the available ActiveX controls

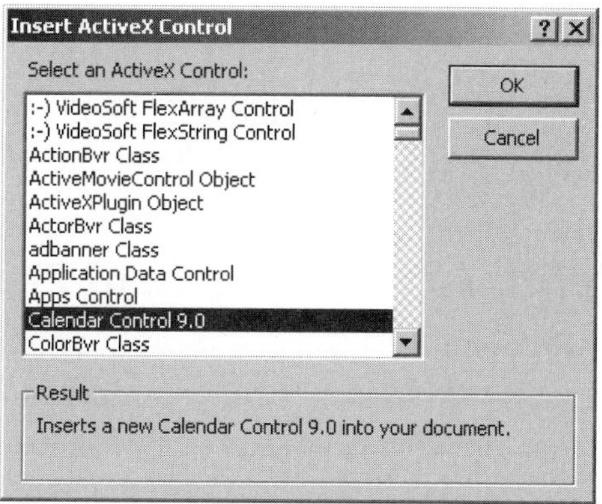

In addition to using the menu, you can create custom command bar buttons for each ActiveX control. To do this, open the Customize dialog by selecting the Customize command from the View ➢ Toolbars menu, select the Commands tab, and select ActiveX Controls from the list of categories. You should see a dialog like the one in Figure 12.26, listing the available controls instead of displaying buttons. To create a custom command bar button, just select an ActiveX control from the list and drag it onto a command bar. Access creates the button using the icon associated with the chosen control.

After creating a custom command bar button, adding the control to a form becomes simply a matter of clicking the button and then dragging a region on the form, just as for any of the built-in controls.

FIGURE 12.26:

Creating a command bar button for an ActiveX control using the Customize dialog

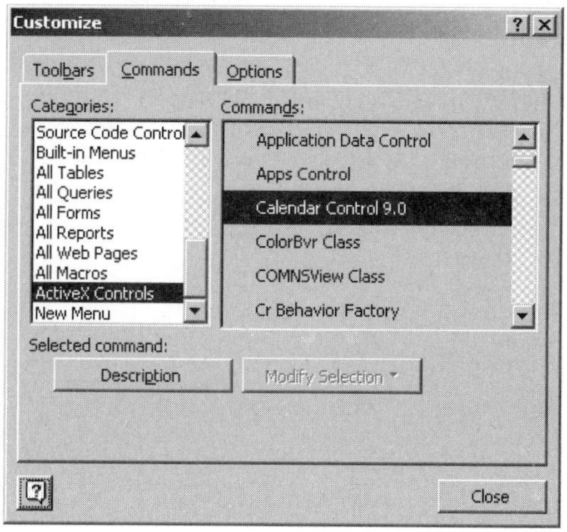

In addition to adding the control to your form, Access automatically adds a reference to the control's type library to your VBA project. You should see a reference for the control listed in the References dialog after inserting it on a form. This allows you to use the control's properties and methods in your VBA code. If you don't see a reference to the control, you'll need to add it yourself.

Modifying ActiveX Control Properties

ActiveX controls have properties, just like built-in controls. Because a special object frame hosts all ActiveX controls, when you select an ActiveX control in Design view, the Access property sheet displays only those properties associated with the object frame. If you want to modify those properties specific to the control, you have two choices. Your first choice is to select the Other (or All) tab from the control's property sheet. Here you will find most of the properties for the ActiveX control. For example, Figure 12.27 shows the property sheet for a copy of the calendar control that ships with Access 2000.

FIGURE 12.27:

Custom properties for a calendar control

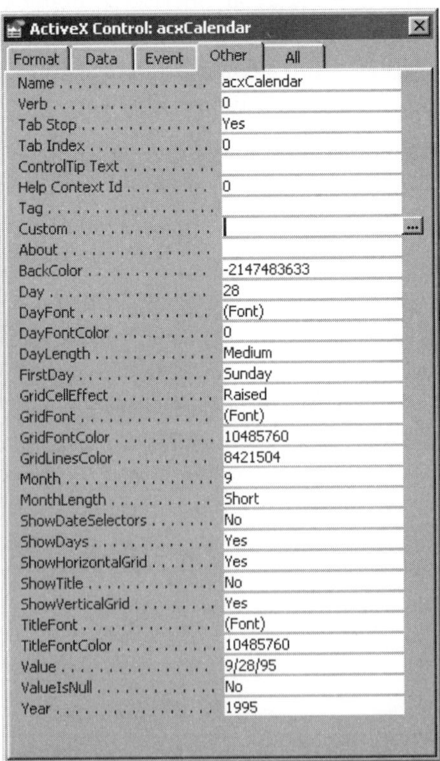

Your other option is to use the control's custom property dialog. Each ActiveX control implements a dialog that lets you modify its properties. Figure 12.28 shows the Calendar Properties dialog for the calendar control. You can display this dialog by clicking the Build button to the right of the Custom property on the Access property sheet (near the top of Figure 12.27) or by right-clicking the control and selecting *ControlType* Object ➢ Properties from the shortcut menu.

FIGURE 12.28:

Calendar Properties dialog for a calendar control

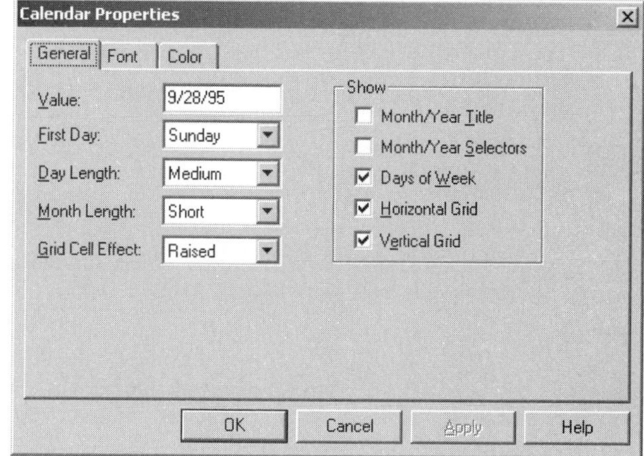

Using ActiveX Control Events

ActiveX controls differ from Access controls in that they do not expose their events through the property sheet. Access controls have properties such as OnClick, which you can use to call a macro, VBA function, or code contained in the form's module. ActiveX control events are available only from the form's module. When you add an ActiveX control to a form, VBA adds event procedure stubs to the form's module that correspond to those supported by the control. To view these event points, you must open the module, select the control from the Object list, and then select the event from the Procedure list. Figure 12.29 shows a module window open to the AfterUpdate event of a calendar control. Note, however, that some of the events in this list belong to the object frame, not to the control itself. These include the Enter, Exit, GotFocus, LostFocus, Click, DblClick, MouseDown, MouseMove, MouseUp, and Updated events.

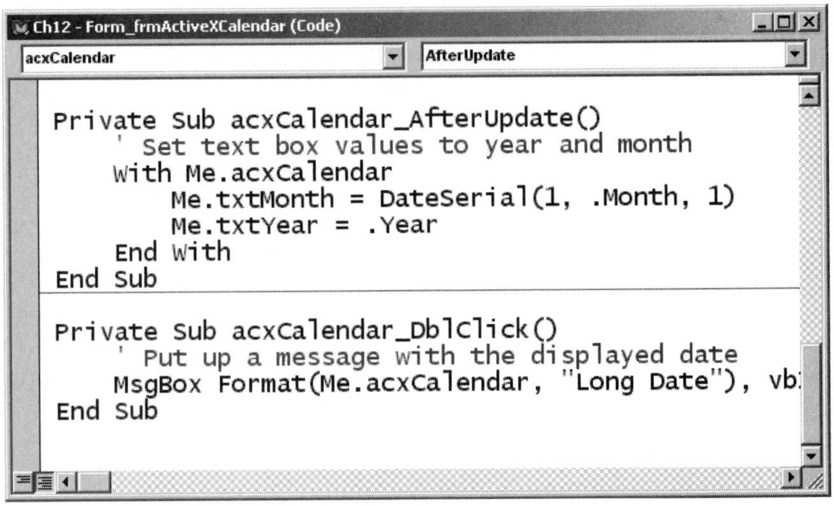

FIGURE 12.29:

Event procedure for a calendar control's AfterUpdate event

```
Ch12 - Form_frmActiveXCalendar (Code)
acxCalendar                    AfterUpdate

Private Sub acxCalendar_AfterUpdate()
    ' Set text box values to year and month
    With Me.acxCalendar
        Me.txtMonth = DateSerial(1, .Month, 1)
        Me.txtYear = .Year
    End With
End Sub

Private Sub acxCalendar_DblClick()
    ' Put up a message with the displayed date
    MsgBox Format(Me.acxCalendar, "Long Date"), vb
End Sub
```

Using Bound ActiveX Controls

A valuable feature of Access 2000 is the support for bound ActiveX controls. For example, you can bind the calendar to a Date/Time field by setting the control's ControlSource property to the field name. There is no need to write any code; you simply choose the control source from the property sheet just as you would for an Access control. We've included a form, frmBoundCalendar, in CH12.MDB, which demonstrates this. This type of binding is called *simple binding* because the control is bound only to a single column. Some ActiveX controls also support *complex binding*—binding to an entire table, with the control managing individual fields. Some of the ActiveX controls that ship with Visual Basic support complex binding. Unfortunately, Access, unlike VB, does not support complex binding from the client side, so you won't be able to use these controls with Access.

Calendar Control Example

To demonstrate the use of ActiveX controls, we have created a simple example using the calendar control that ships with Access 2000. Figure 12.30 shows our sample form, frmActiveXCalendar. It's a rather rudimentary form containing only the calendar control, two text boxes, and four command buttons. We can use it, however, to demonstrate manipulating ActiveX control events and properties.

FIGURE 12.30:

A sample form using the calendar ActiveX control

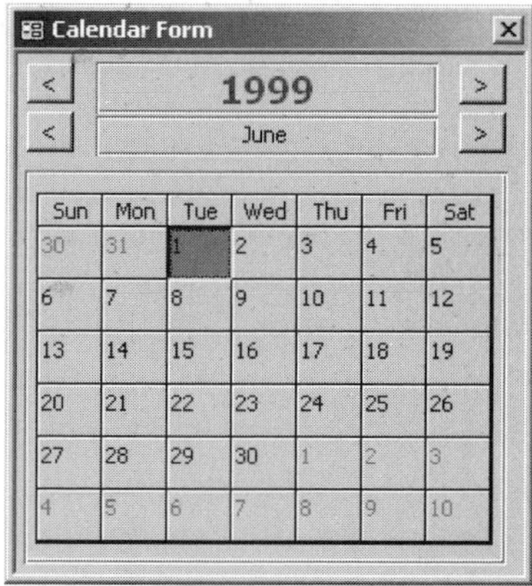

You can use the buttons on the form to move from month to month and year to year. As the date changes, so do the month and year shown in the text boxes at the top of the form. You can use the mouse to click a day on the calendar, and that changes the date as well. Double-clicking the calendar displays a message box containing the current date.

Listing 12.16 shows some of the code contained in frmActiveXCalendar's VBA module. You can view the complete listing by opening the form in Design view. It's not much code, a fact that testifies to the value of ActiveX controls.

Listing 12.16

```
Private Sub Form_Load()
    ' Set the calendar's date to today and update controls
    Me.acxCalendar.Value = Date
    Call acxCalendar_AfterUpdate
End Sub

Private Sub acxCalendar_AfterUpdate()
    ' Set text box values to year and month
    With Me.acxCalendar
        Me.txtMonth = DateSerial(1, .Month, 1)
        Me.txtYear = .Year
    End With
End Sub
```

```
Private Sub acxCalendar_DblClick()
    ' Put up a message with the displayed date
    MsgBox Format(Me.acxCalendar, "Long Date"), vbInformation
End Sub
```

As you can see from the code sample in Listing 12.16, using ActiveX controls is very much like using built-in Access controls. You set their properties the same way and call their methods the same way. You even respond to their events the same way—using the event procedures generated in the form's module (for example, acxCalendar_AfterUpdate). Access and VBA insulate you from the fact that the control is a separate software component.

Using ActiveX Controls from Other Products

As the number of ActiveX controls increases, you will have a wider selection to choose from when building your applications. Be aware, however, that not all ActiveX controls work well with Access. Many of the controls that ship with Microsoft Visual Basic, for example, have features not available through Access. For example, Access does not support the ability to embed one ActiveX control in another, so you won't be able to create the same visual effect with some controls that you can with Visual Basic. As this technology matures, it will be easier to share components among development tools. Until then, treat new ActiveX controls with a degree of caution.

ActiveX Controls—Reusable Components or Not?

One of the benefits of old OLE custom controls was that you could use them in any development tool that supported the custom control architecture. While this was not completely true (for instance, some custom controls that shipped with Visual Basic 4 could not be used with Access 95), the controls were reusable enough to make working with them worthwhile. With the advent of the "new and improved" ActiveX controls, one would think that this situation would, at worst, stay the same and perhaps even improve.

Things are not always as we would like them to be, however. As it turns out, many ActiveX controls are actually *less* reusable than their OLE control counterparts. The reason for this is easy to explain and understand, albeit disappointing.

Continued on next page

The original OLE custom control specification defined a set of programming interfaces that controls, as well as the applications that hosted them, *had* to support. Many of these interfaces, however, were not necessary from the controls' standpoint. Controls implemented the interfaces nonetheless and, as a result, carried around excess baggage in the form of unnecessary program code.

When Microsoft later developed the ActiveX control specification, one driving goal was the ability to make controls available over the Internet via Web browsers such as Microsoft Internet Explorer 3. Since download time is a critical issue for Web-based controls, they need to be as small as possible. Obviously, carrying around excess and unused code increases the time required to download the control to a user's computer. Rather than insist that controls implement every programming interface, Microsoft decided to let developers implement only those that were necessary for the control to function. It is up to the host application (a browser or development tool) to determine which ones the control supports.

The net result of this decision is that you will soon have a plethora of ActiveX controls installed on your computer, only a handful of which you'll be able to use with Access. Keep that in mind as you evaluate controls for use in your applications.

Tapping into Events Using WithEvents

You've just seen how ActiveX controls expose their events to Access and VBA so you can write code in response to them. Have you ever wondered how this works? When Access loads an ActiveX control, it queries the control's type library for the list of events and then registers event sinks with the control for each one. An *event sink* is simply a way for a control to call into VBA rather than VBA calling into the control, which is what happens when you access the control's properties or methods. Until now, the only way Access developers could tap into these event sinks was through event procedures on forms. With the latest version of VBA, however, you can create your own event sinks using the new WithEvents feature.

NOTE WithEvents is also explained in Chapter 3 in regard to custom VBA class modules.

What Is WithEvents?

WithEvents is a VBA keyword used in conjunction with an object variable declaration. It signals to VBA that in addition to exposing the object's properties and methods, you want VBA to notify you of any events that object exposes. WithEvents is most useful when using Automation components like those in Microsoft Office or with your own custom class modules (see Chapter 3 for more information on the latter). After all, ActiveX controls already expose their events through the host form's VBA module. In theory, though, you can use WithEvents with any Automation component that exposes events.

How do you know if an Automation component exposes events? The easiest way to find out is by looking at the component's entries in Object Browser. When you select a class that exposes events, Object Browser lists them along with properties and methods, marking them with a lightning bolt icon. Figure 12.31 shows Object Browser displaying information on Microsoft Word's Application class. Near the bottom of the Members list, you can see the events exposed by the class.

FIGURE 12.31:

Object Browser displaying events exposed by Word's Application class

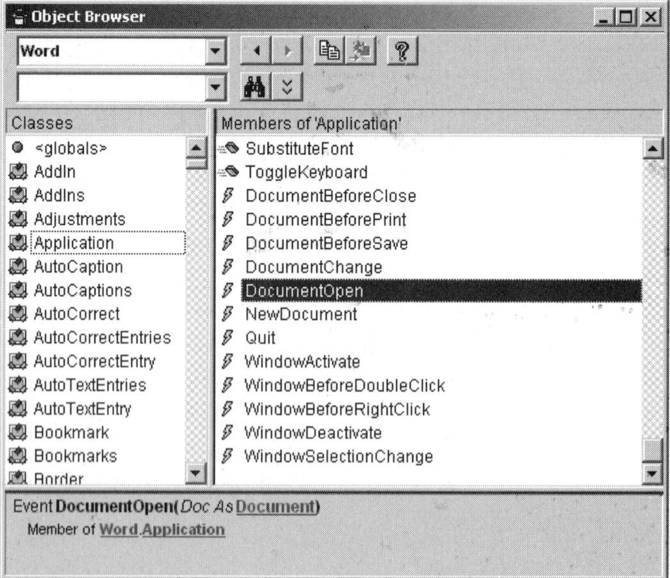

NOTE

The only events that Access exposes in this manner are the ItemAdded and ItemRemoved events of the References collection.

Using WithEvents

You use WithEvents in a variable declaration. There are a couple of catches, however. You can use it only in a class module (including form modules), and it must appear in the declarations section. You can't declare a variable using WithEvents in the body of a procedure. We've included a class module called clsWordEvents in the sample database that contains the following declaration:

```
Private WithEvents mobjWordApp As Word.Application
```

Note that the WithEvents keyword is listed before the object variable name. When you add a declaration using WithEvents to the declarations section of a class module, VBA adds an entry to the Object drop-down list that corresponds to the variable name. This is the same thing that happens when you add a control (ActiveX or otherwise) to an Access form. Selecting that entry from the list displays the object's events in the Procedure list. Figure 12.32 shows clsWordEvents open in Design view with the DocumentChange event procedure selected. You can see that we've responded to the event by opening a dialog that displays the name of the current active document to the VBA Immediate window.

FIGURE 12.32:

Editing mobjWordApp's DocumentChange event procedure

Ch12 - clsWordEvents (Code)

mobjWordApp | DocumentChange

```
Private Sub mobjWordApp_DocumentChange()
    On Error Resume Next
    Debug.Print "Document change. New document is " & _
     mobjWordApp.ActiveDocument.Name
End Sub

Private Sub mobjWordApp_DocumentOpen(ByVal Doc As Word.D
    Debug.Print "Document being opened: " & Doc.Name
End Sub

Private Sub mobjWordApp_NewDocument(ByVal Doc As Word.Do
    Debug.Print "Document being created: " & Doc.Name
End Sub
```

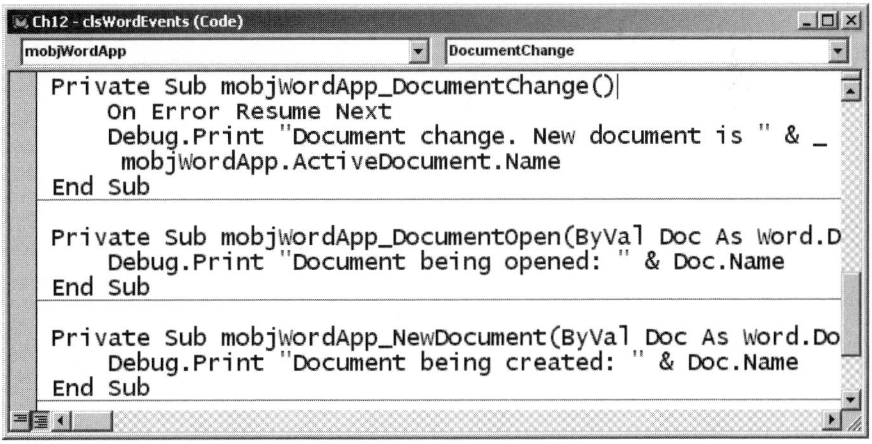

Before you can begin using the event functionality exposed by an Automation component, you must do two things that are normally taken care of for you when using ActiveX controls. You need to instantiate the Automation component class, and you need to create an instance of the VBA class where the component class variable is declared.

We satisfied the first requirement in the Initialize event of our class using the following code:

```
Private Sub Class_Initialize()
    Set mobjWordApp = New Word.Application
    mobjWordApp.Visible = True
End Sub
```

To satisfy the second requirement, you need to create a new instance of the clsWordEvents class. We have included an example in basAutomation:

```
Global gobjWordEvents As clsWordEvents

Sub InitWordEvents()
    Set gobjWordEvents = New clsWordEvents
End Sub
```

That's all you need to create a custom event sink for Microsoft Word. Note that we've declared the object variable as Global. If we had declared it in the body of the InitWordEvents procedure, it would have been destroyed, along with our event sink, when the procedure terminated.

NOTE

If you declare a variable using WithEvents in a form or report module, the event sink will be created as soon as you open the form or report.

Figure 12.33 illustrates how event sinking with VBA works. Our object variable, gobjWordEvents, points to an instance of our VBA class, clsWordEvents. The class instance, in turn, contains another pointer (mobjWordApp) that references an instance of Word's Application class. As the Application class generates events, Word calls our VBA event procedures defined in clsWordEvents. The gobjWord-Events variable is required only to give our event sink "life."

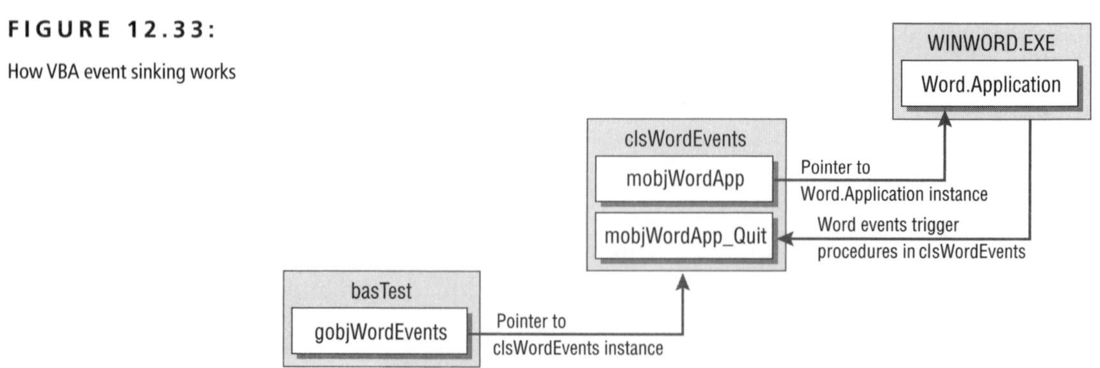

FIGURE 12.33: How VBA event sinking works

Using Event Sinking with Forms

We've included a second example of event sinking in the sample database. This example uses a form, frmWithEventsWatchForm, instead of a VBA class module. Opening the form creates a new instance of Word's Application class and logs each event to a text box. Figure 12.34 shows an example of using the form to monitor the active documents in Word.

FIGURE 12.34:

Using a form to monitor Word events

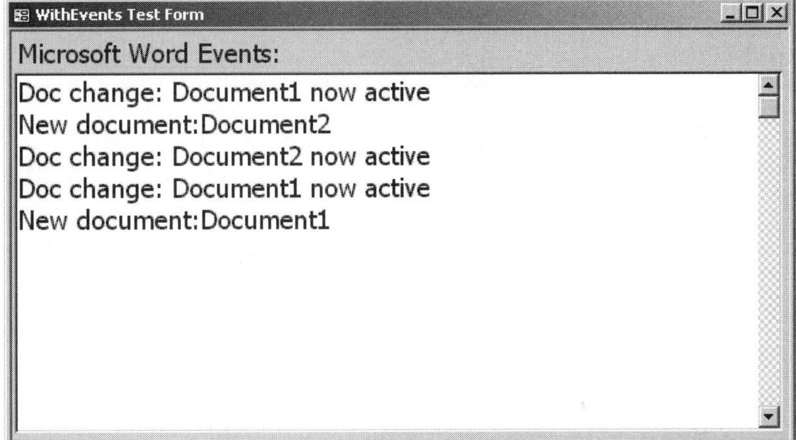

The code behind the form is nearly identical to that explained in the previous section except that we don't need a separate variable to store an instance of the class. Since opening a form automatically creates an instance of the form's class module, this step isn't required.

WARNING Event procedures created using WithEvents are nothing more than functions that an Automation component calls when an event occurs. Just as with normal functions, the Automation component cannot continue processing until an event procedure finishes. Beware of anything that could prevent or delay the completion of an event procedure.

Summary

In this chapter, we explored the basic concepts behind Automation, including:

- The role of Automation clients and servers, the use of type libraries, and the creation of objects in another application
- The similarities between Automation code and the VBA code you write in Access
- How to manipulate other applications using objects, properties, and methods, just as you do Access objects

We used several sample applications that demonstrated how to use the other programs in the Microsoft Office suite in integrated solutions. We also showed how to manipulate ActiveX controls embedded on a form. In each example, we stressed the similarities between Automation code and plain VBA code.

Automation can help you become more productive by giving you the tools to integrate other robust, feature-filled applications into a customized solution. In this chapter, you saw how you can use Access 2000 to control other applications.

CHAPTER

THIRTEEN

13

Access As an Automation Server

- Deciding when to use Access as an Automation server
- Exploring the nuances of Access in the server role
- Designing a VBA class for handling Automation tasks
- Learning to create Automation-friendly applications

Starting with Access 95, Microsoft added a capability long sought by developers who were looking for a way to integrate Access into solutions created with other tools—the ability to control Access from other applications using COM Automation. Having this capability at your disposal opens up a number of interesting possibilities. You can have one Access application that controls another. You can also create applications in Microsoft Visual Basic, or any VBA-enabled application, that use the services of Access to do such things as print reports, create tables and queries, and display forms. In this chapter, we'll examine the reasons to use Access as an Automation server and demonstrate an example of its capabilities by implementing a system that uses Access to preview and print reports. The Automation code in this chapter is encapsulated in a VBA class module on the CD-ROM in text form so you can import it easily into any VBA project.

Working with Access As an Automation Server

One paradox that Access developers must face is that while it is possible to use Access as an Automation server, the need to do so is probably smaller than ever. As companies such as Microsoft move toward a component-based approach built on COM, huge chunks of a program's functionality are now available without the need to actually run the program. A case in point is programmatic data access through ActiveX Data Objects (ADO). Access uses ADO to manipulate both local and server data. You can use ADO directly from any Automation client without going through Access. So, you ask, when does it make sense to use Access as an Automation server? Consider these situations:

- You need to do something that's possible only through Access, such as printing a report.
- You need to create background processes that use information from an active Access session.
- You need to provide seamless integration between Access and another application.

Access provides only one object that you can create using Automation: the Application object. Unlike other Office applications, such as Word and Excel, Access does not feature document objects (for example, Excel.Sheet). As you might expect, the Prog ID for Access' Application object is Access.Application. Using this ID with the New keyword or either CreateObject or GetObject gives you an object pointer to Access' top-level object, from which all other objects can be referenced.

Using the Access Type Library

As with any other COM Automation server, when developing Automation applications, you will find it helpful to include Access 2000's type library, MSACC9.OLB, in the list of references for your project. There are several reasons for this. First, it makes your code more readable by declaring object variables that map directly to the objects in Access. Second, VBA can use the type library to display context-sensitive help when you highlight an Access object name and press the F1 key. Third, if your development tool supports it, you can create an object reference using the New keyword rather than using CreateObject or GetObject. For example, the following code creates a new instance of Access' Application object using the New keyword:

```
' Create a new object of the proper class
Dim objAccess As Access.Application

' Create a new instance of Access
Set objAccess = New Access.Application
```

Finally, if you use the Access type library, VBA can check your code for syntax using the list of objects, properties, and methods exported by Access. VBA would warn you, for example, if you misspelled the HwndAccessApp property or tried to use a property that did not exist.

Differences from Regular Access

Using Access as an Automation server is very much like developing applications the way you do now. The object model, methods, and properties are identical, regardless of whether you call them from a VBA module in an Access database or use Automation from an external application such as Excel or Visual Basic. Subtle differences do exist, however, in the way you use Access objects. First and foremost, all controllable objects descend from the Application object, to which you must create a pointer before using any other object, property, or method. When porting code from Access to another VBA-enabled application, make sure you qualify all "top-level" objects (those for which Access VBA can assume the context) with the object variable holding a pointer to the Access Application object.

For example, the following code snippet executes perfectly well in an Access module:

```
Dim frmAny As Form

Set frmAny = Screen.ActiveForm
frmAny.Visible = False
If frmAny.Caption = Forms(0).Caption Then
    DoCmd.Close acForm, frmAny.Name
End If
```

To mimic the functionality of these statements using Automation in Visual Basic, on the other hand, you would need to declare and initialize an object variable and prefix the Screen, Form, Forms, and DoCmd objects with it, as shown in this code fragment:

```
Dim objAccess As Access.Application
Dim frmAny As Access.Form

Set objAccess = New Access.Application

Set frmAny = objAccess.Screen.ActiveForm
frmAny.Visible = False
If frmAny.Caption = objAccess.Forms(0).Caption Then
    objAccess.DoCmd.Close acForm, frmAny.Name
End If
```

You must also keep in mind that because Access is operating behind the scenes when used as an Automation server, you should not initiate actions that require user intervention. For example, any message box displayed as the result of running a query or macro or opening a form or report will cause your Automation client code to halt while it waits for a response from the user. If Access is not in a state in which it can accept input (if the main window is hidden, for instance), there will be no way for the code to continue executing. In the section "Hiding the Access Main Window" later in this chapter, we will explain how to manage the user interface to display Access forms and dialogs when necessary.

Access Automation Server Behavior

Chapter 12 provided an overview of using COM Automation with Microsoft Office applications. While most of the rules explained in that chapter apply to Access, Access does exhibit some unusual behavior. What's more, Microsoft has changed some of the behavior of Access 2000 to bring it more in line with the rest of Office. The good news is that Access now works more like the other Office applications. The bad news is that some behavior that you may have relied on in Access 97 has changed. The following paragraphs outline Access 2000's idiosyncrasies and changes in its behavior from Access 97.

Access is by default a *single-use* Automation server. As with other single-use servers, using CreateObject or the New keyword will always create a new instance of Access, the result of the function call being a pointer to that instance. With Access 97, when you created a new instance of Access using Automation, you (or your users) could not simply terminate it by selecting File ➢ Exit or clicking the Close button as long as the object reference in your code was still valid. Access forced itself to remain running so that method or property calls made using Automation could execute. Instead of closing, Access closed the current database and minimized its main window, requiring you to call the application's Quit method or destroy the object variable storing the Application object reference.

This behavior has changed in Access 2000 to be more consistent with other applications, not just those in Office. A user can manually terminate most applications that function as Automation servers because other behavior would be unintuitive and annoying. The result of this change is that if you've relied on Access 97's behavior, you'll need to update your procedures with additional error checking to account for the fact that Access may have been terminated by the user. Automation error handling techniques are discussed in Chapter 12.

Another idiosyncrasy you need to be aware of is the behavior of the Visible property. In Access 97, the Visible property did not actually make the Access main window visible or invisible, as it does with most other Office applications; instead, it minimized or restored the main window. Again, Microsoft has changed this behavior to be more consistent with other applications, but it still has its flaws. Unlike other Office applications, you can only change the value of the Visible property if Access' UserControl property is False—that is, if the user is not interacting directly with Access. Attempting to change the property value when UserControl is True results in error 2455, "You entered an expression that has an invalid reference to the property Visible." You can try to change the UserControl property to False, but this also is sometimes an invalid operation. The answer is to continue using the Windows API to hide Access' main window. This technique is discussed later in this chapter in the section "Hiding the Access Main Window."

A Class for Access Automation

Since many of the tasks associated with working with Access as an Automation server (starting an Automation session or opening a database, form, or report) are the same, regardless of purpose, it makes sense to encapsulate much of that behavior in a VBA class module. We've done this in a class called AccessAutomation. Table 13.1 lists the class module's properties and methods. The rest of this section explains how to use Access as an Automation server in the context of describing the class module's implementation.

TABLE 13.1: AccessAutomation Class Module Properties and Methods

Property or Method	Description
AccessInst property	Provides an object pointer to the running instance of Access' Application object obtained by executing the Init method
CreateNewInstance property	True to create a new instance of Access in the Init method, False to use a running instance (if one exists)
FileName property	A text string denoting the name of the Access database or project file opened using Automation
Hide method	Hides the Access main window
Init method	Initializes an Automation session with Access
Initialized property	Returns True if an Automation session with Access has been started
IsAccessRunning method	Returns True if an instance of Access is running, False otherwise
IsProjectLoaded	Returns True if an Access database or data project file has been loaded
IsSecure property	True to start Access using a secure workgroup, False to start Access using the default workgroup, user name, and password
Password property	Password to use when starting Access with a secure workgroup
Show method	Displays the Access main window
UserName property	User name to use when starting Access with a secure workgroup
Version property	Specifies the version of Access to use (default = 9)
Workgroup property	Optional workgroup file to use when starting Access with a secure workgroup

Several of the property and method implementations are described in this chapter. For the complete class module implementation, see the sample application in CH13.XLS or the AccessAutomation.cls file on the accompanying CD-ROM.

TIP

To use the AccessAutomation task in your own applications, just import the AccessAutomation.cls file into your VBA project and set a reference to the Access type library.

Beginning an Automation Session

Beginning an Automation session is comprised of several tasks. First, you must decide whether to use a running instance of Access or create a new one. You then must obtain a pointer to the instance and store it in an object variable. Finally, in nearly all cases, you'll want to open a database or project file. The AccessAutomation class accomplishes all of this in its Init method using property values set prior to calling it. A typical use of the class to begin an Automation session might look like this:

```
Dim objAccAuto As AccessAutomation

Set objAccAuto = New AccessAutomation
With objAccAuto
    .CreateNewInstance = False
    .FileName = "C:\Office\Samples\Northwind.mdb"
    .Init
    .Show
End With
```

In this example, the code instructs an instance of the AccessAutomation class to use a running instance of Access and open the Northwind.mdb after initializing the session. After initializing the Automation session, the code calls the Show method to display Access' main window. Listing 13.1 shows the VBA code for the Init method. Note how it uses the value of the CreateNewInstance property to determine whether to call CreateObject or GetObject.

Listing 13.1

```
Public Function Init() As Boolean
    ' Initializes the Access instance associated
    ' with this instance of the class--uses logic
```

```
' to determine if Access is running and if
' the class should use the running instance

Dim strCmd As String
Dim strProgID As String

On Error GoTo HandleErr

' Only process the method if the instance
' of Access hasn't been initialized
If AccessInst Is Nothing Then

    ' Fix up the ProgID to use the
    ' version specified
    strProgID = conProgID & "." & Me.Version

    ' Special case for secure mode
    If Me.IsSecure Then

        ' Make sure Access isn't already
        ' running because this won't work
        ' if it is
        If Me.IsAccessRunning Then
            Err.Raise _
             vbObjectError + aeErrAccessAlreadyRunning, _
             TypeName(Me) & "::Init", _
             "Access is already running."
        Else
            ' Build a command line including
            ' switches for security information
            strCmd = "MSACCESS.EXE /user " & Me.UserName
            If Len(Me.Password) Then
                strCmd = strCmd & " /pwd " & Me.Password
            End If
            If Len(Me.Workgroup) Then
                strCmd = strCmd & " /wrkgrp " & Me.Workgroup
            End If
            strCmd = strCmd & " /nostartup"

            ' Execute the command and wait a few
            ' milliseconds before attempting
            ' communications (may need adjustment)
            If Shell(strCmd) Then
```

```
                Sleep conWaitIntervalMs
                Set Me.AccessInst = GetObject(, strProgID)
            End If
        End If
    Else
        ' Get appropriate Access instance
        If Me.CreateNewInstance Then
            Set Me.AccessInst = CreateObject(strProgID)
        ElseIf Me.IsAccessRunning Then
            Set Me.AccessInst = GetObject(, strProgID)
        Else
            ' Cannot use existing instance if
            ' there isn't one--raise an error
            Err.Raise _
             vbObjectError + aeErrAccessNotRunning, _
             TypeName(Me) & "::Init", _
             "Running Access instance not found."
        End If
    End If

    ' If database or project name has been
    ' specified, load it
    If Not Me.AccessInst Is Nothing Then
        If Len(Me.FileName) > 3 Then
            If Right(Me.FileName, 3) = "ADP" Then
                Me.AccessInst.OpenAccessProject _
                 Me.FileName
            Else
                Me.AccessInst.OpenCurrentDatabase _
                 Me.FileName
            End If
        End If
    End If
Else
    ' Automation session already initialized--
    ' raise an error
    Err.Raise _
     vbObjectError + aeErrSessionAlreadyInitialized, _
     TypeName(Me) & "::Init", _
     "Automation session already initialized."
End If
```

```
ExitHere:
    Exit Function
HandleErr:
    Select Case Err.Number
        Case Else
            Err.Raise Err.Number, Err.Source, _
             Err.Description, Err.HelpFile, _
             Err.HelpContext
    End Select
End Function
```

Loading a Database or Project

When using Automation to control Access, you'll use a set of methods designed specifically for that purpose that you're unlikely to use anywhere else. These methods open, close, and create Access database or project files. Table 13.2 summarizes these methods.

TABLE 13.2: Methods for Working with Databases and Projects Using Automation

Method	Description
CloseCurrentDatabase	Closes the currently open Access database or project file
CreateAccessProject	Creates a new Access project (ADP) file on disk but does not open it in the Access window
NewAccessProject	Creates a new Access data project file on disk and opens it in the Access window
NewCurrentDatabase	Creates a new Access database (MDB) file on disk and opens it in the Access window
OpenAccessProject	Opens an Access data project file in the Access window
OpenCurrentDatabase	Opens an Access database file in the Access window

As you can see from Table 13.2, you can use Access to create new Access databases and project files. More often than not, however, you'll use the methods for opening and closing existing files.

TIP

If you really need to create a new Access (Jet) database, it's much easier to do so using DAO or ADOX, the ADO Extensions for DDL and Security. With DAO, you use the CreateDatabase method of a Workspace object, while with ADOX you call the Create method of a Catalog object. More information is contained in the online help files included with Access 2000. On the other hand, since ADP files are specific to Access and aren't managed by either DAO or ADO, you will need to use Automation to create them.

The Init method of our AccessAutomation class first checks the file extension of the FileName property to determine if you are working with a database or an Access project file and then calls either OpenCurrentDatabase or OpenAccess-Project, passing the path to the requested file. These methods are also used in the Property Let procedure of FileName property, shown in Listing 13.2. In this case, the class closes an open database when the property value changes. It then opens the newly specified database or project.

NOTE

Unlike some applications, Access does not suppress startup code (the AutoExec macro and/or startup form) when a database is opened using Automation. Startup code that displays dialogs that require a user response such as clicking an OK button may cause your Automation to fail if the user does not respond quickly enough. See the section "The UserControl Property" later in this chapter for ways to make your application respond gracefully to being launched via Automation.

Listing 13.2

```
Property Let FileName(strName As String)

    ' If Access is already open then attempt
    ' to open the database
    If Not Me.AccessInst Is Nothing Then

        ' Close any open database
        If Me.IsProjectLoaded Then
            Me.AccessInst.CloseCurrentDatabase
        End If

        ' Load the new database
        If Len(strName) > 3 Then
            If Right(strName, 3) = "ADP" Then
```

```
                Me.AccessInst.OpenAccessProject _
                 strName
            Else
                Me.AccessInst.OpenCurrentDatabase _
                 strName
            End If
        End If
    End If

    ' Store the new property value
    pstrFileName = strName
End Property
```

NOTE Even though there are two methods for opening files (depending on whether they are Jet databases or Access projects), CloseCurrentDatabase works with both.

WARNING Be careful when calling CloseCurrentDatabase to close a database you didn't open through Automation. If you try to close a user's database that has open, changed objects, the user will have to dismiss a series of confirmation dialogs before Access can close the database. This may cause the CloseCurrentDatabase to time out and fail. Make sure your error handling is set up to cope with this possibility.

Dealing with Secure Workgroups

Working with Automation and Access secure workgroups presents an additional set of challenges. Even though Access 2000 is the third version of Access to support Automation, Access still exhibits a behavior inconsistent with well-behaved Automation servers—it raises a dialog during the Automation process. There are no object model members that enable you bypass this dialog. On one hand, this makes Access more secure by making it harder for hackers to exploit Access applications, but it also can be annoying to the legitimate developer.

When you initiate an Automation session with Access using a secure workgroup, the login dialog appears as soon as you try to open a database. Your Automation code then waits indefinitely for the user to respond. You can see how this can be a problem if you haven't displayed the Access window yet (remember, it starts out hidden). One possible solution is to display the Access main window and then use SendKeys (!) to place a valid user name and password into the keyboard buffer before calling OpenCurrentDatabase. In a multitasking environment like Windows, however, this is likely to produce inconsistent results.

We've chosen to overcome this hurdle by using the one consistent technique for starting Access with a secure workgroup: using command line parameters. Access supports three command line parameters, /user, /pwd, and /wrkgrp, for specifying a user name, password, and workgroup file, respectively, when launching the application. Of course, you can't use command line parameters with Automation; you must launch Access separately using the Shell function.

The code in the Init method constructs a command line based on property settings:

```
' Build a command line including
' switches for security information
strCmd = "MSACCESS.EXE /user " & Me.UserName
If Len(Me.Password) Then
    strCmd = strCmd & " /pwd " & Me.Password
End If
If Len(Me.Workgroup) Then
    strCmd = strCmd & " /wrkgrp " & Me.Workgroup
End If
strCmd = strCmd & " /nostartup"
```

The command line also includes the /nostartup option to suppress Access' opening dialog because this, too, would cause Automation code to halt and wait. After constructing the command line, the Init method calls the Shell function and then makes a call to the Windows API Sleep function. Sleep causes the code to halt for a short time (about a half-second) before the code calls GetObject. This is necessary to give Access enough time to start before attempting to obtain an object reference:

```
' Execute the command and wait a few
' milliseconds before attempting
' communications (may need adjustment)
If Shell(strCmd) Then
    Sleep conWaitIntervalMs
    Set Me.AccessInst = GetObject(, strProgID)
End If
```

If everything goes as planned, you'll have a reference to the secured Access instance stored in the AccessInst property.

NOTE

This technique only works if Access is not already running (notice the call to the internal IsAccessRunning function in the code). That's because GetObject only returns a pointer to the first running instance it finds, which may not be the instance started using the security options.

Controlling Window Visibility

As we mentioned earlier in this chapter (see the section "Access Automation Server Behavior"), Access' Visible property exhibits inconsistent behavior depending on the current UserControl property value. To overcome this behavior, our class implements Show and Hide methods that use the Windows API, which always works. Specifically, the class uses the ShowWindow API function, shown here with two of its associated constants:

```
Private Declare Function ShowWindow Lib "user32" _
 (ByVal hwnd As Long, ByVal nCmdShow As Long) As Long
Private Const SW_HIDE = 0
Private Const SW_NORMAL = 1
```

ShowWindow accepts a window handle and a constant representing the desired window state (hidden or normal in this case). Listing 13.3 shows the implementation of the class' Show and Hide methods.

Listing 13.3

```
Public Sub Show()
    Call ShowAccessWindow(True)
End Sub
Public Sub Hide()
    Call ShowAccessWindow(False)
End Sub
Private Sub ShowAccessWindow(fShow As Boolean)
    ' Control Access main window using ShowWindow
    ' rather than Automation
    If Not AccessInst Is Nothing Then
        If fShow Then
            Call ShowWindow(AccessInst.hWndAccessApp, SW_NORMAL)
        Else
```

```
            Call ShowWindow(AccessInst.hWndAccessApp, SW_HIDE)
        End If
    End If
End Sub
```

NOTE For more information on window handles and Windows API functions, see Chapter 16.

Determining Whether a Project Is Loaded

One important piece of information you may need while using Access as an Automation server is determining whether a database or project file is loaded into the Access application. For example, the CloseCurrentDatabase method will fail if no database is loaded. Unfortunately, there doesn't appear to be a simple way to determine this using the Access object model.

We've implemented an IsProjectLoaded property of our AccessAutomation class that determines the load state by trying to retrieve the name of the currently loaded project. Listing 13.4 shows the property's implementation.

Listing 13.4

```
Public Property Get IsProjectLoaded() As Boolean
    Dim strTemp As String

    On Error GoTo HandleErr

    ' Attempt to retrieve the name of the current project
    strTemp = AccessInst.CurrentProject.Name

    ' No error: a project is loaded
    IsProjectLoaded = True

ExitHere:
    Exit Property
HandleErr:
    Select Case Err.Number
        ' Error 2467: no project is loaded
```

```
            Case conErrNoProjectLoaded
                IsProjectLoaded = False
                Resume ExitHere
            ' Unknown error: send it back to client
            Case Else
                Err.Raise Err.Number, Err.Source, _
                 Err.Description, Err.HelpFile, Err.HelpContext
        End Select
    End Property
```

The property code works by trying to retrieve the name of the currently loaded project into a String variable. If this succeeds with no errors, then a project is in fact loaded. If a runtime error occurs (error 2467), then no project is loaded.

NOTE

You might think we could have simply checked to see if the CurrentProject object was Nothing. This won't work, however, because Access creates a valid object even if no database or project file is loaded.

The AccessAutomation class uses this property in its implementation of the FileName property.

Quitting Access

The final task of the AccessAutomation class is to properly terminate the Automation session with Access. It does this in the class' Terminate event, shown in Listing 13.5. Note how the procedure checks the value of Access' UserControl property. If it returns False, meaning the user has not interacted with Access, the procedure terminates Access using the Quit method. If UserControl returns True, the procedure makes sure the main window is visible (by calling the class' Show method) so the user isn't left with an invisible instance of Access.

Listing 13.5

```
Private Sub Class_Terminate()
    ' Shut down or display Access, depending
    ' on state of UserControl property
    If Not AccessInst Is Nothing Then
        With AccessInst
            If .UserControl Then
```

```
                Me.Show
            Else
                .Quit
            End If
        End With

        Set AccessInst = Nothing
    End If
End Sub
```

Running Access Reports Using Automation

To demonstrate the AccessAutomation class and the general techniques required to use Access as an Automation server, we have written sample code that lets you browse and print reports stored in an Access database. We chose this example for a number of reasons. First, it allows us to demonstrate the very few additional techniques you need to master to use Access effectively as an Automation server. (After all, the rest of this book describes how to write an Access application *in Access*!) Second, printing reports is one thing Access does much better than many other development tools, including other databases. Finally, printing Access reports from other applications, particularly those written in Visual Basic, is a capability a great number of developers, disappointed with those other applications' reporting capabilities, have long sought.

To demonstrate how to use the class (and because we needed something to show), we've included a Microsoft Excel application in CH13.XLS. Figure 13.1 shows the worksheet.

The sample application was written in Microsoft Excel because many of you also have a copy of Excel. Owning a copy of Excel will make it easy to test the sample code without having to write an application of your own.

Finally, we've created several procedures to test different aspects of Access as an Automation server. You'll find these procedures in the basTestFunctions module in the Excel workbook and in a text file called TESTAUTO.BAS on the companion CD-ROM.

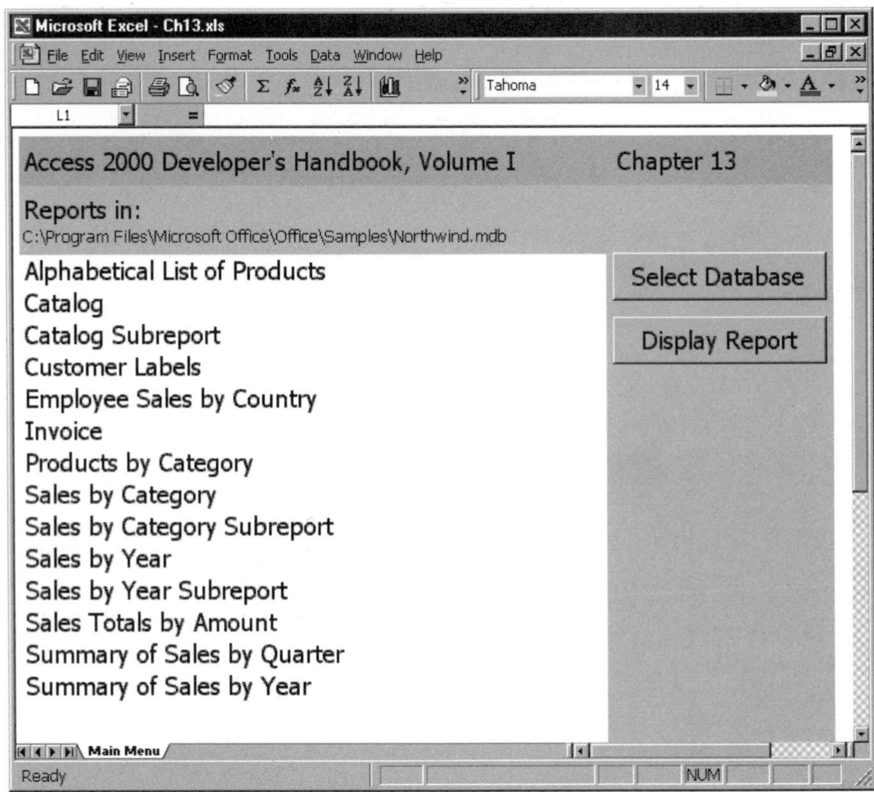

FIGURE 13.1:

A sample Automation application written in Excel

The Sample Application

CH13.XLS contains a worksheet called Main Menu, which holds the application's interface. When the workbook is opened, code in its Open event procedure begins an Automation session with Access. At this point, you can click the Select Database button to select a database or project file using Excel's Open File dialog. The application then opens the file and scans it for reports, which it lists in worksheet cells. To preview a report, simply highlight a cell containing a report name and click the Display Report button.

In summary, these are the tasks that the application performs:

1. Initiating a connection to an instance of Access using Automation in the Workbook_Open event

2. Selecting and opening a database
3. Retrieving a list of reports and displaying the names in the worksheet
4. Previewing a report
5. Shutting down Access by destroying the AccessAutomation object in the Workbook_BeforeClose event

Initiating an Automation Session

Initializing the AccessAutomation class (and in turn an Automation session) is done in the workbook's Open event. For new instances of Access, this distributes the startup time associated with launching a copy of Access when opening the workbook. To increase performance, the code attempts to use a running instance, if possible. The code for the startup procedure is shown below (AccAuto is a module-level variable that holds an instance of the AccessAutomation class):

```
Private Sub Workbook_Open()
    ' Initialize the Access Automation session
    Set AccAuto = New AccessAutomation

    With AccAuto
        ' Use running instance if available
        If .IsAccessRunning Then
            .CreateNewInstance = False
        End If

        ' Initialize the session, display the
        ' Access window and update the report list
        .Init
        .Show
        Call RefreshReportList

        ' Re-activate Excel
        AppActivate "Microsoft Excel"
    End With
End Sub
```

NOTE The IsAccessRunning property uses the Windows API FindWindow function to determine if Access is running.

Opening a Database

The sample application lets you choose a database or Access project file to open. Code behind the command button's Click event calls a Public procedure in the workbook's class module, LoadDatabase, shown in Listing 13.6. Excel implements a very handy GetOpenFileName method that exposes Office's common Open File dialog without having to resort to API functions. GetOpenFileName returns a variant holding the selected file name or the value False if the user cancels the dialog.

Listing 13.6

```
Public Sub LoadDatabase()

    Dim varFileName As Variant

    Const conFilter = "Access Databases,*.mdb;*.adp;" _
     & "*.mda,All files,*.*"
    Const conTitle = "Select Database To Open"

    ' Call the GetOpenFilename method of Excel's Application
    ' object to get the name of database to open--this
    ' method returns a string containing a full path to
    ' a file if the user clicked the OK button.
    varFileName = Application.GetOpenFilename( _
        FileFilter:=conFilter, _
        FilterIndex:=0, _
        Title:=conTitle, _
        MultiSelect:=False)

    ' Check to see if the user chose a database
    If VarType(varFileName) = vbString Then

        ' Make sure class is initialized
        If AccAuto Is Nothing Then
            Call Workbook_Open
        End If

        ' Set the file name property
        AccAuto.FileName = varFileName

        ' Update the worksheet
```

```
        wksMain.Range("DBName") = varFileName

        ' Refresh the report list
        Call RefreshReportList
    End If
End Sub
```

After the user selects a database, the procedure sets the FileName property of AccAuto, the instance of our AccessAutomation class. Note that if the Init method has already been called, then setting the property will load the database immediately. Otherwise, it simply sets the property value for an Init call later on.

TIP

It's interesting to note that implementing LoadDatabase as a custom method of the workbook object eliminates the need for a separate global code module in the project. As long as it's declared as public, you can call it from anywhere in the application using the syntax ThisWorkbook.LoadDatabase.

Getting a List of Reports

After opening a database, the application calls RefreshReportList, a procedure that retrieves report names from the loaded database and writes them to the worksheet. RefreshReportList, shown in Listing 13.7, takes advantage of a new set of objects in Access 2000 to enumerate object names. Specifically, it uses the AllReports collection of the CurrentProject object. The collection is made up of multiple AccessObject objects that expose object names, load state, and additional Access-specific properties. For more information on these new objects, which you should use in place of DAO Document and Container objects, see Chapter 6.

Listing 13.7

```
Sub RefreshReportList()
    Dim rngAny As Range
    Dim objItem As Access.AccessObject

    Const conListStart = "BeginList"

    ' Make sure we have a valid object reference
    If Me.IsReady Then
```

```
            ' Set a reference to the starting range
            ' and clear the current contents
            Set rngAny = wksMain.Range(conListStart)
            rngAny.CurrentRegion.Clear

            ' Loop through each report and copy the
            ' name to the worksheet
            For Each objItem In _
             AccAuto.AccessInst.CurrentProject.AllReports
                rngAny.Value = objItem.Name
                Set rngAny = rngAny.Offset(1)
            Next

            ' Sort the list
            wksMain.Range(conListStart).CurrentRegion.Sort _
             wksMain.Range(conListStart)
        End If
    End Sub
```

NOTE

IsReady is a private method of the workbook's class that checks to see that (a) the AccessAutomation class has been instantiated, (b) an Automation session with Access has been initiated, and (c) a database or project is currently loaded.

There's not much to say about RefreshReportList, because it uses the same technique to build a list of reports that you might use in an Access application. The only difference is the qualification of CurrentProject with the object variable storing a reference to Access (AccAuto.AccessInst in this case).

Retrieving a list of reports in the manner above works with any Access database or project, but it can be slow because of the large number of cross-process method calls. For a faster alternative that requires VBA code in the database you're automating, see the section "Calling User-Defined Functions from an Automation Client" later in this chapter.

Previewing Reports

Printing or previewing a report using Automation is relatively straightforward. Once you know the name of the report, simply call the OpenReport method of Access' DoCmd object. Our application does this in the workbook's OpenReport method, shown in Listing 13.8. You'll also notice that the procedure uses the All-Reports collection again, this time to determine if the selected report is already open. If the IsLoaded property returns True, the procedure closes the report. This ensures that it displays the most recent data.

Listing 13.8

```
Public Sub OpenReport(ReportName As String)
    ' Make sure class is initialized
    If IsReady Then

        With AccAuto.AccessInst

            ' If report is already open, close it before
            ' trying to open it again
            If .CurrentProject.AllReports(ReportName) _
             .IsLoaded Then
                .DoCmd.Close acReport, ReportName
            End If

            ' Call Access' OpenReport method
            ' and maximize the report window
            With .DoCmd
                .OpenReport ReportName, acViewPreview
                .Maximize
            End With
        End With

        ' Activate the Access window
        AppActivate "Microsoft Access"
    End If
End Sub
```

In our sample application, we've chosen to let users preview reports in Access. Obviously, you could modify the code to send reports directly to the printer, if you wish. If you choose to preview them, however, you should make sure to put the Access main window in a position where the user can see it. We do this in our application by first maximizing the report so it fills the Access window. We then call the VBA AppActivate function, passing the window title, Microsoft Access, to bring the Access window to the front.

While the sample application is simple, it does demonstrate a number of key techniques required to use Access as an Automation server, including creating an object reference, calling Access methods and properties, and terminating an Automation session. Given your knowledge of Access, as well as the techniques described in the rest of this book, you should be able to extend the examples here into fully functional Automation applications. The remainder of this chapter discusses additional topics related to using Access as an Automation server, including calling user-defined functions using Automation and creating databases that work equally well whether run from the Access user interface or from Automation.

Calling User-Defined Functions from an Automation Client

In addition to using the properties and methods of Access objects, you can call user-defined subroutines and functions in an Access database via Automation. By using this capability, you can leverage functions already written, eliminating the need to rewrite them in the client application. You use two different methods to call procedures in an Access database, depending on whether they are declared in a global module or a form module.

Global Functions

Public functions are executed using the Run method of Access' Application object. In Access, Run executes functions or subroutines declared in a database that is not referenced by the current database, using the References dialog. When controlling Access through Automation, you can use Run to call a procedure in the current database, just as you would when using Run in VBA in Access or any of the preloaded library databases, such as ACWZTOOL.MDE. Run accepts a variable number of arguments, up to 30, the first of which is the name of the function or subroutine you wish to execute. You use the remaining arguments of Run to pass any arguments the called procedure requires.

NOTE

To call a procedure in a library database, you must precede the procedure name with the library's VBA project name, for example: acwztool.wlib_Hourglass.

To demonstrate, CH13.MDB contains a function called ListReports that returns an array with the names of all reports in the loaded database. You can call the function from an Automation client program by using Access' Run method. Doing so increases performance because the processing is done in VBA in Access' process, rather than making lots of cross-process method calls. For example, the GetReports function in the basTestFunctions module of CH13.XLS (see Listing 13.9) uses this approach to print the names of reports from CH13.MDB to the Immediate window.

NOTE

The ListReports and GetReports functions are included only to demonstrate techniques for calling procedures and passing arguments to user-defined functions through Automation. The sample application does not call these functions, as we designed it to work with any database, not just those that include a ListReports function. As you create your own applications, however, calling VBA code in Access from an Automation client is a valuable technique to use.

Listing 13.9

```
Function ListReports() As Variant
    Dim objRpt As AccessObject
    Dim lngRpt As Long
    Dim varRpt() As Variant

    With Application.CurrentProject

        ' Dimension the array
        ReDim varRpt(1 To .AllReports.Count)

        ' Get all report names
        For Each objRpt In .AllReports
            lngRpt = lngRpt + 1
            varRpt(lngRpt) = objRpt.Name
        Next
    End With

    ' Set return value
    ListReports = varRpt
End Function

Sub GetReports()
    Dim objAccAuto As AccessAutomation
```

```
    Dim varRptList As Variant
    Dim varRpt As Variant
    Dim strProjectName As String
    Dim strProcToRun As String

    ' Initiate an Automation session with Access
    Set objAccAuto = New AccessAutomation
    With objAccAuto
        ' Note: assumes database and workbook are
        ' in the same directory
        .FileName = ThisWorkbook.Path & "\CH13.MDB"
        .Init
        .Show

        ' Get the name of the VBA project, this will be
        ' used to construct the procedure call for
        ' the Run method
        strProjectName = .AccessInst.GetOption("Project Name")

        ' Create the procedure call from the project
        ' name and function name
        strProcToRun = strProjectName & ".ListReports"

        ' NOTE: the next depends on a function
        ' called ListReports in CH13.MDB
        varRptList = .AccessInst.Run(strProcToRun)

        ' Print the report names
        For Each varRpt In varRptList
            Debug.Print varRpt
        Next
    End With

    Set objAccAuto = Nothing
End Sub
```

By using the Run method, you can pass literal values, as well as variables, as arguments to a procedure. If you pass a variable by reference, the called procedure can modify its value.

When using the Run method, it is a good idea to precede the name of the procedure with the name of the database's VBA project (CH13 in CH13.MDB). You can find the name of a database's VBA project in the Project Explorer and Properties window in the VBA IDE. The GetReports procedure uses Access' GetOption method to dynamically retrieve the project name of CH13.MDB.

Form-Level Functions

Form-level functions, those declared in a form's module, are called differently from global functions. First, form-level functions must be explicitly declared as Public in order to be visible to calling programs. Once this is done, they become methods of the form and are called in the same way as any other methods using VBA. That is, you first obtain an object pointer to the form and then call one of its methods. The only difference with Automation is that you must qualify the Forms collection with a pointer to Access' Application object. Listing 13.10 shows a short procedure that calls a function named FormClose, declared in the frmCloseMe form from CH13.MDB. FormClose does nothing more than use the DoCmd.Close method to close the form, but it lets you express this as a built-in method of the form. Listing 13.11 shows the very small bit of code that makes up the FormClose method, as well as an example of how you can call it from VBA code in Access. (We would have liked to call this function Close, but because that's a VBA reserved word, we had to choose something else.)

Listing 13.10

```
Sub TestFormMethod()
    Dim objAccAuto As AccessAutomation
    Dim frm As Access.Form

    ' Get a reference to Access
    Set objAccAuto = New AccessAutomation
    With objAccAuto

        ' Note: assumes database and workbook are
        ' in the same directory
        .FileName = ThisWorkbook.Path & "\CH13.MDB"
        .Init
        .Show

        ' Open the form and set a pointer
        With objAccAuto.AccessInst
            .DoCmd.OpenForm "frmCloseMe"
            Set frm = .Forms("frmCloseMe")
        End With
```

```
            ' Put some code in here that does something

            ' Close the form using its FClose method
            frm.FormClose
        End With

        Set objAccAuto = Nothing
    End Sub
```

Listing 13.11

```
Public Function FormClose()
    ' This public function acts as a new method
    ' of this form object. You can call it from
    ' VBA code in Access (see the cmdClose_Click
    ' procedure) or using Automation
    DoCmd.Close acForm, Me.Name
End Function

Private Sub cmdClose_Click()
    ' Calls the new FormClose method of this form
    Me.FormClose
End Sub
```

TIP

If you've created a method that returns a value, you can capture that in a variable in the Automation client's code just as you would for other methods that return values. Just make sure you include parentheses (as well as any arguments) after the method name.

Writing Automation-Friendly Applications

As you begin to use the Automation server features of Access, you may discover it makes sense to use the same database both as a user application in Access and as the subject of Automation control from another program. The suggestions in this section are aimed at helping you create an application that can serve both purposes well. By keeping in mind that your user may not always be at the helm, you can greatly leverage your time investment.

The UserControl Property

Access exports a property of its Application object that is very useful when creating databases that will be used by both end users and Automation clients. Called UserControl, this property returns True if Access was launched by an end user or False if it was started by a request from an Automation client. UserControl also returns True if a user has interacted with Access after being started by Automation. You should use this property in your own application whenever you need to know whether a user or Automation client is in control. For example, you might use this in your error-handling code to suppress message boxes unless UserControl returns True. The section "Creating Your Own Error Stack" later in this chapter uses this technique.

You should also check the UserControl property in your AutoExec function or the Open event of your startup form and suppress actions that don't make sense for a database being opened by another application. For instance, it is unlikely you'll want to waste time displaying a splash screen during an Automation session. In cases like this, the UserControl property allows you to selectively display forms and messages that make sense for a human user.

Hiding the Access Main Window

One problem with using Access as an Automation server is the inconsistent behavior of Access' main window and problems with the Application object's Visible property (see the section "Access Automation Server Behavior" earlier in this chapter). If the window is visible, there is always a chance a user will activate it and do something that would confuse your Automation code (close the active database, for instance). By default, Access launches as a hidden window when you call it via Automation, so the best approach is to keep the main window hidden whenever possible. However, as you saw in the previous example, this isn't feasible if you want to do something like preview a report. In general, therefore, it's best to keep the window hidden when possible, displaying it only when you need user input or interaction.

Preventing Users from Closing the Database

If you don't want to hide the Access window when using Access as an Automation server (perhaps because you're using an instance of Access launched by the user), another approach to prevent tampering is to keep the database open until your Automation code no longer needs it. You can accomplish this by opening a form that cannot be closed until code is run from your Automation client application. CH13.MDB contains a form called frmLock, which uses a module-level variable to determine whether the form can be closed. Listing 13.12 shows the contents of the form's module.

Listing 13.12

```
' Private variable to control whether form
' (and thus database) can be closed--set by
' public Property Let statement
Private pblnCanClose As Boolean

Property Get CanClose() As Boolean
    ' Property Get for the CanClose property--
    ' returns the value of the form variable
    CanClose = pblnCanClose
End Property

Property Let CanClose(fCanClose As Boolean)
    ' Property Let for the CanClose property--
    ' sets the value of the form variable and
    ' sets the state of the form's check box
    pblnCanClose = fCanClose
    Me.chkCanClose = fCanClose
End Property

Private Sub chkCanClose_AfterUpdate()
    ' Checking the check box lets the user
    ' close the form
    pblnCanClose = Me.chkCanClose
End Sub

Private Sub Form_Unload(Cancel As Integer)
    ' This code prevents the form from closing
    ' if the CanClose poperty is False--to
    ' close the form the user must click the
    ' check box or COM Automation code must
```

```
        ' set the value of CanClose to True
        If Not Me.CanClose Then

            ' If the form cannot be closed display
            ' a warning to the user if UserControl
            ' is True, otherwise just beep once
            If Application.UserControl Then
                MsgBox "Cannot close.", vbCritical
            Else
                Beep
            End If

            ' Cancel the close
            Cancel = True
        End If
    End Sub
```

Code in the form's Unload event checks a user-defined property of the form called CanClose, which is initialized to False. If the property is still False during processing of the Unload event, the event procedure prevents the form from closing. Because Access will not unload the database if the form cannot be closed, preventing the form from closing prevents the database from being closed as well. Code in the TestLock procedure loads frmLock after initializing an Automation session and opening CH13.MDB. TestLock is shown in Listing 13.13.

Listing 13.13

```
Sub TestLock()

    Dim objAccAuto As AccessAutomation

    Const conLockForm = "frmLock"

    ' Get a reference to Access
    Set objAccAuto = New AccessAutomation
    With objAccAuto

        ' Note: assumes database and workbook are
        ' in the same directory
        .FileName = ThisWorkbook.Path & "\CH13.MDB"
        .Init
        .Show
```

```
        ' Open the lock form
        With objAccAuto.AccessInst
            .DoCmd.OpenForm _
             conLockForm, acNormal, , , , acHidden

            ' Go ahead, try and close the database!
            Debug.Assert False

            ' Close the lock form after setting
            ' its CanClose property
            .Forms(conLockForm).CanClose = True
            .DoCmd.Close acForm, conLockForm

            ' Now try, it should close now
            Debug.Assert False
        End With
    End With

    Set objAccAuto = Nothing
End Sub
```

TestLock opens the frmLock form hidden, making it more difficult for the user to locate and close the form manually. This is not foolproof, however. If you really want to hide the form from the user, make sure to set its BorderStyle property to Dialog. That way it won't show up in Access' Unhide dialog. If you want to use the technique described in this section in your applications, be sure to copy the frmLock form from CH13.MDB to your database files.

Being User-Input Aware

When designing your applications, keep in mind that any type of forced user input will interrupt the successful completion of actions initiated via Automation. A good example is the Employee Sales by Country report in NORTHWIND.MDB. It's based on a parameter query that requires users to enter a range of dates before it can print. Launching this report from Automation (especially if the Access main window were hidden) would cause your client code to time out and fail. If you need to use objects that require user input, you should at the very least display and activate the main Access window so users can take action while your Automation code is waiting. Ideally, however, you should not use objects that halt the processing of an object's method.

Creating Your Own Error Stack

If you want to call your own functions from an Automation client, one challenge you face is returning meaningful error information to your application. If a user-defined function called via Automation fails, your client application will receive an Automation error that may or may not be meaningful. An alternative is to maintain your own error stack in the server database that the client can query to determine the status of any runtime errors. CH13.MDB contains code to do this in basErrorStack (see Listing 13.14). It works by opening a form containing a list box and adding error information to the list. Because Access 2000 forms can expose methods and properties, you can retrieve error information from your Automation client application.

WARNING Be careful if you are used to writing Automation server applications using Visual Basic. Generally, you can use the Raise method of VBA's Err object to return error information to an Automation client. However, VBA documentation states that not all host applications support using the Raise method in this fashion and, unfortunately, Access falls into this category. Using the Raise method in your code will produce a runtime error in your Access application, but this error will not be returned to any Automation client application. If you want to see this in action, execute the TestErr procedure in CH13.MDB using the Run method.

Listing 13.14

```
Option Compare Database
Option Explicit

Const conErrForm = "frmErrorStack"

Public Function TestErr()
    Err.Raise vbObjectError + 100, "TestErr", _
     "This is the description."
End Function

Sub InitErrs()
    If SysCmd(acSysCmdGetObjectState, acForm, _
     conErrForm) = acObjStateOpen Then

        Call Forms(conErrForm).ClearErrors
    Else
```

```
        DoCmd.OpenForm _
         FormName:=conErrForm, _
         windowmode:=acHidden
    End If
End Sub

Sub PushError(ByVal lngError As Long, _
 ByVal strError As String, ByVal strProc As String)
    If SysCmd(acSysCmdGetObjectState, acForm, _
     conErrForm) = acObjStateOpen Then

        Call Forms(conErrForm).AddError( _
         lngError, strError, strProc)
    End If
End Sub

Sub TestStack()
    ' Set up error handling
    On Error GoTo TestStack_Error

    ' Flush any exiting errors
    Call InitErrs

    ' Fake an error
    Debug.Print 1 / 0

TestStack_Exit:
    Exit Sub
TestStack_Error:
    ' If Access was launched by the user display
    ' a dialog box, otherwise push the error
    ' information onto our homemade stack
    If UserControl Then
        MsgBox Err.Description, vbExclamation, _
         "Error " & Err.Number
    Else
        Call PushError(Err.Number, _
         Err.Description, "TestStack")
    End If
    Resume TestStack_Exit
End Sub
```

Listing 13.14 shows the contents of basErrorStack, which includes two procedures for managing the error information and one for testing purposes. The first procedure, InitErrs, opens the error stack form (frmErrorStack) and clears existing error information. Note that we open the form hidden so it is not obvious to users who may be working with Access. You should call InitErrs at the head of any procedure within which you want to trap errors.

After calling InitErrors, call PushError in your error handling code to push error information onto the stack. PushError requires three parameters—the error number, the error description, and the procedure name—and calls the AddError method of the error stack form (see Listing 13.15).

TestStack demonstrates the use of the previous two procedures. You'll notice that it calls InitErrors immediately after establishing error handling with the On Error Goto statement. Farther down in the procedure's error handling code, it calls PushError with the error information only if UserControl returns False. If the UserControl property returns True, the procedure displays a message box. This illustrates how an application could be used both interactively by a user and as the server for an Automation client.

Listing 13.15 shows the code contained in frmErrorStack's VBA module that manages the list of errors on the form. It includes public methods to clear the error list (ClearErrors) and add items to it (AddError). It also includes Property Get statements to return error information. You call each of the properties, ErrNo, ErrDesc, and ErrProc, by passing an index into the collection of errors, with 0 being the most recent error. To determine how many errors exist on the stack, you can query the ErrCount property.

Listing 13.15

```
Option Compare Database
Option Explicit

Private Sub cmdClear_Click()
    ' Clear the error stack
    Me.ClearErrors
End Sub

Private Sub cmdClose_Click()
    ' Close the form
    DoCmd.Close acForm, Me.Name
End Sub
```

```
Property Get ErrNo(ByVal intErr As Integer) As Variant
    ' Property Get statement to return a particular
    ' error number--works by changing the BoundColumn
    ' property and returning the data for a given row
    If intErr > Me.lstErrors.ListCount Then
        ErrNo = -1
    Else
        Me.lstErrors.BoundColumn = 1
        ErrNo = Me.lstErrors.ItemData(intErr)
    End If
End Property

Property Get ErrDesc(ByVal intErr As Integer) As Variant
    ' Property Get statement to return a particular
    ' error description--works by changing the BoundColumn
    ' property and returning the data for a given row
    If intErr > Me.lstErrors.ListCount Then
        ErrDesc = "#Error#"
    Else
        Me.lstErrors.BoundColumn = 2
        ErrDesc = Me.lstErrors.ItemData(intErr)
    End If
End Property

Property Get ErrProc(ByVal intErr As Integer) As Variant
    ' Property Get statement to return a particular
    ' error procedure--works by changing the BoundColumn
    ' property and returning the data for a given row
    If intErr > Me.lstErrors.ListCount Then
        ErrProc = "#Error#"
    Else
        Me.lstErrors.BoundColumn = 3
        ErrProc = Me.lstErrors.ItemData(intErr)
    End If
End Property

Property Get ErrCount() As Long
    ' Property Get statement to return the number of
    ' errors--works by returning the ListCount of the
    ' list box
    ErrCount = Me.lstErrors.ListCount
End Property
```

```
Public Sub ClearErrors()
    ' Public method to clear the error list
    Me.lstErrors.RowSource = ""
End Sub

Public Sub AddError(ByVal lngErrNo As Long, _
 ByVal strErrDesc As String, ByVal strProc As String)

    ' Public method to add an error to the list--
    ' works by adding text to the RowSource property
    Me.lstErrors.RowSource = lngErrNo & ";" & strErrDesc & ";" &
strProc & ";" & Me.lstErrors.RowSource
End Sub
```

To demonstrate how this error stack works, we've included a test procedure in the basTestFunctions module of CH13.XLS called TestErrorStack (see Listing 13.16). It calls the TestStack function in basErrorStack using the Application object's Run method. You can see from Listing 13.14 that we've intentionally forced a division-by-zero error in TestStack. After opening CH13.MDB, the procedure then calls the TestStack function, which contains the division-by-zero error. Because UserControl is False, this will place the error information on your custom stack rather than display an error message.

Listing 13.16

```
Sub TestErrorStack()
    Dim objAccAuto As AccessAutomation
    Dim frmErrors As Access.Form
    Dim lngErrors As Long

    ' Get a reference to Access
    Set objAccAuto = New AccessAutomation
    With objAccAuto

        ' Note: assumes database and workbook are
        ' in the same directory
        .FileName = ThisWorkbook.Path & "\CH13.MDB"
        .Init
        .Show

        ' Run the TestStack routine in CH13.MDB--
        ' this will generate an error and put it on
        ' the stack.
```

```
            With objAccAuto.AccessInst
                .Run "TestStack"

                ' Get a pointer to the error stack form
                Set frmErrors = .Forms("frmErrorStack")

                ' Check the error count--if it's greater than
                ' zero loop through each, displaying a message
                If frmErrors.ErrCount > 0 Then

                    For lngErrors = 0 To frmErrors.ErrCount - 1

                        ' Create an error message in this app
                        ' by calling the ErrDesc, ErrNo, and
                        ' ErrProc properties of the error form
                        MsgBox frmErrors.ErrDesc(lngErrors), _
                         vbExclamation, "Error " & _
                         frmErrors.ErrNo(lngErrors) _
                         & " in " & frmErrors.ErrProc(lngErrors)
                    Next

                    ' Clear the error stack now that we're done
                    frmErrors.ClearErrors
                End If
            End With
        End With

        Set objAccAuto = Nothing
    End Sub
```

After calling the test procedure, TestErrorStack gets a reference to the error stack form and stores it in the frmErrors object variable. It then uses this variable to examine the ErrCount property of the form. If there's at least one error (which there will be in this test case), TestErrorStack loops through each one, using the ErrDesc, ErrNo, and ErrProc properties to extract the relevant information and display it in an Excel message box. Finally, the procedure calls the ClearErrors method to flush the error stack. Figure 13.2 shows what your screen might look like if you ran TestErrorStack on your own computer. Figure 13.3, on the other hand, shows frmErrorStack after being made visible with the Window ➢ Unhide command. To view this yourself, you'll have to pause execution before calling the ClearErrors method.

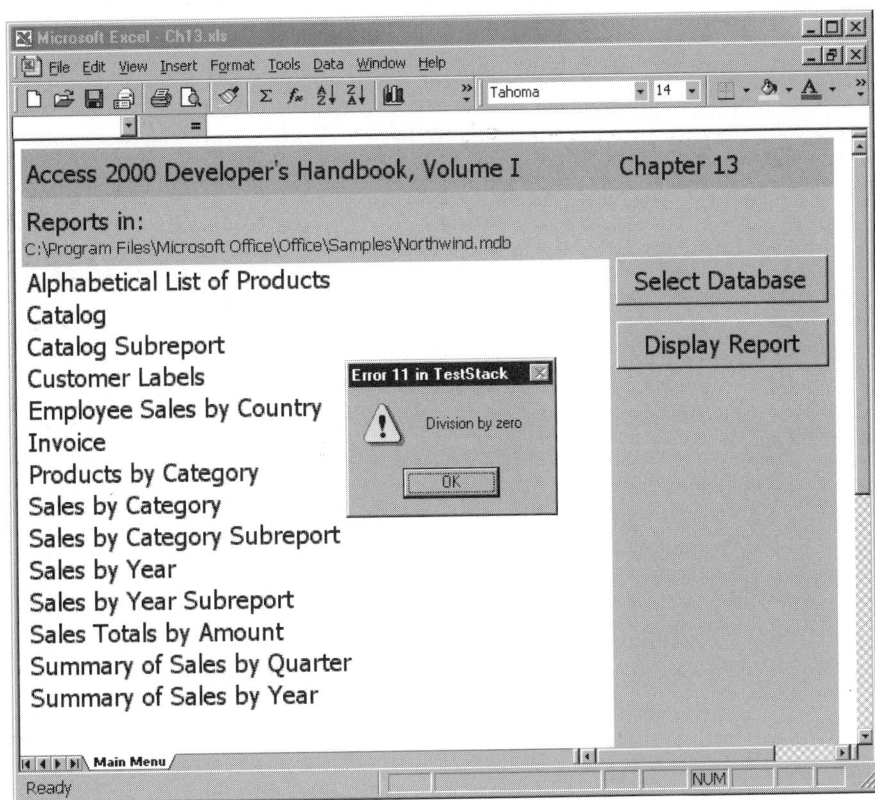

FIGURE 13.2:

Excel session showing error information returned from your custom stack

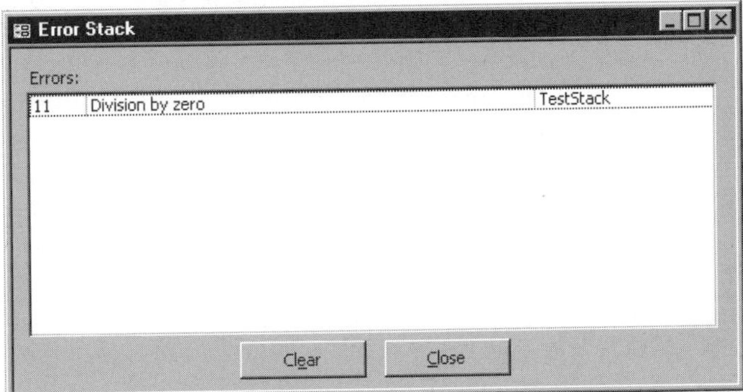

FIGURE 13.3:

Error stack form in Access showing a single error

The downside to this approach is that you must manually query the stack's error count after each call to a user-defined function using Automation. This is because there will be no runtime error in your client application; from your application's perspective, everything will be fine. If you call a lot of user-defined functions with Automation, however, the additional information provided by your error stack may be well worth the effort.

Switching Back to the Client Application

The sample application demonstrates how to preview a report from within Microsoft Excel. At this point, the sample application relinquishes control to the user, who can print the report, close it, or take any number of other actions. For users uncomfortable with the idea of switching between multiple applications, you can provide a way for them to return to your Automation client application from Access.

VBA offers an AppActivate method that accepts a window title as an argument. It activates the first application with a top-level window with a caption matching that title. If it can't find an exact match, it looks for a window with a caption that begins with the string passed as an argument. This is helpful for MDI applications (such as those in Microsoft Office) that include the caption of a child window in the title bar when the child window is maximized. For example, this statement would activate a running instance of Microsoft Excel, no matter which worksheet has the input focus:

```
AppActivate "Microsoft Excel"
```

If you expose the Access user interface to your users, as we do in the sample application, you can give them a way to switch back to your application by calling AppActivate in response to some event. Figure 13.4 shows a report from CH13.MDB in Print Preview view. We've created a custom command bar with a custom button entitled Return to Excel. This button calls ReturnToApp, a function declared in basReturn, which uses AppActivate to switch to Excel. We set the OnAction property of the command bar button to =ReturnToApp("Microsoft Excel"). Using this technique adds to the impression that Access is part of an integrated solution rather than an oddball component.

NOTE The custom command bar is displayed and hidden by code in the Open and Close events of the two reports in CH13.MDB.

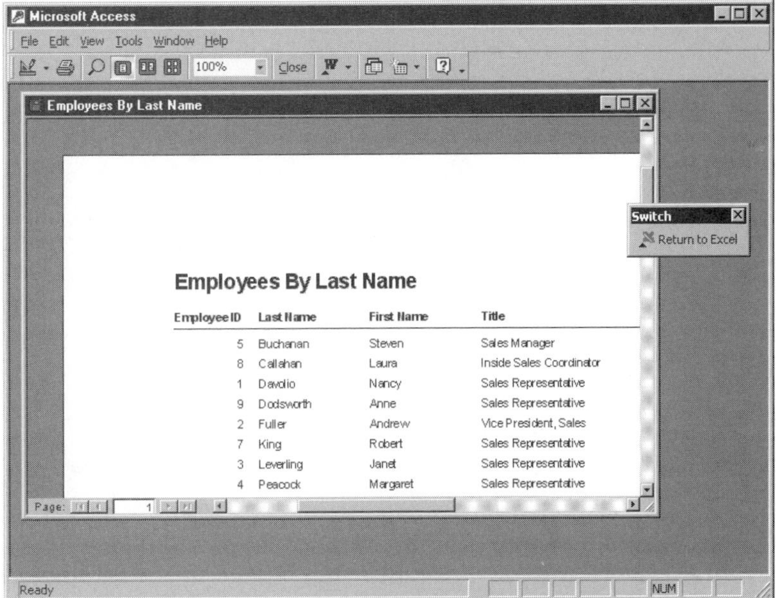

FIGURE 13.4:

A custom toolbar button activates Microsoft Excel.

Summary

In this chapter, we've introduced you to the few concepts you need to be familiar with in order to use Access as an Automation server. Because you can use all the same objects, properties, and methods you can when programming in Access alone, you should be able to write or port code that uses Access as an Automation server very quickly and easily. In summary:

- You create a reference to Access.Application using CreateObject, GetObject, or New.
- All Access properties and methods must be qualified with an object variable.
- You can use the Run method to call user-defined global functions.
- You can use UserControl and other properties to create Automation-friendly applications.
- You can use the AccessAutomation class to simplify Automation tasks by importing it into your applications.

CHAPTER FOURTEEN

14

Error Handling and Debugging

- Dealing with compile-time errors
- Handling runtime errors
- Avoiding and resolving logic errors
- Techniques and strategies for debugging

In any programming environment, you have to deal with errors, and VBA is no different. These errors fall into three categories:

- Compile-time errors
- Runtime errors
- Logic errors

Compile-time errors occur when your code contains incorrect syntax. The compiler requires that these errors be fixed before the code will run. VBA flags the error either when you enter the improper syntax or when the code is compiled, depending on an option you set for the editor.

Runtime errors occur when some condition makes your code invalid. For example, trying to open a table that doesn't exist will trigger a runtime error. If you don't trap runtime errors, VBA displays an error message and stops your code at that point. VBA provides a mechanism using the On Error statement that allows you to trap a runtime error and handle the problem.

Logic errors occur when your code doesn't do what you intended because of improper logic, a misunderstanding of how certain statements and functions work, or outright mistakes. For example, if you use a less-than operator (<) when you mean to have a less-than-or-equal-to operator (<=), you have a logic error. Logic errors are commonly known as *bugs.*

This chapter shows you how to reduce the number of each of these types of errors and how to deal with them when they do occur. All of the sample code shown in this chapter is available in CH14.MDB on the CD-ROM.

Dealing with Syntax Errors

VBA can report syntax errors at two points. If you select Tools ➢ Options in the Visual Basic Editor, you see a check box called Auto Syntax Check. This option controls when VBA will report syntax errors to you. If it is checked, VBA displays a message box as soon as you leave a line of code that has a syntax error in the module editor. If the option is unchecked, VBA merely changes the color to indicate that it doesn't understand the line. In either case, when VBA compiles the code, it reports the error.

Often, you will write half a line of code and then discover you need to move up to the top of the module to declare the variable you are using. At this point, VBA reports the line as having a syntax error if the Auto Syntax Check option is on. Since VBA shows lines with syntax errors in red, you already have immediate feedback that there is a problem, so you may prefer to turn off the option. You can always get complete details on the error by selecting the Debug ➢ Compile menu command.

There are also a number of syntax errors that VBA cannot immediately highlight. These errors occur in multiline constructs, such as If…Then and Select…Case statements. Because a valid statement requires more than one line of code, VBA cannot check the syntax until the module is compiled. To check for these types of errors before running your application, select the Debug ➢ Compile menu command.

Dealing with Runtime Errors

When a runtime error occurs, you have several ways of dealing with it. If you do nothing, VBA responds by displaying an error message and stopping the execution of your code. While this behavior is fine in the development environment, it is rarely acceptable in production applications. For this reason, you will usually want to include error-handling features in your code. Resolving errors that occur at runtime requires three steps:

1. Invoking an error handler
2. Reacting to the error
3. Exiting the error handler

The following sections discuss these steps.

Invoking an Error Handler with the On Error Statement

You invoke an error handler with the On Error statement, which comes in several varieties, as described in the following sections. The On Error statement is actual VBA code that, when executed, tells VBA how to handle runtime errors that occur after the statement. Each procedure can have as many On Error statements as you wish. However, only the most recently executed On Error statement remains in force.

The On Error GoTo Label Statement

On Error GoTo *Label* is the most powerful form of error handling because it gives you the most control over what to do in the event of a runtime error. You use the On Error GoTo *Label* statement to cause VBA to jump to a specific location in your code if an error occurs. When an error occurs in code after an On Error GoTo *Label* statement, control passes to the assigned label. Listing 14.1 shows the most common format for an error handler.

Listing 14.1

```
Sub GenericSubWithHandler()
    ' Stub showing standard way to construct an error handler

    On Error GoTo HandleError

    ' Some code that might generate a run-time error

ExitHere:
    Exit Sub
HandleError:
    ' Error Handler
    Resume ExitHere
End Sub
```

When an error occurs, control immediately passes to the label specified in the On Error GoTo *Label* statement. The label must appear in the same procedure as the On Error GoTo *Label* statement. By convention, the error handler appears at the end of the procedure.

NOTE

Unlike Access 1 and 2, which used Access Basic as the programming language, VBA no longer requires that label names be unique across the entire module.

Use an Exit Sub or Exit Function statement to keep the normal flow of control from passing into the error handler. You can see this in the example, just after the ExitHere label.

Once an error has occurred and control has passed into the error handler, the code is treated as being in a special state. While the code is in this state, the following is true:

- The error handler defined by the On Error GoTo *Label* statement is no longer in effect. This means any runtime error that occurs within the error handler itself is treated as though no error handler exists in this procedure.
- You can use a Resume statement (described in the section "The Resume Statement" later in this chapter) to return control back to the main procedure and resume normal error handling.

The On Error Resume Next Statement

Creating an error handler with the On Error GoTo *Label* statement can require a considerable number of statements. Sometimes you simply want to ignore errors. Other times you know exactly which error to expect and want to handle it without having to write a full error handler. The On Error Resume Next statement informs VBA that you want control to resume at the statement immediately after the statement that generated the error, without any visible intervention from VBA. For example, if you are attempting to delete a file and don't care whether the file actually exists, you might have some code like that shown in Listing 14.2.

Listing 14.2

```
Sub Delfile(ByVal strFileName As String)
    ' Example showing an On Error Resume Next
    'Deletes a file if it exists

    On Error Resume Next

    Kill strFileName
End Sub
```

Normally, the Kill statement generates a runtime error if the file specified as its argument doesn't exist. However, the On Error Resume Next statement in this example causes the runtime error to be ignored, and control passes to the next line (in this case, the End Sub statement).

A slightly more complex example is shown in Listing 14.3.

Listing 14.3

```
Sub SetControlColors(frm As Form, ByVal lngColor As Long)
    ' Changes the color of all the controls on the
    ' form to the color specified by lngColor

    Dim ctl As Control

    On Error Resume Next

    For Each ctl In frm.Controls
        ctl.BackColor = lngColor
    Next
End Sub
```

This procedure loops through all the controls on a form specified by a form variable and changes the BackColor property of the controls to the value specified by the lngColor argument. Some controls, such as command buttons, do not have a BackColor property. When the code reaches these controls, a runtime error is normally generated. The On Error Resume Next statement lets the program ignore the error and continue. See the section "Inline Error Handling" later in this chapter for more on using On Error Resume Next.

The On Error GoTo 0 Statement

When you use an On Error GoTo *Label* or On Error Resume Next statement, it remains in effect until the procedure is exited, another error handler is declared, or the error handler is canceled. The On Error GoTo 0 statement, however, cancels the error handler. VBA (or an error handler in a calling procedure, as described in the section "Hierarchy of Error Handlers" later in this chapter) again traps subsequent errors. This statement also resets the value of the Err object (see the section "Determining Which Error Has Occurred" later in this chapter), so if you need the values it contains, you must store away its properties.

Creating Intelligent Error Handlers

After trapping an error with the On Error GoTo *Label* statement, you will want to take some action. What you do depends on your application. If you are trying to open a table and the table doesn't exist, you might want to report an error to the user. On the other hand, you might decide instead to go ahead and create the table by executing a make-table query. To take action intelligently, you must have some way to determine which specific error (of the literally thousands of possible errors) has occurred. This section explains how to do that using the VBA Err object.

Determining Which Error Has Occurred

VBA has a very convenient method of obtaining runtime error information: the Err object. The Err object has the properties listed in Table 14.1. These properties are set by VBA after a runtime error. By using the properties of the Err object, you can determine exactly which error has occurred.

TABLE 14.1: Err Object Properties

Property	Description
Description	Returns a descriptive string associated with an error.
HelpContext	Returns a context ID for a topic in an online help file.
HelpFile	Returns a fully qualified path to an online help file.
LastDLLError	Returns a system error code produced by a call into a Dynamic Link Library (DLL). The GetLastError Windows API call gives the error code for the most recent Windows API call. When you are calling Windows API calls from VBA, though, you have a problem: VBA itself will make several Windows API calls between the time you make the call through VBA code and when you try to call GetLastError. When VBA does this, it wipes out the information that GetLastError returns. To get around this situation, VBA calls GetLastError for you after every API call.
Number	Returns a numeric value specifying an error. Number is the Err object's default property.
Source	Returns the name of the object or application that originally generated the error.

NOTE

While the error number (Err.Number) associated with a particular error condition is fixed, the text (Err.Description) is not. Microsoft changes it from version to version to clarify error information and provide additional information. Also, if your program is ever run on an international version of Access, the error message will appear in the local language of the version of Access. For these reasons, you should always use the Err.Number property in your error-handling code rather than the description strings from the Err.Description property.

Listing 14.4 shows an example of using the Err object in an error handler. The example tries to open a recordset based on a table that may or may not exist. If the table doesn't exist, VBA invokes the error handler, which examines the Err.Number property for the value -2147217865. Error number -2147217865 indicates that an invalid object name was supplied, in which case a custom error message is displayed. For all other errors, the error handler displays a generic message using the Err.Number and Err.Description properties to provide the user with detailed error information.

WARNING The database examples in this chapter use ADO rather than DAO, which was used in previous versions of the book. Similar errors have drastically different error numbers depending on which data access technology you use. For example, the error number indicating a missing table is 3011 in DAO and –2147217865 in ADO. If you are converting your data access routines to use ADO, make sure you retest them to determine new error codes.

Listing 14.4

```
Sub TypicalErrorHandlerSub()
    Dim rst As Recordset

    ' A constant for the error number
    Const conErrCannotFindObject = -2147217865

    On Error GoTo HandleError

    ' Some code that might generate a runtime error
    Set rst = New Recordset
    rst.Open "SELECT * FROM tblTable", _
     CurrentProject.Connection

    ' You would do some processing with rst here

ExitHere:
    On Error Resume Next
    rst.Close
    Exit Sub
HandleError:
    Select Case Err.Number
```

```
        Case conErrCannotFindObject   'Cannot find object
            MsgBox "tblTable doesn't exist. " _
             & "Call the database administrator.", _
             vbExclamation, "TypicalErrorHandlerSub"
        Case Else
            MsgBox "The application encountered " & _
             "unexpected error #" & Err.Number & _
             " with message string '" & _
             Err.Description & "'", _
             vbExclamation, "TypicalErrorHandlerSub"
    End Select
    Resume ExitHere
End Sub
```

The Select Case statement uses the value in Err.Number to determine which error has occurred. You should use a Select Case statement even if you have only one case you want to handle, since this makes it easy for you to handle other errors later just by inserting another Case statement. Always use a Case Else to trap unexpected errors. You can use a MsgBox statement in the Case Else statement, or an error-reporting routine, as shown in the section "Creating an Error-Reporting Subroutine" later in this chapter.

It's important to realize that two or more statements in your main code can generate the same error (which would have occurred, for instance, if we had used OpenRecordset twice in the above example). If you want different things to happen in your error handler for each of those statements, you must set a flag in your main code and use If statements within the Case statement (or a nested Select Case statement) in your error handler. A more complicated method would define several different error handlers with On Error statements as you reached different parts of your code. Fortunately, most code doesn't require this complexity. If it does, it might be time to consider splitting the procedure into several smaller procedures.

Listing 14.5 shows an example of the use of flags.

Listing 14.5

```
Sub AddLineNumbers()
    Dim intState As Integer
    Dim strInput As String
    Dim lngLineNumber As Long
```

```
    ' State constants
    Const conFStateNone = 0
    Const conFStateOpeningFile1 = 1
    Const conFStateOpeningFile2 = 2

    ' Error constants
    Const conErrFileNotFound = 53
    Const conErrPermissionDenied = 70
    Const conErrPathFileError = 75

    On Error GoTo AddLineNumbersErr

    intState = conFStateOpeningFile1
    Open "c:\file1.txt" For Input As #1

    intState = conFStateOpeningFile2
    Open "c:\file2.txt" For Output As #2

    intState = conFStateNone

    lngLineNumber = 1
    Do Until EOF(1)
        Input #1, strInput
        Print #2, lngLineNumber, strInput
        lngLineNumber = lngLineNumber + 1
    Loop
    Close #2
AddLineNumbersCloseFile1:
    Close #1
AddLineNumbersDone:
    Exit Sub
AddLineNumbersErr:
    Select Case Err.Number
        Case conErrPermissionDenied, _
         conErrPathFileError, conErrFileNotFound

            ' Permission denied or Path/File access error
            Select Case intState
                ' If error occurred trying to open file1...
                Case conFStateOpeningFile1
                    MsgBox "Could not open 'c:\" & _
                      "file1.txt'. Something probably " & _
```

```
                        "has the file locked.", _
                        vbExclamation, "AddLineNumbers"
                       Resume AddLineNumbersDone
                   ' If error occurred trying to open file2...
                   Case conFStateOpeningFile2
                       MsgBox "Could not open 'c:\" & _
                       "file2.txt'. The file may be write" & _
                       " protected or locked.", _
                        vbExclamation, "AddLineNumbers"
                       ' Make sure to close file1!
                       Resume AddLineNumbersCloseFile1
                   Case Else
                       Stop    'Should never reach here.
               End Select
           Case Else
               MsgBox "Unexpected error #" & Err.Number & ".", _
                vbExclamation, "Add Line Numbers"
       End Select
       Resume AddLineNumbersDone
   End Sub
```

This listing shows a procedure that opens an ASCII file named C:\FILE1.TXT. It reads each line, adds a line number to the beginning of the line, and writes a new file, C:\FILE2.TXT, with the changes. There are two Open statements in the procedure that can fail, and you want to show the user two different error messages, depending on which one failed. Also, if an error occurs while the second file is being opened, you need to close the first file before exiting the procedure. The variable intState holds a value indicating which open statement is being processed. When an error occurs, this variable is checked to determine which error message to display. Using the constants conFStateOpeningFile1 and conFStateOpeningFile2 instead of just the numbers 1 and 2 makes the meaning of the current value of intState more explicit.

Another technique for handling the state information uses line numbers. Yes, VBA still allows line numbers, which were required in early versions of Basic, but you don't need them on every line. The Erl function tells you the line number that was most recently executed. For example, the preceding code could be rewritten as shown in Listing 14.6. Note how we added line numbers only to those lines that we thought might cause errors and how the error handler checks the return value of Erl.

Listing 14.6

```
Sub AddLineNumbers2()
    Dim strInput As String
    Dim lngLineNumber As Long

    ' Error constants
    Const conErrFileNotFound = 53
    Const conErrPermissionDenied = 70
    Const conErrPathFileError = 75

    On Error GoTo AddLineNumbers2Err

10  Open "c:\file1.txt" For Input As #1

20  Open "c:\file2.txt" For Output As #2

30  lngLineNumber = 1
    Do Until EOF(1)
        Input #1, strInput
        Print #2, lngLineNumber, strInput
        lngLineNumber = lngLineNumber + 1
    Loop
AddLineNumbers2CloseFile2:
    Close #2

AddLineNumbers2Done:
    Close #1

    Exit Sub
AddLineNumbers2Err:
    Select Case Err.Number
        Case conErrPermissionDenied, _
         conErrPathFileError, conErrFileNotFound

            ' Permission denied or Path/File access error
            Select Case Erl
                ' Error occurred at line 10...
                Case 10
                    MsgBox "Could not open 'c:\" & _
                     "file1.txt'. Something probably " & _
```

```
                    "has the file locked.", _
                    vbExclamation, "AddLineNumbers2"
                   Resume AddLineNumbers2Done
               ' Error occurred at line 20...
               Case 20
                   MsgBox "Could not open 'c:\" & _
                   "file2.txt'. The file may be write" & _
                   " protected or locked.", _
                    vbExclamation, "AddLineNumbers2"
                   Resume AddLineNumbers2CloseFile2
               Case Else
                   Stop    'Should never reach here.
           End Select
       Case Else
           MsgBox "Unexpected error #" & Err.Number & ".", _
            vbExclamation, "Add Line Numbers"
   End Select
   Resume AddLineNumbers2Done
End Sub
```

The Resume Statement

To return to the main part of the procedure from an error handler, you use the Resume statement. The Resume statement has three forms:

- Resume
- Resume Next
- Resume *Label*

They are described in the following sections.

Resume Resume by itself returns control to the statement that caused the error. Use the Resume statement when the error handler fixes the problem that caused the error and you want to continue from the place where you encountered the problem. In the example shown in Listing 14.4, if the error handler ran a make-table query that created tblTable, you would use a Resume statement. Note, however, that if you don't fix the problem that caused the error, an endless loop occurs when the original statement fails again. Use this form of Resume with extreme caution. In most cases, you should provide a dialog where the user can choose to resume or exit the procedure.

Resume Next Use the Resume Next statement inside an error handler when you either want to ignore the statement that caused the error, or have taken other action that was unable to correct the error condition. Control returns to the statement following the one that caused the error, similar to the On Error Resume Next statement.

Resume Label Use the Resume *Label* statement when you want to return to a line other than the one causing the error or the line that follows it. Resume *Label* is similar to a GoTo statement, except you can use it only from inside an error handler. The example in Listing 14.4 shows this use of the Resume statement to jump to the label ExitHere. This approach to exiting a procedure after a runtime error is preferred because there is only one exit point.

Raising Errors

At times, you may want to generate an error yourself rather than wait for one to occur. Other times, you may want to cause the error to happen *again* inside an error handler. You do this by raising an error, using the Err.Raise method. Raise can take as arguments all the properties of the Err object. Thus, you can raise a user-defined error by using this code:

```
Err.Raise Number:=vbObjectError + 65535, _
 Description:="A user-defined error."
```

This code causes VBA to act as though an error occurred at this point in the code and defines the description as being the string "A user defined error." The error number is 65535 (which presumably means something to your application) plus the constant value vbObjectError. You should always add vbObjectError to your custom error numbers because it insures that your error numbers won't override a built-in error code. In your error handler, simply subtract vbObject-Error from the value returned by Err.Number to get your original error number.

With custom errors, the normal handling of the error occurs, so if an On Error GoTo statement is in effect, execution then jumps to the error handler. The Err object's Number and String properties are set to the arguments of the Err.Raise method. If you don't specify an argument to the Raise method, VBA uses the default arguments for the error number.

Why might you actually *cause* an error to occur? Typically, errors are raised in situations where business and program logic rules have been violated. For example, suppose information being read from a text file and inserted into a table contains invalid data. Rather than include code in the body of a procedure to alert the user, you might instead raise a custom error and let your error handler cope with it. Centralizing *all* handling of errors, both runtime and business rule violations, in one part of your procedure makes code management a lot easier.

Inline Error Handling

If you have only one statement in a piece of code that can fail, you might not want to write a full error handler. The Err object used with the On Error Resume Next statement can catch errors in your main code. This is called an *inline error handler.* To use it, lay out your code so it looks like the code in Listing 14.7.

Listing 14.7

```
Sub OnErrorResumeNextExample()
    Dim rst As Recordset
    Dim objError As SavedError

    ' Error constants
    Const conErrNoError = 0
    Const conErrCantFindObject = -2147217865

    ' Suppress normal error messages
    On Error Resume Next

    ' Some code that might generate a runtime error
    Set rst = New Recordset
    rst.Open "SELECT * FROM tblTable", _
     CurrentProject.Connection

    ' Save the error state
    Set objError = New SavedError
    Call objError.Save(Err)

    On Error GoTo 0

    ' Now do something with the saved error info
    Select Case objError.Number
        Case conErrNoError        ' No Error
            ' Do nothing
        Case conErrCantFindObject   'Can't find object
            MsgBox "tblTable doesn't exist. Call the " & _
             "database administrator.", vbExclamation
```

```
            GoTo ExitHere
        Case Else
            ' Stop here with error message
            Call objError.Raise
    End Select

    ' Do some processing with rst
    rst.Close

ExitHere:
End Sub
```

This code contains no error handler. Instead, an On Error Resume Next statement tells VBA to ignore any errors. However, anytime a statement can generate an error, the contents of the Err object are overwritten. If no error occurred, the Err.Number property is 0. Otherwise, the Err object will contain values for the error that occurred.

Because the contents of the Err object are constantly being overwritten, you may want to save the current error to use later. To do this, we've created a custom VBA class called SavedError. It has the same properties as the VBA Err object, and two methods, Save and Raise. After trying to open the recordset based on a nonexistent table, we call the SavedError object's Save method, which accepts the Err object as an argument. The Save method, shown in Listing 14.8, copies the values from the Err object's properties to the SavedError object's. You can find the complete listing of the properties and methods of the class in the SavedError class module in CH14.MDB.

NOTE

If you look in CH14.MDB, you'll also see that we've implemented a SavedErrors (plural) collection class. By declaring a new instance of this class in the declarations section of a module, you can use its Add method to add new SavedError objects to the collection. This lets you collect a number of saved errors and examine their properties later in your code.

Listing 14.8

```
Public Sub Save(objVBAError As ErrObject)
    ' The Save method takes an ErrObject object
    ' and copies its properties to this object's
    ' properties
```

```
    With objVBAError
        mlngNumber = .Number
        mstrSource = .Source
        mstrDescription = .Description
        mstrHelpFile = .HelpFile
        mlngHelpContext = .HelpContext
        mstrLastDLLError = .LastDLLError
    End With
End Sub
```

Note that as soon as you have two different statements that can cause a runtime error, it is usually more efficient to write an error handler using the On Error GoTo *Label* syntax since the overhead of constructing the error handler is encountered only once. If you use the Err object with On Error Resume Next, always use a Select Case statement with a Case Else clause to trap unexpected errors. Otherwise, error numbers without Case statements are ignored and may produce unexpected results.

Hierarchy of Error Handlers

VBA uses a hierarchical approach to error handling when one procedure calls another. If the called procedure generates an error that isn't handled within the procedure, the calling procedure's error handler receives the error. VBA acts as though the procedure call itself generated the error. In effect, VBA looks backward up the call stack until it finds an error handler. If it reaches the top without finding an error handler, it displays its own error message and halts the code.

WARNING

If you have any calls to user-defined functions or subs in your code, you need to be very aware of this feature of VBA's error handlers; it can cause control to unexpectedly jump into your calling procedure's error handler. For this reason, we strongly recommend that you include an error handler in every procedure in your application. This may seem like a lot of work, and it definitely increases the size of your code, but the alternative is worse. You don't want an error in one procedure causing control to unexpectedly jump into another procedure's error handler. This can easily result in bugs in your code. The best way around this problem is to always handle runtime errors locally in *every* procedure. It's worth noting, however, that this does not mean you can't make use of generic error handling/reporting routines. (See the section "Creating an Error-Reporting Subroutine" later in this chapter.)

TIP

Office 2000 Developer includes a VBA add-in that automatically adds error handling to code in a procedure, module, or even the entire project. You can even customize the error-handling code that it adds. This little add-in can be an incredible time-saver when developing large applications. For more information on Office 2000 Developer, visit `http://msdn.microsoft.com/officedev/`.

To demonstrate the hierarchy of error handlers, FunctionA calls SubB in Listing 14.9.

Listing 14.9

```
Function FunctionA()
    ' Sample function to show the hierarchy of
    ' error handlers.
    On Error GoTo HandleError

    Call SubB

    MsgBox "You might expect to get to here, but you don't."
ExitHere:
    Exit Function
HandleError:
    Select Case Err.Number
        Case 1
            MsgBox "You got here from SubB", vbInformation
            Resume ExitHere
        Case Else
            Error Err.Number
        End Select
    Resume ExitHere
End Function

Sub SubB()
    ' Generates an error, but doesn't handle it.

    ' Cause an error in this Sub.
    Err.Raise Number:=1
End Sub
```

VBA generates an error when it raises error number 1 in SubB. Since SubB doesn't contain an error handler, control immediately passes back to FunctionA. FunctionA does contain an error handler, so it processes the error. If FunctionA hadn't contained an error handler, control would have passed to the procedure (if any) that called FunctionA. If VBA gets to the top of the call stack without finding an error handler, it puts up an alert and stops executing the code.

VBA acts as though the Call statement itself generates the error. The Resume Next in FunctionA returns control to the statement following the Call statement; control doesn't return to SubB. If you use a Resume statement instead of a Resume Next in FunctionA, the Resume statement returns control to the Call statement in FunctionA. This calls SubB again, which in this case puts you into an endless loop as the error repeats.

The OnError Property and the Error Event

When you use a bound form or report, Access uses either Jet or MSDE under the covers for all data access. Anytime Access has to populate the fields on a bound form or fill a list box, it is making calls to the database engine. Any of these calls might fail for reasons such as the database being opened exclusively by someone else or a table having been deleted. The On Error statements described earlier in the chapter are in effect only while your code is being executed. But what can you do about errors that happen while Access is manipulating data in a form or report? Access gives you a way to trap those errors through the use of the OnError property and its associated Error event procedure. This property allows you to specify a routine to be executed when an error occurs. When you run the Code Builder (by clicking the ... button for the property and then selecting Code Builder) on this property, you see a procedure stub that looks like the following:

```
Sub Form_Error(DataErr As Integer, Response As Integer)

End Sub
```

DataErr is the value that would be returned by the Err.Number property had the error occurred in code. *Response* is a value you fill in before the procedure terminates. It tells Access whether to report the error to the user. Listing 14.10 shows an example of a routine that handles the Error event in a Jet database.

Listing 14.10

```
Sub Form_Error(DataErr As Integer, Response As Integer)
    ' Reports errors for the form, attached to OnError property
    Const adhcErrNoError = 0
    Const adhcErrFieldNull = 3314
    Const adhcErrDuplicateKey = 3022
    Select Case DataErr
        Case adhcErrNoError       ' No error
        Case adhcErrFieldNull     ' Field '|' can't contain a
                                  ' null value.
            MsgBox "You have left a required field blank.", _
             vbInformation
        Case adhcErrDuplicateKey  ' Duplicate value in index,
                                  ' key, or relationship.
                                  ' Changes were unsuccessful.
            MsgBox "This record contains the same key " _
             & "as another record. Try another value.", _
              vbInformation
        Case Else
            Stop    'Unknown Error
    End Select
    Response = acDataErrContinue
End Sub
```

The Response argument can receive one of two values: acDataErrContinue or acDataErrDisplay. The value acDataErrDisplay causes Access to display the error message that would have appeared if you hadn't had an error handler attached to the form. The value acDataErrContinue causes this error message to be suppressed. By specifying acDataErrContinue, you can substitute your own custom error message.

The function Error(DataErr) returns the Jet error string associated with the error. (For more information on the Form and Report Error events, see Chapter 2.)

NOTE

Due to structural changes to error handling introduced with VBA, many error strings returned by the Error function aren't very helpful. In fact, for most error codes the Error function returns the string "Application or user-defined error". This is because VBA has no knowledge of a specific host's errors. It is up to the host (Access, in this case) to supply the descriptive information when an error occurs. To return error strings for Access errors, Access provides the AccessError method. It works the same way as Error but returns the real error description for a given error number.

Handling Data Access Errors

While the VBA Err object is fine for most runtime error handling, it is limited to reporting only a single error condition—the last error that occurred. When using DAO or ADO to manipulate data, however, error conditions can be more complex, with multiple errors being generated. For instance, if you use DAO to process a query against a SQL Server database and that query generates an error, VBA receives error information from both SQL Server and DAO. For this reason, both DAO and ADO feature ways for you to retrieve the complete error state.

Using the DAO Errors Collection

Anytime Jet is processing data, it can generate runtime errors. Since Jet may report multiple runtime errors from a single operation your code performs (especially when accessing ODBC data), it maintains a collection of those errors. Usually, you are concerned only with determining that an error has occurred and reporting that fact to the end user. In some cases, though, you may want to detail exactly the errors Jet generated. For this, you use the DAO Errors collection.

This collection is a property of the DBEngine object. When you handle an error in an error handler in your code or an Error event handler, you can then browse the DAO Errors collection to determine specifically which Jet errors occurred while processing a statement. The code in Listing 14.11 shows how you do this.

Listing 14.11

```
Sub DAOErrorsCollection()
    Dim errCur As DAO.Error

    On Error GoTo HandleError

    CurrentDb.Execute _
     "qappJetErrorsCollection", dbFailOnError

ExitHere:
    Exit Sub
HandleError:
    ' Loop through the DAO Errors
    For Each errCur In DBEngine.Errors
        Debug.Print errCur.Number, errCur.Description
    Next
    Resume ExitHere
End Sub
```

In this code, when Jet generates a set of errors, each of the error descriptions is printed to the Immediate window. The VBA Err object will reflect the top-most of the objects in the Errors collection. The Errors collection is cleared before the next Jet engine operation is executed.

Using the ADO Errors Collection

Like DAO, ADO also has an Errors collection that lets you determine the complete error state from ADO operations. With a few minor exceptions, using the ADO Errors collection is just like using the DAO Errors collection. Listing 14.12 shows a sample error-handling routine.

Listing 14.12

```
Sub ADOErrorsCollection()
    Dim conThis As ADODB.Connection
    Dim errCur As ADODB.Error
    Dim strSQL As String

    On Error GoTo HandleError

    strSQL = "UPDATE tblNone SET State = 'NY'"

    ' You must declare and use a Connection
    ' object variable for this to work
    Set conThis = CurrentProject.Connection
    conThis.Execute strSQL

    ' You can try this to see what happens
    'CurrentProject.Connection.Execute strSQL

ExitHere:
    Exit Sub
HandleError:
    ' Check ADO Errors collection for contents
    ' and print out if errors exist--otherwise
    ' print the VBA Err object message
    With conThis
        If .Errors.Count > 0 Then
            For Each errCur In conThis.Errors
                Debug.Print "ADO:", errCur.Number, _
                 errCur.Description
            Next
```

```
        Else
            Debug.Print "VBA:", Err.Number, _
             Err.Description
        End If
    End With
    Resume ExitHere
End Sub
```

The major difference between the two collections is that in ADO the Errors collection is associated with a particular ADO Connection object, rather than DBEngine in DAO. ADO doesn't have a concept of a root database engine object. Thus, you must declare a Connection object variable when executing data manipulation methods. In Listing 14.12, the variable conThis stores a reference to the ADO Connection associated with the current database.

If you don't use an object variable but instead execute methods from the default Connection directly, ADO does not populate the Errors collection but uses the VBA Err object instead. To test this out, find ADOErrorsCollection in basChapter14, comment the line of code that reads, "conThis.Execute strSQL", and uncomment the next line of code. If you step through the procedure, you'll see that the ADO Errors collection is empty after the error occurs. That explains the conditional logic in our error handler.

Creating an Error-Reporting Subroutine

Because any robust application will have dozens, if not hundreds, of error handlers in its code, you may want to create a generic way of reporting them. We have created a generic routine you can use to report errors to the user. The error dialog created looks like the one shown in Figure 14.1. Typically, this dialog is used in an error handler to report any unexpected runtime errors. Listing 14.13 shows adhHandleError, the generic error-handling routine that is called to invoke the error dialog.

FIGURE 14.1:

Generic Error Dialog

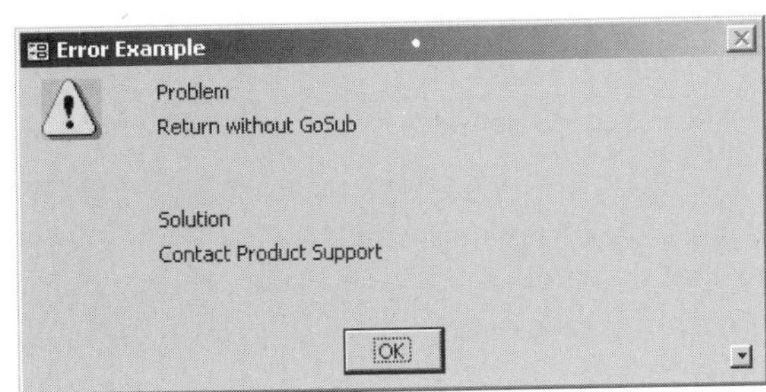

Listing 14.13

```
Public Function adhHandleError() As Integer
    Static fInError As Boolean

    ' Make sure we're not currently in the
    ' error handler; otherwise we'll end up
    ' with an infinite loop
    If fInError Then
        MsgBox "Already in error handler!", vbCritical
        Stop
    Else
        fInError = True

        If CurrentProject.AllForms(conErrorForm) _
         .IsLoaded Then
            DoCmd.Close acForm, conErrorForm
        End If

        ' Open the form in dialog mode--the form will
        ' use the LastError method of the global
        ' SavedErrors collection to get its information
        On Error Resume Next
        DoCmd.OpenForm FormName:=conErrorForm, _
         WindowMode:=acDialog

        ' Set return value and close the form
        If Err.Number = 0 Then
            adhHandleError = Forms(conErrorForm).Action
            DoCmd.Close acForm, conErrorForm
        End If

        ' Reset flag
        fInError = False
    End If
End Function
```

When you call adhHandleErr, it opens the error dialog frmError. During the form's Open event, it sets the value of the controls based on the last saved error that occurred. Listing 14.14 shows the code behind this event procedure. Since the form's Open event uses the SavedErrors collection's LastError property, it is important that when you encounter an error in a procedure, you add it to the collection using the collection's Add method.

Listing 14.14

```
Private Sub Form_Open(Cancel As Integer)
    Dim objLastError As SavedError

    ' Make sure there's an error for us to report on
    If gErrors.Count = 0 Then
        MsgBox "There are no errors to report on!", _
         vbInformation
        Cancel = True
    Else

        ' Set pointer to last error that occurred
        Set objLastError = gErrors.LastError

        With objLastError
            ' Call OverrideError to change property values
            ' to those in error table if one was specified
              Call OverrideError(.Number, .Display)

            ' Use DisplayError object properties to set up
            ' the main information on the form
            With .Display
                Me.Caption = .Title
                mlngButtonMap = .ButtonMap
                Call SetupIcon(.Icon)
                Call SetupButtons(.Buttons)
                Call SetupSolution(.Solution)
            End With
            ' Use SavedError object properties to set up
            ' the extended information on the form
            Me!txtErrorNumber = .Number
            Me!txtDescription = .Description
            Me!txtHelpFile = .HelpFile
            Me!txtHelpContext = .HelpContext
            Me!txtSource = .Source
            Me!txtDLLError = .LastDLLError
```

```
            ' Make sure we've got a valid message
            If .Display.Text = "" Then
                Me!txtDisplayText = .Description
            Else
                Me!txtDisplayText = .Display.Text
            End If
        End With

        ' Enable Log File button if specified
        ' in the SavedErrors collection's property
        Me!cmdLog.Enabled = (gErrors.LogFile <> "")
    End If
End Sub

Private Function OverrideError(lngNumber As Long, _
 objDisplay As DisplayError) As Boolean

    Dim rst As Recordset
    Dim strSQL As String

    ' Build the query based on the error table
    ' and error number
    strSQL = "SELECT * FROM " & objDisplay.ErrorTable & _
     " WHERE Number = " & lngNumber

    ' Look for the error in the current database
    Set rst = New Recordset
    rst.Open strSQL, CurrentProject.Connection, _
     adOpenKeyset, adLockPessimistic

    ' If found, override the error information
    With rst
        If Not .EOF Then
            objDisplay.Text = !Text
            objDisplay.Solution = !Solution
            objDisplay.Icon = !Icon
            objDisplay.Buttons = !Buttons
            objDisplay.ButtonMap = !ButtonMap
            OverrideError = True
        End If
        .Close
    End With
End Function
```

If you look at the definition of the SavedError class in CH14.MDB, you'll see it contains a public declaration of another class called DisplayError. The DisplayError class implements properties such as Title, Icon, and Buttons, which are useful when building a dialog like frmError. The Open event uses these property values to configure the form.

One interesting property of the DisplayError class is ErrorTable. If this property is filled in with the name of a table, the error dialog will look in that table for error information, overriding the property values in the SavedError object. This lets you easily create custom error text for a few select errors. If an error isn't found in the table, the error dialog uses whatever property settings are contained in the SavedError object. Table 14.2 lists the fields the OverrideError procedure expects to find in the table. You can also look at our sample table, tblError, in CH14.MDB.

TIP

If you want to use our SavedError class in your own applications but don't want to create a generic error dialog, you can save a little overhead by deleting the DisplayError declaration from the class module.

TABLE 14.2: Column Names in Error Table

Column	Description
Number	Number of the error message. This is the key value used to find the error in the table.
Description	Description of the error.
Solution	Solution for the error. If this is Null, no solution is displayed and the description box is expanded.
Icon	Icon that should appear. Must be one of the following: vbInformation, vbExclamation, vbQuestion, or vbCritical.
Buttons	Specifies which set of buttons appears in the dialog. Must be one of the following: vbOkOnly, vbOkCancel, vbYesNo, vbYesNoCancel, vbRetryCancel, or vbAbortRetryIgnore.
ButtonMap	Maps the keys specified by varButtonSet to resume status value adhExitSub, adhResumeNext, or adhResume. Must be built by the adhKeyMap function.

The adhHandleError function returns an integer value that will be one of three constants: conExitSub, conResume, or conResumeNext. Based on this return value, your procedure can take appropriate action.

You call the adhHandleError function using code similar to that found in Listing 14.15.

Listing 14.15

```
Public Sub ErrorExample()
    On Error GoTo ErrorExampleErr

    Call gProcStack.EnterProc("ErrorExample")

    ' Error constants
    Const conErrReturnWithoutGosub = 3
    Const conErrWeirdError = 42000
    Const conErrInvalidProcedureCall = 5
    Const conErrOverflow = 6

    ' One example
    err.Raise Number:=conErrReturnWithoutGosub
    ' Another example
    err.Raise Number:=conErrWeirdError
    ' A third example, overriding the description in the table
    err.Raise Number:=conErrInvalidProcedureCall, _
     Description:="Not what you'd expect"
    ' Another example, overriding everything
    err.Raise Number:=conErrOverflow

ErrorExampleDone:
    Call gProcStack.ExitProc("ErrorExample")
    Exit Sub
ErrorExampleErr:
    Dim objError As SavedError

    ' Add error to the errors collection
    Set objError = gErrors.Add(err)

    ' Add error log
    gErrors.LogFile = "C:\Error.log"
```

```
    ' Based on the error number you can change
    ' various property settings if you want
    Select Case objError.Number
        Case conErrOverflow
            With objError
                .Number = 27
                .Description = "Something didn't work!"
                With .Display
                    .Text = "It didn't work!"
                    .Solution = "Fix it!"
                    .Icon = vbCritical
                    .ErrorTable = "tblError"
                    .Title = "Something Happened"
                    .Buttons = vbOKCancel
                    .ButtonMap = adhButtonMap( _
                     conResumeNext, conExitSub, 0)
                End With
            End With
        Case Else
            With objError.Display
                .Title = "Error Example"
                .ErrorTable = "tblError"
                .ButtonMap = adhButtonMap( _
                 conResumeNext, 0, 0)
            End With
    End Select

    ' Now call adhHandleError and take action
    ' based on the value it returns
    Select Case adhHandleError()
        Case conResume
            Resume
        Case conResumeNext
            Resume Next
        Case conExitSub
            Resume ErrorExampleDone
        Case Else
            Call adhAssert(False)
        End Select
    Exit Sub
End Sub
```

This example uses Raise statements to force the invocation of certain errors. Normally, you wouldn't include these types of statements in your code. Instead, you would put in statements that might cause runtime errors.

In order to use the error form, the procedure adds each runtime error to the SavedErrors collection represented by the gErrors object variable. This makes the error information available to the form during its Open event. The procedure also sets the collection's LogFile property. This allows the user to save the error information to a file for later inspection. Finally, a Select Case statement block is used to change the properties of the error before calling adhHandleError. Based on the return value, the procedure executes the errant statement again, moves on to the next statement, or exits.

The user can obtain extended error information by clicking the small button in the lower right-hand corner of the error dialog (see Figure 14.1). Clicking this button expands the form to show information such as the VBA error number and help information, as shown in Figure 14.2. Drop-down lists at the bottom of the display list statistics such as available memory and disk space, along with the call stack. This information could be helpful when debugging your applications. If you're not around to view this information, the user can save it to a text file by clicking the command button at the bottom right of the form.

By using this error-reporting scheme, you can vastly reduce the complexity of your code at any given point because you can handle all generic errors within the errors table. In addition, you can override any of the information in the table to provide information that is specific to any particular error.

FIGURE 14.2:

Generic error dialog with extended error information

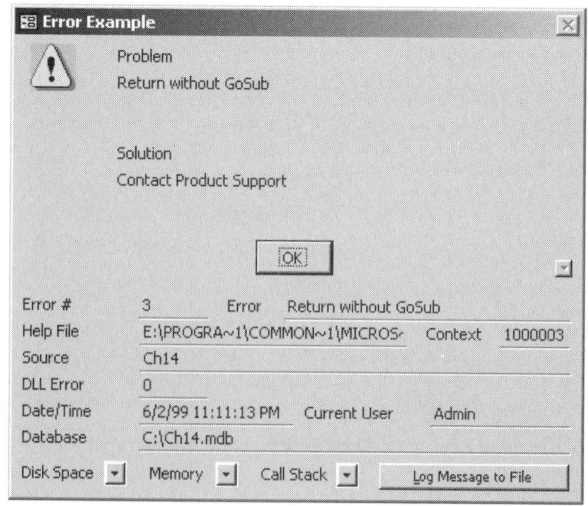

Implementing a Call Stack

When you are in the process of debugging a running procedure, you can select View ➢ Calls to see which function caused the error. Unfortunately, VBA doesn't provide any method for retrieving this information from your code. When you get an unexpected error, it's useful to log what code is being executed at that point and how it got there. Since VBA provides no way to get at the information it keeps internally (that is, the name of the currently executing procedure), you must maintain the information yourself if you need it.

We've implemented several VBA class modules to help with this process. The Procedure and ProcedureStack classes store information on each procedure in VBA's call stack by implementing a stack of their own. The only catch is that you have to write code in your subroutines and functions to add procedures to the stack; VBA can't (and won't) do this for you. Listings 14.16 and 14.17 show the definitions of the Procedure and ProcedureStack classes, respectively.

Listing 14.16

```
' Procedure class
Private mstrName As String
Private mstrModule As String
Private mdatTimeEntered As Date
Private mobjNextProc As Procedure

' Name is the name of the procedure--
' note that it is a write-once property
Property Get Name() As String
    Name = mstrName
End Property
Property Let Name(strName As String)
    If mstrName = "" Then
        mstrName = strName
    End If
End Property

' Module is the name of the module this
' procedure is located in
Property Get Module() As String
    Module = mstrModule
End Property
```

```
Property Let Module(strModule As String)
    If mstrModule = "" Then
        mstrModule = strModule
    End If
End Property

' NextProc is used a pointer to the next
' procedure in the stack
Property Get NextProc() As Procedure
    Set NextProc = mobjNextProc
End Property
Property Set NextProc(objProc As Procedure)
    Set mobjNextProc = objProc
End Property

' TimeEntered is the date/time the class
' instance was created
Property Get TimeEntered() As Date
    TimeEntered = mdatTimeEntered
End Property

Private Sub Class_Initialize()
    ' Set date/time entered
    mdatTimeEntered = Now
End Sub
```

Listing 14.17

```
' ProcedureStack class
Private mobjTopProc As Procedure

Public Function Top() As Procedure
    ' This returns a reference to the top
    ' procedure so a caller can walk the stack
    Set Top = mobjTopProc
End Function

Private Function StackEmpty() As Boolean
    ' This makes sure the stack is not empty
    ' by checking to see if the top proc
    ' pointer is valid
```

```
    StackEmpty = (mobjTopProc Is Nothing)
End Function

Public Function EnterProc(Name As String, _
 Optional Module As String) As Procedure

    ' This pushes a new procedure onto the stack

    Dim objProc As New Procedure

    ' Set the procedure's name and module properties
    objProc.Name = Name
    objProc.Module = Module

    ' Make its NextProc property point to
    ' the one currently at the top of the stack
    Set objProc.NextProc = mobjTopProc

    ' Make the new procedure the one at the top
    Set mobjTopProc = objProc

    ' Return a reference to the new proc
    Set EnterProc = mobjTopProc
End Function

Public Function ExitProc(Name As String) As Boolean
    ' This pops a procedure off the stack.
    ' To enforce FILO behavior we check the
    ' name passed in against that of the top
    ' procedure

    ' Make sure the procedure stack is not empty
    If Not StackEmpty() Then

        ' If the name matches, pop the proc
        ' by making the next proc the top one--
        ' this destroys the pointer to the
        ' proc currently on top and it goes away
        If mobjTopProc.Name = Name Then
            Set mobjTopProc = mobjTopProc.NextProc
            ExitProc = True
        Else
```

```
                MsgBox "Error. Trying to pop wrong procedure. " & _
                "You passed '" & Name & "'. " & _
                 "Current procedure is '" & _
                 mobjTopProc.Name & "'.", vbCritical
                Stop
            End If
        End If
    End Function
```

To implement a call stack using these procedures in your own applications, import the two class modules from CH14.MDB, declare a new instance of the ProcedureStack class in one of your global modules, and then place a call to the EnterProc method of the class at the entry point of every routine in your code. You must also put a call to the ExitProc method of the class at the exit point of every routine. Listing 14.18 shows an example of how to use these methods. It also shows how to print out the contents of the stack. (The VBA code behind the call stack combo box in frmError uses this technique.)

Listing 14.18

```
Sub EnterAndExitExample()
' Call EnterProc to push proc onto the stack
    Call mProcStack.EnterProc("EnterAndExitExample", _
     basChapter14)

    ' Call PrintCallStack which will print call stack
    ' to the Debug window so you can see that it works!
    Call PrintCallStack

    ' Make sure to call ExitProc!!
    Call mProcStack.ExitProc("EnterAndExitExample")
End Sub

Private Sub PrintCallStack()
    Dim objProc As Procedure

    ' Call EnterProc to push proc onto the stack
    Call mProcStack.EnterProc("PrintCallStack"", _
     basChapter14)
```

```
    ' Print it out by walking the stack
    Set objProc = mProcStack.Top
    Do Until objProc Is Nothing
        Debug.Print "Entered procedure '" & objProc.Name & _
         "' at " & objProc.TimeEntered
        Set objProc = objProc.NextProc
    Loop

    ' Make sure to call ExitProc!!
    Call mProcStack.ExitProc("PrintCallStack")
End Sub
```

Because you have to call the ExitProc method at the exit point, you will want to make sure you have only one exit point to your procedures. If you don't, you run the risk of trying to push the wrong procedure off the stack. If this happens, you'll see a dialog like the one in Figure 14.3.

FIGURE 14.3:

Error message indicating you tried to pop the wrong procedure

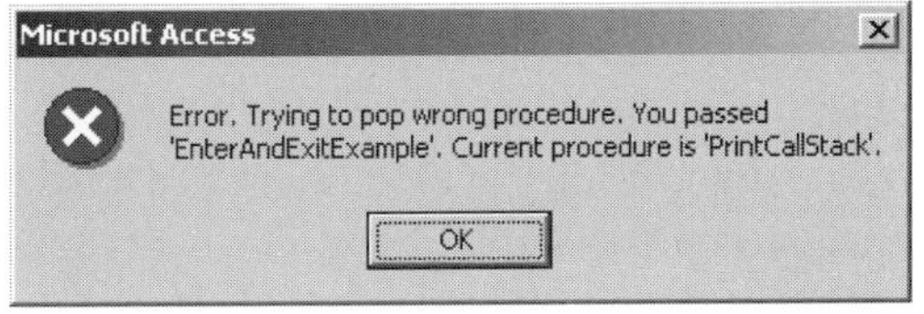

The payoff for using this call stack code comes when you are trying to determine the current application state when an error has occurred. Anytime users get a runtime error, they can press the Log button in the extended info part of your custom dialog, which writes the current state to the log file. The log file is named in the SavedErrors collection's LogFile property. You can then have your user send you the log file, and you can determine exactly what was going on when the error occurred.

Another advantage of having the EnterProc and ExitProc methods surrounding each entry and exit point of your code is that the Procedure class tracks the time it was initialized. Using this information, you can keep track of how much time is spent in the procedure. This is called *profiling*. You can use the profiling information to help determine which routines need optimization work.

Dealing with Logic Errors, aka Bugs!

As stated at the beginning of this chapter, there are three kinds of errors: compile-time errors, runtime errors, and logic errors. VBA informs you of any compile-time errors when you use the Debug ➢ Compile command. Error handlers handle runtime errors. But what can you do about logic errors? If you were a perfect programmer, you'd never have any logic errors, because you'd never make mistakes, you'd always know exactly how Access works, and all your assumptions would always hold true. Professional programmers can't count on perfection, however. Logic errors, also known as *bugs*, are by far the most difficult type of error to find. In the remainder of this chapter, we share some strategies for reducing the number of bugs in your code.

Avoiding Bugs

It's close to impossible to write a substantial application without any bugs, but certain strategies can help you avoid inserting unnecessary bugs. You should develop the necessary discipline to use these strategies whenever you write code, even if you think you're writing a function to use only in testing or for your own internal application. Good habits are hard to develop, but they are also hard to lose once you develop them. The next few sections describe how you can avoid letting bugs slip into your code by following these rules:

- Fix bugs as they appear.
- Use comments.
- Organize your code.
- Modularize your code.
- Use Option Explicit.
- Avoid variants if at all possible.
- Use explicit conversion functions.
- Beware the simple Dim statement.
- Group your Dim statements.
- Use the tightest possible scoping.

- Watch out for "hidden" modules.
- Use consistent naming conventions.
- Use assertions.

Internalizing these suggestions will help you develop a good mind-set for avoiding bugs and for removing the ones that inevitably creep into your code.

As a single rule of thumb, the best bug-avoidance strategy is to take your time and to avoid the urge to make your code "cleverer" than necessary. At times, you simply must use the newest, most complex features of any programming language, but in general, the simpler way is the better way. With this strategy in mind, there are some specific tactics that work well in Access coding to help avoid bugs.

Fixing Bugs As They Appear

It's critical that you fix bugs as they reveal themselves rather than wait until you have more features implemented; hurried cleanup at the end of a project will pressure you to apply bandages instead of real fixes. If your application is failing when the invoice amount is exactly $33.00, don't just patch the procedure like this:

```
If curInvoiceAmt=33 Then
    MyFunction = curTheCorrectValue
Else...
```

Instead, figure out *why* the call is failing and fix its cause instead of the apparent symptom. This requires steady and systematic testing, which is something programmers tend to avoid. Would you rather write 500 lines of code or try 50 test cases on existing code? Most of us would choose the former, since writing code is fun and testing is boring. But if you keep in mind how little fun you'll have if your application doesn't work when it's shipped, you'll buckle down and do the boring testing work, too.

Using Comments

Old code is harder to debug than new code because it is less fresh in your mind. Depending on how busy you are, old code could be two weeks old, two days old, or two hours old! One way to help keep your code from aging rapidly is to insert comments. There's an art to sensible commenting: it depends on adding just enough to tell you what's going on without going overboard and cluttering up your code.

The comment should state the intention of the code rather than tell how the code is implemented. This is an important point. Novice programmers have a tendency to write comments that describe how the code is implemented, as in this example:

```
' Make sure the numbers in the combo box & the text box add up
' to less than the acceptable total
If cboStartTime + CInt(txtSlots) > MAX_SLOTS Then
    ' If not, put up an error message...
    MsgBox "Not enough time in day", vbCritical, _
     "Schedule Error"
    ' ...and exit the application
    GoTo cmdSchedule_Click_Exit
End If
' Find the last slot that needs to be modified
intSlotLast = cboStartTime + CInt(txtSlots) - 1

' Set an object to the current database
Set dbCurrent = CurrentDb()
' Open a querydef object with the Prospective schedule query
' loaded
Set qdfSchedule = _
 dbCurrent.OpenQueryDef("qryScheduleProspective")
' Get the first query parameter from the Installer combo box
qdfSchedule.Parameters(0) = cboInstaller
' Get the second query parameter from the Date combo box
qdfSchedule.Parameters(1) = cboDate
```

Reading through code like this is like trying to understand a telephone conversation with a bad echo on the line. By trimming down the number of comments to a more sensible level, you can highlight the overall structure of the code and note any particularly tricky spots for future programmers, including yourself. Remember, if you've named your variables using a consistent standard, their names will act as minicomments in the code itself. Notice that the comments in this version of the same example describe the intention of the code, not how it is implemented:

```
' Check to see that we have enough hours left in the day
If cboStartTime + CInt(txtSlots) > MAX_SLOTS Then
    MsgBox "Not enough time in day", vbCritical, _
```

```
        "Schedule Error"
      GoTo cmdSchedule_Click_Exit
  End If
  intSlotLast = cboStartTime + CInt(txtSlots) - 1

  ' Get a list of open timeslots to check
  Set dbCurrent = CurrentDb()
  Set qdfSchedule = _
   dbCurrent.OpenQueryDef("qryScheduleProspective")
  qdfSchedule.Parameters(0) = cboInstaller
  qdfSchedule.Parameters(1) = cboDate
```

A comment that is not maintained is worse than no comment at all. Have you ever read a comment and then stared at the code below it and discovered it didn't seem to do what the comment said it did? Now you have to figure out whether it is the comment or the code that is wrong. If your code change requires a comment change, make sure you do it now, because you probably won't get around to doing it later.

To Strip or Not to Strip

One reason for keeping the number of comments to a reasonable level is that comments do take up space in memory while your database is loaded. Some programmers go so far as to encourage comment stripping, the practice of removing all comments from production code. If you choose to do this, make sure you only do it right before shipping and that you don't make changes to the stripped code. Otherwise, you might end up with two different code bases. To facilitate removing comments from code, you can create a COM Add-in for the Visual Basic Editor that programmatically searches for and removes comments. Creating COM Add-ins for Access is covered in Chapter 18. Creating add-ins for the VBE is beyond the scope of this book, however.

Organizing Your Code

In addition to commenting your code, you should do whatever you can to keep it organized. This means you should use indentation to organize the flow of code. It also means you should split large procedures into smaller ones.

Indent your code so that statements that "go together" are at the same indentation level, and statements that are subordinate to others are indented one more tab stop. Although there is room for disagreement, most Access programmers lay out their code something like this:

```
' Initialize the array that governs visibility and
' set up records
For intI = 1 To intTotalTabs
    intShow(intI) = False
    rstLoggedData.AddNew
        rstLoggedData![State] = False
    rstLoggedDate.Update
Next intI
intShow(intTabNumber) = True
```

In VBA, many programmers use indentation both to match up traditional control structures (For…Next, If…Then…Else, Do…Loop, For Each…) and to indicate levels of data access object activity (BeginTrans/CommitTrans, AddNew/Update, and so on).

Modularizing Your Code

Modularization is a fancy term for a simple idea: breaking up your code into a series of relatively small procedures rather than a few mammoth ones. There are several key benefits to writing code this way:

- You make it easier to understand each procedure. Code that is easier to understand is easier to maintain and to keep bug-free.
- You can localize errors to a smaller section of the total code. If a variable is used only in one 10-line function, any error messages referring to that variable are most likely generated within that function.
- You can lessen the dangers of side effects caused by too widely scoping variables. If you use a variable at the top of a 500-line function and again at the bottom for a different loop, you may well forget to reinitialize it.

Using Option Explicit

In the Visual Basic Editor's Tools ➢ Options dialog, you will find a check box labeled Require Variable Declaration. Selecting this check box causes VBA to insert the line "Option Explicit" at the top of any new module it creates. This statement forces you to declare all your variables before referring to them in your code. This will prevent some hard-to-find errors from cropping up in your code. Without Option Explicit, VBA allows you to use any syntactically correct variable in your code, regardless of whether you declare it. This means that any variable you forget to declare will be initialized to a variant and given the value Empty at the point where you first use it. The hours you save in debugging time will make using this option well worth the effort.

Using Option Explicit is an easy way to avoid errors such as the one you'll find in the code in Listing 14.19. Errors like this are almost impossible to catch late in the development cycle, since they're buried in existing code. (Don't feel bad if you don't immediately see the error in the fragment; it's difficult to find.) That's why you'll want to use Option Explicit—to avoid just this sort of error.

Listing 14.19

```
Function UpdateLog(intSeverity As Integer, _
 strProcedure As String, strTracking As String) As Integer
    Dim rstUsageLog As Recordset

    Const conMinSeverity = 1
    ' Don't log activities that aren't severe enough to
    ' bother with
    If intSeverity < conMinSeverity Then
        Exit Function
    End If

    DoCmd.SetWarnings False

    ' Append a new record to the usage log
    Set rstUsageLog = New Recordset
    rstUsageLog.Open "zstblUsageLog", _
     CurrentProject.Connection, adOpenKeyset, _
     adLockPessimistic
    rstUsageLog.AddNew
        rstUsageLog!Severity = intSeverty
        If Err.Number Then
            rstUsageLog!ErrorCode = Err.Number
            rstUsageLog!ErrorText = Err.Description
        End If
        rstUsageLog!User = CurrentUser()
        rstUsageLog!Date = Now
'.
'. etc
'.
End Function
```

In case you missed it, the error occurred on this line of code:

```
rstUsageLog!Severity = intSeverty
```

A small spelling error like this would cause only zeros to be stored in the Severity field and could cause you several hours of debugging time. Option Explicit lets you avoid these kinds of errors.

Avoid Variants If at All Possible

The Variant data type is convenient, but it's not always the best choice. It's tempting to declare all your variables as variants so you don't have to worry about what's in them. The Access and VBA design teams did not put in explicit types to make your life difficult; they put them in because they're useful. If you think something will always be an Integer, declare it as an Integer. If you get an error message later because you've attempted to assign an invalid value to that variable, the error message will point straight to the problem area of your code and give you a good idea of what went wrong. Variants are also slower than explicitly dimensioned variables for the same operations, since they have the overhead of tracking which type of data they are holding at any given time. In addition, variants are larger than almost any other data type and so take longer to move around in memory. These last two reasons alone should be enough to make you reconsider using variants whenever possible.

TIP

In some instances, you have no choice about your data types. If you're assigning values to variables that might, at some point, need to contain a null value, you must use the Variant data type. This is the only data type that can contain a null value, and attempting to assign a null value to a nonvariant variable triggers a runtime error. The same goes for function return values. If a function might need to return a null value, the return value for that function must be a variant.

Use ByVal with Care

You need to be careful about passing information to routines with ByVal parameters. While this is a good way to prevent subroutines from modifying variables passed to them (since ByVal creates a copy), you may lose information when calling the procedure. This is because information passed in is coerced to the data type of the parameter. Therefore, if you pass a variable with the Single data type to a parameter of type Integer, Access truncates the fractional component of the Single when it creates the Integer. You will have no warning of this, however, so make sure you know which data type the procedures expect if you've used ByVal in the declaration.

Beware the Simple Dim Statement

Even the simple Dim statement can introduce subtle bugs into your code. Consider this statement:

```
Dim strFirst, strLast As String
```

The intent here is clearly to define two String variables on one line. If you've ever programmed in C or C++, you know that a similar declaration would do just that. However, this is not the way VBA works. The As clause applies only to the variable it immediately follows, not to all variables on the line. The result of the preceding declaration is that strLast is a String variable but strFirst is a variant variable, with slightly different behavior. For example, strFirst will be initialized to Empty and strLast to a zero-length string. You must explicitly define the data type of every single variable in VBA. The simplest way to ensure this is to get into the habit of declaring only one variable on each Dim statement.

Grouping Your Dim Statements

You can declare your variables anywhere in your procedures, as long you declare them before they are actually used, and VBA will understand and accept the declarations. For the sake of easier debugging, though, you should get into the habit of declaring variables at the top of your procedures. This makes it easy to see exactly what a particular procedure is referring to and to find the declarations when you are in the midst of debugging.

Using the Tightest Possible Scope

Always use the tightest possible scope for your variables. Some beginning programmers discover global variables and promptly declare all their variables as global to avoid the issue of scope altogether. This is a sloppy practice that will backfire the first time you have two procedures, both of which change the same global variable's value. If a variable is used solely in a single procedure, declare it there. If it is used only by procedures in a single module, declare it with module scope. Save global scope for only those few variables you truly need to refer to from widely scattered parts of your code.

If you need a variable to be available globally but want to restrict the scope of procedures that can change that value, you might consider "hiding" it from the rest of your application. To do so, create the variable as a private, module-level variable in a specific module. In that module, place any function that needs to modify the value of the variable. In addition, add one extra function that you'll use to retrieve the value from outside the module. If you want to be able to assign a new value to the variable from a different module, you can also include a procedure that will do that for you. In any case, no procedure in any other module will be able to modify the value of this variable. By hiding the variable in this manner, you can be assured that no other procedures in any other modules can modify your variable without going through your procedures. Listing 14.20 shows a simple case of this mechanism.

Listing 14.20

```
Private pintCurrentValue As Integer

Public Sub SetCurrentValue(intNewValue As Integer)
    pintCurrentValue = intNewValue
End Sub

Public Function GetCurrentValue()
    GetCurrentValue = pintCurrentValue
End Function
```

Given the code in Listing 14.20, any procedure in any module can retrieve the value of pintCurrentValue (by calling the GetCurrentValue function) and can set the value (by calling SetCurrentValue). If you made SetCurrentValue private, however, no procedure outside the current module could change the value of pintCurrentValue. By protecting your *faux*-global variables in this manner, you can avoid errors that can easily occur in multiple-module applications, especially ones written by multiple programmers.

Using Consistent Naming Conventions

In addition to the conventions discussed here that help structure your code, consider adopting a consistent naming convention for objects and variables in your code. We (along with many other programmers) have standardized our naming conventions based on the RVBA naming conventions, which you'll find in Appendix A. A consistent naming standard can make it simple for you to find errors lurking in your programs, in addition to making them simpler for multiple programmers to maintain. By using the RVBA naming convention, you gain two pieces of information about every variable: which data type it is and what scope it has. This information can be very helpful during the debugging process.

Your Friend, the MsgBox Function

As an alternative to setting breakpoints, you can use the MsgBox function to indicate your program's state. With this strategy, you decide what you would like to monitor and call the MsgBox function to return particular information. You can enhance this technique by writing a wrapper for the MsgBox function so that these messages are posted only when you have a conditional compilation constant set to indicate that you want to see debugging messages. This flag controls whether the adhDebugMessageBox function should in fact interrupt execution of your code or whether it should just quietly return to the calling procedure. The adhDebugMessageBox function is shown in Listing 14.21. You'll find this function in the basError module in CH14.MDB. To use it in your own applications, import the module and call adhDebugMessageBox, as described in the following paragraphs.

Listing 14.21

```
#Const conFDebug = True

Function adhDebugMessageBox(ByVal varMessage As Variant, _
 strCaller As String) As Integer
    adhDebugMessageBox = True
#If adhcFDebug Then
    adhDebugMessageBox = (MsgBox(CStr(varMessage), _
     vbOKCancel Or vbQuestion, "Debug: " & strCaller) _
     = vbOK)
#End If
End Function
```

You can sprinkle as many calls to adhDebugMessageBox as you like into your code and make them all active or inactive at once by changing the value of the conFDebug constant. Typically, you can use these message boxes to return news on the state of the program's execution. For example, here's a possible code fragment from your application's AutoExec function (called from the AutoExec macro):

```
If Not adhDebugMessageBox("About to Start Logging", _
 "AutoExec") Then
    Stop
End If

varRet = StartLogging()

If Not adhDebugMessageBox("StartLogging returned " _
 & varRet, "AutoExec") Then
    Stop
End If
```

The adhDebugMessageBox function uses conditional compilation to include or exclude the body of the function. Conditional compilation tells the VBA compiler to include or exclude certain portions of code when it compiles the code. The #Const directive defines a conditional compilation constant. You can also define conditional compilation constants in the VBA Project Properties. The #If and #End If directives define a block that is compiled only if the conditional compilation expression is true. Based on the value of the conFDebug constant, the message box is either displayed or it's not. If the constant is not set, it just returns True, and your code can continue. However, if you are in debug mode instead, the function displays whatever you pass to it, as shown in Figure 14.4.

FIGURE 14.4:

The adhDebugMessageBox function displays anything you send it.

If you click OK, the function returns a True value. If you click Cancel or press the Esc key, the function returns False, which in turn should halt your program execution back at the point where you called the adhDebugMessageBox function. Using debugging message boxes is particularly useful when your code refers to the Screen object and its ActiveForm, ActiveReport, ActiveControl, and ActiveDatasheet properties, because using the Immediate window causes these objects to lose the focus and thus their context.

The VBA Debugging Tools

Once you've recognized that you have a logic error, you will need to track it down. VBA provides a set of tools for debugging your application. These include:

- The Immediate window
- Breakpoints and Single Step mode
- The Call Stack
- Watch expressions
- Quick watches
- Data Tips
- The Locals window
- Debugging options in the Options dialog

This section briefly describes these features. The sections that follow show you how to use them to debug your VBA code.

The Immediate Window

The Immediate window, shown in Figure 14.5, gives you a place to investigate the effects of VBA code directly, without the intervention of macros, forms, or other methods of running the code. Think of the Immediate window as a command line for VBA. You can use it to launch procedures and evaluate expressions. In fact, you can do almost as many things in the Immediate window as you can in VBA procedure code. You open the Immediate window by selecting View ➢ Immediate Window from the VBA Editor menu or pressing Ctrl+G. Immediate window contents are preserved as long as you are in a single session of Access, even if you close one database and open another.

FIGURE 14.5: The Immediate window showing how to call a sub named ErrorExample

The Immediate window displays the last 200 lines of output at all times. As more output is appended to the end, older lines disappear from the top of the list. With the capability to scroll back in the Immediate window, you can position the cursor on an evaluation line and press Enter, and VBA will recalculate the expression and display its value. If you want to remove the lines in the Immediate window above your current location, use Ctrl+Shift+Home to select them all and press Delete. To remove lines below your current location, first select them with Ctrl+Shift+End.

Breakpoints and Single Step Mode

Breakpoints allow you to set locations in your code at which VBA will temporarily halt its execution. Figure 14.6 shows code halted at a breakpoint. Note the highlighted line of code and the small arrow that appears in the left margin. These indicate the line of code *about to be executed.* You set a breakpoint by highlighting a line of code in the editor and pressing F9 or selecting Debug ➢ Toggle Breakpoint.

Once execution has halted at a breakpoint, you can execute one line at a time by using the Single Step mode of VBA's debugger. Single Step mode gives you a great chance to watch, in a very granular way, what's happening with your code.

FIGURE 14.6:

Code halted at a breakpoint

Ch14 - basChapter14 (Code)

(General) | PrintCallStack

```
Private Sub PrintCallStack()
    Dim objProc As Procedure

    ' Call EnterProc to push proc onto the stack
    Call gProcStack.EnterProc("PrintCallStack", _
     "basChapter14")

    ' Print it out by walking the stack
    Set objProc = gProcStack.Top
    Do Until objProc Is Nothing
        Debug.Print "Entered procedure '" & _
         objProc.Module & "::" & objProc.Name & _
         "' at " & objProc.TimeEntered
        Set objProc = objProc.NextProc
    Loop

    ' Make sure to call ExitProc!!
    'Call gProcStack.ExitProc("PrintCallStack")
End Sub
```

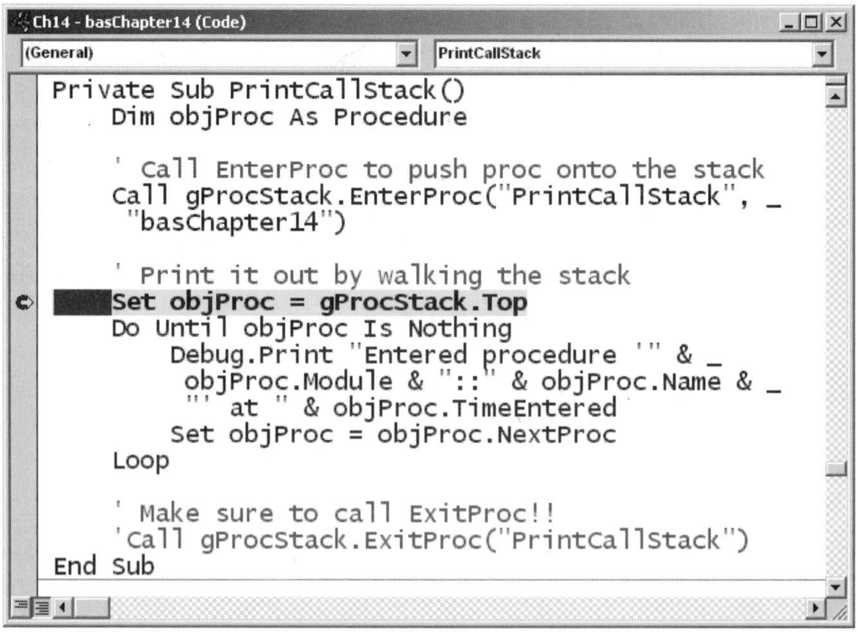

The Call Stack

VBA has the ability to display the call stack when a procedure is paused at a breakpoint. The call stack lists each pending procedure, with the current procedure at the top of the list, the one that called it next on the list, and so on. If the procedure was originally called from the Immediate window, this is noted at the end of the list. If the procedure was called from elsewhere in Access (for example, directly from a Click event or from a RunCode macro action), there is no way to know from where it was called. Figure 14.7 shows the call stack as it might appear at a breakpoint in your code.

FIGURE 14.7:

The VBA Call Stack dialog showing the call stack

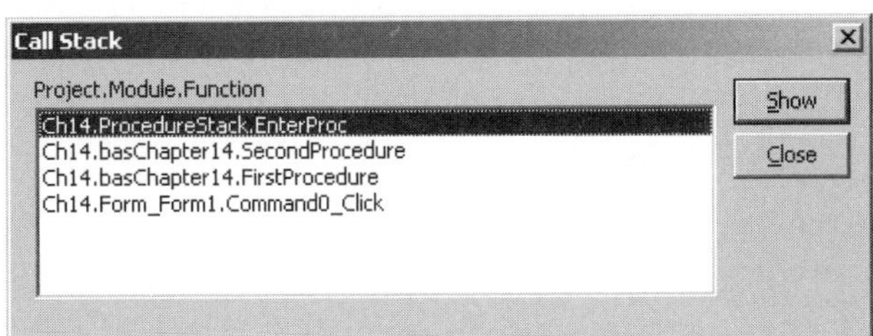

To view the call stack, select the View ➢ Call Stack menu command or press Ctrl+L. Once the Call Stack dialog opens, you can jump to any procedure in the call stack by selecting it from the list and clicking the Show button.

Watch Expressions

You use watches to track the values of expressions as code executes. VBA has implemented a full set of watch functionality. Watches come in three varieties, and you can view them interactively or add them to a list of persistent Watch expressions. You define Watch expressions using commands on the Immediate window. The three types of watches are

- Watch expression
- Break When Expression Is True
- Break When Expression Has Changed

VBA displays Watch expressions in a separate window that you can access by selecting View ➢ Watch Window. Anytime you are debugging in Break mode, all

Watch expressions are evaluated and shown. This is useful if you are single stepping through code and want to watch the contents of a variable or an expression. It is also much more convenient than using the Immediate window to print the contents of variables after each line of code executes.

The Break When Expression Is True and Break When Expression Has Changed functionalities allow you to specify a logical condition or expression. When that condition is true or changes, VBA immediately halts execution and puts you into Break mode. These types of watches are useful for determining when and how a variable's value was changed. For example, say you know that somewhere in your code, a global variable named gintValue is getting set to 0. You can set a Break When Expression Is True watch with the expression "gintValue = 0". Then, as soon as gintValue becomes equal to 0, VBA puts you into Break mode.

Quick Watches

The Quick Watch dialog, shown in Figure 14.8, is useful for quickly seeing the value of a variable. To use this dialog, position the cursor anywhere within a variable name and press Shift+F9. The Quick Watch dialog then shows you the present contents of a variable. You can also select an expression, and VBA will evaluate the expression. Clicking the Add button adds the expression as a regular Watch expression.

FIGURE 14.8:

The Quick Watch dialog

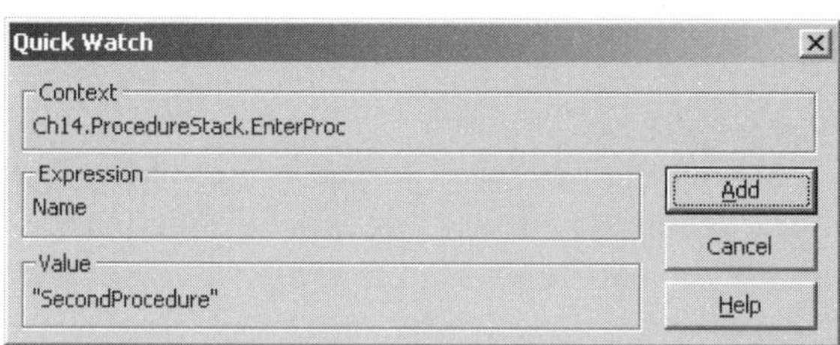

Data Tips

Data Tips work like ToolTips in a code window. To use Data Tips, move the mouse over any variable or property while your code is in Break mode. VBA displays a small ToolTip-type rectangle with the value of the expression. This is even quicker than using a quick watch.

The Locals Window

Similar to the Watch window, the Locals window (see Figure 14.9) displays all objects and variables currently in scope while your code in is Break mode. You can expand and collapse objects to view their properties. In effect, this pane creates Watch expressions for every variable in your code. Select the View ➢ Locals Window command to display the window.

FIGURE 14.9:

The Locals window

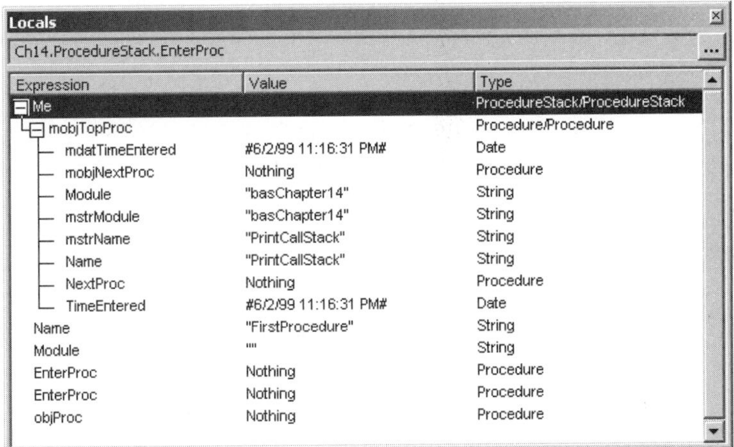

Debugging Options in the Options Dialog

The General tab of the VBA Options dialog has options that let you fine-tune how VBA handles errors and debugging. These concern error trapping and when VBA enters Break mode in response to runtime errors. You can choose among three options:

Break on All Errors Causes VBA to enter Break mode whenever a runtime error occurs, even if you've defined an error handler. Normally, you want to use this option only while debugging an application, not after you distribute it.

Break in Class Module The default setting, this causes VBA to enter Break mode on all untrapped errors in global modules or class modules.

Break on Unhandled Errors Causes VBA to enter Break mode on all untrapped errors in global modules only. If an error occurs in a class module, VBA enters Break mode on the statement in a global module that called the class's property or method code.

Using the Immediate Window

You can use the Immediate window to test parts of an application interactively. From the Immediate window, you can launch procedures, view and change the values of variables, and evaluate expressions. You can also write VBA code to print information to the Immediate window without your intervention.

Running Code from the Immediate Window

You can easily run any function or subroutine that's in scope from the Immediate window. To run a procedure, simply type its name (along with any parameter values) on a blank line in the Immediate window and press Enter. Note that this also returns control to the Immediate window. This technique works for both functions and subroutines. If, on the other hand, you want to run a function and have VBA return the result to the Immediate window, you'll have to use the Print statement. For example, if you enter this expression:

```
Print MyFunction()
```

in the Immediate window, VBA runs the function called MyFunction and prints out the return value.

VBA provides a shortcut for the Print method, as have most previous versions of Basic. In the Immediate window, you can just use the "?" symbol to replace the word *Print*. All our examples use this shortcut. Therefore, the preceding statement could be rewritten as:

```
? MyFunction()
```

Rules of scope apply as in normal code. That is, variables are available from the Immediate window only if they're currently in scope. You can tell what the current scope is by looking at the text box at the top of the Immediate window. It always reflects what VBA sees as the current scope.

Working with Expressions in the Immediate Window

You can use the Immediate window to evaluate expressions, be they simple variables or complex calculations. For example, you can view the current value of the variable intMyVar by typing

```
?intMyVar
```

in the Immediate window and pressing Enter. Of course, the variable must already be declared elsewhere in your code and must be in scope at the time. You cannot enter a Dim statement (or any of its cousins, including ReDim, Public, and Const) in the Immediate window.

In addition to viewing expression results, you can use the Immediate window to change variable values. To change the contents of intMyVar, you could use an expression like this:

```
intMyVar = 97
```

Any code that executes subsequent to your changing the variable value will see the new value.

Any statement you enter for direct execution in the Immediate window must fit on a single line. You cannot, for example, enter a multiline If…Then…Else for evaluation in the Immediate window, although you can execute a single-line If…Then statement. To get around this limitation, you can use the colon (:) character to separate multiple VBA statements on the same line.

For example, the following code will run a loop for you:

```
For intCount = 0 To 10:Debug.Print intCount:Next intCount
```

Printing Information to the Immediate Window

You can use the Immediate window as a way of tracking a running procedure by printing messages or expression values to it while your code is running. You use the Print method of the Debug object to display any expression from within your running code. For example, running the function in Listing 14.22 (from the Fibo procedure in basChapter14 in CH14.MDB) produces the output shown in Figure 14.10. Note the Debug.Print statement inside the For…Next loop.

FIGURE 14.10:

Output from running Fibo

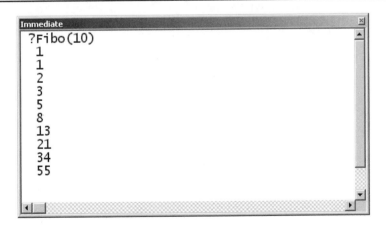

Listing 14.22

```
Function Fibo(intMembers As Integer)
    ' Print the requested number of elements of the
    ' standard Fibonacci series (s(n) = s(n-2) + s(n-1))
    ' to the Debug window.

    Dim intI As Integer
    Dim intCurrent As Integer
    Dim intPrevious As Integer
    Dim intTwoPrevious As Integer

    intPrevious = 1
    intTwoPrevious = 1

    Debug.Print intPrevious
    Debug.Print intTwoPrevious

    For intI = 3 To intMembers
        intCurrent = intPrevious + intTwoPrevious
        Debug.Print intCurrent
        intTwoPrevious = intPrevious
        intPrevious = intCurrent
    Next intI

End Function
```

Handling Remnant Debug.Print Statements

You can safely leave Debug.Print lines in your shipping code if you wish. As long as the user does not for some reason have the Immediate window displayed, these lines will have no visible effect and only a slight performance penalty. However, if you are concerned about the performance hit of these lines, you can surround your debug code with conditional compilation statements. For example:

```
' In the declarations section:
#Const fDebug = True

' In some procedure:
#If fDebug Then
    Debug.Print "Some output"
#End If
```

Using Breakpoints

Using a breakpoint is the equivalent of putting a roadblock in your code. When you set a breakpoint, you tell VBA to stop executing your code at a particular line but to keep the system state in memory. This means that all the variables the function was dealing with are available for your inspection in the Immediate window. You can also use the Step Into and Step Over functionality (using the menu items, the toolbar buttons, or the F8/Shift+F8 key) to move through your code statement by statement so you can watch it execute in slow motion. VBA provides a toolbar with appropriate breakpoint buttons to aid in your debugging efforts. Figure 14.11 shows the Debugging toolbar, with each of the buttons labeled.

FIGURE 14.11:

The VBA Debugging toolbar

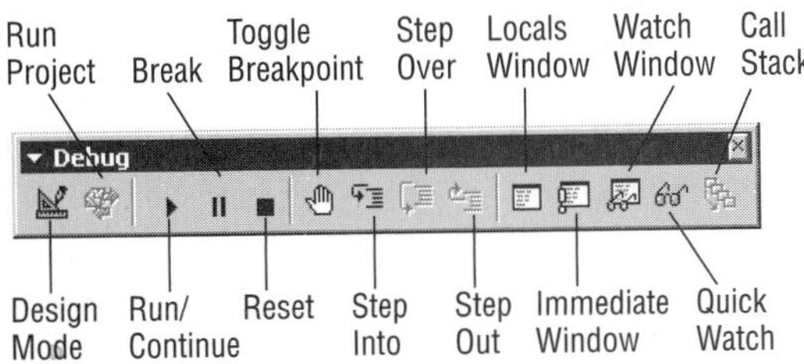

To set a breakpoint on a particular line of code, you can place your cursor anywhere on the line and do one of the following: click the Breakpoint button on the toolbar, choose Debug ➢ Toggle Breakpoint, or press the F9 key. You can also create a breakpoint by clicking the mouse in the margin of the module window. VBA highlights the chosen line in the Module window. (You can control the highlighting colors using the Editor Format tab of the VBA Options dialog.) When you're executing code and you hit a breakpoint, the focus switches to the module window with the breakpoint showing, and a rectangle surrounds the statement where execution is halted. Additionally, if you have the module margin bar shown, VBA displays a small arrow in the left margin indicating the current statement. VBA suspends execution *before* it executes the particular statement. This way, you can check or set the value of variables in your code before executing the chosen line of code.

VBA does not save breakpoints with your code when you close a database. If you close a database and reopen it, any breakpoints you have set in your code vanish. (VBA does, however, preserve breakpoints when the editor window is closed, as long as you don't close the database.) If you need to preserve your breakpoints across sessions, you can use the Stop statement, which acts as a permanent breakpoint and is saved with your module. Just as with a breakpoint, VBA pauses the execution of your code as soon as it encounters the Stop statement. Of course, you'll need to remove Stop statements from your code (or surround them with conditional compilation statements) before you distribute your application, since they will stop the execution of your running code in any environment.

You can clear all breakpoints you have set with the Debug ➢ Clear All Breakpoints item. This resets every breakpoint you have set, including those in global and those in form and report modules.

Single Step Mode

When VBA halts your code at a breakpoint, you can choose how to continue. You can proceed at full speed once again by clicking the Continue button on the toolbar, selecting the Run ➢ Continue menu command, or pressing F5. You can also use *Single Step mode* to execute statements one at a time. To execute the next statement (the one highlighted with the rectangle), click the Step Into button on the toolbar, select the Debug ➢ Step Into menu command, or press F8. After executing the current line of code, VBA will bring you back to Break mode at the next line.

Stepping Into, Over, and Out

When VBA encounters one of your own procedures while in Single Step mode, it continues in one of three ways, depending on which Single Step command you use:

- Choosing Debug ➢ Step Into, pressing the F8 key, or clicking the Step Into toolbar button causes VBA to jump into your procedure, executing it one line at a time.
- Choosing Debug ➢ Step Over, pressing Shift+F8, or clicking the Step Over toolbar button also executes code one line at a time, but only within the context of the current procedure. Calls to other procedures are considered atomic by the Step Over action; it executes the entire procedure at once. This is especially useful if you are calling code you've previously debugged. Rather than take the time to walk through the other procedures, which you're confident are in working order, you can use the Step Over functionality to execute them at full speed while you're debugging.
- Choosing Debug ➢ Step Out, pressing Ctrl+Shift+F8, or clicking the Step Out toolbar button steps out of the current procedure. If it was called from another procedure, VBA returns to the line in that procedure following the call to the current one. This is useful if you have inadvertently stepped into a procedure you don't want to debug and want to return to the procedure from which you called it.

As an alternative to the Single Step commands, you can use the Run to Cursor functionality to continue to a given line. To do so, highlight any line after the currently executing one and select the Debug ➢ Run to Cursor command or press Ctrl+F8. Run to Cursor is also available from the right-click context menu. Run to Cursor causes VBA to continue execution until the line before the selected one is executed and then reenter Break mode.

NOTE

You can never step into code in a DLL. You *can* step into code in an Access code library; however, you cannot set a breakpoint in a code library. To debug a library, you can either set a breakpoint in code in the current database and then single-step into the library code, or open the library code using the Object Browser and set a breakpoint there. This does not work, however, with libraries that have had their source code removed with the Tools ➢ Database Utilities ➢ Make MDE File command.

Other Single Step Options

While in Single Step mode, you can move the current execution point to another location. Placing the insertion point on any statement in the halted procedure and choosing Debug ➢ Set Next Statement causes execution to begin at that statement when you continue the function. This command is also available from the right-click context menu. You can also change the current execution point by clicking and dragging the arrow in the module margin bar. You cannot skip to another procedure in this fashion, though. If you are wading through several open code windows, the Debug ➢ Show Next Statement item brings you back to the one where execution is paused.

Occasionally, your code will become so hopelessly bug-ridden that during the course of single stepping through it, you'll want to throw up your hands and surrender. In this case, you can choose the Run ➢ End command or click the End button on the toolbar to stop executing code. While this stops executing code and takes you out of Break mode, it retains the contents of any module or global variables. To clear the contents of these variables, choose the Run ➢ Reset command, click the Reset toolbar button, or press Shift+F5 instead.

WARNING

While in Break mode it is possible to launch other procedures. VBA maintains the current execution point for the first procedure while other procedures are executed. This can lead to unpredictable results, especially when you are running procedures that use the same data or variables. If you witness unpredictable behavior, make sure you don't have an outstanding Break mode condition by selecting the Show Next Statement command, looking at the call stack, or selecting the Stop or Reset command.

Techniques and Strategies for Debugging

You can start developing a debugging strategy by understanding that bugs, despite the name, are not cute little things that scurry around in your code. Bugs are mistakes, pure and simple. And they're *your* mistakes; the program didn't put them there, and the end user didn't put them there. Removing these mistakes gives you an opportunity to become a better programmer.

Systematic Debugging

The first rule of debugging: *You need a reproducible case to produce the error*. If you cannot reproduce the error, you will have great difficulty tracking down the bug. You may get lucky and be in a situation where you can debug it when it happens, but if you can't reproduce it, your chances of fixing it are small. To reproduce the bug, you need as much information about the conditions that produced the bug as possible, but no more than that. If your users give you the hundred steps they performed that morning before the bug occurred, it makes your job difficult. If users limit the information to the essential three steps that actually cause the bug to occur, you can get somewhere. This isn't always that easy, though. Sometimes you can reproduce a bug only by following numerous steps or, for example, after the user has been using the application for four hours. As you can imagine, these types of bugs are much harder to find and fix.

The second rule of debugging: *Debug data, not code*. This means you should use the debugger and find out what the data is producing instead of staring at the code and speculating as to what it does. This seems a simple rule, but it is very effective at resolving bugs.

After you have found the bug but before you start fixing code, make sure you understand the nature of the problem. For example, a common error occurs when you declare variables to be of a specific simple data type (Integer, Long, String, and so on) and, as part of your application, copy data from a table into these variables. In your own testing, everything works fine. At the client's site your client receives "Invalid Use of Null" messages.

There are two solutions to this problem, and each requires some understanding of the particular application. Clearly, you cannot place null values into Integer, Long, or String variables, so you might consider changing them all to variants. On the other hand, perhaps the solution is to disallow null entries into those particular fields in the table. Your decision on the solution needs to take into account the particular situation.

It seems obvious that you should change code only with a reason, but surprisingly, many programmers ignore this principle. "Experience" often masquerades as a reason when it is really a synonym for "wild guess." Don't just change your loop from

```
For intI = 0 To intCount - 1
```

to

```
For intI = 1 To intCount
```

until and unless you can point to your code and show exactly where and how the off-by-1 error is occurring. Take the time to thoroughly understand the bug before you try fixing it. Otherwise, you'll never know what you're fixing, and the bug will surely crop up somewhere else.

Finally, no matter how good you are and how sure you are of your work, make only one change to your code at a time, and then test it again. It's all too easy to fall into the trap of making multiple fixes without keeping records and then having to junk the current version and reload from a backup because you have no idea which things worked and which only made things worse. Take baby steps, and you'll get there faster. As an added measure, document changes to your code using comments in either individual procedures or the declarations section of a module. By logging changes with the date they were made, you can help track down problems introduced by various "fixes."

TIP

Another way to prevent fixes to one procedure from adversely affecting other parts of your program is to use a source code control program that supports versioning. This lets you fall back to a working version of your code so you can try another debugging tactic. Office 2000 Developer includes an add-in that lets you store Access databases in Visual SourceSafe, a source code control program. We cover source code control for Access in *Access 2000 Developer's Handbook, Volume II.*

There are two more bits of debugging strategy you might want to consider. Many programmers find "confessional debugging" to be one of the most useful techniques around. Confessional debugging works something like this: you grab your printouts and go into the next cubicle, interrupt the programmer working there, and say, "Hey, sorry to bother you, but I've got this function that keeps crashing. See, I pass in the name of a form here and then declare a form variable and then—oh, wait, that's not the form itself, but the form's name. Never mind; thanks for your help." When you get good at it, you can indulge in this sort of debugging with nonprogrammers as the audience or even (in times of desperation) by talking things through with your dog or a sympathetic (but bored) loved one.

Of course, there are times when confessing your code isn't enough. If you have the luxury of working with peers, use them. There's a good chance that other programmers can see the bug that you can't.

If all else fails, take a break. It's easy to get stuck in a mental loop in which you try the same things over and over, even though they didn't work the first time. Take a walk. Have lunch. Get a latte. Take a shower. Your mind's background processing can solve many bugs while the foreground processes are thinking about something else altogether. Many programmers have told stories of waking up in the middle of the night, having just dreamed about a bug they weren't even aware existed until then, along with its solution. Having written down the information during the night, they've gone into work, found the previously unspotted bug, and fixed it on the spot.

Debugging Difficulties

As you debug, you'll come across some particular problems you'll need to watch out for. Most of them equate to the software version of the Heisenberg Uncertainty Principle: Halting code to investigate it can change the state of your program, either introducing spurious bugs or (perhaps worse) hiding actual bugs. Unfortunately, there often isn't much you can do about these problems other than to know they exist. Try using Debug.Print statements to find the program's state when you run into these sorts of bugs.

Resetting the Stopped State

If you set up a function to present the user with a particular environment and then stop it midstream, the application often won't be in the proper environment for you to proceed with your debugging. For example, you may have left screen echo off, warnings off, or the hourglass cursor on. You may also be shipping code with the toolbars turned off and yet want them handy when you're debugging things. The simplest solution to this problem is to have a utility function available, either in your production database or loaded in a library, to reset the environment to a more hospitable state. Listing 14.23 shows a function (from basError in CH14.MDB) you could possibly attach to a keystroke, using an AutoKeys macro that will reset most of your environment. Once you've assigned this function to a keystroke, it's just a simple matter of pressing one key combination whenever you stop the code and can't quite see what you're doing.

Listing 14.23

```
Function adhCleanUp()
    ' Return the application to normal programming mode.
    ' Reinstate screen updating,
    ' reset the cursor to its normal state,
    ' and reset warnings.

    On Error GoTo adhCleanUpErr

    Application.Echo True
    DoCmd.Hourglass False
    DoCmd.SetWarnings True
    Application.SetOption "Built-In Toolbars Available", True

adhCleanUpDone:
    On Error GoTo 0
    Exit Function

adhCleanUpErr:
    MsgBox "Error " & Err.Number & ": " & Err.Description, _
     vbCritical, "adhCleanUp"
    Resume adhCleanUpDone
End Function
```

Using Assertions

An *assertion* is a statement indicating that at a certain point the code should be in a certain state. If the code isn't in the expected state, code execution stops so you can examine the problem.

The adhButtonMap function, shown in Listing 14.24, displays several examples of assertions. This one function has six consecutive assertions.

Listing 14.24

```
Public Function adhButtonMap(ByVal bytButton1 As Byte, _
 ByVal bytButton2 As Byte, ByVal bytButton3 As Byte) As Long

    Debug.Assert (bytButton1 >= 0)
```

```
        Debug.Assert (bytButton1 <= conResumeMax)
        Debug.Assert (bytButton2 >= 0)
        Debug.Assert (bytButton2 <= conResumeMax)
        Debug.Assert (bytButton3 >= 0)
        Debug.Assert (bytButton3 <= conResumeMax)
        adhButtonMap = bytButton1 Or bytButton2 * 2 ^ 8 Or _
         bytButton3 * 2 ^ 16
    End Function
```

These assertions state that the values being passed in fall within a certain range. You use assertions to validate the normal functionality of the program. Use the Assert method of VBA's Debug object to process your assertions. The Assert method evaluates a logical expression and halts code execution if it evaluates to False.

Be sure to precede most assertions with a comment that describes why the assertion might fail: a value is out of range, the procedure name is not the same as the top of the stack, the code should never be reached, and so on. In some cases, the comment might suggest how to fix the assertion. Liberal use of assertions in your code will help in finding many logic errors. The trade-off is that they add slightly to the size and reduce the speed of your code.

WARNING Be sure to thoroughly test your application before distributing it, especially if you use assertions. Assertion failures in a production application will open the Visual Basic Editor and your user will then wonder what to do. This inevitably ends with a support call to you!

Summary

As you develop code, you will run into each of the three types of errors, compile-time, runtime, and logic errors. By using the techniques described in this chapter, you can make your life much simpler by producing robust and easily maintainable code. Follow these suggestions:

- Use a generic error-reporting procedure.
- Plan your code in advance.

- Don't get too "clever."
- Structure and comment your code.
- Use indentation and naming conventions.
- Modularize your code.
- Use Option Explicit.
- Minimize your use of variants.
- Use the tightest scoping possible.
- Use assertions.

When bug avoidance fails, make sure you use a systematic and structured approach to bug removal:

- Reproduce the bug.
- Debug data, not code.
- Confirm your diagnosis before you try to fix it.
- Change code only with a reason.
- Make only one change at a time.

The temptation is always present to attempt a quick-and-dirty fix rather than plod along with the systematic approach. Don't let yourself fall prey to this temptation. It usually wastes much more time than it saves, muddying the waters before it forces you back to the approach outlined in this chapter.

By using these techniques, you can create code that will stand up to the beating your users will give it. If your code does fail, you can quickly locate the problem and resolve it with minimum effort.

CHAPTER

FIFTEEN

15

Application Optimization

- Making your applications run more quickly
- Understanding how the Jet engine optimizes queries
- Understanding and optimizing VBA's module loading
- Timing and comparing methods for solving a problem

As with any large Windows development environment, you can make choices when writing your own Access applications that will affect the performance of your application. How you create your queries, how you organize your tables, and how you write VBA code can all affect your application's speed. This chapter presents a number of issues you need to consider when optimizing your applications.

Tuning Your Application's Performance

The faster your application performs, the more usable it will be. No user (or developer) likes a slow application. Getting extra performance, however, sometimes requires that you make trade-offs, and it may affect other aspects of the application's usability, stability, and maintainability. It's important to keep these other issues in mind as you tune your applications for speed.

Some of the many aspects of performance tuning are outlined here:

- Hardware and memory
- Access configuration
- Database design
- Query design
- Forms design
- Reports design
- Single-user versus multiuser, file-server versus client-server application design
- VBA coding

To create applications that perform well, you will have to address many, if not all, of these areas. Depending on the design of your application, some issues will be less important than others. For example, an application that has only one or two simple reports may not need much attention paid to this component. On the other hand, the same application may need a lot of attention in the areas of query and form tuning.

NOTE

Although we've provided some limited multiuser and client-server performance tips in this chapter, look in *Access 2000 Developer's Handbook, Volume II* for additional performance suggestions specific to those areas. In this chapter, as in this entire book, we've focused on issues involved in using the Jet database engine.

Hardware and Windows Issues

Like most Windows-based programs, Access runs more quickly on a faster machine. Microsoft recommends, at a minimum, a fast Pentium-based PC with 32MB of RAM. This is really the *barest* of minimums, and you and your users will likely be dissatisfied with workstations of this nature. More realistically, the target machine should have

- A reasonably fast (166MHz or higher) Pentium-based processor
- 32MB or more of RAM (64MB is always preferable, especially on Windows NT systems)

If you have to decide whether to get more RAM or a faster processor, we suggest you choose more RAM. For example, a 266MHz Pentium PC with 64MB of RAM may execute your applications more quickly than a 400MHz Pentium with 32MB of RAM.

For all installations you should also consider the following:

- Eliminate the loading of unused drivers and services you rarely use or don't need.
- Remove screen savers, background pictures, and other unnecessary cycle-stealers.
- Eliminate disk-compression software, or at least consider placing your databases on uncompressed partitions. Access databases perform significantly more slowly on compressed partitions. Hard disk prices have fallen dramatically in the last few years; it may be time to buy an additional hard disk drive.
- Clean out your Recycle Bin regularly.
- Use a defrag utility regularly on your hard disks.

Understanding How the Jet Query Engine Works

One of the potentially biggest bottlenecks in your Access applications is query execution. Anytime your application creates a recordset, whether it is by executing a query, opening a form, printing a report, or opening a recordset in code, you are running queries.

The Jet query engine is responsible for the interpretation and execution of queries. Before you can optimize your queries, you need to understand how the Jet query engine works. Jet processes queries in four steps:

1. Definition
2. Compilation
3. Optimization
4. Execution

Query Definition

You can define queries using one of several mechanisms: QBE, SQL, or DAO/ADO. Whichever method you use to create the query definition, the query eventually gets converted to SQL, and it is passed to the Jet query optimizer, which then compiles and optimizes the query.

Query Compilation

Before Jet can optimize a query, it must parse the SQL statement that defines the query and bind the names referenced in the query to columns in the underlying tables. The Jet query engine compiles the SQL string into an internal query object definition format, replacing common parts of the query string with tokens. The internal format can be likened to an inverted tree: the query's result set sits at the top of the tree (the tree's root) and the base tables are at the bottom (the leaves).

Query definitions are parsed into distinct elements when compiled. These elements include the

- Base tables
- Output columns (the fields that will appear in the query's result set)

- Restrictions (in QBE, the criteria; in SQL, WHERE clause elements)
- Join columns (in QBE, the lines connecting two tables; in SQL, the fields in the JOIN clause)
- Sort columns (in QBE, sort fields; in SQL, the fields in the ORDER BY clause)

Each of these elements comes into play as the query optimizer considers different execution strategies, as described in the following sections.

Query Optimization

The query optimizer is the most complex component of Jet. It's responsible for choosing the optimum query execution strategy for the compiled query tree. The Jet query engine uses a cost-based algorithm, costing and comparing each potential execution strategy and choosing the one that's fastest. Jet calculates the cost for two major operations in the execution of queries: base table accesses and joins.

Base Table Access Plans

For each table in the query, the Jet query optimizer must choose a base table access plan. The three ways of accessing the rows in a table are

Table scan Scanning a table record by record without use of an index. This may be necessary if a restriction column is not indexed or if the restriction is not very selective (e.g., a large percentage of the base table rows are being requested). Each data page is read only once for a table scan.

Index range Reading records in a table using an index over one of the single-table restrictions (query criteria). A data page may be read more than once for an index range.

Rushmore restriction A Rushmore restriction is used when there are restrictions on multiple indexed columns. By using multiple indexes, Jet is able to considerably reduce the number of data pages it needs to read. In many cases, Jet can execute Rushmore queries without reading any data pages. (Of course, Jet still has to read index pages, but reading only index pages is almost always more efficient.)

Rushmore Query Optimizations

Jet 4 includes support for Rushmore query optimizations. In Jet 1.*x*, Jet could use only one index for a base table access. Using techniques borrowed from FoxPro, all versions of Jet since 2 have been able to use more than one index to restrict records. Rushmore-based query optimization is used on queries involving restrictions on multiple indexed columns of the following types:

Index Intersection The two indexes are intersected with And. Used on restrictions of the form

WHERE Company = 'Ford' And CarType = 'Sedan'

Index Union The two indexes are unioned with Or. Used on restrictions of the form

WHERE CarType = 'Wagon' Or Year = '1997'

Index Counts Queries that return record counts only (with or without restrictions). Used for queries of the form

SELECT Count(*) FROM Autos

You can execute many queries much more quickly using the Rushmore query optimizer than you can with the other methods. Rushmore can't work, however, if you don't build multiple indexes for each table. It also doesn't come into play for those queries that don't contain index intersections, index unions, or index counts.

Join Strategies

For queries involving more than one table, the optimizer must consider the cost of joins, choosing from the following five types of joins:

- Nested iteration join
- Index join
- Lookup join
- Merge join
- Index-merge join

The Jet query optimizer uses statistics about the tables (discussed in the next section) to determine which join strategy to use. Each possible join combination is considered to determine which will yield the least costly query execution plan. The five join strategies are contrasted in Table 15.1.

TABLE 15.1: Jet Query Join Strategies

Join Strategy	Description	When Used
Nested iteration join	"Brute-force" iteration through the rows in both tables.	Only as a last-ditch effort. May be used when there are few records or no indexes.
Index join	Scans rows in the first table and looks up matching rows in the second table using an index.	When the rows in the second table are small (or no data needs to be retrieved from this table) or when the rows in the first table are small or highly restrictive.
Lookup join	Similar to the index join except that a projection and sort on the second table are done prior to the join.	When rows in the second table are small but not indexed by the join column.
Merge join	Sorts rows in the two tables by the join columns and combines the two tables by scanning down both tables simultaneously.	When the two tables are large and the result set needs to be ordered on the join column.
Index-merge join	Similar to a merge join, except that indexes are used to order the two tables.	Instead of a merge join when each input is a table in native Jet database format. Each input must have an index over its join column, and at least one of the indexes must not allow nulls if there is more than one join column.

Query Statistics

When evaluating various base table access plans and join strategies, the Jet query optimizer looks at the following statistics for each base table:

- Number of records in the base table.
- Number of data pages occupied by the base table. The more data pages that need to be read, the more costly the query.

- Location of the table. Is the table in a local ISAM format or is it from an ODBC database?
- Indexes on the table. When looking at indexes, the optimizer is concerned with

  Selectivity How "unique" is the index? Does the index allow for duplicates? A unique index is the most highly selective index because every value is distinct.

  Number of index pages As with data pages, the more index pages, the more costly the query.

  Whether nulls are allowed in the index Nulls in an index may rule out the usage of an index-merge join.

Putting It All Together

In determining the optimum query execution plan, the Jet query optimizer iterates through the various combinations of base table access plans and join strategies. Before choosing a join strategy, the optimizer selects a base table access plan. The optimizer then stores the estimated number of records returned and a cost indicating how expensive it would be to read the table using that plan. Next, the optimizer generates all combinations of pairs of tables and costs of each join strategy. Finally, the optimizer adds tables to the joins and continues to calculate statistics until it finds the cheapest overall execution plan.

The query optimizer also considers the type of result set when costing various join strategies. When returning a keyset-type recordset (also called a *dynaset*), Jet often favors join strategies that are efficient at returning the first page of records quickly, even if the chosen execution strategy is slower at returning the complete result set. For keyset-type recordsets, this tends to rule out joins that require sorting, such as lookup and merge joins.

For queries based on many tables, the time spent estimating the cost of all potential join combinations could easily exceed the time spent executing any given execution strategy. Because of this, the query optimizer reduces the potential number of joins it needs to consider by using the following rule: Consider joining only the results of a join to a base table. The query optimizer will never consider joining the results of one join to the results of another. This considerably reduces the potential number of joins Jet needs to look at.

After a query has been compiled and optimized by the Jet query optimizer, two additional steps are taken prior to the execution of the query.

For queries involving external data sources, the remote post-processor determines how much of a query can be sent to the back end for processing by the database server application. The goal here is to send as much of the query as possible to the server, taking advantage of the server's abilities in executing queries involving server tables. This reduces the number of records that need to be sent across the network. The remote post-processor identifies those parts of the query tree that can be satisfied by server queries and generates the server SQL strings for each remote query.

Finally, the post-processor takes the compiled query tree and moves it to a new, cleaner, and smaller execution segment. This is the final step prior to query execution.

Query Execution

Once the optimizer has determined the optimum query execution plan, the query engine runs through the final query tree and executes each step to return the recordset.

You can direct Jet to create either a keyset or a static or snapshot type of recordset. When Jet runs a keyset-based query, it creates a set of unique key values called a *keyset* in memory that points back to the rows in the underlying tables. This keyset-driven cursor model is very efficient because Jet needs to read only these key values and store them in memory (overflowing to disk if necessary). The values of the other columns in the keyset aren't read until needed (such as when a user scrolls the datasheet to that screen of keyset rows), minimizing the time needed to execute the query.

For snapshot-based queries, Jet must run the query to completion and extract all the query's columns into the snapshot. When the query contains many columns, it's likely that Jet won't be able to fit the entire snapshot into memory, requiring Jet to overflow the result set to disk, substantially slowing the query. Since Jet reads only the key values of keysets into memory, the same keyset-based query might fit entirely in memory, resulting in a significant performance boost. On the other hand, queries with a small number of columns and rows will likely execute more quickly as snapshots.

Forcing Jet to Recompile and Optimize a Query

Queries are compiled and optimized the first time you run the query. They are not recompiled until you resave and rerun the query. Make sure you run all queries at least once before delivering an application to users. This will eliminate subsequent compilations. Save the query in Design view and then run it without saving it again. You shouldn't save the query *after* running it or it may be saved in an uncompiled state.

Because Jet makes optimization decisions based on the size of source tables and the presence of indexes when you compiled the query, it's a good idea to force Jet to recompile a query after you've altered indexes or significantly changed the schema or number of rows in the tables. You can force recompilation by opening the query in design mode, saving it, and then reexecuting it.

TIP

You may find that simply opening the query in design mode and then saving doesn't reoptimize a query. To be completely sure, you can open the SQL view of the query, modify the SQL (add and then remove a space, for example), and then save the changes.

Taking Advantage of Rushmore

Rushmore is a technology provided by Jet that improves performance by creating bitmaps of index values so that index lookups with multiple fields involved can be extremely fast. There is no way to turn Rushmore on or off. Jet takes advantage of Rushmore optimizations anytime you have criteria that reference multiple indexed columns from the same table. If you have queries that *don't* include multiple restrictions or that contain restrictions on columns for which you haven't created indexes, Rushmore won't be used. Thus, it's important to create indexes on all columns that are used in query restrictions.

Rushmore works for both native and attached Access tables, as well as for attached dBASE tables. Queries involving ODBC, Btrieve, Paradox, or other ISAM tables do not benefit from Rushmore.

Keeping Statistics Accurate

The costing algorithms the query optimizer uses are dependent on the accuracy of the statistics provided by the underlying engine. Statistics for non-native tables will, in general, be less accurate than for native Access tables. For native Access tables, statistics may be inaccurate if many transactions are rolled back. Statistics can also be wrong if Jet (or the database application calling Jet) terminates abnormally without being able to update statistics to disk.

TIP

To force Jet to update the statistics in a Jet database, you should regularly compact the database. Compacting the database may also speed up queries because it forces Jet to write all the data in a table to contiguous pages. This makes scanning sequential pages much faster than when the database is fragmented. Before compacting a database, it's a good idea to also run a disk defrag utility so that Jet can store the newly compacted database in contiguous space on disk.

Configuring the Jet Engine

The Jet 4 engine is an advanced desktop database engine that automatically optimizes many data access operations without user intervention. There are, however, several exposed Jet engine Registry settings you can adjust to help tune Jet for your unique situation. Make any changes to these settings with care because a change to one of the settings may have the exact opposite of your intended effect—that is, it may actually slow down the application. In addition, any change may have side effects that negatively impact concurrency or application robustness.

The Jet 4 Registry settings are summarized in Table 15.2. You can alter the Jet Registry settings in four ways:

- Use RegEdit to directly edit the default Registry settings
- Create a user profile with Registry settings that override the default settings and start Access using the /profile command-line option
- Use the SetOption method of the DAO DBEngine object from your application to temporarily override the default or application Registry settings
- Use a Jet engine-specific property of the ADO Connection object to temporarily override the default or application Registry settings

TABLE 15.2: Jet Engine Registry Settings

Key	Description	Default Value	Key Location	DAO SetOption Constant	ADO Connection property
SystemDB	Path and file name of the security work-group file.	*access_path* \system.mdw	Engines folder*	N/A	Jet OLEDB: System Database
CompactByPKey	If set to 1, Jet reorders records in primary key order during a compact operation; if set to 0, Jet places records in natural order (the order in which the records were originally entered).	1	Engines folder*	N/A	N/A
PrevFormat-CompactWith-UNICODE-Compression	If set to 1, when compacting previous versions of databases to Jet 4, Jet enables the compression attribute on all appropriate string columns. When set to 0, Jet won't set the compression attribute.	1	Engines folder*	N/A	N/A
PageTimeout	Length of time in milliseconds a nonread-locked page is held in the cache before being refreshed.	5000	Jet 4.0 folder**	dbPageTimeout	Jet OLEDB: Page Timeout
UserCommitSync	If set to Yes, the system waits for explicit record write operations to complete before continuing processing; if set to No, Jet operates asynchronously when committing explicit transactions.	Yes	Jet 4.0 folder**	dbUser-CommitSync	Jet OLEDB:User Commit Sync
ImplicitCommitSync	If set to Yes, the system waits for implicit record write operations to complete before continuing processing; if set to No, Jet operates asynchronously when committing implicit transactions***.	No	Jet 4.0 folder**	dbImplicit-CommitSync	Jet OLEDB: Implicit Commit Sync

Continued on next page

TABLE 15.2 CONTINUED: Jet Engine Registry Settings

Key	Description	Default Value	Key Location	DAO SetOption Constant	ADO Connection property
SharedAsyncDelay	Time in milliseconds that Jet waits before committing implicit transactions*** in a shared environment.	0	Jet 4.0 folder**	dbShared-AsyncDelay	Jet OLEDB: Shared Async Delay
ExclusiveAsyncDelay	Time in milliseconds that Jet waits before committing implicit transactions*** when the database is opened exclusively.	2000	Jet 4.0 folder**	dbExclusive-AsyncDelay	Jet OLEDB: Exclusive Async Delay
FlushTransactionTimeout	If nonzero, the number of milliseconds before starting asynchronous writes (if no pages have been added to the cache); a nonzero value disables the ExclusiveAsyncDelay and SharedAsyncDelay settings.	500	Jet 4.0 folder**	dbFlush-Transaction-Timeout	Jet OLEDB:Flush Transaction Timeout
MaxBufferSize	Size of Jet's cache in kilobytes; must be 512 or greater.	((*total available RAM*–12MB) / 4)+ 512KB	Jet 4.0 folder**	dbMax-BufferSize	Jet OLEDB:Max Buffer Size
MaxLocksPerFile	Maximum number of locks requested for a single transaction; if the number of locks exceeds MaxLocksPerFile, the transaction is split and committed partially. This setting prevents problems that can occur with Novell NetWare 3.1 servers.	9500	Jet 4.0 folder**	dbMaxLocks-PerFile	Jet OLEDB:Max Locks Per File
LockDelay	Delay in milliseconds that Jet waits before retrying lock requests.	100	Jet 4.0 folder**	dbLockDelay	Jet OLEDB:Lock Delay
LockRetry	Number of times to repeatedly attempt to lock a page.	20	Jet 4.0 folder**	dbLockRetry	Jet OLEDB:Lock Retry

Continued on next page

TABLE 15.2 CONTINUED: Jet Engine Registry Settings

Key	Description	Default Value	Key Location	DAO SetOption Constant	ADO Connection property
PagesLockedToTableLock	Number of concurrent page locks after which Jet locks the entire table. If set to 50 on the 51st page lock, Jet attempts to lock the entire table. If unsuccessful, Jet attempts again on the 101st page lock.	0	Jet 4.0 folder**	N/A	N/A
RecycleLVs	When set to 1, Jet will recycle long value (memo, OLE, and binary) pages.	0 (disabled)	Jet 4.0 folder**	dbRecycleLVs	Jet OLEDB: Recycle Long-Valued Pages
Threads	Number of background threads Jet uses.	3	Jet 4.0 folder**	N/A	N/A

*The Engines folder is located at the \HKEY_LOCAL_MACHINE\Software\Microsoft\Jet\4.0\Engines key in the Registry.

**The Jet 4.0 folder is located at the \HKEY_LOCAL_MACHINE\Software\Microsoft\Jet\4.0\Engines\Jet 4.0 key in the Registry.

***See Chapter 2 in *Access 2000 Developer's Handbook, Volume II* for a discussion of transactions.

See the User Profiles online help topic for more details on creating and using user profiles.

Using the DAO SetOption Method

You can use the DAO SetOption method to fine-tune performance on an application basis or even within the context of an application. For example, to improve performance for a batch of updates, you might lengthen the SharedAsyncDelay setting to one second using the following:

```
DBEngine.SetOption dbSharedAsyncDelay, 1000
```

There is no corresponding GetOption method.

Using the ADO Jet Engine-Specific Connection Properties

Like the DAO SetOption method, you can use one of the Jet engine-specific Connection properties to fine-tune the performance of an application if you're using ADO. For example, here's the equivalent ADO code to lengthen the SharedAsyncDelay setting to one second:

```
Dim cnn As ADODB.Connection
Set cnn = CurrentProject.Connection
cnn.Properties("Jet OLEDB:Shared Async Delay") = 1000
```

You can read, as well as write, the Jet engine-specific Connection properties; however, the values are not accurate until you first set the properties.

For example, if you execute the following code prior to setting the value of the Jet OLEDB:Shared Async Delay property, Access writes a value of zero to the Immediate window even though the Jet 4 default is a value of 500:

```
Dim cnn As ADODB.Connection
Set cnn = CurrentProject.Connection
Debug.Print cnn.Properties("Jet OLEDB:Shared Async Delay")
```

Not all Registry keys are settable using DAO or ADO. Those keys that can be set have constants listed in Table 15.2. Any settings are in effect until you change them or close DBEngine or the Connection object. In other words, these are temporary settings that affect only for the current session; they are not written to the Registry.

Microsoft's Unsupported Jet Optimization Tools

Microsoft introduced two (officially) undocumented and unsupported Jet optimization tools in Access 95 that are still available but still unsupported:

- The ShowPlan option
- The ISAMStats method

Both these tools are part of Jet itself; you don't need any additional DLLs or other programs to make them work.

The ShowPlan Option

Jet includes an undocumented Registry setting you can use to turn on the logging of query optimization plan information to a text file. To enable this option, you must create the following Registry key using the RegEdit program:

```
HKEY_LOCAL_MACHINE\SOFTWARE\Microsoft\Jet\4.0\Engines\Debug
```

Add the JETSHOWPLAN string value to this key and set it equal to "ON". (The JETSHOWPLAN string is case sensitive; be sure to enter it exactly as it appears here.) When you restart Access and open a database, Jet begins to log query optimization plan information to the file SHOWPLAN.OUT, in the current folder. (Jet only writes information to the SHOWPLAN.OUT file as it creates the query plan. You may need to open a query in Design view, modify it, and save the query, in order to force Jet to recreate the plan for the query.) Figure 15.1 shows the Registry after you've successfully added the appropriate Registry key and value.

FIGURE 15.1:

Add the Debug key and JETSHOWPLAN string value to enable the show plan option.

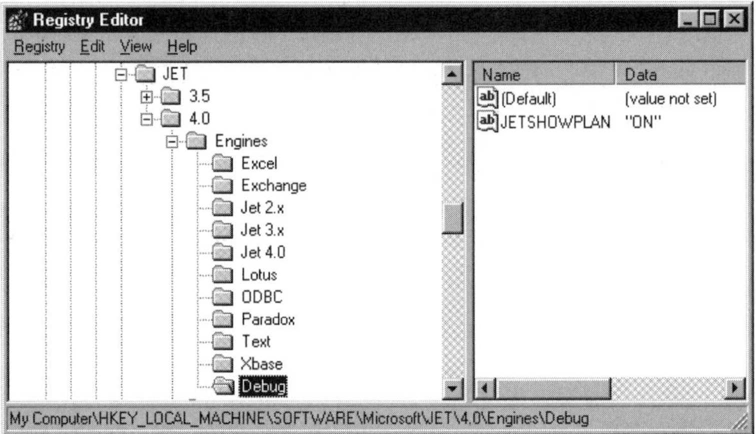

TIP

If you're leery of modifying the Registry yourself, you can simply double-click ShowPlanOn.reg, which is provided on the book's CD. This file adds the appropriate key and value to the Registry for you. To turn off the ShowPlan option, double-click the ShowPlanOff.reg file. This will change the "ON" to "OFF" in the Registry. If you want to remove the Registry key, you'll need to do that manually.

A sampling of a ShowPlan log is shown here:

```
--- qtotEmployeeDinnerSales ---

- Inputs to Query -
Table 'tblMenu'
Table 'tblEmployee'
    Using index 'PrimaryKey'
    Having Indexes:
    PrimaryKey 7 entries, 1 page, 7 values
      which has 1 column, fixed, unique, primary-key, no-nulls
Table 'tblOrder'
    Using index 'PrimaryKey'
    Having Indexes:
    PrimaryKey 171 entries, 1 page, 171 values
      which has 1 column, fixed, unique, clustered and/or counter, _
primary-key, no-nulls
    OrderTakerId 171 entries, 1 page, 7 values
      which has 1 column, fixed
    CustomerId 171 entries, 1 page, 11 values
      which has 1 column, fixed
Table 'tblOrderDetails'
    Using index 'MenuId'
    Having Indexes:
    MenuId 465 entries, 1 page, 18 values
      which has 1 column, fixed
- End inputs to Query -

01) Restrict rows of table tblMenu
      by scanning
      testing expression "Unit="Dinner""
02) Inner Join result of '01)' to table 'tblOrderDetails'
      using index 'tblOrderDetails!MenuId'
      join expression "[tblMenu].[MenuId]=[tblOrderDetails].[MenuId]"
03) Inner Join result of '02)' to table 'tblOrder'
      using index 'tblOrder!PrimaryKey'
      join expression "[tblOrderDetails].[OrderId]=[tblOrder].[OrderId]"
04) Inner Join result of '03)' to table 'tblEmployee'
      using index 'tblEmployee!PrimaryKey'
      join expression "[tblOrder].[OrderTakerId]=[tblEmployee].[EmployeeId]"
05) Group result of '04)'
```

You'll likely find the earlier discussion of Jet query optimization helpful in interpreting the ShowPlan results. Examining the ShowPlan log for poorly performing queries may help you in determining how best to optimize these queries.

ShowPlan is completely undocumented and unsupported by Microsoft and should be treated like any other unsupported feature: with care. Here are some of the issues to consider when using it:

- If you close a database and open another database without exiting and restarting Access, the query plans for the new database will not be logged.
- The plans for some queries Access uses internally will appear in the log.
- The logging of plan information may adversely affect performance.
- The log file may get very large. You'll need to empty it out every so often.
- ShowPlan doesn't log the plan information for parameter queries or subqueries and may incorrectly log the information for other queries.

To stop the logging of ShowPlan information, set the JETSHOWPLAN Registry key to "OFF". (You can also double-click the ShowPlanOff.reg file, as discussed in a previous tip.)

The ISAMStats Method

Jet 4 includes an undocumented technique that you can use to return a variety of pieces of information relating to disk reads and writes. If you're using DAO, you can use the ISAMStats method of the DBEngine object. If you're using ADO, you'll need to create a recordset by calling the OpenSchema method of a Connection.

The ISAMStats method is useful when you use it to compare two possible ways of doing something. For example, if you wished to determine which of two different ways of creating a query was faster, you could use ISAMStats to determine the number of disk reads performed by each version of the query. Of course, you could always just time each query; using ISAMStats, however, may enable you to detect smaller differences that may not show up in timing comparisons. Why would you care about differences that won't show up in timing tests? You may wish to perform tests using a small subset of data or using a fast development machine that you'd like to project to larger recordsets or slower target machines.

Using the ISAMStats DAO method (and its corresponding technique when working with ADO), you can retrieve information on six important statistics:

- Disk reads
- Disk writes
- Reads from cache
- Reads from read-ahead cache
- Locks placed
- Locks released

Working with ISAMStats

To make it simpler for you to retrieve the various ISAMStats values, we've provided an enumerated type (IsamStats) and a user-defined type (IsamStatsType) in basISAMStats:

```
Public Enum IsamStats
    isReads = 0
    isWrites = 1
    isCacheReads = 2
    isReadAheadReads = 3
    isLocksPlaced = 4
    isLocksReleased = 5
End Enum

Public Type IsamStatsType
    Reads As Long
    Writes As Long
    CacheReads As Long
    ReadAheadReads As Long
    LocksPlaced As Long
    LocksReleased As Long
End Type
```

You can use the IsamStats enum with the DAO ISAMStats method to retrieve the particular item you're interested in. (See the section "Using DAO" that follows.) You can also use it with ADO to retrieve the particular field within the ISAMStats recordset you need. (See the section "Using ADO" that follows.)

Using DAO

The basic syntax for the ISAMStats method is as follows:

lngReturn = DBEngine.ISAMStats(*option*, [*reset*])

where *option* is a Long integer representing one of the options from Table 15.3 and *reset* is an optional Boolean value that, when set to True, tells Jet to reset the counter for this particular option.

TABLE 15.3: ISAMStats Options

Value	IsamStats Enum Value	Option
0	isReads	Disk reads
1	isWrites	Disk writes
2	isCacheReads	Reads from cache
3	isReadAheadReads	Reads from read-ahead cache
4	isLocksPlaced	Locks placed
5	isLocksReleased	Locks released

Each of the ISAMStats method options maintains a separate meter that counts the number of times that statistic occurred. The meter is reset back to zero whenever you use the reset option. To make use of ISAMStats, you need to call the method twice: once to get a baseline statistic and once to get a final statistic after running some operation. You determine the actual value of the statistic by then subtracting the baseline statistic from the final statistic. (You can alternatively reset each statistic before you measure it. Either way, you'll need to make two calls to the ISAMStats method for each option you want to measure.) For example, if you wanted to determine the number of disk reads Jet made while executing the qtotEmployeeDinnerSales query, you might use code like this:

```
Public Sub CountReads()

    ' Demonstrate the ISAMStats method,
    ' determining the number of reads involved
    ' in running the qtotEmployeeDinnerSales
    ' query.
```

```
    Dim db As DAO.Database
    Dim rst As DAO.Recordset

    Set db = CurrentDb()

    Call DAO.DBEngine.IsamStats(isReads, True)
    Set rst = db.OpenRecordset( _
     "qtotEmployeeDinnerSales", dbOpenSnapshot)
    Debug.Print "Total reads: " & _
     DAO.DBEngine.IsamStats(isReads)
End Sub
```

NOTE

The previous example resets the ISAMStats "meter" before running the query. You could, instead, retrieve the current setting before and after running the query. In that case, you would need to subtract the before and after values in order to calculate the total disk reads. You might use this technique if you wanted to accumulate all disk reads for a set of queries.

We've also included a simple function, adhGetAllDAOIsamStats (from basISAMStats), which uses the ISAMStats method to retrieve all the statistics at once. This function, shown in Listing 15.1, returns an IsamStatsType data type, with all of its members filled in. You pass in the name of a query or SQL string to execute, and, optionally, a QueryAction value (qaReturnRows or qaExecute) indicating whether the code should attempt to open a recordset or execute the query. The function fills in the IsamStatsType variable and returns it as the function's return value. Listing 15.2 shows a simple test procedure, demonstrating the use of adhGetAllDAOIsamStats. (This procedure also demonstrates the use of the parallel adhGetAllADOIsamStats function.)

Listing 15.1

```
Public Function adhGetAllDAOIsamStats( _
 strQuery As String, _
 Optional qa As QueryAction = qaReturnRows) As IsamStatsType

    Dim lngStat As Long
    Dim db As DAO.Database
    Dim rst As DAO.Recordset
    Dim ist As IsamStatsType
```

```
    Set db = CurrentDb()

    Call DAO.DBEngine.IsamStats(isReads, True)
    Call DAO.DBEngine.IsamStats(isWrites, True)
    Call DAO.DBEngine.IsamStats(isCacheReads, True)
    Call DAO.DBEngine.IsamStats(isReadAheadReads, True)
    Call DAO.DBEngine.IsamStats(isLocksPlaced, True)
    Call DAO.DBEngine.IsamStats(isLocksReleased, True)

    If qa = qaReturnRows Then
        Set rst = db.OpenRecordset(strQuery, dbOpenSnapshot)
    Else
        db.Execute strQuery
    End If

    ist.Reads = DAO.DBEngine.IsamStats(isReads)
    ist.Writes = DAO.DBEngine.IsamStats(isWrites)
    ist.CacheReads = DAO.DBEngine.IsamStats(isCacheReads)
    ist.ReadAheadReads = DAO.DBEngine.IsamStats(isReadAheadReads)
    ist.LocksPlaced = DAO.DBEngine.IsamStats(isLocksPlaced)
    ist.LocksReleased = DAO.DBEngine.IsamStats(isLocksReleased)

    adhGetAllDAOIsamStats = ist
End Function
```

Listing 15.2

```
Public Sub DemoISAMStats()
    Dim ist As IsamStatsType

    ist = adhGetAllDAOIsamStats("qtotEmployeeDinnerSales")
    Debug.Print "qtotEmployeeDinnerSales (DAO)"
    Call ShowInfo(ist)

    ist = adhGetAllDAOIsamStats("qupdIncrementPrice", qaExecute)
    Debug.Print "qupdIncrementPrice (DAO)"
    Call ShowInfo(ist)

    ist = adhGetAllADOIsamStats("qtotEmployeeDinnerSales")
    Debug.Print "qtotEmployeeDinnerSales (ADO)"
    Call ShowInfo(ist)
```

```
    ist = adhGetAllADOIsamStats("qupdIncrementPrice", qaExecute)
    Debug.Print "qupdIncrementPrice (ADO)"
    Call ShowInfo(ist)
End Sub

Private Sub ShowInfo(ist As IsamStatsType)
    Debug.Print "============================="
    Debug.Print "Reads          : " & ist.Reads
    Debug.Print "Writes         : " & ist.Writes
    Debug.Print "CacheReads     : " & ist.CacheReads
    Debug.Print "ReadAheadReads: " & ist.ReadAheadReads
    Debug.Print "LocksPlaced    : " & ist.LocksPlaced
    Debug.Print "LocksReleased : " & ist.LocksReleased
    Debug.Print "============================="
End Sub
```

Using ADO

Because ADO doesn't natively support the ISAMStats method, the Jet OLE DB provider exposes this functionality in a slightly different manner. To retrieve the ISAMStats information using ADO, you must create a special recordset based on the current connection. To do this, use the OpenSchema method of the connection, indicating that you'd like a provider-specific set of information. The OpenSchema method normally requires you to specify which schema you're interested in (tables in a database, fields within a table, and so on) by specifying a constant value. Because the Jet OLE DB provider has made ISAMStats information available "under the covers"—that is, OLE DB knows nothing of this—you must specify a "magic number" (a GUID) rather than a constant value. The OpenSchema method returns a recordset filled with the information you need.

Before you can create the recordset containing the ISAMStats information, however, you'll need to reset all the information. When using DAO, you must reset each statistic individually. Using ADO, you can only reset all the statistics at once. To do that, you set a specific property of the Connection object, like this:

```
Dim cnn As ADODB.Connection
Set cnn = CurrentProject.Connection

' Reset the statistics.
cnn.Properties("Jet OLEDB:Reset ISAM Stats") = 1
```

After you've reset the statistics, you can execute a query to refill the various statistics. Once that's done, you'll want to retrieve the various statistics. To do that, call the OpenSchema method of the Connection object, which returns a one-row Recordset object filled in with the statistics in its various fields:

```
Set rst = cnn.OpenSchema( _
 Schema:=adSchemaProviderSpecific, _
 SchemaID:="{8703b612-5d43-11d1-bdbf-00c04fb92675}")
```

Yes, you must pass that long, seemingly random GUID to the OpenSchema method; obviously, you'll be cutting and pasting this code from the sample module (basISAMStats) rather than typing it in by hand. After this method call, the recordset, rst, contains 12 columns (the values contained in most of which are undocumented), the first 6 of which contain the same information that was returned by the ISAMStats method in the previous section. You might write code like this to retrieve the six values:

```
ist.Reads = rst.Fields(isReads)
ist.Writes = rst.Fields(isWrites)
ist.CacheReads = rst.Fields(isCacheReads)
ist.ReadAheadReads = rst.Fields(isReadAheadReads)
ist.LocksPlaced = rst.Fields(isLocksPlaced)
ist.LocksReleased = rst.Fields(isLocksReleased)
```

To make it easier for you to retrieve this information using ADO, we've provided the adhGetAllADOIsamStats function (from basISAMStats), shown in Listing 15.3. As with the adhGetAllDAOIsamStats function shown in Listing 15.1, this function does the work of running the query for you, retrieves the ISAMStats information, and returns it in an IsamStatsType data structure.

Listing 15.3

```
Public Function adhGetAllADOIsamStats( _
 strQuery As String, _
 Optional qa As QueryAction = qaReturnRows) As IsamStatsType

    Dim rst As ADODB.Recordset
    Dim cnn As ADODB.Connection
    Dim ist As IsamStatsType

    Set cnn = CurrentProject.Connection

    ' Reset the statistics.
```

```
    cnn.Properties("Jet OLEDB:Reset ISAM Stats") = 1
    If qa = qaReturnRows Then
        Set rst = cnn.Execute(strQuery)
    Else
        cnn.Execute strQuery
    End If
    Set rst = cnn.OpenSchema( _
     Schema:=adSchemaProviderSpecific, _
     SchemaID:="{8703b612-5d43-11d1-bdbf-00c04fb92675}")

    ist.Reads = rst.Fields(isReads)
    ist.Writes = rst.Fields(isWrites)
    ist.CacheReads = rst.Fields(isCacheReads)
    ist.ReadAheadReads = rst.Fields(isReadAheadReads)
    ist.LocksPlaced = rst.Fields(isLocksPlaced)
    ist.LocksReleased = rst.Fields(isLocksReleased)

    Set rst = Nothing
    Set cnn = Nothing

    adhGetAllADOIsamStats = ist
End Function
```

Speeding Up Queries and Recordsets

With Jet's sophisticated query optimizer, you don't need to be concerned about the order of columns and tables in queries. The Jet query optimizer decides on the most efficient query strategy and reorders the query's tables and columns to best optimize the query. You can, however, help the optimizer by following these guidelines:

- Create indexes on all columns used in ad hoc query joins (Jet already creates indexes for enforced relationships, so there's no need to create additional indexes for these types of joins), restrictions, and sorts.
- Use primary keys instead of unique indexes whenever possible. Primary key indexes disallow nulls, giving the Jet query optimizer additional join choices.

- Use unique indexes instead of nonunique indexes whenever possible. Jet can then better optimize queries because statistics on unique indexes are more accurate.
- Include as few columns as possible in the result set. The fewer columns returned, the faster the query, especially if you can completely eliminate columns from a table you had included only in order to restrict returned rows.

WARNING If your query includes more than 50 fields or so, you'll see an impact on the speed of running the query. (When using ADO—and therefore, OLE DB—this warning is even more important.) Always limit your queries to the smallest number of fields possible—ADO retrieves all the properties of each field you include in the output of your query (DAO/Jet only retrieves the properties that you specifically access), and this can cause a performance hit.

- Refrain from using expressions, such as those involving the IIf function, in queries. If you are using nested queries (queries based on the results of other queries), try to move up any expressions to the highest (last) query.

WARNING Using expressions in queries may be detrimental to the speed of your queries. Because Jet cannot use an index in any way with a calculated column, you may be causing sequential scans of your data by including an expression in a query. If possible, move these expressions to a form or report where you want to display the information. One more thing to consider: even if a row is excluded from output because of a restriction you've placed on the query, all expressions for that row are still evaluated. This means that if you have a table containing 1000 rows and you've only requested one row back, if your query includes an expression and you're filtering based on that expression, Jet must calculate that expression for all 1000 rows.

- Use Count(*) instead of Count([*column*]). Jet has built-in optimizations that make Count(*) much faster than column-based counts.
- Use the Between operator in restriction clauses rather than open-ended >, >=, <, and <= restrictions. Using Between returns fewer rows. For example, use "Age Between 35 and 50" rather than "Age >= 35".
- When creating restrictions on join columns that are present in both tables in a one-to-many join, it is sometimes more efficient to place the restriction on the one side of the join. Other times, it might be more efficient to place the restriction on the many side. You'll have to test which is more efficient for

each query, because the ratio of the sizes of the tables and the number and type of restrictions determine which is more efficient.

- Normalize your tables, decomposing large tables into smaller normalized ones. Because this reduces the size of tables (and therefore the number of pages required to hold tables), it causes join strategies that involve table scans to execute more quickly.
- In some instances, it might also help to denormalize databases to reduce the number of joins needed to run frequently used queries. (See Chapter 4 for a discussion of denormalization and additional design details.)
- When you have the option of constructing a query using either a join or a subquery, it's worth trying both options. In some cases, you will find the solution that employs the join to be faster; in other cases, the subquery-based solution may be faster.
- Avoid using outer joins if possible because they require a complete scan of the entire preserved table (that is, the "left" table in a left-outer join).
- For nontrivial queries, use saved queries instead of SQL because these queries will have already been optimized. (Access creates hidden querydefs for SQL statements it finds in RecordSource and RowSource properties of forms and reports, but it won't create querydefs for SQL statements you have embedded in VBA code.)

TIP

Although the general consensus is to use stored queries whenever possible, there are times when temporary queries (based on SQL text you enter manually) can be better. When you use a stored query, Jet stores the query plan the first time you run the query, and this plan never changes until you modify the query. If your query contains parameters that can grossly alter the number of rows to be returned by the query (that is, depending on the parameter, you might get 10 or 10 million rows back), a saved query might not be the best solution. Because Jet must always calculate the execution plan for temporary queries, you may get better performance from a temporary query if it's possible that the number of rows may be different each time you run the query.

- If you create a recordset based on a SQL string using ADO, specify the adOpenDynamic CursorType value if possible. Because Jet doesn't support dynamic cursors (even though the constant name would indicate that it does), Jet handles this specifically, giving the best performance with SQL strings. It seems odd, using a constant supporting a specific cursor type that

Jet can't handle to get the best performance with SQL strings, but that's how this particular constant has been mapped internally.

- When you create an ADO recordset retrieving Jet data, do not specify adUseClient for the recordset's CursorLocation property. (The default is adUseServer, so you would have to specify adUseClient intentionally.) Although it may seem that because Jet isn't a client/server database engine, you should choose adUseClient, this logic is incorrect. If you choose adUseClient for the CursorLocation property, you're asking ADO to create its own cursor, in addition to the one Jet always creates. The time difference between using adUseClient and adUseServer is measurable, so don't fall into this trap unless you have some reason to use adUseClient. (Disconnected and in-memory operations, for example, require a client-side cursor, so you won't be able to avoid using adUseClient.)
- Manually recompile queries when the size of tables or the presence or type of indexes has changed. (See the section "Forcing Jet to Recompile and Optimize a Query" earlier in this chapter.)
- When possible, use action queries instead of looping through recordsets in VBA to update or delete batches of data.
- When you need to use a DAO snapshot recordset (or a static recordset using ADO) and you don't need to move backward in the recordset, use a forward-scrolling snapshot (or a forward-only recordset using ADO). If you're using ADO, this is the default type of recordset you'll create. That is, unless you change properties of the recordset, you'll get a static, forward-only recordset.
- When you only wish to add new rows to a recordset, open the recordset using the dbAppendOnly option.

TIP

ADO doesn't support the dbAppendOnly option, so you'll need to devise some other way to open a recordset for appending only. You might want to open the recordset using a WHERE clause that you know will return no rows (for example, asking for all customers whose CustomerID field is –1).

- When creating queries against client-server sources, consider using pass-through queries. (Pass-through queries, however, may not always be faster than regular queries.)
- When running very large action queries, you may wish to set the UseTransaction property of the query to False, which tells Access not to execute

the action query as a single transaction. (For moderately sized action queries, setting UseTransaction to False may actually slow down the query, so be careful using this property.)

- If you're going to add many single rows using DAO or ADO code, try and open the recordset using dbOpenTable flag (or its ADO equivalent, adCmd-TableDirect). This allows Jet to perform the additions as quickly as possible.

The next few tips deal specifically with indexes and their use in your database design. Although indexes can make an enormous difference in the speed of searching and sorting, they aren't *always* a good thing.

- It's usually faster to update data in a nonindexed column. If you're going to be updating or adding many rows to indexed fields, you may want to drop the indexes, perform your changes, and then re-add the indexes. This will, in general, be faster.
- Unless you're using your data in a read-only manner, don't over-index. You should, of course, index fields that will be used for searching, sorting, or joining, but indexing all the fields (up to the 32-field limit) just because you think "one index is good, 32 must be even better" is not wise. Updates to indexed fields require updating both the field and the index and can add substantial overhead to your updates.
- Don't index columns that contain highly duplicated information. For example, indexing a column containing only three different values will cause searching and sorting on that field to be slower than it would be if you didn't have an index at all.

TIP

In previous versions, Jet always created an index on foreign keys in relationships. In some cases, however, such as when your foreign key value is one of just a few values (a small lookup table, for instance), you don't really want an index. In this case, you'll need to use SQL to create your index (or you can do it when you create the table), and you'll need to include the FOREIGN KEY NO INDEX clause when creating a constraint. See Chapter 5 for more information on creating tables using SQL. (This feature isn't available through the Access user interface; it's only available when creating the table using SQL.)

When in doubt, experiment and benchmark various potential solutions. Don't assume one way to do it is faster just because it *should* be or because someone told you it was.

Speeding Up Forms

Most Access applications revolve around forms, so it goes without saying that any improvements to the performance of forms will realize large gains in the usability of your applications. The following sections detail several areas to consider when optimizing your forms.

Limiting a Form's Record Source with Large Recordsets

It's tempting to create forms in Access that are based on a huge recordset of tens or hundreds of thousands of records. However, you will quickly discover a severe performance penalty when opening such forms or attempting to navigate to a different record using the FindFirst method. The problems are exacerbated when you attempt to use these types of forms in a networked file-server or client-server environment, where forms will be retrieving remote data.

The solution is simple. Rather than giving users *all* the records and navigating around the form's dynaset, set up the form to serve up a single record (or some small subset of records) at a time. Then, instead of using the FindFirst method to move to a different record, change the form's RecordSource property.

Speeding Up Combo Boxes with Many Rows

Combo boxes are a great way to present a small or moderately sized list of items to a user, but you shouldn't use combo boxes to present more than a few thousand items. Consider alternative ways of presenting the same data.

Also, consider reworking the form so that the combo box contains fewer rows. You might use other controls on the form to refine the search and reduce the number of rows in the combo box's row source. For example, have the user enter an employee's territory into a territory control to reduce the number of entries in an EmployeeId combo box.

Although the AutoExpand functionality Access provides for combo boxes is very popular with users, it adds a large amount of overhead. Combo boxes will react to keystrokes more quickly if you turn off this property (see Chapter 7 for more information).

Other Form Speed-Up Tricks

Other things you can do to speed up your forms or reduce their memory usage include the following:

- Instead of opening and closing forms, load often-used forms hidden and make them visible and invisible. This uses up more memory and system resources, so you have to balance this technique against memory considerations.
- Consider using lightweight forms and hyperlinks for switchboard forms.
- Reduce the complexity of forms. Break complex forms into multiple pages or multiple forms or use the native tab control.
- Don't use overlapping controls.
- Place controls containing memo and bound OLE objects on pages of a form other than the first page or on ancillary forms that can be popped up using a command button. This allows users to browse quickly through records when they don't need to view these complex objects.
- If your form contains static pictures stored in unbound object frame controls, convert them to use lightweight image controls instead. To do this, right-click the control and select Change To ➢ Image.
- You may find the Performance Analyzer Add-In (Tools ➢ Analyze ➢ Performance) helpful in locating and correcting performance bottlenecks in your application. Although its usefulness is limited, you may find it highlights problems you never thought of checking.

Speeding Up Reports

If you're creating complex reports, they might take longer to print than you'd expect. One reason for this is that Access creates a separate query for each section of the report. Many of the suggestions found in the section "Speeding Up Queries and Recordsets" earlier in this chapter also apply here because the speed of report output (or the lack thereof) is often more an issue of the underlying queries. In addition, you can try the following suggestions to improve report performance:

- Move query expressions onto the report.
- Avoid situations in which one query pulls the data from tables and a second query just filters the data. The more information you can pull together into one query, the better. One query uses less memory.

- Avoid including fields in the query that aren't used in the final output of the report.
- If you're using subreports, look at the queries on which they're based. Generally, you shouldn't use subreports when their record source is the same as the main report's record source. If the main and subform's record sources are the same, try rethinking your design so you can work without the subreport.
- Add subreports to replace multiple expressions that call domain functions such as DLookup or DSum. By using a subreport, you can often get the same functionality you get with the slower domain functions, without using any expressions. On the other hand, if you need to look up only a single value, using a domain function may be faster.

Optimizing VBA's Use of Modules and Compilation

Instead of being a tokenized, interpreted language, as was Access Basic (used in Access 2), VBA is a compiled language. Although this advancement promises a great deal of power, it can be a problem if you aren't aware of the ramifications of using a compiled language. This discussion, through a series of questions and answers, explains the issues involved with compilation of your VBA code and what you can do to control it.

How Does VBA Load Code?

In Access 2, when you loaded an application, Access loaded all the global modules into memory at startup. Form and report modules were loaded as necessary, but the global modules were always available, having been loaded when the application loaded. This meant that although application load time might be longer, form and report loading could, at worst, cause the form or report module to be loaded. Of course, loading a large module takes time; the code must be loaded from disk and read into memory.

VBA loads code when it's needed, at execution time. Only modules called during the application's startup sequence are loaded as the application loads. That is, only modules that are needed by the startup form (or the macro called at startup) are loaded with the application. Then, as your application calls various procedures, VBA loads the appropriate modules. (In Access 95, loading a module caused VBA to also load any modules containing code or variables used by the module. This "call-tree loading" contributed to Access 95's slow load speed for forms.) Certainly, for applications with large amounts of code, this "load on demand" feature allows faster load times. As Access 95 loads each object, it might also need to load global modules called by procedures in the form or report module. This is not true for Access 97 and later: now, VBA loads only the particular module it needs at any given moment to run your code.

VBA always loads an entire module if it needs any portion of the module or if it must use any procedure in a module. The same goes for a variable in a module: if your code attempts to set or retrieve the value of a Public variable in a module, VBA must load the entire module. This, too, can contribute to application slow-downs if you haven't planned accordingly.

TIP

If you'd like Access to load modules the way Access 95 does (that is, all of them in the call tree at once), you can still force this to happen. All you need do is refer to a single variable in each module, and you'll force VBA to load each module. If you want to preload all your modules, add a Public variable to each and attempt to retrieve the value of each in your application's startup code. That way, you'll cause VBA to load each module you reference at that time. This may seem like a lot of work, but at least in Access 97 and later you have the choice of how to handle this; in Access 95, you had no choice at all.

Why Compile Code?

VBA must compile the code at some point before it can run the code. If the code hasn't been previously compiled, VBA must compile it on-the-fly, as needed. That is, as you open forms or reports with uncompiled code, VBA must compile the form/report module before Access can open the object, and compilation takes time. You can certainly see that this would cause your forms or reports to open more slowly.

What Gets Stored When Your Code Is Compiled?

When VBA compiles your code, it stores both the original text (it doesn't store it exactly as you type it but stores a tokenized version) and the compiled version. When Access prepares to run previously compiled code, it loads just the compiled version into memory and runs that compiled code. For uncompiled code, Access must load the original version into memory and then compile the code as needed.

When Should You Compile?

The Debug ➢ Compile <<Project Name>> menu item opens and compiles every module in your application, including the form and report modules. It performs a complete syntax check as well. This is the quickest way to completely compile your application, and you should perform this action before distributing any application. Unlike previous versions of Access, this menu item both compiles all modules and saves the compiled "bits" for each module.

After using this menu item, Access will now have saved both the original tokenized version and the compiled version. In addition, Access will track internally that all the modules are compiled and won't attempt to recompile anything before running your application. If you don't use this menu item, your modules' compiled state will be lost when you quit Access, and VBA will have to recompile before running the application. (If there have been no new changes to the code since it was last compiled, the Compile <<Project Name>> menu item won't be available.)

How Does the Compile On Demand Option Fit In?

When the VBA Tools ➢ Options ➢ General ➢ Compile On Demand option is checked (and that's the default for the option), VBA compiles only the code it must compile in order to run the current procedure. Although this does speed the development process somewhat (VBA isn't compiling code it doesn't need to compile for the current execution path), it's just delaying the inevitable. Sooner or later you must compile all your code. What's more, unless you understand the ramifications of this option, it can get you into trouble by leading you to believe your code is correct when, in fact, it's not.

To see the Compile On Demand option in action, follow these steps:

1. In the VBA editor, Use the Tools ➢ Options ➢ General menu item to make sure the Compile On Demand option is turned on.
2. Create a new module and enter the following code into it:

```
Function Test1()
    Test1 = Test2()
End Function
```

3. Create a second module and enter the following code (which would normally cause a compilation error because the function Test4 doesn't exist):

```
Function Test2()
    Test2 = 1
End Function
```

```
Function Test3()
    Test3 = Test4()
End Function
```

4. In the Immediate window, type the following, causing VBA to run Test1. (Note that this doesn't trigger a compilation error, even though the code is not correct, because you've turned on Compile On Demand and you didn't demand that Test3 be compiled.)

```
? Test1()
```

5. Go back to the Tools ➢ Options ➢ General dialog and turn off the Compile On Demand option.

6. In the Immediate window, repeat step 4. Note that there's still no error, because you're running code that's already compiled.

7. Modify Test1 so it looks like the code below, and then run it in the Immediate window, as in step 4. Now you'll trigger a compile error because you've turned off Compile On Demand and caused the code to be recompiled.

```
Function Test1()
    Test1 = Test2()
    Debug.Print 1
End Function
```

What Causes Code to Be Decompiled?

Decompilation is the VBA programmer's curse. Compiling code can take time, and it's got to happen sometime between code changes and running the application. If you can save your code in a compiled state, you won't have to pay the compilation price at run time. To avoid decompilation of your code, you must know when it occurs and what causes it.

Access marks your VBA, module by module, as being decompiled anytime you save a change to an object that might affect VBA code: forms, reports, controls, or modules. If you modify a form (or a report) or its controls, modify code in a global or class module, or delete or rename any of these objects, you'll cause Access to tell VBA that the specific object needs recompilation. If you make a change but don't save it, you'll preserve the compiled state.

If you change an object or its code, in addition to the object that's been changed, VBA must recompile any module or object that refers to the changed object. That is, decompilation travels "upstream," not "downstream." If module A calls code in module B and you change something in module B that's used in module A, module A will need to be recompiled. If you change something in module A, however, module B will retain its compiled state (assuming that nothing in module B calls code in module A).

VBA stores the project name (the VBA project, a value separate from the database name) as part of its compilation status. When you first create your database, Access assigns the database name as the VBA project name, by default. If you change the project name of a compiled application, Access sees it as being decompiled and forces VBA to recompile the entire application next time it's loaded. From within VBA, you can use the Tools ➢ <<Project Name>> Properties dialog box to change the project name.

TIP

Watch out for partial saves. That is, if you modify multiple VBA objects and deselect one or more items when you save the project, VBA automatically decompiles your project. Unless you're aware of this somewhat unexpected behavior, you might ship uncompiled code without knowing about it.

What Are the Effects of Compilation on Memory and Disk Usage?

Compiled applications require more disk space. As mentioned earlier in this chapter, when you compile all the modules, VBA stores both the decompiled and the compiled code in your database. On the other hand, compiled applications require less memory because VBA loads only the compiled code when it runs the application. If you attempt to compile code-on-the-fly, VBA must load the decompiled code and then compile it as it runs.

Are Modules Ever Removed from Memory?

Modules are not removed from memory until you close the application. VBA loads modules into memory as it needs them, and once a module has been loaded, it's never removed from memory. That is, VBA supports dynamic loading of modules but doesn't support dynamic unloading. Don't forget that VBA will load a module if you reference either a procedure or a variable in that module.

During the development process, this dynamic loading of modules can cause memory usage to grow and free RAM to shrink. You may want to close and reopen the database occasionally to release the memory. Using the Debug ➢ Compile <<Project Name>> menu item causes all the modules to be loaded into memory; make sure you close and reopen the database after compiling all the modules.

WARNING In previous versions of Access (we haven't yet confirmed that this happens with Access 2000, but it's worth knowing anyway), the VBA project for large databases could, on occasion, become corrupted. Weird things happen, and it's not clear why things go wrong. If you find VBA behaving oddly, and you're working with a large application, you may want to try the undocumented /DECOMPILE command-line option. To use this, first back up your database. Then, run Access from the command line, opening your database with the /DECOMPILE flag, like this: "MSACCESS YourDatabase.MDB /DECOMPILE". Access will start, load your database, and along the way, discard all the compiled "bits" of your project. Save your database and quit Access. Start Access again, load your database normally, and immediately compile your project. Quit and restart Access. Your database should be clean and ready to run. Please, back up your database before attempting this undocumented procedure.

What Can You Do to Optimize the Use of Modules?

Once you understand how VBA works with modules, you may want to take some extra steps to make your modules work as efficiently as possible. Although it may sound obvious, try to minimize the amount of extraneous code in each module. Because VBA always loads a full module to reference any procedure in that module, the less code it must load, the more quickly your forms and reports will open. Try to move unnecessary procedures from your modules and group procedures, if possible, by their use. Don't forget that referring to a variable in a module will also cause VBA to load that module. The goal is to load as little code as possible at any given moment.

Unlike its behavior in Access 95, VBA in Access 2000 will not decompile your entire application if a user adds a new form or report. Because of the upstream decompilation, you're guaranteed that no existing code relies on the new form or report, and your application will remain compiled. On the other hand, it's certainly possible for an end user to decompile specific modules by changing an existing form or report: if there's a change to an object that has code dependencies, VBA will have to decompile the code that depends on the object. The code will remain decompiled until the next time Access compiles your code, when it will save the compiled state for you.

One More Consideration: No Circular References in Libraries

Because of a design limitation of VBA, Access projects do not support circular references. No matter how you try to obfuscate the path, no procedure can call a procedure in another project that ends up calling a procedure in the original project. Even if you call procedures in other projects along the way, the procedure call will fail if it eventually calls a procedure in the original project. This will most often occur if you write library databases (add-ins, Wizards, and so on). You will need to design your library database in such a way that you don't require circular references. One unfortunate solution is to place duplicate copies of procedures in multiple modules. (See Chapter 18 for more information on using library databases.)

What Else Can You Do?

There's no simple solution to maintaining the compiled state of your applications. You'll need to take special steps, and this will add extra overhead to your development process. The difference between running compiled code and decompiled code is quite obvious, even for moderate-sized applications, so it's worth taking the time to ensure that your applications are compiled when you need them to be.

Once you've tackled the major issues, you'll want to investigate ways to speed up the VBA code itself. The next portion of this chapter investigates some techniques you can use to improve the performance of the code. No such list could be exhaustive, and we've selected a series of tips that we've accumulated over the past few years. Some are old, some are new, but all can make a difference in how you write efficient VBA code.

TIP

Although the conversion of a database to MDE format (using the Tools ➢ Database Utilities ➢ Make MDE File menu item) doesn't cause your code to run any more quickly, it does strip the source code itself from the database. (Don't let anyone convince you that creating an MDE does something magical that normal usage doesn't—the code's compiled the same way it always was. All creating an MDE does is toss out the source code. No more than that.) That way, Access can load the file more quickly, and, because the database uses less memory (because there's no source code loaded), there's more memory available for your application to use. The more memory, the faster the application, so converting a large application to MDE format should afford one more way of speeding its execution. Of course, once you've converted your application to an MDE file, users can never cause the code to be decompiled, so you'll never again need to worry about the application's compiled state. (For more information on using MDE files, see Chapter 18.)

Speeding Up VBA: Testing Hypotheses

As in any programming language, in VBA there are often many ways to accomplish the same task. Because you're dealing not only with a language but also with the interface and the underlying data all tied together in the programming environment, the choices are often even more complicated than with other, more standard languages. The following sections propose a series of selected optimizations, and some tips are more potent than others. Probably no single application will be able to use each of these, but you can add the ones that help to your bag of tricks as you program in VBA. You'll also find a method for timing those optimizations so you can create your own test cases.

Creating a Stopwatch

Although you could use the built-in VBA Timer function to calculate the time a specific process requires, it's not the wisest choice. Because it measures time in seconds since midnight in a single-precision floating-point value, it's not terribly accurate. Even though you'll most likely be timing intervals larger than a single second, you'll want a bit more accuracy than the Timer function can provide. The Windows API provides the timeGetTime function, which returns the number of milliseconds that have passed since Windows was started, and we recommend that you use this function instead.

NOTE

Not that it matters for testing purposes, but Timer "rolls over" every 24 hours. The timeGetTime function keeps on ticking for up to 49 days before it resets the returned tick count to 0. Most likely, if you're timing something that runs for 49 days, you're not terribly interested in milliseconds, but that's what you get.

To test each of the proposed optimizations, you need some mechanism for starting and stopping the clock. We've provided a class, StopWatch, which includes two useful methods: StartTimer and StopTimer. The StartTimer method stores the current return value from timeGetTime into a private module variable, lngStartTime. You must call this method directly before any code you want to have timed. When you're done with the critical section of code, call the StopTimer method, which returns the difference between the current time and the time when you called the

StartTimer method (the elapsed time). Listing 15.4 shows the declarations and code for the timer functions. To use the StopWatch class, you can write code like this:

```
Dim sw As StopWatch
Set sw = New StopWatch
sw.StartTimer
' Execute the code you want to time.
Debug.Print sw.StopTimer
```

TIP

Although there's no reason the code in the StopWatch class must be in a class module, putting it there adds one extra benefit—you can instantiate multiple StopWatch objects and have each StopWatch instance keep track of its own starting time. This allows you to time multiple concurrent events, if you need to do this. We haven't taken advantage of this capability in this test application, however.

Listing 15.4

```
Private Declare Function timeGetTime _
 Lib "winmm.dll" () As Long

Private lngStartTime As Long

Public Sub StartTimer()
    ' Start the timer, storing the value in
    ' the module global, lngStartTime.

    lngStartTime = timeGetTime()
End Sub

Public Function StopTimer() As Long
    ' End timing, and return the difference between the
    ' current time and lngStartTime

    StopTimer = timeGetTime() - lngStartTime
End Function
```

Getting Reasonable Results

You will find that running any given test only once doesn't provide reliable results. There are just too many external forces in play when you're running under Windows. To get a reasonable idea of the benefit of a given optimization test, you need to run the test code many times within the given test case and then run the test case as many times as necessary, averaging the results, until you get consistent results. For simplicity, each of the tests in this chapter takes as its only parameter a Long value indicating the number of times you want to run the test. Each function loops the specified number of times with the clock running and provides the elapsed time as the return value of the function. Listing 15.5 shows the entire RunTests function.

NOTE

In order to get the most consistent results possible, RunTests continues to run the slower test function until the average amount of time taken to run the function reaches a consistent value. To keep things simple, the function performs a very low-tech analysis: it keeps track of the current average and the previous value. When these values get close enough together, the code stops calling the test function. Once RunTests knows how many times it needs to call the function, it simply loops, calling the faster test code the required number of times. In this way, you can get very consistent results without having to guess at the number of times to call the test functions.

Listing 15.5

```
Public Function RunTests( _
 strFunc1 As String, strFunc2 As String, _
 Optional lngRepeatOp As Long = 100000) As Long

    ' Run two tests cases, comparing their relative timings
    '
    ' The assumption is that strFunc1 will be
    ' slower than strFunc2.

    Dim i As Long
    Dim lngResults1 As Long
    Dim lngResults2 As Long
    Dim lngResult As Long
    Dim lngTemp As Long
```

```
Dim dblAvg As Double
Dim dblPrevAvg As Double
Dim lngCount As Long

On Error GoTo HandleErrors

Dim ot As OptimizingTests
Set ot = New OptimizingTests

' Use this loop to both gather information
' about the slow version of the test, and also
' to figure out how many times to loop in
' order to converge on reasonably consistent
' results. Loop until either the difference
' in the average length of each iteration
' differs from the previous iteration by no more
' than adhcMaxDiff, or until you've hit
' adhcMaxIterations loops.
lngCount = 1
lngResults1 = 0
Do
    Call SetStatus("Running " & strFunc1 & " Pass " & lngCount)
    lngTemp = CallByName(ot, strFunc1, VbMethod, (lngRepeatOp))
    lngResults1 = lngResults1 + lngTemp
    dblAvg = lngResults1 / lngCount
    ' If you've reached the correct difference between
    ' iterations, or you've hit 20 iterations,
    ' just exit the loop.
    If (Abs(dblAvg - dblPrevAvg) <= adhcMaxDiff) Or _
     (lngCount >= adhcMaxIterations) Then
        Exit Do
    Else
        ' Store away the current average
        ' for the next iteration, and bump
        ' the counter.
        dblPrevAvg = dblAvg
        lngCount = lngCount + 1
    End If
Loop

' Now that you know how many times to call
```

```
    ' the function, loop through that many iterations
    ' of the faster function.
    lngResults2 = 0
    For i = 1 To lngCount
        Call SetStatus("Running " & strFunc2 & " Pass " & i)
        lngResults2 = lngResults2 + _
         CallByName(ot, strFunc2, VbMethod, (lngRepeatOp))
    Next i

    ' Don't divide by 0!
    If lngResults1 = 0 Then
        lngResult = 0
    Else
        lngResult = Int(lngResults2 / lngResults1 * 100)
    End If

    ' Show results in the Immediate window.
    Debug.Print strFunc1 & ": " & lngResults1
    Debug.Print strFunc2 & ": " & lngResults2
    Debug.Print strFunc2 & "/" & strFunc1 & " = " & _
     lngResult & "%"
    Debug.Print "=============================="

ExitHere:
    Set ot = Nothing
    RunTests = lngResult
    ' Clear the status line.
    Call SetStatus
    Exit Function

HandleErrors:
    Select Case Err.Number
        Case Else
            MsgBox Err.Description & _
             " (" & Err.Number & ")", _
             vbExclamation, "Error in RunTests"
            lngResult = 0
    End Select
    Resume ExitHere
End Function
```

How It Works

The RunTests procedure, in basRunTests, handles the work of running both of your test cases and of comparing the timings for each. To call RunTests, pass it three parameters:

- strFunc1, a string containing the name of the supposedly slower function.
- strFunc2, a string containing the name of the supposedly faster function.
- lngRepeatOp, a Long containing the number of times to loop, inside each function. (Optional: the default value is 100,000.)

After it has done its work, RunTests displays in the Immediate window the number of milliseconds each test took and the percentage of time the faster function took, as compared to the amount of time the slower function took. For example, you might see the following output in the Immediate window:

```
Call RunTests("Test1a", "Test1b" )
Test1a: 371
Test1b: 130
Test1b/Test1a = 35%
==============================
```

As its return value, RunTests returns the percentage, as a whole number. (That is, in the previous example, the function returned the value 35.)

In order for a procedure to work when called from RunTests, it must follow these rules:

- Each procedure must be exposed as a method (a public function) in a class that includes all your tests. (In the sample, this class is named OptimizingTests.)
- For each test, you must supply two procedures—one for the supposedly slower version, one for the supposedly faster—with the same name, except for an *a* (for slower) or *b* (for faster) appended to the name. For example, Test1a and Test1b would be the slower and faster versions of the Test1 case.
- Each of your functions must accept, as its only parameter, a Long integer indicating how many times you want it to loop, internally.
- Your functions should include a For…Next loop, which loops for as many times as the input parameter indicates.

- As its return value, each function should return the number of milliseconds it took to do its work. In all the examples, the functions use the StopWatch class to do the timings.

To make it easier for you, you'll find the Test00a function, in the Optimizing-Tests class:

```
Public Function Test00a(lngRepeats As Long) As Long
    ' Template for tests.

    Dim i As Long

    sw.StartTimer
    For i = 1 To lngRepeats
        ' Do something in here.
    Next i
    Test00a = sw.StopTimer()
End Function
```

NOTE

If you're really thinking about this methodology, you'll note an important flaw in the testing harness. The For...Next loop itself takes time, and this time is added into the results of each of the slower and faster procedures. Because this extra time is added into each of the two procedures, it skews the results somewhat. Say, for example, a slower test took 1000 milliseconds, and a faster test took 500 milliseconds. Our example would indicate that the faster procedure took 50 percent as long as the slower procedure. In actuality, given (as a guess) that the loop itself consumed 50 milliseconds, the numbers are really 450 and 950 milliseconds, a ratio of around 47 percent. Because this value is always lower than the values we report (meaning that our values are always a little bit on the pessimistic side), we're comfortable with this small error. If you're worried about this, you could modify the test procedures to time a For...Next loop of the correct number of repetitions, and subtract that time from the time taken by the real test. We opted to leave this out to make test procedures more readable.

You can modify this procedure, adding the code you wish to test inside the loop. For example, the first test in the suite we've provided, Test1a, looks like this:

```
Public Function Test1a(lngRepeats As Long) As Long

    ' Use timeGetTime() if possible,
    ' rather than Timer(), to get current
    ' time information.
```

```
    Dim i As Long
    Dim lngTime As Long

    sw.StartTimer
    For i = 1 To lngRepeats
        lngTime = Timer
    Next i
    Test1a = sw.StopTimer()
End Function
```

As you can see, this procedure follows all the rules specified earlier.

TIP

If you look carefully, you'll notice that neither Test1a nor any of the other test procedures instantiates or destroys sw, the StopWatch object. The OptimizingTests class does that itself, in its Initialize and Terminate event procedures. Rather than having each test create and destroy this object, it made sense to have one StopWatch object that all the tests share.

One big question remains: How is it possible for the RunTests procedure, given the names of test procedures as strings, to find and run the procedures? Normally, in VBA, you must know the name of the procedure you want to call at the time you write the code. There's really no late binding available for function calls.

Or is there? In VBA 6 (the version of VBA in Office 2000 and in Visual Basic 6), you'll find a new function: CallByName. This function allows you to specify an object and a string containing the name of the method or property of the object that you want to call (or, for properties, set or retrieve). You must also specify the type of member you're calling (method, Property Get, Property Let, or Property Set, using the constants VbMethod, VbGet, VbLet, or VbSet) and can, optionally, specify a variant—which can contain an array of values—indicating the parameters for the method or property.

You can only use CallByName to work with methods or properties of an object that's in memory, so RunTests must create an instance of the OptimizingTests class before it can do any work. The code that does this, in RunTests, looks like this:

```
Dim ot As OptimizingTests
Set ot = New OptimizingTests
```

Once the object is in memory, RunTests calls its various methods using the CallByName function.

Given that the RunTests procedure receives the four parameters described earlier, it can use CallByName like this (SetStatus is a procedure, in the same module, that displays text on the demonstration form if it's open):

```
For i = 1 To lngReptFunc
    Call SetStatus("Running " & strFunc2 & " Pass " & i)
    lngResults1 = lngResults1 + _
     CallByName(ot, strFunc2, VbMethod, CVar(lngRepeatOp))
Next I
```

VBA Optimization Tips

In this section, we present a series of optimization tips, in no particular order. Some will actually make a difference in your applications; others are interesting programming tips that don't make a huge difference in your code. To test each hypothesis, we've created two similar versions of a simple function. The sample database includes the full source for both versions of each test so you can try them out yourself.

To simplify your experiments with the test cases we present here, you can use frmRunTests. Figure 15.2 shows this form in use. It includes a list box from which you can choose the specific test case to run and spin buttons allowing you to specify how many loops to execute inside the routine, as well as how many times to call each routine. The View Slower and View Faster buttons pop up forms that pull the source code for the functions directly from the OptimizingTests class module, so you can look at the code as you test. Finally, the clock button starts the test, running the slow version as many times as you request and then running the faster version the same number of times.

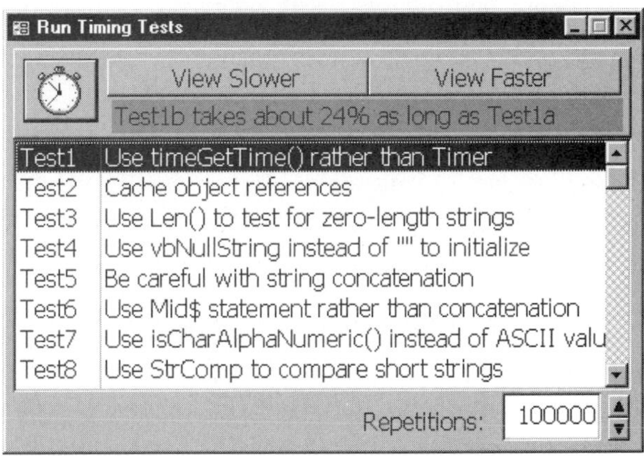

FIGURE 15.2: frmRunTests allows you to choose a specific test and run it, resulting in a comparison between the slow and fast versions.

Clearly, this method of testing is far from perfect. The order in which you run the tests might make a difference, and the host application and the operating system caches all make a difference, too. In our informal testing (and that's all this can be—measurements of relative differences), none of these factors made much difference. Reversing the order of the tests made almost no difference. Remember, the goal of these tests is to determine which of two methods is faster, not to gather exact timings. The ratios we found depend totally on the specific tests we ran and the setup of our system, but we've tried to make them representative of the kinds of improvements you'd see, too.

The results of our performance tests are summarized in Table 15.4.

TABLE 15.4: Summary of the Results of the VBA Performance Tests

Test	Optimization	Ratio of Elapsed Times (Smaller is Better)
1	Use timeGetTime() rather than Timer	25%
2	Cache object references	40%
3	Use Len() to test for zero-length strings	60%
4	Use vbNullString instead of "" to initialize	35%
5	Be careful with string concatenation	15%
6	Use Mid$ statement rather than concatenation	55%
7	Use isCharAlphaNumeric() instead of ASCII values	55%
8	Use StrComp to compare short strings	45%
9	Use Like with wildcards	35%
10	Use "$" string functions when possible	60%
11	Use Integers instead of variants	50%
12	Use Integer division (\) whenever possible	70%
13	Use logical assignments when possible	65%
14	Use Not to toggle between True and False	45%
15	Don't use Byte variables for speed	80%

Continued on next page

TABLE 15.4 CONTINUED: Summary of the Results of the VBA Performance Tests

Test	Optimization	Ratio of Elapsed Times (Smaller is Better)
16	Use For...Next rather than Do...Loop?	50%
17	Be careful with IIf()	50%
18	Use If...Then rather than IIf	30%
19	Don't call DoEvents each time you loop	10%
20	Put the most likely candidate first in Select Case	15%
21	In arrays, For...Next faster than For Each...Next	75%
22	In collections, For Each ... Next faster than For ...Next	2%
23	Set a collection to New collection to clear it	10%
24	Use early binding	10%

Some of the comparisons are more dependent than others on the assumptions made. For example, Test12, which evaluates the difference between using Integer and real division, couldn't be constructed in too many different ways. It's doubtful you'd get results differing much from those in Table 15.4 by rewriting the code. On the other hand, Test17, which compares decisions made using IIf and the If...Then construct, will give widely differing results depending on the details of what you're doing in the True and False cases of the construct. Thus, it's important to be aware of the assumptions made for each test when interpreting the results.

The following sections describe each of the optimization tips tested in the OptimizingTests class module.

NOTE

In general, we haven't listed the test code here. We describe the tests and the concepts involved, but you'll need to investigate the sample database to see the exact details of the tests. In any case, you're very unlikely to use the specific code we've written in your own applications; it's the concepts that count. For each test case, the name of the procedure in the OptimizingTests class is Test*N*a (the presumed slow version) or Test*N*b (the supposedly faster version), where *N* is the test number. For example, the code corresponding to test case 5 is in Test5a and Test5b.

WARNING For each of the following tests, we've provided a percentage; that is, the percentage of time the faster test takes, as compared to the slower test. If the slow test takes 1000 milliseconds, and the fast test takes 250 milliseconds, the percentage will appear as 25 percent. These values can, and will most likely, be different on your machines. We provide these values for comparison only, as a way to judge the effectiveness of the optimization. The lower the number, the better optimization provided by the specific test.

NOTE The effectiveness of each of the optimizations that follow depends on many factors, including the actual code in use at the time, the relative speed of your hard disk versus the processor in your computer, and other programs currently using Windows' memory and resources. There might be a process running in the background that you're not aware of, and Access and the database engine (whether you're using Jet, MSDE, or SQL Server) provide their own internal caching. The only sure way to provide accurate timings would be to remove all background processes and to reboot between each timing. That's not practical, so we'll mention again that the timing results presented here are for comparison purposes only. You'll need to decide for yourself in some of the marginal cases whether the optimization will really help. Therefore, a word of warning: take any suggestions about optimizations with a grain of salt. Try them out in your own applications before swearing by them.

Test 1: Use timeGetTime Instead of Timer

As mentioned earlier, the Windows API function timeGetTime returns the number of milliseconds that have elapsed since you started the current Windows session. The VBA Timer function returns the number of seconds that have elapsed since midnight. If you're interested in measuring elapsed times, you're better off using timeGetTime, for three reasons:

- timeGetTime is more accurate.
- timeGetTime runs longer without "rolling over."
- Calling timeGetTime is significantly faster.

Calling timeGetTime is no more complex than calling Timer, once you've included the proper API declaration for it. In the declarations section of any standard module in your application, you'll need to include the statement

```
Private Declare Function adh_apiGetTime Lib "winmm.dll" _
 Alias "timeGetTime" () As Long
```

With that declaration in place, you can call it from any module in your application, just as though it were an internal Access function. (See Test1a/b for the full test procedures.)

Test 2: Cache Object References

In writing code you often need to retrieve or set properties of the various forms, reports, controls, or other objects in your application. Generally, you refer to these objects with statements like this:

```
strCaption = Forms("frmTest").cmdButton1.Caption
```

For a single reference to an object, there's not much you can do to speed up the reference. If, on the other hand, you're going to be referring to many of the properties of that object or using that object in a loop of some sort, you can achieve a substantial speed increase by pointing an object variable at that object and using that variable to reference the object.

For example, if you were going to reference many of a specific control's properties, you would be well served to use code like this rather than refer to the control with the full syntax each time:

```
Dim ctl as CommandButton
Set ctl = Forms("frmTest").cmdButton1

Debug.Print ctl.Name
Debug.Print ctl.Width
' etc...
```

In addition, using VBA's With...End With syntax affords the same improvements. Your code may end up being more readable if you use cached object references, but if you can use With...End With, it, too, can speed up your code.

In this example, we've used a particular field within an ADO recordset to prove the point. In the slower case, you'll find code like this:

```
Set rst = New ADODB.Recordset
Set rst.ActiveConnection = CurrentProject.Connection
rst.Source = "tblTests"
rst.Open

sw.StartTimer
For i = 1 To lngRepeats
    strName = rst.Fields(0).Name
Next I
```

The faster procedure caches the reference to the field, like this:

```
Set rst = New ADODB.Recordset
Set rst.ActiveConnection = CurrentProject.Connection
rst.Source = "tblTests"
rst.Open

sw.StartTimer
Set fld = rst.Fields(0)
For i = 1 To lngRepeats
    strName = fld.Name
Next i
```

Even in this simple case, where the changed code removes only a single dot within an expression, the code takes about 40 percent of the time it took originally. The more dots you remove by caching references, the bigger improvement you'll see. (See Test2a/b for the full test procedures.)

TIP

Dots in object references will always slow down your code. You should take whatever effort you can to reduce the number of redundant dots, as demonstrated in this test.

Test 3: Use Len() to Test for Zero-Length Strings

There are several ways you can check to see whether the length of a particular string is 0. One method is to compare the string to "", and another is to compare the length of the string to 0. Comparing the results of the Len function to 0 is measurably faster. You might not think that calling a function could be faster than simply comparing the string to "", but it is.

That is, given a choice, use

```
If Len(strValue) = 0 Then
```

rather than

```
If strValue = "" Then
```

to find out if a string contains no characters.

Because of the way VBA stores strings internally, you gain a small advantage if you compare a string's Len to 0—VBA stores the length of the string itself along with a pointer to the string buffer. This means that when you call the Len function,

VBA isn't calculating the length of the string at that point, but rather uses the stored length value. In addition, each time you compare a string to "", you're asking VBA to create a string that contains no characters, in order to compare it to your current string. This action, in itself, takes time. (See Test3a/b for the full test procedures.)

Test 4: Use vbNullString Rather than "" to Initialize Strings

When you want to reinitialize a string value so that it's empty, you normally use code like this:

```
strItem = ""
```

This creates a new string and copies it into the strItem variable. It turns out that a more expeditious solution is to use the vbNullString constant, a *pointer* to an empty string. By using

```
strItem = vbNullString
```

VBA doesn't have to create a new string each time you make the assignment; instead, it uses its own internal pointer to an empty string, saving a substantial amount of work each time you initialize a string variable. (See Test4a/b for the full test procedures.)

NOTE Although you can use vbNullString to initialize a string variable to contain no characters, vbNullString is not itself an empty string. At least, not exactly. The vbNullString constant exists in order to make it easier to call Windows API functions that require a Null pointer (a concept that makes a lot of sense to C programmers, but not as much sense to VBA programmers). When you assign vbNullString to a string variable, VBA sees that you're attempting to assign a Null string pointer into a string variable, and therefore does the right thing—it creates a string that contains no characters for you.

Test 5: Concatenation Is Expensive

Many times, when writing code, you have the choice whether to write a string expression as one long expression or to break it up into multiple expressions concatenated together with the "&" operator. Be careful: concatenation is a slow operation in VBA.

In our example, we've taken a single string ("ABCDEFG") and to test how much time concatenation takes, have broken it up into seven fragments: "A", "B", "C", "D", "E", "F", and "G". The two lines of code:

```
strTest = "A" & "B" & "C" & "D" & "E" & "F" & "G"
```

and

```
strTest = "ABCDEFG"
```

prove that concatenation, if used only to "prettify" your code, is too expensive. In our tests, the faster version (the one without string concatenation) took only around 12 percent or so as long as the slow version. (See Test5a/b for the full test procedures.)

Test 6: Use Mid$ Rather than Concatenation

The often overlooked Mid$ statement allows you to insert text substrings into other text values. For example, if you used the following code:

```
Dim strValue As String
strValue = "I like you"
Mid$(strValue, 3, 4) = "love"
Debug.Print strValue
```

strValue would contain "I love you" once you had finished. The alternative would be to write code like this:

```
Dim strValue As String
strValue = "I like you"
strValue = Left$(strValue, 2) & "love" & Mid$(strValue, 7)
Debug.Print strValue
```

The first alternative is significantly faster than the second. In our test case, either concatenating a series of *X* characters to build an output string, or using the Mid$ statement to replace each character in the output string with *X*, the faster version (using Mid$) took only 50 percent as long as the slower version. Of course, the relative timings might change depending on the action you were taking. In general, concatenation should be avoided in VBA. (See Test6a/b for the full test procedures.)

Test 7: Use IsCharAlphaNumeric Rather than ASCII Values

You may find yourself needing to find out whether a particular character is an alphanumeric character (that is, checking to see whether it falls in the range of characters from A–Z, a–z, or 0–9). One standard method for doing this in VBA is to compare the Asc(UCase(*character*)) to the ANSI values for the ranges. The Windows API provides a function specifically for this purpose, IsCharAlphaNumeric. In addition, you can use a similar API function, IsCharAlpha, to check a character to see whether it's between A and Z. An added bonus of using the Windows API functions is that they're internationalized. Many characters outside the normal A–Z range are considered legal text characters in other countries. The brute-force comparison method would fail on such characters. To top it all off, using the API method is significantly faster than performing the comparisons yourself.

The slow version of the code might look like this:

```
Const cFirstChar = 65
Const cLastChar = 90
Const cFirstDigit = 48
Const cLastDigit = 57

intC = Asc(UCase(strC))
If (intC >= cFirstChar And _
 intC <= cLastChar) _
 Or (intC >= cFirstDigit And _
 intC <= cLastDigit) Then
     ' Do something now that you know the
     ' character is alphanumeric.
End If
```

and the faster version might look like this:

```
If IsCharAlphaNumeric(Asc(strC)) Then
     ' Do something now that you know the
     ' character is alphanumeric.
End If
```

(See Test7a/b for the full test procedures.)

To use IsCharAlphaNumeric, you need to include the following declaration in your application:

```
Private Declare Function IsCharAlphaNumeric _
 Lib "User32" Alias "IsCharAlphaNumericA" _
(ByVal cChar As Byte) As Long
```

Test 8: When Comparing Strings, Use StrComp Rather than Converting with UCase

VBA compares strings based on the Option Compare statement at the top of each module. By default, VBA always assumes Option Compare Binary (in which case all text comparisons are case-sensitive). Because your code can't determine how VBA will compare strings, if you really need to compare a string without regard to case, you need to take extra steps.

One solution is to convert both strings you're comparing to uppercase, using the UCase function. With this technique, once both strings have been converted, you've eliminated upper- and lowercase issues from the comparison. Another alternative is to use the StrComp function. This function allows you to specify two strings to be compared, as well as a constant indicating what method to use for comparisons (vbUseCompareOption [use the Option Compare mode], vbBinaryCompare [compare case-sensitively], vbTextCompare [compare case-insensitively], or vbDatabaseCompare [use the database comparison mode]). StrComp returns 0 if the strings are equal, -1 if the first string is less, or +1 if the first string is greater.

To compare two strings without regard to case, you might write the code this way:

```
If UCase(strValue1) = UCase(strValue2) Then
```

or you might write:

```
If StrComp(strValue, strValue2, vbTextCompare) = 0 Then
```

It turns out that, for short strings, StrComp is faster. As the strings you're comparing grow in size, the difference in speed between the two techniques lessens. For huge strings, both techniques take about the same amount of time. Because most strings you'll work with are rather short, however, we recommend using StrComp for case-insensitive comparisons. (See Test8a/b for the full test procedures.)

Test 9: Use Like Operator Instead of Comparing Individual Characters

Imagine this scenario: you need to allow a variable to contain five characters that must be in a format like this: "W5TGQ", and your code can accept strings in only this format. In this case, you need all letters, except the second character, which must be a digit between 0 and 9. You could work your way through the input string, matching each character against the right conditions and exit the loop if you hit a snag, like this (this example uses the IsCharAlpha API function, which returns 1 if the value sent it represents a character, and 0 otherwise):

```
blnMatch = True
For j = 1 To 5
    intCh = Asc(Mid$(strTest, j, 1))
    Select Case j
```

```
            Case 1, 3, 4, 5
                If (IsCharAlpha(intCh) = 0) Then
                    blnMatch = False
                End If
            Case 2
                If (IsCharAlpha(intCh) <> 0) Then
                    blnMatch = False
                End If
        End Select
        If Not blnMatch Then
            Exit For
        End If
    Next j
```

There are other ways you can do this as well, but one technique stands out. If you investigate the Like operator, you'll see that it provides a simple way to compare two strings using wildcards. (For complete information, check out the online help for this operator.) In this example, you can replace all the code shown above with this simple comparison:

```
blnMatch = _
 strTest Like "[A-Z]#[A-Z][A-Z][A-Z]"
```

In this case, "[A-Z]" matches any character between *A* and *Z* (and takes into account international languages that use the same alphabet as English), and "#" matches any digit (0–9). In our tests, the faster version (using Like) takes only about 35 percent as much time as the original test. Although Like (and its wildcard tests) cannot replace every string comparison, when it can, it does a good job. (See Test9a/b for the full test procedures.)

Test 10: Use $ Functions When Possible

If you investigate all the built-in VBA functions, you'll note something strange about the string-handling functions: any function that returns a String value comes in two "flavors." For example, VBA provides both a Left and a Left$ function. Why both?

NOTE

In early versions of Basic, before you could specify a variable as being of a specific type, programmers had to use type-specification characters—"$" for String, "%" for Integer, "&" for Long, and so on—rather than using specific data type declarations. Basic applied that same concept to function names: functions that return strings ended with "$". We no longer use the characters indicating the data type (some people do, but we don't see any reason that this is a useful habit), but the "$" functions remain.

The Left function returns a variant, and Left$ returns a String. If you're placing the return value into a variant, it makes sense to call Left. On the other hand, you're most likely to place the return value of Left into a string, and by calling Left (rather than Left$), you're forcing VBA to do an extra type conversion.

In our tests, simply running the following code:

```
For i = 1 To lngRepeats
    strValue = Left$(strValue, 3)
Next I
```

first without, and then with, the "$", the faster version (with the "$") took only around 55 percent as much time as the slower one (without the "$"). We recommend always using the "$" version of a string function. (See Test10a/b for the full test procedures.)

Test 11: Use Long Rather than Variant

Unless you specify otherwise, VBA creates all variables using its default type, Variant. To hold data of any simple type, variants must be at least as big and complex as any of the types they can contain. "Big and complex" equates with "slower," so avoid variants if at all possible. Of course, there will be many times when you can't avoid them, but if you're just ill-informed or being lazy, your code will suffer. (See Test11a/b for the full test procedures.)

NOTE

If you're working with data from tables in your code, you generally *must* use variants. Because variants are the only data type that can hold null data, and it's usually possible for data from tables to be null, you'll avoid problems by using variants. In addition, you may find that attempting to use specific data types when working with Jet ends up *slowing* your code. Because Jet uses variants when it communicates with Access, when you place Jet data into specific data types, you're asking VBA to make a data type conversion, and that takes time.

Test 12: Use Integer Division (\) When Possible

Access provides two division operators, the / (floating-point division) and \ (Integer division) operators. To perform floating-point division, Access must convert the operands to floating-point values. This takes time. If you don't care about the fractional portion of the result, you can save some time by using the Integer division operator instead.

The results of this test were decidedly mixed. Using Integer division made almost no difference (although it did make a difference in early versions of Access). In some other examples—working with forms, for instance—it did make a difference. It may be that VBA is smart enough to use Integer math internally if it can tell that that's what will work most quickly. In the test procedure, the code divides each integer value by 7, either using normal or Integer division:

```
Dim intX As Integer

For i = 1 To lngRepeats
    ' In the slow case:
    ' intX = i / 7
    intX = i \ 7
Next I
```

Our take on this: Integer division won't make much of a difference unless you're performing large numbers of divisions in which you care only about the integer portion of the result. But it can't hurt. (See Test12a/b for the full test procedures.)

Test 13: Use Single-Line Logical Assignments

Like many other languages, VBA handles logical values as integers. In addition, Access performs right-to-left expression evaluation. The combination of these two features allows you to make logical assignments directly as part of an expression. For example, to make y contain True if x contains 5, and False otherwise, you could write code like this:

```
If x = 5 Then
    y = True
Else
    y = False
End If
```

This code is wordier than it needs to be. Remember, the intent is to set the variable y to True if x is equal to 5 and False otherwise. The expression (x = 5) has a truth value of its own—that is, it's either True or False. You can assign that value directly to y in a single statement:

```
y = (x = 5)
```

Although it may look confusing, VBA will interpret it correctly. Starting from the right, VBA will calculate the value of the expression x = 5 (either True or

False) and assign that value to the variable y. Other languages, including C and Pascal, use distinct assignment and equality operators, making this expression a little clearer. In C, for example, the statement would read

```
y = (x == 5)
```

with the "=" performing the assignment and the "==" checking the equality.

Any place you use an expression like the If...Then...End If statement above, you should be able to replace it with a single assignment statement.

If you find these logical assignments hard to read, you may choose to skip using them, because the improvement in performance is slight (in the test case, the faster version takes around 66 percent as much time as the slow version). If, however, logical assignments seem natural to use and read, then by all means use them. (See Test13a/b for the full test procedures.)

Test 14: Use Not Operator to Toggle Booleans

In many circumstances, you need to toggle the state of a variable between True and False. You might be tempted to write code like this:

```
If x = True Then
    x = False
Else
    x = True
End If
```

You might think that either of the following solutions would be an improvement over the original:

```
If x Then
    x = False
Else
    x = True
End If
```

or

```
x = IIf(x, False, True)
```

Testing shows that neither is as good as the original expression (and the IIf solution is much slower). But the best solution is to use the following expression:

```
x = Not x
```

That way, if x is currently True, it will become False. If it's False, it will become True. For example, if you want to change the Enabled property of a command button to be True if it's False, and False if it's True, you can use code like this:

```
cmdOK.Enabled = Not cmdOK.Enabled
```

In our tests, using the Not operator takes around 50 percent as much time as the longer If...Then...Else statement. (See Test14a/b for the full test procedures.)

WARNING

Don't even consider using Not to toggle truth values for any type of value other than Boolean. Sooner or later, you'll attempt to use Not with a value that contains something besides True (-1) or False (0), and the result will be different than you would expect. Not is meant to operate only with Boolean values and no other data type.

Test 15: Bytes Aren't Faster than Longs

In an earlier tip, we tried to impress on you that using a smaller data type will result in faster performance then using a larger one, all other things being equal. This isn't always the case, however: if you're performing mathematical operations on integer values, no type will give you the same performance as using a Long variable. That is, given the choice of using a Long, Integer, or Byte data type, using Long will always give you the best performance.

Why is this so? If a Long gives you better performance than a Variant, wouldn't you expect that a Byte would give you better performance than a Long? You might think so, but in reality, your computer's internal architecture uses 32 bits (the same size as a Long) to do all its numerical processing. That is, VBA is optimized for operations involving 32 bits at once. When you use a Long data type, VBA doesn't have to do any extra processing to work with it. When using an Integer, you've added a little overhead, and when using a Byte, you've added substantial overhead. Use Long data types, if you're performing calculations that don't require floating point values. (See Test15a/b for the full test procedures.)

TIP

One place where you'll definitely need to use the Byte data type is when you're working with an array of bytes. In that case, if you're working with individual bytes within a string, or passing a value to the Windows API, you'll need to declare an array of bytes.

Test 16: For ... Next is Faster than Do ... Loop

Although it makes perfect sense, you may not notice that using a Do…Loop in place of a For…Next loop is generally slower than it needs to be. Each pass through a Do…Loop that iterates a specified number of times requires you to also increment or decrement some sort of loop counter, while a For…Next loop does that work for you.

For example, the slower test procedure includes a loop like this:

```
i = 1
Do Until i > lngRepeats
    j = i
    ' Normally, you'd do something with j here.
    i = i + 1

Loop
```

and the faster procedure includes this equivalent loop:

```
For i = 1 To lngRepeats
    j = I
    ' Normally, you'd do something with j here.
Next I
```

The loops provide the same results, yet the second one runs (in our tests) in about 45 percent of the time of the first. Of course, you can't always replace Do…Loop with For…Next: you only want to use For…Next if the number of loop iterations is fixed, not based on some condition. (See Test16a/b for the full test procedures.)

Test 17: Watch Out for IIf—It Doesn't Short-Circuit

Shorter code isn't necessarily faster. Although this fact is documented in the VBA online help, it's easy to miss: in the IIf, Choose, and Switch functions, VBA evaluates any and all expressions it finds, regardless of whether they actually need to be evaluated from a logical point of view. Given an expression like this:

```
varValue = IIf(BooleanExpression, Function1(), Function2())
```

VBA will call both Function1 and Function2. Not only can this lead to undesired side effects, it can just plain slow down your program. In a case like this, you're better off using the standard If…Then…Else construct, which will execute only the portions of the statement that fall within the appropriate clause. Given the statement

```
If BooleanExpression Then
    varValue = Function1()
Else
    varValue = Function2()
End If
```

you can be assured that only Function1 *or* Function2 will end up being called. The same concepts apply for the Choose and Switch functions. If you plan on calling functions from any of these functions, you may be better served by using an If…Then…Else or a Select Case statement.

Beyond any optimization considerations, IIf is very dangerous when dealing with numeric values and division. If this was your expression:

```
dblNew = IIf(intY = 0, 0, intX/intY)
```

it would appear that you had appropriately covered your bases. Your code checks to make sure intY isn't 0 and returns an appropriate value if it is, rather than attempting to divide by 0. Unfortunately, if y is 0, this statement will still cause a runtime error. Because VBA will evaluate both portions of the IIf expression, the division by 0 will occur and will trigger an error. In this case, you need to either trap for the error or use the If…Then…Else statement. (See Test17a/b for the full test procedures.)

NOTE

The IIf function used in queries, forms, or reports doesn't have this same behavior—that is, it works as you'd expect it to in those places. It's only in VBA code, in a module, where you need to avoid IIf because of its over-zealous evaluation tendencies.

TIP

It's also interesting to note that VBA does not short-circuit AND or OR logical expressions. That is, in other languages, when you have an If statement including a compound OR statement (that is, "If x OR y Then"), if it's determined that the first operand is True, the code doesn't even investigate the second operand: the whole expression has to be True. (True OR any expression is True, even True OR Null.) If you write a compound AND statement (that is, "If x AND y Then"), if it's determined that the first operand is False, the code doesn't investigate the second operand: the entire expression must be False. (False AND any expression is False, even False AND Null.) Don't count on this behavior in VBA to avoid runtime errors—it doesn't happen, and VBA will always evaluate both operands in any logical expression before it determines the outcome.

Test 18: If...End If Is Faster than IIf

If the previous tip wasn't enough to make you leery of the IIf function, this one certainly will. In any situation within VBA code, you can always replace a call to the IIf function with a full If...Then...Else...End If statement, and you'll always get better performance. You learned in the previous tip not to ever call functions from the second and third parameters of IIf, but you still pay a price for using IIf, even if you're returning simple literals. For example, you might write an innocuous statement like this:

```
strValue = IIf(i Mod 2 = 0, "Even", "Odd")
```

but you'll find that you'll get better performance by rewriting that single line of code, like this:

```
If i Mod 2 = 0 Then
    strValue = "Even"
Else
    strValue = "Odd"
End If
```

Basically, we see no reason to ever use IIf in VBA code. Because you can always write an equivalent construct without using the function, and the function call is always slower, just avoid it. (See Test18a/b for the full test procedures.)

TIP

Again, the same goes for the Switch and Choose functions. Both can easily be replaced using nested If statements or Select Case statements. Although all three functions have their place when called from queries, forms, or reports (where they cannot be simply replaced), avoid them in VBA code.

Test 19: Don't Call DoEvents on Every Loop Iteration

If you include a tight loop in your VBA code (that is, a loop that runs for a while, and performs calculations without calling any other VBA function) and you want to update the screen or allow mouse clicks or screen activity while the loop is running, you'll find that VBA ties up Access while it runs this loop. A common solution is to insert a call to the VBA DoEvents statement inside the loop. DoEvents effectively yields time to Windows and allows it to update the screen, react to mouse clicks, and perform other background tasks. This would seem to be a perfect solution.

Unfortunately, DoEvents halts your code and doesn't allow it to continue until all the pending Windows activities have been completed. If you call this procedure each time you loop, your code will run significantly slower than it would without DoEvents. In the slower test case, the code calls DoEvents each time through a loop:

```
For i = 1 To lngRepeats
    DoEvents
Next I
```

In the faster case, the code only calls DoEvents every tenth time through the loop:

```
For i = 1 To lngRepeats
    If i Mod 10 = 0 Then
        DoEvents
    End If
Next I
```

Even this small change, calling DoEvents only once every ten times through the loop, makes the loop take only 10 percent of the time it did originally. Of course, that makes sense—the loop is doing nothing besides calling DoEvents, and calling it once every ten times through should take up 10 percent as much time. Even if you add code to the loop that does some processing, that processing won't, in general, take nearly as long as the call to DoEvents, and you'll still end up with code that runs faster. (See Test19a/b for the full procedures.)

Test 20: Put Most Likely Case First in Select Case

When you use a Select Case statement, VBA compares your condition against each of the cases you've provided, from top to bottom, until it finds a case that matches the condition. Say, for example, you wanted to convert a short month name into a month number, and you wrote code like this:

```
Select Case strMonth
    Case "Jan"
        intMonth = 1
    Case "Feb"
        intMonth = 2

    ' Code removed here.

    Case "Nov"
        intMonth = 11
    Case "Dec"
        intMonth = 12
End Select
```

Given a short month name (in English), this code sets intMonth to be the corresponding month number.

The problem is that VBA always starts at the top and looks at each case until it finds a match. If you're most often going to be sending "Dec" in as the month to find, the code will still look, every time, at each of the preceding cases, searching for the specified text.

The answer, then, is to write your code so that the item you're most likely to search for is the first in the list. Ranking the Case statements by their likelihood of occurrence, as opposed to placing them in an otherwise logical order, can speed your code significantly. In our tests, we first tried searching for "Dec", (the last Case statement) and then for "Jan" (the first Case statement). In this example (and the numbers would change, of course, depending on the number of Case statements you have), searching for the first case took only 12 percent as long as searching for the final case. The more Case statements you have, the smaller this value can be. (See Test20a/b for the full procedures.)

Test 21: In Arrays, For...Next is Faster than For Each...Next

If you want to visit each item in an array, you have two alternatives. You can either:

- Use a For…Next loop, looping from the lower bound (determined using the LBound function) to the upper bound (determined using the UBound function) of the array

or

- Use a For Each…Next loop, using a variant to retrieve each value in turn.

For Each…Next seems simpler because you needn't worry about retrieving the lower and upper bounds—the loop simply takes care of that for you:

```
For Each varValue In alngValues
    j = varValue
Next varValue
```

Using For…Next requires a bit more effort on your part because you must write the code that finds the lower and upper bounds:

```
For lngCount = LBound(alngValues) To _
 UBound(alngValues)
    j = alngValues(lngCount)
Next lngCount
```

You might think that For Each...Next would be faster, because it requires less code. That isn't so, in fact. The For...Next loop will give you better performance if you're working with arrays. In our tests, the faster version took about 70 percent as long as the slower version. (See Test21a/b for the full procedures.)

WARNING

It's worth noting that although you can use either of these techniques to read items from an array, you can only use the For...Next loop to write into array elements. The For Each...Next loop retrieves a copy of the data in the array, not the actual array element itself. Although you won't receive an error if you use For Each...Next to write into an array, the data won't actually go into the array.

Test 22: In Collections, For Each...Next Is *Much* Faster than For...Next

Just as with arrays, you can use either of the two techniques listed in the previous section to iterate through a collection. In this case, however, the speed difference is much more pronounced: for collections, using For Each...Next takes about 2 percent as much time as using For...Next. This is a colossal difference in speed. Make sure you consider using For Each...Next to iterate through collections, rather than the commonly used For...Next loop. (The code for this example is almost the same as in the previous example and can be found in Test22a/b.)

TIP

If you have a need to iterate through a collection in any order besides forwards (that is, the order in which items were added to the collection), you have no choice—you won't be able to use the faster For Each...Next loop. In that case, you may be forced to use a For...Next loop instead.

Test 23: Don't Remove Items from a Collection to Empty It

If you use a VBA Collection object within your application, you may have a need to empty the collection and start fresh. It's tempting to simply remove all the items in the collection, one at a time, and then start adding items again once it's empty. To remove items, however, you must specify either an index or a key value (that's the way the Remove method works). And, if you're going to remove the items by their position, you'll need to loop backwards, so that the indexes don't change as you delete items. You might write code like this, to clear your collection:

```
For j = col.Count To 1 Step -1
    col.Remove j
Next j
```

This technique is faster, however:

```
Set col = New Collection
```

By setting the variable equal to a New Collection, you've asked VBA to dispose of the original (since there's no variable referring to the original collection, it will automatically be removed from memory) and make col refer to a new, empty Collection object. (See Test23a/b for the full procedures.) In our tests, the faster version took a miniscule 7 percent of the slower version.

Test 24: Use Early Binding

If you declare an object variable using As Object, you're asking VBA to determine the available characteristics of this object at runtime. If you declare the object variable using a specific type, VBA can do the determination of available members at compile-time. The difference in runtime speed is impressive.

For example, referring to an ADO field either as an Object or as an ADODB.Field makes a huge difference in the speed of accessing that object's properties. The test procedures use the following code:

```
Dim rst As ADODB.Recordset
Dim strName As String
' In the slower case:
' Dim fld As Object
Dim fld As ADODB.Field

Set rst = New ADODB.Recordset
Set rst.ActiveConnection = CurrentProject.Connection
rst.Source = "tblTests"
rst.Open

sw.StartTimer
Set fld = rst.Fields(0)
For i = 1 To lngRepeats
    strName = fld.Name
Next I
```

Declaring fld as ADODB.Field results in times that are around 7 percent of those measured declaring fld as Object.

In every case, if at all possible, declare a variable using the most specific object type that you can. For Access controls, that means using, for example:

```
Dim cmd As CommandButton
```

instead of

```
Dim cmd As Control
```

or, worst of all

```
Dim cmd As Object
```

(See Test24a/b for the full test procedures.)

Summary

This chapter presented a variety of suggestions for improving the performance of your Access applications. We covered the following topics:

- How the Jet engine optimizes and executes queries
- How to make use of the unsupported ISAMStats method and ShowPlan option
- How to optimize Access
- How to optimize queries
- How to speed up forms
- How to improve the performance of reports
- How VBA compiles and loads code and how you can best take advantage of this
- Suggestions for optimizing your VBA code
- How to test your own optimization ideas

At every point in designing any application, you're faced with choices. These choices affect how well your application will work, and you need to be informed about the trade-offs in order to best make these choices. This chapter focused on the major areas in which you can improve the performance of your applications. Although we attempted to cover the major areas of optimization, this chapter is not meant to be comprehensive. On the other hand, it makes for a good start.

CHAPTER

SIXTEEN

16

Accessing DLLs and the Windows API

- Converting 16-bit Windows API calls to 32-bit API calls
- Explaining Dynamic Link Libraries (DLLs)
- Calling DLLs and the Windows API from VBA
- Declaring DLL procedures
- Discovering DLL details

This chapter discusses one of the most powerful features of VBA: the ability to call Dynamic Link Libraries (DLLs) from VBA procedures. DLLs are primarily written in C or C++, but you can also create them using Pascal and Delphi. Calling a DLL provides a method of performing tasks that standard VBA functions and statements do not permit. For example, VBA has no intrinsic ability to retrieve the amount of system resources available, but you can do it easily with the Windows API.

Even if you are not proficient in C or C++, you can use DLLs someone else has written. Windows itself includes a number of DLLs with literally thousands of useful functions. These functions are collectively called the *Windows API. API* is an acronym for Application Programming Interface, and it is the set of functions Windows programs use to manipulate Windows.

Learning how to call the Windows API, and DLLs in general, allows you to vastly extend your ability to manipulate Windows. This chapter is divided into five main sections. The first section describes the basics of calling a DLL or Windows API call. The second section provides some examples of DLL calls. The third section, for more advanced users, shows how to construct a Declare statement to retrieve information from any arbitrary DLL. The fourth section takes a closer look at what goes on during DLL calls. The last section discusses how to convert 16-bit Windows API (from Windows 3.*x*) into 32-bit Windows API calls (for Windows 95, Windows 98, Windows NT, and Windows 2000).

Is COM Replacing the Need for DLLs?

If you are an astute reader (and we assume you are), you are no doubt wondering whether the growing prevalence of COM is eliminating the need to call DLLs. After all, calling a DLL function is not necessarily straightforward when compared with accessing methods of COM objects. Later in this chapter, we'll even tell you about a COM object that wraps up all of the API functions in Windows.

At this point, however, we believe that it still makes sense to keep the knowledge of DLL functions in your developer's toolbox. The reason for this is that, unlike Windows API functions that define Windows itself, COM object model replacements for API functions are not widely available on users' computers. If you want to use them, it means that you will have to be responsible for distributing them with your solution and making sure they get registered properly. As newer operating systems like Windows 2000 begin to ship COM object models as standard features (and as companies widely adopt them), you'll be able to count on them like you do API functions. Until then, however, using API calls is the safest bet for insuring your solutions work when installed on a user's system.

Introducing Dynamic Link Libraries

In traditional compiled languages, every application you create carries around every function it calls and includes exactly the same shared code. For example, when you create a DOS application in standard C, your program probably calls functions from the C runtime library to read a string from a file, get a character from the keyboard, or get the current time. These functions in the libraries are *statically linked* to the program, which means the code for the functions is included in the executable at the time the executable is created. The problem with this scheme is that if you have 200 programs that all write a string to the screen with the printf function, the code for this function is reproduced 200 times on your disk.

Windows uses a different approach: libraries of common functions are usually *dynamically linked* to the program. This means that if you have 200 Windows programs that all write a string to a window, only one copy of the ExtTextOut code resides on your hard disk. Each program includes only a very small amount of overhead to call this common code. These common routines reside in Dynamic Link Libraries, which normally have the extension DLL and are stored in the Windows\System directory if more than one program uses them. It is common practice these days for software vendors that develop multiple applications to place common functions in DLLs.

Programs that run under Windows call functions the operating system provides. These functions provide facilities to create a window, change its size, read and write Registry entries, manipulate a file, and so on. Windows stores most of these functions in three DLLs: USER32.DLL, GDI32.DLL, and KERNEL32.DLL.

To use a DLL, you need to know the procedures in it and the arguments to each of those procedures. The Windows functions are well documented. To make a call to the Windows API, you just need to understand the documentation for the DLL call. For other DLLs, you need to locate and understand the documentation for the DLL itself. Because developers traditionally write DLLs to be called from C or C++, the documentation provided is usually stated in terms of calling functions from C or C++. For this reason, you need to develop some skills in translating the terminology from the C perspective into the VBA perspective. This chapter provides most of the tools necessary to do this and tells you where you can get the rest of the information you need.

NOTE

The Windows API is made up of literally thousands of functions. Describing them all is beyond the scope of this book (whole books have been written on the subject), but they are documented in several places. For example, Office 2000 Developer contains a file named WIN32API.TXT that includes declarations for most Windows API functions. We have put a copy of this file on the CD-ROM that comes with this book. It has the Declare statements for most of the 32-bit Windows API calls, as well as the definition of most of the constants and structures used by the API calls. But to find out what the functions mean, you will need the Win32 documentation. The best source of this information is the Microsoft Developer Network Library CD-ROM. We highly recommend this as a source of information for developing Access applications. You can get more information on the MSDN library (and even view a portion of it online) at `http://msdn.microsoft.com/`.

Calling DLL Procedures from VBA

Calling procedures in DLLs is similar to calling procedures in standard VBA. The difference is that the body of the procedure (the code that makes it work) resides in a DLL instead of inside a VBA module. For this reason, you need to tell VBA where to find a DLL function before calling it. There are two ways to do this:

- By using a Declare statement
- By referencing a type library

Declare statements are the traditional way of calling API functions, having been around since Visual Basic 1. Type libraries provide an easier way of calling functions but are only now becoming prevalent, and they do require you install a separate type library file on your users' workstations.

The next several sections in this chapter discuss using Declare statements. Even if you intend to use a type library to make API calls, you should still read through the sections on Declare statements, because they provide both a fundamental understanding of how DLL functions work as well as requisite techniques, such as string buffer manipulation, that you must know to use type libraries. For a discussion of using type libraries, see the section "Using Type Libraries with DLL Functions" later in the chapter.

Using Declare Statements

A Declare statement is a definition you provide in the declarations section of a module that tells VBA where to find a function and how to call it. (You will find the details on the construction of a Declare statement in the section "How to Construct a Declare Statement" later in this chapter.) The important point here is that you need a Declare statement to be able to call a DLL function that is not specified by a type library. If you intend to call Windows API functions without using a separate type library, you will need to provide Declare statements for every Windows API call you make.

Because every Windows API function needs a Declare statement, someone has already constructed these statements for you. Microsoft provides a file named WIN32API.TXT with Office 2000 Developer that has all the Declare statements you need. (You will also find it on the CD-ROM that comes with this book.) You also need the definition of certain constants and user-defined type declarations. You can find these definitions in WIN32API.TXT, too.

TIP

Microsoft Office 2000 Developer also includes a tool called the API Text Viewer. This tool simply searches the WIN32API.TXT and finds the proper entry. Unfortunately, the user interface on this tool makes it difficult to use; it is often faster to use a text editor with search capabilities to find the Declare statement in the WIN32API.TXT file.

WARNING

Do not include all of WIN32API.TXT in a module. This large file has at least a thousand declarations within it. The amount of resources it consumes will substantially reduce the performance of your application. Because you will probably use at most several dozen of the declarations in your application, just copy the ones you use into your module.

This is an example of a Declare statement:

```
Public Declare Function GetWindowsDirectory Lib "kernel32" _
 Alias "GetWindowsDirectoryA" (ByVal lpBuffer As String, _
 ByVal nSize As Long) As Long
```

As mentioned earlier, you place Declare statements in the declarations section of a module. After you specify the Declare statement, you can use the procedure that has been declared just as though it were an intrinsic part of VBA, with a number of important exceptions. The following sections describe these exceptions.

WARNING VBA provides a very safe environment in which to work. The environment is not as safe, however, when you are calling external DLL functions directly. Because you *will* eventually make a mistake attempting to call a Windows API and cause a General Protection (GP) fault, it is important to save your work before running any code that calls a DLL. The first time you attempt to call any given DLL function or make a change to a Declare statement, you must be extra careful because that is when a GP fault will most likely occur. Keep recent backups of your database just to cover the slight possibility that it becomes corrupt when Access crashes. DLLs are powerful, but they don't provide the protection from your mistakes that VBA normally gives you.

Passing Arguments to DLLs

You pass arguments to DLLs exactly the same way you pass arguments to any built-in function, with two exceptions, described in the sections "Returning Strings from a DLL" and "Using the Any Data Type" later in this chapter. For example, to find out information about the system on which Windows is running, you call the Windows API function GetSystemMetrics. You retrieve the Declare statement and some constants from WIN32API.TXT and place them in the declarations section of a module. The definitions look like this:

```
Declare Function GetSystemMetrics Lib "user32" _
 (ByVal nIndex As Long) As Long
' GetSystemMetrics() codes
Public Const SM_CXSCREEN = 0
Public Const SM_CYSCREEN = 1
Public Const SM_CXVSCROLL = 2
Public Const SM_CYHSCROLL = 3
Public Const SM_CYCAPTION = 4
' etc... There are 75 of them.
```

After putting the Declare statement and constant declarations in the declarations section of the module, you can call the GetSystemMetrics function just as though it were part of VBA. For example:

```
lngCyCaption = GetSystemMetrics(SM_CYCAPTION)
```

The form frmGetSystemMetrics is shown in Figure 16.1. It is based on the tblGetSystemMetrics table, which contains one row for each constant used with the GetSystemMetrics function. It has fields for the constant, its value, and a description. The form calls GetSystemMetrics in a query used as its record source, passing the constant value for each row, and displays the results in the rightmost column.

FIGURE 16.1:

The form frmGetSystemMetrics shows return values using each of the GetSystemMetrics constants.

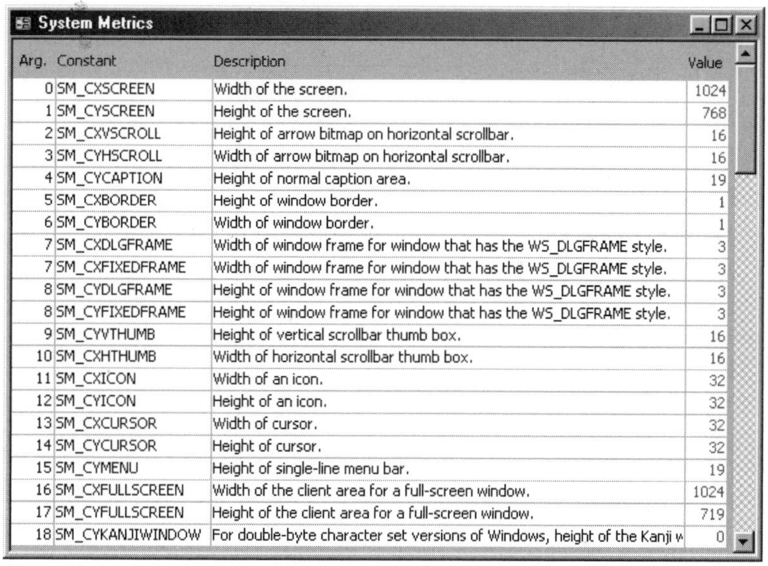

System Metrics

Arg.	Constant	Description	Value
0	SM_CXSCREEN	Width of the screen.	1024
1	SM_CYSCREEN	Height of the screen.	768
2	SM_CXVSCROLL	Height of arrow bitmap on horizontal scrollbar.	16
3	SM_CYHSCROLL	Width of arrow bitmap on horizontal scrollbar.	16
4	SM_CYCAPTION	Height of normal caption area.	19
5	SM_CXBORDER	Height of window border.	1
6	SM_CYBORDER	Width of window border.	1
7	SM_CXDLGFRAME	Width of window frame for window that has the WS_DLGFRAME style.	3
7	SM_CXFIXEDFRAME	Width of window frame for window that has the WS_DLGFRAME style.	3
8	SM_CYDLGFRAME	Height of window frame for window that has the WS_DLGFRAME style.	3
8	SM_CYFIXEDFRAME	Height of window frame for window that has the WS_DLGFRAME style.	3
9	SM_CYVTHUMB	Height of vertical scrollbar thumb box.	16
10	SM_CXHTHUMB	Width of horizontal scrollbar thumb box.	16
11	SM_CXICON	Width of an icon.	32
12	SM_CYICON	Height of an icon.	32
13	SM_CXCURSOR	Width of cursor.	32
14	SM_CYCURSOR	Height of cursor.	32
15	SM_CYMENU	Height of single-line menu bar.	19
16	SM_CXFULLSCREEN	Width of the client area for a full-screen window.	1024
17	SM_CYFULLSCREEN	Height of the client area for a full-screen window.	719
18	SM_CYKANJIWINDOW	For double-byte character set versions of Windows, height of the Kanji w	0

Returning Strings from a DLL

Windows has two ways of storing strings, known to C programmers as BSTR and LPSTR. The section "Passing Strings to a DLL: The Real Story" later in this chapter describes the details of how these are stored internally. All Windows API calls, except those dealing directly with COM, use LPSTRs instead of BSTRs. DLLs cannot change the size of an LPSTR string once it has been created. This causes difficulties when you need the DLL to return a value in a string. In fact, DLL functions that deal with LPSTR strings don't actually return strings but instead modify them in memory.

Because a DLL that accepts an LPSTR cannot change the size of a string that is passed to it, the string needs to be big enough to accept the data to be returned before you pass it to the DLL. This means you need to fill the string with enough characters to create a buffer for the DLL to fill in. You normally accomplish this with the VBA Space function. The DLL must not write past the end of the string, because that can result in a General Protection fault. DLL functions that modify strings normally require that you pass another argument that tells how much space has been allocated for the string. (As odd as it may seem, most DLL functions aren't smart enough to tell how big the buffer is.)

The GetWindowText function is an example of a Windows function that manipulates a string in memory:

```
Declare Function GetWindowText _
 Lib "user32" Alias "GetWindowTextA" _
 (ByVal hwnd As Long, ByVal lpString As String, _
 ByVal cch As Long) As Long
```

You pass it a handle to a window, and it returns the text associated with the window into a buffer.

NOTE

A handle is a Long value that uniquely identifies an object to Windows. The first argument to GetWindowText is a handle to a window, also known as an *hwnd* or *hWnd*. Forms, reports, the Application object, and some ActiveX controls have an hwnd property that will return the handle to a window that you can then pass into the GetWindowText function. You should always retrieve the hwnd property at the time you're calling such a function because Windows will assign a new hwnd to a form each time you reopen it.

When you call GetWindowText, control passes into the Windows API library USER32.DLL. The GetWindowText function inside the DLL looks up the handle in Windows' internal data structures and fills in the lpString parameter with the text that is associated with the window. You call GetWindowText like this:

```
Dim strReturnedString As String
Dim cb As Long

' Allocate enough space for the return value.
strReturnedString = Space(255)

' Call the GetWindowsText function
cb = GetWindowText(Me.hwnd, strReturnedString, _
 Len(strReturnedString)-1)
```

```
' Truncate the string down to the proper size
strReturnedString = Left(strReturnedString, cb)
```

The Space function in this example returns a string of 255 spaces followed by a null character. A null character has the ANSI value 0 and is used in LPSTRs to terminate a string. This allows you to use window captions up to 255 characters. In memory, strReturnedString looks like this:

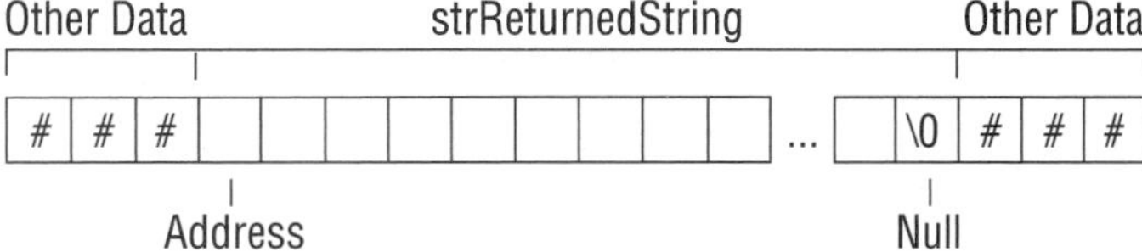

You can see from the illustration that the area in memory corresponding to strReturnedString is identified by an address marking the first byte in the string. You can also see why you don't want to let the DLL function modify too many bytes of memory. Overwriting memory that belongs to other variables or processes can lead to unpredictable results and GP faults.

The code then calls the GetWindowText function. The call has two effects:

- It changes the contents of strReturnedString to be the caption of the window indicated by the hwnd argument, followed by a null character.
- It returns the number of bytes placed into strReturnedString, not counting the terminating null character. (The value is stored in the Long integer variable *cb*, an abbreviation for "count of bytes.")

After the call, strReturnedString looks like this in memory:

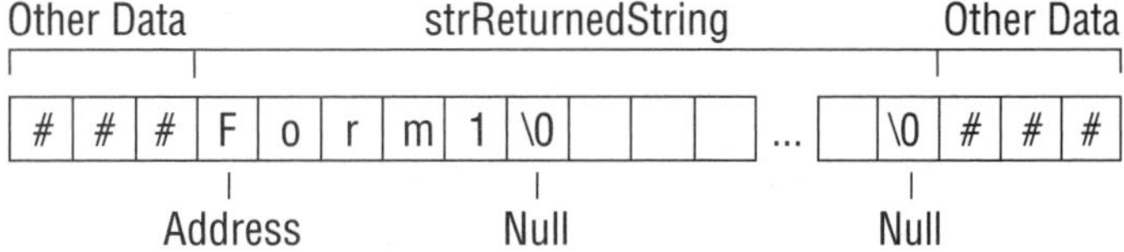

The length of the string hasn't changed, nor has any memory been deallocated—the string is still 255 characters long. Because the DLL cannot make the string shorter, before using strReturnedString you must truncate the string to just before the null character that GetWindowText placed at the end of the string it returned. Fortunately, the return value of the GetWindowText function tells you exactly how many characters should appear in the final string. You then use the Left function to truncate the string. If you pass an invalid value for the hwnd argument, Windows returns a negative value indicating that the API call failed.

If you call a DLL function that doesn't return a value telling you how many characters are in the returned string, you can search for the null character to determine how long the string should be. The Instr function combined with the Left function does the job:

```
strReturnedString = Left(strReturnedString, _
 Instr(1, strReturnedString, vbNullChar) - 1)
```

The GetTextString function is useful, even though you can get the same information by just using the form's Caption property, because the window caption differs depending on which view the form is in. Furthermore, GetTextString works with *any* window in the entire operating system, not just windows that happen to be Access forms. We used the form's hwnd for this example because it was an easy hwnd to get. You can get the hwnd of other windows using other Windows API calls, such as FindWindowEx.

Using the vbNullString Constant

There are times when the documentation for a DLL function indicates that sometimes you need to pass a string and sometimes you need to pass a Null. A Null is a 4-byte zero placed directly on the argument stack. (For a full discussion of what this means, see the section "Understanding Passing by Value and by Reference" later in this chapter.) The main thing you need to know is that to pass a Null, you can use vbNullString.

For example, a Windows API function named SetVolumeLabel sets the label of a disk. The Declare statement for the function is

```
Declare Function SetVolumeLabel _
 Lib "kernel32" Alias "SetVolumeLabelA" _
 (ByVal lpRootPathName As String, _
 ByVal lpVolumeName As String) As Long
```

These are the two arguments to SetVolumeLabel:

Parameter	Meaning
lpRootPathName	Points to a null-terminated string specifying the root directory of a file system volume. This is the volume the function will label. If this parameter is Null, the root of the current directory is used.
lpVolumeName	Points to a string specifying a name for the volume. If this parameter is Null, the function deletes the name of the specified volume.

To set the volume label on the C drive to DRIVE_C, you execute the following code:

```
fRet = SetVolumeLabel("C:\", "DRIVE_C")
```

To delete the volume label using the method documented on the C drive, you need to pass a Null as the second argument. Normally VBA wouldn't allow this, because the arguments are declared as strings, but vbNullString is a special value designed just for this purpose. To delete the volume label, execute the following code:

```
fRet = SetVolumeLabel("C:\", vbNullString)
```

NOTE

Unfortunately, the current shipping version of Windows 95 contains a bug, and the code shown to delete a volume label does not work. (Windows 95 treats a Null as an invalid argument.) However, it does work as documented in Windows NT and Windows 98, and you can work around the bug in Windows 95 by setting the label to an empty string (" ").

Passing a User-Defined Type to a DLL

Sometimes you need to pass a user-defined type to a DLL. For example, many Windows API functions expect complex data structures as arguments. A programmer, rather than the core language being used, defines complex data structures. A common structure is RECT, which represents the boundaries of a rectangle as are used to manipulate screen coordinates. You represent this structure in VBA using a user-defined type or UDT. You can find the declaration in WIN32API.TXT. The RECT UDT is defined like this:

```
Type RECT
    left As Long
    top As Long
```

```
    right As Long
    bottom As Long
End Type
```

You must pass a structure by reference. The declaration of a function that takes a RECT as an argument is

```
Declare Function GetWindowRect Lib "user32" _
 (ByVal hwnd As Long, lpRect As RECT) As Long
```

The form frmGetWindowRect from CH16.MDB uses this function to retrieve the location of the form on the screen (from the upper left-hand corner and measured in pixels). Figure 16.2 shows this form.

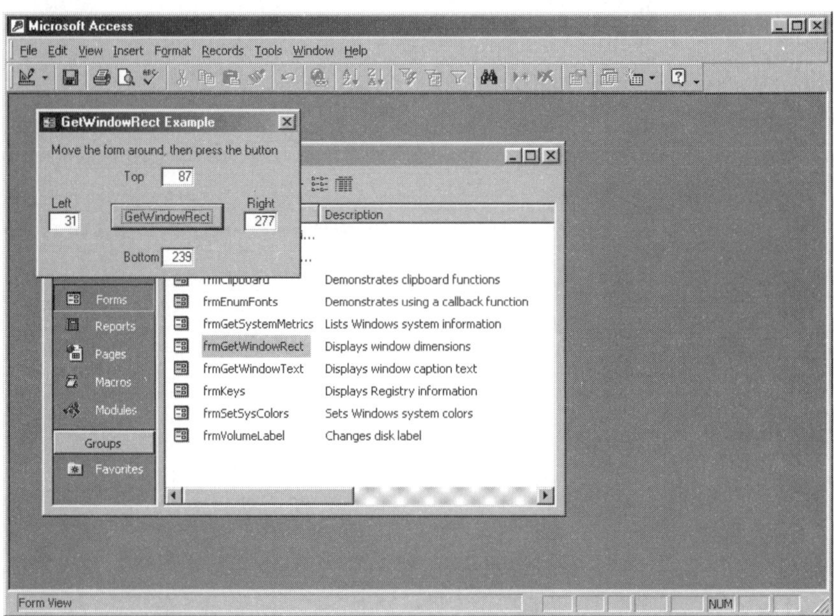

FIGURE 16.2: Using the GetWindowRect Windows API call to determine the location of the window

A call to GetWindowRect looks like this:

```
Dim rectForm As RECT
If GetWindowRect(Me.hwnd, rectForm) Then
    txtLeft.Value = rectForm.left
    txtTop.Value = rectForm.top
    txtRight.Value = rectForm.right
    txtBottom.Value = rectForm.bottom
End If
```

GetWindowRect returns True if it succeeds in filling in the rectForm structure passed in. The sample code then uses the values from the structure to fill in text boxes on the form.

Passing an Array

You can pass individual elements of an array just as you would use any other variable. Sometimes, though, you'll want to pass an entire array to a DLL. You may do this—but only for numeric arrays, not for strings or user-defined arrays, unless the DLL understands a special type called a SAFEARRAY. Documentation of the specific function will indicate when an array is expected. To pass an array, you pass its first element. This, in effect, tells the DLL function the memory address of the first element. Because arrays are always stored in contiguous blocks of memory, the DLL function can deduce the other elements given their size and count. For example, you pass two different arrays to the SetSysColors Windows API as the code from frmSetSysColors in CH16.MDB illustrates:

```
Dim alngDisplayElements() As Long
Dim alngRGBValues() As Long
Dim lngCDisplayElements As Long

' Size the arrays for two elements
lngCDisplayElements = 2
ReDim alngDisplayElements(lngCDisplayElements - 1)
ReDim alngRGBValues(lngCDisplayElements - 1)

' Fill the arrays to set two system colors
alngDisplayElements(0) = COLOR_BTNHIGHLIGHT
alngRGBValues(0) = RGB(&HFF, 0, 0)
alngDisplayElements(1) = COLOR_BTNTEXT
alngRGBValues(1) = RGB(0, 0, &HFF)
Call SetSysColors(lngCDisplayElements, _
 alngDisplayElements(0), alngRGBValues(0))
```

When passing an array to a DLL function, you must give the function some indication of the size of the array. You do this by passing another argument that gives the size of the array. Without this argument, the DLL cannot determine how large the array is and can read beyond the end of the array. If you pass in a size that is larger than the array that has been allocated, you are telling the DLL that more memory has been allocated than really has been. When the DLL tries to access the information past the end of the array, it will get either random bytes or a GP fault, depending on whether the memory it is trying to access actually exists. In other words, be very careful that you pass the correct size in that argument.

Note that while you cannot pass arrays of strings to DLL functions, you can pass what are called *double null terminated* strings. These are strings in which individual fragments are separated by null characters and the entire string is terminated by two nulls. For example, to construct a double null terminated string, you might write code like this:

```
Dim strDblNull As String
strDblNull = "First part" & vbNullChar & "Second part" & _
 vbNullChar & "Third part" & vbNullChar & vbNullChar
```

A few DLL functions require strings of this type. The functions parse data passed to them using the null characters.

An Example: Reading Data from the Registry

To demonstrate the usefulness of the Windows API, we've created an example that shows how to read data from the Windows Registry. While VBA provides functions for this (GetSetting, SaveSetting, GetAllSettings, and DeleteSetting), these only work with a small piece of the Registry. Developers often have a need to obtain information from other parts of the Registry. Due to space limitations, we've shown only a few lines of code. You can find the remainder in the sample database, CH16.MDB.

Registry Functionality

The System Registry is the cache for important data in 32-bit Windows. The Registry is organized as a hierarchical database of information and indexes data-named keys and values. The *key* indicates where within the database it can find the information. The *value* is the name given to a particular piece of information. You can store data of different data types in the Registry, including numbers, strings, and binary information.

You can look at Registry data using the Windows Registry Editor by running REGEDIT.EXE. Figure 16.3 presents a picture of the Registry that REGEDIT shows. The Registry is broken into a number of root entries, also known as *hives*:

- HKEY_CLASSES_ROOT
- HKEY_CURRENT_USER
- HKEY_LOCAL_MACHINE
- HKEY_USERS
- HKEY_CURRENT_CONFIG
- HKEY_DYN_DATA

FIGURE 16.3:

REGEDIT browsing the Registry

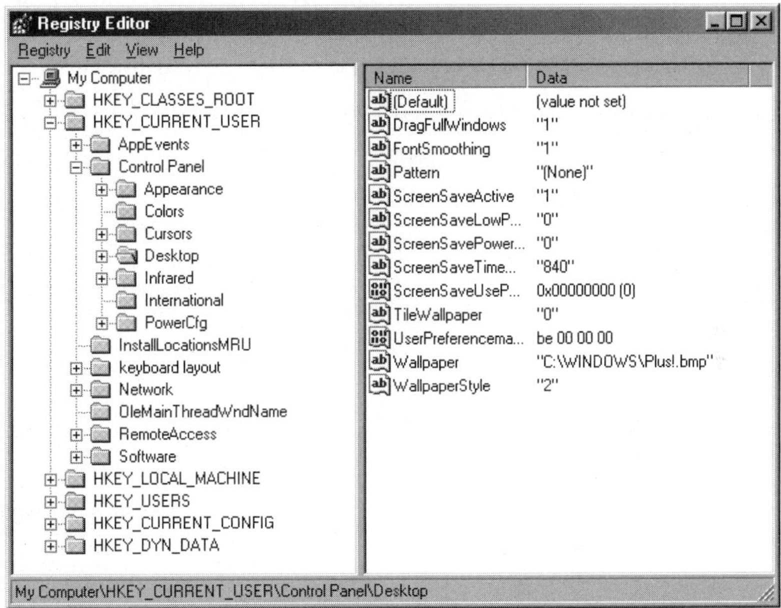

Information about the current system is stored in the HKEY_LOCAL_MACHINE path. Information specific to the currently logged-in user is stored in the HKEY_CURRENT_USER path.

VBA provides some intrinsic functions that get and set some values within the Registry: GetSetting, SaveSetting, GetAllSettings, and DeleteSetting. While these functions are useful for setting and getting information about your program, they let you modify only a small part of the Registry database. Specifically, they let you modify only the HKEY_CURRENT_USER\Software\VB and VBA Program Settings branch of the database. It is often useful to be able to browse and modify other portions of the Registry.

Browsing the Registry

Figure 16.4 shows frmKeys from CH16.MDB. This form allows you to browse the HKEY_CURRENT_USER and HKEY_LOCAL_MACHINE branches of the Registry by selecting an option from the option group on the form. A list of keys is shown in the left-hand list box. When you double-click a key in the left-hand list box, the list is refreshed to show that key's subkeys. Single-clicking a key displays the values assigned to that key in the right-hand list box. Clicking a values name in the right-hand list box displays the contents of that value in the text box at the bottom of the form. Clicking the Reset button takes you back to the root key. This functionality demonstrates traversing the tree and getting values.

FIGURE 16.4:

A Registry browser that allows traversing the Registry tree

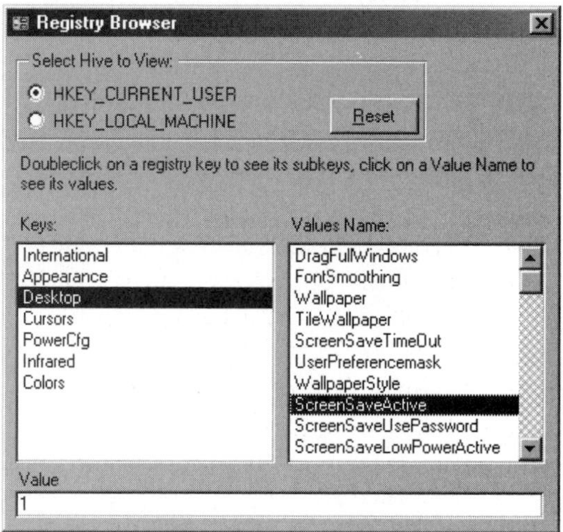

When you open the form, the form initializes the list boxes by calling the cmdRoot_Click event. This function calls adhGetRegistryKeys from the basRegistry module in the same database. adhGetRegistryKeys builds a semicolon-delimited string, which sets the RowSource property of the list box. The function adhGetRegistryKeys is shown in Listing 16.1.

Listing 16.1

```
Public Function adhGetRegistryKeys(ByVal hKey As Long) As String
    ' Returns a semicolon-delimited list of all of
    ' the subkeys of this key
    Dim strRet As String
    Dim lngRet As Long
    Dim strClassName As String
    Dim cchClassName As Long
    Dim lngCSubKeys As Long
    Dim cchMaxSubKey As Long
    Dim cchMaxClass As Long
    Dim lngCValues As Long
    Dim cchMaxValueName As Long
    Dim cbMaxValueData As Long
    Dim cbSecurityDescriptor As Long
    Dim ftLastWrite As FILETIME
    Dim i As Long
    Dim strKey As String
    Dim cchKey As Long
    Dim strClass As String
    Dim cchClass As Long
    Dim retCode As Long

    strRet = ""
    strClassName = Space(256)
    cchClassName = Len(strClassName)
    Call adh_apiRegQueryInfoKey(hKey, strClassName, _
     cchClassName, 0&, lngCSubKeys, cchMaxSubKey, _
     cchMaxClass, lngCValues, cchMaxValueName, _
     cbMaxValueData, cbSecurityDescriptor, ftLastWrite)
    For i = 0 To lngCSubKeys - 1
        strKey = Space(cchMaxSubKey)
        cchKey = Len(strKey) + 1
        strClass = Space(cchMaxClass)
        cchClass = Len(strClass) + 1
        retCode = adh_apiRegEnumKeyEx(hKey, i, strKey, _
         cchKey, 0&, strClass, cchClass, ftLastWrite)

        Select Case retCode And APPLICATION_ERROR_MASK
            Case ERROR_SEVERITY_SUCCESS
```

```
                Case Else
                    Stop
                    Exit For
            End Select
            strKey = Left(strKey, cchKey)
            strRet = strRet & strKey & ";"
        Next i
        adhGetRegistryKeys = strRet
    End Function
```

Each location in the path is a key. The Registry function operates by using handles to these keys. A handle to a key, or hKey, is a Long integer that uniquely identifies a key. Various functions enumerate subkeys and values for keys.

The core functionality works like this:

1. The code retrieves a known handle to a key—in this case, HKEY_ CURRENT_USER, stored in hKeyCurrent.
2. The code calls adhGetRegistryKeys with this handle to a key.
3. adhGetRegistryKeys calls RegQueryInfoKey to find out the number of subkeys under this Registry entry and the maximum length of the keys.
4. For each key, a call is made to RegEnumKeyEx. This gets the name of the key.
5. The code truncates the key down to the proper size, using the Left function.
6. The keys are concatenated together and placed in the RowSource property of the left-hand list box.

When you click an entry in the list box, the code shown in Listing 16.2 is called.

Listing 16.2

```
Private Sub lstKeys_Click()
    ' Fills the lstValues with a list of values based
    ' on the entry clicked on in lstKeys
    Dim hKeyNew As Long
    Dim lngRet As Long

    If hKeySelected Then
        Call adh_apiRegCloseKey(hKeySelected)
```

```
        End If
        lngRet = adh_apiRegOpenKeyEx(hKeyCurrent, lstKeys.Value, _
         0&, KEY_READ, hKeyNew)
        If lngRet = ERROR_SEVERITY_SUCCESS Then
            hKeySelected = hKeyNew
            lstValues.RowSource = adhGetRegistryValues(hKeySelected)
        End If
End Sub
```

NOTE ERROR_SEVERITY_SUCCESS is a constant representing the value 0. It is returned by the Registry functions to indicate that the operation succeeded.

Whenever you select a key in a list box, the code opens the key and stores the hKey in hKeySelected. When you select another key, the code must close the first key, or Windows will continue to keep some memory allocated. The code then calls adhGetRegistryValues. adhGetRegistryValues is virtually the same as adhGetRegistryKeys, except that it calls RegEnumValue to retrieve the names of the values. The difference is that one returns a list of subkeys and the other returns the list of values associated with a key.

When you double-click a key, the code traverses to that subkey. This code is shown in Listing 16.3. It opens the subkey with RegOpenKeyEx, closes the current key with RegCloseKey, and then gets the new values to fill the list box by calling adhGetRegistryKeys again. Finally, the code clears the right-hand list box and closes the currently selected key.

Listing 16.3

```
Private Sub lstKeys_DblClick(Cancel As Integer)
    ' Resets the list boxes to show the new key that
    ' was double-clicked

    Dim lngRet As Long
    Dim hKeyNew As Long

    lngRet = adh_apiRegOpenKeyEx(hKeyCurrent, lstKeys.Value, _
     0&, KEY_READ, hKeyNew)
    If lngRet = ERROR_SEVERITY_SUCCESS Then
```

```
            Call adh_apiRegCloseKey(hKeyCurrent)
            hKeyCurrent = hKeyNew
            lstKeys.RowSource = _
             Left(adhGetRegistryKeys(hKeyCurrent), 1024)
            If hKeySelected Then
                Call adh_apiRegCloseKey(hKeySelected)
            End If
            hKeySelected = 0
            lstValues.RowSource = ""
        End If
    End Sub
```

Retrieving a value when the value name is selected is accomplished by calling adhGetRegistryValue, shown in Listing 16.4. It calls RegQueryValueEx twice. The first time it is called with the lpbData argument set to Null. This is to retrieve the datatype of the key into lngType. The second time it is called in different ways, depending on which type was retrieved. The return value of the function is set to the actual value retrieved.

Listing 16.4

```
Public Function adhGetRegistryValue(ByVal hKey As Long, ByVal _
 strValue As String) As Variant

    ' Returns a Registry value based on an hKey
    ' and a strValue

    Dim retCode As Long
    Dim lngType As Long
    Dim cbData As Long
    Dim strGetValue As String
    Dim lngValue As Long

    adhGetRegistryValue = "<Binary Data>"
    retCode = adh_apiRegQueryValueEx(hKey, strValue, 0&, _
     lngType, ByVal 0&, cbData)

    Select Case retCode And APPLICATION_ERROR_MASK
        Case ERROR_SEVERITY_SUCCESS
            Select Case lngType
                Case REG_NONE
                    adhGetRegistryValue = CVErr(0)
```

```
                Case REG_SZ, REG_EXPAND_SZ
                    strGetValue = Space$(cbData)
                    retCode = adh_apiRegQueryValueEx( _
                     hKey, strValue, 0&, lngType, _
                     ByVal strGetValue, cbData)
                    adhGetRegistryValue = strGetValue
                Case REG_BINARY
                Case REG_DWORD, REG_DWORD_LITTLE_ENDIAN
                    retCode = adh_apiRegQueryValueEx( _
                     hKey, strValue, 0&, lngType, _
                     lngValue, cbData)
                    adhGetRegistryValue = lngValue
                Case REG_DWORD_BIG_ENDIAN
                Case REG_LINK
                Case REG_MULTI_SZ
                Case REG_RESOURCE_LIST
                Case REG_FULL_RESOURCE_DESCRIPTOR
                Case REG_RESOURCE_REQUIREMENTS_LIST
                Case Else
                     Stop
            End Select
        Case Else
            Debug.Assert False   'Should never happen
    End Select
End Function
```

Another Registry Example

The previous example showed you how to walk through the Registry, but what can you use this technique for? It's very useful to be able to retrieve and set Registry entries, given the path through the Registry to a value. For example, you may want to tell the user's screensaver state by retrieving the value in HKEY_CURRENT_USER\Control Panel\Desktop\ScreenSaveActive. You do this by walking down through the various keys. We have provided a generic routine in the sample database, adhGetRegistryValueFromPath, which does the walking for you and returns the value of the key. You would call it with:

```
Dim strValue As String

strValue = adhGetRegistryValueFromPath _
 ("\HKEY_CURRENT_USER\Control Panel\Desktop\ScreenSaveActive")
```

NOTE

Each Registry key has a default entry that has no value name. To retrieve the default entry for a key, follow the key name with a backslash when calling adhGetRegistryValueFromPath. For example, to retrieve the default value of the Desktop key mentioned previously in this chapter, you use \HKEY_CURRENT_USER\Control Panel\Desktop\.

The counterpart to adhGetRegistryValueFromPath is adhSetRegistryValueFromPath, which sets a value based on a path. It executes virtually the same code as adhGetRegistryValueFromPath, except that it looks at the result of the VarType function on the strValue key passed in and calls RegSetValueEx in the appropriate manner to write the value into the Registry. The only data types supported in this code are Strings and Longs. The other data types supported by the Registry (such as binary data) require a bit more code to support and are left as exercises for the reader.

Using Type Libraries with DLL Functions

COM Automation servers use *type libraries* to define their exposed objects, properties, and methods. (For more information on COM Automation see Chapters 12 and 13.) Type libraries can also be used to provide a simplified interface to regular DLL functions. A type library usually has the extension OLB or TLB and is registered with Windows through a set of COM interfaces. The setup program that installs the DLL usually creates the proper entries with the Windows Registry to register the type library. If you select Tools ➢ References from the menus in the VBE, the dialog shows all the registered type libraries that are available to VBA. By placing a check next to the name of a type library, you tell Access that everything within the type library is available to VBA.

If you use a type library, there is no need to use Declare statements because the type library includes all the functionality of the Declare statement. In addition, type libraries avoid the difficulties of passing strings to DLLs. (See the section "Passing Strings to a DLL: The Real Story" later in this chapter.) ADO (ActiveX Data Objects) in VBA is an example of a type library. The type library provides all the functionality of ADO to VBA; none of it is really intrinsic to VBA.

A Type Library for the Windows API

One obvious use for the ability to wrap DLL functions in a type library is harnessing the Windows API. Fortunately Microsoft has done this for you in Windows 98 and NT. They've provided a type library that encapsulates most Windows API calls and included it on the Windows 98 CD-ROM. You'll find it in a file called WIN.TLB in the CD's TOOLS\RESKIT\SYSFILES directory. To use it, you'll need to copy it to your workstation and register it with Windows. To do this:

1. Copy WIN.TLB from the CD to your Windows System directory.
2. Launch Access and open the Visual Basic Editor.
3. Select Tools ➢ References to open the References dialog.
4. Click the Browse button and locate WIN.TLB in the file dialog.
5. Select WIN.TLB and click the Open button.

This will both register the type library on your workstation and add a reference to it to the active VBA project. You'll need to add a reference to the type library to each VBA project in which you want to use it.

Calling API Functions Using WIN.TLB

After referencing the WIN.TLB type library, you can call API functions just as you would any other VBA function. Figure 16.5 shows the VBA Object Browser displaying methods in the type library.

What the type library provides is a simplified way of declaring Windows API functions. What it does not provide is a simplified way of accomplishing tasks using the API. It's merely a one-to-one mapping of API functions to type library definitions. You may still need to call many functions to accomplish a given task. If you want to create higher-level functionality with the simplicity of a type library, you might consider creating a custom VBA class as described in the section "Creating DLL Function Classes" later in this chapter.

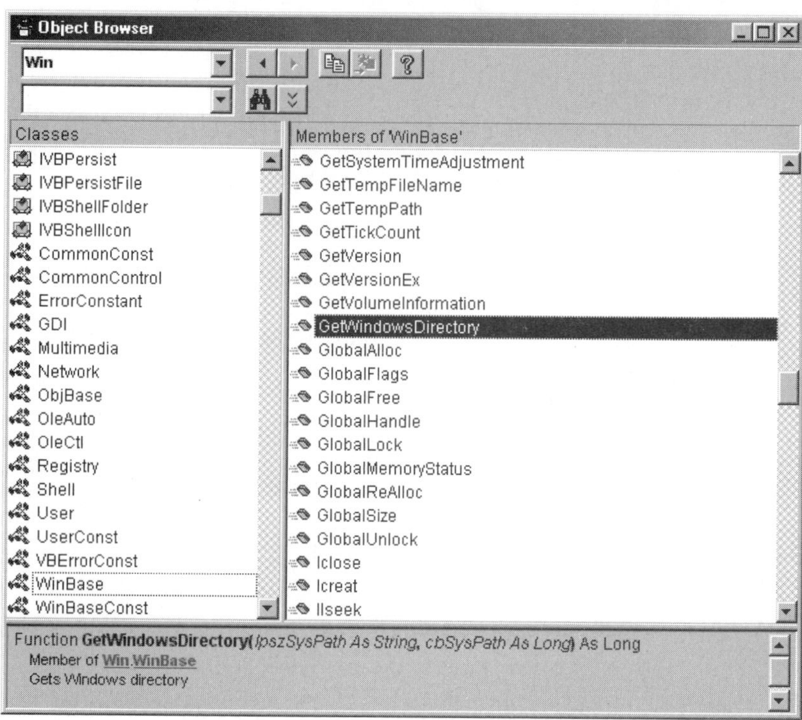

FIGURE 16.5:

The VBA Object Browser shows you Windows API function declarations.

Distributing Solutions That Use Type Libraries

While type libraries may make development easier, they do complicate deployment because you must distribute and register them with your solution in order for the solution to work. The easiest way for you to do this is to use the Package and Deployment Wizard that comes with Office 2000 Developer. It can detect references to type libraries and include them automatically in the setup package it creates. The generated setup program will also register the type library on a user's workstation when your solution is installed.

Creating DLL Function Classes

So far in this chapter, we've discussed calling DLL functions by providing Declare statements in your source code and by using type libraries to provide the declarations. While both are powerful options, they also have their drawbacks. Inline Declarations don't require you to deploy additional files with your solution, but they can be cumbersome to use and difficult to understand. Type libraries, while providing simplified calling conventions, require you to ship and register an additional component. A hybrid solution is to use VBA class modules to encapsulate DLL functionality.

Using class modules offers the benefits of type libraries, namely, a simple way of calling functions, with the deployment benefits of not having to distribute an additional file. Furthermore, class modules let you "roll up" numerous DLL functions required to perform a given task into a set of simplified properties and methods. To illustrate these benefits, we've created a VBA class that manipulates the Windows clipboard.

Using the Clipboard

Unlike Visual Basic, neither Access nor VBA supplies a built-in Clipboard object. This limits your ability to share source code between VB and VBA projects. This section demonstrates how you can use Windows API calls to simulate the same functionality. The example uses the Windows API to produce a class called CClipboard with two methods, SetText and GetText, that correspond to methods of VB's built in Clipboard object. The methods make use of 12 different Windows API calls. Encapsulating these functions in a class module makes it easy to use the clipboard without needing to bother with the excruciating details.

The SetText method performs the following tasks:

1. It uses the GlobalAlloc function to allocate some memory.
2. It moves the passed-in string into it.
3. It opens the clipboard.
4. It empties the current contents of the clipboard.
5. It writes the data onto the clipboard.
6. It closes the clipboard.

The GetText method performs roughly the opposite:

1. It sees whether there is some text on the clipboard that can be read.
2. If so, it opens the clipboard.

3. It gets the current contents of the clipboard.
4. It copies the contents into a string.
5. It truncates the string to the right size.
6. It closes the clipboard.

You can include these clipboard functions in your solution by importing the CClipboard class module from CH16.MDB.

If you look at the functions we've provided, you'll see several things common to working with the Windows API. First and foremost, a *lot* of functions need to be called. The Windows API tends to be very granular, with functions that perform small tasks. Only by combining these functions do you get rich functionality. Second, the clipboard functions use handles, just like other functions dealing with windows. You'll find the Windows API full of handles to just about everything. Individual functions are commonly structured to return a handle as a result or a zero if the function failed. For example, look at the call to the Global Alloc function, which allocates memory to a given program:

```
hMemory = adh_apiGlobalAlloc(GMEM_MOVABLE Or _
 GMEM_DDESHARE, lngSize)
If Not hMemory Then
    varRet = CVErr(adhCANNOTGLOBALALLOC)
    GoTo adhClipboardSetTextDone
End If
```

If GlobalAlloc is successful, it returns a handle to the allocated memory, which is then stored in hMemory. The procedure uses an If...Then test to see whether hMemory contains a valid (nonzero) handle. If it does not, the function returns an error code and exits the function.

Using the CClipboard Class

If the amount of source code in the CClipboard class scares you, don't worry. You needn't be concerned with it after you import the class module into your VBA project. Once there, you can simply use the class' two simple methods.

The form frmClipboard in CH16.MDB, shown in Figure 16.6, demonstrates the two methods. First, you enter some text in the first text box and click the Copy button. This places the contents of the text box in the clipboard. You can then click the Paste button to paste it into the second text box. If you examine the code behind each button, you'll see that it simply calls our two clipboard class methods:

```
Private Clipboard As New CClipboard

Private Sub cmdCopy_Click()
    Clipboard.SetText Me!txtCopy
End Sub

Private Sub cmdPaste_Click()
    Me!txtPaste = Clipboard.GetText()
End Sub
```

FIGURE 16.6:

frmClipboard demonstrates clipboard functionality.

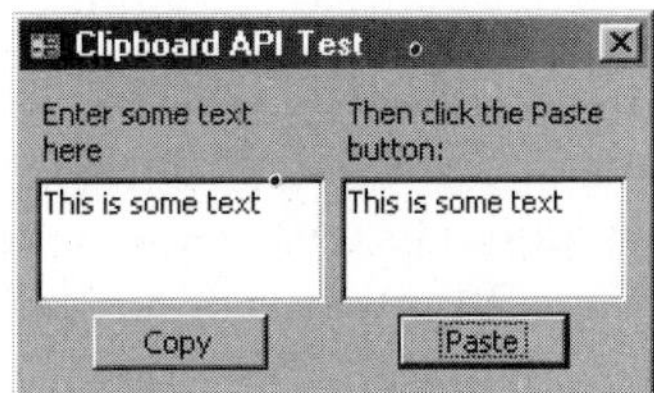

How to Construct a Declare Statement

If you plan on using only Windows API functions, you won't need to construct Declare statements. Instead, you will get them from some source, such as WIN32API.TXT. However, at some point you may call a DLL that doesn't have a Declare statement already prepared for it. In this case, you need to construct a Declare statement from scratch. Also, the file WIN32API.TXT is not perfect. Some of the Declare statements don't allow you to call some of the Windows API calls with arguments of certain types, and we have found bugs in some of the Declare statements as we have worked with them. These may or may not be fixed in your copy of WIN32API.TXT, so understanding how to construct a Declare statement is a useful skill.

The Declare statement gives VBA six pieces of information about a procedure in an external library:

- The scope of the declaration
- The name of the procedure as you want to call it in your code

- The name and path of the containing DLL
- The name of the procedure as it exists in the DLL
- The number and data types of the arguments to the procedure
- If the procedure is a function, the data type of the return value of the function

Given this information, VBA knows how to locate the function on the hard disk and how to arrange the arguments on the stack so they are acceptable to the DLL. The *stack* is a special segment of memory that programs use for storing temporary information. VBA pushes arguments onto the stack, the DLL function is called, and DLL manipulates the arguments. Then the return value is placed on the stack for VBA to return to your program.

The Declare statement defines the size of the arguments to a DLL function and what the arguments mean. It is *crucial* that the declaration be exactly what the DLL expects. Otherwise, you may be giving the DLL incorrect information, and that may cause the DLL to reference information in an invalid memory location. A GP fault results when a program tries to access memory it doesn't have the privilege to read or write. If you receive a GP fault, Access crashes without giving you a chance to save any changed objects. This is what most programmers call "a bad thing."

Defining the VBA Declare statement is similar to defining any other sub or function, except that there is no body to the procedure. The body of the procedure resides in the DLL. Once you have declared a DLL function, you can call it almost as though the code were part of VBA. Declare statements must appear at the module level in the declarations section. The Declare statement takes one of two forms, depending on whether the DLL function being called returns a value:

[Public | Private] Declare Sub subname Lib "*libname*"

[Alias "*aliasname*"] [([*argumentlist*])]

or

[Public | Private] Declare Function *functionname* Lib "*libname*"

[Alias "*aliasname*"] [([*argumentlist*])] [As type]

Here is an example of a Declare statement:

```
Private Declare Function FindWindow Lib "user32" _
  Alias "FindWindowA" _
  (ByVal lpClassName As String, _
  ByVal lpWindowName As String) As Long
```

If the function returns no value (that is, it is declared with the return type *void* in the C programming language), you use the Declare Sub format of the Declare statement. If the function returns a value (and almost all of them do), you use the Declare Function format.

Public versus Private

Just as any normal procedure declaration has a scope that determines what other procedures can call it, procedures defined by Declare statements also have a scope. You can call a DLL procedure from code only within the same form or module as the Declare statement if you prefix the Declare statement with the word *Private.* You can call a DLL function from any code if the Declare statement is prefixed with the word *Public.* Not using either Public or Private is the same as declaring the procedure Public. A Declare statement in the declarations section of a form or class module must have Private scope. A Declare statement in a standard module can have either scope.

Specifying the Procedure Name

The function or sub name given in the Declare statement is the name that is used when you call it in your code. It must follow the same naming rules as for any VBA procedure name:

- It must begin with a letter.
- The other characters must be in the sets A–Z, a–z, 0–9, or an underscore character.
- It must be unique within the same scope.
- It must be no longer than 255 characters.
- It cannot be a VBA keyword.

If you don't supply an Alias clause, the name of the procedure must match the name of the function in the DLL. (See the section "Specifying the Alias" a little later in this chapter.) Keep in mind that API functions in 32-bit Windows are case-sensitive.

Specifying the Lib(rary)

The Lib portion of the declaration tells VBA the DLL's name and also, potentially, its location on the disk. You must enclose the Lib name in quotes. It is not case-sensitive. If the function you are declaring is in one of the main Windows DLLs, you can omit the DLL extension. For example, you can use User32, GDI32, or Kernel32. VBA appends the DLL extension to these names. For other DLLs, you must include the full DLL name, including the file extension.

If you do not include the path on the DLL name, Windows uses this order to search for the DLL:

1. The directory from which the application loaded (for Access, that's the directory from which Access is loaded, not the directory where your MDB is stored).
2. The current directory.
3. Windows NT only: the 32-bit Windows system directory (Windows\System32).
4. The Windows system directory (Windows\System).
5. The Windows directory (Windows).
6. The directories that are listed in the PATH environment variable.

This order can cause some confusion. If you put a DLL in the Windows directory but there is an older version of the DLL in the Windows\System directory, the older version will be called. Furthermore, this order has changed from earlier versions of Windows.

Specifying the Alias

You may include an alias clause when you declare a procedure. The alias clause of the declaration is important because it allows you to change the name of the function from the way it was specified in the DLL to a different name in VBA. There are several reasons why you might use the alias:

- To change an invalid procedure name in the DLL to one that VBA allows
- To change the case of the DLL procedure call
- To set the procedure name to a DLL function that is only exposed by ordinal number
- To have a unique procedure name in an Access library
- To leave off the *A* required by ANSI versions of Windows API calls

These reasons are explained in more detail in the following sections.

Changing the Procedure Name in the DLL to One That VBA Allows

The names that programming languages such as C allow for functions are different from those VBA allows. VBA function names must consist of alphanumeric or underscore characters and begin with a letter. C function names sometimes begin with an underscore. The function name you specify in the Declare statement must be a valid VBA procedure name. If the name in the DLL doesn't match the VBA naming rules, you must use an alias. The name in the DLL might also be a reserved word in VBA, or it might be the name of an existing global variable or function; in these cases, too, you must use an alias.

For example, VBA does not allow function names with a leading underscore. To use the Windows API function _lwrite, then, you might declare the function as

```
Declare Function lwrite Lib "kernel32" Alias "_lwrite" _
 (ByVal hFile As Long, ByVal lpBuffer As String, _
 ByVal wBytes As Long) As Long
```

This defines the function name lwrite as the _lwrite function in the Kernel32 Dynamic Link Library.

NOTE Although the _lwrite function still exists in Win32, it is provided only for backward compatibility with 16-bit Windows. You should use the WriteFile function in your code. We use it here only to illustrate the point regarding function name aliasing.

Changing the Case of the DLL Procedure Call

The name of the procedure given in the Declare statement is case-sensitive. This means it must exactly match the case of the procedure name in the DLL. If you wish to have the procedure name in your code use a different capitalization than that given in the DLL, you must use an alias clause. This wasn't true in 16-bit Windows, so if you are converting Declare statements from old code, you need to be aware of this.

Setting the Procedure Name That Is Exposed by Ordinal Number

Every function in a DLL is assigned a number, called its *ordinal*. Every function in a DLL *may* expose its name but is not required to do so. The programmer writing a DLL chooses which procedures within the DLL can be called from code existing outside the DLL; these functions are *exposed*.

To call a function by ordinal, you must know the ordinal number for the function. You can find this information in the documentation for the DLL (if any) or in the DEF file for the DLL. Tools are also available that can examine a DLL. Whichever way you derive the ordinal, you specify *#ordinalnumber* for the alias name—that is, a pound sign followed by the decimal number of the ordinal. For example, the declaration for the _lwrite function presented earlier might be declared as

```
Declare Function lwrite Lib "Kernel32" Alias "#86" _
 (ByVal hFile As Long, ByVal lpBuffer As String, _
 ByVal wBytes As Long) As Long
```

You may declare any function using its ordinal number, but if the name is exported, we recommend you use the name. This is especially important if you do not maintain the DLL. The DLL developer may assume that people will not call a function by ordinal if it is exported by name. Later versions of the DLL may not keep the same ordinal number for the functions in it but will most likely keep the same name.

Having a Unique Procedure Name in an Access Library

Each declared function at the same level of scope in VBA must have a unique name. Normally, this doesn't have huge implications because you are not likely to give two different functions the same name or declare the same function twice in your own code. But if you are developing a library database that might be included on different systems, and that library calls functions in a DLL (including Windows API calls), this issue becomes important.

Suppose your library calls the GetComputerName Windows API call. If you declare the function in the library with Public scope but without an alias, VBA uses the name GetComputerName. If users then decide to use GetComputerName in their own code and declare it as Public, the name in their code conflicts with the name in your library. For this reason, public declarations in a library should always use an alias. Thus, you might declare GetComputerName in a library as

```
Declare Function MYLB_GetComputerName _
 Lib "kernel32" Alias "GetComputerNameA" _
 (ByVal lpBuffer As String, nSize As Long) As Long
```

When you use the function in the library, you then use MYLB_GetComputerName as the function name. This enables users to avoid conflicts if they also define GetComputerName.

Leaving Off the *A* Required by ANSI Windows API Calls

You can use the Alias clause to do any renaming of functions you wish. One common use is to rename ANSI Windows API calls that have a trailing *A* to the same name without the *A*. The *A* is used in functions such as FindWindowA to indicate that the arguments being passed in are ANSI strings. (You can find a further discussion of ANSI and Unicode functions in the section "Unicode to ANSI and Back" later in this chapter.)

Specifying the Arguments

You pass arguments to a DLL on the stack. The DLL expects those arguments to be placed in a particular order and to have a certain size on the stack. When VBA places arguments on the stack, it looks to the Declare statement for direction. Arguments placed on the stack appear as a series of bytes. The DLL groups and decodes those bytes to use them in the parameters for the DLL call. If the VBA Declare statement and the DLL don't agree on what those bytes mean, incorrect data appears in the parameters for the DLL call. When the DLL tries to use the parameters, it gets the wrong information. Worse, if your program doesn't place enough data on the stack, the DLL will read data left over from previous use of the stack.

Correctly declaring arguments is the trickiest part of using a DLL from VBA. This subject is discussed in the following section.

Converting C Parameters into VBA Declarations

Most DLLs are written in C or C++. The documentation is usually in the form of a C header file (.h file) that provides the type and number of the arguments to the functions in the DLL. Based on the data type required, you will need to convert it to an equivalent VBA data type. Table 16.1 shows how to convert various C data types to VBA.

TABLE 16.1: Conversions between C Data Types and VBA Data Types

C Datatype	VBA Data Type
ATOM	ByVal atom As Integer
BOOL	ByVal fValue As Integer
BYTE	ByVal bytValue As Byte
BYTE	bytValue As Byte
CALLBACK	ByVal lngAddr As Long
char	ByVal bytValue As Byte
char _huge	ByVal strValue As String
char FAR	ByVal strValue As String
char NEAR	ByVal strValue As String
DWORD	ByVal lngValue As Long
FARPROC	ByVal lngAddress As Long
HACCEL	ByVal hAccel As Long
HANDLE	ByVal h As Long

Continued on next page

TABLE 16.1 CONTINUED: Conversions between C Data Types and VBA Data Types

C Datatype	VBA Data Type
HBITMAP	ByVal hBitmap As Long
HBRUSH	ByVal hBrush As Long
HCURSOR	ByVal hCursor As Long
HDC	ByVal hDC As Long
HDRVR	ByVal hDrvr As Long
HDWP	ByVal hDWP As Long
HFILE	ByVal hFile As Integer
HFONT	ByVal hFont As Long
HGDIOBJ	ByVal hGDIObj As Long
HGLOBAL	ByVal hGlobal As Long
HICON	ByVal hIcon As Long
HINSTANCE	ByVal hInstance As Long
HLOCAL	ByVal hLocal As Long
HMENU	ByVal hMenu As Long
HMETAFILE	ByVal hMetafile As Long
HMODULE	ByVal hModule As Long
HPALETTE	ByVal hPalette As Long
HPEN	ByVal hPen As Long
HRGN	ByVal hRgn As Long
HRSRC	ByVal hRsrc As Long
HTASK	ByVal hTask As Long
HWND	ByVal hWnd As Long
int	ByVal intValue As Integer
int FAR	intValue As Integer

Continued on next page

TABLE 16.1 CONTINUED: Conversions between C Data Types and VBA Data Types

C Datatype	VBA Data Type
LONG	ByVal lngValue As Long
long	ByVal lngValue As Long
LPARAM	ByVal lngParam As Long
LPCSTR	ByVal strValue As String
LPSTR	ByVal strValue As String
LPVOID	varValue As Any
LRESULT	ByVal lngResult As Long
UINT	ByVal intValue As Integer
UINT FAR	intValue As Integer
void _huge	bytValue( ) As Byte
void FAR	bytValue( ) As Byte
WORD	ByVal intValue As Integer
WPARAM	ByVal intValue As Integer

More Advanced Details of Calling DLLs

So far, this chapter has discussed most of the details of calling a DLL. Really understanding what is going on, though, requires a fuller understanding of what happens during a DLL call. The following sections will cover this.

Understanding Passing by Value and by Reference

You can pass an argument on the stack to a DLL in one of two ways: by value or by reference. *By value* means that a copy of the actual value of what is being passed is pushed onto the stack. *By reference* means that the address of what is being passed is pushed onto the stack. Unless you tell it otherwise, VBA passes all arguments by reference. On the other hand, most DLLs are written in C, and unless you tell the C compiler otherwise (by passing an address), C passes all arguments by value. The VBA declaration *must* be set up correctly to pass arguments the way the DLL expects them to be passed.

The semantic difference between passing by value and by reference is this:

- When you pass by value, a copy of the value is placed on the stack. Any changes to the value inside the DLL have an effect only on the copy and do not change the value for the calling code.
- When you pass by reference, the address of the original value is placed on the stack. If the DLL makes changes to the value, the calling code will be able to see those changes.

To understand the difference, look at the declaration in C of the function GetFileSize:

```
DWORD GetFileSize
    (
    HANDLE hFile,               // handle of file to get size of
    LPDWORD lpFileSizeHigh,     // address of high-order word
                                // for file size
    );
```

The GetFileSize function takes two arguments:

Parameter	**Meaning**
hFile	Specifies an open handle of the file whose size is being returned. The handle must have been created with either GENERIC_READ or GENERIC_WRITE access to the file.
lpFileSizeHigh	Points to the variable where the high-order word of the file size is returned. This parameter can be Null if the application does not require the high-order word.

The first, hFile, is a handle to a file by value. The second, lpFileSizeHigh, is a Long by reference. The function fills in the second argument. Suppose you call this function with the following code:

```
Function adhGetFileSize(ByVal strFile As String) As Long
    Dim hFile As Long
    Dim lngHigh As Long
    Dim curSize As Currency
```

```
    hFile = CreateFile(strFile, GENERIC_READ, _
     FILE_SHARE_READ, ByVal 0&, OPEN_EXISTING, _
     0&, 0&)

    If Not Err.LastDllError Then
        curSize = GetFileSize(hFile, lngHigh)
        If lngHigh > 0 Then
            curSize = curSize + 2 ^ 32 * lngHigh
        End If
        adhGetFileSize = CLng(curSize)
        Call CloseHandle(hFile)
    Else
        adhGetFileSize = -1
    End If
End Function
```

At the point where GetFileSize is called, a diagram of the stack looks like this:

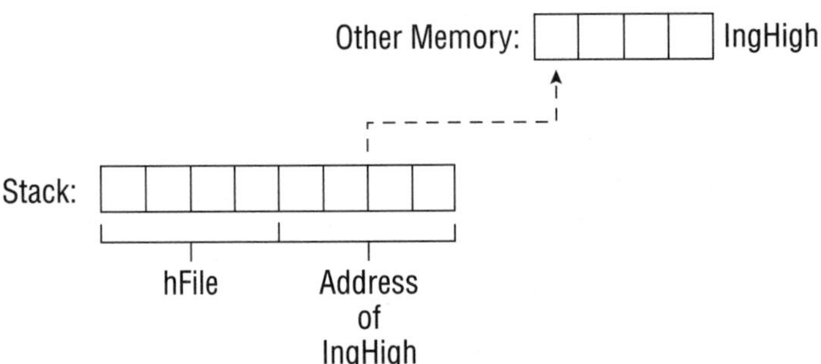

Notice that the value for hFile is directly on the stack (by value) and that a reference to lngHigh is placed on the stack (by reference). The important point to remember is that you must always declare the arguments the way that the function expects to find them.

Passing Strings to a DLL: The Real Story

As mentioned earlier in this chapter, Windows has two ways of storing strings: LPSTR and BSTR. String parameters to DLL functions must specify which kind of string they accept. Internally, VBA uses BSTRs to store strings. If the function accepts an LPSTR as a parameter, the argument must be converted from a BSTR into an LPSTR before being passed in. The vast majority of DLLs that are passed strings expect to be passed LPSTRs, including all the Windows API calls (except COM API calls). This means that you need some method of converting BSTRs to LPSTRs. You should understand how BSTRs and LPSTRs are stored in memory.

An LPSTR is an address of a null-terminated string. A *null-terminated string* is a set of characters followed by a character with the ANSI value 0. An LPSTR is stored in memory like this:

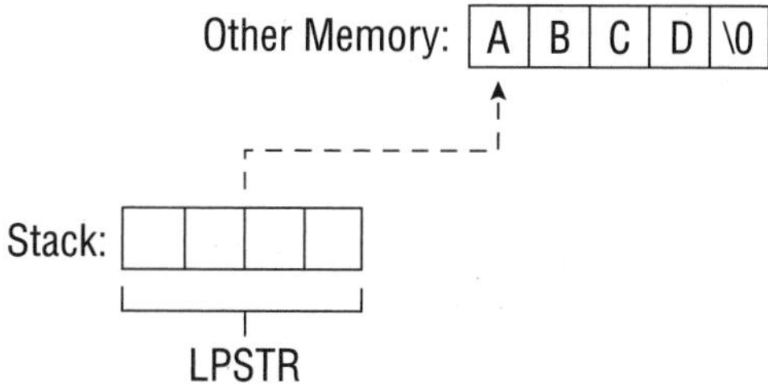

A BSTR is like an LPSTR except that the actual string data is preceded by a 4-byte value representing the size of the string. The address on the stack, however, still points to the first byte in the string. It is stored in memory like this:

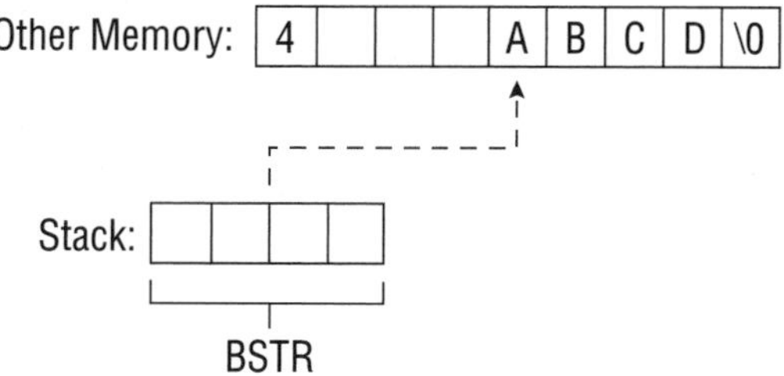

While these might seem like compatible data types, they're not. Unless a DLL function is specifically written to accept a BSTR (and most aren't), you must pass it an LPSTR. How do you tell VBA to pass an LPSTR rather than a BSTR? You declare the argument using the ByVal attribute. Don't worry about VBA placing a string *by value* (that is, all the bytes) on the stack; remember that when it comes to strings, VBA always passes *by reference.* The type of reference (or pointer) it passes, however, differs, depending on whether or not you use ByVal in the declaration. To pass an LPSTR, declare string arguments using ByVal; to pass a BSTR, don't use ByVal.

Using vbNullString—A Closer Look

As shown in the section "Using the vbNullString Constant" earlier in this chapter, you can also pass a Null as the second argument to delete the volume label (at least in Windows NT). How can you pass a null pointer? You cannot pass an empty string, because that would pass a pointer to the empty string. (Remember that strings are passed by reference.) Passing an empty string would result in a stack like this:

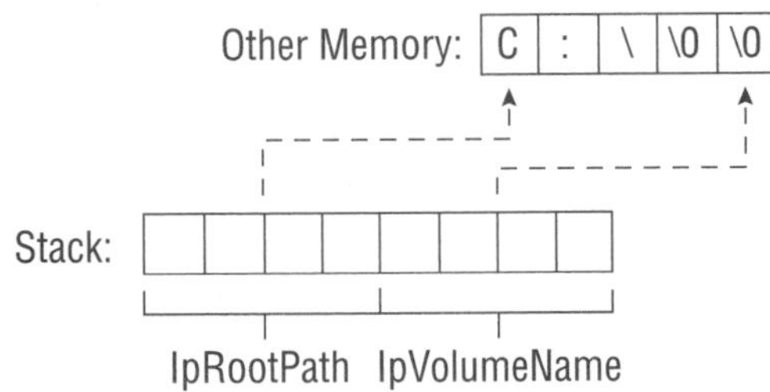

On the other hand, to pass a Null as the second argument, you want the stack to look like this:

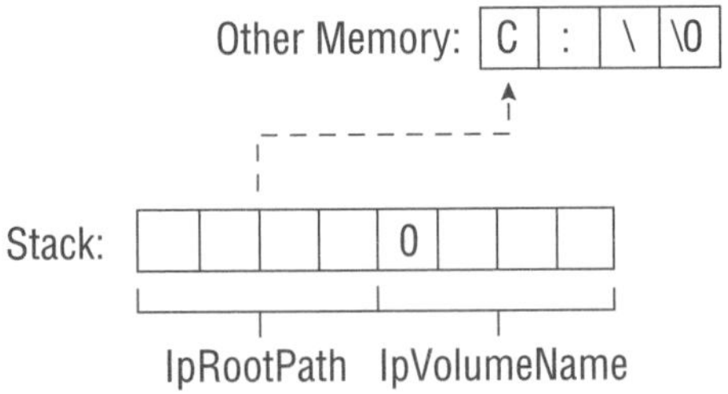

Notice that these two diagrams do not represent the same thing. The first stack passes a pointer to a null character, and the second stack passes a null pointer. How do you pass a null pointer? You pass the vbNullString constant as the second argument. VBA treats the vbNullString constant in a special way. It is a 4-byte–long zero, but no type checking is done on it when it is passed as a string argument. Because the second string argument is declared as being ByVal, passing vbNullString causes a 4-byte–long zero to be placed on the stack. To delete the volume label, you call SetVolumeLabel with:

```
Call SetVolumeLabel("C:\", vbNullString)
```

Unicode to ANSI and Back

The preceding discussion disregards one important subject about passing strings to DLL procedures: VBA stores strings internally as Unicode and converts those strings to ANSI at the time a DLL function call is made. *Unicode* is a character-encoding scheme that uses two bytes to represent each character, allowing representation of 65,536 different characters. The Unicode specification has assigned every character from every major language in the world to one of the Unicode values. ANSI uses only one byte per character and can represent only 256 different characters.

Internally, VBA represents every string in Unicode format. Whenever you make a function call, VBA intercepts the call if any argument is a string or a user-defined structure that contains a string. A temporary buffer is created, and then the strings are converted from Unicode, with the result placed in the temporary buffer. Then the pointers are fixed up to point to the converted strings. When the function returns, all strings are converted back from ANSI to Unicode before VBA returns control to you.

This conversion from ANSI to Unicode has several implications:

- You must never try to represent binary information within strings if you intend to pass these strings to DLL functions. If the information is not human readable as ANSI characters, you must pass an array of bytes. That's why VBA introduced the Byte data type.
- You must call functions that expect ANSI strings. Any Win32 function that has strings as parameters comes in two versions. One ends in the letter *A* and accepts ANSI strings as arguments. The other ends in the letter *W* (for Wide) and accepts Unicode arguments. You must always call the function that ends in the letter *A*. Typically, the Declare statement specifies an alias clause that defines the *A* version to be a generic name without either the *A* or the *W*. For example, GetWindowText is aliased to be the function GetWindowTextA within the DLL.
- VBA translates not only string arguments passed directly, but also strings defined in user-defined types.

TIP

If you receive the error message "DLL function not found" when trying to use a DLL function, check to see whether the function uses string arguments. If so, you must specify the ANSI version of the function using an Alias clause. This error often occurs when you forget to do so.

Using the Any Data Type

Certain API calls require different types of arguments, depending on how they are called. For example, the WinHelp function is defined in the C programming language like this:

```
BOOL WinHelp
    (
    HWND hwnd,           // handle of window requesting Help
    LPCTSTR lpszHelp,    // address of directory-path string
    UINT uCommand,       // type of Help
    DWORD dwData         // additional data
    );
```

The first two arguments are the hWnd of the parent window and the name of the Help file. The uCommand argument defines what you want Windows to do with the Help file. How the dwData argument is used is based on which constant is passed in for the uCommand argument. Two possible values for the uCommand argument are described in the following table.

uCommand	dwData	Meaning
HELP_CONTEXT	Unsigned Long integer containing the context number for the topic	Displays the topic identified by a context number that has been defined in the [MAP] section of the Help project file.
HELP_PARTIALKEY	Long pointer to a string that contains a keyword for the requested topic	Displays the topic in the keyword list that matches the keyword passed in the dwData parameter, if there is one exact match. If there is more than one match, it displays the Search dialog box with the topics listed in the Go To box. If there is no match, it displays the Search dialog box. If you just want to bring up the Search dialog box without passing a keyword (the third result), use a Long pointer to an empty string.

This presents a problem: HELP_CONTEXT wants a Long passed by value on the stack, whereas HELP_PARTIALKEY wants a string passed by reference; the way you call the function determines the data type of the last argument. How can you declare the function so it allows both choices? The answer is the Any data type. The Any data type tells VBA that at the time you declare the function, you don't know what the data type is or how big it is. It defers supplying this information until you call the procedure. This removes compile-time type checking, so all the responsibility for passing reasonable arguments is in your court: you must make sure you actually pass reasonable data to the DLL call. The declaration for this function is

```
Public Declare Function WinHelp _
 Lib "User32" Alias "WinHelpA" _
 (ByVal hwnd As Long, _
 ByVal lpszHelp As String, _
 ByVal uCommand As Long, _
 dwData As Any) As Long
```

Notice that the data type for the dwData argument is Any and that it is not declared using ByVal. At the time the function is called, you need to provide VBA with three pieces of information:

- The data type of the argument
- Whether that data type should be passed by value or by reference
- The contents of the argument

You can include ByVal or ByRef in both the Declare statement and the call. Whatever you use in the call overrides what is in the Declare statement.

You can call this function in two ways:

```
lngRet = WinHelp(Me.hwnd, Me.HelpFile, HELP_CONTEXT, ByVal 3&)
lngRet = WinHelp(Me.hwnd, Me.HelpFile, HELP_PARTIALKEY, _
 ByVal "FindThis")
```

The HELP_CONTEXT call to WinHelp passes a ByVal 3& in the dwData argument. This provides VBA with the following information:

- The information is to be passed by value.
- Four bytes are to be placed onto the stack.
- The contents of the four bytes should be the value 3.

The ByVal indicates that the argument is passed by value. The ampersand (&) is an indication that the constant is a Long, not an Integer. Without the ampersand, only two bytes would be placed on the stack, whereas the function wants four.

The HELP_PARTIALKEY call to the function provides it with the following information:

- The information is to be passed by reference.
- The information is a string.
- The string should be converted from a BSTR to an LPSTR.

All strings are passed by reference, and the data type of the argument is a string constant. The ByVal here performs the conversion between the BSTR and the LPSTR. Because a ByVal wasn't included in the Declare statement for this argument, the ByVal is required in the call statement.

Use the Any data type carefully because VBA is unable to do type checking at compile type. As an alternative, consider declaring the procedure multiple times using different names and specific data types. For example, the following code declares two versions of the WinHelp function—one that accepts a Long value and one that accepts a String value in the dwData argument:

```
Public Declare Function WinHelpContext _
 Lib "User32" Alias "WinHelpA _
 (ByVal hwnd As Long, _
 ByVal lpszHelp As String, _
 ByVal uCommand As Long, _
 ByVal dwData As Long) As Long
Public Declare Function WinHelpPartialKey _
 Lib "User32" Alias "WinHelpA" _
 (ByVal hwnd As Long, _
 ByVal lpszHelp As String, _
 ByVal uCommand As Long, _
 ByVal dwData As String) As Long
```

Using Err.LastDLLError

When you call a Windows API function from Visual Basic, the possibility exists that the call will fail. The function indicates this failure by returning some special value, such as 0 or False. When you are using the Windows API from C, you can then call a function named GetLastError to find out why it failed. Unfortunately, calling GetLastError from VBA doesn't report accurate results. The reason is that

VBA itself is also doing Windows API calls. By the time you get a chance to call GetLastError, VBA has already messed up the result GetLastError would have reported. To get around this problem, VBA implements the LastDLLError property of the Err object. This property is filled in with the error code of the last DLL call you made. You can use this property instead of calling GetLastError. For example:

```
fRet = SetVolumeLabel("C:\", vbNullString)
If Not fRet Then
    If Err.LastDllError = ERROR_INVALID_PARAMETER then
        MsgBox "Due to a Windows '95 bug, you can't delete " _
         & "the volume label. "
    End If
End If
```

Using Callback Functions

A small percentage of the Windows functions requires a callback function. Normally, Windows provides functions that your program calls. A *callback* is a procedure *you* provide for *Windows* to call. Windows calls the callback multiple times, and with each call Windows passes arguments that reference an object in an internal data structure. For example, a call to the EnumWindows function requires a callback. The callback function is called once for each top-level window currently open and is passed a handle to it until they have all been enumerated. In the C declaration, the argument in which you indicate the address of the callback has the data type FARPROC or CALLBACK.

Until now, VBA in Office applications was unable to support callback functions, even though Visual Basic has had this capability since VB 5. VBA 6, on the other hand, inherited this capability from VB, and the two products now share the ability to create and use callback functions. CH16.MDB contains a form, frmEnumFonts, and VBA module, basCallback, which demonstrate how to create a callback function and use it with the VBA AddressOf operator.

AddressOf accepts a VBA procedure name and returns the procedure's address in memory. Your program can then pass this address to a Windows API function that expects a callback function. To illustrate this, we've created a callback function in basCallback that can be passed by address to the EnumFontFamiliesEx

API function. The API function will call the procedure once for each font installed on your system. Here's the declaration for EnumFontFamiliesEx:

```
Private Declare Function EnumFontFamiliesEx Lib _
 "gdi32" Alias "EnumFontFamiliesExA" (ByVal hDC As Long, _
 lpLogFont As LOGFONT, ByVal lpEnumFontProc As Long, _
 ByVal lParam As Long, ByVal dw As Long) As Long
```

The lpEnumFontProc argument is designed to accept the address of a callback function. Here's the callback function we created in the VBA module:

```
Private Function EnumFontFamExProc( _
 lpelfe As ENUMLOGFONTEX, lpntme As NEWTEXTMETRICEX, _
 lngFontType As Long, lngParam As Long) As Long

    Dim strFaceName As String

    ' Grab the font face name from the data structure
    ' passed in by the Windows API add it to the array
    strFaceName = StrConv(lpelfe.elfLogFont.lfFaceName, _
     vbUnicode)
    strFaceName = Left(strFaceName, _
     InStr(strFaceName, vbNullChar) - 1)

    mlngFontCount = mlngFontCount + 1
    ReDim Preserve mavarFontList(1 To mlngFontCount)
    mavarFontList(mlngFontCount) = strFaceName

    EnumFontFamExProc = 1
End Function
```

Note that it's the function's declaration, not its name or contents that matters. Since you pass the function by address, the name is irrelevant. Furthermore, the API function doesn't care what your function does as long as it has the right number and type of arguments and the right return value data type. In this case, our callback function extracts the font name from a data structure passed to it by Windows and adds the name to a module-level array.

With the API function and callback function declared, all that's left to do is call them. This is done by another procedure, adhBuildFontList, shown here:

```
Public Function adhBuildFontList() As Variant
    Dim lf As LOGFONT
    Dim hWnd As Long
    Dim hDC As Long
```

```
    ' Clear the existing list
    ReDim mavarFontList(1 To 1)
    mlngFontCount = 0

    ' Get a device context
    hWnd = Application.hWndAccessApp
    hDC = GetDC(hWnd)

    ' Execute the enumeration function
    Call EnumFontFamiliesEx(hDC, lf, _
     AddressOf EnumFontFamExProc, 0, 0)

    ' Release the device context
    Call ReleaseDC(hWnd, hDC)

    ' Sort and pass back the results
    Call adhQuickSort(mavarFontList)
    adhBuildFontList = mavarFontList
End Function
```

After setting up the array and getting a Windows device context (necessary for retrieving any information related to display or printing), the procedure calls EnumFontFamiliesEx. Notice the AddressOf operator in the function call. This is how the address of EnumFontFamExProc is determined and passed to the API function. After EnumFontFamiliesEx returns, the callback function will have been called numerous times and the array populated with font names. At this point, adhBuildFontList simply sorts the array and returns it to the calling procedure.

Figure 16.7 shows the frmEnumFonts form displaying a list of fonts. The form calls adhBuilfFontList in its Open event.

FIGURE 16.7:

frmEnumFonts demonstrates how to use a callback functions with retrieve information from Windows.

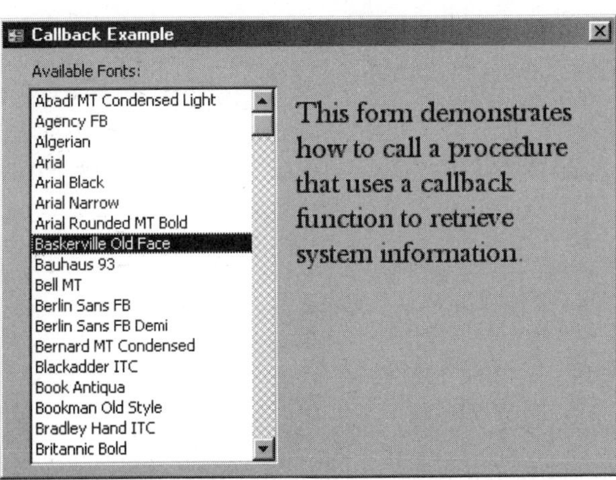

TIP

Chapter 17 has numerous examples of callback functions that are explained in detail.

User-Defined Types and DWORD Packing

When VBA passes a user-defined type to a DLL, it refuses to allow any particular declaration within the structure to cross a DWORD (4-byte) boundary. Instead, it pads out bytes so that the next definition starts on a DWORD boundary. This means that if you compile your own DLL, you must either provide that padding yourself or use the Struct Member Alignment option the C compiler provides. For example, if you have a structure that looks like this:

```
Type TESTSTRUCT
    intTest As Integer
    bytTest As Byte
    lngTest As Long
End Type
```

the structure in memory is represented like this:

```
intTest
bytTest
One byte of padding to make the lngTest align to a DWORD boundary
lngTest
```

so the structure takes up eight bytes in memory. If, instead, the structure is arranged like this:

```
Type TESTSTRUCT
    bytTest As Byte
    lngTest As Long
    intTest As Integer
End Type
```

it is padded out to look like this in memory:

```
bytTest
Three bytes of padding
lngTest
intTest
Two bytes of padding
```

and thus it takes up 12 bytes in memory.

If the DLL is compiled with the Struct Member Alignment option, the C compiler provides the appropriate padding to make the structure members line up with the way the structure is passed from VBA. On the other hand, you would be better off arranging the elements within the structure so they are DWORD-aligned to begin with.

This implicit padding that VBA provides does not cause a problem with the Windows API because the API structures have been DWORD-aligned, but it can cause a problem if you use other DLLs. If the DLL is not compiled with the Struct Member Alignment option and has elements that cross DWORD boundaries, you cannot pass the bytes in the correct arrangement without doing a very tricky manipulation of the bytes within the structure.

Converting Windows API Calls from 16-bit Windows

Even though Access 2000 is the third major 32-bit Access version, there are still many, many 16-bit Access 2 applications still in use. Windows API functions represent a particularly tricky conversion issue since the transition from 16-bit to 32-bit functions is both necessary and often tedious. Many Access 2 applications use API functions to make up for functionality lacking in that version of the product. If you are converting code from Access 2, you will need to revisit all your Windows API calls; many of them have changed. At a minimum, you'll need to update the Declare statements to refer to 32-bit DLLs and, possibly, adjust those requiring String arguments so that ANSI DLL functions are used. This is a significant amount of work.

Windows API conversion issues come in five classes:

- Calls that merely have to reference the Win32 libraries instead of the Win16 libraries.
- Calls that must be modified to use the ANSI versions of Win32 API functions.
- Calls that now have additional functionality under Win32.
- Calls that have a new extended version (for example, GetWindowExt has a new extended version, GetWindowExtEx).
- Calls that are not supported under Win32.

Use the following steps as a guideline to make the conversion:

1. Start by finding each of your Declare statements in existing code.
2. Look in the Win32 documentation to determine in which one of the five classes of conversions the call falls.
3. Replace the Declare statement with the new Declare statement (unless the call is no longer supported in Win32).
4. Examine every function call to your Windows API calls. Make sure the arguments match the data type of the parameters in the Declare statement. A great many of the arguments will need to be changed from Integers to Longs. Make sure these changes propagate throughout your code.
5. Save your database and make a backup copy.
6. Set a breakpoint on each of your API calls. Run your code. When you reach the breakpoint, verify that the arguments are both the correct value and the correct size. Then step through the call.

This is a lot of work, but it is absolutely necessary to get your code to work reliably under Win32.

Table 16.2 is not exhaustive, but it may help with some of the conversions.

TABLE 16.2: Some Windows 3.1 Calls That Need to Be Changed for 32-bit Windows

Win16 Call	Replace With
GetWindowWord	GetWindowLong
SetWindowWord	SetWindowLong
GetClassWord	GetClassLong
SetClassWord	SetClassLong
GetPrivateProfileString	(VBA built-in function GetSetting or GetAllSettings)
GetPrivateProfileInt	(VBA built-in function GetSetting)
WritePrivateProfileString	(VBA built-in statement SaveSetting)
MoveTo	MoveToEx
OffsetViewportOrg	OffsetViewportOrgEx

Continued on next page

TABLE 16.2 CONTINUED: Some Windows 3.1 Calls That Need to Be Changed for 32-bit Windows

Win16 Call	Replace With
OffsetWindowOrg	OffsetWindowOrgEx
GetAspectRatioFilter	GetAspectRatioFilterEx
GetBitmapDimension	GetBitmapDimensionEx
GetBrushOrg	GetBrushOrgEx
GetCurrentPosition	GetCurrentPositionEx
GetTextExtent	GetTextExtentPoint
GetViewportExt	GetViewportExtEx
GetViewportOrg	GetViewportOrgEx
GetWindowExt	GetWindowExtEx
GetWindowOrg	GetWindowOrgEx
ScaleViewportExt	ScaleViewportExtEx
ScaleWindowExt	ScaleWindowExtEx
SetBitmapDimension	SetBitmapDimensionEx
SetMetaFileBits	SetMetaFileBitsEx
SetViewportExt	SetViewportExtEx
SetViewportOrg	SetViewportOrgEx
SetWindowExt	SetWindowExtEx
SetWindowOrg	SetWindowOrgEx
AccessResource	(No longer exists in Win32)
AllocDSToCSAlias	(No longer exists in Win32)
AllocResource	(No longer exists in Win32)
AllocSelector	(No longer exists in Win32)
Catch	(No longer exists in Win32)
ChangeSelector	(No longer exists in Win32)
FreeSelector	(No longer exists in Win32)

Continued on next page

TABLE 16.2 CONTINUED: Some Windows 3.1 Calls That Need to Be Changed for 32-bit Windows

Win16 Call	Replace With
GetCodeHandle	(No longer exists in Win32)
GetCodeInfo	(No longer exists in Win32)
GetCurrentPDB	(No longer exists in Win32)
GetEnvironment	(No longer exists in Win32)
GetInstanceData	(No longer exists in Win32)
GetKBCodePage	(No longer exists in Win32)
GetModuleUsage	(No longer exists in Win32)
GlobalDOSAlloc	(No longer exists in Win32)
GlobalDOSFree	(No longer exists in Win32)
GlobalNotify	(No longer exists in Win32)
GlobalPageLock	(No longer exists in Win32)
LockData	(No longer exists in Win32)
NetBIOSCall	(No longer exists in Win32)
Throw	(No longer exists in Win32)
SetEnvironment	(No longer exists in Win32)
SetResourceHandler	(No longer exists in Win32)
SwitchStackBack	(No longer exists in Win32)
SwitchStackTo	(No longer exists in Win32)
UnlockData	(No longer exists in Win32)
ValidateCodeSegments	(No longer exists in Win32)
ValidateFreeSpaces	(No longer exists in Win32)
Yield	(No longer exists in Win32)
IsGdiObject	(No longer exists in Win32)
IsTask	(No longer exists in Win32)
DefineHandleTable	(No longer exists in Win32)

Continued on next page

TABLE 16.2 CONTINUED: Some Windows 3.1 Calls That Need to Be Changed for 32-bit Windows

Win16 Call	Replace With
MakeProcInstance	(No longer exists in Win32)
FreeProcInstance	(No longer exists in Win32)
GetFreeSpace	(No longer exists in Win32)
GlobalCompact	(No longer exists in Win32)
GlobalFix	(No longer exists in Win32)
GlobalUnfix	(No longer exists in Win32)
GlobalUnwire	(No longer exists in Win32)
LocalCompact	(No longer exists in Win32)
LocalShrink	(No longer exists in Win32)
LockSegment	(No longer exists in Win32)
UnlockSegment	(No longer exists in Win32)
SetSwapAreaSize	(No longer exists in Win32)

Summary

This chapter covered the following topics:

- Declaring a DLL procedure from VBA
- Specifying the DLL function arguments
- Understanding passing by value and passing by reference
- Converting C parameters into VBA declarations
- Using callback functions
- Returning strings from a DLL
- Understanding the Unicode-to-ANSI issue

- Using the vbNullString constant
- Using the Any data type
- Passing a user-defined type to a DLL
- User-defined types and DWORD packing
- Passing an array
- Using type libraries
- Using the Windows API
- Converting Windows API calls from Access 2
- Examples using the Windows API

DLLs are one of the three ways by which you can reach outside the bounds of Access into other Windows programs, the other two being DDE and COM Automation. Automation is covered in Chapter 12. Due to space limitations, information on DDE has been moved to the CD-ROM (or you can refer to Chapter 20 of our *Microsoft Access 95 Developer's Handbook*). The DLL interface allows you to manipulate Windows directly through the Windows API, as well as to call your own DLLs. Combined with a C or C++ compiler and the appropriate knowledge, DLLs allow you to do virtually anything that is possible with Windows. However, even without the use of C or C++, the ability to call the Windows API vastly extends the power of Access.

CHAPTER

SEVENTEEN

17

Harnessing Wizard Magic

- File-handling functions
- Interfaces to Windows' common dialogs
- Font-handling functions
- Reading/writing values in the Registry
- Database object listing functions
- Screen and file version information classes

In previous editions of this book, we were able to explicitly discuss undocumented features provided by the Access team that allowed the Access Wizards to perform their work. In Access 2 and Access 95, the Access team provided a DLL (MSAU200.DLL and then MSAU7032.DLL). For Access 97, the Access team moved the code from the DLL into the MSACCESS.EXE executable and provided public entry points accessible like Windows API calls, which we documented in the previous edition of this book.

For Access 2000, the Access team has pulled the plug—many of the previously undocumented functions are no longer available for VBA developers to use. Some are still there, and some aren't. Most of the ones that are still exposed will go away in a future version. Therefore, this chapter is no longer solely about calling undocumented functions exposed by Access directly. Instead, this chapter serves three purposes:

- It provides replacement functions, with the same names, parameters, and return types, as the exposed Access functions we discussed in previous editions. (We couldn't provide replacements for all the functions, but we got very close.) Using these drop-in procedures, you should be able to take code you wrote for Access 97 that used the old undocumented procedures and have your application run just as it did before. This way, you're no longer dependent on the Access team to support undocumented behaviors.
- It provides standard and class modules that allow you to gather information about file versions, use the Windows common file Open/Save, Color, and Font dialog boxes, browse for folders, and much more. In other words, starting with the ideas of the previous edition's chapter, we've added new useful functionality to this chapter.
- It describes the undocumented procedures that were available in Access 97 and are still available in Access 2000 that aren't easily replaceable with VBA code. There's no guarantee that these procedures will be available in any future version of Access, but you may need their functionality now, and they are available.

The modules we've provided here break down into seven basic categories:

- File-handling functions: Check for file existence; split file name components; retrieve a full path given a relative path
- Interfaces to common dialogs: File Open/Save, Font, and Color Choosers, and a folder/printer/machine browser

- Read and write Registry values: Retrieve the number of subkeys and values for a given key; read and write keys and their values. In addition, replace the built-in GetSetting, SaveSetting, DeleteSetting, and GetAllSettings procedures with procedures that read or write from any registry location
- Font-handling functions: List available fonts and their sizes; retrieve the height and width of a given string in a specified font
- Object-listing functions: Retrieve a list of object names or a list of objects along with their types; sort an array of strings; sort an array of objects either by name or by type
- File version information: Retrieve file language, code page, target operating system, copyright, version number, file type, and product name
- Screen information: Retrieve screen size, color depth, twips per pixel, screen fonts, available font sizes, display settings and the ability to change settings (such as screen size and color depth) from within your application

WARNING

Microsoft makes a point that documented functionality will not change from one version to the next. They make no such claim for undocumented functionality. If nothing else, the contents of this chapter should prove that using undocumented technology can, and usually will, lead to issues of some sort in future versions. Just because Microsoft provided the MSAU7032 DLL in Access 95 and made public entry points in MSACESS.EXE available in Access 97, doesn't mean that they'll offer similar functionality in current or future versions—and they don't. Therefore, almost everything provided in this current chapter is documented, proven, and standard technology—that is, we've simply used the old chapter as a starting point, rewritten as many of the old functions as possible using the Windows API or DAO, and expanded from there.

TIP

The code provided in this chapter started out as a simple replacement for the undocumented procedures we discussed in the previous edition of the book. Along the way, however, the scope of the chapter grew and grew and grew. We've included direct replacements for as many of the old functions as possible, but, in many cases, we've provided better ways to get at the same information, generally using class modules. If you have existing code using the adh_acc* procedures documented in the Access 97 version of this book, you should be able to use them without modifying your code. On the other hand, you may find it useful to peruse this chapter to see how you might better use the code we've provided here.

Using the Procedures

Unlike almost any other chapter in this book, this chapter dwells less on how the provided code works and more on how you can take advantage of that code. If you dig into the sample project we've provided, you'll find a ton of Windows API declarations, types, and constants, and many lines of often-complex VBA code. Explaining how all that code works is beyond the scope of, and is mostly unnecessary for, this book. You're welcome to dig in, investigate, and figure out how all the code in the sample database works, if you like. On the other hand, this chapter focuses on showing you how to use the code you'll find there.

The sample database contains a number of standard and class modules and a number of demonstration forms. None of the forms is required for your own projects. That is, if you want to use these techniques in your own applications, you won't need to import any of the forms, but you will need to import modules. In each section, we'll indicate which modules you need to import (it usually will require more than a single module to get the functionality you want).

TIP

The code in this chapter's database makes heavy use of both class modules and the Windows API. If you're not familiar with those concepts, we suggest that you work through the chapters covering those topics (Chapters 3 and 16, respectively) before attempting to modify the code provided in this chapter.

File-Handling Functions

Most Access applications need to work with file paths, in one way or another. The sample project provides this set of capabilities:

- Check for the existence of a file
- Split a full path into its component pieces
- Get the full path associated with a file
- Retrieve the path of the current database

The following sections deal individually with each of these functions.

TIP

To use the procedures discussed in this section in your own project, import the basFileHandling module.

Checking for the Existence of a File

You can check for the existence of a file by calling the adh_accFileExists function. To call it, use syntax like this:

```
fRetval = adh_accFileExists(strFileName)
```

This function returns True if the file exists or False otherwise.

For example, to check for the existence of C:\AUTOEXEC.BAT, you could use the following code:

```
If adh_accFileExists("C:\AUTOEXEC.BAT") Then
    ' You know that C:\AUTOEXEC.BAT exists.
End If
```

NOTE

The Access 97 version of this function returned 0 if the file didn't exist, or 1 if it did. We've modified the function to be more VBA-like, so that it now returns True if the file exists, and False if it doesn't. This may affect converted Access 97 code. Check for existing code that counted on the old behavior, and modify it to use the new return values.

If you're writing new code, use the adhFileExists function instead of the adh_accFileExists function (which is provided, with its odd name, only for backward compatibility). The adh_accFileExists function ends up calling adhFileExists anyway, so calling adhFileExists directly will cause your code to execute a tiny bit faster.

How It Works

The adhFileExists function makes use of the built-in Dir function, which returns the filename portion of any file specification you send it, if the file exists. (We've specified attributes associated with the file name, so that Dir will find hidden, system, and read-only files in addition to normal files.) If the return value is an empty string, or if the call triggered an error, you're guaranteed that the file doesn't exist. Therefore, the following simple procedure does the job:

```
Public Function adhFileExists(strName As String) As Boolean
    ' From basFileHandling.
    On Error Resume Next
    Dim strTemp As String
    ' Search for files with any attributes set.
    strTemp = Dir(strName, _
     vbHidden Or vbSystem Or _
     vbArchive Or vbReadOnly)
    adhFileExists = ((Len(strTemp) > 0) And _
     (Err.Number = 0))
End Function
```

Splitting a Full Path Reference into Components

As part of many applications, you'll need to take a full path reference, in the format

Drive:\Path\FileName.Ext

and retrieve any one of the single parts of the name (the drive, the path, the file name, or the extension) as a separate piece. The adhSplitPath subroutine will do the work for you, filling in each of the various pieces. You pass in a full path name and four string variables to contain all the pieces of information. The adhSplitPath procedure fills in the four pieces of information from the full path.

NOTE

The adhSplitPath procedure doesn't check to make sure that the path you've specified is valid. It does its work using brute force, breaking apart the string based on "\" and "." delimiters it finds within your input value. Don't count on this procedure to validate file names for you.

For example, running the code in Listing 17.1 produces the output shown in Figure 17.1.

Listing 17.1

```
Public Sub TestSplitPath()
    ' From basTestFileHandling
    Dim strDrive As String
    Dim strPath As String
```

```
    Dim strFileName As String
    Dim strExt As String

    adhSplitPath "C:\Windows\System\FOO.INI", strDrive, _
     strPath, strFileName, strExt
    Debug.Print "=========================================="
    Debug.Print "Full : " & "C:\Windows\System\FOO.INI"
    Debug.Print "=========================================="
    Debug.Print "Drive: " & strDrive
    Debug.Print "Path : " & strPath
    Debug.Print "File : " & strFileName
    Debug.Print "Ext  : " & strExt

    adhSplitPath "C:\", strDrive, strPath, strFileName, strExt
    Debug.Print "=========================================="
    Debug.Print "Full : " & "C:\"
    Debug.Print "=========================================="
    Debug.Print "Drive: " & strDrive
    Debug.Print "Path : " & strPath
    Debug.Print "File : " & strFileName
    Debug.Print "Ext  : " & strExt
End Sub
```

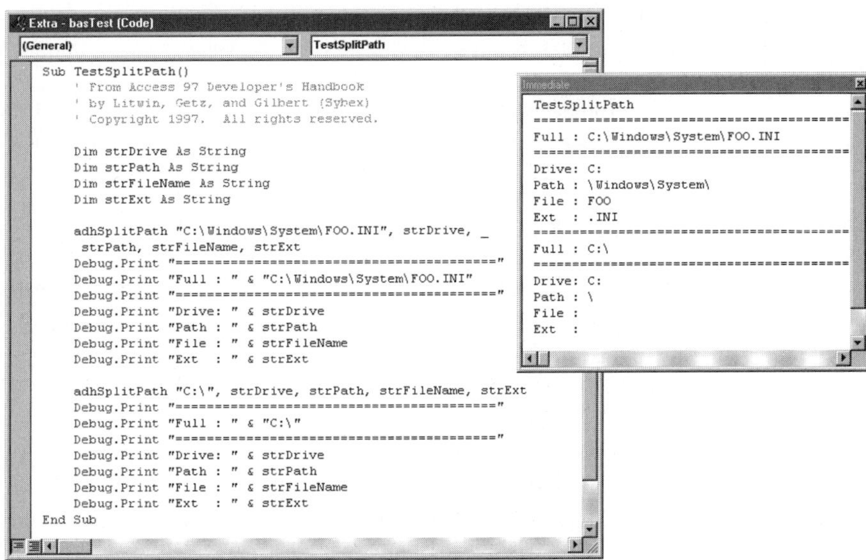

FIGURE 17.1: The adhSplitPath procedure breaks a full path name into its components.

How It Works

The adhSplitPath procedure accepts five parameters; one is passed by value (using the ByVal keyword), and the rest are passed by reference (using the ByRef keyword) and are optional. The procedure returns no value. Because you pass the final four parameters by reference, adhSplitPath fills in their values given the full path you specified in the first parameter. If all you need is a file's folder, for example, you could call adhSplitPath like this:

```
' The following fragment assumes that
' strFullPath contains a full path,
' and that strPath is a string
' variable that will contain the folder
' portion.
adhSplitPath strFullPath, Folder:=strPath
Debug.Print strPath
```

In this case, the code in adhSplitPath will do all the work it normally would, but only returns the value for the Folder parameter.

If you want to investigate exactly how adhSplitPath does its work, look in basFileHandling. It's interesting if you're excited by string manipulations, but otherwise, it's unenlightening.

TIP

If you haven't used the new Split function available in Access 2000, you might want to take a look at the code in adhSplitPath to see how it works. This useful function takes in a string and a delimiter value, splits your input string every time it finds the delimiter you've specified, and returns an array of substrings. We've used this function to parse out the various parts of the input path.

Getting the Full Path for a File

You can use the adhFullPath function to retrieve the full path for a file, based on a relative path. For example, if your current directory is the C:\Windows directory, the following function call

```
adhFullPath("..\SAMPLES\TESTAPP.EXE")
```

returns the value C:\SAMPLES\ TESTAPP.EXE, a fully qualified path name for the file. This function can be useful if you need to display a full path but only have a relative path. For example, if you want to retrieve the folder name for a file, knowing only its relative location, you can call adhFullPath to get the full path, and then pass the results to the adhSplitPath procedure.

NOTE

This function can be confusing in its intent. It looks at the current directory and the relative path name you've sent it and creates a complete path name for the file based on that information. It does nothing more; it does not check for the existence of the file (you can pass it anything you wish for the file name), nor does it check to see whether the actual directories exist. Its only purpose is to turn relative paths into absolute paths.

How It Works

The adhFullPath function calls the Windows API function, GetFullPathName. This function accepts a relative path and, based on the current folder, returns the fully qualified path to the specified file. Like most other API functions that operate on VBA strings, this function requires that you send it a string buffer to be filled in, along with the length of that buffer. This function is friendly, however, in that if you pass in a buffer that's too short for the return value, it tells you how many characters you need. This gives you the opportunity to call the function again, with a correctly sized buffer. Listing 17.2 shows the entire adhFullPath function.

Listing 17.2

```
Public Function adhFullPath(strName As String) _
As String
    ' MAX_PATH is defined by the Windows API.
    Const MAX_PATH = 260
    Dim lngLen As Long
    Dim lngFilled As Long
    Dim strBuffer As String

    lngLen = MAX_PATH
    Do
        strBuffer = Space(lngLen)
        lngFilled = GetFullPathName( _
         strName, lngLen, strBuffer, vbNullString)
        ' If the buffer was too small (and
        ' this ought not happen, given that
        ' we've used the maximum path length
        ' for the variable), lngFilled will
```

```
        ' now contain the length needed.
        ' So do it again.
        If lngFilled > lngLen Then
            lngLen = lngFilled
        End If
    Loop Until lngFilled < lngLen
    adhFullPath = Left$(strBuffer, lngFilled)
End Function
```

Using Windows' Dialog Boxes

To standardize specific often-needed dialogs, Windows provides a group of common dialogs all applications can use. If you want to allow your users to select a file name for opening, saving, or selecting a color or font, Windows has a common dialog box to handle the selection. Access provides no mechanism for you to get to any of the common dialogs except the printing common dialog for your own applications, but the Windows API makes it possible to use any of these standard dialogs.

Using these API functions is somewhat daunting, however, so we've wrapped up much of the code in a simpler-to-use class module, CommonDlg, and have provided several examples of using this class. The following sections discuss how you can use the CommonDlg class, making it easy for you to take advantage of these common dialogs in your own applications.

Access provides the undocumented ability to use the Microsoft Office file open dialog, and we've provided a module here that makes using this dialog box easy. If you've opened or saved files in any Office application, you've become acquainted with this tool. Using the code provided in basOfficeFileOpen, you can take advantage of this dialog box in your own applications.

WARNING

As with any undocumented tool (as evidenced with several procedures we covered in the previous edition of this book that no longer exist in Access), you never know whether you'll be able to migrate code using basOfficeFileOpen to a future version. Our guess is that the capability to call any of the undocumented Access functions, such as this one, will go away in the next version. But the code works for now. And perhaps they'll expose a public technique for accessing the Office dialog box next time.

We've also included code that's not part of the common dialogs but satisfies a common need in Access applications: the ability to select a folder. Windows provides this functionality, but it's not part of the standard common dialog set. Using the code in the ShellBrowse class module, you'll be able to pop up a dialog box allowing users to browse for a folder, a machine, a printer, or any other virtual folder.

NOTE Because of the scale of the project involved and its lack of usefulness from within Access, we haven't implemented the Printer common dialog box within the CommonDlg class. This dialog box allows you to choose printer settings, but once it's been dismissed, it's still up to you to assign the settings to your objects. Because Access provides the acCmdPrint option for the RunCommand method, you can easily get to the Printer common dialog without using this class.

Using the CommonDlg Class

The CommonDlg class contains code that allows you to easily display the File Save, File Open, Font, and Color common dialogs. The class takes care of all the communication between VBA and the Windows API. It takes advantage of a number of user-defined types, enums, and API calls, and provides a large number of methods and properties. In particular, the four methods you'll need to use, in order to display the common dialogs, are as follows:

Method	Action
ShowColor	Displays the Color chooser common dialog
ShowFont	Displays the Font chooser common dialog
ShowOpen	Displays the File Open common dialog
ShowSave	Displays the File Save common dialog

To use the dialogs in the simplest case, you can instantiate a new CommonDlg object and then call one of these methods. That is, the simplest usage for displaying the Font common dialog might look like this:

```
Dim cdl As CommonDlg
Set cdl = New CommonDlg
cdl.ShowFont
Debug.Print cdl.FontName
```

How About the Common Dialog ActiveX Control?

If you have the Windows Common Dialog ActiveX control available, you're welcome to use that in place of the CommonDlg class we've provided here. We've encountered several issues using that control, however, including the following:

- The control must be placed on a form. If you want to use the common dialogs from multiple locations in your application, you'll either need to place the control on every form where you might need it, or make sure that the form hosting the control is always open. Using the class module has no similar requirements.
- The control does not allow you to specify a callback function. It's in this callback function (that is, a function you supply that's called by the common dialog while it's displayed on screen) that you can position the dialog box where you want it, change the captions of controls on the dialog (in the case of the File Open/Save dialog boxes) or react to other actions taken on the dialog box. Our class can take advantage of this callback mechanism and includes an example callback function that centers the dialog box on the screen.
- The control does not allow you to specify the owner of the dialog box. Without this capability, it's difficult to manage what happens when you use the Alt+Tab keystroke to move to a different application while the dialog box is displayed. The CommonDlg class provides an hWndOwner property, which allows you to specify which window "owns" the dialog box.
- The control doesn't include source code. If you want to add features or modify the behavior of existing features, you're out of luck. Using the CommonDlg class, you have full control over the source code.

Common Steps

No matter which of the common dialogs you want to use, the steps are similar:

1. Make sure your project contains the CommonDlg class. (If you want to use a callback function described later, you might also want to import basCommonDlg and basCommon. These modules make it possible to use the sample callback functions.)
2. Create a variable of type CommonDlg to refer to the CommonDlg object in memory, like this:

```
Dim cdl As CommonDlg
```

3. Instantiate the variable:

```
Set cdl = New CommonDlg
```

4. Set properties of the CommonDlg object. You needn't set any properties at all, but you'll normally set the appropriate flags property (OpenFlags, ColorFlags, FontFlags), indicating specific preferences you have about the behavior of the dialog box. Use the Or operator to combine various settings. You might see code like this:

```
cdl.InitDir = "C:\"
cdl.OpenFlags = cdlOFNAllowMultiSelect Or _
 cdlOFNNoChangeDir
```

5. Call the appropriate method of the object (ShowOpen, ShowSave, ShowColor, or ShowFont) to display the selected dialog box. This will halt your code until the user has dismissed the dialog box. Your code might look like this:

```
cdl.ShowOpen
```

6. Once the user has dismissed the dialog box, retrieve the appropriate information from the CommonDlg object. For example, to retrieve the selected file name, you might write code like this:

```
Me.txtFileName = cdl.FileName
```

7. When you're done, destroy the CommonDlg object:

```
Set cdl = Nothing
```

TIP

Generally, you'll also want to add a bit of code to determine whether the user clicked the Cancel button. To do this, you must set the CancelError property of the CommonDlg object to True, and then you must add error handling to trap for the error raised by the control when the user cancels the dialog box by clicking Cancel. See the section "Checking for Cancellation" later in the chapter for more information on using this technique.

All that's left to take care of are the details. Describing those details is the job of the following sections, which show how to use each of the common dialog boxes. Make sure you take the time to investigate all of the options, and check out the sample forms frmTestCommonDlg and frmTestFileOpenSave to see how the dialog boxes work.

Compatibility of Existing Code

To make it easier for you to migrate code that you may have already written using the Common Dialog ActiveX control, we decided to make the CommonDlg class compatible with the Common Dialog ActiveX control. That is, if you have code written using the ActiveX control, you should be able to remove the control from your project and use the CommonDlg class instead. Although we've added new options and properties, existing code that uses the ShowOpen, ShowSave, ShowColor, or ShowFont methods of the ActiveX control should work with this class as well. If you have code from a previous edition of this book that uses the Office File Open or Save common dialog, you may want to use that dialog box in Access 2000, as discussed in a later section.

Setting Options

Besides the basic properties of the CommonDlg class that you'll see described in the next few sections, the Windows common dialogs allow you to specify detailed properties all rolled into a single value. Internally, the CommonDlg class sends a user-defined type full of information to the Windows API, and one of the elements of that structure is named Flags. This Long integer consists of 32 possible bits worth of information. By turning on various bits within the 32 available bits, you indicate to Windows exactly how you want the common dialog to behave.

We've mirrored that same behavior in the Flags property of the CommonDlg object. Each different type of dialog box (Open, Save, Color, and Font) interprets the bits in the Flags property differently, and we've provided groups of constants as enums to make your choice of bits easier. In the CommonDlg class module, you'll find the adhFileOpenConstants (for both the File Open and Save dialogs), adhFontsConstants, and adhColorConstants enums. So that you can select values from IntelliSense-provided drop-down lists of values, we've created three separate properties (OpenFlags [used for both File Open and File Save], ColorFlags, and FontFlags) corresponding to each of the enums. Internally, the CommonDlg class copies these individual values into the general Flags property for you. This makes it easier for you to type code without losing the flexibility of the flags values. For example, the CommonDlg class contains the following enum, allowing you to select behavior for the File Open and Save dialogs. The specific values aren't of interest to you—all you care about are the constants themselves:

```
Public Enum adhFileOpenConstants
    cdlOFNAllowMultiselect = 512
    cdlOFNCreatePrompt = 8192
```

```
    cdlOFNEnableHook = 32
    cdlOFNEnableSizing = 8388608
    cdlOFNExplorer = 524288
    cdlOFNExtensionDifferent = 1024
    cdlOFNFileMustExist = 4096
    cdlOFNHelpButton = 16
    cdlOFNHideReadOnly = 4
    cdlOFNLongNames = 2097152
    cdlOFNNoChangeDir = 8
    cdlOFNNoDereferenceLinks = 1048576
    cdlOFNNoLongNames = 262144
    cdlOFNNoNetworkButton = 131072
    cdlOFNNoReadOnlyReturn = 32768
    cdlOFNNoValidate = 256
    cdlOFNOverwritePrompt = 2
    cdlOFNPathMustExist = 2048
    cdlOFNReadOnly = 1
    cdlOFNShareAware = 16384
End Enum
```

Because the various flags properties can consist of combinations of zero or more of these constants, you'll need to combine them together to specify multiple values. To do this, you can either use the "+" or Or operator. Mathematically, these accomplish the same goal. We use Or in our code because that makes it clearer that we're combining bits together to create a Long integer value. If you're more comfortable using "+", however, your code will still work fine. Figure 17.2 shows how you might select from available lists of constants to supply the value for the OpenFlags property.

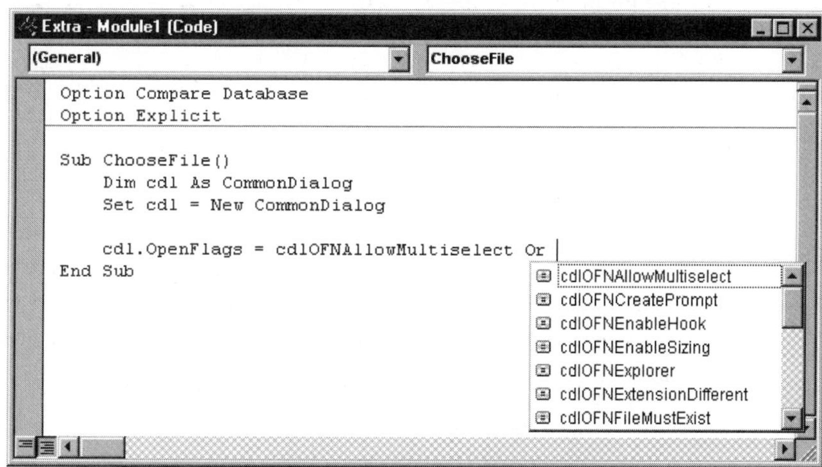

FIGURE 17.2: Use IntelliSense to choose from lists of possible flag values combined with Or.

TIP

Each of the sections describing the individual common dialogs includes a table defining the available values for the Flags property that apply to that particular dialog box.

Using a Callback Function

The ability to have your own code executing while the Windows common dialog is onscreen is a powerful feature, and it's available to you using the CommonDlg class. We've supplied a simple callback function (it centers the dialog box on the screen after the dialog has been initialized), but this technique is powerful—and potentially dangerous—once you've studied the API documentation.

NOTE

For more information on using callback functions with Windows API procedures, see Chapter 16.

In order to use a callback procedure with the Windows common dialogs, you must work through four issues:

- How do you indicate to the CommonDlg class that it should call your callback function?
- How do you declare the callback function so that the Windows common dialog can send information to it correctly?
- How do you supply the address of the procedure as a property of the CommonDlg class?
- What do you do from within the callback function?

The first question is the simplest: set the appropriate flag property to include the flag that enables a hook (that is, a callback) procedure. These flag values all include the text "EnableHook". If you don't set this flag, Windows will never call your procedure.

How do you specify the parameters for the callback function? When you create the procedure called by the common dialog, it's imperative that you get the data types, return type, and parameter passing information correct. Because Windows calls your procedure directly with no intervention from Visual Basic, any mistakes in the declaration of the procedure will generally cause your application to crash. For the common dialogs, your callback function must be declared like this:

```
Public Function SampleCallback( _
```

```
ByVal hWnd As Long, ByVal uiMsg As Long, _
ByVal wParam As Long, ByVal lParam As Long) As Long
```

The exact name of the procedure is inconsequential, as are the names of the parameters, but the data types, the parameter passing (that is, the use of ByVal), and the return type must match this example. If you use our sample callback functions, you won't have any trouble.

How do you tell Windows about this procedure? The CallBack property of the CommonDlg object requires you to send it the address of a VBA procedure. To do that, you use the AddressOf modifier (previously available only in Visual Basic, now available in all VBA hosts), which converts a procedure name into its address in memory. For this mechanism to work, this procedure must be a public procedure in a standard module—it can't be private, and it can't be within a class module. (For more information on using the AddressOf modifier, see Chapter 16.) One small problem: AddressOf only works within a procedure call. You can't write code like this:

```
cdl.CallBack = AddressOf SampleCallBack
```

because VBA won't compile this code. You need to supply the address of a procedure in the Callback property, however. To get around this problem, we've supplied the adhFnPtrToLong function in basCommon, which takes one Long parameter and simply returns that value:

```
Public Function adhFnPtrToLong(lngAddress As Long) As Long
    adhFnPtrToLong = lngAddress
End Function
```

How is this useful? Although it looks like adhFnPtrToLong isn't really doing anything, it allows you to call it using the AddressOf modifier, and it returns the address you've sent it. With a procedure like this, you can now write

```
cdl.CallBack = adhFnPtrToLong(AddressOf SampleCallBack)
```

and get the address you need in the CallBack property of the class. If you look at the samples that use the CommonDlg class, you'll see that they all use code similar to this in order to set the CallBack property.

What can you do within the callback procedure? From within the function itself, you react to messages sent to the callback function from Windows. These messages indicate the current state of the dialog box and allow you to make decisions about what to do. (You can think of messages in Windows as constants—they're actually Long integers—which Windows uses to communicate between windows.) Windows passes to your procedure a message value and the window handle for the open dialog box. Although, with enough research into the Windows API documentation, you can perform major tricks with the common dialogs, our example simply waits to receive the WM_INITDIALOG message (indicating that the dialog box has finished its initialization process) and then centers the dialog box on the screen. Listing 17.3 shows the callback function for the Font and Color dialogs. (You'll find both this and the CenterWindow procedure in the basCommonDlg module.)

TIP

For more information on using callback functions with common dialogs, you'll need to consult a good Windows API reference. If you have a subscription to the Microsoft Developer Network (MSDN), that's a good place to start.

Listing 17.3:

```
Public Function CDCallback( _
 ByVal hWnd As Long, ByVal uiMsg As Long, _
 ByVal wParam As Long, ByVal lParam As Long) As Long

    Select Case uiMsg
        Case WM_INITDIALOG
            ' On initialization, center the dialog.
            Call CenterWindow(hWnd)

            ' You could get many other messages here, too.
            ' All the normal window messages get
            ' filtered through here, and you can
            ' react to any that you like.
    End Select
    ' Tell the original code to handle the message, too.
    ' Otherwise, things get pretty ugly.
    ' To do that, return 0.
    CDCallback = 0
End Function
```

Using the Windows File Open/Save Common Dialogs

The Window File Open and File Save dialogs make it easy for you to allow users to select a file for opening or saving. The programmatic interface to these common dialogs requires you to send Windows some information, and then Windows will do its job, pop up the dialog, and return information to you.

No matter what options you choose and no matter what file you select, the dialog box does no more than return to your application the choices made while the dialog box was visible. It does not open or save a file—it merely allows you to make choices. What you do with the information gathered by the dialog box is up to you.

In order to use the File Open or File Save common dialogs, you may want to set properties of the CommonDlg object that pertain to these dialogs. Table 17.1 lists the properties that apply to the File Open and Save dialogs.

NOTE

In Windows 98 and Windows 2000, you can modify the size and position of the File Open and Save dialog boxes, and Windows will "remember" those settings for subsequent uses of the dialog box. See the notes in Table 17.2 on specific flags that alter this behavior. We've also noticed that if any VBA error occurs (if the user presses Cancel on the dialog box, for example, and you've got the CancelError property set to True), Windows seems to "forget" the size and location.

TABLE 17.1: Properties of the CommonDlg Class That Pertain to the File Open and Save Dialogs

Field Name	Datatype	Description
CallBack	Long	Address of a procedure to be called while the dialog is displayed. This procedure can position the dialog box or take other actions, depending on the particular dialog box.
CancelError	Boolean	If True, pressing the Cancel button on the common dialog triggers a runtime error in the class. Check for the cdlCancel error if you've set this property to True.
DefaultExt	String	If you don't supply an extension, the dialog appends this to your file name. See also the cdlOFNExtensionDifferent value in Table 17.2.
DialogTitle	String	Text that appears in the dialog caption.
FileExtOffset	Long	After returning from the call to ShowOpen or ShowSave, contains the offset, in characters, to the file extension. This makes it easy to parse the file name.
FileList	String()	If you've specified the cdlOFNAllowMultiSelect flag setting, the user may have selected multiple files. After dismissing the dialog box, this array of strings will contain one element for each selected file. FileList(0) always contains the folder in which the user selected files, and FileList(1) through FileList(n) (where n is the total number of selected files) contain the names of the selected files. If the user only selected a single file, FileList(0) contains the folder, and FileList(1) contains the single file name.

Continued on next page

TABLE 17.1 CONTINUED: Properties of the CommonDlg Class That Pertain to the File Open and Save Dialogs

Field Name	Datatype	Description
FileName	String	The full name (including path) of the selected file. If you specify this value before calling ShowOpen or ShowSave, the dialog will display this file name as the default file to be selected.
FileNameBufferSize	Long	When you call the Open or Save dialog boxes, the CommonDlg class must allocate space for the returned file name(s). The default size allocated is 20,000 bytes. If you think you may need more space, you can specify your own size. Unless you know users are going to be choosing lots of files at once, the default should be sufficient.
FileOffset	Long	After returning from the call to ShowOpen or ShowSave, contains the offset, in characters, to the name of the file (that is, the offset of the beginning of the filename portion of the full path).
FileTitle	String	After returning from the call to ShowOpen or ShowSave, contains the file name and extension (no path information) of the selected file. If you've selected multiple files, this property will contain no text.

Filter	String	List of pairs of filter values, separated with "|". For example, you can use a string like the following:
		`"Text Files (*.txt)|`
		`*.txt|`
		`Database Files (*.mdb,*.mda,.mde)|`
		`*.mdb;*.mda;*.mde|`
		`All Files (*.*)|`
		`*.*"`
		The first half of each pair contains the text the user sees in the Files of type combo box, and the second half of each pair indicates to Windows the file specification it should look for. (For multiple wildcards in the second half of a pair, use a semicolon to separate the items). Supplying no filter is the same as requesting all files.

FilterIndex	Integer	One-based index of the filter item that you want to be selected when the dialog box opens (the default value is 1). After the dialog has been dismissed, contains the index of the currently selected filter.

Continued on next page

TABLE 17.1 CONTINUED: Properties of the CommonDlg Class That Pertain to the File Open and Save Dialogs

Field Name	Datatype	Description
Flags	Long	Zero or more values from Table 17.2, combined with the Or operator, indicating how you want the dialog box to be initialized and how it should behave. You can set the value of this or the OpenFlags property, but using the OpenFlags property supplies a drop-down list of values based on adcFileOpen-Constants enumeration. We suggest you use the OpenFlags property instead of this property, which is provided for compatibility with the Common Dialog ActiveX control.
hWndOwner	Long	Windows handle for the parent of the dialog. Normally, supply a form's hWnd property. If you're not using a form, supply Application.hWndAccessApp for this property.
InitDir	String	The folder in which you want the dialog to first show files. If you don't specify this property, the dialog box will start in the current folder. Once you make a selection, Windows makes the selected file's folder the new current folder, unless you also specify the cdlOFNNoChangeDir flag.
OpenFlags	adhFileOpenConstants	Zero or more values from Table 17.2, combined with the Or operator, indicating how you want the dialog box to be initialized and how it should behave. You can set the value of this or the Flags property, but using the OpenFlags property supplies a drop-down list of values based on adcFileOpen-Constants enumeration. We suggest you use the OpenFlags property instead of the Flags property, which is provided for compatibility with the Common Dialog ActiveX control.

TABLE 17.2: Possible Values for the Flags or OpenFlags Properties

Constant Name	Description
cdlOFNAllowMultiselect	Specifies that the File Name list box allows multiple selections. If you include this flag, use the FileList property to investigate the array of selected file names (see Table 17.1).
cdlOFNCreatePrompt	If the user selects a file that doesn't exist, this flag causes the dialog box for permission to create the file to appear. It doesn't actually create the file, however. If the user chooses to create the file, the dialog box closes and the FileName property contains the name of the selected file. Without this flag set, specifying a nonexistent file requires no intervention from the user. If you use this flag with the cdlOFNAllowMultiselect flag, only one nonexistent file is allowed.

Continued on next page

TABLE 17.2 CONTINUED: Possible Values for the Flags or OpenFlags Properties

Constant Name	Description
cdlOFNEnableHook	If you include this flag, Windows will call the function specified in the CallBack property as it processes the dialog box. In Windows 98 or Windows 2000, setting this property causes the dialog box to not be sizable, unless you also set the cldOFNEnableSizing flag.
cdEnableSizing	(Windows 98 and Windows 2000 only) The ability to resize the dialog box is the default behavior, and Windows remembers the last position/size of the dialog box between uses. Generally, you won't need this flag, but if you also specify the cdlOFNEnableHook flag, Windows thinks that you're providing your own form template for the dialog and disables sizing. Using this class, you cannot supply your own template, so if you specify the cdlOFNEnableHook flag, you'll also want to include this flag. This flag is ignored (and you cannot resize the dialog box) under Windows 95 and Windows NT.
cdlOFNExplorer	Causes the dialog box to use the newer "explorer-style" interface. The CommonDlg class always adds this flag to the value you specify for the Flags or OpenFlags property. If you want to alter this behavior, you'll need to modify the code in the CommonDlg class.

cdlOFNExtensionDifferent	On return from the dialog box, indicates that the user chose a file with an extension different from that in the DefaultExt property. If you haven't specified a value for DefaultExt, this flag will never be set. Use the And operator, like this, to check for this flag:
	`If cdl.OpenFlags And _`
	` cdlOFNExtensionDifferent <> 0 Then`
	`    ' You know that you selected a`
	`    ' file whose extension is different`
	`    ' than that specified in the`
	`    ' DefaultExt property.`
	`End If`

cdlOFNFileMustExist	Specifies that the user can enter only names of existing files in the File Name entry field. If the user enters an invalid name, the dialog box displays a warning in a message box. If you specify this flag, the common dialog works as if you'd also specified the cdlOFNPathMustExist flag.
cdlOFNHelpButton	Displays a Help button on the dialog box. Although it's possible to react to the user clicking this button, it requires subclassing a form and reacting to Windows registered messages to make it work. Doing this is beyond the scope of this book, and this constant is only supplied for compatibility with the ActiveX control*.
cdlOFNHideReadOnly	If selected, this flag hides the Read Only check box on the dialog box.

Continued on next page

TABLE 17.2 CONTINUED: Possible Values for the Flags or OpenFlags Properties

Constant Name	Description
cdlOFNLongNames	For old-style dialog boxes (see cdlOFNExplorer), causes the dialog to use long file names. Has no effect in the CommonDlg class and is included for compatibility only.
cdlOFNNoChangeDir	If specified, Windows restores the directory to its original value if the user changed the directory while searching for a file.
cdlOFNNoDereferenceLinks	Causes the dialog box to return the path and file name of the selected shortcut (.LNK) file. If not specified, the dialog box returns the path and file name of the file referenced by the selected shortcut.
cdlOFNNoLongNames	If you're using the old-style dialog box, causes the dialog to display all file names using 8.3 format. Has no effect in the CommonDlg class and is included for compatibility only.
cdlOFNNoNetworkButton	If you're using the old-style dialog box (see the cdlOFNExplorer flag), setting this flag removes the Network button from the dialog box. Has no effect in the CommonDlg class and is included for compatibility only.
cdlOFNNoReadOnlyReturn	On return from the dialog box, if this flag is set, the returned file does not have the Read Only check box checked and is not in a write-protected folder. Use the And operator (see the example shown in the cdlOFNExtensionDifferent flag) to find out if this flag has been set.
cdlOFNNoValidate	Specifies that the dialog box allows invalid characters in the file name. Generally, it's not a good idea to use this flag setting*.
cdlOFNOverwritePrompt	Causes the Save As dialog box to generate a message box if the selected file already exists. The developer can decide whether to allow the selection of this file.
cdlOFNPathMustExist	Specifies that the user can select only valid paths and file names. If selected, this flag causes the dialog box to display a message box if the entered file name and path are invalid.
cdlOFNReadOnly	Causes the Read Only check box to be checked when the dialog box opens. After the dialog box has been dismissed, indicates whether the check box was checked at the time the user closed the dialog box. Use the And operator (see the example shown in the cdlOFNExtensionDifferent flag) to find out if this flag has been set.
cdlOFNShareAware	Specifies that if the user specifies a file that's in use, the error is ignored and the dialog box returns the selected name anyway*.

*Will require extra Windows API coding to fully support, so we recommend that you know what you're doing when using these flags

You needn't set any of the CommonDlg properties, if you're happy with the default behavior. When you're ready to select a file for opening or saving, call the appropriate method of the CommonDlg object (either ShowOpen or ShowSave). That is, if you simply write code like this, you'll see the name of the file you select from the dialog box:

```
Dim cdl As CommonDlg
Set cdl = New CommonDlg
cdl.ShowOpen
MsgBox cdl.FileName
```

On the other hand, if you want to control which files are offered to the user, which folder the dialog starts in, whether the Read Only check box is displayed, or any other specific attributes of the dialog box, you'll want to investigate the many properties and flags shown in Tables 17.1 and 17.2. To demonstrate the use of many of the properties of the CommonDlg class, Listing 17.4 shows a procedure from the sample form, frmTestCommonDlg.

TIP

To run this procedure, open frmTestCommonDlg in Form view. Click the Test File Open button and select a file. If you select a file with an extension other than BAT, you'll get an alert indicating that you chose a file with an extension other than the default extension. See the code in Listing 17.4 for the full cmdFileOpen_Click event procedure.

This procedure takes the following actions:

- Declares and instantiates the CommonDlg object:

```
Dim cdl As CommonDlg
Set cdl = New CommonDlg
```

- Sets the owner of the dialog to be the current form:

```
cdl.hwndOwner = Me.hWnd
```

- Sets up the filter text, and selects a particular filter to be displayed when the dialog appears:

```
' Set three pairs of values for the Filter.
cdl.Filter = _
 "Text files (*.txt)|" & _
 "*.txt|" & _
 "Database files (*.mdb, *.mde, *.mda)|" & _
```

```
    "*.mdb;*.mde;*.mda|" & _
    "All files (*.*)|" & _
    "*.*"

  ' Select filter 2 (Database files) when
  ' the dialog opens.
  cdl.FilterIndex = 2
```

- Sets the OpenFlags property, indicating how you want the dialog box to behave:

```
cdl.OpenFlags = cdlOFNEnableHook Or _
 cdlOFNNoChangeDir Or cdlOFNFileMustExist
```

- Sets up the callback function, pointing to our sample callback function (stored in basCommonDlg). This callback function must be a public function in a standard module and must meet the requirements described in the previous section, "Using a Callback Function." Note that you must call the adhFnPtrToLong function in order to store the address of the procedure into a variable:

```
cdl.CallBack = adhFnPtrToLong(AddressOf GFNCallback)
```

- Sets up other miscellaneous properties:

```
cdl.InitDir = "C:\"
cdl.FileName = "autoexec.bat"
cdl.DefaultExt = "bat"
```

- Calls the ShowOpen method of the object. This causes your code to halt, waiting for the dialog box to be dismissed:

```
cdl.ShowOpen
```

- After the dialog has been dismissed, retrieves the selected file name:

```
txtFileOpen = cdl.FileName
```

- Checks to see if the selected file had a different extension than that provided in the DefaultExt property. If so, handles that situation:

```
If (cdl.OpenFlags And _
 cdlOFNExtensionDifferent) <> 0 Then
    MsgBox "You chose a different extension!"
End If
```

Listing 17.4 shows the entire procedure.

TIP

To use this functionality in your own applications, make sure you've imported the CommonDlg class module. If you want to use callbacks, you'll also want to import basCommonDlg and basCommon.

TIP

For information on using the CancelError property to trap when a user cancels the dialog box, see the next section, "Checking for Cancellation."

Listing 17.4:

```
Private Sub cmdFileOpen_Click()

    ' From Access 2000 Developer's Handbook, Volume I
    ' by Getz, Litwin, and Gilbert. (Sybex)
    ' Copyright 1999. All rights reserved.

    ' Test the CommonDlg class' FileOpen common dialog.

    Dim cdl As CommonDlg
    Set cdl = New CommonDlg

    cdl.hWndOwner = Me.hWnd
    cdl.CancelError = True

    On Error GoTo HandleErrors

    ' Set three pairs of values for the Filter.
    cdl.Filter = _
     "Text files (*.txt)|" & _
     "*.txt|" & _
     "Database files (*.mdb, *.mde, *.mda)|" & _
     "*.mdb;*.mde;*.mda|" & _
     "All files (*.*)|" & _
     "*.*"

    ' Select filter 2 (Database files) when
    ' the dialog opens.
    cdl.FilterIndex = 2

    ' Indicate that you want to use a callback function,
    ' change back to the original directory when
```

```
    ' you're done, and require that the selected
    ' file actually exists.
    cdl.OpenFlags = cdlOFNEnableHook Or _
     cdlOFNNoChangeDir Or cdlOFNFileMustExist

    ' Select the callback function.
    cdl.CallBack = adhFnPtrToLong(AddressOf GFNCallback)

    ' Set up miscellaneous properties.
    cdl.InitDir = "C:\"
    cdl.FileName = "autoexec.bat"
    cdl.DefaultExt = "bat"

    ' Open the file open dialog box,
    ' and wait for it to be dismissed.
    cdl.ShowOpen

    ' Retrieve the selected file na
    txtFileOpen = cdl.FileName

    ' Check the OpenFlags (or Flags) property to
    ' see if the selected extension is different than
    ' the default extension.
    If (cdl.OpenFlags And _
     cdlOFNExtensionDifferent) <> 0 Then
        MsgBox "You chose a different extension!"
    End If

ExitHere:
    Set cdl = Nothing
    Exit Sub

HandleErrors:
    Select Case Err.Number
        Case cdlCancel
            ' Cancelled!
            Resume ExitHere
        Case Else
            MsgBox "Error: " & Err.Description & _
             "(" & Err.Number & ")"
    End Select
    Resume ExitHere
End Sub
```

NOTE

The only real difference between the File Open and File Save dialog boxes is the interpretation of some of the flag values shown in Table 17.2. Otherwise, the usage and behavior of the common dialog is the same whether you use the ShowOpen or ShowSave methods. In either case, use the OpenFlags property to specify the flags you'd like to apply.

TIP

If you'd rather have this all wrapped up for you, check out the adhCommon-FileOpenSave procedure, in the basFileOpen module. This procedure allows you to pass in parameters indicating the behavior you'd like, and the procedure does all the work of instantiating the object for you. It returns, as its return value, the file name that was selected.

Checking for Cancellation

If you want to know whether the user pressed the Cancel button (as opposed to clicking OK with no file selected), you'll need to add code to handle this. Specifically, follow these steps:

1. Set the CancelError property of your CommonDlg object to True.
2. Add an error handler to your procedure, and specifically check for the error cdlCancel (32755). This is the error the CommonDlg class will raise if the user clicks on the Cancel button (or presses Escape) while the dialog is displayed.

In your error handler, you may decide to do something if the user pressed Cancel. Most of the time, however, you'll simply go on with your application without taking any action. For example, the following code, excerpted from the cmdChooseColor_Click event procedure in frmTestCommonDlg, reacts to the user pressing Cancel by doing nothing at all (for more information on using the color-choosing dialog, see the appropriate section later in this chapter):

```
Private Sub cmdChooseColor_Click()
    Dim cdl As CommonDlg

    On Error GoTo HandleErrors
    Set cdl = New CommonDlg

    ' Trigger a run-time error if the user
    ' presses Cancel.
```

```
    cdl.CancelError = True

    ' Code removed here...
    cdl.ShowColor
    ' Code removed here...

ExitHere:
    Set cdl = Nothing
    Exit Sub

HandleErrors:
    Select Case Err.Number
        Case cdlCancel
            ' Do nothing at all.
        Case Else
            MsgBox "Error: " & Err.Description & _
             " (" & Err.Number & ")"
    End Select
    Resume ExitHere
End Sub
```

WARNING

Make sure you investigate the value of the VBA Tools ➢ Options ➢ Error Trapping property. If it's set to be Break in Class Module, none of these classes will work correctly. If this setting is checked, that means that even if you have error handling in a class module, the code will drop into break mode if a runtime error occurs. Although this setting may make sense when you're working in Visual Basic, which creates standalone executables, it never makes sense when you distribute Access applications. You must make sure to set this option to be Break on Unhandled Errors, or you won't be able to make use of the CancelError property of this class. To try this out, open a module, make sure the setting is set to Break in Class Module, and then try the code in frmTestCommonDlg, pressing the Cancel button. Although you wouldn't expect it, you'll hit a breakpoint in the error handler. Not cool. If you use error handling, make sure you verify this option setting for each and every project you distribute.

Trying Out All the Options

To make it easier for you to try out all the available options, we've supplied frmTestFileOpenSave, shown in Figure 17.3. This form allows you to choose the flags you want set and the text you'd like to use. Once you've made all your choices, click Test the Dialog to give it a try. The example places the selected file (or files) in the Results text box. Figure 17.4 shows the sample form after the common dialog has been dismissed.

FIGURE 17.3:

Use frmTestFileOpenSave to try out all the options for the CommonDlg class' File Open dialog box.

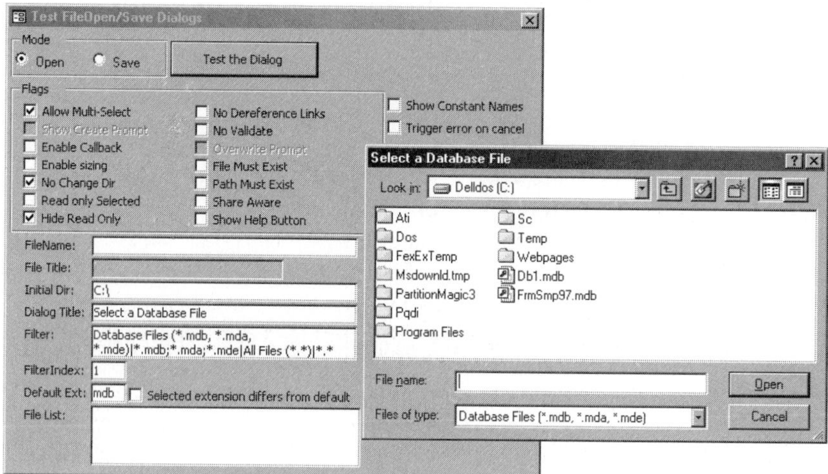

FIGURE 17.4:

After dismissing the File Open dialog box, frmTestFileOpen-Save might look like this.

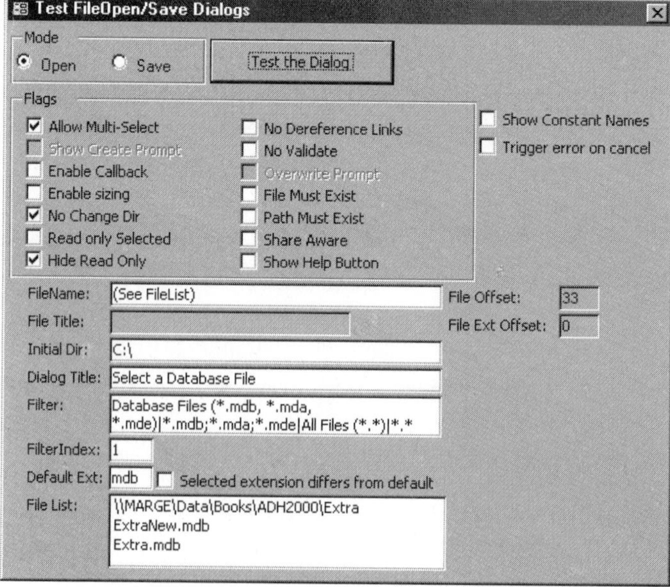

Modifying the Look of the File Open or Save Common Dialog Box

Although it's not simple, you can modify the text displayed in any command button or label on the common dialog boxes, and you can control the visibility of any item on the form, as well. To accomplish these goals, you'll need to modify code in the callback function used by the dialog. Modifying the layout of the dialog box requires sending messages, using the Windows API SendMessage function, to the dialog box, indicating what you want to change. Windows provides a Long integer that uniquely identifies each of the controls on the form, and you can find an enumeration of those values in the adhFileOpenSaveControls enum, in the CommonDlg class. To change the text of a control, call the SendMessageText variation on the SendMessage API (see the code in basCommonDlg), specifying the window handle for the dialog box, the CDM_SETCONTROLTEXT message, the identifier of the control you want to change, and the new text. The following example shows how you might do this:

```
Call SendMessageText(hWndParent, CDM_SETCONTROLTEXT, _
 fosOKButton, "&Select")
```

To change the visibility of a control on the dialog box, call the SendMessageLong variation on the SendMessage API, passing the window handle, the CDM_HIDECONTROL message, the identifier of the control, and 0, like this:

```
Call SendMessageLong(hWndParent, CDM_HIDECONTROL, _
 fosFilterListLabel, 0)
```

(Note that there's no message available to redisplay a hidden control.) Remove the conditional compilation statements in the GFNCallBack procedure (in basCommonDlg) to see this code working. When you make this change and click the Test File Open button on frmTestCommonDlg, you'll see that the label for the Open button is now Select, and the Files of Type label is invisible.

Using the Office File Open/File Save Common Dialog

If you've used Office for long, you've noticed that its File Open/Save dialog is different from the one Windows provides. This dialog adds an Outlook-like menu bar along the left, making it easy to get to specific folders like Personal, Desktop, and Favorites. The dialog also makes it possible for you to allow users to select a path, rather than both a path and file (the standard Windows dialog doesn't supply this feature). From your perspective as a developer, using this dialog is similar to using the standard common dialogs. In this case, however, we haven't supplied a class wrapper around the technology. Whether you are opening or saving a file, you must create a variable of the adh_accOfficeGetFileNameInfo datatype. (We've defined this structure for you in basOfficeFileOpen.) You fill out certain fields in the structure and then send it off to the adhOfficeGetFileName function. This function either requests a file to open or a name under which to save (depending on the value in one of its parameters) and returns the structure to you, all filled out with the information the user chose from the dialog. Figure 17.5 shows the Office File Open/Save dialog at work.

WARNING

The Office common dialog is not available if you distribute your application using the Access runtime version. Unless you can guarantee that your users are running the full copy of Access, you should avoid using this functionality. If you are using this dialog box because it makes it possible for you to prompt your users for a path (and not a file), see the section "Using the ShellBrowse Class" later in this chapter for an alternative. If you're using this dialog box to allow users to select a file, you'll want to use the standard Windows common dialog, unless you're sure that your users all have a full copy of Access.

FIGURE 17.5:

The Office File Open dialog looks radically different from the standard Windows common dialog.

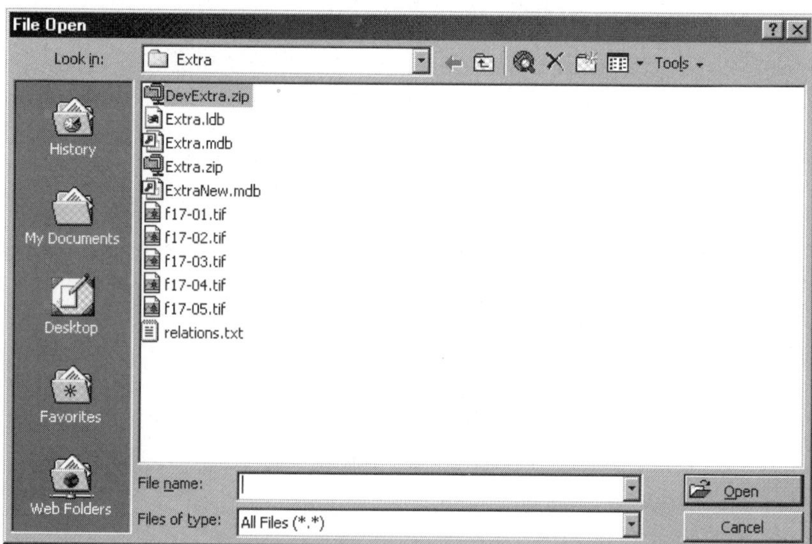

Because readers of our previous editions may have existing code using the Office common dialog box, we haven't changed the interface to this functionality or wrapped its usage up in a class for this edition. Therefore, to use the Office File Open (or Save) dialog box, you must follow slightly different steps than you might if using the CommonDlg class discussed earlier. In order to use the Office File Open or Save dialog boxes, you'll need to follow these steps:

1. Make sure your project contains the basOfficeFileOpen module.
2. Create a variable, of type adh_accOfficeGetFileNameInfo, to contain all the information you'll send to the function call.
3. Supply values for the members of the adh_accOfficeGetFileNameInfo data structure, as shown in Tables 17.3 through 17.5.
4. Call the adhOfficeGetFileName function, passing as parameters the data structure you filled in in the previous step and a Boolean value indicating whether you want to select a file for opening (True) or saving (False). This causes your code to halt, waiting for the dialog to be dismissed.
5. After the dialog box has been dismissed, check the return value from the call to adhOfficeGetFileName. If it indicates success (adhcAccErrGFN-Success) the adh_accOfficeGetFileNameInfo will contain information returned from the dialog, including the name of the selected file (or files). You might also receive other return values, as shown in Table 17.6.

Table 17.3 lists all the fields in the adh_accOfficeGetFileNameInfo structure, along with information on using those fields. Table 17.4 lists the possible values for the lngFlags field in this structure, and Table 17.5 lists the possible values for the lngView field. Table 17.6 lists the possible return values you might receive from calling the adhOfficeGetFileName function.

NOTE

Just as when working with the Windows common dialogs, neither the Office File Open nor the File Save dialog actually *does* anything with the file you select. These dialogs just return a file name to your application so you can decide what you wish to do with that file. It's up to you to actually open or save the file.

TABLE 17.3: Fields in the adh_accOfficeGetFileNameInfo Structure

Field Name	Datatype	Description
hWndOwner	Long	Windows handle for the parent of the dialog. Normally, supply a form's hWnd property, or Application.hWndAccessApp for this value.
strAppName	String*255	Describes the application. Not currently used.
strDlgTitle	String*255	Text that appears in a dialog caption.
strOpenTitle	String*255	Text that appears on the Open button when choosing a file to open.
strFile	String*4096	On input, contains the name of a file to have selected initially. On output, contains the file name or path of the selected item. If you've allowed multiple selections, contains the list of selected items delimited with a tab character. Use the Split function to break the names apart.
strInitialDir	String*255	Initial directory.
strFilter	String*255	List of filter values, separated with "|". For example: Text Files (*.txt)|Database Files (*.mdb)|All Files (*.*). Note that this filter list does not contain name/filespec pairs, as would a filter value for the CommonDlg class. The dialog finds the file specification within the single string you specify.
lngFilterIndex	Long	Zero-based index into the array of filters, indicating which is to be selected when the dialog opens (note that the corresponding value for the normal File open/Save dialog box is 1-based).
lngView	Long	One of the values from Table 17.5, indicating which view of the directory is to be displayed when the dialog opens. This value is disregarded unless the lngFlags field includes the adhcGfniInitializeView constant.
lngFlags	Long	Zero or more values from Table 17.4, combined together with the Or (or "+") operator to control the behavior of the dialog box.

TABLE 17.4: Possible Values for the lngFlags Field in the adh_accOfficeGetFileNameInfo Structure

Constant Name	Description
adhcGfniConfirmReplace	When choosing a file name in which to save, confirms with a dialog if the file already exists.
adhcGfniNoChangeDir	Instead of changing the current directory to the selected directory, maintains the original directory after using the dialog.

Continued on next page

TABLE 17.4 CONTINUED: Possible Values for the lngFlags Field in the adh_accOfficeGetFile-NameInfo Structure

Constant Name	Description
adhcGfniAllowMultiSelect	Allows the user to select multiple items. Office returns multiple items in the strFile field delimited with a tab character (vbTab). Use the Split function to break this value apart into its individual file names. If you're choosing a file name for saving, the dialog returns only the first selected file name.
adhcGfniDirectoryOnly	Limits the user to selecting directories only. This flag overrides all others and turns the dialog into a directory picker.
adhcGfniInitializeView	Allows the setting for the initial view to override the user's most recent choice. If this flag isn't set, the value in the lngView field is disregarded.

TABLE 17.5: Possible Values for the lngView Field in the adh_accOfficeGetFileNameInfo Structure

Constant Name	Description
adhcGfniViewDetails	Displays file details
adhcGfniViewPreview	Displays file preview, if available
adhcGfniViewProperties	Displays file properties, if available
adhcGfniViewList	Displays the file list (the standard view)

TABLE 17.6: Possible Return Values for the adhOfficeGetFileName Function

Constant Name	Value	Description
adhcAccErrGFNSuccess	0	The dialog box succeeded
adhcAccErrGFNCantOpenDialog	-301	Properties specified for the dialog box made it impossible for the dialog box to be displayed
adhcAccErrGFNUserCancelledDialog	-302	The user canceled the dialog box

TIP

None of the values in the lngView field (chosen from Table 17.5) will have any effect unless the value in the lngFlags field includes the adhcGfniInitializeView flag. Make sure your code uses the Or operator to include this value if you want to specify the view.

To call the adhOfficeGetFileName function, you needn't supply values for all the fields in Table 17.3. Listing 17.5 shows a simple example of using the Office common dialog to retrieve a file name. Figure 17.6 shows the dialog box this function pops up. (If you're interested in exactly what the adhOfficeGetFileName function is doing, you can check out its code in basOfficeFileOpen.)

TIP

To run this procedure, open frmTestCommonDlg in Form view. Click the Test Office File Open button and select a file. See the code in Listing 17.5 for the full procedure.

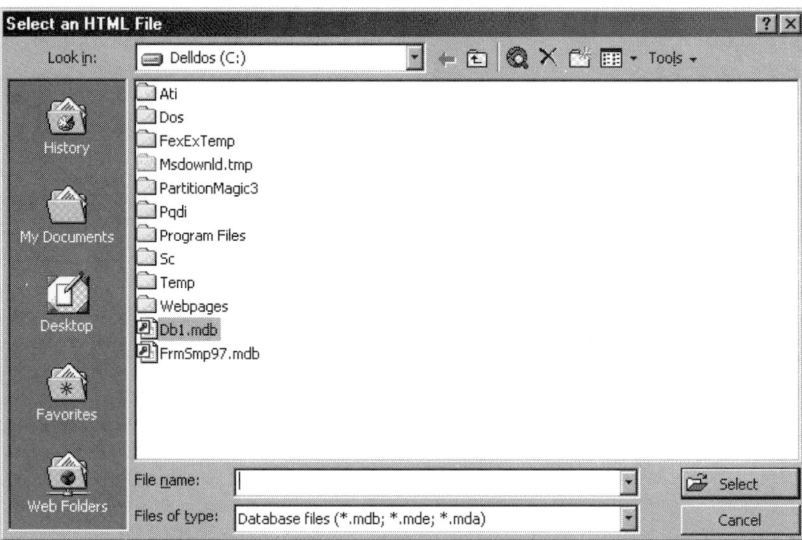

FIGURE 17.6:

The code in Listing 17.5 causes this dialog to be displayed.

Listing 17.5

```
Private Sub cmdOfficeFileOpen_Click()

    ' Test the Office file open common dialog.
    Dim gfni As adh_accOfficeGetFileNameInfo
    With gfni
        .hWndOwner = Me.hWnd
        .strDlgTitle = "Select a File"
        .strOpenTitle = "Select"
        .strFile = ""
        .strInitialDir = "C:\"
        .strFilter = _
         "Text files (*.txt)|" & _
         "Database files (*.mdb; *.mde; *.mda)|" & _
         "All files (*.*)"
        .lngFilterIndex = 1
        .lngView = adhcGfniViewList
        .lngFlags = adhcGfniNoChangeDir Or _
         adhcGfniInitializeView
    End With
    If adhOfficeGetFileName(gfni, True) = _
     adhcAccErrGFNSuccess Then
        txtOfficeFileOpen = Trim$(gfni.strFile)
    End If
End Sub
```

There are a few items to note about this function:

- Because all the strings in the data type are fixed-length strings, you need to use the Trim function to remove trailing spaces when you want to use the data that's in those strings.
- If you want to initialize the view (Details, Preview, List, or Properties) in the lngView field, you must also specify the adhcGfniInitializeView flag in the lngFlags field. The example in Listing 17.5 does this.
- Most likely, you'll want to at least supply values for the fields used in Listing 17.5: strInitialDir, strDlgTitle, and strFilter. You can, of course, supply other values, but those will be the most useful ones. Note that you must end each entry in the strFilter field with a vertical bar and that each entry must

consist of two parts: the text description of the filter item and, within parentheses, the file specification that will select that group. In addition, if you want to use two or more different filespecs within a group (as we did in Listing 17.5), separate them with a comma or a semicolon (;) inside the parentheses.

- Calling the adhOfficeGetFileName function will return one of three values: adhcAccErrGFNSuccess (0), indicating success; adhcAccErrGFNCantOpenDialog (–301), indicating there was some error in the parameters making it impossible to open the dialog; or adhcAccErrGFNUserCancelledDialog (–302), indicating that the user canceled the dialog (with the Cancel button).

To choose a file name for saving, set the second parameter to adhOfficeGetFileName to False. That way, you've indicated that you're trying to save a file rather than load it.

Trying Out All the Options

To make it easier for you to try out all the available options, we've supplied frmTestOfficeFileOpen, shown in Figure 17.7. This form allows you to choose the flags you want set, the text you'd like to use, and the initial view. Once you've made all your choices, you can click Test the Dialog to give it a try. The example places the selected file (or files) in the Results text box. Figure 17.7 shows the sample form set up to display the same dialog as the code in Listing 17.5.

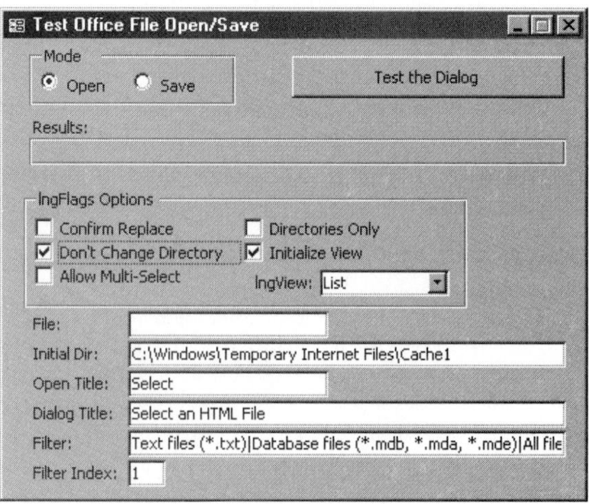

FIGURE 17.7:

Use frmTestOfficeFileOpen to try out all the options for adhOfficeGetFileName.

TIP

To use this functionality in your own applications, make sure you've imported the basOfficeFileOpen module.

WARNING

Chances are good that the ability to use the Office File Open/Save dialog box will either be provided by a different mechanism, or unavailable altogether, in a future version of Access. As with any undocumented feature, you should be aware that you're using it at your own risk. It works fine in this version, but it may make upgrading to the next a challenge.

Selecting Colors

If you need to allow your users to choose colors within your application, the easiest solution is to use the Windows common dialog Color Chooser. Figure 17.8 shows the Color dialog in action.

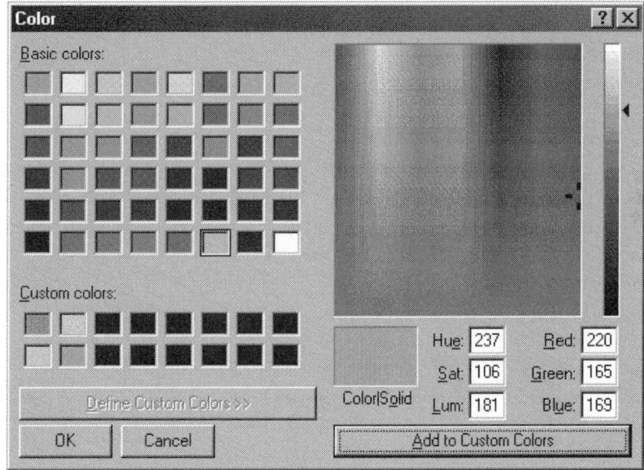

FIGURE 17.8: Windows color-choosing common dialog

Just as with the file name-choosing dialog, you can use the CommonDlg class to provide access to the color-choosing dialog box. For information on using this class, see the earlier section "Using the CommonDlg Class."

TIP

If you were using the adhChooseColor function provided in previous editions of this book, you still can—we've provided a function with this name that uses the CommonDlg class (see basCommonDlg for information on calling this function). If you're writing new code, however, you'll probably want to use the CommonDlg class directly. You get more options and capabilities using the class directly. If you want to use the adhChooseColor function, you'll need to import both the CommonDlg class module and the basCommonDlg standard module into your project.

The CommonDlg class includes several properties and flags that are specific to calling the Color common dialog. Table 17.7 lists the properties you're likely to use, and Table 17.8 lists the options for the ColorFlags property.

TABLE 17.7: Properties of the CommonDlg Class That Pertain to the Color-Choosing Dialog

Field Name	Datatype	Description
CallBack	Long	Address of a procedure to be called while the dialog is displayed. This procedure can position the dialog box or take other actions, depending on the particular dialog box.
CancelError	Boolean	If True, pressing the Cancel button on the common dialog triggers a runtime error in the class. Check for the cdlCancel error if you've set this property to True.
Color	Long	Before calling the ShowColor method, you can use this property to specify the color to be selected when the dialog is displayed. After the dialog has been dismissed, this property contains a Long integer corresponding to the selected color. The value of this property will be 0 if the user presses Escape or clicks on the Cancel button (see the CancelError property for more information).
ColorFlags	adhColorConstants	Zero or more values from Table 17.8, combined with the Or operator, indicating to Windows how you want the dialog box to be initialized and how it should behave. You can set the value of this or the Flags property, but using the ColorFlags property supplies a drop-down list of values based on adcColorConstants enumeration. We suggest you use the ColorFlags property instead of the Flags property, which is provided for compatibility with the Common Dialog ActiveX control.

Continued on next page

TABLE 17.7 CONTINUED: Properties of the CommonDlg Class That Pertain to the Color-Choosing Dialog

Field Name	Datatype	Description
CustomColors	Long()	An array of up to 16 colors (indexed starting with 0) displayed in the Custom Colors section at the bottom of the dialog box. You can create a dynamically sized array of up to 16 values and set the CustomColors property before displaying the dialog box, and/or you can retrieve the custom colors selected by the user, store it away, and use it on subsequent calls to the dialog box. The dialog box itself does not preserve these values, so if you want to maintain the custom colors, make sure you create a static array variable in which to store the values. On return from the dialog box, the CustomColors property will contain an array of Long integers, indexed from 0 through 15, containing one value for each selected custom color. The setting of the cdlCCRGBInit flag has no bearing on the initialization of this property (see Table 17.8 for more information).
Flags	Long	Zero or more values from Table 17.8, combined with the Or operator, indicating to Windows how you want the dialog box to be initialized and how it should behave. You can set the value of this or the ColorFlags property, but using the ColorFlags property supplies a drop-down list of values based on adcColorConstants enumeration. We suggest you use the ColorFlags property instead of this property, which is provided for compatibility with the Common Dialog ActiveX control.
hWndOwner	Long	Windows handle for the parent of the dialog. Normally, supply a form's hWnd property. If you're not using a form, supply Application.hWndAccessApp for this property.

TABLE 17.8: Possible Values for the Flags or ColorFlags Properties

Constant Name	Description
cdlCCAnyColor	Causes the dialog to display all available colors in the set of basic colors.
cdlCCEnableHook	If you include this flag, Windows will call the function specified in the CallBack property as it processes the dialog box.
cdlCCFullOpen	Causes the dialog box to display with both "halves" displayed, allowing users to create custom colors without having to first click the Define Custom Color button.

Continued on next page

TABLE 17.8 CONTINUED: Possible Values for the Flags or ColorFlags Properties

Constant Name	Description
cdlCCHelpButton	Displays a Help button on the dialog box. Although it's possible to react to the user clicking this button, it requires subclassing a form and reacting to Windows registered messages to make it work. Doing this is beyond the scope of this book, and this constant is only supplied for compatibility with the ActiveX control.
cdlCCPreventFullOpen	Disables the Define Custom Colors button.
cdlCCRGBInit	Causes the dialog box to use the color specified in the Color property as the initial color selection.
cdlCCSolidColor	Causes the dialog box to display only solid (nondithered) colors in the set of basic colors.

To test out the color-chooser dialog box, you can run code like this, taken from frmTestCommonDlg. (For information on reacting to the error canceling the dialog, see the section "Checking for Cancellation," earlier in the chapter):

```
Private Sub cmdChooseColor_Click()
    Dim cdl As CommonDlg

    On Error GoTo HandleErrors
    Set cdl = New CommonDlg

    ' Trigger a run-time error if the user
    ' presses Cancel.
    cdl.CancelError = True
    ' You should usually set the hwndOwner property
    ' to be an open form.
    cdl.hWndOwner = Me.hWnd
    ' Initialize the dialog from the Color property,
    ' and enable callbacks.
    cdl.ColorFlags = cdlCCRGBInit Or cdlCCEnableHook
    ' Set the callback address.
    cdl.CallBack = adhFnPtrToLong(AddressOf CDCallback)
    ' Get the 16 custom colors from the local static
    ' array of colors.
    cdl.CustomColors = alngCustom
    ' Get a starting color from the label control.
    cdl.Color = lblColor.BackColor
    ' Show the dialog, and wait for it to be dismissed.
    cdl.ShowColor
    ' Set the label control's backcolor.
```

```
        lblColor.BackColor = cdl.Color
        ' Store away the array of 16 custom colors.
        alngCustom = cdl.CustomColors

ExitHere:
        Set cdl = Nothing
        Exit Sub

HandleErrors:
        Select Case Err.Number
            Case cdlCancel
                ' Do nothing at all.
            Case Else
                MsgBox "Error: " & Err.Description & _
                 " (" & Err.Number & ")"
        End Select
        Resume ExitHere
End Sub
```

Selecting Fonts

You may need to allow users to select a font (name, size, weight, and so on) within an application. The easiest way to do this is to use the CommonDlg class, which includes code that can call the Windows font-selecting dialog box. This dialog box, shown in Figure 17.9, allows you to preselect font information and to retrieve the information the user selects in the dialog, as well.

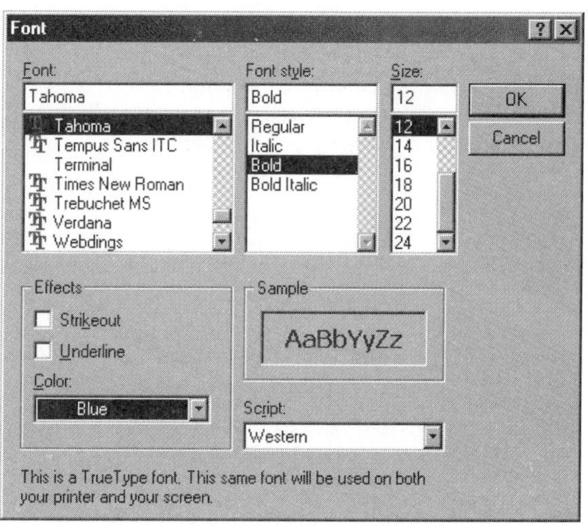

FIGURE 17.9:

The font-choosing common dialog allows you to retrieve complete font information.

Using the font-choosing common dialog box entails the same basic steps as using the file or color choosing dialogs. See the section "Using the CommonDlg Class" for more information on these basic steps. In order to take advantage of this dialog box, however, you'll need to know which properties and flag settings in the CommonDlg class to use. Table 17.9 lists all the properties of the CommonDlg class that apply, and Table 17.10 lists the values available for the FontFlags property.

TABLE 17.9: Properties of the CommonDlg Class That Pertain to the Font-Choosing Dialog

Field Name	Datatype	Description
CallBack	Long	Address of a procedure to be called while the dialog is displayed. This procedure can position the dialog box or take other actions, depending on the particular dialog box.
CancelError	Boolean	If True, pressing the Cancel button on the common dialog triggers a runtime error in the class. Check for the cdlCancel error if you've set this property to True.
Flags	Long	Zero or more values from Table 17.10, combined with the Or operator, indicating to Windows how you want the dialog box to be initialized and how it should behave. You can set the value of this or the FontFlags property, but using the FontFlags property supplies a drop-down list of values based on adcFontsConstants enumeration. We suggest you use the FontFlags property instead of this property, which is provided for compatibility with the Common Dialog ActiveX control.
FontBold	Boolean	Is the font bold? (If so, its FontWeight property should be 700.)
FontColor	Long	Long integer representing the selected color.
FontFlags	adhFontsConstants	Zero or more values from Table 17.10, combined with the Or operator, indicating to Windows how you want the dialog box to be initialized and how it should behave. You can set the value of this or the Flags property, but using the FontFlags property supplies a drop-down list of values based on adcFontsConstants enumeration. We suggest you use the FontFlags property instead of the Flags property, which is provided for compatibility with the Common Dialog ActiveX control.

Continued on next page

TABLE 17.9 CONTINUED: Properties of the CommonDlg Class That Pertain to the Font-Choosing Dialog

Field Name	Datatype	Description
FontItalic	Boolean	Is the font italicized?
FontName	String	Name of the font face.
FontScript	adhFontFaceAPI	Defines the character set for the font. See the adhFont-FaceAPI enum in CommonDlg for a list of possible values.
FontSize	Single	Size, in points, for the font. Although this is a Single, for compatibility with the ActiveX control, Access uses only integer values for font sizes.
FontStrikeThrough	Boolean	Is the strikethrough attribute set for the font?
FontStyle	String	A string containing information from the Font Style combo box on the dialog. Might be text like "Italic", or "Bold Italic". (You can use this property to specify font style before calling the dialog box, but we don't recommend it.)
FontType	adhCDFontType	On return from the dialog box, specifies the font type for the selected font. It can be a combination of any of the adhCDFontType values. For example, you could use this property to determine if the selected font is a screen or printer font.
FontUnderline	Boolean	Is the font underlined?
FontWeight	Long	Font weight, given as an integer between 100 and 900. For normal fonts, the FontWeight is 400; for bold fonts, the FontWeight is 700.
hWndOwner	Long	Windows handle for the parent of the dialog. Normally, supply a form's hWnd property. If you're not using a form, supply Application.hWndAccessApp for this property.
Max	Integer	Specifies the maximum point size a user can select. The dialog box recognizes this value only if you've set the cdl-CFLimitSize flag (see Table 17.10 for more information).
Min	Integer	Specifies the minimum point size a user can select. The dialog box recognizes this value only if you've set the cdl-CFLimitSize flag (see Table 17.10 for more information).

TABLE 17.10: Possible Values for the Flags or FontFlags Properties

Constant Name	Description
cdlCFANSIOnly	Obsolete. Included only for compatibility with the Common Dialog ActiveX control.
cdlCFApply	Causes the dialog to display the Apply button. To support this functionality, you'll need to do a great deal more work with the Windows API. We recommend you not use this flag unless you've studied the API documentation carefully.
cdlCFBoth	Causes the dialog box to display both printer and screen fonts (this flag is included for you if you don't specify any of cdlCFScreenFonts, cdlCF-PrinterFonts, or cdlCFBoth).
cdlCFEffects	Causes the dialog box to display the controls that allow the user to specify strikeout, underline, and text color options. With this option set, you can use the FontColor property to set the font color and retrieve the selected font color.
cdlCFEnableHook	If you include this flag, Windows will call the function specified in the CallBack property as it processes the dialog box.
cdlCFFixedPitchOnly	Specifies that the dialog box should display fixed-pitch fonts only.
cdlCFForceFontExist	Specifies that the dialog box should trigger an error condition if you attempt to select a font or style that doesn't exist.
cdlCFInitToLogFontStruct	Causes the dialog box to initialize its values based on property settings you've made. Always assumed by the CommonDlg class. Included here only for compatibility with the Common Dialog ActiveX control.
cdlCFLimitSize	Specifies that the dialog should select only font sizes within the range specified by the Min and Max properties.
cdlCFNoFaceSel	Causes the dialog box to not select a face name when it first appears, even if you've specified a font name.
cdlCFNoSimulations	Specifies that the dialog box should not allow GDI font simulations.
cdlCFNoSizeSel	Causes the dialog box to not select a font size when it first appears, even if you've specified a font size.
cdlCFNoStyleSel	Causes the dialog box to not select a font style when it first appears, even if you've specified a font style.
cdlCFNoVectorFonts	Specifies that the dialog box should not allow vector font selections.
cdlCFNoVertFonts	Causes the dialog box to list only horizontally-oriented fonts.

Continued on next page

TABLE 17.10 CONTINUED: Possible Values for the Flags or FontFlags Properties

Constant Name	Description
cdlCFPrinterFonts	Causes the dialog box to list only the font supported by the printer associated with the current device context.
cdlCFScalableOnly	Specifies that the dialog box should display only scalable (such as TrueType) fonts.
cdlCFScreenFonts	Causes the dialog box to list only the screen fonts supported by the system.
cdlCFShowHelp	Displays a Help button on the dialog box. Although it's possible to react to the user clicking this button, it requires subclassing a form and reacting to Windows registered messages to make it work. Doing this is beyond the scope of this book, and this constant is only supplied for compatibility with the ActiveX control.
cdlCFTTOnly	Specifies that the dialog box should list only TrueType fonts.
cdlCFUseStyle	Specifies that the FontStyle property should be used to initialize the Font Style combo box on the dialog. When the user closes the dialog box, the font style information is copied back to the FontStyle property.
cdlCFWYSIWYG	Specifies that the dialog box should allow only the selection of fonts available on both the printer and the display. If you use this flag, you should also specify the cdlCFBoth and cdlCFScalableOnly flags.

To test out the Font common dialog box, open frmTestCommonDlg in Form view and click the Test Font Dialog button. This example initializes the dialog box based on the font it finds in the text box on the sample form, displays the dialog allowing you to select a font, and then sets the font properties of the sample text box. Listing 17.6 displays the test procedure in its entirety.

Listing 17.6

```
Private Sub cmdChooseFont_Click()

    Dim cdl As CommonDlg
    Set cdl = New CommonDlg

    cdl.hWndOwner = Me.hWnd
    cdl.FontFlags = cdlCFEnableHook Or _
     cdlCFEffects Or cdlCFLimitSize Or cdlCFBoth
```

```
        With txtFont
            cdl.FontName = .FontName
            cdl.FontItalic = .FontItalic
            cdl.FontSize = .FontSize
            cdl.FontUnderline = .FontUnderline
            cdl.FontWeight = .FontWeight
            cdl.FontColor = .ForeColor
        End With
        cdl.Min = 8
        cdl.Max = 24

        cdl.hWndOwner = Application.hWndAccessApp
        cdl.CallBack = adhFnPtrToLong(AddressOf CDCallback)
        cdl.ShowFont

        With txtFont
            .FontName = cdl.FontName
            .FontItalic = cdl.FontItalic
            .FontSize = cdl.FontSize
            .FontUnderline = cdl.FontUnderline
            .FontWeight = cdl.FontWeight
            .ForeColor = cdl.FontColor
        End With
        Set cdl = Nothing
    End Sub
```

NOTE

To use the font common dialog (or any of the common dialogs based on the CommonDlg class), you'll need to import the CommonDlg class into your own project. If you're going to be using callback functions, you'll also need to import the basCommonDlg and basCommon modules.

Using the ShellBrowse Class

If you've ever needed to prompt your users to supply a folder, printer, or machine name, you know that relying on them to type in a value is risky, at best. Although you can use the Office common dialog to allow users to select a folder, you have very little control over the dialog. In addition, this dialog doesn't work in applications distributed with the Access runtime version. We've found the Windows ShellBrowse common dialog to be very useful, allowing users to select folders, machines, or printers. Figures 17.10, 17.11, and 17.12 demonstrate three different uses for the same common dialog.

FIGURE 17.10:

You can use the ShellBrowse dialog to select a folder.

FIGURE 17.11:

You can also use the Shell-Browse dialog to select a printer.

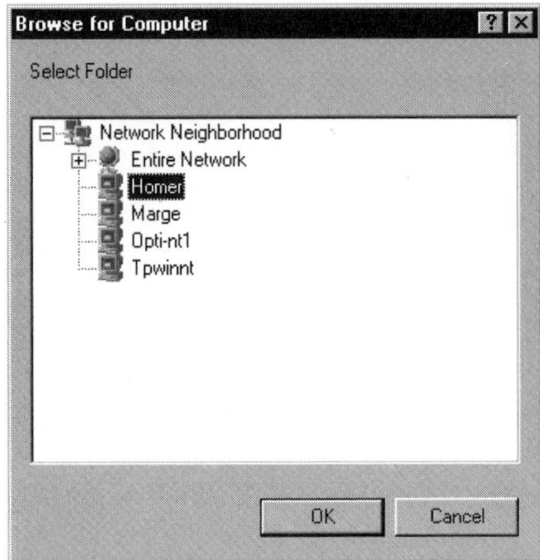

FIGURE 17.12:

You can force the ShellBrowse dialog to only allow selection of machines.

The ShellBrowse dialog gives you great flexibility in the type of object you're seeking, the starting location of the browse, and the types of objects whose choice will enable the OK button. We can't begin to document all the options here—in fact, we'll only explain how to use the ShellBrowse class and demonstrate its features with a sample form. If you want to dig further, you'll need to investigate the sample code.

In its simplest case, you can use the ShellBrowse class like this, to request a path from a user:

```
Dim sb As ShellBrowse
Set sb = New ShellBrowse
sb.BrowseForFolder
Debug.Print sb.Result
Set sb = Nothing
```

Using the BrowseForFolder method this way allows you to select a folder, as shown in Figure 17.10. You can also specify properties, as shown in Table 17.11, which modify the behavior of the ShellBrowse object. Two properties, RootFolder and InitialFolder, require you to select from a provided list of constant values. Table 17.12 describes the options available for those two properties.

TIP

In order to use the ShellBrowse class in your own applications, you'll need to import the ShellBrowse class itself, along with the basShellBrowse and basCommon modules.

TABLE 17.11: Properties of the ShellBrowse Class

Property	Type	Description
Caption	String	Text to be displayed about the tree view control on the browse dialog. You can use this text to specify instructions for the user.
ComputersOnly	Boolean	Allows the user to select only a computer.
DontGoBelowDomain	Boolean	Does not include network folders below the domain level in the tree view control. Local folders appear in the browser, but no network folders appear below the domain level.
FileSystemAncestorsOnly	Boolean	Allows the user to select only file system ancestors, or so says the Windows documentation. We're not completely sure what a "file system ancestor" is, so we include this option for compatibility's sake only.
FileSystemDirsOnly	Boolean	Allows the user to select file system directories only. If the user selects folders that are not part of the file system (that is, a virtual folder), the OK button is grayed. Note that this also allows the user to select computers.
hWndOwner	Long	Handle to the owner window for the dialog box. The window you select will control the placement and modality of the browse dialog box.
IncludeFiles	Boolean	(Available in Windows 98/2000 only) The Browse dialog displays files as well as folders, so you can use this dialog to select files, if you wish.
InitialFolder	adhRootFolders	A virtual folder, indicating what the Browse dialog should select when it first appears. Choose a value from Table 17.12. Specify either InitialFolder or InitialPath. You can specify neither value, but not both. If you specify both, the InitialPath value will override the InitialFolder setting.
InitialPath	String	A file-system folder, indicating the folder the browse dialog should select when it first appears. Specify either InitialFolder or InitialPath. You can specify neither value, but not both. If you specify both, the InitialPath value will override the InitialFolder setting.
PrintersOnly	Boolean	Allows the user to select only a printer.
Result	String	(On return from the dialog) The selected folder, printer, or machine, if it's a fiie-system object. If the value represents a virtual folder, it's surrounded with "<>".

Continued on next page

TABLE 17.11 CONTINUED: Properties of the ShellBrowse Class

Property	Type	Description
RootFolder	adhRootFolders	The root folder from which to browse. Only the specified folder and its subfolders appear in the dialog box. If you don't specify this value, the browse dialog will start at the desktop folder. Choose a value for this property from the values shown in Table 17.12.
ShowStatusText	Boolean	If this flag is set, a callback function can set the status text in reaction to a change in selection or the browser's initialization. You must provide the callback function that does the work yourself (and the example does provide such a callback function), but setting this flag on merely enables the callback function to update the status area.

TABLE 17.12: Values for the RootFolder and InitialFolder Properties

Constant	Description
rfWindowsDesktop	Virtual folder that is the Windows desktop.
rfProgramsUser	File system folder that contains the user's program groups. A common path is C:\WINNT\Profiles*username*\Start Menu\Programs.
rfProgramsCommon	File system folder that contains the directories for the common program groups that appear on the Start menu for all users. A common path is C:\WINNT\Profiles\All Users\Start Menu\Programs.
rfPersonal	File system directory that serves as a common repository for documents. A common path is C:\WINNT\Profiles*username*\My Documents.
rfFavorites	File system directory that serves as a common repository for the user's favorite items. A common path is C:\WINNT\Profiles*username*\Favorites.
rfStartupUser	File system directory that corresponds to the user's Startup program group. The system starts these programs whenever any user logs into Windows 95/98 or logs into Windows NT or Windows 2000. A common path is C:\WINNT\Profiles*username*\Start Menu\Programs\Startup.
rfStartupCommon	File system directory that corresponds to the Startup folder for all users. A common path is C:\WINNT\Profiles\All Users\Start Menu\Programs\Startup.
rfRecent	File system directory that contains the user's most recently used documents. A common path is C:\WINNT\Profiles*username*\Recent.

Continued on next page

TABLE 17.12 CONTINUED: Values for the RootFolder and InitialFolder Properties

Constant	Description
rfSendTo	File system directory that contains Send To menu items. A common path is C:\WINNT\Profiles*username*\SendTo.
rfStartMenuUser	File system directory containing Start menu items. A common path is C:\WINNT\Profiles\username\Start Menu.
rfStartMenuCommon	File system directory containing Start menu items for all users. A common path is C:\WINNT\Profiles\All Users\Start Menu.
rfDesktopFolderUser	File system directory used to physically store file objects on the desktop (not to be confused with the desktop folder itself, from which you can browse to all objects displayed on the Windows desktop). A common path is C:\WINNT\Profiles*username*\Desktop.
rfDesktopFolderCommon	File system directory used to physically store file objects on the desktop for all users. A common path is C:\WINNT\Profiles\All Users\Desktop.
rfMyComputer	My Computer—virtual folder containing everything on the local computer: storage devices, printers, and Control Panel. This folder may also include mapped network drives.
rfNetwork	Network Neighborhood—virtual folder representing the top level of the network hierarchy.
rfTemplates	File system directory that serves as common repository for document templates.
rfAppData	File system directory that serves as a common repository for application-specific data. A common path is C:\WINNT\Profiles*username*\Application Data.

NOTE

Table 17.12's list of possible folders isn't all-inclusive. The class module itself has a few more, commented out, which you're unlikely to use. You can enable any of those options that you need. In addition, as new versions of Windows arrive, the list of available virtual and special folders grows. You'll need to check a good API reference (such as Microsoft Developer Network) for more information. For example, Windows 2000 offers several new virtual folders that aren't available at the time of this writing. We weren't able to find constants corresponding to these new folders, so we'll leave their discovery to you, as you need them.

To demonstrate the use of the ShellBrowse dialog, we've included frmTestShellBrowse. This form, shown in Figure 17.13, exercises all the options and properties for the dialog box. Give the ShellBrowse class a workout using this form. You'll get a feel for combinations of root folders and starting folders that make sense, as well as which of the properties provide the return values you need. Beware: not all of the combinations of options and properties make sense, and often you won't get exactly what you need without doing some experimenting.

NOTE

Some folders displayed in the dialog box aren't real folders—they're "virtual" folders. For example, the Network Neighborhood folder, available on the dialog, doesn't map to a physical folder. To make that clear, frmTestShellBrowse displays virtual folders surrounded with angle brackets ("<>").

The sample form does little more than use your choices to set properties of an instance of the ShellBrowse class. If you're interested, peruse the code in frmTest-ShellBrowse's module. The interesting code is in the cmdTest_Click event procedure, shown in Listing 17.7.

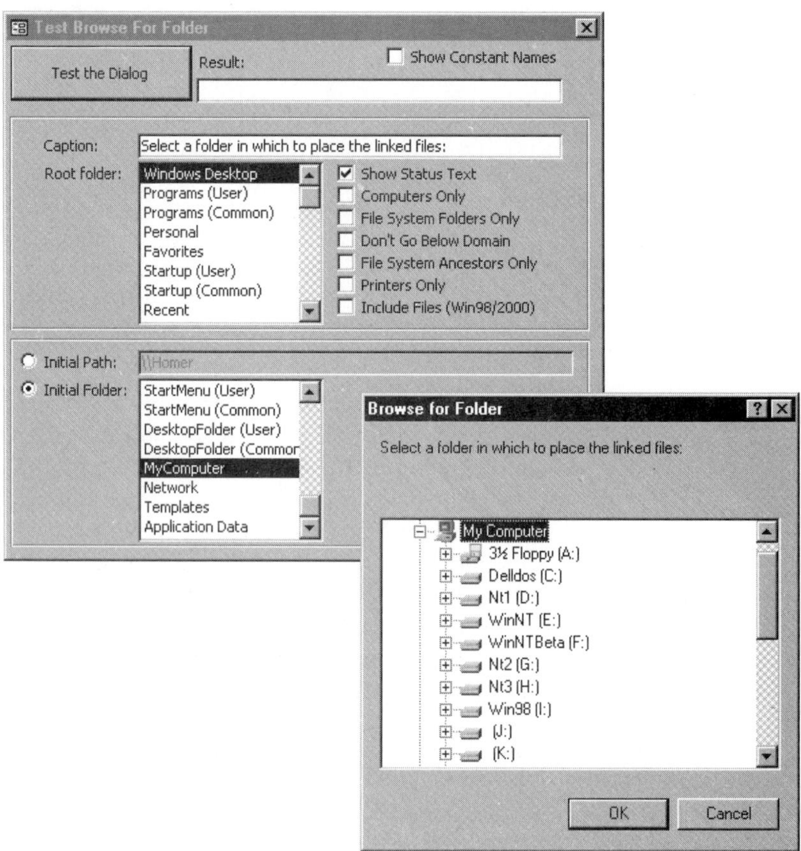

FIGURE 17.13: Use frmTestShellBrowse to try out the ShellBrowse class.

Listing 17.7

```
Private Sub cmdTest_Click()
    ' Test the browser.
    On Error GoTo HandleErrors

    Dim sb As ShellBrowse
    Set sb = New ShellBrowse

    ' Clear out the Result text box.
    txtResult = Null

    ' Set up the initial path/folder.
    ' If the frame's value is ioInitPath,
    ' then use the Initial Path value.
    ' Otherwise, use the Initial Folder
    ' value.
    If fraInit = ioInitPath Then
        sb.InitialPath = txtInitialPath
    Else
        sb.InitialFolder = lstInitialFolder
    End If
    ' If you've specified a caption,
    ' set that property now.
    If Len(txtCaption & "") > 0 Then
        sb.Caption = txtCaption
    End If

    ' Use the current form as the hWndOwner.
    sb.hWndOwner = Me.hWnd

    ' Copy in the rest of the property
    ' values.
    sb.ComputersOnly = chkComputersOnly
    sb.DontGoBelowDomain = chkDontGoBelowDomain
    sb.FileSystemAncestorsOnly = chkFSAncestorsOnly
    sb.FileSystemDirsOnly = chkFileSystemFoldersOnly
    sb.IncludeFiles = chkIncludeFiles
    sb.PrintersOnly = chkPrintersOnly
    sb.RootFolder = lstRootFolder
    sb.ShowStatusText = chkShowStatusText
```

```
        ' Display the dialog box.
        ' Wait for it to be dismissed.
        Call sb.BrowseForFolder

        ' Place the result in the output
        ' text box.
        txtResult = sb.Result

    ExitHere:
        On Error Resume Next
        Set sb = Nothing
        Exit Sub

    HandleErrors:
        Resume ExitHere
    End Sub
```

NOTE

In order to set the original selection and to display status text, the ShellBrowse class relies on an API callback function mechanism. Because the callback function must exist in a standard module, you'll find (if you examine the code) that the ShellBrowse class specifies a callback function in basShellBrowse. This callback function does nothing more than call directly back into a method of the ShellBrowse class itself. We've employed this mechanism so that the real callback function (that is, the CallBack method of the ShellBrowse class) can share variables and code with the rest of the class. This is a common technique, and you might want to give it a look to see how you can implement classes yourself that require callback functions.

Reading and Writing Registry Values

Although you can use the Windows API directly to read and write Registry values, doing so isn't much fun. In the previous edition of this book, we documented six functions exposed by MSACCESS.EXE that made working with the Registry much simpler. Although those undocumented functions are still available in this version, we've opted to write them ourselves in VBA code and replace the need to use undocumented functionality exposed by MSACCESS.EXE. This way, you needn't worry about their disappearance in a future version, and you get the source code, so you can modify them yourself should you ever have the need. These six functions make working with the Registry a little easier, although they still require a bit of effort on your part. The following sections explain how you can use these functions to make your work with the Registry simpler.

TIP

If you simply intend to store your own application information in the Registry, you needn't fight with these functions. VBA supplies the GetSetting, SaveSetting, GetAllSettings, and DeleteSetting procedures, which allow you to get and set Registry values in a limited manner. If, on the other hand, you like the way these functions work but want to write or read data from any location in the Registry, check out the adhGetRegSetting, adhSaveRegSetting, adhGetAllRegSettings, and adhDeleteRegSetting functions provided in basRegistry. We won't discuss these functions here in the book, but they're available in the sample project, and you can import the module (along with basCommon) into your own projects to use them.

WARNING

Although the examples in this section make heavy use of the Registry, this book does not intend to, nor can it, provide a reference or instructions on using the System Registry. Anytime you modify settings in the Registry, if you're not sure of what you're doing, you risk making your system unusable. Before you modify anything in the Registry, programmatically or manually, make sure you've backed up.

To use any of the procedures in this section, you'll need to import the standard modules basRegistry and basCommon into your own project. Once you've imported those two modules, you have all the code you need to work with the Registry programmatically.

TIP

All the examples for this section can be found in the basTestRegistry module. In addition, if you're running Windows 95 or Windows NT 4, you can test these procedures using frmStartupTips, which allows you to view and edit Windows' startup tips. This form won't work in Windows 98 or Windows 2000, however, because those environments don't include startup tips, at least not in the same way. If you have sound installed on your computer, you can also try out frmSoundList, which demonstrates a few of the other functions.

Retrieving Information about a Key

If you're interested in working your way through all the subkeys or values associated with a key in the Registry, you will need to know, before you start, how many of each exist. The adh_accRegGetKeyInfo function retrieves, for a given root key and path to a key, the number of subkeys and values associated with that key. In addition, as you'll see, it can also retrieve the maximum size of the values and/or subkeys, so you can allocate space to hold them if necessary.

NOTE

The terminology surrounding the Registry can get confusing. From the Registry's point of view, a *key* is a node within the Registry, at any level within the hierarchy. A *subkey* of that key is any key located at the next lower level in the hierarchy. A *value* is a named quantity, displayed in the right pane of the Registry Editor, and can be text, numeric, or binary. The Registry includes a number of root keys as well, including HKEY_LOCAL_MACHINE and HKEY_CURRENT_USER.

In this example, you want to retrieve information from the specific key:

```
HKEY_CURRENT_USER
    Software
        Microsoft
            Office
               9.0
                   Access
                       Settings
```

as shown in Figure 17.14. The root key is HKEY_CURRENT_USER, and the key to check on is

```
Software\Microsoft\Office\9.0\Access\Settings
```

You may need to know, in this case, how many values (Access program settings) are associated with this key. To do this, call adh_accRegGetKeyInfo, passing to it the value for the handle to the root key, HKEY_CURRENT_USER (defined as the constant adhcHKEY_CURRENT_USER), a string containing the path to the key in question, and two Long integer variables that the function will fill in with the number of subkeys and values:

```
lngRetval = adh_accRegGetKeyInfo(adhcHKEY_CURRENT_USER, _
 "Software\Microsoft\Office\9.0\Access\Settings", _
 lngSubKeys, lngValues)
```

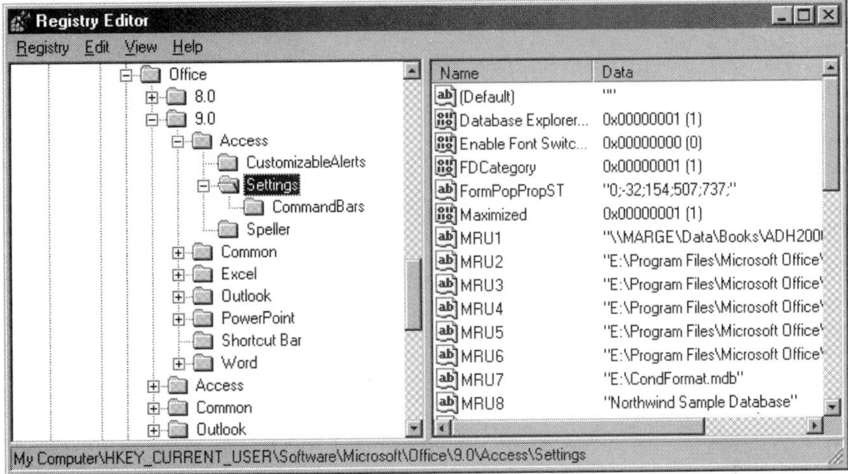

FIGURE 17.14: Access stores all its program settings in the Registry, at this location.

The adh_accRegGetKeyInfo function will retrieve the information for you and pass it back in those final two variables. The syntax for calling adh_accRegGetKeyInfo is shown in Table 17.13.

TABLE 17.13: Syntax for Calling adh_accRegGetKeyInfo

Parameter	Type	Description	Comments
hkeyRoot	Long	Key to use as the root	Use one of the constants defined in basRegistry: adhcHKEY_LOCAL_MACHINE or adhcHKEY_CURRENT_USER, normally.
strSubKey	String	Path to the key in question	Do not include the root key name or a leading backslash (\).
lngSubKeys	Long	(Optional) Filled in by the function call with the number of subkeys underneath the specified key	Only subkeys located at the next lower level in the hierarchy are counted.
lngValues	Long	(Optional) Filled in by the function call with the number of values associated with the specified key	

Continued on next page

TABLE 17.13 CONTINUED: Syntax for Calling adh_accRegGetKeyInfo

Parameter	Type	Description	Comments
lngMaxSubKeyLen	Long	(Optional) Filled in by the function call with the maximum length of a subkey	If you're going to make further function calls to determine information about this key, you may need to allocate buffer space for the subkey. This value lets you know the size of the largest subkey.
lngMaxValueNameLen	Long	(Optional) Filled in by the function call with the maximum length of a value name	If you're going to make further function calls to determine information about this key, you may need to allocate buffer space for the value names. This value lets you know the size of the largest value name.
lngMaxValueDataLen	Long	(Optional) Filled in by the function call with the maximum length of any value data	If you're going to make further function calls to determine information about this key, you may need to allocate buffer space for the value data. This value lets you know the size of the largest data.
Return Value	Long	Error code	adhcAccErrSuccess, adhcAccErrRegKeyNotFound, or adhcAccErrUnknown.

For example, here's code that retrieves information about the number and sizes of subkeys, values, and data for the Access program settings:

```
Public Sub TestGetKeyInfo()
    Dim lngRetVal As adhRegErrors
    Dim lngSubKeys As Long
    Dim lngValues As Long
    Dim lngMaxSubKeyLen As Long
    Dim lngMaxValueNameLen As Long
    Dim lngMaxValueDataLen As Long

    lngRetVal = adh_accRegGetKeyInfo( _
     adhcHKEY_CURRENT_USER, _
     "Software\Microsoft\Office\9.0\Access\Settings", _
     lngSubKeys, lngValues, _
     lngMaxSubKeyLen, lngMaxValueNameLen, _
     lngMaxValueDataLen)
```

```
    If lngRetVal = adhcAccErrSuccess Then
        Debug.Print "SubKeys: " & lngSubKeys
        Debug.Print "Values : " & lngValues
        Debug.Print "Max Value Name Len: " & _
         lngMaxValueNameLen
        Debug.Print "Max SubKey Len: " & lngMaxSubKeyLen
        Debug.Print "Max Value Data Len: " & _
         lngMaxValueDataLen
    End If
End Sub
```

Retrieving a Value Name

To retrieve value data for a particular value using this set of functions, you must know the name of the value. (You can get around this restriction using the Windows API directly, but this chapter attempts to solve problems using the wrappers previously exposed by Access, with as few "raw" API calls as possible. For more information on using the API to get to the Registry, see Chapter 16.)

To retrieve the name of a value, use the adh_accRegGetValName function. As in the previous function, you supply it with a root key and a path to the key in question. You must also give it the index for the value for which you want to retrieve the name, a buffer in which to place the returned value, the size of that buffer, and a Long integer into which the function can place the type of value (Text, Numeric, and so on) it retrieved. Table 17.14 shows the syntax for calling adh_accRegGetValName.

TABLE 17.14: Syntax for Calling adh_accRegGetValName

Parameter	Type	Description	Comments
hkeyRoot	Long	Key to use as the root	Use one of the constants defined in basRegistry: adhcHKEY_LOCAL_MACHINE or adhcHKEY_CURRENT_USER, normally.
strSubKey	String	Path to the key in question	Do not include the root key name or a leading backslash (\).
lngIndex	Long	Index of the value to retrieve	The index is zero-based.
strValName	String	Buffer to contain the value name	Must be large enough to contain the string before you call the function. (Use the Space function to "puff" it out, or use a fixed-length string.)

Continued on next page

TABLE 17.14 CONTINUED: Syntax for Calling adh_accRegGetValName

Parameter	Type	Description	Comments
lngMaxLen	Long	Maximum characters in the output buffer	Initialize the output buffer with this much space before calling the function.
lngType	Long	On return from the function, filled in with the datatype of the value	For a list of possible types, see the constants starting with adhcREG_ in basRegistry. In general, the only datatypes you'll care about are adhcREG_SZ (null-terminated string) and adhcREG_DWORD (Long integer).
Return Value	Long	Error code	adhcAccErrSuccess, adhcAccErr-RegKeyNotFound, or adhcAcc-ErrRegValueNotFound.

For example, once you've retrieved the number of values associated with the Access program settings key, you can walk through them all, retrieving their names and types, with the following code:

```
Public Sub TestGetValName()
    Dim lngRetval As adhRegErrors
    Dim lngSubKeys As Long
    Dim lngValues As Long
    Dim i As Long
    Dim strValName As String
    Dim lngType As Long

    Const conSubKey = "Software\Microsoft\" & _
     "Office\9.0\Access\Settings"

    lngRetval = adh_accRegGetKeyInfo( _
     adhcHKEY_CURRENT_USER, _
     conSubKey, lngSubKeys, lngValues)

    If lngRetval = adhcAccErrSuccess Then
        For i = 0 To lngValues - 1
            strValName = Space(adhcMaxDataSize)
            lngRetval = adh_accRegGetValName( _
             adhcHKEY_CURRENT_USER, _
             conSubKey, i, strValName, _
             Len(strValName), lngType)
```

```
                If lngRetval = adhcAccErrSuccess Then
                    If Len(strValName) = 0 Then
                        strValName = "(Default)"
                    End If
                    Debug.Print strValName, lngType
                End If
            Next i
        End If
    End Sub
```

Retrieving a Value from the Registry

Given the name of a key's value, you can retrieve its actual data using the adh_accRegGetVal function, like this:

```
strValue = Space(adhcMaxSize)
lngRetval = adh_accRegGetVal(adhcHKEY_CURRENT_USER, _
 "Software\Microsoft\Office\9.0\Access\Settings", _
 strValueName, strValue, adhcMaxSize)
```

TIP

If you're converting calls to this function from a previous version of the code, you must remove any ByVal keywords you've placed in your function calls. In previous versions of this code, that ByVal keyword was necessary. Using this code, your function calls will fail with that keyword included. See the varData parameter described in Table 17.15 for more information.

This function, as well as all the other Registry functions discussed in this section, requires that you tell it the root key and the path to the specific key. You must also specify the name of the value to be retrieved, a buffer in which to place the value, and the size of that buffer. The function places the value into the buffer and returns a status code. Table 17.15 explains the syntax for calling adh_accRegGetVal.

TABLE 17.15: Syntax for Calling adh_accRegGetVal

Parameter	Type	Description	Comments
hkeyRoot	Long	Key to use as the root	Use one of the constants defined in basRegistry: adhcHKEY_LOCAL_ MACHINE or adhcHKEY_CURRENT_ USER, normally.
strSubKey	String	Path to the key in question	Do not include the root key name or a leading backslash (\).

Continued on next page

TABLE 17.15 CONTINUED: Syntax for Calling adh_accRegGetVal

Parameter	Type	Description	Comments
strValName	String	Name of the value to retrieve	
varData	Variant	Buffer to contain the returned data	If you're converting code from a previous version of this function, you should remove the ByVal in front of this parameter's value. Previously, the ByVal keyword was necessary, but it will not work with the current incarnation of the code.
lngMaxLen	Long	Maximum characters in the output buffer	Initialize the output buffer with this much space before calling the function if you're retrieving text, or place the length of the buffer if you're retrieving a Numeric type. (You can use the LenB function to find the length of the datatype.)
Return Value	Long	Error code	adhcAccErrSuccess, adhcAccErrRegKeyNotFound, adhcAccErrRegValueNotFound, or adhcAccErrBufferTooSmall.

The following example attempts to retrieve the MRU1 value (the first item in the most recently used list, from Access' file menu):

```
Sub TestRegGetVal()
    Dim lngRetVal As adhRegErrors
    Dim strValue As String

    strValue = Space(adhcMaxDataSize)
    lngRetVal = adh_accRegGetVal(adhcHKEY_CURRENT_USER, _
     "Software\Microsoft\Office\9.0\Access\Settings", _
     "MRU1", strValue, Len(strValue))
    If lngRetVal = adhcAccErrSuccess Then
        Debug.Print strValue
    End If
End Sub
```

Writing a Value to the Registry

You may need to write a value to the Registry in a location other than that allowed by the SaveSetting function. The basRegistry module provides the adh_accReg-WriteVal function to write data to a value associated with a given key. You tell it the (by now familiar) root key and path to the key, as well as the name of the value, the data, and the datatype.

Table 17.16 describes the syntax for calling adh_accRegWriteVal.

TABLE 17.16: Syntax for Calling adh_accRegWriteVal

Parameter	Type	Description	Comments
hkeyRoot	Long	Key to use as the root.	Use one of the constants defined in basRegistry: adhcHKEY_LOCAL_MACHINE or adhcHKEY_CURRENT_USER, normally.
strSubKey	String	Path to the key in question.	Do not include the root key name or a leading backslash (\).
strValName	String	Name of the value to be written to.	If the value does not exist, the function will create it.
varData	Variant	Buffer containing the output data.	If you're converting code from a previous version of this function, you should remove the ByVal in front of this parameter's value. Previously, the ByVal keyword was necessary, but it will not work with the current incarnation of the code.
lngType	Long	Data type for the value in lpData. Must be either adhcREG_SZ (null-terminated string) or adhcREG_DWORD (Long integer). Any other data type will cause the function to return an error.	If you need to support other data types (and you will need to only in very few situations), you can modify the code to handle whatever data types you need.
Return Value	Long	Error code.	adhcAccErrSuccess, adhcAccErrRegTypeNotSupported, adhcAccErrRegKeyNotFound, or adhcAccErrRegCantSetValue.

The following example uses the adh_accRegWriteVal function to modify the Maximized setting for Access (note that this code won't really do anything useful if you call it from within Access. That is, every time you quit Access, it stores away the current maximized state so that it can use it the next time it starts up. We've selected this value, even though it's a fruitless change, because it's so completely harmless.)

```
Public Sub TestRegWriteVal()
    Dim lngRetVal As adhRegErrors
    lngRetVal = adh_accRegWriteVal( _
     adhcHKEY_CURRENT_USER, _
     "Software\Microsoft\Office\9.0\Access\Settings", _
     "Maximized", 1, adhcREG_DWORD)
End Sub
```

Retrieving the Name of a Registry Subkey

At times, you may need to retrieve the name of a Registry subkey associated with a given key, given the subkey's index. You can call adh_accRegGetKeyInfo to find out how many subkeys there are, and then you can loop through them, retrieving the name of each with adh_accRegGetKey. To call adh_accRegGetKey, use the syntax shown in Table 17.17.

TABLE 17.17: Syntax for Calling adh_accRegGetKey

Parameter	Type	Description	Comments
hkeyRoot	Long	Key to use as the root	Use one of the constants defined in basRegistry: adhcHKEY_LOCAL_MACHINE or adhcHKEY_CURRENT_USER, normally.
strSubKey	String	Path to the key in question	Do not include the root key name or a leading backslash (\).
lngIndex	Long	Zero-based index of the subkey name to retrieve	
strName	String	Buffer to contain the subkey name	Must be large enough to contain the string before you call the function. (Use the Space function to "puff" it out, or use a fixed-length string.)

Continued on next page

TABLE 17.17 CONTINUED: Syntax for Calling adh_accRegGetKey

Parameter	Type	Description	Comments
lngMaxLen	Long	Maximum characters in the output buffer	Initializes the output buffer with this much space before calling the function if you're retrieving text, or places the length of the buffer if you're retrieving a numeric type. (You can use the LenB function to find the length of the datatype.)
Return Value	Long	Error code	adhcAccErrSuccess, adhcAccErr-KeyNotFound, or adhcAccErr-SubkeyNotFound.

NOTE

You might want to try out frmSoundList, which uses several of the functions described in this section, to retrieve a list of available events to which Windows attaches sounds. Once you've selected a sound event, if there is an associated sound, you can play that sound from the sample form. If your computer does not support sound, however, you will not be able to test frmSoundList. If it can't find the requisite Registry keys, it will fail and display an alert. In order for the keys to exist, you must have the hardware installed, and you must have selected a sound scheme. Run the Control Panel applet, Sounds, to set up the sound scheme.

The following example loops through all the subkeys of the Office 9 Registry key and lists out each of the subkey names.

```
Public Sub TestRegGetKey()
    Dim i As Long
    Dim lngRetVal As adhRegErrors
    Dim lngSubKeys As Long
    Dim strKeyName As String

    lngRetVal = adh_accRegGetKeyInfo( _
    adhcHKEY_CURRENT_USER, _
    "Software\Microsoft\Office\9.0", _
    lngSubKeys)
    If lngRetVal = adhcAccErrSuccess Then
        For i = 0 To lngSubKeys - 1
            strKeyName = Space(adhcMaxDataSize)
```

```
                lngRetVal = adh_accRegGetKey( _
                 adhcHKEY_CURRENT_USER, _
                 "Software\Microsoft\Office\9.0", _
                 i, strKeyName, Len(strKeyName))
                If lngRetVal = adhcAccErrSuccess Then
                    Debug.Print strKeyName
                End If
            Next i
        End If
    End Sub
```

Creating a New Key

The final Registry-focused procedure is also the simplest to use. It allows you to create a new key in the Registry. The adh_accRegWriteKey function is as user-friendly as a function can be: it creates the key and, if the key is nested beneath other keys that need to be created, it creates those keys as well. In addition, if the key already exists, the function just leaves it alone.

For example, to create this scenario:

```
HKEY_CURRENT_USER
   Software
      KPM and Associates
         Marketing
            Application
```

you could call adh_accRegWriteKey like this:

```
Public Sub TestRegWriteKey()
    Dim lngRetval As Long
    lngRetval = adh_accRegWriteKey( _
     adhcHKEY_CURRENT_USER, _
     "Software\KPM and Associates\Marketing\Application", _
     "")
End Sub
```

Windows will create the Application key, as well as any keys above it in the Registry that it must create in order to supply the path you've requested. Figure 17.15 shows the Registry after calling the code in the example. Table 17.18 shows the syntax for calling adh_accRegWriteKey.

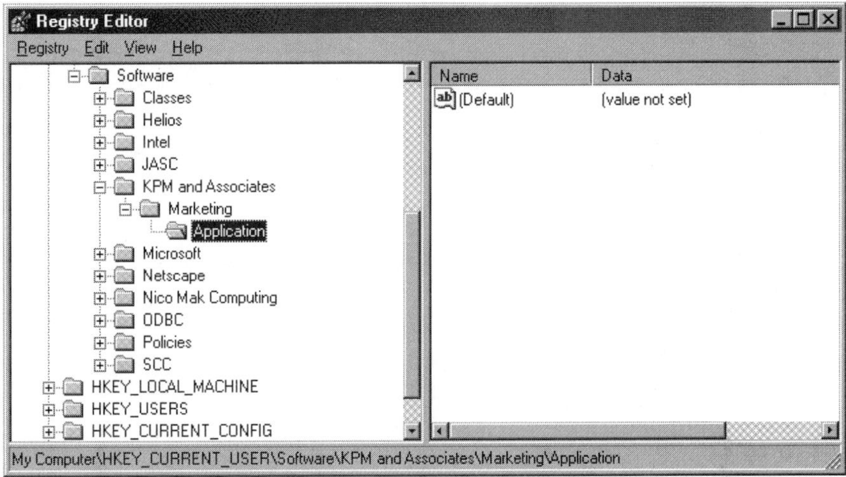

FIGURE 17.15: Call adh_accRegWriteKey to create new Registry keys.

TABLE 17.18: Syntax for Calling adh_accRegWriteKey

Parameter	Type	Description	Comments
hkeyRoot	Long	Key to use as the root.	Use one of the constants defined in basRegistry: adhcHKEY_LOCAL_MACHINE or adhcHKEY_CURRENT_USER, normally.
strSubKey	String	Full path of the key you want to create.	Do not include the root key name or a leading backslash (\). Windows will create any keys necessary to get to your new key if they don't already exist.
strClass	String	Specifies the class (object type) of this key. Ignored if the key already exists. Normally unused.	The Microsoft documentation (if you look up the RegCreateKeyEx API function) for this parameter is cloudy, to say the least. Until you can find more information about what this parameter is really for, perhaps it's best to leave it as an empty string.
Return Value	Long	Error code.	Either adhcAccErrSuccess or adhcAccErrRegCantCreateKey.

TIP

If you want to see all these functions working together, don't forget to check out the two sample forms, frmStartupTips (which only works in Windows 95 or Windows NT 4) and frmSoundList (which only works if you have sound installed on your system).

Emulating VBA's Registry Functions

VBA provides four limited functions that work with the Registry: GetSetting, SaveSetting, GetAllSettings, and DeleteSetting. These functions can work only with a very small "corner" of the Registry. That is, it can only work with keys under the HKEY_CURRENT_USER\Software\VB and VBA Program Settings key. If you want to use these functions to work with any general Registry keys, you're out of luck. In basRegistry, you'll find four parallel functions: adhGetRegSetting, adhSaveRegSetting, adhGetAllRegSettings, and adhDeleteRegSetting. These functions emulate the built-in functions (mostly using the functions described previously in this section to do their work), except for one big difference: you can work with any Registry key simply by providing the full path as a string. Check out the test functions in basTestRegistry to see how to use these useful replacements. Each of the new functions works just like the original VBA function, so you can refer to the VBA help file to find out more about how to use the replacement.

One shortcut that's worth noting: rather than requiring you to type out HKEY_CURRENT_USER or HKEY_LOCAL_MACHINE, these functions accept abbreviations, like HKCU or HKLM for those key names. If you look at the private procedure, GetHKeyFromPath (in basRegistry), you'll find the code that takes care of this translation.

Make sure you read the comments for each of the four replacement procedures in basRegistry before using them. Some of the procedures are potentially dangerous (especially the adhDeleteRegSetting procedure, which can decimate your entire Registry in one function call).

Font-Handling Functions

If you need to supply users with a list of available fonts and their sizes, this chapter's sample project can help you out. Performing this task in previous versions of Access without external help was difficult, if not impossible. Providing this information requires using a callback function from an API call, and that technique was not available from VBA in Office 97. In that version, MSACCESS.EXE provided functions to retrieve the count of installed fonts; a list of those fonts; and for each raster (bitmapped) font, a count of the available sizes and a list of those sizes. In this version, we've rewritten these functions purely in VBA (using the new AddressOf capability to allow for Windows API callback functions). The next few sections cover the use of these font information functions. In addition, we've provided a sample form (frmListFonts) that ties together all these techniques. Because these topics will be much clearer with a real example to discuss, you might want to take a moment to exercise frmListFonts before digging into this material. Figure 17.16 shows the form in use.

FIGURE 17.16:

frmListFonts allows you to view any font in any available point size.

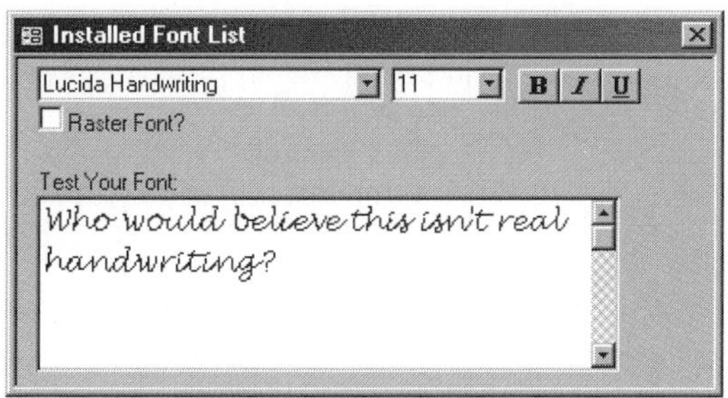

TIP

We've included these particular functions because previous editions of the book included them. We've rewritten them totally in VBA, so you needn't worry about them disappearing in future versions, but they're somewhat cumbersome to use. We've also included a class, ScreenInfo, which provides useful information about your screen. This class provides a Fonts array (emulating the Visual Basic 6 Screen object's Fonts property), and a FontInfo property, which allows you to retrieve information about a specific font. We think it's easier to use this class rather than the functions converted from the previous edition. To prove this, we've included a second version of the form shown in Figure 17.16, frmListFontsScreenInfo, the source code of which you may find interesting. For more information on using the ScreenInfo class, see the examples in the sample project.

Retrieving a List of Fonts

We've provided two functions (in basFontHandling) that you need in order to fill an array with a list of all the available fonts. The adh_accGetFontCount function returns the number of fonts, and adh_accGetFontList fills a passed array with the names of all those fonts. The code attached to frmListFonts' Open event calls both of these functions directly in order to fill the combo box on the form with a list of fonts. Listing 17.8 shows the portion of the code that handles this process.

Listing 17.8

```
Dim hdc As Long
hdc = GetDC(HWND_DESKTOP)

If hdc <> 0 Then
    ' Get the number of fonts.
    mlngCountFonts = adh_accGetFontCount(hdc)
    ' If there are fonts, dimension the array
    ' to be the right size.
    If mlngCountFonts > 0 Then
        ReDim mafiFonts(0 To mlngCountFonts - 1)
        ' Fill mafiFonts() with the font names.
        mlngCountFonts = adh_accGetFontList( _
         hdc, mafiFonts())
    End If
    '
    ' the code continues...
    '
    ' Clean up.
    Call ReleaseDC(HWND_DESKTOP, hdc)
    hdc = 0
End If
```

When working with fonts, the first step is to retrieve information about the current display device. To do this, call the Windows API function GetDC. This function returns a Long integer acting as a handle referring to a device context (information about a hardware device). Asking for the device context of the Windows desktop gets you the information you need, a device handle referring to the current display device, as shown in the following code fragment:

```
Dim hDC As Long

hDC = GetDC(HWND_DESKTOP)
```

Once you have a device context, you can request the number of installed fonts. To call adh_accGetFontCount, just send it the device context as a parameter, and it will return the number of fonts installed for that device:

```
If hdc <> 0 Then
    ' Get the number of fonts.
    mlngCountFonts = adh_accGetFontCount(hdc)
```

Given the number of installed fonts, you can create an array to hold the list. That array will need to be made up of elements of the type adhFontInfo, as shown here:

```
Type adhFontInfo
    fRasterFont As Long
    strName As String * 32
End Type
```

where each element stores both a Long value, indicating whether the font is a raster font, as well as the name of the font. The code to resize the array looks like this:

```
ReDim mafiFonts(0 To mlngCountFonts - 1)
```

To fill in the list of font information, call adh_accGetFontList, passing to it the device context and the array. The function returns the actual number of fonts it filled in and fills in the entire array:

```
mlngCountFonts = adh_accGetFontList(hdc, mafiFonts())
```

Last but not least, you should always release the device context handle when you're done with it. Although there's only a very small chance that not releasing the handle would cause trouble, it's always best to release Windows resources that you use:

```
Call ReleaseDC(HWND_DESKTOP, hDC)
hDC = 0
```

This code both releases the handle and resets the variable's value back to 0. That way, subsequent code that checks the value of hDC knows it doesn't represent a valid device context anymore.

Retrieving a List of Sizes

For TrueType fonts, Windows generally presents you with a standardized list of font sizes:

```
8,9,10,11,12,14,16,18,20,22,24,26,28,36,48,72
```

The code attached to frmListFonts maintains an array, maintTTSizes, which contains those standard sizes. For raster fonts, however, it is the font itself that determines the available sizes. Therefore, for raster fonts, the code needs to retrieve the list of specific sizes for the font. The procedure in Listing 17.9, FillFontSizes, fills the global array malngRasterSizes with the available font sizes for the specified font.

Listing 17.9

```
Private Sub FillFontSizes(hdc As Long, _
 ByVal strName As String)

    If Len(strName) > 0 Then
        mlngCountRasterSizes = _
         adh_accGetSizeCount(hdc, strName)
        If mlngCountRasterSizes > 0 Then
            ReDim malngRasterSizes( _
             0 To mlngCountRasterSizes - 1)
            mlngCountRasterSizes = adh_accGetSizeList( _
             hdc, strName, malngRasterSizes())
        End If
    End If
End Sub
```

To call FillFontSizes, you pass to it the device context you previously created and the name of the specific font. If the face name is an empty string, of course, the procedure can't do its work and will need to just exit.

Next, the procedure needs to determine how many sizes are available for the given font. To do this, it can call the adh_accGetSizeCount function. This function takes the device context and a font name and returns the number of available font sizes:

```
mlngCountRasterSizes = adh_accGetSizeCount(hdc, strName)
```

Once you have the number of fonts, all you need to do is redimension the global array to be large enough to contain the list of font sizes, and then retrieve them. To fill the array with the list of available font sizes, you can call the adh_accGetSizeList function:

```
If mlngCountRasterSizes > 0 Then
    ReDim malngRasterSizes(0 To mlngCountRasterSizes - 1)
```

```
        mlngCountRasterSizes = adh_accGetSizeList(hdc, _
         strName, malngRasterSizes())
    End If
```

That's basically all there is to frmListFonts. When the user chooses a font from the list, the AfterUpdate event code requeries the list containing the available sizes for that font. In addition, it sets the properties of the text box that displays the same text to match the chosen values.

Using Font Information in Your Own Projects

To take advantage of this functionality, you'll need to import the following modules into your project:

- basFontHandling
- basFontCommon
- basCommon

Remember, before you can use any of these functions, you'll need to call the GetDC API function, as shown earlier, to retrieve a device context. When you're done, you should call the ReleaseDC function to release the device context.

Using the ScreenInfo Class

If you want to make this all a bit easier, you can use the ScreenInfo class that's included in the sample project. Using this class, the code to provide a list of fonts and their sizes is somewhat simpler. To verify this, look at the form module for the sample form, frmListFontsScreenInfo. This form does the same work as the form discussed earlier (frmListFonts), but uses the ScreenInfo class to gather information about fonts.

To use this class, you must import the following modules into your own project:

- ScreenInfo
- basCommon
- basFontCommon
- basScreenInfo

Once you've imported these modules, you can use the methods and properties of the ScreenInfo class to make it easy to work with fonts. Table 17.19 lists the properties and methods of this object that are focused on fonts. (See Table 17.21 for a list of all the properties and methods of the ScreenInfo class.) One of the properties, FontInfo, requires you to specify the exact information you need to retrieve about a font. Table 17.20 lists the options you can use when using the FontInfo property.

TABLE 17.19: Font-Oriented Properties in ScreenInfo Class

Name	Parameters	Return Value	Description
FontCount		Integer	Returns the number of installed screen fonts.
FontInfo	Item As Variant, fi as adhFontDataInfo	Variant	Given a numeric index or the name of a font, along with a specific item to retrieve (selected from Table 17.20), returns information about a specific font. Because the fonts are stored as an array (and not as a collection) retrieving information given the font's name is slow. If you don't know the index, use FontInfo to retrieve the index, and then use the index in subsequent calls to the FontInfo property.
Fonts	Item as Long	String	Given an index, returns the name of the corresponding screen font. Basically, acts as an array of strings, indexed starting with 0.

TABLE 17.20: Options for the FontInfo Property of the ScreenInfo Class

Constant	Description
fiFaceName	Causes FontInfo to return the name of the face corresponding to the requested index. This is equivalent to using the Fonts property directly, given an index.
fiSizes	For raster fonts, returns an array of Longs, containing all the available sizes for this font. For nonraster fonts, this array is empty.
fiSizeCount	For raster fonts, returns the number of available sizes. For nonraster fonts, returns 0.
fiIndex	Given a font name as the first parameter and this constant as the second parameter, the FontInfo property will find the font name in its array of fonts and return the corresponding index.

Continued on next page

TABLE 17.20 CONTINUED: Options for the FontInfo Property of the ScreenInfo Class

Constant	Description
fiType	Returns a Long integer containing one or more values from the adhFontTypeAPI enumeration, indicating the type of font.
fiIsRaster	Returns a Boolean value indicating whether the type of the font includes the RASTER_FONTTYPE bit. This just makes it easier for code that needs to determine easily whether a font is a raster font.

The code in Listing 17.10 (from basTestFonts) demonstrates some of the font-related features of the ScreenInfo class. This procedure lists out, to the Immediate window, all the available screen fonts. For raster fonts, it also displays the number of available sizes, and lists out the sizes.

Listing 17.10

```
Sub TestScreenInfoFonts()
    Dim si As ScreenInfo
    Dim i As Long
    Dim j As Long
    Dim lngSizes As Long
    Dim alngSizes() As Long

    ' Instantiate the ScreenInfo object.
    Set si = New ScreenInfo

    ' Loop through all the screen fonts.
    For i = 0 To si.FontCount - 1
        ' Print out the font name.
        Debug.Print si.Fonts(i);
        ' If this is a raster font,
        ' then list out the number of
        ' font sizes, and the list of sizes.
        If si.FontInfo(i, fiIsRaster) Then
            lngSizes = si.FontInfo(i, fiSizeCount)
            Debug.Print " (" & lngSizes & " size(s)): ";
            alngSizes = si.FontInfo(i, fiSizes)
            ' Loop through all the available sizes.
            For j = 0 To lngSizes - 1
                Debug.Print alngSizes(j);
```

```
            Next j
        End If
        Debug.Print
    Next i
    Set si = Nothing
End Sub
```

What Else Is in That ScreenInfo Class?

Although there's too much code in the ScreenInfo class to discuss it all here, you may be interested in the other properties and methods provided by the class besides the ones you've seen that apply to fonts. Table 17.21 lists all the properties and methods of the class, along with a description of each.

TABLE 17.21: Members of the ScreenInfo Class

Member	Type	Property/Method	Description
BitsPerPixel	Integer	Property	Returns the number of bits per pixel—that is, the color depth. The number of colors is generally 2 to this power. High Color corresponds to a value of 24 and True Color to a value of 32.
CurrentResolution	Long	Property	Index, within the array of available screen resolution/color depth combinations, of the current screen resolution. You can use this value to indicate current settings if you display a list of all the available settings.
DisplaySettingsCount	Long	Property	The number of available screen settings.
DisplaySettingsText	String	Property	Given an integer index, provides a string containing the width, height, color depth, and, if available, frequency for a specific screen setting. If the index is out of range, returns an empty string.

Continued on next page

TABLE 17.21 CONTINUED: Members of the ScreenInfo Class

Member	Type	Property/Method	Description
FontCount	Long	Property	Returns the number of installed screen fonts.
FontInfo	Variant	Property	Given a numeric index or the name of a font, along with a specific item to retrieve (selected from Table 17.20), returns information about a specific font. Because the fonts are stored as an array (and not as a collection), retrieving information given the font's name is slow. If you don't know the index, use FontInfo to retrieve the index, and then use the index in subsequent calls to the FontInfo property.
Fonts	String	Property	Given an index, returns the name of the corresponding screen font. Basically, acts as an array of strings, indexed starting with 0.
Height	Single	Property	Returns the height of the screen, in twips.
HeightInPixels	Long	Property	Returns the height of the screen, in pixels (the normal unit for measuring screen size).
TwipsPerPixelX	Single	Property	Number of twips per pixel in the horizontal direction.
TwipsPerPixelY	Single	Property	Number of twips per pixel in the vertical direction.
VerticalRefresh	Integer	Property	Refresh rate (in Hz) for the display device. Not available for all operating systems/devices. If unavailable, the value will be 0.
Width	Single	Property	Width of the screen, in twips.
WidthInPixels	Single	Property	Width of the screen, in pixels (the normal unit for measuring screen size).

Continued on next page

TABLE 17.21 CONTINUED: Members of the ScreenInfo Class

Member	Type	Property/Method	Description
ChangeResolution	Long	Method	Given an index into the available screen settings, attempts to change the screen setting to the selected value. Depending on the value selected, you may need to restart Windows before your setting takes effect. Use this method only if absolutely required, as it's not good form to change the user's screen resolution or color depth. Depending on the results of the attempt to change the screen settings, this method may display an alert, telling the user what to do. For a completely "silent" way to change resolution, see the SetDisplaySettings method, which this method calls internally.
SetDisplaySettings	Long	Method	Given an index into the available screen settings, attempts to change the screen setting to the selected value. Depending on the value selected, you may need to restart Windows before your setting takes effect. Use this method only if absolutely required, as it's not good form to change the user's screen resolution or color depth. This method will never display any user interface, but will silently take action or fail. If you want a more "polite" wrapper, see the ChangeResolution method.

As a simple introduction to using the ScreenInfo class, you might write code that looks like this:

```
Dim si As ScreenInfo
Set si = New ScreenInfo
Debug.Print "Screen size in pixels: " & _
 si.WidthInPixels & " by " & si.HeightInPixels
Set si = Nothing
```

To demonstrate more of the capabilities of the ScreenInfo class, try out the frmTestScreenInfo form. This form, shown in Figure 17.17, provides a list of available screen settings for your hardware and allows you to select one and switch to that setting.

FIGURE 17.17:

Use frmTestScreenInfo to test out the screen setting properties and methods of the ScreenInfo class.

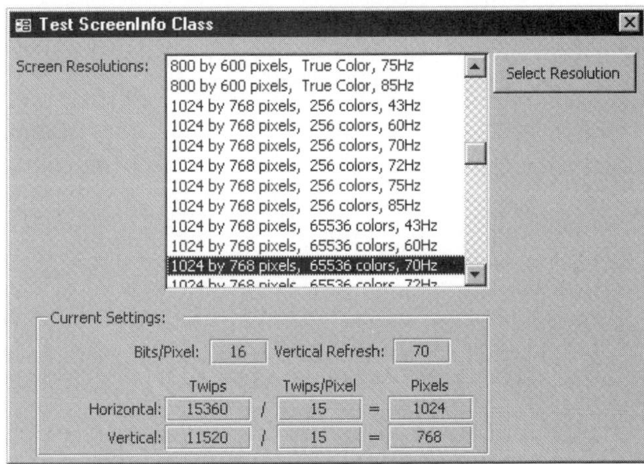

WARNING It's generally not a good idea to switch the user's screen resolution from within your application. We've provided the functionality here because we could (as good a reason as any), but you should use this power only when absolutely necessary. When you do switch resolutions using the ChangeResolution method, your users may need to reboot in order to see the change. Beware that this affects other portions of your application (what if they reboot without shutting down your application gracefully?), and please heed the warning to be circumspect about using this technology.

Finding the Screen Size for Text in a Given Font

At times, you'll need to know the screen size for a piece of text, given a font name, its size, and its attributes. For example, you might want to set the size of a text box so that it just fits the text inside it, in which case you need to know how much space the text will take up. Or, imagine you'd like to set the width of a combo box so that it can display all the text of all its items. The function adh_accTwipsFromFont, in basFontHandling, can do the job for you. Figure 17.18 shows a sample form (frm-FontWidth) that calculates the width of the text for each value in a combo box's list and resizes the combo to match, based on the font being used in the control.

FIGURE 17.18:

Calculate the maximum width of items in a combo box's list and resize accordingly.

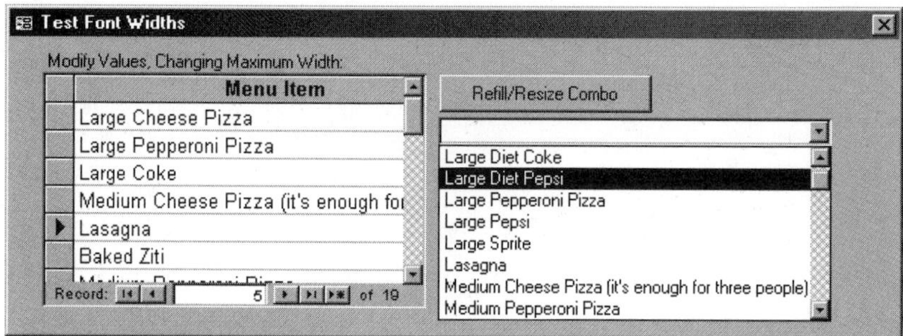

To call adh_accTwipsFromFont, use the parameters described in Table 17.22.

TABLE 17.22: Syntax for Calling adh_accTwipsFromFont

Parameter	Type	Description	Comments
FontName	String	Name of the font.	Must match one of the installed font names, or Windows will make a substitution.
Size	Long	Size, in points (as shown in the font size drop-down list in Access).	The point size must be between 1 and 127.
Weight (Optional)	Long	Weight of the font, chosen from the following list: 100 (Thin), 200 (Extra Light), 300 (Light), 400 (Normal), 500 (Medium), 600 (Semi-bold), 700 (Bold), 800 (Extra Bold), 900 (Heavy).	The default value is 400 (Normal).
Italic (Optional)	Long	Logical value indicating whether the text is italicized.	The default value is False.
Underline (Optional)	Long	Logical value indicating whether the text is underlined.	The default value is False.

Continued on next page

TABLE 17.22 CONTINUED: Syntax for Calling adh_accTwipsFromFont

Parameter	Type	Description	Comments
TotalChars	Long	To use the average character width for the font in the calculations, specify the number of characters in this parameter.	Fill in either Caption or TotalChars. If you fill in both, TotalChars will take priority. This parameter interacts with the UseMaxWidthCount parameter: the function will use the maximum character width for the UseMaxWidthCount of the characters and use the average width for the rest, up to TotalChars. Unless you supply a value larger than 0 for this parameter, the function disregards the value in UseMaxWidthCount. The default value is 0.
Caption	String	Text for which you wish to calculate the width and height. Either supply the text here (the function will calculate the actual width, based on your character string) or supply a length in the TotalChars parameter (the function will use the average character width).	
UseMaxWidthCount	Long	Number of characters for which you'd like to use the maximum character width for the font when making calculations.	If you supply a value for TotalChars, the function will use the average character width for the requested font when making its calculations. Supply a value in this parameter to specify for how many of those characters you'd like to use the maximum character width. This is useful if you want to display abbreviations, part numbers, and so on, which are short and must display all the characters, no matter what. The function will use the maximum character width for the first UseMaxWidthCount characters and the average width for TotalChars—UseMaxWidthCount characters. This parameter is ignored if TotalChars isn't greater than 0. The default value is 0.
Width	Long	Filled in by the function with the width, in twips, of the text.	This value doesn't take into account the width of the border, nor the extra space Access always adds to the text in a control. Therefore, we've found that adding 70 twips to this value will allow for a near-perfect fit.

Continued on next page

TABLE 17.22 CONTINUED: Syntax for Calling adh_accTwipsFromFont

Parameter	Type	Description	Comments
Height	Long	Filled in by the function with the height, in twips, of the text.	
Return Value	Boolean	True if the function succeeded, False otherwise.	

The sample form, frmFontWidth, uses the code in Listing 17.11 to set the size for the combo box, based on the values in the MenuDescription field of tblMenu. It loops through each item in the combo's list, calling adh_accTwipsFromFont with the attributes of the control's font, and sets the width of the combo box to match the maximum width of the field. (The sample form uses the ScreenInfo class to figure out how much room the scroll bar takes up on the screen. It uses the GetSystem-Metrics API function to find the width of scroll bars in pixels, and then multiplies by the ScreenInfo class' TwipsPerPixelX property, to convert to twips.)

Listing 17.11

```
Private Function GetMaxWidth(cbo As ComboBox)

    Dim lngMax As Long
    Dim lngWidth As Long
    Dim fOK As Boolean
    Dim strFont As String
    Dim intWeight As Integer
    Dim fItalic As Boolean
    Dim fUnderline As Boolean
    Dim lngHeight As Long
    Dim intSize As Integer
    Dim strText As String
    Dim intI As Integer
    Dim si As ScreenInfo

    With cbo
        intSize = .FontSize
        strFont = .FontName
```

```
        intWeight = .FontWeight
        fItalic = .FontItalic
        fUnderline = .FontUnderline
    End With
    ' Loop through all the values, and
    ' calculate the length of the longest one.
    For intI = 0 To cbo.ListCount - 1
        strText = cbo.Column(0, intI)
        If adh_accTwipsFromFont(strFont, intSize, _
         intWeight, fItalic, fUnderline, 0, strText, _
         False, lngWidth, lngHeight) Then
            If lngWidth > lngMax Then
                lngMax = lngWidth
            End If
        End If
    Next intI

    ' Add in the width of the scrollbar,
    ' which we get in pixels.
    ' Convert it to twips for use in Access.
    Set si = New ScreenInfo
    GetMaxWidth = lngMax + adhcAdjustForScreen + _
     GetSystemMetrics(SM_CXVSCROLL) * si.TwipsPerPixelX
    Set si = Nothing
End Function
```

Object-Handling Functions

Many of the Access Wizards need to display lists of database objects. There are many factors to take into account when deciding which items you want to see on those lists: Are system objects visible? Are hidden objects visible? Exactly which types of queries do you want to see? Which kinds of tables (local, ISAM, ODBC) do you want to see?

You can make all these decisions using brute-force DAO or ADO (as shown in Chapter 6) to provide the list, but it's a lot of work. To simplify this process, we've included four functions (previously exported from MSACCESS.EXE, now written in VBA, using DAO) to help you supply lists of objects. You can retrieve a list of names of objects and sort that list. You can retrieve a list of data structures that includes names and object types, and you can sort that list. Each of the next sections details one of the four functions.

NOTE

The functions outlined here are all written using DAO. Although they could have been rewritten using ADO, we figured that most people using them will be doing so as an upgrade to a previous edition of this book's code, and their databases will naturally be using DAO. You can convert these to use ADO, but it would take considerable effort. We've left this task as an exercise for the reader.

Retrieving a List of Object Names

If you need to provide a list of object names in your applications, you can certainly use simple DAO code to create the list (see Chapter 6 for more information). On the other hand, you generally need to make a large number of decisions about exactly what objects to list. The adh_accGetObjNames function makes it easy: you specify the object type and specify some parameters describing which subsets of that object you want, and the function fills in an array with a list of the items.

The sample form, frmDBCTab (see Figure 17.19), attempts to display all the Access objects in a rational manner. That is, what about hidden or system objects? What if you've told Access to display hidden objects, but not system objects? Instead of using simple DAO or ADO to fill its lists, frmDBCTab uses the adh_accGetObjNames function, which handles all the decisions for you. Table 17.23 describes the syntax for calling adh_accGetObjNames.

TIP

In order to use the procedures in this section, you'll need to import the two modules basObjList and basCommon from the sample project into your own project. You'll also need to make sure your project includes a reference to DAO (as opposed to the default ADO), as the code uses DAO objects, such as Database and Recordset. Chapter 6 includes a similar form that uses ADO to fill the appropriate lists. It doesn't, on the other hand, use the wrapper functions we've provided here.

FIGURE 17.19:

frmDBC, using a function call rather than simple DAO to fill itself

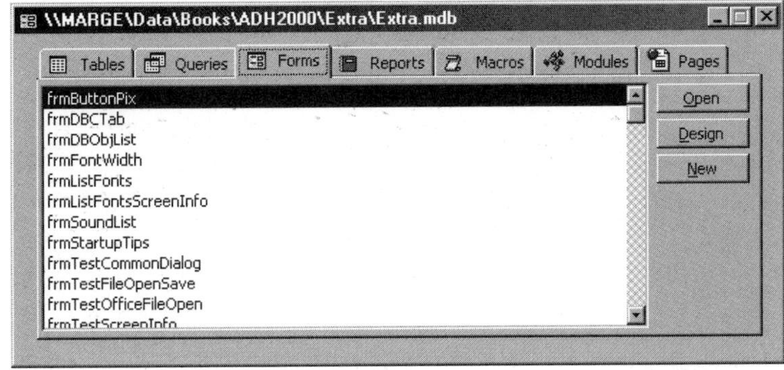

TABLE 17.23: Syntax for Calling adh_accGetObjNames

Parameter	Type	Description	Comments
varWrk	Variant	Reference to the workspace containing the database from which you want to retrieve object names.	This parameter is vestigial and not used in this code. It was used in the Access 97 version of the procedure, so we left it in so as to be compatible. If you're using this function in new development, you might want to remove this parameter.
varDB	Variant	Reference to the database from which you want to retrieve object names.	
intObjType	Integer	One of the standard object types: acTable, acQuery, acForm, acReport, acMacro, acModule, acDataPage.	
lngFlags	Long	One or more values, combined with the Or operator, indicating which subset of objects you want to retrieve. For tables, use one or more of adhcBitTblLocal, adhcBitTblAttachedISAM, adhcBitTbl-AttachedODBC, and adhcBitTblAll. For queries, use the standard DAO Type constants (dbQSelect, dbQCrossTab, and so on), passed through the adhcvtQryType-ToBitfunction, or use adhcBitQryAll to get all queries. For any type of object, use adhcBitObjSystem and adhcBitObjHidden to control the display of Hidden and System objects.	

Continued on next page

TABLE 17.23 CONTINUED: Syntax for Calling adh_accGetObjNames

Parameter	Type	Description	Comments
astrObjects	String array	Zero-based array of strings. On return, filled in with the list of objects you requested.	Before you call the function, you must dimension the array to hold as many elements as the maximum number of items to be returned. That is, if you're asking for a subset of the queries, make the array large enough to hold all the queries. On return, the intItemsFilled parameter will contain the number of items the function actually placed into the array, so you can dimension the array again at that point.
intStart	Integer	Zero-based index, indicating where to start placing items into the array. (Optional, default value is 0.)	Useful if you need to put more than one type of object into the array (if you want to list tables and queries at the same time, for instance).
intItemsFilled	Integer	Filled in, on return, with the number of items the function placed into the array. (Optional: if you don't supply a parameter, you simply don't get this information back.)	Make sure you dimension astrObjects large enough to hold all possible items.
Return Value	Long	adhcAccErrSuccess or adhcAccErrUnknown.	

In frmDBCTab, look in the ListObjects list-filling function to find the interesting code. Listing 17.12, excerpted from the ListObjects procedure in frmDBCTab's module, shows the initialization step of the function.

Listing 17.12

```
Dim db As DAO.Database
Static sastrItems() As String
Static slngCount As Integer
Dim lngFlags As Long
Dim intSize As Integer
```

```
Select Case intCode
    Case acLBInitialize
        Set db = CurrentDb()

        ' Fill in sastrItems() with the list of
        ' object names.
        slngCount = db.Containers(GetContainer( _
         Me.tabObjects)).Documents.Count
        If slngCount > 0 Then
            ' Set up the array.  It might be too
            ' many elements, but the code will resize
            ' the array at the end.
            ReDim sastrItems(0 To slngCount - 1)

            ' Set up the flags, so you just open the
            ' items you want.  Assume you want all the
            ' tables (attached or otherwise), and then
            ' check on whether or not to show
            ' hidden/system objects.
            Select Case Me.tabObjects
                Case acTable
                    lngFlags = adhGetAppInfo(adhcBitTblAll)
                Case acQuery
                    lngFlags = adhGetAppInfo(adhcBitQryAll)
                Case Else
                    lngFlags = adhGetAppInfo(0)
            End Select
            Call adh_accGetObjNames(DBEngine(0), db, _
             Me.tabObjects.Value, lngFlags, sastrItems(), _
             0, slngCount)
            ' If it returned any items, resize the array to
            ' just the right size.
            If slngCount > 0 Then
                ReDim Preserve sastrItems( _
                 0 To slngCount - 1)
                Call adh_accSortStringArray(sastrItems())
            End If
  ' code continues...
```

This code works in a series of steps that you'll also need to follow when using adh_accGetObjNames in your own applications.

1. Dimension the array: The array must be able to hold enough rows for all possible items. In this case, the code just retrieves the count of documents in the appropriate container. (The GetContainer function simply converts container constant values into the appropriate names.) Of course, when the code gets the count of documents in the Tables container, it's going to get tabledefs and querydefs (they're both referenced from the same Container object), but that's not a problem. Once the code has executed, you'll resize the array to just the right size.

```
Static sastrItems() As String
' ...
slngCount = db.Containers(GetContainer( _
 Me.tabObjects)).Documents.Count
If slngCount > 0 Then
    ReDim sastrItems(0 To slngCount - 1)
    ' code continues...
```

2. Set the flags correctly: In this example, you want to see all items honoring the system settings (Show System Objects/Show Hidden Objects). Therefore, call the adhGetAppInfo function, which combines its incoming parameter with the appropriate flags (adhcBitObjHidden and adhcBitObjSystem) indicating whether or not to show system and hidden objects.

```
' From the list-filling function...
Select Case Me.tabObjects
    Case acTable
        lngFlags = adhGetAppInfo(adhcBitTblAll)
    Case acQuery
        lngFlags = adhGetAppInfo(adhcBitQryAll)
    Case Else
        lngFlags = adhGetAppInfo(0)
End Select
' the code continues...

Public Function adhGetAppInfo( _
 lngFlags As Long) As Long

    If Application.GetOption( _
     "Show Hidden Objects") Then
```

```
            lngFlags = lngFlags Or adhcBitObjHidden
        Else
            lngFlags = lngFlags And Not adhcBitObjHidden
        End If
        If Application.GetOption( _
         "Show System Objects") Then
            lngFlags = lngFlags Or adhcBitObjSystem
        Else
            lngFlags = lngFlags And Not adhcBitObjSystem
        End If
        adhGetAppInfo = lngFlags
    End Function
```

TIP

These functions do not use the built-in DAO constants (dbQSelect, dbQCrosstab, and so on) to specify the query types you want to see. To make it possible to work with the bits involved in the representation of the query type, they use a slightly different flag to represent each query type. To convert from the normal DAO query types to the flags these functions expect to find, use the adhCvtQryTypeToBit function, in basObjList. This function takes in DAO constants and returns the appropriate bit-mapped flag value.

3. Call adh_accGetObjNames: Now that everything is all set up, call the function. This fills slngCount with the number of items the function actually placed into the array.

```
Call adh_accGetObjNames(DBEngine(0), db, _
 Me.tabObjects.Value, lngFlags, sastrItems(), _
 0, slngCount)
```

4. Resize the array: Once you've placed the data in the array, you must resize it so that it's just large enough to hold the items placed in it. If you're not going to sort it or you're going to add more elements, you can skip this step, but if you're sorting the array, this step is crucial. (See the next section for information on sorting the array.)

```
If slngCount > 0 Then
    ReDim Preserve sastrItems( _
     0 To slngCount - 1)
    Call adh_accSortStringArray(sastrItems())
End If
```

Sorting a String Array

To support the adh_accGetObjNames function, we've included adh_accSortString-Array. This function is a simple wrapper around the adhQuickSort procedure, called from several other procedures in this chapter. We've assigned adh_accGet-ObjNames its unusual name only for compatibility with previous editions of this book. This function is useful in its own right: it can sort any array of strings you care to send it, not just object names.

TIP

You can also call the adhQuickSort procedure directly, if you prefer. It's in bas-Common, and that's the only module you'd need to import if all you need to do is sort an array.

Calling adh_accSortStringArray is simple: pass it an array filled with strings, and it will sort them in place. It returns adhcAccErrUnknown if anything goes wrong or adhcAccErrSuccess if it succeeds. You can use this function with any array of strings.

Retrieving a List of Objects and Their Types

At times, you'll need to retrieve lists of multiple object types stored in the same array and be able to discern between them (as when the Wizards provide a list of tables and queries in the same control). We've included a function, adh_accGet-DbObjList, which fills an array with data structures:

```
Type adhDBObj
    intObjType As Integer
    strName As String
    lngFlags As Long
End Type
```

Because this structure contains both the object's name and its type, you can tell the different object types apart once they're in your array.

NOTE

Although this structure contains a lngFlags field, our functions disregard this field. You can remove it from the structure if you like—we've included it here for compatibility with previous versions. It's vestigial and can easily (and should, for new development) be removed.

The sample form, frmDBObjList, shown in Figure 17.20, allows you to experiment with all the options available for the lngFlags parameter to adh_accGetDBObjList. (The flags work just the same for adh_accGetObjNames.) As you make choices, the form requeries the list box and shows the items in the array that has been filled by adh_accGetDBObjList.

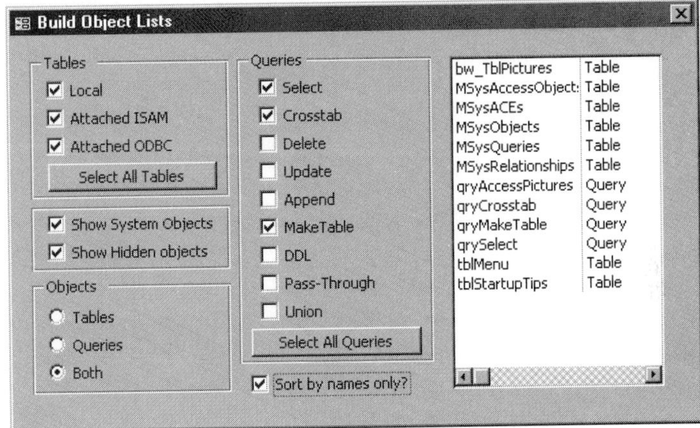

FIGURE 17.20: Use frmDBObjList to test the functions that create lists of objects.

Table 17.24 shows the syntax you use to call adh_accGetDBObjList. You may find it interesting to dig in and see how frmDBObjList works, but in general, it follows the same set of steps outlined for working with adh_accGetObjNames.

TABLE 17.24: Syntax for Calling adh_accGetDBObjList

Parameter	Type	Description	Comments
varWrk	Variant	Reference to the workspace containing the database from which you want to retrieve object names.	This parameter is vestigial, and not used in this code. It was used in the Access 97 version of the procedure, so we left it in so as to be compatible. If you're using this function in new development, you can remove this parameter.
varDB	Variant	Reference to the database from which you want to retrieve object names.	

Continued on next page

TABLE 17.24 CONTINUED: Syntax for Calling adh_accGetDBObjList

Parameter	Type	Description	Comments
intObjType	Integer	One of the standard object types: acTable, acQuery, acForm, acReport, acMacro, acModule, acDataPage.	
lngFlags	Long	One or more values, combined with the Or operator, indicating which subset of objects you want to retrieve. For tables, use one or more of adhcBitTblLocal, adhcBitTblAttachedISAM, adhcBitTbl-AttachedODBC, and adhcBitTblAll. For queries, use the standard DAO Type constants (dbQSelect, dbQCrossTab, and so on), passed through the adhcvt-QryTypeToBitfunction, or use adhcBit-QryAll to get all queries. For any type of object, use adhcBitObjSystem and adhcBitObjHidden to control the display of Hidden and System objects.	
adboObjects	Array of adhDBObj data structures	On return, filled in with the list of objects you requested.	You must dimension the array before you call this function to hold as many elements as the maximum number of items to be returned. That is, if you're asking for a subset of the queries, make the array large enough to hold all the queries. On return, the intItemsFilled parameter will contain the number of items the function actually placed into the array, so you can dimension the array again at that point.
intStart	Integer	Zero-based index, indicating where to start placing items into the array. (Optional, default value is 0.)	Useful if you need to put more than one type of object into the array (if you want to list tables and queries at the same time, for instance).
intItemsFilled	Integer	Filled in, on return, with the number of items the function placed into the array. (Optional: if you don't supply a parameter, you simply don't get this information back.)	Make sure you dimension astrObjects large enough to hold all possible items.
Return Value	Long	adhcAccErrSuccess or adhcAccErrUnknown.	

Sorting the Array of DBObj Structures

To sort the array of structures, we've provided the adh_accSortDBObjArray function. This function is simple to call: pass to it an array of adhDBObj structures all filled in and a Boolean flag, NamesOnly, indicating whether you want to sort by object type and then names, or just by names. For example,

```
fSuccess = adh_accSortDBObjArray(atypNames(), True)
```

sorts atypNames in order of names only, disregarding the object types. If you pass False for the NamesOnly parameter, the function sorts the array first by object type and then by name. Try out this feature on frmDBObjList (check and uncheck the Sort by Names Only? check box) to get a feel for the differences. The function returns either adhcAccErrSuccess or adhcAccErrUnknown, indicating the success or failure of the function.

TIP

To use the four object-handling functions discussed in this chapter, you'll need to import both basObjList and basCommon from the sample project.

Miscellaneous Functions

To round out your whirlwind tour of functions that were, at one point, exported by MSACCESS.EXE, this final section includes a few functions that didn't fit any of the other categories. These functions include retrieving the current national language and using toolbar bitmaps in your own applications.

Retrieving National Language Info

You may have a need to find out the national language version of Access that's currently running, and that information isn't easy to recover using VBA alone. We've provided a simple function, adh_accGetLanguage (in the basGetLanguage module), which can tell you the specific language version of Access that is currently running. It returns a number, indicating the current language. Table 17.25 lists some of the language code numbers defined by Windows—you can figure out which language is current by using the values in this table, along with the constants provided in the VersionInfo class module.

NOTE

Most of the language enumeration constants are commented out in the VersionInfo class module to save a small bit of memory. If you're going to need these, you might want to uncomment some or all of the constants as your own needs dictate. In addition, this list isn't exhaustive. You'll need to investigate new language constants in MSDN, or some other Microsoft documentation, as you're working on your internationalized application.

TABLE 17.25: A Subset of Windows Language Codes

ID	Language	ID	Language
1046	Brazilian Portuguese	2058	Mexican Spanish
3084	Canadian French	1045	Polish
1034	Castilian Spanish	2070	Portuguese
1027	Catalan	1048	Romanian
1050	Croato-Serbian (Latin)	1049	Russian
1029	Czech	2074	Serbo-Croatian (Cyrillic)
1030	Danish	2052	Simplified Chinese
1043	Dutch	1051	Slovak
1035	Finnish	1053	Swedish
1036	French	4108	Swiss French
1031	German	2055	Swiss German
1032	Greek	2064	Swiss Italian
1037	Hebrew	1054	Thai
1038	Hungarian	1028	Traditional Chinese
1039	Icelandic	1055	Turkish
1040	Italian	2057	U.K. English
1041	Japanese	1033	U.S. English
1042	Korean	1056	Urdu

Although it's tricky to retrieve this information using API calls directly from Access, it is possible. This function wraps all the work up and makes it simple. To find out the language version, just call adh_accGetLanguage directly, perhaps like this:

```
Select Case adh_accGetLanguage()
    Case adhcUSEnglish
        ' You're running the US version
    Case adhcFrench
        ' You're running the French version
    ' and so on...
End Select
```

NOTE

To use the adh_accGetLanguage function, you'll need to import the basGet-Language, VersionInfo, and basCommon modules.

TIP

Office 9 also provides a technique that you can use to determine the language used in a given installation of Access. In your application, set a reference to the Microsoft Office 9.0 Object Library, and then check out the LanguageSettings object. Using this object, you can find out the user interface language, the install language, the help language, and the language preferred for editing.

Retrieving Complete Version Information

When we took on the task of converting the previously undocumented functions exported by MSACCESS.EXE, we knew we'd have to write a great deal of VBA code to replace the original functions. As we worked through the issues, however, it became clear that simply replacing the existing functions wouldn't be enough. If we were going to take the effort to retrieve the language information, it would be silly not to take it all the way—providing a VersionInfo class that could provide a great deal of information about any file or module loaded in memory.

Therefore, you'll find the VersionInfo class in the sample project for this chapter. This class includes a number of properties that you can use to retrieve information about almost any executable file, DLL, or driver. Table 17.26 lists all the properties of the VersionInfo class. Some of the properties are supplied by the application's developer and may be empty. This table has a special column

(Optional) indicating which of the properties are programmer-supplied. Table 17.27 lists all the possible values for the FileFlags and FileFlagsRaw properties. The actual contents of those properties can contain 0 or more of these constants, combined with the Or or "+" operator.

TABLE 17.26: Properties of the VersionInfo Class

Property	Type	Optional	Description
CodePage	Long		A code page is a character set that can include numbers, punctuation marks, and other symbols. Different languages and locales may use different code pages. For example, the ANSI code page 1252 is used for American English and most European languages; OEM code page 932 is used for Japanese Kanji. This property returns the first code page assigned to the file.
Comments	String	✓	Supplied by the developer. Normally, comments about the file.
CompanyName	String	✓	Supplied by the developer. Normally, information about the company.
FileDescription	String	✓	Supplied by the developer. Normally, information about the file.
FileFlags	String		Text describing the file. See Table 17.27 for the possible values, which may be combined into a single string.
FileFlagsRaw	adhFileFlags		Numeric value describing the file. See Table 17.27 for the possible values, which may be combined into a single number, using the Or operator. You can use the And operator to determine if any particular flag is set.
FileName	String		The name of the file being investigated. You can either specify the FileName property, or the ModuleName property. Use the ModuleName property if you want information about a loaded application or DLL (providing the developer-supplied module name, such as MSAIN900, used on the sample form) or the FileName property to gather information about a file on disk. Once you specify the ModuleName property, you can retrieve the FileName property to see which disk file is associated with the module in memory.

Continued on next page

TABLE 17.26 CONTINUED: Properties of the VersionInfo Class

Property	Type	Optional	Description
FileOS	String		Text indicating both the targeted API (Win16, PM [Presentation Manager on OS/2], or Win32) and possibly the target operating system (DOS, OS/2 16, OS/2 32, or Windows NT).
FileOSRaw	adhTargetOS		Long integer containing information about the target API and operating system. See the adhTargetOS enum in the VersionInfo class for more information.
FileSubType	String		If the file's type (see the FileType property) is a driver or font, returns text describing the driver or font. For drivers, the possible values are Communications, Display, Input Method, Installatable, Keyboard, Language, Mouse, Network, Printer, Sound, System, or Unknown. For fonts, the possible values are Raster, TrueType, Vector, or Unknown.
FileSubTypeRaw	adhFileSubType		One of the Long integers included in the adhFileSubType enum, in the VersionInfo class module.
FileType	String		Text describing the type of file you've selected. The possible options are Application, DLL, Driver, Font, Static-link Library, Unknown, or VXD. For more information about drivers or fonts, see the FileSubType property.
FileTypeRaw	adhFileType		One of the Long integers included in the adhFileType enum in the VersionInfo class module.
FileVersion	String	✓	Supplied by the developer (in Visual Basic applications, the developer supplies major, minor, and revision values individually). Normally contains information about the version number of the application.
InternalName	String	✓	Supplied by the developer. Normally, information about the internal name of the application.
Language	Long		The primary language identifier associated with the file. Table 17.25 lists some of the possible values for this property.
LegalCopyright	String	✓	Supplied by the developer. Normally, information about the legal copyright information.

Continued on next page

TABLE 17.26 CONTINUED: Properties of the VersionInfo Class

Property	Type	Optional	Description
LegalTrademarks	String	✓	Supplied by the developer. Normally, information about the legal trademarks.
LegalTrademarks1	String	✓	Supplied by the developer. Normally, information about the legal trademarks.
LegalTrademarks2	String	✓	Supplied by the developer. Normally, information about the legal trademarks.
ModuleName	String		The name of the module in memory being investigated. You can either specify the FileName property, or the ModuleName property. Use the ModuleName property if you want information about a loaded application or DLL (providing the developer-supplied module name, such as MSAIN900, used on the sample form) or the FileName property to gather information about a file on disk. Once you specify the ModuleName property, you can retrieve the FileName property to see which disk file is associated with the module in memory.
OriginalFileName	String	✓	Supplied by the developer. Normally, information about the original file name.
PrivateBuild	String	✓	Supplied by the developer. Normally, information about the build, if it's private.
ProductName	String	✓	Supplied by the developer. Normally, information about the product name.
ProductVersion	String	✓	Supplied by the developer. Normally, information about the product version.
SpecialBuild	String	✓	Supplied by the developer. Normally, information about the build, if it's special.

TABLE 17.27: Values Available for the FileFlags and FileFlagsRaw Properties

FileFlags Value	FileFlagsRaw Value	Description
Debug	VS_FF_DEBUG	The file contains debugging information or is compiled with debugging features enabled.

Continued on next page

TABLE 17.27 CONTINUED: Values Available for the FileFlags and FileFlagsRaw Properties

FileFlags Value	FileFlagsRaw Value	Description
Patched	VS_FF_PATCHED	The file has been modified and is not identical to the original shipping file of the same version number.
Pre-Release	VS_FF_PRERELEASE	The file is a development version, not a commercially released product.
Private	VS_FF_PRIVATEBUILD	The file was not built using standard release procedures. If this flag is set, you should also find data in the PrivateBuild property.
Special	VS_FF_SPECIALBUILD	The file was built by the original company using standard release procedures but is a variation of the normal file of the same version number. If this flag is set, you should also find data in the SpecialBuild property.

Using the VersionInfo class is a bit unusual because it works both with program files on disk (specified in the FileName property) and with program files already loaded into memory (specified in the ModuleName property). When you use the VersionInfo class, you'll specify one or the other of these properties, but not both, before retrieving any other properties. Whichever you set last before retrieving other properties controls what values you'll receive.

TIP

For the ModuleName property to be able to retrieve information, it first asks Windows for the name of the file associated with the in-memory module and then acts as if you'd specified the file name yourself. Therefore, once you specify the ModuleName property, you can retrieve the FileName property to find out the actual disk file name for the loaded module. If you investigate the code in the VersionInfo class, you'll see that setting the ModuleName property ends up doing the same thing as if you'd specified the FileName property, except that it must find the file name first.

If anything goes wrong while attempting to retrieve version information, the VersionInfo class raises an error, which your code should handle. Table 17.28 lists the error codes that the VersionInfo class might raise and what they mean.

TABLE 17.28: Possible Error Codes Returned from the VersionInfo Class

Constant	Error Code	Description
adhcErrNoModuleHandle	-2127660987	You specified the ModuleName property, and the code was unable to find the module (perhaps it's not in memory?).
adhcErrNoModule	-2127660986	You specified the ModuleName property, and the code was unable to find the associated file name.
adhcErrNoFileName	-2127660985	Either you specified an invalid file name, or the module you specified couldn't be associated with a valid file.
adhcErrNoVersionInfoSize	-2127660984	Unable to retrieve the version info size from the specified file. If you specify a file that isn't a valid executable or DLL, you'll get this error.
adhcErrNoVersionInfo	-2127660983	Unable to retrieve the version information.
adhcErrNoLangCPInfo	-2127660982	Unable to retrieve language and code page information.
adhcNoFixedFileInfo	-2127660981	Unable to retrieve the fixed file information.
adhcErrUnknown	-2127660980	Unknown error.

As a simple example of using the VersionInfo object, you might write code to determine the location of the Access international DLL, MSAIN900.DLL. If Access is running, you're guaranteed that this DLL is loaded into memory, so the following code will tell you the location of the file associated with this module in memory:

```
Dim vi As VersionInfo
Set vi = New VersionInfo

vi.ModuleName = "MSAIN900"
Debug.Print vi.FileName
Set vi = Nothing
```

To test the VersionInfo class more fully, try out the sample form, frmTestVersionInfo. This form starts out displaying information about the MSAIN900 module, but you can select any disk file, as well, and display the version information about that file. Figure 17.21 shows the default information, all about the MSAIN900 module that's always loaded while you're running Access.

NOTE To use the VersionInfo class, you'll need to import both the VersionInfo and basCommon modules into your application.

FIGURE 17.21: Use frmTestVersionInfo to display information about any Windows executable, DLL, driver, or font, and to exercise the VersionInfo class.

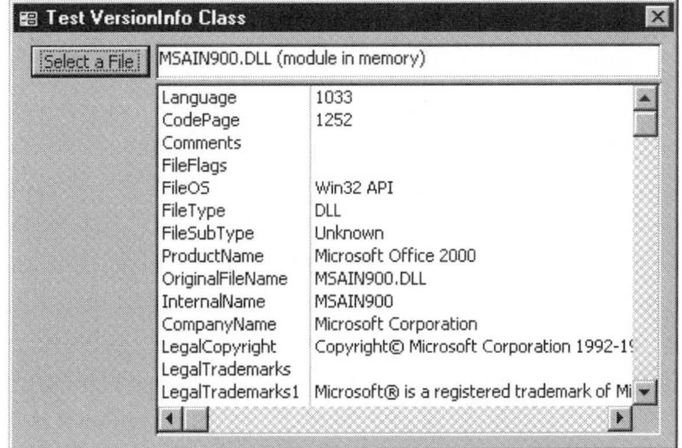

Working with Toolbar Bitmaps

As you've noticed if you've modified the button face of a toolbar button, Access provides a limited set of bitmaps from which to choose. More bitmaps are available for you to use on buttons through the Button Wizard.

Office 2000 stores this collection of bitmaps as a single "slab" in one of its DLLs. (We mention Office 2000 here, as opposed to Access 2000, because all the bitmaps are stored as part of an Office-wide resource.) Storing the bitmaps this way saves on graphics resources, which are in short enough supply with major Windows applications running! In addition, Access provides its own set of extra button bitmaps (mostly for historical purposes).

To do their work, the Access Command Button Wizard and the tools working with menus require some method of retrieving a single bitmap from the slab, and MSACCESS.EXE provides the code necessary to retrieve that bitmap. Given an index into the group of bitmaps, the function, adh_accGetTBDib, fills a byte array with the requested bitmap.

WARNING

Yes, this is one of the dreaded undocumented, exposed-by-Access-for-who-knows-how-long functions. It worked in Access 97, and it continues to work in Access 2000. All bets are off whether this will work in the next version, but because we documented this function in the previous edition of this book and it continues to work in Access 2000, it's here.

To add its own set of bitmaps to the ones Office supplies, the Access Wizards use a table (bw_TblPictures) that includes offsets into the slab of images mentioned above, and additionally, actual bitmaps (stored in the table) for other images. You need this table, listing all the pictures and their ID values (which indicate to the function where to start pulling data, inside the bitmap), in order to emulate the Command Button Wizard in Access. (Investigate the RetrieveDIB function in frmButtonPix for information on how the form uses the bitmaps stored directly in the table, as opposed to those stored in the bitmap slab. This form requires a reference to ADO in order to do its work, as well.) You must include bw_TblPictures in any application for which you'd like to supply this functionality. If you just want to retrieve a bitmap from the Office supply of bitmaps, you don't need to use this table—its only purpose is to supply captions and pointers to the bitmaps used by the Access Wizards.

WARNING

Because you're including the bw_TblPictures table in your application, you must be careful to keep the table updated to match the current version of Access. The table we've supplied matched Access 2000 at the time of this writing. Anytime the version of Access changes, you'll need to import bw_TblPictures from whichever library it's currently in. (In Access 2000, it's in ACWZDAT.MDT.) Because Microsoft maintains complete control over both the table and the bitmap slab, (which is hidden away in some Office 2000 DLL), you have to make sure you have them synchronized. You could, of course, just link the table bw_TblPictures from ACWZDAT.MDT and use it externally. The problem with this solution is that if you use a linked table, you must worry about relinking it on users' machines. We decided to import the table and not worry about the relinking issues.

The adh_accGetTBDib function fills a byte array containing the selected portion of the bitmap slab. Although the imported table, bw_TblPictures, contains information about all the images available on Access buttons, the bitmap slab contains many other images. In fact, it contains all of the bitmaps used on all the toolbars for all the Office 2000 applications. Therefore, although you can use bw_tblPictures to get at the bitmaps that Access uses for command buttons by name, you can also get at the bitmaps in the table, or not, by number only. The sample form, frmButton-Pix, gives you both options. Table 17.29 describes the three parameters for adh_accGetTBDib.

TABLE 17.29: Parameters for adh_accGetTBDib

Parameter	Datatype	Description
lngBmp	Long	The ID of the bitmap to retrieve.
fLarge	Long	True to use large bitmaps, False to use small bitmaps. It appears that this parameter is vestigial and no longer has any effect. Bitmaps are all small.
abytBuffer	Array of bytes	Buffer to hold the bitmap information.
Return Value	Long	Zero on failure, non-zero otherwise.

The lngBmp parameter indicates which particular bitmap chunk you'd like to retrieve. They're all the same size (the fLarge parameter isn't used, apparently, and is included for compatibility with previous versions), and this value simply indicates an offset into the full set of bitmaps available. Access only uses a small portion of the available bitmaps in its Command Button Wizard.

It's up to you to make sure abytBuffer is large enough to hold all the bitmap information before you call adh_accGetTBDib. For large bitmaps, you'll need 488 bytes, and for small bitmaps you'll need 296 bytes. You might use code like the following to set this up:

```
Const adhcLargeBitmapSize = 488
Const adhcSmallBitmapSize = 296

ReDim abytBuffer(0 To _
 IIf(fUseLargePictures, adhcLargeBitmapSize, _
 adhcSmallBitmapSize) - 1)
```

To make it easy to retrieve a specific bitmap, we've provided the GetPicture function, shown in Listing 17.13. This function retrieves the requested bitmap, places its bytes into a byte array, and returns that byte array. You'll find this function in the module for frmButtonPix.

NOTE

You may ask for large bitmaps, but you won't get them. All bitmaps in Office 2000 are small. We've left the adhcLargeBitmapSize in the code so that code you import from previous versions will still compile, but its use won't get you large bitmaps.

Listing 17.13

```
Private Function GetPicture(lngID As Long, _
 Optional fUseLargePictures = True) As Byte()
    Dim abytBuffer() As Byte

    ' If you just want to retrieve a portion of the
    ' image "slab" by number, this is the procedure to call.
    ' This procedure returns a byte array full of the
    ' bytes required to place an image into an Image
    ' control, or onto a button.

    Const adhcLargeBitmapSize = 488
    Const adhcSmallBitmapSize = 296

    ReDim abytBuffer(0 To _
     IIf(fUseLargePictures,  _
      adhcLargeBitmapSize, adhcSmallBitmapSize) - 1)
    If adh_accGetTbDIB(lngID, _
     fUseLargePictures, abytBuffer()) <> 0 Then
        GetPicture = abytBuffer()
    End If
End Function
```

Once you've got the array of bytes, you can use it by assigning it into the PictureData property of any object that supports this property—a form, report, command button, toggle button, image, or page. For this example, we're assigning the byte array into the PictureData property of a command button, using code like this:

```
ctl.PictureData = GetPicture(13, True)
```

Using adh_accGetTbDIB

We've created a small tool, frmButtonPix, which demonstrates the use of the adh_accGetTbDIB function for you. Using the code shown below, the function can place any bitmap provided by Office (or one of the extra bitmaps provided by

Access in bw_TblPictures) onto any button on any form you have loaded. This can be a useful design-time tool, and it works fine at runtime, too. Figure 17.22 shows frmButtonPix running. In addition to pulling information from the table provided by the Access Wizards, you can also scan through all the (greater than 6000 possible) bitmaps provided by Office by choosing the Office Pictures tab. Many of the indexed bitmaps aren't used (they're simply empty gray squares), but frmButtonPix also allows you to browse through all the Office bitmaps you'd like and to copy them onto a button on any form.

FIGURE 17.22:

frmButtonPix can change the picture on any button on any form.

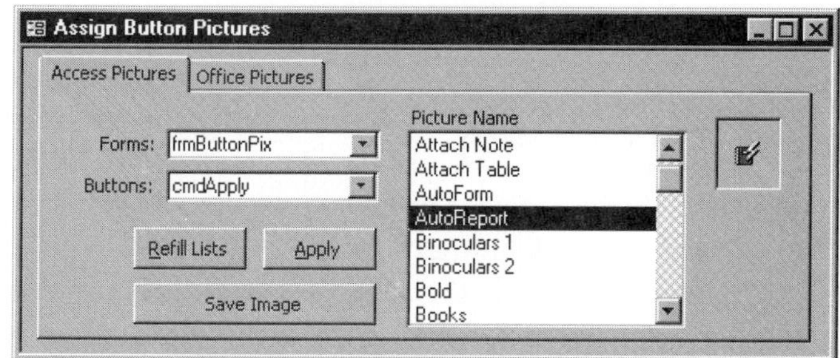

NOTE

If you wish to use frmButtonPix to change the picture on a button permanently, you need to open the form containing that button in Design view, use frmButtonPix to change the button face, and then save the changed form. Programmatic changes made to forms at runtime are not saved with the form.

Because there's no simple way for frmButtonPix to know that you've loaded or closed forms around it, we've supplied the Refill Lists button on the form. This button allows you to open and close forms and then tell frmButtonPix about it.

Once you've selected a form and a button on that form, you can click the Apply button (or double-click the picture image on the form), and the code will apply the chosen image to the chosen button:

```
Private Sub cmdApply_Click()
    On Error Resume Next
    Forms(lstForms)(lstButtons).PictureData = _
     imgSample.PictureData
End Sub
```

To use frmButtonPix in your own applications, import the form, the query qry-AccessPictures, and the table bw_TblPictures.

WARNING Importing this form into a new database causes a small problem. The form uses an ActiveX control, the MSForms 2.0 Scrollbar control. When you import the form into a new database, the form imports correctly, but the reference to the MSForms library is lost. To fix this problem, you can place another MSForms control (any of the possible controls will do) on the form once you've imported the form into its new home. This is categorized as "working as designed," but it's a pain to work around each time you import a form that contains an ActiveX control.

Some Interesting Points

This adh_accGetTbDIB example brings up two interesting and undocumented features of Access. First, if you take a look at bw_TblPictures (see Figure 17.23), you'll note that the PictureName column contains only a series of long integers. Using these integer identifiers, Access looks up the actual text of the messages in an file of text messages—this way, the Wizard won't require recoding for different languages. (If you're running this form on a German version of Access, for example, this one form will automatically be translated into German.) How does the Wizard (and frmButtonPix) find the correct text? The answer is an undocumented method of the Application object: AppLoadString. Given a Long integer, AppLoadString returns the associated text message that Access uses. Of course, we have no way of knowing which text message is associated, in general, with which number. For fun, you could write code that iterates through all two billion or so possible ID values and see what text you get back. If you look at qryAccessPictures in the sample project, you'll see that it creates a calculated field from the PictureName field, containing the actual, translated text.

In addition, Access provides an undocumented use of the SysCmd function that allows you to retrieve the picture displayed in an image control, on a command button, or any other place that Access displays images, as a special data type: IPictureDisp (provided by the stdole type library, which is always available, in Access). If you have a picture available in the standard IPictureDisp format, then you can call the SavePicture method to save it as an individual BMP file, on disk. This way, you can cut a bitmap from the slab of available bitmaps, save it to an individual bitmap file, and use it anywhere you need BMP files. (This is exactly what the Access Wizards use to convert forms into Web pages for you.) Figure 17.24 shows the Object Browser displaying information about the SavePicture method.

FIGURE 17.23:

The Access Wizards don't store text—they get it from Access at runtime.

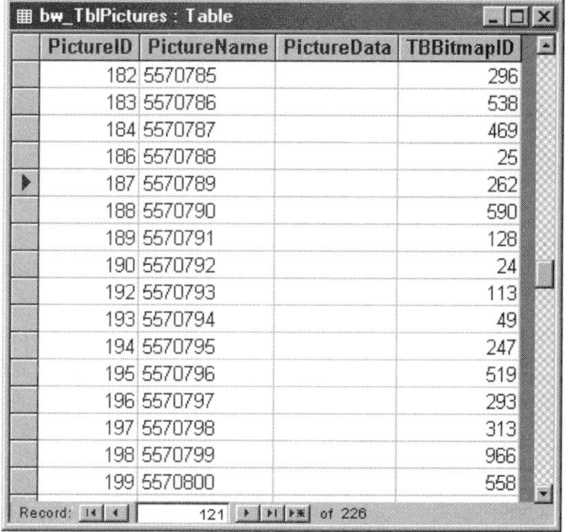

bw_TblPictures : Table

PictureID	PictureName	PictureData	TBBitmapID
182	5570785		296
183	5570786		538
184	5570787		469
186	5570788		25
187	5570789		262
188	5570790		590
189	5570791		128
190	5570792		24
192	5570793		113
193	5570794		49
194	5570795		247
195	5570796		519
196	5570797		293
197	5570798		313
198	5570799		966
199	5570800		558

Record: 121 of 226

FIGURE 17.24:

Given the extra SysCmd help, you can use the SavePicture method to store bitmaps on disk.

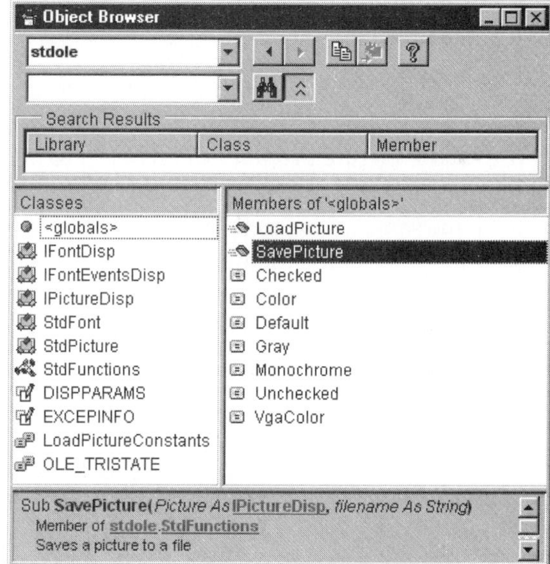

To try this out, select an image on frmButtonPix, and then click the Save Image button on the form. The following code fragment, from the cmdSaveImage_Click event procedure, saves the image displayed in imgSample to a disk file:

```
' strFileName contains the name to use
' for the saved bitmap.
' imgSample contains the image to be saved.
Dim img As stdole.IPictureDisp
Set img = SysCmd(712, imgSample)
Call stdole.SavePicture(img, strFileName)
```

In this example, the code first declares an IPictureDisp object to contain the image, then calls SysCmd (passing the value 712 and an Image control from which to retrieve the image) to get the picture. Finally, the code calls the Save-Picture method, passing the IPictureDisp object and a file name. This saves the image to a disk file (with a BMP extension).

NOTE To create the file name used in this sample, the code uses the descriptive text from the list box if you've selected the Access Pictures page. If you've selected the Office Pictures page, the code uses the index of the image as its file name.

To load an image into the Picture property of a control or a form, you could use the LoadPicture method of the stdole object, but it's not necessary. You can simply set the Picture property of an object to be the name of the disk file, and Access will load the image for you. (If you want to set the Picture property of one object to be the same as the picture displayed in another object at runtime, the simplest solution is to set the PictureData property of one object equal to the PictureData property of the other object.)

Summary

This chapter served three purposes:

- To introduce VBA replacements for undocumented Access functions. These functions were exposed as API calls into MSACCESS.EXE in Access 97 and aren't generally available in the current version.

- To provide expanded user-interface functionality for your Access applications, including the ability to work with the screen, fonts, Registry, and common dialogs.
- To describe the undocumented user-interface function exposed directly by MSACCESS.EXE that are still available in this version.

Specifically, the sections in this chapter demonstrated these areas:

File-handling functions:

- Check for the existence of a file
- Split a full path reference into component pieces
- Retrieve the full path name for a file
- Find the path of the running database

Common dialogs:

- Use the File Open and Save common dialogs
- Use the Color Chooser dialog
- Use the Font Chooser dialog
- Use the Office File Open/File Save dialogs

Work with the Registry:

- Retrieve the number of subkeys and values for a given Registry key
- Get a subkey name by its index
- Get a key value
- Get a value's name given its index
- Create a Registry key
- Write a key's value
- Use the GetRegSetting, SaveRegSetting, DeleteRegSetting, GetAllRegSettings procedures for working with any Registry setting

Work with installed fonts:

- Retrieve the count of available fonts
- Retrieve the list of available fonts
- Retrieve the count of available font sizes for a font
- Retrieve the list of available font sizes for a font
- Use the ScreenInfo class to work with fonts

Work with DAO objects:

- Retrieve a list of object names
- Retrieve a list of objects and their types
- Sort an array of strings
- Sort an array of database objects, either by type or by name

Miscellaneous:

- Retrieve the current running version of Access' national language
- Retrieve file information using the VersionInfo class
- Retrieve a bitmap from the common button bitmaps
- Retrieve information about your screen (size, color depth, installed fonts) and change screen resolution dynamically using the ScreenInfo class

In addition, we've provided sample forms that demonstrate a number of these techniques. You can easily import these forms directly from CH17.MDB into your own applications.

CHAPTER EIGHTEEN

Building Add-Ins

- Understanding what Access add-ins are
- Creating library databases, including menu add-ins
- Developing property builders
- Designing and implementing custom Wizards
- Building COM Add-ins for Access 2000

Access is a unique product in that it is aimed both at end users seeking an easy-to-use database and at developers looking for a powerful development platform. Somewhere in between is a group of users who demand more than a simple list manager but don't have the level of expertise required to call themselves developers. For this group of people, Microsoft has provided extensions to Access generally known as *add-ins.* Add-ins are designed to simplify complex tasks by walking the user through various steps using easy-to-understand dialogs. You can create your own add-ins to assist your users or make working with Access easier for yourself. If you're really ambitious, you can create add-ins that can be sold commercially. In this chapter, we explain how to create a variety of add-ins, and we give a number of examples to get you started. We also explain some exciting new Access 2000 features: managing references using VBA, programmatic control of modules, and the ability to distribute your add-ins *without the source code* using the Make MDE function. Lastly, we'll examine the new, unified add-in architecture shared among each Office 2000 application and how to leverage it for creating Access add-ins.

NOTE

In this chapter, we stress the use of traditional Access databases (MDB files). The concepts we explain also apply to the new Access Data Project (ADP) file format of Access 2000.

Libraries and Wizards and Builders, Oh My!

In this chapter, we discuss several categories of add-ins:

- *Libraries* are add-ins that contain functions users can call from VBA code in their database. Access documentation often refers to any type of add-in as a library database. In this book, we use this term for databases that contain nothing but VBA code called from procedures in other databases.
- *Builders* are add-ins that assist the user in setting a property of a database object, usually through some type of dialog. Access' property sheets feature Build buttons (the small buttons with an ellipsis [...] that appear next to property values) that launch a builder when clicked.

- *Wizards* are add-ins that create new objects in a user's database. You can build Wizards that create new tables, queries, forms, and reports. You can also build Wizards that create new form and report controls.

In the following sections, we explain some of the common elements of Access add-ins. We follow this up with extensive discussions of each type of add-in, including how to create, install, and distribute them. With the exception of COM Add-ins, all types of Access add-ins are created using Access databases and VBA code. COM Add-ins are compiled COM components—either executables or COM DLLs. The bulk of this chapter covers Access database–based add-ins because they can be used in instances where COM Add-ins cannot be.

Entry Points for Add-Ins

Access provides five default ways for a user to launch an add-in. This chapter explains how to write add-ins to take advantage of these entry points, shown in Table 18.1. You can also add your own custom menu commands using a COM Add-in. This gives you unlimited user interface flexibility. COM Add-ins are discussed later in the chapter.

TABLE 18.1: Entry Points for Access Add-Ins

Entry Point	Remarks
Menu add-in	You can find these on the Tools ➢ Add-ins menu.
Wizard	Table, Query, Form, and Report Wizards are available from the list of Wizards Access displays when a user creates a new object.
Control Wizard	Users launch Control Wizards when they create a new control on a form or report. Users can disable Control Wizards by toggling the Control Wizard button in the toolbox.
Builder	Builders help users set property values. Users initiate builders by clicking the Build button on an Access property sheet.
Library functions	Users call library functions directly from their own VBA code.

All add-ins, with the exception of COM Add-ins, are initiated by a function call. With the exception of library functions, Access calls all add-in functions directly in response to the events listed in Table 18.1, and the declaration of these functions is predetermined. The sections that follow detail the proper way to declare each type of function.

Data Access and Add-Ins

Just as in regular user applications, you may need to read and/or write data to an add-ins database. One important difference between writing data access code in library databases versus normal databases is your use of the CurrentDB or CurrentProject methods. In a normal Access database, CurrentDB returns a pointer to the Jet database in which the executing code is located. CurrentProject.Connection returns a pointer to the ADO Connection object associated with the current database or project file. This is merely a coincidence, however, because CurrentDB and CurrentProject are actually designed to return a reference to the database that is loaded in Access' user interface. Using either one in a library database can be problematic if you are trying to reference the library database, not the current user database.

To reference a library database, use the CodeDB or CodeProject methods instead. CodeDB returns a pointer to the database that contains the executing code while CodeProject.Connection returns a pointer to the library database's ADO Connection. When you are developing your library databases in Access' user interface, they both work just like CurrentDB and CurrentProject. When running in a library database, however, they will reference it, not the user database. You'll see an example of using CodeProject in the section "A Sample Form Wizard" later in this chapter.

Add-Ins and the Registry

Access 2000 depends heavily on settings in the Windows Registry, and add-ins are no exception. Add-in information is stored in the Registry tree in several locations. Figure 18.1 shows the Registry open to the Access 2000 branch (HKEY_LOCAL_MACHINE\Software\Microsoft\Office\9.0\Access). Normally, Access stores add-in information directly under the Access key. If you're using Access user profiles, however, Access may also store add-in information on a user-by-user basis under the profile key for each user.

The following sections on libraries, builders, and Wizards explain how to create Registry entries for each type of add-in.

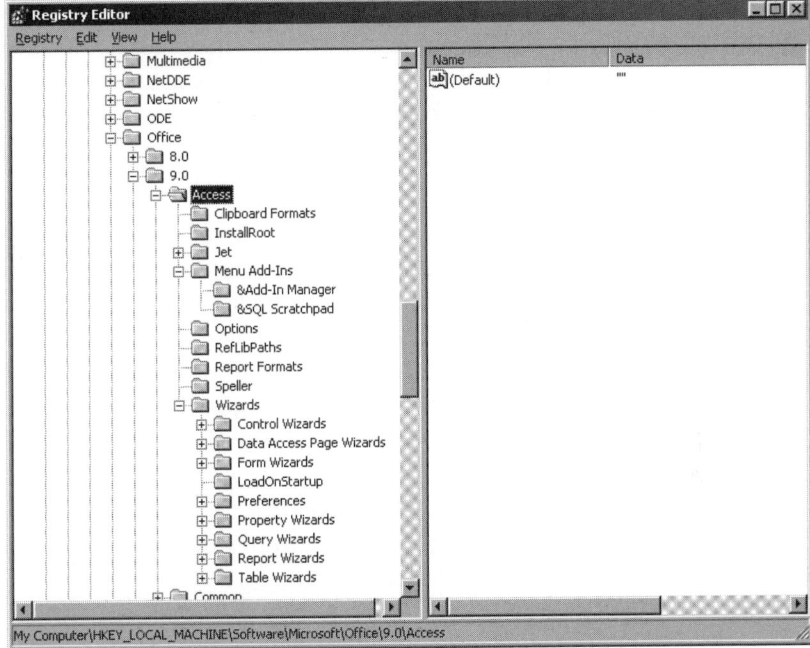

FIGURE 18.1:

Windows Registry settings showing keys for add-ins and Wizards

Creating Library Databases

Library databases are those that contain code modules with common functions shared by a number of applications. The benefit of creating a code library is that it relieves you from having to create and maintain a separate version of a function in each database where it is called. Creating library databases in Access 2000 is relatively straightforward. The trick is making them available to other applications. (The concept of references, introduced in Chapter 12, comes into play here.) In this section, we explain a number of issues related to creating library databases, including structuring library code modules, using library databases, and some of the reference issues involved.

Structuring Library Code Modules

What you put in an Access library database is really up to you. As you write more and more applications, you will find common functions on which you depend.

These are all good candidates for library databases. How you structure your library databases, though, is important; it will dictate how well your applications perform and the amount of memory they require. Assuming that a "good" library database is one that loads quickly and consumes little memory, you can make decisions on how to structure library databases to meet these goals. To determine the best way to structure library databases, you need to understand how VBA treats the code they contain.

One improvement in VBA, starting with VBA 5 in Access 97, is *dynamic loading* of VBA code. In previous versions of Access, all global modules (as opposed to form and report modules) were loaded into memory when a database was opened. This applied to library databases, as well as to user databases opened through the user interface. As a result, users paid a penalty of increased load time, especially of large applications, even if they never called a function in a global module. VBA in Access 2000, on the other hand, does not load a module until it is needed. Users still suffer slightly during the initial load process, but now this takes place incrementally rather than all at once. The important thing to understand about this process, from a developer's standpoint, is how VBA determines when a module is needed.

Obviously, if your code calls a function in a particular VBA module, VBA must load that module into memory. VBA loads the entire module, even if you're going to call only a single function. The same holds true if you reference a global variable declared in a VBA module. Therefore, the first rule for creating library databases is to separate those functions that are called frequently from those that are called infrequently. By putting infrequently called procedures in separate modules, you will prevent VBA from loading them until they are actually used. In fact, it is not too outrageous to suggest placing procedures that are called extremely infrequently in individual modules of their own. Alternatively, by centralizing frequently used functions in one module, you virtually ensure that the module will already be loaded into memory when you call a function it contains.

Using a Library Database

In Chapter 12, we introduced the concept of code references as a way for you to write VBA code that called methods and used properties implemented by Automation servers. Access library databases are subject to the same reference requirements as Automation server type libraries. That is, before you can call a function in a library database, you must establish a reference to it.

We've included a sample library database called CH18LIB.MDA that contains two small but useful functions, adhMin and adhMax, which compute the minimum and maximum values, respectively, within a list of numbers. The module basLibFunctions, in CH18LIB.MDA on the companion CD, shows the definition of these two procedures. Both use a ParamArray argument to accept a variable number of parameters. We can use CH18LIB.MDA to demonstrate the process of setting a library reference and calling a library function.

To demonstrate the referencing process, you'll need to create a new database. Then, follow these steps:

1. Open the Visual Basic Editor and create a new code module.
2. Select Tools ➢ References to display the References dialog.
3. Click the Browse button on the References dialog.
4. Select "Add-ins (*.mda)" from the list of file types on the Add Reference dialog that appears.
5. Locate the CH18LIB.MDA file and click OK. You should now see CH18LIB in the Available References list box on the References dialog.
6. Click OK to close the References dialog.

TIP

Unless you've password-protected your source code or created an MDE file, VBA will display the library database's VBA project in the VB Editor. You can browse, edit, and debug code in the library database at the same time as you work on the user database.

You can now call adhMin and adhMax from the new database. To test this, enter the subroutine shown here (or something similar) in the new module and run it from the Immediate window:

```
Sub TestFunctions()
    MsgBox "Minimum: " & adhMin(3, 7, 8.9, -3, 10)
    MsgBox "Maximum: " & adhMax(3, 7, 8.9, -3, 10)
End Sub
```

As long as you maintain the reference to CH18LIB.MDA, the test procedure will continue to compile and work. If you break the link by either moving or renaming the library database, Access complains that the reference to CH18LIB.MDA cannot be found. If this happens, you must reestablish the reference either manually, using the References dialog, or through VBA code. For more information on the latter, see the section "Restoring References Using VBA" later in this chapter.

NOTE

The entry that appears in the References dialog is the name of the database's VBA project. If you are converting a database from previous versions of Access, the project name will be the same as the database name, including the file extension. New Access 2000 databases use the database name without the file extension. You can change the project name to be whatever you want using the Project Properties command on the Visual Basic Editor Tools menu.

Library Database Reference Issues

When VBA cannot resolve a reference to a library database, VBA issues an error stating that the "Project or library cannot be found" and then displays the line of code calling into the library (see Figure 18.2). When this happens, you have two options when you open the References dialog (see Figure 18.3): you can either use the Browse button to find the missing database, or uncheck the box next to the reference to remove it from the project. If you opt for the latter, you must remove or comment out all references to procedures or variables declared in the missing library.

Lost references become an issue if you plan to distribute your library database to other users who might not install it in the same directory. Of course, you can insist that they install it to a particular directory, but most users don't take kindly to developers who insist on anything. Fortunately, there are several alternatives that will prevent references from becoming lost. First, if VBA is unable to locate a reference based on the *absolute path* that is saved with the project, it automatically tries to find the library using the same *relative path* as the database in which it is referenced. This means that VBA will be able to find library databases if they are in the same directory as the database that uses them or in the same relative location. For example, if you create a database in C:\Test\Libs and reference it from a database in C:\Test\Apps, you can easily move them to C:\Prod\Libs and C:\Prod\Apps, respectively, with no problem.

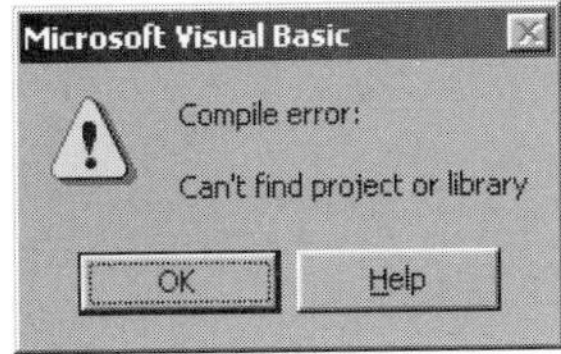

FIGURE 18.2:

You see this warning message when compiling a module after moving or renaming a library database.

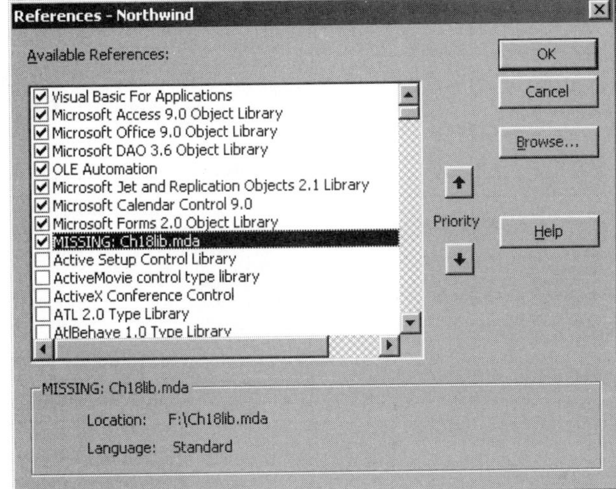

FIGURE 18.3:

References dialog showing that the reference to CH18LIB.MDA is missing

If a relative path search proves unsuccessful, VBA searches for the library database in the following places:

- The directory where Access is installed
- The Windows and Windows\System directories
- Any directory included in the environmental PATH variable

Finally, you can create a Registry entry that specifies another secondary location. This is a good idea if you plan to distribute several library databases because it lets you choose one distinct location for installing all of them. To create these entries, add a Registry key called RefLibPaths under the HKEY_LOCAL_MACHINE\Software\Microsoft\Office\9.0\Access key. For each library, create a new string value with the name of the library database and a value indicating the path to that database. Figure 18.4 shows an example of this Registry setting.

Circular References Are Not Allowed

Due to changes imposed by the integration of VBA into Access, you can no longer create circular references among libraries and databases. This was never an issue in Access 2 because all public functions shared the same global name space. Procedures in any library could call procedures in any other. This is no longer the case. Any level of circularity is illegal. For example, Figure 18.5 shows two scenarios of references.

FIGURE 18.4:

This Registry key specifies an alternative location for library databases

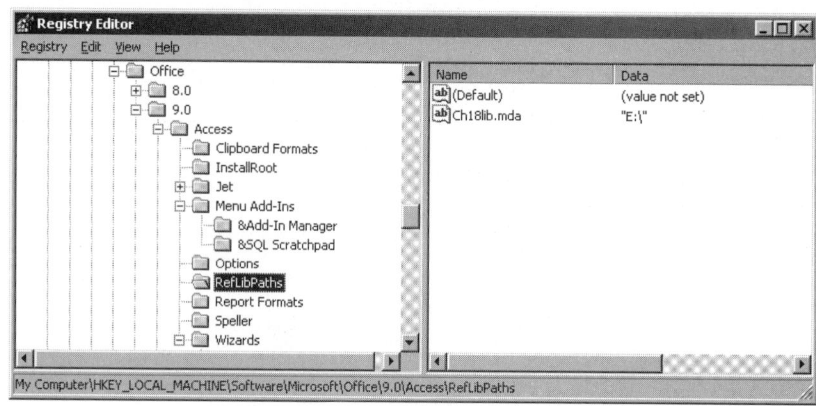

FIGURE 18.5:

Stacked, but not circular, references are allowed.

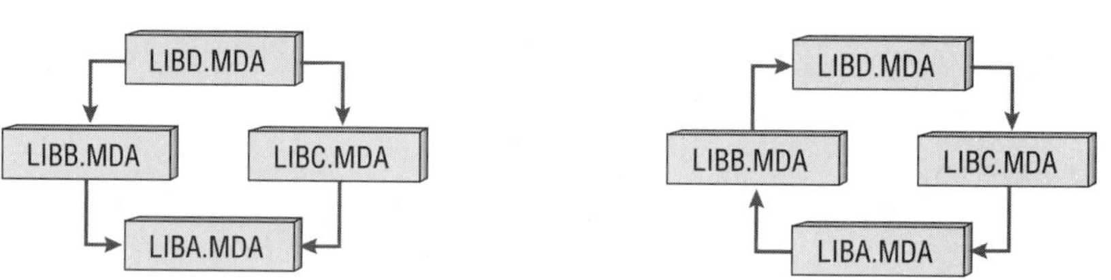

Given the first scenario in Figure 18.5, procedures in libraries LIBB.MDA and LIBC.MDA can call procedures in library LIBA.MDA. Procedures in library LIBD.MDA, in turn, can call procedures in libraries LIBB.MDA and LIBC.MDA. The second scenario is not allowed, however, because the referencing of LIBA.MDA to LIBB.MDA to LIBD.MDA to LIBC.MDA and back to LIBA.MDA results in a circular reference.

Editing Loaded Library Code

Once you've created a library database, you should install it as described in the previous sections and test it by calling library functions from a user database. If you find problems in your code, you can easily make modifications without unloading the library and restarting Access. All you need to do is set a reference to your library from another database. VBA displays the library project in the Visual Basic Editor (see Figure 18.6) and you can access its source code just like any other project.

TIP

You can edit any form or report objects in library databases that have a VBA module associated with them by clicking the View Object button on the VBA Project Explorer window.

FIGURE 18.6:

Viewing library databases in the Visual Basic Editor Project Explorer

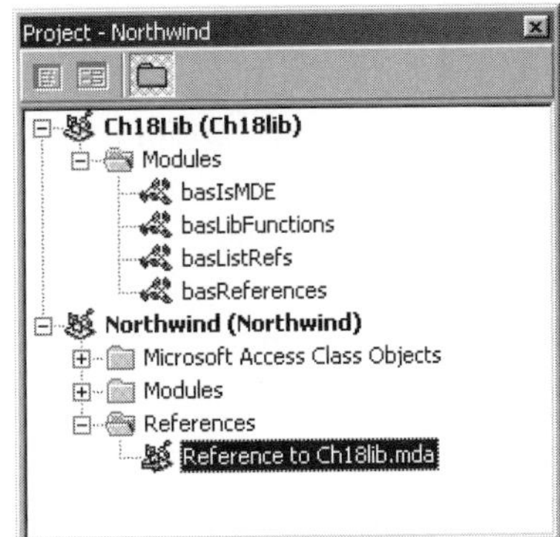

NOTE

If you converted the library to an MDE file (see the section "Creating MDE Files" near the end of this chapter for more information) you will not be able to view or edit any code.

Using Application.Run to Run Procedures

You saw in Chapter 12 how you could use the Run method of Access' Application object to execute procedures in an Access database using Automation. You can use the same technique to call procedures in library databases. The advantage of this approach is that VBA does not require a reference until runtime. You will, however, need to load the library into memory. The next section describes how to do this automatically.

Run accepts the name of a procedure and up to 30 of the procedure's arguments. You can use it to execute both subroutines and functions. For example, you could modify the TestFunctions procedure shown earlier in this chapter to use the Run method. The sample procedure shown below demonstrates this. (Note that the first argument to Run is the name of the procedure and that it is preceded by the VBA project name of the library.)

```
Sub TestFunctionsUsingRun()
    MsgBox "Minimum: " & Application.Run( _
     "CH18Lib.adhMin", 3, 7, 8.9, -3, 10)
End Sub
```

Using the LoadOnStartup Key with Application.Run

If you want to use Application.Run, you must give Access a way of finding the database containing the procedure you're calling. You do this either by installing the database in one of the locations described earlier in section "Library Database Reference Issues" or by using the LoadOnStartup Registry key. When you use the Run method and Access cannot find the specified procedure in any of the loaded or referenced libraries, it searches for it in any databases listed under this key. Figure 18.7 shows the key and two sample entries. You must add this key yourself (it is not created by default) under the HKEY_LOCAL_MACHINE\Software\Microsoft\Office\9.0\Access\Wizards key and add string values for each of the libraries in which you want Access to look.

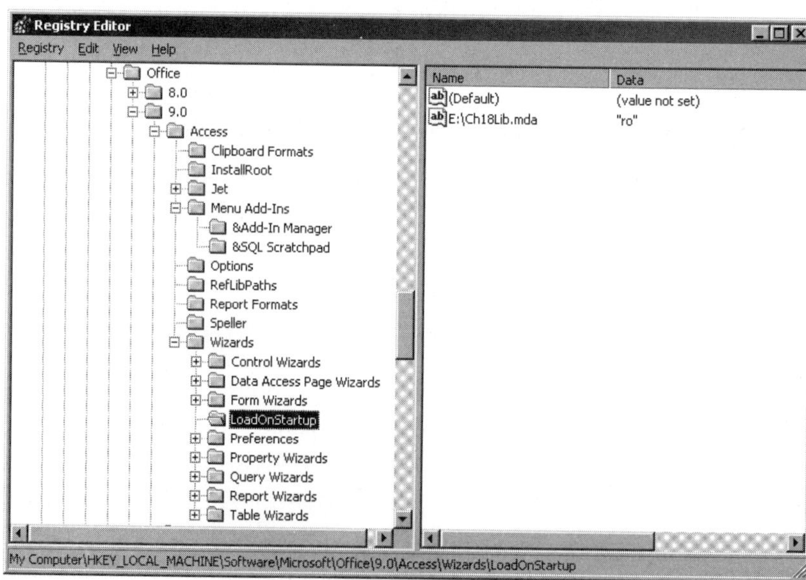

FIGURE 18.7: LoadOnStartup Registry key showing additional libraries to search

LoadOnStartup uses a format similar to the Libraries section of Access 2's initialization file, MSACC20.INI. Each string value contained in the key is named after a library database, including the complete path if it is *not* located in the Access 2000 directory. The value must be either "rw", for read/write, or "ro", for read-only. Unless you have code in the library that needs to update tables that are also in the library, you should specify "ro". Unlike Access 2 libraries, however, databases listed under the LoadOnStartup key are not loaded into memory when Access 2000 starts, as the key name implies. Instead, Access loads only the module and procedure lists. The modules themselves are not loaded until a procedure is executed using Application.Run.

WARNING Library databases loaded using the LoadOnStartup key will appear in the Visual Basic Editor. If you don't want users to modify your library code, make sure to password-protect the project or compile it into an MDE file.

Always Compile Your Libraries

One final topic regarding library databases relates to VBA code compilation: Because a library database contains nothing but code, you don't have to worry about the database becoming decompiled once you have compiled it. Therefore, since compiled VBA code loads and executes more quickly than uncompiled code, be sure to compile and save all modules prior to distributing it to users. You can ensure the compiled state by creating an MDE file, as covered in the section "Creating MDE Files" later in this chapter.

Menu Add-Ins: the Simplest Add-Ins

Perhaps the simplest add-in you can create is a menu add-in. Menu add-ins are functions that are called by a menu command under Access' Tools ➢ Add-ins menu. You can call any function from a menu command by making a few entries in the Windows Registry. Figure 18.8 shows the Registry keys for the default add-ins, along with the Registry values for our sample SQL Scratchpad add-in.

To create a menu add-in, you first add a new Registry key beneath the Menu Add-ins key shown in Figure 18.8. Access will use the name of the key as the menu command on the Add-ins fly-out menu. As shown in Figure 18.8, you can precede a character with an ampersand to make that character the access key for the menu command. After creating the key, you must create two String values, named Library and Expression.

FIGURE 18.8:

Registry entries for menu add-ins

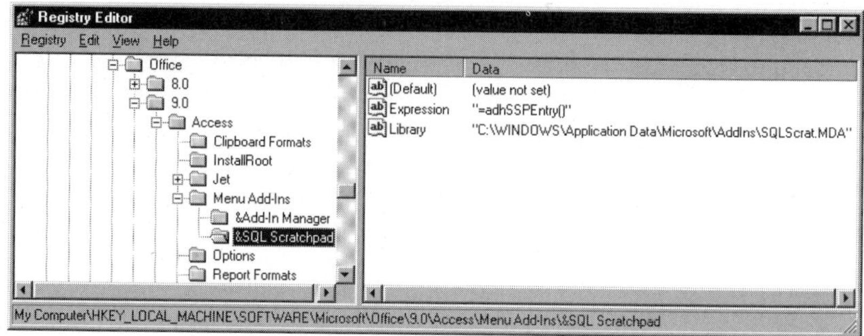

Access uses the Library value to identify which database contains the add-in's main function. The Expression value contains the code fragment that Access must evaluate to invoke the add-in itself. In Figure 18.8, the value for Expression, "=LoadSQLForm()", is a function call, including the equal sign and parentheses. You can create your own menu add-ins very simply by calling a function in a library database.

Building Your Own Builders

Builders (sometimes called Property Wizards) are functions in library databases that assist you in setting properties of objects in an Access database. When you select a property in an Access property sheet and the Build button appears, that's your cue that a builder is available for that property. Access ships with a number of builders. In addition, you can write your own builders by following the few simple rules outlined in the following sections. We also describe a sample builder that we included with this book's sample files.

The Sample Builder

We've created a sample builder, called the System Color Builder, to demonstrate the basic requirements for creating your own builders. You can use the System Color Builder to set Access color properties to Windows system colors by selecting them from a dialog that emulates Windows' Display Properties dialog. Because there are three properties that relate to color, you'll need to install this builder to work with each one of them.

NOTE

Access 2000 is much better than version 2 was about using system colors. The default background color for new forms, for example, is the system color for 3D objects (like command buttons). When a user makes changes to these colors through the Control Panel, Access automatically updates each form. This was not the case in Access 2. You will find the System Color Builder useful when updating forms created in version 2 to make them compatible with Access 2000 forms.

NOTE

The previous edition of this book included instructions on creating a code builder—a builder that helped you write VBA code. Now that Access is using the same Visual Basic Editor as the other Office applications (instead of its own editor), it no longer supports code builders. The Visual Basic Editor has an add-in architecture, however, so you could create an add-in with similar functionality.

Writing a Builder Function

You create builders by writing VBA functions that Access uses to set property values. Access requires that builder functions follow a strict set of rules. These rules can be summarized as follows:

- Builder functions must be declared with a specific set of three arguments.
- Builder functions must return the new property value as a string.
- Any forms opened through code in the builder function must be opened in dialog mode.

The following table lists the required builder function arguments:

Argument	Data Type	Description
strObject	String	Name of the table, query, form, report, or data access page object on which the builder function is operating
strControl	String	Name of the control to which the property applies
strCurVal	String	Current property value

Note that the argument names are arbitrary. Only their position in the declaration is important. When you initiate a builder, Access calls the builder function, passing it values in the three arguments.

In the body of your builder function, you can use the information provided by the arguments to decide how your builder function should continue. Once you've computed the new value for the property, you must return it as a String result of the builder function.

How you compute the new value is where writing builder functions gets interesting. You can do just about anything you wish inside the builder function: open dialogs, call other procedures, or query databases. The only restriction Access places on you is that you must open forms as dialogs. This ensures that code execution in your builder function will halt until the dialog form is closed or hidden. Access requires, when a builder function terminates, that the screen be left in the same state it was in when the function was called. Leaving nonmodal forms hanging around would violate this rule.

The structure of builder functions will become clear as we explain the sample builder we've included with this book. First, however, we must explain how Access knows a builder has been installed. For that, we'll need to take yet another trip into the Windows Registry.

Builder Registry Entries

The Registry settings for Access include a host of keys and values that relate to builder functions. Access maintains individual builder keys beneath HKEY_LOCAL_MACHINE\Software\Microsoft\Office\9.0\Access\Wizards\ Property Wizards. Each Registry key is named after the property to which it applies. When Access starts up, it reads the list of keys from the Registry and makes the Build button available for properties that have builders defined. Access does not attempt to execute a builder function, however, until a user actually clicks the Build button. Although only a small number of properties are assigned builders when you install Access, you can create builders for every built-in Access property. See the next section, "Creating New Builder Entries," for information on how to add Registry keys to do this.

Access allows more than one builder for each property. Separate Registry keys beneath the key that corresponds to a property denote each individual builder. Figure 18.9 displays the Registry tree expanded to show the settings for our System Color Builder. When Access finds two builders defined for the same property, it displays a dialog like the one shown in Figure 18.10 that allows the user to choose which builder to use.

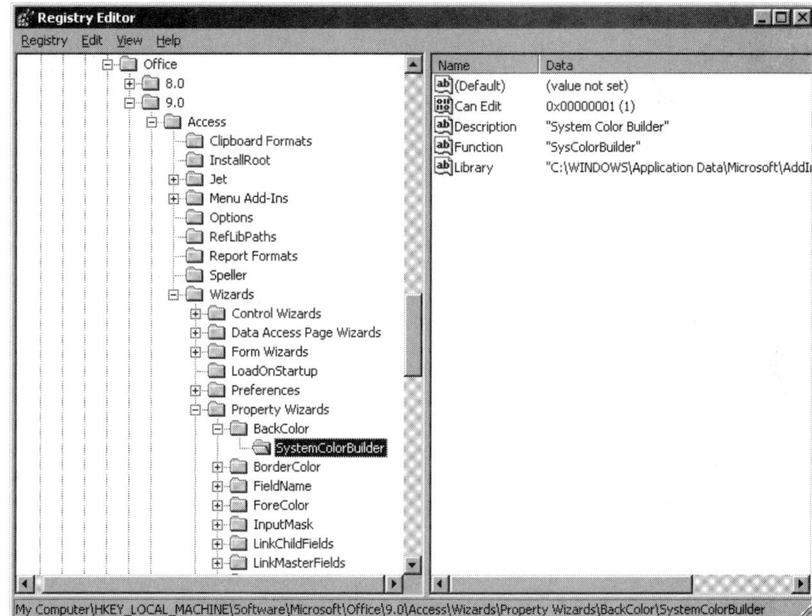

FIGURE 18.9:

Registry settings for our sample System Color Builder

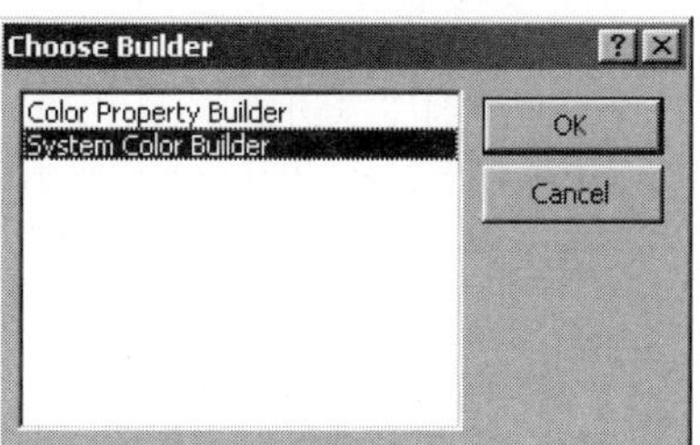

FIGURE 18.10:

Access dialog for selecting which builder to use

NOTE

Some builders, like the default color builders, are implemented as part of Access itself, not as part of a separate library database. In these cases, you'll see a dialog like the one in Figure 18.10 even though there is only one builder entry in the Registry.

The key name for each builder (SystemColorBuilder in this example) is arbitrary and serves only to identify the builder to Access. Each separate key needs to be unique, however. When deciding on names for your builders, be sure to keep that in mind.

Each individual builder key must contain four values: Can Edit, Description, Function, and Library. You can see them in the right pane of the Registry Editor window in Figure 18.9. Each of these values is explained in Table 18.2 along with two other values (Feature and Version) that are used exclusively by the Office setup program and are not necessary for your own builders.

TABLE 18.2: Registry Values for Property Builders

Value Name	Value Type	Remarks
Can Edit	DWORD	Set to 1 to allow a builder to operate on an existing value. It is hard to imagine an Access property with no existing value (even a null), but if you ever find one and don't want your builder to change it, make the Can Edit value 0.
Description	String	Set to the description of your builder. Access will use this description in the builder dialog when more than one builder is defined for the same property.
Function	String	Set to the name of your builder function with no arguments or parentheses. Remember that builder functions have a fixed set of arguments that Access will supply when the function is called.
Library	String	Set to the path to the library database that contains the builder function. You can omit the path if your library database is located in the Access directory.
Feature	String	Name of the Office feature that the builder belongs to.
Version	DWORD	Feature version number.

Creating New Builder Entries

To add a new builder and have Access recognize it, you must create a new set of entries. In this section, we show you how to make the entries to install the sample builders. Normally, though, you won't have to do this manually. The section "Distributing and Installing Add-Ins" later in this chapter discusses how to set up your library database so Access' Add-in Manager can automatically create the entries for you.

To install the sample builder, you'll need to create a set of Registry entries for it. To install the System Color Builder, create an entry for the BackColor property, as shown in Figure 18.9. Then add an entry under the BackColor key (our example uses SystemColorBuilder) and add the values listed in Table 18.3. When you're finished your Registry should look like the one shown in Figure 18.9.

WARNING Before making any changes to the Registry, it's a good idea to make a backup. You can do this by creating a Startup disk or by using the Registry Editor to export the entire Registry database as a text file.

TABLE 18.3: Registry Values for the System Color Builder

Value Name	Value Type	Value
Can Edit	DWORD	1
Description	String	System Color Builder
Function	String	SysColorBuilder
Library	String	Set this to indicate the path to CH18BLD.MDA on your computer, for example: C:\ADH\CH18BLD.MDA

That's all it takes to install the System Color Builder to work with any BackColor property in Access. If you want to install the builder to use the other color properties, ForeColor and BorderColor, you will need to repeat the preceding steps to create new builder keys beneath each property key. If you find this too tedious, wait for the section "Using Add-In Manager" later in this chapter, where we'll explain how you can use the Access Add-in Manager to create these keys.

If you do not follow this Registry structure exactly, Access issues an "Invalid add-in entry for *addinname*" message when you first launch it, where *addinname* is the name of the Registry key with invalid entries. Access does not provide any information in addition to the Registry key causing the problem, however. (For instance, it would be helpful to know the property key where the errant add-in was located.) If you see this error and can't find the problem, you can use the Registry Editor's search capability to look for a key with the name of the errant add-in.

Now that the builder is installed, we can look at how it works.

The System Color Builder

Have you ever consulted the Access Help file to find the values for Windows system colors? While VBA provides constants for these values, you still need to enter the literal numbers in Access property sheets. The System Color Builder (shown in Figure 18.11) is a simple tool that sets these values using a dialog. Listing 18.1 shows the tool's builder function, SysColorBuilder. (You can find this function in basBuilders in CH18BLD.MDA.)

FIGURE 18.11:

Sample System Color Builder

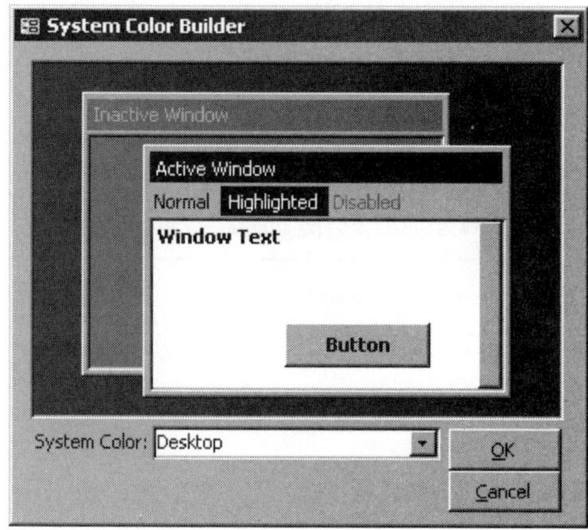

Listing 18.1

```
Function SysColorBuilder(strObjName As String, _
 strControl As String, strCurVal As String) As String

    On Error GoTo HandleError

    ' Constant holds the name of builder form
    Const conFrmSysColBld = "frmSysColorBuilder"

    ' Open the builder form in dialog mode--this
    ' halts the code until the form is closed
    ' (by the Cancel button) or hidden (by the
    ' OK button)--note that we pass the current
    ' property value in the OpenArgs argument
    DoCmd.OpenForm FormName:=conFrmSysColBld, _
```

```
         windowmode:=acDialog, _
         OpenArgs:=strCurVal

        ' Check to see if the form is still open--
        ' if so then the user clicked OK
        If CodeProject.AllForms( _
         conFrmSysColBld).IsLoaded Then

            ' Set the return value to the value
            ' of the color combo box
            SysColorBuilder = CStr(Forms( _
             conFrmSysColBld).Controls("cboColors"))

            ' Close the builder form
            DoCmd.Close acForm, conFrmSysColBld
        Else
            SysColorBuilder = strCurVal
        End If

ExitHere:
    Exit Function

HandleError:
    MsgBox Err.Description, vbExclamation, _
     "Error " & Err.Number
    Resume ExitHere
End Function
```

SysColorBuilder simply opens the builder form, frmSysColorBuilder, in dialog mode and waits for the user to take some action. It passes the current property value (stored in the strCurVal argument) to the form in its OpenArgs property. Code in the form's Load event procedure sets the initial value of the system color combo box to this value. If the user clicks OK, VBA code in the form's module hides the form by setting its Visible property to False. Alternatively, if the user clicks the Cancel button, the form is closed. At this point, SysColorBuilder continues executing and uses the AllForms collection to determine whether the form is still open (but hidden).

If the form is still open, SysColorBuilder reads the value of the system color combo box and returns it to Access. It then closes the form. If, on the other hand, the user canceled the dialog, SysColorBuilder returns the original property value.

NOTE

You must return something as the result of a builder function; otherwise, the property will be set to an empty string.

SysColorBuilder is an example of a basic procedure that demonstrates the minimum requirements for an Access builder function. It accepts the current value of a property, changes it in the body of the procedure (in this case, using a dialog form), and returns the changed value as a result.

NOTE

The System Color Builder form, which actually manages the process of accepting user input, contains a good deal of rather uninteresting code. Most of the VBA code is contained in Click and DblClick event procedures and is used to set the value of the combo box in response to mouse clicks. We have chosen not to include the actual code here.

TIP

You can test builder functions like SysColorBuilder by executing them from the VBA Immediate window.

Developing Custom Wizards

One of the most interesting areas of Access development is the creation of custom Wizards. Wizards let you extend the product in a way that is both unique and tightly integrated. In a sense, your Wizards become part of the product itself. In this section, we show you how to create new Wizards using a framework that manages the mechanics of wizardry and lets you focus on defining the functionality of your Wizards. We demonstrate this framework using a sample Form Wizard that lets you create simple dialog boxes.

Access Wizard Functions

Before digging into creating custom Wizards, we must explain the built-in functions Access provides for creating new objects. Objects you can create with Wizards generally fall into two categories: data objects and user-interface objects. You create data objects—tables and queries—using data definition objects and methods. Chapter 6 provides a detailed discussion of ADO and how to use it to create and modify tables and queries. If you want to create Wizards that build data objects, you'll need to integrate code from Chapter 6 into the Wizard framework we describe in the following section.

User-interface objects—forms and reports—are handled by a completely different set of functions. Access provides seven functions that create and delete forms, reports, data access pages, and controls. Table 18.4 lists each function. In this section, we provide a brief overview of each function. The section "Finishing the Process" later in this chapter gives examples of how to use them.

TABLE 18.4: Access Wizard Functions

Function	Description
CreateForm	Creates a new form based on the current form template
CreateReport	Creates a new report based on the current report template
CreateDataAccessPage	Creates a new data access page based on an HTML file
CreateControl	Creates a new control on a form
CreateReportControl	Creates a new control on a report
DeleteControl	Removes a control from a form
DeleteReportControl	Removes a control from a report

CreateForm and CreateReport both take two optional String arguments that let you select a form or report template to use as the basis for the new object. The first argument is the path to a database containing the desired template, and the second argument is the name of the template. If you leave both arguments blank, the default template will be used (the form or report specified in the Forms/Reports tab of Access' Options dialog). Using templates lets you create new objects that already have a number of properties, such as size and color, predefined. Both functions return a pointer to the newly created object.

CreateDataAccessPage works a bit differently. It also accepts two arguments, but the first is the path to an HTML file. The second is a Boolean value. If the second argument is False, Access uses the HTML file specified in the first argument as the data access page, saving any changes back to the original file. If the second argument is True, Access creates a new, unsaved HTML file based on the one passed as the first argument.

CreateControl and CreateReportControl take a relatively large number of arguments and create a form or report control as a result. Like the previously mentioned functions, both also return a pointer to the new control object. Table 18.5 lists the arguments for each. Note that only the first two, FormName/ReportName and ControlType, are required.

TABLE 18.5: CreateControl/CreateReportControl Arguments

Argument	Type	Remarks
FormName/ReportName	String	Specifies the name of the form or report on which Access should create the new control.
ControlType	Integer	Specifies the type of control to create. It should be one of the control type constants listed in online help (for example, acTextbox).
Section	Integer	Number of the section where Access should create the control. It defaults to 0 (the Detail section) but can be any section (including report group levels) on the form or report.
Parent	String	Specifies the parent of the new control. Controls that have parents, such as attached labels, move with them.
ColumnName	String	Specifies the name of the field to which the control should be bound. For unbound controls, this should be an empty string (the default).
Left, Top, Height, Width	Integer	Sets the location and size of the control in twips. There are 1,440 twips per inch. If you omit any of these arguments, the default property for the control type is used.

NOTE

If you want to modify the contents of a newly created data access page, you'll need to use the Document Object Model exposed by the Internet Explorer HTML editor, which is what the Access data access page designer uses. For more information on creating data access pages, see *Access 2000 Developer's Handbook, Volume II*.

When you create a new control using either of these two functions, it is automatically endowed with the default properties for that control type. If you want to change any of these values, you can do so using the control object returned by the function. You will see, in the section "Finishing the Process" later in this chapter, that we do not use any of the optional arguments in our sample Form Wizard. Instead, we use the control object returned by the functions to set properties of the new control individually. We think using explicit property names makes code more readable.

DeleteControl and DeleteReportControl are subroutines that accept two mandatory String arguments, the first being the name of a form or report and the second being the name of a control. If successful, these procedures remove the specified control permanently. Finally, although it should be obvious, you can use these functions, as well as CreateControl and CreateReportControl, only when a form or report is open in Design view.

One thing you should notice about these procedures is that they are not very object-oriented. For instance, wouldn't it make more sense for CreateControl to be a method of form and report objects? Unfortunately, we are still bearing the burden of the original, undocumented (not to mention unobject-oriented) Wizard functions from Access 1. As you read through the rest of this chapter, though, it should become clear how to use these procedures effectively in your own Wizards.

Defining a Wizard Framework

There are many ways to create Access Wizards or programs that use the Wizard functions. In this chapter, we've chosen to develop a framework that we think is both powerful and flexible for writing Wizards. Our framework concentrates on the mechanics of a Wizard—eliciting user input and moving between pages on a dialog—freeing you to focus on writing code to make the Wizard do what you want.

Our Wizard framework is premised on the idea of using one main Wizard dialog to store information provided by the user and manage navigation using standard Next, Back, Cancel, and Finish buttons. Individual Wizard options are set by controls on one or more subforms that are dynamically loaded and unloaded in response to navigation commands. Each Wizard page corresponds to a different Wizard state. An Access table manages each state, including which subform object to load, as well as which buttons to enable or disable.

A Sample Form Wizard

To demonstrate both our framework and the Access Wizard functions, we've created a simple Form Wizard in CH18WIZ.MDA for creating input dialogs like the one shown in Figure 18.12. You can use this Wizard to create forms that ask simple questions or accept typed input. This example demonstrates a variety of Wizard techniques. Not only will you see how to create forms and controls, you will see how our Wizard framework lets us respond to choices the user makes.

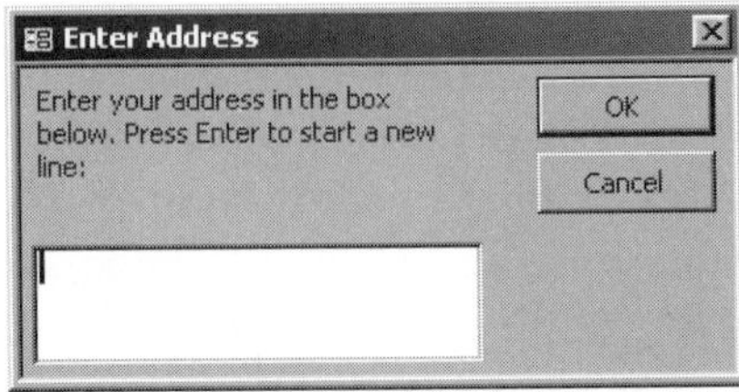

FIGURE 18.12: Dialog created using the sample Form Wizard

Our Wizard has three distinct states, each of which is represented by options on a separate subform. The first Wizard state requires the user to choose a dialog type—either a simple prompt or an input box. Depending on the user's selection, the Wizard can then proceed directly to the last state, where final choices are made before creating the form, or to an intermediate state, where details for the input box are specified.

We will control the program flow by making entries in the state table and by adding decision logic to the VBA modules for each Wizard page. Figures 18.13, 18.14, and 18.15 show the sample Wizard's three states, each of which is implemented as a separate form.

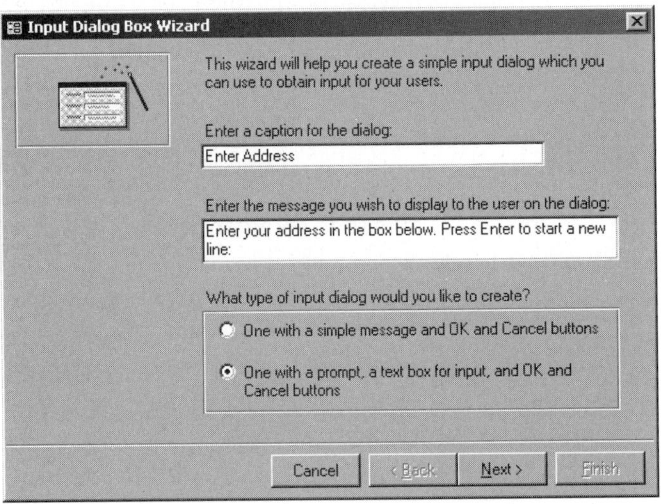

FIGURE 18.13: The first Wizard state uses sbfWizDialog1 to set caption, message, and type information.

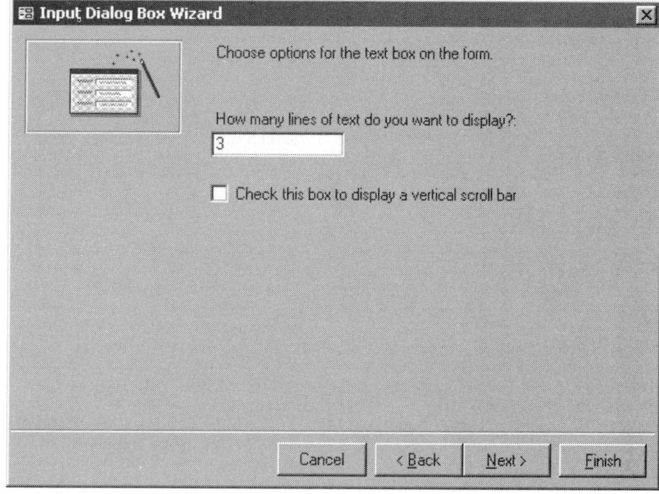

FIGURE 18.14:

The second Wizard state uses sbfDialog2 to set input box properties.

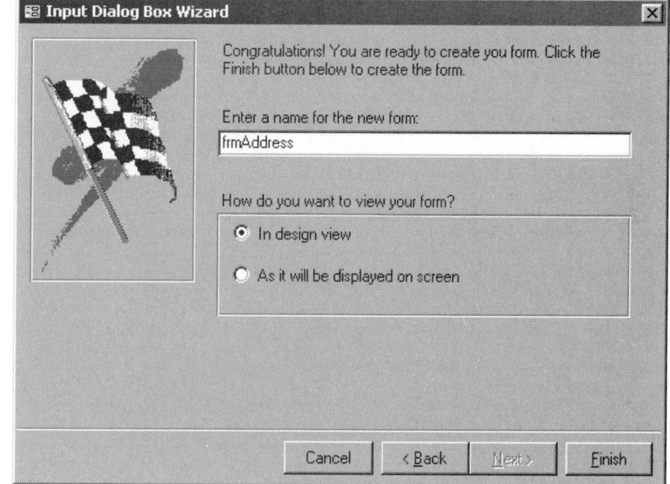

FIGURE 18.15:

The third Wizard state uses sbfWizDialog3 to save and display the completed forms.

How to Use the State Table

Each Wizard state can be represented by a set of values that controls such things as which subform to display and which buttons to enable. Also crucial is the state to which a Wizard should move if the user clicks either the Next or Back button. We've chosen to store this information in an Access table (called tblWizState in CH18WIZ.MDA) because this makes it very easy to add new Wizards and states, as well as to modify existing state information. Table 18.6 lists the fields in tblWizState.

TABLE 18.6: Field Definitions for tblWizState

Name	Type	Purpose
Wizard	Text	Wizard identifier
WizardState	Integer	State number
WizardForm	Text	Subform to load for this state
Comment	Text	Descriptive comments of the Wizard state
BackState	Integer	State reached by clicking the Back button
NextState	Integer	State reached by clicking the Next button
OptionalState	Text	State reached by clicking the optional button or the name of a function to call when the button is pressed
OptionalLabel	Text	Caption to display on the optional button
ShowOptional	Yes/No	Indicates whether the optional button should be displayed
EnableBack	Yes/No	Indicates whether the Back button should be enabled
EnableNext	Yes/No	Indicates whether the Next button should be enabled
EnableFinish	Yes/No	Indicates whether the Finish button should be enabled
ConfirmCancel	Yes/No	Prompts the user to confirm canceling the Wizard

When adding your own Wizards to our framework, you'll need to create one record in the table that represents each Wizard state. To describe which values to enter, let's look at the records in the table for our sample Form Wizard. Table 18.7 lists the most important field values.

TABLE 18.7: State Table Values for Our Sample Form Wizard

WizardState	WizardForm	BackState	NextState	EnableBack	EnableNext	EnableFinish
1	sbfWizDialog1	–1	2	No	Yes	No
2	sbfWizDialog2	1	3	Yes	Yes	Yes
3	sbfWizDialog3	2	–1	Yes	No	Yes

Our Wizard uses three sequentially numbered states. The state numbers need not be sequential, but it is easier to follow the program logic if they are. The first state uses sbfWizDialog1 as the source object for the Wizard's subform control. From state 1, the user can enter a caption for the dialog and a message to display on the form and can choose between a simple dialog or one with a text box for user input. You can see from the values in the state table that the only choice of movement is forward. An EnableBack setting of No disables the Wizard form's Back button, and a BackState value of –1 ensures that even if the button were enabled, no state information would be found in the table.

By default, if the user clicks the Next button, the Wizard moves to state 2 (determined by the NextState value). Later on, in the section titled "Creating Wizard Pages," we'll show how to adjust this logic using VBA code to skip state 2. In this state, which uses sbfWizDialog2 to elicit input on how the input box should appear, the user can move either backward or forward. (EnableBack and EnableNext are both Yes.) Finally, in state 3 the Next button is disabled, preventing the user from overrunning the Wizard. Also notice that the Finish button is enabled only in states 2 and 3. This forces the user to enter information on the first Wizard page before building the form.

You should be able to see a pattern in how the Wizard state values are specified. When you create your own Wizards, you will need to map their logic to records in the state table.

Looking at the Wizard Host Form

Our Wizard framework uses one form that acts as the host for the subforms that make up individual Wizard states. Figure 18.16 shows the sample host form, frmWizardFrame, in Design view. The entire Detail section of the form is filled with a subform object. Our Wizard code will dynamically change the control's SourceObject property, depending on which state the Wizard is in.

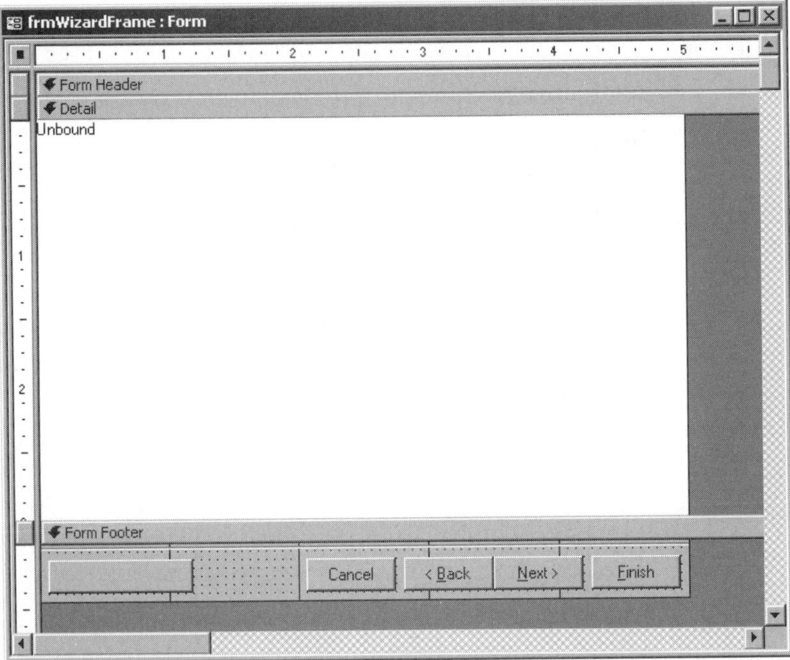

FIGURE 18.16: Sample Wizard host form in Design view

Command buttons in the form's footer are used for Wizard navigation (Back, Next) and control (Cancel, Finish). You can use the button on the left, which has no caption, for an optional command. For example, it might make sense to include an Advanced or Options button in a particular form state. Our Wizard functions will dynamically update this control based on settings in the state table.

Code behind the Host Form

If you open frmWizFrame in CH18WIZ.MDA on the companion disk in Design view, you can browse the contents of the host form's VBA module. To save space, we have chosen not to include all of it here, so you may find it helpful to view the code on screen or print it out to have while reading this section. If you examine it, you will see that it is a very small amount of code. Generic code in the basWizards module handles most of the navigation tasks. The code that resides in the form itself is mainly responsible for initializing the Wizard and maintaining its current state. Several module-level variables are defined in the declarations section of the frmWizFrame's module. CurrentState is defined as a Public Integer, and we use it to store the Wizard's current state number. NextState is another Public Integer, which we use to store the state to which the Wizard moves when the user clicks the Back or Next button. We have declared these as Public so we can access them from other procedures. Similarly, StateTable is a Public Recordset variable, which we use as a pointer to records in tblWizState that apply to the current Wizard. We use a Private Boolean variable, mfCanceled, to denote whether a user has canceled the Wizard by clicking the Cancel button. We will use this variable later when processing the form's Unload event. When creating your own Wizards using our host form as a template, you should not change or delete any of these variables. You should, however, change the value of the conWizID constant. This is the Wizard identifier specified by the Wizard field in tblWizState, and it should correspond to the value you use in that table to identify your Wizard.

Code in the form's Load event (see Listing 18.2) establishes the recordset used to retrieve state information. We use a SQL statement to query the tblWizState table based on the conWizID constant declared in the form. Once we have a pointer to the recordset, we can retrieve information about individual states and take some action, such as enabling or disabling buttons, and so on. If the SQL statement produces a valid recordset (that is, one containing records), we set the value of the form's CurrentState property to 1 and call the global function adhWizGotoState, described in the section "Global Wizard Functions" later in this chapter.

Listing 18.2

```
Private Sub Form_Load()
    ' ********************************************
    ' ** Required wizard code -- do not change **
    ' ********************************************

    Dim strSQL As String

    ' Set up the form's state table recordset by
    ' querying the table based on the wizard id
    strSQL = "SELECT * FROM tblWizState WHERE " & _
     "Wizard = '" & conWizID & "'"
    Set StateTable = New ADODB.Recordset
    StateTable.Open strSQL, CodeProject.Connection, _
     adOpenKeyset, adLockPessimistic

    ' Make sure we've got at least one record in
    ' the recordset and, if so, go to the first state
```

```
    If Not StateTable.EOF Then
        Me.CurrentState = 1
        Call adhSetWizardControls(Me)
    End If

    ' ************************************
    ' ** Add your own start up code here **
    ' ************************************

End Sub
```

Code in the form's Unload event performs clean-up duties by closing the Recordset object. It is also responsible for issuing a message box dialog if the user tries to cancel the form and the current Wizard state calls for a confirmation. Code in the Click event for the cmdCancel button sets mfCanceled to True and calls DoCmd.Close to close the form. If the recordset's ConfirmCancel field is set to True when the user cancels the Wizard and the user does not answer Yes to the prompt, the procedure cancels the Unload event and resets the mfCanceled flag.

Code that responds to the Click events for the Back and Next buttons (cmdBack and cmdNext, respectively) calls a global function, adhWizGotoPage. Each passes a reference to the Wizard form using the Me object, as well as a Boolean value. Which state to go to is determined by the value in the state table's BackState and NextState fields.

Finally, there is no code attached to the Finish button's Click event. This is where you place code that is specific to your Wizard. As we look at the sample Form Wizard, it will become clear how to use this button's event.

An Example Wizard Form

The code behind frmWizardFrame showed the VBA code contained in our template host form. When you create your own Wizard forms, you will need to add code to the existing module that is specific to your Wizard. Listing 18.3 shows the additional code contained in our sample Form Wizard. It is composed of nothing more than several form-level variables we will use to store values the user selected. The reason there isn't much code is that all the work of eliciting and validating user input is handled by the subforms that make up individual Wizard pages.

Listing 18.3

```
' ************************************************
' ** Add your own properties here              **
' ************************************************
' Change this constant to reflect your wizard id
' as set in the state table
Const adhcWizID = "SimpFormWiz"

' Public properties to store user selections
Public DialogType As ftFormType
Public DialogCaption As String
Public DialogMessage As String
Public LinesOfText As Integer
Public VerticalScrollbar As Boolean
Public OpenMode As ftFormView
Public NewFormName As Variant

Private Sub Form_Load()
    ' See frmWizardFrame for the rest of the code

    ' ************************************
    ' ** Add your own startup code here **
    ' ************************************
    ' This sets an initial value for LinesOfText
    Me.LinesOfText = 1
End Sub

Private Sub cmdFinish_Click()
    If Me.sbfWizard.Form.StateExit(True) Then

        ' ***********************************
        ' ** Add your own Finish code here **
        ' ***********************************
        If FormWizFinish(Me) Then
            DoCmd.Close acForm, Me.Name
        End If
    End If
End Sub
```

The most relevant code is in the declarations section of the form's module. Here we've declared a number of Public variables we will use to store selections the user makes. These variables, described in Table 18.8, map directly to the user input controls on our Wizard pages. As the user leaves each page, values in the controls are saved in the Public variables. When the user clicks the Finish button, our Wizard uses these values to create a new form.

TABLE 18.8: Sample Form Wizard Variables

Variable	Purpose
DialogType	Type of dialog to create—simple message (ftMessage) or text input (ftInput)
DialogCaption	Caption for dialog box
DialogMessage	Text message to appear on the dialog
LinesOfText	For input dialogs, how many lines of text to allow
VerticalScrollbar	For input dialogs, whether the text box should have a vertical scroll bar
OpenMode	Whether the new form should be displayed in Design view (fvDesign) or Form view (ftForm)
NewFormName	Name for the new form

You'll also notice that code in the form's Load event sets an initial value for the LinesOfText property (1). A validation rule on the text box for this property restricts user input to values between 1 and 10. You'll want to initialize any variables your own Wizard uses in the Load event, as well.

NOTE The values for DialogType and OpenMode are enumerated types defined in basFormWizEntry. For more information on enumerated types, see Chapter 3.

Global Wizard Functions

While each Wizard you create requires a separate copy of the host form, all Wizards share a set of common functions in a global VBA module (basWizards). These functions handle the mechanics of Wizard navigation and control. Listing 18.4 shows the first of these functions, adhWizGotoState. The adhWizGotoState function accepts two arguments: frmWiz, a pointer to a Wizard form, and fForward, a flag indicating whether the user is moving forward or backward in the Wizard process.

Listing 18.4

```
Function adhWizGotoState(frmWiz As Form, _
 ByVal fForward As Boolean) As Boolean

    Dim strBookmark As String
    Dim strCurrentForm As String
    Dim frmWizPage As Form

    ' Record the current position in the recordset
    ' in case we have to go back
    strBookmark = frmWiz.StateTable.Bookmark
    strCurrentForm = frmWiz.sbfWizard.SourceObject

    ' Call the StateExit method of the current
    ' subform to make sure it's okay to leave it
    If frmWiz.sbfWizard.Form. _
     StateExit(fForward) Then

        frmWiz.StateTable.MoveFirst
        frmWiz.StateTable.Find _
         "WizardState = " & frmWiz.NextState

        ' Make sure there's a match
        If Not frmWiz.StateTable.EOF Then

            ' Turn off form painting
            frmWiz.Painting = False

            ' If so, then bring up the next subform
            ' based on the entry in the state table
            frmWiz.sbfWizard.SourceObject = _
             frmWiz.StateTable!WizardForm

            ' Now call the StateEnter method of the
            ' new subform to make sure it's okay
            ' to proceed
            If frmWiz.sbfWizard.Form. _
             StateEnter(fForward) Then
```

```
                    ' If so, call adhSetWizardControls
                    ' to set the state of the host
                    ' form's navigation controls
                    Call adhSetWizardControls(frmWiz)

                    ' Set the host form's CurrentState
                    ' property to the new state
                    frmWiz.CurrentState = frmWiz.NextState
                Else

                    ' Otherwise restore the current
                    ' state by reloading the original
                    ' subform and resetting the recordset
                    ' to its original location
                    frmWiz.StateTable.Bookmark = _
                     strBookmark
                    frmWiz.sbfWizard.SourceObject = _
                     strCurrentForm
                End If

                ' Restore form painting
                frmWiz.Painting = True
            End If
        End If
    End Function
```

The adhWizGotoState function is responsible for moving between Wizard states, a process comprising several steps. First, the procedure records data on the current Wizard state, including the position in the Wizard's recordset and the current subform SourceObject property. The procedure may need to use this information later to return to the current state if an error occurs. After we've collected this information, the procedure executes the recordset's Find method to jump to the row containing state settings for the given state. Once we have this information, we can update the Wizard's host form to reflect the new state by loading the appropriate subform.

Before doing that, however, we must make sure it is okay to do so. Why wouldn't it be okay? There are a number of situations in which you would not want a user to leave or enter a particular Wizard state until certain tasks had been completed or options selected. For example, suppose one Wizard state features a list of database objects from which the user must pick. Until the user actually makes a selection, we need a way to prevent the user from going forward. The adhWizGotoState function verifies that it is okay to leave the current state by calling a custom method of the currently loaded subform called StateExit (see the next section, "Creating Wizard Pages," for more information).

We pass the fForward flag to StateExit so the method knows the direction in which the user is moving. If StateExit returns False, the procedure terminates; otherwise, it loads the subform acting as the desired state's Wizard page into the host form by setting the SourceObject property to the value of the recordset's WizardForm field. Immediately after the form is loaded, we call a complementary method of the new subform object, StateEnter. Similar to StateExit, StateEnter determines whether it is okay to enter the desired state. If this method returns True, adhWizGotoState calls adhSetWizardControls (which enables or disables the host forms' command buttons) and updates the host form's CurrentState property. If, on the other hand, the method returns False, the procedure restores the previous state's subform SourceObject setting and recordset position (by resetting its Bookmark property).

Creating Wizard Pages

Now that we've explained the code behind the host form and the global Wizard functions module, we can discuss the creation of individual Wizard pages using Access forms. Creating a new Wizard page involves making a copy of the sbfWizardPage form in CH18WIZ.MDA. SbfWizardPage contains sample image and label controls, and it is the correct size to fit in the Detail section of the host form. Its VBA module also includes function stubs for the StateEnter and StateExit methods. After making a copy of this form, you should edit the form and its VBA module to add controls and code particular to your Wizard page. You will need to include the following bits of code:

- Code in the Form_Load event that reads current values from the host form into local variables.
- A Public function called StateEnter that returns True if state entry is allowed and False if it is not.
- A Public function called StateExit that returns True if state exit is allowed and False if it is not. If state exit is allowed, this function should transfer data from any local variables to the host form's variables.

Because the module in sbfWizardPage is only a shell for your own Wizard code, it is easier to describe the requirements of our framework if we look at the module of one of the sample Wizard pages. Listing 18.5 shows the code in sbfWizDialog1, the first page of our sample Form Wizard. The code listing contains the minimum amount of code you will need to provide as part of your own Wizard pages.

Listing 18.5

```
Const conWizStateFirst = 1
Const conWizStateLast = 3

Private Sub Form_Load()
    ' Enter intialization code here
    Me.txtMessage = Me.Parent.DialogMessage
    Me.txtCaption = Me.Parent.DialogCaption
    Me.grpType = Me.Parent.DialogType
End Sub

Public Function StateEnter(fForward As Boolean) As Boolean
    ' Enter code to accept or prevent state entry here
    StateEnter = True
End Function

Public Function StateExit(fForward As Boolean) As Boolean
    ' Enter code to accept or prevent state exit here
    StateExit = True

    ' This makes sure the user entered some text for
    ' the dialog message
    If fForward And Len(Me.txtMessage & "") = 0 Then
        MsgBox "You must provide a message to display.", _
         vbExclamation
        Me.txtMessage.SetFocus
        StateExit = False
        Exit Function
    End If

    ' This is logic to jump to the final state if the
    ' user selected the simple dialog option
    If Me.grpType = ftMessage And fForward Then
        Me.Parent.NextState = conWizStateLast
    End If
```

```
    ' Enter termination code here
    Me.Parent.DialogMessage = Me.txtMessage
    Me.Parent.DialogCaption = Me.txtCaption & ""
    Me.Parent.DialogType = Me.grpType
End Function
```

When the user moves to this page in our sample Form Wizard, we need to update the controls on the form with the current dialog properties. We do this in the Form_Load event procedure by examining the value using the subform's Parent property. Parent returns a pointer to the form in which the subform is embedded.

NOTE Form_Load will be executed when we set the SourceObject property of the subform object to sbfWizDialog1.

After the subform loads, the adhWizGotoState procedure calls its StateEnter method. Note that we have declared both StateEnter and StateExit as Public functions, thus making them accessible to procedures outside the form's VBA module. In our example, we don't need to perform any validation before allowing entry to this particular state, so StateEnter simply returns True.

Our StateExit function, on the other hand, is slightly more complex. Before moving to the next Wizard state, the user must enter a value for the dialog text. An If…Then statement examines the length of the text in txtMessage to determine whether it is greater than 0. If the user has not entered any text and is trying to move to the next state, the procedure issues a warning message, sets its return value to False, and terminates. This prevents adhWizGotoState from moving to a new state. If, on the other hand, all the conditions for leaving the current state are met (the user has entered a message), StateExit returns True. This allows adhWizGotoState to load the next Wizard page.

Finally, another If…Then statement examines the value in the dialog type control (grpType) that determines whether the new form will be a simple message dialog or will accept user input. If the user selects a simple dialog, it does make sense to display the second Wizard page—the one that lets the user set properties for the input box control. In this case, the procedure sets the NextState property to the final Wizard state number. This has the effect of bypassing the logic in the state table and jumping to a different state. You can use similar logic in your own Wizards to alter the user's path through your dialogs.

Finishing the Process

After working with various Wizard pages to make selections, users can click the Finish button to have the Wizard transform their choices into a beautiful new object. Depending on the complexity of your Wizard, this may require large amounts of VBA code. The code attached to the Finish button on our sample Form Wizard, shown in Listing 18.6, is extremely simple, however.

Listing 18.6

```
Private Sub cmdFinish_Click()
    If Me.sbfWizard.Form.StateExit(True) Then

        ' ************************************
        ' ** Add your own Finish code here **
        ' ************************************
        If FormWizFinish(Me) Then
            DoCmd.Close acForm, Me.Name
        End If
    End If
End Sub
```

You should notice two things about this code. First, we are calling a separate function (FormWizFinish) to create the new form, and second, the function is located in a separate module in the database (basFormWizFinish). Since the form creation process could involve a large amount of VBA code, it would be nice if we could delay loading this into memory until the user actually clicks the Finish button. Placing FormWizFinish in a separate module prevents Access from loading the module until the procedure statement is executed. This technique provides better Wizard load time because Access does not need to load basFormWizFinish along with the Wizard form itself. And, of course, if the user cancels the Wizard process, we never waste time loading this Finish code at all.

Creating Forms and Controls

As we just mentioned, we use a separate function, FormWizFinish, to create the dialog form defined by the user's selections in our Wizard. The module basFormWizFinish, in CH18WIZ.MDA on the companion disk, shows FormWizFinish, a procedure that uses Access' Wizard functions to create the dialog form and its controls. To save space, we've included only the highlights in this section. FormWizFinish accepts a single argument, frmWiz, which points to the Wizard form. Because we have defined the variables that hold Wizard settings as Public, frmWiz is all that's required to reference them from this global procedure.

Logically, the first thing FormWizFinish does is create the form that will be used as our dialog box, using the CreateForm function and no arguments. Access creates a new form in the current database based on the default form template and returns a pointer to it in the frmNew variable. We can now use frmNew to set several form properties appropriate for a dialog box. For example, we remove the record selector, navigation buttons, and scroll bars and change the form's size to three inches wide by one inch tall. As the following code fragment shows, we also change its grid settings and caption. We set the latter to the Wizard form's DialogCaption property:

```
' Build the form
Set frmNew = CreateForm()
frmNew.Width = 3 * conTwipsPerInch
frmNew.Section(0).Height = 1 * conTwipsPerInch
frmNew.Caption = frmWiz.DialogCaption
frmNew.GridX = 16
frmNew.GridY = 16
frmNew.AutoCenter = True
frmNew.AutoResize = True
frmNew.RecordSelectors = False
frmNew.ScrollBars = 0
frmNew.NavigationButtons = False
frmNew.MinMaxButtons = 0
```

After creating the form, the procedure goes on to create a label control and, if the user chose an input dialog, a text box. The following code fragment shows our use of the CreateControl function, passing it the name of the form to create the control using our new form variable, frmNew, and the control type. The return value, a pointer to the newly created control, is stored in ctlNew:

```
Set ctlNew = CreateControl(frmNew.Name, acTextBox)
```

Although we could have passed additional arguments to indicate its control source, position, and size, we did not, opting instead to set these properties individually. Using specific property names makes the code easier to understand:

```
With ctlNew
    .Height = frmWiz.LinesOfText * _
      conLineHeight * conTwipsPerInch
```

```
        .Width = 1.875 * conTwipsPerInch
        .Top = 0.75 * conTwipsPerInch
        .Left = 0.0625 * conTwipsPerInch
    End With
```

After the procedure creates the text box and adjusts the height of the form accordingly, it creates two command buttons—one labeled OK and the other Cancel. It places these on the right-hand side of the form. Once the command buttons have been created and their property values assigned, we must also insert some VBA code to make the controls work. We do this by calling a function, InsertCode, which we describe in the next section. If the user chose to create an input dialog, we call InsertCode to insert VBA code for the form's Load event to set an initial value of the control when the form is opened.

Finally, after the procedure creates the form and its controls and all the VBA code has been inserted, we can display and, optionally, save the form. The code that does this, shown below, first makes sure the new form is the active object by calling its SetFocus method. It then uses the Save method of the DoCmd object to save the active object (the new form) using the name provided by the Wizard form's NewFormName property. Finally, it calls the OpenForm method to display the new form in Form view if the user selected that option.

```
frmNew.SetFocus
If Not IsNull(frmWiz.NewFormName) Then
    DoCmd.Save , frmWiz.NewFormName
End If
DoCmd.Restore

If frmWiz.OpenMode = fvForm Then
    DoCmd.OpenForm frmNew.Name, acNormal
End If
```

Form Wizard code that you write is likely to be very different from the code in our sample Wizard because your code is specific to your Wizard's function. It should, however, have a similar structure—that is, a CreateForm statement followed by one or more CreateControl statements, finishing with an action that saves and/or displays the completed object.

Using an Access Table to Store Code

Our sample Wizard must insert code into the newly created form's VBA module to enable the two command buttons. Rather than embed large amounts of code in the Wizard module, we store it in an Access table. This lets us modify it easily, without having to edit the Wizard code. The code table, tblWizCode, contains three fields,

CodeID, CodeText, and CodeDesc. CodeID is a text field that acts as the unique identifier for each code fragment in the table. CodeText is a memo field containing the actual VBA code. CodeDesc lets you specify a descriptive comment for the code fragment. Figure 18.17 shows tblWizCode open in Datasheet view. You can see that it contains VBA code fragments that we will use in our Form Wizard.

FIGURE 18.17: VBA code stored in tblWizCode

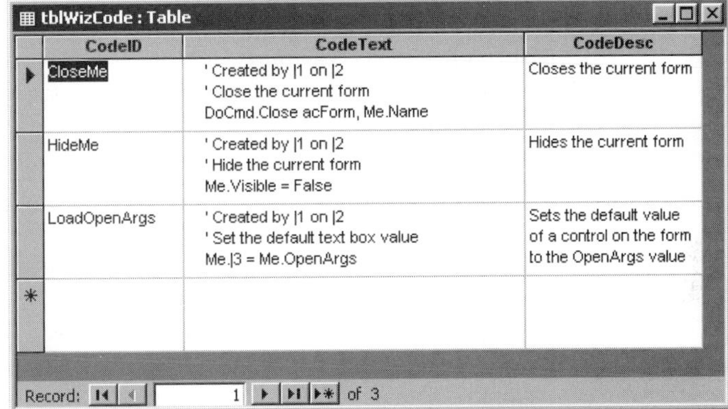

We've also created a function, InsertCode, shown in Listing 18.7, that inserts the code into a form's VBA module. InsertCode accepts five arguments and returns a Boolean value indicating success or failure. Table 18.9 lists each of these arguments and its purpose.

TABLE 18.9: Arguments to InsertCode

Argument	Type	Remarks
strCodeID	String	Should be a value in the CodeID field of tblWizCode; finds the block of text to insert into the form's VBA module.
frmAny	Form	Specifies the form containing the module into which we will insert code.
ctlAny	Control	Specifies the control to which the event code applies. Note that this can be Nothing, indicating that the code applies to the form itself, not a control.
strEvent	String	Specifies the name of the event to which the code applies (for example, "Click").
avarTokens	Variant	This ParamArray argument lets you pass substitution strings to the procedure that the procedure, in turn, will insert into the code.

Listing 18.7

```
Function InsertCode(ByVal strCodeID As String, _
 frmAny As Form, ctlAny As Control, ByVal strEvent _
 As String, ParamArray avarTokens() As Variant) _
 As Boolean

    Dim rstCode As ADODB.Recordset
    Dim varToken As Variant
    Dim intToken As Integer
    Dim strCode As String

    Const conTokenChar = "|"

    ' Query the code table to get the code for the
    ' selected CodeID
    Set rstCode = New ADODB.Recordset
    rstCode.Open "SELECT CodeText FROM tblWizCode " & _
     "WHERE CodeID = '" & strCodeID & "'", _
     CodeProject.Connection

    ' If we found a match go ahead and build the code
    If Not rstCode.EOF Then

        ' Build the declaration using the form
        ' or the control name--if we didn't
        ' supply a control reference then
        ' we must want to add code to the form's
        ' event procedures
        If ctlAny Is Nothing Then
            strCode = "Sub Form"
        Else
            strCode = "Sub " & ctlAny.Name
        End If

        ' Add the '()' and a carriage return
        strCode = strCode & "_" & strEvent & _
         "()" & vbCrLf

        ' Add the code from the table
        strCode = strCode & rstCode![CodeText]
```

```
            ' For each token replacement call Replace
            ' to insert the replacement text
            For Each varToken In avarTokens
                intToken = intToken + 1
                strCode = Replace(strCode, _
                 conTokenChar & intToken, _
                 varToken)
            Next

            ' Add a carriage return and 'End Sub'
            strCode = strCode & vbCrLf & "End Sub"

            ' Insert the code into the form's module
            frmAny.Module.InsertText strCode

            InsertCode = True
        End If

        rstCode.Close
    End Function
    InsertCodeInsertCode
```

The bulk of the code that makes up InsertCode handles the task of building a text string that will eventually be inserted into the form's module using the module's InsertText method. You will notice that InsertCode adds "Sub" and "End Sub" strings to the text it retrieves from tblWizCode. You should not, therefore, include an event procedure's declaration in tblWizCode.

InsertCode uses a For Each… loop to iterate through any additional arguments passed to the procedure using the ParamArray argument, avarTokens. It calls Replace (new in VBA 6) to replace all instances of a token (the pipe symbol, |, followed by a number) in the VBA code with an argument from the array.

NOTE

As it is written, InsertCode works only with event procedures that do not require arguments. If you wish to use it with those that do (for example, BeforeUpdate), you will need to modify InsertCode so that it appends the argument list to the procedure declaration instead of empty parentheses.

If you refer to the FormWizFinish procedure in CH18WIZ.MDA, you'll see how we use InsertCode in our sample Form Wizard. The statement that inserts code for the form's Load event is repeated here:

```
Call InsertCode("LoadOpenArgs", frmNew, _
 Nothing, "Load", CurrentUser, Now, strInputControl)
```

In this example, the string "LoadOpenArgs" identifies the code fragment in tblWizCode. Once InsertCode has retrieved it from the table, it is inserted into the form's module. Passing the symbolic constant Nothing as the control argument forces InsertCode to create an event procedure for the form, as opposed to a specific control. Finally, three additional arguments are passed to the function. Tokens in the code stored in tblWizCode (you can see the tokens, |1, |2, and |3, in the code in Figure 18.17) will be replaced with these values.

Launching the Wizard

Like builders, Wizards are normally initiated by a function call from Access. While you can launch your Wizards any way you wish, if you want to integrate them into the list of standard Access Wizards, you must create a function with a specific declaration. There are two varieties of Access Wizard functions—one for tables and queries and one for forms and reports. Wizard functions for forms and reports must define at least one argument, regardless of whether you use it in your code. No arguments are required for Table and Query Wizards. Listing 18.8 shows the function used to initiate our sample Form Wizard, adhFrmWizEntry.

Listing 18.8

```
Function FormWizEntry(strRecordSource _
 As String) As Variant

    ' Name of wizard form
    Const conFrmWizForm = "frmWizDialog"

    ' Open wizard form and let it do its stuff
    DoCmd.OpenForm FormName:=conFrmWizForm, _
     Windowmode:=acDialog

End Function
```

The argument to a Form or Report Wizard function such as FormWizEntry must be a string, which Access will fill in with the name of a record source for the new object. This could be the name of either a table or a query. Access gets this value from the combo box on the initial Wizard dialog. Our sample Wizard creates an unbound form, so we ignore this argument. If you were creating a bound form, however, you would use this to examine the record source for field names and types. Access does not pass anything to Wizard functions that create new tables or queries.

You can define additional arguments to your Wizard functions if you plan on calling them from elsewhere in your application. For example, you might create a common Wizard function that handles both forms and reports, depending on the value of a second argument. (In fact, this is how the Access Wizards work.) If you do this, however, you need to tell Access about the additional argument; otherwise, the normal Wizard functionality will be impaired. Informing Access of additional arguments requires making additional Registry entries, as explained in the next section.

WARNING

You must adhere exactly to the rules for declaring Wizard functions. Any error in your Wizard function, including declaration, syntax, and compile errors, will result in Access issuing a "This feature is not installed" error when you attempt to invoke your Wizard. As you can see, this is far from being the most descriptive Access error message ever written. If you receive this error, you will need to shut down Access before attempting to edit your code. This is because, once an Access database has been loaded as a library, it cannot be opened in the user interface.

The only task that remains is to tell Access about our Wizard so that our users have the option of selecting it from the standard list of Form Wizards. To do that, we'll need to make some more (you guessed it) Registry entries.

Wizard Registry Entries

Access separates Wizard entries into groups based on the type of object the Wizard creates. Figure 18.18 shows the Registry keys for Control Wizards and Form Wizards. Not visible are the keys for Table Wizards, Query Wizards, Data Access Page Wizards, and Report Wizards. Figure 18.18 also shows the Form Wizard subkeys that define the individual Wizards themselves. To add a new Wizard to Access' list of installed Wizards, you must add a new subkey beneath the appropriate Wizard type key. Access will use the name you give to the subkey in the list of Wizards displayed to the user, so choose something short but descriptive. For example, to install our sample Form Wizard, create a new subkey called Dialog Form Wizard beneath the Form Wizards key.

FIGURE 18.18:

Registry entries that define Access Wizards

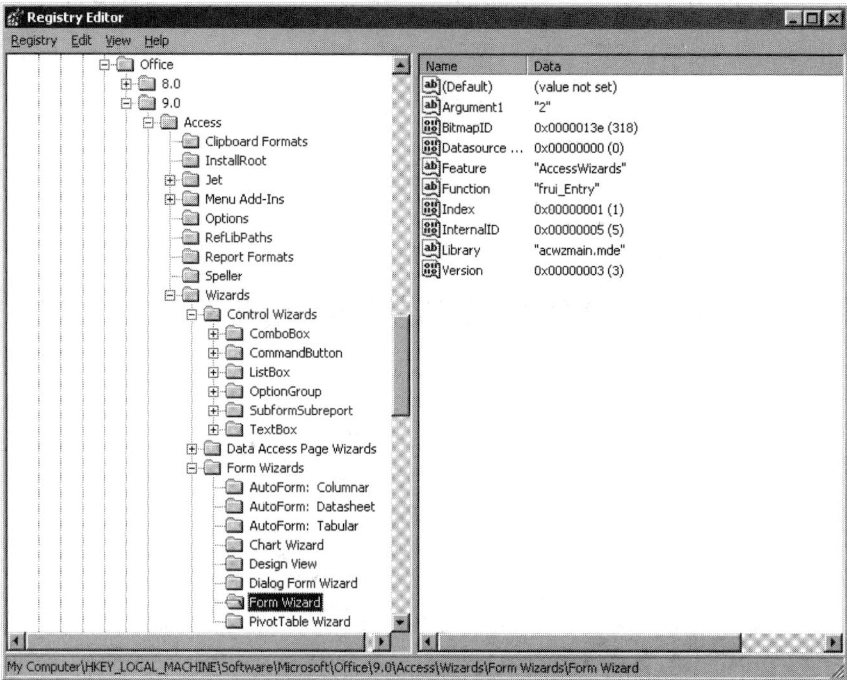

In addition to the subkey, you'll need to create several Registry values. Table 18.10 lists the required value names for Table, Query, Form, and Report Wizards, along with the values for our sample Wizard. To complete the installation of our Wizard, you'll need to add these values to the Dialog Form Wizard Registry key.

TABLE 18.10: Object Wizard Registry Key Values

Value Name	Value Type	Sample Value	Remarks
Bitmap	String	Path to ADHWIZ.BMP	Defines the path to a bitmap (BMP) file containing an image that Access displays in the new object dialog when the Wizard is selected.

Continued on next page

TABLE 18.10 CONTINUED: Object Wizard Registry Key Values

Value Name	Value Type	Sample Value	Remarks
BitmapID	DWORD	N/A	Resource ID of the bitmap to use for this Wizard. Access Wizards use resource IDs to reference bitmaps included as part of the MSACCESS .EXE executable file.
Datasource Required	DWORD	0	If set to 1, Access requires the user to select a data source for the object. A value of 0 means a data source is optional.
Description	String	"Creates a simple dialog that displays a message or accepts input"	Lets you create a description of the Wizard that Access will display in the new object dialog.
Function	String	FormWizEntry	Defines the name of the Wizard function Access calls to initiate the Wizard.
Index	DWORD	N/A	Defines the position of the Wizard in the list of Wizards. Must be between 0 (the first in the list) and 1 less than the number of installed Wizards. Must also be unique among other Wizards. If omitted, Access adds the Wizard at the end of the list.
InternalID	DWORD	N/A	Marks the Wizard as one implemented by MSACCESS.EXE, not a library database, and indicates which internal Wizard function to use. (You can't really use this setting; we've included it here for the sake of completeness.)
Library	String	Path to CH18WIZ.MDA	Defines the path to the library database containing the Wizard function. You can omit the path if the library is located in the Access directory.

If you have declared additional arguments to your Wizard function, you also need to create values for each one in the Wizard's Registry key. You can see in Figure 18.18 the values for Access' built-in Form Wizard and an additional String value named

Argument1. In addition to the required String argument, Access' Wizard function, frui_Entry, declares an Integer argument denoting which type of object is being created. Since, by default, Access will pass the Wizard function only one argument (the record source), this Registry value forces Access to pass a second one (in this case, with the value 2). If your Wizard function accepts more than one argument, you must define additional Registry values named Argument1, Argument2, and so on, one for each additional argument. After creating the additional Registry entries, assign them the values you want Access to pass to the additional arguments when Access invokes your Wizard function. These must be hard-coded as strings and cannot be evaluated at runtime.

FIGURE 18.19:

Registry entries for the sample Form Wizard

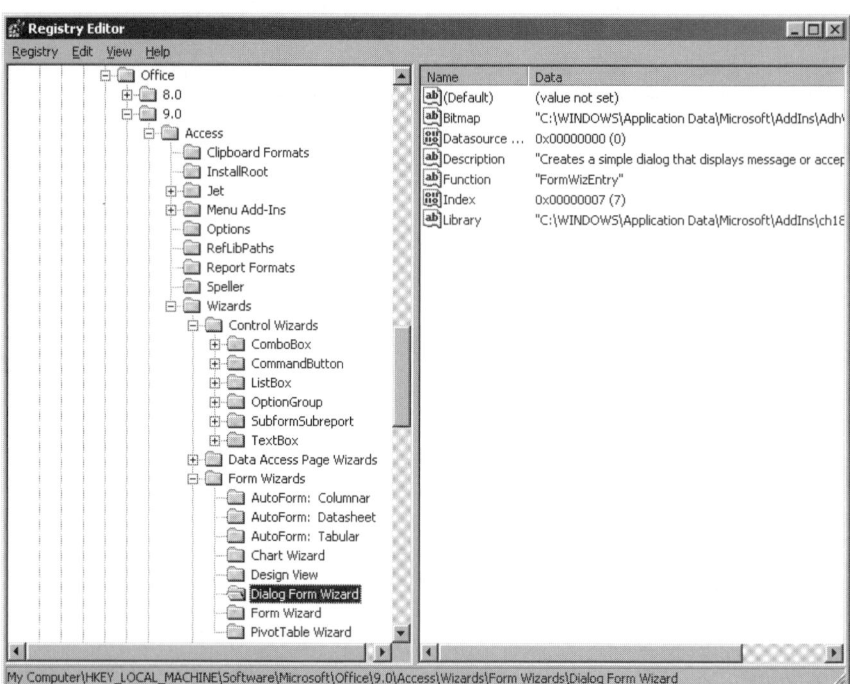

Figure 18.19 shows the Registry updated to reflect settings for our sample Form Wizard. To test the Wizard, open any Access database and click the New Form button on the toolbar or select the Insert ➢ Form menu command. Figure 18.20 shows the New Form dialog with the sample Wizard selected. Note the Wizard's name, description, and bitmap. These are all defined using the Registry entries described earlier in this chapter.

FIGURE 18.20:

New Form dialog showing details for the sample Form Wizard

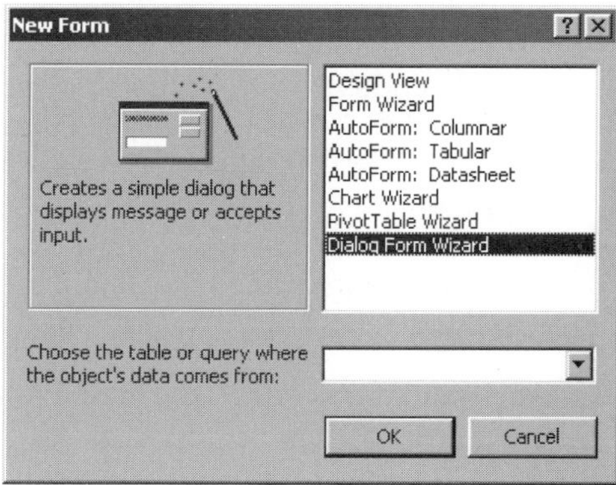

NOTE

If you want our custom bitmap to appear in the New Form dialog, you must copy ADHWIZ.BMP from the CD-ROM to your hard disk and set the Bitmap Registry value appropriately.

Our Framework in Summary

We have presented a great deal of information in this chapter describing how to create Access Wizards. The discussion included both the Access Wizard functions and our framework for creating Wizard dialogs. Try not to confuse the two. You can use the Access Wizard functions (CreateForm, CreateControl, and so on) in any VBA procedure to create new objects. We have included a description of our framework because we believe it is a powerful yet easy-to-implement way of creating Wizards that look and act like those that come with Access.

If you choose to use our framework, there are a number of things you need to do. We have described them in detail in this chapter. To summarize, the steps for creating new Wizards using our framework are

1. Create a copy of frmWizardFrame. This will act as the host form for your Wizard.
2. Change the conWizID constant to the unique ID for your Wizard.
3. Add Public variables to the host form's declarations section to hold user choices.

4. Add code to the Load event of the host form to initialize the Wizard.
5. Add code to the cmdFinish_Click procedure that calls your object-creation code.
6. For each Wizard page, create a copy of sbfWizardPage.
7. Add code to the subform's Load event to initialize that page.
8. Add validation code to the StateEnter procedure to restrict entry to that state.
9. Add validation code to the StateExit procedure to prevent users from leaving that state.
10. Add code to the StateExit procedure to save values from the subform to the host form's Public variables.
11. Set the SourceObject property for the subform object on your host form to the name of the first Wizard page.
12. Add a record to tblWizState that defines the subform and options for that state.
13. Create a function that accepts a pointer to the host form and uses the form's custom properties to create a new object.
14. Create a Wizard function that opens the host form in dialog mode.
15. Register your Wizard so Access can display it to users and call its Wizard function.

Control Wizards: A Hybrid

In addition to object Wizards such as our sample Form Wizard, Access supports Control Wizards that are invoked when a user creates a new control on a form or report. Access' Combo Box Wizard is an example of a Control Wizard. Additionally, you can create ActiveX Control Wizards that are called when a user adds a new custom control to a form or report. We briefly describe how to create a Control Wizard in this section. You will find, however, that the overall process differs little from regular Wizards and builders.

To use a Control Wizard, the user must have enabled this option by clicking the Control Wizards button on the form design command bar. We've created an extremely simple Wizard that is invoked when a user creates a new text box. In fact, we've reused the second page of our Form Wizard. Figure 18.21 shows the Wizard's main form, frmTBWiz.

FIGURE 18.21:

Sample Text Box Wizard

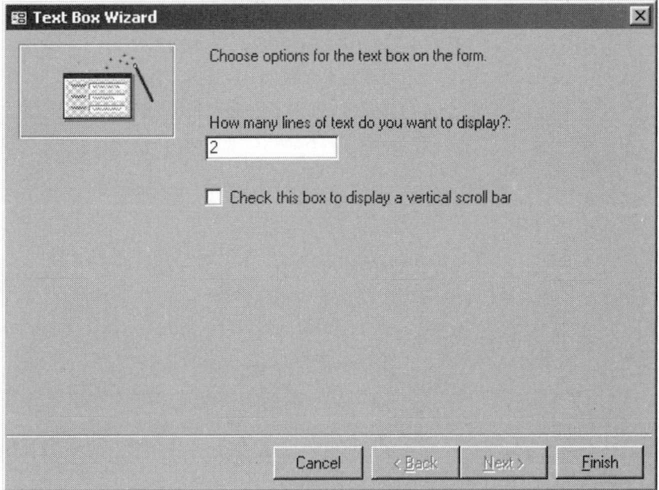

Control Wizard Functions

Like regular Wizards, Control Wizards must be invoked by a function. Access passes the name of the newly created control and its label (if it has one) as String arguments to the Wizard function. Listing 18.9 shows the function for the Text Box Wizard that we've included with this book.

Listing 18.9

```
Function TextBoxWizEntry(strControlName As _
 String, strLabelName As String) As Variant

    Dim ctlNew As Control
    Dim frmWiz As Form

    ' Constants for line height
    Const conTwipsPerInch = 1440
    Const conLineHeight = 0.1575
    ' Name of wizard form
    Const conTextBoxWizForm = "frmTBWiz"
```

```
    ' Check the active object and make sure it's
    ' a form (scrollbars don't make sense
    ' for reports)
    If Application.CurrentObjectType = acForm Then

        ' Get a reference to the newly
        ' created control
        Set ctlNew = Forms(Application. _
         CurrentObjectName).Controls( _
         strControlName)

        ' Make sure it's a text box
        If ctlNew.ControlType <> acTextBox Then
            MsgBox "You can only use this wizard " _
             & "with text boxes.", vbExclamation
        Else
            ' Open wizard form and let it do its stuff
            DoCmd.OpenForm FormName:=conTextBoxWizForm, _
             Windowmode:=acDialog

            ' If form is still open, proceed
            If CodeProject.AllForms(conTextBoxWizForm). _
             IsLoaded Then

                ' Get reference to wizard form
                Set frmWiz = Forms(conTextBoxWizForm)

                ' Set control properties
                ctlNew.Height = frmWiz.LinesOfText * _
                 conLineHeight * conTwipsPerInch

                ' Text box scroll bars
                ctlNew.ScrollBars = ( _
                 Abs(frmWiz.VerticalScrollbar) * 2)

                ' Close the wizard form
                DoCmd.Close acForm, conTextBoxWizForm
            End If
        End If
    End If
End Function
```

There are several things to note about this function. First, before any substantial processing begins, the procedure checks the return value of Access' CurrentObjectType method to ensure that the active object is a form. You can use this technique (as we have in this case) to take a different action if the active object is a report rather than a form. Next, this procedure sets a reference to the newly created control (stored in the ctlNew Control variable) using the control name Access passes to the function. You could use Screen.ActiveControl, but using the control's name is much safer and more intuitive. Once the reference is set, the procedure checks to make sure the control is, in fact, a text box and then opens the Wizard form.

Code attached to the cmdFinish button on the Wizard's host form simply hides the form and lets TextBoxWizEntry continue. TextBoxWizEntry then sets the Height and ScrollBars properties of the newly created control. Keep in mind that Access has already added the control to the form or report before it invokes your Wizard. The only thing your Wizard needs to do is set its properties.

Control Wizard Registry Entries

The Registry entries for Control Wizards are similar to those for builders. Figure 18.22 shows the entries for our sample Text Box Wizard. You can have more than one Wizard for each control, and these are grouped under the Control Wizards Registry key. There is a subkey for each control type (you can also add ones that are not created by default), and each of these has subkeys for each Wizard that applies to the control. If you wanted to add a second text box builder, for example, you would create a new, unique subkey beneath the TextBox key shown in Figure 18.22.

The Registry values themselves (in the right-hand pane in Figure 18.22) are the same for builders and were listed in Table 18.2 earlier in this chapter. The only significant difference is in the use of the Can Edit value. In the case of builders, you almost always want this value to be 1, indicating that the builder can be invoked for an existing property value. Control Wizards, on the other hand, are normally used to create new objects. In this case, it may not make sense to invoke the builder on an existing control. For this reason, the Can Edit value should be 0. You can have reentrant Control Wizards, of course, but you may have to write extra code to account for this.

FIGURE 18.22:

Registry entries for Control Wizards

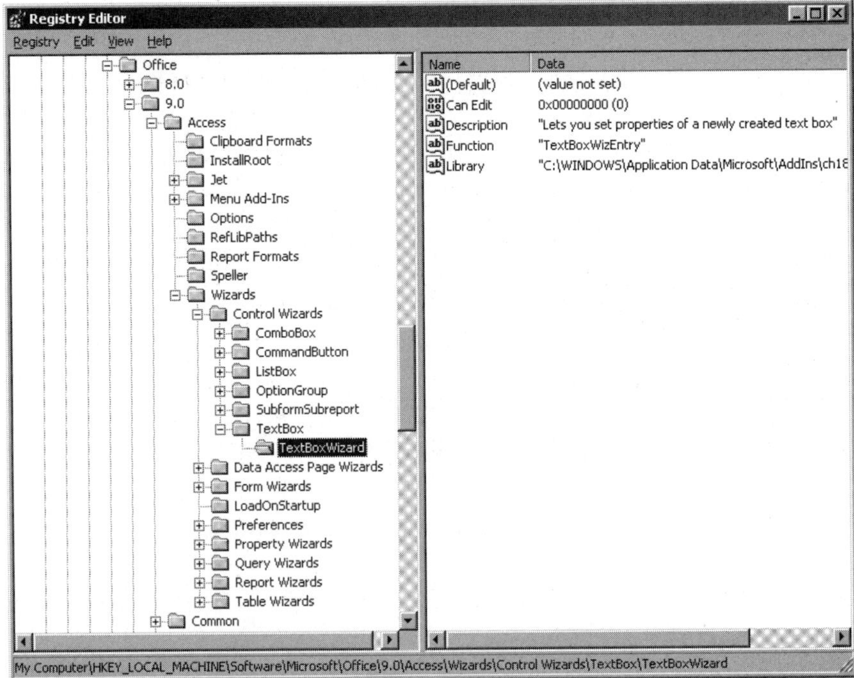

ActiveX Control Wizards

We have one final word on Wizards. If you develop and distribute your own ActiveX controls, you can also install special Wizards to work with them. Access will recognize a Registry key for custom controls that follows the same rules as for normal Control Wizards, with a few exceptions.

First, before you install your Wizard, you must create a new Registry key called OLE CONTROL WIZARDS (it must be uppercase) beneath the normal Access Wizards key. Then, instead of a control type, you must create a new subkey beneath the OLE CONTROL WIZARDS key using the ProgID of the custom control. For example, DBOutl.DataOutline is the ProgID for the data outline control.

From here, the rules are the same as for regular Control Wizards. Create a new subkey beneath the control subkey with the values listed in Table 18.2.

Distributing and Installing Add-Ins

Once you've created an add-in, builder, or Wizard, you can easily distribute it to others by providing them with a copy of the library database. The only complication involves installing it on another person's computer and making the appropriate Registry entries. Fortunately, Access provides two mechanisms to ease this task: Add-in Manager and the USysRegInfo table. In this section, we describe each of these and how to use them to distribute your own custom add-ins.

Using Add-In Manager

Using the Access Add-in Manager is usually the easiest way to install and uninstall Access Wizards, builders, and add-ins. Add-in Manager uses a special table in the Wizard database called USysRegInfo to create or delete the Registry entries required for the add-in to operate. You invoke Add-in Manager by selecting Tools ➢ Add-ins ➢ Add-in Manager from the Access menus. Figure 18.23 shows the Add-in Manager dialog.

FIGURE 18.23:

Access' Add-in Manager dialog

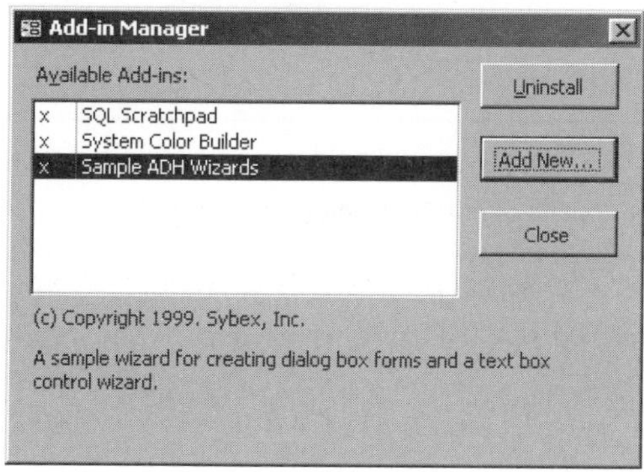

The list box displays all the add-ins Add-in Manager knows about. Access builds this list by looking at all the library databases in the \Microsoft\Addins directory of your user profile (C:\Windows\Application Data\ by default on Windows 98) and examining their database properties. Add-in Manager examines three properties for each library database in the Access directory: Title, Company, and Comments. Figure 18.24 shows the Summary tab of the Database Properties dialog for our sample Form Wizard database, CH18WIZ.MDA. You can see how values in these three properties are displayed in the Add-in Manager dialog in Figure 18.23.

FIGURE 18.24:

Document properties used by Add-in Manager

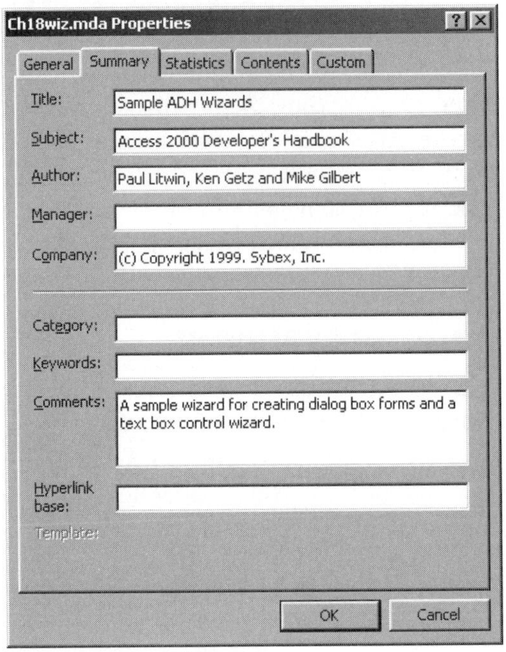

NOTE

You must have Open/Run permission on a library database for Add-in Manager to read its properties. If you do not have permission to open the database, Add-in Manager displays a warning dialog and omits the add-in from the list.

A check box next to the add-in description in the Add-in Manager dialog tells you whether the add-in is currently installed. Add-in Manager makes this determination by looking for values in the Registry that match those in the add-in's USysRegInfo table (which we describe in the next section). If the library database does not have a USysRegInfo table, Add-in Manager cannot determine its installed state. You can toggle the installed state of an existing add-in by double-clicking the add-in on the list or by selecting it and clicking the Uninstall button. For add-ins that are not currently installed, the caption of this button changes to Install, and clicking it installs the selected add-in.

You can also install new add-ins that aren't in the list by clicking the Add New button. This opens a browse dialog with which you can locate the library database containing the add-in. After you have found the add-in, Add-in Manager automatically copies it to the Addins directory and installs it. There is no way to prevent

Add-in Manager from copying the file. You can have add-ins in other directories, but your users will not be able to use Add-in Manager to administer them.

Creating the USysRegInfo Table

Add-in Manager depends on the existence of a table called USysRegInfo in your library database that contains your add-in's required Registry entries. USysRegInfo is composed of four fields. Table 18.11 lists each of these fields and its data type.

TABLE 18.11: Field Layout for the USysRegInfo Table

Field	Type	Remarks
Subkey	Text	Contains the name of the Registry subkey containing a specific Registry setting
Type	Number	Defines the type of entry to create: key (0), string (1), or DWORD (4)
ValName	Text	For Registry values, defines the name of the value
Value	Text	For Registry values, the actual value as text

The value in the Subkey field is the name of the Registry subkey you want Add-in Manager to create when it installs your add-in. Previous sections of this chapter described the keys that are necessary to install each of the various add-in types. You can have as many sets of entries in USysRegInfo as you wish. However, Registry entries that apply to a given add-in must all have the same value in the Subkey field.

When adding records to the USysRegInfo table for your own add-ins, the first record in each group should consist of the subkey name and the value 0 in the Type field. A Type of 0 instructs Add-in Manager to create the subkey. You must do this prior to adding values to it. Once you have created the subkey, you add values to it by adding more records to USysRegInfo.

The format of the Subkey value is important. All values in this field must begin with either "HKEY_LOCAL_MACHINE" or "HKEY_CURRENT_ACCESS_PROFILE". These strings have an identical effect when installing your add-in, except when you are using Access User Profiles. In this case, the latter string instructs Add-in Manager to create Registry entries beneath the current profile instead of beneath Access' normal Registry structure. Normally, you should use HKEY_CURRENT_ACCESS_ PROFILE unless you want to force Add-in

Manager to create entries under HKEY_LOCAL_MACHINE\Software\Microsoft\Office\8.0\Access. The remainder of the Subkey value is the Registry key structure beginning with the Access Registry key, including any preexisting keys.

Figure 18.25 shows the USysRegInfo table from our sample Form Wizard. Note the Subkey values that point to a new Registry key called Dialog Form Wizard. The first entry in the table creates the key (Type equals 0) and the rest add appropriate values for Library, Description, and so on. Note the string " | ACCDIR" in the Library entry's Value field. This is a token Add-in Manager will replace with the full path to the Addins directory when it installs the add-in.

FIGURE 18.25:

USysRegInfo values for the sample Form Wizard

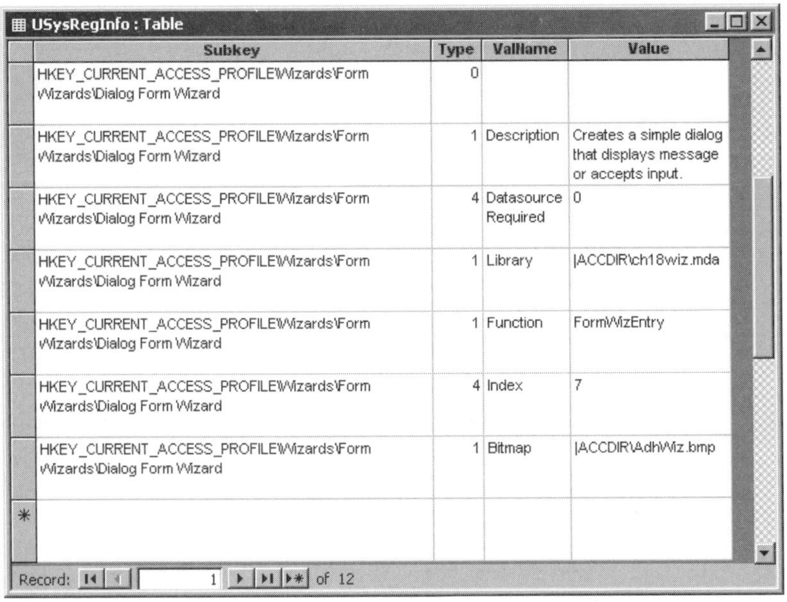

USysRegInfo : Table

Subkey	Type	ValName	Value
HKEY_CURRENT_ACCESS_PROFILE\Wizards\Form Wizards\Dialog Form Wizard	0		
HKEY_CURRENT_ACCESS_PROFILE\Wizards\Form Wizards\Dialog Form Wizard	1	Description	Creates a simple dialog that displays message or accepts input.
HKEY_CURRENT_ACCESS_PROFILE\Wizards\Form Wizards\Dialog Form Wizard	4	Datasource Required	0
HKEY_CURRENT_ACCESS_PROFILE\Wizards\Form Wizards\Dialog Form Wizard	1	Library	|ACCDIR\ch18wiz.mda
HKEY_CURRENT_ACCESS_PROFILE\Wizards\Form Wizards\Dialog Form Wizard	1	Function	FormWizEntry
HKEY_CURRENT_ACCESS_PROFILE\Wizards\Form Wizards\Dialog Form Wizard	4	Index	7
HKEY_CURRENT_ACCESS_PROFILE\Wizards\Form Wizards\Dialog Form Wizard	1	Bitmap	|ACCDIR\AdhWiz.bmp
*			

Record: 1 of 12

Examine the USysRegInfo tables in the other sample add-ins to see how to create Registry entries for every type of Wizard, builder, and add-in.

Advanced Add-In Topics

Finally, there are a few advanced Access 2000 features that relate to the development and distribution of add-ins. We discuss those in this section.

Restoring References Using VBA

In Access 95, references were, to say the least, troublesome. They were necessary due to the new architecture of VBA, yet developers had no programmatic control over them. The only way for an end user to use a library database was to add the reference manually. Fortunately, that changed for the better starting with Access 97. Access' Application object now contains a References collection populated with one Reference object for each reference in the current VBA project. You can use the collection and objects to view and even change VBA references. This gives you the capability to install and rebuild references using VBA code.

Table 18.12 lists the properties of a Reference object. You can use these to examine the characteristics of existing references using VBA code as follows. (You can find this code in the basListRefs module in CH18LIB.MDA.)

```
Dim ref As Reference

For Each ref In Application.References
    With ref
        Debug.Print .Name,
        Debug.Print .FullPath,
        Debug.Print IIf(.BuiltIn, "Required", ""),
        Debug.Print IIf(.Kind, "Project", "TypeLib: " _
         & .Guid),
        Debug.Print .Major & "." & .Minor,
        Debug.Print IIf(.IsBroken, "Missing!", "")
    End With
Next
```

TABLE 18.12: Properties of a Reference Object

Property	Description
BuiltIn	True if the reference is required for Access to operate. (For example, Access and VBA are both required.) Required references cannot be removed.
Collection	Pointer to the parent References collection.
FullPath	Full path to the type library, executable, or Access database the reference is linked to.
Guid	The GUID (Globally Unique Identifier) for the reference. Only type libraries and executable programs have GUIDs.
IsBroken	True if the reference has been broken (shown as Missing in the References dialog).

Continued on next page

TABLE 18.12 CONTINUED: Properties of a Reference Object

Property	Description
Kind	Type of reference. Returns 0 for a type library or executable and 1 for a VBA project (that is, an Access database).
Major	Major version number. Always 0 for VBA projects.
Minor	Minor version number. Always 0 for VBA projects.
Name	Reference name. For VBA projects, this is the project name unless the reference is broken. In this case, it will be the full path to the database (that is, the same as the FullPath property).

All the properties listed in Table 18.12 are read-only. You make changes to references using methods of the References collection. In addition to a Remove method, which you can use to remove broken references, the collection has two methods for adding references. AddFromFile accepts the path to an Access database as its only argument and adds a reference to it to the current project. AddFromGuid accepts a type library's GUID (Globally Unique Identifier) plus major and minor version numbers. This method looks up the GUID in the Windows Registry and adds a reference to the type library associated with it.

We've provided code in CH18LIB.MDA that adds a reference to the sample library to a user database. The function that accomplishes this, AddReference, is shown in Listing 18.10.

Listing 18.10

```
Function AddReference() As Variant
    Dim ref As Reference
    Dim strDBName As String
    Dim fOK As Boolean

    ' VBA project name
    Const conProject = "CH18Lib"

    On Error GoTo HandleError

    ' Get the name of this database
    strDBName = GetJustMDBName(CurrentDb.Name)
```

```
    ' Make sure reference isn't already added
    For Each ref In Application.References

        ' If reference name equals project name
        ' then we're okay!
        If ref.Name = conProject Then
            fOK = True
            Exit For

        ' If database name is contained in reference
        ' name then we've got a broken reference
        ElseIf GetJustMDBName(ref.Name) = strDBName Then

            ' Delete the bad reference
            References.Remove ref
            Exit For
        End If
    Next

    ' If we haven't fixed it then we have to add it
    If Not fOK Then
        References.AddFromFile CodeProject.Name
        MsgBox "Reference to " & CodeProject.Name & _
         " added.", vbInformation
    End If
ExitProc:
    Exit Function
HandleError:
    MsgBox Err.Description, vbExclamation, _
     "Error " & Err.Number
    Resume ExitProc
End Function
```

AddReference works by examining each of the references in the current project, comparing its name with the library's project name, CH18Lib. If a match is found, the reference exists and is valid. If, on the other hand, the database name is found, the reference exists but is currently broken. (When a reference to a database is broken, the Name property returns the last known path to the database.) In this case, the bad reference is removed.

After removing the missing reference (or failing to find any reference to the database at all), AddReference uses the AddFromFile method to create a new reference to the library.

So how does a user call this function if there is no reference to the library? Our sample library database contains a USysRegInfo table that establishes a Menu Add-in command to call the function. With this approach, end users can install the library once using Add-in Manager and then select the menu command to add a reference to any database they want!

Creating MDE Files

MDE files are Access databases containing modules that have been saved without the VBA source code. Instead, only the compiled VBA pseudocode is stored. This makes for a much smaller database than a normal MDB file, and one that is inherently much more secure. Since the source code is not included, there is no danger of an unscrupulous individual breaking in and stealing it.

NOTE This is actually how the Wizards in Access 95 were secured. At the time, Microsoft said they were secured using "an undocumented technique." Since the functionality was developed late in the development cycle, Microsoft chose not to make it available in Access 95 but instead to use it only to secure the Wizards.

Creating an MDE file is simple. Select Make MDE File from the Tools ➢ Database Utilities menu. At the prompt, you enter a new file name, to which Access appends the .MDE extension. When Access creates an MDE file, it compiles all the VBA source code and saves only the compiled state, discarding the source code itself. Access also compacts the database during the save process.

The database you use to create an MDE file must meet certain criteria:

- The code must be free of compile errors.
- If the database has been secured, you must have Read Design privileges for all objects.
- The database cannot be a replica or design master. (Once you create the MDE file, however, you can replicate it.)
- If the database references other Access databases, they must first be compiled into MDE files.

After conversion, some of the functionality of your database is altered due to the removal of VBA source code:

- You cannot view any module in the database.
- You cannot create any new forms, reports, or modules.
- You cannot use the Module methods described in the previous section to view or alter source code.
- You cannot change any references in the VBA project.
- You cannot change the VBA project name.
- You cannot export or import forms, reports, or modules; however, you can export and import tables, queries, and macros.
- The View Definition button in the Object Browser will be disabled if you examine modules and procedures in an MDE file.

Since creating an MDE file alters your database dramatically, be sure to keep a copy of the original MDB or MDA file. This copy will be necessary should you have to fix any errors in your VBA code.

WARNING

MDE files are version-specific. That is, if you create an MDE file using Access 2000, there is no guarantee that it will work with future major versions of Access. If you want to use your MDE with Access 2002 (or whatever the next version is called), you'll need to retain the original version of the database, convert it to the new version of Access, and then use the new version to create another MDE. What about minor releases (for example, 9.0a, 9.1, and so on), if there are any? Microsoft has stated they will make every effort not to break MDE functionality with minor (sometimes called *point*) releases, but they're not making any promises. In any event, make sure you keep a copy of the original database, just in case.

To programmatically determine whether a database has been converted to the MDE format, you can check a user-defined property of the database that Access adds during the conversion process. This property, called MDE, will return the letter *T* if the database is an MDE file. If the database is not an MDE file, the property will not exist. Listing 18.11 shows the adhIsMDE function, which accepts a database object pointer and returns True or False, depending on whether the database is an MDE.

Listing 18.11

```
Function adhIsMDE(dbAny As Database) As Boolean
    Dim varRet As Variant

    On Error Resume Next
    varRet = dbAny.Properties("MDE")
    adhIsMDE = (varRet = "T") And (Err.Number = 0)
End Function
```

WARNING

Be careful when creating MDE files from libraries containing a USysRegInfo table. If you create an MDE file, make sure you change the library name in the table to reflect the MDE file extension. Otherwise, Access will be unable to locate your add-in.

COM Add-Ins

With Office 2000, Microsoft has taken a bold step towards unifying the programming experience for developers working with Office. Prior to Office 2000, if you wanted to write add-ins for multiple Office applications, you needed to cope not only with object model differences but also with differences in project, storage, and deployment models. These differences manifested themselves particularly fiercely in the way add-ins were created for Office. Despite the fact that there are only five applications that make up the Office suite, Office 97 had nine different add-in models! This has all changed, however, with the COM Add-in architecture in Office 2000. We close this chapter with a discussion of this architecture and the benefits it provides. We will also demonstrate how to create and deploy a simple add-in.

NOTE

This section assumes some level of familiarity with COM and creating COM components. If you've never written a COM component with, say, Visual Basic, you may want to consult any of the following resources, all available from Sybex in Fall/Winter 1999: *Mastering COM and COM+* by Ash Rofail and Yasser Shohoud, *VB Developer's Guide to COM/COM+* by Wane S. Freeze, or *COM and COM+ Developer's Handbook* by Kate Gregory.

COM Add-In Pros and Cons

The primary benefit of the new COM Add-in architecture is that it's the same, regardless of application. Defined around a COM interface called IDTExtensibility2, the architecture defines how an add-in is registered with an application, how the add-in gets loaded, and what information is passed to the add-in regarding the application in which it is running. What this means is that the add-in need only worry about the application's object model, not the idiosyncrasies of how it gets loaded, unloaded, and so on.

What this also means is that it's perfectly feasible to create a single add-in that works in more than one application. As long as the add-in has code to detect the host application and respond to its object model you no longer have to create separate add-ins to add the same functionality to multiple applications. For instance, if you wanted to create an add-in that formatted tables of data in Word 97 and Excel 97, you would need two distinct add-ins, a Word DOT file and an Excel XLA file. In Office 2000, you can create a single add-in.

Lastly, since the new architecture is based on COM, you can use any COM-enabled tool, such as Microsoft Visual Basic, to create COM Add-ins. COM Add-ins are really nothing more than COM EXEs or DLLs that you can create with VB, C++, Delphi, or a host of other tools. (Of course, if the only development tool you know is Access you may be out of luck, since Access and VBA alone can't create COM components.)

So, why have we spent the bulk of this chapter discussing Access add-ins instead of COM Add-ins? The reason is that COM Add-ins are really only as useful as the events exposed by the host application and Access exposes almost no events. Think about how an add-in works. The host application loads the add-in and the add-in must decide what it will respond to and how. It could simply put a custom command bar button on the menu and wait for it to be clicked. If the application exposes interesting events, however, the add-in can create event sinks on those and respond when they occur. For instance, an Outlook COM Add-in could take action when new mail arrives in the Inbox. Since Access doesn't expose any useful events (save for those of forms and reports), COM Add-ins can only respond to menu commands.

Perhaps in the future Access will expose interesting events, such as when a new form is being created or when a property value is being changed. Until then, you must continue to use specialized Access builders and Wizards.

Using the COM Add-Ins Dialog

You may find it helpful while working through this part of the book to enable Access' COM Add-ins dialog. You'll need to dig for it, because it's not exposed on the menu structure by default. This is true for all Office applications, the rationale being that most users won't need to use the dialog if developers manage the loading and unloading of add-ins.

You'll find the menu command that opens the dialog in the Command Bar well. Just right-click on any Command Bar and choose Customize or select the Tools ➢ Customize menu command. Select the Commands tab on the Customize dialog and scroll the Categories list until you see the Tools category. Then scroll the Command list to locate the COM Add-ins command (it's at the very bottom—see Figure 18.26). Finally, drag the command onto the menu bar somewhere.

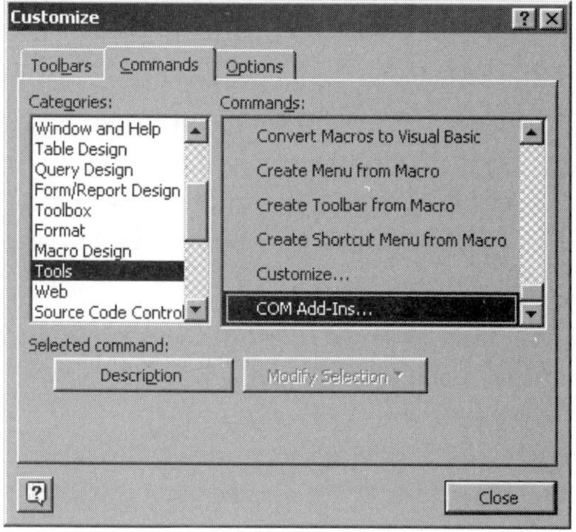

FIGURE 18.26: Locating the COM Add-ins menu command in the Customize dialog

Figure 18.27 shows the Office 2000 COM Add-ins dialog. The dialog lists each add-in registered with Access and displays a check box indicating whether it's loaded. You can use this to load or unload individual add-ins. You can also do this programmatically. See the section "The COMAddIns Collection" later on this chapter for more information on programmatically controlling add-ins.

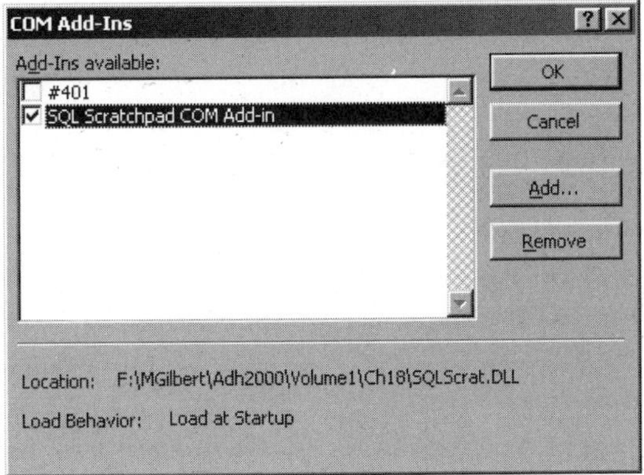

FIGURE 18.27: The COM Add-ins dialog shows those add-ins registered with Access.

Exploring IDTExtensibility2

The Office 2000 COM Add-in model is based on a COM interface called IDT-Extensibility2. A COM interface is a defined set of properties and methods that a COM component must support. In this case, IDTExtensibility2 defines a set of methods that allows an Office application to load and unload add-ins and pass them useful information. Table 18.13 lists the methods that make up IDTExtensibilty2. When you create your own COM Add-ins they must implement these methods.

TABLE 18.13: Methods Defined by IDTExtensibility2

Method	Description
OnAddinsUpdate	Called when an application's list of add-ins changes; for instance, if another add-in is loaded or unloaded
OnBeginShutdown	Called by the application prior to shutting down
OnConnection	Called when the add-in is loaded
OnDisconnection	Called when the add-in is unloaded
OnStartupComplete	Called by the application when it finishes its startup routines (i.e., when the application is in a ready state)

The two methods you'll use most often are OnConnection and OnDisconnection, as they denote the life span of an instance of your add-in. The others also have interesting uses.

OnConnection

When an application loads a COM Add-in that you've created and installed, it first creates an instance of your add-in using the COM CoCreateInstance function call. Once it has a pointer to an instance of your add-in, it attempts to call the OnConnection method. OnConnection accepts a number of parameters, as you can see from its prototype:

```
Private Sub AddinInstance_OnConnection( _
 ByVal Application As Object, _
 ByVal ConnectMode As AddInDesignerObjects.ext_ConnectMode, _
 ByVal AddInInst As Object, _
 custom() As Variant)

End Sub
```

The first argument, Application, is a pointer to the host application that's loading the add-in. In the case of Office, this will be the Application object of Access, Excel, Word, etc. You use this to determine what application you're running in and set up the mechanism for responding to events. (We'll explore this later in the section "Coding the Add-In.")

Additionally, OnConnection accepts a value indicating when the add-in was loaded. Table 18.14 lists the possible values for this argument.

TABLE 18.14: Startup Methods for a COM Add-In

Constant	Value	Description
ext_cm_AfterStartup	0	Add-in was loaded after the application was already running, either by selecting it in the COM Add-ins dialog or by programmatically controlling the host application's COMAddIns collection.
ext_cm_CommandLine	3	Not used for Office add-ins.
ext_cm_External	2	Not used for Office add-ins.
ext_cm_Startup	1	Add-in was loaded at application startup.

NOTE Two of the startup modes are not supported by COM Add-ins that work with Microsoft Office. They are used with add-ins for Visual Basic and the Microsoft Development Environment (the shell for Visual J++), which also support IDTExtensibility2.

NOTE The enumerated constants in Table 18.14 are defined by the COM Add-in Designer DLL that ships with Visual Basic and Microsoft Office 2000 Developer. We used the Designer to create our sample add-in. If you choose not to use the Designer or create your add-in using other tools like C++ or Delphi, you'll need to either define these constants yourself or use the numeric values in Table 18.14.

The AddInInst argument is a pointer to the instance of the add-in itself. It's useful for determining properties of the add-in at runtime. We'll use this later to show you how to create a command button that loads an add-in automatically.

Finally, the last argument, custom, is a Variant array that contains additional information that may be passed by the application. Currently only one piece of information is passed by Office applications. It tells you how the host application was started and is stored in the first element of the array. Custom(1) will return 1 if the application was loaded normally (i.e., from the Start menu or by opening an Office document), 2 if the application was started by embedding one document inside another, and 3 if the application was started via Automation. You can use this to decide not to enable your add-in's functionality if, for instance, the host application was started by activating an embedded document.

OnDisconnection

OnDisconnection is the counterpart to OnConnection. It's called when an add-in is being unloaded from the host application. It's your chance to perform housekeeping tasks like deleting menu items or dropping database connections. OnDisconnection is similar to OnConnection in that your add-in will be passed information during the event. Take a look at the procedure definition:

```
Private Sub AddinInstance_OnDisconnection( _
 ByVal RemoveMode As AddInDesignerObjects.ext_DisconnectMode, _
 custom() As Variant)

End Sub
```

RemoveMode will be one of two values: ext_dm_HostShutdown (0) if the host application itself is shutting down, or ext_dm_UserClosed (1) if the user deselected the add-in using the COM Add-ins dialog. (RemoveMode will also be ext_dm_UserClosed if an application programmatically unloads the add-in using the COMAddIns collection.)

The custom argument contains the same information as the argument of the same name in OnConnection.

Other Add-In Methods

While you'll probably use OnConnection and OnDisconnection the most, you may occasionally write code for the other add-in methods. For instance, if your add-in depends on the host application being in a completely ready state, you may delay taking any action until the OnStartupComplete method is called.

Likewise, if your add-in depends on other add-ins, you can write code in the OnAddInsUpdate method to check to see if the add-ins are still loaded. OnAddIns-Update is called whenever an application's list of loaded add-ins changes, either by the user selecting or deselecting them from the COM Add-ins dialog or through code. All Office applications implement a COMAddIns collection that your add-in can query for the existence of other add-ins (and even load or unload them).

The COMAddIns Collection

To help you manage COM Add-ins, every Office application implements a COMAddIns collection. You can use this as you would any other collection to iterate through the list of add-ins registered with the application. For example, you can run the following VBA code in Access to view its add-ins:

```
Sub ListAddins()
    Dim objAddIn As COMAddIn

    ' Iterate through list of add-ins
    For Each objAddIn In COMAddIns
        With objAddIn
            Debug.Print .Description, .Connect
        End With
    Next
End Sub
```

NOTE

Before running the code shown above, you'll need to add a reference to the Office 9 type library, since that's where the COMAddIn object is declared.

Table 18.15 lists the collection's properties and methods. You'll notice that while you can iterate through existing add-ins, there is no way to add new ones. That's because the only way to add new COM Add-ins is to make Registry entries. Normally, this happens automatically when the add-in itself is registered. See the section "COM Add-In Registry Entries" later in the chapter for more information on COM Add-in Registry entries.

TABLE 18.15: Properties and Methods of the Application's COMAddIns Collection

Property or Method	Description
Application property	Returns a pointer to the host application.
Count	Returns the number of add-ins in the collection.
Parent	Same as Application.
Item	Returns a particular COMAddIn object.
Update	Updates the collection. This should be used after an add-in has been added or removed from the system while an application is running.

It's no surprise that the COMAddIns is a collection of COMAddIn objects. Table 18.16 lists the properties for the COMAddIn class.

TABLE 18.16: Properties of the COMAddIn Class

Property	Description
Application	Returns a pointer to the host application.
Connect	True/False value indicating whether the add-in is loaded. You use this to load or unload individual add-ins.
Description	Description of the add-in as it appears in the COM Add-ins dialog.
Guid	Global unique identifier of the COM component that implements the add-in.
Object	Returns a pointer to the running instance of the add-in if it's loaded.
Parent	Same as Application.
ProgId	Returns the ProgId for the add-in (e.g., "MyAddin.Init").

In addition to being able to see the description of each add-in, you can use the Connect property to load or unload individual add-ins. You might use this, say, to load a series of add-ins required by one of yours. Once loaded, you can use the Object property to return the running instance of each add-in. This lets your add-in communicate with other add-ins using any public properties or methods they expose.

Building a Simple COM Add-In

There's no better way to explore the ins and outs of COM Add-ins than by building a sample add-in. We've created an add-in that replicates the functionality of the SQL Scratchpad add-in described earlier in this chapter so you can see how they differ. Remember that the Scratchpad add-in described earlier was implemented as an Access library database and registered with Access as a menu add-in using the Add-in Manager and USysRegInfo table. While much of the code was salvageable, our COM Add-in version required a completely new user interface and new code to manipulate Access' Command Bar structure.

NOTE

We've included two versions of the add-in on the companion CD-ROM. One uses the COM Add-in Designer that ships as part of Microsoft Office 2000 Developer, and the other is implemented using Visual Basic 6. If you want to compile and test these, you'll need a copy of MOD or VB.

Using the COM Add-In Designer

The easiest way to create COM Add-ins is by using the COM Add-in Designer that ships as part of Visual Basic 6 or Microsoft Office 2000 Developer. The Designer takes care of implementing the IDTExtensibility2 COM interface and includes a user interface for specifying options that enable the add-in to register itself with an Office application. If you don't use the Designer, you'll need to handle all these details yourself. Figure 18.28 shows the Designer window open in our SQL Scratchpad add-in project.

TIP

To load the project in Visual Basic 6, open the SQLSCRAT.VBP project file. To load the project using the Office 2000 Developer COM Add-in Designer, open the SQLSCRAT.VBA file from the VBA Editor in Microsoft Excel. Note that you must use Excel since Access does not allow the insertion of MSForms dialogs into VBA projects. The add-in uses an MSForms dialog for its user interface.

FIGURE 18.28:

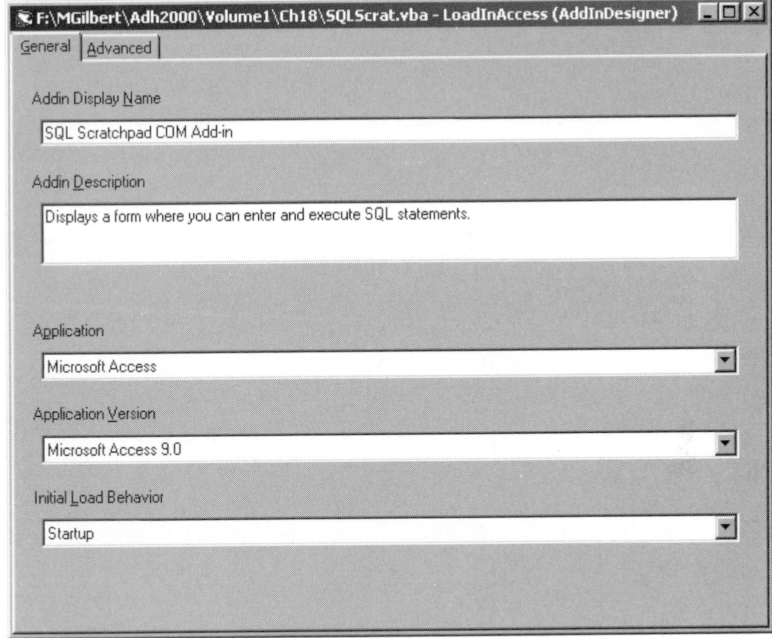

COM Add-in Designer window showing options for the SQL Scratchpad project

You use the Designer's UI to set basic options for the add-in. Table 18.17 lists each field and its purpose.

TABLE 18.17: Settable Options in the COM Add-In Designer

Option	Description
Addin Display Name	Sets the display name as it will appear in the COM Add-ins dialog; also sets the value of the COMAddIn object's Description property
Addin Description	Sets the description as it will appear in the COM Add-ins dialog when a user selects the add-in from the list
Application	Defines the host application for this instance of the designer
Application Version	Controls the version for which this add-in is intended; only version 9 is currently supported
Initial Load Behavior	Sets the initial load behavior of the add-in (see below)

The Advanced tab of the Designer lets you supply additional information that will be compiled into the add-in. Figure 18.29 shows the Advanced tab. Using this tab, you can specify a satellite DLL for your project. Satellite DLLs are used to provide localized resources separate from the add-in to aid developers distributing solutions in multiple languages. For more information on satellite DLLs, consult a Visual Basic resource such as the MSDN online library (`http://msdn.microsoft.com/`).

FIGURE 18.29:

Advanced COM Add-in properties

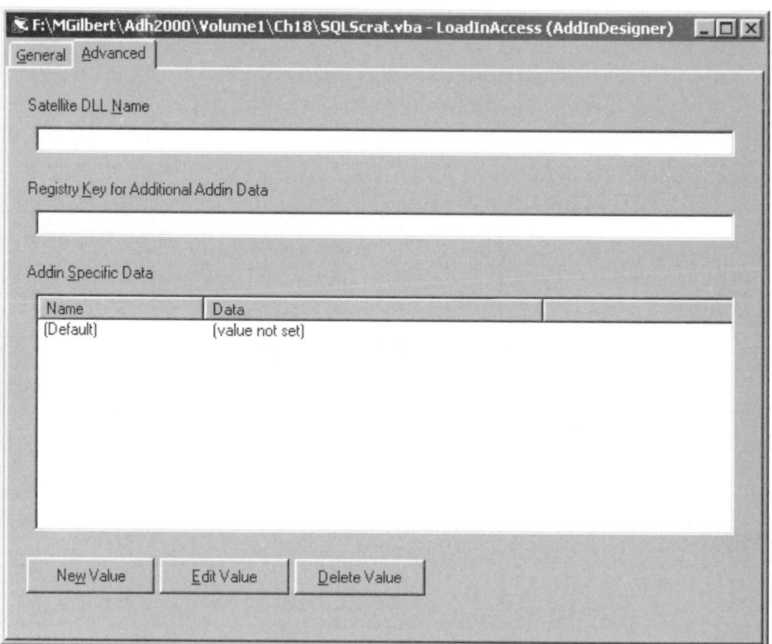

The Advanced tab also lets you specify additional Registry values under a key of your choosing that the add-in will create when it's registered with the operating system. You could use this, for instance, to set preference data into the Registry when the add-in is first installed. Simply set the Registry you want to use to store the data (e.g., HKEY_CURRENT_USER\Software\VB & VBA Program Settings) and then use the command buttons to add, edit, or delete Registry values.

Specifying Add-In Load Behavior

Add-in load behavior is probably the most important setting on the Designer's dialog because it controls how and when your add-in gets loaded into the host application. There are four possible settings for this option: None, Startup, Load at Startup Only, and Load on Demand.

None When you choose None as the load behavior, your add-in will not be loaded automatically by the host application. It will, however, still show up in the COM Add-ins dialog so the user can load it. You can also load it programmatically by setting the add-in's Connect property to True using the object model.

Startup Loading an add-in at startup will likely be the option you choose most often. When an add-in loads at startup, it appears as if it's part of the host application—a new feature—and the user never has to deal with the COM Add-ins dialog.

Load on Next Startup Only You may decide to load an add-in automatically the next time the host application starts but not thereafter. This allows you to create an add-in that is loaded *on demand*. (See the section titled "Creating a Demand-Loaded Add-In" later in this chapter.) After loading the first time, the add-in automatically reverts to a Load on Demand state (described next).

Load on Demand This last option is not one you should choose directly. It exists only to report on an add-in that has been set to this state by a previous setting of Load on Next Startup Only.

Our sample add-in is set to load at startup.

Coding the Add-In

Once you've set the initial load behavior and other options, it's time to write some code. The COM Add-in Designer that ships with Office 2000 Developer does not include any code for you to work from, although the code you need is pretty simple. Visual Basic 6 ships with an add-in template project with some sample code, although you'll need to modify it to work with Office applications.

The most important coding task is writing code in the OnConnection event to "hook" your add-in into the host application somehow. This can be done through a custom menu command or toolbar button or through sinking to one of the application's events. As we stated earlier, Access supplies virtually no events to work with, so our example uses a custom Command Bar button.

Listing 18.12 shows the code behind our Designer. (To view this code in the Visual Basic Editor, just activate the Designer and select the View ➢ Code menu command, or press F7.)

Listing 18.12

```
Public WithEvents MenuCommand As Office.CommandBarButton

Private Sub AddinInstance_OnConnection( _
 ByVal Application As Object, _
 ByVal ConnectMode As AddInDesignerObjects.ext_ConnectMode, _
 ByVal AddInInst As Object, custom() As Variant)

    ' Set a reference to the host application
    Set AccessInst = Application

    ' Add the custom menu command
    Set MenuCommand = AddMenuCommand(Application, AddInInst)
End Sub

Private Sub AddinInstance_OnDisconnection( _
 ByVal RemoveMode As AddInDesignerObjects.ext_DisconnectMode, _
 custom() As Variant)

    ' Remove the custom menu command
    MenuCommand.Delete

End Sub

Private Sub MenuCommand_Click( _
 ByVal Ctrl As Office.CommandBarButton, _
 CancelDefault As Boolean)

    ' Show the SQL Scratchpad form
    frmSQLScratchPad.Show vbModeless
End Sub
```

There are several things to note in this code. First, we use a custom function, AddMenuCommand, to add the custom menu command. This makes our code more manageable by moving it out of the OnConnection event. Second, the menu command we add in the OnConnection event is removed in the OnDisconnection event by calling its Delete method. Finally, we've declared the module-level CommandBarButton variable using the WithEvents keyword. This provides our sink into the button's Click event. We respond to this event by showing the scratchpad form.

Listing 18.13 shows the code that makes up the AddMenuCommand function, which is defined in basCommandBars. (Note that we've also included the constant declarations for readability, even though they're declared in a different module.)

Listing 18.13

```
Private Const conMenuIDTools = 30007
Private Const conMenuName = "SQL Scratchpad"

Function AddMenuCommand(cbrMenu As Office.CommandBar, _
 AddInInst As Object) _
 As Office.CommandBarButton

    Dim cbcTools As Office.CommandBarPopup
    Dim cbcSQL As Office.CommandBarButton

    ' Get a pointer to the Tools menu
    Set cbcTools = cbrMenu.FindControl( _
     ID:=conMenuIDTools, Recursive:=False)

    ' If we found the Tools menu then add
    ' a new menu command (but only if it doesn't
    ' already exist!)
    If Not cbcTools Is Nothing Then

        ' Try to find the command based on its tag
        Set cbcSQL = cbcTools.CommandBar.FindControl( _
         Tag:=conMenuName, Recursive:=False)

        ' If we didn't find it, add a new command
        If cbcSQL Is Nothing Then
            Set cbcSQL = cbcTools.Controls.Add( _
             Type:=msoControlButton)
            With cbcSQL
                .Caption = conMenuName
                .Style = msoButtonCaption
                .Tag = conMenuName

                ' This enables demand loading
                .OnAction = "!<" & AddInInst.ProgId & ">"
            End With
        End If
```

```
        ' Return pointer to menu command
        Set AddMenuCommand = cbcSQL
    End If

End Function
```

This procedure adds a custom menu command to the bottom of the Tools menu (specified by the control ID 30007) and sets its Caption, Style, and Tag properties. Setting the Tag property is critical because it enables the procedure to search for the menu command before trying to add it. If it did not do this, it would risk adding multiple menu commands if the add-in terminated abnormally or otherwise failed to clean up after itself properly.

NOTE For more information on manipulating command bars, see Chapter 11.

From here on out, the code behind the SQL Scratchpad form is pretty similar to our Access library-based add-in, and we'll leave it to you to explore if you'd like.

Debugging, Compiling, and Distributing

The added twist to debugging COM Add-ins is that because they are developed using a traditional programming tool, you must explicitly execute the add-in before you can debug it. In the case of the Office 2000 Developer COM Add-in Designer, you do this by clicking the Run Project button on the toolbar (as opposed to the Run Sub/Userform button). With add-ins created using Visual Basic, you simply click the Run button. Other than that, debugging works just like it does with regular VBA projects. For instance, you can add a breakpoint in the OnConnection event to step through the startup code.

After you've tested and debugged your add-in, it's time to compile it. To do so, select the File ➢ Make command from the Visual Basic Editor. This creates a COM DLL (or potentially a COM EXE if you're using Visual Basic) on your hard disk. It also creates the required Registry entries that associate the add-in with a host application on your development machine. You still need to cope with deploying the add-in to your users.

Once you've created the add-in, you can distribute it to others. Since it's a COM component, you'll need to register the component of each user's computer. If you want to do this manually, for instance, to test your add-in on another developer's computer, you can use the REGSVR32 program. Just copy your add-in to a directory on the hard drive and run REGSVR32 from a DOS prompt as follows:

```
REGSVR32 <addinpath>\<addinfile>
```

REGSVR32 is normally installed in the Windows\System directory. If this directory is not in your PATH statement, you'll need to modify the command line. You can also unregister the add-in using the /u flag:

```
REGSVR32 /u <addinpath>\<addinfile>
```

It's unlikely you'll want to install your add-in manually on every user's workstation. Instead, you'll want to use a setup program that will automatically install and register the add-in. The Package and Deployment Wizard that ships with both Visual Basic and Microsoft Office 2000 Developer creates setup programs that will do this.

COM Add-In Registry Entries

One thing that differentiates an Office COM Add-in from regular COM components is the set of Registry entries that associates it with a particular host application. We'll document these here, although if you use the COM Add-in Designer to create your add-ins, you probably won't need to worry about them unless you need to troubleshoot a misbehaving add-in.

Office applications look in two related locations in the Registry to determine which add-ins they should load. Add-in information is stored under \Software\Microsoft\Office\<*application*>\Addins for both the HKEY_LOCAL_MACHINE and HKEY_CURRENT_USER hives. The difference is that those add-ins listed under the former hive are available to all users of a workstation, while those listed under the latter hive are only available to the current user.

NOTE Another difference between the two hives is that only those add-ins listed under HKEY_CURRENT_USER show up in the COM Add-ins dialog.

When you register a COM Add-in, it creates a subkey that is its Prog ID. Figure 18.30 shows the Windows Registry Editor open to the add-ins key for Access. You can see the subkey for our SQL Scratchpad add-in—its Prog ID is SQLScratchpad.LoadInAccess.

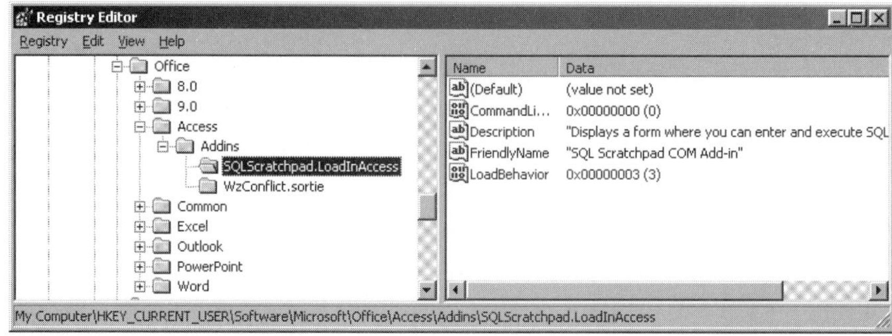

FIGURE 18.30: Registry entries for the sample SQL Scratchpad COM Add-in

At load time, Access, or any other Office application, reads the subkeys, looking for registered add-ins. It then looks at values for each key to determine whether to load the add-in. Table 18.18 lists the Registry values defined for COM Add-ins. LoadBehavior is the value that controls whether an Office application loads the add-in at startup or not.

TABLE 18.18: Registry Values for COM Add-Ins

Value Name	Data Type	Description
CommandLineSafe	DWORD	Determines whether the add-in can be launched from a command line—not applicable to Office COM Add-ins and should be set to 0
Description	String	Description of the add-in that will appear in the COM Add-ins dialog when a user selects the add-in
FriendlyName	String	Name of the add-in that will appear in the list of add-ins in the COM Add-ins dialog
LoadBehavior	DWORD	Load behavior of the add-in: 0 = none 3 = startup 9 = on demand 16 = next startup only
SatelliteDLLName	String	Name of add-in's satellite DLL, if it has one

Targeting Multiple Applications

We mentioned earlier in the chapter that one benefit of the COM Add-in architecture is that you can create a single add-in that targets multiple applications. In fact, if you've examined our sample add-in, you'll see that it does just that. Not only does it work within Access but it works in Excel, too.

To create an add-in that works in multiple applications, all you need to do is add an additional COM Add-in Designer to the project and choose the application you want to target.

Creating a Demand-Loaded Add-In

One final topic with regard to COM Add-ins is the creation of *demand-loaded* add-ins. A demand-loaded add-in is one that is not loaded into memory until the user clicks on a menu command. If you're creating an add-in that your users will seldom use, you can cause Access to load it on demand to reduce startup time associated with loading the add-in each time Access is started.

The key to creating demand-loaded add-ins is setting the OnAction property of a Command Bar button to a specially formatted string that contains an add-in's Prog ID. When a user clicks the button, Access reads the Prog ID, loads the add-in, and calls its OnConnection method. Our sample add-in actually does this when it's loaded at startup. Here's the line of code from the AddMenuCommand procedure that does it:

```
' This enables demand loading
.OnAction = "!<" & AddInInst.ProgId & ">"
```

Note that the OnAction string begins with "!<", ends with ">", and includes the add-in's Prog ID. The full string would look something like "!<SQLScratchpad.LoadInAccess>".

To turn our startup-loaded add-in into a demand-loaded add-in, all you need to do is change the Designer's Load Behavior setting to Load on Next Startup Only and then remove the line of code in the OnDisconnection event that removes the custom menu command. If you don't do the latter, there will be no way for your user to load your add-in!

Summary

In this chapter, we explored the very powerful capabilities of Access Wizards. Creating custom Wizards allows you to invest your users with specialized tools that appear as built-in features of Access. Specifically, we covered the following topics:

- Where Wizard Registry entries are stored
- How to launch a function from the Add-ins menu
- How to create a builder to help users change property settings
- How to design a custom Wizard using our Wizard framework
- How to make it easy for your users to install your add-in using Add-in Manager
- How to change references using VBA code
- How to manipulate module code using VBA
- How to create an MDE file
- How to create and use COM Add-ins with Access

The information contained in this chapter should help you create your own custom Wizards easily and quickly.

APPENDIX A

The Reddick VBA Naming Conventions, Version 6

The purpose of the Reddick VBA (RVBA) Naming Conventions is to provide a guideline for naming objects in the Visual Basic for Applications (VBA) language. Having conventions is valuable in any programming project. When you use them, the name of the object conveys information about the meaning of the object. These conventions attempt to provide a way of standardizing that meaning across the body of VBA programmers.

VBA is implemented to interact with a host application—for example, Microsoft Access, Microsoft Visual Basic, AutoCAD, and Visio. The RVBA conventions cover all implementations of the VBA language, regardless of the host application. Some of the tags described in this appendix may not necessarily have an implementation within some of the particular host programs for VBA. The word *object,* in the context of this appendix, refers to simple variables and VBA objects, as well as to objects made available by the VBA host program.

While I am the editor of these conventions, they are the work of many people, including Charles Simonyi, who invented the Hungarian conventions on which these are based, and Stan Leszynski, who co-authored several versions of the conventions. Many others, too numerous to mention, have also contributed to the development and distribution of these conventions.

These conventions are intended as a guideline. If you disagree with a particular part of the conventions, simply replace that part with what you think works better. However, keep in mind that future generations of programmers may need to understand those changes, and place a comment in the header of a module indicating what changes have been made. The conventions are presented without rationalizations for how they were derived, although each of the ideas presented has a considerable history to it.

Changes to the Conventions

Some of the tags in the version of the conventions presented here have changed from previous versions. Consider all previous tags to be grandfathered into the conventions—you don't need to go back and make changes. For new development work, I leave it up to you to decide whether to use the older tags or the ones suggested here. In a few places in this appendix, older tags are shown in {braces}. As updates to this appendix are made, the current version can be found at `http://www.xoc.net`.

An Introduction to Hungarian

The RVBA conventions are based on the Hungarian conventions for constructing object names (they were named for the native country of the inventor, Charles Simonyi). The objective of Hungarian is to convey information about the object concisely and efficiently. Hungarian takes some getting used to, but once adopted, it quickly becomes second nature. The format of a Hungarian object name is

```
[prefixes]tag[BaseName[Suffixes]]
```

The square brackets indicate optional parts of the object name. These components have the following meanings:

Component	**Meaning**
Prefixes	Modify the tag to indicate additional information. Prefixes are all lowercase. They are usually picked from a standardized list of prefixes, given later in this appendix.
Tag	Short set of characters, usually mnemonic, that indicates the type of the object. The tag is all lowercase. It is usually selected from a standardized list of tags, given later in this appendix.
BaseName	One or more words that indicate what the object represents. The first letter of each word in the BaseName is capitalized.
Suffixes	Additional information about the meaning of the BaseName. The first letter of each word in the Suffix is capitalized. They are usually picked from a standardized list of suffixes, given later in this appendix.

Notice that the only required part of the object name is the tag. This may seem counterintuitive; you may feel that the BaseName is the most important part of the object name. However, consider a generic procedure that operates on any form. The fact that the routine operates on a form is the important thing, not what that form represents. Because the routine may operate on forms of many different types, you do not necessarily need a BaseName. However, if you have more than one object of a type referenced in the routine, you must have a BaseName on all but one of the object names to differentiate them. Also, unless the routine is generic, the BaseName conveys information about the variable. In most cases, a variable should include a BaseName.

Tags

You use tags to indicate the data type of an object, and you construct them using the techniques described in the following sections.

Variable Tags

Use the tags listed in Table A.1 for VBA data types. You can also use a specific tag instead of *obj* for any data type defined by the host application or one of its objects. (See the section "Host Application and Component Extensions to the Conventions" later in this appendix.)

TABLE A.1: Tables for VBA Variables

Tag	Object Type
bool {f, bln}	Boolean
byte {byt}	Byte
cur	Currency
date {dtm}	Date
dec	Decimal
dbl	Double
int	Integer
lng	Long
obj	Object
sng	Single
str	String
stf	String (fixed length)
var	Variant

Here are several examples:

```
lngCount
intValue
strInput
```

You should explicitly declare all variables, each on a line by itself. Do not use the old-type declaration characters, such as %, &, and $. They are extraneous if you use the naming conventions, and there is no character for some of the data types, such as Boolean. You should always explicitly declare all variables of type Variant using the *As Variant* clause, even though it is the default in VBA. For example:

```
Dim intTotal As Integer
Dim varField As Variant
Dim strName As String
```

Constructing Properties Names

Properties of a class present a particular problem: Should they include the naming convention to indicate the type? To be consistent with the rest of these naming conventions, they should. However, it is permitted to have property names without the tags, especially if the class is to be made available to customers who may not be familiar with these naming conventions.

Collection Tags

You treat a collection object with a special tag. You construct the tag using the data type of the collection followed by the letter *s*. For example, if you had a collection of Longs, the tag would be lngs. If it were a collection of forms, the collection would be frms. Although, in theory, a collection can hold objects of different data types, in practice, each of the data types in the collection is the same. If you do want to use different data types in a collection, use the tag objs. For example:

```
intsEntries
frmsCustomerData
objsMisc
```

Constants

Constants always have a data type in VBA. Because VBA will choose this data type for you if you don't specify it, you should always specify the data type for a constant. Constants declared in the General Declarations section of a module should always have a scope keyword of Private or Public and be prefixed by the scope prefixes *m* or *g*, respectively. A constant is indicated by appending the letter *c* to the end of the data type for the constant. For example:

```
Const intcGray As Integer = 3
Private Const mdblcPi As Double = 3.14159265358979
```

Although this technique is the recommended method of naming constants, if you are more concerned about specifying that you are dealing with constants rather than their data type, you can alternatively use the generic tag *con* instead. For example:

```
Const conPi As Double = 3.14159265358979
```

Menu Items

The names of menu items should reflect their position in the menu hierarchy. All menu items should use the tag mnu, but the BaseName should indicate where in the hierarchy the menu item falls. Use *Sep* in the BaseName to indicate a menu separator bar, followed by an ordinal. For example:

```
mnuFile (on menu bar)
mnuFileNew (on File popup menu)
mnuFileNewForm (on File New flyout menu)
mnuFileNewReport (on File New flyout menu)
mnuFileSep1 (first separator bar on file popup menu)
mnuFileSaveAs (on File popup menu)
mnuFileSep2 (second separator bar on file popup menu)
mnuFileExit (on File popup menu)
mnuEdit (on menu bar)
```

Creating Data Types

VBA gives you three ways to create new data types: enumerated types, classes, and user-defined types. In each case, you will need to invent a new tag that represents the data type that you create.

Enumerated Types

Groups of constants of the *Long* data type should be made an enumerated type. Invent a tag for the type, append a *c*, then define the enumerated constants using that tag. Because the name used in the Enum line is seen in the object browser, you can add a BaseName to the tag to spell out the abbreviation indicated by the tag. For example:

```
Public Enum ervcErrorValue
    ervcInvalidType = 205
    ervcValueOutOfBounds
End Enum
```

The BaseName should be singular, so that the enumerated type should be ervcErrorValue, not ervcErrorValues. The tag that you invent for enumerated types can then be used for variables that can contain values of that type. For example:

```
Dim erv As ervcErrorValue
Private Sub Example(ByVal ervCur As ervcErrorValue)
```

While VBA only provides enumerated types of groups of the Long type, you can still create groups of constants of other types. Just create a set of constant definitions using an invented tag. For example:

```
Public Const estcError205 As String = "Invalid type"
Public Const estcError206 As String = "Value out of bounds"
```

Unfortunately, because this technique doesn't actually create a new type, you don't get the benefit of the VBA compiler performing type checking for you. You create variables that will hold constants using a similar syntax to variables meant to hold instances of enumerated types. For example:

```
Dim estError As String
```

Tags for Classes and User-Defined Types

A class defines a user-defined object. Because these invent a new data type, you will need to invent a new tag for the object. You can add a BaseName to the tag to spell out the abbreviation indicated by the tag. User-defined types are considered a simple class with only properties, but in all other ways are used the same as class modules. For example:

```
gphGlyph
edtEdit
Public Type grbGrabber
```

You then define variables to refer to instances of the class using the same tag: For example:

```
Dim gphNext As New gphGlyph
Dim edtCurrent as edtEdit
Dim grbHandle as grbGrabber
```

Polymorphism

In VBA, you use the *Implements* statement to derive classes from a base class. The tag for the derived class should use the same tag as the base class. The derived classes, though, should use a different BaseName from the base class. For example:

```
anmAnimal (base class)
anmZebra (derived class of anmAnimal)
anmElephant (derived class of anmAnimal)
```

This logic of naming derived classes is used with forms, which are all derived from the predefined Form base class and use the frm tag. If a variable is defined to be of the type of the base class, then use the tag, as usual. For example:

```
Dim anmArbitrary As anmAnimal
Dim frmNew As Form
```

On the other hand, if you define a variable as an instance of a derived class, include the complete derived class name in the variable name. For example:

```
Dim anmZebraInstance As anmZebra
Dim anmElephantExample As anmElephant
Dim frmCustomerData As frmCustomer
```

Constructing Procedures

VBA procedures require you to name various items: procedure names, parameters, and labels. These objects are described in the following sections.

Constructing Procedure Names

VBA names event procedures, and you cannot change them. You should use the capitalization defined by the system. For user-defined procedure names, capitalize the first letter of each word in the name. For example:

```
cmdOK_Click
GetTitleBarString
PerformInitialization
```

Procedures should always have a scope keyword, Public or Private, when they are declared. For example:

```
Public Function GetTitleBarString() As String
Private Sub PerformInitialization
```

Naming Parameters

You should prefix all parameters in a procedure definition with ByVal or ByRef, even though ByRef is optional and redundant. Procedure parameters are named the same as simple variables of the same type, except that arguments passed by reference use the prefix *r*. For example:

```
Public Sub TestValue(ByVal intInput As Integer, ByRef rlngOutput As Long)
Private Function GetReturnValue(ByVal strKey As String, ByRef rgph As
Glyph) As Boolean
```

Naming Labels

Labels are named using upper- and lowercase, capitalizing the first letter of each word. For example:

```
ErrorHandler:
ExitProcedure:
```

Prefixes

Prefixes modify an object tag to indicate more information about an object.

Arrays of Objects Prefix

Arrays of an object type use the prefix *a*. For example:

```
aintFontSizes
astrNames
```

Index Prefix

You indicate an index into an array by the prefix *i*, and, for consistency, the data type should always be a Long. You may also use the index prefix to index into other enumerated objects, such as a collection of user-defined classes. For example:

```
iaintFontSizes
iastrNames
igphsGlyphCollection
```

Prefixes for Scope and Lifetime

Three levels of scope exist for each variable in VBA: Public, Private, and Local. A variable also has a lifetime of the current procedure or the lifetime of the object in which it is defined. Use the prefixes in Table A.2 to indicate scope and lifetime.

TABLE A.2: Scope Prefixes

Prefix	Object Type
(none)	Local variable, procedure-level lifetime, declared with *Dim*
s	Local variable, object lifetime, declared with *Static*
m	Private (module) variable, object lifetime, declared with *Private*
g	Public (global) variable, object lifetime, declared with *Public*

You also use the *m* and *g* constants with other objects, such as constants, to indicate their scope. For example:

```
intLocalVariable
mintPrivateVariable
gintPublicVariable
mdblcPi
```

VBA allows several type declaration words for backward compatibility. The older keyword Global should always be replaced by Public, and the Dim keyword in the General Declarations section should be replaced by Private.

Other Prefixes

Table A.3 lists and describes some other prefixes:

TABLE A.3: Other Commonly Used Prefixes

Prefix	Object Type
c	Count of some object type
h	Handle to a Windows object
r	Parameter passed by reference

Here are some examples:

```
castrArray
hWndForm
```

Suffixes

Suffixes modify the base name of an object, indicating additional information about a variable. You'll likely create your own suffixes that are specific to your development work. Table A.4 lists some generic VBA suffixes.

TABLE A.4: Commonly Used Suffixes

Suffix	Object Type
Min	The absolute first element in an array or other kind of list.
First	The first element to be used in an array or list during the current operation.
Last	The last element to be used in an array or list during the current operation.
Lim	The upper limit of elements to be used in an array or list. Lim is not a valid index. Generally, Lim equals Last + 1.
Max	The absolutely last element in an array or other kind of list.
Cnt	Used with database elements to indicate that the item is a Counter. Counter fields are incremented by the system and are numbers of either type Long or type Replication Id.

Here are some examples:

```
iastrNamesMin
iastrNamesMax
iaintFontSizesFirst
igphsGlyphCollectionLast
lngCustomerIdCnt
varOrderIdCnt
```

File Names

When naming items stored on the disk, no tag is needed because the extension already gives the object type. For example:

```
Test.Frm (frmTest form)
Globals.Bas (globals module)
Glyph.Cls (gphGlyph class module)
```

Host Application and Component Extensions to the Conventions

Each host application for VBA, as well as each component that can be installed, has a set of objects it can use. This section defines tags for the objects in the various host applications and components.

Access 2000, Version 9 Objects

Table A.5 lists Access object variable tags. Besides being used in code to refer to these object types, these same tags are used to name these kinds of objects in the form and report designers.

TABLE A.5: Access Object Variable Tags

Tag	Object Type
aob	AccessObject
aops	AccessObjectProperties
aop	AccessObjectProperty
app	Application
bfr	BoundObjectFrame
chk	CheckBox
cbo	ComboBox
cmd	CommandButton
ctl	Control
ctls	Controls
ocx	CustomControl
dap	DataAccessPage
dcm	DoCmd
frm	Form
fcd	FormatCondition
fcds	FormatConditions
frms	Forms

Continued on next page

TABLE A.5 CONTINUED: Access Object Variable Tags

Tag	Object Type
grl	GroupLevel
hyp	Hyperlink
img	Image
lbl	Label
lin	Line
lst	ListBox
bas	Module
ole	ObjectFrame
opt	OptionButton
fra	OptionGroup (frame)
brk	PageBreak
pal	PaletteButton
prps	Properties
shp	Rectangle
ref	Reference
refs	References
rpt	Report
rpts	Reports
scr	Screen
sec	Section
sfr	SubForm
srp	SubReport
tab	TabControl
txt	TextBox
tgl	ToggleButton

Some examples:

```
txtName
lblInput
```

For ActiveX custom controls, you can use the tag ocx as specified in Table A.5 or more specific object tags that are listed later in this appendix in Tables A.14 and A.15. For an ActiveX control that doesn't appear in the Tables A.14 or A.15, you can either use ocx or invent a new tag.

DAO 3.6 Objects

DAO is the programmatic interface to the Jet database engine shared by Access, Visual Basic, and Visual C++. The tags for DAO 3.6 objects are shown in Table A.6.

TABLE A.6: DAO Object Tags

Tag	Object Type
cnt	Container
cnts	Containers
db	Database
dbs	Databases
dbe	DBEngine
doc	Document
docs	Documents
err	Error
errs	Errors
fld	Field
flds	Fields
grp	Group
grps	Groups
idx	Index
idxs	Indexes
prm	Parameter

Continued on next page

TABLE A.6 CONTINUED: DAO Object Tags

Tag	Object Type
prms	Parameters
pdbe	PrivDBEngine
prp	Property
prps	Properties
qry	QueryDef
qrys	QueryDefs
rst	Recordset
rsts	Recordsets
rel	Relation
rels	Relations
tbl	TableDef
tbls	TableDefs
usr	User
usrs	Users
wrk	Workspace
wrks	Workspaces

Here are some examples:

```
rstCustomers
idxPrimaryKey
```

Table A.7 lists the tags used to identify types of objects in a database.

TABLE A.7: Access Database Explorer Object Tags

Tag	Object Type
tbl	Table
qry	Query

Continued on next page

TABLE A.7 CONTINUED: Access Database Explorer Object Tags

Tag	Object Type
frm	Form
rpt	Report
mcr	Macro
bas	Module
dap	DataAccessPage

If you wish, you can use more exact tags or suffixes to identify the purpose and type of a database object. If you use the suffix, use the tag given from Table A.7 to indicate the type. Use either the tag or the suffix found along with the more general tag, but not both. The tags and suffixes are shown in Table A.8.

TABLE A.8: Specific Object Tags and Suffixes for Access Database Explorer Objects

Tag	Suffix	Object Type
tlkp	Lookup	Table (lookup)
qsel	(none)	Query (select)
qapp	Append	Query (append)
qxtb	XTab	Query (crosstab)
qddl	DDL	Query (DDL)
qdel	Delete	Query (delete)
qflt	Filter	Query (filter)
qlkp	Lookup	Query (lookup)
qmak	MakeTable	Query (make table)
qspt	PassThru	Query (SQL pass-through)
qtot	Totals	Query (totals)
quni	Union	Query (union)
qupd	Update	Query (update)

Continued on next page

TABLE A.8 CONTINUED: Specific Object Tags and Suffixes for Access Database Explorer Objects

Tag	Suffix	Object Type
fdlg	Dlg	Form (dialog)
fmnu	Mnu	Form (menu)
fmsg	Msg	Form (message)
fsfr	SubForm	Form (subform)
rsrp	SubReport	Form (subreport)
mmnu	Mnu	Macro (menu)

Here are some examples:

```
tblValidNamesLookup
tlkpValidNames
fmsgError
mmnuFileMnu
```

When naming objects in a database, do not use spaces. Instead, capitalize the first letter of each word. For example, instead of Quarterly Sales Values Table, use tblQuarterlySalesValues.

There is strong debate over whether fields in a table should have tags. Whether you use them is up to you. However, if you do use them, use the tags from Table A.9.

TABLE A.9: Field Tags (If You Decide to Use Them)

Tag	Object Type
lng	Autoincrementing (either sequential or random) Long (used with the suffix Cnt)
bin	Binary
byte	Byte
cur	Currency
date	Date/time
dbl	Double
guid	Globally unique identified (GUID) used for replication AutoIncrement fields

Continued on next page

TABLE A.9 CONTINUED: Field Tags (If You Decide to Use Them)

Tag	Object Type
int	Integer
lng	Long
mem	Memo
ole	OLE
sng	Single
str	Text
bool	Yes/No

Visual Basic 6 Objects

Table A.10 shows the tags for Visual Basic 6 objects.

TABLE A.10: Visual Basic 6 Object Tags

Tag	Object Type
app	App
chk	CheckBox
clp	Clipboard
cbo	ComboBox
cmd	CommandButton
ctl	Control
dat	Data
dir	DirListBox
drv	DriveListBox
fil	FileListBox
frm	Form
fra	Frame

Continued on next page

TABLE A.10 CONTINUED: Visual Basic 6 Object Tags

Tag	Object Type
glb	Global
hsb	HScrollBar
img	Image
lbl	Label
lics	Licenses
lin	Line
lst	ListBox
mdi	MDIForm
mnu	Menu
ole	OLE
opt	OptionButton
pic	PictureBox
prt	Printer
prp	PropertyPage
scr	Screen
shp	Shape
txt	TextBox
tmr	Timer
uctl	UserControl
udoc	UserDocument
vsb	VscrollBar

Microsoft ActiveX Data Objects 2.1 Tags

Office 2000 provides version 2.1 of the ActiveX Data Objects library. Table A.11 lists the recommended tags for this version of ADO.

TABLE A.11: ADO 2.1 Object Tags

Tag	Object Type
cmn {cmd}	Command
cnn {cnx}	Connection
err	Error
errs	Errors
fld	Field
flds	Fields
prm	Parameter
prms	Parameters
prps	Properties
prp	Property
rst	Recordset

Avoiding Object Confusion

Many of the ADO, ADOX, and JRO tags overlap with existing DAO tags. Make sure you include the object library name in all references in your code, so there's never any possibility of confusion. For example, use

```
Dim rst As ADODB.Recordset
```

or

```
Dim cat As ADOX.Catalog
```

rather than using the object types without the library name. This will not only make your code more explicit and avoid confusion about the source of the object, but will also make your code run a bit faster.

Microsoft ADO Ext. 2.1 for DDL and Security (ADOX) Tags

In order to support DDL and security objects within Jet database, Microsoft provides ADOX, an additional ADO library of objects. Table A.12 lists tags for the ADOX objects.

TABLE A.12: ADOX Object Tags

Tag	Object Type
cat	Catalog
clms	Column
clm	Columns
cmd	Command
grp	Group
grps	Groups
idx	Index
idxs	Indexes
key	Key
keys	Keys
prc	Procedure
prcs	Procedures
prps	Properties
prp	Property
tbl	Table
tbls	Tables
usr	User
usrs	Users
vw	View
vws	Views

Microsoft Jet and Replication Objects 2.1

In order to support Jet's replication features, ADO provides another library, JRO. Table A.13 lists suggested tags for the JRO objects.

TABLE A.13: JRO Object Tags

Tag	Object Type
flt	Filter
flts	Filters
jet	JetEngine
rpl	Replica

Microsoft SQL Server and Microsoft Data Engine (MSDE) Objects

Table A.14 lists tags for Microsoft SQL Server and the Microsoft Data Engine (a limited-connection version of SQL Server 7) objects.

TABLE A.14: SQL Server/MSDE Object Tags

Tag	Object Type
tbl	table
proc	stored procedure
trg	trigger
qry	view
dgm	database diagram
pk	primary key
fk	foreign key
idx	other (nonkey) index
rul	check constraint
def	default

Microsoft Common Control Objects

Windows 95 and Windows NT have a set of common controls that are accessible from VBA. Table A.15 lists the tags for objects created using these controls.

TABLE A.15: Microsoft Common Control Object Tags

Tag	Object Type
ani	Animation
btn	Button (Toolbar)
bmn	ButtonMenu (Toolbar)
bmns	ButtonMenus (Toolbar)
bnd	Band (CoolBar)
bnds	Bands (CoolBar)
bnp	BandsPage (CoolBar)
btns	Buttons (Toolbar)
cbr	CoolBar
cbp	CoolBarPage (CoolBar)
hdr	ColumnHeader (ListView)
hdrs	ColumnHeaders (ListView)
cbi	ComboItem (ImageCombo)
cbis	ComboItems (ImageCombo)
ctls	Controls
dto	DataObject
dtf	DataObjectFiles
dtp	DTPicker
fsb	FlatScrollBar
imc	ImageCombo
iml	ImageList
lim	ListImage
lims	ListImages
lit	ListItem (ListView)

Continued on next page

TABLE A.15 CONTINUED: Microsoft Common Control Object Tags

Tag	Object Type
lits	ListItems (ListView)
lsi	ListSubItem (ListView)
lsis	ListSubItems (ListView)
lvw	ListView
mvw	MonthView
nod	Node (TreeView)
nods	Nodes (TreeView)
pnl	Panel (Status Bar)
pnls	Panels (Status Bar)
prb	ProgressBar
sld	Slider
sbr	StatusBar
tab	Tab (Tab Strip)
tabs	Tabs (Tab Strip)
tbs	TabStrip
tbr	Toolbar
tvw	TreeView
udn	UpDown

Other Custom Controls and Objects

Finally, Table A.16 lists the tags for other commonly used custom controls and objects.

TABLE A.16: Tags for Commonly Used Custom Controls

Tag	Object Type
cdl	CommonDialog (Common Dialog)
dbc	DBCombo (Data Bound Combo Box)
dbg	DBGrid (Data Bound Grid)

Continued on next page

TABLE A.16 CONTINUED: Tags for Commonly Used Custom Controls

Tag	Object Type
dls	DBList (Data Bound List Box)
gau	Gauge (Gauge)
gph	Graph (Graph)
grd	Grid (Grid)
msg	MAPIMessages (Messaging API Message Control)
ses	MAPISession (Messaging API Session Control)
msk	MaskEdBox (Masked Edit Textbox)
key	MhState (Key State)
mmc	MMControl (Multimedia Control)
com	MSComm (Communication Port)
out	Outline (Outline Control)
pcl	PictureClip (Picture Clip Control)
rtf	RichTextBox (Rich Textbox)
spn	SpinButton (Spin Button)

Summary

Using a naming convention requires a considerable initial effort on your part. The payoff comes when either you or another programmer has to revisit your code at a later time. Using the conventions given here will make your code more readable and maintainable.

Greg Reddick is the President of Xoc Software, a software development company developing programs in Visual Basic, Microsoft Access, and C/C++. He leads training seminars in Visual Basic for Application Developers Training Company and is a co-author of Microsoft Access 95 Developer's Handbook, *published by Sybex. He worked for four years on the Access development team at Microsoft. Greg can be reached at* `grr@xoc.net` *or at the Xoc Software Web site at* `http://www.xoc.net`.

APPENDIX B

Startup and Global Options

- Setting startup options
- Setting and retrieving global options

This appendix covers the Access startup options and the global options used with Application.SetOption and GetOption. Although the options covered in this appendix are crucial for your professional applications, there really wasn't any clear location for them in the body of the book. The following sections describe, in detail, each of the allowable settings and its use. In addition, the final section presents several undocumented settings that you may find useful in your applications.

Controlling Startup Options

For most applications, you want Access to take a specific action automatically every time a user loads your application. To make this possible, Access provides the Tools ➢ Startup dialog box, allowing you to specify most settings you will ever need to set at your application's startup. Table B.1 shows the options you can set, with a short description of each.

TABLE B.1: Automatic Startup Options

Option	Description	Database Property
Application Title	Access' main window title bar caption.	AppTitle
Application Icon	File name for icon to be displayed when Access is minimized.	AppIcon
Display Form	Name of the form to be displayed automatically on startup. Code attached to the form's Open events (Open, Load, Activate, and so on) runs, of course.	StartupForm
Display Database Window	If false, Access automatically hides the Database container when your application loads. (If you choose this option, the database window is still available—you must use the Window ➢ Unhide menu or press the F11 key to display it.)	StartupShowDBWindow
Display Status Bar	If false, Access hides the status bar that normally appears at the bottom of the Access window.	StartupShowStatusBar

Continued on next page

TABLE B.1 CONTINUED: Automatic Startup Options

Option	Description	Database Property
Menu Bar	Name of the default menu bar to be used when not overridden by a specific form or report menu bar.	StartupMenuBar
Shortcut Menu Bar	Name of the default shortcut menu to be used when not overridden by a specific form, report, or control menu.	StartupShortcutMenuBar
Allow Full Menus	If false, Access will not allow the full menus to be used.	AllowFullMenus
Allow Default Shortcut Menus	If false, Access will not display the default shortcut menus.	AllowShortcutMenus
Allow Built-In Toolbars	If false, Access hides the built-in toolbars. (If you're using the runtime version of Access, default toolbars are never available.)	AllowBuiltInToolbars
Allow Toolbar Changes	If false, users cannot make changes to toolbars.	AllowToolbarChanges
Use Access Special Keys	If false, Access disregards the special keys it normally traps (Ctrl+Break to break executing code, F11 to select the database container, and so on). This makes your running application simulate the runtime environment.	AllowSpecialKeys
(No UI equivalent)	If false, Access treats code errors as though you were running the runtime version. That is, it unceremoniously dumps your application back to Windows. (Note: This option existed in Access 97, but doesn't appear on the Access 2000 dialog box. In addition, although setting this property programmatically doesn't fail, it also doesn't appear to do anything.)	AllowBreakIntoCode
(No UI equivalent)	This option allows the Access retail product to disregard the Shift key (the bypass key) as your application loads. Has no effect until the next time you load the application. Make sure this is set to True when you're debugging your application.	AllowBypassKey

Setting Startup Options Programmatically

You can change any of the options in Table B.1 programmatically, but the techniques are different depending on whether you're using an MDB file or an ADP file. In either case, all the items in that table are properties of either a database (for MDB files), or the current project (for ADP files). As with all other properties that aren't built in, you must create the properties if they don't already exist. For example, if you try to set the AppTitle property for the current database, it may fail because that property doesn't yet exist. (If you haven't yet created the property in the Tools ➢ Startup dialog box, it won't exist.)

Setting MDB Startup Options

In an MDB file, the simplest possible code for setting a database property might look like this code, from basAppTitle (see Appendix C for information on using DAO to create new properties):

```
Private Const adhcErrPropNotFound as Long = 3270

Public Sub adhSetAppTitleMDB(strTitle As String)

    ' Given a text string, set the application title.
    ' At this point, there's no way to use this to reset
    ' the title back to its default state.

    Dim db As DAO.Database
    Dim prp As DAO.Property

    On Error Resume Next
    Set db = CurrentDb()
    db.Properties("AppTitle") = strTitle
    If Err.Number = adhcErrPropNotFound Then
        Set prp = db.CreateProperty("AppTitle", _
         dbText, strTitle)
        db.Properties.Append prp
    End If
    Application.RefreshTitleBar
End Sub
```

TIP

If you set the AppTitle property, you must also call the Application.RefreshTitleBar method to force Access to redisplay the title bar.

WARNING

If you set the AppTitle property, there's no way to force it to revert to its original value. You just have to know that the original value was "Microsoft Access," if you ever want to revert to the original setting programmatically. Odd, however, that the Access user interface does this for you if you delete your setting in the Startup dialog box.

You could write similar procedures to set any of the other database properties. Note that this technique requires DAO, and even for newly created databases (with no reference set to DAO), you'll need to set a reference to DAO and use DAO's methods to append a property to an MDB file.

TIP

Actually, you needn't set a reference to DAO in order to add properties to the database. Even if you've referenced only ADO, you can still add properties, but you'll need to use generic Object variables and define your own constants for the CreateProperty method. If you're doing this sort of work, the overhead of adding a reference to DAO doesn't seem like a terribly onerous price to pay for early binding and predefined constants.

In addition to the properties listed in Table B.1, every new MDB file automatically has the following properties added to it by Access:

Connect

Transactions

Updatable

CollatingOrder

QueryTimeout

Version

RecordsAffected

ReplicaID

DesignMasterID

AccessVersion

Build

For more information on working with Access object properties, see Appendix C.

WARNING

Access' behavior concerning these database properties is different, depending on where you set them. If you set the value of any of these properties from the Access user interface, Access may also set other startup properties to coincide with your property setting. If you set them programmatically, however, you're on your own—you'll need to set each property manually.

Setting ADP Startup Options

If you're working in an Access project (ADP file), it's slightly simpler to set the Access startup properties. In an ADP file, you can use the Properties collection of the CurrentProject object, adding the properties you need. In this case, however, you can simply add the property, without worrying about whether it's already been added. If it's already in the Properties collection, Access overwrites its value.

Therefore, you can use code like the following (from basAppTitle) to set the AppTitle property of an ADP file:

```
Public Sub adhSetAppTitleADP(strTitle As String)
    ' This won't work in this MDB file - you
    ' need to have an ADP file in order to
    ' use this technique.
    CurrentProject.Properties.Add "AppTitle", strTitle
    Application.RefreshTitleBar
End Sub
```

In addition to the properties listed in Table B.1, every new ADP file automatically has the following properties added to it by Access:

AccessVersion

Build

Running Code at Startup

Most often, the options Access provides in the Tools ➢ Startup menu will give you all the flexibility you need. On the other hand, you may still need to specify a set of steps you'd like executed when your application starts up. (Perhaps you need to perform some steps not associated with any form.) Although it would be helpful if Access provided a facility for executing a VBA procedure at startup, it does not. Instead, you must use a macro if you don't want to display a form. Therefore, you have two choices:

- If your application contains a macro named AutoExec, Access executes that macro after it loads the database. Because of the limitations of macros, we suggest that this macro do nothing more than use the RunCode action to execute a VBA procedure.
- A better alternative, because almost all Access applications start up by displaying a form, is to call any startup code you need to execute from the Open event of your startup form. You can specify a form that will be loaded automatically when a user opens your database (see Table B.1), and Access will execute your code as it loads that form. In almost all cases, this is the preferable method.

Choosing Your Own Startup Macro

If you'd like to be able to specify a particular macro to be run when your application loads, you have another choice. You may have a particular application you use for varying circumstances. In one instance, you'd like to start it and run Macro1. In other instances, you'd like to start it and run a different macro, Macro2. To make this happen, you need to tell Access, from the command line, which macro to run. You can specify both a database and a startup macro from the command line, as in:

```
MSACCESS YourApp.MDB /xYourMacro
```

Access runs the macro name that follows the /x (with or without a separating space) as soon as it loads the application. By setting up different icons that run Access with various startup macros, you can control exactly which portion of your application is executed when the user clicks a given icon.

WARNING

If your application includes an AutoExec macro and your command line tells Access to run a different macro when it loads your application (using the /x option), Access first runs the AutoExec macro and then your specified macro. This certainly isn't a bug, but it is something to be aware of. In addition, if the application's startup options indicate a form to open automatically, that form's Open and Load event procedures will run before either macro.

Skipping the AutoExec Macro

If you have a macro running automatically every time you start your application, sooner or later you're going to want to run the application *without* running that macro. To bypass the AutoExec macro, press and hold the Shift key when you load the database. This is a standard keypress, used in (at least) Access, Word, and Excel to bypass autoexecuting code, and in Windows itself to bypass the Startup group/folder.

If your application is running in the Access runtime environment, your users won't be able to bypass the AutoExec (or the command line–specified) macro at all. The runtime environment disregards the Shift key at load time. If your users are running your application in the retail version of Access, you can still disable the Shift key by setting the AllowBypassKey property of the database to be False. See Table B.1 for more information. The following procedures, from basByPassKey, show how you can enable and disable this option (for both an MDB and ADP file):

```
Public Sub adhSetBypassKeyMDB(AllowIt As Boolean)

    Dim db As DAO.Database
    Dim prp As DAO.Property

    On Error Resume Next
    Set db = CurrentDb()
    db.Properties("AllowByPassKey") = AllowIt
    If Err.Number = adhcErrPropNotFound Then
        Set prp = db.CreateProperty("AllowByPassKey", _
         dbBoolean, AllowIt)
        db.Properties.Append prp
    End If
End Sub

Public Sub adhSetByPassKeyADP(AllowIt As Boolean)
    CurrentProject.Properties.Add "AllowByPassKey", AllowIt
End Sub
```

Controlling Global Options

Access provides two methods of the Application object, GetOption (a function) and SetOption (a subroutine), which can set and retrieve global options. Most of the settings mentioned here correlate to settings available in the Tools ➢ Options dialog box in Access. The few remaining correspond to options you can set within VBA, from the Tools ➢ Options ➢ General (Error Trapping) dialog box. The syntax necessary to call them is

Application.SetOption *optionName*, *Setting*

Setting = Application.GetOption(*optionName*)

The only catch is that the *optionName* value must be the exact text shown in the first column of Table B.2. (Misspellings and abbreviations will fail.) In addition, Table B.2 lists all the possible values for each option, as well as properties (defined in the OptionValues class module) you can use to refer to each option instead of having to type the text strings explicitly.

TIP

Because SetOption and GetOption are methods of the Application object, you actually don't need to mention Application in your code at all. Simply calling GetOption or SetOption makes it clear to Access that you're using a method of the top-level Application object.

TABLE B.2: Application.GetOption/SetOption Options and Constants

Option	Property Name	Values	Comments	Settable	MDB/ADP
		Advanced Tab			
Break On All Errors	BreakOnErrors	–1 (True); 0 (False)	Available, but use Error Trapping instead. This setting is left over from Access 95 and should not be used.	Read/write	Both
CommandLine Arguments	CommandLineArgs	(Valid command-line arguments)		Read/write	Both
Conditional Compilation Arguments	CondCompArgs	(Conditional compilation arguments, in the format: arg1=value1: arg2=value2)		Read/write	Both
Default Open Mode for Databases	OpenMode	0 (Shared); 1 (Exclusive)		Read/write	MDB Only

Continued on next page

TABLE B.2 CONTINUED: Application.GetOption/SetOption Options and Constants

Option	Property Name	Values	Comments	Settable	MDB/ADP
		Advanced Tab			
Default Record Locking	RecordLocking	0 (No locks); 1 (All records); 2 (Edited record)		Read/write	Both
Enable DDE Refresh	EnableDDERefresh	–1 (True); 0 (False)		Read/write	Both
Error Trapping	ErrorTrapping	0 (Break on all errors); 1 (Break in class module); 2 (Break on unhandled errors)	Make absolutely sure this option is set to 2 when you deliver your application.	Read/write	Both
Ignore DDE Requests	IgnoreDDE	–1 (True); 0 (False)		Read/write	Both
Number of Update Retries	RetryCount	0 to 10		Read/write	MDB Only
ODBC Refresh Interval (sec)	ODBCRefresh	1 to 3600		Read/write	MDB Only
OLE/DDE Timeout (sec)	OLEDDETimeout	0 to 300		Read/write	Both
Project Name	ProjectName	(Valid project name)	Changing this value at runtime is guaranteed to decompile the entire project.	Read/write	Both
Refresh Interval (sec)	RefreshInterval	1 to 32766		Read/write	Both
Row Limit	RowLimit	0 To 32766	In the UI, Access doesn't check this value—you can enter anything. Behavior is undefined if you do.	Read/write	ADP Only
Update Retry Interval (msec)	RetryInterval	0 to 1000		Read/write	MDB Only
Use Row Level Locking	UseRowLevelLocking	–1 (True); 0 (False)	Incorrect in online help (refers to "Use Record Level Locking").	Read/write	MDB Only

Continued on next page

TABLE B.2 CONTINUED: Application.GetOption/SetOption Options and Constants

Option	Property Name	Values	Comments	Settable	MDB/ADP
		Datasheet Tab			
Default Background Color	BackgroundColor	0 (Black); 1 (Maroon); 2 (Green); 3 (Olive); 4 (Navy); 5 (Purple); 6 (Teal); 7 (Gray); 8 (Silver); 9 (Red); 10 (Lime); 11 (Yellow); 12 (Blue); 13 (Fuchsia); 14 (Aqua); 15 (White)		Read/write	Both
Default Cell Effect	CellEffect	0 (Sunken); 1 (Raised); 2 (Flat)		Read/write	Both
Default Column Width	ColumnWidth	0.1 to 22.75 inches (up to 32,767 twips), as a string, including units ("1 in," for example)		Read/write	Both
Default Font Color	FontColor	0 (Black); 1 (Maroon); 2 (Green); 3 (Olive); 4 (Navy); 5 (Purple); 6 (Teal); 7 (Gray); 8 (Silver); 9 (Red); 10 (Lime); 11 (Yellow); 12 (Blue); 13 (Fuchsia); 14 (Aqua); 15 (White)		Read/write	Both
Default Font Italic	FontItalic	–1 (True); 0 (False)		Read/write	Both
Default Font Name	FontName	(Any installed font name)		Read/write	Both
Default Font Size	FontSize	(Any integer value between 1 and 127, inclusive)		Read/write	Both
Default Font Underline	FontUnderline	–1 (True); 0 (False)		Read/write	Both
Default Font Weight	FontWeight	0 (Thin); 1 (Extra Light); 2 (Light); 3 (Normal); 4 (Medium); 5 (Semi-Bold); 6 (Bold); 7 (Extra Bold); 8 (Heavy)		Read/write	Both
Default Gridlines Color	GridlinesColor	0 to 15 (see Default Font Color)		Read/write	Both

Continued on next page

TABLE B.2 CONTINUED: Application.GetOption/SetOption Options and Constants

Option	Property Name	Values	Comments	Settable	MDB/ADP
		Datasheet Tab			
Default Gridlines Horizontal	GridlinesHorizontal	–1 (True); 0 (False)		Read/write	Both
Default Gridlines Vertical	GridlinesVertical	–1 (True); 0 (False)		Read/write	Both
Show Animations	ShowAnimations	–1 (True); 0 (False)		Read/write	Both
		Edit/Find Tab			
Confirm Action Queries	ConfirmQueries	–1 (True); 0 (False)		Read/write	MDB Only
Confirm Document Deletions	ConfirmDeletions	–1 (True); 0 (False)		Read/write	Both
Confirm Record Changes	ConfirmChanges	–1 (True); 0 (False)		Read/write	Both
Default Find/ Replace Behavior	FindReplace	0 (Fast Search); 1 (General Search); 2 (Start of Field Search)		Read/write	Both
Show Values in Indexed	ShowLocalIndexed	–1 (True); 0 (False)		Read/write	MDB Only
Show Values in Nonindexed	ShowLocalNonIndexed	–1 (True); 0 (False)		Read/write	MDB Only
Show Values in Remote	ShowRemote	–1 (True); 0 (False)		Read/write	MDB Only
Show Values in Server	ShowValuesInServer	–1 (True); 0 (False)		Read/write	ADP Only
Show Values in Snapshot	ShowValuesInSnapshot	–1 (True); 0 (False)		Read/write	ADP Only
Show Values Limit	ShowValuesLimit	0 to 32766		Read/write	Both
		Forms/Reports Tab			
Always Use Event Procedures	UseEventProcs	–1 (True); 0 (False)		Read/write	Both
Form Template	FormTemplate	(Name of any form in the current database)		Read/write	Both

Continued on next page

TABLE B.2 CONTINUED: Application.GetOption/SetOption Options and Constants

Option	Property Name	Values	Comments	Settable	MDB/ADP
		Forms/Reports Tab			
Report Template	ReportTemplate	(Name of any report in the current database)		Read/write	Both
Selection Behavior	SelectionBehavior	0 (Partially enclosed); 1 (Fully enclosed)		Read/write	Both
		General Tab			
Auto Compact	AutoCompact	–1 (True); 0 (False)		Read/write	Both
Bottom Margin	BottomMargin	0 to the height of the printed page (see Left Margin)		Read/write	Both
Default Database Directory	DefaultDirectory	(Any valid path, including ".")		Read/write	Both
Enable MRU File List	EnableMRU	–1 (True); 0 (False)		Read/write	Both
Four-Digit Year Formatting	FourDigitYear	–1 (True); 0 (False)	Undocumented in online help.	Read/write	Both
Four-Digit Year Formatting All Databases	FourDigitYearAllDatabases	–1 (True); 0 (False)	Undocumented in online help.	Read/write	Both
Left Margin	LeftMargin	0 to the width of the printed page, as a string, including units ("3 cm" or "1 in," for example)		Read/write	Both
Log Name AutoCorrect Changes	LogNameAutocorrectChanges	–1 (True); 0 (False)		Read/write	MDB Only
New Database Sort Order	SortOrder	0 (General); 1 (Chinese Pronounciation); 2 (Chinese Stroke Count); 3 (Chinese Stroke Count [Taiwan]); 4 (Chinese Bopomofo ([Taiwan]); 5 (Croatian); 6 (Czech); 7 (Estonian); 8 (French); 9 (Georgian Modern); 0 (German Phone Book); 11 (Hungarian); 12 (Hungarian)		Read/write	MDB Only

Continued on next page

TABLE B.2 CONTINUED: Application.GetOption/SetOption Options and Constants

Option	Property Name	Values	Comments	Settable	MDB/ADP
		General Tab			
Perform Name AutoCorrect	PerformName-AutoCorrect	–1 (True); 0 (False)		Read/write	MDB Only
Provide Feedback with Sound	ProvideFeedback-WithSound	–1 (True); 0 (False)		Read/write	Both
Right Margin	RightMargin	0 to the width of the printed page (see Left Margin)		Read/write	Both
Size of MRU File List	SizeOfMRU	0 to 9		Read/write	Both
Top Margin	TopMargin	0 to the height of the printed page (see Left Margin)		Read/write	Both
Track Name Auto-Correct Info	TrackNameAuto-Correct	–1 (True); 0 (False)		Read/write	MDB Only
		General Tab/Web Options			
Followed Hyperlink Color	Followed-HyperlinkColor	0 (Black); 1 (Maroon); 2 (Green); 3 (Olive); 4 (Navy); 5 (Purple); 6 (Teal); 7 (Gray); 8 (Silver); 9 (Red); 10 (Lime); 11 (Yellow); 12 (Blue); 13 (Fuchsia); 14 (Aqua); 15 (White)		Read/write	Both
Hyperlink Color	HyperlinkColor	0 (Black); 1 (Maroon); 2 (Green); 3 (Olive); 4 (Navy); 5 (Purple); 6 (Teal); 7 (Gray); 8 (Silver); 9 (Red); 10 (Lime); 11 (Yellow); 12 (Blue); 13 (Fuchsia); 14 (Aqua); 15 (White)		Read/write	Both
Underline Hyperlinks	UnderlineHyperlinks	–1 (True); 0 (False)		Read/write	Both

Continued on next page

TABLE B.2 CONTINUED: Application.GetOption/SetOption Options and Constants

Option	Property Name	Values	Comments	Settable	MDB/ADP
		Keyboard Tab			
Arrow Key Behavior	ArrowKeys	0 (Next field); 1 (Next character)		Read/write	Both
Behavior Entering Field	EnterField	0 (Entire field); 1 (End of field); 2 (Beginning of field)		Read/write	Both
Cursor Stops at First/Last Field	CursorStops	–1 (True); 0 (False)		Read/write	Both
Move After Enter	MoveAfterEnter	0 (Don't move); 1 (Next field); 2 (Next record)		Read/write	Both
		Tables/Queries Tab			
AutoIndex on Import/Create	AutoIndex	(A semicolon-delimited list of field names)		Read/write	MDB Only
Default Field Type	DefaultFieldType	0 (Text); 1 (Memo); 2 (Number); 3 (Date/Time); 4 (Currency); 5 (AutoNumber); 6 (Yes/No); 7 (OLE Object); 8 (Hyperlink)		Read/write	MDB Only
Default Number Field Size	DefaultNumberField	0 (Double); 1 (Integer); 2 (Long Integer); 3 (Single); 4 (Byte); 5 (Replication ID)		Read/write	MDB Only
Default Text Field Size	DefaultTextField	1 to 255		Read/write	MDB Only
Enable AutoJoin	EnableAutoJoin	–1 (True); 0 (False)		Read/write	MDB Only
Output All Fields	OutputAllFields	–1 (True); 0 (False)		Read/write	MDB Only
Run Permissions	RunPermissions	0 (User's); 1 (Owner's)		Read/write	MDB Only
Show Table Names	ShowTableNames	–1 (True); 0 (False)		Read/write	MDB Only

Continued on next page

TABLE B.2 CONTINUED: Application.GetOption/SetOption Options and Constants

Option	Property Name	Values	Comments	Settable	MDB/ADP
		View Tab			
Database Explorer Click Behavior	Database-ExplorerClick	0 (Single-click open); 1 (Double-click open)		Read/write	Both
Enable Font Switching	EnableFontSwitching	–1 (True); 0 (False)		Read/write	Both
Show Conditions Column	MacroConditions	–1 (True); 0 (False)		Read/write	Both
Show Hidden Objects	ShowHidden	–1 (True); 0 (False)		Read/write	Both
Show Macro Names Column	MacroNames	–1 (True); 0 (False)		Read/write	Both
Show New Object Shortcuts	ShowNewObject-Shortcuts	–1 (True); 0 (False)		Read/write	Both
Show Startup Dialog Box	StartupDialog	–1 (True); 0 (False)		Read/write	Both
Show Status Bar	ShowStatusBar	–1 (True); 0 (False)		Read/write	Both
Show System Objects	ShowSystemObjects	–1 (True); 0 (False)		Read/write	Both
Show Windows In Taskbar	ShowWindows-InTaskbar	–1 (True); 0 (False)	Incorrect in online help.	Read/write	Both
Substitute Font Name	SubstituteFontName	Valid font name		Read/write	Both
		Undocumented or No Tab			
Auto Compact Percentage	AutoCompact-Percentage	0 to 100	Apparently, Access doesn't check this value when you set it, nor is this documented. We're not sure if it actually is hooked up. If it is, this value specifies the minimum decrease in size before Access automatically compacts your database on closing.	Read/write	Both
Built-In Toolbars Available	BuiltInToolbars	–1 (True); 0 (False)		Read/write	Both

Continued on next page

TABLE B.2 CONTINUED: Application.GetOption/SetOption Options and Constants

Option	Property Name	Values	Comments	Settable	MDB/ADP
		Undocumented or No Tab			
Can Customize Toolbars	CustomizeToolbars	–1 (True); 0 (False)		Read/write	Both
Control Wizards	ControlWizards	–1 (True); 0 (False)		Read/write	Both
Cursor	Cursor	0 or 1	Unknown behavior.	Read/write	Both
Data Assistant	DataAssistantCoords	Coordinates for the Data Assistant window, in the format: Open?;Left;Top;Width ;Height. For example: 0;275;150;650;325.		Read/write	Both
Debug Window on Top	DebugOnTop	–1 (True); 0 (False)	Has no effect in Access 2000.	Read/write	Both
General Alignment	GeneralAlignment	0 or 1	Unknown behavior.	Read/write	Both
HlinkTab	HlinkTab	0 to 32766	Unknown behavior.	Read/write	Both
Key Assignment Macro	KeyAssignment	(Any valid macro name)		Read/write	Both
Large Toolbar Buttons	LargeButtons	–1 (True); 0 (False)	Turns on or off display of large icons on toolbars.	Read/write	Both
Last User	LastUser	Any text string	Unknown behavior.	Read/write	Both
Maximized	Maximized	–1 (True); 0 (False)	Was the main Access window maximized when you last quit? If False, check the values in the Window Width, etc., settings, to find the exact coordinates where Access was started. If True, the four coordinate settings are invalid.	Read-only	Both
Move Enclosed Controls	MoveEnclosed	–1 (True); 0 (False)	If set to True, moving any control in design view will also move any controls it contains. By default, this is set to False.	Read/write	Both

Continued on next page

TABLE B.2 CONTINUED: Application.GetOption/SetOption Options and Constants

Option	Property Name	Values	Comments	Settable	MDB/ADP
		Undocumented or No Tab			
MRU1	MRU1		Returns the first item in the File menu's most-recently used list.	Read-only	Both
MRU2	MRU2		Returns the second item in the File menu's most-recently used list.	Read-only	Both
MRU3	MRU3		Returns the third item in the File menu's most-recently used list.	Read-only	Both
MRU4	MRU4		Returns the fourth item in the File menu's most-recently used list.	Read-only	Both
MRU5	MRU5		Returns the fourth item in the File menu's most-recently used list.	Read-only	Both
MRU6	MRU6		Returns the sixth item in the File menu's most-recently used list.	Read-only	Both
MRU7	MRU7		Returns the seventh item in the File menu's most-recently used list.	Read-only	Both
MRU8	MRU8		Returns the eighth item in the File menu's most-recently used list.	Read-only	Both
MRU9	MRU9		Returns the ninth item in the File menu's most-recently used list.	Read-only	Both
New Tables/Queries/ Forms/Reports	NewTablesEtc	0 or 1	Unknown behavior.	Read/write	Both
Objects Snap To Grid	SnapToGrid	–1 (True); 0 (False)		Read/write	Both
Save Login and Password	SaveLoginAnd-Password	–1 (True); 0 (False)		Read/write	ADP Only
Show Grid	ShowGrid	–1 (True); 0 (False)	Show the form/report design grid?	Read/write	Both

Continued on next page

TABLE B.2 CONTINUED: Application.GetOption/SetOption Options and Constants

Option	Property Name	Values	Comments	Settable	MDB/ADP
		Undocumented or No Tab			
Show Ruler	ShowRuler	–1 (True); 0 (False)	Show form/report design ruler?	Read/write	Both
Syntax Checking	SyntaxChecking	–32768 to 32767	Doesn't raise an error, but doesn't do anything.	Read/write	Both
Use Default Printer Setup	UseDefaultPrinter	–1 (True); 0 (False)	Forces Access to print all documents to the Windows Default printer, even if the object has been set to print to a specific printer. Only takes effect when you quit and then restart Access (it has no effect in the current session).	Read/write	Both
Warn Width	WarnWidth	–1 (True); 0 (False)	Enables/disables the warning Access displays when you attempt to print a report that's too wide to print without tiling.	Read/write	Both
Window Height	WindowHeight	0 to 32766	If the Maximized setting is False, indicates the height of the main Access window (in pixels) when it was last closed.	Read-only	Both
Window Left	WindowLeft	0 to 32766	If the Maximized setting is False, indicates the width of the main Access window (in pixels) when it was last closed.	Read-only	Both

Continued on next page

TABLE B.2 CONTINUED: Application.GetOption/SetOption Options and Constants

Option	Property Name	Values	Comments	Settable	MDB/ADP
		Undocumented or No Tab			
Window Top	WindowTop	0 to 32766	If the Maximized setting is False, indicates the top of the main Access window (in pixels) when it was last closed.	Read-only	Both
Window Width	WindowWidth	0 to 32766	If the Maximized setting is False, indicates the width of the main Access window (in pixels) when it was last closed.	Read-only	Both
		Coordinates			
Datapage Sorting-Grouping State	DataPageSorting-Coords	Coordinates for the Data Page sorting/grouping window, in the format: Open?;Left;Top;Width;Height. For example: 0;275;150;650;325.		Read/write until used	Both
DP Pop Prop ST	DataPageProperty-SheetCoords	Coordinates for the data page property sheet, in the format: Open?;Left;Top;Width;Height. For example: 0;275;150;650;325.		Read/write until used	Both
ECLST	FieldListCoords	Coordinates for the Form/Report design fields list, in the format: Open?;Left;Top;Width;Height. For example: 0;275;150;650;325.	Use 1 in the first position to force the window open at startup. For this window, the final coordinate is disregarded if it would force the window to be taller than the number of fields in the list would require.	Read/write until used	Both

Continued on next page

TABLE B.2 CONTINUED: Application.GetOption/SetOption Options and Constants

Option	Property Name	Values	Comments	Settable	MDB/ADP
		Coordinates			
FD Category	PropCategory	-1 (All), 1 (Format), 2 (Data), 4 (Event), 8 (Other)	Like coordinate settings, this value only affects the tab on the property sheet before you open a form in Design view. Once you've opened a form for design, Access never looks at this setting again.	Read/write until used	Both
FormPopPropST	PropertiesCoords	Coordinates for the form design property sheet, in the format: Open?;Left;Top;Width; Height. For example: 0;275;150;650;325.		Read/write until used	Both
IndexesST	IndexCoords	Coordinates for the table design indexes list, in the format: Open?;Left;Top;Width; Height. For example: 0;275;150;650;325.		Read/write until used	Both
IPaneST	DebugCoords	Coordinates for the Immediate window, in the format: Open?; Left;Top;Width; Height. For example: 0;275;150;650;325.		Read/write until used	Both
QueryPopPropST	QueryPropsCoords	Coordinates for the query design property sheet, in the format: Open?;Left;Top;Width; Height. For example: 0;275;150;650;325.		Read/write until used	Both
ReportPopPropST	ReportPropsCoords	Coordinates for the Report design property sheet, in the format: Open?;Left;Top;Width; Height. For example: 0;275;150;650;325.		Read/write until used	Both

Continued on next page

TABLE B.2 CONTINUED: Application.GetOption/SetOption Options and Constants

Option	Property Name	Values	Comments	Settable	MDB/ADP
		Coordinates			
SGST	SortingGrouping-Coords	Coordinates for the report Sorting/Grouping dialog box, in the format: Open?;Left;Top;Width;Height. For example: 0;275;150;650;325.		Read/write until used	Both
TDPopPropST	TablePropsCoords	Coordinates for the table design property sheet, in the format: Open?;Left;Top;Width;Height. For example: 0;275;150;650;325.		Read/write until used	Both
		Unused			
Active Server Pages Session Timeout	ActiveXTimeout	Number of minutes before timing out	Apparently, Access does no checking on this value. Make sure to enter a valid number of minutes.	Read/write	Both
Active Server Pages URL	ActiveXServerURL Read/write	(Any valid URL) Both			
Data Source Name	DataSourceName	(Any valid DSN)		Read/write	Both
HTML Template	HTMLTemplate	(Any HTML file name)		Read/write	Both
Password	ODBCPassword	(Valid ODBC password)		Read/write	Both
Show Hyperlink Addresses In Status Bar	ShowHLinkIn-StatusBar	–1 (True); 0 (False)	Not valid for Access 2000—Access 2000 shows hyperlinks in tool tips. Using this option will trigger a runtime error. Nice backward compatibility, eh?	Read/write	Both
User Name	ODBCUserName	(Any valid ODBC user name)		Read/write	Both

TIP

If you're developing applications for other people to use, there's one setting in Table B.2 you'll want to incorporate into every application you write: you'll need to set the Error Trapping option to 2 (Break on Unhandled Errors) when you start up and put it back the way it was when you're done. If you leave this option as 0 (Break on All Errors), any time your application triggers any sort of runtime error, whether or not you've trapped for and handled that error, your code will halt. This option is great for developers who want to watch every error occur, but for end users it's the fastest way there is to kill any application. Do not bypass this step or, sooner or later, you'll be sorry.

Remember that the options settings are both global and persistent. That is, if you make a change to the global options from within one database and then load another, your options still apply. In addition, if you quit Access, your changes are stored in the Registry, so that they apply to the next Access session you start up. The moral: If you make a change, be sure to set it back. Certainly, if you change any settings using Application.SetOption, you must make an effort to reset the values when your application exits. Whether your user exits through an error handler or through the normal shutdown procedures, you should reset any options your application changed. That is, your application might contain code to set the value for the OLE/DDE Timeout to be 100 seconds. In the application's startup routine you might include code like this (the variable gintTimeOut is Public):

```
pintTimeOut = GetOption("OLE/DDE TimeOut (sec)")
SetOption "OLE/DDE TimeOut (sec)", 100
```

Then, in the code that's executed when your application shuts down, include a statement like this:

```
SetOption "OLE/DDE TimeOut (sec)", pintTimeOut
```

If you don't reset the value when your application shuts down, your user will find the settings as your application left them the next time Access starts up.

In the sample database, you'll find tblOptions, a table containing all the information in Table B.2. You may want to try out the test procedure, TestOptions, from basTestOptions, which runs through all the items in the table and prints the value of each option to the Immediate window:

```
Public Sub TestOptions()
    Dim rst As ADODB.Recordset
    Set rst = New ADODB.Recordset
    Set rst.ActiveConnection = CurrentProject.Connection
```

```
    rst.Source = _
     "SELECT Option FROM tblOptions " & _
     "ORDER BY Option"
    rst.Open

    On Error Resume Next
    Do Until rst.EOF
        Debug.Print rst("Option") & ":",
        Debug.Print GetOption(rst("Option"))
        If Err.Number <> 0 Then
            Debug.Print "<<< ERROR"
            Err.Clear
        End If
        rst.MoveNext
    Loop
    rst.Close
    Set rst = Nothing
End Sub
```

Making It a Bit Simpler

To make it a bit simpler for you to use the GetOption and SetOption methods, we've supplied a class module containing properties representing all the possible options. This way, rather than use the exact strings each time you set or retrieve options, you can use the properties of this class, treated just like enumerated constants. This saves your typing the strings, which can introduce errors. Instead of using this expression:

```
SetOption "Update Retry Interval (msec)", 100
```

you can use

```
SetOption pov.RetryInterval, 100
```

Table B.2 includes a list of all the options, their associated properties, and the allowed values for each. To use these in your own applications, import the class named OptionValues from APDXB.MDB. In addition, you'll need to declare, in some standard module, a Public variable that will refer to the OptionValues object you need:

```
Public pov As New OptionValues
```

Once you've declared this variable, you can use pov anywhere in you application where you need to call the GetOption or SetOption methods.

NOTE

Although we've repeatedly steered you away from using the single-line declaration/instantiation mechanism, this is one place where it actually makes sense. By including the New keyword in the declaration for pov, you can use the variable anywhere you like, even in the Immediate window, without needing to explicitly instantiate the variable. Because there's really no code in the class, and you don't care when this object gets created or destroyed, this is one time where we can safely suggest that you use the simpler technique for declaring and instantiating an object.

A Few Undocumented Options

Besides the documented options for Application.SetOption and GetOption that correspond to settings in the Tools ➢ Options dialog, Access supports a few extra options that have no user-interface equivalents. As a matter of fact, these options offer the only way in Access to change the associated settings! In addition, there are several other undocumented settings you can use with GetOption and SetOption. We recognize that they're of limited use and have never been mentioned in the documentation for any version of Access, so we've placed them together at the end of Table B.2.

Using the Undocumented Settings

Many of the undocumented settings in Table B.2 include "Read/write until used" in the Settable column. This option indicates that for this setting, you can set the value only until Access first uses the value. From then on, Access doesn't look again at the value you've set (it uses its own internal settings) until you restart. For example, the SGST value allows you to set or get the location and visibility of the Sorting/Grouping window in Report Design view. Until you actually open a report in Design view, you can set the value of this property and control the location and visibility of the window. When you first open any report in Design view, Access looks at the value in the SGST setting and uses the value it finds there. From then on, it disregards that value until the next time you start Access. This same logic applies to all the values in Table B.2 set as "Read/write until used."

In each set of coordinates, the first position indicates whether the window is visible by default, and the other coordinates indicate the left, top, width, and height for the window. In each case, Access reads these values only the first time it loads each of the windows. Once you've loaded each window so it's visible, Access no longer notices the settings in these options, and changing them once the window is open would be a waste of time.

So, you ask, what's the point? For the most part, these are interesting factoids, but they're not terribly useful. One very important use for these, however, is the ability they give you to ensure that the Report property sheet isn't visible when you open a report in Design view. You can't open a report invisibly, and if you want to perform some modifications to a report in Design view, you'll want to hide the property sheet while you're working. You can use the ReportPopPropST setting to make sure that when you first open a report in your application, Access won't display the property sheet, and your application will look much smoother because of it.

To make this change, you could use code like this:

```
Dim strOpt As String
strOpt = GetOption("ReportPopPropST")
' Make sure the first character is a 0.
strOpt = "0" & Mid$ (strOpt, 2)
SetOption "ReportPopPropST", strOpt
' Now, open the report in Design view.
```

Certainly, this technique is not for everyone, and it is subject to change. But if you're attempting to write a clean add-in that works on reports in Design view, this could finally make your application appear seamless.

APPENDIX C

Data Access Objects

- Handling Access objects programmatically with DAO
- Creating, deleting, and modifying database objects from VBA using DAO
- Working with DAO recordsets

NOTE

This appendix is, for the most part, an exact reprint of the chapter we included in the *Access 97 Developer's Handbook*. It's included here for new Access developers who need help getting started with DAO. Much of the text included here is the same as, or similar to, text in the current Chapter 6, which discusses ADO. If you're working with MDB files, you can choose whether you want to use ADO or DAO to work with your objects, programmatically. If you're using ADP files, you'll want to use ADO exclusively. This appendix attempts only to explain how you can use DAO, if you've made the choice to work that way.

Using DAO in Your Applications

If you create a new database in Access 2000, Access will assume that you want to use ADO and will include a reference only to the ADO type library. If you want to use DAO, you'll need to use the Tools ➢ References dialog box from within VBA and add Microsoft DAO 3.6 Object Library to the list of selected references.

If you convert an existing Access 97 (or previous) application to Access 2000, Access will maintain the existing reference to DAO—updated to DAO 3.6—and you can continue to use DAO as you did previously.

Because both ADO and DAO provide some similar objects (Recordset and Field, for example), you'll need to make it clear in your code exactly which type of object you're creating. We recommend that you start prefacing each declaration with the object library providing the object, like this:

```
Dim rst As DAO.Recordset
Dim fld As DAO.Field
```

When you have a project that uses both DAO and ADO, you'll be glad you did this. (This technique, called *disambiguation*, is discussed in more detail in Chapter 6.)

DBEngine and the Workspaces Collection

The DBEngine object is the top-level object in any DAO reference. To refer to any object in the Jet hierarchy, you'll always start by referring to the DBEngine object. As you can see in Figure C.1, the DBEngine object contains two collections: the collection of open workspaces and the Errors collection.

If you're using DAO from outside Access, you have no choice: the DBEngine object is the only way to get to any DAO object. From within Access, you can and should use the CurrentDb function to obtain a reference to the current database. (See the section "CurrentDb versus DBEngine(0)(0)" later in this appendix for more information.) To reference objects that aren't part of the current database, however, you'll need to start with a reference to DBEngine even within Access.

NOTE

We could list, in this appendix, all the properties and methods of each object. However, this information is neatly encapsulated in Access' online help. For each object type, search through online help and choose the object summary page for a complete list of the properties and methods each object exposes.

FIGURE C.1:

The Jet engine DAO hierarchy

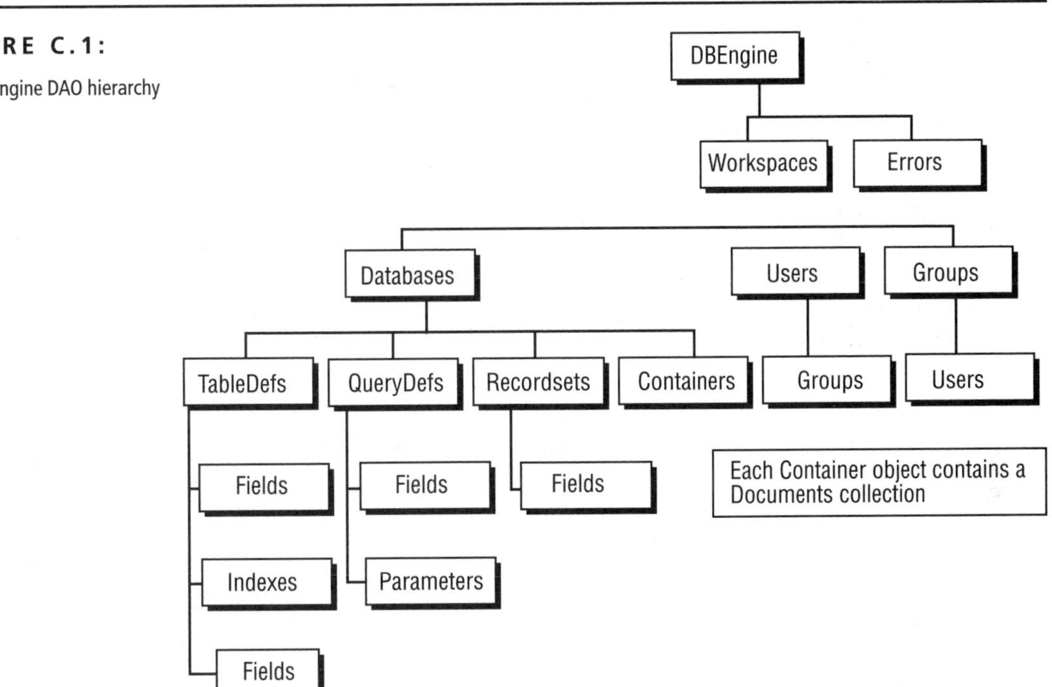

A workspace object represents a user's session. It contains all the open databases and provides for transaction processing and a secure workgroup. The Workspaces collection (of the DBEngine object) is the collection of all active workspaces. Unless you need to open an additional workspace, you'll rarely have any interaction with any workspace besides the default workspace Access opens for you.

As you can see in Figure C.1, each workspace object contains three collections: Databases, Users, and Groups. The Databases collection contains all the opened databases, and the Users and Groups collections contain information about (you guessed it) all the users and groups in the current workgroup.

Referring to Objects

You refer to data access objects by following the hierarchy presented in the preceding section. Start with the DBEngine object and work your way down. The general format for referring to objects is

DBEngine.*ParentCollectionItem.ChildCollection!ChildObject*

where it may take several iterations through parent collections before you get to the child collection you're interested in.

Access provides a special way to refer to the current user database: the CurrentDb function. (See the next section, "CurrentDb versus DBEngine(0)(0)," for more information.) From code, we'll almost always refer to the user's database with the CurrentDb function, because this is the preferred method. In addition, you can use the CurrentDb function when retrieving properties, like this (the parentheses following CurrentDb are optional and seldom used in this syntax):

```
Debug.Print CurrentDb.TableDefs(0).Name
```

To refer to any member of any collection, you can use one of four syntactical constructs. Table C.1 lists the four available methods. (In each example you're attempting to refer to the database named Sales that you'd previously opened as the only database in the default workspace—the one with the ordinal position 0).

TABLE C.1: Methods for Referring to Objects

Syntax	Details	Example
collection("name")		DBEngine.Workspaces(0).Databases("Sales")
collection(*var*)	Where *var* is a string or variant variable	strDatabase="Sales"DBEngine. Workspaces(0).Databases(strDatabase)
collection(*ordinal position*)	Where *ordinal position* is the object's position within its collection	DBEngine.Workspaces(0).Databases(0)
collection!*name*collection![*name*]	Brackets are necessary if *name* contains a nonstandard character, such as a space	DBEngine.Workspaces(0).Databases!Sales

WARNING

Access and DAO number all built-in collections with ordinal values beginning with 0. Almost all other components in the Microsoft "world" number their collections starting with 1, and user-defined collections within Access are also numbered starting with 1. This is a point about which you'll want to be very careful.

All objects except DBEngine have an associated collection that contains all the objects of the given type. For example, the TableDefs collection contains a TableDef object for each table saved in the database. Collections make it easy to "visit" all the objects of a specific type, looping through all the items in the collection. Because you can refer to all the items in a collection either by name or by position, you have the best of both worlds. If you know the specific object's name, you can find it by name, as in the following code fragment:

```
Debug.Print CurrentDb.TableDefs("tblCompanies").RecordCount
```

If you want to refer to an object by number, you can do that, too:

```
Debug.Print CurrentDb.TableDefs(0).Name
```

By the way, in Access 2, a subtle problem made it impossible to chain together references below the current database in the DAO hierarchy until you had already referred to the current database itself at least once. Therefore, in Access 2, your code had to declare a database variable, set it equal to a database, and then create references from there:

```
Dim db As DAO.Database
Dim tdf As DAO.Tabledef
Set db = DBEngine.Workspaces(0).Databases(0)
Set tdf = db.TableDefs(0)
Debug.Print tdf.RecordCount
```

This problem was fixed in Access 95, and you can now create references in one long string, if you wish. Either of the following statements will work:

```
Debug.Print DBEngine.Workspaces(0).Databases(0). _
 Tabledefs(0).RecordCount
```

or

```
Debug.Print CurrentDb.TableDefs(0).RecordCount
```

TIP

The "strung-out" reference using CurrentDb is useful only for retrieving properties; you cannot use it reliably to retrieve object references. In some situations it will work, but you're best off creating a variable that refers to the database and then using that variable for retrieving other references, just as you did in Access 2. You can use DBEngine.Workspaces(0).Databases(0) or CurrentDb to retrieve references directly in one statement, but it's simpler to subscribe to the old technique: get an object variable that refers to the current database and work from there.

CurrentDb versus DBEngine(0)(0)

To retrieve a reference to the current user's database, the DAO solution is to start with the DBEngine object, work your way through the Workspaces collection (Access creates Workspaces(0) for you when you log in to Access) and through the Databases collection (Access opens the user database as Databases(0)), all the way to:

```
DBEngine.Workspaces(0).Databases(0)
```

which you can shorten to:

```
DBEngine(0)(0)
```

if you count on default collections. (See the section "Using Default Collections" later in this appendix.)

Why, then, does Access *also* provide the CurrentDb function, which returns a reference to the current user's database? And why, when Microsoft stated quite clearly in Access 2 that CurrentDb was to be phased out and that the DAO reference was the preferred method for referencing the user's database, have they turned around and stated that CurrentDb is again the preferred method?

It all boils down to this: Jet and Access are two separate products. Jet provides the database services that Access requires, but Access provides its own layer on top of Jet, which you're using if you're designing applications inside Access. Access provides CurrentDb as a reference to the current database, and Jet provides DBEngine.Workspaces(0).Databases(0) (which can be condensed to DBEngine(0)(0)).

Certainly, the DBEngine(0)(0) syntax is required if you're working outside of Access. That is, if you're using OLE automation to control DAO, this is the only way to get a reference to the user's database in Access. On the other hand, Access provides the CurrentDb function, which will always refer to the current database from within Access.

Access presents some rather subtle problems having to do with the currency of the reference to the user's database. CurrentDb and DBEngine(0)(0) are not the same object internally, although they do both refer to the same database. Every time you retrieve a reference using CurrentDb, you're asking Access to create a new internal object that refers to the current database. On the other hand, Jet maintains only a single reference to the current database, DBEngine(0)(0). This explains why you can't create references using CurrentDb in a single long string: as VBA executes the line of code, Access creates a new database reference and gives you an object reference in that database. It's as though you've executed an explicit OpenDatabase on the current database. As soon as the line of code has finished executing, Access closes the database reference it just opened. For certain types of objects (Recordsets, in particular), Access attempts to keep the reference to the recordset viable. For other types of objects, however, Access does not maintain the open reference, and further attempts at using the object will fail.

For example, attempting to run this procedure:

```
Sub ThisDoesntWork()
    Dim doc As DAO.Document
    Set doc = CurrentDb.Containers!Tables.Documents(0)
    Debug.Print doc.Name
End Sub
```

will fail with an error when the code attempts to print doc.Name. The database object that was used to reference that particular document is long gone, and *doc* becomes an invalid reference. Note, however, that if you were to replace CurrentDb with DBEngine(0)(0), this procedure would work fine. If you change the code to use a database variable instead of a single long reference, it will also work fine:

```
Sub ThisDoesWork()
    Dim db As DAO.Database
    Dim doc As DAO.Document

    Set db = CurrentDb()
    Set doc = db.Containers!Tables.Documents(0)
    Debug.Print doc.Name
End Sub
```

How do you choose between CurrentDb and DBEngine(0)(0) in your applications? If you're working with Jet using Automation, your answer is simple: you use DBEngine(0)(0) to refer to the current database. If you're working in Access, however, you can use either CurrentDb or DBEngine(0)(0) to refer to the current database. Certainly, using CurrentDb is simpler, and it is easier to understand as you peruse code. On the other hand, it's slower. (Experimentation has shown that retrieving a reference using CurrentDb can be an order of magnitude slower than using DBEngine(0)(0).) There's one big difference between the two that may make your decision for you: the database referred to by CurrentDb is always up to date with the user interface. However, you must call the Refresh method before you use any collection retrieved using a reference through DBEngine(0)(0). The Refresh method is quite expensive (slow, that is) and will immediately obviate any speed gains you made by choosing DBEngine(0)(0) over CurrentDb. Almost every example in this book that refers to the current database (using DAO) uses CurrentDb.

Bang (!) versus Dot (.)

The bang ("!") and dot (".") identifier operators help describe the relationships among collections, objects, and properties in an expression. They indicate that one part of an expression belongs to another.

In general, you follow the bang with the name of something you created: a form, report, or control. The bang also indicates that the item to follow is an element of a collection. You'll usually follow the dot with a property, collection, or method name.

You can also think of the uses of these operators this way: a bang separates an object from the collection it's in (a field in a table, a form in the Forms collection, a control on a form), while a dot separates an object from a property, method, or collection of that object.

Ordinal Positions

As you've seen, you can refer to an object using the ordinal position within its collection. Jet assigns and maintains these ordinal positions, and they always start with position number 0. For the Workspaces and Databases objects, ordinal position 0 always refers to the current workspace and the current database (the one that's open in the user interface). For example, when you start Microsoft Access, it opens a Jet engine session, creates a workspace, and assigns it to the first ordinal position in the Workspaces collection. When you open a database through the user interface (using the File ➢ Open Database menu item), Access assigns the database to the first ordinal position in the Databases collection.

For objects other than workspaces and databases, an object's ordinal position is dependent on the order in which it was added to its collection. The first table you create will have a lower ordinal position than tables that you create later. As you create and delete objects, an object's ordinal position changes within its collection. Additionally, Access creates objects (such as the system tables) that may preclude your objects from starting at ordinal position 0. For this reason, it is not a good idea to refer to a specific object using its ordinal position. You should use the ordinal position of objects only as loop indexes, for iterating through all the objects in a collection.

NOTE

Using an object's ordinal position has become less important since Access 2, with the addition of the For Each...Next construct. There are times, however, when you must loop through the entries in a collection. If your action changes the number of elements in the collection, using For Each...Next will, in general, fail. In cases when you're closing objects or deleting them from their collection, use a For...Next loop, using the objects' ordinal position to refer to them.

Using Default Collections

You can see from previous examples that a simple object reference can result in a long line of code. Fortunately, DAO provides default collections for most object types: if you don't specify a collection, Access assumes you're referring to the default collection for the parent object. You can use the default collection behavior of objects to make your code more compact (but somewhat less readable). Table C.2 lists the default collection within each object type.

TABLE C.2: Default Collections for DAO Objects

Object	Default Collection
Container	Documents
Database	TableDefs
DBEngine	Workspaces
Group	Users
Index	Fields
QueryDef	Parameters
Recordset	Fields
Relation	Fields
TableDef	Fields
User	Groups
Workspace	Databases

Using default collections, you can shorten this expression:

```
DBEngine.Workspaces(0).Databases(0).TableDefs(0)
```

to

```
DBEngine(0)(0)(0)
```

This expression means, "Refer to the first tabledef within the first database within the first workspace" because the default collection for DBEngine is the Workspaces collection, the default collection for a workspace object is the Databases collection, and the default collection for a database object is the TableDefs collection.

You can use similar contractions to simplify your code. Be aware, though, that using default collections to reduce your code also makes it less readable: whoever is reading the code will have to understand the meaning of the expression without any visual clues.

Enumerating Objects in Collections

Because you can access any object in any collection by its position in the collection, you can use a loop to look at or modify any object in the collection. Use the Count property of a collection to determine the size of the collection. Remember that the ordinal position of objects within a DAO collection starts at 0; if a collection contains three elements, they'll be numbered 0 through 2.

For example, you could use code like this to print out the names of all the tables in your database:

```
Dim db As DAO.Database
Dim intI As Integer
Dim tdf As DAO.Tabledef

Set db = CurrentDb()
For intI = 0 To db.TableDefs.Count - 1
    Set tdf = db.TableDefs(intI)
    Debug.Print tdf.Name
Next intI
```

The simplest way to loop through any collection, however, is to use the For Each...Next syntax. This syntax requires you to create a variable that can refer to the object type in the collection you're looping through and then use code like this to do the work:

```
Dim db As DAO.Database
Dim tdf As DAO.TableDef

Set db = CurrentDb()
For Each tdf In db.TableDefs
    Debug.Print tdf.Name
Next tdf
```

In this case, For Each...Next does the "Set" operation for you.

Working with Properties

If you have worked with forms, reports, and controls, you are already familiar with referencing properties. (See Chapters 7 through 9 for more information on user interface objects.) However, the interaction between the Jet engine and Microsoft Access introduces new subtleties when you are working with properties.

Properties for data access objects behave somewhat differently from Microsoft Access properties. As you saw earlier in this appendix, every object has a collection of properties. For Access objects (forms and reports, for example), every property in the Properties collection that will ever exist for the object exists when you create the object. This is not necessarily the case for data access objects. Properties may not exist in the collection until you set them to a value, depending on the specific object. Therefore, it's important that you understand the differences among the different types of properties used in DAO.

Types of Properties

DAO properties can be either built-in or user-defined.

Built-in properties always exist for an object. They define the basic characteristics of an object and are available to any application that uses the Jet engine. For example, for Field objects, *Name* and *Type* are built-in properties. They define the basic characteristics of a field.

User-defined properties are added to the Properties collection of an object. These properties may be added either by Microsoft Access as a client of the Jet engine or by you as an application developer. If Microsoft Access added the property to the object, it's treated as a special case of a user-defined property. The properties Access adds are properties it needs in order to do its job. The Jet engine can't provide them, because they're specific to Access.

User-defined properties do not exist until they are added to the object's Properties collection. While this may seem obvious, it does cause some unexpected behavior. For example, a field's description is not a built-in property. Even though you can enter a field's description while defining the table, the Jet engine doesn't know about it until you've actually typed it into the property list for the field. If you try to retrieve the Description property of an object that has not yet had this property set, you will get a trappable runtime error.

Referring to Data Access Object Properties

As in referencing any other property, you can use the standard

object.property

syntax for referring to a built-in property of an object. On the other hand, to refer to a user-defined property (whether the "user" is you, your application, or Access as a client of the Jet engine), you must refer to the property through the Properties collection of the object (and this syntax always works, even for built-in properties):

object.Properties("property")

or

object.Properties!property

For example, to retrieve the Description property for the tblClients table, you could use code like the following. (Note that this code will fail with a runtime error if the Description property hasn't already been set.)

```
Dim db As DAO.Database
Dim tdf As DAO.TableDef
Dim strDescription As String

Set db = CurrentDb()
Set tdf = db.TableDefs!tblCustomers
strDescription = tdf.Properties!Description
```

(For more information on adding user-defined properties, see the section "Creating Your Own Properties" later in this appendix.)

Enumerating the Properties

Listing C.1 shows code you could use to print out all the properties of any table:

Listing C.1

```
Function ListProperties(strTable As String)

    Dim db As DAO.Database
    Dim tdf As DAO.TableDef
    Dim prp As DAO.Property

    Set db = CurrentDb()
    ' You could use the following expression:
    ' Set tdf = db.TableDefs(strTable)
    ' but the TableDefs collection is the default collection
    ' for a Database object.  So its use is unnecessary
    ' in the expression.
    Set tdf = db(strTable)

    For Each prp In tdf.Properties
        Debug.Print prp.Name, prp.Value
    Next prp
End Function
```

You'll find ListProperties in basTestProperties (in APDXC.MDB). The output from the preceding code might look something like the output shown in Figure C.2.

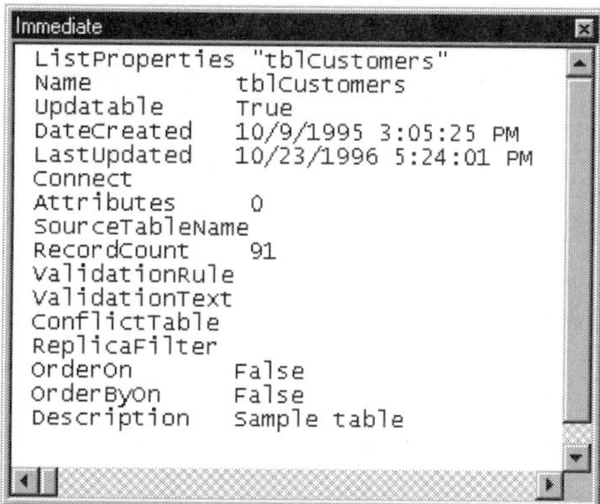

FIGURE C.2: Sample property listing for tblCustomers

Setting and Retrieving Properties

To make it simpler to set and get properties of objects, we've provided the adhGetProp and adhSetProp functions in basHandleProps (in APDXC.MDB). The adhSetProp function takes as its parameters an object reference, a property name, and a value. It attempts to set the property, and if it fails, it attempts to create the property and then set its value. Of course, this feature can work only for objects that allow you to create user-defined properties (Database, Field, Index, QueryDef, or TableDef). For example:

```
Set db = CurrentDb()
varRetval = adhSetProp(db.TableDefs("tblCustomers"), _
 "Description", "This is the customer table")
If Not IsError(varRetval) Then
    MsgBox "Description set successfully!"
End If
```

will set the Description property. If that property hadn't existed before the function call, adhSetProp would have created it and then set it. (See basHandleProps for the details.)

The adhGetProp function is simpler: it just attempts to retrieve the requested property, and it returns the value if the property exists or an error value otherwise. For example:

```
Set db = CurrentDb()
varRetval = adhGetProp( _
 db.TableDefs("tblCustomers").Fields("CustomerID"), _
 "Description")
If Not IsError(varRetval) Then
    MsgBox "The Description property was: " & varRetval
End If
```

will return either the Description property for the CustomerID field in tblCustomers or an error value if that property doesn't exist.

Data Definition Using DAO

The previous sections have been using data access objects to refer to existing objects and properties. A large portion of DAO's power, though, lies in its ability to programmatically create and manipulate objects. Using the Create… and Append methods, you can create and modify virtually any data access object.

Creating Objects

To create a new object using DAO, follow these three steps:

1. Use one of the Create… methods to create the object (CreateTable, Create-Index, and so on).
2. Define the new object's characteristics by setting its properties. Some properties (such as its name) are essential to its existence and must be specified when you create the object. Others may be specified later. (In most cases, this step can be rolled up into the previous one. All the Create… methods accept optional parameters that let you specify essential properties of the new object.)
3. Append the object to its collection to make it a permanent part of your database.

In cases where the new object contains other objects (a table contains fields, for instance), you must create the main object, then create the subordinate objects, append them to the appropriate collection, and then append the main object to its collection. You can use this same technique when creating a new table, index, or relation programmatically. Each operation is unique in one way or another, so consult the online help for more information on the CreateTable, CreateField, CreateIndex, CreateProperty, and CreateRelation methods. The following sections demonstrate how to create these complex objects.

Creating a New Table

The following example creates a new table called tblOrders and adds two fields to it. You'll find the complete function in basCreateTable in APDXC.MDB.

```
Public Function CreateOrdersTable()

    Dim db As DAO.Database
    Dim tdfOrders As DAO.TableDef
    Dim fld1 As DAO.Field
    Dim fld2 As DAO.Field

    Set db = CurrentDb()

    On Error Resume Next
    ' Delete the table if it already exists.
```

```
db.TableDefs.Delete "tblOrders"
On Error GoTo 0

Set tdfOrders = db.CreateTableDef()
tdfOrders.Name = "tblOrders"

Set fld1 = tdfOrders.CreateField("OrderID", dbLong)
Set fld2 = tdfOrders.CreateField("CustomerName", _
 dbText, 30)
```

At this point, the new table and its two fields exist only in memory. To make the new objects a permanent part of the database, you must use the Append method. If you do not append a new object to a collection, it will not be saved as an object in the database.

WARNING Creating objects and giving them properties is not enough. You must take the step of appending them to the correct collection, or Access will never know of their existence. If your program exits before you've used the Append method to add them to a collection, they will be discarded.

The next lines save the new objects to the database:

```
With tdfOrders.Fields
    .Append fld1
    .Append fld2
End With

With db.TableDefs
    .Append tdfOrders
    .Refresh
End With
```

Finally, you can refresh the TableDefs collection to ensure that the new objects are included in it. In a multiuser environment, the new table may not be immediately available to other users unless you refresh the collection. The following line refreshes the TableDefs collection:

```
db.TableDefs.Refresh
```

Even using the Refresh method, Access won't update the database window itself until it must. It will only show the new table you've created once you move to a different collection and then back to the list of tables. To solve this problem,

Access 97 added the RefreshDatabaseWindow method of the Application object. Adding this line of code will refresh the database window's display:

```
Application.RefreshDatabaseWindow
```

TIP

The With...End With syntax can make it simpler to modify multiple properties or use multiple methods of an object. The previous example used the syntax only for the purpose of introducing it, but it can both simplify your code and make its intent clearer. You'll want to use it whenever possible.

You can also use the

Dim objectVar As New *Object*

syntax to create the objects. When you do this, Access creates the reference and then instantiates the object automatically. Rather than having to call CreateTable explicitly, Access creates the TableDef object for you when you write

```
Dim tdf As New DAO.TableDef
```

This syntax creates, at the same time, both the object variable and the object to which it points. Once you've created an object this way (by running the procedure that includes the declaration), you still need to assign the values of the properties of the object, and you need to append it to the appropriate collection.

For example, you could rewrite the preceding function as shown here. Note that this function will fail if you attempt to run it twice or if you've already run CreateOrdersTable—if you want to rerun it, manually delete the table from the database.

```
Public Function CreateOrdersTable2()

    Dim db As DAO.Database

    ' Create the objects RIGHT NOW, as opposed
    ' to creating variables to point to objects that
    ' you'll create later.
    Dim tdfOrders As New DAO.TableDef
    Dim fld1 As New DAO.Field
    Dim fld2 As New DAO.Field
```

```
    Set db = CurrentDb()
    ' The tabledef's already created, so
    ' just assign the properties.
    tdfOrders.Name = "tblOrders"

    ' The fields are already created, so just
    ' assign the properties.
    With fld1
        .Type = dbLong
        .Name = "OrderID"
    End With

    With fld2
        .Type = dbText
        .Size = 30
        .Name = "CustomerName"
    End With
    With tdfOrders.Fields
        .Append fld1
        .Append fld2
    End With

    With db.TableDefs
        .Append tdfOrders
        .Refresh
    End With
    Application.RefreshDatabaseWindow
End Function
```

We can't recommend a real preference for either method, except that calling the Create… methods directly makes your code more *explicit:* on viewing the code, it's easier to see exactly what it's doing. In addition, using a Create… method allows you greater control over when the object comes into being: when you use the New keyword, Jet creates the object the first time you attempt to set or retrieve a property of the object.

The Create... Methods

For each data access object that you can create programmatically, there's an associated *Create* method. Table C.3 summarizes the methods and their syntax.

TABLE C.3: Object Creation Methods

Object	Method	Arguments	Data Type	Description
Table	CreateTableDef	Name	String	Name of the new table.
		Attributes	Integer	Settings for attached, system, and hidden tables.
		Source	String	An attached table's base table type information.
		Connect	String	An attached table's base table path and file name.
Field	CreateField	Name	String	Name of the new field.
		Type	Integer	Data type of the new field.
		Size	Integer	Size of the field if it is a text field.
Index	CreateIndex	Name	String	Name of the new index.
Query	CreateQueryDef	Name	String	Name of the new query.
		SQLText	String	Valid SQL string that defines the new query.
Relation	CreateRelation	Name	String	Name of the new relation.
		Table	String	Name of the relation's primary table.
		ForeignTable	String	Name of the relation's foreign table.
		Attributes	Integer	Settings for relationship type, enforced referential integrity, and cascaded updates and deletes.
Workspace	CreateWorkspace	Name	String	Name of the new workspace.
		User	String	Name of an existing user. This user will become the owner of the new workspace object. For code that references the new workspace object, *User* will, in effect, be the user executing the code.

Continued on next page

TABLE C.3 CONTINUED: Object Creation Methods

Object	Method	Arguments	Data Type	Description
Workspace	CreateWorkspace	Password	String	Password for the new workspace object. Can contain any characters except ASCII null (Chr$(0)).
		Type	Long	Value indicating the data source (dbUseJet for Jet, or dbUseODBC for ODBCDirect).
Database	CreateDatabase	DatabaseName	String	Name of the file that contains the database.
		Locale	String	Collating order of the database.
		Options	Integer	Options for the new database. You can specify whether or not the database is to be encrypted and which version (2.0 or 3.0) of the file format to use when saving the database.
Group	CreateGroup	Name	String	Name of the new group.
		PID	String	Personal identifier for the new group.
User	CreateUser	Name	String	Name of the new user.
		PID	String	Personal identifier for the new user.
		Password	String	Password for the new User object (up to 14 characters).

Creating an Index

As part of your applications, you may need to create an index programmatically. Follow these steps to create a new index:

1. Use the CreateIndex method of a TableDef object to create the index object and set its Name property (either in the function call itself or by assigning a

value to the Name property sometime before you append the index to the Indexes collection).

2. Assign values to the new index's properties, as appropriate. All the properties are read/write for an index object that hasn't yet been appended to the Indexes collection but are read-only once that has occurred. The properties you'll most likely be interested in are Name, Primary, Unique, and Required.
3. Use the CreateField method to create a field object for each field that makes up part of the index, and append each to the index's Fields collection. This collection of fields indicates to the index the fields for which it must maintain values in order to keep itself current.
4. Use the Append method of the original TableDef object to append the index object to its Indexes collection.

NOTE

Because all the properties of an index object are read-only once the object has been appended to its collection, if you need to modify a property of an index once it's been created, you must delete the object and then create a new one.

TIP

In Access, using DAO, you can name your indexes any way you wish. However, if you have code you're using that counts on your primary key being named PrimaryKey (and almost any place you're using the Seek method in your code, you will), you must ensure that your primary keys are named with the standard value, PrimaryKey. Otherwise, existing code might break.

The adhCreatePrimaryKey function in Listing C.2 creates the primary key for any specified table. You pass to this function the name of the table, the name of the primary key, and a variant that may contain an array of field names or just a single field name to use as part of the primary key. Along the way, adhCreatePrimaryKey calls the FindPrimaryKey function, which returns the name of the primary key if it exists or Null if it doesn't. If a primary key already exists, adhCreatePrimaryKey deletes the primary key so it can create a new one. We've also included a test procedure, TestCreatePK, to test the functionality. You'll find all these examples in the module basPK in APDXC.MDB.

Listing C.2

```
Public Function adhCreatePrimaryKey( _
 strTableName As String, strKeyName As String, _
 ParamArray varFields() As Variant) As Boolean

    Dim idx As DAO.Index
    Dim tdf As DAO.TableDef
    Dim fld As DAO.Field
    Dim varPK As Variant
    Dim varIdx As Variant
    Dim idxs As DAO.Indexes
    Dim db As DAO.Database

    On Error GoTo CreatePrimaryKey_Err

    Set db = CurrentDb()
    Set tdf = db.TableDefs(strTableName)
    Set idxs = tdf.Indexes

    ' Find out if the table currently has a primary key.
    ' If so, delete it now.
    varPK = FindPrimaryKey(tdf)
    If Not IsNull(varPK) Then
        idxs.Delete varPK
    End If
    ' Create the new index object.
    Set idx = tdf.CreateIndex(strKeyName)

    ' Set the new index up as the primary key.
    ' This will also set:
    '   IgnoreNulls property to False,
    '   Required property to True,
    '   Unique property to True.
    idx.Primary = True

    ' Now create the fields that make up the index,
    ' and append each to the collection of fields.
    For Each varIdx In varFields
        AddField idx, varIdx
    Next varIdx

    ' Now append the index to the TableDef's
```

```
    ' index collection
    idxs.Append idx
    adhCreatePrimaryKey = True

CreatePrimaryKey_Exit:
    Exit Function

CreatePrimaryKey_Err:
    MsgBox "Error: " & Err.Description & _
     " (" & Err.Number & ")"
    adhCreatePrimaryKey = False
    Resume CreatePrimaryKey_Exit
End Function

Private Function FindPrimaryKey( _
 tdf As DAO.TableDef) As Variant

    ' Given a particular tabledef, find the
    ' primary key name, if it exists.

    ' Return the name of the primary key's index, if
    ' it exists, or Null if there wasn't a primary key.

    Dim idx As DAO.Index

    For Each idx In tdf.Indexes
        If idx.Primary Then
            FindPrimaryKey = idx.Name
            Exit Function
        End If
    Next idx
    FindPrimaryKey = Null
End Function

Private Function AddField( _
 idx As DAO.Index, varIdx As Variant) As Boolean

    ' Given an index object, and a field name, add
    ' the field to the index.
    ' Return True on success, False otherwise.

    Dim fld As DAO.Field
```

```
    On Error GoTo AddIndex_Err
    If Len(varIdx & "") > 0 Then
        Set fld = idx.CreateField(varIdx)
        idx.Fields.Append fld
    End If
    AddField = True

AddIndex_Exit:
    Exit Function

AddIndex_Err:
    AddField = False
    Resume AddIndex_Exit
End Function

Public Sub TestCreatePK()
    Debug.Print adhCreatePrimaryKey( _
     "tblCustomerItems", "PrimaryKey", _
     "CustomerID", "ItemID")
End Sub
```

Creating Relationships

To create a relationship, use the CreateRelation method of a database object. Follow these steps to create a new relation:

1. Open the database that will be the basis for your relation.
2. Verify that the referenced table (the primary table in the relation) has a primary key in place.
3. Use the CreateRelation method of the database to create the relation object. Either set the relation's properties when you create it or set them one by one after the fact. These properties include the Table, ForeignTable, and Attributes properties.
4. Create a field object for each primary key field from the primary table involved in the relationship. For each field object, supply the ForeignName property, which corresponds to the name of the matching key field in the secondary table. Append each new field object to the relationship's Fields collection.

5. Use the Append method to append the new relation object to the database's Relations collection.

The following table lists all the possible values for the Attributes property of a relation object:

Constant	Description
dbRelationUnique	Relationship is one-to-one
dbRelationDontEnforce	Relationship isn't enforced (no referential integrity)
dbRelationInherited	Relationship exists in the database that contains the two attached tables
dbRelationLeft	Relationship is a left outer join
dbRelationRight	Relationship is a right outer join
dbRelationUpdateCascade	Updates will cascade
dbRelationDeleteCascade	Deletions will cascade

Set the property to be the sum of any of these constants. (Most programmers use the Or operator to combine these sorts of flags, just to make it clear they're working with flag values and not doing some sort of arithmetic.) If you set no value for the Attributes property, Access attempts to create a one-to-many inner-joined relationship with referential integrity enabled.

Listing C.3 demonstrates, in the simplest case, the steps involved in creating a relationship. This function (from basRelations in APDXC.MDB) creates a left outer join between tblCustomers and tblCustomerItems and enables cascading deletes. Just to make sure the function succeeds, if it finds that the relation already exists, it deletes that relation and recreates it.

Listing C.3

```
Const adhcErrObjectExists = 3012

Function CreateRelationship() As Boolean

    ' Create a relationship between tblCustomers
    ' and tblCustomerItems.
```

```
' The relation will be a left outer join, with cascading
' deletes enabled.

Dim db As DAO.Database
Dim rel As DAO.Relation
Dim fld As DAO.Field

On Error GoTo CreateRelationship_Err

Set db = CurrentDb()

' Create the new relation object.
Set rel = db.CreateRelation()

' Set the relation's properties.
With rel
    .Name = "Relation1"
    .Table = "tblCustomers"
    .ForeignTable = "tblCustomerItems"

    ' Create a left outer join containing
    ' tblCustomers and tblItems,
    ' with cascading updates enabled.
    .Attributes = dbRelationLeft Or _
     dbRelationDeleteCascade
End With
' Or, you could set all the properties when
' you create the object:
' Set rel = db.CreateRelation( _
'  "Relation1", "tblCustomers", "tblCustomerItems", _
'   dbRelationLeft Or dbRelationDeleteCascade)

' Set the relation's field collection.
Set fld = rel.CreateField("CustomerID")
' What field does this map to in the OTHER table?
fld.ForeignName = "CustomerID"
rel.Fields.Append fld
' You could append more fields, if you needed to.

' Append the relation to the database's
' relations collection.
```

```
    db.Relations.Append rel
    CreateRelationship = True

CreateRelationship_Exit:
    Exit Function

CreateRelationship_Err:
    Select Case Err.Number
        Case adhcErrObjectExists
            ' If the relationship already exists,
            ' just delete it, and then try to
            ' append it again.
            db.Relations.Delete rel.Name
            Resume
        Case Else
            MsgBox "Error: " & Err.Description & _
             " (" & Err.Number & ")"
            CreateRelationship = False
            Resume CreateRelationship_Exit
    End Select
End Function
```

Creating Your Own Properties

Access support for DAO makes it possible for you to create your own properties and append them to the Properties collection for an object. For example, you might like to add a LastChanged property to a table to keep track of the last time a user touched the table. Just as for adding an object of any other type, you take three steps:

1. Use the CreateProperty method to create the new property.
2. Define the new property's characteristics by setting its properties. (You may have done this in step 1.)
3. Append the object to the Properties collection to make it a permanent part of your database.

The code in Listing C.4 creates the LastChanged and LastUser properties and appends them to the tblCustomers table. (You can find the function in basTest-Properties in APDXC.MDB.) The following paragraphs examine the function in detail.

The function's caller has passed in the name of the table on which to operate, so the first step is to set up a reference to the correct TableDef object:

```
Dim db As DAO.Database
Dim tdf As DAO.TableDef
Dim prpLastChanged As DAO.Property
Dim prpLastUser As DAO.Property
Dim prp As DAO.Property

Set db = CurrentDb()
Set tdf = db.TableDefs(strName)
```

Then, you need to create the new Property objects. When you call CreateProperty, you may supply the property's name, type, and initial value. You may also set those properties later, before you append the property to the table's Properties collection. In this case, it's simpler just to do it all in the call to CreateProperty. You set the LastChanged property to contain the current time and the LastUser property to contain the current user ("Admin", unless you've logged in as someone else). (This step corresponds to steps 1 and 2 in the previous list of steps necessary to create new properties.)

```
' Create the two new properties.
Set prpLastChanged = tdf.CreateProperty("LastChanged", _
 dbDate, Now)
Set prpLastUser = tdf.CreateProperty("LastUser", _
 dbText, CurrentUser())
```

Use the Append method to add the properties to the table so they become persistent. Because the Append method triggers a runtime error if you've already appended the properties, you can avoid the problem by turning off error checking while appending:

```
On Error Resume Next
With tdf.Properties
    .Append prpLastChanged
    .Append prpLastUser
End With

On Error GoTo 0
```

To list the properties, you can loop through the Properties collection:

```
Dim prp As DAO.Property
For Each prp In tdf.Properties
    Debug.Print prp.Name, prp.Value
Next prp
```

To modify the LastChanged property, use one of the two possible syntax variations:

```
tdf.Properties!LastChanged = Now
```

or

```
tdf.Properties("LastChanged") = Now
```

Listing C.4

```
Sub TestAddProps(strName As String)
    Dim db As DAO.Database
    Dim tdf As DAO.TableDef
    Dim prpLastChanged As DAO.Property
    Dim prpLastUser As DAO.Property
    Dim prp As DAO.Property

    Set db = CurrentDb()
    Set tdf = db.TableDefs(strName)

    ' Create the two new properties.
    Set prpLastChanged = tdf.CreateProperty("LastChanged", _
     dbDate, Now)
    Set prpLastUser = tdf.CreateProperty("LastUser", _
     dbText, CurrentUser())

    ' This code will fail if the properties have already
    ' been added, so just let the errors occur,
    ' and keep on going.
    On Error Resume Next
    With tdf.Properties
        .Append prpLastChanged
        .Append prpLastUser
    End With
    On Error GoTo 0

    ' Now list out all the properties.
    ' This syntax works, no matter whether
    ' the property is built-in or user-defined.
    For Each prp In tdf.Properties
        Debug.Print prp.Name, prp.Value
    Next prp
```

```
    ' Reset the LastChanged property, just to show how:
    tdf.Properties("LastChanged") = Now
End Sub
```

Modifying Objects

You can modify an existing object using DAO methods and properties without having to open the object in Design view. There are, however, other restrictions to keep in mind when setting properties of data access objects. Some properties can be set only when the object is created and cannot be changed after the object has been appended to its collection. The Attributes property of TableDef objects is an example of this restriction: you cannot change the Attributes property of an existing TableDef object but must set this value when you first create the object. If you must alter the Attributes property for a given tabledef, you need to create a new one, copy in all the information from the existing one, and set the Attributes property before you use the Append method to add the tabledef to your database. Also, you need to be aware that some properties do not exist for a data access object until they have been set to a value. (See the section "Types of Properties" earlier in this appendix for a reminder about this limitation.)

Working with Recordsets

In almost any Access application, sooner or later you'll need to manipulate data from VBA. DAO provides a rich set of data access objects to allow you to view, edit, add, and delete fields, rows, and tables. In its attempt to be as flexible as possible, Jet provides three separate means of working with data: tables, dynasets, and snapshots. Each has its own uses and capabilities. The following sections discuss these issues.

Meet the Recordsets

Although DAO provides three types of recordset objects, the one you use in any given situation depends on the source of the data being referenced and the methods you need to use to access the data. Table C.4 lists each recordset type, along with its benefits and drawbacks.

TABLE C.4: Recordset Types and Their Benefits/Drawbacks

Recordset Type	Description	Benefits	Drawbacks
Table	Set of records in a table in a database	Can use indexes for quick searches. Data can be edited.	Works only for local Access tables, not attached tables.
Dynaset	Set of pointers (bookmarks) referring to data in tables or queries in a database	Can include data from multiple tables, either local or attached. Can be based on a SQL string. Data can be edited in most cases.	Some dynasets may not be editable. Cannot perform indexed searches using the faster Seek method.
Snapshot	Copy of a set of records as it exists at the time the snapshot is created	Can optionally be set to scroll forward only, allowing faster operations.	Data cannot be edited. All records in a recordset's data source are read before control is returned to the program. Doesn't reflect changes to data made in a multiuser environment. A snapshot is a picture of the data at the time the snapshot is created, and no updates will be reflected in its set of rows. Cannot perform indexed searches using the faster Seek method.

Creating a Recordset

You use an expression such as one of the following to create a recordset:

Dim rst As DAO.Recordset

Set rst = db.OpenRecordset(*Source*, *Type* , *Options*, *LockEdits*)

or

Set rst = *object*.OpenRecordset(*Type*, *Options*, *LockEdits*)

(The Type, Options, and LockEdits parameters are optional.)

In the first example, you're creating a new recordset based on something in the database referred to by the database variable db. The *Source* parameter indicates where the data will come from and must be one of the following:

- Name of an existing table
- Name of an existing query that returns rows
- A SQL statement that returns rows

For table-type recordsets, the source can only be the name of an existing table.

In the second example, *object* can be any previously opened database object that returns rows, such as a table, a query, or even another recordset variable. Because you've already specified the source of the data, you needn't specify it again when creating a recordset based on an existing object.

In both cases, the *Type* parameter specifies the type of the recordset. It should be one of the following built-in constant values:

- dbOpenTable, to open a table recordset
- dbOpenDynaset, to open a dynaset recordset
- dbOpenSnapshot, to open a snapshot recordset
- dbOpenForwardOnly, to open a forward-only type recordset (cannot be cloned and supports only the MoveNext method)

If you don't specify a type, Access automatically chooses the type it will open for the given *Source.* For example, if you create a recordset based on a table in the current database and don't specify *Type,* Access automatically opens a table-type recordset. Likewise, if *Source* is an attached table, a query, or a SQL string and you haven't specified the *Type* parameter, Access automatically opens a dynaset recordset. In addition, you cannot specify dbOpenTable unless the *Source* parameter is the name of a local table. If you do, Access triggers trappable error 3011, "Couldn't find object…," for SQL expressions, or 3219, "Invalid operation," for attached tables.

The *Options* parameter controls the multiuser access and update behavior of the recordset. It can be one of the values listed in Table C.5.

TABLE C.5: Options for Recordsets

Constant	Description
dbAppendOnly	You can only append new records. (Applies only to dynaset-type recordsets.)
dbSQLPassThrough	Causes the SQL to be passed through directly to the back-end server for processing. (Applies only to snapshot-type recordsets.)
dbSeeChanges	Jet triggers a runtime error if another user changes data you're currently editing. (Applies only to dynaset-type recordsets.)
dbDenyWrite	Other users can't modify or add records. This effectively write-locks the recordset's underlying data source(s). Note that when you lock a dynaset recordset, you are locking all the underlying tables.
dbDenyRead	Other users can't view records. By setting this option, you are completely locking other users out of viewing the table. (Applies only to table-type recordsets.)
dbForwardOnly	The recordset is a forward-scrolling snapshot. Use this type of recordset when you are making only one pass through the records. Since a forward-only snapshot does not copy data into a scrollable buffer, it can run much more quickly. Supplied for backward compatibility—see the dbOpenForwardOnly option. (Applies only to snapshot-type recordsets and cannot be used in conjunction with the dbOpenForwardOnly option.)
dbReadOnly	You can only view records; other users can modify them. This is a useful safeguard that can keep your code from inadvertently modifying data.
dbInconsistent	Inconsistent updates are allowed. (Applies only to dynaset-type recordsets, and only one of dbConsistent and dbInconsistent is allowed.)
dbConsistent	Only consistent updates are allowed. (Applies only to dynaset-type recordsets, and only one of dbConsistent and dbInconsistent is allowed.)

The *LockEdits* parameter controls the concurrency of multiple users' access to the new recordset. Choose one or more of the following values:

dbReadOnly You can only view records; other users can modify them. Use this flag in either the Options parameter or the LockEdits parameter, but not both.

dbPessimistic Use pessimistic locking. A page is locked as soon as you use the Edit method and stays locked as long as you're editing any data in the page. This is the default for Jet.

dbOptimistic Use optimistic locking. A page is locked only when you use the Update method and is therefore only locked long enough to write the data to the table.

See online help for more information on interactions between the various settings.

Consistent versus Inconsistent Updates

When you create a recordset object based on more than one table, Access by default allows you to make changes only to the "many" side of a join. This is known as a *consistent update.* At times, you may want to update both sides of a join. To do this, set the dbInconsistent option. Note that this may violate the relationships between tables that your application needs. It is up to you to provide the necessary code to ensure that any "implied" referential integrity is maintained.

If you've turned on referential integrity for a relationship and enabled cascading updates, the dbInconsistent and dbConsistent options will cause identical behavior. In this case, the referential integrity takes control, and the cascading updates will update the "many" side of the relationship when you update the "one" side.

Creating Recordset Objects

The following examples show a number of ways you can create recordset objects. This list isn't exhaustive, but it does show some representative cases.

- To create a recordset based on a table or a saved query:

```
Dim db As DAO.Database
Dim rstCustomers As DAO.Recordset
Dim rstSales As DAO.Recordset

Set db = CurrentDb()

' This will create a table-type Recordset.
Set rstCustomers = db.OpenRecordset("tblCustomers", _
 dbOpenTable)

' This will create a dynaset-type Recordset.
Set rstSales = db.OpenRecordset("qryCustSales", dbOpenDynaset)
```

- To create a dynaset-type recordset based on a SQL string:

```
Dim db As DAO.Database
Dim rstCustomers As DAO.Recordset
Dim strSQL As String

strSQL = "SELECT [Contact Name] AS Name " & _
 "FROM Customers ORDER BY [Contact Name]"
Set db = CurrentDb()
Set rstCustomers = db.OpenRecordset(strSQL, dbOpenDynaset)
```

- To create a table-type recordset that locks other users out of the source's records:

```
Dim db As DAO.Database
Dim rstCustomers As DAO.Recordset

Set db = CurrentDb()
Set rstCustomers = db.OpenRecordset( _
 "tblCustomers", dbOpenTable, dbDenyRead)
```

- To create a snapshot-type recordset based on a table:

```
Dim db As DAO.Database
Dim rstCustomers As DAO.Recordset

Set db = CurrentDb()
Set rstCustomers = db.OpenRecordset("tblCustomers", _
 dbOpenSnapshot)
```

Moving through a Recordset

Once you've created a recordset, Access provides a variety of methods for navigating through the rows: MoveFirst, MoveLast, MovePrevious, and MoveNext. Each of these works in the manner you would expect, based on the name. In addition, Access provides the Move method, which can move a specified number of rows forward or backward, either from the current row or from a stored bookmark. If the object is a table-type recordset, the movement follows the order of the active index, which you can set using the Index property of the recordset. If you have not specified the index for table-type recordsets, the row order is undefined. Recordsets also support the AbsolutePosition and PercentPosition properties, which allow you to read and write the current position within the recordset, based on the data in the current set of rows. (Neither forward-scrolling nor table-type recordsets support the AbsolutePosition property, but the other types do. Forward-scrolling recordsets also don't support the PercentPosition property, although table-type recordsets allow you to use this property.)

Using the Move Method

Although the actions of the other Move… methods are obvious, based on their names, the Move method is a bit more ambiguous. The Move method of a recordset accepts one or two parameters:

rst.Move *rows*[, *start*]

The *rows* parameter indicates the number of rows to move (greater than 0 for forward, less than 0 for negative), and the optional *start* parameter can contain a saved bookmark. If you supply the value for the bookmark, Access starts there and moves the appropriate number of rows from that spot. If you don't specify the start location, Access assumes you want to start moving from the current row. See the section "Adding New Rows to a Recordset" later in this appendix for an example of using the Move method.

NOTE

When working with a forward-only recordset, the *rows* parameter must be a positive integer, and you can't specify a bookmark. You can only move forward a specific number of rows from the current location.

Using the AbsolutePosition and PercentPosition Properties

You can set the value of either the AbsolutePosition property or the PercentPosition property to move to a specific row in the recordset. If you wanted to move to the row approximately 50 percent of the way through your rows, you could use code like this:

```
rst.PercentPosition = 50
```

To move to the 35th row in the rows currently in the recordset, given the current filtering and sorting, you could try this:

```
rst.AbsolutePosition = 35
```

You can also use these two properties to tell where you are in the recordset.

TIP

Table-type recordsets do not support the AbsolutePosition property. That's just one more reason not to use table-type recordsets for anything but lookups. In addition, forward-scrolling recordsets do not support either the AbsolutePosition or the PercentPosition property.

WARNING

The AbsolutePosition property is *not* a record number and should not be thought of as such. It simply returns the current row's position within the current set of rows, and it will change as you modify the filter or the sort order of the rows. To be able to find a row, no matter how you've modified the sorting or filtering, you'll need to use a bookmark (see the section "Using Bookmarks" later in this appendix) or store the primary key for later retrieval.

Finding the Number of Rows in a Recordset

In spite of any implication made by its name, the RecordCount property of recordsets may not return the actual number of rows in a given recordset. This common misconception leads to a lot of confusion. The RecordCount property actually returns the number of rows *accessed so far* in the recordset if the recordset is not a table-type recordset. To find the actual number of rows in a recordset, you must first use the MoveLast method (and then move somewhere else, if you like) before checking the value of the RecordCount property. If you don't move to the last row, the RecordCount property returns either 0 (if there are no rows) or 1 (if one or more rows exist) when you first create the recordset.

NOTE

Table-type recordsets maintain their RecordCount property, so you needn't move to the last row. When you work with linked TableDef objects (not recordsets based on them), Jet always returns –1 for the RecordCount property.

WARNING

ADO recordsets don't require you to move to the last row in order to populate the RecordCount property, if the recordset supports the property. If you convert from DAO to ADO, you'll need to be aware of this difference in behavior.

In a single-user environment, the RecordCount property always correctly returns the number of rows in the recordset, once you've let Access calculate how many there are by moving to the last row. If you delete a row, either interactively or programmatically, the RecordCount property stays in sync. In a multiuser environment, things are a bit more complex. If you're sharing data with another user and you both have a recordset open that's based on the same data, deletions made on the other machine won't immediately show up on your machine. Access won't update the RecordCount value until the code actually accesses the deleted row, at which point Access decrements the RecordCount. Therefore, in a multiuser environment, if you must know exactly how many rows are currently in the recordset, you should take the following steps:

1. Use the Requery method on the recordset object.
2. Use the MoveLast method to move to the end of the recordset.
3. Check the RecordCount property for the current value.

You could use the GetRecordCount function in Listing C.5 as a simple example. (You'll find GetRecordCount in basRecordset in APDXC.MDB.) It uses the Restartable property of the recordset to make sure it can requery the recordset and just returns –1 if it can't. In that case, the caller would know that the GetRecordCount function wasn't able to requery the recordset and that it needs to find a less generic means of solving the problem. Once GetRecordCount knows it can requery the recordset, it follows the steps outlined above, preserving and resetting the position in the recordset using the recordset's Bookmark property. (See the section "Using Bookmarks" later in this appendix for more information.) This function is actually useful only for dynaset-type recordsets because table-type recordsets can't be requeried and snapshot-type recordsets don't need to be requeried. Because a snapshot-type recordset won't reflect any changes made by other users, its RecordCount property won't change once it's created.

Listing C.5

```
Public Function GetRecordCount( _
 rst As DAO.Recordset) As Long

     ' Return the current record count for a RecordSet.
     ' If the RecordSet isn't Restartable (and table-type
     ' RecordSets aren't) then just return -1, indicating
     ' that the caller needs to reopen the RecordSet in order
     ' to pick up any foreign changes.
```

```
    Dim varBookmark As Variant
    With rst
        If .Restartable Then
            .Requery
            If .Bookmarkable Then
                varBookmark = .Bookmark
            End If
            .MoveLast
            GetRecordCount = .RecordCount
            If .Bookmarkable Then
                .Bookmark = varBookmark
            End If
        Else
            GetRecordCount = -1
        End If
    End With
End Function
```

Testing for Boundaries

Every recordset supports two properties, BOF and EOF, that indicate whether the current row is currently at the end of the recordset (EOF) or at the beginning of the recordset (BOF):

- If you use MovePrevious while the first row is current, BOF becomes True and there is no current row.
- If you use MovePrevious again, BOF stays True but a runtime error occurs.
- If you use MoveNext while the last row is current, EOF becomes True and there is no current row.
- If you use MoveNext again, EOF stays True but a runtime error occurs.

Testing for an Empty Recordset

Often, when you create a recordset, you want to know immediately whether that recordset actually contains any rows. It's quite possible to create a recordset that doesn't return any rows, and you might need to take different steps based on whether the result contained any rows.

You can test for an empty recordset in a number of ways, but the two methods that follow ought to serve your needs. The following expression:

```
Set rst = db.OpenRecordset("qryCust")
If Not rst.BOF And Not rst.EOF Then
    ' You'll only be in here if there are some rows.
End If
```

checks to see whether both the BOF and the EOF properties for the recordset are True. If so, there must *not* be any rows, because that's the only way the current position could be at both the beginning and the end of the recordset. In addition, you often will want to loop through the rows of your recordset. In that case, you needn't check; just write the loop so that it won't even start if there are no rows:

```
Set rst = db.OpenRecordset("qryCust")
Do Until rst.EOF
    ' Process rows in here
Loop
```

You can also check the RecordCount property of a recordset: if it's 0, you know there aren't any records in the recordset. For example, you might use code like this:

```
Set rst = db.OpenRecordset("qryCust")
If rst.RecordCount > 0 Then
    ' You'll only be in here if there are some rows.
End If
```

You may find this technique easier to use.

Looping through All the Rows

Although you're likely to have less reason than you'd think to loop through all the rows of a recordset (that's what action queries are for), the syntax is quite simple. The code in Listing C.6 walks through a recordset backward, from the end to the beginning and, if there are any records to be had, prints out one of the fields in the underlying data. (Look for ListNames in basRecordset.)

Listing C.6

```
Public Sub ListNames()

    Dim db As DAO.Database
    Dim rst As DAO.Recordset
```

```
    Set db = CurrentDb()
    Set rst = db.OpenRecordset("tblCustomers")
    ' Check first to see if there are any rows.
    With rst
        If .RecordCount > 0 Then
            ' Move to the end.
            .MoveLast
            ' Loop back towards the beginning.
            Do Until .BOF
                Debug.Print ![ContactName]
                .MovePrevious
            Loop
        End If
        .Close
    End With
End Function
```

Using Arrays to Hold Recordset Data

You can use the GetRows method of any recordset to copy its data into a variant variable. Access will create a two-dimensional array with enough space to hold the data:

```
varData = rst.GetRows(intRowsToGrab)
```

You don't have to dimension or size the array; Access will do that for you. Because arrays give you random access to any row or column within the array, you may find it more convenient to work with arrays than with the recordset itself. For example, if you want the fastest access to data that you don't need to write to, you might want to use a forward-only recordset. But using this type of snapshot limits your movement in the data. If you create a forward-only recordset and copy its data to an array, you've got the best of both worlds: fast access *and* random access.

If you ask for more rows than exist, Access returns as many as there are. Use the UBound function to find out how many rows were actually returned:

```
intRows = UBound(varData, 2) + 1
```

The ", 2" tells UBound to find the number of rows (the second dimension of the array); then you must add 1 to the result, because the array is zero-based.

TIP

Be careful when creating your recordset before calling the GetRows method. Because Access will copy all the columns, including memos and long binary fields, you may want to exclude large fields from the recordset before you create the array; they can consume large amounts of memory and can be slow to load.

The following code (from basRecordset in APDXC.MDB) fills an array with data and then prints it out backward:

```
Public Sub TryGetRows()

    ' Use an array to process data in a recordset.

    Dim db As DAO.Database
    Dim rst As DAO.Recordset
    Dim varData As Variant
    Dim intCount As Integer
    Dim intI As Integer

    Set db = CurrentDb()
    Set rst = db.OpenRecordset( _
     "tblCustomers", dbOpenSnapshot, dbForwardOnly)
    ' Pick some arbitrary large number of rows to retrieve.
    varData = rst.GetRows(1000)

    ' How many rows did it actually send back?
    intCount = UBound(varData, 2) + 1
    ' Loop through all the rows, printing out the
    ' data from the second column.
    For intI = intCount - 1 To 0 Step -1
        Debug.Print varData(1, intI)
    Next intI

End Sub
```

Creating a Recordset Based on a Querydef

If you need to create a recordset based on any select query (about which you might know nothing at all until your program is running), you must be prepared to supply the recordset with all the parameters the querydef requires. Without DAO, doing so requires knowing in advance what the parameters are and supplying their values in your code. Using DAO, you can loop through all the parameters of your querydef and evaluate the necessary parameters. QueryDef objects provide a useful Parameters collection, each element of which represents a single query parameter.

A problem occurs because Access cannot fill in the parameters' values for you when you're creating a recordset based on a querydef, even if the parameter values are available to Access. It's up to you to supply those values for the querydef before you attempt to create the recordset.

TIP

Your query won't be able to run at all unless all the necessary parameters are available. If your query uses form objects as parameters, for example, you need to make sure the appropriate form is open and running, with appropriate values filled in, before you attempt to run a query based on those parameters.

The following code works with any QueryDef object that represents a select query:

```
Dim db As DAO.Database
Dim qdf As DAO.QueryDef
Dim prm As DAO.Parameter
Dim rst As DAO.Recordset

Set db = CurrentDb()
Set qdf = db.QueryDefs("qrySomeQuery")
For Each prm In qdf.Parameters
    prm.Value = Eval(prm.Name)
Next prm
Set rst = qdf.OpenRecordset(dbOpenDynaset)
```

The code loops through all the parameters of the object (and there may be none, in which case the loop won't ever execute), pointing a parameter variable at each of the parameters for the querydef, one at a time. For each parameter, the code evaluates the Name property using the Eval function and assigns the return value to the Value property of the parameter. This retrieves the value of each parameter, without your having to know in advance where the parameter is getting its value.

For example, if your query has a single parameter, on the City field:

```
Forms!frmInfo!CityField
```

the QueryDef container contains a single parameter object, for which the Name property is Forms!frmInfo!CityField. Through the use of the Eval function, the code in the previous example retrieves the value stored in that field and assigns it to the *Value* property of the specific parameter object. This satisfies the needs of the QueryDef object, and you'll be able to create the recordset you need based on that querydef.

Finding Specific Records

You handle the task of finding specific data in a recordset in different ways, depending on the type of the recordset. Table-type recordsets can use an indexed search to find data, but dynaset- and snapshot-type recordsets often cannot.

Finding Data in Table-Type Recordsets

If you've created a table-type recordset object, you can use the fast Seek method to locate specific rows. (Attempting to use the Seek method with any recordset other than a table-type recordset results in runtime error 3219, "Invalid Operation.") You must take two specific steps to use the Seek method to find data:

1. Set the recordset's Index property. This tells Access through which index you'd like it to search. If you want to use the primary key for searching, you must know the name of the primary key. (It's usually PrimaryKey, unless your application has changed it.)
2. Use the Seek method to find the value you want, given a search operator and one or more values for which to search. The search operator must be <, <=, =, >=, or >, indicating how you want Access to search. If the operator is =, >=, or >, Access searches from the beginning of the recordset. Otherwise, it starts at the end and works its way backward. To indicate to Access what it needs to search for, you supply one or more values, corresponding to the keys in the index you selected. If you based your index on one value, you need to supply only one value here. If your index includes multiple columns, you must supply all the values unless your search operator is something other than =.

For example, if your database contained an index named OrderIndex consisting of three columns—OrderNumber, OrderItem, and OrderDate—and you wanted to find the first item for order number 3, order item 17, for any date, the following fragment could get you to the correct row:

```
rst.Index = "OrderIndex"
rst.Seek ">=", 3, 17
```

The values you send to the Seek method must match the data types of the values in the index. In this case, the values were numeric. Had they been strings or dates, you would have needed to use matching data types in the call to the Seek method.

Once you've used the Seek method to find a row, you must, *without fail*, use the recordset's NoMatch property to check that you actually found a row. The following code expands on the previous fragment, handling the success or failure of the seek:

```
rst.Index = "OrderIndex"
rst.Seek ">=", 3, 17
If rst.NoMatch Then
    MsgBox "Unable to find a match!"
Else
    MsgBox "The item name is: " & rst![ItemName]
End If
```

TIP

The Seek method always starts at the beginning (or end) of the recordset when it searches. Therefore, using Seek inside a loop, searching for subsequent rows that match the criteria, is generally fruitless. Unless you modify the value once you find it so that further searches no longer find a match on that row, your loop will continually find the same row.

Finding Data in Dynaset- and Snapshot-Type Recordsets

Unlike table-type recordsets, dynaset- and snapshot-type recordsets cannot use the Seek method for finding data. Because these recordsets might well be based on ordered subsets of the original data, Access can't always use an index to speed up the search. Therefore, a search involving dynasets or snapshots might be a linear search, visiting every row in the recordset until it finds a match. Access will use an index if it can.

On a bright note, however, Access provides much greater flexibility in dynaset/snapshot searches. The four different methods (FindFirst, FindNext, FindPrevious, and FindLast) allow you to optimize the search so it has to look through the smallest number of rows to find the data it needs. Because you can use FindNext with these searches, you won't need to start back at the beginning of the recordset to find subsequent matches. In addition, you can use loops to walk your way through the records because you can restart the search without going back to the first row.

You use the same syntax for each of these methods:

Recordset.{FindFirst | FindPrevious | FindNext | FindLast} *criteria*

where *Recordset* is an open dynaset- or snapshot-type recordset variable and *criteria* is a WHERE clause formatted as though in a SQL expression, without the word *WHERE*. For example, the following fragment searches for a last name of "Smith".

```
rst.FindFirst "[LastName] = 'Smith'"
```

Just as with the Seek method, you must follow every call to a Find method with a check of the recordset's NoMatch property. If that property is True, there is no current row, and the search fails. Often, when performing some operation that requires looping through all the rows that match some criteria, you can use code like this:

```
strCriteria = "[LastName] = 'Smith'"
With rst
    .FindFirst strCriteria
    Do While Not .NoMatch
        ' Since you know you found a match,
        ' do something with the current row.
        Debug.Print ![FirstName]
        .FindNext strCriteria
    Loop
End With
```

Of course, many such loops can be replaced with action queries, which are almost always a better solution to the given programming problem.

Using Variables in Strings

In building criteria for Find methods and in several other places in VBA (when calling domain functions and when creating SQL strings, for example), you often need to embed variable values into a string. Because Jet has no way of finding the value of VBA variables, you need to supply their values before you ask it to do any work for you. This can cause trouble because Access requires delimiters (quotes for strings, # for dates) around those values, but they aren't part of the variables themselves. This causes many Access developers, experts and neophytes alike, a great deal of anguish.

Numeric values require no delimiters at all, and you can simply represent a string variable using an expression like this:

```
"[NumericField] = " & intNumber
```

Date variables need to be delimited with # in an expression. The general solution for the date problem would be

```
"[DateField] = #" & varDate & "#"
```

That's not so bad!

The difficulty arises when you attempt to embed a variable containing a string value inside a string. For example, imagine you have a variable named strName that contains the name you'd like to match in your call to the FindFirst method (for the sake of simplicity here, "Smith"). You need to build a string that represents the required WHERE clause:

```
[LastName] = "Smith"
```

As a first attempt, you might try this:

```
strCriteria = "[LastName] = strName"
```

When you attempt to run the search, Access complains with a runtime error. The problem is that the expression in strCriteria was this:

```
[LastName] = strName
```

Most likely, no one in your table has that particular last name.

As a second attempt, you might try a new approach:

```
strCriteria = "[LastName] = " & strName
```

When you attempt to run the search this time, Access again complains with a runtime error. In this case, it was using the value

```
[LastName] = Smith
```

which won't work because Access expects string values to be enclosed in quotes.

It should be clear by now that you need to get the quotes into that string. Access provides no fewer than three solutions to this problem.

All the solutions need to arrive at a value for strCriteria that looks like this:

```
[LastName] = "Smith"
```

or like this:

```
[LastName] = 'Smith'
```

Following are several solutions to this particular problem. These exercises are actually easier to envision if you do the work in reverse order.

The first solution is based on the fact that Access treats two quote characters side by side inside a string as representing one quote character. Remembering that every string expression must be enclosed in a pair of quotes, the first step in the first solution involves enclosing the final expression in those quotes. When enclosed in quotes, each internal quote needs to be replaced with two. The expression then becomes

```
"[LastName] = ""Smith"""
```

With the name separated out, the expression becomes

```
"[LastName] = """ & "Smith" & """"
```

Finally, with the constant replaced with the variable, the expression becomes

```
"[LastName] = """ & strName & """"
```

This last expression is the one you'd use with the FindFirst method.

You could also replace each quote with its ANSI representation, Chr$(34). If you go to the Immediate window and ask Access to print out the value

```
? Chr$(34)
```

it responds by printing a double-quote symbol. Therefore, again working backward:

```
[LastName] = "Smith"
```

becomes

```
"[LastName] = " & Chr$(34) & "Smith" & Chr$(34)
```

which becomes

```
"[LastName] = " & Chr$(34) & strName & Chr$(34)
```

If you create a string variable (perhaps named strQuote) and assign to it the value Chr$(34), you can use this expression:

```
"[LastName] = " & strQuote & strName & strQuote
```

You can also create a constant and assign to it a value that will resolve to be the string that is just a quotation mark. You can't use the Chr$ function when creating a constant, so this is the only way to create a constant value that does what you need:

```
Const QUOTE = """"
```

This might be the most straightforward solution to the problem.

The third solution involves replacing each internal quote with an apostrophe. That is, following the same backward steps:

```
[LastName] = "Smith"
```

becomes

```
[LastName] = 'Smith'
```

which becomes

```
"[LastName] = 'Smith'"
```

which becomes

```
"[LastName] = '" & "Smith" & "'"
```

which becomes (finally)

```
"[LastName] = '" & strName & "'"
```

The main problem with this solution (which many developers use) is that the value stored in strName cannot contain an apostrophe. If it did, you'd end up with an apostrophe embedded within a string that's enclosed in apostrophes. That's not allowed in Access' syntax. Therefore, you can use this method only when strName contains a value that could never contain an apostrophe. (Of course, the previous two solutions will fail if the string in question contains a double quote ("). But that's far less likely to happen than to have a string contain an apostrophe.)

To summarize, when building a string expression in Access that needs to contain a variable that represents a string, you must ensure that the final expression includes the quotes that enclose that string variable. The three suggested solutions are

```
Const QUOTE = """"
strCriteria = "[LastName] = """ & strName & """"
strCriteria = "[LastName] = " & QUOTE & strName & QUOTE
strCriteria = "[LastName] = '" & strName & "'"
```

In each case, the important issue is that you place the *value* of the variable into the string being sent off to FindFirst rather than the *name* of the variable. The Jet engine (which ultimately receives the request to find a row) has no clue as to what to do with an Access variable. It's up to your code to supply the value before requesting help from the Jet engine.

A General Solution for Strings

If you want to completely generalize this problem, what about the case in which you have both apostrophes and quotes inside the text you're trying to embed in a string? This can't work:

```
strName = Forms!txtStoreName
strCriteria = "StoreName = " & QUOTE & strName & QUOTE
```

if the text box on the form happens to contain the string

Joe's "Pizza" Store

because the string itself contains a quote. This won't work, either:

```
strCriteria = "StoreName = '" & strName & "'"
```

because the string contains an apostrophe, too.

You won't be able to use either quotes or apostrophes as delimiters, so what's the solution? In this case, and if you wish to be as general as possible in your solution, the answer is always to modify the delimited value by doubling any occurrences of whatever delimiter you choose. To do this, you'll need a function that accepts a string value and the delimiter character as parameters and returns the string with any occurrences of the delimiter inside it "doubled up." You'll find that function, adhHandleQuotes, in basHandleQuotes in APDXC.MDB. It can solve the previous problem:

```
strCriteria = "StoreName = " & _
 adhHandleQuotes(strName, QUOTE)
```

or

```
strCriteria = "StoreName = " & _
 adhHandleQuotes(strName, "'")
```

The adhHandleQuotes function looks for all the delimiter characters inside strName, fixes them up, surrounds the string with the requested delimiter, and returns the string. Because Access allows doubled quotes inside a quoted string, all will be well, no matter what the delimiter and the string. If you're interested in seeing how adhHandleQuotes works, look in basHandleQuotes; the code uses brute-force string manipulations. If you want to use this technique in your own applications, just import the basHandleQuotes module and call adhHandleQuotes yourself.

Using Bookmarks

One of the primary functions needed in any database product is the ability to move quickly to a specified row. Access provides a number of ways to move about in recordsets, as seen in the section "Moving through a Recordset" earlier in this appendix. In addition to the methods presented there, Jet provides the Bookmark property, which allows you to quickly preserve and restore the current location within a recordset.

What Is a Bookmark?

Every active recordset maintains a single current row. To retrieve a reference to that row, you can store the bookmark for that row. The bookmark itself is a 4-byte long integer, the exact value of which is of no particular importance to you. Access uses the value, but under no circumstances can you use the value in any sort of calculation. You can perform two basic operations with bookmarks:

- Retrieve the value of the bookmark, in order to store it for later retrieval.
- Set the value of the bookmark to a previously stored value, effectively setting the current row to be the row where you were when you originally saved the bookmark.

You can retrieve and store as many bookmarks for a given recordset as you wish to maintain. Manipulating bookmarks in Access is the fastest way to maneuver through rows. For example, if you need to move from the current row and then move back to it, you can use one of two methods:

Store the primary key value Move from the row and use the Seek or FindFirst method to move back to the original row, using the saved primary key value to find the row.

Store the bookmark Move from the row and then use the bookmark to move back to the original row.

The second method, using the bookmark, is much faster than the first. (For proof of this, see Chapter 17.) The code to do this might look something like the following example:

```
Dim varBookmark as Variant

varBookmark = rst.Bookmark
' Move to the first row.
rst.MoveFirst
'
' Now do whatever you moved from the current row to do.
'
' Then move back to the original row.
rst.Bookmark = varBookmark
```

Bookmarks and Record Numbers

If you're moving to Access from an Xbase environment, you might be tempted to think of bookmarks as a replacement for record numbers. In reality, that's not the case. Because Access is set-based, row numbers really have no validity here. Access neither stores nor maintains a record number in its data, and you can't count on a bookmark to act as a permanent locator for any given row. Once you close a recordset, the bookmark value is no longer valid. In addition, you cannot use bookmarks as locators across different recordsets, even though the recordsets might be based on the same data and might contain the same rows in the same order. On the other hand, as stated in the preceding section, bookmarks provide an excellent means of moving about in an open recordset.

To Bookmark or Not to Bookmark

Not all recordsets in Access support the Bookmark property. Some data sources make it impossible for Access to maintain bookmarks, so it is your responsibility as a developer to check the Bookmarkable property of a recordset before attempting to use bookmarks with that recordset. Any recordset based on native Access data always supports bookmarks, but external data may not. If the recordset does not support bookmarks, attempting to use the Bookmark property results in trappable error 3159, "Not a valid bookmark."

Also be aware that there is no valid bookmark when you've positioned the current row to be the "new" row in a recordset. That is, the following code will trigger runtime error 3021, "No Current Record":

```
rst.MoveLast
' Move to the "new" row.
rst.MoveNext
varBookmark = rst.Bookmark
```

TIP

In 16-bit versions of Access, one of the few ways to know you were currently working with the "new" row on a form was to count on the fact that retrieving a bookmark for the new row would fail. Access forms now provide the NewRecord property, making this technique unnecessary.

The Clone Method

For bookmarkable recordsets, you can use the Bookmark property to set and retrieve a marker for the current row. If you need to refer to the same recordset in two different ways with two different current rows, you can use the Clone method to create a clone of a recordset. (To retrieve a clone of a form's recordset, use the form's RecordsetClone property instead of the Clone method. See the next section for more information.) With a clone of the original recordset, you can effectively maintain two separate "current" rows. This way you can compare the values in two of the rows in the recordset, for example.

You might be tempted to ask, "Why use the Clone method instead of just creating a new recordset based on the same source?" The answer is clear: creating a recordset clone is faster, in most cases, than creating a new recordset object. When the source of the data is a querydef, the difference can be enormous. Rather than reexecuting the entire query to produce the new recordset, the Clone method just points a separate object variable at the original set of rows. This effectively gives you two current rows and two bookmarks, based on the same data. You can also assign the bookmark from one recordset to its clone because they really are the same recordset.

Be aware of these two issues:

- A recordset created with the Clone method is documented as not having a current row. (Experimentation has shown that the clone does, in fact, inherit the original recordset's current position. Because this is explicitly documented as not being so, however, don't count on it!) To set a specific row as the current row, use any of the Find or Move methods (FindFirst, MoveFirst, and so on) or set the recordset's Bookmark property with a value retrieved from the original recordset. Remember that bookmark assignments work only when applied to identical recordsets (as are the original and its clone).
- Using the Close method on either the original recordset or its clone doesn't affect the other recordset.

As an example of using the Clone method, imagine the following situation: you'd like to create a function to compare certain columns in the current row to see whether they have the same value as the same columns in the previous row. You could use the Clone method to handle this problem, as you'll see in Listing C.7. In this case, you just check the value in the Country field. This example also uses the form's RecordsetClone property to retrieve the underlying recordset, which is covered in the next section. The sample form, frmLookup in APDXC.MDB, uses the function in Listing C.7 (CheckPreviousRow, from basClone) in the Current event of the form to display or hide a label if the current Country field has the same value as the field in the previous row. Figure C.3 shows this form in action.

FIGURE C.3:

frmLookup displays or hides a label, based on the comparison of the current and previous values in the Country field.

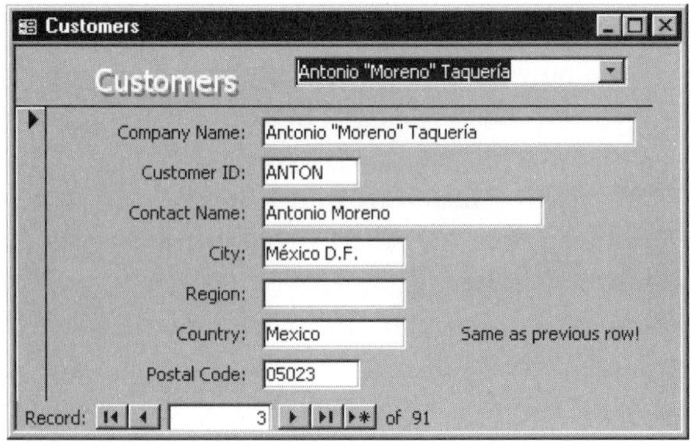

Listing C.7

```
Public Function CheckPreviousRow( _
 frm As Form, strFieldName As String) As Boolean

    Dim rst As DAO.Recordset
    Dim rstClone As DAO.Recordset

    ' Set rst to refer to the form's recordset,
    ' and set its bookmark to match the form's.
    Set rst = frm.RecordsetClone
    rst.Bookmark = frm.Bookmark

    ' Now create the record set clone, and make it
    ' refer to the same row as rst, which is on the same
    ' row as the form.
    Set rstClone = rst.Clone()
    rstClone.Bookmark = rst.Bookmark

    ' Move the clone record set to the previous row.
    ' If this puts us at the BOF, then the result has to be
    ' FALSE, and leave the function.
    rstClone.MovePrevious
    If rstClone.BOF Then
        CheckPreviousRow = False
    Else
        ' If you're not at BOF, then retrieve the
        ' necessary info.
        CheckPreviousRow = _
         (rst(strFieldName) = rstClone(strFieldName))
    End If

    rstClone.Close
End Function
```

The RecordsetClone Property

You use the RecordsetClone property to retrieve a reference to a form's recordset. Any bound form maintains its own recordset, the set of rows onto which the form provides a window. You'll often need to manipulate that set of rows without showing your work on the visible form. To do this, you create a recordset based on the form's recordset and do your manipulations there. For example, the code in Listing C.8, called from the AfterUpdate event of a combo box, searches for a specific company name on a form and sets the form to show the correct row once it finds a match. To see this form in action, try out frmLookup in APDXC.MDB. Figure C.4 shows this form in use.

FIGURE C.4:

Choosing a name from the combo box forces the code in Listing C.8 to locate the correct row.

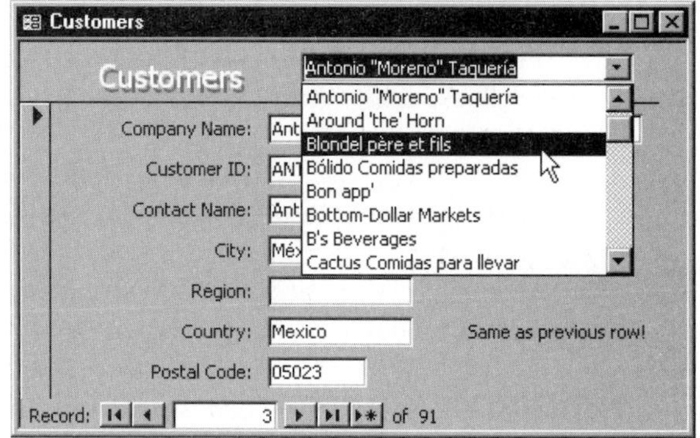

Listing C.8

```
Const adhcQuote = """"
Private Sub cboCompany_AfterUpdate()
    Dim rst As DAO.Recordset

    Set rst = Me.RecordsetClone
    rst.FindFirst "[CompanyName] = " & _
     adhHandleQuotes(Me!cboCompany, adhcQuote)

    If rst.NoMatch Then
        MsgBox "No match was found."
    Else
        Me.Bookmark = rst.Bookmark
    End If
    rst.Close
End Sub
```

NOTE

Assigning a recordset variable using the RecordsetClone property is the only time you set a recordset object without using the standard syntax, starting with a database object. Because you're retrieving a special kind of recordset, Access treats this case a bit differently. The results are almost the same, though: you end up with a recordset object variable referring to the set of rows filling the form. The recordset you're pointing to, however, doesn't support all the same properties as a real recordset. You can't set a form recordset's Filter or Sort property, for example. (For more information on using a form's RecordsetClone property, see Chapter 8. For more information on a recordset's Filter and Sort properties, see the next few sections.) Because you're not creating a new recordset but obtaining a reference to an existing one, the current row is undefined once you return the reference.

Sorting Recordsets

When using recordsets as part of your applications, you'll often need to present the rows in a specific order. Again, Access treats table-type recordsets differently from dynaset- and snapshot-type recordsets. For all objects, however, remember that if you want a particular sort order, you must specify it yourself.

Sorting Table-Type Recordsets

For table-type recordsets, you can specify the ordering by setting the Index property. (Access does not allow you to set the Index property of any other type of recordset. Attempting to do so will only get you a runtime error. As soon as you set that property, the rows appear in their new ordering. After applying an index, Access appears to set the first row as the current row. This behavior is not documented, however, and you would be wise to explicitly set the current row after setting the Index property.)

Listing C.9 shows a procedure that lists the fields in the index, in index order, for each index in a specified table. ListIndexFields does its work by looping through the TableDef object's collection of indexes. For each index in the collection, it gathers up the index name and the field names and uses them to set the index and to print out the value of each field for each row in the recordset. To test ListIndexFields, you might want to create a table with just a few rows and create an index for a few of the columns. Then, in the Immediate window, enter

? ListIndexFields("*YourTableName*")

replacing *YourTableName* with the name of your table. This should show all the indexes in your table, with the first indexed field in indexed order. (Look for ListIndexFields in basRecordset in APDXC.MDB.)

Listing C.9

```
Public Sub ListIndexFields(strTable As String)

    Dim rst As DAO.Recordset
    Dim db As DAO.Database
    Dim tdf As DAO.TableDef
    Dim idx As DAO.Index
    Dim fld As DAO.Field

    Dim strField As String

    Set db = CurrentDb()
    Set tdf = db.TableDefs(strTable)
    Set rst = db.OpenRecordset(strTable, dbOpenTable)

    ' List values for each index in the collection.
    For Each idx In tdf.Indexes
        ' Set the index to use in the recordset
        rst.Index = idx.Name
        ' The index object contains a collection of fields,
        ' one for each field the index contains.
        Debug.Print
        Debug.Print "Index: " & rst.Index
        Debug.Print "=========================="
        ' Move through the whole RecordSet, in
        ' index order, printing out the index
        ' fields, separated with tabs.
        rst.MoveFirst
        Do While Not rst.EOF
            For Each fld In idx.Fields
                strField = strField & vbTab & rst(fld.Name)
            Next fld
            If Len(strField) > 0 Then
                strField = Mid(strField, 2)
            End If
            Debug.Print strField
```

```
                strField = ""
                rst.MoveNext
            Loop
        Next idx
        rst.Close
    End Sub
```

Sorting Dynaset- and Snapshot-Type Recordsets

Just as with table-type recordsets, unless you specify a sorting order for dynaset- and snapshot-type recordsets, the rows will show up in an indeterminate order. The natural order for these derived recordsets is a bit more complex because it might depend on more than one table. In any case, if you need a specific ordering, you must set up that ordering yourself.

To create sorted dynaset- or snapshot-type recordsets, you have two choices, outlined in the next two sections.

Using a SQL ORDER BY Clause

You can create a recordset object using a SQL statement including an ORDER BY clause. To do so, specify the SQL expression as the row source for the OpenRecordset method. For example, this fragment:

```
Set db = CurrentDb()
Set rstSorted = db.OpenRecordset( _
 "SELECT * FROM tblCustomers ORDER BY [ContactName];")
```

creates a recordset based on tblCustomers, including all the columns, sorted by the LastName column. You can base a recordset on a SQL string only when creating recordsets based on a database object (as opposed to other uses of OpenRecordset, which can be based on tables, queries, or other recordsets). Attempting to do so will get you a runtime error. Creating a recordset using a SQL expression creates a dynaset-type recordset (unless you request a snapshot-type recordset).

Using the Sort Property

You can set the Sort property of any non-table-based recordset to change its sort order. The Sort property must be a string, in the same style as the ORDER BY clause of a SQL expression. You must specify the column on which to sort and, optionally, the ordering. The next time you create a recordset based on this recordset, the new sort order will take effect. (This is different from the way table-type recordset sorting works; there, the sorting takes effect immediately.) The following fragments show how to set the Sort property:

```
rst.Sort = "[LastName]"          ' Defaults to ascending
rst.Sort = "[LastName] Asc"      ' Ascending sort
rst.Sort = "[LastName] Desc"     ' Descending sort
```

Here are some items to remember when using the Sort property:

- The new sort order doesn't take effect until you create a new recordset, based on the old one.
- The Sort property doesn't apply to table-type recordsets. Use the Index property for them.
- It might be faster to open a new recordset based on a SQL expression than to use the Sort property.

The following code shows two methods for creating a sorted dynaset-type recordset:

```
Dim db As DAO.Database
Dim rst As DAO.Recordset
Dim rstSorted1 As DAO.Recordset
Dim rstSorted2 As DAO.Recordset

Set db = CurrentDb()
' Create a sorted Recordset using SQL.
Set rstSorted1 = db.OpenRecordset( _
 "SELECT * FROM tblCustomers ORDER BY [ContactName];")
' Create a sorted Recordset based on an existing Recordset.
Set rst = db.OpenRecordset("tblCustomers", dbOpenDynaset)
rst.Sort = "[CompanyName]"
Set rstSorted2 = rst.OpenRecordset()
'
' Do whatever you need to do here with the sorted recordsets
'
rst.Close
rstSorted1.Close
rstSorted2.Close
```

Filtering Non-Table Recordsets

Just as with sorting a recordset, you have two choices if you want to create a filtered subset of rows. These choices are outlined in the next two sections. You'll need to decide which method to use based on the circumstances of your application.

Using a SQL WHERE Clause

You can create a recordset by using a SQL statement including a WHERE clause. To do so, specify the SQL expression as the row source for the OpenRecordset method. For example, this fragment:

```
Set db = CurrentDb()
Set rstSorted = db.OpenRecordset( _
 "SELECT * FROM tblCustomers WHERE [ZipCode] = '90210'")
```

creates a recordset based on all the columns in tblCustomers, including only the rows where the ZipCode field is "90210". You can use this method only when creating recordsets based on a database object (as opposed to other uses of OpenRecordset, which can be based on tables, queries, or other recordsets). Attempting to do otherwise will get you a runtime error.

Using the Filter Property

You can also set the Filter property of any dynaset- or snapshot-type recordset to change the set of rows it contains. The Filter property must be a string, in the same style as the WHERE clause of a SQL expression. The next time you create a recordset based on this recordset, the new filtering will take effect. For example, you generally use the Filter property like this:

```
' rst is an existing recordset.
rst.Filter = "[Age] > 35"
Set rstFiltered = rst.OpenRecordset()
' Now rstFiltered contains all the rows from rst that
' have an [Age] field greater than 35.
```

Here are some items to remember when using the Filter property:

- The new filtering doesn't take effect until you create a new recordset based on the old one.

- The Filter property doesn't apply to table-type recordsets.
- It might be faster to open a new recordset based on a SQL expression than to use the Filter property.
- The new filtering will never retrieve additional rows from the original source tables. It will filter only rows that are in the base recordset you are filtering.

The following code shows two methods for creating a filtered dynaset-type recordset:

```
Dim db As DAO.Database
Dim rst As DAO.Recordset
Dim rstSQL as DAO.Recordset
Dim rstFiltered As DAO.Recordset

Set db = CurrentDb()
Set rstSQL = db.OpenRecordset( _
 "SELECT * FROM tblCustomers WHERE [PostalCode] = '90210';")
Set rst = db.OpenRecordset("tblCustomers", dbOpenDynaset)
rst.Filter = "[PostalCode] = '90210'"
Set rstFiltered = rst.OpenRecordset()
```

Editing Data in a Recordset Object

Of course, almost any database application needs to be able to add, update, and delete data. Access provides methods for accomplishing each of these tasks. The next few sections discuss the various data-manipulation methods that Access supports.

When Is a Recordset Modifiable?

You can modify data only if you have permission to do so, of course. When you open a recordset, you may be able to retrieve the data for viewing only. If so, your attempts to modify the data will result in a runtime trappable error. You can always edit table-type recordsets unless someone else has placed a lock on that table (by opening it exclusively or creating a recordset based on it with an option that precludes others from changing its data). You can edit dynaset-type recordsets unless locks have been placed by other users, just as with table-type recordsets. In addition, join rules may prevent editing of certain fields. Snapshot-type recordsets are never modifiable, because they're read-only by definition.

Changing Data in a Recordset

To programmatically change the data in any recordset (assuming the recordset is updatable), take the following steps:

1. Move to the desired row.
2. Use the Edit method to put the current row in edit mode.
3. Make changes.
4. Use the Update method to save the edits.

Don't skip any of these steps, or your data won't be saved. The most important step, however, is the final one. If you make changes to the row but forget to use the Update method to commit those changes, Access treats the row as though you'd never made any changes at all. (If you want to explicitly discard a change, you can do so with the recordset's CancelUpdate method.)

WARNING If you use ADO, you'll find that its behavior when modifying data is exactly the opposite of DAO's. That is, in DAO, unless you explicitly save your data, your changes are discarded when you move to a new row. In ADO, however, your changes are saved unless you explicitly request the changes to be discarded. Beware of this difference if you migrate between the two.

The following code finds the first row in the recordset in which the LastName field contains "Smith" and changes it to "Smythe":

```
With rst
    .FindFirst "[LastName] = 'Smith'"
    If .NoMatch Then
        MsgBox "No Match was Found!"
    Else
        .Edit
            ![LastName] = "Smythe"
        .Update
    End If
End With
```

Adding New Rows to a Recordset

To programmatically add new rows to a recordset (assuming neither updatability nor security keeps you from doing so), follow these steps:

1. Use the AddNew method to add a new row. All fields will be set to their default values.
2. Fill in fields as needed.
3. Use the Update method to save the new row.

As in the preceding section, if you neglect to call the Update method before you leave the current row, Access discards any changes you've made and does not add the new row.

When you use the AddNew method, the current row remains the row that was current before you added the new row. If you want the new row to be the current row, employ the Move method, using as its parameter the bookmark returned from the LastModified property of the recordset.

The following example adds a new row to the recordset and fills in a few of the fields. Once it's done, it makes the new row the current row:

```
With rst
    .AddNew
        ![LastName] = "Smith"
        ![FirstName] = "Tommy"
    .Update

    .Move 0, .LastModified
End With
```

Dynaset-type recordsets treat new rows a bit differently than do table-type recordsets. For a dynaset-type recordset object, Access always places the new row at the end of the recordset. For table-type recordsets, if you've set the Index property, Access places the row at its correct spot in the index. For dynaset-type recordsets, Access adds the new row to the end of the underlying table. If you're working with a table-type recordset, though, new rows added to the table won't be seen by users who have based a recordset on that table until they refresh their rows.

In early versions of Access (and the Jet database engine), adding new rows could result in page-lock collisions. With pessimistic locking, the final page of a table might have been locked, and your attempts to add a row would have failed. Starting with Access 95 (and Jet 3), these sorts of collisions should be a thing of the past. (See Chapter 2 in *Access 2000 Developer's Handbook, Volume II* for more information on inserting new rows and page locking.)

Deleting Data from a Recordset

To delete a row from a recordset, follow these steps:

1. Move to the desired row.
2. Use the Delete method to delete it.

TIP

You don't need to use the Update methods when deleting a row, unlike the other methods of modifying rows. Once you delete it, it's gone—unless, of course, you wrapped the entire thing in a transaction. In that case, you can roll back the transaction to retrieve the deleted row.

TIP

After you delete a record, it is still the current record. The previous row is still the previous row, and the next row is still the next row. Use MoveNext to move to the next row, if that's where you'd like to be.

The code in Listing C.10 deletes all the rows from a table, although it is not necessarily the best way to solve the problem. In reality, you'd use a delete query to do the work. To try this function out, check in basRecordset in APDXC.MDB.

Listing C.10

```
Public Sub ZapTable(strTable As String)

    ' Delete all the rows from a table, the
    ' slowest way possible!

    Dim db As DAO.Database
    Dim rst As DAO.Recordset

    Set db = CurrentDb()
    Set rst = db.OpenRecordset(strTable)
```

```
    With rst
        If rst.RecordCount > 0 Then
            .MoveFirst
            Do
                .Delete
                ' Without this MoveNext, Access would
                ' continually try to delete the same row,
                ' the first one.
                .MoveNext
            Loop Until .EOF
        End If
        .Close
    End With
End Sub
```

Using Containers to Handle Saved Documents

A *container* object contains information about saved database objects. Its main purpose is to provide the Jet engine with some mechanism for knowing about all the Access UI objects. Because Jet provides security for Access, it must maintain information about ownership and permissions, and it does so in these containers. Some of the containers are provided by the Jet engine and some by the application. Table C.6 lists the useful containers, the parent for each container, and what each contains.

TABLE C.6: Containers and Their Parents

Container	Parent	Contains Information About
Databases	Jet database engine	Containing database, database properties
Tables	Jet database engine	Saved tables and queries
Relationships	Jet database engine	Saved relationships
SysRel	Jet database engine	Saved relationship layout information

Continued on next page

TABLE C.6 CONTINUED: Containers and Their Parents

Container	Parent	Contains Information About
Forms	Microsoft Access	Saved forms
Reports	Microsoft Access	Saved reports
Scripts	Microsoft Access	Saved macros
Modules	Microsoft Access	Saved modules
DataAccessPages	Microsoft Access	Saved data access pages

Each container object contains a collection of Document objects, each of which is a saved object in the database. The Document objects contain information about the saved objects, but not about the data they contain. For example, the Tables container includes a Document object for each table and query in the database. Each document stores information about the permissions, creation date, and owner of the stored object. But documents in the Tables container don't store the actual data. The same goes for documents in the Forms container: each document object contains information about the form object but provides no information about the structure or content of the form itself. The Containers collection, and each container's collection of Documents, makes it possible to retrieve information about the documents in the database; this is how you can find out what exactly is *in* the database, when it was last modified, and so on.

Each container object is a collection that contains nonengine objects. The Jet engine can get very limited information about them, such as their creator and creation time, through DAO. This allows the engine to know, in a limited sense, about the objects that are application specific. The main significance of containers is that they

- Give you information about the live Access objects; that is, they give you a mechanism you can use to walk through collections of non-DAO objects
- Provide the only method for retrieving information about your saved macros, modules, reports, and forms
- Let you treat nonengine objects as though they were data access objects instead of application-provided objects; that is, they let you use the set of DAO rules and tools with non-DAO objects

Because security is provided at the engine level, Jet has to know about non-DAO objects so it can handle their security.

To refer to a particular container, use the syntax

Containers("*name*")

or

Containers!name

or

Containers(index)

where *name* is one of the items in the first column from Table C.6.

NOTE

The Forms, Reports, DataAccessPages, and Modules *containers* are very different from the Forms, Reports, DataAccessPages, and Modules *collections*. Using the containers, you can work with any forms or reports in the database but can only retrieve information such as the owner, permissions, and date of creation. Using the collections, you can refer only to currently opened forms and reports, but you can retrieve information about the controls on the form, their layout, and so on.

To examine the various containers and their contents, run the function ListContainers in basContainers in APDXC.MDB. This function can display, in the Immediate window, a list of containers and the documents within them and, if you like, all the properties and their values for each document. To make the function a bit more useful, you can pass it parameters that limit the output. (See the header comments for more information.) Listing C.11 shows the function, and Figure C.5 shows sample output.

Listing C.11

```
Public Sub ListContainers( _
 Optional ListProps As Boolean = False, _
 Optional ContainerName As String = "ALL")

    Dim db As DAO.Database
    Dim con As DAO.Container
    Dim doc As DAO.Document
    Dim prp As DAO.Property

    Set db = CurrentDb()
```

```
    For Each con In db.Containers
        If ContainerName = "ALL" Or _
         (ContainerName = con.Name) Then
            Debug.Print con.Name
            For Each doc In con.Documents
                Debug.Print , doc.Name
                If ListProps Then
                    For Each prp In doc.Properties
                        Debug.Print , , prp.Name, prp.Value
                    Next prp
                End If
            Next doc
        End If
    Next con
End Sub
```

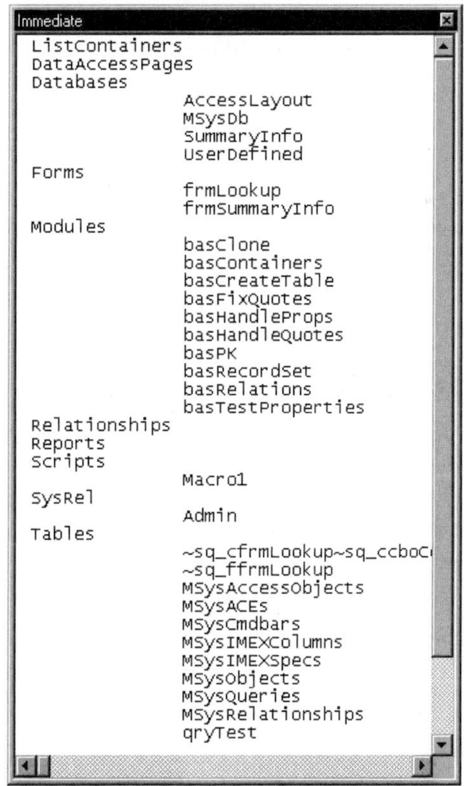

FIGURE C.5:

ListContainers can display lists of all the containers and their properties.

Database Properties

Access allows you to set database properties with the File ➢ Database Properties menu. Those properties are stored as properties of the SummaryInfo document in the Databases container. If you set up user-defined properties for your database (choose the Custom tab on the File ➢ Database Properties dialog box to set these properties), they're stored as properties of the UserDefined document within the Databases container.

You may need to supply an interface for setting and retrieving your database's summary information from within your application. To get you started, we've supplied a simple form, frmSummaryInfo in APDXC.MDB, that does the work for you and looks very similar to the built-in dialog box (see Figure C.6).

FIGURE C.6:

frmSummaryInfo allows you to set and retrieve database summary info from your applications.

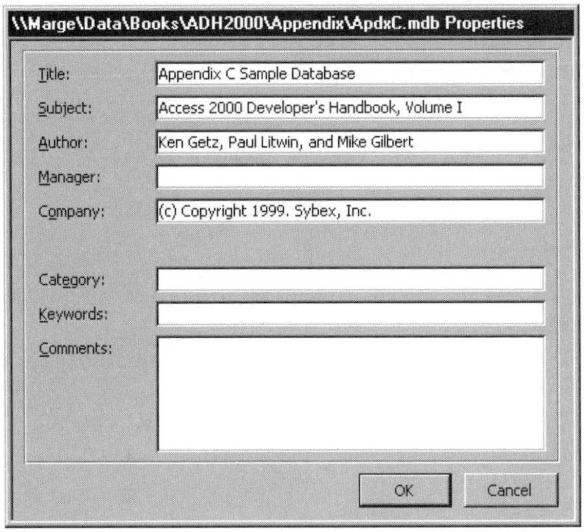

To use this form within your own applications, import it (frmSummaryInfo) and the module containing the property-handling functions, basHandleProps, from APDXC.MDB. You may find it interesting to study the code in frmSummaryInfo's module. It makes several calls to the adhGetProp and adhSetProp functions, handling the various database summary information properties.

Summary

This appendix presented a broad introduction to programming Jet's object model using DAO. Although we've made attempts to bring our own personal perspectives into this appendix, a full understanding of this material requires far more depth than we can cover here.

This appendix covered these major topics:

- Access' support for DAO with Jet
- Objects that Jet provides
- Referring to objects
- Iterating through collections
- Using properties
- Jet data definition using DAO
- Working with Jet's recordsets
- Using Access' application-supplied containers

Our main goal in this appendix is to present enough information so that you'll be able to use DAO in the several places it's still required in Access 2000. Refer to Chapter 6 for information about ADO—that's the current data access programming model you'll want to use. On the other hand, no matter how much Microsoft would like to force all data access to use ADO, there are still a few situations in Access where you'll be forced to use DAO.

INDEX

Note to the Reader: Throughout this index **boldfaced** page numbers indicate primary discussions of a topic. *Italicized* page numbers indicate illustrations.

A

B

C

D

E

F

G

H

I

J

K

L

M

N

O

Q

R

S

T

U

V

W

Y

Z

What's on the CD

This CD is a valuable companion to the book. It provides a wealth of information in a readily usable format to aid in your Access development efforts. We've included every significant example presented in the text—not just the VBA code. We've also included all the tables (with sample data), queries, forms, reports, and so on—everything you need to get up and running instantly. The CD also contains a white paper on converting from DAO to ADO, several free and shareware utility programs, and demonstrations of commercial products.

Here's just a sampling of what you'll find on the CD:

- An Access add-in that serves as a scratchpad facility for entering SQL statements on-the-fly and then viewing the output.
- Demos of all the award-winning Access add-ins from FMS, Inc.
- Classes to make your development work easier. From scaling and sizing controls on forms, to providing a list of installed printers, to investigating file version information, to working with the Windows screen—you'll find many tools that you can just drop into your own applications and use.
- Ready-to-use pop-up calendar and calculator forms that you can use in your own applications.
- Windows shareware programming for zipping and unzipping files.
- Demo versions of ClickBook (a printing utility that makes it easy to print code listings or anything else, in a compact, easy-to-carry format) and WebWhacker, both from BlueSquirrel Software.

For more information about the CD, including installation instructions, see the section entitled "About the CD" in the Introduction of this book and the README.TXT file in the root folder of the CD.

NOTE

If you use Windows Explorer to copy the sample database files directly from the CD to your hard disk, the files will be marked as read-only. Either run the supplied Chapter.exe self-extracting zip file, or, after you've copied files manually, use Windows Explorer to clear the Read-Only attribute of the file.